The Soar Papers

Artificial Intelligence

Patrick Henry Winston, founding editor

J. Michael Brady, Daniel G. Bobrow, and Randall Davis, current editors

Artificial intelligence is the study of intelligence using the ideas and methods of computation. Unfortunately, a definition of intelligence seems impossible at the moment because intelligence appears to be an amalgam of so many information-processing and information-representation abilities.

Of course psychology, philosophy, linguistics, and related disciplines offer various perspectives and methodologies for studying intelligence. For the most part, however, the theories proposed in these fields are too incomplete and too vaguely stated to be realized in computational terms. Something more is needed, even though valuable ideas, relationships, and constraints can be gleaned from traditional studies of what are, after all, impressive existence proofs that intelligence is in fact possible.

Artificial intelligence offers a new perspective and a new methodology. Its central goal is to make computers intelligent, both to make them more useful and to understand the principles that make intelligence possible. That intelligent computers will be extremely useful is obvious. The more profound point is that artificial intelligence aims to understand intelligence using the ideas and methods of computation, thus offering a radically new and different basis for theory formation. Most of the people doing work in artificial intelligence believe that these theories will apply to any intelligent information processor, whether biological or solid state.

There are side effects that deserve attention, too. Any program that will successfully model even a small part of intelligence will be inherently massive and complex. Consequently, artificial intelligence continually confronts the limits of computer-science technology. The problems encountered have been hard enough and interesting enough to seduce artificial intelligence people into working on them with enthusiasm. It is natural, then, that there has been a steady flow of ideas from artificial intelligence to computer science, and the flow shows no sign of abating.

The purpose of this series in artificial intelligence is to provide people in many areas, both professionals and students, with timely, detailed information about what is happening on the frontiers in research centers all over the world.

J. Michael Brady
Daniel Bobrow
Randall Davis

The Soar Papers

Research on Integrated Intelligence

Volume Two

Edited by

Paul S. Rosenbloom, John E. Laird, and Allen Newell

THE MIT PRESS
CAMBRIDGE, MASSACHUSETTS
LONDON, ENGLAND

Printed and bound in the United States of America.

Library of Congress Cataloging-in-Publication Data

The Soar papers : research on integrated intelligence / edited by Paul S. Rosenbloom, John E. Laird, and Allen Newell.

p. cm.

Includes bibliographical references and index.

ISBN 0-262-18152-5 (hc)—ISBN 0-262-68071-8 (pbk)

1. Artificial intelligence. I. Rosenbloom, Paul S. II. Laird, John, 1954- . III. Newell, Allen.

Q335.S63 1992

006.3--dc20 91-48463

CIP

Contents

Volume One: 1969-1988

1988

Volume Two: 1989-1991

1989

The Soar Papers

1989

CHAPTER 31

A Discussion of "The Chunking of Skill and Knowledge" by Paul S. Rosenbloom, John E. Laird and Allen Newell

*T. Bösser**

1 Introduction

From the viewpoint of psychology, the remarkable generality claimed for SOAR by its authors (*"a system to perform the full range of cognitive tasks"*, Laird, Rosenbloom and Newell, 1986), which can be understood to cover not only human cognition, but all cognition which has evolved, is bold and provocative. SOAR descends from Newell and Simon's (1972) general problem solver and finally puts some of the promises made early in the history of artificial intelligence and cognitive science to a conclusive test. But there are also other ancestors: What Rosenbloom, Laird and Newell call a cognitive architecture corresponds to what used to be put forward as psychological theories with equal aspirations to generality, but none was ever implemented as a comprehensive, computable model.

I will remark on some technical aspects of SOAR which, if claimed to be representative of human cognition, may indicate that there are some limits to generality, also due to the fact that the modelling must refer to a basis of facts to model, and can only be as comprehensive as the data available. The main question is: Is the 'cognitive architecture' engineering artefact or psychological theory?

2 Cognitive architecture versus psychological theory

An architecture is a structure for combining all functions and components which are needed for a purpose – SOAR combines all the functions needed for intelligent behaviour, but it is not designed to represent the exact structure and functional organization of human intelligence. There are some

* Psychologisches Institut, Westfälische Wilhelms-Universität, Schlaunstrasse 2, D-4400 Münster, Federal Republic of Germany.

WORKING MODELS OF HUMAN PERCEPTION
ISBN 0-12-238050-9

further requirements for a cognitive architecture: It must be computable, well structured – which is a subjective criterion – and it must correspond to Einstein's principle (*"Everything should be made as simple as possible, but not simpler"*).

There is an obstacle to the application of Einstein's principle: What initially seems to be a good design may later need to be patched up with some additional functions. This, especially if done by an architect with less of an overview, may result in a questionable overall design. I will discuss functions which are not presently included in SOAR, but may be needed later.

SOAR is similar to the family of GOMS models (Card, Moran and Newell, 1983), 'GOMS' being short for the elements in the models: GOALS, OPERATORS, METHODS and SELECTION rules. SOAR stands out as a much more comprehensive effort to provide a generally practicable model. The specific aspects of SOAR are:

- The architecture is based on a production memory, but is extended by the powerful constructs of subgoaling and chunking.
- The performance aspect is represented by assumptions about Choice Reaction Time.
- Unique learning capabilities are provided by the chunking mechanism.

SOAR, however, does not have some architectural features of other models thought to be characteristic of human cognition, i.e. limited size of working memory.

The primitives or atomic structures of SOAR determine the explanatory power of the model in a psychological, empirical sense. The primitives of SOAR are operations and methods (called plans in another context). The precise definition is the technical implementation. To obtain a realistic model of human cognition, care would have to be taken to choose the right primitives, because learning starts from the primitive operations – pure inductive learning, without any preassumptions, is not possible. In SOAR the primitives are defined by the author of the model in such a way as to be convenient for his application.

Experimental psychologists see their science as reductionist, i.e. they assume that the elementary structures and functions of what they are modelling can be individually identified and then synthesized into an overall design. Cognitive processes are not separable into constituent elements and, due to the large number of parameters, not identifiable by 'black-box' methods. Consequently, psychological theories require axiomatic assumptions to limit the space of models (the architecture), which also guides experimentation (usually called a paradigm). The architecture can be seen as a language with which different means to build models generating the same behaviours can be built. SOAR is designed to be a programming language which is universally applicable for modelling intelligent behaviour. Steier, Laird, Newell, Rosenbloom, Flynn, Golding, Polk, Shivers, Unruh and Yost (1987) list the models implemented so far.

In this sense, comparable languages are ACT* (Anderson, 1983), but also connectionism (Thorndike, 1898), associationism (Guthrie, 1952) and operant conditioning (Skinner, 1938). They are comparable in their attempt to provide a structure to integrate experimental data, theoretical assumptions and structural and computational mechanisms, but none of them has been realized as a comprehensive computable system like SOAR. A successful attempt to transform these classical psychological theories into working models might have been similar, but most likely simpler than SOAR.

How can we compare the intelligent behaviour of such an architecture with human cognition with any confidence? Only falsification is possible: We can test for differences, but not similarities, and a model cannot be shown to be the only one capable of modelling a data set. The 'architecture' is a special-purpose high-level programming language with facilities for expressing certain phenomena conveniently, comparable to an expert system shell. In the current state of knowledge the primary objective is not to design the most elegant architecture, but to demonstrate that the principles can actually be implemented.

A psychological theory would generally be thought of as having structural isomorphy to reality. A precondition is that the data which are modelled are representative of human cognition ('the full range'), but the in most instances structural isomorphy will still resist a test by falsification.

3 Implementation issues

Since any formal language can be translated into any other, provided both can represent a Turing machine, there can be no doubt, in principle, that SOAR can be made to represent any process which can be implemented on a similar system. The issue really is whether the design of SOAR allows to construct working models of all or many cognitive tasks in practice.

The language of SOAR is computer science, not psychology. This tends to draw it towards axiomatic and formal language rather than towards describing cognitive processes in terms of psychologically meaningful component processes. Much effort seems to be needed for the efficient implementation of SOAR in terms of time and memory. Such considerations introduce architectural details which lead away from a model of human cognition. Evolution, working with different components, is likely to have found different solutions. The decision cycle and chunking are two examples.

Decision cycle. The decision cycle presented in SOAR does not accommodate responses to events occurring in real time (a dynamic world). Active perception of the human updates the world model continuously, and external events can bring about an instantaneous rearrangement of the goal structure, i.e. do multiprocessing by time sharing. The implementation of the decision cycle in SOAR precludes the representation of this type of behaviour in tasks with real-time constraints.

The implementation of chunking as 'all-or-none' learning has a very axiomatic quality. An implementation of these parameters with continuous variation might be less efficient, but is closer to psychological thinking.

4 Modularity of functional elements

The need to modularize complex systems may stem entirely from our inability to understand them *in toto*, rather than from the structure properties of these systems themselves. In order to arrive at a model with separable functional elements, the clusters of separable elements have to be found. In SOAR there are separate blocks of general and specific knowledge for task domains. Human knowledge is additive, and different forms of knowledge can coexist. It would be interesting to see how SOAR functions when a number of working models are integrated into one.

In order to test which functional modules are needed to achieve a desired performance, models must be modular, so that it can be shown that by including a particular module a certain performance is possible. But how do we show that without this module it is not? Modularization must therefore rely on plausibility and is quite arbitrary.

Model validation by simulation and experimentation (the connection to psychology), also relies on the separability of functions, because experimentation implies that separable tasks can be defined. Experimental psychology has not been successful in separating out clear-cut functional blocks of cognition which can be recognized unambiguously as components of complex tasks. The non-additive and nonlinear interactions of subtasks are often referred to in order to explain unexpected observations. Can this be different for cognitive models? This shows both the advantage and the weakness of a computable cognitive model: It gives the means to combine functions and test the performance of the complete system by simulation, sensitivity analysis and parameter fitting, but does not lead conclusively to a structure.

5 Parallelism

There is considerable parallelism in SOAR, which should be interesting to explore, considering that cognitive functions in biology are implemented with many inefficient biological chips connected in parallel. The combination of symbolic processing with a highly parallel architecture and a form of inductive learning is a very exciting idea. There may be more similarity to the fashionable Parallel Distributed Processing (PDP) (Rumelhart and McClelland, 1986) models than is obvious at first sight.

6 Experimental data and SOAR

Some selective features of SOAR are designed on the basis of experimental data and paradigms, primarily choice reaction time and the learning curve. Although there can be no doubt about the capability of SOAR to model these, the phenomena themselves are not as unambiguous and stable as they seem to be at first sight.

Choice reaction time (CRT). Both the experimental data cited and simulation in SOAR are based on choice situations which, compared with real-life situations, contain a limited number of alternatives of roughly equal probability. The generalization of these results to choice situations with many alternatives, some of them with low probability, is hypothetical, and also the quantitative effect of including prior knowledge is not well understood. The appropriateness of the CRT model has not really been shown for human choice in situations of this type. It is hard to devise experimental procedures to test this question conclusively; simulation might even go ahead and indicate which hypotheses should be tested empirically.

The practice and learning curves used for describing experimental data and simulation results for chunking are overparametrized and therefore not uniquely identifiable, i.e. more than one curve can be fitted to the data set. This has been discussed more extensively by Bösser (1987), where it is argued that not too much can be inferred about the underlying mechanisms on the basis of curve fitting, and the curves should extend as far as possible into the asymptotic range in order to give reliable estimates. Fitting learning curves cannot give strong support to the hypothesis that SOAR models structural properties of the mechanism of human learning.

Both the capability to model human performance in choice reaction time tasks and to generate learning curves have been put forward to support the claim for SOAR's capability to represent human cognitive performance – which it can, but limited to the extent that the empirical data are representative of these human functions. Modelling cannot substitute experimental data and observations, and only as far as data realistically represent human behaviour can the model which generates the same data represent these cognitive functions. The validity of any statement relating to data rests on

- ingenious and valid experimental procedures and
- the fact that the process under study is representative of the domain to which the results are to be generalized.

7 Motivation

SOAR, like GPS (General Problem Solver) and other GOMS (Goals, Operators, Methods, Selection) models, is based on a representation of the problem space in terms of operations, where states are only defined as the states reachable by operations. This is efficient for a sparsely covered state space, but I can conceive of problems where similarities between states are relevant, and consequently the dimensions of the state space need to be known. One instance is motivation which I see as a mechanism for choosing an optimal alternative from a set of achievable states.

Motivation is not represented in SOAR, in my opinion a very important omission. Motivation guides behaviour, and behaviour is the basis of learning in SOAR. I believe that motivation must be appropriately represented in a model of general intelligence. The preferences implemented in SOAR are functions for the efficient internal execution of SOAR functions, i.e. the motivation to utilize internal resources efficiently, but in human cognition there are many other motivational factors. A state-space representation of motivation has been advocated in a different field of study by Sibly and McFarland (1974) who have shown that it can be constructed from decision data. It could probably be integrated into a model like SOAR, if desired.

8 Representation of the external world (and the task space)

In order to compare the simulated performance of a model to that of the human (or any other existing system), behaviour is studied under controlled conditions in experiments, which are simulations where one of the components is the human. The validity of this test depends upon the ability to present the right tasks to both model and human. In other words: We need a representation of the world and the task. For psychology, reality is represented by experimental data, which must be collected from the appropriate subset of reality in order to be meaningful. Cognitive performance in a number of different tasks has been successfully modelled by SOAR, and it is a sound principle to start with the topics which are likely to lead to success. It will be interesting, however, to see what types of cognitive behaviour can be represented by SOAR, and what is outside its limits. It has been shown that SOAR models can be constructed for a number of task domains, but in order to see how complete the field of cognitive processes can be covered, more needs to be known about the mapping of the space of all cognitive activity onto tasks modelled in SOAR.

9 Conclusion from a subjective point of view

Psychology leaves much to be desired, especially in the provision of models with fairly comprehensive capabilities, and in making useful contributions, based on scientific method and theory, for solving real-world problems. One main criticism is that psychological theories and data are too limited and fragmented into unrelated pieces, and need to be more closely integrated.

I would like to predict that what we see in SOAR today gives us a glimpse of what psychology will be like in the future. SOAR, and all similar efforts, will have to overcome the problem of model identification. The final test as a model for psychology is the mapping of observed intelligent behaviour into a scientific language. This language should be as universal as possible, in the same way as geometry, differential calculus and predicate logic. A single person cannot work out everything from scratch. We therefore need a common language which will give us a means to communicate and compare models – as it is, we only look at verbal reports, often very long, of what models, expert systems and other artificial-intelligence constructs can do. The first test, of course, is the implementation of some interesting models, but to proceed to a generally useful cognitive architecture, it will be necessary to compare architectures, models and data, as well as to identify the required features. The form such a tool can take must resemble SOAR, which has been made available as a tool to program cognitive models.

But in order to test whether we really have a *"system to perform the full range of cognitive tasks"* data are needed which represent these tasks. Experimental data, for well-known reasons, are often collected from simple experimental tasks. To test a working model against such data is not trivial, but a conclusive test based on equally reliable data (covering *"...the full range of cognitive tasks"*) must be available – experimental psychology and the building of models really must coexist.

References

Anderson, J.R. (1983) *The architecture of Cognition*, Cambridge, MA: Harvard University Press.

Bösser, T. (1987) Learning in man-computer interaction. A review of the literature, *Esprit Research Reports, Vol. 1*, Heidelberg: Springer Verlag.

Card, S.K., Moran, T.P. and Newell, A. (1983) *The psychology of human-computer interaction*, Hillsdale, NJ: Lawrence Erlbaum Associates.

Guthrie, E.R. (1952) *The psychology of learning*, New York: Harper.

Laird, J.E., Rosenbloom, P.S. and Newell, A. (1986) Chunking in SOAR: The anatomy of a general learning mechanism, *Machine Learning, 1*, 11-46.

Newell, A and Simon, H.A. (1972) *Human problem solving*, Englewood Cliffs, NJ: Prentice Hall.

Rumelhart, D.E. and McClelland, J.L. (eds) (1986) *Parallel distributed processing*, Cambridge, MA: MIT Press.

Sibly, R. and McFarland, D.J. (1974) A state-space approach to motivation. In: D.J. McFarland (ed.), *Motivational control systems analysis*, London: Academic Press, 213-250.

Skinner, E.F. (1938) *The behaviour of organisms*, New York: Appleton-Century Crofts.

Steier, D.M., Laird, J.E., Newell, A., Rosenbloom, P.S., Flynn, R.A., Golding, A., Polk, T.A., Shivers, O.G., Unruh, A. and Yost, G.R. (1987) Varieties of learning in SOAR, paper presented at the 4th International Workshop on Machine Learning.

Thorndike, E.L. (1898) Animal intelligence, *Psychological Review, Monograph Supplement 2, No. 8.*

CHAPTER 32

A Comparative Analysis of Chunking and Decision-Analytic Control

O. Etzioni, University of Washington, and T. M. Mitchell, Carnegie Mellon University

1 Introduction

An increasing number of AI researchers are being seduced by visions of an adaptive, domain-independent, and meta-level uniform architecture for an autonomous agent [Laird *et al.*, 1987, Russell and Wefald, 1989, Mitchell *et al.*, 1991]. A fundamental problem facing any such agent is the problem of controlling its search processes. The above conceptions agree that the agent ought to utilize its problem-solving experiences to reduce its search in a given task-environment.

The visions differ widely, however, in the mechanisms they propose for achieving this compilation of past experience, the representations proposed for learned knowledge, and the decision procedures that operate over the representations. A central point of divergence is the role of decision theory in controlling an agent's reasoning or planning. Several researchers (e.g., [Russell and Wefald, 1989, Smith, 1988]) are developing decision-analytic control mechanisms, whereas for others (e.g., [Laird *et al.*, 1987, Mitchell *et al.*, 1991]) decision-theoretic notions are conspicuously absent. This paper suggests that the key property by which to evaluate a compilation/control mechanism is its convergence towards a quickly computable function from problems to optimal (or merely acceptable) solutions. The paper explores the differences between exemplars of the two approaches by focusing on the convergence properties of each, and concludes by suggesting a simple combination of the two mechanisms that retains the desirable features of both, and ameliorates their weaknesses.

*This paper originally appeared in the Working Notes of the 1989 AAAI Spring Symposium on AI and Limited Rationality. The reader is referred to [Etzioni, 1991] for a more comprehensive treatment of many of the issues raised here.

2 The General Picture

Below we sketch in simple and general terms the picture that most if not all of the researchers working on domain-independent architectures for autonomous agents seem to share. An agent has a set of actions at its disposal represented by a set of operators that transform the state of the world. Given an initial state and a set of goal states, the agent attempts to find a sequence of operators that will allow it to transform the world from the initial state to a goal state. We may view the agent as computing a function from problem specifications (initial state, and goal set pairs) to operator sequences that solve the problems.[1] If no solution exists to the problem then the agent indicates this to be the case. We refer to this function as the *problem-solving function*. A central concern in developing adaptive architectures is enabling the agent to compute this function more efficiently with experience.

We can abstract away from the details of computing the problem-solving function by modeling the computation as a function that given a problem specification and the agent's current state outputs the agent's next (mental) action. We refer to this function as the agent's *control function*. A good control function enables the agent to quickly compute the problem-solving function. An adaptive architecture begins problem solving in a given domain with some default control function—depth-first search for Soar, Theo, and Prodigy ([Laird *et al.*, 1987, Mitchell *et al.*, 1991, Minton *et al.*, 1989]). Problem-solving experiences enable the architecture to modify its control function so that the problem-solving function is computed more quickly. The following sections explore two distinct approaches to computing the control function.

[1]Strictly speaking we have not specified a function because more than one solution is possible for some problems, but this lacuna is easily filled.

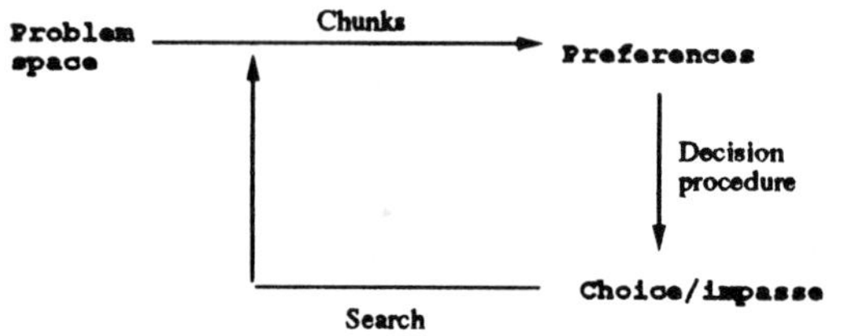

Figure 1: Chunking

3 Preferential Control

Architectures such as Prodigy and Soar compile their problem-solving experiences into preference rules. A preference rule is an if-then rule whose antecedent specifies the class of problems to which it applies, and whose consequent side specifies a preference relation between one object (Such as an operator or a goal) and others. A preference rule to travel from New York to San Francisco by air could be represented as follows: "if goal=San Francisco and state=New York then select(fly)". The consequent may be absolute as in this example, or relative as in prefer(fly,walk). Preference rules may be learned as a result of a variety of problem-solving experiences including success and failure. A preference rule for rejection is learned as a result of failure.

For concreteness this paper will focus on Soar as an exemplar of architectures that employ a preferential control mechanisms. Using Soar's terminology we will refer to preference rules as chunks. When Soar terminates search in a problem space it creates a chunk that compiles that problem-solving experience for future use. Thus, once Soar has solved a problem it has chunks corresponding to the successful solution of that problem and to the solutions of any subgoals posed in the course of solving the problem. Consequently, if Soar encounters a similar subsequent problem it can apply its learned chunks to the new problem. If none of Soar's chunks apply to a problem, it faces an impasse that is resolved by its default search mechanisms.

What does this amount to in terms of the control and problem-solving functions introduced earlier? Each newly acquired chunk modifies the control function and thus speeds up the computation of the problem-solving function for problems that match the antecedents of the learned chunks. Given N options, a selection preference (compiled after a success) provides an immediate choice so that the N options are reduced to 1. A rejection preference (compiled after a failure) reduces the number of choices available by the number of choices that match its antecedent. A schematic depiction of Soar's control mechanism appears in Figure 1.

3.1 Analyzing Preferential Control

The best case for a preferential control mechanism occurs when all the problems it will encounter are subsumed by one top level chunk. Then, having solved one problem the agent is able to speedily solve all other problems. The worst case occurs when the chunks acquired by the agent never apply. Then, the agent pays the computational overhead of trying to match its chunks to the world without any benefit. By and large, of course, neither case will hold and the efficacy of preferential compilation will depend on the number of chunks required to subsume a significant portion of the problems that the agent will be asked to solve.

An important feature of preferential control is the agent's ability to exert a measure of control over its world, and thereby influence the distribution of problem instances that it will encounter. If the agent is able to decompose new problems with which it is presented into subproblems that it already knows how to solve, it will increase the coverage of the compiled portions of the problem-solving function.

On the negative side, preferential control architectures have generally assumed that their operators provide a complete and correct model of a static world. Consequently, little attention has been paid to the problem of incorrect or uncertain compilation of problem-solving experience. Noisy domains, uncertain, contradictory, or incomplete information, and changing environments raise serious problems for a preferential compilation mechanism. Although the mechanisms for coping with these problems seem to be available in Soar ([Laird, 1988]) no well-motivated policy has been put forth for utilizing the mechanisms. Furthermore, it is not clear how a preferential control mechanism will take account of the agent's resource limitations and risk-taking policy in a principled manner. The above considerations suggest that a preferential control mechanism may be fruitfully augmented with a decision-analytic one.

4 Decision-Analytic Control

Decision-analytic control schemes employ heuristic approximations to decision theoretic formulae in order to compute the control function. We chose the SE system [Etzioni, 1988, Mitchell *et al.*, 1991] as our exemplar of decision-analytic control since we are most familiar with it. We believe that our analysis applies equally well to the decision-analytic control mechanisms reported by [Simon and Kadane, 1975, Sproull, 1977, Smith, 1988, Russell and Wefald, 1989].

SE is a decision-analytic control mechanism that operates within the Theo software framework for constructing autonomous agents. Like Soar's chunking mechanism, SE proceeds by mapping problem instances to classes and using beliefs formed about these classes to guide problem solving behavior. SE differs from

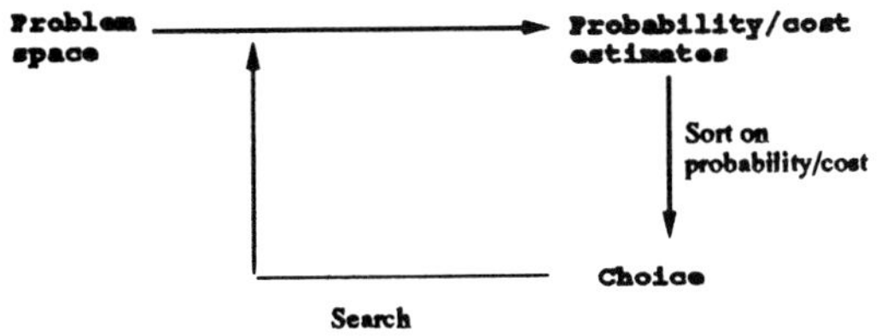

Figure 2: Decision-Analytic Compilation/Control

chunking, however, in how it maps problem instances to classes, in the beliefs associated with the problem classes, and in the decision procedure that uses the beliefs to choose an action.

SE's operation is best illustrated by an example. Consider the problem of inferring the volume of Cube1. Suppose that two methods are available for solving problems of this sort: inheriting the volume from a superclass, and computing it from its definition. Suppose further that SE maps this problem to the class of problems of inferring geometrical properties of polygonal objects. Based on its experience with this class SE estimates the probability of success and expected cost of each method. SE sorts the two methods on the ratio of the estimated probability of success to the expected cost[2] and executes them in that order.

Thus, SE's decision procedure is fixed (just sorting the methods). It corresponds to Soar's decision procedure. SE's estimates of cost and probability of success are what SE extracts from Theo's previous problem-solving experiences. SE's mapping of problem instances to problem classes corresponds to the matching of the antecedent of Soar's chunks. SE's estimates correspond to the consequents of Soar's chunks, because both represent what each compilation mechanism extracts from its problem solver's past experiences. A depiction of SE's control mechanism appears in Figure 2.

4.1 Analyzing Decision-Analytic Control

It is instructive to think of SE in statistical terms. SE maps problem instances to populations of problems, and uses samples from these populations to estimate the cost and probability of success for the problem instances. Sample means are used to form the estimates. The mean of a population is a good predictor for points in that population when the variance of the population is low [Etzioni, 1988]. We refer to such populations as homogeneous.

One best case for decision-analytic control occurs when it is able to find homogeneous populations. In that case even small samples yield highly reliable estimates that may be used to control the problem solver. Another best case occurs when the options are very clearly differentiated. Suppose one method is considerably cheaper and more likely to succeed than another in a given context. The first method is said to strongly *dominate* the second. When this is the case, even small samples are likely to result in appropriate control of the problem solver. The worst case for the decision-analytic mechanism occurs when it is unable to find either homogeneous populations or dominating methods. Then, its estimates will frequently lead it to choose suboptimal methods, and the problem-solving function will be computed slowly.

5 Decision-Analytic Control versus Preferential Control

We are now in a position to compare the two mechanisms. Both compilation mechanisms attempt to use past problem solving to guide future problem solving. Both mechanisms do so by mapping each new problem instance to problem classes, and by using beliefs about the problem classes to guide the solution of the instance. However, each mechanism represents the "lessons" of past problem-solving in a different fashion. The preferential mechanism extracts chunks that apply to classes of problems from single problem-solving episodes. In contrast, the decision-analytic mechanism acquires estimates of the cost and probability of success of methods over problem classes.

Whereas the class to which a chunk applies is (more or less) determined by the problem-solving episode from which it was extracted, estimated costs and probabilities can be computed for arbitrary classes. They simply represent the average of experiences from the given class. This observation points to two key differences between preferential and decision-analytic compilation. First, preferential compilation generates classes of problems, whereas decision-analytic compilation does not. Second, the "advice" of the preferential control mechanism extends to the generated classes of problems, and to no others. In contrast, the decision-analytic mechanism can offer advice for any problem class.

Consequently, the different compilation/control mechanisms will have different modes of convergence to the optimal control function. Over time, the preferential mechanism increases its coverage over the domain of the problem-solving function—the function can be computed quickly for increasingly large portions of the domain as the agent accumulates experience. If the preferential mechanism encounters a problem (or subproblem) not covered by its chunks, however, it offers no guidance to the computation of the problem-solving function. The control function is computed in the architecture's default manner. In contrast, the decision-analytic mechanism rapidly covers any control decision

[2]See [Etzioni, 1989] for a theoretical analysis of this formula.

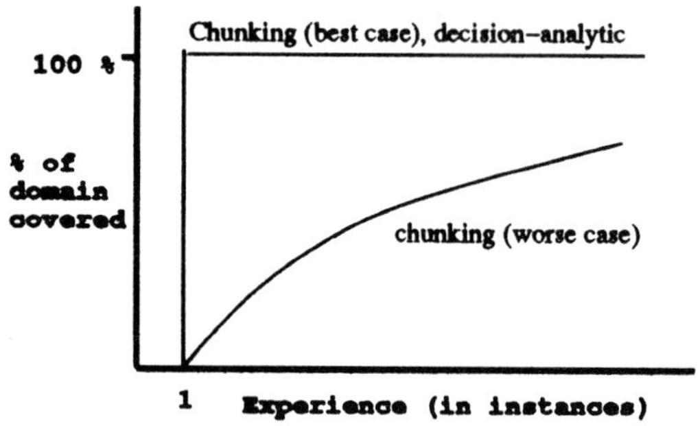

Figure 3: How the coverage of the control mechanisms improves with experience.

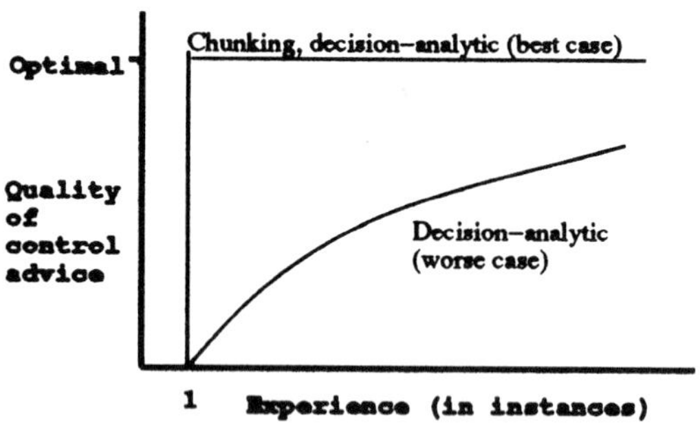

Figure 4: How the quality of the control advice improves with experience.

the architecture needs to make (see Figure 3).

The quality of the mechanism's advice improves, however, with the proximity of the estimates on which it is based to the truth, and with the refinement of the advice to different problem-classes. Additional data points enable the mechanism to refine its estimates, to converge to the optimal control function, and thus to speed up the computation of the problem-solving function. In contrast, the quality of the chunks' control advice is uniformly high, assuming that a correct and complete model produces the chunks (see Figure 4). It is important to note that the decision-analytic mechanism is not committed to a particular discipline for forming classes over the problem-solving function's domain. The decision-analytic mechanism may even use chunking to suggest homogeneous problem classes. We return to this idea in Section 5.2.

The implementations of the control mechanisms we have described differ in a variety of ways. For example, Theo indexes control knowledge by placing the knowledge in the appropriate locations on its object generalization hierarchies, whereas Soar uses a Rete network to find applicable chunks. Furthermore, the two architectures employ different impasses to move from ground-level problem solving to the meta-level. While these are clearly important architectural issues, we view them as orthogonal to the issue of decision-analytic control simply because SE's control mechanism could have been implemented in Soar. Likewise, a chunking mechanism is built into Theo. We have focused, therefore, on the convergence properties of Soar and Theo's distinct compilation/control mechanisms.

5.1 Convergence

On the one hand, we do not expect a domain-independent architecture to efficiently solve problems in a given task-environment at the outset. On the other hand, even a rote learner will *eventually* display significantly improved performance on a population of problems. Hence, it seems that the meaningful measure by which to assess a compilation/control mechanism is its ability to converge to a quickly computable problem-solving function. Figures 3 and 4 provide a rough and ready vocabulary for analyzing convergence. While we are not ready to report on a formal analysis of convergence, some general observations can be made:

- The efficacy of the preferential mechanism depends on its ability to provide guidance for portions of the problem-solving function's domain from which future problems will be drawn. This idea may be formalized in terms of the probability of encountering an instance that matches the antecedent of a learned chunk. This probability increases with three factors:

- Nonuniformity in the distribution of problems (as pointed out in [Mitchell *et al.*, 1986]).
- The correspondence between the chunk's antecedent and the skew in the problem distribution. Chunks are most useful when they cover instances that are likely to be encountered.
- The antecedent's ability to cover many distinct problem instances with nonzero probabilities of occurrence. Thus, even if the probability of encountering each individual instance is low, the cumulative probability of matching the antecedent may be high.

- Powerful generalization is sufficient to guarantee successful preferential compilation. On a uniform distribution of problems, generalization appears to be the only way in which preferential compilation can achieve significant coverage.
- Unless the distribution is so nonuniform that caching of solution sequences will succeed, the ability to generalize to 'likely' problems is necessary. Otherwise, even on a nonuniform distribution, the compilation mechanism may generalize to problems that have zero probability of appearing.
- The preferential mechanism offers no guidance at all on portions of the problem-solving function's domain for which chunks have not yet been compiled (Figure 3).
- The performance of the preferential mechanism degrades as the correctness and completeness of its world model deteriorate.

Additional observations can be made regarding decision-analytic mechanisms:

- The decision-analytic mechanism is likely to rapidly lead to some improvement in the performance of the architecture over the entire domain of the problem-solving function.
- However, converging towards optimal problem-solving requires that the decision-analytic mechanism decompose the problem-solving function's domain into homogeneous subdomains, or at least subdomains in which clearly dominant methods emerge.
- The decision-analytic mechanism offers little insight for generating the desired subdomains, but is able to recognize them once they are generated.
- The decision-analytic mechanism is robust to noisy, changing, and uncertain domains. It will tolerate contradictions in its data and an imperfect world model with gracefully degraded performance.

5.2 Synergy

The above observations suggest that the two compilation/control mechanisms are in fact complementary. Indeed, the Theo framework currently supports prototypes of both. The decision-analytic mechanism augments the preferential mechanism in three important ways. First, the decision-analytic mechanism provides guidance when no chunks apply. Second, keeping statistical records enables the agent to evaluate (and thus to discard or strengthen) the preferences formed.[3] Third, the decision-analytic mechanism provides the ability to handle noisy data and imperfect theories. The preferential mechanism, in turn, serves the critical role of generating problem classes for which statistical averages may be kept.

6 Conclusion

This paper has contrasted preferential control with decision-analytic control. We have argued that the two mechanisms ought to be evaluated in terms of their ability to converge to rapid problem-solving behavior in a variety of task environments—an issue that requires further study. Our preliminary analysis indicates that, over time, preferential compilation/control covers an increasing portion of the environment, whereas decision-analytic compilation/control covers the whole environment increasingly well (Figures 3 and 4). The complementary nature of the two mechanisms suggests that they may be crossed to yield synergistic fruit.

Acknowledgments

We would like to thank Jonathan Amsterdam, Haym Hirsh, Craig Knoblock, Dan Kuokka, Lije Millgram, Milind Tambe, and especially David Steier for helpful comments on a previous draft. The first author was supported by an AT&T Bell Labs Ph.D. Scholarship. This research was sponsored by the National Science Foundation under contract IRI-8740522.

References

[Etzioni, 1988] Etzioni, Oren 1988. Hypothesis filtering: A practical approach to reliable learning. In *Proceedings of the Fifth International Conference on Machine Learning*, Ann Arbor, MI. Morgan Kaufmann. 416–429.

[Etzioni, 1989] Etzioni, Oren 1989. Tractable decision-analytic control. In *Proceedings of the First International Conference on Principles of Knowledge Representation and Reasoning*. Morgan Kaufmann. An expanded version is available as technical report CMU-CS-89-119.

[3] This idea was originally propounded by Minton [1987].

[Etzioni, 1991] Etzioni, Oren 1991. Embedding decision-analytic control in a learning architecture. *Artificial Intelligence* 49(1–3):129–160.

[Laird *et al.*, 1987] Laird, J. E.; Newell, A.; and Rosenbloom, P. S. 1987. Soar: An architecture for general intelligence. *Artificial Intelligence* 33:1–64.

[Laird, 1988] Laird, John E. 1988. Recovery from incorrect knowledge in soar. In *Proceedings of the Seventh National Conference on Artificial Intelligence*. Morgan Kaufmann.

[Minton *et al.*, 1987] Minton, Steven; Carbonell, Jaime G.; Etzioni, Oren; Knoblock, Craig A.; and Kuokka, Daniel R. 1987. Acquiring effective search control rules: Explanation-based learning in the Prodigy system. In *Proceedings of the Fourth International Workshop on Machine Learning*.

[Minton *et al.*, 1989] Minton, Steven; Carbonell, Jaime G.; Knoblock, Craig A.; Kuokka, Daniel R.; Etzioni, Oren; and Gil, Yolanda 1989. Explanation-based learning: A problem-solving perspective. *Artificial Intelligence* 40:63–118. Available as technical report CMU-CS-89-103.

[Mitchell *et al.*, 1986] Mitchell, Tom M.; Keller, Rich; and Kedar-Cabelli, Smadar 1986. Explanation-based generalization: A unifying view. *Machine Learning* 1(1).

[Mitchell *et al.*, 1991] Mitchell, Tom M.; Allen, John; Chalasani, Prasad; Cheng, John; Etzioni, Oren; Ringuette, Marc; and Schlimmer, Jeffrey C. 1991. Theo: A framework for self-improving systems. In VanLehn, K., editor 1991, *Architectures for Intelligence*. Erlbaum.

[Russell and Wefald, 1989] Russell, Stuart and Wefald, Eric 1989. Principles of metareasoning. In *Proceedings of the First International Conference on Principles of Knowledge Representation and Reasoning*, Toronto, Canada. Morgan Kaufmann. 400–411.

[Simon and Kadane, 1975] Simon, Herbert A. and Kadane, Joseph B. 1975. Optimal problem-solving search: All-or-none solutions. *Artificial Intelligence* 6(3):235–247.

[Smith, 1988] Smith, David E. 1988. A decision-theoretic approach to the control of planning search. Technical Report LOGIC-87-11, Stanford Logic Group. Draft.

[Sproull, 1977] Sproull, Robert F. 1977. Strategy construction using a synthesis of heuristic and decision-theoretic methods. Technical Report CSL-77-2, Xerox PARC.

CHAPTER 33

Toward a Soar Theory of Taking Instructions for Immediate Reasoning Tasks

R. L. Lewis, A. Newell, and T. A. Polk, Carnegie Mellon University

Abstract
Soar is a theory of the human cognitive architecture. We present here the Soar theory of taking instructions for *immediate reasoning* tasks, which involve extracting implicit information from simple situations in a few tens of seconds. This theory is realized in a computer system that comprehends simple English instructions and organizes itself to perform a required task. Comprehending instructions produces a *model of future behavior* that is interpretively executed to yield task behavior. Soar thereby acquires task-specific problem spaces that, together with basic reasoning capabilities, model human performance in multiple immediate reasoning tasks. By providing an account of taking instructions, we reduce the *degrees of freedom* available to our theory of immediate reasoning, and also give more support for Soar as a unified theory of cognition.

Soar is a theory of human cognition (Newell, 1989), embodied in a computer system. Soar specifies the cognitive architecture, which is the relatively fixed set of mechanisms that permit goals and knowledge of the task environment to be encoded in memory and brought to bear to produce behavior. Soar is proposed as a unified theory of cognition, and it has been applied to human behavior in a broad spectrum of domains. This paper reports progress in getting Soar to take instructions and organize itself to perform a required task.

There are three important reasons for wanting a theory of instructions. First, taking instructions is a domain of cognitive activity, with interesting phenomena and practical importance. Any unified theory of cognition must ultimately provide such a theory. Second, a major issue for psychology has always been the radical underdetermination of theory by data. Though an issue for all sciences, it is particularly irksome for psychology (and the social sciences) because humans bring massive knowledge to a task and dynamically organize themselves accordingly. Taking instructions to perform tasks is an important instance of such self-organization (e.g., as it takes place in psychological experiments). By specifying how task specific organization arises from instructions, a theory of instruction comprehension would go some way toward removing what can be called *theory degrees of freedom*. Instructions are only one source of knowledge determining behavior, but understanding them could pave the way for dealing with other sources. Third, including both instruction taking and task performance in the same theoretical account provides mutual constraint. This constraint is an instance of the gains to be made from a unified theory of cognition.

In this paper we take some steps toward a theory of instruction taking.[1] The system we present here, NL-Soar, comprehends instructions given in elementary English for *immediate reasoning* tasks, such as the *relational reasoning* task (Johnson-Laird, 1988) shown in Figure 1. This comprehension is part of a system, IR-Soar, that models the way humans perform immediate reasoning (reported in a companion paper (Polk, Newell & Lewis, 1989)). Here we focus on the internal representation of instructions, how

[1]Building on earlier work in (Newell, 1989, Chap. 7; Yost & Newell, 1988).

Instructions

Read four premises. Then read a statement. If the statement is true say "true". Then stop.

Task input

Premises	A plate is left of a knife. A fork is left of the plate. A jug is above the knife. The fork is below a cup.
Statement	The cup is left of the jug.

Figure 1: **Relational reasoning task.**

Soar organizes itself to do the task, and the associated psychological claims. The process of comprehending the language of instructions to create these representations is also part of the total theory, and involves both linguistic and psycholinguistic issues. Although we do not deal with these issues here, NL-Soar does embody a theory of language comprehension (Newell, 1989, Chap. 8). We also do not present direct behavioral evidence for instruction taking. For the moment, the psychological relevance of the instruction taking is that it leads to an organization of IR-Soar that explains how people do immediate reasoning tasks.

There has been relatively little work on the psychology of instruction taking. The most notable was the UNDERSTAND program (Simon & Hayes, 1979), which took instructions for the Tower of Hanoi and constructed a problem space in which to do the task. Our account is consonant with the broad thrust of that work, the main advances being in the plausibility of the processes and representations used, and in the embedding of this in a unified theory. Our account is also consonant with the implications from ACT* (Anderson, 1983): that conversion from declarative to procedural form occurs by an interpretive process that leads to creating chunks of conditional behavior (productions).

We first present the psychological claims of the Soar theory of taking instructions, and in passing review the basic assumptions of the Soar architecture. We then illustrate the theory by tracing the behavior of the system in detail on the relational reasoning task in Figure 1. Finally, we briefly describe how the theory has been applied to two other immediate reasoning tasks.

THE SOAR THEORY OF TAKING INSTRUCTIONS

Soar as a cognitive architecture has been described in several places (Laird, Newell & Rosenbloom, 1987) and we will take its major outlines to be familiar. All tasks are formulated in *problem spaces*; all long term knowledge is held in a *recognition memory* (realized as productions); processing proceeds by a sequence of *decision cycles* that accumulate knowledge about what spaces, states and operators to select; *subgoals* are generated in an attempt to resolve *impasses* that occur when the decision-making knowledge is insufficient or conflicting; and the experience gained in resolving impasses is learned in the form of *chunks* (new productions in recognition memory).

One additional assumption is that states in problem spaces are *annotated models*.[2] Models consist of

[2]This is not yet an architectural assumption for Soar, which only assumes a representation consisting of attributes and values.

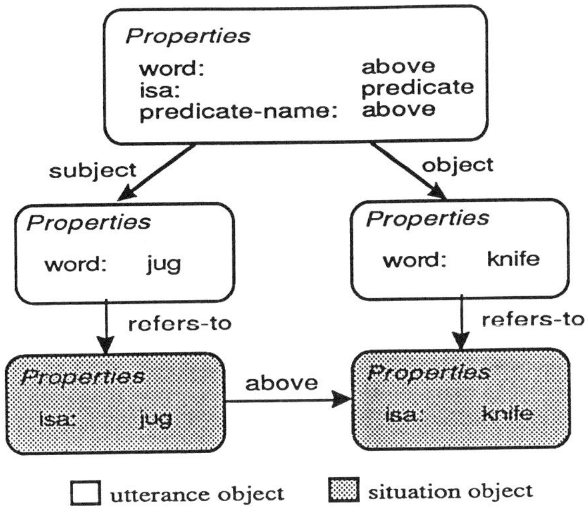

Figure 2: **Utterance and situation models for "A jug is above the knife."**

objects, properties, and relations (model elements) and satisfy the semantic assumption that each element in the representation corresponds to an element in the referent. This assumption may be violated in principled ways by attaching annotations to model elements. An annotation specifies a non-standard interpretation for the single element to which it is attached (e.g., an element annotated **many** corresponds to multiple elements in the referent). There are computational advantages to processing annotated models and there is also evidence that humans use them (Johnson-Laird, 1983; Polk & Newell, 1988). We do not review these considerations, but simply assume annotated models. Beyond these assumptions, the Soar theory of taking instructions embodies the following psychological claims:

1. **Situation model.** The objective of comprehending an utterance is to represent the situation that the utterance is about. To do so, comprehension builds a *model of the situation.*
2. **Utterance model.** As a processing side effect, comprehension produces a *model of the utterance*—a model that reflects the logical form of the utterance, and that can be interpreted as the abstract proposition or description asserted by the utterance.
3. **Behavior model.** If instructions are comprehended, the situation model that comprehension produces is a *model of the subject's future behavior.*
4. **Performance by interpretation.** Task performance proceeds initially by *interpretively executing* the behavior model. During this interpretation process, chunks are learned that directly perform the task.

The theory of comprehension

Comprehension (construction of the situation model) occurs in the **comprehend** problem space by applying a *comprehension operator* to each incoming word (Newell, 1989). These operators iteratively

---

Nevertheless, the current work in Soar on human cognition assumes models (Newell, 1989, Chap. 7; Polk & Newell, 1988).

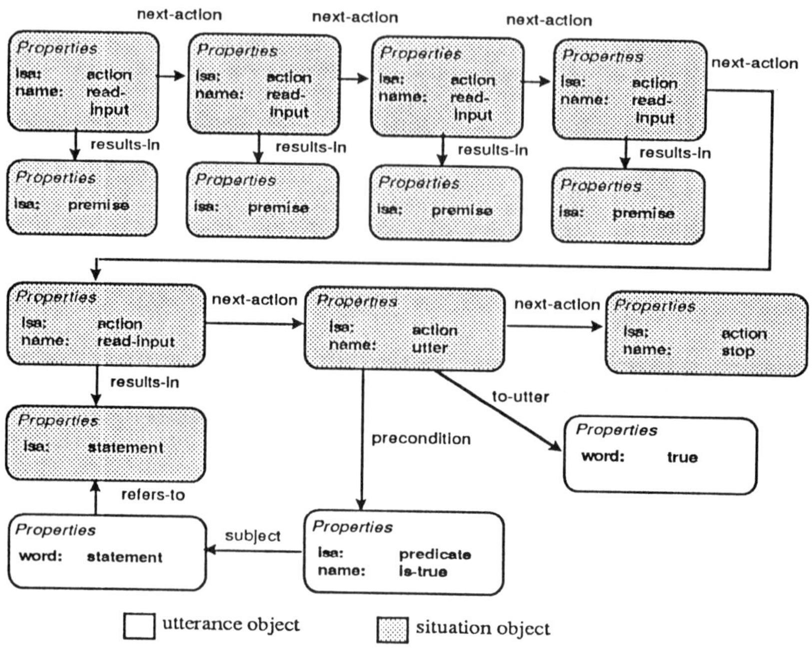

Figure 3: **Behavior model for the relational reasoning task of Figure 1.**

augment and refine the situation model as the utterance is comprehended. Figure 2, bottom, shows a simple situation model produced by **comprehend** for the third premise of Figure 1.

Since all the knowledge that a word contributes to an utterance may not be available at the moment the word is read, the comprehension process must have some means of holding partial comprehension knowledge. In the **comprehend** space, this knowledge is held by *expectation* data structures. Expectations can be syntactic, semantic, or pragmatic. In particular, part of what is delivered by a comprehension operator for a word is knowledge about what is expected to come in the rest of the utterance. Thus, there must be some way of modeling the utterance itself. The utterance model that serves this processing requirement is a structured linguistic form. As comprehension proceeds, it evolves into a model that reflects the underlying logical form of the utterance. In contrast to the situation model, the utterance model is closer to a predicate calculus-like language.

As an example, Figure 2, top, gives the final utterance model for "A jug is above the knife." [3] It is useful to compare the two models in this figure. The objects in the situation model correspond to the jug and knife in the situation, and the relation "above" corresponds to the spatial relation in the situation. In contrast, the objects in the utterance model correspond to linguistic objects that can be interpreted as predicates and arguments. Thus, "above" in the utterance model corresponds to the predicate "above", and the relations correspond to relations between the predicate and its arguments. Since objects in the utterance model originate as words, the language of predicates is as rich as the

[3]The utterance model in this figure is actually somewhat simplified for expository purposes.

natural language expressing the utterance.

The utterance model is not a deliberate product of comprehension; it is the means by which **comprehend** deals with language. However, since some knowledge cannot be encoded in the situation model (e.g., universal quantification), the total knowledge provided by an utterance may reside jointly in both models.

The theory of task performance

Comprehending instructions produces a model that represents future actions to be taken. An element in a behavior model corresponds to an action or an object related to an action (such as the expected input or output). For example, the model in Figure 3, produced by NL-Soar for the task of Figure 1, specifies that the task begins with four acts of reading input, and that each act should yield a premise.

After reading the instructions, the system attempts to perform the task. It is initially unable to proceed, because it lacks operational knowledge of the task in recognition memory (the knowledge is in the static data structures of the behavior model). This leads to interpreting the behavior model. Earlier work with Soar has shown how such processes can yield chunks that directly implement the task and bypass interpretation (Yost & Newell, 1988; Newell, 1989). Currently, this capability is embodied in BI-Soar (behavior-model interpretation), a set of problem spaces that are independent of NL-Soar and IR-Soar. For immediate reasoning tasks, the interpretation of the behavior model gives rise to problem spaces whose operators are implemented in the three basic IR-Soar spaces (**comprehend**, **test-proposition**, and **build-proposition**). Polk, Newell & Lewis (1989) show that the task spaces so acquired can indeed be used to model human performance.

AN EXAMPLE: RELATIONAL REASONING

We illustrate the theory by tracing through the task of Figure 1. Figure 4 shows the behavior of the system as it comprehends the instructions and attempts to perform the task. The system begins in the **read** problem space (see (1) in Figure 4), and applies a series of comprehend-input operators to read the instructions. Each operator application comprehends one statement, and builds up the behavior model accordingly. (2) The comprehend-input operator is implemented in the **comprehend** space, where a series of comprehension operators fire for each incoming word. These operators actually fire multiple times as expectations build up and are satisfied.

(3) Processing continues until comprehension of the word "begin," which the system takes to mean it should start the task. (4) It deliberately sets the goal of doing the task by selecting the do-new-task operator. (5) Since the knowledge required to perform the task is not directly available in recognition memory, Soar impasses and creates a new problem space (**relation**) to implement the operator.

(6) Once in the **relation** space, Soar impasses again because it has no operators to propose for this new space. Resolving the impasse requires consulting the behavior model for what to do next. (7) This is the function of the **fetch-operator** problem space (a space of BI-Soar), which contains the knowledge required to locate the next action in the behavior model and interpret it as an operator in the task space. (8) In this case, the impasse is resolved by selecting read-input, an instantiation of the comprehend-input operator that will yield a premise (Figure 3). (9) The premise object from the behavior model is set up

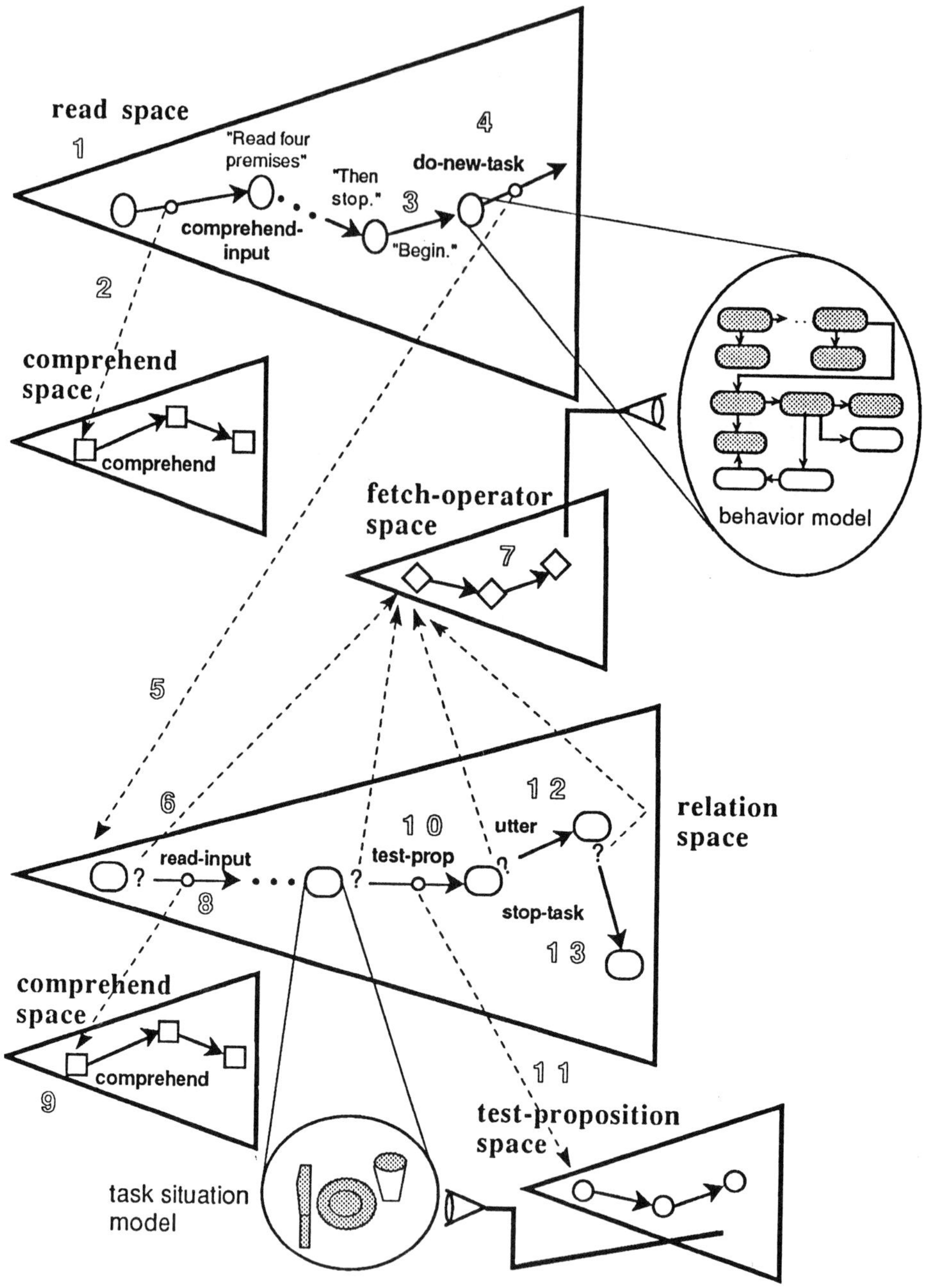

Figure 4: **Acquiring and performing the relational reasoning task.**

Categorical Syllogisms

Instructions	Syllogism space operators
1. Read two premises that share a term.	1. Read-input [comprehend]
2. Then produce a statement that follows from the premises.	2. Make-conclusion [build-proposition]
3. The statement relates the unique terms of the premises.	3. Make-conclusion (goal-test)
4. Then stop.	4. Stop-task

Elementary Sentence Verification

Instructions	ESV space operators
1. Examine the picture.	1. Read-input [comprehend]
2. Then read a statement.	2. Read-input [comprehend]
3. If the statement is true press the t-button.	3. Test-prop [test-proposition]
4. If the statement is false press the f-button.	4. Test-prop [test-proposition]
5. Then stop.	5. Stop-task

Figure 5: **Other immediate reasoning tasks.**

as an expectation in the **comprehend** space, and thus provides the goal test for read-input.

This *impasse-fetch-apply* cycle continues until Soar arrives at the utter action in the behavior model. This action has a precondition (namely, that the statement just read is true), interpreted as a proposition (Figure 3). This proposition originated as part of the utterance model for one of the comprehended instructions. (10) Determining if this action should be taken requires verifying the proposition, so the impasse in the **relation** space is resolved by selecting the test-prop operator. (11) This operator is implemented in the **test-proposition** space, one of the three basic IR-Soar problem spaces (Polk, Newell & Lewis, 1989). (12) Once the proposition has been verified by consulting the situation model, the **fetch-operator** space selects and instantiates the utter operator in the next fetch cycle. (13) Finally, the stop-task operator is selected and terminates the task.

OTHER TASKS

NL-BI-Soar has acquired two other immediate reasoning tasks. Figure 5 shows the instructions and problem-spaces for the elementary sentence verification task (Clark & Chase, 1972), and the categorical syllogisms task. As in the relational reasoning task, task-specific behavior arises by interpreting the behavior model, and applying operators in the new task space that are implemented in IR-Soar's **comprehend, test-proposition,** or **build-proposition** problem spaces[4].

The elementary sentence verification task differs from relational reasoning in the simplicity of the initial situation, and the form used to present the situation (a picture). The latter difference shows up in the behavior model as a comprehend-input action that expects a picture rather than a linguistic utterance. The difference in simplicity is a function of the task input, not the task instructions.

The syllogisms task (Polk, Newell & Lewis, 1989) is interesting because the subject must utter a conclusion that conforms to a particular specification given in the instructions— namely, that the conclusion relate the *unique terms of the premises.* Soar realizes this as an application of the build-proposition operator instantiated to relate the correct terms. Knowledge in the comprehension operators for the words "unique" and "relate" leads to construction of the appropriate behavior model

[4]NL-Soar will deal with the conditional reasoning and Wason tasks, which are the additional examples in (Polk, Newell & Lewis, 1989); as of submission of this paper, the runs are not completed, but no difficulties are expected.

that captures this constraint.

CONCLUSION

We have presented a Soar theory of taking instructions for immediate reasoning tasks. This theory is implemented in two collections of Soar problem spaces, NL-Soar and BI-Soar. NL-Soar uses the **comprehend** problem space to read simple English statements and produce an annotated model of the situation being described. As a side effect of comprehending these statements, **comprehend** produces a model that reflects the logical form of the utterance. When reading task instructions, **comprehend** creates a model of the behavior described by the instructions. By repeatedly consulting this behavior model, BI-Soar can acquire the problem spaces necessary to perform the task.

Besides being interesting in its own right, this theory opens up some interesting possibilities. For one, it begins to significantly alleviate the problem of the underdetermination of theories by data. In a companion paper (Polk, Newell & Lewis, 1989), we have presented a theory of immediate reasoning that depends on the task-specific problem spaces that arise from the instructions given to NL-Soar. The degrees of freedom available to that theory are significantly reduced as a result. Further, the two subtheories of taking instructions and immediate reasoning mutually constrain each other, making both significantly stronger. For instance, it is not an independent assumption of the immediate reasoning theory that both the utterance model and the situation model are available as sources of knowledge to do the task. Similarly, the problem spaces acquired through task instructions must be used to model behavior in immediate reasoning tasks, significantly constraining the theory presented here. Finally, this theory represents another step toward making Soar a unified theory of cognition.

Acknowledgements

Many thanks to Erik Altmann, Norma Pribadi, Kathryn Swedlow, and Shirley Tessler for useful comments and invaluable assistance in preparing the draft and the figures, as well as to Chris Tuck for helping bridge the Pittsburgh-Ann Arbor gap. This work was supported by the Information Sciences Division, Office of Naval Research, under contract N00014-86-K-0678, and by the National Science Foundation and Kodak fellowship programs in which Richard Lewis and Thad Polk, respectively, participate. The views expressed in this paper are those of the authors and do not necessarily reflect those of the supporting agencies. Reproduction in whole or in part is permitted for any purpose of the United States government. Approved for public release; distribution unlimited.

References

Anderson, J. R. (1983). *The Architecture of Cognition.* Harvard University Press, Cambridge, Massachusetts.

Clark, H. and Chase, W. (1972). On the process of comparing sentences against pictures. *Cognitive Psychology, 3*, 472–517.

Johnson-Laird, P. (1988). Reasoning by rule or model? In *Proceedings of the Annual Conference of the Cognitive Science Society*, pages 765–771.

Johnson-Laird, P. N. (1983). *Mental models: Towards a cognitive science of language, inference and consciousness.* Harvard University Press, Cambridge, Massachusetts.

Laird, J. E., Newell, A., and Rosenbloom, P. S. (1987). Soar: An architecture for general intelligence. *Artificial Intelligence, 33(1)*, 1–64.

Newell, A. (1989). *Unified Theories of Cognition.* Harvard University Press, Cambridge, Massachusetts. In press.

Polk, T., Newell, A., and Lewis, R. (1989). Toward a Unified Theory of Immediate Reasoning in Soar. To appear in the Proceedings of the Annual Conference of the Cognitive Science Society, August, 1989.

Polk, T. A. and Newell, A. (1988). Modeling human syllogistic reasoning in Soar. In *Proceedings of the Annual Conference of the Cognitive Science Society*, pages 181–187.

Simon, H. and Hayes, J. (1979). Understanding written problem instructions. In Simon, H., editor, *Models of Thought*, pages 451–476, Yale University Press, New Haven, Conneticut.

Yost, G. R. and Newell, A. (1988). Learning New Tasks in Soar. Unpublished.

Integrating Learning and Problem Solving Within a Chemical Process Designer

A. K. Modi and A. W. Westerberg, Carnegie Mellon University

Abstract. Process design is a complex activity that requires the design agent to possess characteristics currently missing in most artificial design systems. Recent work in cognitive science has resulted in the development of Soar, an integrated software architecture to support the full range of capabilities required of intelligent behaviour. We describe two systems we have developed within the Soar framework to take but a very small step at understanding how learning is accomplished and how it could become a part of future design aids. CPD-Soar is a system for the design of distillation-based separation systems. It demonstrates the chunking mechanism of Soar, showing its usefulness for remembering already solved subproblems within a given problem, but also indicating that the learning is too specific to be of use for a different problem. Interval-Soar is the first system tried in Soar that can learn in situations where decisions are based on quantitative information. It is a system that can learn the intersection point of two arbitrary functions whose forms are unknown to it. We discuss the performance of both systems and indicate how the functionality of a system like Interval-Soar could be used to further improve the performance of a system such as CPD-Soar whose domain is highly quantitative.

1 Introduction

Design is a significant activity within all industry, including that dealing with chemical processes. Every year, enormous amounts of resources are committed to design and design-related activities. Westerberg [Westerberg 88, p. 2] states, "Several industrial studies have shown that design typically consumes about 10 to 15 per cent of the resources used to create a new product, but the decisions made in this step generally fix 70 to 80 per cent of the final product costs." Automating the design process, i.e., moving it into the machine, even partly, offers two main types of benefits. The more obvious kind concerns economics, reliability and quality. The cost of performing design could be reduced, serious design flaws that could result in enormous penalties may be avoided and the quality of design solutions could be improved. The second kind of benefit concerns understanding. Design is still as yet an incompletely characterised activity. Attempting to automate it may help to understand it better.

In an effort to mechanise the design process, many computer-aided design (CAD) tools have been and continue to be developed to address the myriad of tasks that routinely arise in the execution of a typical design scenario. Such tasks include modelling the artifact that is to be designed, synthesizing or generating alternative design solutions, analysing and evaluating these solutions, managing the large quantities of information required for the design and displaying the results of the design at different stages of the process. For complex structures such as chemical plants, the number of these tasks can be staggeringly large. However, existing CAD tools cover only a few tasks. Talukdar *et al* [Talukdar *et al* 88, p. 2] describe this situation as "islands of automation in a sea of human activity." Furthermore, very few systems have been developed to perform the synthesis task in design, which may be considered to be the core of the entire process. Before the level of automation can be significantly increased over current levels, integrated systems that can perform many more of the tasks required for design than is possible with existing artificial systems, will have to be developed.

The knowledge requirements of a complex activity such as chemical process design are enormous. Endowing a system with the knowledge needed to perform this activity, an enterprise referred to as knowledge engineering, can be a laborious, time-consuming and costly effort. Many person-years of work may be required. Furthermore, it is a task that never really ends. The knowledge required to perform design, as is needed to perform any other activity, is dynamic. That which is imparted to a system at creation time may not be adequate at problem solution time. This implies a need by a design system of an ability to learn. Learning can aid in two ways. First, it can help alleviate the knowledge acquisition bottleneck alluded to above, thereby significantly reducing, and perhaps even completely eliminating, the knowledge engineering effort. Second, it can allow design systems to improve with experience, thus enabling them to increase the efficiency and effectiveness with which they perform their tasks.

Recent work in the fields of artificial intelligence (AI) and cognitive science has resulted in the development of a number of integrated software architectures that combine problem solving and learning in their functionality. One of these systems, Soar [Laird *et al* 87] has already demonstrated its potential in both these functions.

The primary motivation of our research has been to understand the issues involved in building artificial design systems that integrate both learning and problem solving in their performance. This is crucial if machine learning is ever to play a role in chemical process design. Since Soar has already shown itself to be a powerful problem-solving engine and its learning mechanism, chunking, has been applied in a wide variety of learning situations, it was decided to conduct our experiments within the framework provided by this architecture. The work presented here describes our experiences thus far in this arena. We report on two systems that were constructed using the Soar architecture. The first, CPD-Soar, is a system for the design of unintegrated distillation sequences. The second, Interval-Soar, is a system that can learn the intersection point of two arbitrary and unknown functions. In this latter system, we solve what appears to be an extremely easy problem and discover that we need a few hundred production rules to do it. We will try to make clear the actual complexity of the learning activity required. A description of each system is provided together with its performance. We also indicate how the functionality of a system like Interval-Soar could be used to further improve the performance of a chemical design system such as CPD-Soar.

2 The Soar Architecture

Soar is a general model of human cognition [Newell 89] that has been implemented as a software system. Problems ranging from traditional AI "toy" problems such as the eight-puzzle and the Tower of Hanoi to complex real world knowledge-intensive tasks such as a portion of the computer configuration performed by the R1 (XCON) expert system [Rosenbloom *et al* 85] have been solved by Soar systems. The system has five key architectural features: problem spaces, recognition memory, decision cycle, impasse-driven subgoaling and chunking. We shall illustrate these features later when we step through the execution of CPD-Soar and Interval-Soar.

2.1 Problem Spaces

All tasks in Soar are formulated as search in problem spaces. A problem space consists of a set of states and a set of operators. Applying an operator to the current state generates a new state and a goal is achieved when a desired state is reached. The task is accomplished when the top-level goal is attained. Multiple goals correspond to a task decomposition and each of these may require different problem spaces to be searched. All search is realised by two generic functions: task-implementation and search-control. Task-implementation functions involve the retrieval or generation of problem spaces, states and operators. Search-control functions, on the other hand, involve the selection of objects (problem spaces, states, operators) from among those competing.

2.2 Recognition Memory

All long-term knowledge in Soar is stored in an associative recognition memory, realised as a production system. All knowledge about the current problem-solving situation is stored in working memory as a collection of data elements. Each production consists of a set of conditions and a set of actions. The conditions test working memory for the presence or absence of simple patterns (attribute-value elements) whereas the actions add new elements to it. Productions encode all knowledge required to perform a task. This knowledge can pertain to either task implementation or search control. An important characteristic of Soar as a production system is the absence of any conflict resolution. All productions that are instantiated, i.e., have their conditions satisfied, are selected to fire, thus allowing the retrieval of knowledge in parallel. Although the attribute-value representational scheme employed by Soar is basic, both attributes and values may be other objects, hence complex frame-like structures can be constructed.

2.3 Decision Cycle

All problem solving in Soar revolves around a number of decisions; what goal should be attained, what problem space should be searched to attain the goal, what state should the search proceed from and what operator should be applied to the state. These decisions occur in a sequence of decision cycles, each of which consists of two phases. During the first phase, the elaboration phase, all instantiated productions fire. Since productions may create working memory elements that satisfy other productions, this process could continue for many elaboration cycles. It terminates when it runs to quiescence, i.e., when no more productions can fire. Elaboration results in two kinds of data elements being added to working memory. The first kind are new task-implementation objects such as problem spaces, states and operators or augmentations to existing objects. The second kind are preferences. Preferences are special elements that encode knowledge about the acceptability and desirability of problem spaces, states and operators for any role in the total problem-solving context. This selection of an object for a role is made during the second phase of the decision cycle, the decision procedure phase. Begining with the oldest goal, the decision procedure considers each slot in the goal-context-stack. Within a context, the problem-space role is considered first, followed by the state and operator roles respectively. All preferences relevant to a slot are gathered and interpreted to determine an object for its role. If a unique decision can be made for an object for one of the slots in the context hierarchy, that object will be selected. This act signifies the end of the current decision cycle and problem solving then proceeds with the elaboration phase of the next cycle.

2.4 Subgoals

A situation may arise in the problem solving when a unique decision cannot be made for any of the slots in the current context. This may be due to either incomplete or inconsistent information. Soar deals with such a situation, known as an impasse, by subgoaling. This happens dynamically. Furthermore, subgoals may occur within subgoals, thus resulting in a hierarchy. The architecture recognises four kinds of impasses: rejection, no-change, tie and conflict. To illustrate some of these, consider the following examples. An operator tie impasse occurs when several operators have been made acceptable, but not enough knowledge exists to select one. A state no-change impasse occurs when a state has been selected, but no operators are proposed to apply to it. The operator tie impasse would be resolved when preferences that allow Soar to uniquely select one of the candidate operators are thrown into working memory. The state no-change impasse would be resolved when a preference for an operator that can be applied to the state is generated.

2.5 Chunking

Soar learns from its experiences in resolving impasses by constructing productions, known as chunks, for insertion into its long-term or recognition memory. The chunks summarise the problem solving that occurred in the subgoals and are created whenever results are generated. These results form the actions of the chunks. The conditions are the pre-impasse situation upon which these results depend. This requirement that the chunk conditions only be working memory elements that existed prior to the subgoal that were instrumental in generating the results is one way the chunks are generalised. Another involves converting identifiers to variables, a process known as variablization. Also, results created in a subgoal whose function is solely to guide the research, i.e., search-control knowledge, are not used in the creation of chunks. These generalisation processes thus ensure that the chunks learned may apply in future problem-solving situations that aren't exactly the same as the ones they were created under, only similar. Like any other learning system, it is possible for Soar to acquire incorrect knowledge. This may result if the system either makes an incorrect inference or receives incorrect information. Laird [Laird 88] has described how Soar systems can recover from any incorrect knowledge they may have captured in their long-term memories.

3 CPD-Soar

CPD-Soar is a system for the design of distillation sequences. It can currently create unintegrated sequences of sharp-splitting columns only. Given a feed specification, it first generates the splits that have to be applied to the feed stream to create the desired products and then sequences these splits. Multicomponent products can be handled. Search is controlled through the application of a number of heuristics commonly used in distillation sequence design.

3.1 Problem Spaces

There are eight problem spaces in CPD-Soar: **design**[1], **feed**, **order**, **split**, **sequence**, **update**, **output** and **selection**. All of them, except **design** and **selection** are operator-implementation spaces. The top space, **design**, has eight operators: ***get-feed***, ***order-components***, ***link-components***, ***make-splits***, ***identify-forbidden***, ***sequence-split***, ***update-stream*** and ***write***. Figure 1 shows the decomposition of the system into its problem spaces and operators.

The ***get-feed*** operator interacts with the user to obtain the feed specifications. This operator is implemented as a problem space called **feed** which contains two operators, ***make-feed*** and ***get-comp***. ***Make-feed*** prompts the user for the name of the feed stream and the number of components. ***Get-comp*** obtains the following information about each component from the user: flowrate, volatility and product in which it is desired.

Order-components ranks the components in a stream in descending order according to volatility. The lightest component, i.e., the one with the highest volatility, is given a rank one. The ***order-components*** operator is instantiated for all streams that are unordered and is implemented as a problem space called **order**. This space contains a single operator, ***rank***, which is instantiated for all unranked components in the selected stream.

Streams are represented as linked lists and columns are modelled as list-splitters, i.e., as perfect splitters. Each component in a stream, other than the one with the highest rank, has an attribute "lighter-than" whose value is the identifier of the component that is adjacent to and

---

[1]We will use the convention of **boldface TimesRoman** font to denote problem spaces and ***boldface italics*** font to denote operators.

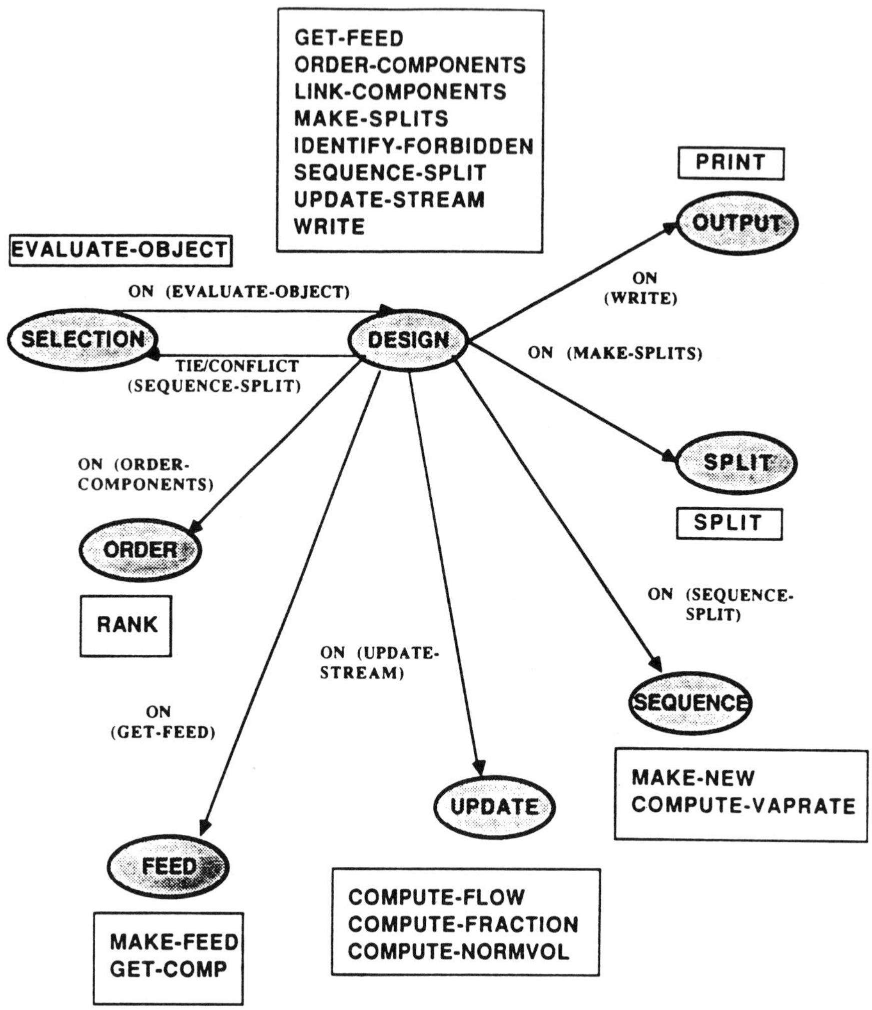

Figure 1: Hierarchy of Problem Spaces and Operators in CPD-Soar[2]

heavier than it. The operator ***link-components*** links all the components in a stream that has already had its components ordered.

[2]Each problem space is depicted by an oval and the operators it contains are listed in the box next to it. Impasses are noted next to the directed lines linking problem spaces. (ON refers to an Operator No-change impasse).

Make-splits generates all the possible sharp splits that can be applied to the feed stream. For a stream with N components, the number of possible sharp splits is (N - 1). Each split is characterised by a light and heavy key. The **split** problem space implements the ***make-splits*** operator. This space also contains a single operator with the same name which generates a split and computes the ratio of the volatilities of the light and heavy keys. ***Identify-forbidden*** tags each of the splits generated by ***make-splits*** as either allowed or forbidden. A split is forbidden if its two keys coexist in the same product.

The operator ***update-stream*** computes the mole fractions of a stream's components, normalises their volatilities with respect to the heaviest component and computes the total flowrate of the stream. It is implemented as a problem space called **update**, which contains three operators: ***compute-flow***, ***compute-fraction*** and ***compute-normvol***.

When all the allowable splits have been sequenced, the ***write*** operator writes them to the screen in the order they are to be applied. The operator is implemented as a problem-space called **output**. This space contains a single operator called ***print*** which outputs a split to the screen.

The **selection** space is selected to resolve ties or conflicts among competing problem spaces, states or operators. It contains one operator, ***evaluate-object***, whose function is to compute an evaluation for a competing object. The next section describes the use of the **selection** space to resolve ties or conflicts among competing ***sequence-split*** operators in CPD-Soar.

3.2 Resolving Ties and Conflicts among Splits

The above described operators are all concerned with routine book-keeping and input/output functions required by the design problem. The most important operator is ***sequence-split***. This ranks all the allowable splits in the order they are to be applied. It is implemented as a problem space called **sequence** which contains two operators, ***make-new*** and ***compute-vaprate***. The ***make-new*** operator performs a number of functions. It generates two new streams corresponding to the distillate and bottoms products and augments these streams with their components. It also generates a column that is augmented with its feed and product streams. ***Compute-vaprate*** computes the vapour flowrate in the column using a simplied function that Douglas [Douglas 88, p. 463] has proposed for a binary column.

The ***sequence-split*** operator is made acceptable for all unranked allowable splits that may be applied to streams that have not already been split and are not products. Splits that apply to different streams are made indifferent to each other. The following heuristics are used to select among splits that apply to the same stream: easiest separation best (similar to hardest separation worst), removal of lightest key best and removal of component with largest flowrate best. Since these heuristics discriminate on the basis of different attributes, conflicts are to be expected in many cases. Most previous works in the field have dealt with this problem in one of a number of ways. One approach involves ranking the heuristics in order of importance. In all cases however, the ranking function used is very subjective and usually does not have any basis. A second approach does away with the use of heuristics altogether. Instead, evaluation functions are employed to rate all the competing splits. However, this is a policy that can prove to be computationally expensive for even moderately sized problems. A third approach uses only a small subset of all the heuristics that have been shown to be useful. This subset is selected carefully so as to avoid the possiblity of conflicts arising. However, this approach loses out in situations where the weeded-out heuristics could have applied. Soar's ability to deal with inconsistent and incomplete information by subgoaling avoids the weaknesses of all these approaches. The power of using heuristics as a means of controlling search is exploited, and only when the heuristics are in conflict, or result in ties, are the evaluation functions employed. CPD-Soar resolves conflicting and tieing splits by applying in turn, each split to the stream, generating the product streams and the column, and computing the vapour flowrate in the column. The split resulting in the column with the lowest vapour rate is selected. In other words, the search strategy employed in tie or conflict instances is a simple one-step lookahead.

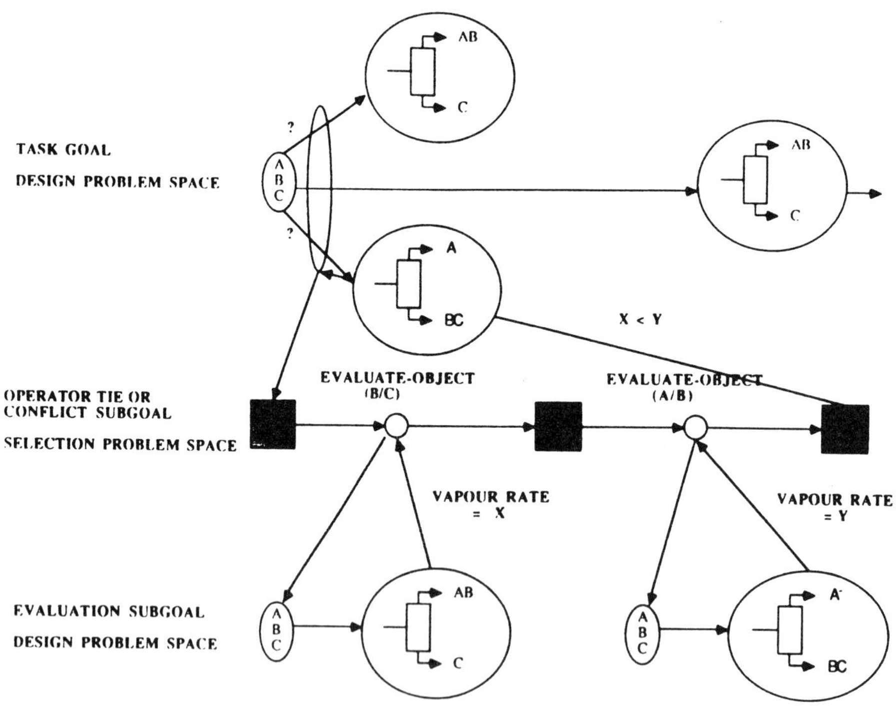

Figure 2: Selecting among Competing Splits in CPD-Soar

Figure 2 depicts the subgoaling CPD-Soar would undergo in the case of a tie or conflict impasse. Consider the simple, but representative, situation in which a stream consisting of three components, A, B and C, is to be split. Suppose that CPD-Soar, on the basis of its current knowledge, i.e., its heuristics, is unable to decide between the two possible splits, A/B or B/C. This could be due to one of two reasons. Either its knowledge indicates both splits are equally good, in which case a tie impasse will be encountered, or its knowledge is conflicting, with one piece of information stating A/B is better and another stating B/C is better, in which case a conflict impasse will arise.

In both cases, CPD-Soar subgoals into the **selection** space to generate the knowledge required to resolve the impasse. In the **selection** space, the ***evaluate-object*** operator is made acceptable for each of the tieing or conflicting objects; in this case, the two **sequence-split** operators. Since it does not matter in which order the splits are evaluated, the ***evaluate-object*** operators are made indifferent to each other. CPD-Soar evaluates the competing splits by trying each one out in turn and comparing the results. Suppose the B/C split is selected first to be evaluated. If CPD-Soar encounters an operator no-change impasse in trying to apply the ***evaluate-object*** operator, the **design** space is made acceptable. The B/C split is applied to the stream and the vapour flowrate of the resulting column computed. Suppose it is X in this case. This knowledge is passed back to the **selection** space. CPD-Soar next performs the same sequence of operations for the second split. Suppose the vapour flowrate for the A/B split is Y. The two evaluations, i.e., flowrates, are then compared in the selection space and a better-than preference is generated for the split corresponding to the smaller one with respect to the other. Since in this case X is smaller than Y, the split B/C is chosen.

3.3 Performance of CPD-Soar

CPD-Soar is an attempt to emulate the behaviour of a human process designer working without the use of any external computational aids except a device to perform simple arithmetic calculations. Hence its performance should not be measured relative to man-machine computing systems where the machine is an extremely powerful number cruncher. With this in mind, it would probably be fair to state that CPD-Soar's performance is acceptable.

Two points will be made concerning the strategy used by CPD-Soar to resolve ties or conflicts among competing splits. The first concerns the one-step lookahead search and the second concerns the vapour flowrate evaluation function.

The one-step lookahead search employed was decided upon for the following reasons. Since the heuristics are employed to select the next step, i.e., operator, to be applied, using each operator in turn and selecting which resulted in the best state was deemed sufficient in providing a functional equivalence to the knowledge encoded in the heuristics. Of course, the decision resulting from such a limited lookahead is only optimal locally. Searches that look beyond the first step are certainly possible. One potential search would be a lookahead to the completion of a sequence. It should be noted however, that the deeper a search is, the more expensive it will be computationally. The main motivation, however, for resorting to the one-step lookahead in the current version of CPD-Soar was to get an appreciation of the sort of chunks that would be generated.

In many instances the vapour flowrate is a good indicator of the cost, both construction and operating, of a column. Lower vapour rates result in smaller columns and lower utility usage. Hence, it was decided to use this parameter as being indicative of the quality of the state generated. However, this does not imply that the strategy employed by CPD-Soar is dependent upon this evaluation function. For the design of heat-integrated sequences, this will probably change.

The chunks generated in response to the above-described impasses are too specific, i.e., their condition elements have numeric attributes whose values are specific constants. An example chunk is presented in Figure 3[3]. Such a chunk can be extremely useful within the same problem-solving trial. A chunk acquired earlier on in the problem solving can fire during later stages of the same trial. Such a transfer can help in making much larger design problems (than are routinely attempted today) tractable. In process design problems, it is usually the case that many computations have to be repeated several times over during the same problem instance. Also, decisions among the same competing choices may also be repeated. An example from the domain of distillation-sequence design would be the calculation of the column parameters for a particular split. A search down one branch of the tree may require the A/B split to be evaluated. However, further down the branch a decision may be made not to explore it any further and to switch the search to another branch. This new branch may now also require the A/B split to be evaluated. However, since the design system would have chunked away the results of the A/B evaluation carried out during the search of the previous branch, this evaluation will not have to be repeated. In process design problems, it is also often the case that decisions from among the same competing choices may also have to be remade several times within a single problem instance. For example, while searching a particular branch of a tree, a decision may have to be made between two competing splits, say, A/B and B/C, which in turn may require their full evaluations. Later, when some other branch of the tree is being searched, it is possible that a decision may again be required between A/B and B/C. This time however, the system would be able to make a decision straight away based on the knowledge it had acquired the previous time. The example chunk presented encodes such knowledge.

However, the power of a learning mechanism lies in its ability to acquire knowledge that can be employed in a situation that is not exactly the same as the situation it was acquired in, i.e., its ability to generalize. Chunks that are more general in their applicability than those currently learned by CPD-Soar are possible. One kind include those that would refer to intervals or ranges rather than specific values of numbers. Such chunks, it is conceived, would

---

[3]The syntax of the production presented here differs from those presented later since CPD-Soar was developed using Soar 4, whereas Interval-Soar employs a newer version, Soar 5

```
(sp p43 elaborate
    (goal <g1> ^problem-space { <> undecided <p1> }
     ^state { <> undecided <n1> } ^desired <d1>)
    (desired <d1> ^better lower)
    (operator <o2> ^name sequence-split ^split <s1>
     ^stream <s3>)
    (split <s1> ^hk <h1> ^lk <l1> ^relvol 3/2)
    (hk <h1> ^name b)
    (stream <s3> ^component <c1> { <> <c1> <c2> }
     { <> <c2> <> <c1> <c3> })
    (component <c1> ^name b ^flowrate 2)
    (lk <l1> ^name c)
    (component <c2> ^name c ^flowrate 3)
    (operator { <> <o2> <o1> } ^name sequence-split)
    (operator <o1> ^split { <> <s1> <s2> } ^stream <s3>)
    (split <s2> ^hk { <> <h1> <h2> } ^lk { <> <l1> <l2> }
     ^relvol 2)
    (hk <h2> ^name a)
    (component <c3> ^name a ^flowrate 1)
    (lk <l2> ^name b)
  -->
    (preference <o2> ^role operator ^value worse
     ^reference <o1> ^goal <g1>  ^problem-space <p1>
     ^state <n1>))
```

```
 If    there is a sequence-split operator <o2> that
       implements split <s1>
and    split <s1> has light key C and heavy key B
and    the ratio of volatilities between B and C is 1.5
and    C has flowrate 3
and    B has flowrate 2
and    there is a sequence-split operator <o1> that implements
       split <s2>
and    split <s2> has light key B and heavy key A
and    the ratio of volatilities between A and B is 2
and    A has flowrate 1

then   create a worse preference for operator <o2> with
       respect to operator <o1>
```

Figure 3: Example of a Chunk Learned by CPD-Soar and its English Description.

prescribe domains within which volatilities, for instance, or flowrates, would have to fall in order for the chunks to apply. However, before CPD-Soar can acquire such chunks, an understanding of how intervals of numbers may be learned and represented within Soar systems has to be acquired. The following section describes another system, Interval-Soar, that possesses the ability to learn ranges for relatively simple problems. It is one of a series of systems we are developing within the Soar framework to explore the issues involved in understanding and developing systems that can perform useful learning in highly quantitative domains.

Our experiences with CPD-Soar have indicated that Soar as a problem-solving engine seems to provide all that has thus far been sought in an architecture for design. As noted earlier, the performance of CPD-Soar, as a system that attempts to emulate a human designer, is acceptable and its performance will certainly be better than a corresponding non-learning system.

4 Interval-Soar

Interval-Soar is a system that can learn the intersection point between two arbitrary and unknown functions, f1 and f2. This learning is performed as a welcome side-effect of performing another task. The task consists of applying one of the two functions to each element in a set of data points and computing the result. The data point, a scalar denoted by x, is then labelled with the function that was applied to it. When all data points have been labelled, the task is considered accomplished.

Each function is characterized by a parameter called its bound. For function f1, this is ub-o1 (upper bound of operator 1) and for function f2, it is lb-o2 (lower bound of operator 2)[4]. The bounds of the operators thus demarcate the intervals or regions that the operators should be applied in. The value at which the two bounds, ub-o1 and lb-o2, are equal, will correspond to the intersection or crossover point between the two functions.

If a data point falls within a particular interval, then the operator to which that interval corresponds can be selected to apply to the data point. If a data point does not fall within an interval, then both operators will have to be fully evaluated in order to make a decision about which to select. If, after a full evaluation, ***op1*** is selected as the operator to apply, the data point will be learned as the new value of ub-o1. Conversely, if ***op2*** is selected, the value of lb-o2 will be updated to the data point. By such a process of refining the values of the bounds, it is possible for Interval-Soar to incrementally converge to the intersection point of the two intervals.

To perform the above-described task is not as simple as it may seem to be. The main reason for this is that Interval-Soar must carry out this task without any knowledge of the functions themselves[5]. Thus, it should be emphasized, it is not a question of solving two equations in two unknowns. Instead, it is a problem of determining the intersection using

[4]The lower bound of operator 1 is assumed to be minus infinity and the upper bound of operator two is assumed to be plus infinity.

[5]The example problem described later shows the two functions since they are used for the purposes of illustration. However, Interval-Soar does not have accesss to this knowledge per se.

knowledge of a sample set of data points only. One assumption that Interval-Soar currently makes is that the functions only intersect at a single point. It is expected that future versions of the system will relax this assumption. In order to perform this task, as will become clearer later, the system must possess the ability to recognize and recall declarative knowledge. However, since chunking is the only learning mechanism within Soar, this memorizing of declarative knowledge must be performed using it, and this is not so straightforward.

The problem spaces in Interval-Soar can be categorized into three major groups: the task spaces, the function spaces and the **memory** space. Figure 4 shows the decomposition of the system into its problem spaces.

4.1 Task Spaces

There are three task spaces in Interval-Soar: the **interval** space, the **selection** space and the **refine** space.

The **interval** space is the top-level space. It contains three operators: ***select-x***, ***op1*** and ***op2***. ***Select-x*** selects a data point to be classified from among all those still unlabelled. ***Op1*** and ***op2*** implement functions f1 and f2 respectively.

The **selection** space is chosen in response to a tie between operators ***op1*** and ***op2*** in the **interval** space. It has four operators: ***memory***, ***x-lte-ub-o1***, ***x-gte-lb-o2*** and ***refine-interval***. ***Memory*** is used to retrieve the current values of the bounds, ub-o1 and lb-o2. ***X-lte-ub-o1*** and ***x-gte-lb-o2*** are comparison operators. The first compares x to ub-o1 and if it is less than or equal to the bound, returns the value true. The second compares x to lb-o2 and in this case returns true if x is greater than or equal to the bound. The operator ***refine-interval*** is used to refine the values of the bounds on the intervals. It does this by carrying out a full evaluation of the operators ***op1*** and ***op2***, comparing the evaluations and updating the bound of the operator that has the higher evaluation.

The **refine** space, which implements the ***refine-interval*** operator, contains five operators: ***op1***, ***op2***, ***f1-eq-f2***, ***f1-gt-f2*** and ***memory***. ***F1-eq-f2*** returns a value of true if f1 is equal to f2. Likewise, ***f1-gt-f2*** returns a value of true if f1 is greater than f2. In contrast to the ***memory*** operator in the **selection** space, the ***memory*** operator in the **refine** space associates the value of a bound with its corresponding cue, i.e., it learns a new bound value.

4.2 Memory Space

The chunking mechanism within the Soar architecture has been demonstrated to be adequate for the acquisition of procedural knowledge[7]. On the other hand, the acquisition of

[7]Procedural knowledge includes knowledge about which actions the system can perform, when certain actions should be preferred over others and how to carry out the actions.

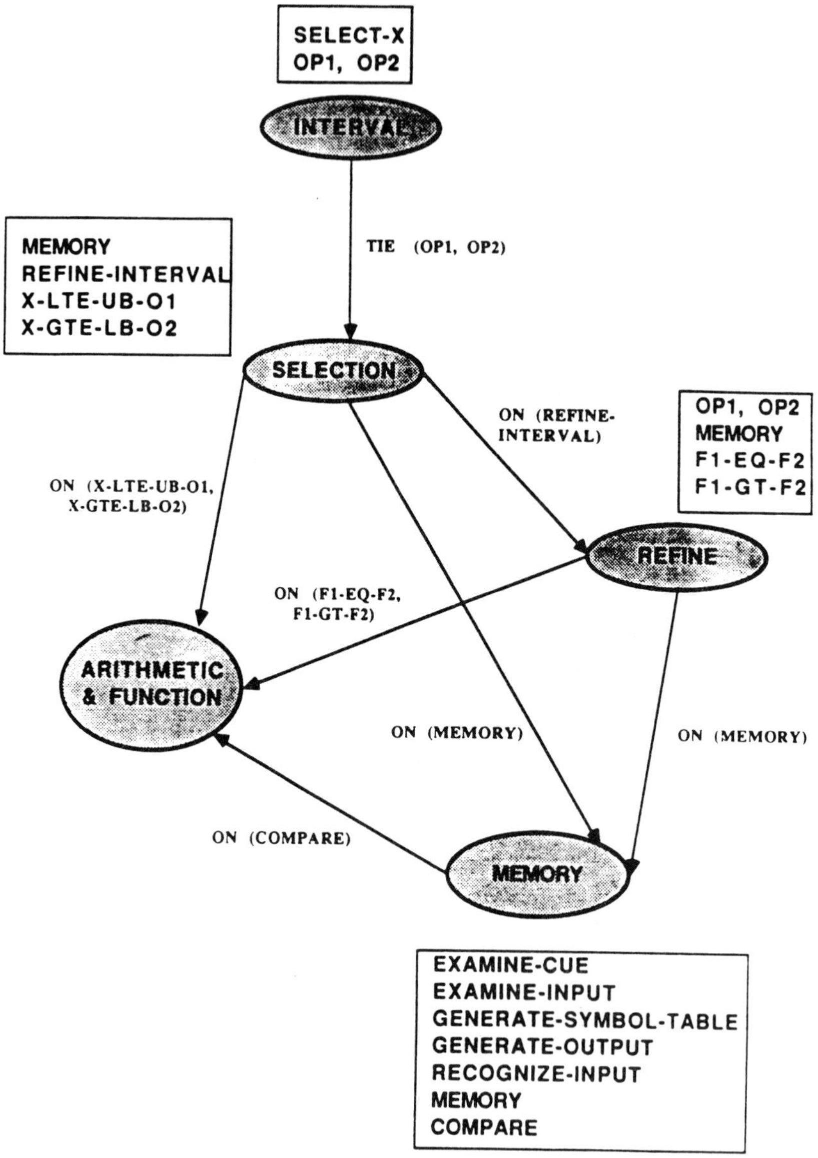

Figure 4: Hierarchy of Problem Spaces in Interval-Soar[6]

[6]Each problem space is depicted by an oval and the operators it contains are listed in the box next to it. Impasses are noted next to the directed lines linking problem spaces. (ON refers to an Operator No-change impasse).

declarative knowledge[8] is not so straightforward. Although the chunking mechanism can be used to acquire such knowledge, the system must first perform some deliberate processing in order to do so. This processing occurs in the **memory** space, which implements the ***memory*** operator. An involved discussion of representing, storing, retrieving, using and acquiring different forms of knowledge, including both procedural and declarative, has been provided by Rosenbloom *et al* [Rosenbloom *et al* 89].

The ***memory*** operator provides Interval-Soar with the means to memorize and retrieve declarative knowledge. It provides an ability to learn to recognize and learn to recall objects. The operator takes two arguments: an input object (the object to be learned) and a cue object. The cue constrains the situations in which the input object is to be retrieved. When the ***memory*** operator is applied, all objects that were previously associated with the given cue are recalled. If the input object is not among those retrieved, then it is learned (and will thus be retrieved the next time the ***memory*** operator is applied with the same cue). The absence of a cue is effectively taken to be the cue if the memory operator is applied without one. The operator will only perform retrieval of earlier memorized objects if it applied without an input object. However, if no objects had been previously associated with the cue, then nothing is retrieved and the operator is simply terminated.

The following example will hopefully serve to provide a clearer description of the functioning of the ***memory*** operator. Suppose we wish to associate the objects "Fido" and "Bozo" with the cue "dog." This means that whenever the system is presented with the cue "dog," the objects "Fido" and "Bozo" should be recalled. This association, which is a form of memorization, is carried out by selecting and applying the ***memory*** operator, in this case, twice. Suppose the first time the operator is applied with the cue "dog" and the input object (or object to be learned) "Fido." The result of applying the ***memory*** operator will be a chunk that delivers, i.e., retrieves, the object "Fido" on any future occasion that the operator is applied with the cue "dog." Suppose the operator is applied for a second time. However, this time we wish to associate the object "Bozo" with the cue "dog." This application will result in the object "Fido" being retrieved (since it was previously associated with the given cue) and the object "Bozo" being memorized, i.e., a chunk being created that will, on future occasions, deliver the object "Bozo" when the cue "dog" is presented. If the ***memory*** operator is applied for a third time with the cue "dog" and no object to be learned, then only retrieval of the objects "Fido" and "Bozo" will occur. An application of the ***memory*** operator with the cue "cat" will not retrieve anything since no objects have been associated with that cue. In Interval-Soar, the cues are "ub-o1" and "lb-o2" and the learned objects are the values of the bounds.

The application of the ***memory*** operator results in the learning of two kinds of chunks: recognition chunks and recall chunks. The recognition chunks allow the system to determine if it has seen an object before and the recall chunks allow it to generate a representation of an

---

[8]Declarative knowledge includes facts. It is knowledge about what is true in the world.

object seen before.

The ***memory*** operator is implemented as the **memory** space. This problem space contains seven operators: ***examine-input***, ***examine-cue***, ***generate-symbol-table***, ***generate-output***, ***recognize-input***, ***memory*** and ***compare***. The ***examine-input*** and ***examine-cue*** operators cycle through all the symbols the input and cue objects are respectively constructed of so that tests of these symbols appear in the recognition chunks learned. ***Generate-symbol-table*** creates a symbol table relating the input symbols to the output symbols, which ***generate-output*** uses to construct the output object from. ***Recognize-input*** recognizes the input object and the input-cue pair. The ***memory*** operator augments the parent ***memory*** operator (which was implemented as the **memory** space) with the recalled object. The ***compare*** operator compares the previously learned bound (which has now been retrieved) with the current bound to be learned. If they are not equal (which will always be the case since the interval is being refined), a reject preference is generated for the old bound. The **memory** space is complex and subtle and the above is a very basic description of the functions of its operators. A more detailed description of the space has been provided by Rosenbloom [Rosenbloom 89].

4.3 Function Spaces

The function spaces contain knowledge about performing basic logical, arithmetic and control functions. This knowledge allows Interval-Soar to symbolically execute the mathematical functions it needs, such as computing f1 and f2, comparing f1 to f2, comparing x to ub-o1 and ub-o2 and comparing the new value of a bound with an old one, all without recourse to an external computing device. A detailed description of the function spaces has been given by Rosenbloom & Lee [Rosenbloom & Lee 89].

4.4 Example Task

The functioning of Interval-Soar will now be illustrated by a simple example. Consider the two functions, $f1 = 7 - x$ and $f2 = x + 1$, and consider three data points: $x = 1.3$, $x = 3.0$ and $x = 5.8$. As described earlier, the task is to apply one of the functions to each of the data points, compute the results and label the points with the names of the operators corresponding to the functions that were applied to them. As a by-product of this problem solving, the system must learn the values of two bounds, ub-o1 and lb-o2. These parameters demarcate the intervals where the functions should be selected. If a data point has a value less than or equal to ub-o1, f1 should be applied. If it has a value greater than or equal to lb-o2, f2 should be applied.

Problem solving begins in the **interval** space. The initial state consists of a set of (three in this case) unlabelled data points. The desired state is one in which each data point has had its function value computed and is labelled. The operator ***select-x*** is first applied to choose a data point to be worked on. Since the order in which the data points are selected is irrelevant, they are all made indifferent to each other. Once a point has been selected (suppose in this case it is $x = 5.8$), operators ***op1*** and ***op2*** are proposed to apply. ***Op1*** implements f1 and ***op2*** implements f2. Since both operators are equally acceptable at this stage, a tie impasse results.

To resolve the tie between ***op1*** and ***op2*** in the **interval** space, a subgoal is created and the **selection** space is chosen. In the **selection** space, Interval-Soar first tries to retrieve any existing bounds on the tieing operators. It does this by proposing the ***memory*** operator twice, one with the cue ub-o1 and the other with the cue lb-o2. Since the order in which the bounds are retrieved is irrelevant, the two memory operators are made indifferent to each other. However, nothing is retrieved because no values have yet been associated with the cues since this is the first time Interval-Soar is solving the problem.

Thus, to make a decision that resolves the impasse, a full evaluation of the tieing operators must be made. To do this, Interval-Soar selects the ***refine-interval*** operator. If there is an operator no-change impasse in attempting to apply the ***refine-interval*** operator, the **refine** space is selected. The schemes used to evaluate the operators ***op1*** and ***op2*** are just the functions themselves. Thus, ***op1*** and ***op2*** are first applied in random order to the data point. In this case f1 = 1.2 and f2 = 6.8. Next, the comparison operators ***f1-eq-f2*** and ***f1-gt-f2*** are selected and applied in turn to determine the relative magnitude of f1 with respect to f2. ***F1-eq-f2*** returns a value of false (indicating the two parameters are not equal) and ***f1-gt-g2*** returns a value of false (indicating that f1 is not greater than f2). Before this knowledge is passed back to the higher-level spaces, the value of lb-o2 (since f2 is greater than f1) is memorized as 5.8. Interval-Soar carries this out by selecting and applying the ***memory*** operator with the cue object as lb-o2 and the learned object as 5.8. The knowledge that f2 is greater than f1 is now passed back to the higher spaces to resolve the initial tie between ***op1*** and ***op2***. Interval-Soar thus applies ***op2*** to the data point x = 5.8, which is consequently labelled op2. The state of affairs at this stage of the problem solving is depicted in Figure 5.

The entire problem-solving behaviour is now repeated for another data point. There are a few differences since Interval-Soar uses some of the knowledge it had chunked away when running the first point. Suppose the point x = 3.0 is selected this time. The **selection** space is again chosen in response to a tie between ***op1*** and ***op2*** in the **interval** space. In the **selection** space, the ***memory*** operators first apply to retrieve any bounds, i.e., any numbers associated with the cues ub-o1 and lb-o2. Since 5.8 has been associated with lb-o2, it is recalled instantly. The comparison operator ***x-gte-lb-o2*** is next selected and applied to determine the relative magnitude of the data point with respect to the bound. Since x is not greater than or equal to lb-o2 in this case, a value of false is returned. This knowledge does not allow a decision to be made between the competing operators; hence, the ***refine-interval*** operator is selected to compute a full evaluation once again. ***Op1*** and ***op2*** are applied in random order in the **refine** space. In this case, both f1 and f2 are determined to be 4.0. The operator ***f1-eq-f2*** is next applied and returns a value of true. Again, before this knowledge is passed back to the higher spaces to resolve the tie, the values of the bounds are updated by applying the ***memory*** operator. The value of ub-o1 is memorized to be 3.0 by associating the number 3.0 with the cue ub-o1. In the case of lb-o2, the process is slightly different. Since the number 5.8 is already associated with the cue lb-o2 (from the previous run), the number associated with the

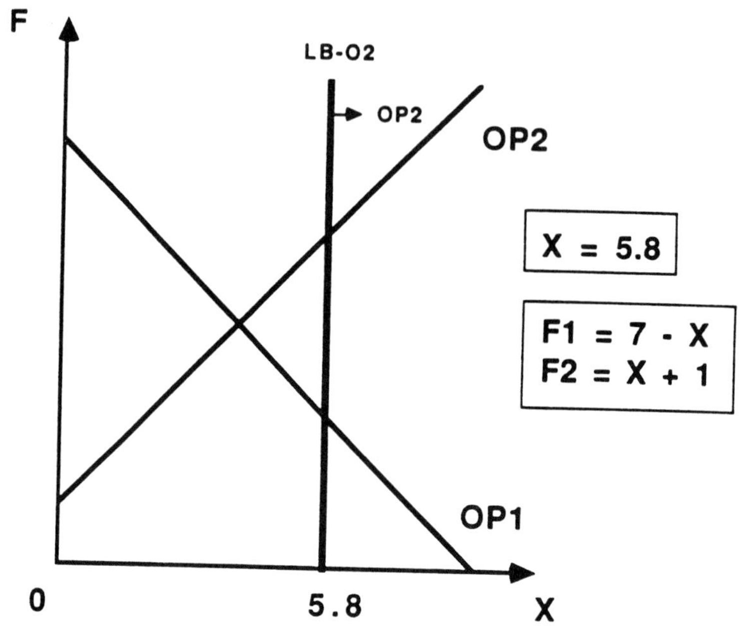

Figure 5: Location of Bounds after First Data Point is Employed

cue is updated to 3.0[9]. This updating is performed in the **memory** space (which is selected in response to a no-change impasse for the ***memory*** operator) by applying the ***compare*** operator. This operator compares the new value of the bound (the number to be learned) with its old value. If they are not equal (which, as noted earlier, will always be the case since the interval is being refined), a reject preference is generated for the old bound. After the memorization process is completed, the knowledge that f1 is equal to f2 is passed up to the higher spaces. In this situation, ***op1*** and ***op2*** will be made indifferent to each other and one will be picked at random. Figure 6 depicts the problem solving situation at this stage.

The final point from the set to be labelled is x = 1.3. By now the sequence of steps taken to achieve this should hopefully be clear. In the **selection** space, ***memory*** operators are first applied to retrieve the current values of the bounds. In this case, both ub-o1 and lb-o2 are associated with the number 3.0. Next, the comparison operators, ***x-lte-ub-o1*** and ***x-gte-lb-o2***

[9]In Soar, this is equivalent to having a chunk that generates a reject preference for 5.8 and another chunk that generates an acceptable preference for 3.0.

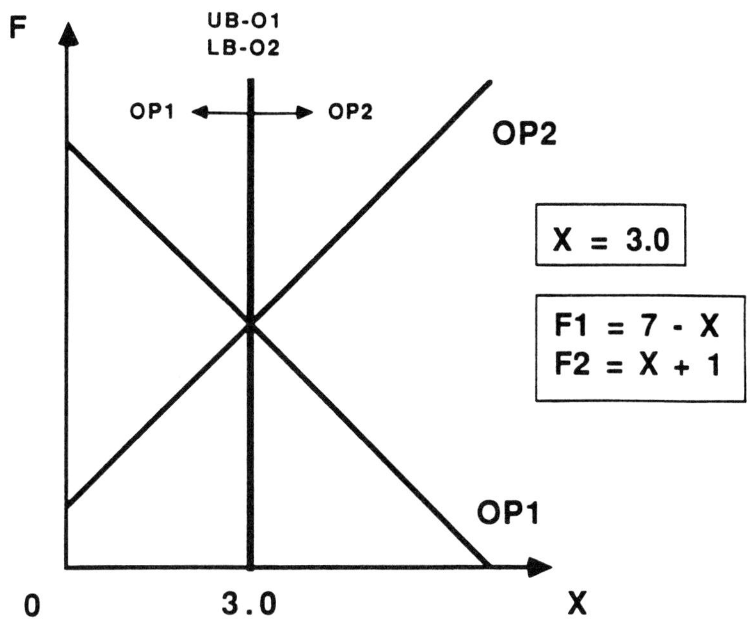

Figure 6: Location of Bounds after Second Data Point is Employed

are selected to apply. The first returns a value of true since x is less than ub-o1, while the second returns a value of false since x is less than lb-o2. Since Interval-Soar possesses the knowledge that if a data point is less than the bound ub-o1, operator ***op1*** should be selected, a better-than preference is generated for ***op1*** with respect to ***op2***. Hence, in this case, the tie impasse in the **interval** space can be resolved without resorting to a full evaluation of the competing operators, as was done during the two previous trials. The situation at this stage is depicted in Figure 7.

It should be noted that operator no-change impasses are encountered when attempting to apply ***op1***, ***op2***, the comparison operators (***f1-eq-f2***, ***f1-gt-f2***, ***x-lte-ub-o1***, ***x-gte-lb-o2*** and ***compare***) and the ***memory*** operator. The **memory** space is selected in the case of the ***memory*** operator and the function spaces are selected for the others.

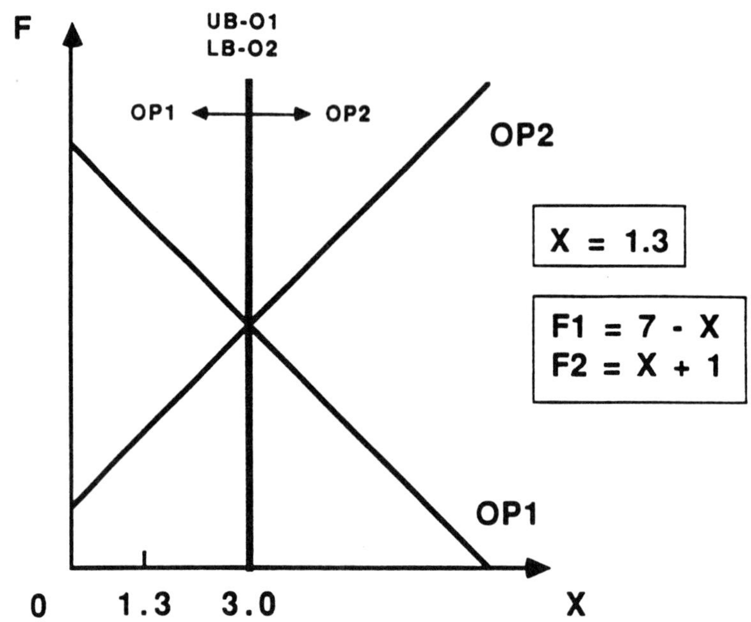

Figure 7: Location of Bounds after Third Data Point is Employed

4.5 Performance of Interval-Soar

To illustrate the performance of Interval-Soar, the results from running the system using three different sets of data points will be presented. Each set consists of three points: set 1 is (1.3, 3.0, 5.8), set 2 is (1.8, 3.7, 6.6) and set 3 is (2.4, 4.5, 6.9).

Across-trial transfer occurs when chunks acquired when solving one instance of a problem apply when another instance of the same problem is executed. Table 1 illustrates the effects of across-trial transfer. The results presented there include the changes in decision cycle numbers for each test case as well as the average over all three sets. As can be seen, the benefits of learning are encouraging. For the first trial, the average number of decision cycles required was 355. For trial two, this dropped to 73, a percentage drop of 79.4 and for trial three, this further dropped to 9 for a total percentage drop of 97.5 over the first trial.

Table 2 shows the number of productions learned by the system over the course of each

Trial Case	1	2	3
1	317	57	9
2	374	81	9
3	374	81	9
Ave	355	73	9

Table 1: Effects of Across-Trial Transfer of Chunks: Changes in Numbers of Decision Cycles

of the three trials. In all cases the system begins with 934 productions. A Soar system that learns on all goals during a trial will normally not acquire additional knowledge during subsequent trials. This is because the system will have learned all that it can during the first trial. The behaviour of Interval-Soar however, is an interesting example of how a system that learns on all goals during a first trial can learn additional knowledge during a second trial. This occurs in Interval-Soar since knowledge acquired during the first trial causes it to carry out a different problem-solving process in the second trial. This new process creates a different goal hierarchy, thus allowing the system to acquire knowledge that was not acquired through the original problem-solving process. To illustrate this, consider the data points in example set 1. At the end of the first trial, Interval-Soar learns that the values of ub-o1 and lb-o2 are both 3. During the second trial, this knowledge is brought to bear. When Interval-Soar attempts to decide which function to apply to 5.8, the first point in the set, it compares this number with the retrieved bounds instead of carrying out a complete evaluation as it did during the first trial. This comparison process requires Interval-Soar to subgoal into the arithmetic and function spaces (rather than the **refine** space) and the chunking that takes place over these spaces thus allows the system to acquire additional knowledge during a second trial. For case 1, the system acquires 65 chunks during the first trial and 10 chunks during the second trial. No chunks are acquired during the third trial since the system has learned all that it can. During this trial, no subgoaling occurs since productions learned in the previous trials fire to prevent all impasses.

Trial Case	1	2	3
1	65	10	0
2	76	15	0
3	76	15	0

Table 2: Numbers of Productions Learned during Different Trials

Table 3 illustrates the effects of across-task transfer. This occurs when chunks learned when solving a problem in a particular domain apply during the solution of another problem within the same domain. In the case of Interval-Soar, chunks acquired when using the data from set 1, for instance, fire when performing the task using the data from set 2 or set 3. Again, the benefits of learning are encouraging. Each data set was run independently with the chunks acquired during the running of the other two data sets and in each case, the number of decision cycles required was less than the number needed when no imported chunks were used. The percentage decrease in decision cycles ranged from 12.6 (when running set 1 with chunks learned during the running of set 3) to 71.4 (when running set 2 with chunks learned during the running of set 1). The average decrease over all 6 runs was 38.1%.

Case	No. Decision Cycles	% Decrease in DC
1 with no imported chunks	317	
1 with chunks imported from 2	252	20.5
1 with chunks imported from 3	277	12.6
2 with no imported chunks	374	
2 with chunks imported from 1	107	71.4
2 with chunks imported from 3	257	31.3
3 with no imported chunks	374	
3 with chunks imported from 1	169	54.8
3 with chunks imported from 2	232	38.0

Table 3: Effects of Across-Task Transfer of Chunks

4.6 Analysis of Knowledge Learned by Interval-Soar

As described earlier, chunks acquired during problem solving prevent the system from subgoaling should the same or similar situations arise in the future. Most of the chunks learned in Interval-Soar are operator-implementation productions. These are productions that fire to directly implement an operator in particular situations. Before learning, such an operator, because of its complexity, would require subgoaling in order to be applied. Table 4 is a summary of the number of operator-implementation productions learned for the different operators in Interval-Soar.

The ***memory*** operator-implementation chunks deserve special attention. As noted earlier, the purpose of applying the ***memory*** operator is to either recall or memorize declarative knowledge. These chunks allow the system to recognize the input object, i.e., the object to be learned, to recognize the combination of cue and input objects and to retrieve any previously learned objects associated with the given cue. Typical examples of these chunks are presented in Figure 8.

Operator	No. Implementation Chunks Learned
op1	7
op2	5
x-lte-ub-o1	4
x-gte-lb-o2	4
memory	3
f1-eq-f2	3
f1-gt-f2	4
compare	3

Table 4: Numbers of Operator-Implementation Chunks Learned for Different Operators

Chunks are also acquired that reject previously learned values of the bounds. An example of such a chunk is given in Figure 9.

Besides operator-implentation chunks, search-control productions are also acquired by Interval-Soar to resolve the tie impasses encountered between ***op1*** and ***op2*** in the **Interval** space. An example of such a chunk is presented in Figure 10.

4.7 Potential Application to Chemical Process Design

The functionality of a system such as Interval-Soar could be employed in two areas to improve the performance of a design system such as CPD-Soar. One area, which was first alluded to in Section 3.3, is the learning of chunks whose condition elements refer to ranges of numbers rather than specific values. Such chunks could then be used in situations that are different from those under which they were created. This would be equivalent to learning an "approximation" of the model used to evaluate the partial or total design solutions generated.

A second area where a design system could employ the functionality of a system like Interval-Soar is in learning to discriminate among the use of competing models. The example used to illustrate the behaviour of Interval-Soar employs evaluation functions that are the same as the operators they are evaluating. This simple example was used since the intention was to convey an unambiguous description of the functioning of Interval-Soar. However, nothing precludes the system from having a different evaluation function (than the operator itself) or even a set of evaluation functions from which to select. Furthermore, there is also no restriction on the use of an external device to compute the evaluation. Since the functions employed in the example are really simple, these can be computed by Interval-Soar itself using the knowledge it possesses about basic arithmetic.

```
;; Recognize the combination of cue and input objects if the
;; cue is lb-o2 and the object to be learned is the number 5.
(sp p293 elaborate
   (goal <g1> ^operator <o1>)
   (operator <o1> ^name memory ^cue <c2> ^learn <y1>)
   (class <c2> ^name lb-o2)
   (param <y1> ^value <i1>)
   (integer <i1> ^sign positive ^head <c1> ^tail <c1>)
   (column <c1> ^anchor head tail ^digit <d1>)
   (digit <d1> ^name 5)
 -->
   (operator <o1> ^recognized cue-input &, cue-input +))

;; Recognize the object to be learned if it is the number 5.
(sp p294 elaborate
   (goal <g1> ^operator <o1>)
   (operator <o1> -^recognized input ^name memory
    ^learn <y1>)
   (param <y1> ^value <i1>)
   (integer <i1> ^sign positive ^head <c1> ^tail <c1>)
   (column <c1> ^anchor head tail ^digit <d1>)
   (digit <d1> ^name 5)
 -->
   (operator <o1> ^recognized input &, input +))

;; Augment the memory operator with the recalled object, which
;; is the number 5.
(sp p295 elaborate
   (goal <g1> ^operator <o1>)
   (operator <o1> ^name memory ^cue <c1>)
   (class <c1> ^name lb-o2)
 -->
   (integer <x3> ^sign positive + ^head <x1> + ^tail <x1> +)
   (digit <x2> ^name 5 +)
   (column <x1> ^digit <x2> +
    ^anchor head + head &, tail &, tail +)
   (param <x4> ^value <x3> +)
   (operator <o1> ^recalled <x4> =, <x4> +))
```

Figure 8: Example Memory Operator-Implementation Chunks

In fact, the existence of a suite of models for evaluating designs, some of which could be computationally very expensive, accurately depicts the state of affairs in chemical process design. For example, in the area of distillation sequence design, models can range from simple list-splitters to those based on rigorous stage-by-stage calculations. Multiple models exist not only for the unit operations and equipment, but also for the materials themselves. For instance, a vapour could be analyzed using the ideal gas law or it could be subjected to extremely

```
;; Reject the recalled object if it is the number 5.
(sp p593 elaborate
   (goal <g1> ^operator <o1>)
   (operator <o1> ^name memory ^cue <c1> ^recalled <x4>)
   (class <c1> ^name lb-o2)
   (param <x4> ^value <x1>)
   (integer <x1> ^tail <x3>)
   (column <x3> ^anchor tail ^digit <x2>)
   (digit <x2> ^name 5)
 -->
   (operator <o1> ^recalled <x4> - <x4> @))
```

Figure 9: Example Chunk to Reject a (Previously Learned) Bound

```
;; Prefer op1 over op2 for the data point x = 2.
(sp p1051 elaborate
   (goal <g1> ^operator <o2> + { <> <o2> <o1> } +)
   (operator <o2> ^name op1 ^param <x1>)
   (operator <o1> ^name op2)
   (param <x1> ^value <i1>)
   (integer <i1> ^sign positive ^tail <c1> ^head <c1>)
   (column <c1> ^anchor head ^digit <d1>)
   (digit <d1> ^name 2)
 -->
   (goal <g1> ^operator <o2> > <o1>))
```

Figure 10: Example Search-Control Chunk

detailed molecular theory. Of course these are extremes, but the point trying to be made is that it is usually the case that choices exist. Thus, a critical design decision that often has to be made is what model to use. Factors such as resources available and quality of solution desired are usually taken into consideration when making such a decision. The use of a more detailed model can result in a better quality solution, but at a dearer price.

Useful knowledge to acquire is that which would allow a design agent to decide what situations warrant the use of what models. The ability to make such discriminations could enhance the performance of a design agent considerably. Valuable resources could be saved by selecting and employing simpler models in situations where the use of more complex models would have yielded the same decisions.

It is possible to conceive that a design system such as CPD-Soar could learn to discriminate among the use of multiple competing models if it were endowed with a functionality that was similar to the one possessed by Interval-Soar in learning the intersection point of two functions.

5 Conclusions

We have presented two Soar systems: CPD-Soar, for the design of distillation sequences and Interval-Soar, for learning the intersection point of two functions. With CPD-Soar, we have successfully demonstrated how a process design problem can be carried out within the Soar framework. This is the first application of a cognitive architecture to chemical process design problems.

With Interval-Soar, we have shown how the learning of declarative knowledge could be used to discretize a space of real numbers into two intervals. This learning is performed as a beneficial by-product of performing another task, that of computing the function values of a set of data points.

We have also described how the functionality of a system such as Interval-Soar could be used by a system such as CPD-Soar either to acquire an approximate model of the domain or to discriminate among competing models. Such abilities, it is hypothesized, could significantly enhance the performance of the design system over its current levels.

6 Acknowledgements

We would like to thank David Steier for his extremely useful guidance in conducting this research and Allen Newell for his occasional insightful comments. We would also like to thank Paul Rosenbloom for the use of the ***memory*** operator and, along with Soowon Lee, for the use of the arithmetic and function spaces. This work was supported by the Engineering Design Research Center at Carnegie Mellon University through a grant from the National Science Foundation.

References

[Douglas 88] Douglas, J. M.
Conceptual Design of Chemical Processes.
McGraw-Hill, San Francisco, CA, 1988.

[Laird 88] Laird, J. E.
Recovery from Incorrect Knowledge in Soar.
In *Proceedings of the National Conference on Artificial Intelligence*, pages 618-623. August, 1988.

[Laird *et al* 87] Laird, J. E., A. Newell & P. S. Rosenbloom.
SOAR: An Architecture for General Intelligence.
Artificial Intelligence 33(1):1-64, 1987.

[Newell 89] Newell, A.
Unified Theories of Cognition.
Harvard University Press, Cambridge, MA, 1989.
In press.

[Rosenbloom 89] Rosenbloom, P. S.
A Memory Operator for Soar.
1989.
Unpublished code and working notes.

[Rosenbloom & Lee 89]
Rosenbloom, P. S. & S. Lee.
Soar Arithmetic and Functional Capability.
1989.
Unpublished code and working notes.

[Rosenbloom *et al* 85]
Rosenbloom, P. S., J. E. Laird, J. McDermott, A. Newell & E. Orciuch.
R1-Soar: An Experiment in Knowledge-Intensive Programming in a Problem-Solving Architecture.
IEEE Trans. Patt. Anal. 75(5):561-569, 1985.

[Rosenbloom *et al* 89]
Rosenbloom, P. S., A. Newell & J. E. Laird.
Towards the Knowledge Level in Soar: The Role of the Architecture in the Use of Knowledge.
In K. VanLehn (editor), *Architectures for Intelligence.* Lawrence Erlbaum Associates, Hillsdale, NJ, 1989.
In press.

[Talukdar *et al* 88]
Talukdar, S., J. Rehg & A. Elfes.
Descriptive Models for Design Projects.
1988.
Unpublished paper.

[Westerberg 88] Westerberg, A. W.
Synthesis in Engineering Design.
In *Proceedings of Chemdata88.* Gothenburg, Sweden, June, 1988.

CHAPTER 35

Symbolic Architectures for Cognition

A. Newell, Carnegie Mellon University, P. S. Rosenbloom, USC–ISI, and J. E. Laird, University of Michigan

In this chapter we treat the fixed structure that provides the frame within which cognitive processing in the mind takes place. This structure is called the *architecture.* It will be our task to indicate what an architecture is and how it enters into cognitive theories of the mind. Some boundaries for this chapter are set by the existence of other chapters in this book. We will not address the basic foundations of the computational view of mind that is central to cognitive science, but assume the view presented by Pylyshyn in chapter 2. In addition to the groundwork Pylyshyn also deals with several aspects of the architecture. Chapter 1, the overview by Simon and Kaplan, also touches on the architecture at several points and also in the service of the larger picture. Both treatments are consistent with ours and provide useful redundancy.

This chapter considers only *symbolic architectures* and, more particularly, architectures whose structure is reasonably close to that analyzed in computer science. The space of all architectures is not well understood, and the extent and sense to which all architectures must be symbolic architectures is a matter of contention. Chapter 4 by Rumelhart covers nonsymbolic architectures, or more precisely the particular species under investigation by the connectionists.

First, we sketch the role the architecture plays in cognitive science. Second, we describe the requirements the cognitive architecture must meet. Third, we treat in detail the nature of the cognitive architecture. Fourth, we illustrate the concepts with two cognitive architectures: Act* and Soar. Fifth, we indicate briefly how theories of the architecture enter into other studies in cognitive science. We close with some open questions.

3.1 The Role of the Architecture in Cognitive Science

Viewing the world as constituted of *systems of mechanisms* whose *behavior* we observe is part of the common conceptual apparatus of science. When the systems are engineered or teleological, we talk about *structure* and *function*—a system of a given structure producing behavior that performs a given function in the encompassing system. The term *architecture* is used to indicate that the structure in question has some sort of primary, permanent, or originating character. As such one can talk about the architecture of the mind or a part of the mind in a general and descriptive way—the architecture of the visual system, an architecture for the conceptual system, and so on.

In cognitive science the notion of architecture has come to take on a quite specific and technical meaning, deriving from computer science. There the term stands for the hardware structure that produces a system that can be programmed. It is the design of a machine that admits the distinction between hardware and software.[1] The concept of an architecture for cognitive science then is the appropriate generalization and abstraction of the concept of computer architecture applied to human cognition: the fixed system of mechanisms that underlies and produces cognitive behavior. As such, an appropriate starting place is a description of an ordinary computer architecture.

The Architecture of Computers

Consider a simple (uniprocessor) digital computer. The top of figure 3.1 shows the gross physical configuration of the system. There is a set of components—a processor, a primary memory, and so on—joined by communication links (the link connecting almost everything together is called the bus). Over the links flow streams of bits. A look inside the processor (the lower-left portion of the figure) reveals more anatomical detail of components connected by links—a number of register memories; a data unit for carrying out various operations such as addition, intersection, shifting, and the like; and an interpreter unit for carrying out the instructions of the program. The primary memory contains a few instructions from a program. The address in the program address register points to one of them, which is brought into the program register and decoded. The left part of the instruction is used to select one of the basic operations of the computer, and the right part is used to address a cell of the primary memory, whose content is retrieved to become an argument for the operation. The repeated acts of obtaining the next instruction, interpreting it, and performing the operation on the argument are called the *fetch-execute cycle.*

Figure 3.1 specifies the architecture of a digital computer (given literary license). It describes a mechanistic system that behaves in a definite way. The language used to describe it takes much for granted, referring to registers, links, decoders, and so on. These components and how they operate require further specification—to say how they are to be realized in circuit technology and ultimately in electron physics—all of which can be taken for granted here.

The behavior of this machine depends on the program and data stored in the memory. Indeed the machine can exhibit essentially any behavior whatsoever depending on the content. By now we are all well ac-

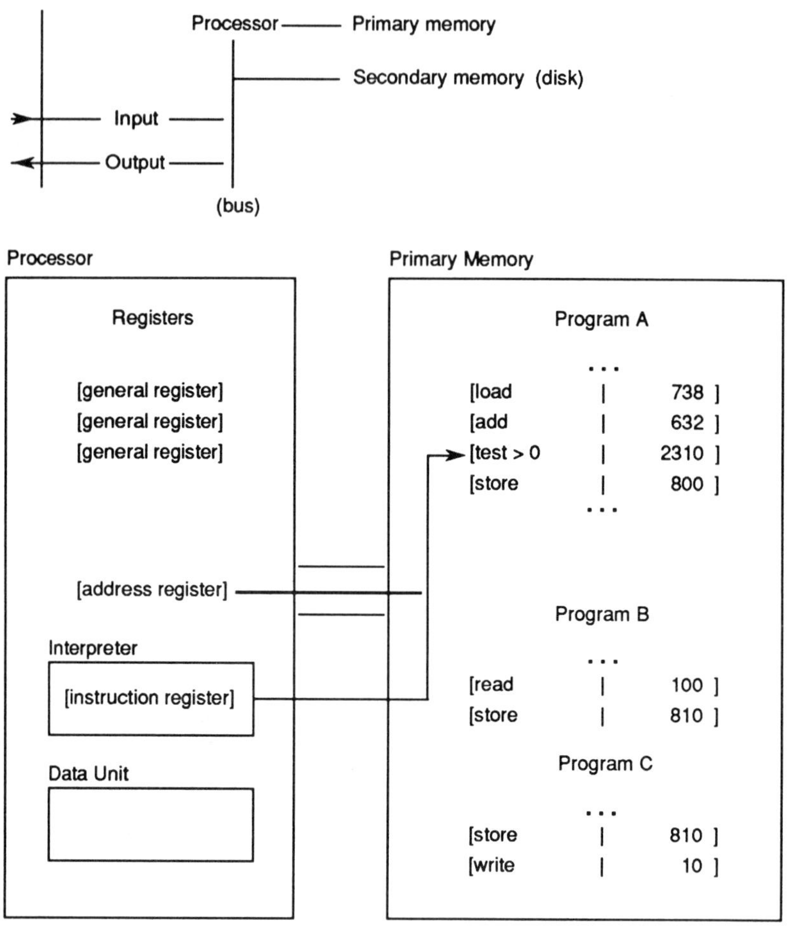

Figure 3.1 Structure of a simple digital computer

quainted with the amazing variety of such programs—computing statistics, keeping inventories, playing games, editing manuscripts, running machine tools, and so on—but also converting the machine's interaction with its environment to occur by a wide variety of languages, graphic displays, and the like. All this happens because of three things taken jointly: the computer architecture, which enables the interpretation of programs; the flexibility of programs to specify behavior, both for external consumption and for creating additional programs to be used in the future; and lots of memory to hold lots of programs with their required data so that a wide variety of behavior can occur.

Figure 3.1 is only the tip of the iceberg of computer architectures. It contains the essential ideas, however, and serves to introduce them in concrete form.

The Architecture of Cognition

Figure 3.1 epitomizes the invention of the computer, a mechanism that can exhibit indefinitely flexible, complex, responsive, and task-oriented behavior. We observe in humans flexible and adaptive behavior in seemingly limitless abundance and variety. A natural hypothesis is that systems such as that of figure 3.1 reveal the essential mechanisms of how humans attain their own flexibility and therefore of how the mind works.

A chief burden of chapter 2 (and a theme in chapter 1) is to show how this observation has been transformed into a major foundation of cognitive science. The empirical basis for this transformation has come from the immense diversity of tasks that have been accomplished by computers, including, but not limited to, the stream of artificial intelligence (AI) systems. Compelling force has been added to this transformation from the theory of computational mechanisms (Hopcroft and Ullman 1979), which abstracts from much that seems special in figure 3.1 and shows both the sufficiency and the necessity of computational mechanisms and how such mechanisms relate to systems having representations of their external world (that is, having semantics). The architectures that arise from this theory are called symbolic architectures.

As laid out in chapter 2, the human can be described at different system levels. At the top is the *knowledge level*, which describes the person as having goals and knowing things about the world, in which knowledge is used in the service of its goals (by the principle of rationality). The person can operate at the knowledge level only because it is also a *symbol level* system, which is a system that operates in terms of representations and information-processing operations on these representations. The symbol level must also be realized in terms of some substrate, and the architecture is that substrate defined in an appropriate descriptive language. For computers this turns out to be the *register-*

transfer level, in which bit-vectors are transported from one functional unit (such as an adder) to another, subject to gating by control bits. For humans it is the neural-circuit level, which currently seems well described as highly parallel interconnected networks of inhibitory and excitatory connections that process a medium of continuous signals. Below that of course are other levels of description—neurons, organelles, macromolecules, and on down.

This arrangement of system levels seems very special—it is after all the eye of the needle through which systems have to pass to be able to be intelligent. Nevertheless there is an immense variety of architectures and an immense variety of physical substrates in which they can be implemented. No real appreciation exists yet for this full double variety or its consequences, except that they are exceedingly large and diverse. It is relatively easy to understand a given architecture when presented, though there may be a fair amount of detail to wade through. However, it is difficult to see the behavioral consequences of an architecture, because it is so overlaid by the programs it executes. And it is extremely difficult to compare different architectures, for each presents its own total framework that can carve up the world in radically different ways. Despite these difficulties cognitive science needs to determine the architecture that underlies and supports human cognition.

The architecture does not by itself determine behavior. The other main contributors are the goal the person is attempting to attain, the task environment within which the person is performing, and the knowledge the person has. The first is not only the knowledge of the conditions or situation desired, but also the commitment to govern behavior to obtain such conditions. The second is the objective situation, along with the objective constraints about how the person can interact with the situation. The third is the subjective situation of the person in relation to the task. The knowledge involved in accomplishing any task is diverse and extensive and derives from multiple sources. These sources include the statement or presenting indications of the task, the immediately prior interaction with the task situation, the long-term experience with analogous or similar situations, prior education including the acquisition of skills, and the socialization and enculturation that provide the background orientation. All these sources of knowledge make their contribution.

The goal, task, and knowledge of course constitute the knowledge-level characterization of a person. The architecture's primary role is to make that possible by supporting the processing of the symbolic representations that hold the knowledge. If it did so perfectly, then the architecture would not appear as an independent factor in the determination of behavior any more than would acetylcholine or sulfur atoms. It would simply be the scaffolding that explains how the actual determinants (task and knowledge) are realized in our physical world.

But the knowledge-level characterization is far from perfect. As the linguists used to be fond of saying, there can be a large gap between competence and performance. The architecture shows through in many ways, both large and small. Indeed much of cognitive psychology is counting these ways—speed of processing, memory errors, linguistic slips, perceptual illusions, failures of rationality in decision making, interference effects of learned material, and on and on. These factors are grounded in part in the architecture. Aspects of behavior can also have their source in mechanisms and structure defined at lower levels—neural functioning, properties of muscle, imperfections in the corneal lens, macromolecular structure of drugs, the effects of raised temperature, and so on. When the architecture fails to support adequately knowledge-based goal-oriented behavior, however, it gives rise by and large to characteristics we see as psychological. Viewed this way, much of psychology involves the investigation of the architecture.

What the notion of the architecture supplies is the concept of the *total* system of mechanisms that are required to attain flexible intelligent behavior. Normally psychological investigations operate in isolation, though with a justified sense that the mechanisms investigated (memory, learning, memory retrieval, whatever) are necessary and important. The architecture adds the total system context within which such separate mechanisms operate, providing additional constraints that determine behavior. The architecture also brings to the fore additional mechanisms that must be involved and that have received less attention in experimental psychology, for instance, elementary operations and control. This requirement of integration is not just a pleasant condiment. Every complete human performance invokes most of the psychological functions we investigate piecemeal—perception, encoding, retrieval, memory, composition and selection of symbolic responses, decision making, motor commands, and actual motor responses. Substantial risks are incurred by psychological theory and experimentation when they focus on a slice of behavior, leaving all the rest as inarticulated background.

A theory of the architecture is a proposal for the total cognitive mechanism, rather than for a single aspect or mechanism. A proposed embodiment of an architecture, such as a simulation system, purports to be a complete mechanism for human cognition. The form of its memory embodies a hypothesis of the form of human symbolic specifications for action; the way its programs are created or modified embodies a hypothesis of the way human action specifications are created or modified; and so on (Newell 1987).

To summarize, the role of the architecture in cognitive science is to be the central element in a theory of human cognition. It is not the sole or even the predominant determinant of the behavior of the person, but it is the determinant of what makes that behavior psychological rather than a reflection of the person's goals in the light of their knowledge. To have a theory of cognition is to have a theory of the architecture.

3.2 Requirements on the Cognitive Architecture

Why should the cognitive architecture be one way or the other? All architectures provide programmability, which yields indefinitely flexible behavior. Why wouldn't one architecture do as well as another? We need to address this question as a preliminary to discussing the nature of the cognitive architecture. We need to understand the requirements that shape human cognition, especially beyond the need for universal computation. The cognitive architecture must provide the support necessary for all these requirements. The following is a list of requirements that could shape the architecture (adapted from Newell 1980):

1. Behave flexibly as a function of the environment
2. Exhibit adaptive (rational, goal-oriented) behavior
3. Operate in real time
4. Operate in a rich, complex, detailed environment
   a. perceive an immense amount of changing detail
   b. use vast amounts of knowledge
   c. control a motor system of many degrees of freedom
5. Use symbols and abstractions
6. Use language, both natural and artificial
7. Learn from the environment and from experience
8. Acquire capabilities through development
9. Live autonomously within a social community
10. Exhibit self-awareness and a sense of self

These requirements express our common though scientifically informed knowledge about human beings in their habitat. There is no way to know how complete the list is, but many relevant requirements are certainly included.

(1) We list first the requirement to behave flexibly as a function of the environment, since that is the central capability that architectures provide. If a system cannot make itself respond in whatever way is needed, it can hardly be intelligent. The whole purpose of this list, of course, is to go beyond this first item. (2) Flexibility by itself is only a means; it must be in the service of goals and rationally related to obtaining the things and conditions that let the organism survive and propagate. (3) Cognition must operate in real time. This demand of the environment is both important and pervasive. It runs directly counter to the requirements for flexibility, where time to compute is an essential resource. (4) The environment that humans inhabit has important characteristics

beyond just being dynamic: it is combinatorially rich and detailed, changing simultaneously on many fronts, but with many regularities at every time scale. This affects the cognitive system in several ways. (a) There must be multiple perceptual systems to tap the multiple dynamic aspects; they must all operate concurrently and dynamically, and some must have high bandwidth. (b) There must be very large memories because the environment provides the opportunity to know many relevant things, and in an evolutionary, hence competitive, world opportunity for some produces requirements for all. (c) For the motor system to move around and influence a complex world requires continual determination of many degrees of freedom at a rate dictated by the environment.

(5) Human cognition is able to use symbols and abstractions. (6) It is also able to use language, both natural and artificial. These two requirements might come to the same thing or they might impose somewhat distinct demands. Both are intimately related to the requirement for flexibility and might be redundant with it. But there might be important additional aspects in each. All this need not be settled for the list, which attempts coverage rather than parsimony or independence.

(7) Humans must learn from the environment, not occasionally but continuously and not a little but a lot. This also flows from the multitude of regularities at diverse time scales available to be learned. (8) Furthermore many of our capabilities are acquired through development. When the neonate first arrives, it is surely without many capabilities, but these seem to be exactly the high-level capabilities required to acquire the additional capabilities it needs. Thus there is a chicken-and-egg constraint, which hints at a significant specialization to make development possible. As with the requirements for symbols and language, the relation between learning and development is obscure. Whatever it turns out to be, both requirements belong in the list.

(9) Humans must live autonomously within a social community. This requirement combines two aspects. One aspect of autonomy is greater capability to be free of dependencies on the environment. Relative to the autonomy of current computers and robots, this implies the need for substantially increased capabilities. On the other hand much that we have learned from ethology and social theory speaks to the dependence of individuals on the communities in which they are raised and reside (von Cranach, Foppa, Lepinies, and Ploog 1979). The additional capabilities for low-level autonomy do not negate the extent to which socialization and embedding in a supportive social structure are necessary. If humans leave their communities, they become inept and dysfunctional in many ways. (10) The requirement for self-awareness is somewhat obscure. We surely have a sense of self. But it is not evident what functional role self-awareness plays in the total scheme of mind. Research has made clear the importance of metacognition—considering the capabilities of the self in relation to the task environ-

ment. But the link from metacognition to the full notion of a sense of self remains obscure.

Human cognition can be taken to be an information-processing system that is a solution to all of the listed requirements plus perhaps others that we have not learned about. Flexibility, the grounds for claiming that human cognition is built on an architecture, is certainly a prominent item, but it is far from the only one. Each of the others plays some role in making human cognition what it is.

The problem of this chapter is *not* what shape cognition as a whole takes in response to these requirements—that is the problem of cognitive science as a whole. Our problem is what is implied by the list for the shape of the architecture. For each requirement there exists a body of general and scientific knowledge, more or less well developed. But cognition is always the resultant of the architecture plus the content of the memories, combined under the impress of being adaptive. This tends to conceal the inner structure and reveal only knowledge-level behavior. Thus extracting the implications for the architecture requires analysis.

Several approaches are possible for such analyses, although we can only touch on them here. The most important one is to get temporally close to the architecture; if there is little time for programmed behavior to act, then the architecture has a chance to shine through. A good example is the exploration of immediate-response behavior that has established an arena of *automatic* behavior, distinguished from an arena of more deliberate *controlled* behavior (Schneider and Shiffrin 1977, Shiffrin and Schneider 1977). Another approach is to look for universal regularities. If some regularity shows through despite all sorts of variation, it may reflect some aspect of the architecture. A good example is the power law of practice, in which the time to perform repeated tasks, almost no matter what the task, improves according to a power law of the number of trials (Newell and Rosenbloom 1981). Architectural mechanisms have been hypothesized to account for it (Rosenbloom and Newell 1986). Yet another approach is to construct experimental architectures that support a number of the requirements in the list. These help to generate candidate mechanisms that will meet various requirements, but also reveal the real nature of the requirement. Many of the efforts in AI and in the development of AI software tools and environments fit this mold (a recent conference (VanLehn 1989) provides a good sampling).

Functional requirements are not the only sources of knowledge about the cognitive architecture. We know the cognitive architecture is realized in neural technology and that it was created by evolution. Both of these have major effects on the architecture. We do not treat either. The implications of the neural structure of the brain are treated in other chapters of this volume, and the implications of evolution, though tantalizing, are difficult to discern.

3.3 The Nature of the Architecture

We now describe the nature of the cognitive architecture. This is to be given in terms of functions rather than structures and mechanisms. In part this is because the architecture is defined in terms of what it does for cognition. But it is also because, as we have discovered from computer science, an extremely wide variety of structures and mechanisms have proved capable of providing the central functions. Thus no set of structures and mechanisms has emerged as sufficiently necessary to become the criterial features. The purely functional character of architectures is especially important when we move from current digital computers to human cognition. There the underlying system technology (neural circuits) and construction technology (evolution) are very different, so we can expect to see the functions realized in ways quite different from that in current digital technology.

In general the architecture provides support for a given function rather than the entire function. Because an architecture provides a way in which software (that is, content) can guide behavior in flexible ways, essentially all intellectual or control functions can be provided by software. Only in various limiting conditions—of speed, reliability, access to the architectural mechanisms themselves, and the like—is it *necessary* to perform all of the certain functions directly in the architecture. It may, of course, be *efficient* to perform functions in the architecture that could also be provided by software. From either a biological or engineering perspective there is no intrinsic reason to prefer one way of accomplishing a function rather than another. Issues of efficiency, modifiability, constructibility, resource cost, and resource availability join to determine what mechanisms are used to perform a function and how they divide between architectural support, and program and data.

The following list gives known functions of the architecture.

1. Memory
   a. Contains structures that contain symbol tokens
   b. Independently modifiable at some grain size
   c. Sufficient memory
2. Symbols
   a. Patterns that provide access to distal symbol structures
   b. A symbol token in the occurrence of a pattern in a structure
   c. Sufficient symbols
3. Operations
   a. Processes that take symbol structures as input and produce symbol structures as output
   b. Complete composibility

4. Interpretation
   a. Processes that take symbol structures as input and produce behavior by executing operations
   b. Complete interpretability
5. Interaction with the external world
   a. Perceptual and motor interfaces
   b. Buffering and interrupts
   c. Real-time demands for action
   d. Continuous acquisition of knowledge

We stress that these functions are only what are known currently. Especially with natural systems such as human cognition, but even with artificial systems, we do not know all the functions that are being performed.[2] The basic sources of our knowledge of the functions of the architecture is exactly what was skipped over in the previous section, namely the evolution of digital computer architectures and the corresponding abstract theory of machines that has developed in computer science. We do not ground the list in detail in this background, but anyone who wants to work seriously in cognitive architectures should have a fair acquaintance with it (Minsky 1967, Bell and Newell 1971, Hopcroft and Ullman 1979, Siewiorek, Bell, and Newell 1981, Agrawal 1986, Fernandez and Lang 1986, Gajski, Milutinovic, Siegel, and Furht 1987). We now take up the items of this list.

Symbol Systems

The central function of the architecture is to support a system capable of universal computation. Thus the initial functions in our list are those required to provide this capability. We should be able to generate the list simply by an analysis of existing universal machines. However, there are many varieties of universal systems. Indeed a striking feature of the history of investigation of universal computation has been the creation of many alternative independent formulations of universality, all of which have turned out to be equivalent. Turing machines, Markov algorithms, register machines, recursive functions, Pitts-McCulloch neural nets, Post productions, tag systems, plus all manner of digital computer organizations—all include within them a way of formulating a universal machine. These universal machines are all equivalent in flexibility and can all simulate each other. But like architectures (and for the same reasons) each formulation is a framework unto itself, and they often present a quite specific and idiosyncratic design, such as the tape, reading head, and five-tuple instruction format of a Turing machine. Although not without a certain charm (special but very general!), this tends to obscure the general functions that are required. The formulation we choose is the *symbol system*[3] (Newell 1980), which is equivalent to all the others. The prominent role it gives to symbols has proved useful in discussions of human cognition, however, and its avoidance of specific details of operation makes it less idiosyncratic than other formulations.

The first four items of the list of functions provide the capability for being a symbol system: *memory, symbols, operations,* and *interpretation.* However, none of these functions (not even symbols) is the function of *representation* of the external world. Symbols do provide an internal representation function, but representation of the external world is a function of the computational system as a whole, so that the architecture supports such representation, but does not itself provide it. (See chapter 2 for how this is possible, and how one moves from the knowledge level, which is *about* the external world, to the symbol level, which contains the mechanisms that provide *aboutness.*)

Memory and Memory Structures The first requirement is for *memory,* which is to say, structures that persist over time. In computers there is a memory hierarchy ranging from working registers within the central processor (such as the address register) to registers used for temporary state (such as an accumulator or operand stack), to primary memory (which is randomly addressed and holds active programs and data), to secondary memory (disks), to tertiary memory (magnetic tapes). This hierarchy is characterized by time constants (speed of access, speed of writing, and expected residency time) and memory capacity, in inverse relation—the slower the memory the more of it is available. The faster memory is an integral part of the operational dynamics of the system and is to be considered in conjunction with it. The larger-capacity, longer-term memory satisfies the requirement for the large amounts of memory needed for human cognition.

Memory is composed of structures, called *symbol structures* because they contain *symbol tokens.* In computers all of the memories hold the same kinds of structures, namely, vectors of bits (bytes and words), although occasionally larger multiples of such units occur (blocks and records). At some sufficiently large grain size the memory structures must be independently modifiable. There are two reasons for this. First, the variety of the external world is combinatorial—it comprises many independent multivalued dimensions located (and iterated) throughout space and time. Only a combinatorial memory structure can hold information about such a world. Second, built-in dependencies in the memory structure, while facilitating certain computations, must ultimately interfere with the ability of the system to compute according to the dictates of the environment. Dependencies in the memory, being unresponsive to dependencies in the environment, then become a drag, even though it may be possible to compensate by additional computation. Within some limits (here called the grain size) of course structures may exhibit various dependencies, which may be useful.[4]

Symbols and Symbol Tokens Symbol tokens are patterns in symbol structures that provide *access* to distal memory structures, that is, to structures elsewhere in memory.[5] In standard computer architectures a symbol is a memory address and a symbol token is a particular string of bits in a particular word that can be used as an address (by being shipped to the memory-address register, as in figure 3.1). The need for symbols[6] arises because it is not possible for all of the structure involved in a computation to be assembled ahead of time at the physical site of the computation. Thus it is necessary to travel out to other (distal) parts of the memory to obtain the additional structure. In terms of the knowledge level this is what is required to bring all of the system's knowledge to bear on achieving a goal. It is not possible generally to know in advance all the knowledge that will be used in a computation (for that would imply that the computation had already been carried out). Thus the ingredients for a symbol mechanism are some pattern within the structures being processed (the token), which can be used to open an access path to a distal structure (and which may involve search of the memory) and a retrieval path by means of which the distal structure can be communicated to inform the local site of the computation.[7]

Operations The system is capable of performing *operations* on symbol structures to compose new symbol structures. There are many variations on such operations in terms of what they do in building new structures or modifying old structures and in terms of how they depend on other symbol structures. The form such operations take in standard computers is the application of an operator to a set of operands, as specified in a fixed instruction format (see figure 3.1). Higher-level programming languages generalize this to the full scope of an applicative formalism, where ($F\ x_1, x_2, \ldots, x_n$) commands the system to apply the function F to operands $x_1, \ldots, x_n$ to produce a new structure.

Interpretation Some structures (not all) have the property of determining that a sequence of symbol operations occurs on specific symbol structures. These structures are called variously *codes, programs, procedures, routines,* or *plans.* The process of applying the operations is called *interpreting* the symbol structure. In standard computers this occurs by the fetch-execute cycle (compare figure 3.1), whereby each instruction is accessed, its operands decoded and distributed to various registers, and the operation executed. The simplicity of this scheme corresponds to the simplicity of machine language and is dictated by the complexity of what can be efficiently and reliably realized directly in hardware. More complex procedural (high-level) languages can be compiled into an elaborate program in the simpler machine language or executed on the fly (that is, interpretively) by the microcode of a simple subcomputer. Other alternatives are possible, for example, constructing a specific special-purpose machine that embodies the operations of the program and then activating the machine. All these come to the same thing—the ability to convert from symbol structures to behavior.

The Integrated System We now have all the ingredients of a symbol system. These are sufficient to produce indefinitely flexible behavior (requirement 1 in the first list). Figure 3.2 gives the essential interaction. Operations can construct symbol structures that can be interpreted to specify further operations to construct yet further symbol structures. This loop provides for the construction of arbitrary behavior as a function of other demands. The only additional requirements are some properties of sufficiency and completeness. Without sufficient memory and sufficient symbols the system will be unable to do tasks demanding sufficiently voluminous intermediate references and data, just because it will run out of resources. Without completeness in the loop some sequences of behavior will not be producible. This has two faces: complete composability, so operators can construct any symbol structure, and complete interpretability, so interpretable symbols structures are possible for any arrangement of operations. Under completeness should also be included reliability—if the mechanisms do not operate as posited (including memory), then results need not follow.

Universality is a simple and elegant way to state what it takes to be flexible, by taking flexibility to its limit.[8] Failures of sufficiency and completeness do not necessarily threaten flexibility in critical ways. In a finite world all resources are finite, but so is the organism's sojourn on earth. Failures of completeness are a little harder to assess because their satisfaction can be extremely devious and indirect (including the uses of error-detecting and correcting mechanisms to deal with finite reliability). But in general there is a continuum of effect in real terms with the severity and extent of the failure. However, no theory is available to inform us about approximations to universality.

In addition to providing flexibility, symbol systems provide important support for several of the other requirements in the first list. For adapt-

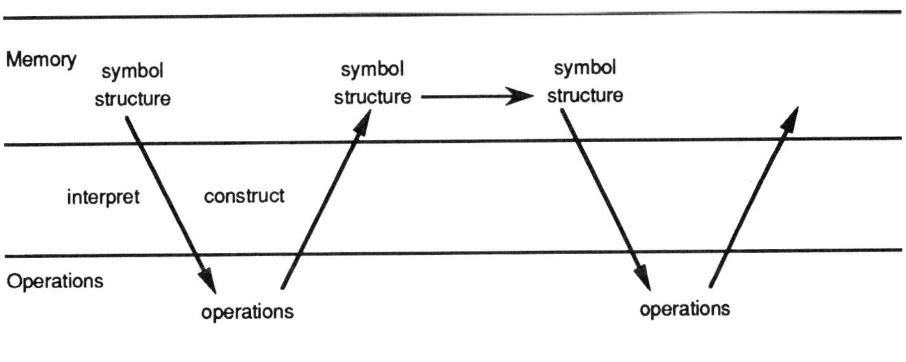

Figure 3.2 The basic loop of interpretation and construction

ability (requirement 2) they provide the ability to represent goals and to conditionalize action off of them. For using vast amounts of knowledge (requirement 4.b), they provide symbol structures in which the knowledge can be encoded and arbitrarily large memories with the accompanying ability to access distal knowledge as necessary. For symbols, abstractions, and language (requirements 5 and 6) they provide the ability to manipulate representations. For learning (requirement 7) they provide the ability to create long-term symbol structures.

Interaction with the External World

Symbol systems are components of a larger embedding system that lives in a real dynamic world, and their overall function is to create appropriate interactions of this larger system with that world. The interfaces of the large system to the world are sensory and motor devices. Exactly where it makes sense to say the architecture ends and distinct input/output subsystems begin depends on the particular system. All information processing right up to the energy transducers at the skin might be constructed on a common design and be part of a single architecture, multiple peripheral architectures of distinct design might exist, or multiple specialized systems for transduction and communication might exist that are not architectures according to our definition. Despite all this variability several common functions can be identified: The first is relatively obvious—the architecture must provide for the interfaces that connect the sensory and motor devices to the symbol system. Just what these interfaces do and where they are located is a function of how the boundary is drawn between the central cognitive system (the symbol system) and the peripheral systems.

The second arises from the asynchrony between the internal and external worlds. Symbol systems are an interior milieu, protected from the external world, in which information processing in the service of the organism can proceed. One implication is that the external world and the internal symbolic world proceed asynchronously. Thus there must be *buffering* of information between the two in both directions. How many buffer memories and of what characteristics depends on the time constants and rates of the multiple inputs and outputs. If transducers are much slower than internal processing, of course the transducer itself becomes a sufficiently accurate memory. In addition there must be *interrupt* mechanisms to cope with the transfer of processing between the multiple asynchronous sources of information.

The third function arises from the real-time demand characteristics of the external world (requirement 3 in the first list). The environment provides a continually changing kaleidoscope of opportunities and threats, with their own time constants. One implication for the architecture is for an interrupt capability, so that processing can be switched in time to new demands. The mechanics of interruption has already been posited, but the real-time demand also makes clear a requirement for precognitive assessment, that is, for assessment that occurs before assessment by the cognitive system. A demand that is more difficult to specify sharply, but is nonetheless real, is that processing be oriented toward getting answers rapidly. This cannot be an unconditional demand, if we take the time constants of the implementation technology as fixed (neural circuits for human cognition), because computing some things faster implies computing other things slower, and more generally there are intrinsic computational complexities. Still, architectures that provide effective time-limited computation are indicated.

The fourth function arises from an implication of a changing environment—the system cannot know in advance everything it needs to know about such an environment. Therefore the system must continually acquire knowledge from the environment (part of requirement 7) and do so at time constants dictated by the environment (a less obvious form of requirement 3). Symbol systems have the capability of acquiring knowledge, so in this respect at least no new architectural function is involved. The knowledge to be acquired flows in from the environment in real time, however, and not under the control of the system. It follows that learning must also occur essentially in real time. In part this is just the dynamics of the bathtub—on average the inflow to a bathtub (here encoded experience) must equal the outflow from the bathtub (here experience processed to become knowledge). But it is coupled with the fact that the water never stops flowing in, so that there is no opportunity to process at leisure.

Summary

We have attempted to list the functions of the cognitive architecture, which is to provide the support for human cognition, as characterized in the list of requirements for shaping the architecture. Together the symbol-system and real-time functions cover a large part of the primitive functionality needed for requirements 1 through 7. They do not ensure that the requirements are met, but they do provide needed support.

There is little to say for now about architectural support for development (requirement 8). The difficulty is our minimal knowledge of the mechanisms involved in enabling developmental transitions, even at a psychological level (Klahr 1989). It makes a significant difference whether development occurs through the type of general learning that is supported by symbol systems—that is, the creation of long-term symbol structures—or by distinct mechanisms. Even if development were a part of general learning after the first several years, it might require special architectural mechanisms at the beginning of life. Such requirements might shape the architecture in many other ways.

Autonomy in a social environment is another requirement (number 9 in the list) where we cannot yet pin down additional functions for the architecture to support. On the more general issue of autonomy, however, issues that have proved important in computer architecture include protection, resource allocation, and exception handling. Protection enables multiple components of a system to behave concurrently without interfering with each other. Resource allocation enables a system to work within its finite resources of time and memory, recycling resources as they are freed. Exception handling enables a system to recover from error situations that would otherwise require intervention by a programmer (for example, a division by zero or the detection of an inconsistency in a logic data base).

Issues of self-awareness (requirement 10) have recently been an active research topic in computer science, under the banner of metalevel architecture and reflection (the articles in Maes and Nardi 1988 provide a good sampling). Functionalities studied include how a system can model, reason about, control, and modify itself. Techniques for exception handling turn out to be a special case of the ability of a system to reason about and modify itself. On the psychological side the work on metacognition has made us aware of the way knowledge of a person's own capabilities (or lack of) affects performance (Brown 1978). As yet this work does not seem to have clear implications for the architecture, because it is focused on the development and use of adaptive strategies that do not seem to require special access to the instantaneous running state of the system, which is the obvious architectural support issue.

3.4 Example Architectures: Act* and Soar

We now have an analysis of the functions of a cognitive architecture and the general way it responds to the requirements of our first list. To make this analysis concrete, we examine two cognitive architectures, Act* (Anderson 1983) and Soar (Laird, Newell, and Rosenbloom 1987). Act* is the first theory of the cognitive architecture with sufficient detail and completeness to be worthy of the name. It represents a long development (Anderson and Bower 1973, Anderson 1976), and further developments have occurred since the definitive book was written (Anderson 1986, Anderson and Thompson 1988). Soar is a more recent entry as a cognitive theory (Newell 1987, Polk and Newell 1988, Rosenbloom, Laird, and Newell 1988). Its immediate prior history is as an AI architecture (Laird, Rosenbloom, and Newell 1986, Steir et al. 1987), but it has roots in earlier psychological work (Newell and Simon 1972, Newell 1973, Rosenbloom and Newell 1988). Using two architectures provides some variety to help clarify points and also permits a certain amount of comparison. Our purpose is to make clear the nature of the cognitive architecture, however, rather than to produce a judgment between the architectures.

Overview

Let us start with a quick overview of the two systems and then proceed to iterate through the functions in the second list. Figure 3.3 gives the

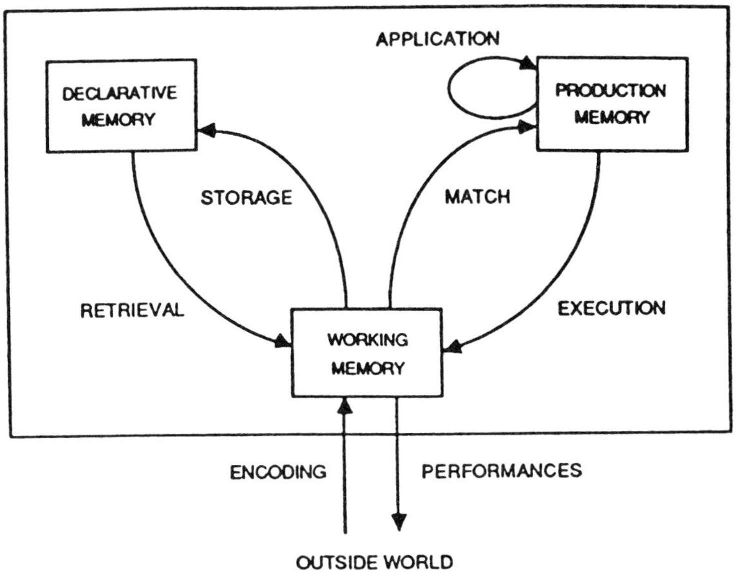

Figure 3.3 Overview of the Act* cognitive architecture (Anderson 1983)

basic structure of Act*. There is a long-term declarative memory in the form of a semantic net. There is a long-term procedural memory in the form of productions. Strengths are associated with each long-term memory element (both network nodes and productions) as a function of its use. Each production has a set of conditions that test elements of a working memory and a set of actions that create new structures in the working memory. The working memory is activation based; it contains the activated portion of the declarative memory plus declarative structures generated by production firings and perception.[9] Activation spreads automatically (as a function of node strength) through working memory and from there to other connected nodes in the declarative memory. Working memory may contain goals that serve as large sources of activation. Activation, along with production strength, determines how fast the matching of productions proceeds. Selection of productions to fire is a competitive process between productions matching the same data. New productions are created by compiling the effects of a sequence of production firings and retrievals from declarative memory so that the new productions can move directly from initial situations to final results.[10] Whenever a new element is created in working memory, there is a fixed probability it will be stored in declarative memory.

Figure 3.4 provides a corresponding overview of Soar. There is a single long-term memory—a production system—that is used for both declarative and procedural knowledge. There is a working memory that contains a goal hierarchy, information associated with the goal hierarchy, preferences about what should be done, perceptual information, and motor commands. Interaction with the outside world occurs via

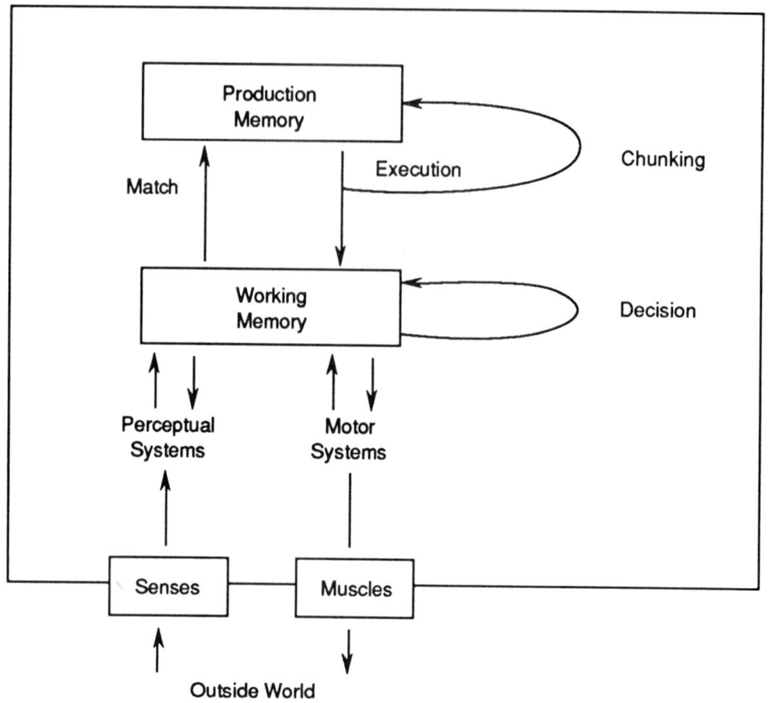

Figure 3.4 Overview of the Soar cognitive architecture

interfaces between working memory and one or more perceptual and motor systems. All tasks are formulated as searches in problem spaces, that is, as starting from some initial state in a space and finding a desired state by the application of the operators that comprise the space. Instead of making decisions about what productions to execute—all productions that successfully match are fired in parallel—decisions are made about what problem spaces, states, and operators to utilize. These decisions are based on preferences retrieved from production memory into working memory. When a decision proves problematic (because of incomplete or inconsistent knowledge), a subgoal is automatically created by the architecture and problem solving recurses on the task of resolving the impasse in decision making. This generates a hierarchy of goals and thus problem spaces. New productions are created continuously from the traces of Soar's experience in goal-based problem solving (a process called chunking).

Memory

Memory is to be identified by asking what persists over time that can be created and modified by the system. Both Act* and Soar have memory hierarchies that range in both time constants and volume. At the small, rapid end both have working memories. Working memory is a temporary memory that cannot hold data over any extended duration. In Act* this is manifest because working memory is an activated subset of declarative memory and thus ebbs and flows with the processing of activation. In Soar working memory appears as a distinct memory. Its short-term character derives from its being linked with goals and their problem spaces, so that it disappears automatically as these goals are resolved.

Beyond working memory both architectures have permanent memories of unbounded size, as required for universality. Act* has two such memories—declarative memory and production memory—with strengths associated with each element in each memory. The normal path taken by new knowledge in Act* is from working memory to declarative memory to production memory. Declarative memory comes before production memory in the hierarchy because it has shorter storage and access times (though it cannot lead directly to action). Soar has only one permanent memory of unbounded size—production memory—which is used for both declarative and procedural knowledge. Soar does not utilize strengths.

The above picture is that Act* has two totally distinct memories, and Soar has one that is similar to one of Act*'s memories. However, this conventional surface description conceals some important aspects. One is that Act* and Soar productions do not function in the same way in their respective systems (despite having essentially the same condition-action form). Act* productions correspond to problem-solving operators. This is essentially the way productions are used throughout the AI and expert-systems world. Soar productions operate as an associative memory. The action side of a production contains the symbol structures that are held in the memory; the condition side provides the access path to these symbol structures. Firing a Soar production is the act of retrieval of its symbol structures. Operators in Soar are implemented by collections of productions (or search in subgoals). Another hidden feature is that Act*'s production memory is realized as a network structure similar in many ways to its semantic net. The main effect is that activation governs the rate of matching of productions in the same way that activation spreads through the declarative network. Thus these two memories are not as distinct as it might seem.

In both Act* and Soar the granularity of long-term memory (the independently modifiable unit) is relatively fine, being the individual production and, for Act*'s declarative memory, the node and link. This is a much larger unit than the word in conventional computers (by about two orders of magnitude) but much smaller than the frame or schema (again by about two orders of magnitude). This is an important architectural feature. The frame and schema have been introduced on the hypothesis that the unit of memory organization needs to be relatively large to express the organized character of human thought (Minsky 1975). It is not easy to make size comparisons between units of memory organization because this is one place where the idiosyncratic world-view character of architectures is most in evidence, and all memory organization have various larger and smaller hierarchical units. Nevertheless both Act* and Soar are on the fine-grained side.

The memory structures of both Act* and Soar are the discrete symbolic structures familiar from systems such as Lisp. There are differences in detail. Soar has a uniform scheme of objects with sets of attributes and values. Act* has several primitive data structures: attributes and values (taken to be the abstract propositional code), strings (taken to be the temporal code), and metric arrays (taken to be the spatial code). The primary requirement of a data structure is combinatorial variability, and all these structures possess it. The secondary considerations are on the operations that are required to read and manipulate the data structures, corresponding to what the structures are to represent. Thus standard computers invariably have multiple data structures, each with associated primitive operations, for example, for arithmetic or text processing. Act* here is taking a clue from this standard practice.

Symbols

Symbols are to be identified by finding the mechanisms that provide distal access to memory structures that are not already involved in processing. For both Act* and Soar this is the pattern match of the production system, which is a process that starts with symbolic structures in working memory and determines that a production anywhere in the long-term memory will fire. The symbol tokens here are the combinations of working memory elements that match production conditions. Each production's left-hand side is a symbol.

For Soar this is the only mechanism for distal access (working memory being essentially local). For Act* there is also a mechanism for distal access to its declarative memory, in fact a combination of two mechanisms. First, each token brought into working memory by firing a production (or by perception) makes contact with its corresponding node in the declarative semantic net. Second, spreading activation then operates to provide access to associated nodes.

It is useful to identify the pair of features that gives symbolic access in production systems its particular flavor. The first feature is the context-dependent nature of the production match. Simple machine addresses act as context-independent symbols. No matter what other structures exist, the address causes information to be retrieved from the same location.[11] In a production system a particular pattern can be a symbol that results in context-independent access to memory structures, or (more typically) it can be conjoined with additional context patterns to form a more complex symbol that constrains access to occur only when the context is present.

The second feature is the recognition nature of the production match. Traditional computers access memory either by pointers to arbitrary memory locations (random access) or by sequential access to adjacent locations (large secondary stores). In production systems symbols are constructed out of the same material that is being processed for the task, so memory access has a *recognition, associative,* or *content-addressed* nature. All schemes can support universality; however, the recognition scheme is responsive to two additional cognitive requirements. First, (approximately) constant-time access to the whole of memory is responsive to the real-time requirement. This includes random-access and recognition memories, but excludes sequential access systems such as Turing machines. But specific task-relevant accessing schemes must be constructed, or the system is doomed to operate by generate and test (and might as well be a tape machine). Recognition memories construct the accessing paths from the ingredients of the task and thus avoid deliberate acts of construction, which are required by location-pointer schemes. This may actually be an essential requirement for a learning system that has to develop entirely on its own. Standard programming involves intelligent programmers who invent specific accessing schemes based on deep analysis of a task.[12]

Operations

The operations are to be identified by asking how new structures get built and established in the long-term memory. In standard computer systems the form in which the operations are given is dictated by the needs of interpretation, that is, by the structure of the programming language. Typically everything is fit within an operation-operand structure, and there is a single, heterogeneous set of all primitive operation codes—load, store, add, subtract, and, or, branch-on-zero, execute, and so on. Some of these are operations that produce new symbol structures in memory, but others affect control or deal with input/output.

Production systems, as classically defined, also operate this way. The right-hand-side actions are operation-operand structures that can specify general procedures, although a standard set of operations are predefined (make, replace, delete, write . . .). In some it is possible to execute a specified production or production system on the right-hand side, thus providing substantial right-hand-side control. But Act* and Soar use a quite different scheme.

The right-hand-side action becomes essentially just the operation of creating structures in working memory. This operation combines focusing, modifying, and creating—it brings existing structures into working memory, it creates working memory structures that relate existing structures, and it creates new structures if they do not exist. This operation is coextensive with the retrieval of knowledge from long-term memory (production firing). The dependence of the operation on existing structures (that is, its inputs) occurs by the matching of the production conditions. It is this matching against what is already in working memory that permits the multiple functions of focusing, modifying, and creating to be distinguished and to occur in the appropriate circumstances, automatically, so to speak. Along with this the act of retrieval from long-term memory (into working memory) does not happen as a distinct operation that reproduces the content of long-term memory in working memory. Rather each retrieval is an act of computation (indeed computation takes place only in concert with such retrievals), so that working memory is never the same as stored memory and is always to some extent an adaptation of the past to the present.

In Act* and Soar storing information in long-term memory is separated from the act of computation in working memory. It is incorporated as learning new productions, called *production compilation* in Act* and *chunking* in Soar, but similar operations nonetheless. The context of production acquisition is the occasion of goal satisfaction or termination, and the constructed production spans from the conditions holding before the goal to the actions that caused the final resolution. The production is simply added to the long-term production memory and becomes indistinguishable from any other production. Such a production is functional, producing in one step what took many steps originally. It also constitutes an implicit form of generalization in that its conditions are extracted from the total context of working memory at learning time, and so can be evoked in situations that can be arbitrarily different in ways that are irrelevant to these conditions. Production compilation and chunking go considerably beyond the minimal support for experiential learning provided by a standard symbol system. Without deliberate effort or choice they automatically acquire new knowledge that is a function of their experiences.

Act* has other forms of memory aside from the productions and necessarily must have operations for storing in each of them. They are all automatic operations that do not occur under deliberate control of the system. One is the strength of productions, which governs how fast they are processed and hence whether they become active in an actual situation. Every successful firing of a production raises its strength a little and hence increases the likelihood that if satisfied it will actually fire (another form of experiential learning). The second is storage in declarative memory. Here there is simply a constant probability that a newly created element will become a permanent part of declarative memory. Declarative learning is responsive to the requirement of learning from the environment. In Soar chunking performs this function in addition to its function of learning from experience.

Interpretation

Interpretation is to be identified by finding where a system makes its behavior dependent on the symbolic structures in its long-term memory, in particular, on structures that it itself created earlier. A seemingly equivalent way is to find what memory structures correspond to the program in typical computer systems, namely, the symbol structures that specify a sequence of operations: do this, then do that, then do this, although also admitting conditionals and calls to subprocedures. Namely, one seeks compact symbol structures that control behavior over an extended interval.

One looks in vain for such symbol structures in the basic descriptions of the Act* and Soar architectures. (Program structures can exist of course, but they require software interpreters.) Memory-dependent behavior clearly occurs, however, and is derived from multiple sources—production systems, problem-solving control knowledge, and goal structures.

The first source in both systems is the form of interpretation inherent in production systems. A production system shreds control out into independent fragments (the individual productions) spread out all over production memory, with data elements in working memory entering in at every cycle. This control regime is often referred to as *data directed*, in contrast to *goal directed*, but this characterization misses some important aspects. Another way to look at it is as a *recognize-act cycle* in contrast to the classical *fetch-execute cycle* that characterizes standard computers. According to this view, an important dimension of interpretation is the amount of decision making that goes on between steps. The fetch-execute cycle essentially has only a pointer into a plan and has to take deliberate steps (doing tests and branches) to obtain any conditionality at all. The recognize-act cycle opens up the interpretation at every point to anything that the present working memory can suggest. This puts the production match *inside* the interpretation cycle.

The second source is the control knowledge used to select problem-solving operators. In Act* the productions are the problem-solving operators. As described in the previous paragraph, production selection is a function of the match between working memory elements and production conditions. Several additional factors, however, also come into play in determining the rate of matching and thus whether a production is selected for execution. One factor is the activation of the working memory elements being matched. A second factor is the strength of the production being matched. A third factor is the competition between productions that match the same working memory elements in different ways.

In Soar problem-solving operators are selected through a two-phase *decision cycle*. First, during the elaboration phase the long-term production memory is accessed repeatedly—initial retrievals may evoke additional retrievals—in parallel (there is no conflict resolution) until quiescence. Any elements can be retrieved, but among these are *preferences* that state which of the operators are acceptable, rejectable, or preferable to others. When all the information possible has been accumulated, the decision procedure winnows the available preferences and makes the next decision, which then moves the system to the next cycle.

In fact Soar uses this same basic interpreter for more than just selecting what operator to execute. It is always trying to make the decisions required to operate in a problem space: to decide what problem space to use, what state to use in that problem space, what operator to use at that state, and what state to use as the result of the operator. This is what forces all activity to take place in problem spaces. This contrasts with the standard computer, which assumes all activity occurs by following an arbitrary program.

The third source of memory-dependent behavior is the use of goal structures. Act* provides special architectural support for a goal hierarchy in its working memory. The current goal is a high source of activation, which therefore operates to focus attention by giving prominence to productions that have it as one of their conditions. The architecture takes care of the tasks of popping successful subgoals and moving the focus to subsequent subgoals, providing a depth-first traversal of the goal hierarchy. Thus the characterization of data- versus goal-directed processing is somewhat wide of the mark. Act* is a paradigm example of an AI system that uses goals and methods to achieve adaptability (requirement 2 in the first list). Complex tasks are controlled by productions that build up the goal hierarchy by adding conjunctions of goals to be achieved in the future.

Soar uses a much less deliberate strategy for the generation of goals. When the decision procedure cannot produce a single decision from the collection of preferences that happen to accumulate—because, for example, no options remain acceptable or several indistinguishable options remain—an impasse is reached. Soar assumes this indicates lack of knowledge—given additional knowledge of its preferences, a decision could have been reached. It thus creates a subgoal to resolve this impasse. An impasse is resolved just when preferences are generated, of whatever nature, that lead to a decision at the higher level. Thus Soar generates its own subgoals out of the impasses the architecture can detect, in contrast to Act*, which generates its subgoals by deliberate action on the part of its productions. The effect of deliberate subgoals is achieved in Soar by the combination of an operator, which is deliberately generated and selected, and an impasse that occurs if productions do not exist that implement the operator. In the subgoal for this impasse the operator acts as the specification of a goal to be achieved.

Interaction with the External World

Act*, as is typical of many theories of cognition, focuses on the central architecture. Perception and motor behavior are assumed to take place in additional processing systems off stage. Input arrives in working, which thus acts as a buffer between the unpredictable stream of environmental events and the cognitive system. Beyond this, however, the architecture has simply not been elaborated on in these directions.

Soar has the beginnings of a complete architecture, which embeds the central architecture within a structure for interacting with the external world. As shown in figure 3.4, Soar is taken as a controller of a dynamic system interacting with a dynamic external environment (located across the bottom of the figure). There are processes that transduce the energies in the environment into signals for the system. Collectively they are called *perception,* although they are tied down only on the sensory side (transduction from the environment). Similarly there are processes that affect the environment. Collectively they are called the *motor system,* although they are tied down only on the physical action side. As in Act* working memory serves as the buffer between the environment and central cognition.

The total system consists of more than perception to central cognition to the motor system. There are productions, called *encoding productions* and *decoding productions.* These are identical in form and structure to the productions of central cognition. They differ only in being independent of the decision cycle—they just run free. On the input side, as elements arrive autonomously from the perceptual system, encoding productions provide what could be termed perceptual parsing, putting the elements into a form to be considered by central cognition. On the output side decoding productions provide what could be called motor-program decoding of commands produced by the cognitive system into the form used by the motor system. The motor system itself may produce elements back into the working memory (possibly parsed by encoding productions), permitting monitoring and adjustment.

All this activity is not under control; these productions recognize and execute at will, concurrently with each other and central cognition. Control is exercised by central cognition, which can now be seen to consist essentially of just the architecture of the decision mechanism, from which flows the decision cycle, impasses, the goal stack, and the problem-space organization. Further, central cognition operates essentially as a form of localized supervisory control over autonomous and continuing activities in working memory generated by the perception systems, the motor systems, and their coupled encoding and decoding productions.

This permits an understanding of an architectural question that has consumed a lot of attention, namely, wherein lies the serial character of cognition? Central cognition is indeed serial, which is what the decision mechanism enforces, and so it can consider only some of what goes on in the working memory. The serial system is imposed on a sea of autonomous parallel activity to attain control, that is, for the system to be able to prevent from occurring actions that are not in its interests. Thus seriality is a designed feature of the system. Seriality can occur for other reasons as well, which can be summarized generally as resource constraints or bottlenecks. Such bottlenecks can arise from the nature of the underlying technology and thus be a limitation on the system.

Interrupt capabilities are to be identified by finding where behavior can switch from one course to another that is radically different. For Act* switching occurs by the basic maximum-selecting property of an activation mechanism—whatever process can manage the highest activation can take over the control of behavior. For Soar switching occurs by the decision cycle—whatever can marshal the right preferences compared with competing alternatives can control behavior. Switching can thus occur at a fine grain. For both Act* and Soar their basic switching mechanism is also an interrupt mechanism, because alternatives from throughout the system compete on an equal basis. This arises from the open character of production systems that contact all of memory at each cycle. Thus radical changes of course can occur at any instant. This contrasts with standard computers. Although arbitrary switching is possible at each instruction (for example, branch on zero to an arbitrary program), such shifts must be determined deliberately and by the (preconstructed) program that already has control. Thus the issue for the standard computer is how to be interrupted, whereas the issue for Soar and Act* (and presumably for human cognition) is how to keep focused.

Learning from the environment involves the long-term storage of structures that are based on inputs to the system. Act* stores new inputs into declarative memory with a fixed probability, from which inputs can get into production memory via compilation, a process that should be able to keep pace with the demands of a changing environment. Soar stores new inputs in production memory via chunking. This implies that an input must be used in a subgoal for it to be stored, and that the bandwidth from the environment into long-term memory will be a function of the rate at which environmental inputs can be used.

Summary

We have now instantiated the functions of the cognitive architecture for two architectures, Soar and Act*, using their commonalities and differences to make evident how their structures realize these functions. The communalities of Act* and Soar are appreciable, mostly because both are built around production systems. We have seen that production systems, or more generally, recognition-based architectures, are a species of architecture that is responsive to the real-time requirement, which is clearly one of the most powerful shapers of the architecture beyond the basic need for symbolic computation.

The move to production systems, however, is only the first of three major steps that have moved Act* and Soar jointly into a very different part of the architecture space from all of the classical computers. The second step is the abandonment of the application formalism of applying operations to operands. This abandonment is not an intrinsic part of production systems, as evidenced by the almost universal use of application on the action side of productions. This second step locks the operations on symbolic structures into the acts of memory retrieval.

The third step is the separation of the act of storing symbolic structures in long-term memory—the learning mechanisms of Act* and Soar—from the deliberate acts of performing tasks.

There are some architectural differences between Act* and Soar, though not all appear to be major differences when examined carefully. One example is the dual declarative and procedural memory of Act* versus the single production memory of Soar. Another is the use of activation in Act* versus the use of accumulated production executions (the elaboration phase) in Soar. A third is the commitment to multiple problem spaces and the impasse mechanism in Soar versus the single-space environment with deliberate subgoals in Act*. Thus these architectures differ enough to explore a region of the architecture space.

The downside of using two closely related architectures for the exposition is that we fail to convey an appreciation of how varied and rich in alternatives the space of architecture is. With a slight stretch we might contend we have touched three points in the architecture space: classical (von Neumann) architectures, classical production systems, and Act* and Soar. But we could have profitably examined applicative languages (for example, Lisp; see Steele 1984), logic programming languages (for example, Prolog; see Clocksin and Mellish 1984), frame (or schema) systems (for example, KLONE; see Brachman 1979), blackboard architectures (for example, BB1; see Hayes-Roth 1985), and others as well. Also we could have explored the effect of parallelism, which itself has many architectural dimensions. This was excluded because it is primarily driven by the need to exploit or compensate for implementation technology, although (as has been pointed out many times) it can also serve as a response to the real-time requirement.

3.5 The Uses of the Architecture

Given that the architecture is a component of the human cognitive system, it requires no justification to spend scientific effort on it. Understanding the architecture is a scientific project in its own right. The architecture, however, as the frame in terms of which all processing is done and the locus of the structural constraints on human cognition, would appear to be the central element in a general theory of cognition. This would seem to imply that the architecture enters into all aspects of cognition. What keeps this implication at bay is the fact (oft noted, by now) that architectures hide themselves beneath the knowledge level. For many aspects of human cognitive life, what counts are the goals, the task situation, and the background knowledge (including education, socialization, and enculturation). So the architecture may be critical for cognition, just as biochemistry is, but with only circumscribed consequences for ongoing behavior and its study.

How then is a detailed theory of the architecture to be used in cognitive science, other than simply filling in its own part of the picture?

There are four partial answers to this question, which we take up in turn.

Establishing Gross Parameters

The first answer presupposes that the architecture has large effects on cognition, but that these effects can be summarized in a small set of gross parameters. The following list assembles one set of such parameters, which are familiar to all cognitive scientists—the size of short-term memory, the time for an elementary operation, the time to make a move in a problem space, and the rate of acquisition into long-term memory:

1. Memory Unit: 1 chunk composed of 3 subchunks
2. Short-term memory size: 3 chunks plus 4 chunks from long-term memory
3. Time per elementary operation: 100 ms
4. Time per step in a problem space: 2 s
5. Time to learn new material: 1 chunk per 2 s

It is not possible to reason from parameters alone. Parameters always imply a background model. Even to fill in the list it is necessary to define a unit of memory (the chunk), which then already implies a hierarchical memory structure. Likewise to put a sequence of elementary operations together and sum their times is already to define a functionally serial processing structure.

The block diagrams that have been a standard feature in cognitive psychology since the mid-1950s (Broadbent 1954) express the sort of minimal architectural structure involved. Mostly they are too sketchy, in particular, providing only a picture of the memories and their transfer paths. A somewhat more complete version, called the *model human processor* (Card, Moran, and Newell 1983), is shown in figure 3.5, which indicates not only the memories but a processor structure of three parallel processors—perceptual, cognitive, and motor. Perception and motor systems involve multiple concurrent processors for different modalities and muscle systems, but there is only a single cognitive processor. The parameters of the two figures have much in common. Figure 3.5 is of course a static picture. By its very lack of detail it implies the simplest of processing structures. In fact it can be supplemented by some moderately explicit general principles of operation (Card, Moran, and Newell 1983), such as that uncertainty always increases processing time. These principles provide some help in using it, but are a long way from making the scheme into a complete architecture. In particular the elementary operations and the details of interpretation remain essentially undefined.

If the way the architecture influences behavior can be summarized by a small set of parameters plus a simple abstract background model,

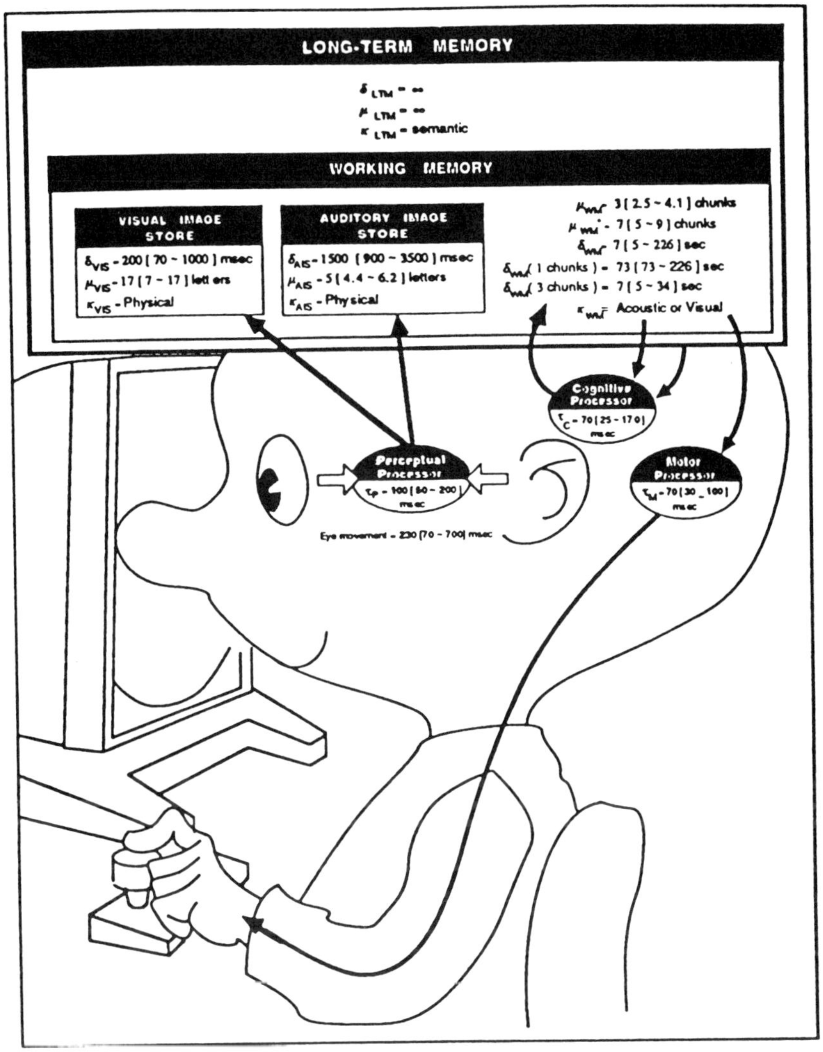

Figure 3.5 The model human processor block diagram (Card, Moran, and Newell 1983)

then the contribution from studying the architecture is twofold. First, given an established scheme such as figure 3.5, the parameters need to be pinned down, their variability understood, their mutability discovered, their limits of use assessed, and so on. Second, the gross processing model can be wrong, not in being a gross approximation (which is presumed) but in being the wrong sort of formulation. If it were replaced with a quite different formulation, then inferences might become easier, a broader set of inferences might be possible, and so forth. One such example from the mid-1970s is the replacement of the multistore model of memory with a model containing only a single memory within which information is distinguished only by the depth to which it has been processed (Craik and Lockhart 1972).

The Form of Simple Cognitive Behavior

To perform a complex task involves doing a sequence of basic operations in an arrangement conditional on the input data. Much of psychological interest depends on knowing the sequence of operations that humans perform for a given task, and much psychological effort, both experimental and theoretical, is focused on finding such sequences. This is especially true for tasks that are primarily cognitive, in which perceptual and motor operations play only a small role in the total sequence.

The architecture dictates both the basic operations and the form in which arrangements of operations are specified, namely, the way behavior specifications are encoded symbolically. Thus the architecture plays some role in determining such sequences. For tasks of any complexity, however, successful behavior can be realized in many different ways. At bottom this is simply the brute fact that different methods or algorithms exist for a given task, as when a space can be searched depth first, breadth first, or best first, or a column of numbers can be added from the top or the bottom. Thus writing down the sequence of operations followed by a subject for a complex task, given just the architecture and the task, is nearly impossible. It is far too underdetermined, and the other factors, which we summarize as the subject's knowledge, are all important.

As the time to perform the task gets shorter, however, the options get fewer for what sequences could perform a task. Indeed suppose the time constant of the primitive data operations of the architecture is about 100 ms, and we ask for a task to be performed in about 0.1 ms, then the answer is clear without further ado: it cannot be done. It makes no difference how simple the task is (for example, are two names the same?). Suppose the task is to be performed in about 100 ms. Then a scan of the architecture's basic processes will reveal what can be done in a single operation time. If the performance is possible at all, it is likely to be unique—there is only one way to test for name equality in a single basic operation, though conceivably an architecture might offer some small finite number of alternatives. As the time available grows, what can be accomplished grows and the number of ways of accomplishing a given task grow. If 100 s is available, then there are probably several ways to determine whether two names are the same. The constraint comes back, however, if the demands of the performance grow apace.

Thus there is a region in which knowing the architecture makes possible plausible guesses about what operation sequences humans will use on a task. Consider the memory-scanning task explored by Sternberg and discussed by Bower and Clapper in chapter 7 in connection with the additive-factors methodology. The subject first sees a set of items H, P, Z and then a probe item Q and must say as quickly as possible whether the probe was one of the sequence. Three regularities made this experiment famous. First, the time to answer is linear in the size of the test set (response time = 400 + 3 · 40 = 520 ms for the case above), strongly suggesting the use of a serial scan (and test) at 40 ms per item. Second, the same linear relation with the same slope of 40 ms per item holds whether the probe is or is not in the list. This contradicts the obvious strategy of terminating the scan when an item is found that matches the probe, which would lead to an apparent average search rate for positive probes that is half as large as that for negative probes—on average only half of the list would be scanned for a positive probe before the item is found. Third, the scan rate (40 ms per item) is *very* fast—humans take more than 100 ms per letter to say the alphabet to themselves.

As Bower and Clapper (chapter 7) report, this experimental situation has been explored in many different ways and has given rise to an important experimental method (*additive factors*) to assess how different factors entered into the phenomena. For us the focus is on the speed with which things seem to happen. Speeded reaction times of about 400 ms already get close to the architecture, and phenomena that happen an order of magnitude faster (40 ms per item) must be getting close to the architecture floor. This is especially true when one considers that neurons are essentially 1-ms devices, so that neural circuits are 10-ms devices.

Just given the Sternberg phenomena, including these tight bounds, one cannot infer the mechanisms that perform it. In fact the Sternberg situation has been studied to show that one cannot even infer whether the "search" is going on in series or in parallel. Given an architecture, however, the picture becomes quite different. For instance, given Act*, the time constants imply that productions take a relatively long time to fire, on the order of 100 ms. Thus the Sternberg effect cannot be due to multiple production firings. Hence it must be a spreading activation phenomenon. Indeed the explanation that Anderson offers for the Sternberg effect is based on spreading activation (Anderson 1983, pp. 119–120). Two productions, one to say yes if the probe is there and one to say no if the probe is not, define the subject's way of doing the task, and then a calculation based on the flow of activation shows that it approximates the effect. The important point for us is that the two productions are the obvious way to specify the task in Act*, and there are few if any alternatives.

If we turn to Soar, there is an analogous analysis. First, general timing constraints imply that productions must be 10-ms mechanisms, so that the decision cycle is essentially a 100-ms mechanism, although speeded tasks would force it down (Newell 1987). Thus selecting and executing operators will take too long to be used to search and process the items of the set (at 40 ms each). Thus the Sternberg effect must be occurring within a single decision cycle, and processing the set must occur by executing a small number of productions (one to three) on each item. The fact that the decision cycle runs to quiescence would seem to be related to all items of the set being processed, whether the probe matches or not. These constraints do not pin down the exact program for the memory-scanning task as completely as in Act*, but they do specify many features of it. Again the important point here is that the closer the task is to the architecture, the more the actual program used by humans can be predicted from the structure of the architecture.

Hidden Connections

An architecture provides a form of unification for cognitive science, which arises, as we have seen, from all humans accomplishing all activities by means of the same set of mechanisms. As we have also seen, these common mechanisms work through content (that is, knowledge), which varies over persons, tasks, occasions, and history. Thus there is immense variability in behavior, and many phenomena of cognitive life are due to these other sources.

One important potential role for studies of the architecture is to reveal hidden connections between activities that on the basis of content and situation seem quite distant from each other. The connections arise, of course, because of the grounding in the same mechanisms of the architecture, so that, given the architecture, they may be neither subtle nor obscure. One such example is the way chunking has turned out to play a central role in many different forms of learning—such as the acquisition of macrooperators, the acquisition of search-control heuristics, the acquisition of new knowledge, constraint compilation, learning from external advice, and so on—and even in such traditionally nonlearning behaviors as the creation of abstract plans (Steier et al. 1987). Previously, special-purpose mechanisms were developed for these various activities.

In addition to the joy that comes directly from discovering the cause of any scientific regularity, revealing distal connections is useful in adding to the constraint that is available in discovering the explanation for phenomena. An example—again from the domain of Soar—is how chunking, whose route into Soar was via a model of human practice, has provided the beginnings of a highly constrained model of verbal learning (Rosenbloom, Laird, and Newell 1988). Using chunking as the basis for verbal learning forces it to proceed in a reconstructive fashion—learning to recall a presented item requires the construction of an internal representation of the item from structures that can already be recalled—and is driving the model, for functional reasons, to where it has many similarities to the EPAM model of verbal learning (Feigenbaum and Simon 1984).

Removing Theoretical Degrees of Freedom

One of the itches of cognitive scientists ever since the early days of computer simulation of cognition is that to get a simulation to run, it is necessary to specify many procedures and data structures that have no psychological justification. There is nothing in the structure of the simulation program that indicates which procedures (or more generally which aspects) make psychological claims and which do not.

One small but real result of complete architectures is to provide relief for this itch. A proposal for an architecture is a proposal for a complete operational system. No additional processes are required or indeed even possible. Thus when a simulation occurs within such an architecture, all aspects of the system represent empirical claims. This can be seen in the case of Soar—the decision cycle is claimed to be how humans make choices about what to do, and impasses are claimed to be real and to lead to chunking. Each production is claimed to be psychologically real and to correspond to an accessible bit of knowledge of the human. And the claims go on. A similar set of claims can be made for Act*. Many of these claims (for Act* or Soar) can be, and indeed no doubt are, false. That is simply the fate of inadequate and wrong theories that fail to correspond to reality. But there is no special status of aspects that are not supposed to represent what goes on in the mind.

All this does is remove the somewhat peculiar special status of simulation-based theory and return such theories to the arena occupied by all other scientific theories. Aspects of architectures are often unknown and are covered by explicit assumptions, which are subject to analysis. Important aspects of a total theory are often simply posited, such as the initial contents of the mind resulting from prior learning and external conditions, and behavior is invariably extremely sensitive to this. Analysis copes as best it can with such uncertainties, and the issue is not different with architectures.

3.6 Conclusions

An appropriate way to end this chapter is by raising some issues that reveal additional major steps required to pursue an adequate theory of the cognitive architecture. These questions have their roots in more general issues of cognitive science, but our attention is on the implications for the cognitive architecture.

The list of requirements that could shape the architecture contains a number of items whose effects on the architecture we do not yet know, in particular the issues of acquiring capabilities through development, of living autonomously in a social community, and of exhibiting self-awareness and a sense of self (requirements 8 through 10).

Another issue is the effect on the architecture of its being a creation of biological evolution that grew out of prior structures shaped by the requirements of prior function. Thus we would expect the architecture to be shaped strongly by the structure of the perceptual and motor systems. Indeed we know from anatomical and physiological studies that vast amounts of the brain and spinal cord are devoted to these aspects. The question is what sort of architecture develops if it evolves out of the mammalian perceptual and motor systems, existing as sophisticated controllers but not yet fully capable of the flexibility that comes from full programmability. Beneath the level of the organization of the perceptual and motor systems, of course, is their realization in large, highly connected neural circuits. Here with the connectionist efforts (chapter 4) there is a vigorous attempt to understand what the implications are for the architecture.

An analogous issue is the relationship of emotion, feeling, and affect to cognition. Despite recent stirrings and a long history within psychology (Frijda 1986), no satisfactory integration yet exists of these phenomena into cognitive science. But the mammalian system is clearly constructed as an emotional system, and we need to understand in what way this shapes the architecture, if indeed it does so at all.[13]

We close by noting that the largest open issue with respect to the architecture in cognitive science is not all these phenomena whose impact on the architecture remains obscure. Rather it is our almost total lack of experience in working with complete cognitive architectures. Our quantitative and reasonably precise theories have been narrow; our general theories have been broad and vague. Even where we have approached a reasonably comprehensive architecture (Act* being the principal existing example), working with it has been sufficiently arcane and difficult that communities of scientists skilled in its art have not emerged. Thus we know little about what features of an architecture account for what phenomena, what aspects of an architecture connect what phenomena with others, and how sensitive various explanations are to variations in the architecture. About the only experience we have with the uses for architectures described in section 3.5 is analysis using gross parameters.

Such understandings do not emerge by a single study or by many studies by a single investigator. They come from many people exploring and tuning the architecture for many different purposes until derivations of various phenomena from the architecture become standard and understood. They come, as with so many aspects of life, from living them.

Notes

1. This technical use of the term is often extended to include combinations of software and hardware that produce a system that can be programmed. This broad usage is encouraged by the fact that software systems often present a structure that is meant to be fixed, so that the computer plus software operates just as if it were cast in hardware. In this chapter, however, we always take *architecture* in the narrow technical sense.

2. In part this is because functions are conceptual elements in an analysis of natural systems, and so what functions exist depends on the scheme of analysis.

3. They have been called *physical symbol systems* (Newell and Simon 1976) to emphasize that their notion of symbol derives from computer science and artificial intelligence, in contradistinction to the notion of symbol in the arts and humanities, which may or may not prove to be the same. The shorter phrase will do here.

4. Note, however, that it has proved functional in existing computers to drive the independence down as far as possible, to the bit.

5. Access structures can be (and are in plenitude) built up within the software of a system; we discuss the basic capability in the architecture that supports all such software mechanisms.

6. Note that the term *symbol* is used here for a type of structure and mechanism within a symbol system and not, as in *to symbolize*, as a synonym for something that represents. This notion of symbol, however, does at least require internal representation—addresses designate memory structures, input stimuli must map to fixed internal structures, and operator codes designate operations.

7. Conceivably this could be extended to include the external world as a distal level in the system's memory hierarchy (beyond the tertiary level). Symbol tokens would specify addresses in the external world, and the access and retrieval paths would involve perceptual and motor acts.

8. As the famous results of Turing, Church, and others have shown, this limit does not include all possible functional dependencies but only a large subclass of them, called the *computable functions*.

9. Another way to view the relationship of working memory to the long-term declarative memory is as two manifestations of a single underlying declarative memory. Each element in this underlying memory has two independently settable bits associated with it: whether the element is active (determines whether it is in working memory), and whether it is permanent (determines whether it is in long-term declarative memory).

10. In Anderson 1983 Act* is described as having two additional methods for creating new productions—generalization and discrimination—but they were later shown to be unnecessary (Anderson 1986).

11. *Virtual addressing* is a mechanism that introduces a small fixed amount of context, namely, a base address.

12. As always, however, there is a trade-off. Recognition schemes are less flexible compared with location-pointer schemes, which are a genuinely task-independent medium for constructing accessing schemes, and hence can be completely adapted to the task at hand.

13. Feelings and emotions can be treated as analogous to sensations so they could affect the content of the cognitive system, even to including insistent signals, but still not affect the shape of the architecture.

References

Agrawal, D. P. 1986. *Advanced Computer Architecture*. Washington, DC: Computer Society Press.

Anderson, J. R. 1976. *Language, Memory and Thought*. Hillsdale, NJ: Erlbaum.

Anderson, J. R. 1983. *The Architecture of Cognition*. Cambridge, MA: Harvard University Press.

Anderson, J. R. 1986. Knowledge compilation: The general learning mechanism. In R. S. Michalski, J. G. Carbonell, and T. M. Mitchell, eds. *Machine Learning: An Artificial Intelligence Approach*. Vol. 2. Los Altos, CA: Morgan Kaufmann Publishers, Inc.

Anderson, J. R., and Bower, G. 1973. *Human Associative Memory*. Washington, DC: Winston.

Anderson, J. R., and Thompson, R. 1988. Use of analogy in a production system architecture. In S. Vosniadou and A. Ortony, eds. *Similarity and Analogical Reasoning*. New York: Cambridge University Press.

Bell, C. G., and Newell, A. 1971. *Computer Structures: Readings and Examples*. New York: McGraw-Hill.

Brachman, R. J. 1979. On the epistemological status of semantic networks. In N. V. Findler, ed. *Associative Networks: Representation and Use of Knowledge by Computers*. New York: Academic Press.

Broadbent, D. E. 1954. A mechanical model for human attention and immediate memory. *Psychological Review* 64:205.

Brown, A. L. 1978. Knowing when, where, and how to remember: A problem in metacognition. In R. Glaser, ed. *Advances in Instructional Psychology*. Hillsdale, NJ: Erlbaum.

Card, S., Moran, T. P., and Newell, A. 1983. *The Psychology of Human-Computer Interaction*. Hillsdale, NJ: Erlbaum.

Clocksin, W. F., and Mellish, C. S. 1984. *Programming in Prolog*. 2nd ed. New York: Springer-Verlag.

Craik, F. I. M., and Lockhart, R. S. 1972. Levels of processing: A framework for memory research. *Journal of Verbal Learning and Verbal Behavior* 11:671–684.

Feigenbaum, E. A., and Simon, H. A. 1984. EPAM-like models of recognition and learning. *Cognitive Science* 8:305–336.

Fernandez, E. B., & Lang, T. 1986. *Software-Oriented Computer Architecture*. Washington, DC: Computer Society Press.

Frijda, N. H. 1986. *The Emotions*. Cambridge, Engl.: Cambridge University Press.

Gajski, D. D., Milutinovic, V. M., Siegel, H. J., and Furht, B. P. 1987. *Computer Architecture*. Washington, DC: Computer Society Press.

Hayes-Roth, B. 1985. A blackboard architecture for control. *Artificial Intelligence* 26:251–321.

Hopcroft, J. E., and Ullman, J. D. 1979. *Introduction to Automata Theory, Languages, and Computation*. Reading, MA: Addison-Wesley.

Klahr, D. 1989. Information processing approaches to cognitive development. In R. Vasta, ed. *Annals of Child Development*. Greenwich, CT: JAI Press, pp. 131–183.

Laird, J. E., Newell, A., & Rosenbloom, P. S. 1987. Soar: An architecture for general intelligence. *Artificial Intelligence* 33(1):1–64.

Laird, J. E., Rosenbloom, P. S., and Newell, A. 1986. Chunking in Soar: The anatomy of a general learning mechanism. *Machine Learning* 1:11–46.

Maes, P., and Nardi, D., eds. 1988. *Meta-Level Architectures and Reflection*. Amsterdam: North-Holland.

Minsky, M. 1967. *Computation: Finite and infinite machines*. Englewood Cliffs, NJ: Prentice-Hall.

Minsky, M. 1975. A framework for the representation of knowledge. In P. Winston, ed. *The Psychology of Computer Vision*. New York: McGraw-Hill.

Newell, A. 1973. Production systems: Models of control structures. In W. C. Chase, ed. *Visual Information Processing*. New York: Academic Press.

Newell, A. 1980. Physical symbol systems. *Cognitive Science* 4:135–183.

Newell, A. 1987 (Spring). Unified theories of cognition. The William James lectures. Available in videocassette, Psychology Department, Harvard University, Cambridge, MA.

Newell, A., and Rosenbloom, P. S. 1981. Mechanisms of skill acquisition and the law of practice. In J. R. Anderson, ed. *Cognitive Skills and their Acquisition*. Hillsdale, NJ: Erlbaum.

Newell, A., and Simon, H. A. 1972. *Human Problem Solving*. Englewood Cliffs, NJ: Prentice-Hall.

Newell, A., and Simon, H. A. 1976. Computer science as empirical inquiry: Symbols and search. *Communications of the ACM* 19(3):113–126.

Polk, T. A., and Newell, A. 1988 (August). Modeling human syllogistic reasoning in Soar. In *Proceedings Cognitive Science Annual Conference—1988*. Cognitive Science Society, pp. 181–187.

Rosenbloom, P. S., and Newell, A. 1986. The chunking of goal hierarchies: A generalized model of practice. In R. S. Michalski, J. G. Carbonell, and T. M. Mitchell, eds. *Machine Learning: An Artificial Intelligence Approach*. Vol. 2. Los Altos, CA: Morgan Kaufmann Publishers, Inc.

Rosenbloom, P. S., and Newell, A. 1988. An integrated computational model of stimulus–response compatibility and practice. In G. H. Bower, ed. *The Psychology of Learning and Motivation*. Vol. 21. New York: Academic Press.

Rosenbloom, P. S., Laird, J. E., and Newell, A. 1988. The chunking of skill and knowledge. In H. Bouma and B. A. G. Elsendoorn, ed. *Working Models of Human Perception*. London: Academic Press, pp. 391–440.

Schneider, W., and Shiffrin, R. M. 1977. Controlled and automatic human information processing: I. Detection, search and attention. *Psychological Review* 84:1–66.

Shiffrin, R. M., and Schneider, W. 1977. Controlled and automatic human information processing: II. Perceptual learning, automatic attending, and a general theory. *Psychological Review* 84:127–190.

Siewiorek, D., Bell, G., and Newell, A. 1981. *Computer Structures: Principles and Examples*. New York: McGraw-Hill.

Steele, G. L., Jr., ed., with contributors Fahlman, S. E., Gabriel, R. P., Moon, D. A., and Weinreb, D. L. 1984. *Common Lisp: The Language*. Marlboro, MA: Digital Press.

Steier, D. E., Laird, J. E., Newell, A., Rosenbloom, P. S., Flynn, R. A., Golding, A., Polk, T. A., Shivers, O. G., Unruh, A., and Yost, G. R. 1987 (June). Varieties of learning in Soar: 1987. In *Proceedings of the Fourth International Workshop on Machine Learning*. Los Altos, CA: Morgan Kaufmann.

VanLehn, K., ed. 1989. *Architectures for Intelligence*. Hillsdale, NJ: Erlbaum.

von Cranach, M., Foppa, K., Lepinies, W., and Ploog, D., eds. 1979. *Human Ethology: Claims and Limits of a New Discipline*. Cambridge, Engl.: Cambridge University Press.

CHAPTER 36

Approaches to the Study of Intelligence

D. A. Norman, University of California, San Diego

Abstract

Norman, D.A., Approaches to the study of intelligence, Artificial Intelligence 47 (1991) 327–346.

How can human and artificial intelligence be understood? This paper reviews Rosenbloom, Laird, Newell, and McCarl's overview of Soar, their powerful symbol-processing simulation of human intelligence. Along the way, the paper addresses some of the general issues to be faced by those who would model human intelligence and suggests that the methods most effective for creating an artificial intelligence might differ from those for modeling human intelligence. Soar is an impressive piece of work, unmatched in scope and power, but it is based in fundamental ways upon Newell's "physical symbol system hypothesis"—any weaknesses in the power or generality of this hypothesis as a fundamental, general characteristic of human intelligence will affect the interpretation of Soar. But our understanding of the mechanisms underlying human intelligence is now undergoing rapid change as new, neurally-inspired computational methods become available that are dramatically different from the symbol-processing approaches that form the basis for Soar. Before we can reach a final conclusion about Soar we need more evidence about the nature of human intelligence. Meanwhile, Soar provides an impressive standard for others to follow. Those who disagree with Soar's assumptions need to develop models based upon alternative hypotheses that match Soar's achievements. Whatever the outcome, Soar represents a major advance in our understanding of intelligent systems.

Introduction

> Human intelligence . . . stands before us like a holy Grail—Rosenbloom, Laird, Newell, and McCarl. [17]

How can human intelligence be understood? The question is an old one, but age does not necessarily lead to wisdom, at least not in the sense that long-standing interest has led to a large body of accumulated knowledge and understanding. The work under discussion here, Soar, attempts to provide an advance in our understanding by providing a tool for the simulation of thought,

0004-3702/91/$03.50 © 1991 — Elsevier Science Publishers B.V.

thereby providing a theoretical structure of how human intelligence might operate.

Soar has a lofty mission: providing a critical tool for the study of human cognition. The goal is most clearly stated by Allen Newell in his William James lectures "Unified theories of cognition". Newell thought the statement important enough to present it twice, both as the first paragraph of the first chapter and then as the final paragraph of the final chapter:

> Psychology has arrived at the possibility of unified theories of cognition—theories that gain their power by having a single system of mechanisms that operate together to produce the full range of cognition.
>
> I do not say they are here. But they are within reach and we should strive to attain them. (Newell [11])

Soar represents the striving. Among other things, Soar hopes to provide a coherent set of tools that can then be used by the research community in a variety of ways. Soar is built upon a number of fundamental assumptions about the nature of human cognition: within the broad range of theories subsumed under these assumptions, Soar can provide powerful and important benefits. Prime among the assumptions is that the fundamental basis for intelligent behavior is a physical symbol system.

In this paper I examine the power and promise of Soar from the point of view of a cognitive scientist interested in human cognition. The emphasis, therefore, is not on Soar's capabilities as a system of artificial intelligence as much as its ability to simulate the behavior of humans and to enhance our understanding of human cognition. The goal is to provide a friendly, constructive critique, for the goal of Soar is one all cognitive scientists must share, even if there is disagreement about the underlying assumptions. Because of the wide scope and generality of Soar, it can only be examined by asking about fundamental issues in the study of intelligence, issues that lie at the foundations of artificial intelligence, of psychology, and of cognitive science.

1. Psychology and the study of human cognition

Psychology tends to be a critical science. It has grown up in a rich and sophisticated tradition of carefully controlled experimentation, the power of the analysis of variance as the statistical tool, and counterbalanced conditions as the experimental tool. Occam's Razor is held in esteem—no theory is allowed to be more complex than it need be. This is a reasonable criterion if several competing theories all attempt to account for the same phenomena. However, because of psychology's emphasis on a theory for every experimental result, the interpretation has caused a proliferation of very simple theories for very simple phenomena. There is a strong bias against theories such as Soar—they are more complex than the community is willing to accept, even when the range is extremely broad and comprehensive.

There is another negative tendency within psychology. Students are taught to be critics of experimental design: give students any experiment and they will find flaws. Graduate seminars in universities are usually devoted to detailed analyses of papers, ripping them apart point-by-point. Each paper provides the stimulation for new experimental work, each responding to the perceived flaws in the previous work. As a result, the field is self-critical, self-sustaining. Experiments seem mainly to be responses to other experiments. It is rare for someone to look back over the whole body of previous work in order to find some overall synthesis, rare to look over the whole field and ask where it is going.

With so much careful experimentation in psychology, surely there ought to be a place for compiling and understanding the systematic body of knowledge. This goal is shared by many, but it is especially difficult in psychology for there has been no systematic effort to compile these data, and the data are often collected through experimental methods different enough from one another to confound any simple compilation.

Why do we have this state of affairs? In part because of the extreme difficulties faced by those who study human behavior. The phenomena are subtle, for people are sensitive to an amazing range of variables. Experimental scientists over the years have found themselves fooled by apparent phenomena that turned out to be laboratory artifacts. We are trained to beware of "Clever Hans", the nineteenth century counting horse, certified as legitimate by a committee of eminent scientists. Alas, Hans couldn't count at all: he responded to subtle, unconscious cues from his audience. Modern experimental rigor is designed to avoid these and countless other pitfalls.

The resulting caution may, however, be an over-reaction. Complete control can only be found in the laboratory, but of necessity, a laboratory experiment has to simplify the conditions that are to be studied, both in order to control all the factors that are not of immediate interest and so that one can make precise measurements of behavior. But the simplification of the environment may have eliminated critical environmental structure, thereby changing the task that the person is performing. And the simplifications of the response measure may mean that the real behavior of interest is missed. Perhaps the emphasis on experimental rigor and control has led to measurements of the wrong variables?

Soar wades into the psychological arena by proposing a coherent, systematic way to evaluate the experimental data that now exist. It takes those data seriously and suggests that the difficulty in providing cohesion in the past has more to do with the limited theoretical tools available than with the nature of the data. Soar proposes to provide a "unified theory of cognition".

2. Toward a unified theory of cognition[1]

The lack of systematic, rich data in psychology has led many in AI to rely on introspection and "common sense" as evidence. But common sense is "folk-psychology" and it does not have a good reputation among behavioral scientists as a source of legitimate measures of behaviour. In order to improve the quality of theory in cognitive science in general, there needs to be a systematic, cumulative set of reliable and relevant experimental data. Yet in psychology, there has been surprisingly little building upon previous work, little "cumulative science". Why this lack? The developers of Soar suggest that the difficulty results from the lack of good theoretical tools that would allow one generation of researchers to build upon the work of the previous generation. One important gap is a set of modeling tools, tools that permit one to evaluate theoretical assumptions against empirical research in a systematic, constructive fashion.

Soar is really an attempt to do psychology differently than the way it has usually been done. It provides a set of general mechanisms that are postulated to range over all the relevant phenomena of cognition. The idea is to provide concrete mechanisms that can be tested against the known phenomena and data of psychology. When Soar fails, this will point to a deficiency in the theory, leading to refinement of the mechanisms: truly a cumulative approach to theory building. In this method, not only the data, but also the inner structure of the theory has its say (see Newell's famous analysis "You can't play 20 questions with nature and win" [9]).

The problem for such theory-building in psychology is that any given theory never quite gets the phenomenon right. That would normally be alright if there was agreement that the attempt provides useful information. But in the culture of modern day psychology, the response to such theories is "See, it doesn't account for *Y*, so it's wrong." The developers of Soar advocate the more constructive approach of using the misfits to guide the future development: "Yes, it accounts for *X*, but not for *Y*—I wonder what we would need to change to make it handle *Y* better?" "Don't bite my finger", says Allen Newell, "but look at where it is pointing."

In this review I follow the spirit of Newell's admonition: I do not bite at Soar, but rather, I examine the direction in which it points. Of course, I was also trained as a psychologist, so at times, the review may seem more critical than supportive. But the critiques are meant to be constructive, to state where I feel the more fundamental problems lie.

I do not examine the details of the (very) large number of papers and demonstrations of Soar that have now appeared. Rather I focus on the

[1] This section has gained much from discussions with Paul Rosenbloom, Allen Newell, and Stu Card. Some of the material was inspired by an e-mail interaction with Stu Card.

overriding philosophy and method of approach. I conclude that for those who travel in this direction, Soar provides the most systematic, most thoughtful approach to the terrain. However, I will also question whether the direction of travel is appropriate, or perhaps, whether it might not be important to examine several different paths along the terrain of human cognition.

3. Soar

3.1. *An overview of Soar*

The study of human intelligence requires the expertise of many disciplines ranging in level from that of the individual cell to that of societies and cultures. Soar aims at an in-between level, one that it calls the *cognitive band*. Soar is built upon a foundation of cognitive theory, and even the choice of levels at which it operates has a theoretical basis, in this case an analysis of the time-frame of intelligent systems. Newell ([10]; also see [12]) has argued that different levels of scientific disciplines study phenomena that lie within different time frames. According to this argument, cognitive events take place in the time bands that lie between 10 msec and 10 sec., and it is in this region that Soar aims to provide an appropriate theoretical basis (see [17, Fig. 1]). Not all events relevant to human intelligence lie within this band, of course. Events that occur with a time scale less than 10 msec. are relevant to the computational or neural base. Thus, this is the region studied by those interested in architecture; it is where the connectionist systems work. Events that take place with a time scale greater than 10 sec. are most relevant to rational cognition, to the use of logic or rule-following, as in expert systems where the system operates by following rules stated within its knowledge base.

Soar stakes out the middle ground, that of the cognitive band. At the lower levels of its operation it overlaps within studies of the neural band: Soar makes no claims about this level and tries to be compatible with all approaches, including (especially?) connectionist approaches (e.g., [16]). At the higher levels, Soar attempts to match up with the rational band and the logicist and expert system communities.

3.2. *Soar's assumptions*

Soar builds upon a number of assumptions and like all theories, how you evaluate it depends to a large extent upon how well you accept these basic premises. The basic premises are these:

(1) That psychological evidence should be taken seriously.
(2) That intelligence must be realized through a representational system based upon a physical symbol system.

(3) That intelligent activity is goal-oriented, symbolic activity.
(4) That all intelligent activity can be characterized as search through a problem space.
(5) That there is a single, universal architecture.
(6) That the architecture is uniform, with but a single form of long-term memory.
(7) That there is a single, universal learning mechanism.
(8) That much of the general power can come from an automatic subgoal mechanism.
(9) That the system derives its power from a combination of weak methods plus integration into a single system.

In addition, research on Soar is driven by four methodological assumptions:

(M1) That in the search for a general understanding of cognition, one should focus on the cognitive band, not on the neural or rational bands.
(M2) That general intelligence can be studied most usefully by not distinguishing between human and artificial intelligence.
(M3) That the architecture should consist of a small set of orthogonal mechanisms, with all intelligent behavior involving all or nearly all of these basic mechanisms.
(M4) Architectures should be pushed to the extreme to see how much general intelligence they can cover.

These assumptions arise for a combination of reasons. First, some are derived from behavioral evidence from psychology. Second, some are "natural" processing and representational decisions based on concepts from computer and information sciences. Thus, the assumptions of a physical symbol system drives the representations and processing. And third, some assumptions seem to be made for convenience, or personal preferences rather than for well-grounded reasons. An example of this is the exclusion of partial information, not even ubiquitous "activation values", or "connection strengths", concepts that have pervaded psychological theorizing for many decades, and that are the mainstay of connectionist modeling.

4. Soar as a model of human intelligence

4.1. Assessing the experimental evidence

Soar takes psychological data seriously. Its developers have culled the experimental literature for data in a form amenable to test. On the whole, Soar does pretty well at this, and a major portion of its claim to success is the ability to mimic psychological phenomena. But what are we to make of this claim?

The answer rests upon how well we think those phenomena get at the core issues of human intelligence and cognition.

There appear to be four assumptions that are critical:

(1) That there is a uniform computational architecture, including a single, uniform long-term memory structure.
(2) That there is a single form of learning (*chunking*).
(3) That all intelligent operations are performed by symbol manipulation—the physical symbol system hypothesis.
(4) That all reasoning and problem solving is done through search within a uniform problem space.

Assumption (1), the notion of uniform computational structure seems suspect. Now, this is simply not the sort of issue one can decide by experimental, behavioral observation. Whatever behavior is observed, one could postulate an underlying uniformity or non-uniformity: behavioral evidence can never distinguish between the two. But what of biological evidence? What do we know about the neurological basis of cognition? The brain is composed of different structures, each apparently specialized for different kinds of operations. The cortex is surely not the only place where cognitive operations take place, and although it is the largest relatively uniform structure in the brain, even it differs in appearance and structure from place to place. The cortex differs from the cerebellum which differs from the hippocampus and the thalmus, much as the liver differs from the pancreas and the kidney. We do not expect the organs of the body to have a common underlying chemical or biological structure, why would we expect uniformity in the biology of computational structures?

4.2. *Semantic and episodic memory*

The assumption of a single long-term memory seems unwarranted. Now, back in the days when all we had to go on was psychological, behavioral evidence, we talked of long-term memory, short-term memory, and various sensory (iconic) memories. I was even responsible for some of this. But now that we have a larger accumulation of evidence, especially evidence from neurologically impaired patients, this simple division no longer seems to apply.

A good example of the difficulty of assessing human cognitive architecture from behavioral data alone comes from the distinction in the psychological literature between semantic and episodic memory [25]. Tulving has suggested that we distinguish between semantic and episodic memory. Semantic memory is generalized, abstracted knowledge (e.g., "a dog has four legs, is a mammal, and is a member of the canine family"). Episodic memory is experiential in nature (e.g., the memory for the event when Sam, my family's dog, got stuck in the fence and it took three of us to extricate him). Tulving and other have claimed that these distinctions are more than simply a different representational format, but rather that they represent separate memory systems [26]. This, of course, would violate a basic postulate of Soar, and so, in his William James lectures, Newell reports upon a test of this idea [11, Chapter 6].

Soar passes the test, for the existing mechanisms of Soar seem quite capable of producing behavior of the sort seen for both episodic and semantic memory, and although the test is not made, it probably produces the right behavior under the right conditions. Newell is justifiably proud of this performance: "a unified theory contains the answer to a question, such as the episodic/semantic distinction. One does not add new information to the theory to obtain it. One simply goes to the theory and reads out the solution."

This demonstration is an excellent example of the power of Soar (or any other unified theory of cognition, Newell is careful to point out), but it also shows the weaknesses. For the scientific judgment on the distinction of memory types cannot rest on behavioral evidence alone: in fact, I believe the behavioral evidence will almost always be too weak to distinguish among theoretical variants. Much stronger evidence comes by combining behavioral observations with neuropsychological evidence, both by examining patients with brain abnormalities and through measurements of neural activity in the human brain. Neurological studies (see [23, 27]) strongly support the notion of separate memory structures. Tulving points out that some forms of brain damage produce amnesiacs that are more damaged in episodic memory than semantic; and measurement of regional cerebral blood flow in normal humans doing two different memory tasks that involve the two classes of memory activate different regions of the brain. Tulving uses these studies to argue specifically for the distinct neurological, psychological, and functional nature of episodic and semantic memory. Squire and Zola-Morgan [23] suggest that in addition to the differences found by Tulving, declarative and nondeclarative memories reside in different brain areas (both episodic and semantic memories are forms of declarative memory). If these studies are verified, they provide persuasive evidence against the uniform memory hypothesis, even though the behavioral performance of Soar is just fine.

These studies illustrate the difficulty faced by the theorist in this area: Behavioral studies are really not precise enough to distinguish among different biological mechanisms. Any theory that attempts to model the functional behavior of the human must also take into account different biological bases for these mechanisms. Presumably different biological mechanisms will also lead to different kinds of observable behavior, but the distinctions may not be noticed until one knows what to look for.

4.3. Learning

Is there a single form of learning—assumption (2)? Today's answer is that we do not know. Many psychologists distinguish among several kinds. Rumelhart and I claimed there were three: accretion, structuring, and tuning

[19]. Anderson [2] has claimed a similar three. What about the fundamental distinction between operant and classical learning, or any of the many forms of learning identified within the animal literature? Of course, it is quite possible that all these forms of learning rely upon a single primitive mechanism, so that something like "chunking" could be the substratum upon which all of these apparently disparate properties of the learning system are created. My personal opinion is that there probably is a simple primitive of learning, but that it is apt to be very low-level, more like a mechanism for strengthening a bond or link in an association than like the higher-level concept of chunking.

Note that other systems have other assumptions about the nature of learning. Connectionist models use one or another variant of hill climbing to adjust their weights, most frequently guided by a teacher, but under appropriate circumstances guided by other criteria. Weight adjustment provides an excellent mechanism for handling constraint-satisfaction tasks, for performing generalizations, and for systems that do not require exact matches, but will accept closest matches. There really is still not enough work exploring connectionist architectures with the sort of tasks done by Soar. However, connectionist architectures are especially well suited for skill learning, and at least one system does also produce the power law of performance [8].

Holland, Holyoak, Nisbett and Thagard's system of genetic algorithms provides another form of learning mechanism, one more rapid and efficient than the simple weight adjustment of connectionist systems [5]. This system is well-suited for a wide range of cognitive tasks, especially that of induction.

Explanation-based learning systems use several procedures: generalization, chunking, operationalization, and analogy (an excellent review and comparison of systems is provided by Ellman [4]). Soar, which is a form of explanation-based system, only uses chunking, which appears to limit its powers, especially in its lack of ability to learn from observation and to perform induction.

What of the power of Soar's learning? Learning is impasse-driven: new operators result when an impasse in processing occurs, forcing the generation of new subgoals or other mechanisms. New operators are created through chunking, when a sequence of operators reaches some desired state, the sequence can be "chunked" together into one new operator, creating the appropriate establishing conditions and output conditions to working memory. Chunking has obvious problems in forming just the right level of generalization. It can easily construct a chunk appropriate to the exact conditions which started the sequence, but this would be too specific for future use. Deciding which variables to generalize, which to make explicit is a major problem faced by all such learning mechanisms, and Soar is no exception.

As a result, Soar chunks can be "expensive" (in that there will soon be multiple, highly specialized chunks requiring analysis and search): new procedures have overcome this expense, but they had to be added for the purpose [24].

Soar also has trouble with induction: If I say the series is 1, 2, 4, what is the next number? Humans have no trouble with this task. In fact, humans do it too often, including when it is inappropriate and when the induced information is wrong: if Soar is to be a model of human performance, it too must have the same biases. My preference would be for a system where these "natural" errors of people fall naturally out of the system, not one where special mechanisms have to be added to produce the behavior. Chunking is really a limited mechanism: learning takes place only after a satisfactory solution is reached, and the learning occurs by collapsing the operator sequence into a single operator that is more efficient.

What about dealing with impasses? The normal way leads to a fairly logical, orderly pursuit through subgoal space. VanLehn, Ball, and Kowalski [28] have presented experimental evidence against the last-in-first-out constraint on the selection of goals that is present in Soar (and many other problem-solving theories): this is the assumption that leads to the problem solver working only on the unsatisfied goal that was created most recently. Are the mechanisms of Soar flexible enough to get around this assumption? Probably.

What can one conclude? As usual, the jury is still out. Chunking is clearly a powerful mechanism and the range of problems to which it can be applied is broad. It is not the only possible mechanism, however, and it is clearly not so well suited for some tasks as for others. But a systematic comparison of learning mechanisms and tasks has yet to be performed.

4.4. Symbol processing

Assumption (3) is that of symbol processing and the unified nature of intelligent processing. Again, this is so fundamental that it is difficult to get evidence. Some of us believe it necessary to distinguish between two very different kinds of processing. One, subconscious, takes place by means of constraint-satisfaction, pattern-matching structures, perhaps implemented in the form of connectionist nets. These are non-symbolic modes of computation (often called sub-symbolic[2]). The other kind of processing is that of higher-level conscious mechanisms, and it is only here that we have the classical symbol processing mechanisms that Soar attempts to model because this higher, symbolic level of processing also exists within the brain, it too must be constructed from neural circuits. The well-known difficulties that neural networks have with symbol manipulation, for maintaining variables and bindings, and for even such basic symbolic distinctions as that between type and token, lead to strong limitations on the power of this symbolic level of processing: it is

[2] I am fully aware of the controversy over the term "sub-symbolic", with the critics saying it has no meaning. Either something is symbolic or it is not. The term is, therefore, vague and ill-defined. It gives the pretense of a well-defined sense, but in fact, means quite different things to different people. And, therefore, it exactly suits my purpose.

slow, serial, and with limited memory size. This suggestion of a dual processing structure is in accord with the experimental evidence. In particular, the limits in the symbolic processor are consistent with human data. Thus, human ability to do formal symbolic reasoning (e.g., logical reasoning) without the aid of external devices is extremely limited.

The view I just proposed, with both sub-conscious and conscious processing, is a minority one, shared neither by the strong connectionists nor the strong symbolists. Moreover, Soar may not need to take a stance: it could argue (and it has done so) that any sub-conscious processing that might take place lies in the neural band, beneath the region of its interest, that these operations take place within the time domains faster than 100 msec. where hardware issues dominate. Soar is concerned only with symbolic representations and if these are constructed on top of underlying, more primitive computational structures, that is quite compatible with its structures (see [16]).

But it may very well be that the physical symbol system hypothesis does not hold for much of human cognition. Perhaps much of our performance is indeed done "without representation" as Brooks [3], among others, have suggested. It will be quite a while before the various cognitive sciences have settled on any consensus, but this assumption is so fundamental to Soar, that if the evidence beneath it is weakened, Soar's claims to a general model of human cognition must suffer.

Where do I stand on this? Mixed. As I said, I believe we probably do lower-level processing in a sub-symbolic mode, with symbols restricted to higher-order (conscious?) processing. Conscious processing is heavily restricted by the limits of working memory. I give part of this argument in an early paper of connectionism [14] and another useful view of these distinctions is given by Smolensky [21]. The dual-view is probably consistent with Soar, or at least some modification of Soar that takes into account new developments about the borderline of lower-level (neural band?) processing and symbolic processing.

4.5. Search within a uniform problem space

Finally, we have assumption (4), that not only is there a uniform representational and processing structure, but that all reasoning and problem solving is done through search within a uniform problem space. Again, who knows? Can a single representational and a single processing structure handle the differences among perception, problem solving, motor control? Among language, reasoning, analogies, deduction and inference? Maybe, or maybe not. We simply do not know.

This assumption is the one that gives many of my colleagues in AI the most trouble. I am not so certain, for the problem space of Soar is very powerful, and by appropriate coding of the symbols, it can act as if it were partitioned and structured.

Is a problem space appropriate for all tasks? Again, it isn't clear, but I am not convinced that this poses any fundamental difficulty for Soar. Thus, many of us have argued that physical constraints and information in the environment plays a major role in human planning, decision making and problem solving. But if so, this information is readily accommodated by Soar. Thus, in the current version, the formulation of the problem space automatically encodes physical constraints [17, Section 2.3]. And when Soar gets the appropriate I/O sensors, it should be just as capable of using environmental information as any other model of behavior. Here the only restriction is the state of today's technology, but in principle, these factors are readily accounted for.

5. Soar as artificial intelligence

How well does Soar do as a mechanism for AI? Here, Soar falls between the cracks. It is neither logic, nor frames, nor semantic nets. Soar classifies itself as a production system, but it is not like the traditional forms that we have become used to and that fill the basic texts on AI. As theoretical AI, Soar has several weaknesses, many shared by other approaches as well. In particular, Soar suffers from:

- weak knowledge representation;
- unstructured memory;
- the characterization of everything as search through a problem space.

Weak knowledge representation certainly stands out as one of the major deficits. In this era of highly sophisticated representational schemes and knowledge representation languages, it is somewhat of a shock to see an AI system that has no inheritance, no logic, no quantification: Soar provides only triples and a general purpose processing structure. How does Soar handle reasoning that requires counterfactuals and hypotheticals and quantifiers? How will it fare with language, real language? What about other forms of learning, for example, learning by being told, learning by reflection, learning by restructuring, or learning by analogy? How will Soar recover from errors? All unanswered questions, but never underestimate the sophistication of a dedicated team of computer professionals. Soar will master many or even all of these areas. In fact, in the time that elapsed between the oral presentation of the Soar paper under review and now, the final writing of the review, Soar has made considerable progress in just these areas.

What about other methods of deduction and inference? We have already noted Soar's weaknesses in doing inference.

Technically, Soar has all the power it needs. It is, after all, Turing-equivalent, and with the basic structure of triples it can represent anything that it needs. In fact, one of the assumptions of Soar is that it should start with only the minimum of representation and process: everything else that might be needed is learned. It gains considerable speed with experience—through chunking—and in any event, speed was never a prerequisite of a theoretical structure.

Soar gets its main strength by virtue of its uniformity of architecture, representation, and learning. It can solve anything because it is so general, so unspecialized. It then gets its power through the learning mechanism: the assumption is:

- weak methods + chunking → strong methods;
- the tuning of preferences → strength.

Soar has many positive features. It is a production system, but with a major difference. Conflict resolution, a critical feature of traditional production systems, has disappeared. All relevant Soar productions are executed in parallel. The execution puts all their memory data into working memory, where the decision procedure selects a relevant action to be performed from the information in working memory. Soar can be both goal-driven and data-driven. And the strategy of action is flexibly determined by the kind of information available within working memory.

5.1. Soar and its competition

How does Soar compare to other AI systems? Restricting the consideration to those that aspire to a unified theory of intelligence, and then further restricting it to evaluate the systems in terms of their relevance to human cognition, the answer is that there really isn't much competition. Of the more traditional AI systems, only Soar is viable. Soar's principles and structure seem much more in harmony with what we know of human processing than systems such as the traditional expert system approach to reasoning, or the decision processes of knowledge representation languages, various database systems and truth-maintenance systems, and logic programming. Work on explanation-based learning [4] could potentially be compared, but for the moment, there are no unified, grand systems to come out of this tradition (with the exception of Soar itself, which is a variant of explanation-based learning).

Psychologists have a history of system building as well that should be considered. Thus, Soar could be compared to the approach followed by Anderson in his continual refinements of his computer models (e.g., ACT*, [1]), or by the earlier work of Norman, Rumelhart, and the LNR Research Group [15]. But of these, only ACT* is active today. Here, I would probably conclude that ACT* is superior in the way it models the finer details of the psychological processes that it covers, but that its scope is quite restricted: ACT* is an important influential theory, but it has never been intended as a general, unified theory of all cognitive behavior.

There are numerous small systems, each devoted to the detailed modeling of restricted phenomena. Connectionist modeling fits this description, with perhaps the largest and most detailed simulation studies being those of Rumelhart and McClelland in their simulation of a wide variety of data on word recognition and perception [6, 18, 20]. In all these cases, although the work provides major contributions to our understanding of the phenomena being modeled, they are restricted in scope, hand-crafted for the task (even if the underlying representational structures are learned) and no single system is intended to be taken as a unified theory, applicable to a wide range of phenomena.

There is one major system, however, which does attempt the same range of generality—the genetic algorithm approach of Holland, Holyoak, Nisbett, and Thagard [5]. This work comes from a strong interdisciplinary group examining the nature of cognition and its experimental and philosophical basis. Its computer modeling tools do provide an alternative, a kind of cross between connectionist modeling and symbolic representation, with an emphasis on learning. How do these two systems compare? So far, Soar has the edge, in part because of the immense amount of effort to the development of a wide-ranging, coherent model. But the approach of Holland et al. [5] has the capability to become a second unified theory of cognition, one that would allow more precise comparison with the assumptions of Soar. It will be a good day for science when two similar systems are available, for comparisons of the performance on the same tasks by these two systems with very different underlying assumptions can only be beneficial. Indeed, this is one of the hopes of the Soar enterprise: the development of competing models that can inform one another.

6. Reflections and summary

6.1. Soar's stengths and weaknesses

The strength of Soar is that it starts with fundamental ideas and principles and pushes them hard. It derives strength and generality from a uniform architecture, uniform methods, and uniform learning. Weak methods are general methods, and although they may be slow, they apply to a wide range of problems: the combination of weak methods plus a general learning mechanism gives Soar great power. The learning method allows for specialization, for the chunking of procedures into efficient steps, tuned for the problem upon which it is working.

Learning within Soar is impressive. I was prepared to see Soar gradually improve with practice, but I was surprised to discover that it could take advantage of learning even within its first experience with a problem: routines learned (chunked) in the early phases of a problem aided it in the solution of the later phases, even within its first exposure. Soar may indeed have taken advantage of both worlds of generality and specialization: an initial generality that gives it scope and breadth, at the tradeoff of being slow and inefficient, plus chunking that provides a learned specialization for speed and efficiency.

The weaknesses of Soar derive from its strengths. It has a weak knowledge representation language and a weak memory structure. It has no formalism for higher-order reasoning, for productions, for rules, or for preferences. It is not clear how well Soar will do with natural language (where reasoning and quantification seem essential), or with argumentation, or for that matter, with simple input and output control. Everything in Soar is search: how far can that be carried?

6.2. *Soar as a theoretical tool for psychology*

Soar claims to be grounded upon psychological principles, but the psychology is weak. As I have pointed out, this is no fault of Soar, but it reflects the general status of psychological theory, which in turn reflects the difficulty of that scientific endeavor. Still, unsettled science provides shaky grounds for construction. How can I, as a psychologist, complain when someone takes psychological data seriously?

The problem is the sort of psychological evidence that is considered. As I indicated at the start of this review, there are different ideas about the nature of the appropriate evidence from psychology. The Soar team takes the evidence much more seriously than do I.

One basic piece of psychological evidence offered as support for the chunking hypothesis is the power law of learning, that the relationship between speed of performance and number of trials of experience follows a power law of the form $Time = k(trials)^P$ over very many studies, and with the number of trials as large as 50,000 (or more: see [13]). Yes, the ability of Soar to produce the power law of learning is impressive. At the time, it was the only model that could do so (now however, Miyata [8] has shown how a connectionist model can also yield the power law of learning).

Soar handles well the data from the standard sets of problem-solving tasks, for inference, and for other tasks of think-aloud problem solving. But how much of real cognition do these tasks reflect? There is a growing body of evidence to suggest that these are the sorts of tasks done primarily within the psychological laboratory or the classroom, and that they may have surprisingly little transfer to everyday cognition. For example, consider the set of problems against which Soar tests its ability to mimic human problem solving: the Eight Puzzle, tic-tac-toe, Towers of Hanoi, missionaries and cannibals, algebraic equations, satisfying local constraint networks, logical syllogisms, balance beam problems, blocks world problems, monkey-and-bananas, and the waterjug problems. These are indeed the traditional problems studied in both the human and artificial intelligence literature. But, I contend, these are not the typical problems of everyday life. They are not problems people are particularly good at. One reason psychologists study them is that they do offer so many difficulties: they thereby provide us something to study.

But if this is not how people perform in everyday life, then perhaps these should not be the baseline studies on which to judge intelligent behavior. If I am right, this stands as an indictment of human psychology, not of Soar, except that Soar has based its case on data from the human experimental literature.

6.3. The choice of phenomena to be modeled

How has Soar chosen the set of phenomena that it wishes to consider? Not clear. Thus, there is a well-established and rich core of knowledge about human short-term memory, and although the current theoretical status of the concept is unclear, the phenomena and data are still valid. The literature is well known to the developers of Soar, and key items are summarized in Newell's William James lectures. One of the major developments over the years is the finding that items in STM decay: not that less and less items are available, but that only partial information is available from any given item. Two major methods have been developed for representing this decay, one to allow each item to have some "activation value" that decreases with time or interference from other items (thus decreasing its signal-to-noise ratio), the other that each item is composed of numerous "micro-features", and each of the features drops out probabilistically as a function of time or interference from other items, so the main item gets noisier and noisier with time.

Soar decides to use neither of these mechanisms of memory loss. Why? Loss of activation is rejected, probably because activation values are simply not within the spirit of representation chosen for Soar ("The simplest decay law for a discrete system such as Soar is not gradual extinction, but probabilistic decay", Chapter 6 of the William James lectures [11]). And loss of microfeatures is not possible because the Soar representation is wholistic: internal components cannot be lost.

Does this difference matter? It is always difficult to assess the impact of low-level decisions upon the resulting global behavior. Clearly, the choice rules out the simulation of recognition-memory operating characteristics (e.g., [29]). This kind of decision permeates the model-building activity, and it isn't always easy to detect where a basic assumption is absolutely forced by the phenomena or universal processing constraints, where selected for more arbitrary reasons.

In general Soar seems on strongest ground when it discusses the highest-order of the cognitive band: tasks that clearly make use of symbol processing, especially problem-solving tasks. At the lowest level, it is weak on time-ordered tasks, both on the effects of time and activity rate on performance and cognition, and also on the simulation of tasks that require controlled rates of production. At the middle level, it is weakest on issues related to knowledge representation: the existing representation has little overall structure and none of the common organizational structures or inference rules of knowledge representation languages.

Soar also espouses the software-independence approach to modeling. That is, psychological functions are assumed to be independent of hardware implementation, so it is safe to study the cognitive band without examination of the implementation methods of the neural band, without consideration of the physical body in which the organism is imbedded, and without consideration of non-cognitive aspects of behavior. How big a role does the biological implementation of cognition play? What constraints, powers, and weaknesses result? What of the body, does it affect cognition? How about motivation, culture, social interaction. What about emotions? The separation of these aspects into separate compartments is the common approach to cognition of the information processing psychologist of an earlier era, but the psychologist of the 1990s is very apt to think the separation cannot be maintained. Certainly the connectionist takes as given that:

(1) There is continuous activation.
(2) The implementation makes a major difference.
(3) Time is important.
(4) Major biases and processing differences can result from extra-cognitive influences.

How do we weigh these various considerations? The field is young, the amount of knowledge low. Soar may be right. But it does not implement the only possible set of alternatives.

And how does Soar react to criticisms of this sort? Properly: Soar aspires to set the framework for general models of cognition. It tests one set of operating assumptions. The goal, in part, is to inspire others to do similar tasks, perhaps with different sets of assumptions and mechanisms. But then they are all to be assessed with the same data. The goal is not to show Soar right or wrong, the goal is to advance the general state of knowledge. With this attitude, Soar—and the science of cognition—can only win.

6.4. Soar as a modeling tool for AI

Maybe Soar should be evaluated separately for its role as a tool for artificial intelligence and for psychological modeling. Personally, that is my view, but the Soar community has soundly rejected this idea. One of the basic methodological assumptions, (M2), is that general intelligence can be studied most usefully by not distinguishing between human and artificial intelligence. But I am not convinced. Human intelligence has evolved to meet the demands of the situations encountered through evolutionary history, where survival and reproduction were critical aims. The brain has a biological basis and the sensory, motor, and regulatory structures reflect the evolutionary history and the demands made upon them over a time course measured in millions of years. Human intelligence is powerful, but restricted, specialized for creativity, adaptivity, and robustness, with powerful perceptual apparatus that probably dominates the mechanisms of thought. Human language is also the product of an evolutionary struggle, and its properties are still not understood by the scientific community, even though virtually all humans master their native, spoken language. The properties of biological and artificial systems are so dramatically different at the hardware level (the neural band), that this must certainly also be reflected at the cognitive level (see [7]).

Good artificial intelligence may not be good psychology. Soar attempts to be both, but by so doing, I fear it weakens its abilities on all counts. By attempting to account for the known experimental results on cognition, it is forced to adopt certain computational strategies that may hamper its performance on traditional tasks of artificial intelligence. And by being developed from the traditional framework of information processing artificial intelligence, it may limit the scope of human mechanisms that it tries to duplicate.

6.5. How should Soar be judged?

How should Soar—or any other model of intelligence—be judged? On the criteria of practical and theoretical AI I think the answer is clear. One uses a standard set of benchmarks, probably similar to what Soar has done. Here the answer is given by how well the system performs. On the issue of the simulation of human cognition, the answer is far from clear. We don't have a set of benchmark problems. If I am to be a constructive critic (look where Soar is pointing), I have to conclude that what it does, it does well: in this domain it has no competiton.

Soar does not aspire to be *the* tool for human simulation. Rather, it hopes to set an example of what can be done. Others are urged to follow, either by building upon Soar or by providing their own, unified theory of cognition, to be tested and compared by attempting to account for exactly the same set of data.

One practical barrier stands in the way of the systematic use and evaluation of Soar by the research community: the difficulty of learning this system. Today, this is not an easy task. There is no standard system, no easy introduction. Programming manuals do not exist. Until Soar is as easy to master as, say, LISP or PROLOG, there will never be sufficient people with enough expertise to put it to the test. If Soar usage is to go beyond the dedicated few there needs to be a standard system, some tutorial methods, and a standard text.

6.6. Conclusion: Powerful and impressive

In conclusion, Soar is a powerful, impressive system. It is still too early to assess Soar on either theoretical or practical grounds, for either AI or psychology, but already it has shown that it must be taken seriously on both counts. The chunking mechanism is a major contribution to our understanding of learning. The exploitation of weak methods provides a valuable lesson for system builders. And the use of uniform structures may very well provide more benefits than deficits. I am not so certain that we are yet ready for unified theory, for there are many uncertainties in our knowledge of human behavior and of the underlying mechanisms—our understanding of the biological structure of processing is just beginning to be developed, but already it has added to and changed some of our ideas about the memory systems. But for those who disagree or who wish to explore the terrain anyway, Soar has set a standard for all others to follow.

Acknowledgement

This article has benefited from the aid of several reviewers as well as through discussions and correspondence with Stu Card, David Kirsh, Allen Newell, Paul Rosenbloom, and Richard Young. My research was supported by grant NCC 2-591 to Donald Norman and Edwin Hutchins from the Ames Research Center of the National Aeronautics and Space Agency in the Aviation Safety/ Automation Program. Everett Palmer served as technical monitor. Additional support was provided by funds from the Apple Computer Company and Digital Equipment Corporation to the Affiliates of Cognitive Science at UCSD.

References

[1] J.R. Anderson, *The Architecture of Cognition* (Harvard University Press, Cambridge, MA, 1983).
[2] J.R. Anderson, *Cognitive Psychology and Its Implications* (Freeman, New York, 1985).
[3] R.A. Brooks, Intelligence without representation, *Artif. Intell.* **47** (1991) 139–159, this volume.
[4] T. Ellman, Explanation-based learning: a survey of programs and perspectives, *ACM Comput. Surv.* **21** (1989) 163–221.
[5] J.H. Holland, K.J. Holyoak, R.E. Nisbett and P.R. Thagard, *Induction: Processes of Inference, Learning, and Discovery* (MIT Press, Cambridge, MA, 1987).
[6] J.L. McClelland and D.E. Rumelhart, An interactive activation model of context effects in letter perception, Part I: An account of basic findings, *Psychol. Rev.* **88** (1981) 375–407.
[7] C. Mead, *Analog VLSI and Neural Systems* (Addison-Wesley, Reading, MA, 1989).
[8] Y. Miyata, A PDP model of sequence learning that exhibits the power law, in: *Proceedings 11th Annual Conference of the Cognitive Science Society*, Ann Arbor, MI (1989) 9–16.

[9] A. Newell, You can't play 20 questions with nature and win, in: W.G. Case, ed., *Visual Information Processing* (Academic Press, San Diego, CA, 1973).

[10] A. Newell, Scale counts in cognition, 1986 American Psychological Association Distinguished Scientific Award Lecture.

[11] A. Newell, *Unified Theories of Cognition* (Harvard University Press, Cambridge, MA, 1990); 1987 William James lectures at Harvard University.

[12] A. Newell and S.K. Card, The prospects for psychological science in human-computer interaction, *Hum.-Comput. Interaction* **1** (1985) 209–242.

[13] A. Newell and P.S. Rosenbloom, Mechanisms of skill acquisition and the law of practice, in: J.R. Anderson, ed., *Cognitive Skills and Their Acquisition* (Erlbaum, Hillsdale, NJ, 1981).

[14] D.A. Norman, Reflections on cognition and parallel distributed processing, in: J.L. McClelland, D.E. Rumelhart and the PDP Research Group, eds., *Parallel Distributed Processing: Explorations in the Microstructure of Cognition* **2**: *Psychological and Biological Models* (MIT Press/Bradford, Cambridge, MA, 1986).

[15] D.A. Norman, and D.E. Rumelhart, The LNR Research Group, *Explorations in Cognition* (Freeman, New York, 1975).

[16] P.S. Rosenbloom, A symbolic goal-oriented perspective on connectionism and Soar, in: R. Pfeifer, Z. Schreter, F. Fogelman-Soulie and L. Steels, eds., *Connectionism in Perspective* (Elsevier, Amsterdam, 1989).

[17] P.S. Rosenbloom, J.E. Laird, A. Newell and R. McCarl, A preliminary analysis of the Soar architecture as a basis for general intelligence, *Artif. Intell.* **47** (1991) 289–325, this volume.

[18] D.E. Rumelhart and J.L. McClelland, An interactive activation model of context effects in letter perception, Part II: The contextual enhancement effect and some tests and extensions of the model, *Psychol. Rev.* **89** (1982) 60–94.

[19] D.E. Rumelhart and D.A. Norman, Accretion, tuning and restructuring: three modes of learning, in: J.W. Cotton and R. Klatzky, eds., *Semantic Factors in Cognition* (Erlbaum, Hillsdale, NJ, 1978).

[20] M.S. Siedenberg and J.L. McClelland, A distributed, developmental model of word recognition and naming, *Psychol. Rev.* **96** (1989) 523–568.

[21] P. Smolensky, On the proper treatment of connectionism, *Brain Behav. Sci.* **11** (1988) 1–74.

[22] L.R. Squire, *Memory and Brain* (Oxford University Press, New York, 1987).

[23] L.R. Squire, and S. Zola-Morgan, Memory: Brain systems and behavior, *Trends Neurosci.* **11** (4) (1988) 170–175.

[24] M. Tambe and P.S. Rosenbloom, Eliminating expensive chunks by restricting expressiveness, in: *Proceedings IJCAI-89*, Detroit, MI (1989).

[25] E. Tulving, Episodic and semantic memory, in: E. Tulving and W. Donaldson, eds., *Organization of Memory* (Academic Press, San Diego, 1969).

[26] E. Tulving, *Elements of Episodic Memory* (Oxford University Press, New York, 1983).

[27] E. Tulving, Remembering and knowing the past, *Am. Sci.* **77** (1989) 361–367.

[28] K. VanLehn, W. Ball and B. Kowalski, Non-LIFO execution of cognitive procedures, *Cogn. Sci.* **13** (1989) 415–465.

[29] W.A. Wickelgren and D.A. Norman, Stength models and serial position in short-term recognition memory, *J. Math. Psychol.* **3** (1966) 316–347.

CHAPTER 37

Toward a Unified Theory of Immediate Reasoning in Soar

T. A. Polk, A. Newell, and R. L. Lewis, Carnegie Mellon University

Abstract

Soar is an architecture for general intelligence that has been proposed as a unified theory of human cognition (UTC) (Newell, 1989) and has been shown to be capable of supporting a wide range of intelligent behavior (Laird, Newell & Rosenbloom, 1987; Steier *et al.*, 1987). Polk & Newell (1988) showed that a Soar theory could account for human data in syllogistic reasoning. In this paper, we begin to generalize this theory into a unified theory of immediate reasoning based on Soar and some assumptions about subjects' representation and knowledge. The theory, embodied in a Soar system (IR-Soar), posits three basic problem spaces (**comprehend**, **test-proposition**, and **build-proposition**) that construct annotated models and extract knowledge from them, learn (via chunking) from experience and use an attention mechanism to guide search. Acquiring task specific knowledge is modeled with the **comprehend** space, thus reducing the degrees of freedom available to fit data. The theory explains the qualitative phenomena in four immediate reasoning tasks and accounts for an individual's responses in syllogistic reasoning. It represents a first step toward a unified theory of immediate reasoning and moves Soar another step closer to being a unified theory of all of cognition.

IMMEDIATE REASONING TASKS

An immediate reasoning task involves extracting implicit information from a given situation within a few tens of seconds. The examples addressed here are relational reasoning, categorical syllogisms, the Wason selection task, and conditional reasoning. Typically, they involve testing the validity of a statement about the situation or generating a new statement about it. The situation, and often the task instructions, are novel and require comprehension. Usually, but not invariably, they are presented verbally. All the specific knowledge required to perform the task is available in the situation and the instructions and need not be consistent with other knowledge about the world (hence the task can be about unlikely or imaginary states of affairs).

THE SOAR THEORY OF IMMEDIATE REASONING

The Soar theory of immediate reasoning makes the following assumptions (elaborated below):

1. **Problem spaces.** All tasks, routine or difficult, are formulated as search in problem spaces. Behavior is always occurring in some problem space.
2. **Recognition memory.** All long-term knowledge is held in an associative recognition memory (realized as a production system).
3. **Decision cycle.** All available knowledge about the acceptability and desirability of problem spaces, states, or operators for any role in the current total context is accumulated, and the best choice made within the acceptable alternatives.

4. **Impasse driven subgoals.** Incomplete or conflicting knowledge at a decision cycle produces an impasse. The architecture creates a subgoal to resolve the impasse. Cascaded impasses create a subgoal hierarchy.
5. **Chunking.** The experience in resolving impasses continually becomes new knowledge in recognition memory, in the form of chunks (constructed productions).
6. **Annotated models.** Problem space states are annotated models whose structure corresponds to that of the situation they represent.
7. **Focus of attention.** Attention can be focused on a small number of model objects. Operators are triggered by objects in the focus. When no operators are triggered, an impasse occurs and attention operators add other objects to the focus. Matching and related objects are added first.
8. **Model manipulation spaces.** Immediate reasoning occurs by heuristic search in model manipulation spaces that support comprehension, proposition construction, and proposition testing.
9. **Distribution of errors.** The main sources of errors are interpretation, carefulness and independent knowledge.

The first five assumptions are part of the Soar architecture. Annotated models and attention embody a discipline that is used for modeling cognition (and may become part of the architecture). The last two assumptions are specific to immediate reasoning.

A Soar system consists of a collection of problem spaces with states and operators. At each step during problem solving, the recognition memory brings all relevant knowledge to bear and the decision cycle determines how to proceed. An impasse arises if the decision cycle is unable to make a unique choice. This leads to the creation of a subgoal to resolve the impasse. Upon resolving the impasse, a chunk that summarizes the relevant problem solving is added to recognition memory, obviating the need for similar problem solving in the future.

The states in problem spaces are represented as *annotated models*. A *model* is a representation that satisfies the *structure correspondence condition*: parts, properties, and relations in the model (model elements) correspond to parts, properties, and relations in the represented situation, without completeness (Johnson-Laird, 1983). By exploiting the correspondence condition, processing of models can be match-like and efficient. The price paid is limited expressibility (e.g., models cannot directly represent disjunction or universal quantification). Arbitrary propositions can be represented, but only indirectly, by building a model of a proposition — a model interpretable as an abstract proposition, rather than a concrete object. Some expressibility can be regained without losing efficiency by attaching *annotations* to model elements. An annotation asserts a variant interpretation for the element to which it is attached, but is local to that element and does not admit unbounded processing (e.g., **optional** means that the model element *may* correspond to an element in the situation, but not necessarily).

Problem space states maintain a *focus of attention* that points to a small set of model objects. An operator is proposed when attention is focused on model objects that match its proposal conditions. When no operators are proposed, an impasse occurs and the system searches for a focus of attention that triggers one. Objects that share properties with a current focus of attention or are linked by a relation to one are tried first (others are implicitly assumed to be less relevant). When attention focuses on an object that triggers an operator, the impasse is resolved and problem solving continues.

Immediate reasoning occurs by heuristic search in *model manipulation spaces* (**comprehend, build-proposition**, and **test-proposition**). These spaces provide the basic capabilities necessary for immediate reasoning tasks, namely, constructing representations and generating and testing conclusions (Johnson-Laird, 1988). We assume that normal adults possess these spaces before they are confronted with these tasks. All of these problem spaces use the attention mechanism described above. **Comprehend** reads language and generates models that correspond to situations. It produces a model both of what is described (a *situation model*) and of the linguistic structure of the utterance itself (an *utterance model*). **Build-proposition** searches the space of possible propositions until it finds a proposition that is consistent with the situation model and that satisfies any added constraints in the goal test (e.g., its subject is "fork"). It works by combining properties and relations of model objects into constructed propositions. If attention is focused on an existing proposition, the attention mechanism biases the problem solving toward using parts of it. As a result, constructed propositions tend to be similar to existing propositions on which attention is focused. **Test-proposition** tests models of propositions against models of situations to see if they are valid. It does so by searching for objects in the situation model that correspond to those described in the proposition, and checking if the proposition is true of them. A proposition is considered true or false only if the situation model explicitly confirms or denies the proposition in question (i.e., there are objects in the situation model that correspond to the subject and object of the proposition that are (not) related in the way specified by the proposition). If a proposition is about an object(s) that does not match anything in the situation model, the proposition is considered irrelevant. If a proposition is about an object(s) that does appear in the situation model, but is neither explicitly confirmed nor denied, the proposition is considered relevant but unknown.

Individual subjects respond quite differently from each other in many immediate reasoning tasks. The theory predicts that these differences arise mainly from four sources: (1) the interpretation of certain words and phrases (e.g., quantifiers, connectives), (2) the care taken during reasoning (e.g., completeness of search, testing candidate solutions), (3) knowledge from sources outside the task (such as familiarity with the subject matter), and (4) the order in which attention is focused on model objects. We propose that most errors arise from interpretation mistakes (failing to consider all of the implicit ramifications of the premises or making unwarranted assumptions), incomplete search for conclusions (including the generation of other models if necessary), and less frequently from the inappropriate use of independent knowledge. This predicts that better subjects will interpret premises more completely and correctly or will search more exhaustively for a conclusion. Immediate reasoning tasks are difficult to the extent that they present opportunities for these errors.

ACQUIRING TASKS FROM INSTRUCTIONS

Immediate reasoning is so intimately involved in acquiring knowledge, both of the situation to be reasoned about and the task to be performed, that a theory of immediate reasoning needs to include a theory of acquisition. A companion paper (Lewis, Newell & Polk, 1989) describes NL-BI-Soar, a Soar system that acquires tasks from simple natural language utterances. NL-BI-Soar provides the **comprehend** problem space for IR-Soar, producing both the situation model and the utterance model. It also comprehends the instructions for these tasks. This leads to the creation of a problem space that is unique to the task, whose operators make use of the pre-existing spaces, **comprehend, test-proposition** and **build-proposition**. It is usual in cognitive theories for this structuring of the task to be posited by the theory — to be, in effect, added degrees of freedom in fitting the theory to the data. In the Soar

Relational Reasoning

Instructions	Relation Problem Space
1. Read four premises.	1. Read-input [**comprehend**]
2. Then read a statement.	2. Read-input [**comprehend**]
3. If the statement is "true", say "true".	3. Test-prop [**test-proposition**]
4. Then produce a statement ...	4. Make-conclusion [**build-proposition**]
5. ...that relates the fork to the knife	5. [goal-test]

Categorical Syllogisms

Instructions	Syllogism Problem Space
1. Read two premises that share a term.	1. Read-input [**comprehend**]
2. Then produce a statement that follows from the premises.	2. Make-conclusion [**build-proposition**]
3. The statement relates the unique terms of the premises.	3. [goal-test]

Wason Selection Task

Instructions	Wason Problem Space
1. Examine four cards that have a number on one side and a letter on the other side.	1. Read-input [**comprehend**]
2. Then read a statement.	2. Read-input [**comprehend**]
3. For each card, does deciding if the statement is true require turning over the card?	3. Test-prop [**test-proposition**]

Conditional Reasoning

Instructions	Conditional Problem Space
1. Read two premises.	1. Read-input [**comprehend**]
2. Then read a statement.	2. Read-input [**comprehend**]
3. Then decide if the statement is true.	3. Test-prop [**test-proposition**]
OR	
1. Read two premises.	1. Read-input [**comprehend**]
2. Then produce a statement that follows from the premises.	2. Make-conclusion [**build-proposition**]

Figure 1: Task instructions and the corresponding problem spaces.

theory, comprising NL-BI-Soar and IR-Soar jointly, these degrees of freedom no longer exist. The instructions do not specify all details of IR-Soar versions (there are still substantial individual differences among subjects), but do add a major constraint.

Figure 1 lists the English instructions and the corresponding operators for each task. The subspace used to implement each operator is given in brackets next to the operator name. As NL-BI-Soar reads the instructions it builds a model of what they describe (i.e., the required behavior). When the described task is attempted, impasses arise and NL-BI-Soar consults the behavior model to determine how to proceed, leading to the construction of the problem space (see Lewis, Newell, and Polk (1989) for details).

RELATIONAL REASONING

Relational reasoning involves deducing implicit relationships between objects given explicit relationships (e.g., 3-term series problems). Figure 2 illustrates a version similar to that in Johnson-Laird (1988). Given a set of premises (Figure 2, left) that describe a spatial configuration of objects, the task is to answer questions or make conclusions about the described situation (Figure 2, right).

Premises
1. A plate is left of a knife.
2. A fork is left of the plate.
3. A jug is above the knife.
4. The fork is below a cup.

Read this statement and say if it is true:
"The cup is left of the jug"
then
Produce a statement that relates the fork to the knife

Figure 2: Relational reasoning task (after Johnson-Laird, 1988).

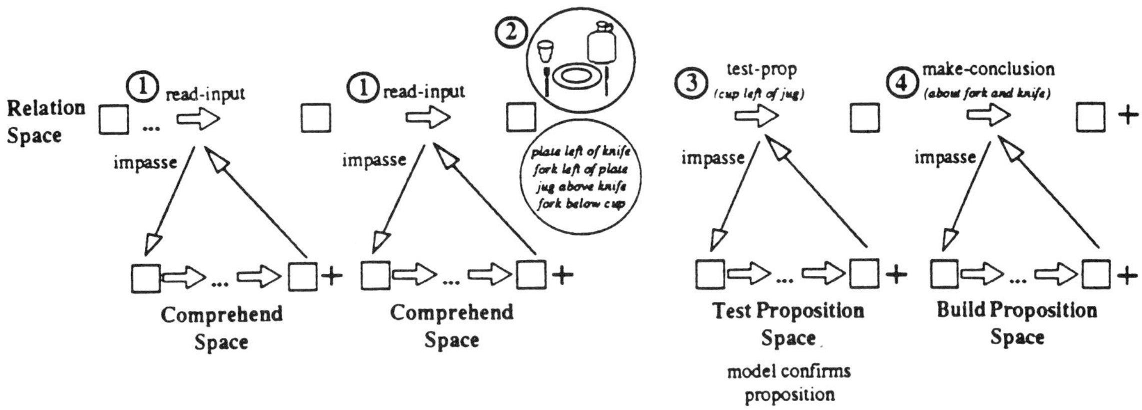

Figure 3: **Behavior of IR-Soar on the relational reasoning task.**

Reading the instructions for this task (Figure 1, top left) leads to a model of the required behavior. The objects in this behavior model are actions that need to be performed for this task. When the task is attempted, NL-BI-Soar consults this behavior model and evokes the operators listed in the figure, instantiating them with the appropriate arguments and goal tests.

Figure 3 illustrates the system's behavior on this task.. (1) After acquiring the task from the instructions, the system starts in **relation** and applies read-input, implemented in **comprehend**, to each of the premises describing the situation. (2) This results in an initial model of the situation as well as a model of the premises (the utterance model). (3) The third instruction triggers the test-prop operator for the proposition "The cup is left of the jug". This operator is implemented in **test-proposition**. Since the situation model contains an object with property cup that is related via a left-of relation to an object with property jug, the proposition is considered true. (4) Instructions four and five call for generating a proposition about the fork and knife so make-conclusion is chosen, implemented in **build-proposition**. **Build-proposition**'s initial state is focused on a proposition with subject fork and object knife but no relation. Attending to the proposition's fork leads to focusing on the fork in the situation model (which is left of the situation's knife). This leads to constructing the proposition "A fork is left of a knife".

The theory predicts the same relative difficulty of problems of this type as Johnson-Laird (1988). It predicts that problems that have an unambiguous interpretation (i.e., admit only a single model) will be the easiest since they do not present opportunities for interpretational errors (assumption nine). Further, since a single model cannot represent disjunction (assumption six), realizing that a relation holds in some situations while not in others requires using multiple models in searching for a conclusion. Hence, problems without valid conclusions will be the hardest since they invite incomplete search (assumption nine). Ambiguous problems that support a valid conclusion will be of intermediate difficulty since conclusions based on considering only a single model may be correct. The percentage of correct responses for each of these problem types confirms these predictions (70%, 8%, and 46% correct, respectively). Many relational reasoning studies have focused on response latencies (Huttenlocher, 1968) and we have not yet addressed this data. The emphasis here is on accounting for major phenomena from many different tasks rather than explaining a single task in its entirety. Eventually we

Premise 1 : No archers are bowlers
Premise 2 : Some bowlers are clowns

Conclusion : Some clowns are not archers
(classified as EabIbc Oca)

A : All a are b
I : Some a are b
E : No a are b
O : Some a are not b

#1 ab #2 bc (EabIbc)	#1 ba #2 bc (AbaObc)
#1 ab #2 cb (OabAcb)	#1 ba #2 cb (IbaEcb)

Figure 4: **Syllogism task.**

expect deep coverage in all of them.

CATEGORICAL SYLLOGISMS

Syllogisms are reasoning tasks consisting of two premises and a conclusion (Figure 4, left). Each premise relates two sets of objects (a and b) in one of four ways (Figure 4, middle), and they share a common set (*bowlers*). A conclusion states a relation between the two sets of objects that are not common (the end-terms, *archers* and *clowns*) or that no valid conclusion exists. The three terms a,b,c can occur in four different orders, called *figures* (Figure 4, right, examples in parentheses), producing 64 distinct premise pairs.

In addition to the basic model manipulation spaces, the task-specific **syllogism** space is used in syllogistic reasoning. Figure 1 shows the correspondence between this problem space and the instructions. This problem space arises directly from the English instructions via NL-BI-Soar. After acquiring the task from the instructions, the system reads both premises and builds a situation model and a model of each of the premises (the utterance model) via **comprehend**. It then attempts to make a conclusion in the **build-proposition** problem space. The attention mechanism biases the form of the constructed conclusion to be similar to that of existing propositions (the premises) (assumptions seven and eight), leading to both the *atmosphere* and *figural* effects. The system may then test the proposition in **test-proposition** and construct additional models, though we have not found this necessary in modeling subjects in the Johnson-Laird & Bara (1984) data.

Polk & Newell (1988) showed how an earlier version of this theory could account for the main trends in group data. Our coverage with the more general theory is almost identical. We have also modeled the individual responses of a randomly chosen subject (subject 16 from Johnson-Laird & Bara (1984)). This subject was modeled by assuming the following processing errors (assumption nine): (1) *all x are y* implies *all y are x* (interpretation), (2) *no x are y* does *not* imply *no y are x* (interpretation), and (3) if neither premise has an end-term as subject, the search is abandoned (carefulness). The focus of attention was treated as a degree of freedom in fitting the subject. For this subject, we were able to predict 55/64 responses (86%).

THE WASON SELECTION TASK

The Wason selection task involves deciding which of four cards (Figure 5, left) *must* be turned over to decide whether or not a particular rule (Figure 5, right) is true (Wason, 1966). This task has been much studied mainly because very few subjects solve it correctly.

Figure 1 shows the top-level **wason** problem space and its correspondence with the instructions. For

E	K	4	7

Given:	Every card has a number on one side and a letter on the other side.
Rule:	Every card with an 'E' on one side has a '4' on the other side.

Figure 5: **Wason selection task.**

each of the four cards, this problem space uses the **test-proposition** problem space to try to decide whether it must be turned over. Since the model will not directly answer this question, the system impasses and tries to augment the model. It does so by watching itself decide whether the rule is true while only turning over relevant cards (again using the **test-proposition** problem space). The system will often mistakenly consider cards that do not match the rule to be irrelevant (assumptions seven and eight) and will not select them. The model of deciding whether the rule is true is then inspected to see if the card was in fact turned over, thus resolving the initial impasse of deciding if it must be.

In this task, the cards can be classified into four cases: (1) those that satisfy the antecendent of the rule (the 'E'), (2) those that deny the antecedent of the rule (the 'K'), (3) those that affirm the consequent of the rule (the '4'), and (4) those that deny the consequent of the rule (the '7'). Cards in cases (1) and (4) are the only ones that must be turned over. The theory predicts that, ceteris paribus, cards that do not match the rule will be selected less frequently than those that do (assumptions seven and eight). Evans & Lynch (1973) demonstrated this *matching bias* in an experiment in which they varied the presence of negatives while holding the logical case constant (e.g., they used rules like "Every card with an E on one side does *not* have a '4' on the other side"). In all four logical cases, cards that did not match the rule were selected less frequently than those that did (56% vs. 90%, 6% vs 38%, 19% vs. 54%, and 38% vs. 67%). The standard task is difficult because the correct solution requires overcoming this matching bias to select the '7' (which does not match and hence seems irrelevant) and to reject the '4' (which does match and hence does seem relevant). These mistakes are indeed the two most common made by subjects. A number of other phenomena (e.g., facilitation) arise in variants of this task and the theory has not yet been applied to these.

CONDITIONAL REASONING

Conditional reasoning tasks involve deriving or testing the validity of a conclusion, given a conditional rule and a proposition affirming or denying either the rule's antecedent or consequent (Figure 6).

Figure 1 shows the correspondence between the top-level problem space and the instructions. For this task, the system comprehends the conditional rule and the proposition. It then either constructs a conclusion or tests one that is given, depending on the instructions (using **build-proposition** or **test-proposition**, respectively). In the absence of other knowledge, the system will consider given

Conditional Rule:	If the letter is 'A' then the number is '4'.
Assumed Proposition:	The number is not '4'.
Derive or Test:	The letter is not 'A'.

Figure 6: **Conditional reasoning task.**

conclusions that do not match the conditional to be less relevant (assumptions seven and eight). When constructing conclusions, the system is similarly biased toward conclusions that match (share one or more terms with) the rule (assumptions seven and eight).

Thus, as in the selection task, the theory predicts a matching bias. For conditional reasoning, this implies that conclusions that do not match the conditional will be less frequently constructed and considered relevant than those that do. Evans (1972) showed that when the logical case was factored out, conclusions whose terms did not match the rule were indeed less likely to be constructed than those that share one or both terms (the percentage of subjects constructing conclusions with zero, one, and two shared terms were 39%, 70%, and 86% respectively). Further, when Evans & Newstead (1977) asked subjects to classify conclusions as 'true', 'false', or 'irrelevant', mismatching conclusions were indeed often considered irrelevant.

CONCLUSION

We have presented a theory of human behavior in immediate reasoning tasks based on Soar. The theory uses model manipulation spaces (**comprehend**, **test-proposition**, and **build-proposition**) to construct and extract knowledge from annotated models and is guided by an attention mechanism. Though not reported on here, it includes a theory of learning (chunking). The theory accounts for qualitative phenomena in multiple immediate reasoning tasks and for detailed individual behavior in syllogistic reasoning. This theory is joined by the Soar subtheory for taking instructions in moving Soar to be a unified theory of cognition that deals in depth with a wide range of psychological phenomena.

Acknowledgements

Thanks to Norma Pribadi for making the intricate figures and to Kathy Swedlow for technical editing. Thanks to Erik Altmann and Shirley Tessler for comment and criticism. This work was supported by the Information Sciences Division, Office of Naval Research, under contract N00014-86-K-0678, and by the Kodak and NSF fellowship programs in which Thad Polk and Richard Lewis, respectively, participate. The views expressed in this paper are those of the authors and do not necessarily reflect those of the supporting agencies. Reproduction in whole or in part is permitted for any purpose of the United States government. Approved for public release; distribution unlimited.

References

Evans, J. S. B. (1972). Interpretation and 'matching bias' in a reasoning task. *Quartlerly Journal of Experimental Psychology, 24(2)*, 193–199.

Evans, J. S. B. and Lynch, J. (1973). Matching bias on the selection task. *British Journal of Psychology, 64*, 391–397.

Evans, J. S. B. and Newstead, S. (1977). Language and reasoning: A study of temporal factors. *Cognition, 5(3)*, 265–283.

Huttenlocher, J. (1968). Constructing spatial images: A strategy in reasoning. *Psychological Review, 75(6)*, 550–560.

Johnson-Laird, P. (1988). Reasoning by rule or model? In *Proceedings of the Annual Conference of the Cognitive Science Society*, pages 765–771.

Johnson-Laird, P. and Bara, B. (1984). Syllogistic Inference. *Cognition, 16*, 1–61.

Johnson-Laird, P. N. (1983). *Mental models: Towards a cognitive science of language, inference and consciousness*. Harvard University Press, Cambridge, Massachusetts.

Laird, J. E., Newell, A., and Rosenbloom, P. S. (1987). Soar: An architecture for general intelligence. *Artificial Intelligence, 33(1)*, 1–64.

Lewis, R., Newell, A., and Polk, T. (1989). Toward a Soar Theory of Taking Instructions for Immediate Reasoning Tasks. To appear in the Proceedings of the Annual Conference of the Cognitive Science Society, August, 1989.

Newell, A. (1989). *Unified Theories of Cognition*. Harvard University Press, Cambridge, Massachusetts. In press.

Polk, T. A. and Newell, A. (1988). Modeling human syllogistic reasoning in Soar. In *Proceedings of the Annual Conference of the Cognitive Science Society*, pages 181–187.

Steier, D. M., Laird, J. E., Newell, A., Rosenbloom, P. S., Flynn, R. A., Golding, A., Polk, T. A., Shivers, O. G., Unruh, A., and Yost, G. R. (1987). Varieties of learning in Soar: 1987. In *Proceedings of the Fourth International Workshop on Machine Learning*, pages 300–311.

Wason, P. C. (1966). Reasoning. In Foss, B. M., editor, *New Horizons in Psychology I*, Penguin, Harmondsworth, England.

CHAPTER 38

A Symbolic Goal-Oriented Perspective on Connectionism and Soar

P. S. Rosenbloom, USC–ISI

Abstract—*In this article we examine connectionism from the perspective of symbolic goal-oriented behavior. We present a functional analysis of the capabilities underlying symbolic-goal oriented behavior, map it onto Soar — a prototypical symbolic problem solver — and onto both basic and extended connectionist systems. This analysis reveals that connectionist systems have progressed only a fraction of the way towards general goal-oriented behavior, but that no fundamental roadblocks would appear to be in the way. We also speculate on how a hybrid connectionist Soar system might be constructed.*

Keywords—Connectionism, goals, hybrid systems, neural networks, problem solving, search, Soar, symbolic processing

The ability to set and achieve a wide range of goals is one of the principal hallmarks of intelligence. The goals faced by an intelligent system can range over a variety of external tasks, from solving simple puzzles, such as the Eight Puzzle, to accomplishing everyday tasks, such as getting home from work, to performing complex intellectual tasks, such as diagnosing medical diseases or configuring computers. They can also range over a variety of desired situations that are internal to the intelligent system itself; that is, to reflective processing. For example, one important type of internal goal is a goal to make a decision about what action to perform next.

The issue of goals, and of how they can be achieved, has been one of the major research foci of Artificial Intelligence (AI), and the understanding of how to construct systems that can accomplish a wide range of goals has been one of the major breakthroughs provided by the study of symbolic processing in AI. Soar — a symbolic architecture for intelligence that integrates together basic mechanisms for problem solving, use of knowledge, learning, and perceptual-motor behavior (Laird, Newell, & Rosenbloom, 1987) — is a prototypical example of a system constructed within this paradigm. Soar can work on the full range of goals mentioned above.

Connectionism[1], on the other hand, has not shared this focus on goals to any significant extent, choosing so far to concentrate primarily on issues of knowledge acquisition, storage and use. This article is based on the assumption that connectionist systems, if they are ever to be serious contenders for complete models of cognition, must eventually incorporate the ability to set and achieve the full range of goals faced by intelligent systems. Our primary purpose here is to analyze connectionist systems from the perspective of symbolic goal-oriented behavior. In the process we hope to provide a better understanding of what is needed, how far connectionist systems have come to date, and what is still left to be done. We also hope that this will further meaningful comparisons between connectionist and symbolic systems, by providing a functional framework within which both must fit, and which can therefore be mapped onto both types of systems. Our secondary purpose here is to begin the process of investigating a hybrid architecture — a connectionist Soar — by speculating about what such an architecture would look like, what issues would arise in constructing it, and what utility it might have.

The starting point for the analysis is a hierarchy of functional capabilities that has been abstracted out from the AI research on symbolic goal-oriented behavior (Section 1). We utilize a hierarchy that has been influenced by experience with Soar. Not all researchers will agree with all of the details of this hierarchy, but the main points should still hold true. Following the presentation of the functional hierarchy, it will be mapped onto the Soar system to concretely illustrate the abstract capabilities (Section 2), and to provide the basis for the later speculations on a connectionist Soar. In Section 3, we analyze connectionist systems with respect to the functional capabilities underlying symbolic goal-oriented behavior. In Section 4 we speculate about a potential synthesis of Soar and connectionism. Finally, in Section 5 we conclude with final remarks about connectionism and symbolic goal-oriented behavior.

1. FUNCTIONAL CAPABILITIES

Figure 1-1 shows a simplified functional hierarchy of the capabilities underlying symbolic goal-oriented behavior. In the figure, arrows represent functional dependencies between capabilities; for example, the performance of a sequence of task steps depends on being able to select and perform individual steps. Loops represent recursive uses of the functional hierarchy, allowing subcapabilities, such as the selection of task steps, to utilize the full power and flexibility of goal-oriented behavior. Terminals represent capabilities that, though clearly important, will not be focused on in detail here.

At the top of the hierarchy is a goal, which can be to reach one of a wide variety of desired internal and external situations. Satisfactory goal-oriented behavior requires that the goal be achieved, and that the system be able to detect that the goal has been achieved. Goal detection is necessary so that the system can behave differentially according to whether the

[1]As there is not yet a single universally accepted name for the broad study of neural (and neurally-inspired) network models, we will use connectionism as a stand-in generic name for the field.

goal has been achieved or not — for example, by ending the attempt to achieve it. We will not discuss goal detection in detail, but simply note that some form of it is required. Instead we focus on goal achievement, which can be accomplished in three distinct ways: by knowledge access, by performing a sequence of task steps, or by decomposing the goal into subgoals which then must themselves be achieved. In the remainder of this section we examine these three options, starting with knowledge access.

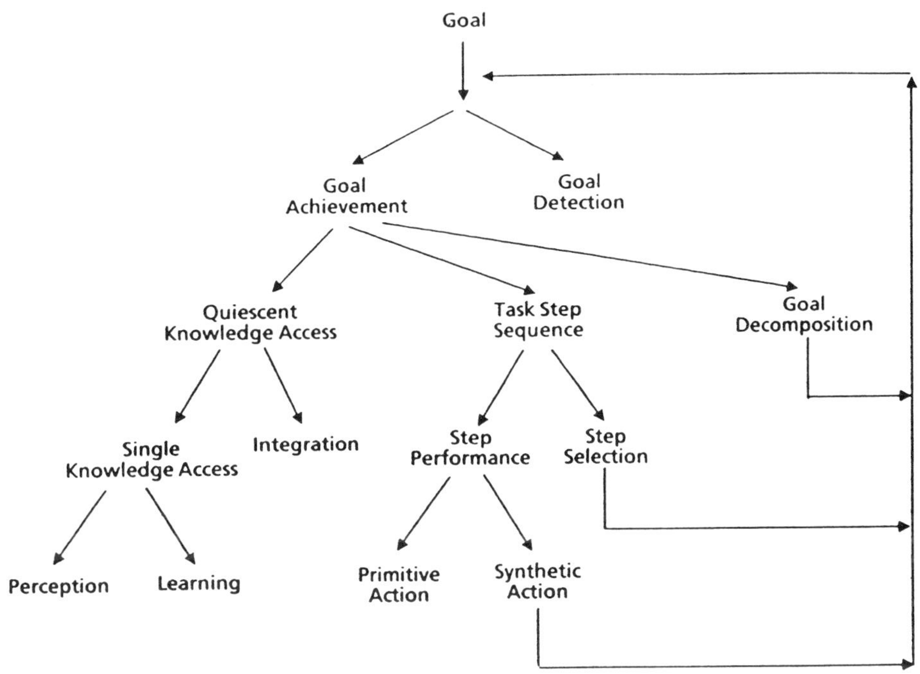

Figure 1-1: Simplified functional hierarchy for goal-oriented behavior.

1.1. Knowledge Access

Familiar internal goals — such as determining what move to make in Tic-Tac-Toe (for a system that has played the game repeatedly) — can be achieved directly by knowledge access. The goal must be internal because knowledge access does not directly affect the outside world. The goal must be familiar for the system to have been able to acquire previously the knowledge that achieves the goal. Consider, for instance, the internal goal of determining which Tic-Tac-Toe move is best for player O in Figure 1-2. An intelligent system that is familiar with Tic-Tac-Toe will have a variety of knowledge in its memory about which moves are better than which others in this situation. It might know that move 1 is better than move 9 because move 1 blocks two of X's one-in-a-rows and creates a two-in-a-row. Likewise it might know that move 6 is better than move 9 because move 6 blocks a two-in-a-row. If enough of this comparative knowledge can be retrieved from memory, along with knowledge about the relationships among the elements of comparative knowledge, the goal can be achieved directly by knowledge access. Even when knowledge access is insufficient by itself for the achievement of a goal, it can play a critical subrole via the recursive loops in the hierarchy.

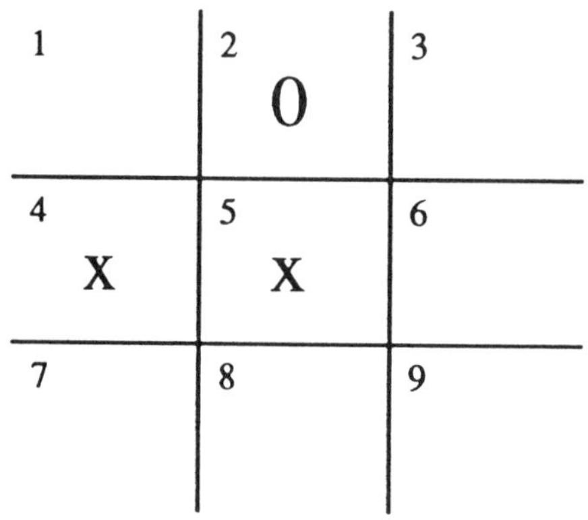

Figure 1-2: A Tic-Tac-Toe position

In an ideal world, all of the knowledge required to achieve a goal would be immediately available where and when it is required. However, the nature of the real world dictates otherwise. One problem with the real world is that any suitably large body of knowledge must be physically distributed over a region of space — the larger the body of knowledge, the larger the region of space.[2] Moreover, because of the variability in the range of goals that can arise, it is impossible to always guarantee that all of the knowledge required for any particular goal is proximally situated. Thus there is a need to transmit knowledge from distal regions of the system; that is, to access the distal memory in which the knowledge is located. What knowledge needs to be transmitted is a function of the current situation and the goal.

In Figure 1-1, knowledge access is partitioned into two distinguishable capabilities: single knowledge access and quiescent knowledge access. Single knowledge access consists of a single cycle of transmission of information from one part of the system to another — multiple parallel transmissions can all be considered as a single access. One effect of a single knowledge access is to augment the knowledge available about the current situation and goal. A second effect is to enable a second access that is based on the augmented situation and goal. Quiescent knowledge access involves repeated cycles of single knowledge access, continuing until no new knowledge about the situation or goal is accessed[3] . It also involves the integration of the independent pieces of retrieved knowledge into a coherent whole.

---

[2] The arguments in this paragraph are largely derived from Newell (1989).

[3] Another way of viewing this is that a single knowledge access is a single sample of what is known. The first sample allows a second, more informed sample to be made, and so on until the sampling process reaches quiescence. The sampling process could be either discrete or continuous.

Consider the example goal in Tic-Tac-Toe of selecting the right move to make in the position shown in Figure 1-2. The first cycle of transmission might access information about where there are one-in-a-rows, two-in-a-rows, etc. Based on this information, the second cycle would then access the comparative information about which moves are better than which other moves. The third cycle would then access the information about the relationships among the comparative information. Quiescence would then be reached. When this information is integrated together, it achieves the goal by determining that move 6 is the one to select. Quiescent knowledge access thus provides an approximation to the ideal situation, by allowing the relevant stored knowledge to be brought to bear on achieving the goal.

As described in this example, quiescence is purely a function of retrieval — when nothing more can be retrieved, quiescence is reached, and then integration occurs. It should be clear though that quiescence could equally well have been applied to the integration process, with retrieval and integration possibly being tightly interleaved. Under such circumstances, quiescence occurs when the results of the integration process are no longer changing.

Another problem with the real world is that in many cases the requisite knowledge will not already exist within the system's memory. Dealing with this problem requires perceptual and learning capabilities. Perception performs distal transmission of knowledge from outside of the system to the inside. It thus increases the knowledge that is immediately available for use, though only transiently (during the extent of the perceptual event). Learning results in an augmentation of the knowledge in the system's long-term memory, thus increasing what can be accessed for later goals. Both perception and learning need, and deserve, entire functional analyses of their own, but the important aspect here is how they support knowledge access, and thus goal-oriented behavior.

1.2. Task Step Sequence

The second way to achieve a goal is to perform a sequence of task steps. Each step in the sequence is a task-relevant action which modifies the current situation, yielding a new situation. The new situation may or may not have ever been previously experienced. In a game like Tic-Tac-Toe the task steps are the allowable moves — the placement of an X or an O in an empty position. In a task like computer configuration, the task steps are the configuration operations of putting two components, such as a box and a cabinet, together in an appropriate way. A sequence of task steps achieves a goal by starting with the initial situation and generating a sequence of intermediate situations, until ultimately the desired situation is reached.

Performance of task sequences is supported by two further capabilities: step performance, and step selection. Step performance consists of the execution of a single task-relevant action. The action can be a primitive one which directly alters the external or internal situation — for example, a primitive motor action — or it can be a synthetic one which is performed by a recursive use of the functional hierarchy. This recursive use of subgoals implies that, in addition to being able to perform the basic activities of goal achievement and detection, the system must also be able to suspend goals while their subgoals are being pursued, and to reactivate goals when their subgoals are achieved. The benefit of using subgoals for synthetic actions is the freedom it allows in the creation of task-relevant actions. Synthetic actions enable hierarchical action performance, with higher-level actions occurring via sequences of lower-level actions. They enable actions to be performed by knowledge access (at least for actions that need not directly affect the outside world). They also enable actions to be performed by the interpretation of declarative structures that describe the actions — that is, what is classically referred to as "rule-following behavior".

Step selection consists of determining which task-relevant actions should be performed in which situations. As with synthetic actions, step selection occurs via a recursive use of the functional hierarchy. Some decisions, such as the Tic-Tac-Toe one described earlier, can be made directly by quiescent knowledge access. Another example of using knowledge access for step selection occurs in following a deliberate plan, where a selection is made by accessing the portion of the plan relevant to the current situation.

When simple knowledge access is insufficient to make a selection, the system has three options: (1) it can make a possibly incorrect selection based on insufficient knowledge, while being prepared to recover if the choice does turn out to be wrong, (2) it can perform a sequence of actions that results in having sufficient knowledge to make the correct selection, or (3) it can attempt to decompose the problem into subgoals. The first two options intrinsically involve search (the third option is discussed in the following section). With the first option, search occurs in the process of trying options and recovering when they fail. With the second option, search occurs in the process of determining which option is correct; for example, by a lookahead search using a simulation of the task. Search arises not because it is the best way to achieve goals, but because of the uncertainty that arises from a lack of knowledge about what to do.

The necessity of performing effective search demands the ability to control the search. Consider, for example, the second option above, where the system attempts to perform a sequence of steps in service of determining what action to select. If the system is not to perform brute-force search, intelligent decisions must be made about which steps to select for this sequence. This, in turn, involves a second-level of recursion on the functional hierarchy, so that the search can be controlled by knowledge access — including knowledge about the weak methods (see, for example, Rich, 1983, Part 1) — or by further information-gathering search.

1.3. Goal Decomposition

Decomposing a goal into a set of independent subgoals is one of the principal ways to reduce complexity. Without goal decomposition, if there is a goal that requires a sequence of steps of length N for achievement, and if there are B potential task steps available at each point, then finding the sequence of task steps that achieves the goal requires a search of size B^N. However, if the goal can be decomposed into M independent subgoals, the cost of finding the desired sequence of task steps can be reduced to $M*B^{N/M}$. Not all goals can be decomposed into independent subgoals, but when they can, problem solving effort can be greatly reduced (see, for example, Korf, 1987).

2. AN EXAMPLE: SOAR

Soar is an attempt to bring together in one system as much of the basic functionality required for general intelligence as is currently possible. It is firmly rooted in the classic symbolic problem-solving tradition, and serves well as a prototype of state-of-the-art research on symbolic goal-oriented behavior. Our primary purposes here are to use Soar as an illustrative instantiation of the abstract functional hierarchy described in the previous section, and to provide the basis for speculations about what a combination of connectionism and Soar might look like (Section 4). However, by providing a somewhat non-standard analysis of Soar, it also provides new insight into the structure of Soar itself.

2.1. The Soar Architecture

Soar is based on formulating all symbolic goal-oriented behavior as search in problem spaces. The problem space determines the set of states and operators that can be used during the processing to attain a goal. The states represent situations. There is an initial state, representing the initial situation, and a set of desired states that represent the goal. An operator, when applied to a state in the problem space, yields another state in the problem space. The goal is achieved when a desired state is reached as the result of a sequence of operator applications starting from the initial state. Each goal defines a problem solving context ("context" for short) that contains, in addition to a goal, roles for a problem space, state, and an operator. The combination of a particular context and a particular role within the context is referred to as a "context slot", or just "slot".

Problem solving for a goal is driven by decisions that result in the selection of problem spaces, states, and operators for the appropriate roles in the context. Decisions are made by the retrieval and integration of preferences — special architecturally interpretable elements that describe the acceptability, desirability, and necessity of selecting particular problem spaces, states, and operators. Acceptability preferences determine which objects are candidates for selection. Desirability preferences establish a partial order on the set of candidates. Necessity preferences specify objects that must (or must not) be selected for the goal to be achieved.

All long-term knowledge is stored in a recognition-based memory — a production system. Each production is a cued-retrieval procedure that retrieves the contents of its actions when the pattern in its conditions is successfully matched. By sharing variables between conditions and actions, productions can retrieve information that is a function of what was matched. By having variables in actions that are not in conditions, new objects can be generated/retrieved.

Transient process state is contained in a working memory. This includes information retrieved from long-term memory (problem spaces, states, operators, etc.), results of decisions made by the architecture, information currently perceived from the external environment, and motor commands. Structurally, working memory consists of a set of objects and preferences about objects.

For each problem solving decision, an elaboration phase occurs in which long-term memory is accessed, retrieving into working memory new objects, new information about existing objects, and preferences. Elaboration proceeds in a sequence of synchronous cycles, during each of which all successfully matched productions are fired in parallel. When this process quiesces — that is, when no more productions can fire on a cycle — an architectural decision procedure is invoked that interpets the preferences in working memory according to their fixed semantics. If the preferences uniquely specify an object to be selected for a role in a context, then a decision can be made, and the specified object becomes the current value of the role. The whole process then repeats.

If the decision procedure is ever unable to make a selection — because the preferences in working memory are either incomplete or inconsistent — an impasse occurs in problem solving because the system does not know how to proceed. When an impasse occurs, a subgoal with an associated problem solving context is automatically generated for the task of resolving the impasse. The impasses, and thus their subgoals, vary from problems of selection (of problem spaces, states, and operators) to problems of generation (e.g., operator application). Given a subgoal, Soar can bring its full problem solving capability and knowledge to bear on resolving the impasse that caused the subgoal. When impasses occur within impasses — if, for example, there is insufficient knowledge about how to evaluate a competing alternative — then subgoals occur within subgoals, and a goal hierarchy results (which therefore defines a hierarchy of contexts). A subgoal terminates when its impasse (or some higher impasse) is resolved. Soar learns by acquiring new productions which summarize the processing that leads to results of subgoals, a process called chunking. The actions of the new productions are based on the results of the subgoal. The conditions are based on those working memory elements in supergoals that were relevant to the determination of the results. Chunking is a form of explanation-based learning (Rosenbloom & Laird, 1986).

Soar's perceptual-motor behavior is mediated through the state in the top context (Wiesmeyer, 1988). Each perceptual and motor system has its own field in the state. Perceptual systems behave by autonomously adding perceived information to their fields of the top state. This information is then available for examination by productions, until it is overwritten by later information arriving from the same system. Motor systems behave by autonomously executing commands that are placed (by the firing of productions) in their fields of the top state.

2.2. Mapping Symbolic Goal-Oriented Behavior onto Soar

Figure 2-1 shows the mapping of functional capabilities onto Soar (including capabilities mentioned in the text, but not explicitly in Figure 1-1). This mapping is relatively straightforward, as it should be, given that the hierarchy was strongly influenced by abstracting from the experience with Soar. However, the first step is a bit complicated: functional goals — that is, the kinds of goals that are included in the functional hierarchy — are mapped onto a combination of context slots and (Soar) goals.

In the traditional Soar view, goals only occur when an impasse occurs; that is, when a context slot cannot be filled by direct knowledge access. At that point there is a declarative structure in working memory that represents the goal of resolving the impasse. The non-standard mapping arises because in the functional hierarchy, knowledge access is considered one of the ways of achieving a goal, rather than a means of accomplishing things directly; that is, without requiring goal structures as intermediaries.

Symbolic Goal-Oriented Behavior	Soar
Goal	Determine value for context slot
Goal achievement	Determining value
Goal detection	Value determined (decision procedure)
Goal recursion	Impasse/goal/context creation
Goal suspension	Implicit (when can't make progress)
Goal reactivation	Automatic (when can make progress)
Goal decomposition	Decomposition into independent operators
Quiescent knowledge access	Elaboration phase
Integration	Preference combination (decision procedure)
Single knowledge access	Elaboration cycle
Perception	Input system
Learning	Chunking
Task step sequence	Operator sequence
Step performance	Operator application
Primitive action	Motor action
Synthetic action	Operator
Step selection	Operator selection
Search	Subgoal-based lookahead and reselection

Figure 2-1: Mapping of goal-oriented capabilities onto Soar.

Thus, in this mapping, the creation of a context slot is the act of creating a goal to have an appropriate value selected for that slot.[4] A problem-space slot is the goal of determining what problem space should be used in the context. A state slot is the goal of determining what the current state is in the context. An operator slot is the goal of determining what operator should be applied in the context. Consider, for example, what happens during medical diagnosis when a diagnose-illness operator is selected in a context. As a result of this selection, the state slot becomes the goal of selecting the state that results from applying the operator to the previous state; that is, the state slot is the goal of having a state representing the correct diagnosis.

An impasse provides a refinement of the goal defined by a context slot, incorporating additional information about the way in which quiescent knowledge access failed to accomplish the goal — whether there are no candidates remaining under consideration for selection or multiple candidates. The impasse also provides the new context that allows full recursive use of the functional hierarchy. Without this additional structure, only memory access could be used for the achievement of goals. With this additional structure, goal achievement can also be pursued by task step sequences and goal decomposition (as

[4] It is not clear whether this shift in view has any major implications for Soar, or even if it will necessarily prove a more useful way to describe Soar than existing ways. However, it is appropriate for this analysis, and it does have the side benefit of emphasizing the relationship of Soar to such slot-based architectures as Eurisko (Lenat, 1983) and Theo (Mitchell et al, 1989).

described below). The combination of context slots and impasses (with their associated goals and contexts) thus seems to provide the best mapping of the functional hierarchy onto Soar.

Goal detection occurs via the decision procedure — if the preferences available in working memory determine a unique object to be selected for a slot, then the goal is achieved. However, once a decision results in a change in the context hierarchy, the situation has changed, and each slot represents anew the goal of selecting the appropriate value given the (changed) situation.

Goal suspension occurs implicitly. Whenever nothing more can be done for a goal, it is effectively suspended. It is automatically reactivated whenever additional progress can be made on it. Reactivation usually occurs when a subgoal completes, providing the altered situation (or information) upon which the goal was waiting. However, goal reactivation can occur any time the required situation exists, whether as a direct result of subgoal completion or not.

2.2.1. Knowledge Access

Soar accesses its knowledge by the firing of productions. A single knowledge access consists of a single cycle of elaboration, during which all of the successfully matched productions fire in parallel. The result of a single access is the context-dependent augmentation of the local environment — the contents of working memory — with additional information.

A quiescent knowledge access consists of a single decision cycle — the combination of an elaboration phase followed by an application of the decision procedure. During the elaboration phase, single knowledge accesses are performed repeatedly until exhaustion (that is, until no more productions are able to fire). At exhaustion, all of the accessible knowledge about the goal and situation have been retrieved. Quiescence is purely a function of this retrieval process. Integration occurs immediately following quiescence, when the decision procedure interprets the set of preferences in working memory to determine what they jointly imply. This integration actually covers not just information retrieved by memory access, but all preferences in working memory, whether they are retrieved by memory access, or generated by perception, a sequence of task steps, or decomposed subgoals. Quiescent memory access occurs for each context slot in parallel, and is repeated each time a context slot is changed. It thus occurs for each functional goal.

Perception occurs in Soar by the autonomous input-driven creation of structures in working memory. Once in working memory, perceptual information acts just as if it were retrieved from memory (though it is possible to distinguish the two by their location in working memory).

Learning occurs by the chunking of Soar's experience. This places new productions in memory, which are then available for use during later goal-oriented behavior. Chunking learns both from the system's own behavior and from the outside world (Rosenbloom, Laird, & Newell, 1988).

2.2.2. Task Step Sequence

Problem space operators are the synthetic actions, and motor commands are the primitive actions. These two types of actions are closely coupled in Soar — motor commands (primitive actions) are generated by production firing (knowledge access) in service of applying operators (synthetic actions). This lets us focus on the selection and application of operators, while leaving motor commands in the background. In fact, most Soar operators actually bottom out in knowledge access anyway, rather than in primitive actions; or in other terms, operators tend to be synthetic actions which lead to subgoals that are achieved via knowledge access. Both operator selection and application, and thus step selection and performance, occur via a functional goal — an operator slot and a state slot, respectively (as discussed above). This enables Soar's full goal-oriented behavior to be available for both, allowing them to be performed by knowledge access, task step sequences, and decomposition. Search occurs when knowledge access is inadequate, usually as a lookahead search in service of determining which of several options is preferred. Backtracking on error can also occur by the reselection of objects (problem spaces, states, and operators) that were previously selected.

Soar has several other features that, though not mentioned explicitly in the functional hierarchy, are important to its production of goal-oriented behavior. One feature is that Soar embodies the notion of problem spaces — sets of states and operators. Problem spaces allow Soar to pursue goal achievement within an appropriately restricted context. This wasn't included as an essential capability in the functional hierarchy, but does appear to be implicated in effective goal-oriented behavior. The other feature is that Soar allows states to be selected, in addition to problem spaces and operators. This enables easy recovery from bad task step sequences by the reselection of previous states, and allows the use of search methods — such as best-first search — which require state selection.

2.2.3. Goal Decomposition

In Soar, a goal decomposition is indistinguishable from a task step sequence. This occurs because an operator is a deliberately generated structure whose selection leads to a subgoal to apply it. A goal can thus be decomposed by the generation, selection, and application of a set of operators which jointly accomplish the goal. The issue of how to automatically decompose goals into a set of independent operators has not been addressed in any great detail in Soar. However, if the knowledge about such decompositions are in Soar's memory, it can use them.

3. CONNECTIONISM

Now that the groundwork has been laid, it is time to examine connectionism, and its relationship to symbolic goal-oriented behavior. We start by reviewing basic connectionist architectures, then proceed to analyze how symbolic goal-oriented behavior maps onto this basic structure, and then look beyond the basic architecture to systems that embody additional high-level structure for goal-oriented behavior.

3.1. Basic Connectionist Architecture

A basic connectionist architecture – as described, for example, in Rumelhart, Hinton, & McClelland (1986) – consists of units and connections between units. Units have activations, and connections have weights (either positive or negative). During each unit of time, activation passes from each individual unit over connections to its neighbors as determined by an output function (a function of the unit's output and the connection's weight), and an activation rule (a function of the unit's input and current activation). In a simple linear system, the activation of a unit at time $t+1$ is the sum of the products of its neighbors' activations at time t and the weights of the connections to the neighbors, though many more sophisticated possibilities also exist.

Performance occurs by activating a set of input units, propagating activation through the network until it settles down, and then reading the results off as the activations of a set of output units. Learning occurs by experience-driven modification of connection weights.

At the level of detail at which this basic architecture is described, it abstracts away from many of the important distinctions among connectionist systems — single-level versus multi-level networks, feedforward versus feedback networks, supervised versus unsupervised learning, and local versus distributed representations. For most of goal-oriented behavior, these distinctions are not critical.

3.2. Mapping Symbolic Goal-Oriented Behavior onto Basic Connectionism

Figure 3-1 shows the mapping of the hierarchy of functional capabilities onto the basic connectionist architecture. The mapping is close to trivial, because the basic connectionist architecture provides only quiescent knowledge access. The structure and weights in the network embody the long-term knowledge in the system. The propagation of activation which occurs during a single time step corresponds to a single knowledge access — activation is a short-term reflection of the long-term structure of the system (and its input). Activation propagation transmits this information to distal parts of the network. Transmission occurs in parallel over the set of connections, but it still amounts to just a single knowledge access. Repeated propagation until the network has settled corresponds to quiescent knowledge access. This ensures that all relevant information has been transmitted to where it might be needed. It also performs knowledge integration during every cycle of propagation, by the addition and subtraction of activation, and possibly additional nonlinear transformations. Quiescence is a function of the integration process settling down, rather than purely the transmission (retrieval) process.

Perception occurs via the activation of special input units. This changes the short-term activation of the system, without changing its long-term structure. Learning occurs via the adjustment of connection weights, thus allowing the network to be more knowledgeable at later points in time.

Two main classes of capabilities are missing from the basic architecture. The first class includes the goal-centered capabilities: achievement, detection, recursion, suspension, reactivation, and decomposition. The second class includes the capabilities required for performing task step sequences. This includes step performance and selection, synthetic and primitive actions, and search. Without such capabilities, general goal-oriented behavior is impossible.

Symbolic Goal-Oriented Behavior	Basic Connectionism
Goal	
Goal achievement	
Goal detection	
Goal recursion	
Goal suspension	
Goal reactivation	
Goal decomposition	
Quiescent knowledge access	Activation passing until quiescence
Integration	Activation combination
Single knowledge access	One cycle of activation passing
Perception	Activation of input units
Learning	Adjustment of connection weights
Task step sequence	
Step performance	
Primitive action	
Synthetic action	
Step selection	
Search	

Figure 3-1: Mapping of goal-oriented capabilities onto basic connectionism.

3.3. Beyond the Basic Architecture

It should not be too surprising that the basic connectionist architecture does not by itself provide symbolic goal-oriented behavior, any more than would Soar with just its production memory (even when augmented a bit). As in Soar, additional structure is required. For goal-oriented behavior, it does not matter whether this structure is implemented in "symbolic matter" outside of the connectionist memory, or by a set of special purpose connectionist memories that interact via hard-wired connections, or by structure (or weights) in a single connectionist memory — though, such considerations will certainly interact with other important issues, such as learning and simplicity. What does matter is the functionality provided.

Bits and pieces of the required structure can be found in some existing connectionist systems. One of the more straightforward approaches, taken from Rumelhart, Smolensky, McClelland, & Hinton (1986), is shown in Figure 3-2. This system, which is specialized to the domain of Tic-Tac-Toe, is able to select and execute a sequence of task steps. The task steps can be either primitive actions which result in actually playing the game, or synthetic actions which simulate the results of real actions. Distinct memories are used for step performance and selection.

Though this system does represent significant progress, much is still missing. One problem is that the system has no goals; or alternatively, it has only one hard-wired implicitly-represented goal: playing Tic-Tac-Toe. The ability to have multiple goals, and to achieve, detect, suspend, reactivate, and decompose them, is missing. A second problem is that the system does not learn. This may not be a fundamental problem, since connectionist systems definitely do learn, but this particular system did not learn. A third problem is that the system cannot recursively use the hierarchy for step selection and performance. One consequence of this is that, though it can perform sequences of task steps, it cannot use such sequences as lookahead searches in service of determining what steps to select.

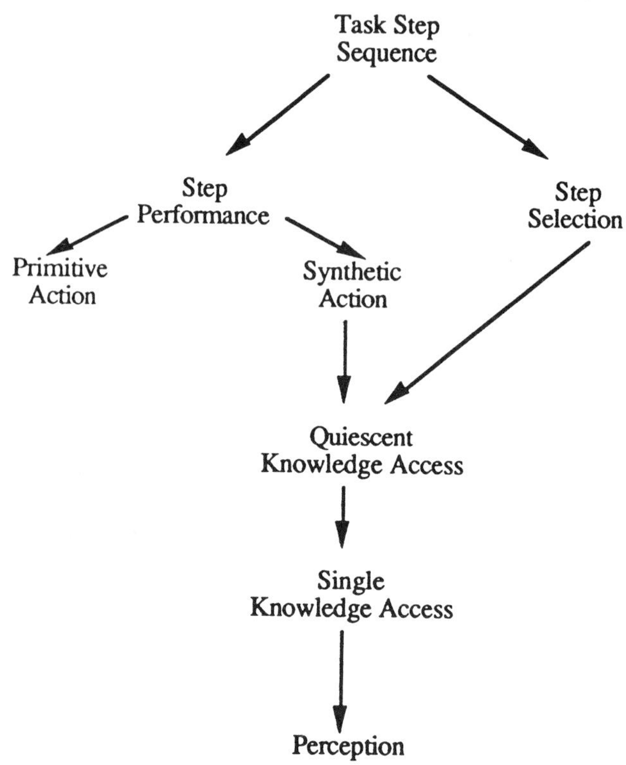

Figure 3-2: Functional capabilities provided by Tic-Tac-Toe system in Rumelhart, Smolensky, McClelland, & Hinton (1986).

Other systems provide fragments of related functionality, such as the explicit representation of the goal, and its use in hill-climbing (Kawamoto, 1986); the explicit representation of evaluation functions for states (Sutton & Barto, 1981, Anderson, 1987); traversal of hierarchical structures (Hinton, 1981, Touretzky, 1986); and the use of limited forms of lookahead search in service of step selection (Sutton & Barto, 1981). However, no connectionist system yet provides all of the requisite functionality.

4. A CONNECTIONIST SOAR

One possible approach to creating a connectionist system capable of general goal-oriented behavior is to combine Soar's well-developed capabilities for the use of goals and task step sequences, with a connectionist model of knowledge access. In addition to providing the necessary structure that is missing from connectionist systems, the creation of such a hybrid could help focus comparisons between symbolic and connectionist memories, by asking how well each supports the needs of symbolic goal-oriented behavior. This could shift the focus of the discussion from more peripheral topics, such as the binding of values to variables, to what is clearly one of the central issues in general intelligence.

Another benefit of creating such a hybrid is the promise it provides of solving some of the extant problems with Soar's current model of memory. A number of sources of evidence have recently come together to imply that Soar's existing production system memory is too powerful: the problem of expensive chunks, where learned rules severely degrade the performance of the system by requiring exponential match time (Tambe & Newell, 1988, Tambe & Rosenbloom, 1988); the difficulties in implementing Soar on highly parallel computers such as the Connection machine (Flynn, 1988); the limits on the forms of declarative knowledge that are learnable by chunking (Rosenbloom, Newell, & Laird, 1989); and work on mental models (Polk & Newell, 1988). The vector of change clearly points in the direction of more restricted models of memory. Connectionist memories, along with various forms of simpler symbolic memories, are major candidates for the new Soar memory model.

A first cut at what a connectionist Soar would look like can be obtained by combining the relevant portions of the functional mappings in Figures 2-1 and 3-1 to yield the hybrid functional mapping in Figure 4-1. When viewed from the Soar perspective, this mapping involves four substitutions of major components (Figure 4-2): production memory is replaced by a network with units and weighted links; working memory is replaced by unit activations; the chunking mechanism is replaced by a weight adjustment mechanism, such as (but not limited to) back-propagation (Rumelhart, Hinton, & Williams, 1986); and the decision procedure is replaced by functions which combine units' input activations.

Symbolic Goal-Oriented Behavior	Connectionist Soar
Goal	Determine value for context slot
Goal achievement	Determining value
Goal detection	Value determined (decision procedure)
Goal recursion	Impasse/goal/context creation
Goal suspension	Implicit (when can't make progress)
Goal reactivation	Automatic (when can make progress)
Goal decomposition	Decomposition into independent operators
Quiescent knowledge access	Activation passing until quiescence
Integration	Activation combination
Single knowledge access	One cycle of activation passing
Perception	Activation of input units
Learning	Adjustment of connection weights
Task step sequence	Operator sequence
Step performance	Operator application
Primitive action	Motor action
Synthetic action	Operator
Step selection	Operator selection
Search	Subgoal-based lookahead and reselection

Figure 4-1: Mapping of goal-oriented capabilities onto a connectionist Soar.

Symbolic Soar		Connectionist Soar
Production memory	→	Units with weighted links
Working memory	→	Unit activations
Chunking	→	Adjustment of connection weights
Decision procedure	→	Activation combination

Figure 4-2: Component substitution from symbolic to connectionist Soar.

Actually building such a hybrid is considerably more complicated than this simple set of substitutions suggests. At least six issues need to be resolved. The first issue is the expressibility of connectionist memories as associative memories; that is, what is the power of the language connectionist memories embody for describing when particular pieces of knowledge are to be accessed. Our investigations of restricted symbolic memories for Soar have revealed a number of expressibility issues that arise for various simple memory models: the representation of object cohesion, which assures that there is no confusion about which features go with which objects; the representation of undifferentiated sets of objects, which enables a rapid search over the objects in working memory during quiescent knowledge access; and the representation (and performance) of equality and inequality tests between objects in working memory. These particular issues may not be the ones that arise in using a connectionist memory, but expressibility issues are certain to arise. For each expressibility limitation that does arise, either: the memory model must be extended to overcome it; it must be possible to overcome the limitation some other way, such as by a sequence of task steps or by subgoal decomposition; or it must be shown that the additional expressibility is unnecessary.

The second issue is how to base knowledge access on an arbitrary number of cues (the knowledge in working memory), and how to access an arbitrary amount of knowledge in parallel. This is an issue that has been addressed in local connectionist systems, but not yet in a general way in completely distributed systems (Feldman, 1987).

The third issue is the adequacy of activation combination as a mechanism for decision making. Soar currently makes decisions based on a partial ordering among the alternatives (as encoded in the preferences), rather than by a total ordering (as encoded in activation levels). It needs to be determined whether a total ordering is sufficient, and if not, how a partial ordering could be implemented. One possible strategy might be to use asymmetric negative weights to implement a partial ordering: if object A is better than object B, then object A differentially inhibits object B. Another possibility is to directly store preferences in the memory and use an external decision procedure, as is currently done in Soar.

The fourth issue is how impasses are detected and classified — at least to determine whether at quiescence there are no candidates still being considered for selection, or multiple candidates. This requires that the system be able to distinguish objects that are candidates from those that are not, that it be able to detect that no unique candidate is left after quiescence is reached, and that it be able to determine whether the problem is caused by there being no candidates left or multiple candidates left. If a way is found to distinguish candidates — some structural distinction, for example — detection may be possible by determining how many candidates are above threshold at quiescence.

The fifth issue is how new problem solving contexts are created once an impasse has been detected. In the current version of Soar, the creation of a new context increases the number of slots about which decisions are to be simultaneously made. This in turn increases the amount of knowledge in working memory upon which further knowledge access is based, and may increase the amount of knowledge that will be retrieved before quiescence is reached (the second issue, above). One possible approach to this issue is to use a programmable connectionist system (McClelland, 1985). In such a system there is a single central store of knowledge, represented as a connectionist network, that controls the weights in an arbitrary number of identical programmable networks. By allocating one programmable network per subgoal, it may be possible to dynamically increase the number of slots about which decisions can be simultaneously made (at the price of some cross-talk).

The sixth issue is the relationship between Soar's learning mechanism — chunking — and connectionist learning mechanisms. Both are experiential learning mechanisms, but of different character. Chunking is an explanation-based learning mechanism that bases its generalizations on dependency analyses of single examples. Connectionist learning algorithms are more empirical, basing their generalizations on statistical regularities among sets of examples. While these differences are real, they may not be of quite the magnitude that they initially seem. The modifications made by connectionist learning algorithms — such as back-propagation — are a function of the paths by which, during performance, activation proceeded from the input units to the output units; that is, on dependency analyses of the outputs. Thus such learning algorithms may actually be performing some combination of explanation-based and empirical learning. In the field of symbolic machine learning, the combination of these two types of learning — explanation-based and empirical — is currently a major research topic (see, for instance, Flann & Dietterich, 1986).

Together, these six issues make the construction of a connectionist Soar far from the relatively trivial enterprise of just substituting the analogous connectionist mechanisms for Soar's production memory, working memory, decision procedure, and chunking mechanism. Nonetheless, there are potentially a variety of interesting payoffs from constructing such a system.

5. CONCLUSION

In this article we have presented a functional analysis of the capabilities underlying symbolic-goal oriented behavior, and mapped it onto Soar — a prototypical symbolic problem solver — and onto both basic and extended connectionist systems. From this analysis it is clear that the basic connectionist system, consisting solely of quiescent knowledge access, is missing many of the structures required to support general goal-oriented behavior. Fragments of the required structures do show up in several experimental systems, but no system yet comes close to the complete functionality that is required. Nonetheless, no fundamental roadblocks became apparent which would imply that this is impossible to do.

If the requisite structure were added to a connectionist system, the overall system is likely to resemble its symbolic cousins fairly closely, but with some interesting differences in the details. Contrasting two such systems — one connectionist and one symbolic — could provide needed focus in comparing connectionist and symbolic systems, by asking what the trade-offs are for the overall system from differences in the models of knowledge access. One concrete way of doing this is to attempt to create a connectionist Soar by replacing Soar's model of knowledge access with a connectionist model. We have provided some speculations on what such a hybrid might look like. A number of key issues make the construction of such a system far from trivial, but it does offer potential for overcoming existing problems with both Soar and connectionist systems.

ACKNOWLEDGEMENT

I would like to thank John Laird and Allen Newell for their helpful comments on an earlier draft of this article — and for a variety of useful conversations related to this material. I would also like to thank Rex Flynn and Milind Tambe for their provocative conversations on Soar's computational (that is, memory) model. Much of the inspiration, and a number of the ideas, underlying this article originated in conversations with these four people. I would also like to thank Rolf Pfeifer for prompting me to write this article.

This research was sponsored by the Defense Advanced Research Projects Agency (DOD) under contract numbered N00039-86C-0033 (via subcontract from the Knowledge Systems Laboratory, Stanford University) and by the National Aeronautics and Space Administration under cooperative agreement number NCC 2-538.

REFERENCES

Anderson, C.W. (1987). Strategy learning with multilayer connectionist representations. P. Langley (Ed.)., *Proceedings of the Fourth International Workshop on Machine Learning*. Irvine, CA, Morgan Kaufmann.

Feldman, J.A. (1987). Connectionist representation of concepts. In D. Waltz & J.A. Feldman (Eds.), *Connectionist Models and their Applications*. Ablex.

Flann, N.S. & Dietterich, T.G. (1986). Selecting appropriate representations for learning from examples. *Proceedings of AAAI-86*. Philadelphia, PA.

Flynn, R. (1988). Placing Soar on the Connection Machine 'Prepared for and distributed at the AAAI Mini-Symposium "How Can Slow Components Think So Fast'.

Hinton, G.E. (1981). Implementing semantic networks in parallel hardware. In G.E. Hinton & J.A. Anderson (Eds.), *Parallel Models of Associative Memory*. Hillsdale, NJ: Erlbaum.

Kawamoto, A.H. (1986). Solving puzzles with a connectionist network using a hillclimbing heuristic. *Proceedings of the Eighth Annual Conference of the Cognitive Science Society*. Amherst, MA.

Korf, R.E. (1987). Planning as search: A quantitative approach. *Artificial Intelligence*,**33**, 65-88.

Laird, J.E., Newell, A., & Rosenbloom, P.S. (1987). Soar: An architecture for general intelligence. *Artificial Intelligence*, **33**, 1-64.

Lenat, D.B. (1983). EURISKO: A program that learns new heuristics and domain concepts. The nature of heuristics III: program design and results.*Artificial Intelligence*, **21**, 61-98.

McClelland, J.L. (1985). Putting knowledge in its place: A scheme for programming parallel processing structures on the fly. *Cognitive Science*, **9**, 113-146.

Mitchell, T.M., Allen, J., Chalasani, P., Cheng, J., Etzioni, O., Ringuette, M., & Schlimmer, J.C. (1989). Theo: A framework for self-improving systems. In K. VanLehn (Ed.), *Architectures for Intelligence*. Hillsdale, NJ: Erlbaum. In press.

Newell, A. (1989). Unified Theories of Cognition. Cambridge, MA: Harvard University Press. In preparation.

Polk, T.A. & Newell, A (1988). Modelling human syllogistic reasoning in Soar. *Proceedings of the 10th Annual Conference of the Cognitive Science Society,* Montreal.

Rich, E. (1983). *Artificial Intelligence*. New York: McGraw-Hill.

Rosenbloom, P.S., & Laird, J.E. (1986). Mapping explanation-based generalization onto Soar. *Proceedings of AAAI-86*, Philadelphia.

Rosenbloom, P.S., Laird, J.E., & Newell, A. (1988). The chunking of skill and knowledge. In H. Bouma & B.A.G. Elsendoorn (Eds.), *Working Models of Human Perception*. London: Academic Press.

Rosenbloom, P.S., Newell, A., & Laird, J.E. (1989). Towards the knowledge level in Soar: The role of the architecture in the use of knowledge. In K. VanLehn (Ed.), *Architectures for Intelligence*. Hillsdale, NJ: Erlbaum. In preparation.

Rumelhart, D.E., Hinton, G.E., & McClelland, J.L. (1986). A general framework for parallel distributed processing. In D.E. Rumelhart, J.L. McClelland, and the PDP Research Group (Eds.), *Parallel Distributed Processing: Explorations in the Microstructure of Cognition, Volume 1: Foundations*. Cambridge, MA: Bradford Books/ MIT Press.

Rumelhart, D.E., Hinton, G.E., & Williams, R.J. (1986). Learning internal representations by error propagation. In D.E. Rumelhart, J.L. McClelland, and the PDP Research Group (Eds.), *Parallel Distributed Processing: Explorations in the Microstructure of Cognition, Volume 1: Foundations*. Cambridge, MA: Bradford Books/ MIT Press.

Rumelhart, D.E., Smolensky, P., McClelland, J.L., & Hinton, G.E. (1986). Schemata and sequential thought processes in PDP models. In J.L. McClelland, D.E. Rumelhart, and the PDP Research Group (Eds.), *Parallel Distributed Processing: Explorations in the Microstructure of Cognition, Volume 2: Psychological and Biological Models*. Cambridge, MA: Bradford Books/ MIT Press.

Sutton, R.S. & Barto, A.G. (1981). An adaptive network that constructs and uses an internal model of its world. *Cognition and Brain Theory,* **4,** 217-246.

Tambe, M. & Newell, A. (1988). Some chunks are expensive. J. Laird (Ed.), *Proceedings of the Fifth International Conference on Machine Learning*. Ann Arbor, MI.

Tambe, M. & Rosenbloom, P.S. (1989). Eliminating Expensive Chunks by Restricting Expressiveness. *Proceedings of IJCAI-89*, Detroit, MI. In press.

Touretzky, D.S. (1986). BoltzCONS: Reconciling connectionism with the recursive nature of stacks and trees. *Proceedings of the Eight Annual Conference of the Cognitive Science Society*. Amherst, MA.

Wiesmeyer, M. (1988). *Soar I/O Reference Manual, Version 2*.Department of EECS, University of Michigan.

CHAPTER 39

The Chunking of Skill and Knowledge

P. S. Rosenbloom*, J. E. Laird°, and A. Newell‡

1 Introduction

The concept of chunking has played a major theoretical role in cognitive psychology ever since Miller's classic paper (Miller, 1956). Through much of this history it has been used primarily in models of memory organization. According to this view, chunking is a process of creating symbols (chunks) which represent the combination of several other symbols. In this long and productive tradition, chunking has been used to model a wide variety of memory phenomena (Miller, 1956; De Groot, 1965; Bower and Winzenz, 1969; Johnson, 1972; Chase and Simon, 1973; Chase and Ericsson, 1981).

In recent years, chunking has also been proposed as the basis for a model of human practice (Newell and Rosenbloom, 1981; Rosenbloom, 1983; Rosenbloom and Newell, 1987*a*). According to this view, chunking is a process that acquires new productions (chunks) by the catching of goal-based performance. This version of chunking was successfully able to model the ubiquitous power law shape of human practice curves. In building on these results, chunking has been reimplemented as a learning mechanism within an artificial intelligence problem solver called SOAR (Laird, 1983;

* This research was sponsored by the Defense Advanced Research Projects Agency (DOD) under contract N00039-86-C-0133 and by the Sloan Foundation. Computer facilities were partially provided by NIH grant RR-00785 to Sumex-Aim. The views and conclusions contained in this document are those of the authors and should not be interpreted as representing the official policies, either expressed or implied, of the Defense Advanced Research Projects Agency, the US Government, the Sloan Foundation, or the National Institutes of Health.

* Knowledge Systems Laboratory, Departments of Computer Science and Psychology, Stanford University, Palo Alto, California, USA. Present address: University of Southern California, Information Sciences Institute, 4676 Admiralty Way, Marina del Rey, California, USA.

° Department of Electrical Engineering and Computer Science, University of Michigan, Ann Arbor, Michigan, USA.

‡ Department of Computer Science, Carnegie-Mellon University, Pittsburgh, Pensylvania, USA.

Laird, 1986; Laird, Newell and Rosenbloom, 1987). This combination of SOAR and chunking has provided a learning architecture with the flexibility and power needed to demonstrate learning behaviours that go considerably beyond simple practice effects (Steier, Laird, Newell, Rosenbloom, Flynn, Golding, Polk, Shivers, Unruh and Yost, 1987). The results have been good enough for chunking to be proposed as a general learning mechanism for artificially-intelligent systems (Laird, Rosenbloom and Newell, 1984; Laird, Rosenbloom and Newell, 1986).

The generality of the combination of chunking and SOAR as an AI learning system raises the possibility that this combination can be transferred back into psychology to provide the basis for a general model of human learning. In this article we report on a preliminary examination of this possibility that involves the application of SOAR to two major domains of human learning: skill acquisition and knowledge acquisition. Within skill acquisition we return to the subdomain of practice, asking whether SOAR can replicate the earlier results by producing power-law practice curves. Within knowledge acquisition we look within the subdomain of verbal learning at simple recognition, recall, and cued recall tasks. In this preliminary investigation we are not yet looking for close matches to experimental data. Instead, we focus on the nature of the processing that allows these tasks to be performed by chunking.

In the next two sections we give brief descriptions of SOAR and chunking. This background material is followed by sections on skill acquisition and knowledge acquisition in SOAR, and then by a section containing concluding remarks.

2 SOAR

SOAR is based on formulating all symbolic goal-oriented processing as search in problem spaces (Newell, 1980). The problem space determines the set of states and operators that can be used during the processing to attain a goal. The states represent situations. There is an initial state, representing the initial situation, and a set of desired states that represent the goal. An operator, when applied to a state in the problem space, yields another state in the problem space. The goal is achieved when a desired state is reached as the result of a sequence of operator applications starting from the initial state.

Each goal defines a problem-solving context ('context' for short). A context is a data structure in SOAR's working memory – a short-term declarative memory – that contains, in addition to a goal, roles for a problem space, a state, and an operator. Problem solving for a goal is driven by the acts of selecting problem spaces, states, and operators for the appropriate roles in the context. Each deliberate act of the SOAR architecture – a selection of a problem space, a state or an operator – is accomplished via a two-phase decision cycle. First, during the elaboration phase, the description of the current situation (that is, the contents of working memory) is elaborated with relevant information from SOAR's production memory – a long-term procedural memory. The elaboration phase proceeds in a sequence of synchronous cycles. During each cycle of the elaboration phase, all of the productions in the production memory are matched against working memory, and then all of the resulting production instantiations are executed. The net effect of these production firings is to add information to the working memory. New objects are created, new knowledge is added about existing objects, and preferences are generated.

There is a fixed language of preferences that is used to describe the acceptability and desirability of the alternative being considered for selection. By using different preferences, it is possible to assert that a particular problem space, state, or operator is acceptable (should be considered for selection), rejected (should not be considered for selection), better than another alternative, and so on. When the elaboration phase reaches quiescence – that is, no more productions can fire – the second phase of the decision cycle, the decision procedure, is entered. The decision procedure is a fixed body of code that interprets the preferences in working memory according to their fixed semantics. If the preferences uniquely specify an object to be selected for a role in a context, then a decision can be made, and the specified object becomes the current value of the role. The decision cycle then repeats, starting with another elaboration phase.

If, when the elaboration phase reaches quiescence, the preferences in working memory are either incomplete or inconsistent, an impasse occurs in problem solving because the system does not know how to proceed. When an impasse occurs, a subgoal with an associated problem-solving context is automatically generated for the task of resolving the impasse. The impasses, and thus their subgoals, vary from problems of generation (e.g., operator application). Given a subgoal, SOAR can bring its full problem-solving capability and knowledge to bear on resolving the impasse that caused the subgoal. When impasses occur within impasses, then subgoals occur within subgoals and a goal hierarchy results (which therefore defines a hierarchy of contexts). The top goal in the hierarchy is a task goal; such as, to recognize an item. The subgoals below it are all generated as the result of impasses in problem solving. A subgoal terminates when its impasse (or some higher impasse) is resolved.

3 Chunking

The traditional view of chunks is that they are symbols representing the combination of several other symbols (Miller, 1956). Newell and Rosenbloom (1981) turned this concept into a model of practice by describing how performance could be improved by the acquisition of chunks that represent patterns of objects in the task environment. This model was instantiated in a production-system architecture, first in a domain-specific form (Rosenbloom and Newell, 1987*b*), and then in a domain-independent form (Rosenbloom, 1983; Rosenbloom and Newell, 1987*a*). A modified version of the domain-independent chunking mechanism was then implemented as part of the SOAR architecture (Laird, Rosenbloom and Newell, 1986).

In its SOAR implementation, chunking is a learning mechanism that acquires new productions which summarize the processing that leads to results of subgoals. The conditions are based on those aspects of the pre-goal situation that were relevant to the determination of the results. Relevance is determined by using the traces of the productions that fired during the subgoal. Starting from the production trace that generated the subgoal's result, those production traces that generated the working-memory elements in the conditions of the trace are found, and then the traces that generated their condition elements are found, and so on, until elements are reached that existed prior to the subgoal. Productions that only generate preferences do not participate in this backtracking process – preferences only affect the efficiency with which a goal is achieved, and not the correctness of the goal's results.

An example of this chunking process is shown schematically in figure 1. The circled letters are objects in working memory. The two striped vertical bars mark the beginning and ending of the subgoal. The objects to the left of the first bar (A, B, C, D, E, and F) exist prior to the creation of the subgoal. The objects between the two bars (G, H, and I) are internal to the subgoal. The objects to the right of the second bar (J) are results of the subgoal. $P1, P2, P3$, and $P4$ are production traces; for example, production trace $P1$ records the fact that a production fired which examined objects A

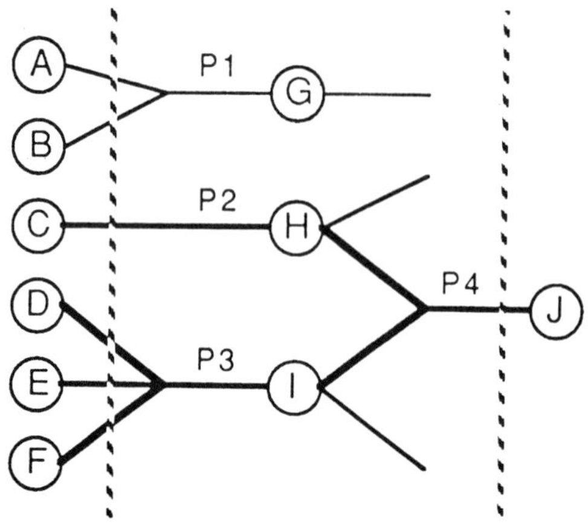

Figure 1: Schematic view of the chunking process in SOAR.

and B and generated object G. The highlighted production traces are those that are involved in the backtracking process.

Chunking in this figure begins by making the result object (J) the basis for the action of the chunk. The condition-finding process then begins with object J, and determines which production trace produced it – trace $P4$. It then determines that the conditions of trace $P4$ (objects H and I) are generated by traces $P2$ and $P3$, respectively. The condition elements of traces $P2$ and $P3$ (objects C, D, E, and F) existed prior to the subgoal, so they form the basis for the conditions of the chunk. The resulting chunk is

$$C \wedge D \wedge E \wedge F \longrightarrow J \quad (1)$$

Once a chunk has been learned, the new production will fire during the elaboration phase in relevantly similar situations in the future, directly producing the required information. No impasse wil occur, and problem solving will proceed smoothly. Chunking is thus a form of goal-based caching which avoids redundant future effort by directly producing a result that once required problem solving to determine. It bears a family resemblance to other learning mechanisms which move the system along the store-versus-compute trade-off, such as production composition (Lewis, 1978; Neves and Anderson, 1981; Anderson, 1982; Anderson, 1983), memo functions (Michie, 1968), macro-operators (Fikes, Hart and Nilsson, 1972; Korf, 1985), and explanation-based generalization (Mitchell, Keller and Kedar-Cabelli, 1986).

In the pre-SOAR implementation of chunking, chunks were learned bottom-up in the goal hierarchy, reflecting the accepted view of human chunking. On any trial, only the terminal subgoals – the subgoals that did not themselves have subgoals – were chunked. Higher-level subgoals could be chunked only after all of their subgoals had been chunked. This bottom-up approach was critical in producing power-law practice curves. However, chunking has been implemented in SOAR with a settable option. Chunking can proceed for only the terminal subgoals (bottom-up chunking) or for all of the goals in the hierarchy (all-goals chunking). Given a sufficient number of trials, the results of the two approaches should be essentially indistinguishable. However, because all-goals chunking yields faster learning, most research on learning in SOAR has employed it. In this article, all results except for those specifically intended to model practice curves were generated with all-goals chunking. Practice curves were generated with bottom-up chunking.

4 Skill acquisition

There is a ubiquitous regularity in human practice – *the power law of practice* – that states that the time to perform a task (T) decreases as a power-law function of the number of times the task has been performed (that is, the number of trials, N):

$$T = BN^{-\alpha} \tag{2}$$

While the power law of practice was originally recognized in the domain of motor skills (Snoddy, 1926), it has recently become clear that it holds over a much wider range of human tasks – possibly extending to the full range of human performance (Newell and Rosenbloom, 1981).

The driving force behind the initial development of chunking as a learning mechanism was a desire to develop a model of practice that would produce power law practice curves. The experimental task used during these early investigations was a 1023-choice reaction-time task (Seibel, 1963). This is a perceptual-motor task in which there is a stimulus display of ten lights, arranged horizontally, and a response apparatus of ten buttons, arranged horizontally in such a way that each finger rests on one of them. The stimulus and response environments are set up so that there is a highly compatible one-to-one correspondence between the lights and buttons, each light directly above a button. On each trial of the experiment, some of the lights are on and some are off. The subject's task is to respond as quickly as possible by pressing the buttons corresponding to the lights that are on.

The performance algorithm used in modelling this task is based on a top-down divide-and-conquer algorithm. The top goal is to process a horizontal region of the display, containing a pattern of on and off lights. This goal is recursively decomposed into subgoals to process smaller and smaller regions until patterns are reached which can be directly converted into corresponding patterns of button presses. Chunking works in a bottom-up fashion in this goal hierarchy. Productions are first learned for the bottom-most level of subgoals. These chunks relate small patterns of lights to their corresponding patterns of button presses. In later trials, these chunks can be used in place of problem solving in the low-level subgoals, speeding up task performance. This also allows chunking to proceed up the goal hierarchy, acquiring chunks which relate increasingly larger patterns of lights to patterns of button presses.

A simple analysis of this learning process suggests exponential speed-ups with practice. Each time a task is practised, a new and higher level of chunks can be acquired, reducing the time to perform the task by a constant factor (the size of the chunks). However, learning slows down because the larger chunks that are learned later in practice are encountered less often – for example, in the Seibel task, a chunk that contains three lights is encountered half as often as a chunk that contains two lights – and therefore contributes less to the overall speedup than do the smaller chunks which are encountered more often. Learning (chunk acquisition) actually continues at a constant pace, but what is learned becomes progressively less helpful. The net result is a slow down of the learning process to the point where it becomes more like a power law than an exponential. Approximate mathematical analyses of this process can be found in Newell and Rosenbloom (1981) and Rosenbloom (1983).

In addition to the mathematical analyses, the pre-SOAR implementation of chunking was evaluated by generating and analysing simulated practice curves (Rosenbloom, 1983; Rosenbloom and Newell, 1987*a*). For the Seibel task, the simulated practice curves were shown to provide close approximations to power laws. To determine whether these results continue to hold for the implementation of chunking in SOAR, a version of Seibel's task has been implemented in SOAR. The divide-and-conquer algorithm is implemented by having a problem space with a single operator – process-a-region-of-lights – which can be instantiated for different regions. In the top goal, two instances of this operator are generated, one for each half of the display. When one of these operators is selected, an impasse occurs because there is no knowledge directly available in productions about how to process regions that contain more than one light. In the subgoal for this impasse, two more instances of the operator are generated, this time for the two halves of the region that the higher-level operator was processing. This recursion continues until operator instances are generated for regions that contain only a single light. Such operators can be processed directly by productions.

With practice on this task, chunks are learned which summarize the processing that goes on in the subgoals. These chunks directly implement particular instances of the process-a-region-of-lights operator, avoiding the need for problem solving in a subgoal. Figure 2 shows a log-log plot – power laws plot as straight lines in log-log plots – of 125 trials of the Seibel task, as performed by SOAR. In this figure, the data have been aggregated at

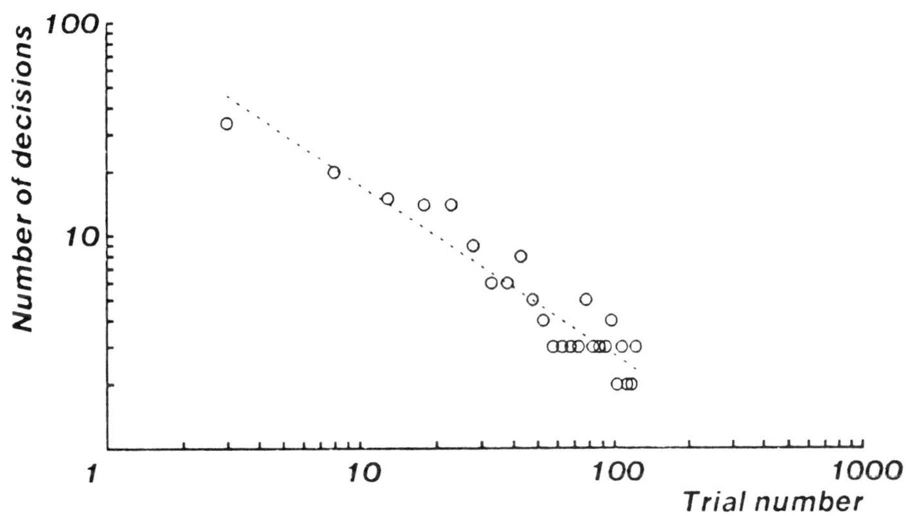

Figure 2: Simulated practice curve for a 1023-choice RT task.

a rate of five trials per point. Simulated time is computed by counting the number of decisions required to perform the task. The best-fit power law curve for these data is:

$$T = 110N^{-0.80} \tag{3}$$

In addition to the Seibel task, well over twenty other tasks have been implemented in SOAR. Practice curves have not been generated for most of these tasks, but one does exist for the task of computer configuration. This is a difficult task that involves configuring a working computer by assembling a list of components that have been ordered by a customer. About

25% of the R1/XCON computer-configuration expert system (McDermott, 1982) has been reimplemented in SOAR by designing and implementing a set of problem spaces in which the computer components can be assembled (Rosenbloom, Laird, McDermott, Newell and Orciuch, 1985; van de Brug, Rosenbloom and Newell, 1987). The final system had nine task-problem spaces with a total of 34 operators.

One interesting phenomenon that shows up in this task (as well as in others) is that chunks can transfer within a single trial (improving performance the first time a problem is solved), across trials (to later instances of the same problem), and across tasks (to other configuration problems). As long as two subproblems are relevantly similar, chunks can transfer between them. Figure 3 shows a thirty-trial practice curve generated by SOAR for this task[1]. The data presented in this figure are unaggregated (accounting

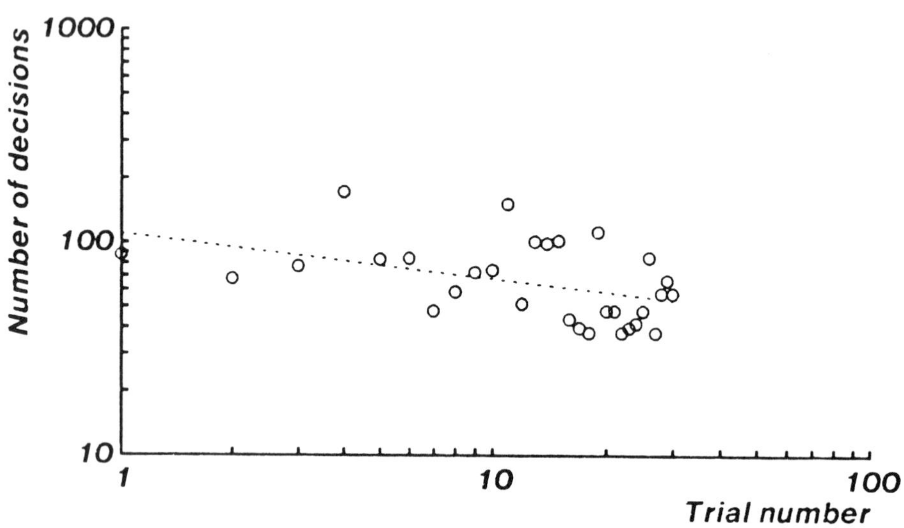

Figure 3: Simulated practice curve for a computer configuration task.

for the apparent increase in variance). The thirty-trial sequence consists of two complete passes through a sequence of 15 orders. The best-fit power law curve for these data is:

$$T = 111N^{-0.21} \tag{4}$$

The chunks that SOAR learns while performing these two tasks fall into two categories. The first category of chunks are for operator implementation. In

[1]Interestingly, this curve was produced by plotting existing data generated for a different purpose. This was not a deliberate experiment to produce power-law practice curves.

the Seibel task, chunks are learned which directly relate patterns of lights to patterns of button presses. These chunks act as implementation productions for the process-a-region-of-lights operator. In the computer configuration domain there is a single top-level problem space for the task. All of the other task-problem spaces are used as subspaces for the implementation of the operators in this space, or at lower levels to implement operators of subspaces. Implementation chunks are acquired for all of these complex operators.

The second category of chunks are for selection – usually of operators, but also potentially of states and problem spaces. When it is unclear which among several operators should be selected for a state in a problem space, an impasse and subgoal are generated. The results of problem solving in the subgoal should be preferences that lead to the selection of one of the alternatives. Chunking this type of subgoal leads to the acquisition of search control productions; that is, productions which generate preferences that can be used to control the problem-space search. This category of chunks does not appear in the relatively simple implementation of the Seibel task, but does appear in the computer-configuration task. In other tasks, such as Tic-Tac-Toe, for which we do not yet have practice curves, search-control chunks are the dominating factor in learning.

5 Knowledge acquisition

In the previous section it was demonstrated how the acquisition of chunks could lead to improvements in performance. Procedural chunks were learned that performed operator implementation, and control chunks were learned which helped in selection. However, chunking originated as a model of declarative memory, and only later was it converted into a model of skill learning. Given this conversion, the question naturally arises as to whether it can, in its current form, be used to acquire declarative chunks which represent new knowledge. For example, can chunking support the types of learning that are required in simple verbal learning experiments? There have been good reasons for doubting that this form of *data chunking* is possible. Chunking, as a skill-acquisition mechanism, improves performance by creating productions which cache the effects of subgoal-based problem solving. The new productions thus summarize processing that the system can already perform. They do not, at least in any obvious fashion, lead to qualitatively new behaviours or to the acquisition of new knowledge that is not already known to the problem solver. Nonetheless, as was demonstrated in Rosenbloom, Laird and Newell (1987), chunking can be used as the basis for a data-chunking capability in SOAR.

Consider one of the simplest of the verbal learning tasks, a recognition task. Let us assume that the object to be learned are strings of letters, such as "*ab*", and that the performance task is to recognize whether a string has ever been seen before[2]. There are two types of trials: training and performance. On each training trial the system must perceive a new string, and then store into its long-term memory a representation of the string that will enable it to perform an old-versus-new judgment on a performance trial. Thus, the first step in SOAR's learning to recognize a new string is for it to use its perceptual capabilities to generate a representation of the string in its working memory[3]. At this point, the new string is available for use by the system, but it has not yet been learned – working memory is only a temporary memory which holds the current data upon which the system is working. The learning act occurs when a production is created which can, at appropriate points in the future, recognize the string. If SOAR is to use its chunking mechanism to do this, it must take advantage of the fact that chunking learns from goal-based experience. The key is for it to set up the right internal tasks so that its problem-solving experience in subgoals leads to the creation of chunks that represent the new knowledge.

To learn to recognize a new string, an internal task is set up in which, in a subgoal, the system first examines each of the letters out of which the string is composed, and then generates a name for the string. The name is an internally generated symbol for the new string; for example, $G3297$. The name becomes the result of the subgoal, and thus forms the basis for the action of a chunk. The conditions of the chunk explicitly test for the contents of the string. For example, when the system learned to recognize the string "*ab*", the following production was acquired that augments (/) the string with its name.[4]

$$\text{“}ab\text{”} \longrightarrow /G3297 \tag{5}$$

On a performance trial, a string is presented and an old-versus-new judgment must be made. This judgment is made by determining whether a name for

[2]The system described in Rosenbloom, Laird and Newell (1987) actually learns about hierarchically structured objects that are grounded in a set of primitive objects that represent letters. However, in this article only one-level strings of letters are discussed.

[3]SOAR does not yet have an appropriate I/O interface, so in the current implementation this perceptual phase is performed by special-purpose Lisp code.

[4]This is a simplified representation of the actual production.

the string has been retrieved from long-term memory. There is one tricky aspect to this judgment. Suppose a name does appear for the string in working memory. Was the name retrieved from long-term memory by the execution of a recognition chunk, or was it just now invented? An 'old' response should only be produced for a string if a recognition chunk has been learned for it on a previous training trial. The key to making this discrimination lies in realizing that the data generated by a production can be used in more than one way. The most straightforward way to use a recognition chunk is as a means of speeding up the generation of a name for a string – it allows a name to be generated during the elaboration phase, rather than via problem solving in a subgoal. However, the task at hand is to determine whether the string has been seen before, not to generate a name for it.

To actually use the chunk for the recognition task it needs to be treated as episodic knowledge representing the fact that the string has been perceived. This involves a small inductive leap in assuming that chunks are only created for strings that are perceived – it can be wrong if the system learns about a string that it has imagined rather than perceived. To use the recognition chunk as episodic knowledge in SOAR, responses on performance trials are based on the contents of working memory after the completion of one elaboration phase. If a recognition chunk has been learned for the string, its name will be retrieved during elaboration. If, on the other hand, quiescence is reached without a name appearing, then the string is not recognized. This recognition task is described in detail in Rosenbloom, Laird and Newell (1987).

Also described in Rosenbloom, Laird and Newell(1987, A.) is a simple recall task which involves the memorization of a set of strings, which are later to be generated on demand. From the point of view of the internal task, it is the dual of the recognition task. Instead of incorporating information about a new string into the conditions of a production, the information must be incorporated into the actions. As with recognition, there are training and performance trials. On each training trial the system is presented with a new string, and it must learn to generate it on demand. On a performance trial, the system receives a recall request, and must respond by producing the strings that it learned to generate on the training trials.

To accomplish this, on training trials chunks need to be acquired that can generate the presented strings when the demand arises. The appropriate internal task for this problem would appear to be simply to copy a presented string in a subgoal. The chunk that is learned from this experience has actions which generate a string that is a copy of the presented string. The problem with this simple solution is that, if the copy is based on an examination of the presented string, then the conditions of the chunk will test for the existence of the presented string before generating the copy, thus allowing the string to be recalled in only those circumstances where it is already available. The solution to this problem that we have discovered is to split recall learning into separate generate and test phases. Generation is performed in a problem space that contains operators which generate (and combine) a primitive set of known letters. The result of the generation process is a new string constructed from known objects, rather than a copy of the input string. As with other generate-and-test models of recall, a recognition capability – a recognition chunk – is used as the basis for the test (see, for example, Watkins and Gardiner, 1979), but in contrast with other models, generate-and-test is being used here during training trials rather than performance trials.

The entire training trial consists of three steps:

1. learn to recognize the presented string;

2. in a subgoal, generate a new string by selecting and executing a sequence of operators that build up a string one letter at a time (without examining the presented string in the process);

3. if the generated string is recognized, return it as a result of the subgoal and learn a chunk which will generate the string.

Constructing the new string from scratch ensures that the chunk will not test the presented string. However, it does introduce an additional problem of how to control the generation process so that the to-be-learned string will be generated rather than any of the other infinite possibilities. The solution to this problem is to use the presented string as search-control knowledge during the process of generating the new string. As described in the section entitled 'SOAR', search control knowledge (productions which generate preferences) does not enter into the chunking process because it only affects the efficiency with which a problem is solved, and not its correctness. The goal test – that is, the recognition chunk – determines correctness. In consequence, the generation process can proceed efficiently, but the chunk created for it will not depend on the presented object.

The following production is a typical recall chunk. It generates a string and its name if there is not already a string with that name in working memory. The *'s denote wildcards which can match any letter.

$$\neg\text{“}**\text{”}/G3297 \longrightarrow \text{“}ab\text{”}/G3297 \quad (6)$$

On a performance trial, all of the available recall chunks execute, retrieving into working memory representations of all of the strings that the system has so far learned to recall. To satisfy the recall request, all of these retrieved objects must then be produced.

One peculiarity of this recall task is that to recall a single object (or a subset of the learned objects), all known objects must be retrieved from long-term memory into working memory. To solve this problem, and to lead up to more complex verbal learning tasks, such as paired-associate learning, a form of cued recall has been implemented. In cued recall there are a set of cues associated with each string to be learned. A string can only be retrieved from long-term memory if its cues are present in working memory. When a new string is to be learned, its features may provide cues which lead to the retrieval of old strings from long-term memory. The cues acquired for the new string are determined by finding the features which will discriminate it from these old strings.

The procedure followed during a cued recall training trial is similar to that used for the simple recall task. The principal difference is that during the generation phase search control is used to suggest both the letters used in the presented string, and the letters used in any of the old strings that are retrieved but not rejected. An impasse will get generated whenever the letter has been suggested. To resolve this impasse, the presented string is first examined to determine which letter it contains. Then, based on this examination, the conflicting letter and string are rejected, and the letter from the presented string is selected. Below are some of the chunks that are acquired as the system learns to recall the sequence of strings “*ab*”, “*ba*”, “*aa*”, “*bb*”, “*ca*”, “*cb*”, “*cc*”, “*bc*”, and “*ac*” (not shown are the recognition chunks that are also acquired and the chunks which reject the incorrect letters). When more than one chunk is learned on the same trial, they are shown on two consecutive lines, separated by a semicolon. Single quotes denote a pattern which is to match the input string, while double quotes denote a pattern that is to match a retrieved string.

$$\neg\text{“}**\text{”}/G3297 \longrightarrow \text{“}ab\text{”}/G3297 \quad (7)$$

$$\text{‘}b*\text{’} \wedge \text{“}a*\text{”} \wedge \neg\text{“}**\text{”}/G3298 \longrightarrow \text{“}ba\text{”}/G3298;$$

$$\text{‘}b*\text{’} \wedge \text{“}a*\text{”} \longrightarrow Reject(\text{“}a*\text{”}) \quad (8)$$

$$\text{‘}*a\text{’} \wedge \text{“}*b\text{”} \wedge \neg\text{“}**\text{”}/G3299 \longrightarrow \text{“}aa\text{”}/G3299;$$

$$`*a' \wedge ``*b" \longrightarrow Reject(``*b") \tag{9}$$

$$`*b' \wedge ``*a" \wedge \neg``**"/G3300 \longrightarrow ``bb"/G3298;$$

$$`*b' \wedge ``*a" \longrightarrow Reject(``*a") \tag{10}$$

$$`c*' \wedge ``a*" \wedge \neg``**"/G3301 \longrightarrow ``ca"/G3301;$$

$$`c*' \wedge ``a*" \longrightarrow Reject(``a*") \tag{11}$$

$$`c*' \wedge ``b*" \wedge \neg``**"/G3302 \longrightarrow ``cb"/G3302;$$

$$`c*' \wedge ``b*" \longrightarrow Reject(``b*") \tag{12}$$

$$`*c' \wedge ``*a" \wedge \neg``**"/G3303 \longrightarrow ``cc"/G3303;$$

$$`*c' \wedge ``*a" \longrightarrow Reject(``*a") \tag{13}$$

$$`b*' \wedge ``c*" \wedge \neg``**"/G3304 \longrightarrow ``bc"/G3304;$$

$$`b*' \wedge ``c*" \longrightarrow Reject(``c*") \tag{14}$$

$$`*c' \wedge ``*b" \wedge \neg``**"/G3305 \longrightarrow ``ac"/G3305;$$

$$`*c' \wedge ``*b" \longrightarrow Reject(``*b") \tag{15}$$

On the first learning trial, the string "*ab*" is presented, and production 7 is learned. It looks just like the corresponding simple recall chunk, production 6, because there are no previously learned strings from which it must be discriminated. On the second learning trial, the string "*ba*" is presented, resulting in the retrieval of string "*ab*" (because production 7 retrieves "*ab*" for every string). The two strings are then discriminated based on their first letters, resulting in the creation of the two productions on line 8. The first production generates "*ba*" if:

1. the first letter of the input string is "*b*";

2. a string has been retrieved that has "*a*" as its first letter, and

3. no string named *G*3298 has already been retrieved into working memory.

The second production rejects any string beginning with "*a*" if the first letter of the input string is "*b*". Consider what happens when the cue "*b*∗" (or "*ba*", for that matter) is presented on a training trial after these two strings have been learned. First production 7 fires, retrieving "*ab*". Then the productions on line 8 fire in parallel, retrieving "*ba*" and rejecting "*ab*". The string "*ba*" is then recalled because it is the only non-rejected string that has been retrieved.

As more strings are learned, multiple cycles of retrieval and rejection often occur before a desired string is recalled. The following lines show the sequences of retrievals that occur, as a function of input cue, after all of the strings have been learned. Sets of strings are bracketed when they are retrieved in parallel.

$$Input(\text{``}{*}{*}\text{''}) \vee Input(\text{``}a{*}\text{''}) \vee Input(\text{``}{*}b\text{''}) \vee Input(\text{``}ab\text{''}) : \text{``}ab\text{''}$$
$$Input(\text{``}b{*}\text{''}) : \text{``}ab\text{''}, \text{``}ba\text{''}$$
$$Input(\text{``}{*}a\text{''}) : \text{``}ab\text{''}, \text{``}aa\text{''}$$
$$Input(\text{``}c{*}\text{''}) : \text{``}ab\text{''}, \text{``}ca\text{''}$$
$$Input(\text{``}ba\text{''}) : \text{``}ab\text{''}, \{\text{``}ba\text{''}, \text{``}aa\text{''}\}$$
$$Input(\text{``}aa\text{''}) : \text{``}ab\text{''}, \text{``}aa\text{''}$$
$$Input(\text{``}bb\text{''}) : \text{``}ab\text{''}, \text{``}ba\text{''}, \text{``}bb\text{''}$$
$$Input(\text{``}ca\text{''}) : \text{``}ab\text{''}, \{\text{``}aa\text{''}, \text{``}ca\text{''}\}$$
$$Input(\text{``}cb\text{''}) : \text{``}ab\text{''}, \text{``}ca\text{''}, \text{``}bb\text{''}, \text{``}cb\text{''}$$
$$Input(\text{``}cc\text{''}) : \text{``}ab\text{''}, \{\text{``}ca\text{''}, \text{``}ac\text{''}\}, \text{``}cc\text{''}$$
$$Input(\text{``}bc\text{''}) : \text{``}ab\text{''}, \{\text{``}ba\text{''}, \text{``}ac\text{''}\}, \text{``}cc\text{''}, \text{``}bc\text{''}$$
$$Input(\text{``}{*}c\text{''}) \vee Input(\text{``}ac\text{''}) : \text{``}ab\text{''}, \text{``}ac\text{''}$$

Another way to look at the set of productions that have been learned in this cued recall situation is as the implementation of a discrimination network, as in EPAM (Feigenbaum and Simon, 1984). In EPAM, the discrimination network was a tree in which objects were stored at the leaf nodes, and tests were stored at the internal nodes. Given a set of features, tests would be performed and branches would be followed until a leaf node was reached. In the SOAR version of cued recall, every node in the network contains an object (a string), and each pair of productions performs a test and branches to a new node (rejecting the old node in the process). Discrimination stops when there are no further branches to follow – essentially, a node acts like a leaf when it has been retrieved but not rejected. In this discrimination network, multiple tests can be pursued in parallel on one or more features, and multiple branches can be followed in parallel. However, for each string, there is only one path through the network that results in that string appearing as a leaf.

This network can potentially support at least three distinct types of behaviour (only the first has so far been demonstrated). First, given a set of letter features, it can be used to retrieve the string which is the 'best' match to those features. The evaluation of what match is 'best' is not based on some ideal notion of a closest match; rather, it is based on the structure of the network, which has been built up in response to the need to make the necessary discriminations. For example, given "xc" as input, the network retrieves "ac" as the best match. Second, if the recognition chunk fails – because, for example, some of the input string's features are missing or modified – an old-versus-new judgment could be made by comparing the input string with the string that it causes to be retrieved from the network. Third, strings could be recalled in a free-recall task by repeatedly prompting the network with potential cues.

6 Conclusions

In this article we have taken a step toward an integrated model of human learning that is based on the concept of chunking. All learning occurs via the acquisition of chunks (productions) that summarize goal-based problem-solving experiences. Chunking has been shown to produce forms of both skill acquisition and knowledge acquisition.

In skill acquisition, chunks speed up task performance by directly implementing operators (procedural knowledge) and by controlling problem-space search (control knowledge). Chunks can transfer within a trial, across trials, and across tasks. For both a simple perceptual-motor task and a complex cognitive task, the practice curves do appear to be power law in form. However, we have not yet performed a careful comparison between these curves and alternative functional forms. Future work along these lines should include a more careful look at practice curves from a wider variety of tasks, particularly tasks in which most of the chunks are learned for search control rather than operator implementation, and an expansion of the coverage of the model to other aspects of skill acquisition.

In knowledge acquisition, chunking can be used to support verbal learning. Procedural knowledge that is learned through experience is used to answer episodic questions about what the system has perceived. The result is successful performance in simple recognition and recall tasks. The most complex form of verbal learning presented, cued recall, involves discrimination, generation, and test (recognition) processes. Future work along these lines should include extending the model to deal with more complex forms of verbal learning, such as paired-associate learning, and with other domains, such as semantic memory. Also required is a more detailed comparison of the model to human experimental data. Until this is done, these results must be considered tentative. As such comparisons are made, and as the scope of the model is extended, the model will undoubtedly need to be refined in a variety of ways.

In addition to the fact that the model has qualitatively reasonable properties in the domains of practice and verbal learning, it is important to note that it is embedded in a total architecture that is capable of a wide variety of cognitive activities. For instance, the chunking mechanism which does these two types of learning also does other types of learning. This larger context provides additional support for the model from outside of the experimental domains explicitly covered here.

References

Anderson, J.R. (1982) Acquisition of cognitive skill, *Psychological Review, 89*, 369-406.

Anderson, J.R. (1983) Knowledge compilation: The general learning mechanism. In: R.S. Michalski, J.G. Carbonell, and T.M. Mitchell (eds), *Proceedings of the 1983 Machine Learning Workshop.*

Bower, G.H. and Winzenz, D. (1969) Group structure, coding, and memory for digit series, *Journal of Experimental Psychology, Monograph 80*, 1-17.

Brug, A. van de, Rosenbloom, P.S. and Newell, A. (1987) Some experiments with R1-SOAR (in preparation).

Chase, W.G. and Ericsson, K.A. (1981) Skilled memory. In: J.R. Anderson (ed.), *Cognitive skills and their acquisition.* Hillsdale, NJ: Lawrence Erlbaum Associates.

Chase, W.G. and Simon, H.A. (1973) Perception in chess, *Cognitive Psychology, 4*, 5-81.

Feigenbaum, E.A. and Simon, H.A. (1984) EPAM-like models of recognition and learning, *Cognitive Sciences, 8*, 305-336.

Fikes, R.E., Hart, P.E. and Nilsson, N.J. (1972) Learning and executing generalized robot plans, *Artificial Intelligence, 3*, 251-288.

Groot, A.D. de (1965) *Thought and choice in chess.* The Hague: Mouton.

Johnson, N.F. (1972) Organization and the concept of a memory code. In: A.W. Melton and E. Martin (eds), *Coding processes in human memory.* Washington, DC: Winston.

Korf, R.E. (1985) Macro-operators: A weak method for learning. *Artificial Intelligence, 26*, 35-77.

Laird, J.E. (1983) *Universal subgoaling.* Doctoral dissertation, Carnegie-Mellon University. (Available in: J.E. Laird, P.S. Rosenbloom, A. Newell, *Universal subgoaling and chunking: The automatic generation and learning of goal hierarchies*). Hingham, MA: Kluwer.

Laird, J.E. (1986) SOAR user's manual (version 4), *Technical Report, ISL-15.* Xerox Palo Alto Research Center.

Laird, J.E., Newell, A. and Rosenbloom, P.S. (1987) SOAR: An architecture for general intelligence, *Artificial Intelligence, 33*, 1-64.

Laird, J.E., Rosenbloom, P.S. and Newell, A. (1984) Towards chunking as a general learning mechanism, *Proceedings of AAAI-84*. Austin.

Laird, J.E., Rosenbloom, P.S. and Newell, A. (1986) Chunking in SOAR: The anatomy of a general learning mechanism, *Machine Learning, 1*, 11-46.

Lewis, C.H. (1978) *Production system models of practice effects.* Doctoral dissertation, University of Michigan.

McDermott, J. (1982) R1: A rule-based configurer of computer systems, *Artificial Intelligence, 19*, 39-88.

Michie, D. (1968) 'Memo' functions and machine learning, *Nature, 218*, 19-22.

Miller, G.A. (1956) The magic number seven plus or minus two: Some limits on our capacity for processing information, *Psychological Review, 63*, 81-97.

Mitchell, T.M., Keller, R.M. and Kedar-Cabelli, S.T. (1986) Explanation-based generalization: A unifying view, *Machine Learning, 1*, 47-80.

Neves, D.M. and Anderson, J.R. (1981) Mechanisms for the automatization of cognitive skills. In: J.R. Anderson (ed.), *Cognitive skills and their acquisition.* Hillsdale, NJ: Lawrence Erlbaum Associates.

Newell, A. (1980) Reasoning, problem solving and decision processes: The problem space as a fundamental category. In: R. Nickerson (ed.), *Attention and Performance VIII.* Hillsdale, NJ: Lawrence Erlbaum Associates.

Newell, A. and Rosenbloom, P.S. (1981) Mechanisms of skill acquisition and the law of practice. In: J.R. Anderson (ed.), *Cognitive skills and their acquisition.* Hillsdale, NJ: Lawrence Erlbaum Associates.

Rosenbloom, P.S. (1986) *The chunking of goal hierarchies: A model of practice and stimulus-response compatibility.* Doctoral dissertation, Carnegie-Mellon University. (Available in: J.E. Laird, P.S. Rosenbloom, and A. Newell, *Universal subgoaling and chunking: The automatic generation and learning of goal hierarchies*). Hingham, Mass.: Kluwer.

Rosenbloom, P.S. and Newell, A. (1987) An integrated computational model of stimulus-response compatibility and practice. In: G.H. Bower (ed.), *The psychology of learning and motivation, Vol. 21.* Academic Press, in press.

Rosenbloom, P.S. and Newell, A. (1987) Learning by chunking: A production-system model of practice. In: D. Klahr, P. Langley, R. Neches (eds): *Production system models of learning and development.* Cambridge, Mass.: Bradford Books/MIT Press.

Rosenbloom, P.S., Laird, J.E. and Newell, A. (1987) Knowledge level learning in SOAR. In: *Proceedings of AAAI-87.* Seattle.

Rosenbloom, P.S., Laird, J.E., McDermott, J., Newell, A. and Orciuch, E. (1985) R1-SOAR: An experiment in knowledge-intensive programming in a problem-solving architecture, *IEEE Transactions on Pattern Analysis and Machine Intelligence, 7*, 561-569.

Seibel, R. (1963) Discrimination reaction time for a 1,023 alternative task, *Journal of Experimental Psychology, 66*, 215-226.

Snoddy, G.S. (1926) Learning and stability, *Journal of Applied Psychology, 10*, 1-36.

Steier, D.M., Laird, J.E., Newell, A., Rosenbloom, P.S., Flynn, R., Golding, A., Polk, T.A., Shivers, O.G., Unruh, A. and Yost, G.R. (1987) Varieties of learning in SOAR: 1987. In: P. Langley (ed.), *Proceedings of the fourth International Workshop on Machine Learning.* Los Altos, CA: Morgan Kaufmann Publishers, Inc.

Watkins, M.J. and Gardiner, J.M. (1979) An appreciation of generate-recognize theory of recall, *Journal of Verbal Learning and Verbal Behaviour, 18*, 687-704.

CHAPTER 40

A Preliminary Analysis of the Soar Architecture as a Basis for General Intelligence

P. S. Rosenbloom, USC–ISI, J. E. Laird, University of Michigan, A. Newell, Carnegie Mellon University, and R. McCarl, University of Michigan*

Abstract

Rosenbloom, P.S., J.E. Laird, A. Newell and R. McCarl, A primary analysis of the Soar architecture as a basis for general intelligence, Artificial Intelligence 47 (1991) 289–325.

In this article we take a step towards providing an analysis of the Soar architecture as a basis for general intelligence. Included are discussions of the basic assumptions underlying the development of Soar, a description of Soar cast in terms of the theoretical idea of multiple levels of description, an example of Soar performing multi-column subtraction, and three analyses of Soar: its natural tasks, the sources of its power, and its scope and limits

Introduction

The central scientific problem of artificial intelligence (AI) is to understand what constitutes intelligent action and what processing organizations are

* Much of the work on this article was done while the first author was affiliated with the Knowledge Systems Laboratory, Department of Computer Science, Stanford University.

capable of such action. Human intelligence—which stands before us like a holy grail—shows to first observation what can only be termed *general intelligence*. A single human exhibits a bewildering diversity of intelligent behavior. The types of goals that humans can set for themselves or accept from the environment seem boundless. Further observation, of course, shows limits to this capacity in any individual—problems range from easy to hard, and problems can always be found that are too hard to be solved. But the general point is still compelling.

Work in AI has already contributed substantially to our knowledge of what functions are required to produce general intelligence. There is substantial, though certainly not unanimous, agreement about some functions that need to be supported: symbols and goal structures, for example. Less agreement exists about what mechanisms are appropriate to support these functions, in large part because such matters depend strongly on the rest of the system and on cost-benefit tradeoffs. Much of this work has been done under the rubric of AI tools and languages, rather than AI systems themselves. However, it takes only a slight shift of viewpoint to change from what is an aid for the programmer to what is structure for the intelligent system itself. Not all features survive this transformation, but enough do to make the development of AI languages as much substantive research as tool building. These proposals provide substantial ground on which to build.

The Soar project has been building on this foundation in an attempt to understand the functionality required to support general intelligence. Our current understanding is embodied in the Soar architecture [22, 26]. This article represents an attempt at describing and analyzing the structure of the Soar system. We will take a particular point of view—the description of Soar as a hierarchy of levels—in an attempt to bring coherence to this discussion.

The idea of analyzing systems in terms of multiple levels of description is a familiar one in computer science. In one version, computer systems are described as a sequence of levels that starts at the bottom with the device level and works up through the circuit level, the logic level, and then one or more program levels. Each level provides a description of the system at some level of abstraction. The sequence is built up by defining each higher level in terms of the structure provided at the lower levels. This idea has also recently been used to analyze human cognition in terms of levels of description [38]. Each level corresponds to a particular time scale, such as ~100 msec. and ~1 sec., with a new level occurring for each new order of magnitude. The four levels between ~10 msec. and ~10 sec. comprise the cognitive band (Fig. 1). The lowest cognitive level—at ~10 msec.—is the symbol-accessing level, where the knowledge referred to by symbols is retrievable. The second cognitive level—at ~100 msec.—is the level at which elementary deliberate operations occur; that is, the level at which encoded knowledge is brought to bear, and the most elementary choices are made. The third and fourth cognitive levels—at ~1 sec.

Rational Band	...	
	~10 sec.	Goal attainment
Cognitive Band	~1 sec.	Simple operator composition
	~100 msec.	Elementary deliberate operations
	~10 msec.	Symbol accessing
Neural Band	...	

Fig. 1. Partial hierarchy of time scales in human cognition.

and ~10 sec.—are the simple-operator-composition and goal-attainment levels. At these levels, sequences of deliberations can be composed to achieve goals. Above the cognitive band is the rational band, at which the system can be described as being goal oriented, knowledge-based, and strongly adaptive. Below the cognitive band is the neural band.

In Section 2 we describe Soar as a sequence of three cognitive levels: the memory level, at which symbol accessing occurs; the decision level, at which elementary deliberate operations occur; and the goal level, at which goals are set and achieved via sequences of decisions. The goal level is an amalgamation of the top two cognitive levels from the analysis of human cognition.

In this description we will often have call to describe mechanisms that are built into the architecture of Soar. The architecture consists of all of the fixed structure of the Soar system. According to the levels analysis, the correct view to be taken of this fixed structure is that it comprises the set of mechanisms provided by the levels underneath the cognitive band. For human cognition this is the neural band. For artificial cognition, this may be a connectionist band, though it need not be. This view notwithstanding, it should be remembered that it is the Soar architecture which is primary in our research. The use of the levels viewpoint is simply an attempt at imposing a particular, hopefully illuminating, theoretical structure on top of the existing architecture.

In the remainder of this paper we describe the methodological assumptions underlying Soar, the structure of Soar, an illustrative example of Soar's performance on the task of multi-column subtraction, and a set of preliminary analyses of Soar as an architecture for general intelligence.

1. Methodological assumptions

The development of Soar is driven by four methodological assumptions. It is not expected that these assumptions will be shared by all researchers in the field. However, the assumptions do help explain why the Soar system and project have the shapes that they do.

The first assumption is the utility of focusing on the cognitive band, as opposed to the neural or rational bands. This is a view that has traditionally been shared by a large segment of the cognitive science community; it is not, however, shared by the connectionist community, which focuses on the neural band (plus the lower levels of the cognitive band), or by the logicist and expert-systems communities, which focus on the rational band. This assumption is not meant to be exclusionary, as a complete understanding of general intelligence requires the understanding of all of these descriptive bands.[1] Instead the assumption is that there is important work to be done by focusing on the cognitive band. One reason is that, as just mentioned, a complete model of general intelligence will require a model of the cognitive band. A second reason is that an understanding of the cognitive band can constrain models of the neural and rational bands. A third, more applied reason, is that a model of the cognitive band is required in order to be able to build practical intelligent systems. Neural-band models need the higher levels of organization that are provided by the cognitive band in order to reach complex task performance. Rational-band models need the heuristic adequacy provided by the cognitive band in order to be computationally feasible. A fourth reason is that there is a wealth of both psychological and AI data about the cognitive band that can be used as the basis for elucidating the structure of its levels. This data can help us understand what type of symbolic architecture is required to support general intelligence.

The second assumption is that general intelligence can most usefully be studied by not making a distinction between human and artificial intelligence. The advantage of this assumption is that it allows wider ranges of research methodologies and data to be brought to bear to mutually constrain the structure of the system. Our research methodology includes a mixture of experimental data, theoretical justifications, and comparative studies in both artificial intelligence and cognitive psychology. Human experiments provide data about performance universals and limitations that may reflect the structure of the architecture. For example, the ubiquitous power law of practice—the time to perform a task is a power-law function of the number of times the task has been performed—was used to generate a model of human practice [39, 55], which was later converted into a proposal for a general artificial learning mechanism [27, 28, 61]. Artificial experiments—the application of implemented systems to a variety of tasks requiring intelligence—provide sufficiency feedback about the mechanisms embodied in the architecture and their interactions [16, 51, 60, 62, 73]. Theoretical justifications attempt to provide an abstract analysis of the requirements of intelligence, and of how various architectural mechanisms fulfill those requirements [38, 40, 49, 54, 56]. Comparative studies, pitting one system against another, provide an evaluation of how well the respective systems perform, as well as insight about how the capabilities of one of the systems can be incorporated in the other [6, 50].

[1] Investigations of the relationship of Soar to the neural and rational bands can be found in [38, 49, 56].

The third assumption is that the architecture should consist of a small set of orthogonal mechanisms. All intelligent behaviors should involve all, or nearly all, of these basic mechanisms. This assumption biases the development of Soar strongly in the direction of uniformity and simplicity, and away from modularity [10] and toolkit approaches. When attempting to achieve a new functionality in Soar, the first step is to determine in what ways the existing mechanisms can already provide the functionality. This can force the development of new solutions to old problems, and reveal new connections—through the common underlying mechanisms—among previously distinct capabilities [53]. Only if there is no appropriate way to achieve the new functionality are new mechanisms considered.

The fourth assumption is that architectures should be pushed to the extreme to evaluate how much of general intelligence they can cover. A serious attempt at evaluating the coverage of an architecture involves a long-term commitment by an extensive research group. Much of the research involves the apparently mundane activity of replicating classical results within the architecture. Sometimes these demonstrations will by necessity be strict replications, but often the architecture will reveal novel approaches, provide a deeper understanding of the result and its relationship to other results, or provide the means of going beyond what was done in the classical work. As these results accumulate over time, along with other more novel results, the system gradually approaches the ultimate goal of general intelligence.

2. Structure of Soar

In this section we build up much of Soar's structure in levels, starting at the bottom with memory and proceeding up to decisions and goals. We then describe how learning and perceptual-motor behavior fit into this picture, and wrap up with a discussion of the default knowledge that has been incorporated into the system.

2.1. Level 1: Memory

A general intelligence requires a memory with a large capacity for the storage of knowledge. A variety of types of knowledge must be stored, including declarative knowledge (facts about the world, including facts about actions that can be performed), procedural knowledge (facts about how to perform actions, and control knowledge about which actions to perform when), and episodic knowledge (which actions were done when). Any particular task will require some subset of the knowledge stored in the memory. Memory access is the process by which this subset is retrieved for use in task performance.

The lowest level of the Soar architecture is the level at which these memory phenomena occur. All of Soar's long-term knowledge is stored in a single production memory. Whether a piece of knowledge represents procedural, declarative, or episodic knowledge, it is stored in one or more productions. Each production is a condition-action structure that performs its actions when its conditions are met. Memory access consists of the execution of these productions. During the execution of a production, variables in its actions are instantiated with values. Action variables that existed in the conditions are instantiated with the values bound in the conditions. Action variables that did not exist in the conditions act as generators of new symbols.

The result of memory access is the retrieval of information into a global working memory. The working memory is a temporary memory that contains all of Soar's short-term processing context. Working memory consists of an interrelated set of objects with attribute-value pairs. For example, an object representing a green cat named Fred might look like (object o025 ^name fred ^type cat ^color green). The symbol o025 is the identifier of the object, a short-term symbol for the object that exists only as long as the object is in working memory. Objects are related by using the identifiers of some objects as attributes and values of other objects.

There is one special type of working memory structure, the preference. Preferences encode control knowledge about the acceptability and desirability of actions, according to a fixed semantics of preference types. Acceptability preferences determine which actions should be considered as candidates. Desirability preferences define a partial ordering on the candidate actions. For example, a better (or alternatively, worse) preference can be used to represent the knowledge that one action is more (or less) desirable than another action, and a best (or worst) preference can be used to represent the knowledge that an action is at least as good (or as bad) as every other action.

In a traditional production-system architecture, each production is a problem-solving operator (see, for example, [42]). The right-hand side of the production represents some action to be performed, and the left-hand side represents the preconditions for correct application of the action (plus possibly some desirability conditions). One consequence of this view of productions is that the productions must also be the locus of behavioral control. If productions are going to act, it must be possible to control which one executes at each moment; a process known as conflict resolution. In a logic architecture, each production is a logical implication. The meaning of such a production is that if the left-hand side (the antecedent) is true, then so is the right-hand side (the consequent).[2] Soar's productions are neither operators nor implications. Instead, Soar's productions perform (parallel) memory retrieval. Each produc-

[2] The directionality of the implication is reversed in logic programming languages such as Prolog, but the point still holds.

tion is a retrieval structure for an item in long-term memory. The right-hand side of the rule represents a long-term datum, and the left-hand side represents the situations in which it is appropriate to retrieve that datum into working memory. The traditional production-system and logic notions of action, control, and truth are not directly applicable to Soar's productions. All control in Soar is performed at the decision level. Thus, there is no conflict resolution process in the Soar production system, and all productions execute in parallel. This all flows directly from the production system being a long-term memory. Soar separates the retrieval of long-term information from the control of which act to perform next.

Of course it is possible to encode knowledge of operators and logical implications in the production memory. For example, the knowledge about how to implement a typical operator can be stored procedurally as a set of productions which retrieve the state resulting from the operator's application. The productions' conditions determine when the state is to be retrieved—for example, when the operator is being applied and its preconditions are met. An alternative way to store operator implementation knowledge is declaratively as a set of structures that are completely contained in the actions of one or more productions. The structures describe not only the results of the operator, but also its preconditions. The productions' conditions determine when to retrieve this declarative operator description into working memory. A retrieved operator description must be interpreted by other productions to actually have an affect.

In general, there are these two distinct ways to encode knowledge in the production memory: procedurally and declaratively. If the knowledge is procedurally encoded, then the execution of the production reflects the knowledge, but does not actually retrieve it into working memory—it only retrieves the structures encoded in the actions. On the other hand, if a piece of knowledge is encoded declaratively in the actions of a production, then it is retrievable in its entirety. This distinction between procedural and declarative *encodings* of knowledge is distinct from whether the knowledge is declarative (represents facts about the world) or procedural (represents facts about procedures). Moreover, each production can be viewed in either way, either as a procedure which implicitly represents conditional information, or as the indexed storage of declarative structures.

2.2. Level 2: Decisions

In addition to a memory, a general intelligence requires the ability to generate and/or select a course of action that is responsive to the current situation. The second level of the Soar architecture, the decision level, is the level at which this processing is performed. The decision level is based on the memory level plus an architecturally provided, fixed, decision procedure. The decision level proceeds in a two phase elaborate-decide cycle. During elaboration, the memory is accessed repeatedly, in parallel, until quiescence is reached; that is, until no more productions can execute. This results in the retrieval into working memory of all of the accessible knowledge that is relevant to the current decision. This may include a variety of types of information, but of most direct relevance here is knowledge about actions that can be performed and preference knowledge about what actions are acceptable and desirable. After quiescence has occurred, the decision procedure selects one of the retrieved actions based on the preferences that were retrieved into working memory and their fixed semantics.

The decision level is open both with respect to the consideration of arbitrary actions, and with respect to the utilization of arbitrary knowledge in making a selection. This openness allows Soar to behave in both plan-following and reactive fashions. Soar is following a plan when a decision is primarily based on previously generated knowledge about what to do. Soar is being reactive when a decision is based primarily on knowledge about the current situation (as reflected in the working memory).

2.3. Level 3: Goals

In addition to being able to make decisions, a general intelligence must also be able to direct this behavior towards some end; that is, it must be able to set and work towards goals. The third level of the Soar architecture, the goal level, is the level at which goals are processed. This level is based on the decision level. Goals are set whenever a decision cannot be made; that is, when the decision procedure reaches an impasse. Impasses occur when there are no alternatives that can be selected (*no-change* and *rejection* impasses) or when there are multiple alternatives that can be selected, but insufficient discriminating preferences exist to allow a choice to be made among them (*tie* and *conflict* impasses). Whenever an impasse occurs, the architecture generates the goal of resolving the impasse. Along with this goal, a new *performance context* is created. The creation of a new context allows decisions to continue to be made in the service of achieving the goal of resolving the impasse—nothing can be done in the original context because it is at an impasse. If an impasse now occurs in this subgoal, another new subgoal and performance context are created. This leads to a goal (and context) stack in which the top-level goal is to perform some task, and lower-level goals are to resolve impasses in problem solving. A subgoal is terminated when either its impasse is resolved, or some higher impasse in the stack is resolved (making the subgoal superfluous).

In Soar, all symbolic goal-oriented tasks are formulated in problem spaces. A problem space consists of a set of states and a set of operators. The states represent situations, and the operators represent actions which when applied to states yield other states. Each performance context consists of a goal, plus roles for a problem state, a state, and an operator. Problem solving is driven by decisions that result in the selection of problem spaces, states, and operators for their respective context roles. Given a goal, a problem space should be selected in which goal achievement can be pursued. Then an initial state should be selected that represents the initial situation. Then an operator should be selected for application to the initial state. Then another state should be selected (most likely the result of applying the operator to the previous state). This process continues until a sequence of operators has been discovered that transforms the initial state into a state in which the goal has been achieved. One subtle consequence of the use of problem spaces is that each one implicitly defines a set of constraints on how the task is to be performed. For example, if the Eight Puzzle is attempted in a problem space containing only a slide-tile operator, all solution paths maintain the constraint that the tiles are never picked up off of the board. Thus, such conditions need not be tested for explicitly in desired states.

Each problem solving decision—the selection of a problem space, a state, or an operator—is based on the knowledge accessible in the production memory. If the knowledge is both correct and sufficient, Soar exhibits highly controlled behavior; at each decision point the right alternative is selected. Such behavior is accurately described as being algorithmic or knowledge-intensive. However, for a general intelligence faced with a broad array of unpredictable tasks, situations will arise—inevitably and indeed frequently—in which the accessible knowledge is either incorrect or insufficient. It is possible that correct decisions will fortuitously be made, but it is more likely that either incorrect decisions will be made or that impasses will occur. Under such circumstances search is the likely outcome. If an incorrect decision is made, the system must eventually recover and get itself back on a path to the goal, for example, by backtracking. If instead an impasse occurs, the system must execute a sequence of problem space operators in the resulting subgoal to find (or generate) the information that will allow a decision to be made. This processing may itself be highly algorithmic, if enough control knowledge is available to uniquely determine what to do, or it may involve a large amount of further search.

As described earlier, operator implementation knowledge can be represented procedurally in the production memory, enabling operator implementation to be performed directly by memory retrieval. When the operator is selected, a set of productions execute that collectively build up the representation of the result state by combining data from long-term memory and the previous state. This type of implementation is comparable to the conventional implementation of an operator as a fixed piece of code. However, if operator implementation knowledge is stored declaratively, or if no operator implementation knowledge is stored, then a subgoal occurs, and the operator must be implemented by the execution of a sequence of problem space operators in the subgoal. If a declarative description of the to-be-implemented operator is available, then these lower operators may implement the operator by interpreting its declarative description (as was demonstrated in work on task acquisition in Soar [61]). Otherwise the operator can be implemented by decomposing it into a set of simpler operators for which operator implementation knowledge is available, or which can in turn be decomposed further.

When an operator is implemented in a subgoal, the combination of the operator and the subgoal correspond to the type of deliberately created subgoal common in AI problem solvers. The operator specifies a task to be performed, while the subgoal indicates that accomplishing the task should be treated as a goal for further problem solving. In complex problems, like computer configuration, it is common for there to be complex high-level operators, such as Configure-computer which are implemented by selecting problem spaces in which they can be decomposed into simpler tasks. Many of the traditional goal management issues—such as conjunction, conflict, and selection—show up as operator management issues in Soar. For example, a set of conjunctive subgoals can be ordered by ordering operators that later lead to impasses (and subgoals).

As described in [54], a subgoal not only represents a subtask to be performed, but it also represents an introspective act that allows unlimited amounts of meta-level problem-space processing to be performed. The entire working memory—the goal stack and all information linked to it—is available for examination and augmentation in a subgoal. At any time a production can examine and augment any part of the goal stack. Likewise, a decision can be made at any time for any of the goals in the hierarchy. This allows subgoal problem solving to analyze the situation that led to the impasse, and even to change the subgoal, should it be appropriate. One not uncommon occurrence is for information to be generated within a subgoal that instead of satisfying the subgoal, causes the subgoal to become irrelevant and consequently to disappear. Processing tends to focus on the bottom-most goal because all of the others have reached impasses. However, the processing is completely opportunistic, so that when appropriate information becomes available at a higher level, processing at that level continues immediately and all lower subgoals are terminated.

2.4. *Learning*

All learning occurs by the acquisition of chunks—productions that summarize the problem solving that occurs in subgoals [28]. The actions of a chunk represent the knowledge generated during the subgoal; that is, the results of the subgoal. The conditions of the chunk represent an access path to this knowledge, consisting of those elements of the parent goals upon which the results depended. The results of the subgoal are determined by finding the elements generated in the subgoal that are available for use in subgoals—an element is a result of a subgoal precisely because it is available to processes outside of the subgoal. The access path is computed by analyzing the traces of the productions that fired in the subgoal—each production trace effectively states that its actions depended on its conditions. This dependency analysis yields a set of conditions that have been implicitly generalized to ignore irrelevant aspects of the situation. The resulting generality allows chunks to transfer to situations other than the one in which it was learned. The primary system-wide effect of chunking is to move Soar along the space-time trade-off by allowing relevantly similar future decisions to be based on direct retrieval of information from memory rather than on problem solving within a subgoal. If the chunk is used, an impasse will not occur, because the required information is already available.

Care must be taken to not confuse the power of chunking as a learning mechanism with the power of Soar as a learning system. Chunking is a simple goal-based, dependency-tracing, caching scheme, analogous to explanation-based learning [4, 36, 50] and a variety of other schemes [55]. What allows Soar to exhibit a wide variety of learning behaviors are the variations in the types of subgoals that are chunked; the types of problem solving, in conjunction with the types and sources of knowledge, used in the subgoals; and the ways the chunks are used in later problem solving. The role that a chunk will play is determined by the type of subgoal for which it was learned. State-no-change, operator-tie, and operator-no-change subgoals lead respectively to state augmentation, operator selection, and operator implementation productions. The content of a chunk is determined by the types of problem solving and knowledge used in the subgoal. A chunk can lead to skill acquisition if it is used as a more efficient means of generating an already generatable result. A chunk can lead to knowledge acquisition (or knowledge level learning [5]) if it is used to make old/new judgments; that is, to distinguish what has been learned from what has not been learned [52, 53, 56].

2.5. Perception and motor control

One of the most recent functional additions to the Soar architecture is a perceptual-motor interface [75, 76]. All perceptual and motor behavior is mediated through working memory; specifically, through the state in the top problem solving context. Each distinct perceptual field has a designated attribute of this state to which it adds its information. Likewise, each distinct motor field has a designated attribute of the state from which it takes its commands. The perceptual and motor systems are autonomous with respect to each other and the cognitive system.

Encoding and decoding productions can be used to convert between the high-level structures used by the cognitive system, and the low-level structures used by the perceptual and motor systems. These productions are like ordinary productions, except that they examine only the perceptual and motor fields, and not any of the rest of the context stack. This autonomy from the context stack is critical, because it allows the decision procedure to proceed without waiting for quiescence among the encoding and decoding productions, which may never happen in a rapidly changing environment.

2.6. *Default knowledge*

Soar has a set of productions (55 in all) that provide default responses to each of the possible impasses that can arise, and thus prevent the system from dropping into a bottomless pit in which it generates an unbounded number of content-free performance contexts. Figure 2 shows the default production that allows the system to continue if it has no idea how to resolve a conflict impasse among a set of operators. When the production executes, it rejects all of the conflicting operators. This allows another candidate operator to be selected, if there is one, or for a different impasse to arise if there are no additional candidates. This default response, as with all of them, can be overridden by additional knowledge if it is available.

One large part of the default knowledge (10 productions) is responsible for setting up operator subgoaling as the default response to no-change impasses on operators. That is, it attempts to find some other state in the problem space to which the selected operators can be applied. This is accomplished by generating acceptable and worst preferences in the subgoal for the parent problem space. If another problem space is suggested, possibly for implementing the operator, it will be selected. Otherwise, the selection of the parent problem space in the subgoal enables operator subgoaling. A sequence of operators is then applied in the subgoal until a state is generated that satisfies the preconditions of an operator higher in the goal stack.

Another large part of the default knowledge (33 productions) is responsible for setting up lookahead search as the default response to tie impasses. This is accomplished by generating acceptable and worst preferences for the *selection* problem space. The selection problem space consists of operators that evaluate the tied alternatives. Based on the evaluations produced by these operators, default productions create preferences that break the tie and resolve the impasse. In order to apply the evaluation operators, domain knowledge must exist that can create an evaluation. If no such knowledge is available, a second impasse arises—a no-change on the evaluation operator. As mentioned earlier,

---

If there is an impasse because of an operator conflict
  and there are no candidate problem spaces available
then reject the conflicting operators.

Fig. 2. A default production.

the default response to an operator no-change impasse is to perform operator subgoaling. However, for a no-change impasse on an evaluation operator this is overridden and a lookahead search is performed instead. The results of the lookahead search are used to evaluate the tied alternatives.

As Soar is developed, it is expected that more and more knowledge will be included as part of the basic system about how to deal with a variety of situations. For example, one area on which we are currently working is the provision of Soar with a basic arithmetical capability, including problem spaces for addition, multiplication, subtraction, division, and comparison. One way of looking at the existing default knowledge is as the tip of this large iceberg of background knowledge. However, another way to look at the default knowledge is as part of the architecture itself. Some of the default knowledge—how much is still unclear—must be innate rather than learned. The rest of the system's knowledge, such as the arithmetic spaces, should then be learnable from there.

3. Example: multi-column subtraction

Multi-column subtraction is the task we will use to demonstrate Soar. This task has three advantages. First, it is a familiar and simple task. This allows the details of Soar not to be lost in the complexities of understanding the task. Second, previous work has been done on modeling human learning of subtraction in the Sierra architecture [71]. Our implementation is inspired by the Sierra framework. Third, this task appears to be quite different from many standard search-intensive tasks common in AI. On the surface, it appears difficult to cast subtraction within the problem-space framework of Soar—it is, after all, a procedure. One might also think that chunking could not learn such a procedure. However, in this example, we will demonstrate that multi-column subtraction can be performed by Soar and that important parts of the procedure can be learned through chunking.

There exist many different procedures for performing multi-column subtraction. Different procedures result in different behaviors, both in the order in which scratch marks—such as borrowing notations—are made and in the type of mistakes that might be generated while learning [72]. For simplicity, we will demonstrate the implementation of just one of the many possible procedures. This procedure uses a borrowing technique that recursively borrows from a higher-order column into a lower-order column when the top number in the lower-order column is less than the bottom number.

3.1. A hierarchical subtraction procedure

One way to implement this procedure is via the processing of a goal hierarchy that encodes what must be done. Figure 3 shows a subtraction goal

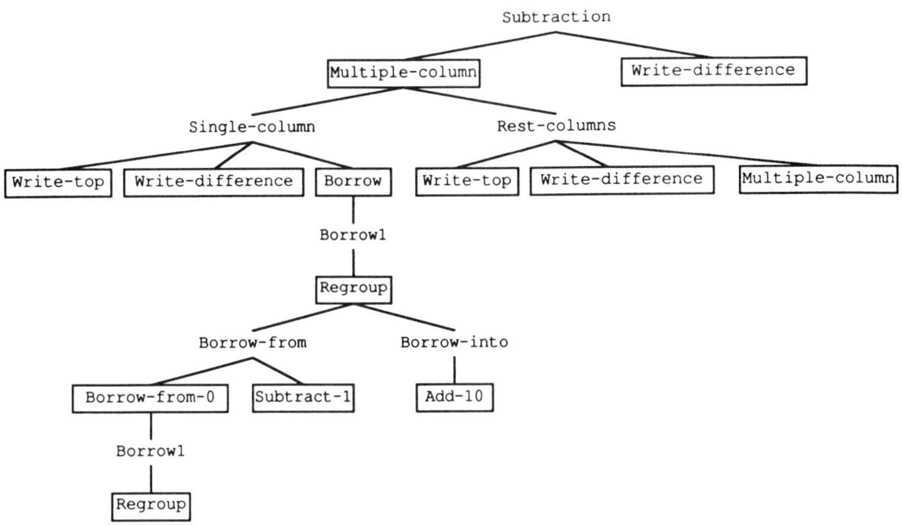

Fig. 3. A goal hierarchy for multi-column subtraction.

hierarchy that is similar to the one learned by Sierra.[3] Under each goal are shown the subgoals that may be generated while trying to achieve it. This Sierra goal hierarchy is mapped onto a hierarchy of operators and problem spaces in Soar (as described in Section 2). The boxed goals map onto operators and the unboxed goals map onto problem spaces. Each problem space consists of the operators linked to it from below in the figure. Operators that have problem spaces below them are implemented by problem solving in those problem spaces. The other operators are implemented directly at the memory level by productions (except for multiple-column and regroup, which are recursive). These are the primitive acts of subtraction, such as writing numbers or subtracting digits.

The states in these problem spaces contain symbolic representations of the subtraction problem and the scratch marks made on the page during problem solving. The representation is very simple and direct, being based on the spatial relationships among the digits as they would appear on a page. The state consists of a set of columns. Each column has pointers to its top and bottom digits. Additional pointers are generated when an answer for a column is produced, or when a scratch mark is made as the result of borrowing. The physical orientation of the columns on the page is represented by having "left" and "right" pointers from columns to their left and right neighbors. There is no inherent notion of multi-digit numbers except for these left and right relations between columns. This representation is consistent with the operators, which

[3] Sierra learned a slightly more elaborate, but computationally equivalent, procedure.

treat the problem symbolically and never manipulate multi-digit numbers as a whole.

Using this implementation of the subtraction procedure, Soar is able to solve all multi-column subtraction problems that result in positive answers. Unfortunately, there is little role for learning. Most of the control knowledge is already embedded in the productions that select problem spaces and operators. Within each problem space there are only a few operators from which to select. The preconditions of the few operators in each problem space are sufficient for perfect behavior. Therefore, goals arise only to implement operators. Chunking these goals produces productions that are able to compute answers without the intermediate subgoals.[4]

3.2. A single-space approach

One way to loosen up the strict control provided by the detailed problem-space/operator hierarchy in Fig. 3, and thus to enable the learning of the control knowledge underlying the subtraction procedure, is to have only a single subtraction problem space that contains all of the primitive acts (writing results, changing columns, and so on). Figure 4 contains a description of the

- *Operators*:
  - **Write-difference:** If the difference between the top digit and the bottom digit of the current column is known, then write the difference as an answer to the current column.
  - **Write-top:** If the lower digit of the current column is blank, then write the top digit as the answer to the current column.
  - **Borrow-into:** If the result of adding 10 to the top digit of the current column is known, and the digit to the left of it has a scratch mark on it, then replace the top digit with the result.
  - **Borrow-from:** If the result of subtracting 1 from the top digit in the current column is known, then replace that top digit with the result, augment it with a scratch mark and shift the current column to the right.
  - **Move-left:** If the current column has an answer in it, shift the current column left.
  - **Move-borrow-left:** If the current column does not have a scratch mark in it, shift the current column left.
  - **Subtract-two-digits:** If the top digit is greater than or equal to the lower digit, then produce a result that is the difference.
  - **Subtract-1:** If the top digit is not zero, then produce a result that is the top digit minus one.
  - **Add 10:** Produce a result that is the top digit plus ten.
- *Goal Test*: If each column has an answer, then succeed.

Fig. 4. Primitive subtraction problem space.

[4] This work on subtraction was done in an earlier version of Soar that did not have the perceptual-motor interface described in Section 2. In that version, these chunks caused Soar to write out all of the column results and scratch marks in parallel—not very realistic motor behavior. To work around this problem, chunking was disabled for goals in this task during which environmental interactions occurred.

problem space operators and the goal test used in this second implementation. The operators can be grouped into four classes: the basic acts of writing answers to a single column problem (write-difference, write-top); borrow actions on the upper digits (borrow-into, borrow-from); moving from one column to the next (move-left, move-borrow-left); and performing very simple arithmetic computations (subtract-two-digits, subtract-1, add-10). With this simple problem space, Soar must learn the subtraction procedure by acquiring control knowledge that correctly selects operators.

Every operator in the subtraction problem space is considered for every state in the space. This is accomplished by having a production for each operator that generates an acceptable preference for it. The conditions of the production only test that the appropriate problem space (subtraction) is selected. Similar productions existed in the original implementation, except that those productions also contained additional tests which ensured that the operators would only be considered when they were the appropriate ones to apply.

In addition to productions which generate acceptable preferences, each operator has one or more productions which implement it. Although every operator is made acceptable for every state, an operator will actually be applied only if all of the conditions in the productions that implement it are satisfied. For example, write-difference will only apply if the difference between the top and bottom numbers is known. If an operator is selected, but the conditions of the productions that implement it are not satisfied, an impasse arises. As described in Section 2, the default response to this type of impasse is to perform operator subgoaling.

Figure 5 shows a trace of Soar's problem solving as it performs a simple two-column subtraction problem, after the learning of control knowledge has been completed. Because Soar's performance prior to learning on this problem is considerably more complicated, it is described after this simpler case. The

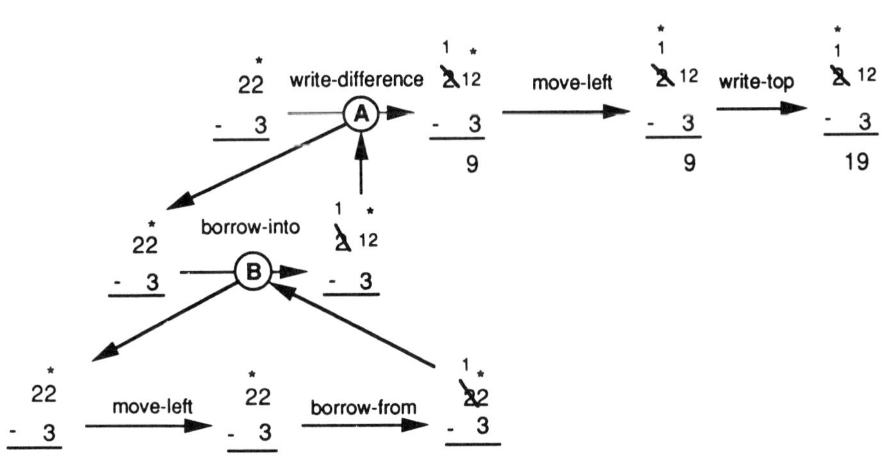

Fig. 5. Trace of problem solving after learning for 22 – 3.

top goal in this figure is to have the result of subtracting 3 from 22. Problem solving in the top goal proceeds from left to right, diving to a lower level whenever a subgoal is created in response to an impasse. Each state is a partially solved subtraction problem, consisting of the statement of the subtraction problem, a * designating the current column, and possibly column results and/or scratch marks for borrowing. Operator applications are represented by arrows going from left to right. The only impasses that occur in this trace are a result of the failure of operator preconditions—a form of operator no-change impasse. These impasses are designated by circles disrupting the operator-application arrows, and are labeled in the order they arise (A and B). For example, impasse A arises because write-difference cannot apply unless the lower digit in the current column (3) is less than the top digit (2).

For impasse A, operator subgoaling occurs when the subtraction problem space is selected in the subgoal. The preconditions of the write-difference operator are met when a state has been generated whose top digit has been changed from 2 to 12 (by borrowing). Once this occurs, the subgoal terminates and the operator applies, in this case writing the difference between 12 and 3. In this implementation of subtraction, operator subgoaling dynamically creates a goal hierarchy that is similar to the one programmed into the original implementation.

3.3. *Performance prior to learning*

Prior to learning, Soar's problem solving on this task is considerably more complicated. This added complexity arises because of an initial lack of knowledge about the results of simple arithmetic computations and a lack of knowledge about which operators should be selected for which states. Figure 6

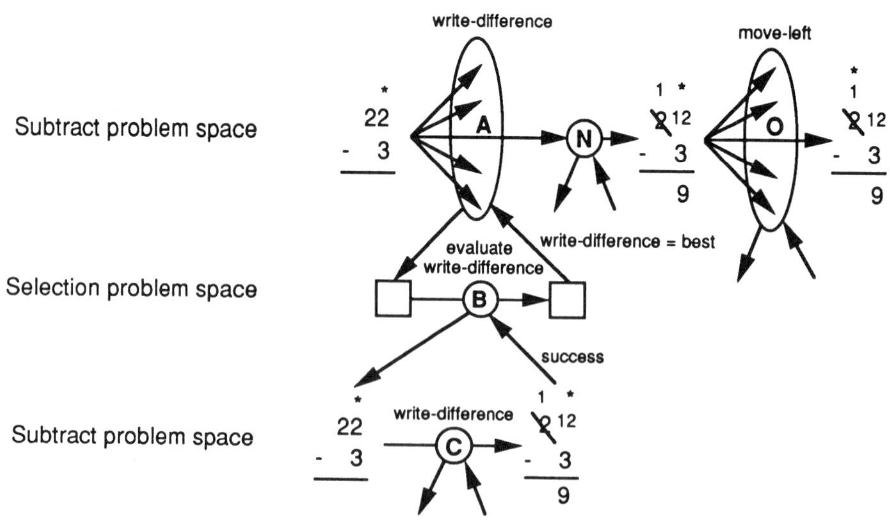

Fig. 6. Trace of problem solving before learning for 22 – 3.

shows a partial trace of Soar's pre-learning problem solving. Although many of the subgoals are missing, this small snapshot of the problem solving is characteristic of the impasses and subgoals that arise at all levels.

As before, the problem solving starts at the upper left with the initial state. As soon as the initial state is selected, a tie impasse (A) arises because all of the operators are acceptable and there are no additional preferences that distinguish between them. Default productions cause the selection space to be selected for this impasse. Within this space, operators are created to evaluate the tied operators. This example assumes that evaluate-object(write-difference) is selected, possibly based on advice from a teacher. Then, because there is no knowledge available about how to evaluate the subtraction operators, a no-change impasse (B) occurs for the evaluation operator. More default productions lead to a lookahead search by suggesting the original problem space (subtraction) and state and then selecting the operator that is being evaluated. The operator then applies, if it can, creating a new state. In this example, an operator subgoal impasse (C) arises when the attempt is made to apply the write-difference operator—its preconditions are not satisfied. Problem solving continues in this subgoal, requiring many additional impasses, until the write-difference operator can finally be applied. The lookahead search then continues until an evaluation is generated for the write-difference operator. Here, this happens shortly after impasse C is resolved. The system was given the knowledge that a state containing an answer for the current column is a (partial) success—such states are on the path to the goal. This state evaluation is then converted by default productions into an evaluation of "success" for the operator, and from there into a best preference for the operator. The creation of this preference breaks the operator tie, terminating the subgoals, and leading to the selection of the preferred operator (write-difference). The overall behavior of the system during this lookahead search is that of depth-first search—where backtracking occurs by subgoal termination—intertwined with operator subgoaling. Once this search is completed, further impasses (N) arise to actually apply the selected operator, but eventually, a solution is found.

One way in which multi-column subtraction differs from the classic AI search tasks is that the goal test is underspecified. As shown in Fig. 4, the goal test used here is that a result has been generated for each column of the problem. This determines whether some answer has been given for the problem, but is inadequate to determine whether the correct answer has been generated. The reason for this is that when solving a subtraction problem, the answer is in general not already available. It is theoretically (and practically) possible to use an addition procedure to test whether the subtraction procedure has generated the correct result. However, that corresponds to a deliberate strategy of "checking your work", rather than to the normal procedural goal test of determining whether the sequence of steps has been completed.

One consequence of having an underspecified goal test is that the combination of the problem space and goal test are not sufficient to ensure correct performance. Additional knowledge—the control knowledge which underlies the subtraction procedure—must also be provided in some form. VanLehn provided Sierra with worked-out examples which included the order in which the primitive external actions were to be performed [71]. The approach that we have taken is to provide advice to Soar [12] about which task operators it should evaluate first in the selection problem space. This ensures that the first answer generated during the lookahead search is the correct one.

3.4. Learning in subtraction

When chunking is used during subtraction problem solving, productions are created which reproduce the results of the subgoals in similar future situations. For the subgoals created because of tie impasses, the chunks create best preferences for the operators that led to the solution. These chunks essentially cache the results of the lookahead searches. A set of such chunks corresponds to a plan (or procedure)—they determine at every step what should be done—thus chunking converts Soar's behavior from search into plan (or procedure) following. When Soar is rerun on the same problem, the tie impasses do not arise and the solution is found directly, as in Fig. 5.

One important issue concerning the chunked productions is their generality. Does Soar only learn chunks that can apply to the exact same problem, or are the chunks general enough so that advice is no longer needed after a few subtraction problems have been completed? The answer is that the learned control chunks are quite general—so general that only one or two are required per operator. Once these chunks are acquired, Soar is able to solve perfectly all multi-column subtraction problems that have a positive answer. One sample control chunk for the borrow-into operator is shown in Fig. 7. Similar chunks are learned for each of the other major operators.

One reason for this generality is that operator subgoaling leads to a fine-grained goal hierarchy. There are a large number of relatively simple goals having to do with satisfying the preconditions of an operator. Because the problem solving for these goals is relatively minimal, the resulting chunks are quite general. A second reason for the generality of the learning is that the

If the super-operator is write-difference,
  and the bottom digit is greater than the top digit,
then make a best preference for borrow-into.

Fig. 7. A control chunk for borrow-into.

control chunks do not test for the specific digits used in the problems—if such tests were included, the chunks would transfer to many fewer problems.[5]

Though the control chunks that are learned are quite general, many specialized implementation chunks are also learned for the simple arithmetic operators. For example, the set of chunks that are eventually learned for the subtract-two-digits operator comprise a partial subtraction table for one- and two-digit numbers. Conceivably, these chunks could have been learned before multi-column subtraction is ever attempted—one may imagine that most of these simple digit manipulations are learned during earlier lessons on addition and single-column subtraction. Alternatively, these chunks can continue to be acquired as more multi-column subtraction problems are solved. The control chunks would all be acquired after a few trials, but learning of arithmetic knowledge would continue through later problems.

4. Analysis of Soar

There are a variety of analyses that could be performed for Soar. In this section we take our cue from the issues provided by the organizers of the 1987 Workshop on the Foundations of Artificial Intelligence [14]. We examine the set of tasks that are natural for Soar, the sources of its power, and its scope and limits.

4.1. Natural tasks

What does it mean for a task to be natural for an architecture? To answer this question we first must understand what a task is, and then what it means for such a task to be natural. By "task" we will mean any identifiable function, whether externally specified, or completely internal to the system. Computer configuration and maneuvering through an obstacle course are both tasks, and so are inheritance and skill acquisition. One way to define the idea of naturalness for a combination of a task and architecture is to say that a task is natural for an architecture if the task can be performed within the architecture without adding an extra level of interpretation within the software. This definition is appealing because it allows a distinction to be made between the tasks that the architecture can perform directly and those that can be done, but for which the architecture does not provide direct support. However, applying

[5] Chunking would include tests for the digits if their specific values were examined during the lookahead searches. However, the actual manipulation of the numbers is performed by the simple arithmetic operators: add-10, subtract-1 and subtract-two-digits. Before an operator such as write-difference is applied, an operator subgoal is created in which subtract-two-digits is selected and applied. The chunk for this subgoal reproduces the result whenever the same two digits are to be subtracted, eliminating the need for subtract-two-digits in such situations in the future. In the following lookahead searches, only pointers to the digits rather than the actual digits are ever tested, thereby leading to control chunks that are independent of the actual digits.

this definition is not without its problems. One problem is that, for any particular task, it is possible to replace the combination of an interpreter and its interpreted structures with a procedure that has the same effect. Some forms of learning—chunking, for example—do exactly this, by compiling interpreted structures into the structure of the interpreter. This has the effect of converting an unnatural task implementation into a natural one. Such a capability causes problems for the definition of naturalness—naturalness cannot be a fixed property of the combination of a task and an architecture—but it is actually a point is favor of architectures that can do such learning.

A second problem is that in a system that is itself built up in levels, as is Soar, different tasks will be performed at different levels. In Soar, tasks can be performed directly by the architecture, by memory retrieval, by a decision, or by goal-based problem solving. A task is implemented at a particular level if that level and all lower levels are involved, but the higher levels are not. For example, consider the task of inheritance. Inheritance is not directly implemented by the Soar architecture, but it can be implemented at the memory level by the firing of productions. This implementation involves the memory level plus the architecture (which implements the memory level), but not the decision or goal levels. Alternatively, inheritance could be implemented at the decision level, or even higher up at goal level. As the level of implementation increases, performance becomes more interpretive, but the model of computation explicitly includes all of these levels as natural for the system.

One way out of this problem is to have pre-theoretic notions about the level at which a particular task ought to be performable. The system is then natural for the task if it can be performed at that level, and unnatural if it must be implemented at a higher level. If, for example, the way inheritance works should be a function of the knowledge in the system, then the natural level for the capability is at the memory level (or higher).

In the remainder of this section we describe the major types of tasks that appear to us to be natural in Soar. Lacking any fundamental ways of partitioning the set of all tasks into principled categories, we will use a categorization based on four of the major functional capabilities of Soar: search-based tasks, knowledge-based tasks, learning tasks, and robotic tasks. The naturalness judgments for these task types are always based on assumptions about the natural level of implementation for a variety of subtasks within each type of task. We will try to be as clear as possible about the levels at which the subtasks are being performed, so that others may also be able to make these judgments for themselves.

4.1.1. Search-based tasks

Soar performs search in two qualitatively different ways: within context and across context. Within-context search occurs when Soar "knows" what to do at every step, and thus selects a sequence of operators and states without going into a subgoal. If it needs to backtrack in within-context search, and the states in the problem space are internal (rather than states of the outside world), it can do so by reselecting a previously visited state. Within-context search corresponds to doing the task, without lookahead, and recovering if anything goes wrong. Across-context search occurs when the system doesn't know what to do, and impasses arise. Successive states in the search show up in successively lower contexts. Backtracking occurs by terminating subgoals. Across-context search corresponds to lookahead search, hypothetical scenario generation, or simulation.

Various versions of Soar have been demonstrated to be able to perform over 30 different search methods [21, 25, 26]. Soar can also exhibit hybrid methods—such as a combination of hill-climbing and depth-first search or of operator subgoaling and depth-first search—and use different search methods for different problem spaces within the same problem.

Search methods are represented in Soar as method increments—productions that contain a small chunk of knowledge about some aspect of a task and its action consequences. For example, a method increment might include knowledge about how to compute an evaluation function for a task, along with the knowledge that states with better evaluations should be preferred. Such an increment leads to a form of hill climbing. Other increments lead to other search methods. Combinations of increments lead to mixed methods.

The basic search abilities of making choices and generating subgoals are provided by the architecture. Individual method increments are at the memory level, but control occurs at the decision level, where the results of all of the method increments can be integrated into a single choice. Some search knowledge, such as the selection problem space, exists at the goal level.

4.1.2. Knowledge-based tasks

Knowledge-based tasks are represented in Soar as a collection of interacting problem spaces (as are all symbolic goal-oriented tasks). Each problem space is responsible for a part of the task. Problem spaces interact according to the different goal-subgoal relationships that can exist in Soar. Within each problem space, the knowledge is further decomposed into a set of problem space components, such as goal testing, state initialization, and operator proposal [77]. These components, along with additional communication constructs, can then be encoded directly as productions, or can be described in a high-level problem space language called TAQL [77], which is then compiled down into productions. Within this overall problem space organization, other forms of organization—such as object hierarchies with inheritance—are implementable at the memory level by multiple memory accesses. Task performance is represented at the goal level as search in problem spaces.

Several knowledge-based tasks have been implemented in Soar, including the R1-Soar computer configuration system [51], the Cypress-Soar and Designer-Soar algorithm design systems [60, 62], the Neomycin-Soar medical diagnosis system [73], and the Merl-Soar job-shop scheduling system [16].

These five knowledge-based systems cover a variety of forms of both construction and classification tasks. Construction tasks involve assembling an object from pieces. R1-Soar—in which the task is to construct a computer configuration—is a good example of a construction task. Classification tasks involve selecting from among a set of objects. Neomycin-Soar—in which the task is to diagnose an illness—is a good example of a classification task.[6] In their simplest forms, both construction and classification occur at the decision level. In fact, they both occur to some extent within every decision in Soar—alternatives must be assembled in working-memory and then selected. These capabilities can require trivial amounts of processing, as when an object is constructed by instantiating and retrieving it from memory. They can also involve arbitrary amounts of problem solving and knowledge, as when the process of operator-implementation (or, equivalently, state-construction) is performed via problem solving in a subgoal.

4.1.3. Learning tasks

The architecture directly supports a form of experiential learning in which chunking compiles goal-level problem solving into memory-level productions. Execution of the productions should have the same effect as the problem solving would have had, just more quickly. The varieties of subgoals for which chunks are learned lead to varieties in types of productions learned: problem space creation and selection; state creation and selection; and operator creation, selection, and execution. An alternative classification for this same set of behaviors is that it covers procedural, episodic and declarative knowledge [56]. The variations in goal outcomes lead to both learning from success and learning from failure. The ability to learn about all subgoal results leads to learning about important intermediate results, in addition to learning about goal success and failure. The implicit generalization of chunks leads to transfer of learned knowledge to other subtasks within the same problem (within-trial transfer), other instances of the same problem (across-trial transfer), and other problems (across-task transfer). Variations in the types of problems performed in Soar lead to chunking in knowledge-based tasks, search-based, and robotic tasks. Variations in sources of knowledge lead to learning from both internal and external knowledge sources. A summary of many of the types of learning that have so far been demonstrated in Soar can be found in [61].

The apparent naturalness of these various forms of learning depends primarily on the appropriateness of the required problem solving. Towards the natural end of the spectrum is the acquisition of operator selection productions, in

[6] In a related development, as part of an effort to map the Generic Task approach to expert system construction onto Soar, the Generic Task for classification by establish-refine has been implemented in Soar as a general problem space [17].

which the problem solving consists simply of a search with the set of operators for which selection knowledge is to be learned. Towards the unnatural end of the spectrum is the acquisition of new declarative knowledge from the outside environment. Many systems employ a simple store command for such learning, effectively placing the capability at the memory level. In Soar, the capability is situated two levels further up, at the goal level. This occurs because the knowledge must be stored by chunking, which can only happen if the knowledge is used in subgoal-based problem solving. The naturalness of this learning in Soar thus depends on whether this extra level of interpretation is appropriate or not. It turns out that the problem solving that enables declarative learning in Soar takes the form of an understanding process that relates the new knowledge to what is already known. The chunking of this understanding process yields the chunks that encode the new knowledge. If it is assumed that new knowledge should always be understood to be learned, then Soar's approach starts to look more natural, and verbatim storage starts to look more inappropriate.

4.1.4. Robotic tasks

Robotic tasks are performed in Soar via its perceptual-motor interface. Sensors autonomously generate working memory structures representing what is being sensed, and motor systems autonomously take commands from working memory and execute them. The work on robotics in Soar is still very much in its infancy; however, in Robo-Soar [30], Soar has been successfully hooked up to the combination of a camera and a Puma arm, and then applied to several simple blocks-world tasks.[7] Low-level software converts the camera signal into information about the positions, orientations and identifying characteristics of the blocks. This perceptual information is then input to working memory, and further interpreted by encoding productions. Decoding productions convert the high-level robot commands generated by the cognitive system to the low-level commands that are directly understood by the controller for the robot arm. These low-level commands are then executed through Soar's motor interface.

Given a set of operators which generate motor commands, and knowledge about how to simulate the operators and about the expected positions of blocks following the actions, Robo-Soar is able to successfully solve simple blocks-world problems and to learn from its own behavior and from externally provided advice. It also can make use of a general scheme for recovering from incorrect knowledge [23] to recover when the unexpected occurs—such as when the system fails in its attempt to pick up a triangular prism—and to learn to avoid the failure in the future. Robo-Soar thus mixes planning (lookahead

[7] The work on Robo-Soar has been done in the newest major release of Soar (version 5) [24, 63], which differs in a number of interesting ways from the earlier versions upon which the rest of the results in this article are based.

search with chunking), plan execution and monitoring, reactivity, and error recovery (with replanning). This performance depends on all of the major components of the architecture, plus general background knowledge—such as how to do lookahead search and how to recover from errors—and specific problem spaces for the task.

4.2. Where the power resides

Soar's power and flexibility arise from at least four identifiable sources. The first source of power is the universality of the architecture. While it may seem that this should go without saying, it is in fact a crucial factor, and thus important to mention explicitly. Universality provides the primitive capability to perform any computable task, but does not by itself explain why Soar is more appropriate than any other universal architecture for knowledge-based, search-based, learning, and robotic tasks.

The second source of power is the uniformity of the architecture. Having only one type of long-term memory structure allows a single, relatively simple, learning mechanism to behave as a general learning mechanism. Having only one type of task representation (problem spaces) allows Soar to move continuously from one extreme of brute-force search to the other extreme of knowledge-intensive (or procedural) behavior without having to make any representational decisions. Having only one type of decision procedure allows a single, relatively simple, subgoal mechanism to generate all of the types of subgoals needed by the system.

The traditional downside of uniformity is weakness and inefficiency. If instead the system were built up as a set of specialized modules or agents, as proposed in [10, 34], then each of the modules could be optimized for its own narrow task. Our approach to this issue in Soar has been to go strongly with uniformity—for all of the benefits listed above—but to achieve efficiency (power) through the addition of knowledge. This knowledge can either be added by hand (programming) or by chunking.

The third source of power is the specific mechanisms incorporated into the architecture. The production memory provides pattern-directed access to large amounts of knowledge; provides the ability to use strong problem solving methods; and provides a memory structure with a small-grained modularity. The working memory allows global access to processing state. The decision procedure provides an open control loop that can react immediately to new situations and knowledge; contributes to the modularity of the memory by allowing memory access to proceed in an uncontrolled fashion (conflict resolution was a major source of nonmodularity in earlier production systems); provides a flexible control language (preferences); and provides a notion of impasse that is used as the basis for the generation of subgoals. Subgoals focus the system's resources on situations where the accessible knowledge is inadequate; and allow flexible meta-level processing. Problem spaces separate control from action, allowing them (control and action) to be reasoned about independently; provide a constrained context within which the search for a desired state can occur; provide the ability to use weak problem solving methods; and provide for straightforward responses to uncertainty and error (search and backtracking). Chunking acquires long-term knowledge from experience; compiles interpreted procedures into non-interpreted ones; and provides generalization and transfer. The perceptual-motor system provides the ability to observe and affect the external world in parallel with the cognitive activity.

The fourth source of power is the interaction effects that result from the integration of all of the capabilities within a single system. The most compelling results generated so far come about from these interactions. One example comes from the mixture of weak methods, strong methods, and learning that is found in systems like R1-Soar. Strong methods are based on having knowledge about what to do at each step. Because strong methods tend to be efficient and to produce high-quality solutions, they should be used whenever possible. Weak methods are based on searching to make up for a lack of knowledge about what should be done. Such methods contribute robustness and scope by providing the system with a fall-back approach for situations in which the available strong methods do not work. Learning results in the addition of knowledge, turning weak methods into strong ones. For example, in R1-Soar it was demonstrated how computer configuration could be cast as a search problem, how strong methods (knowledge) could be used to reduce search, how weak methods (subgoals and search) could be used to make up for a lack of knowledge, and how learning could add knowledge as the result of search.

Another interesting interaction effect comes from work on abstraction planning, in which a difficult problem is solved by first learning a plan for an abstract version of the problem, and then using the abstract plan to aid in finding a plan for the full problem [41, 57, 70, 69]. Chunking helps the abstraction planning process by recording the abstract plan as a set of operator-selection productions, and by acquiring other productions that reduce the amount of search required in generating a plan. Abstraction helps the learning process by allowing chunks to be learned more quickly—abstract searches tend to be shorter than normal ones. Abstraction also helps learning by enabling chunks to be more general than they would otherwise be—the chunks ignore the details that were abstracted away—thus allowing more transfer and potentially decreasing the cost of matching the chunks (because there are now fewer conditions).

4.3. Scope and limits

The original work on Soar demonstrated its capabilities as a general problem solver that could use any of the weak methods when appropriate, across a wide range of tasks. Later, we came to understand how to use Soar as the basis for knowledge-based systems, and how to incorporate appropriate learning and perceptual-motor capabilities into the architecture. These developments increased Soar's scope considerably beyond its origins as a weak-method problem solver. Our ultimate goal has always been to develop the system to the point where its scope includes everything required of a general intelligence. In this section we examine how far Soar has come from its relatively limited initial demonstrations towards its relatively unlimited goal. This discussion is divided up according to the major components of the Soar architecture, as presented in Section 2: memory, decisions, goals, learning, and perception and motor control.

4.3.1. Level 1: Memory

The scope of Soar's memory level can be evaluated in terms of the amount of knowledge that can be stored, the types of knowledge that can be represented, and the organization of the knowledge.

Amount of knowledge. Using current technology, Soar's production memory can support the storage of thousands of independent chunks of knowledge. The size is primarily limited by the cost of processing larger numbers of productions. Faster machines, improved match algorithms and parallel implementations [13, 65, 66] may raise this effective limit by several orders of magnitude over the next few years.

Types of knowledge. The representation of procedural and propositional declarative knowledge is well developed in Soar. However, we don't have well worked-out approaches to many other knowledge representation problems, such as the representation of quantified, uncertain, temporal, and episodic knowledge. The critical question is whether architectural support is required to adequately represent these types of knowledge, or whether such knowledge can be adequately treated as additional objects and/or attributes. Preliminary work on quantified [43] and episodic [56] knowledge is looking promising.

Memory organization. An issue which often gets raised with respect to the organization of Soar's memory, and with respect to the organization of production memories in general, is the apparent lack of a higher-order memory organization. There are no scripts [59], frames [33], or schemas [1] to tie fragments of related memory together. Nor are there any obvious hierarchical structures which limit what sets of knowledge will be retrieved at any point in time. However, Soar's memory does have an organization, which is derived from the structure of productions, objects, and working memory (especially the context hierarchy).

What corresponds to a schema in Soar is an object, or a structured collection of objects. Such a structure can be stored entirely in the actions of a single production, or it can be stored in a piecemeal fashion across multiple productions. If multiple productions are used, the schema as a unit only comes into existence when the pieces are all retrieved contemporaneously into working memory. The advantage of this approach is that it allows novel schemas to be created from fragments of separately learned ones. The disadvantage is that it may not be possible to determine whether a set of fragments all originated from a single schema.

What corresponds to a hierarchy of retrieval contexts in Soar are the production conditions. Each combination of conditions implicitly defines a retrieval context, with a hierarchical structure induced by the subset relationship among the combinations. The contents of working memory determines which retrieval contexts are currently in force. For example, problem spaces are used extensively as retrieval contexts. Whenever there is a problem solving context that has a particular problem space selected within it, productions that test for other problem space names are not eligible to fire in that context. This approach has worked quite well for procedural knowledge, where it is clear when the knowledge is needed. We have just begun to work on appropriate organizational schemes for episodic and declarative knowledge, where it is much less clear when the knowledge should be retrieved. Our initial approach has been based on the incremental construction, via chunking, of multi-production discrimination networks [53, 56]. Though this work is too premature for a thorough evaluation in the context of Soar, the effectiveness of discrimination networks in systems like Epam [7] and Cyrus [19] bodes well.

4.3.2. Level 2: Decisions

The scope of Soar's decision level can be evaluated in terms of its speed, the knowledge brought to bear, and the language of control.

Speed. Soar currently runs at approximately 10 decisions/second on current workstations such as a Sun4/280. This is adequate for most of the types of tasks we currently implement, but is too slow for tasks requiring large amounts of search or very large knowledge bases (the number of decisions per second would get even smaller than it is now). The principal bottleneck is the speed of memory access, which is a function of two factors: the cost of processing individually expensive productions (the *expensive chunks* problem) [67], and the cost of processing a large number of productions (the *average growth effect* problem) [64]. We now have a solution to the problem of expensive chunks which can guarantee that all productions will be cheap—the match cost of a production is at worst linear in the number of conditions [68]—and are working on other potential solutions. Parallelism looks to be an effective solution to the average growth effect problem [64].

Bringing knowledge to bear. Iterated, parallel, indexed access to the contents of long-term memory has proven to be an effective means of bringing knowledge to bear on the decision process. The limited power provided by this process is offset by the ability to use subgoals when the accessible knowledge is inadequate. The issue of devising good access paths for episodic and declarative knowledge is also relevant here.

Control language. Preferences have proven to be a flexible means of specifying a partial order among contending objects. However, we cannot yet state with certainty that the set of preference types embodied in Soar is complete with respect to all the types of information which ultimately may need to be communicated to the decision procedure.

4.3.3. Level 3: Goals

The scope of Soar's goal level can be evaluated in terms of the types of goals that can be generated and the types of problem solving that can be performed in goals. Soar's subgoaling mechanism has been demonstrated to be able to create subgoals for all of the types of difficulties that can arise in problem solving in problem spaces [21]. This leaves three areas open. The first area is how top-level goals are generated; that is, how the top-level task is picked. Currently this is done by the programmer, but a general intelligence must clearly have grounds—that is, motivations—for selecting tasks on its own. The second area is how goal interactions are handled. Goal interactions show up in Soar as operator interactions, and are normally dealt with by adding explicit knowledge to avoid them, or by backtracking (with learning) when they happen. It is not yet clear the extent to which Soar could easily make use of more sophisticated approaches, such as non-linear planning [2]. The third area is the sufficiency of impasse-driven subgoaling as a means for determining when meta-level processing is needed. Two of the activities that might fall under this area are goal tests and monitoring. Both of these activities can be performed at the memory or decision level, but when they are complicated activities it may be necessary to perform them by problem solving at the goal level. Either activity can be called for explicitly by selecting a "monitor" or "goal-test" operator, which can then lead to the generation of a subgoal. However, goals for these tasks do not arise automatically, without deliberation. Should they? It is not completely clear.

The scope of the problem solving that can be performed in goals can itself be evaluated in terms of whether problem spaces cover all of the types of performance required, the limits on the ability of subgoal-based problem solving to access and modify aspects of the system, and whether parallelism is possible. These points are addressed in the next three paragraphs.

Problem space scope. Problem spaces are a very general performance model. They have been hypothesized to underlie all human, symbolic, goal-oriented behavior [37]. The breadth of tasks that have so far been represented in problem spaces over the whole field of AI attests to this generality. One way of pushing this evaluation further is to ask how well probem spaces account for the types of problem solving performed by two of the principal competing paradigms: planning [2] and case-based reasoning [20].[8] Both of these paradigms involve the creation (or retrieval) and use of a data structure that represents a sequence of actions. In planning, the data structure represents the sequence of actions that the system expects to use for the current problem. In case-based reasoning, the data structure represents the sequence of actions used on some previous, presumably related, problem. In both, the data structure is used to decide what sequence of actions to perform in the current problem. Soar straightforwardly performs procedural analogues of these two processes. When it performs a lookahead search to determine what operator to apply to a particular state, it acquires (by chunking) a set of search control productions which collectively tell it which operator should be applied to each subsequent state. This set of chunks forms a procedural plan for the current problem. When a search control chunk transfers between tasks, a form of procedural case-based reasoning is occurring.

Simple forms of declarative planning and case-based reasoning have also been demonstrated in Soar in the context of an expert system that designs floor systems [47]. When this system discovers, via lookahead search, a sequence of operators that achieves a goal, it creates a declarative structure representing the sequence and returns it as a subgoal result (plan creation). This plan can then be used interpretively to guide performance on the immediate problem (plan following). The plan can also be retrieved during later problems and used to guide the selection of operators (case-based reasoning). This research does not demonstrate the variety of operations one could conceivably use to modify a partial or complete plan, but it does demonstrate the basics.

Meta-level access. Subgoal-based problem solving has access to all of the information in working memory—including the goal stack, problem spaces, states, operators, preferences, and other facts that have been retrieved or generated—plus any of the other knowledge in long-term memory that it can access. It does not have direct access to the productions, or to any of the data structures internal to the architecture. Nonetheless, it should be able to indirectly examine the contents of any productions that were acquired by chunking, which in the long run should be just about all of them. The idea is to reconstruct the contents of the production by going down into a subgoal and retracing the problem solving that was done when the chunk was learned. In this way it should be possible to determine what knowledge the production cached. This idea has not yet been explicitly demonstrated in Soar, but research on the recovery from incorrect knowledge has used a closely related approach [23].

The effects of problem solving are limited to the addition of information to

[8] The work on Robo-Soar also reveals Soar's potential to exhibit reactive planning [11]. The current version of Soar still has problems with raw speed and with the unbounded nature of the production match (the expensive chunks problem), but it is expected that these problems will be solved in the near future.

working memory. Deletion of working memory elements is accomplished by a garbage collector provided by the architecture. Productions are added by chunking, rather than by problem solving, and are never deleted by the system. The limitation on production creation—that it only occurs via chunking—is dealt with by varying the nature of the problem solving over which chunking occurs [56]. The limitation on production deletion is dealt with by learning new productions which overcome the effects of old ones [23].

Parallelism. Two principal sources of parallelism in Soar are at the memory level: production match and execution. On each cycle of elaboration, all productions are matched in parallel to the working memory, and then all of the successful instantiations are executed in parallel. This lets tasks that can be performed at the memory level proceed in parallel, but not so for decision-level and goal-level tasks.

Another principal source of parallelism is provided by the motor systems. All motor systems behave in parallel with respect to each other, and with respect to the cognitive system. This enables one form of task-level parallelism in which non-interfering external tasks can be performed in parallel. To enable further research on task-level parallelism we have added the experimental ability to simultaneously select multiple problem space operators within a single problem solving context. Each of these operators can then proceed to execute in parallel, yielding parallel subgoals, and ultimately an entire tree of problem solving contexts in which all of the branches are being processed in parallel. We do not yet have enough experience with this capability to evaluate its scope and limits.

Despite all of these forms of parallelism embodied in Soar, most implementations of the architecture have been on serial machines, with the parallelism being simulated. However, there is an active research effort to implement Soar on parallel computers. A parallelized version of the production match has been successfully implemented on an Encore Multimax, which has a small number (2–20) of large-grained processors [66], and unsuccessfully implemented on a Connection Machine [15], which has a large number (16 K–64 K) of small-grained processors [9]. The Connection Machine implementation failed primarily because a complete parallelization of the current match algorithm can lead to exponential space requirements. Research on restricted match algorithms may fix this problem in the future. Work is also in progress towards implementing Soar on message-passing computers [65].

4.3.4. Learning

In [61] we broke down the problem of evaluating the scope of Soar's learning capabilities into four parts: when can the architecture learn; from what can the architecture learn; what can the architecture learn; and when can the architecture apply learned knowledge. These points are discussed in Section 4.1, and need not be elaborated further here.

One important additional issue is whether Soar acquires knowledge that is at the appropriate level of generalization or specialization. Chunking provides a level of generality that is determined by a combination of the representation used and the problem solving performed. Under varying circumstances, this can lead to both overgeneralization [29] and overspecialization. The acquisition of overgeneral knowledge implies that the system must be able to recover from any errors caused by its use. One solution to this problem that has been implemented in Soar involves detecting that a performance error has occurred, determining what should have been done instead, and acquiring a new chunk which leads to correct performance in the future [23]. This is accomplished without examining or modifying the overgeneral production; instead it goes back down into the subgoals for which the overgeneral productions were learned.

One way to deal with overspecialization is to patch the resulting knowledge gaps with additional knowledge. This is what Soar does constantly—if a production is overspecialized, it doesn't fire in circumstances when it should, causing an impasse to occur, and providing the opportunity to learn an additional chunk that covers the missing case (plus possibly other cases). Another way to deal with overspecialized knowledge is to work towards acquiring more general productions. A standard approach is to induce general rules from a sequence of positive and negative examples [35, 45]. This form of generalization must occur in Soar by search in problem spaces, and though there has been some initial work on doing this [48, 58], we have not yet provided Soar with a set of problem spaces that will allow it to generate appropriate generalizations from a variety of sets of examples. So, Soar cannot yet be described as a system of choice for doing induction from multiple examples. On the other hand, Soar does generalize quite naturally and effectively when abstraction occurs [69]. The learned rules reflect whatever abstraction was made during problem solving.

Learning behaviors that have not yet been attempted in Soar include the construction of a model of the environment from experimentation in it [46], scientific discovery and theory formation [31], and conceptual clustering [8].

4.3.5. Perception and motor control

The scope of Soar's perception and motor control can be evaluated in terms of both its low-level I/O mechanisms and its high-level language capabilities. Both of these capabilities are quite new, so the evaluation must be even more tentative than for the preceding components.

At the low-level, Soar can be hooked up to multiple perceptual modalities (and multiple fields within each modality) and can control multiple effectors. The critical low-level aspects of perception and motor control are currently done in a standard procedural language outside of the cognitive system. The resulting system appears to be an effective testbed for research on high-level aspects of perception and motor-control. It also appears to be an effective testbed for research on the interactions of perception and motor control with other cognitive capabilities, such as memory, problem solving, and learning. However, it does finesse many of the hard issues in perception and motor control, such as selective attention, shape determination, object identification, and temporal coordination. Work is actively in progress on selective attention [74].

At the high end of I/O capabilities is the processing of natural language. An early attempt to implement a semantic grammar parser in Soar was only a limited success [44]. It worked, but did not appear to be the right long-term solution to language understanding in Soar. More recent work on NL-Soar has focused on the incremental construction of a model of the situation by applying comprehension operators to each incoming word [32]. Comprehension operators iteratively augment and refine the situation model, setting up expectations for the part of the utterance still to be seen, and satisfying earlier expectations. As a side effect of constructing the situation model, an utterance model is constructed to represent the linguistic structure of the sentence. This approach to language understanding has been successfully applied to acquiring task-specific problem spaces for three immediate reasoning tasks: relational reasoning [18], categorical syllogisms, and sentence verification [3]. It has also been used to process the input for these tasks as they are performed. Though NL-Soar is still far from providing a general linguistic capability, the approach has proven promising.

5. Conclusion

In this article we have taken a step towards providing an analysis of the Soar architecture as a basis for general intelligence. In order to increase understanding of the structure of the architecture we have provided a theoretical framework within which the architecture can be described, a discussion of methodological assumptions underlying the project and the system, and an illustrative example of its performance on a multi-column subtraction task. In order to facilitate comparisons between the capabilities of the current version of Soar and the capabilities required to achieve its ultimate goal as an architecture for general intelligence, we have described the natural tasks for the architecture, the sources of its power, and its scope and limits. If this article has succeeded, it should be clear that progress has been made, but that more work is still required. This applies equally to the tasks of developing Soar and analyzing it.

Acknowledgement

This research was sponsored by the Defense Advanced Research Projects Agency (DOD) under contract N00039-86-C-0133 and by the Sloan Foundation. Computer facilities were partially provided by NIH grant RR-00785 to Sumex-Aim. The views and conclusions contained in this document are those of the authors and should not be interpreted as representing the official policies, either expressed or implied, of the Defense Advanced Research Projects Agency, the US Government, the Sloan Foundation, or the National Institutes of Health.

We would like to thank Beth Adelson, David Kirsh, and David McAllester for their helpful comments on an earlier draft of this article.

References

[1] F.C. Bartlett, *Remembering: A Study in Experimental and Social Psychology* (Cambridge University Press, Cambridge, England, 1932).

[2] D. Chapman, Planning for conjunctive goals, *Artif. Intell.* **32** (1987) 333–377.

[3] H.H. Clark and W.G. Chase, On the process of comparing sentences against pictures, *Cogn. Psychol.* **3** (1972) 472–517.

[4] G. DeJong and R.J. Mooney, Explanation-based learning: an alternative view, *Mach. Learn.* **1** (1986) 145–176.

[5] T.G. Dietterich, Learning at the knowledge level, *Mach. Learn.* **1** (1986) 287–315.

[6] O. Etzioni and T.M. Mitchell, A comparative analysis of chunking and decision analytic control, in: *Proceedings AAAI Spring Symposium on Limited Rationality and AI*, Stanford, CA (1989).

[7] E.A. Feigenbaum and H.A. Simon, Epam-like models of recognition and learning, *Cogn. Sci.* **8** (1984) 305–336.

[8] D.H. Fisher and P. Langley, Approaches to conceptual clustering, in: *Proceedings IJCAI-85*, Los Angeles, CA (1985) 691–697.

[9] R. Flynn, Placing Soar on the connection machine, Prepared for and distributed at the AAAI Mini-Symposium "How Can Slow Components Think So Fast" (1988).

[10] J.A. Fodor, *The Modularity of Mind* (Bradford Books/MIT Press, Cambridge, MA, 1983).

[11] M.P. Georgeff and A.L. Lansky, Reactive reasoning and planning, in: *Proceedings AAAI-87*, Seattle, WA (1987) 677–682.

[12] A. Golding, P.S. Rosenbloom and J.E. Laird, Learning general search control from outside guidance, in: *Proceedings IJCAI-87*, Milan, Italy (1987).

[13] A. Gupta and M. Tambe, Suitability of message passing computers for implementing production systems, in: *Proceedings AAAI-88*, St. Paul, MN (1988) 687–692.

[14] C. Hewitt and D. Kirsh, Personal communication (1987).

[15] W.D. Hillis, *The Connection Machine* (MIT Press, Cambridge, MA, 1985).

[16] W. Hsu, M. Prietula and D. Steier, Merl-Soar: applying Soar to scheduling, in: *Proceedings Workshop on Artificial Intelligence Simulation, AAAI-88*, St. Paul, MN (1988) 81–84.

[17] T.R. Johnson, J.W. Smith Jr and B. Chandrasekaran, Generic Tasks and Soar, in: *Working Notes AAAI Spring Symposium on Knowledge System Development Tools and Languages*, Stanford, CA (1989) 25–28.

[18] P.N. Johnson-Laird, Reasoning by rule or model? in: *Proceedings 10th Annual Conference of the Cognitive Science Society*, Montreal, Que. (1988) 765–771.

[19] J.L. Kolodner, Maintaining order in a dynamic long-term memory, *Cogn. Sci.* **7** (1983) 243–280.

[20] J.L. Kolodner, ed., *Proceedings DARPA Workshop on Case-Based Reasoning*, Clearwater Beach, FL (1988).
[21] J.E. Laird, Universal subgoaling, Ph.D. thesis, Carnegie-Mellon University, Pittsburgh, PA (1983); also in: J.E. Laird, P.S. Rosenbloom and A. Newell, *Universal Subgoaling and Chunking: The Automatic Generation and Learning of Goal Hierarchies* (Kluwer, Hingham, MA, 1986).
[22] J.E. Laird, Soar user's manual (version 4), Tech. Rept. ISL-15, Xerox Palo Alto Research Center, Palo Alto, CA (1986).
[23] J.E. Laird, Recovery from incorrect knowledge in Soar, in: *Proceedings AAAI-88*, St. Paul, MN (1988) 618–623.
[24] J.E. Laird and K.A. McMahon, Destructive state modification in Soar, Draft V, Department of EECS, University of Michigan, Ann Arbor, MI (1989).
[25] J.E. Laird and A. Newell, A universal weak method, Tech. Rept. 83-141, Department of Computer Science, Carnegie-Mellon University, Pittsburgh, PA (1983).
[26] J.E. Laird, A. Newell and P.S. Rosenbloom, SOAR: an architecture for general intelligence, *Artif. Intell.* **33** (1987) 1–64.
[27] J.E. Laird, P.S. Rosenbloom and A. Newell, Towards chunking as a general learning mechanism, in: *Proceedings AAAI-84*, Austin, TX (1984) 188–192.
[28] J.E. Laird, P.S. Rosenbloom and A. Newell, Chunking in Soar: the anatomy of a general learning mechanism, *Mach. Learn.* **1** (1986) 11–46.
[29] J.E. Laird, P.S. Rosenbloom and A. Newell, Overgeneralization during knowledge compilation in Soar, in: T.G. Dietterich, ed., *Proceedings Workshop on Knowledge Compilation*, Otter Crest, OR (1986).
[30] J.E. Laird, E.S. Yager, C.M. Tuck and M. Hucka, Learning in tele-autonomous systems using Soar, in: *Proceedings NASA Conference on Space Telerobotics*, Pasadena, CA (1989).
[31] P. Langley, H.A. Simon, G.L. Bradshaw and J.M. Zytkow, *Scientific Discovery: Computational Explorations of the Creative Processes* (MIT Press, Cambridge, MA, 1987).
[32] R.L. Lewis, A. Newell and T.A. Polk, Toward a Soar theory of taking instructions for immediate reasoning tasks, in: *Proceedings 11th Annual Conference of the Cognitive Science Society*, Ann Arbor, MI (1989).
[33] M. Minsky, A framework for the representation of knowledge, in: P. Winston, ed., *The Psychology of Computer Vision* (McGraw-Hill, New York, 1975).
[34] M. Minsky, *The Society of Mind* (Simon and Schuster, New York, 1986).
[35] T.M. Mitchell, Generalization as search, *Artif. Intell.* **18** (1982) 203–226.
[36] T.M. Mitchell, R.M. Keller and S.T. Kedar-Cabelli, Explanation-based generalization: a unifying view, *Mach. Learn.* **1** (1986) 47–80.
[37] A. Newell, Reasoning, problem solving and decision processes: the problem space as a fundamental category, in: R. Nickerson, ed., *Attention and performance* **8** (Erlbaum, Hillsdale, NJ, 1980).
[38] A. Newell, *Unified Theories of Cognition* (Harvard University Press, Cambridge, MA, 1990).
[39] A. Newell and P.S. Rosenbloom, Mechanisms of skill acquisition and the law of practice, in: J.R. Anderson, ed., *Cognitive Skills and Their Acquisition* (Erlbaum, Hillsdale, NJ, 1981) 1–55.
[40] A. Newell, P.S. Rosenbloom and J.E. Laird, Symbolic architectures for cognition, in: M.I. Posner, ed., *Foundations of Cognitive Science* (Bradford Books/MIT Press, Cambridge, MA, 1989).
[41] A. Newell and H.A. Simon, *Human Problem Solving* (Prentice-Hall, Englewood Cliffs, NJ, 1972).
[42] N.J. Nilsson, *Principles of Artificial Intelligence* (Tioga, Palo Alto, CA, 1980).
[43] T.A. Polk and A. Newell, Modeling human syllogistic reasoning in Soar, in: *Proceedings 10th Annual Conference of the Cognitive Science Society*, Montreal, Que. (1988) 181–187.
[44] L. Powell, Parsing the picnic problem with a Soar3 implementation of Dypar-1, Department of Computer Science, Carnegie-Mellon University, Pittsburgh, PA (1984).
[45] J.R. Quinlan, Induction of decision trees, *Mach. Learn.* **1** (1986) 81–106.
[46] S. Rajamoney, G.F. DeJong, and B. Faltings, Towards a model of conceptual knowledge

acquisition through directed experimentation, in: *Proceedings IJCAI-85*, Los Angeles, CA (1985) 688–690.

[47] Y. Reich, Learning plans as a weak method for design, Department of Civil Engineering, Carnegie-Mellon University, Pittsburgh, PA (1988).

[48] P.S. Rosenbloom, Beyond generalization as search: towards a unified framework for the acquisition of new knowledge, in: G.F. DeJong, ed., *Proceedings AAAI Symposium on Explanation-Based Learning*, Stanford, CA (1988) 17–21.

[49] P.S. Rosenbloom, A symbolic goal-oriented perspective on connectionism and Soar, in: R. Pfeifer, Z. Schreter, F. Fogelman-Soulie and L. Steels, eds., *Connectionism in Perspective* (Elsevier, Amsterdam, 1989).

[50] P.S. Rosenboom and J.E. Laird., Mapping explanation-based generalization onto Soar, in: *Proceedings AAAI-86*, Philadelphia, PA (1986) 561–567.

[51] P.S. Rosenbloom, J.E. Laird, J. McDermott, A. Newell and E. Orciuch, R1-Soar: an experiment in knowledge-intensive programming in a problem-solving architecture, *IEEE Trans. Pattern Anal. Mach. Intell.* **7** (1985) 561–569.

[52] P.S. Rosenbloom, J.E. Laird and A. Newell, Knowledge level leaning in Soar, in: *Proceedings AAAI-87*, Seattle, WA (1987) 499–504.

[53] P.S. Rosenbloom, J.E. Laird and A. Newell, The chunking of skill and knowledge, in: B.A.G. Elsendoorn and H. Bouma, eds., *Working Models of Human Perception* (Academic Press, London, 1988) 391–410.

[54] P.S. Rosenbloom, J.E. Laird and A. Newell, Meta-levels in Soar, in: P. Maes and D. Nardi, eds., *Meta-Level Architectures and Reflection* (North-Holland, Amsterdam, 1988) 227–240.

[55] P.S. Rosenbloom and A. Newell, The chunking of goal hierarchies: a generalized model of practice, in: R.S. Michalski, J.G. Carbonnell and T.M. Mitchell, eds., *Machine Learning: An Artificial Intelligence Approach* **2** (Morgan Kaufmann, Los Altos, CA, 1986) 247–288.

[56] P.S. Rosenbloom, A. Newell and J.E. Laird, Towards the knowledge level in Soar: the role of the architecture in the use of knowledge, in: K. VanLehn, ed., *Architectures for Intelligence* (Erlbaum, Hillsdale, NJ, 1990).

[57] E.D. Sacerdoti, Planning in a hierarchy of abstraction spaces, *Artif. Intell.* **5** (1974) 115–135.

[58] R.H. Saul, A Soar2 implementation of version-space inductive learning, Department of Computer Science, Carnegie-Mellon University, Pittsburgh, PA (1984).

[59] R. Schank and R. Ableson, *Scripts, Plans, Goals and Understanding* (Erlbaum, Hillsdale, NJ, 1977).

[60] D. Steier, Cypress-Soar: a case study in search and learning in algorithm design, in: *Proceedings IJCAI-87*, Milan, Italy (1987) 327–330.

[61] D.M. Steier, J.E. Laird, A. Newell, P.S. Rosenbloom, R. Flynn, A Golding, T.A. Polk, O.G. Shivers, A. Unruh and G.R. Yost, Varieties of learning in Soar: 1987, in: P. Langley, ed., *Proceedings Fourth International Workshop on Machine Learning*, Irvine, CA (1987) 300–311.

[62] D.M. Steier and A. Newell, Integrating multiple sources of knowledge in Designer-Soar: an automatic algorithm designer, in: *Proceedings AAAI-88*, St. Paul, MN (1988) 8–13.

[63] K.R. Swedlow and D.M. Steier, Soar 5.0 user's manual, School of Computer Science, Carnegie Mellon University, Pittsburgh, PA (1989).

[64] M. Tambe, Speculations on the computational effects of chunking, Department of Computer Science, Carnegie Mellon University, Pittsburgh, PA (1988).

[65] M. Tambe, A. Acharya and A. Gupta, Implementation of production systems on message passing computers: Simulation results and analysis, Tech. Rept. CMU-CS-89-129, School of Computer Science, Carnegie Mellon University, Pittsburgh, PA (1989).

[66] M. Tambe, D. Kalp, A. Gupta, C.L. Forgy, B. Milnes and A. Newell, Soar/PSM-E: Investigating match parallelism in a learning production system, in: *Proceedings ACM/SIGPLAN Symposium on Parallel Programming: Experience with Applications, Languages, and Systems* (1988) 146–161.

[67] M. Tambe and A. Newell, Some chunks are expensive, in: J. Laird, ed., *Proceedings Fifth International Conference on Machine Learning* Ann Arbor, MI (1988) 451–458.

[68] M. Tambe and P.S. Rosenbloom, Eliminating expensive chunks by restricting expressiveness, in: *Proceedings IJCAI-89*, Detroit, MI (1989).

[69] A. Unruh and P.S. Rosenbloom, Abstraction in problem solving and learning, in: *Proceedings IJCAI-89*, Detroit, MI (1989).

[70] A. Unruh, P.S. Rosenbloom and J.E. Laird, Dynamic abstraction problem solving in Soar, in: *Proceedings Third Annual Aerospace Applications of Artificial Intelligence Conference*, Dayton, OH (1987) 245–256.

[71] K. VanLehn, *Mind Bugs: The Origins of Procedural Misconceptions* (MIT Press, Cambridge, MA, 1990).

[72] K. VanLehn and W. Ball, Non-LIFO execution of cognitive procedures, *Cogn. Sci.* **13** (1989) 415–465.

[73] R. Washington and P.S. Rosenbloom, Applying problem solving and learning to diagnosis, Department of Computer Science, Stanford University, CA (1988).

[74] M. Wiesmeyer, Personal communication (1988).

[75] M. Wiesmeyer, Soar I/O reference manual, version 2, Department of EECS, University of Michigan, Ann Arbor, MI (1988).

[76] M. Wiesmeyer, New and improved Soar IO, Department of EECS, University of Michigan, Ann Arbor, MI (1989).

[77] G.R. Yost and A. Newell, A problem space approach to expert system specification, in: *Proceedings IJCAI-89*, Detroit, MI (1989).

CHAPTER 41

Towards the Knowledge Level in Soar: The Role of the Architecture in the Use of Knowledge

P. S. Rosenbloom, USC–ISI, A. Newell, Carnegie Mellon University, and J. E. Laird, University of Michigan

Soar has been described as an architecture for a system that is to be capable of general intelligence (Laird, Newell, & Rosenbloom, 1987). One way to specify what this might mean is to enumerate the set of capabilities that, based on the field's cumulative experience, appear to be required for general intelligence: to be able to work on the full range of tasks, to be able to use the full range of problem-solving methods and varieties of knowledge, to be able to interact with the outside world in real time, and to learn about the world and the system's own performance. Progress can then be evaluated by determining the degree to which the architecture supports such capabilities. For Soar, such an evaluation reveals significant progress in the areas of tasks (Laird, Newell, & Rosenbloom, 1987), problem-solving methods (Laird & Newell, 1983, Laird, 1983) and learning (Steier et al., 1987); some progress in the area of outside interaction (Laird, Hucka, Yager & Tuck, in press); and an unclear situation in the area of knowledge.

The problem with such an approach to specifying (and evaluating progress towards) general intelligence is the lack of theoretical justifications for the set of capabilities included. Without such justifications it is unclear, for example, whether some new form of learning that is developed is necessary for general intelligence, or just an interesting oddity. In addition, whole categories of critical capabilities may be unknowingly omitted. What is needed is a more fundamental definition of general intelligence from which the required capabilities can be derived (or at least justified).

One idea that shows promise towards providing such a definition is the *knowledge level* (Newell, 1982). The idea of the knowledge level is based on earlier developments in the area of computer systems levels (Bell & Newell, 1971). A computer systems level consists of a *medium* that is processed, *components* that provide primitive processing, *laws of composition* that permit components to be assembled into *systems,* and *laws of behavior* that determine how system behavior depends on the component behavior and the structure of the system. Existing levels (and their media) include the device level (electrons), the circuit level (current), the logic level (bits), the register-transfer level (bit-vectors), and the program (or symbol) level (symbols, expressions). In terms of these levels, an *architecture* is a register-transfer level system that defines a symbol level.

The knowledge level is a distinct computer systems level that lies immediately above the symbol level. The medium processed at the knowledge level is knowledge. An agent—a system at the knowledge level—consists of a physical body that can interact with an environment, knowledge, and a set of goals. The law of behavior is the *Principle of Rationality:* "If an agent has knowledge that one of its actions will lead to one of its goals, then the agent will select that action" (Newell, 1982, p. 102). Once knowledge is acquired, it is available for all future goals. There are no capacity limitations on the amount of knowledge that can be available or on the agent's ability to bring it to bear in the selection of actions that achieve its goals. An essential feature of the knowledge level is that the agent's behavior is determined by the content of its knowledge, not by any aspects of its internal structure. It abstracts away from the processing and representation of the lower levels. This lack of significant internal structure implies that there are no laws of composition at the knowledge level.

The knowledge level provides a straightforward, though not uncontroversial, definition for intelligence. A system is intelligent to the degree that it approximates a knowledge-level system (Newell, In press). Perfect intelligence requires a complete lack of internal resource limitations. However, this ideal is unreachable in physically realizable systems that are required to make decisions using bounded resources over a sufficiently wide range of goals using large bodies of knowledge. Such systems can at best only approximate a knowledge-level system, and thus achieve some level of intelligence that is less than perfect. The ideal of perfect intelligence also does not entail the generality of that intelligence. A system's behavior is characterized both by its intelligence and by its generality. Generality for a knowledge-level system is the range of interactions that it can have with the environment, the range of goals it can have, and the range of knowledge that it can acquire and use. Intelligence is how well the system applies its knowledge to the tasks within its scope.

Assuming this knowledge-level definition of general intelligence, the key question for the architecture is how it supports the knowledge level for a sufficiently broad set of goals and knowledge. How does it approximate rationality with bounded resources? How does it support the acquisition and use of knowledge? A complete answer to the key question requires answering a number of such subquestions. In (Newell, in press), a beginning was made at answering the first subquestion. In this chapter we provide the beginnings of an answer to the second subquestion. We examine how the Soar architecture supports and constrains the representation, storage, retrieval, use and acquisition of three pervasive forms of knowledge.

The first form of knowledge to be examined is *procedural* knowledge. Procedural knowledge is knowledge about the agent's actions. It includes knowledge about which actions can be performed, which actions should be performed when (control knowledge), and how actions are performed. The second form of knowledge to be examined is *episodic* knowledge. Episodic knowledge is knowledge about what objects, actions, and action sequences have occurred in the agent's past. It allows answering such questions as "Did this object, action, or action sequence occur (in this context)?" and "What objects, actions, or action sequences occurred (in this context)?" The third and final form of knowledge to be examined is *declarative knowledge*. Declarative knowledge is knowledge about what is true in the world. These final two forms of knowledge have often been referred to collectively as propositional knowledge, with the term "semantic knowledge" used in place of declarative knowledge (Tulving, 1983).

The plan for this chapter is to start with a brief conventional description of the Soar architecture, followed by its redescription in terms of the direct support it provides for knowledge. The core of the chapter then consists of in-depth analyses of how procedural, episodic, and declarative knowledge are represented, stored, retrieved, used, and acquired in Soar. Special emphasis is placed on how the architecture supports and constrains these abilities. The chapter is concluded with a summary of key points and important directions for future work.

SOAR[1]

Research on Soar to date has focused on the development (and application) of an architecture for intelligence that is based on formulating all symbolic goal–oriented behavior as search in problem spaces. The problem space determines the set of states and operators that can be used during the processing to attain a goal. The states represent situations. There is an initial state, representing the initial situation, and a set of desired states that represent the goal. An operator, when applied to a state in the problem space, yields another state in the problem space. The goal is achieved when a desired state is reached as the result of a sequence of operator applications starting from the initial state. Each goal defines a problem-solving context ("context" for short) that contains, in addition to a goal, roles for a problem space, a state, and an operator.

[1]This section describes Soar 4.5 (Laird et al., 1989), which is the basis for the analyses in this chapter.

Problem solving for a goal is driven by decisions that result in the selection of problem spaces, states, and operators for the appropriate roles in the context. Decisions are made by the retrieval and integration of preferences—special architecturally interpretable elements that describe the acceptability, desirability, and necessity of selecting particular problem spaces, states, and operators. The context in which a preference is applicable is specified by its goal, problem-space, state, and operator attributes. When present, they specify the objects that must already be selected in the context for the preference to be valid. For example, the following is a desirability preference stating that operator *o1* is at least as good as any other operator—that is, it is *best*—for state *s1*, problem space *p1*, and goal *g1*.

(preference *o1* ^role operator ^value best
 ^goal *g1* ^problem-space *p1* ^state *s1*)

There are two types of acceptability preferences—acceptable and reject—to rule an operator into and out of consideration for selection. A reject preference overrides an acceptable preference. There are five types of desirability preferences—worst, worse, indifferent, better, and best—to determine the relative desirability of considered objects. Worst and best are unary preferences. Worse and better are binary preferences. Indifferent can be binary or unary, in which case the object is indifferent to all other competing objects with indifferent preferences. There are two types of necessity preferences—require and prohibit—for asserting that an object must or must not be selected for a goal to be achieved. Details on the semantics of preferences can be found in Laird et al., 1987.

All long-term knowledge is stored in a recognition-based memory—a production system. Each production is a cued-retrieval unit that retrieves the contents of its actions when the pattern in its conditions is successfully matched. By sharing variables between conditions and actions, productions can retrieve information that is a function of what was matched. By having variables in actions that are not in conditions, new objects can be generated/retrieved.

Transient process state is contained in a working memory. This includes information retrieved from long-term memory, results of decisions made by the architecture, information currently perceived from the external environment, and motor commands. It should be clear that this process state is much more than just a single state in a problem space. The process state is the entire transient state of the system, which includes as components, states in problem spaces, and in fact whole problem-solving contexts. It provides the cues for retrieving additional information from long-term memory.

Structurally, working memory consists of a set of objects and preferences about objects. Each object in working memory has a class name, a unique identifier, and a set of attributes with associated values, which may be constants or identifiers (allowing a graph structure of objects). For example, a particular box could be represented by the following object.

(box *b1* ^name box1 ^height 10 ^width 4 ^depth 2)

The class is "box," the identifier is "*b1,*" the name of the box is "box1," and the box has a height of 10 a width of 4 and a depth of 2.

For each problem-solving decision, the contents of working memory is elaborated by parallel access of long-term memory to exhaustion. All productions that match the current working memory are fired in parallel, and this repeats until no productions match. This elaboration process retrieves into working memory new objects, new information about existing objects, and new preferences. When quiescence is reached—that is, when no more productions can fire—an architectural decision procedure interprets the preferences in working memory according to their fixed semantics. If the preferences uniquely specify an object to be selected for a role in a context, such as selecting the current operator for a state, then a decision can be made, and the specified object becomes the current value of the role. The whole process, an elaboration phase followed by a decision, then repeats.

If the decision procedure is ever unable to make a selection—because the preferences in working memory are either incomplete or inconsistent—an *impasse* occurs in problem solving because the system does not know how to proceed. When an impasse occurs, a subgoal with an associated problem-solving context is automatically generated for the task of resolving the impasse. The impasses, and thus their subgoals, vary from problems of selection (of problem spaces, states, and operators) to problems of generation (e.g., operator application). Given a subgoal, Soar can bring its full problem-solving capability and knowledge to bear on resolving the impasse that caused the subgoal. For example, if an operator-tie impasse occurs because multiple operators are competing for selection with insufficiently distinguishing preferences, then a subgoal is created in which Soar can (among other things) execute operators to evaluate the competing alternatives. Productions can then create preferences based on these evaluations, allowing the decision to be made.

When impasses occur within impasses—if, for example, there is insufficient knowledge about how to evaluate a competing alternative—then subgoals occur within subgoals, and a goal hierarchy results (which therefore defines a hierarchy of contexts). The top problem space consists of task operators; such as, to recognize an item. The subgoals are generated as the result of impasses in problem solving. A subgoal terminates when the impasse is resolved.

Soar learns by acquiring new productions that summarize the processing that leads to the results of subgoals, a process called *chunking*. The actions of the new productions are based on the results of the subgoal. The conditions are based on those working memory elements in supergoals that were relevant to the determination of the results. Relevance is determined by using the traces of the productions that fired during the subgoal. Starting from the production trace that generated the subgoal's result, those production traces that generated the working-memory elements in the conditions of the trace are found, and then the traces that generated their condition elements are found, and so on until elements are reached that are in supergoals. Productions that only generate desirability preferences do not participate in this backtracing process—desirability preferences only affect the efficiency with which a goal is achieved, and not the correctness of the goal's results.

Soar's perceptual–motor behavior is driven by a set of asynchronous modules, and mediated through the state in the top context. Each perceptual and motor modality (module) has its own state attribute to which perceptual information is added and/or motor commands are taken. New sensory information arrives in working memory whenever it is available, and motor commands are sent to the appropriate motor modules as soon as they are added to working memory. Sensory information can be retained by explicitly attaching it to other existing structures. Otherwise, it will be displaced when new information arrives.

Figure 4.1 summarizes the major functional and structural components of the Soar architecture—its memories, basic computational cycle, learning, and interfaces.

- Purpose of Research: Architecture for general intelligence.
- Organizing Framework: Goals and problem spaces.
- Long-term Memory: Recognition–based productions.
- Short-term Memory: Objects and attributes.
- Basic Computation Cycle: Elaboration (access LTM until quiescence) and decision.
- Decisions: Preference–based for problem spaces, states, and operators.
- Subgoal Creation: Impasses in decision scheme.
- Learning: Chunking—summarize processing of subgoal as a production.
- Interface to External Environment: Asynchronous through top state.

FIG. 4.1. Summary of Soar.

ARCHITECTURAL SUPPORT FOR KNOWLEDGE

The conventional description of Soar provided in the previous section does not always make clear the ways in which the architecture directly supports knowledge. That is the task for this section—to make explicit the ways the architecture directly supports knowledge in general, and procedural, episodic, and declarative knowledge in particular. The question of indirect architectural support is left to the later sections, which examine each of these three types of knowledge in detail.

General support is provided by productions, the elaboration phase, impasses, subgoals, problem space search, working memory, and chunking. Productions provide for the explicit storage of knowledge. The knowledge is stored in the actions of productions, while the conditions act as access paths to the knowledge. The process of retrieving knowledge by the matching and firing of a production comprises a search of the system's explicitly stored long-term knowledge. It is thus termed *knowledge search* (or *k–search*). Knowledge retrievable by k-search—that is, by the firing of a production—is termed *k–retrievable knowledge*. K-search is efficient, but relatively limited in its capabilities.

Knowledge that is not retrievable by the firing of a single production may still be retrievable by the firing of multiple productions in a single elaboration phase. This happens when information retrieved early in an elaboration phase provides the cues that allow the desired information to be retrieved by a later production firing. It also happens when the desired information is distributed among the actions of multiple productions, which retrieve it by firing jointly within the same elaboration phase. This is termed *k*–search,* and knowledge retrievable through elaboration is termed *k*–retrievable knowledge.* k*–search is exhaustive but efficient, allowing the system to use a significant body of knowledge in its decisions even under relatively stringent time constraints.

The creation of impasses provides a means for determining when the k*–retrievable knowledge is an inadequate basis for making a decision. The decision procedure can detect incompleteness and inconsistency in the set of k*–retrievable preferences, but cannot directly detect incorrect or suboptimal knowledge.

Subgoals provide contexts in which knowledge that is not k*-retrievable can be retrieved by *problem–space search* (or *ps-search*). Knowledge that is retrievable by ps–search is termed *ps–retrievable knowledge*. Because problem-space search (ps–search) is always eventually grounded in production firings (k*–search), there is a fairly direct relationship between ps–retrievable knowledge and k*-retrievable knowledge.[2] Knowledge that is ps–retrievable in the current context is constructed from pieces of knowledge which are independently k*–retrievable in other contexts, but not jointly k*–retrievable in the current context. Ps–search allows for the consideration of alternatives and the deliberate construction of information, whereas k*–search provides for only the monotonic accumulation of knowledge. Problem–space search is selective and slow, but can with sufficient resources retrieve any knowledge in the system's knowledge level.

---

[2]Here, and in the remainder of this chapter the terms k*-search and k*-retrievable knowledge will be assumed to subsume the terms k-search and k-retrievable knowledge, respectively, except where the distinction is particularly crucial.

Working memory provides a locus where retrieved knowledge can be examined and used. It also provides a locus where new knowledge can reside temporarily before it is stored into long-term memory by chunking. Chunking provides a means of creating new productions, thus directly augmenting the system's store of k*–retrievable knowledge, and indirectly augmenting its store of ps–retrievable knowledge. Chunking is the mechanism for converting ps–search to k*-search.

Procedural knowledge is specifically supported by the architecture in four ways. First, production execution is a primitive form of controlled action. Executing a production performs a form of retrieval in which the retrieved information is adapted to the current situation before being retrieved. The nature of the adaptation is determined by the production's variables. Variables that are shared between conditions and actions result in the retrieved information being instantiated to be about existing objects. Variables that exist only in actions result in the creation of new objects. Control is exerted on production execution by the match. Production conditions specify situations that must hold in working memory in order for the retrieval actions to be executed (Newell, Rosenbloom, & Laird, 1989). Unlike traditional production systems, there is no additional conflict resolution process that participates in the control of production execution.

Second, the selection of an object for a context slot is also a primitive form of controlled action. Selections are actions performed by the architecture that change the focus of problem solving in working memory. For example, the selection of a new operator changes what the system is attempting to accomplish. Preferences represent architecturally interpretable control information for the selection process.

Third, the concept of a problem-solving operator is partially supported by the architecture. The architecture provides an operator role in contexts and the decision procedure that enables the selection of operators for operator roles. It also provides for the generation of impasses when there is insufficient knowledge about how to select or execute an operator. An important form of support not provided is an architecturally interpretable operator language. Instead, operator execution always eventually grounds out in memory retrieval (and motor behavior). How this happens may be quite complicated, involving numerous subgoals, or the interpretation by productions—that is, by further memory retrieval—of an arbitrary operator language.

Fourth, the architecture provides motor commands that perform primitive actions in the external environment. There is not yet a complete and standard set of motor commands in Soar. Instead, what exists is a text-output module, providing basic text-output commands, and a flexible mechanism for adding new modules to, for example, control robot arms (Laird et al., in press) and mobile robots. Selection of motor commands is not provided directly by the architecture. It is under the control of the knowledge (productions) which retrieve the motor commands into working memory, usually under the aegis of operator execution.

Episodic knowledge is specifically supported by the chunking and execution of new productions. Chunking acquires new productions based on problem-solving episodes. The actions of a chunk correspond to information that was generated as the result of an episode. When the chunk executes it retrieves information that is similar to that generated during the episode—though, as mentioned above, the retrieved information is generally adapted to the current situation rather than being a verbatim record of the earlier episode's results. The conditions of the chunk ensure that the adapted results are only retrieved in similar situations. Not provided by the architecture is a mechanism that creates verbatim records of the system's experiences for later examination.

Declarative knowledge is specifically supported by the working and production memories. Working memory is a transient memory of objects, with associated attributes and values. These objects are declarative in that they are examinable (by productions), but they need not have a fixed semantics. Production memory provides for long-term storage of declarative structures—in the actions of productions—which can be retrieved (and adapted) by production execution.

PROCEDURAL KNOWLEDGE

As mentioned in the introduction, procedural knowledge is knowledge about the agent's actions, which includes knowledge about which actions can be performed, which actions should be performed when (control knowledge), and how actions are performed. Procedural knowledge is already one of the most well developed and understood parts of Soar. Soar was, after all, originally developed as a general problem-solving architecture. Thus this section primarily serves as a review, but it also serves to develop a number of the basic concepts used in the subsequent sections on episodic and declarative knowledge. The discussion is divided into subsections covering the three subdomains mentioned above: performable actions, action control, and action performance. For each of these subdomains we discuss how the knowledge is represented, stored, retrieved, used, and acquired. This same suborganization will be followed in later sections on episodic and declarative knowledge.

Performable Actions

Performable actions are represented as operators, along with acceptable preferences that can cause the operators to be considered in some set of situations. Each operator is represented in working memory as an object—a declarative structure—rather than a production. For example, an operator in the Eight Puzzle that slides a tile from one cell on the board to an adjacent one could be represented as (operator *o1* ^name slide). When augmented with parameters specifying the source and destination cells for the tile, the operator can be represented as (operator *o1* ^name slide ^source *c1* ^destination *c2*), where the symbols *c1* and *c2* are the identifiers of the two cells.

The declarative structure for operators, and their acceptable preferences, are stored in the actions of productions. The entire object can be stored in the actions of a single production (k–retrievable); it can be distributed across the actions of a group of productions that all fire within a single decision cycle (k*–retrievable); or it can be distributed across multiple productions that fire in a subgoal that constructs the operator, bit by bit (ps–retrievable).

Problem spaces are a major source of context for operator retrieval. The production in which the above Eight Puzzle operator is stored will have a condition which tests that the Eight Puzzle problem space is the one currently selected in a context before retrieving the operator for the context. It is also often useful to utilize the operator's preconditions as a source of retrieval context. If this is done, then the operator is only retrieved in situations for which it is applicable. An alternative is to retrieve the operator according to means–ends analysis, that is, when the operator will reduce the difference between the current state and the desired state. With means-ends analysis, an operator may be retrieved even when its preconditions are not satisfied by the current state.

Operators by themselves do nothing. The architecture does not understand the language(s) in which operators are written, and therefore does not know how, based just on the operators themselves, to either select among them or to perform them. The best the architecture can do without additional knowledge is to perform various default actions based on its understanding of their acceptable preferences. It can select an operator if it is the only candidate available, and generate an impasse if there is more than one operator, or if the selected one cannot be executed.

Operators, and their acceptable preferences, are cues for retrieving a variety of additional knowledge. The operator structure can trigger knowledge about how to select and perform operators. The acceptable preferences can trigger knowledge in both prospective and retrospective fashions. Prospectively, acceptable preferences for operators determine what operators are being considered for the next selection. Retrospectively, acceptable preferences for operators act as episodic knowledge about what operators were considered for what states.

Operators, and their acceptable preferences, are acquired by the chunking of problem-solving episodes that generate them as results. Chunking does not by itself generate new operators, but it can convert ps–retrievable operators into k*–retrievable ones, as well as store away in production memory new operators that are generated. The conversion of operator knowledge from ps–retrievable to k*–retrievable is the obvious caching effect produced by chunking. Storage of newly generated operators factors into two cases. If the new operators are generated internally, then they must have already been ps–retrievable—that is, retrievable by problem space search—thus reducing this case to the previous caching situation. If the new operators are based on external information, chunking can turn unretrievable operators into k*–retrievable operators. This is a more subtle consequence of chunking that is worth looking at in some detail.

Yost and Newell (1988) demonstrated how new operators could be acquired from external information, in the context of a system called TAQ (Yost, 1987) that acquires new tasks (i.e., problem spaces) from external descriptions. In more recent work, this approach has been extended to take simple English instructions for a range of immediate-reasoning tasks, such as categorical syllogisms and sentence verification (Lewis, Newell, & Polk, 1989). Figure 4.2 shows the two basic steps. The first step in task acquisition is to comprehend an externally provided description of the task to be acquired. This description can conceptually take a variety of forms—versions of TAQ have accepted descriptions in simple English sentences and in a formal problem space notation. The outcome of the comprehension process is the presence in working memory of a declarative description of a problem space for the task. The second step is to solve the problem using the declarative description interpretively. That is, at each point in task performance, if the next required activity—such as the generation of an operator—is not directly performable by k*–search, then a subgoal occurs. Within the subgoal, the declarative task description is examined and interpreted by a set of pre-existing problem spaces that search through the declarative task description for information about what to do in the current situation.

The chunks acquired for these interpretation subgoals directly implement the required activity. Chunking the comprehension process converts unretrievable operators into ps-retrievable operators—using memorization techniques described later—and chunking of the interpretation process makes the ps–retrievable knowledge k*–retrievable.

Action Control

Control knowledge—that is, knowledge about how to select among performable actions—is represented to the architecture by operator preferences. The three types of preferences described previously in this chapter—acceptability, desir-

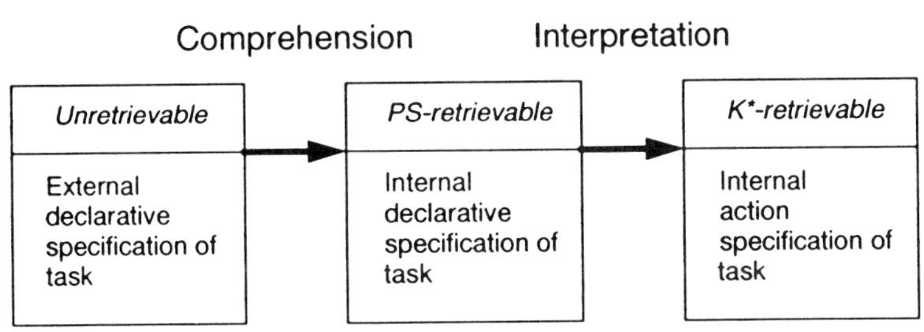

FIG. 4.2. The two stages of acquiring operator knowledge.

ability, and necessity—are used to represent three qualitatively different types of control knowledge. Acceptability preferences represent knowledge about whether an operator is to be considered for execution. Unconsidered operators have no effect on the decision procedure; they cannot be selected, nor can they cause an impasse to occur. Desirability preferences represent heuristic information that can be brought to bear in determining what operator is likely to lead towards goal satisfaction. Necessity preferences represent constraints derived from the goal. They can be used to guarantee that certain conditions are always (or never true) during the search, thus eliminating the need to explicitly test them at the end. In the extreme, necessity preferences can be used to explicitly represent the entire sequence of steps in a procedure that achieves some goal, eliminating the need for an explicit goal test at the end.

Preferences are stored in the actions of productions. In any particular situation an arbitrary preference can be k–retrievable, k*–retrievable, ps-retrievable, or unretrievable. The primary context for preference retrieval is the object being considered and the objects already selected as part of the problem solving context. For example, the retrieval context for operator preferences in the Eight Puzzle includes the operator being considered (to slide a tile from cell *c1* into cell *c2*), the goal to be achieved (a solution to the Eight Puzzle), the problem space (Eight Puzzle), and the state to which the operator is to be applied. For binary preferences, such as better worse and indifferent preferences, the retrieval context includes multiple contending objects.

Preferences are used both by the architecture—the decision procedure—and by other knowledge. The architecture uses preferences to determine what selection to make, or what type of subgoal to generate if no selection can be made. As mentioned previously in this chapter, preferences can act as cues about what the decision procedure is going to do, and to reconstruct what it did in the past.

Preferences are acquired by the chunking of problem-solving episodes that generate preferences as their results. Most of our experience in acquiring preferences involves the acquisition of desirability preferences and that is all that will be discussed here, though the acquisition of acceptable preferences is covered under the discussion of operator acquisition.

As with knowledge about performable actions, chunking can turn ps–retrievable preferences into k*–retrievable preferences, and convert unretrievable preferences into ps-retrievable and k*–retrievable preferences. The most common way to turn ps-retrievable preferences into k*–retrievable ones involves a look-ahead search. This process has been described in detail elsewhere (Laird, Newell, & Rosenbloom, 1987), but the essence is to use Soar's basic search capability along with knowledge—about how to evaluate states, how to back up evaluations to earlier operators and states, and how to generate preferences from evaluations—to generate, and thus learn via chunking, preferences about operators that have tied for selection.

As demonstrated in (Golding, Rosenbloom, & Laird, 1987), it is possible to use external advice to assist in the process of converting ps–retrievable knowledge into k*–retrievable knowledge. If advice is given about what alternatives are good (or bad, for that matter), the advice can be turned into preferences which guide the look-ahead search. This can reduce the amount of search required without changing the chunks that are learned for the search. Externally provided knowledge can also be used to shift a piece of control knowledge from unretrievable to k*–retrievable using the techniques described in the section on "Performable Actions." (Yost & Newell, 1988).

Action Performance

As mentioned previously, Soar does not have a single, architecturally interpretable language for action performance. Instead, there are several distinct ways of representing action performance. One way to represent action performance, at least for external actions, is as some combination of motor commands. Retrieval of motor commands into working memory causes the associated motor systems to behave in appropriate fashions. There is a fixed language of motor commands, as determined by the available motor systems.

A second way to represent action performance is as a subprocedure that performs the action when executed. In Soar terms, the subprocedure is the processing in a subgoal that arises when the results of performing the action are not k*–retrievable. Within the subprocedure, the types of procedural knowledge described in this section would be applied recursively.

A third way to represent action performance is as the state that results from applying the operator representing the action. As with operators, the entire state can be stored in the actions of a single production (k–retrievable), it can be distributed across the actions of a group of productions that all fire within a single decision cycle (k*–retrievable), or it can be distributed across multiple productions that fire under different circumstances (ps–retrievable). The ps-retrievable case corresponds to the representation of action performance as subprocedures that is described above. Such a procedural representation—that is, representation as a subprocedure, rather than representation of a procedure—can actually be used for any piece of knowledge, whether the knowledge is itself about procedures or not.

The primary context for the retrieval of a result state is the conjunction of relevant features of the previous state and the operator. The result state is used as the basis for further problem solving, by serving as part of the retrieval context for goal testing, result generation, state and operator evaluation, and operator generation, selection, and application. The result state's acceptable preference is used by the decision procedure to select the state as the current state. As mentioned in the previous subsections, other knowledge may also use the preference prospectively to determine what state is going to be selected, and retrospectively to determine what state was selected, and what operator and state preceded it.

Acquisition of result states occurs by the chunking of problem-solving episodes that generate such states. One of the most common ways to acquire a k*–retrievable result state is to chunk over the process of executing a procedure that represents an action. As with the acquisition of knowledge about control, external advice can be utilized to speed up the process of acquiring knowledge about action performance. In one version, demonstrated for subtraction, Tic-Tac-Toe, and simple block manipulation, the system starts out with a set of primitive operators that are sufficient to implement the individual tests and modifications made by any operator. Advice is then used to determine which elements the action should test and generate for the specific operator being acquired. Given the primitive operators, this approach allows arbitrary operators to be acquired from advice.

Another way to acquire knowledge about action performance is to chunk over the process of interpreting an externally provided description of the action, as in (Yost & Newell, 1988). The process proceeds much as did the corresponding one in the earlier section on "Performable Actions," where in this case, one or more chunks are learned that can retrieve the result state in the future.

Summary

Procedural knowledge appears to be adequately supported by the current architecture. This should not be too surprising as it was originally designed for this; or at least for representing problem-solving knowledge. One aspect that might come as a surprise is that productions, though they are a primitive form of action, are not the model for action—operators are. Another possibly surprising aspect is that there is no single architecturally interpreted operator language. The fixed operator language common to most systems is replaced by the ability to perform operators by memory retrieval—either k*–retrieval or ps-retrieval—in conjunction with motor commands. The flexibility of this approach allows performance knowledge to be represented either directly in action form or as declarative structures that are interpreted. In fact, with the aid of software interpreters it should be possible to construct arbitrary operator languages. One example of such an approach is the language and interpreter used in the task acquisition work.

Learning has an important place in the use of procedural knowledge. By converting ps-retrievable knowledge into k*–retrievable knowledge, it can improve the system's ability to retrieve relevant knowledge under real-time constraints, and thus improve the system's approximation to the principle of rationality. It can convert interpreted behavior into direct action. It can also acquire new knowledge from the outside world, allowing the system to expand the tasks it can work on and the knowledge that it can use on those tasks.

EPISODIC KNOWLEDGE

Episodic knowledge is knowledge about what has occurred. In general, the individual elements of episodic knowledge can be viewed as instances of a binary predicate, Occurred(x, y), where x is an object, action, or sequence of actions that has occurred—for simplicity we will refer to all such members of the class of things that can occur as *events*—and y is a context in which the event occurred. Two loose but illustrative examples are Occurred("gaf," "List 1 of Experiment 2"), which denotes that a particular object (the nonsense trigram "gaf") occurred in a particular context (during the first list of experiment 2), and Occurred("pull-knob then turn-knob," "setting time on watch"), which denotes that a particular sequence of actions (pulling out of the watch's knob followed by turning of it) occurred in a particular context (the setting of the watch).

There are two notable features about the role or episodic knowledge in Soar. First, episodic knowledge can be represented at many different levels of explicitness. Second, although the representation, storage, retrieval, and use of episodic knowledge is rather straightforward, the acquisition of some forms of episodic knowledge is quite challenging. It leads us to posit the existence of comparatively complex strategies for acquiring these forms of episodic knowledge.

Representation

One way to represent episodic knowledge is completely as declarative structures; that is, as objects with attributes and values. In such a representation, the above two examples might appear as follows.

(occurred *e1* ^event *o1* ^context *c1*)
(object *o1* ^name gaf)
(context *c1* ^experiment 2 ^list 1)

(occurred *e2* ^event *s1* ^context *c2*)
(sequence *s1* ^action1 *a1* ^action2 *a2*)
(action *a1* ^name pull–knob)
(action *a2* ^name turn–knob)
(context *c2* ^name setting–time–on–watch)

However, not all of this knowledge need be represented directly as declarative structures. The alternative is to omit some of the components from the explicit representation, and assume them implicitly by default. The key to making this work is an understanding of the episodic nature of chunking; that is, that chunks are acquired as the result of problem-solving episodes, and execute in contexts that are similar to the ones in which they were learned. Spinning out the consequences of this understanding leads to a sequence of ways of omitting and modifying components of the representation.

The first component that can be omitted is the context. The conditions of a chunk represent both the context in which the information was learned and the contexts in which it should be retrieved. Therefore, when information is retrieved from long-term memory it can be assumed that it was learned in a situation that was similar to the retrieval situation. Eliminating the explicit context from the example above leaves the following explicit structures.

(occurred *e1* ^event *o1*)
(object *o1* ^name gaf)

(occurred *e2* ^event *s1*)
(sequence *s1* ^action1 *a1* ^action2 *a2*)
(action *a1* ^name pull-knob)
(action *a2* ^name turn-knob)

The next component that can be omitted is the occurred predicate, which, now that the context is removed, just states that its event occurred. If it is assumed that all knowledge that is retrieved from long-term memory got there via chunking—even if the system starts out with a number of productions, after sufficient time nearly all of its productions should have been acquired by chunking—then it can be assumed that any structures retrieved from long-term memory must have been seen before. Therefore, the explicit predicate can be eliminated in favor of the assumption that anything that is retrieved has occurred. Eliminating the occurred predicate from the example leaves the following explicit structures.

(object *o1* ^name gaf)

(sequence *s1* ^action1 *a1* ^action2 *a2*)
(action *a1* ^name pull–knob)
(action *a2* ^name turn–knob)

The episodic knowledge about the gaf event is now represented quite simply as a typical Soar object—all structures that were introduced solely for their role in representing episodic knowledge have been deleted. This is thus its final form. However, for the watch event, two additional steps are needed to convert its action sequence into its final form. The first step involves a change in nomenclature to replace actions with operators. Operators are intended to represent actions that can be performed rather than actions that were performed, but the assumptions made so far imply that if an operator is retrieved in a context then it must have been learned in a similar context. Operators can therefore stand in for actions that have occurred. Making this change eliminates the need for creating new structures to explicitly represent actions that have occurred, using the existing operator structures instead.

(sequence *s1* ^operator1 *a1* ^operator2 *a2*)
(operator *a1* ^name pull-knob)
(operator *a2* ^name turn-knob)

The second, and final, step is to replace the explicit representation of operator sequences with preferences. As mentioned previously, preferences can be used retrospectively to determine what objects were selected. Through their context fields—the goal, problem-space, state, and operator fields—they can also be used to determine what objects were current in the context at the time the object was selected. The following recoding of the example represents that operator *a1* was acceptable in the situation characterized by *g1*, *p1*, and *s1*; that state *s2* was acceptable in the situation where operator *a1* was additionally selected (it is *a1*'s result); and that operator *a2* was acceptable in the situation where state *s1* has been replaced by state *s2*.

```
(preference a1 ^value acceptable ^role operator
  ^goal g1 problem-space p1 ^state s1)
(operator a1 ^name pull-knob)
(preference s2 ^value acceptable ^role state
  ^goal g1 problem-space p1 ^state s1 ^operator a1)
(preference a2 ^value acceptable ^role operator
  ^goal g1 problem-space p1 ^state s2)
(operator a2 ^name turn-knob)
```

As was true of the gaf event earlier, the watch event is now represented without the use of any structures introduced solely for their role in representing episodic knowledge. The explicit structures that are left may actually be larger than some of the previous (this is not true of the gaf example), but they are structures that are already available because of their role in problem solving. This is thus Soar's native form of episodic knowledge. The significance of this is three-fold. First, this is the form of episodic knowledge which is available without positing additional semantics (or apparatus). Second, this form of episodic knowledge will always be around anyway, so it needs to be taken into consideration. Third, because it posits no additional apparatus, it should automatically compose well with the other capabilities in the system.

Storage

The manner of storage of episodic knowledge is a function of the representation that is used. Components that are directly represented as declarative structures are stored in the actions of productions. The "gaf" example might be stored in a production like the following (or across multiple productions).[3]

```
→
(occurred <e1> ^event <o1> ^context <c1>)
(object <o1> ^name gaf)
(context <c1> ^experiment 2 ^list 1)
```

[3] Symbols enclosed in angle brackets, such as <e1>, are variables.

Though this production is shown without conditions, as described later in this chapter, it is necessary (and possible) to add additional conditions to restrict the situations in which such declarative structures are retrieved.

Assumed parts are simply omitted from the actions. However, for the context assumption to work, a representation of the context must appear in the conditions of the production. This doesn't allow the context to be retrieved as an explicit structure, but does constrain the explicit structures to be retrieved only in contexts similar to the ones in which they were learned. The "gaf" example above would be stored as a production like the following one.

(context <*c1*> ^experiment 2 ^list 1)
→ (object <*o1*> ^name gaf)

Retrieval

Explicit episodic knowledge is retrieved in the same way as are other declarative structures; that is, by a combination of k*–search and ps-search. Omitted components are retrieved by assumption. If the context of occurrence is omitted, then it is assumed to share critical features with the retrieval context. If the predicate is omitted, occurrence is assumed for retrieved information. If actions are omitted, operator retrieval is assumed to denote an action that was executed. If sequence information is omitted, preferences are assumed to denote sequences of operators and states that occurred.

Use

There has not yet been a great need for episodic knowledge in the tasks that have so far been implemented in Soar. Nonetheless, it has been used in several distinct ways. One way is the use of preferences as the basis for a form of chronological backtracking—a short-term episodic use in which the preferences remain in working memory throughout. Soar normally backtracks in look-ahead search by terminating subgoals that lead to failure. However, there are times when Soar thinks it knows what it is doing—so no look-ahead search is being performed—yet failure still occurs. Backtracking under these circumstances involves examining the acceptable preference for the state at which failure occurred to find out which state was current when the failed state was selected. This prior state is then reselected, and problem solving is continued.

A second use is as the basis for recognition and recall tasks (Rosenbloom, Laird, & Newell, 1987, 1988a). In a recognition task the system is presented with a list of items to be memorized. It is then prompted with an item which may or may not be in the list. Its task is to say *yes* if the item was in the list and *no* if it wasn't. A recall task is similar, but instead of being prompted with an item, the system must produce as many of the items in the list as it can, without producing items not in the list. These tasks require episodic knowledge because they ask questions about what happened in the system's past.

A third use is as the basis for the transfer of procedural knowledge. The procedural knowledge that Soar learns can be viewed as really being episodic knowledge about the past behavior of the system. To use this episodic knowledge as procedural knowledge, there is an implicit assumption that what is descriptive of the past is normative for the future. This assumption is maintained until it leads to an error, at which point the system attempts to recover by doing something other than what is directly dictated by its past experience (Laird, 1988).

The issue of errors is actually a key one when native episodic knowledge is used, because, whenever an assumption is made, the possibility for error creeps in. There are four classes of situations that can lead to errors. Some of these are intrinsic in the nature of the world, while others arise because of specific architectural commitments in Soar. The first class of errors arises because of mistakes in credit assignment. Soar cannot examine the conditions of productions, so when knowledge is retrieved it can only guess as to which aspects of the retrieval context were shared with the context in which the knowledge was learned. This can lead to both errors of commission and omission. Suppose, for example, that the system is winding a watch at the same time it is trying to recall the elements that occurred in list 1 of experiment 2. It will retrieve both "gaf" and "pull-knob then turn-knob." The problem is that there is no a priori reason to assume that one of these events is in the list and that the other is not. In this particular case it might be able to use background or other contextual knowledge to reason that the watch events were not part of the list, but in other cases it may not be so lucky.

The second class of situations arises because of mistakes in context generalization. There is a trade-off between the scope of applicability of knowledge and its utility as episodic knowledge. The more general is the context, the more situations in which the knowledge can be retrieved, and thus be available for use. However, increasing the generality also decreases the ability to discriminate the situations in which the knowledge was originally learned from related situations. This can be seen clearly in the acquisition and use of control knowledge. The more general is the control knowledge, the more search is eliminated, assuming the generalization is correct. However, generality also implies that the knowledge will be retrieved in a variety of contexts, many of which are only remotely like the one in which the knowledge was learned.

The third class of situations arises because of mistakes in memory attribution. The only examinable structures in Soar are those in its working memory. Such structures could arise from memory retrieval, from intervention by the architecture (the decision procedure), or from perception. Only those that arise from memory retrieval embody episodic knowledge. Normally this shouldn't be a problem because the decision procedure and perceptual systems each create structures in a characteristic fashion: the decision procedure only modifies certain special attributes of goals; perception always adds its structures to special attributes of the state in the top context. However, the possibility remains.

The fourth, and final class of situations can be caused by any of the first three. It occurs because of mistakes in co-occurrence attribution. Such failures occur when the system mistakenly thinks it has previously experienced an event because it has experienced all of its individual pieces, though never all as part of a single event. Suppose, for example, that in one context the system sees a large ball, and in a similar context it sees a green ball. A co-occurrence error occurs if the system thinks that it saw both in the same context, or worse, that it has seen a single large green ball. In the recognition and recall tasks this problem is partially dealt with by assuming that k*–retrievable objects have been experienced, while ps-retrievable and unretrievable objects have not. The rationale is that k*–retrieval, being a limited computational mechanism, has a limited ability to put things together in novel ways, while ps-retrieval allows arbitrary structures to be created.

Acquisition

Episodic knowledge is acquired by chunking problem-solving episodes. Though this is somewhat of a tautology for Soar, it is not always as simple as it sounds. The simple case is the acquisition of episodic knowledge about objects generated in subgoals. If such objects are returned as results of their subgoals, then chunks are created which can later be used as episodic knowledge about the objects. The variety of subgoal results—objects, operators, preferences, and so on—leads directly to variety in the episodic knowledge that can be learned.

Under normal circumstances this episodic knowledge is represented in what we have referred to as native form; that is, predicates, contexts, actions, and sequences are represented respectively by chunk existence, production conditions, operators, and preferences. However, if the system monitors its own performance, and creates declarative structures representing what has transpired, then the chunks created for such structures can be used as explicit declarative-form episodic knowledge about what has transpired. In addition, such chunks can be used as native episodic knowledge about the monitoring process itself.

One form of episodic knowledge that cannot be handled this easily is knowledge about what has happened to the system; that is, knowledge about what the system has perceived rather than knowledge about what the system has generated. The "gaf" example presented above is a typical perceptual event. The episodic knowledge to be acquired is about the perception of "gaf" in a particular context (experiment 2, list 1). As described previously, Soar's input mechanism attaches perceptual information to the state in the top problem–solving context. In order for information about the event to be stored into long-term memory by chunking, an internal episode must be generated in which this perceptual information is used.

For perceptual events it is relatively easy to acquire a form of episodic knowledge akin to a familiarity test. The system must simply chunk over a subgoal in which it examines a representation of the perceptual event and the context, and generates as a subgoal result an occurred predicate covering them (Rosenbloom Laird, & Newell, 1987). A familiarity chunk for this example might look like one of the following two productions, depending on whether the context is explicit or not.

```
(object <o1> ^name gaf)
(context <c1> ^experiment 2 ^list 1)
→
(occurred <e1> ^event <o1> ^context <c1>)

(object <o1> ^name gaf)
(context <c1> ^experiment 2 ^list 1)
→
(occurred <e1> ^event <o1>)
```

In the systems so far implemented, context is actually ignored in the learning of episodic knowledge. By having no explicit representation of context in either the conditions or the actions of the chunks, the context is effectively the entire history of the system. In this form, the "gaf" familiarity chunk looks like the following:

```
(object <o1> ^name gaf)
→
(occurred <e1> ^event <o1>)
```

Familiarity chunks allow the determination of whether an event has occurred before in a particular context. Whenever a representation of the event appears in working memory along with a representation of the context, an occurred predicate will be retrieved for them. Familiarity chunks can thus support performance in recognition tasks, where the task is to determine whether a presented object has been seen before.

What familiarity chunks do not directly support is the retrieval of events that occurred in a particular context. For an event to be retrieved by the execution of a chunk, the event must be stored in the actions of the chunk, and not tested in its conditions. A retrieval chunk for the "gaf" example should look something like the following (with an assumed context and predicate):

```
(context <c1> ^experiment 2 ^list 1)
→
(object <o1> ^name gaf)
```

For such productions to be learned by Soar, they must be created by chunking over some form of problem solving. But chunking is not an indefinitely flexible mechanism. A chunk's actions are always based on the results of a subgoal, and its conditions are always based on a dependency analysis of the results. This immediately imposes two constraints on the nature of the problem solving that can underly the acquisition of retrieval chunks.

1. For the event to appear in the actions of a chunk, it must be generated as a result of a subgoal.
2. For the event to not appear in the conditions of the chunk, the subgoal results must not depend on an examination of the event.

The first constraint is relatively easy to meet; for example, by creating a copy of the perceptual event in a subgoal, and returning the copy as a result. However, attempting to meet both constraints at once leads to the *data chunking problem:* if the result is based on examining the object to be learned, then the conditions of the chunk will also test the object, allowing it to only be retrieved when it is already available. For example, using the copying strategy for the "gaf" example would lead to a chunk like the following:

```
(context <c1> ^experiment 2 ^list 1)
(object <o1> ^name gaf)
→
(object <o1> ^name gaf)
```

In contrast to the desired retrieval chunk, this one tests that "gaf" is already in working memory before it will retrieve it. So it doesn't do the job.

The solution to the data chunking problem is to separate the result generation process from the use of the perceptual event. Result generation must be based on what the system already knows, rather than on the perceptual event. One approach involves assembling the result from components that the system can already retrieve (Rosenbloom, Laird, & Newell, 1987). For example, if the letters "g," "a," and "f" are retrievable, then "gaf" can be generated by retrieving and assembling them. This is a syntactic compositional process which may or may not respect any specific semantic rules in performing the assembly. Another approach is to start with the context and to chain through a sequence of productions which form a pre-existing, though possibly indirect, link between the context and the event (Rosenbloom, 1988). For example, (object *o1* ^name gaf) can be generated if (context *c1* ^experiment 2 ^list 1) is already in working memory, and if the following two retrieval chunks exist.

```
(context <c1> ^experiment 2 ^list 1)
→
(object <o1> ^name fem)

(object <o1> ^name fem)
→
(object <o1> ^name gaf)
```

Either approach requires the system to start out with a set of primitive elements that can be generated. Other more complex structures can then be built up out of compositions of these primitive elements. For the work on recognition and recall, the system was initialized with the ability to generate the 26 letters. Conceivably, Soar could have been initialized with an even lower level of primitives, such as simple lines, curves, and points, from which it would construct the letters. It could also have been initialized with more meaningful primitives, such as the primitive ACTs in Conceptual Dependency Theory (Schank, 1975) or the epistemological primitives in KL-ONE (Brachman, 1979).

Though the perceptual event cannot be used directly in the generation process, it is still used in two critical ways. The first is as the basis of a goal test for the generation process. The generation process can conceivably return any event that it can either assemble or chain to, so a goal test is necessary to determine when the desired event has been generated. The straightforward approach of comparing the perceptual and generated events does not work. Instead, it leads to a secondary version of the data chunking problem in which the comparison causes tests of the perceptual event to appear in the conditions of the chunk.

To avoid this secondary data chunking problem, the goal test is based on a familiarity chunk for the perceptual event rather than directly on the event. Given a familiarity chunk for the perceptual event, the generation goal test is satisfied when a familiar but unretrieved event is generated. The test of familiarity guarantees that the event has been seen in the current context (or a similar one). If the event is unretrieved, it is one that the system has not previously learned to generate. This test is somewhat overgeneral in that it can't guarantee that the generated event is a copy of the current perceptual event. However, at worst it will only generate a different event that is familiar in the same context. If this happens, it is always possible to try again to generate an event that corresponds to the input event. The use of a familiarity chunk as the goal test for the generation process makes this is a generate-recognize approach to recall (see, for example, Watkins & Gardiner, 1979), though focused on the acquisition phase rather than the retrieval phase.

The second way that the perceptual event is used is as the basis for controlling the search through the space of events that can be generated. The goal test determines the correctness of the result, but does not affect the efficiency of the search. Using the perceptual event as control knowledge makes the search tractable, potentially removing all backtracking, without affecting the correctness of the result. Thus the result technically does not depend on such control knowledge. The bottom line is that the use of search control knowledge can speed up performance without introducing additional conditions into chunks (recall from earlier in this chapter that chunking does not backtrace through the use of desirability preferences by the decision procedure). Of secondary importance is that the use of the perceptual event as search control increases the likelihood that the first event generated will correspond to the perceptual event rather than to another familiar but unretrieved event.

When the generation, goal testing, and control processes are all put together, a retrieval chunk can be learned that is identical to the one that was desired. Context can be treated in the same ways that it is for familiarity chunks. It can be explicit (in the actions), assumed (in the conditions), or completely ignored (nowhere). The systems so far implemented have ignored context.

One consequence of this approach to the acquisition of retrieval chunks is that it forces information storage to be based on an understanding process. The understanding may be only of syntax (surface structure), or it may be of a deeper semantic (deep structure) nature, but without it, learning will not occur. There is no simple assignment operation—such as the SETQ operation in Lisp—that allows an unanalyzed structure to be stored in long-term memory. A second consequence is that the understanding process must be a reconstructive—or analysis-by-synthesis—process (Bartlett, 1982; Neisser, 1967), in which events are reconstructed in terms of known structures. A third consequence is that the storage process is semantically penetrable. Other knowledge can potentially alter the reconstruction process, and thus what is stored, leading to generalization and other forms of bias in the memory structures that are stored.

Summary

Soar can represent, store, retrieve, use, and acquire episodic knowledge. However, the situation is nowhere near as clean and simple as it was for procedural knowledge. In fact, if we were to sit down to design a capability for episodic knowledge from scratch, with no constraints, we would be unlikely to design it as currently embodied by Soar. What the architecture most directly supports is native episodic knowledge about structures generated by the system itself. Such knowledge is represented, stored, retrieved, and acquired without requiring additional cognitive effort. However, the assumptions required to use such knowledge can lead to errors. By increasing cognitive effort, more explicit forms of episodic knowledge can be acquired that require fewer assumptions for use, and thus hopefully lead to fewer errors. Such structures are not terribly dissimilar to the structures used in other episodic memory proposals, such as Scripts (Schank & Ableson, 1977) and E-Mops (Kolodner, 1985).

The situation is even more complicated for episodic knowledge about perceptual events. Three features of the architecture yield strong constraints on how the knowledge is acquired.

1. Chunk actions are based on subgoal results.
2. Chunk conditions are based on the supergoal structures upon which the results depend.
3. Perceptual information arrives in the top goal.

Together these features force a reconstructive approach to knowledge acquisition. Though this approach is considerably more complicated than simple verbatim storage of what has transpired, it does have a number of promising properties.

Given the overall picture of episodic knowledge, as relatively complicated and messy, it is important to ask whether this signals a need for modification of the architecture. One key question is the appropriateness of the levels of support and constraint that are provided by the architecture. For psychology, this is a matter of the extent to which the level of support models human capabilities, and the level of constraint models human limitations. For AI, this is a matter of whether the system achieves an appropriate level of episodic functionality. A second key question is whether there are more appropriate mechanisms—for either definition of "appropriate"—for the support of episodic knowledge which could be integrated cleanly into the architecture. Providing detailed answers to these two key questions remains for future work.

DECLARATIVE KNOWLEDGE

Declarative knowledge is knowledge about what is true in the world. Examples include the facts that dogs have four legs and that Fido is a dog. Declarative representation comes in many forms, such as natural language, diagrams, maps, charts, tables, and graphs. This is also the area with which logic is classically concerned. A logic has a syntax specifying the form that statements take, and a semantics which relates logical statements to an abstract conceptualization of the world. For first order predicate calculus (FOPC) the syntax is based on constants, variables, predicates, connectives ($\wedge$, $\vee$, $\neg$, and $\supset$), and quantifiers ($\forall$ and $\exists$). The mapping between the syntax and the semantics, called the interpretation, is used to determine the truth of statements expressed in the syntax of the logic.

In this section we are primarily concerned with the syntactic side of declarative knowledge, taking advantage of logic's privileged role in AI as a language for representing declarative knowledge. We examine how declarative knowledge is represented (its syntax), stored, retrieved, used, and acquired. On the issue of semantics, we assume that the meaning of a structures is determined by a combination of two factors: its relationship to the outside world, as mediated by the perceptual and motor systems, and how it is used by internal processes.

As with episodic knowledge, the main challenge is in the acquisition of declarative knowledge. The data chunking techniques described earlier are extended to handle declarative representations.

Representation

As with episodic and procedural knowledge, there are several different ways that declarative knowledge can be represented in Soar.[4] The most flexible and general approach is to represent each syntactic component—whether it be a constant,

[4]In this section we focus on derivation-based representations for logic. Other representations are possible, such as validity-based techniques—see, for example, (Polk & Newell, 1988) and (Polk, Newell, & Lewis, 1989) for research on mental models in Soar. These have somewhat different properties, but much of the discussion would remain the same.

variable, predicate, connective, or quantifier—as an object. The details of exactly how this is done are not crucial, but the general flavor should be clear from the following example which shows a statement in FOPC and how it could be translated into a set of objects in Soar.

$\forall x\ [P(x) \supset Q(x)]$

(quantifier *q1* ^name forall ^variable *v1* ^body *b1*)
(variable *v1* ^name x)
(connective *b1* ^name implies ^antecedent *a1* ^consequent *c1*)
(predicate *a1* ^name p ^argument *v1*)
(predicate *c1* ^name q ^argument *v1*)

For simple statements containing no quantifiers or variables, no predicates with more than two arguments, and no connectives except for $\wedge$, there is a simpler native representation that takes direct advantage of Soar's object structure. Constants are represented as objects, predicates as attributes, and conjunction as simultaneous occurrence. Here's a simple example about Fido.

Category(Fido, Dog) $\wedge$ Alive(Fido)

(object *o1* ^name fido ^category *o2* ^alive)
(object *o2* ^name dog)

This native representation is more succinct than the previous one, but in exchange it lacks expressibility.

Another variation is to use productions as a representation for a subclass of implications. A production can represent a universally quantified implication in which the antecedent is a conjunction of predicates, and the consequent is an existentially quantified conjunction of predicates.

$$\forall(x_1,\ldots,x_n)[C_1(x_1,\ldots,x_n) \wedge \ldots \wedge C_j(x_1,\ldots,x_n) \supset$$
$$\exists(y_1,\ldots,y_m)\ [A_1(x_1,\ldots,x_n,y_1,\ldots,y_m) \wedge \ldots \wedge A_k(x_1,\ldots,x_n,y_1,\ldots,y_m)]]$$

The existential quantifier in the consequent arises from the ability to create new objects when variables appear in actions that are not in conditions. A form of negation as failure is also available in the antecedent which allows a predicate to be assumed false unless it is explicitly known to be true (that is, available in working memory).

Implications encoded as productions are non-examinable and can only be used to forward chain. We do not discuss them further here. Instead we focus on examinable structures of either of the first two types.

Storage

Storage of declarative knowledge is straightforward. As with declaratively represented procedural and episodic knowledge, declarative knowledge is stored in the actions of productions.

Retrieval

Declarative knowledge is retrieved by k*–search and ps-search. If the knowledge is stored directly in productions, k*–search can retrieve it, otherwise ps-search is required. Hopefully, by this point, this is obvious. However, less obvious is what the context should be for retrieval of declarative knowledge. The retrieval contexts for both procedural and episodic knowledge are straightforward. An element of procedural knowledge is retrieved when it may be needed to produce behavior. An element of episodic knowledge is retrieved when a context is established that is similar to the one in which the episode occurred (at least if the context is tested in production conditions rather than stored in production actions). In contrast, declarative knowledge is by its essence not associated with a particular context. The knowledge is true, independent of context, and should be usable in any context requiring it.

On the other hand, if declarative knowledge is stored with no context—that is, with a null set of production conditions—the knowledge will not only be retrievable in all contexts, it will in fact be retrieved in all contexts, swamping the system with true but irrelevant information. One approach to controlling the retrieval of declarative knowledge is to use the connectedness among facts as a co-relevance heuristic. This is often implemented by the mechanism of spreading activation, which retrieves facts close to those that are already retrieved (Anderson, 1983; Collins & Loftus, 1975). Another approach is to control the retrieval of declarative knowledge by providing a partial description of the knowledge to be retrieved (Norman & Bobrow, 1979). The partial description then delineates the set of things which appear to be relevant.

The approach that we have taken is to store declarative knowledge in a discrimination network that allows retrieval of objects by partial description (Rosenbloom, Laird, & Newell, 1988a). Given any partial description, a single object is retrieved along with the facts about it. The construction of this discrimination network is discussed below, under acquisition.

One last important aspect of the retrieval of declarative knowledge concerns the basis for believing that structures retrieved from long-term memory represent true facts about the world. This belief must be based on the implicit assumption that the system knew what it was doing during the episode in which the structures were acquired. In other words, the system must trust its past behavior. This is one form of assumption that cannot be completely avoided by adding more explicit structure. Even if explicit true-in-world annotations are added to all structures representing true facts about the world, the system must still trust that in the past it only added such annotations when the facts were true. It might be more "careful" about adding such annotations than it is about adding structures to working memory in general, but since there is no oracle for truth, it is still assuming that these annotations were added correctly. This assumption that the annotations are true is of the same type as the original one. It may localize the assignment of trust, but can not completely eliminate it.

Use

Declarative knowledge has a multitude of uses. It can be used to describe procedures so that they can be reasoned about, or followed interpretively (from which native procedures can be compiled). It can be used to explicitly describe episodes. It can be used to describe knowledge whose function is not yet clear. It can be used as the basis for memorization tasks. A complete list would go on considerably longer, but this gives a sampling of typical uses.

Acquisition

The acquisition of declarative knowledge has much in common with the acquisition of episodic knowledge. Declarative knowledge that is generated as the result of a problem solving episode is directly acquired by chunking, with a retrieval context that corresponds to those elements of the situation on which creation of the knowledge depended. Likewise, the acquisition of perceptually originating declarative knowledge utilizes the data chunking solution described previously in this chapter. Though, to go beyond the types of structures acquired in the research on episodic knowledge, Soar was initialized with primitive elements for the 26 letters, plus a set of primitive attributes (isa, has, color, response, letter1, letter2, letter3, letter4, letter5, letter6, letter7, letter8, letter9, letter10).[5] Using these primitives, facts are represented by attributes relating named objects. For example Isa(Fido, Dog) is represented by the following structures.

```
(object <f> ^letter1 <f1> ^letter2 <f2> ^letter3 <f3>
  ^letter4 <f4> ^isa <d>)
(letter <f1> ^name f)
(letter <f2> ^name i)
(letter <f3> ^name d)
(letter <f4> ^name o)
(object <d> ^letter1 <d1> ^letter2 <d2> ^letter3 <d3>)
(letter <d1> ^name d)
(letter <d2> ^name o)
(letter <d3> ^name g)
```

This is a variation on the native representation described previously in this chapter. The primary difference is that names, which were unanalyzable atoms in the earlier representation, have been expanded out to where their internal structure is open for examination and creation.

There are a number of ways in which the acquisition of declarative knowledge is more complicated than the acquisition of episodic knowledge in Soar. We have

[5]In future work we will be examining how to loosen up the requirement that attributes be preexisting primitives as well as investigating different levels of primitive elements.

so far isolated three additional issues that must be resolved in the acquisition of perceptually originating declarative knowledge. (a) How is a discrimination network to be acquired that can control the retrieval of declarative knowledge? (b) How is knowledge about objects acquired incrementally? (c) How do chunks store the components of an object?

As mentioned earlier, utilizing the data chunking solution alone results in the acquisition of context-free declarative knowledge.[6] Acquiring a discrimination network thus requires an augmentation of the basic data chunking solution. Abstractly, the approach is to modify the simple memorization strategy underlying data chunking so that the acquisition of new knowledge involves relating the new knowledge to what is already known. If in the process of establishing relations, an explanation is created as to why the new knowledge is different from similar existing knowledge, this should lead to discrimination. Similar processing could lead to generalization, or other alterations of the new knowledge prior to its being stored (Anderson, 1986; Rosenbloom 1988).

The current implementation in Soar uses such a strategy to perform object-centered discrimination. Given a new fact, such as Isa(Fido, Dog), the system uses the features of Fido to see what object is retrieved from the discrimination network. If Fido is retrieved, no discrimination is necessary. If some other object, such as Fred, is retrieved, Fido's features are compared with Fred's to find a difference, such as the letter "d" in the third position of the name.[7] This difference is then used as the justification for generating a new symbol representing Fido, and for rejecting Fred as the object to be retrieved. If there is more than one difference, one is picked indifferently.

By thus loosening the prohibition against examining perceptual knowledge during result generation, discriminating conditions are added to retrieval chunks which control when the acquired knowledge is retrieved. Schematically, the production resulting from this process looks like the following.

$$\text{Retrieved(g35)} \wedge \neg\ \text{Rejected(g35)} \wedge \text{letter3(g35, e)} \wedge \text{Perceived}(p) \wedge \text{letter3}(p, \text{d}) \rightarrow \text{Reject(g35)} \wedge \text{Retrieve(g37)} \quad (1)$$

This production says that if there is a retrieved, but not yet rejected, object with symbol g35 and an "e" as its third letter, and the perceived object's third letter is "d," then reject the retrieved object and create a new symbol (g37) for the perceived object. Each such retrieval production forms one link in the discrimination network that is constructed as new objects are perceived. This discrimination network supports k*-retrievability—that is, retrievability by a combination

[6]There is a corresponding, but not identical, issue for perceptually originating episodic knowledge which has not yet been addressed: how the situational context is incorporated into chunk conditions.

[7]In the current implementation, discrimination is always based on features of object names, rather than on other facts known about the object.

of production firings within a single elaboration phase—rather than the k-retrievability that is possible for knowledge stored with no context.

Consider what happens when the following three facts are learned in sequence, ignoring for now all of the learning except for the creation of the discrimination network.

Isa(Fred, Cat)
Isa(Fido, Dog)
Isa(Carl, Dog)

First, Fred is processed. Because no object has been learned previously, no discrimination is necessary, and the only action to be taken is the creation of a new symbol for Fred. This results in the acquisition of a production which generates the symbol for Fred if no object has already been retrieved.

$$\neg \text{Retrieved}() \rightarrow \text{Retrieve}(\text{g35}) \qquad (2)$$

Second, Cat is processed. Given the features of Cat, the symbol for Fred (g35) is retrieved by production 2. As described, the information about Fred is cued off of Fred's symbol, so the retrieval of g35 leads to the retrieval of what is known about Fred. Once this knowledge is retrieved, Cat is discriminated from Fred. The system chooses indifferently one of the discriminating letters of the objects' names—in this case the second letter—yielding the following production.

$$\begin{aligned}&\text{Retrieved}(\text{g35}) \wedge \neg \text{Rejected}(\text{g35}) \wedge \text{letter2}(\text{g35, r})\\&\quad \wedge \text{Perceived}(p) \wedge \text{letter2}(p, \text{a}) \rightarrow \text{Reject}(\text{g35}) \wedge \text{Retrieve}(\text{g36}) \qquad (3)\end{aligned}$$

Third, Fido is processed. Fred is retrieved and discriminated from Fido by the third letter, yielding production 1. Fourth, Dog is processed, Once again, Fred is retrieved, and the discrimination is again based on the third letter, yielding the following production:

$$\begin{aligned}&\text{Retrieved}(\text{g35}) \wedge \neg \text{Rejected}(\text{g35}) \wedge \text{letter3}(\text{g35, e})\\&\quad \wedge \text{Perceived}(p) \wedge \text{letter3}(p, \text{g}) \rightarrow \text{Reject}(\text{g35}) \wedge \text{Retrieve}(\text{g38}) \qquad (4)\end{aligned}$$

Fifth, Carl is processed. This time Fred is retrieved and then immediately rejected by production 3, which also retrieves Cat. Carl is then discriminated from Cat by the third letter, yielding the following production:

$$\begin{aligned}&\text{Retrieved}(\text{g36}) \wedge \neg \text{Rejected}(\text{g36}) \wedge \text{letter3}(\text{g35, t})\\&\quad \wedge \text{Perceived}(p) \wedge \text{letter3}(p, \text{r}) \rightarrow \text{Reject}(\text{g36}) \wedge \text{Retrieve}(\text{g39}) \qquad (5)\end{aligned}$$

Sixth, Dog is processed. Fred is retrieved, and then immediately rejected by production 4, which also retrieves the symbol for Dog. Because there is no mismatch between the perceived and retrieved objects, no discrimination is necessary, no new symbol is generated, and no new production is created. At this point the discrimination network has the shape shown in Figure 4.3.

Given a partial specification of an object name, the symbol for the object whose name matches most closely—according to the structure of the discrimina-

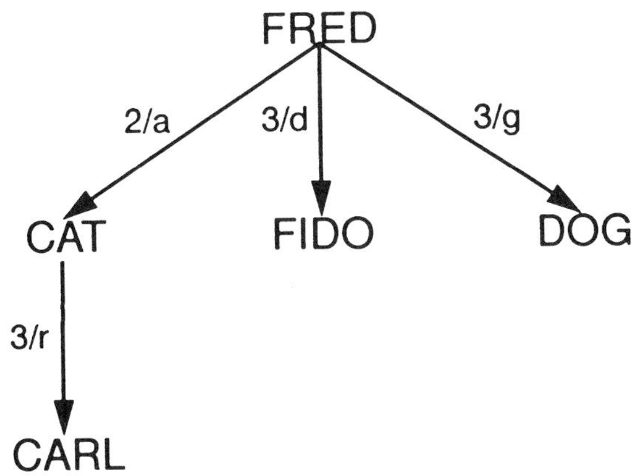

FIG. 4.3. Discrimination network acquired from sequence of facts.

tion network—is retrieved. The knowledge associated with the object is acquired with a retrieval context consisting of the object's symbol. As with episodic knowledge, this occurs by first acquiring a familiarity chunk for the new knowledge, and then acquiring a retrieval chunk which depends on the object's symbol.

Unfortunately, this approach depends on having all of the knowledge about the object available at once, which raises the second issue: How to incrementally acquire knowledge about objects. If the familiarity chunk must recognize the entire object, as it does in the previously published approaches, no learning can occur about an object until all of the knowledge about it is available. Conceptually, the solution to this problem is straightforward. Data chunking is applied to each fragment of an object individually. The processes of familiarization and generation are performed independently for each letter of the object's name, and for each fact about the object. As an example, the individual familiarity and retrieval productions for the first letter of Fred's name look like the following:

$$\text{letter1(g35, f)} \rightarrow \text{Familiar[letter1(g35, f)]} \tag{6}$$

$$\text{Retrieved(g35)} \wedge \neg\, \text{Rejected(g35)} \rightarrow \text{letter1(g35, f)} \tag{7}$$

The implementation of this solution allows new facts to be acquired about known objects, for example, that Color(Fido, Red). However, what is given up in going with this solution is the ability to use familiarity chunks to directly perform recognition tasks. Object recognition must now be based on multiple productions. The obvious way to do this is to sort the object through the discrimination network. If the new object is the same as the one stored in the node at which discrimination ends, then it is recognized.

The third issue is how references to learned objects should be stored in retrieval chunks. For primitive objects, such as the letters, the answer is simple. The value is stored directly in the actions of the retrieval chunk, as shown in production 7. However, for values that are objects, the situation is more complicated and leads to a sequenced pair of discriminations, similar to the approach taken by EPAM (Feigenbaum & Simon, 1984).

Suppose the system has already learned about the object bej, a nonsense trigram, and that the retrieval cue associated with bej is its first letter (b). Then suppose that the system is presented with a paired associate (a stimulus–response pair) in which bej is the response, for example Response(gaf, bej). This pair would be represented as follows:

(object *s* ^letter1 *s1* ^letter2 *s2* ^letter3 *s3* ^response *r*)
(letter *s1* ^name g)
(letter *s2* ^name a)
(letter *s3* ^name f)
(object *r* ^letter1 *r1* ^letter2 *r2* ^letter3 *r3*)
(letter *r1* ^name b)
(letter *r2* ^name e)
(letter *r3* ^name j)

If g41 is the symbol for gaf and g42 is the symbol for bej, the obvious retrieval production to create for this pair (ignoring for now the retrieval productions for the objects' names) is the following.

$$\text{Retrieved(g41)} \wedge \neg\ \text{Rejected(g41)} \rightarrow \text{Response(g41, g42)} \qquad (8)$$

However, the rule that is actually created will have an additional condition which tests bej's retrieval cue (b).

$$\text{Retrieved(g41)} \wedge \neg\ \text{Rejected(g41)} \wedge \text{Letter1(g42, b)} \rightarrow \text{Response(g41, g42)} \qquad (9)$$

This happens because the retrieval cue is examined in order to retrieve g42 from the discrimination network. Therefore, the appearance of g42 in the chunk's actions leads to the cue appearing in the chunk's conditions. Such a retrieval production cannot support performance in paired–associate tasks, where after studying a list of stimulus–response pairs, the subject must generate responses when given just the corresponding stimuli.

One solution to this problem is to include a (partial) description of the value object in the retrieval production rather than the object itself. If the description is created anew, by data chunking, from the information provided in the paired associate, no additional retrieval cues get incorporated. With this change, the following chunk is learned.

$$\text{Retrieved(g41)} \wedge \neg\ \text{Rejected(g41)} \rightarrow \text{response(g41, letter1(}-\text{, b))} \qquad (10)$$

Given such a chunk (or set of chunks), the paired associate task can be performed by using the stimulus features to retrieve its symbol (g41), using the stimulus symbol to retrieve a (possibly partial) description of the response (letter1(−, b)), using the description of the response to retrieve the response symbol (g42), and then using the response symbol to retrieve the information about the response (bej).

Using this strategy the task now requires two independent retrievals from the discrimination network—one to retrieve the stimulus symbol and one to retrieve the response symbol. This is similar to the double discrimination performed by EPAM during paired associate tasks (Feigenbaum & Simon, 1984). However, it occurs in Soar not because of a need to match the data, but as a means of enabling responses to be retrieved from stimuli in the absence of any additional response cues.

Summary

The representation, storage and use of declarative knowledge are relatively straightforward in Soar. The architecture provides some support for these capabilities through the primitive attribute–value representation, the ability to store declarative structure in productions, and the ability to examine declarative structures in working memory. The architecture does not enforce a fixed semantics for declarative knowledge, nor does it provide default inference mechanisms that automatically generate structures representing knowledge that is implied by its existing structures. Both of these, if part of the architecture, would imply excessive rigidity in how the system could behave. To the extent they are needed, provision should be made by adding knowledge and problem spaces on top of the fixed architecture.

The acquisition and retrieval of declarative knowledge is considerably less straightforward. Chunking is provided as a means for acquiring declarative knowledge, but the problem solver must be put through a number of contortions for the system to acquire the appropriate chunks from externally provided knowledge. In addition to the constraint imposed by the data chunking problem, a related architectural constraint restricts how known objects can be used in the acquisition of new knowledge. The solution to the problem posed by this constraint leads to an approach which is increasingly like the discrimination network structure of the EPAM model of memory.

Retrieval of declarative knowledge is supported by production firing, but considerable additional complexity arises from the need to constrain retrieval to what might be relevant. The discrimination network we have employed provides one approach to this. Though the approach currently seems somewhat ad hoc, the abstract characterization of the process as relating the new knowledge to existing knowledge, leads to the hope that it will eventually be placed on a principled footing.

Further work is clearly called for in developing and evaluating the acquisition and retrieval mechanisms that have been proposed (and implemented).

CONCLUSIONS

Taking an architecture seriously means living within its constraints and using what support it provides, at least until it is clear that the architecture must be modified. In this chapter we have taken a step towards evaluating the level of support and constraint which the Soar architecture provides for the knowledge level, a concept that is closely related to the idea of general intelligence. This helps us to understand the extent to which the architecture's current levels of support and constraint are adequate for achieving general intelligence. It also provides an alternative way of viewing Soar in which its architectural mechanisms are subjugated to their role in supporting knowledge. This complements other efforts that view Soar as a set of mechanisms (Laird, Newell, & Rosenbloom, 1987), a hierarchy of meta-levels (Rosenbloom, Laird, & Newell, 1988b), a hierarchy of cognitive levels at different time scales (Newell, in press; Rosenbloom, Laird, Newell, & McCarl, in press), a physical symbol system (Newell, Rosenbloom, & Laird, 1989), and a general goal–oriented system (Rosenbloom, 1989).

Our particular focus in this step has been on how the Soar architecture supports and constrains the representation, storage, retrieval, use, and acquisition of three pervasive forms of knowledge: procedural, episodic, and declarative. The analysis reveals that Soar adequately supports procedural knowledge—to some extent it was designed for this—but that there are still significant questions about episodic and declarative knowledge. These questions arise primarily because of consequences of the principle source of constraint in Soar, the fact that all learning occurs via chunking. Chunking can support the acquisition of episodic and declarative knowledge, but in so doing it imposes significant requirements on how the problem solving underlying this acquisition proceeds. These requirements amount to architecturally-derived hypotheses about how learning occurs. We have reported here some new results that elaborate on these hypotheses in the acquisition of declarative knowledge, but considerable future work is still called for in both the development and testing of these hypotheses.

One obvious question at this point is why not just add new architectural mechanisms that directly support the acquisition of episodic and declarative knowledge? Assuming that appropriate mechanisms could be developed, there are still at least two critical reasons not to rush into adding them to the architecture. The first reason is that the integration of new mechanisms into an existing architecture can have major consequences. An integrated architecture is more than just a collection of useful mechanisms. It must be constructed so that its mechanisms compose appropriately with each other. The number of potential interactions that need to be worried about increases rapidly—exponentially, if there can be interactions among all possible subsets—with the number of mechanisms. Frequently, the addition of a perfectly reasonable new mechanism will cause strongly dysfunctional behavior in others of the existing mechanisms.

Though there are times when an architectural addition is absolutely required, and a research effort must be engendered to get the interactions right (as recently occurred for perceptual–motor behavior in Soar (Wiesmeyer, 1988)), almost always a conservative strategy is what is required.

The second reason is that rushing to add new mechanisms discourages learning about the limits of the existing mechanisms, and their combinations. This is essential to understanding the scope and limits of the architecture. It is also essential to discovering the deeper, nonobvious consequences of the architecture. If we had jumped to add new learning mechanisms to Soar, we would never have discovered how the current mechanisms inherently imply a reconstructive learning strategy. The discovery of such nonobvious consequences is some of the most interesting research that can be done with architectures.

This being said, much additional work is still needed. One issue to be addressed is the origins of the bootstrap knowledge that allows new procedural, episodic, and declarative knowledge to be acquired. The acquisition of perceived procedural knowledge requires the existence of an interpreter for the knowledge. The acquisition of perceived episodic and declarative knowledge requires a set of pre-existing primitive elements plus the knowledge about how to familiarize, discriminate, and construct object representations. It appears necessary to add some of this to the architecture, such as the ability to generate a set of primitive elements. Other parts may just be specific instances of more general capabilities, which of course must themselves be either innate or learned. For example, the interpreter for procedural knowledge may be just an instantiation of a more general comprehension process. The same may also be true of the discrimination and construction processes for declarative and episodic knowledge. The current implementation does not quite look like this, and architectural changes may be required before it does, but this is one promising path to pursue.

Finally, a number of additional steps must still be taken before the relationship of the Soar architecture to the knowledge level is completely tied down. The most important missing aspect is the relationship between Soar's mechanisms and the principle of rationality. The key issue is how its architectural mechanisms, such as its decision procedure and subgoal generator, allow Soar to approximate rationality even under the constraints of its being a physical system with time and space bounds. We have commented briefly on how chunking increases Soar's ability to bring knowledge to bear under real-time constraints, but much more is left to be done.

ACKNOWLEDGMENTS

This research was sponsored by the Defense Advanced Research Projects Agency (DOD) under contract numbers N00039-86C-0033 (via subcontract from the Knowledge Systems Laboratory, Stanford University), and F33615-87-C-1499

(ARPA Order No. 4976, monitored by the Air Force Avionics Laboratory), by the National Aeronautics and Space Administration under cooperative agreement numbers NCC 2-538 and NCC 2-517, and the Office of Naval Research under contract numbers N00014-86-K-0678 (Information Sciences Division) and N00014-88-K-0554 (Computer Science Division). The views and conclusions contained in this document are those of the authors and should not be interpreted as representing the official policies, either expressed or implied, of the Defense Advanced Research Projects Agency, the National Aeronautics and Space Administration, the Office of Naval Research or the US Government.

REFERENCES

Anderson, J. R. (1983). A spreading-activation theory of memory. *Journal of Verbal Learning and Verbal Behavior, 22,* 261–295.

Anderson, J. R. (1986). Knowledge compilation: The general learning mechanism. In R. S. Michalski, J. G. Carbonell, & T. M. Mitchell (Eds.), *Machine learning: An artificial intelligence approach* (Vol. II). Los Altos, CA: Morgan Kaufmann.

Bartlett, F. C. (1932). *Remembering: A study in experimental and social psychology.* Cambridge, England: Cambridge University Press.

Bell, C. G. & Newell, A. (1971). *Computer structures: Readings and examples.* New York: McGraw-Hill.

Brachman, R. J. (1979). On the epistemological status of semantic nets. In N. V. Findler (Ed.), *Associative networks.* New York: Academic Press.

Collins, A. M., & Loftus, E. F. (1975). A spreading-activation theory of semantic processing. *Psychological Review, 82,* 407–428.

Feigenbaum, E. A., & Simon, H. A. (1984). EPAM-like models of recognition and learning. *Cognitive Science, 8,* 305–336.

Golding, A., Rosenbloom, P. S., & Laird, J. E. (1987). Learning general search control from outside guidance. *Proceedings of IJCAI-87.* Milan. Los Altos, CA: Morgan Kaufman.

Kolodner, J. L. (1985). Memory for experience. In G. Bower (Ed.), *Psychology of learning and motivation* (Vol. 19). New York: Academic Press.

Laird, J. E. (1983). *Universal subgoaling.* Doctoral dissertation, Carnegie-Mellon University. (Available in Laird, J. E., Rosenbloom, P. S., & Newell, A. (1986). *Universal subgoaling and chunking: The automatic generation and learning of goal hierarchies,* Hingham, MA: Kluwer.

Laird, J. E. (1988). Recovery from incorrect knowledge in Soar. *Proceedings of AAAI-88.* St. Paul. Los Altos, CA: Morgan Kaufman.

Laird, J. E., Hucka, M., Yager, E. S., & Tuck, C. M. (in press). Robo-Soar: An integration of external interaction, planning and learning using Soar. *Robotics and autonomous systems.*

Laird, J. E., & Newell, A. (1983). A universal weak method: Summary of results. *Proceedings of IJCAI-83.* Karlsruhe. Los Altos, CA: William Kaufman.

Laird, J. E., Swedlow, K. R., Altmann, E., Congdon, C. B., & Wiesmeyer, M. (1989). *Soar User's Manual: Version 4.5.* (Unpublished).

Laird, J. E., Newell, A., & Rosenbloom, P. S. (1987). Soar: An architecture for general intelligence. *Artificial Intelligence, 33,* 1–64.

Lewis, R. L., Newell, A., & Polk, T. A. (1989). Toward a Soar theory of taking instructions for immediate reasoning tasks. *Proceedings of the 11th Annual Conference of the Cognitive Science Society.* Ann Arbor, MI. Hillsdale, NJ: Lawrence Erlbaum Associates.

Neisser, U. (1967). *Cognitive Psychology.* New York: Appleton-Century-Crofts.

Newell, A. (1981). The knowledge level. *Artificial Intelligence 18*, 18–127.
Newell, A. (in press). *Unified theories of cognition*. Cambridge, MA: Harvard University Press.
Newell, A., Rosenbloom, P. S., & Laird, J. E. (1989). Symbolic architectures for cognition. In M. I. Posner (Ed.), *Foundations of cognitive science* (pp. 93–131). Cambridge, MA: MIT Press.
Norman, D. A., & Bobrow, D. G. (1979). Descriptions: An intermediate stage in memory retrieval. *Cognitive Psychology, 11*, 107–123.
Polk, T. A. & Newell, A. (1988). Modeling human syllogistic reasoning in Soar. *Proceedings of the 10th Annual Conference of the Cognitive Science Society*. Montreal. Hillsdale, NJ: Lawrence Erlbaum Associates.
Polk, T. A., Newell, A., & Lewis, R. L. (1989). Toward a unified theory of immediate reasoning in Soar. *Proceedings of the 11th Annual Conference of the Cognitive Science Society*. Ann Arbor, MI. Hillsdale, NJ: Lawrence Erlbaum Associates.
Rosenbloom, P. S. (1988). Beyond generalization as search: Towards a unified framework for the acquisition of new knowledge. In G. F. DeJong (Ed.), *Proceedings of the AAAI Symposium on Explanation-Based Learning*. Stanford, CA: AAAI.
Rosenbloom, P. S. (1989). A symbolic goal-oriented perspective on connectionism and Soar. In R. Pfeifer, Z. Schreter, F. Fogelman-Soulie, & L. Steels (Eds.), *Connectionism in perspective*, (pp. 245–263). Amsterdam: Elsevier.
Rosenbloom, P. S., Laird, J. E., & Newell, A. (1987). Knowledge level learning in Soar. *Proceedings of AAAI-87*. Seattle. Los Altos, CA: Morgan Kaufmann.
Rosenbloom, P. S., Laird, J. E., & Newell, A. (1988). The chunking of skill and knowledge. In B. A. G. Elsendoorn & H. Bouma (Eds.), *Working models of human perception*. London: Academic Press.
Rosenbloom, P. S., Laird, J. E., & Newell, A. (1988). Meta-levels in Soar. In P. Maes & D. Nardi (Eds.), *Meta-level architectures and reflection*. Amsterdam: North Holland.
Rosenbloom, P. S., Laird, J. E., Newell, A., & McCarl, R. (in press). A preliminary analysis of the foundations of the Soar architecture as a basis for general intelligence. *Artificial Intelligence*.
Schank, R. C. (1975). *Conceptual information processing*. Amsterdam: North Holland.
Schank, R., & Ableson, R. (1977). *Scripts, plans, goals and understanding*. Hillsdale, NJ: Lawrence Erlbaum Associates.
Steier, D. M., Laird, J. E., Newell, A., Rosenbloom, P. S., Flynn, R., Golding, A., Polk, T. A., Shivers, O. G., Unruh, A., & Yost, G. R. (1987). Varieties of Learning in Soar: 1987. P. Langley (Ed.), *Proceedings of the Fourth International Workshop on Machine Learning*. Los Altos, CA, Morgan Kaufmann.
Tulving, E. (1983). *Elements of episodic memory*. New York: Oxford University Press.
Watkins, M. J., & Gardiner, J. M. (1979). An appreciation of generate-recognize theory of recall. *Journal of Verbal Learning and Verbal Behavior, 18*, 687–704.
Wiesmeyer, M. (1988). *Soar I/O Reference Manual, Version 2*. Unpublished manual.
Yost, G. R. (1987). *TAQ: Soar Task Acquisition System, Version 2*.
Yost, G. R., & Newell, A. (1988). *Learning new tasks in Soar*. Unpublished manual.

CHAPTER 42

Tower-Noticing Triggers Strategy-Change in the Tower of Hanoi: A Soar Model

D. Ruiz and A. Newell, Carnegie Mellon University

People who solve the Tower of Hanoi start out with a guided trial-and-error strategy and later acquire a recursive strategy, the generally most effective strategy. Protocol data shows that noticing and using subtowers in problem-solving differentiates two subjects who acquired the recursive strategy from one who did not. A working Soar model explains Tower of Hanoi strategy-acquisition by first assuming the basic ability to notice and use subtowers, and then charting the process by which this new knowledge is integrated with existing knowledge to produce the recursive strategy. Of particular importance in the integration is learning to see *nested* subtowers and using simple spatial-manipulation reasoning to figure out how to move those subtowers. The model shows a good qualitative fit to the data, providing support for Soar as a unified theory of human cognition.

THE PHENOMENON

How are new problem-solving strategies acquired? In particular, what new information triggers the acquisition process, and how is that information integrated into problem-solving to produce a new strategy? We address this question within the Tower of Hanoi domain. The puzzle (Figure 1) consists of five disks of graded sizes which in the initial state are sitting on one peg (the Source) to form a tower. The object is to move the disks to the Destination peg while moving only one disk at a time from peg to peg and never placing a larger disk on a smaller. Much is already known about this problem. In particular, it has been found that the Tower of Hanoi can be solved with a small number of well-defined, easily detectable strategies and that people tend to learn new strategies while solving it (Simon, 1975; Anzai & Simon, 1979). These characteristics make the problem ideal for studying strategy-acquisition.

Subjects start out solving the Tower of Hanoi using a guided trial-and-error (GTE) strategy and frequently end up using a recursive strategy (Egan & Greeno, 1974; Simon, 1975; Anzai & Simon, 1979; Ruiz, 1988; VanLehn, 1989). The GTE strategy consists of never moving the same disk twice in a row and never returning a disk to the peg from which it most recently came. The recursive strategy consists of setting a goal to move the largest disk that is not yet on the Destination to the Destination, followed by recursively setting subgoals to move blocking disks out of the way. Prior speculations and models of this change have typically relied on three assumptions (Egan & Greeno, 1974; Simon, 1975; Anzai & Simon, 1979). First, search takes place only in the Tower of Hanoi problem-space. Second, prior knowledge of (domain-independent) means-ends analyses (MEA) is necessary either to guide the acquisition of new

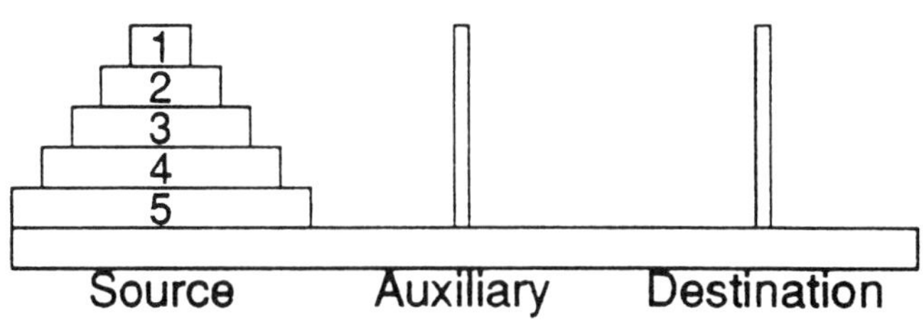

Figure 1: The Five-Disk Tower of Hanoi.

information that will later lead to the development of the recursive strategy, or to directly provide a template for building the recursive strategy. Third, little prior knowledge, drawn from other domains, is assumed. (VanLehn's model sets aside the MEA assumption, but retains the assumptions of a single problem-space and little prior knowledge.) Our theory, a working Soar model (Newell, in press), provides a new explanation of Tower of Hanoi strategy acquisition without having to make these sometimes overly restrictive assumptions.

HUMAN DATA

Our model is based on thinking-aloud protocols taken from three subjects solving the five-disk Tower of Hanoi problem: AS, RN, and PD. AS is Anzai and Simon's well-known (1979) subject, who did the following trials using a physical problem: part of a five-disk, a complete five-disk, a one-disk, a two-disk, a three-disk, a four-disk (these last four problems were experiments initiated by AS), and then two more five-disks. RN and PD were run in our laboratory on an IBM PC; they used special keys to pick up and drop disks. Numbers were printed on the disks to aid identification. They each did five complete trials of the five-disk Tower of Hanoi. Their moves and times were recorded. The following regularities were observed in the protocols:

1. All three subjects initially used the GTE strategy; RN and AS later acquired the recursive strategy. AS acquired it upon starting her three-disk experiment; RN acquired it during his first trial at state _,1234,5 (the Source is blank, Auxiliary has disks 1-4, and 5 is on Destination). While PD was able to solve the Tower of Hanoi, he did not acquire the recursive strategy; he did use lookahead, but that only infrequently (six times).
2. Solving one-disk and two-disk subtowers was trivial for all subjects.
3. Before acquiring the recursive strategy, RN set five subgoals and AS set six. Two of RN's subgoals and three of AS's subgoals were to move a two-disk subtower. In both, the two-disk tower was then planned out and moved. The remaining goals were to move larger towers; they were abandoned in favor of a move generated according to the GTE strategy.
4. Upon or after placing disk 4 on the Destination, all three subjects realized they had made an error and tried to rectify it.
5. Subtowers figured prominently in RN's and AS's pre-recursive problem-solving, but not in PD's pre lookahead problem-solving. (A subtower is defined as a stack of *k* consecutive-sized disks, with disk 1 as the first disk.) RN mentioned them explicitly in six statements such as "Now I need to move disks one, two, and three [to the] auxiliary." AS did her aforementioned four experiments solving subtowers. PD did mention subtowers five times in his pre-lookahead problem-solving. These mentionings were either vague or were comments on a tower just about to be completed; they never occurred while planning a move.
6. Recursion was displayed suddenly by both AS and RN, within one move.
7. Recursive reasoning occurred when AS and RN were confronted with subtowers (e.g., the state 5,4,123); there was little mention of goals while moving between subtowers.

SOAR

The theory we shall present is a subtheory within Soar. Soar provides the general theoretical constructs (learning, problem-spaces, memory structure, etc) that support and realize our strategy-change explanation. To understand the subtheory, it is necessary to first understand Soar.

Soar is a general cognitive architecture which models the human cognitive architecture (Newell, in press). Soar has an associative, recognition-based long-term memory (LTM), realized by productions, and a working memory to hold intermediate results of computation. As with humans, the *problem-space* (the problem-states and operators that can be used to solve the problem) is the basis of Soar's cognition (Newell, 1980). Given a goal to solve a problem, Soar makes progress by first deciding on a problem-space for that goal, then deciding on a problem-state, and then deciding on an *operator* to apply to that state. The operator is used to create a new state, to which new operators are applied, and so on. Each decision (problem-space, state, and operator) takes place within a *decision-cycle*, during which candidates are first generated via production match from LTM, followed by the selection of the best candidate. The selection is done by collecting desirability information about each candidate from LTM, and then applying a fixed decision procedure to this information. If Soar has conflicting or insufficient information to make a decision, it sets up a subgoal to resolve the *impasse*. By searching in one or more problem-spaces, Soar generates the needed information and resolves the impasse. Impasses can occur within impasses, leading to a subgoal hierarchy. Soar learns from its experience in resolving impasses by determining which working-memory elements were responsible for generating the results that resolved the most recent impasse in the stack. The responsible elements and the generated results become the condition and action, respectively, of a new production, a *chunk*. The chunk will fire when the impasse situation (or any other sufficiently similar situation) occurs in the future. Thus the chunk both avoids impasses and causes transfer of learning. Soar has no pre-built procedures for handling faulty chunks: they must be detected and overriden by deliberate problem-solving.

THE MODEL

The model consists of productions that provide the knowledge Soar needs to use the various problem-spaces. Each problem-space corresponds to a particular cognitive function (e.g., how to generate operators, and how to reason about generated operators). Our description of the model will first be problem-space oriented, with the exception of subtower-noticing, which does not occur in its own problem-space (Figure 2). Then, we will describe the mechanics of the individual models for RN and AS, and finally their general behavior. (PD is not modeled here, but is used simply to supply contrasting data.)

TOH

Tower Of Hanoi moves disks in the real world. TOH is assumed to arise from comprehending the

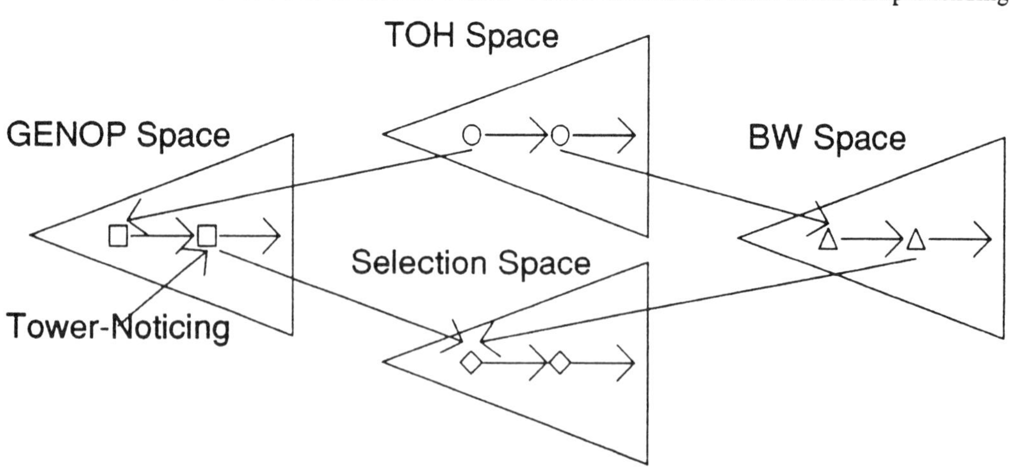

Figure 2: Summary of Problem-Spaces.

problem instructions, which specify how disks may be moved. (Future versions of this model will actually comprehend problem instructions, using the language comprehension system developed by Lewis, Newell & Polk (1989).) TOH translates the physically realizable results of operator generation and reasoning into disk movements. TOH is implemented in Soar with the move-disk operator, which transfers a disk from one peg to another.

GENOP

GENerate OPerator generates move-disk operators for TOH by first choosing a disk to move and then choosing a peg to which to move it. Operator generation is given a separate problem-space because it is a complex cognitive activity, as indicated by the fact that subjects employ several heuristics in generating operators. GENOP uses two heuristics to select disks for movement: do not repetitively move an object, and prefer the largest (non-repetitive) object which can be moved. GENOP employs three heuristics to select pegs: do not block the goal on the first move, do not move an object to the location from which it was last moved, and prefer to move an object to its final location (the Destination peg). Prior to the problem-solver perceiving a stack of consecutive-sized disks as both a unit (a subtower) and as movable, GENOP generates move-disk operators from the tops of the stacks, as they are the only movable disks. This effectively implements the GTE strategy. After a problem-solver has started seeing stacks of disks as movable subtowers, GENOP will generate operators to move the bottom disk of an encountered subtower. This effectively generates the operators needed to begin the recursive strategy. In the Soar model, GENOP has two operators: choose-disk and choose-to-peg. The results of these operators are recorded on the problem-state and then used to form a move-disk operator for TOH.

BW

Blocks World reasons about TOH's unimplementable move-disk operators. BW is so named because it reflects people's ability to do simple spatial-manipulation reasoning, of which blocks-world type problems are a paradigmatic case. This reasoning capability is called into use by the Tower of Hanoi's spatial character. Since spatial-manipulation reasoning is at least able to solve a two-disk problem, BW was built with enough knowledge to do that. BW does three things. First, given an unimplementable move, it determines the *blocking* object using two heuristics: prefer the largest movable object, and prefer the object that blocks the unimplementable move's desired location. Second, BW chooses a peg to which to move the blocking object, using the heuristic that it is best to move the blocking object out of the way of the desired move. Third, BW tries out the assembled move-disk operator. If this results in a new state, then the move-disk operator is implementable and is used to resolve the unimplementable operator's impasse. If no new state is produced, an impasse has occurred and BW is used again to resolve this new impasse. The final result of BW's reasoning is returned to TOH and executed. In the Soar model, BW has one operator for each action: a mark-blocking-disk operator, a mark-receiving-peg operator, and an operator called try-operator. The results of the first two operators are recorded on the state. Try-operator tries out the assembled operator as discussed above. When BW finally reasons out a move, it provides TOH with both the move and the operator it should use next, as determined in the reasoning chain.

Selection

Selection is a default, domain-independent problem-space that collects information about alternatives (usually, operators) and uses that information to choose one of them. The selection-space is derived from people's ability to use heuristics and to make simple choices as a result of applying those heuristics. The selection-space is used when a problem-space encounters an impasse in which it has insufficient information to directly choose between several alternatives. The selection-space applies all relevant heuristics for each alternative separately, and then integrates the results of those heuristics into a single choice, thus resolving the original problem-space's impasse. (The selection-space does not generate heuristics; it only applies them.) The selection-space has one operator: evaluate-object, which evaluates each alternative and records the results of each evaluation on the selection-space's problem-state.

Subtower-Noticing

Subtower-noticing distinguished RN and AS from PD, and thus is postulated to be the crucial variable in discovering the recursive strategy. Subtower-noticing occurs when the subject realizes that a series of consecutive, stacked disks (starting with disk 1) forms a tower, and makes the assumption that this tower might be moved as a unit. The subject's ability to see consecutive disks as a tower is derived from his/her prior knowledge of such things as towers, pyramids and triangles. The impetus to apply this knowledge to the problem comes from the problem name (the TOWER of Hanoi) plus the frequency with which subtowers occur in the problem. For example, in a perfect solution to a 5-disk problem, 12 of the 32 problem-states will have a subtower sitting by itself on a peg. Most important, the subject will, during his/her solution, encounter these subtowers in order of size. For example, s/he may see a two-disk tower followed by a three-disk tower, followed by a four-disk tower. This experience should lead the subject to see the subtowers as being nested, i.e., that a three-disk tower really consists of a two-disk tower sitting on top of disk 3. Seeing subtowers as nested is important because it effectively breaks a subtower down into components about which BW can reason. For, a nested subtower of k disks is really just a two-disk subtower: a $(k - 1)$-disk subtower sitting on disk k. (Of course, the $(k - 1)$-disk tower must itself be a two-disk tower for reasoning to proceed.) In Soar, tower-noticing occurs in the GENOP problem-space upon seeing a k-disk subtower sitting by itself on a peg. The noticing (implemented via productions) results in a minor change to the problem-state: the tower's bottom disk is marked as a tower and as movable. A chunk gets built that can then label that tower in any context, including when it is the subtower of another tower. Repeated experience with single subtowers thus gives Soar the ability (i.e., the chunks) to see nested subtowers. Since these chunks allow the use of BW, they (and not the subtower-noticing productions) are directly responsible for the development of the recursive strategy.

Model Mechanics

Two variant models were created, one each for RN and AS. The GENOP, BW, and TOH problem-spaces were the same in the two models. The productions constituting these problem-spaces were integrated into LTM before solving the Tower of Hanoi. The two models differed in three areas. First, RN's model was given the ability to label subtowers as subtowers before it was given the ability to label them as movable, while AS' model was given the two abilities simultaneously. This corresponds to the fact that RN noticed subtowers well before trying to move them, whereas AS noticed and used subtowers at the same time. In both models, the relevant productions were integrated into LTM at the indicated point in the human subjects' problem-solving. Second, AS required several additional productions to model the different initial states in her one-disk through four-disk problems. These were integrated into LTM before the start of each problem. Third, a small set of special-case productions (two for AS and one for RN) modeled instances in which the subjects used reasoning processes outside of the scope of the GENOP, BW, and TOH problem-spaces. In AS' model, one production was used to halt her simulation after placing disk 4 on the Destination in the first trial, mimicking AS' giving up midway on her first trial. Another production mimicked AS' second-trial realization that disk 1 had to go to the Destination on the first move. Finally, one production mimicked RN's violation of the disk non-repetition heuristic at state 5,_,1234. The first of these productions was introduced along with the three problem-spaces; the last two were introduced at the appropriate points in the problem-solving. Effectively, the two models only explained moves that corresponded to a strict use of the recursive and GTE strategies. Learning was always on; the models therefore learned continuously from their experience.

Model Behavior

Upon starting to solve the problem, the models used the TOH problem-space. Since TOH cannot generate operators, it encountered impasses and used GENOP to supply the needed move-disk operators. At this point, the models did not notice subtowers, and therefore generated implementable operators according to the GTE strategy. Upon learning about subtowers, GENOP began generating operators to move (the bottom disks of) subtowers. Since such operators were not directly implementable, impasses resulted and BW was used to reason out how to make progress towards applying the operators. BW tried to generate an operator to move the blocking disk/tower out of the way. If BW produced an implementable move-disk operator, the new operator was used in TOH. If BW produced an unimplementable operator, another impasse resulted and BW was once again used to reason about the new unimplementable operator. This successive use of BW on a single move produced the observed recursion. BW's first implementable result was used to continue progress in TOH. The selection-space was used every time GENOP or BW had to choose between several versions of an operator. The selection-space applied the heuristics discussed above to make the choices. Learning had three major effects on the model's behavior. First, it produced the chunks that noticed nested subtowers. Second, it abbreviated, with time, the amount of processing needed to use both the GTE and recursive strategies. Third, it eventually built chunks that directly generated move-disk operators in TOH, thus bypassing strategic processing.

MODEL AND DATA: THE FIT

Problem-Solving Fit

The models show a good quantitative fit to the subjects' external problem-solving behavior. Moves made by the model corresponded to 77% and 67% of AS's and RN's first-trial moves, respectively. In the remaining trials, the correspondence was almost always 100% with the exception of AS's second trial (94%) and RN's last trial (97%). Unmodeled moves were the result of errors or error-recovery on the subjects' part, both of which deviated from a perfect GTE or recursive sequence; these moves either had no analog in the models, or were mimicked with the special-purpose productions described above. (Both types of moves were counted against the models.) To test the models further, RN's move-times were correlated with the number of decision-cycles that his model required to make the corresponding moves. (Unmodeled moves were not included in this correlation.) The correlations, in order of trials, were r = 0.69, 0.61, 0.85, 0.45 (0.75), and 0.01. The Trial 4 correlation was low because RN remembered the first move and executed it directly, whereas the model reasoned it out; without this outlier, the correlation goes to 0.75. The final correlation was nil (and should be), because both RN and the model had low variance. Move-time data was not reported for AS in Anzai & Simon (1979) so no correlations could be calculated.

The models' problem-solving strategies displayed a good qualitative fit to the subjects'. We simulated a pure form of the GTE and recursive strategies. Therefore, the models showed some differences: their GTE showed no occasional goal-setting and their recursive strategy showed excess goal-setting between subtowers. Within these boundaries, the models' GTE and recursive strategies showed the same type of reasoning and behavior as AS and RN. The protocols might be fit more closely by remembering more of BW's reasoning chain or using the BW problem-space earlier. However, a closer fit would not change the basic result, i.e., that the recursive strategy arises from noticing and using (nested) subtowers in problem-solving.

Strategy-Change Fit

The models closely fit the qualitative aspects of the subjects' strategy-change. AS's and RN's models acquired the recursive strategy at the same point that AS and RN did. RN's model, like RN, acquires the recursive strategy at state _,1234,5; AS's model, like AS, acquires it during its 3-disk experiment. In both cases, the model's acquisition was the result of having correctly mimicked subtower-noticing and use. RN's model had been learning to notice subtowers for the same amount of time that

RN did; upon acquiring the ability to mark labeled towers as movable, the model was immediately able to make use of that information. AS's model had had previous experience with a two-disk tower, and thus saw the three-disk tower as a nested tower (a two-disk tower sitting on disk 3), allowing it to apply BW. Thus, the switch to the recursive strategy is not due to the subtower-noticing productions per se, but to the chunks that allow the models to see the subtowers as nested and to Soar's ability to recursively use problem-spaces. Finally, the models, like RN and AS, acquired the recursive strategy suddenly. This is because the models treat movable objects (disks or subtowers) alike: as soon as subtowers are noticed, they can immediately be reasoned about.

Learning Fit

The learning displayed by the models showed a good qualitative fit to the subjects'. Besides noticing subtowers, the models' learning did two major things: it abbreviated strategic processing and it eventually caused well-learned moves to be executed directly, without the need for any strategic processing. The abbreviation of strategic processing appeared in the protocols as decreased verbalization over trials, as well as corresponding decreases of move-times in RN's protocol. Making well-learned moves directly executable brought the model more in line with the sparse recursive reasoning displayed by the subjects. After the moves between major subtowers had been well-learned, the model, like the subjects, only reasoned out moves when confronted with a subtower.

CONCLUSIONS

Our model has provided a simple answer to the question of Tower of Hanoi strategy-acquisition. It comes about because people notice nested subtowers and use spatial-manipulation reasoning to move them. This latter capability is cast in terms of physical objects in general, and so is able to work with either disks or towers once these have been noted as relevant to the task at hand. In positing this answer, our model has bypassed the need for some of the basic assumptions of previous models and speculations. Our model, like previous models, works by problem-space search. However, our model works in multiple problem-spaces, not one, and thus claims that people (who can use multiple types of reasoning on a single task) do likewise. The claim of multiple problem-spaces is both a specific claim of our model and a general claim of Soar, which processes information in many problem-spaces.

Second, we have reduced the types of information that prior models claimed had to be learned. Like previous models, ours learns continuously from its experience. But, the crucial information that allows the switch to the recursive strategy is noticing (nested) subtowers. This paper has described how this knowledge is incorporated into problem-solving to produce a new strategy; future work will tackle the mechanics of subtower-noticing per se.

Third, our model has eliminated prior knowledge of domain-independent MEA as the cause of strategy-change. While our model certainly behaves according to MEA in the BW problem-space, that MEA is a direct result of domain-specific knowledge, and is not necessarily transferable to non-spatial-manipulation domains. The recursion characteristic of Tower of Hanoi solutions comes about because of Soar's ability to recursively use problem-spaces to resolve impasses. We have therefore set up a strong alternative hypothesis to strategy-adaptation: strategy-building. This claim about MEA is a general Soar claim, as Soar has nothing corresponding to a domain-independent MEA. Rather, Soar's use of weak methods stems from its task knowledge against the background of its use of multiple problem-spaces (Laird & Newell, 1983)

Fourth, our model directly relies on prior knowledge of a specific domain: spatial-manipulation problems. We have therefore taken this task out of the realm of knowledge-lean tasks, and made it more knowledge-intensive, where the knowledge used is knowledge of spatial relationships and operators. In so doing, we have blurred the boundaries of the traditional toy-task category.

Finally, the work done here will generalize to other task domains. The fundamental insight, that strategy-change comes about via noticing aggregate problem features and attempting to operate on them, is certainly empirically verifiable, and therefore amenable to modeling, in other tasks. The GENOP problem-space might be easily extended to other tasks, thus providing a source of models and ideas about people's default strategies. Finally, the BW problem-space might be expanded to include many other spatial-manipulation tasks, and thus might be the starting point for a single Soar theory of puzzle problem-solving.

To conclude, this model derives its explanatory power from being a subtheory of Soar. Soar provides the ability to search in problem-spaces, the learning, and the theory of how knowledge is transmitted between problem-spaces. Our task as theorists has been to carefully specify the knowledge people have about the Tower of Hanoi. What Soar has thus done is not only ease our burden as theorists, but reduce our theoretical degrees of freedom as well. In return, the success of this model supports Soar as a unified theory of human cognition.

ACKNOWLEDGEMENTS

We thank the members of the Soar group and the Carnegie-Mellon Department of Psychology, particularly David Klahr, Kenneth Kotovsky, and Kurt VanLehn for helpful criticism and insights on this work. We offer special thanks to two anonymous reviewers for their helpful comments. This work was supported by the Information Sciences Division, Office of Naval Research, under contract N00014-86-K-0678, and by a Ford Foundation Minority Postdoctoral Fellowship awarded to Dirk Ruiz. The views expressed in this paper are those of the authors and do not necessarily reflect those of the supporting agencies.

REFERENCES

Anzai, Y., & Simon, H. A. (1979). The theory of learning by doing. *Psychological Review, 86(2)*, 124-140.

Egan, D. E., & Greeno, J. G. (1974). Theory of rule induction: Knowledge acquired in concept learning, serial pattern learning, and problem solving. In L. W. Gregg (Ed.), *Knowledge and cognition*, Hillsdale, New Jersey: Lawrence Erlbaum Associates.

Laird, J. & Newell, A. (1983) A universal weak method: Summary of results. In *Proceedings of IJCAI-83*, Los Altos, CA: Kaufman.

Lewis, R., Newell, A. & Polk, T. (1989). *Towards a Soar theory of taking instructions for immediate reasoning tasks*. Manuscript submitted for publication.

Newell, A. (1980). Reasoning, problem solving, and decision processes: The problem space as a fundamental category. In R. Nickerson (Ed.), *Attention and Performance VIII*, Hillsdale, New Jersey: Lawrence Erlbaum Associates.

Newell, A. (in press). *Unified theories of cognition*. Cambridge, MA: Harvard University Press.

Ruiz, D. (1988). Learning and problem-solving: What is learned while solving the Towers of Hanoi (Doctoral dissertation, Stanford University, 1987). *Dissertation Abstracts International, 42*, 3438B.

Simon, H. A. (1975). The functional equivalence of problem-solving skills. *Cognitive Psychology, 7*, 268-288.

VanLehn, K. (1989). *Learning events in the discovery of problem solving strategies*. Manuscript submitted for publication.

CHAPTER 43

"But How Did You Know To Do That?": What a Theory of Algorithm Design Process Can Tell Us

D. M. Steier, Carnegie Mellon University

1. Motivation

An algorithm is a procedure, decribed in terms of some abstract computational model, to be implemented in a program. The design of such a procedure is usually a creative act, involving the integration of substantial amounts of knowledge about algorithms and the application domain in new ways to make design decisions. For most of the last decade, I (along with Elaine Kant, Allen Newell, and a host of students) have been involved in an effort to build an automatic algorithm designer. We have analyzed the design task, studied the behavior of human algorithm designers, and built several automatic systems embodying different approaches to algorithm design. This paper will focus on the theory of the algorithm design process that resulted from the research, and what that theory has to say about knowledge-based creative design. The paper argues for the following:

1. We have most of a computational theory of the design process and have built systems that implement most of that theory, using an architecture for general intelligence as a framework.
2. Within that theory, creativity can usefully be described as the application of knowledge in a task environment that is significantly different from the environment in which the knowledge was acquired.
3. Although incomplete, the current theory is sufficiently well-defined so that issues can at least be formulated in a precise way, providing sorely-needed structure on the research effort to understand creativity.

To the extent that there is any consensus at all among AI and design researchers, we all seem to agree that it would be nice to have a theory of design. What does that really mean? Ideally, a scientific theory both *explains* previous observations and *predicts* future observations of phenomena that fall within some well-defined scope. Such theories are commonplace in natural sciences such as physics, but not as common in "sciences of the artificial" [21], such as computer science. For understanding the performance of difficult intellectual tasks such as algorithm design, theories that both explain and predict in a non-trivial way are extremely rare.

This paper therefore first considers what is desired, in terms of the scope, form, and expected benefits of the theory. Then, some observations about algorithm design, obtained from analyzing both the design task directly and the behavior of human algorithm designers, are presented. We then summarize a theory of the algorithm design process that accounts for these observations. The theory permits us to draw some preliminary conclusions about creativity, which are then compared with the model of creative design of Maher, Zhao & Gero [14].

We are interested in understanding the process of going from an understanding of the problem to be solved by the algorithm to a description of the computational method for solving it. Since we seek an understanding of the *design* of algorithms, an understanding of the algorithms themselves, e.g. their computational complexity, etc., must be a part of the theory. The large body of knowledge about algorithms can simply be incorporated wholesale into the theory, leaving us free to concentrate in this paper on the manner in which a designer acquires and applies this knowledge. For human designers, the process may take from a few minutes for simple problems, to months or years for the research problems at the frontier of the field. The theory is primarily concerned with performance on the lower end of this time scale, minutes to hours, for which one can get both detailed data on human behavior, and reasonably detailed automatic design runs.

Within these boundaries of both subject and time scale, a theory of the algorithm design process can embody any of a number of approaches to design. Much of the research in automatic algorithm design has been devoted to developing and refining such approaches. For example, Manna and Waldinger [15] have long been advocating a deductive approach to design based on the extraction of an algorithm from a constructive proof of the existence of the algorithm's output. More recently, Lowry [13] has cast algorithm design in the framework of instantiation of parametrized theories.

Neither of these approaches has explicitly considered factors that we believe to be crucial in real design situations: constraints on resources and the availability of knowledge in usable form. Algorithm design, like any type of problem-solving, is difficult because designers are limited, both in the amount of resources (time, memory, etc.) that can be expended, and in the access to relevant knowledge, which may be of a variety of types, and come from diverse sources. The existence of such limitations is not dependent on whether the designer is a human being or a computer program; they stem from the need of a finite intelligent agent to cope with the diversity inherent in its environment and the necessity to act in real time. It is for this reason that the intended scope of the present theory is the behavior of algorithm designers on modestly difficult problems, given the need to cope both with bounded resources and diverse knowledge about the task.

What should a theory of this scope look like? It should be content-oriented, describing mechanisms sufficient to design algorithms in accordance with the assumptions of the theory. As an information-processing theory, it must posit representations capable of expressing different types of knowledge, as well as processes for accessing that knowledge, for integrating the knowledge to make decisions, and for acquiring new knowledge based on experience. This means that the theory must incorporate a theory of algorithm designers themselves. Although that requirement appears at first glance to put the desired theory out of our grasp, we find that much of the structure required is generic to all intelligent behavior, and has been described and implemented in the work on Soar, an architecture intended to realize such behavior [12]. Thus our theory is actually to be composed of a number of sub-theories: the theory of Soar, the theory of Soar-based design behavior, and the theory of the artifacts to be designed, including theories about algorithms themselves, techniques for their analysis, etc.

What is a theory of this scope and form good for? If the theory is precise enough, then its mechanisms can be embodied in practical automatic algorithm designers, or perhaps in algorithm design assistants. It may change the way novices are taught to design algorithms, and the methods experts apply to difficult algorithm design problems. Ideally, one would like use the theory as a scientific tool to predict how a designer with given resource constraints and access to particular bits of knowledge will perform on a given task. Performance could be measured in terms of success or failure, design time, decisions made, etc. Cognitive psychology is just now beginning to build such theories for humans engaged in short tasks (requiring response on the order of seconds), such as transcription typing [8]. For longer and more complex tasks such as algorithm design, it is extremely difficult to assess the initial state of a human designer in terms of knowledge available or to know exactly the computational constraints, so precise predictions can't be made. However, the theory we will present does permit relatively detailed explanations for observed human protocols, and the prediction of certain gross features of future human protocols. In this respect, it is similar in power (though not in scope) to Newell and Simon's theory of human problem solving [17]. Finally, one might also use the theory to make predictions about phenomena not strictly covered by the scope of the theory, but which are closely related; in this case, design of artifacts similar to algorithms, such as programs.

We are now ready to exhibit the data to be explained by the theory. Two kinds of data will be presented in the next two sections, respectively: 1) descriptions of what knowledge is relevant to the algorithm design task, and 2) observations of algorithm designers in action. The need for both of these becomes evident when we consider designers in terms of the *knowledge level* [16]. An agent such as a designer that functions perfectly at the knowledge level, one who is perfectly intelligent, will apply all available knowledge to achieve its goals. The total pool of knowledge upon which such an ideal designer could draw is specified by the first kind of data. The second kind of data is necessary because actual designers working in real-time, whether human or machine, can only approximate perfect knowledge-level behavior. Real design tasks are characterized by a complex environment in which knowledge is not immediately available and by limited designers who can't afford to reason indefinitely to make decisions [21]. Given that the research goal is to build a theory of design that accounts for behavior under such conditions, and since humans are currently the most robust and expert designers, then the second type of data will be obtained by studying human designers.

2. An analysis of the knowledge used in algorithm design

The available publications and most courses on the subject of algorithms give relatively little insight into how algorithms could be designed. Consequently, the design of a particular algorithm may first appear to be a magical act, not even amenable to decomposition into motivated steps, much less automation. But the design of any artifact, including an algorithm, involves a series of choices. At each choice point, alternatives must be proposed, evaluated (if there are more than one), and a selection made between the proposed alternatives. One way to make these proposals, evaluations, and selections explicit is to create a rational reconstruction of the algorithm in the form of an *idealized design history*. An example of an idealized design history for Graham's convex hull algorithm [7] is shown in Appendix I; it is one of seven convex hull algorithm design histories we constructed [23]. Other examples, compiled from 23 presentations in the literature on algorithms and program transformations, can be found in [25]. The main advantage of constructing idealized design histories is that they force one to be explicit about the rationale for each deliberate act in the design, and therefore permits a detailed assessment of the knowledge used. The assessment resulted in the following observations:

There is substantial regularity in design goals: In the presentations surveyed in [25], most of the goals upon which design decisions were based pertained to functional correctness (in terms of desired input-output relationships). Other considerations (in order of decreasing frequency) were time complexity, simplicity, space complexity, and algorithm termination. Together with correctness, these categories accounted for over 90% of the goals. This does not imply that progress towards these goals is always easily measured, but it does show that the goals most commonly targeted in algorithm design form a fairly small set.

The process of deciding between alternatives is often simple and well-defined, if only because the work has been done in proposing the alternatives: This conclusion is based on studying the 59 selection rationales in the idealized design histories for the seven convex hull algorithms. In some cases, such as in measuring expected-case complexity or simplicity, some effort is required to formalize and apply the appropriate metrics, but this happens infrequently. This is due in large part to the fact that in over half the decisions, the decision is practically forced because the right set of alternatives is proposed. Infeasibility of the other proposed alternatives, where a successful algorithm can not be designed given the previous design path, accounts for about one-sixth of the rationales. Over a third of the choices were forced because there was only one candidate, and a little under a fourth of the choices were essentially arbitrary, since all alternatives met the specification for the subproblem equally well. Based on these facts, we conclude that selection between design alternatives is generally not a creative process.

Relatively little is understood about how design alternatives are proposed. This was noticed in studying the convex hull algorithms. The vast majority of the proposal rationales for these designs is that a given geometric fact, or in some cases, a given algorithmic refinement, happens to be known and is used at the right time. Often, these facts can be proven formally given the right axioms or induced, given the right diagram, as mentioned earlier. But the provability of such facts is unhelpful, since these facts are needed for *proposal* of actions, where the desired fact is unknown. In some cases, the existence of a design scheme, such as divide-and-conquer [22], suggests functional roles for refinements to play. For example, the divide step in a divide-and-conquer algorithm should produce smaller subproblems, with subproblem size being a mapping from subproblems to elements in some well-founded ordering. But the designer must still discover that the candidate refinements possess the required properties. This is where any additional effort at analyzing the application domain, e.g. geometry in the case of convex hull algorithms, will have the greatest payoff in facilitating creative design.

A wide variety of types of knowledge are considered in design. We cast the knowledge used in the idealized design histories for the convex hull algorithms into rule form, e.g. *If an algorithm is to find the extreme member of a set by generating them all, require the set to have a finite number of elements.* Over the design of the seven algorithms, 80 such rules were generated. The rules are used a total of 206 times for all the designs, since many rules (49 of the 80) are used more than once. To determine the set of concepts that were used in the rules, each rule was abstracted into keywords, and the total sum collected. For example, the rule above was abstracted into: *extreme-member, set, generate-and-test --> require, set, cardinality, finite.* Performing this abstraction for all the rules yields 134 concept terms, with an average of 3.3 occurrences per term, that can be classified into sixteen broader categories: specification, problem-solving, design, efficiency, parallelizability, simplicity, inputs-and-outputs, algorithm schemes, algorithm refinements, data structures, order, number, arithmetic, sets, sequences, and geometry.

The diversity of knowledge is apparent even at the level of individual rules: Continuing the analysis above, the keywords in each abstracted rule were replaced by the conceptual categories listed above to get a further abstraction of the knowledge, e.g. *order, sets, algorithm-schemes --> problem-solving, sets, number.* The purpose of this further abstraction is to study the rules in terms of how they connect different types of knowledge. One can count the number of distinct conceptual areas referenced in the conditions of each rule, in the actions, and the union of the conditions and actions. The distributions of the number of references are shown in Figure 2-1. The average number of references to distinct conceptual areas per left-hand-side is 2.8, per right-hand-side, 1.6, and per rule total is 3.5 (so there is an overlap of about one area between left- and right-hand-sides). One could do a similar analysis on the knowledge in program synthesis systems, with rules stating, for example, that a given abstract data structure can be refined into a given concrete data structure. I conjecture that for those systems, and in fact most current knowledge-based programming tools, all three averages would be closer to one. It is perhaps no accident that such systems are focused on routine, rather than creative design.

3. Results of protocol analyses

Considering the variety of knowledge needed to design algorithms, it is impressive that people can succeed at the task in relatively short periods of time, even knowing that they're being taped for careful study later. We made audio- (and in some cases video-) tape recordings of fifteen computer science undergraduate students, graduate students, and faculty who were instructed to talk aloud as they worked on algorithm design problems. The problems ranged in difficulty from verifying the correctness of a given implementation of binary search to the design of convex hull algorithms; the length of the resulting protocols ranged from ten minutes to over an hour. The protocols of these recordings were analyzed to produce models of the processes used by the designers. The protocol analysis consisted of hypothesizing that a designer works in particular problem spaces (using certain representations and operators), and studying the protocol, phrase-by-phrase, to refine the hypotheses. In three cases, the analysis produced a graph of the subject's problem space search. Constructing such a *problem behavior graph* [17] is perhaps the most detailed analysis possible on data of this type. The results of the studies have been published and discussed in detail in [9, 10, 11]. They are summarized here:

Abstract algorithm representation: Designers have a representation for algorithms and algorithm fragments that is not tied to a particular programming language (though it may be influenced by languages they know). The key features of this representation are its data flow character, object (or data) oriented control, and a small set of

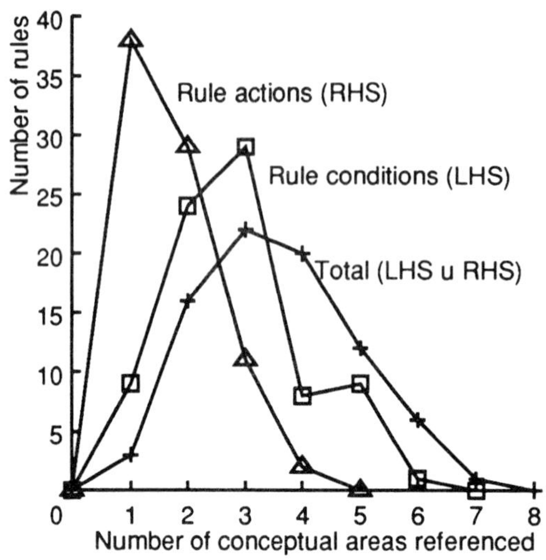

Figure 2-1: Number of distinct conceptual references per rule

primitive steps of general functional character (e.g. *generate*, *compare*).

Refinement of schemes: In almost all cases, designers chose a basic scheme, or kernel idea, for the algorithm relatively quickly, and devoted the remainder of the time to refining the initial scheme. Occasionally, a basic scheme is abandoned and a new one selected. An example of a scheme is *divide-and-conquer*, and a sample refinement of that scheme is the choice of partitioning a set of numbers about its median to divide a problem into subproblems.

Means-ends-analysis (MEA) for control: Usually, design is guided by difficulties and opportunities for refinement detected in the current design. This locally-driven process often results in differing levels of refinement for different parts of the algorithm. Unless a problem is very routine for a designer, there is almost never strict adherence to a top-down refinement strategy.

Execution to drive MEA: Given that design is fundamentally driven by MEA, execution of partial algorithms is the method to find differences between the desired properties of the algorithm and the properties present in the current design. The execution works on inputs at a variety of levels of detail, so that the inputs may be symbolic, yielding *symbolic execution*, or actual data items (such as the set {2, 5, 7}), yielding *test-case execution*.

Test-case execution sets the stage for discoveries: During test-case execution, designers will often draw figures or use methods that they later realize can be used to satisfy accomplish some unsatisfied algorithm refinement goal. In the case of figures, visual noticing operations, which may perceive some symmetry or complete the missing edge of a polygon, are often automatically applied, and result in structures later recognized to be useful. We say that discovery occurs when a designer "does the right thing for the wrong reasons."

Progressive deepening behavior: The pattern of execution during design displays much repetition, with the analysis slightly varied or extended on each repetition, in a manner determined by prior knowledge. Evidence of progressive deepening is seen in the problem behavior graphs, and is similar to that encountered by DeGroot [4], and Newell and Simon in protocol analyses of chess players [17].

Explanation is another iteration of progressive deepening: When explaining an algorithm to somebody else, designers do not seem to be just reading off an internal data structure representing the algorithm. Rather, they explain what is happening as they reconstruct the algorithm by execution. The execution process is the same as used for design, so much so that designers often detect bugs during their explanations, and interrupt themselves to repair these bugs as if they were still in the "design phase."

4. A theory of the algorithm design process

We have seen that the ability to design interesting algorithms not to stem as much from the quantity of the knowledge possessed (measured in terms of numbers of rules) as from the scope. The rules generated from the idealized design histories use a conceptual vocabulary with on the order of 100 distinct terms, falling into 10 or 20 conceptual categories. People often integrate ideas from different categories to make design decisions, and an analysis of the rules derived from the idealized design histories shows that rules that reference several categories are by far the norm rather than the exception. Thus a a major constraint on a theory of the algorithm design process is that the mechanisms it describes must be capable of combining knowledge of diverse types. The theory described in this section incorporates such mechanisms in a cognitively plausible manner, relying on execution and progressive deepening search to retrieve and apply the relevant knowledge in developing algorithms.

As mentioned before, we base our theory of design on the mechanisms present in the Soar architecture [12]. Soar is ultimately intended to function automonomously, capable of acquiring and applying knowledge to work on the entire range of tasks requiring intelligent behavior. Although such functionality requires Soar to interact with its environment, we do not focus on that interaction here[1], except to note the constraint it imposes for a theory of design: the necessity to act in real-time excludes any theory requiring potentially unbounded amounts of computation to make decisions.

Our focus here will be on the internal cognitive processing, which for Soar means to understand how problem spaces are searched to design algorithms. A problem space is a collection of states, operators that move from state to state, a state representing the initial situation of the problem solver, and one or more desired states representing task accomplishment. Problem spaces are distinguished from ordinary state spaces in that they preserve a problem space invariant: any path from initial state to desired state obtained by application of operators in that space consitutes an acceptable solution to the problem. In Soar, every decision is formulated in terms of problem space search: what problem space to use, what initial state in the space should be used, what operators to apply, and how new states in the space should be generated when an operator is applied. The knowledge to make these decisions is stored in a long-term recognition memory as productions. These productions are matched against objects describing the short-term problem solving situation, stored in working memory. Those productions that are determined to be relevant fire to add information to working memory, including preferences about what actions to perform. Examples of such preferences include those of the form that a given problem space is acceptable, a given state is required for the current space, or that one operator should be preferred to another for application to the current state. These preferences are accumulated during the elaboration phase of a two-phase decision cycle. When no further productions can fire in an elaboration phase, Soar continues with the decision procedure, which uses the available preferences to make a new selection for a problem space, state or operator in the total problem solving context. If insufficient knowledge is available to make such a choice, an impasse is encountered, and Soar generates a subgoal to resolve the impasse. For example, if Soar knows that two operators are acceptable, but neither is known to be

[1]A complete theory of the design process must also account for such interaction, which would explain how the designer draws figures, perceives patterns and consults outside sources for advice.

preferable to the other, a tie impasse results. In working on the subgoal to resolve such an impasse, Soar will select problem spaces, states and operators, just as it did in the previous contexts. In this way, Soar generates subgoal hierarchies, and recursively applies its knowledge to terminate those goals.

Soar also has a mechanism that uses the subgoal hierarchy to learn from experience. Those working memory elements added to higher-level spaces, states or operators based on the elements in lower-level contexts are considered subgoal results. Soar learns to generate those results in future similar situations without subgoaling by building new productions, known as chunks. Similar situations are recognized by chunks because the chunks test those attributes of the problem solving context that existed prior to the impasse and were examined in order to generate the result of the subgoal. Chunking, which is Soar's only learning mechanism, thus can generalize from irrelevant attributes of problem solving situations and lead to transfer of knowledge under a variety of conditions [26].

Given the major elements of Soar (problem spaces, recognition memory, the decision cycle, impasse-driven subgoals, and chunking) as a basis, we are finally ready to present our theory of the algorithm design process, summarized in the following propositions:

1. Design takes place in multiple problem spaces. A subset of these spaces embodies the target model of computation, and another set embodies the model of the application domain.
2. The task of design is to use knowledge of the application domain to build a procedure for computing the desired output in the computational spaces.
3. The computational spaces have functional operators corresponding to steps in an algorithm, at whatever level of abstraction is necessary for the design.
4. Means-ends analysis on the results of execution drives the design, with the resulting series of execution passes in a design session exhibiting the pattern of progressive deepening.
5. Any part of the knowledge necessary for accomplishing the design task may be acquired by learning. The algorithm itself is represented as learned knowledge for navigating through the computational spaces.

The remainder of this section expands on this summary.

The basic concepts of the theory are taken straight from algorithm design texts [2]. A *model of computation* specifies the set of executable primitive operations and their associated costs. An *algorithm* is a procedure that is executable under some model of computation and that terminates for some class of valid inputs.

The model of computation defines the space of possible alorithms that could serve as candidate solutions to an algorithm design problem. Theoretically, one could solve algorithm design problems by searching this space, generating and testing candidate solutions until finding one satisfying the specifications. Unfortunately, the space of procedures defined directly in terms of primitives at the level of machine instructions is too large to solve problems in a reasonable amount of time (though it has been tried [6]). In general, the way to make search tractable is to apply knowledge to decrease the number of candidate solutions that need to be tested. In this instance, we know that certain designs can be considered together, because the differences between them do not matter at the functional level at which algorithm design normally takes place. What is needed is a representation that groups functionally equivalent designs together, forming an abstracted version of the original computational model.

The theory incorporates such a representation: algorithms are represented procedurally in terms of functional operators corresponding to the conceptual building blocks of algorithm design. These operators include: repeatedly *generate* elements of a set, *test* a data item for the truth of some predicate, *compare* two data items, *select* a data item from a set, *apply* some function to data (perhaps recursively), *store* data into memory, and *retrieve* data from memory. These operators are in some sense "natural" set, in that people who design algorithms use these terms, and that alternatives would not vary radically from these. These operators may be composed into higher level operators, and so on. For example, in designing divide-and-conquer algorithms, it is often useful to speak of an operation to *decompose* the problem into subproblems, and an operation to *compose* the solutions to the subproblems to get the answer to the original problem. So these steps can become operators in the language. The point is that the level of abstraction adapts as appropriate to the goals of the design process, allowing the designer to focus only on relevant details.

A theory of the algorithm design process must also define how a designer determines what the desired algorithm is to compute; this information is provided in the problem *specification*. We assume that, at a minimum, a specification provides (perhaps implicitly) a procedure that exhibits the desired behavior if executed in a model of the application domain. Even a specification that specifies the form of the output and the conditions for recognizing when an output is valid contains enough information for a generate and test procedure (assuming the output domain is recursively enumerable). Another way to state this is that given a specification and some input, a designer has enough information to compute the desired outputs of the algorithm using primitive operations that may be distinct from those for which the algorithm is being designed. For example, a designer who understands a convex hull problem specification will be able to find the convex hull of a given set of points, perhaps by using visual operations, without necessarily knowing an algorithm for finding hulls on a conventional computer.

Additional constraints may come from performance requirements on the algorithm or from resource limitations on the design process itself. An example of a constraint on the algorithm is that the number of times a particular operation is performed should not be more than a given function of the input size. An example of a constraint on the design process is a limitation on the resources that may be expended to solve the design problem. The task of the designer is to find an algorithm for the target computational model that is functionally equivalent to the algorithm for the application model, while satisfying the given constraints.

Any theory of problem-solving processes must stipulate some mechanism for determining when the problem-solving is finished. For the algorithm design task, there must be some way to tell if the algorithm satisfies the specification. The difficulty, given the theory so far, is that testing for equivalent functionality of two procedures (one for the application domain and one for the computational model) is undecidable in the general case. However, we desire only a mechanism that works for the cases that occur in practice, which are usually simple. A direct match suffices if the relevant functional properties can be represented so that similarities and differences are easily detectable. If procedures for both the domain model and the computational model are always executable, a possible strategy is to execute both models so that the features of interest can be read off directly from the results of the executions. For example, one could check if the behavior of the algorithm designed so far is equivalent to that of the specification for a given class of inputs by running both the domain model and the computational model on a representative of that class and checking to see if the outputs match. If the input class includes all valid inputs to the algorithm, the execution is equivalent to verification if carried out in full generality. Specialized execution procedures have many applications in design, including testing for correctness in specific cases, checking for type clashes, even efficiency analysis and explanation. These variations on a theme arise from changing the input and the processing of the interpreter doing the execution in accordance with the goals of the designer.

Assuming an execution-based design process, an issue remains of how the process is guided, since designs can be executed on many examples and at varying levels of abstraction. The purpose of execution is to make all the information necessary to make the next design decision available *locally*, in the immediate context in which the designer is working. Given the right input and attention to detail, execution can propagate relevant constraints imposed as a result of previous design decisions to a single context for inspection. Familiar patterns can then be recognized in the context by a simple match. The next design step can focus on whatever problems or opportunities are found by such recognition. Execution therefore occurs in the context of *means-ends analysis*: the current state of the design is compared to the desired state, and operators are applied to reduce those discrepancies deemed most critical to the success of the design. The comparison is done by execution and inspection of the results, while recognition of familiar patterns helps to make the decision about the relative importance of problems and the remedies to be applied. The execution takes place as a series of runs, with the partial design being executed each time until something unexpected is noticed, such as a bug or opportunity for refinement, or the algorithm is completely executed and design is considered finished. Much of the algorithm structure is traversed repeatedly, but each run examines a slightly different aspect of the design, resulting in the behavior known as *progressive deepening*.

Note that we have not posited a sophisticated, intelligent, fixed control mechanism specific to algorithm design to guide execution. Instead, the theory claims that the patterns of execution behavior arise when rather simple problem-solving methods are applied in the context of available knowledge about algorithms and the application domain. This is a consequence of the embedding of the design theory within an adaptive architecture for intelligence, and in fact the variety of strategies one would expect from this theory are exhibited in protocols of human algorithm designers.

Finally, learning from experience plays an important role in the design theory. The algorithm designed is represented as procedural knowledge, which is acquired in the process of learning to execute the algorithm in the computational space. The design terminates when enough such knowledge has been learned so that the algorithm can be executed directly without consulting other sources of knowledge to resolve operator selection and implementation impasses. The learned knowledge constituting the design is stored along with all other knowledge in long-term memory and is evoked when relevant attributes of the problem-solving context have the same values as existed in the situtation in which the knowledge was acquired. Thus learned knowledge can transfer both within a design, as in repeated executions, and across designs, as in when the current design problem is appropriately similar to one seen previously. With a general-purpose learning mechanism such as Soar's chunking, learning can be used not only to design the algorithms themselves, but also to acquire specifications and to augment the designer's knowledge about the application domain and algorithm design techniques.

Much of the theory has been shaped by the constraints of diversity of knowledge and bounded design resources. Algorithms are represented in spaces of abstract functional operators because such spaces are easiest to search for the design task. Specifications are cast in procedures for searching application domain spaces because this is the form in which knowledge about the problem is initially available in the environment. Model-based representations are used because purely propositional representations may necessitate large amounts of computation to guarantee correct inferences, when such a guarantee is possible at all. Execution in the context of means-ends analysis seems to be the most natural way to inspect models so that any potentially relevant knowledge may be brought to bear. Progressive deepening is useful because the entire state of the design need not be kept continuously in working memory since the relevant parts can be regenerated on each execution pass. Learning ties all this together by shifting knowledge between spaces, by minimizing the expense of repeated execution, and by lessening the load on limited working memory by transferring the knowledge to long-term memory. Thus virtually every important aspect of the theory is affected by these constraints.

Almost all of the mechanisms posited by this theory have been implemented in a program, called Designer-Soar. The operation of Designer-Soar in creating a variant of insertion sort (first created by the CYPRESS system [22]) is summarized in Table 4-1 (further details of the design are given in [24]). The same format is used as for the idealized design histories, so unfortunately, the progressive deepening nature of the search is not evident from the table. C1 and C2 occur on a first pass of abstracted symbolic execution. C3 and C4 occur on a second execution pass, this time using the empty sequence as input to test-case execution. C5 through C8 occur on a single element sequence, and C9 through C14 occur as a result of execution on two large sequences. Each execution pass allows refinement of a different aspect of the algorithm. The entire run takes 883 decision cycles, requiring about 35 minutes on a Sun3/260.

Choice	Alternatives considered (selected alts. *italicized*)	Rationale for choice
C1. **Specification**	`Sort` *integer sequence*	Domain procedure acquired by TAQ
C2. **Sort scheme**	*Divide-and-conquer* Generate-and-test, Other functional operators	Abstract lookahead
C3. **Sort decomposability test**	`Length`(*Input*) > 0 *true*	Can't decompose empty sequences
C4. **Sort directly-solve**	`Id`	Domain op says empty sequence is sorted
C5. **Sort DivConq form**	*Simple decompose* Simple compose	Pre-selected preference
C6. **Sort decomposition**	`FirstRest` ListSplit	Pre-selected preference
C7. **Insertion scheme**	*Divide-and-conquer* Generate-and-test Other functional operators	Abstract lookahead
C8. **Insertion decomposability test**	`Length`*(seq-param)* > 0 *true*	Can't decompose empty sequences
C9. **Insertion DivConq form**	*Simple compose* Simple decompose	Pre-selected preference
C10. **Insertion directly-solve**	`Cons` `Second-in-pair`	`Cons` returns desired result
C11. **Insertion decompose scheme**	*Conditional* Non-conditional function	Domain execution shows two possibilities for returning results
C12. **Insertion decompose predicate**	*int-param* ≥ `First`*(seq-param)* *int param* ≤ `First`*(seq-param)*	Need ordered result for composition
C13. **Insertion decompose action**	*Smallest first in returned result* Largest first in returned result	Ensure smallest element moved to front in example
C14. **Insertion composition**	`Cons` `Id`	`Cons` returns desired result

Table 4-1: Insertion-sort design in Designer-Soar.

The fact that the program actually designs algorithms allows us to make the claim of sufficiency for the mechanisms. The claim can not yet be made that these mechanisms are necessary (although we are developing some strong opinions based on our experience, e.g. for the use of annotated models, progressive deepening, etc.).

5. Creativity in the Context of the Theory

A relatively detailed theory of the computational design process has been presented and implemented; what does this all have to do with creative design? To answer this question, we must define creativity, since the standard view of creativity as "the process of coming up with something new in a way we don't really understand yet" automatically puts creativity beyond the reach of scientific inquiry.

It seem that the adjective "creative" must refer to the use of knowledge, rather than the final artifact produced by the design process. The first time a particular designer produces a design, we may call the design creative. If the designer learns from the experience and produces the same design in the future, it would be considered routine rather than creative design (if it would be considered design at all). Also, what may be an instance of creative behavior in a novice may not be considered creative at all in an expert; the classification seems to depend crucially on the past experience of the designer as well as the design task itself. Therefore, we will define creativity as *the use of knowledge in a task environment that is significantly different from the environment in which the knowledge was acquired.*

Our previous studies of human algorithm designers noted that discovery occurs when a structure previously created for one purpose is found to satisfy another previously unsatisfied goal. This definition of discovery complements the one we have presented for creativity. Further, it suggests that differences between task environments should be measured in terms of the functionality a given structure is known to provide. Designers' knowledge of objects includes information about common functional roles as well as structural properties [5]. Routine design selects objects to be design refinements based on functional roles the objects are already known to fulfill. In creative design, in contrast, objects are selected by their structural properties to fulfill new functional roles.

A simple example will illustrate: If a designer with some experience in computational geometric algorithms is told to design an algorithm to find the convex hull of a set of point, the designer will usually assume a target computational model with generators, tests, function applications, etc. described above. If the designer is then told that the primitives to be used are not those at all, but rather operations using a hammer, a board, a rubber band, and some nails, some surprise may be expected, because those items are not normally thought to be useful for algorithm design. A creative designer will use the knowledge that a convex hull is the smallest polygon that encloses a set of points, and that a rubber band stretched around one or more objects of sufficient size will contract to enclose the smallest area it can. This area is easily defined if the objects can be fixed so that their position and boundaries are not deformed. Eventually the designer may hit on the solution of hammering in the nails to correspond to coordinates in the plane and stretching a rubber bound around the perimeter formed by the group of nails. Exclusive of preprocessing, this is a constant-time algorithm, and the designer who discovers this procedure can be considered to have exhibited creativity.

Designer-Soar (nor any other automatic algorithm designer) does not currently perform this kind of creative problem-solving. The design of algorithms such as insertion sort uses knowledge in relatively routine fashion. Yet, we have sufficient experience, both in system implementation and in observing human designers that do exhibit creativity [11], to offer some speculation on two developments that might be required:

Conceptual organizations of problem spaces accessible in multiple contexts: Knowledge is retrieved in two ways in Soar: By automatic recognition, as production firings, or by deliberate search through operator application and subgoaling. Creativity arises precisely in those cases where knowledge is not available directly by recognition, or even by application of operators in a single space. An impasse and corresponding subgoal are generated, and Soar must then select a problem space in which to work on the subgoal. Nearly all current Soar systems do not engage in extensive problem-solving to determine what problem space to use; the knowledge has usually been hand-coded as productions that dictate this decision. We expect that for creative design, Soar must be able to use a variety of problem spaces, and hence representations, to solve a problem. Thus, the problem of problem space selection needs to be cast itself as problem space search. The knowledge of what problem spaces are available must be explicitly represented and reasoned about, in the same way that a person can list what concepts are relevant to a problem, even in some of the cases where the problem can't be solved yet. In design, the concepts would be retrieved by functional roles, structural properties, or a combination thereof. The nature of such concepts and their associated indices is therefore an important research topic for us.

Increased use of progressive deepening: As previously stated, discoveries seem to involve re-examination of a previously created structure with respect to a new goal. It appears that this behavior could be produced by employing the strategy of progressive deepening, but further research will be required to understand this completely. Currently, progressive deepening behavior in Designer-Soar is produced by applying the same execution operator sequence at different levels of abstraction or on slightly different examples. This mechanism is only partially succesful at this point, as some of the chunks used to transfer knowledge to successive execution passes do not fire when needed. These chunks are overspecific, being dependent on the context in which they were generated, that is, the example being used as input to the algorithm. What seems to be required is a capability to generate a structure, remember it, and retrieve it in a variety of contexts. Fortuantely, such a capability has been implemented in Soar in the work on *data chunking* [19], originally used to model psychological data on verbal learning. Using data chunking, we expect to be able to store arbitrary structures and reproduce them for re-examination in contexts that are not just re-executions of the same operator sequence.

While both of these extensions may be difficult to implement, they do not seem infeasible, as they extend existing mechanisms in Soar. We also expect to obtain additional leverage and constraint from other researchers in Soar currently working on similar problems in different applications.

6. Discussion and comparison with related work

This paper has proposed a theory of knowledge-based creative design, based on detailed analyses of the knowledge involved in design and of human design behavior. Although we have grounded our theory in the domain of algorithm design, it can be generalized to other design domains. The theory can be restated in more general terms as follows: Design takes place in multiple spaces. One space or set of spaces defines the requirements to be fulfilled by the designed artifact. The requirements specify the intended functionality for the artifact with respect to some environment. Another space or set of spaces is defined by the primitive objects out of which the artifact is to be built. There exists some inspection-based method for assessing the state of the partial design in the space of primitives with respect to the requirements. This method, which is execution in the case of algorithms, is used to bring together information for a locally-driven means-ends analysis process. The structure of the artifact being produced is explored by repeated inspection, with additional details of the design being specified on each repetition. Any information relevant to the design process that must persist for more than a few seconds (the span of working memory) will be stored in long-term memory by the designer's learning mechanism: this includes the specifications, any record of the design decisions made, as well as the final design produced. This theory has been applied in some to detail to the analysis of protocols of software designers [1]. We also believe it can fruitfully be applied to non-software related domains. For example, a problem behavior graph displayed by Akin in [3] shows clear evidence of progressive deepening in architectural design.

To conclude we will briefly compare this theory to the model of knowledge-based creative design offered by Maher, Zhao, and Gero [14]. Their model of design is based on state-space search, in which the operators transform partial design descriptions into new descriptions. These operators are based on design prototypes, which encapsulate knowledge relating function and structure in the design domain. Creative design is characterized by the incorporation of knowledge from outside the space. This external knowledge is used to modify or generate prototypes that expand the set of design descriptions reachable within the space. The two operations they suggest to make use of this external knowledge are mutation (syntactic modifications to structural descriptions that don't adhere to semantic constraints on the representations), and analogy (the use of a prototype despite a mismatch to the functional requirements of the situation). A system applying these methods to structural engineering problems has been partially implemented.

We see the mechanisms of mutation and analogy (they are closely related) as being entirely compatible with the theory of the algorithm design process presented in this paper. Algorithm designers often combine computational steps in novel ways to see what happens in the context of execution, and the results may form the basis for new discoveries. The problem of control of analogy maps directly into the question of how to identify useful concepts from other spaces, which still to be addressed in a subtantial way in the work on Soar. In the reverse direction, we see the method of means-ends-analysis based on the results of execution (or rather, its equivalent in structural engineering) and the strategy of progressive deepening to be applicable to their model.

Perhaps the major difference is in the problem spaces searched. We do not assume an explicit search of a space of partial design descriptions as do Maher, et.al., since previous experiments found that this led to unacceptably high overhead in maintaining such descriptions [24]. Rather, such design descriptions are the paths learned from execution in a space of the computational primitive operations. Thus what is creative is the use of knowledge from other spaces to control search in the computational space. The model of Maher, et.al. incorporates external knowledge to expand a single space, and therefore assumes human guidance in formulating the initial design prototypes as well as insuring useful external knowledge is available. Our goal is to model the entire process, rather than provide interactive tools, hence the different strategies.

In both cases, though, the commitment to a problem-space based framework seems to have provided useful structure for our research into understanding knowledge-based creative design. Eventually we hope that those frustrated design students who ask "But how did you know to do that?" may receive operational answers as a result of this research.

I. A case study in algorithm design: the convex hull problem

This appendix examines a particular problem of the type we are trying to build a system to solve, designing an algorithm to compute the convex hull of a set of points,

Figure I-1 shows a point set and its convex hull, which may be thought of as the smallest "fence" enclosing all the points in the input. More mathematically, given an arbitrary subset L of points E^d, the *convex hull* conv(L) of L, is the smallest convex set containing L. A point p of a convex set S is an *extreme point* if no two points $a,b \in S$ exist such that p lies on the open line segment $\overline{ab}$. This paper considers only the two-dimensional case; the problem becomes much harder when generalized to three and higher dimensions.

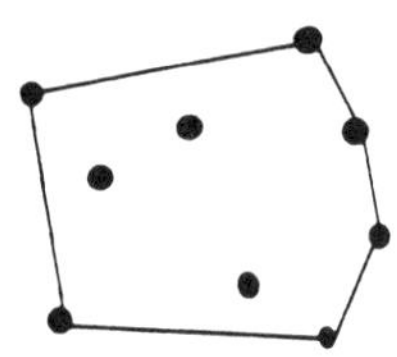

Figure I-1: A set of points and its convex hull

Although the mathematical definitions are precise, they are nonconstructive, and thus do not even lead to a naive algorithm for finding the convex hull or the extreme points of a point set. In each case, the number of possibilities that would have to be tested by the simplest generate-and-test algorithm is infinite. The key insight for designing an algorithm for this problem is that in two dimensions, the hull of a point set is a convex polygon. Considering the output as a polygon transforms the problem because only a finite number of possibilities need be examined to determine the polygon's vertices and edges.

A number of algorithms may be used to find the structure of the polygon, described in textbooks such as [18] and [20]. One of the best known is Graham's scan, which sorts the points in the input by polar angle about some internal point, then scan through the sorted list to eliminate those points which form a reflex angle with their neighbors (making the polygon non-convex). The scan is performed in linear time, so the cost of the sort dominates the runtime, resulting in an $O(N \log N)$ algorithm. Table I-1 is an idealized design history for Graham's scan. The table gives the choice number and subject of the choice in the first column, the alternatives considered, with the one selected in italics, in the second column, and the rationale for the choice in the third column. When more than one alternative was proposed in the second column, the rationale gives the reason one alternative was selected from among all the candidate. When only one alternative was proposed, as in GS8, the rationale refers to reasons why that alternative was generated for the choice. One could in fact decompose each deliberate act further, as the result of solving some subproblem, but in this table, the choices and rationale will all be presented at a single level.

Choice	Alternatives considered (selected alt. in *italics*)	Rationale for choice
GS1. Method at top-level	*Construct hull polygon*; Find smallest convex set containing input	Uncountable number of convex sets containing input
GS2. Method to construct polygon	*Find vertices, then order into polygon*; Find edges, then order them	Arbitrary
GS3. Method to compute extreme points	*Generate-and-test*; Divide-and-conquer	Arbitrary
GS4. Point generation order	*Increasing polar angle and distance*; Random order	Sacrifice simplicity in hopes of eliminating redundant tests
GS5. Method of finding interior point	*Centroid of three points*; Centroid of all points	Finding 3 non-collinear points almost always constant time, beats $O(N)$.
GS6. Comparisons for polar angle	*Areas of signed triangles*; Convert to polar coordinates	No trigonometric operations necessary
GS7. Comparisons for distance	*Compare when angles tied*; Compute all distances; Compute squared distances	Finding greatest distance easiest when points collinear
GS8. Storage of sorted points	*Doubly-linked circular list*	Low-cost predecessor, successor, and deletion operations
GS9. Direction of test	*Exclude non-extreme points*; Include extreme points	Exclusion-based algorithm feasible (lookahead)
GS10. Exact test used	*Eliminate points inside specific triangle*; Eliminate points inside any triangle	Constant time test beats $O(N^3)$ cost
GS11. Method of using test	*Repeatedly examine triples for right turn, then eliminate point or advance scan*; Add candidate points and eliminate previously placed points that create non-hull edges	Arbitrary (linear complexity achieved both ways)

Table I-1: GS algorithm design summary

References

[1] Adelson, B.
Modeling software design in a problem-space architecture.
In *Proceedings of the Annual Conference of the Cognitive Science Society*, pages 174-180. August, 1988.

[2] Aho, A.V. , Hopcroft, J.E., & Ullman, J.D.
The Design and Analysis of Computer Algorithms.
Addison-Wesley, Reading, Massachusetts, 1974.

[3] Akin, O.
The Psychology of Architectural Design.
Pion Limited, London, 1986.

[4] de Groot, A.D.
Thought and Choice in Chess.
Mouton, The Hague, 1965.

[5] Freeman, P. & Newell, A.
A model for functional reasoning in design.
In *Proceedings of the Second International Joint Conference on Artificial Intelligence*, pages 621-640. August, 1971.

[6] Friedberg, R.
A learning machine: Part 1.
IBM Journal 2:2-13, 1958.

[7] Graham, R. L.
An efficient algorithm for determining the convex hull of a finite planar set.
Information Processing Letters 1, 1972.

[8] John, B.E.
Contributions to Engineering Models of Human-Computer Interaction.
PhD thesis, Department of Psychology, Carnegie Mellon University, May, 1988.

[9] Kant, E.
Understanding and automating algorithm design.
IEEE Transactions on Software Engineering SE-11(11):1361-1374, 1985.

[10] Kant, E. & Newell, A.
Naive algorithm design techniques: A case study.
In *Proceedings of the European Conference on Artificial Intelligence.* Orsay, France, July, 1982.
Reprinted in *Progress in Artificial Intelligence*, L. Steels and J.A. Campbell (editors), Ellis Horwood Limited, 1985.

[11] Kant, E. & Newell, A.
Problem solving techniques for the design of algorithms.
Information Processing and Management 20(1-2):97-118, 1984.

[12] Laird, J. E., Newell, A., & Rosenbloom, P. S.
Soar: An architecture for general intelligence.
Artificial Intelligence 33(1):1-64, 1987.

[13] Lowry, M.R.
The structure and design of local search algorithms.
In *Proceedings of the Workshop on Automating Software Design*, pages 138-145. August, 1988.

[14] Maher, M. L., Zhao, F., & Gero, J. S.
An approach to knowledge-based creative design.
In *Preprints of the NSF Engineering Design Research Conference*, pages 333-346. June, 1989.

[15] Manna, Z. & Waldinger, R.
Synthesis: Dreams $\rightarrow$ programs.
IEEE Transactions on Software Engineering SE-5(4):294-328, July, 1979.

[16] Newell, A.
The knowledge level.
Artificial Intelligence 19(2):87-127, 1982.

[17] Newell, A. & Simon, H. A.
Human Problem Solving.
Prentice-Hall, Englewood Cliffs, New Jersey, 1972.

[18] Preparata, F. P. & Shamos, M. I.
Computational Geometry: An Introduction.
Springer-Verlag, New York, NY, 1985.

[19] Rosenbloom, P. S., Laird, J. E. & Newell, A.
Knowledge-level learning in Soar.
In *Proceedings of the National Conference on Artificial Intelligence*, pages 499-504. August, 1987.

[20] Sedgewick, R.
Algorithms.
Addison-Wesley, Reading, Massachusetts, 1983.

[21] Simon, H. A.
The Sciences of the Artificial.
MIT Press, Cambridge, MA, 1969.

[22] Smith, D. R.
Top-down synthesis of divide-and-conquer algorithms.
Artificial Intelligence 27(1):43-96, 1985.

[23] Steier, D. M.
The quest for the holy hull: Progress and challenges in automating algorithm design.
Technical Report, School of Computer Science, Carnegie-Mellon University, 1989.
Technical report, in preparation.

[24] Steier, D.M.
Automating Algorithm Design Within an Architecture for General Intelligence.
PhD thesis, School of Computer Science, Carnegie Mellon University, March, 1989.
Available as Technical Report CMU-CS-89-128.

[25] Steier, D. M. & Anderson, A. P.
Algorithm Synthesis: A Comparative Study.
Springer-Verlag, New York, NY, 1989.

[26] Steier, D. M., Laird, J. E., Newell, A., Rosenbloom, P. S., Flynn, R. A., Golding, A., Polk, T. A., Shivers, O. G., Unruh, A., & Yost, G. R.
Varieties of learning in Soar: 1987.
In *Proceedings of the Fourth International Workshop on Machine Learning*, pages 300-311. June, 1987.

CHAPTER 44

Abstraction in Problem Solving and Learning

A. Unruh, Stanford University, and P. S. Rosenbloom, USC–ISI

Abstract

Abstraction has proven to be a powerful tool for controlling the combinatorics of a problem-solving search. It is also of critical importance for learning systems. In this article we present, and evaluate experimentally, a general abstraction method — *impasse-driven abstraction* — which is able to provide necessary assistance to both problem solving and learning. It reduces the amount of time required to solve problems, and the time required to learn new rules. In addition, it results in the acquisition of rules that are more general than would have otherwise been learned.

1 Introduction

Abstraction has proven to be a powerful tool for controlling the combinatorics of a problem-solving search [Kor87]. Problem solving using abstract versions of tasks can provide cost-effective search heuristics and evaluations for the original, or "full", tasks which significantly reduce their computational complexity, and thus make large problems tractable [Gas79, Kib85, Pea83, Val81].

Abstraction is also of critical importance for learning systems. Creating abstract rules can reduce the cost of matching the rules, thus improving their operationality [Kel90, Zwe88]. Abstract rules can transfer to a wider range of situations, thus potentially increasing their usability and utility. Abstract

*We would like to thank John Laird and Rich Keller for providing valuable ideas and discussions about this research, and Gregg Yost for his help in re-conceptualizing and rewriting R1-Soar. This research was sponsored by the Hughes Aircraft Company Artificial Intelligence Center, and by the Defense Advanced Research Projects Agency (DOD) under contract number N00039-86C-0033. The views and conclusions contained in this document are those of the authors and should not be interpreted as representing the official policies, either expressed or implied, of the Hughes Aircraft Company, the Defense Advanced Research Projects Agency, or the US Government.

rules may also be easier and/or cheaper to create, thus simplifying the learning process and/or making it more tractable.

In this article we are concerned with abstraction techniques that assist in both problem solving and learning. The four key requirements such a technique should satisfy are:

1. Apply in any domain.

2. Reduce problem solving time.

3. Reduce learning time (therefore help in intractable domains).

4. Increase the transfer of learned rules.

The first requirement implies that the technique must be a *general weak method* that is applicable to domains without additional domain-specific knowledge about how to perform the abstraction. Most problem solvers that utilize abstractions do so only when the appropriate abstractions have been prespecified for them. The second requirement implies that, on average, the time to solve problems with abstraction should be less than the time without. Implicit in this requirement is also that this should be true even if only one problem is being solved; that is, abstraction should help immediately, on the first problem seen in the domain. The third requirement implies that abstraction should be integral to the rule creation process. If the problem-solving time necessary to learn a rule is to be reduced, an approach that simply abstracts the output of the normal learning algorithm will not be sufficient. The fourth requirement implies that abstraction should result in the creation of generalized rules. Even if the rule creation process is a justified method, such as explanation-based learning [MKKC86], this can lead to a form of unjustified induction (though a useful one).

In this article we describe and evaluate an abstraction method which meets these four requirements. The following sections provide a description of the basic method, a discussion of how abstraction propagates through a problem, experimental results from an implementation of the method in two domains, and a set of conclusions and future work.

2 The Abstraction Method

The abstraction method is based on the integration of learning and problem solving found in the Soar system [LNR87]. In Soar, problems are solved by search in problem spaces. Decisions are made about how to select problem spaces, states, and operators, plus how to apply operators to states to yield new states (operator implementation). Decisions are normally based on knowledge retrieved from memory by the firing of productions. However, if this knowledge is inadequate, an *impasse* occurs, which the system then tries to resolve by recursive search in

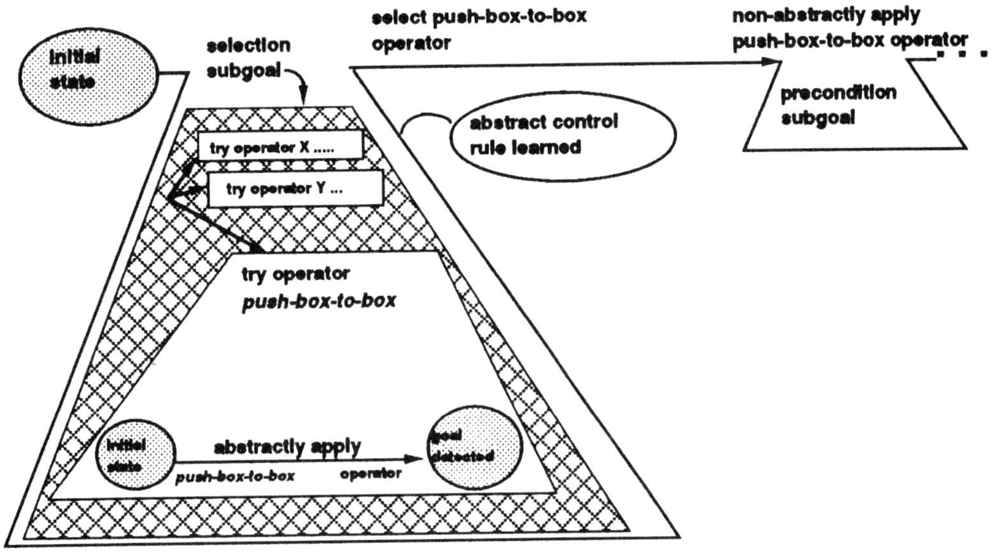

Figure 1: Abstract problem solving and learning (toy robot example).

subgoals. This leads to hierarchical processing in which control decisions can be based on multiple levels of look-ahead searches, and complex operators can be implemented by multiple levels of simpler operators (an operator aggregation hierarchy). Learning occurs by converting subgoal-based search into rules that generate comparable results under similar conditions. This *chunking* process is a form of explanation-based learning in which the explanation is derived from a trace of the search that led to the results of the subgoal [RL86].

Abstraction occurs in this framework in the service of control decisions. If an impasse occurs because of a lack of knowledge about how to make a selection, the resulting search is performed abstractly. Consider a simple example from a toy robot domain. Suppose that among the operators in the domain are ones that allow a robot to push a box to a box (*push-box-to-box*(BOX1,BOX2)) and go to a box (*goto*(BOX)). The preconditions of the *push-box-to-box* operator are that the robot is next to the first box and that the boxes are in the same room. The precondition of the *goto* operator is that the robot is in the same room as the box that it wants to reach. The goal is to reach a state where the two boxes (**box1** and **box2**) are next to each other. In the initial state, the robot and the two boxes are in the same room together, but at different locations.

Given this initial state, a control decision must be made that will result in the selection of an operator. With partial means-ends control knowledge (encoded as rules), the system can determine that the *push-box-to-box*(**box1**,**box2**) operator is one of the possible alternatives, but it may not be able to eliminate all of the other alternatives, leading to an impasse, and thus a subgoal. In the subgoal, a search will be performed by trying out each alternative until one is found that leads to the goal. When the *push-box-to-box* operator is tried, it will fail to apply because one of its preconditions — that the robot is next to the first box — is not met. However, if this precondition is abstracted away, then the operator can apply — abstractly, as the robot itself couldn't actually do this — and the goal of the abstract search will be achieved. ¿From this abstract search, the information that the *push-box-to-box* operator is the right one to select is returned, and used to make the original control decision. Simultaneously, a control rule is learned which summarizes the lesson of the abstract search. Figure 1 illustrates this process.

Though the basic idea of abstracting within control searches is simple, its consequences are far-reaching. One consequence is that the abstract search is likely to be shorter than the full search would have been because less now needs to be done. If the abstract searches are shorter, yet still return adequate control knowledge, then the time to solve the problem will be reduced (Requirement 2) — as in the toy robot example. Additional consequences arise because learning occurs via the chunking of subgoal-based search. If chunking is done over an abstract search, then the time required to learn about the task is reduced because of the reduced time to generate the explanation (Req. 3). In addition, because abstract searches lead to abstract explanations, the rules acquired by chunking abstract searches will themselves be abstract, and thus be able to transfer to more situations (Req. 4). These generalized control rules effectively form an *abstract plan* for the task. Though these rules may not always be completely correct, limiting abstraction to control decisions ensures that unjustified abstractions will not lead to incorrect behavior — control knowledge in the Soar framework affects only the efficiency with which a goal is achieved, not the correctness.

The actual abstraction of the control search occurs by *impasse-driven abstraction*. When an impasse occurs during the control search, it is resolved by making an assumption, instead of by further problem solving in another level of subgoals. Impasse-driven abstraction belongs to the general class of abstractions that involve *removing*, or abstracting away, some aspects of the problem in question. (In the taxonomy provided by [Doy86], our techniques fall under the category of *approximation*.) For example, in the toy robot example above, when the precondition of the *push-box-to-box* operator failed during the control search, leading to an impasse, the system simply assumed that the precondition was met, and continued the abstract search as best it could. (Another way of looking at this is that the system didn't care if the precondition was met). Without abstraction, the impasse would lead to a subgoal in which the system would search for a state to which the operator could legally apply (by applying the *goto* operator).

Impasse-driven abstraction is a general technique that can be applied to arbitrary domains without domain-specific abstraction knowledge; that is, it is a general weak method (Requirement 1). With it, the default abstraction behavior for the problem solver is to abstract away those parts of an operator

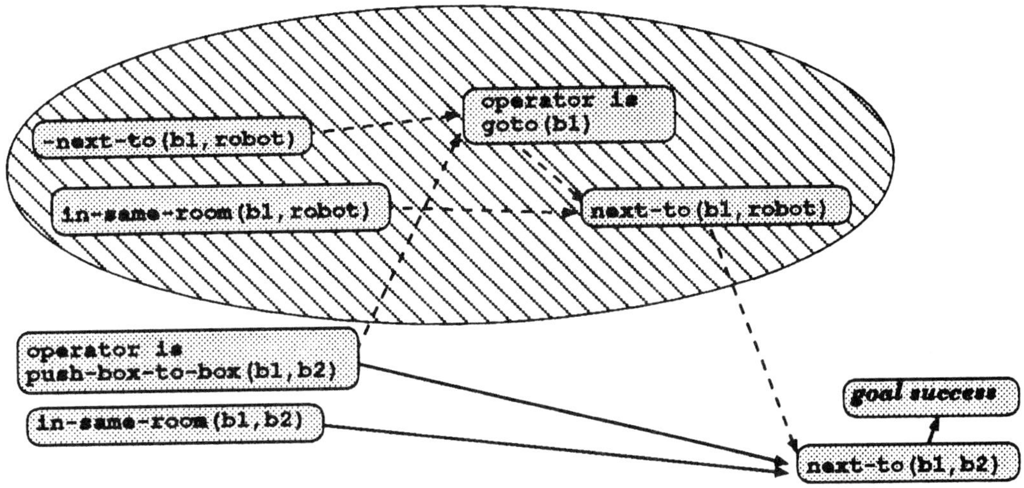

Figure 2: An explanation structure for the *next-to*(**box1**, **box2**) goal.

which are not already compiled into rules, and which therefore generate impasses and require subgoals to achieve. This behavior results in abstraction of operator preconditions and abstraction of operator implementations. The former leads to a form of abstraction similar to that obtained in ABStrips [Sac74], while the latter leads to behavior that is best described as successive refinement [Ste81]. As an example of the latter, consider what happens when there is a complex operator for which a complete set of rules does not exist a priori about how to perform it. When such an operator is selected, some rules may fire, but an impasse will still occur because of what is left undone. Without abstraction the system would enter a subgoal where it would complete the implementation by a search with a set of sub-operators. With abstraction, the system assumes that what was done by the rules was all that needed to be done. It then proceeds from the abstract state produced by this abstract operator implementation.

Another way to understand what impasse-driven abstraction is doing is to look at its effect on the explanation structure created as a byproduct of abstract search (and upon which the learning is based). Figure 2 shows a simplified version of the explanation structure for the toy robot example. Without abstraction, the rule learned from this explanation is:

```
operator is push-box-to-box(b1,b2) ∧
  in-same-room(b1,b2) ∧
  in-same-room(b1,robot) ∧
  ¬ next-to(b1,robot)
⇒ goal success.
```

With abstraction, information that would normally be needed for the generation of the result is essentially ignored, and some subtrees of the unabstracted explanation tree — the circled substructure in the figure — no longer need to be expanded for the goal to be "proved". (Another way of looking at this is that some nodes in the proof tree are effectively replaced with the value *TRUE*. Alteration of a proof tree in this manner has been proposed by [Kel90] as a method of forming approximate concepts.) The abstracted rule becomes:

```
operator is push-box-to-box(b1,b2) ∧
  in-same-room(b1,b2)
⇒ goal success.
```

Alteration of the explanation structure in this way has made the rule more general, and thus able to apply to a larger number of situations.

The same abstraction techniques extend, with no additional mechanism, to multi-level abstraction of both preconditions and implementations. The levels of refinement grow naturally out of the dynamic hierarchy of subgoals that are created during problem solving. Consider multi-level precondition abstraction, for example. In the toy robot problem above, the abstract search that was performed was at the most abstract level — the search was cut off at the highest level of precondition subgoals. Once this search is done, and the *push-box-to-box* operator is selected, it is necessary to do another search to determine what sequence of operators will satisfy its preconditions. In this particular example, the *goto* operator would be among the candidates. Here no impasse of the *goto* operator application would occur, because its preconditions are already met. However, if an impasse did occur during this new search, it would lead to abstraction in the search. This new abstract search is one level more detailed than was the original one. The same cycle continues until a complete plan is generated in which nothing has been abstracted.

Note that there is nothing in the impasse-driven abstraction techniques which prevents the problem solver from making use of additional domain-specific knowledge about what to abstract. The existence of such knowledge can certainly improve performance. However, domain-specific abstraction knowledge is not often available. If it is not, then the impasse-driven techniques, as a weak method, are able to provide useful abstract problem-solving behavior when it would not otherwise have been possible.

3 Abstraction Propagation

Thus far, we have presented the effects of impasse-driven abstraction on problem solving and learning. However, this is only part of the picture. An important feature of impasse-driven abstraction is the way in which the abstraction occurs *dynamically* during problem solving. Each time an impasse occurs during a control search, some aspect of the problem gets abstracted. However, these bits of abstraction initially happen only locally — just because part of one particular operator application gets abstracted during one search step does not necessarily mean that the rest of the problem space will automatically be abstracted in a compatible fashion. Once some part of a problem has been abstracted away, the effects must be *propagated* to later aspects of the problem, including the goal test. Consider, for example, what would happen if the goal in the toy robot domain was to have two boxes adjacent and in the same room, but all of the "in-room" information in the problem space was abstracted away. If the "full", non-abstract goal test was used during abstract search, it would never succeed, and the abstract search would never terminate (unless all options became exhausted, or some monitoring process decided to kill it). It would be more desirable if the goal test of the abstract search was to be compatibly abstracted, so that it cared only about whether the two boxes were adjacent.

The general approach that we have taken is to develop a set of restrictions on the construction of problem spaces which, if followed, ensure appropriate propagation of the abstraction. The two restrictions — *problem-space factorization* and *assumption-based goal tests* — do not limit what can be expressed, only how it is expressed.

A problem space is factored if it is designed so that the descriptions of problem space components (states, operators, or goals) are separated into any independent sub-parts which compose them; for example, by creating one production per sub-part. When problem-space components are factored, they may still be partially applicable to the task at hand, even if some of the problem-space knowledge is missing or ignored. For example, if an operator is composed of a number of sub-actions, and if each sub-action is described separately, some of the sub-actions may be able to apply even though there is not enough information available to allow the operator to apply in its entirety. In this way the operator applies abstractly.

For an example of operator factorization, consider the following simplified "robot domain" operator, which moves a robot through a door to a new room, and in the process keeps track of how many robots are currently in each room. The operator's preconditions are not shown here. If it is true that the operator "may apply", its preconditions are either met or have been ignored through abstraction. Unfactored, the operator is:

```
operator is go-through-door(robot,door,new-room)
  ∧ the operator may apply
  ∧ inroom(robot,old-room)
  ∧ #-of-robots-in-room(old-room,n1)
  ∧ #-of-robots-in-room(new-room,n2)
 ⇒ add(inroom(robot,new-room))
  ∧ delete(inroom(robot,old-room))
  ∧ change(#-of-robots-in-room(new-room,n2+1))
  ∧ change(#-of-robots-in-room(old-room,n1-1))
```

If the operator is factored, then each independent sub-action is considered separately:

```
operator is go-through-door(robot,door,new-room)
  ∧ the operator may apply
  ∧ inroom(robot,old-room)
```

```
   ⇒ delete(inroom(robot,old-room))
and:
   operator is go-through-door(robot,door,new-room)
    ∧ the operator may apply
   ⇒ add(inroom(robot,new-room))
and:
   operator is go-through-door(robot,door,new-room)
    ∧ the operator may apply
    ∧ #-of-robots-in-room(new-room,n2)
   ⇒ change(#-of-robots-in-room(new-room,n2+1))
and:
   operator is go-through-door(robot,door,new-room)
    ∧ the operator may apply
    ∧ #-of-robots-in-room(old-room,n1)
   ⇒ change(#-of-robots-in-room(old-room,n1-1))
```

Thus, if information about the number of robots in either room is not available, the rest of the operator can still apply. Additionally, if because of abstraction the previous location of the robot was unknown, it can still be "moved" to its new room. Factorization enables abstract problem-solving behavior to be propagated dynamically; whatever can be done will be done, while what can't be done because of previously abstracted information is simply ignored. Then, when part of a process is ignored, this in turn may cause new problem-space information to become abstracted. (There is some indication that factorization is not specifically an abstraction issue — if a problem space is factored, then more generalized learning can occur regardless of whether or not abstraction takes place). Note that a factorization determines what *may* be abstracted in a problem space — the set of possible abstractions. It is the impasses that arise during problem solving which determine what actually *is* abstracted.

Assumption-based goal testing refers to the problem-solver's ability to make assumptions about whether or not goals have been achieved during abstract problem solving. To do this, it is necessary to be able to detect that a goal has *not* been met, in addition to being able to detect that it has been met. Under normal circumstances, the problem solver has enough information about a state to determine one or the other; that is, that the state either does or does not achieve the goal. However, when the problem is abstracted, neither test may succeed. Under these conditions, the problem solver needs to make a default assumption as to whether the goal is met or not. Such default assumptions can be made about a goal as a whole, or if it is factored, about individual conjuncts of the goal. To do this properly, the problem solver needs to be supplied with additional information about which goals, and goal conjuncts, should be assumed true and which should be assumed false. Rare termination conditions, for example, should be assumed by default to be unmet. This additional assumption information is not knowledge about what to abstract, or any particular abstraction. Rather, it plays a part in determining the behavior of the system once abstraction has occurred.

The restrictions which support abstraction propagation are independent of *what* is abstracted, or what is expected to be abstracted. In fact, they are independent of whether problem information is missing because of deliberate abstraction, or because of some other reason (such as bad instrument readings, etc.). Therefore, the problem spaces in which these restrictions have been followed could provide a more robust support for problem solving in noisy domains, and make assumptions based on the best data at hand, regardless of whether or not abstraction is deliberately used.

4 Experimental Results

Experiments have been run with impasse-driven abstraction in two distinct task domains: a Strips-like robot domain and a computer-configuration domain (R1-Soar) [RLM+85]. The robot domain is similar to the one in the example presented earlier, but slightly more complicated: there are two robots and two rooms, with two doors between them, as well as two boxes. The R1-Soar computer-configuration domain was based on a re-implementation of a portion of the classic R1 expert-system [McD82]. The two domains were chosen because they cover both a classical search/planning domain (the robot domain) and a classical expert system domain (computer configuration). Moreover, the domains also differ in that the robot domain stresses abstractions based on operator preconditions, while the R1-Soar domain stresses abstractions based on operator implementations.

To achieve further variation, two different problems were run in the robot domain, with the same goal, but with different initial states. In both problems the conjunctive goal was to have the two boxes pushed next to each other, and to have the two robots "shake hands" (to do this the robots had to be next to each other). The key difference in the initial states was that in the second problem one of the doors was locked, and there was no key. (This second problem should cause some additional complexity if the system abstracts away whether the doors are unlocked.) For each problem, the amount of search-control knowledge that was directly available to the problem solver was also varied. In one version, the problem solver started with means-ends knowledge that allowed it to directly recognize which operators helped solve which subgoals. In the other version, the problem solver could detect when a subgoal had been solved, but knew nothing directly about which operators helped solve which subgoals. In the R1-Soar domain, two computer-configuration problems were also run. Once again, the goal was the same — to have a configured computer — but the initial states were varied.

The problem spaces for these domains were designed according to the restrictions discussed in Section 3. The key issues to be addressed by these experiments are the degree to which impasse-driven abstraction meets the four abstraction

	No Abstr. (dec.)	Abstr. (dec.)	Abstr./ No Abstr.
ROBOT DOMAIN:			
Problem 1			
Means-ends knowl.	99	80	.81
No means-ends knowl.	> 3000	599	< .20
Problem 2			
Means-ends knowl.	120	97	.81
No means-ends knowl.	> 3000	> 3000	
R1-SOAR:			
Problem 3	1260	707	.56
Problem 4	1255	900	.72

Table 1: Number of decisions to solve problems.

requirements presented in the introduction.

The first requirement was that the method should be applicable in any domain. The evidence to date is that the abstraction method has been applied to these two quite different domains. In both domains it was possible to apply the impasse-driven abstraction techniques. In the robot domain it was not necessary to add any abstraction-specific knowledge. With R1-Soar, it turned out that although the method was applicable, it was necessary to add a small amount of additional knowledge about the abstraction, to prevent random behavior. R1-Soar is designed so that complex operators are implemented by multiple levels of simpler operators, to form an operator aggregation hierarchy. If abstraction occurred at the level of the top operator, then there was not enough information remaining in the problem space (all configuration work occurred in lower subgoals) to make an informed control decision. That is, the decisions became random. Therefore, we instructed the problem-solver not to abstract at the top level in R1-Soar. Default abstraction behavior at other levels of the operator hierarchy was not affected. It would be preferable for the problem-solver to be able to determine more intelligently (through experimentation, and the current amount of chunked vs. unchunked knowledge in the system), a useful level at which to begin abstraction. We are currently working on an abstraction method which builds on the impasse-driven abstraction techniques, and allows the problem solver to make such a determination.

The second requirement on the abstraction method was that abstraction should reduce the problem solving time required. Table 1 shows the number of decisions that the problem solver required to solve each of the problems, and the ratio of the performance with abstraction to that without[1]. Because several of the problems were completely intractable, an arbitrary cutoff was set at 3000 decisions.

[1]In the R1-Soar runs, a few chunks learned were altered to avoid problems generated by the way the current version of Soar copies information to new states. This difficulty is unrelated to the abstraction issues, and will be fixed in the next version of Soar.

	No Abstr. (secs.)	Abstr. (secs.)	Abstr./ No Abstr.
Problem 3	4,161	1,535	.37
Problem 4	4,641	2,146	.46

Table 2: Time (seconds) to solve R1-Soar problems.

The overall trend revealed by these results is that abstraction does reduce the problem solving time, when measured in terms of number of decisions. Moreover, the harder the problem, in terms of the amount of search required without abstraction, the more abstraction helps. Even in the second robot problem, where the problem solver does indeed abstract away the test of whether it can get through the locked door, abstraction helps. It turns out that this abstraction does not make the problem solver noticeably less efficient when doors are locked, since when it does not use abstraction it is still forced, during its search, to go to the door and try to open it before it realizes this is not possible. What abstraction was not able to do was to make all of the intractable tasks tractable.

Hidden in the R1-Soar numbers is another interesting phenomenon. In problem 4, abstraction reduced the amount of time required to generate a configuration, but the configuration was not as good as the one generated without abstraction. The goal test for R1-Soar is that there be a complete and correct configuration. Not tested is the cost of the configuration. Instead, R1-Soar uses control knowledge to guide it through the space of partial configurations so that the first complete configuration it reaches is likely to be a cheap one. This use of control knowledge to determine optimality is a soft violation of the constraint that control knowledge not determine correctness, and thus abstraction can (and does) have a negative impact on it. A recoding of R1-Soar to incorporate optimality testing into the goal test could avoid this, or it could simply be lived with as an effort/quality trade-off.

To return to requirement 2, the normal assumption in Soar is that the time per decision is fairly constant, so the decision numbers should be directly convertible into times. However, it turns out that decisions for deep searches are considerable more expensive than ones for shallow searches because of the amount of additional information in the system's working memory. Table 2 shows the actual problem solving times for the two R1-Soar problems, with and without abstraction. These numbers show that when actual run times are compared, the advantage of abstraction is even greater.

The third requirement was that abstraction should reduce the time required to learn. To evaluate this, we need to look at how long it takes to acquire control chunks, with and without abstraction. Table 3 presents the relevant data. It shows the number of decisions that occurred before the control chunk for the first operator tie was learned, for one robot problem and one R1-Soar problem.

	No Abstr. (decisions)	Abstr. (decisions)	Abstr./ No Abstr.
ROBOT DOMAIN: *Problem 1* Means-ends knowl.	92	19	.21
R1-SOAR: *Problem 3*	1248	101	.08

Table 3: Number of decisions to learn control rule for first operator tie.

ABSTRACT:
If a push-box-to-box operator has been suggested,
and its boxes are pushable,
and the two boxes and one robot are all in the same room,
and the desired state is to have the two boxes adjacent
and to have the robots shake hands,
then mark the operator as being "best".

NON-ABSTRACT:
If a push-box-to-box operator has been suggested,
and its boxes are pushable,
and the two boxes and one robot are all in the same room,
and the desired state is to have the tow boxes adjacent
and to have the robots shake hands
and the operator has the precondition that
the robot be next to the box to be pushed,
and the other robot is in the other room,
and there is a door that connects the two rooms,
and the door is closed and unlocked,
then mark the operator as being "best".

Figure 3: Abstract and non-abstract chunks from the robot domain.

In both cases, abstraction greatly reduced the amount of effort required before the control rule could be learned.

The fourth requirement was that abstraction should increase the transfer of learned rules. Rather than evaluate transfer directly, what we shall do is illustrate this effect by comparing a corresponding pair of abstract and non-abstract chunks from the robot domain (Figure 3). The two have identical tests up to a point; however, the non-abstract chunk cares whether the robot is next to the box to be pushed, and whether the robots, rooms, and doors are arranged so that the robots will later be able to get together to shake hands. These extra conditions limit the domain of applicability of the non-abstract rule with respect to the abstract rule.

Together these experimental results provide support, though not yet conclusive support, for the ability of impasse-driven abstraction to meet the four key requirements on an abstraction method.

5 Conclusions and Future Work

In earlier work we showed how an abstraction, once chosen, could be made to dynamically propagate through a problem space [URL87]. In this article we have built on that work, by turning it into a general weak method that does not require manual specification of how the problem spaces and goal tests are to be abstracted; the key ideas being impasse-driven abstraction and restrictions on problem space construction. We have also shown how this technique can yield multi-level abstraction and successive refinement.

Another important way that the earlier results have been extended is by the performance of a set of experiments in two task domains. These experiments provided evidence for the satisfaction of four key requirements on an abstraction mechanism: that it should be applicable in any domain, that it should reduce problem solving time, that it should reduce learning time, and that it should increase the transfer of learned rules. However, in the R1-Soar domain, the problem solver was provided with additional abstraction knowledge beyond the default which prevented it from abstracting at the highest level of the domain's operator hierarchy. This knowledge was necessary to make the abstraction useful; it prevented random control decisions stemming from too little information.

Despite progress with the general weak method presented here, a number of issues remain to be addressed. The most important issue is how the weak method can be strengthened by using additional knowledge about domains and their abstractions. Impasse-driven abstraction does appear to be a plausible technique to use in many situations. Due to the experiential nature of chunking, those parts of the problem space that are familiar will be encoded as compiled knowledge, and thus won't generate the impasses which initiate abstractions. If the heuristic holds that "familiar" is "important", the default abstraction behavior may be quite useful.

But because the current method is weak, there must be many circumstances in which it will not cause the most appropriate behavior to occur. We plan to try to use the combination of the weak method and experiential learning (chunking) to bootstrap the system to a richer theory of abstractions by learning about the utility of the abstractions that the system tries. One promising avenue of current research is the technique referred to in Section 4, by which the system tries to determine through experimentation a helpful level of abstraction for a given problem context. There are many other ways to learn about an abstraction's utility as well. One possibility is empirical observation over a sequence of related tasks. Alternatively, the problem solver might notice that an abstraction has caused a problem in a particular context, and "explain" to itself why this is the case, using its domain knowledge (failure-driven refinement of the abstraction "theory".) A final option would be for the problem solver to analyze its domain, if it has time to do so, and attempt to come up with a partially pre-processed abstraction theory, as in [Ben89, Ell88, Kno89, Ten88].

A second item of future work is the extension of the experiments, both in breadth and depth. We will be looking at abstraction in a number of domains, and trying to empirically evaluate how domain characteristics impact the utility of abstraction.

A final item will be to evaluate the extent to which the restrictions on problem space construction presented in Section 3 can improve the robustness of problem solving in noisy domains.

References

[Ben89] D. P. Benjamin. Learning problem-solving abstractions via enablement. In *AAAI Spring Symposium Series: Planning and Search*, 1989.

[Doy86] R. Doyle. Constructing and refining causal explanations from an inconsistent domain theory. In *Proceedings of AAAI-86*, pages 538–544, 1986.

[Ell88] T. Ellman. Approximate theory formation: An explanation-based approach. In *Proceedings of the Seventh National Conference on Artifical Intelligence*, 1988.

[Gas79] J. Gaschnig. A problem simililarity approach to devising heuristics. In *Proceedings of IJCAI-79*, pages 301–307, 1979.

[Kel90] R. Keller. Learning approximate concept descriptions. In *Proceedings of the AAAI Workshop on Automatic Generation of Approximations and Abstractions*, 1990.

[Kib85] D. Kibler. Generation of heuristics by transforming the problem representation. Technical Report TR-85-20, ICS, 1985.

[Kno89] Craig A. Knoblock. Learning hierarchies of abstraction spaces. In *Proceedings of the Sixth International Workshop on Machine Learning*. Morgan Kaufmann, 1989.

[Kor87] R. E. Korf. Planning as search: A quantitative approach. *Artificial Intelligence*, 33:65–88, 1987.

[LNR87] J. E. Laird, A. Newell, , and P. S. Rosenbloom. Soar: An architecture for general intelligence. *Artificial Intelligence*, 33:1–64, 1987.

[McD82] J. McDermott. R1: A rule-based configurer of computer systems. *Artificial Intelligence*, 19:39–88, 1982.

[MKKC86] T. Mitchell, R. Keller, and S. Kedar-Cabelli. Explanation-based generalization: A unifying view. *Machine Learning*, 1, 1986.

[Pea83] J. Pearl. On the discovery and generation of certain heuristics. *AI Magazine*, pages 23–33, 1983.

[RL86] P. S. Rosenbloom and J. E. Laird. Mapping explanation-based generalization onto Soar. In *Proceedings of AAAI-86*, Philadelphia, 1986.

[RLM+85] P. S. Rosenbloom, J. E. Laird, J. McDermott, A. Newell, and E. Orciuch. R1-Soar: An experiment in knowledge-intensive programming in a problem-solving architecture. *IEEE Transactions on Pattern Analysis and Machine Intelligence*, 7(5):561–569, 1985.

[Sac74] E. D. Sacerdoti. Planning in a hierarchy of abstraction spaces. *Artificial Intelligence*, 5:115–135, 1974.

[Ste81] M. Stefik. Planning and meta-planning (molgen: Part 2). *Artificial Intelligence*, 16:141–169, 1981.

[Ten88] J. Tenenberg. *Abstraction in Planning.* PhD thesis, University of Rochester, 1988.

[URL87] A. Unruh, P. S. Rosenbloom, and J. E. Laird. Dynamic abstraction problem solving in Soar. In *Proceedings of the AOG/AAAIC Joint Conference*, Dayton, OH, 1987.

[Val81] M. Valtorta. A result on the computational complexity of heuristic estimates for the A* algorithm. Technical report, University of North Carolina, 1981.

[Zwe88] M. Zweben. Improving operationality with approximate heuristics. In *AAAI Spring Symposium Series: Explanation-Based Learning*, 1988.

CHAPTER 45

A Computational Model of Musical Creativity†
(Extended Abstract)

S. Vicinanza and M. J. Prietula, Carnegie Mellon University

(Extended Abstract)

1. Introduction

Creativity has long been viewed as a form of problem solving (Newell, Shaw & Simon, 1962). Similar assertions have been put forth for related, if not equivalent, phenomena such as insight and intuition (Kaplan & Simon, 1988; Simon, 1986) and scientific discovery (Langley, Simon, Bradshaw & Zytkow, 1987; Qin & Simon, 1988). The primary tenet of these theories is that all cognitive behavior can be described by general mechanisms of problem representation and learning. Musical creativity, as a form of human cognition, can also be described in these terms. In this work we investigate how a crucial component of the musical creative process, melody generation, may be simulated through software which emboides a view of musical creativity as heuristic search through multiple problem spaces.

While cognitive models of music composition have been proposed (e.g., Gardner, 1982; Pressing, 1984; Sloboda, 1985), these models make no attempt to explain the process of melody generation and have treated it as a block box, referring to it as an "unconscious process" or a "creative impulse." We postulate that such a process is a form of problem solving and, consequently, can be explained in terms of the problem solving machinery generally available — problem spaces and operators. Before delving into the specifics of the model, we must first agree upon what we expect it to produce. As there is no clear concensus as to what represents music, we will articulate our definition.

2. The Structure of Music

At the most elemental level, music is a series of pitches that have dynamics, envelopes, durations, and timbres. For our purposes a *pitch* is the fundamental frequency of the sound produced by an instrument. The *dynamics* of the pitch refer to its amplitude, relative to other pitches in the music. The *envelope* refers to the change in the amplitude over time and is partially dependent on the instrument and partially controlled by the performer. The *duration* is the

---

† Prepared for the *AI and Music Workshop, International Joint Conference on Artificial Intelligence*, Detroit MI, August 20-25, 1989

pitch's time span. The *timbre* is the harmonic content of the pitch which helps us distinguish one instrument from another and is almost entirely a function of the instrument itself.

In modeling melody generation, it is convenient to disregard those features that assume a role of lesser importance. Such simplifying assumptions enable the model to retain both simplicity and power. The distinguishing features of a melody are the pitches and their durations. We will refer to a pitch-duration combination as a *musical note.* One would recognize a sequence of (musical) notes as a particular melody whether it was performed on a clarinet, harmonica, or piano, even though the three instruments sound quite different from one another (a function of their respective envelopes and timbres). Our interest, therefore, will be only in the notes that comprise melody.

When a sequence of notes are appropriately organized, we perceive the result as music instead of as some incoherent collection of pitches. There is evidence that the appropriate structure for this organization is a hierarchy (Stoffer, 1985). In fact, hierarchical decomposition of tonal music has served as the basis for a complete theory of music perception and generation (Lerdahl & Jackendoff, 1983). According to this theory, music is perceived in segments or groups which are arranged so that the most basic groups are combined into higher level perceptual groups which are themselves perceived as parts of still higher level groups and so on. Thus, notes are combined to form *motives,* the lowest level group. Motives are perceived as parts of themes or melodies. Themes are perceived as parts of sections which form the musical piece.

Our focus is on the *generation of motives* and their integration into higher level melodies. Music is formed when notes are arranged into a hierarchical structure in accordance wth the constraining rules of tonal music. Musical style is determined by the constraints imposed by the generative rules (Sundberg & Lindblom, 1976). These rules determine which sequences of notes may be considered "musical" and which may not. The generation or modification of a set of constraining rules (creation of musical style) can itself be considered a problem solving task, although we will not address this issue here.

A melody is thus defined as a hierarchical structure, perceived as a unit and comprising one or more phrases, related to one another both harmonically and rhythmically. Similarly, a phrase is composed of related motifs. A motif is the most basic compound structure, being the shortest sequence of notes which may be perceived as a unit. The task of any melody generation system, whether human or machine, is thus to create a sequence of notes that form a multi-level hierarchical structure which exhibits the appropriate relationships among the different sub-structures. The rules governing the relationship between sub-structures and even the format of the different sub-structures determine the style of music being generated. The hierarchical nature of the melody, however, is consistent.

3. Soar: A Problem Solving Architecture

The system described in this paper is based on a general architecture for cognition called *Soar*. Soar is a system which characterizes all symbolic goal-oriented behavior as search in problem spaces and serves as an architecture for general intelligent behavior (Laird, Newell & Rosenbloom, 1987). *Decisions* are the primitive acts of the system used for the search (i.e., generation and selection) of appropriate problem spaces, states and operators as well as the application of operators for new state configuration, in the pursuit of goals. The information required to drive correct decisions (i.e., effective and efficient search paths) require knowledge and this knowledge is acquired in one of two ways in Soar.

First, the knowledge may be directly available in long term memory as productions (all long term memory knowledge in Soar is realized as productions) and, when the antecedent conditions are deemed sufficient, the relevant productions fire and the results are added to a globally accessable working memory structure. On the other hand, for some decisions the knowledge required is not directly available (such as the selection of which operator of several might be "best" to apply) and further problem solving ensues. The mechanisms which are brought to bear to resolve ambiguous decisions are simple and universal in the Soar architecture — subgoaling. In essence, such decisions are described as *impasses* and result in the specification of a new goal and a new problem space to which attention must be immediately paid — the resolution of the impasse. As all goal-driven behavior in Soar is characterized in the same manner, the mechanisms embodied in the entire Soar architecture are available for the resolution of the impasse — it is simply another goal to achieve (Laird, 1984). †

4. Melody-Soar: Modeling Creativity

Melody-Soar is a model based on Soar which generates the structure of a melody from the fundamental components of music — notes. Melody-Soar describes the task of melody creation as a set of problem spaces and search control knowledge. The search control knowledge, in the form of productions, causes different search paths to be traced through the hierarchy of problem spaces, where each different path results in a final state representing a unique melody.

Knowledge in Melody-Soar is organized into a series of *hierarchical problem spaces* that parallel the hierarchical structure of a melody (see Figure 1). A melody is created by achieving the series of sub-goals that is represented by these problem spaces. When Melody-Soar begins to create a melody it sets as a goal the creation of a series of phrases. An initial state is added to working memory that contains a number of "empty" phrases. The goal is to transform

† Another property of Soar is its ability to learn (Laird, Rosenbloom & Newell, 1986); however, in this version of the model we have not yet exploited that capability.

this state into one in which the phrases have been filled in with motifs. To satisfy this goal an *operator* is proposed that can fill in the phrase. Because there is no knowledge in the top-level problem space regarding how this operator accomplishes this task, an impasse occurs and a sub-goal is created to implement the operator. This impasse causes the *phrase-problem-space* to be invoked.

The goal of the *phrase-problem-space* is to build a single phrase from motifs. The knowledge that this problem space contains is that phrases are composed of motifs and that motifs are rhythmic patterns that have pitches associated with each note in the pattern. Each motif in the phrase must be augmented with a sequence of notes. The notes are composed of pitches and durations. The knowledge present in the phrase problem space is that a phrase is made of motifs and to create a motif entails creating a rhythm pattern for it then assigning pitches to each note in the pattern.

An operator is proposed in the *phrase-problem-space* to create a rhythmic pattern. Because there is no knowledge in the phrase space to directly perform this operation on the state, another impasse occurs which deepens the goal stack yet another level. The *rhythm-problem-space* is now invoked in the new context frame. Multiple operators are instantiated in this space, one for each rhythmic pattern in the repertoire that meets the duration requirements of the motif. Melody-Soar randomly selects one of these operators and applies it to the state, achieving the goal of adding a rhythmic pattern to the motif. When the goal is achieved in the *rhythm-problem-space,* control returns to the *phrase-problem-space.* The next operator applied to the state attempts to add a pitch to each note in the motif. An impasse occurs at this point and a new problem space, the *pitch-problem-space,* is invoked.

The goal that must be achieved in the *pitch-problem-space* is the assignment of pitches to the notes of the rhythm pattern in a method that makes "musical sense." To accomplish this task, pitches are assigned to notes one by one, as a probabilistic function of the current chord and the pitch assigned to the preceding note. There are three basic methods of assigning pitches. The first method is to *step* to the next or previous pitch. The second method is a *jump* to any note in the current chord. The final and most interesting method is to select pitches by *analogy* to a previous motif in the melody.

Pitch assignment by analogy works by examining the relationships between notes in a previously assigned motif and duplicating those relationships, without necessarily duplicating the actual notes, in the current motif. This operator is powerful and is capable of creating many common melodic devices such as echoed and repeated motifs. One of the three methods is selected at random. In addition, there are usually multiple operators that can assign the next note in a series and the choice of which operator to apply is made at random as well. When all of the notes have been assigned, the impasse in the *pitch-problem-space* is resolved and Melody-Soar continues working on the goal of completing the phrase. Similarly, when all of the motifs in the phrase have been completed, the *phrase-problem-space* is terminated and work on the next phrase can begin.

In this manner, Melody-Soar is able to construct a coherent melody out of pitches and rhythms (see Figure 2). It has direct knowledge of scales, chords, rhythmic patterns, and a few simple heuristics of how to go about selecting a pitch for a note. What is surprising is that very few rules are needed to generate many different and acceptable melodies. This is because even under the constraints of the heuristic rules, the combinatorics of the problem provide a very large number of possible paths through the problem space. By randomizing operator selection whenever mutually acceptable operators are applicable, Melody-Soar is able to generate many different melodies from the same knowledge base. This behavior can be viewed as analogous to that of a human composer who also creates many different melodies from the same knowledge base. The random selection of mutually acceptable state operators at all levels in the problem space hierarchy ensures that the model meets the requirements of musical diversity and productivity.

5.Conclusion

Though the current version of Melody-Soar is quite limited in the depth of its knowledge and by many simplifying assumptions, the architecture demonstrates that the problem space approach is both a feasible and extensible model that can account for one aspect of musical creativity. Furthermore, this model is consistent with recent research on expertise which suggests that the foundations for expert performance lie in the nature of practice and experience (Bloom, 1985). Both of which underly the development of the appropriate problem spaces and operators permitting reasoning diversity, speedup, and accuracy through a general mechanism of skill acquisition. In the future we hope to verify this by incorporating the capability which permits musical knowledge and talent to develop — learning.

6. References

Bloom, B. (1985). (Ed.) *Developing Talent in Young People.* New York, NY: Ballantine Books.

Gardner, H., (1982). *Art, Mind, and Brain: A Cognitive Approach to Creativity.* New York, NY: Basic Books.

Kaplan, C. & Simon, H. (1988). *In Search of Insight.* Department of Psychology, Carnegie-Mellon University, Pittsburgh, PA.

Langley, P., Simon, H., Bradshaw, G. & Zytkow, J. (1987). *Scientific Discovery: Computational Exploarations of the Creative Processes.* Cambridge, MA: MIT Press.

Laird, J. (1984). *Universal Subgoaling.* Doctoral Dissertation, Computer Science Department, Carnegie Mellon University, Pittsburgh, PA.

Laird, J.E., Newell, A. & Rosenbloom, P.S. (1987). Soar: An Architecture of General Intelligence, *Artificial Intelligence,* 33, 1-64.

Laird, J.E., Rosenbloom, P.S., and Newell, A. (1986). Chunking in SOAR: The anatomy of a general learning mechanism, *Machine Learning,* 1(1), 11-46.

Lerdahl F. & Jackendoff, R. (1983). *A Generative Theory of Tonal Music.* Cambridge, MA: MIT Press.

Newell A., Shaw J.C. & Simon H. (1962). The Process of Creative Thinking, In Gruber, Terrell & Wertheimer (Eds.), *Contemporary Approaches to Creative Thinking.* New York, NY: Atherton Press.

Pressing, J. (1984). Cognitive Processes in Improvisation. In W. Crozier & A. Chapman (Eds.), *Cognitive Processes in the Perception of Art.* New York, NY: Elsevier Science Publishers.

Qin, Y. & Simon, H. (1988). *Laboratory Replication of Scientific Discovery Processes.* Department of Psychology, Carnegie-Mellon University, Pittsburgh, PA.

Simon, H. (1986). The information processing explanation of Gestalt phenomena, *Computers in Human Behavior,* 2, 241-255.

Sloboda, J.A. (1985). *The Musical Mind: The Cognitive Psychology of Music.* New York, NY: Oxford University Press.

Stoffer, Thomas H. (1985). Representation of Phrase Structure in the Perception of Music, *Perception,* 3(2), 191-220.

Sundberg, J. & Lindblom, B. (1976). Generative Theories in Language and Music Descriptions, *Cognition,* 4, 99-122.

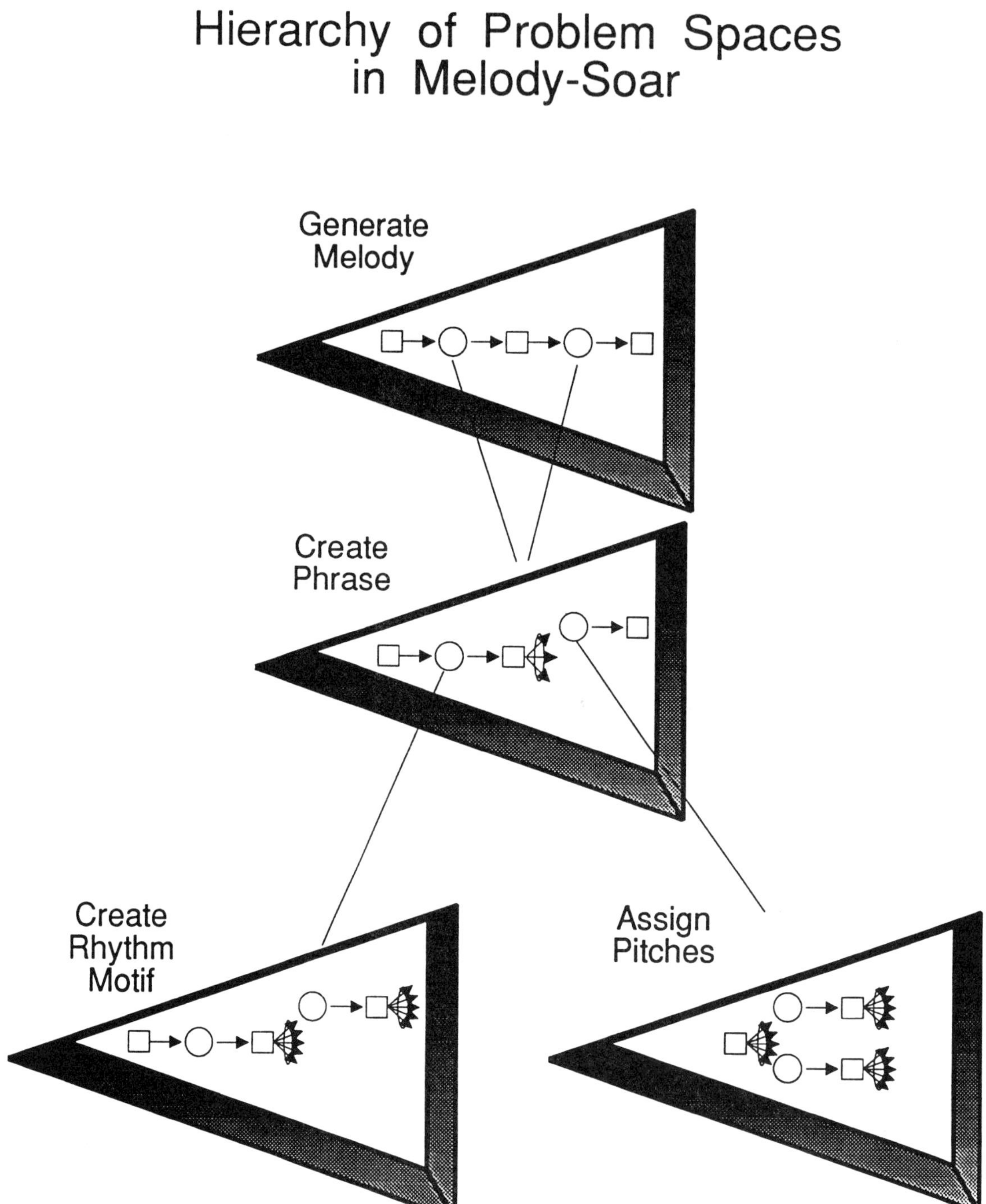
Hierarchy of Problem Spaces in Melody-Soar
Generate Melody
Create Phrase
Create Rhythm Motif
Assign Pitches

FIGURE 1

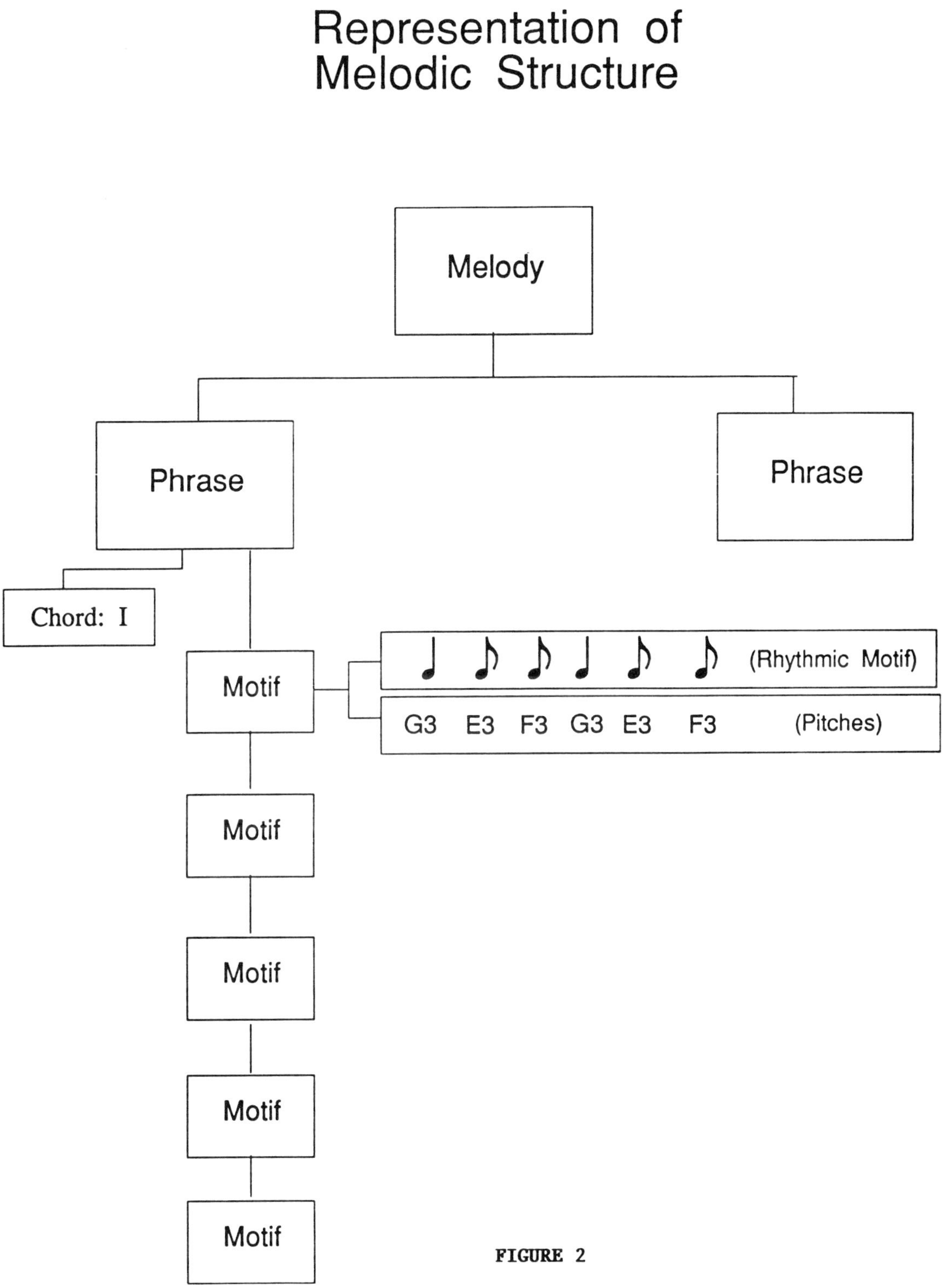
Representation of
Melodic Structure
Melody
Phrase
Phrase
Chord: I
Motif
(Rhythmic Motif)
G3 E3 F3 G3 E3 F3
(Pitches)
Motif
Motif
Motif
Motif

FIGURE 2

CHAPTER 46

A Problem Space Approach to Expert System Specification

G. R. Yost and A. Newell, Carnegie Mellon University

Abstract

One view of expert system development separates the endeavor into two parts. First, a domain expert, with the aid of a knowledge engineer, articulates a procedure for performing the desired task in some external form. Next, the knowledge engineer operationalizes the external description within some computer language. This paper examines the nature of the processes that operationalize natural task descriptions. We exhibit a language based on a computational model of problem spaces for which these processes are quite simple. We describe the processes in detail, and discuss which aspects of our computational model determine the simplicity of these processes.[1]

1. Introduction

Viewed abstractly and somewhat simplistically (Figure 1, top), one fundamental paradigm of expert system development starts with a domain expert who *articulates* the means of performing the task in some language T. A knowledge engineer then comprehends the task knowledge expressed in T, resulting in a conceptualization of the knowledge in terms of the task domain TD. Next, the knowledge engineer maps the task knowledge from the terms of TD to the terms of some computational domain CM (called a *computational model*). Finally, the knowledge engineer composes a set of statements that express the computational conceptualization of the task in a computer language L. Together, the comprehension, domain mapping, and composition are referred to as *operationalization* of the task knowledge. This description does not imply that all task knowledge is articulated before operationalization begins. In practice, these phases are highly interleaved and incremental. The processes described apply to individual knowledge fragments, not to the body of task knowledge as a whole.

T must be a language that both the domain expert and the knowledge engineer are familiar with, and that permits clear and concise description of the task knowledge. Thus, T is usually a natural language. In the remainder of this paper we assume that T is English. Operationalization remains a task for humans, rather than computers, because natural language comprehension is routine for humans but is much too difficult to perform automatically. Further, operationalization remains a task for knowledge engineers, rather than domain experts, because the latter rarely are skilled in the use of computer languages. Thus, this paper assumes a human knowledge engineer and an appropriate level of language skills in T and in L (it also assumes that the description of task knowledge in T does not pose its own difficulties by being a confusing or obscure text). The remainder of this paper focuses on the third component of operationalization: the conceptual mapping from the task domain to the computation domain.

By separating the notion of a language from the domains it describes, we see that improving the state of the art in expert system development is not simply an issue of making language improvements. We may modify a language so that it describes its domains more perspicuously, but the fundamental conceptual mismatch between the task domain and the computation domain remains. This conceptual mismatch accounts for most of the difficulty of operationalization. If the processes that perform the mapping are complex and open ended, then operationalization will be a difficult intellectually-creative task. If these processes are simple and routine, then design of expert systems will be routine. Different computational models could require quite different processes, and thus could present quite different degrees of difficulty.

This paper illustrates this thesis by describing PSCM (*Problem Space Computational Model*), a computational model with a small set of clearly-describable operationalization processes (Figure 1, bottom). PSCM is a computational model of problem spaces based on the Soar architecture (Laird, Newell & Rosenbloom, 1987, Laird, 1986). TAQL (*Task Acquisition Language*) is the language (L) that is based on PSCM; it has a compiler that

[1]This research was sponsored by the Defense Advanced Research Projects Agency (DOD), ARPA Order No. 4976 under contract F33615-87-C-1499, and monitored by the Air Force Avionics Laboratory. The research was also supported in part by Digital Equipment Corporation. The views and conclusions contained in this document are those of the authors and should not be interpreted as representing the official policies, either expressed or implied, of the Defense Advanced Research Projects Agency, Digital Equipment Corporation, or the U.S. Government.

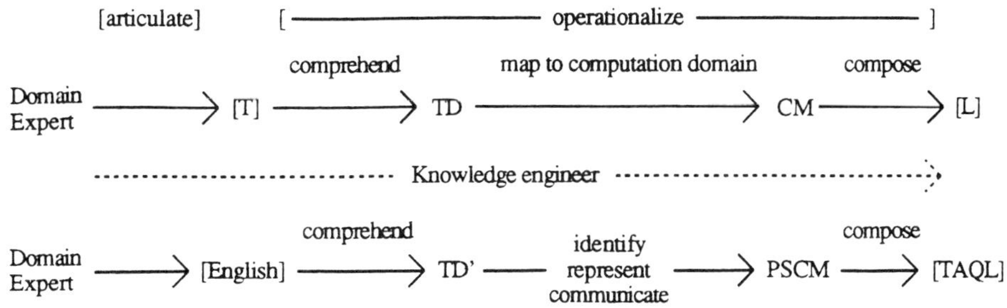

Figure 1: A fundamental paradigm of expert system development (simplified).

converts systems described in TAQL into Soar, hence into running expert systems. Only three types of processes are required to operationalize an English task knowledge description into TAQL: *identification*, *representation* and *communication*, each of limited character and complexity (given adequate language skills in English and in TAQL).

Section 2 describes PSCM. Section 3 describes the operationalization processes. Section 4 describes TAQL and gives a brief example of operationalization. Section 5 discusses the role of the computational model in determining the operationalization processes.

2. The Computational Model

A computational model is a set of entities, some of which perform operations on other domain entities. Thus a computational model has two kinds of domain entities: *structural* entities, and *functional* entities. Structural entities are the basic objects in the domain. Functional entities perform operations on structural entities. Some entities may be both structural and functional. For example, in the computational model underlying Lisp, certain lists may be treated as either programs or data.

PSCM is a computational model of problem spaces abstracted from the Soar problem solving architecture. In PSCM, as in Soar, all tasks are represented as finding a desired state in a problem space.

Table 1 lists the entities that comprise PSCM. The first row of the table lists the structural entities: tasks, problem spaces, states, and operators. Tasks are particular problems to be solved. Problem spaces are organizing structures that group related knowledge. States consist of the data objects relevant to the task. Operators manipulate states with their associated data objects. The rest of the table lists the functional PSCM entities. They are grouped by the structural entity with which they are most closely associated. In the rest of this paper, these structural and functional entities are collectively referred to as *PSCM components*.

Each PSCM component has a set of aspects that must be defined for the component to be meaningful. For example, an operator proposal component has three such aspects: which problem space the component belongs to; the conditions under which the operator should be proposed; and the operator object to be proposed, expressed in terms of objects in the current problem-solving context.

A task is represented as a collection of interacting problem spaces, each of which performs some portion of the task. Problem spaces interact in a variety of ways. For example, one problem space may implement an operator invoked in another problem space. During problem solving, problem spaces are situated within a goal hierarchy. Whenever a new goal is created, problem solving proceeds in that goal as follows:

Select a problem space and initialize it
Select an initial state for the problem space
While no goal test is satisfied:
  Propose operators to apply to the current state
  Select a single operator designated as better than all others by the available operator selection components
  Apply the operator to the current state, producing a new current state.

Subgoals are generated whenever problem solving in the current problem space cannot proceed until another problem space has performed some subtask on its behalf. For example, when the available operator selection components do not uniquely determine which operator should be applied next, PSCM creates a subgoal to choose one of the candidate operators.

Problem solving in PSCM proceeds in general without knowledge of a global control structure for the task. Rather, PSCM assembles a solution dynamically through the application of a sequence of localized problem-solving components. Some sets of PSCM components may lead PSCM to exhibit the behavior produced by a well-known problem solving method. Other sets of components may exhibit no easily-characterizable global behavior. However, PSCM admits problem-solving methods that influence the overall behavior of an entire set of components. Such method-based behavior is easily produced, but is not required.

While PSCM and Soar are both computational models of problem spaces, PSCM describes tasks at a higher level of abstraction than Soar. Soar expresses problem space computations in terms of concepts such as productions,

Tasks	Problem Spaces	States	Operators
Goal testing Methods	Problem space proposal Problem space initialization	State initialization Elaboration Evaluation	Operator proposal Operator selection Operator implementation Operator failure Evaluation

Table 1: Components of the PSCM computational model

working memory, preferences, and impasses. PSCM abstracts away from these architectural mechanisms and describes problem spaces in their own terms.[2]

3. The Operationalization Processes

The processes that operationalize English descriptions of domain knowledge into a given computational model are determined by the computational model. As displayed in the lower half of Figure 1, the operationalization of English task knowledge into TAQL is produced by a knowledge engineer who comprehends the knowledge description, maps the comprehended task concepts to components of PSCM, and composes a set of TAQL language statements expressing those PSCM components. For PSCM, the mapping between domain and computational model performs three functions: *identify* a PSCM component; *represent* a data object; and *communicate* some information from one PSCM component to another.

In general, while the operationalization processes themselves are determined by the computational model, their instantiation and application to a given knowledge description is strongly determined by the forms of expression used in that description. For PSCM, we can make an even stronger statement: *for descriptions of real-world tasks expressed naturally and in their own terms, the operationalization processes yield a set of PSCM components that directly model the forms of expression used in the description.* In other words, to a large extent, the processes involve not design and creative reformulation, but comprehension and re-expression of English knowledge descriptions in the terms of PSCM. This is particularly true for the identification and representation processes. The remainder of this paper explicates this claim.

To begin, we describe the three processes in more detail.[3] Let E denote an English description of the task knowledge for a particular task. The first function to be performed is to identify PSCM components in E. All types of PSCM components are identified at this stage, including organizational components such as problem spaces; data-object components that make up the problem solving state; and problem-solving methods, which determine the behavior of an entire set of PSCM components. The identification proceeds by labeling paragraphs, sentences, or phrases in E with the PSCM components that will encode the knowledge in those parts of E. In essence, it involves segmentation of the text in E.

The labels are assigned based on comprehension of the functional roles of parts of E. For example, a description of how to perform some subtask would be labeled with the name of an operator to perform that subtask, and would be classified as an operator-implementation component. Components created for related subtasks are grouped into problem spaces. A method is identified when E describes behaviors that match the behaviors known to be produced by the method. A structure that is the target of some action described in E is identified as a data object (part of a state). The identification of a data object may be further refined by classifying it as an instance of an abstract data type: such an identification is made when E describes manipulations of the identified data object that match the computational operations defined on the abstract data type.

After identification, the next function to be performed in the operationalization of E is to *represent* data objects. The identification process yields a conceptualization of the task knowledge in terms of abstract problem spaces. At this stage, most of the procedural structure of the final PSCM solution has been determined. Tasks have been assigned to operators, related subtasks have been grouped into problem spaces, and the relationships among problem spaces have been determined at an abstract level. The interactions among operators within a space are also known at an abstract level. However, the interactions among problem spaces and operators cannot be completely determined until data representations have been selected. Immediately after identification has completed, objects are still in terms of the task domain, except for the occasional appearance of abstract data type terms.

Data representations require raw materials out of which they can be constructed. The choice of raw materials depends to some extent on what is appropriate for the computational model. For example, representations built from machine-level units such as bytes (e.g., records and arrays) have proved appropriate for the computational models underlying conventional programming languages such as C and Pascal. For PSCM, the representations are in terms of attribute/value structures, which have

[2] Soar also provides a learning mechanism (chunking). PSCM does not.

[3] An example of these processes in action appears in Section 4.

historically proved useful in computational models for expert systems (e.g., OPS5 (Forgy, 1981)) and are used in Soar.

The representations of data objects described in E are developed in the same way as the PSCM components were assembled. That is, the attribute/value structures are not so much *designed* as they are *identified* from the structure of their descriptions in E. Thus, if E mentions a backplane with nine slots, it might be represented as an object of class *backplane* with a *slots* attribute whose value is *9*. These structures can be hierarchical. For example, if E mentions individual backplane slots and their widths, the backplane object may be given a *slot* attribute, the value of which is an object of class *slot* having a *width* attribute. In the cases where the abstract data type of an object has been identified, representation is even easier: it is assumed that the knowledge engineer is skilled in the expression of common abstract data types in the terms of PSCM; thus, creativity is not required.

Once the representation process has been completed, the operationalization of E in PSCM is almost finished. Most of the interactions among PSCM components are known by the time the identification process completes, and the components need only be restated in terms of the chosen attribute/value representations to become operational in PSCM. However, since the components were identified at an abstract level (before data representations were known), some of these components may now need to be modified or refined.

This fine-tuning of interactions is the province of the *communicate* process. Communication comes in two forms: inter-space communication, and inter-operator communication. Both forms of communication are driven by the need to make available the information operators must have to apply correctly and in the proper order.

The abstract problem space descriptions classify the connections among problem spaces. For example, they may state that the problem space in a subgoal implements a specific operator in the superspace. However, they do not indicate in any detail what information in the current goal needs to be made available in the subgoal, or what information produced by the subgoal needs to be returned to the supergoal when the subgoal exits. The *communicate* process fills in the details of this inter-space communication.

Data objects are copied *to* a subgoal to make them readily available to the problem space operating in the subgoal, or to any of its subspaces. This is particularly important for data objects that are modified by operators in the subspace. Data objects are copied *from* a subgoal to the superspace either to make a result available to operators in the superspace, or to preserve the value of a data object for a future invocation of the same problem space or one of its subspaces.

Inter-operator communication must be refined in two situations:

1. When an operator needs data in a form other than the form created by the operator that produces the data.
2. When an operator needs data that was available at some point during prior computation, but that would not otherwise be preserved in the current state.

The first situation can be resolved by either modifying the operators involved so that they represent the data in the same way, or by introducing a new operator or elaboration component that translates between the two forms. The second situation can be resolved by modifying operators that had access to the required information in the past so that they make this information part of their result states, thus preserving it for future use.

4. The TAQL Specification

The operationalization processes described in Section 3 map task knowledge from the terms of the task domain into the terms of PSCM. The final requirement in the operationalization is to express these computational model structures in a formal, compilable language: namely, TAQL.[4] The stages of the complete operationalization process are displayed graphically in the left-hand column of Figure 2 (we will describe the rest of that figure below).

TAQL directly reflects the structure of PSCM. Thus, a TAQL specification consists of a set of *TAQL constructs*, called TCs, each of which describes some aspect of a PSCM component. A Common Lisp program compiles TCs into Soar productions. When loaded into Soar along with a small set of runtime support productions, these productions implement the task described by the TCs. This compilation is fully automated and very efficient: it does not take noticeably longer to load a file of TCs than it does to load the productions generated by those TCs.

Each TC is a list consisting of the TC type and a name for the TC instance, followed by a list of keyword arguments. Each keyword specifies some aspect of the related PSCM component. An operator-proposal TC appears at the bottom of Figure 2. In terms of PSCM, the aspects that must be defined for an operator-proposal component are the problem space it applies in, the operator object to be proposed, and the conditions under which the operator should be proposed. These aspects are specified directly in the *propose-operator* TC as the values of the *:space*, *:op*, and *:when* keywords, respectively. Data is represented in TAQL using attribute/value structures of the form produced by the representation process during operationalization.[5]

We now provide a detailed example of the operationalization of a small piece of English task

[4]See the TAQL User Manual (Yost, 1988) for a more detailed description of TAQL than is given here.

[5]The current version of TAQL makes no attempt at graceful syntactic forms, as the emphasis so far has been on the operationalization processes.

description. The domain is computer configuration, as performed by the R1/XCON expert system (McDermott, 1982). R1 was coded in OPS5. Several years ago, the unibus-configuration subtask of R1 was recoded in Soar (Rosenbloom, Laird, McDermott, Newell & Orciuch, 1985). R1-Soar is an expert system of about 340 rules. Since its creation, it has served as a testbed for a number of efforts within the Soar project.

We have produced an English description of the unibus configuration task, and have realized this task in TAQL by applying the operationalization processes to that description. Figure 2 illustrates how the operationalization processes apply to a small piece of the description. The two English sentences at the top of the figure express when specific instances of an action (backplane cabling) should be performed. This is exactly the kind of information a PSCM operator-proposal component expresses. Thus, the identification process yields two operator-proposal components, one for each of the two cable lengths. Only the component for cables of length ten is shown in detail in the figure. Next, the representation process applies to the conditions in the abstract component, and also to the operator object that is to be proposed. A straightforward mapping from the English description of the abstract component yields the attribute/value representations shown.[6]

The condition that determines whether or not the backplane has been filled with modules is naturally expressed as a test for the presence of a *^modules-configured* attribute on the state. However, the operationalization of the modules-into-backplane operator, which fills the backplane[7], does not generate this information. Thus, the communication process must build a link between the modules-into-backplane and cable-bp operators. It does so by modifying modules-into-backplane to return the required modules-configured attribute, in addition to any other actions the operator already performs.

Before leaving this example, we say a few words about how R1-TAQL compares to R1-Soar. For the comparisons given here, we use an updated version of R1-Soar that reflects the task-oriented conceptual structure of unibus configuration more closely than the original R1-Soar did.[8]

Both R1-TAQL and R1-Soar use the same seven problem spaces. R1-TAQL has 153 TCs, and R1-Soar has 337 hand-coded Soar productions. The 153 TCs compile into 352 Soar productions. A more useful measure of size is the number of *words* in each description, where a word is defined to be the smallest unit that has meaning to the TAQL compiler or to the Soar production compiler. Words include attribute names, variables, and parentheses, among other things. The English description of R1 has 756 words; R1-TAQL has 5774 words, and R1-Soar has 21752 words. Thus the number of words in R1-TAQL is 26% of the number of words in R1-Soar, a significant reduction.

5. The Role of the Computational Model

We have described PSCM and TAQL, a computational model and associated language that require only simple processes of operationalization. Existing practice takes the creation of expert systems to be a difficult task, although the development of knowledge acquisition tools and expert system shells has simplified the task for some classes of systems at the expense of generality in the tool (Clancey, 1983, McDermott, 1988). Much of this difficulty resides in operationalization, although articulation of domain knowledge (which is outside the scope of this paper) clearly contributes as well.

The desirable course would be to describe the operationalization processes for existing expert system specification languages, and compare them with the processes for TAQL. However, this course is not presently feasible, because the operationalization processes for other languages cannot yet be specified. All that is known is the overall complexity of the language in practice. For example, Common Lisp, a standard, highly effective, general purpose system-building language, still requires substantial effort when used to build medium-sized expert systems. But to give the operationalization processes for coding expert systems in Common Lisp would be to describe how to do program synthesis of very substantial and complex programs — well beyond current understanding. That operationalization processes can be described when they are simple (as they are for TAQL) does not imply that they can be described when they are more complex.

However, some things can be said. For most specification systems, the basic computational model is some variant of procedural semantics: data types with associated sets of operations, on top of which is provided a set of procedural control constructs, built out of the notions of execution, sequence, and conditionality. Production systems, object-oriented programming, conventional programming, and a number of other schemes are all variations on this theme. All such specification systems require specifying such things as programs, methods, strategies, reasoning schemes, executives, etc. For simple applications, this may be easy, but as the complexity of the application grows this becomes a genuine program design task. The operationalization processes for using these languages must include some way to synthesize the required methods, executive organizations and so forth. Let us call this operationalization process *method-design*.

Method-design is not required for operationalizing into TAQL. This is surely a major factor in the simplicity of its operationalization processes. Some of the reasons for this are presented in Section 2: the mutually supporting problem space structure of PSCM provides the

[6]Part of the representation of the configuration structure is determined by other parts of the R1 English task description (not shown), and is simply reused here.

[7]This operator is described in a part of the R1 description not shown here.

[8]This was the joint work of Amy Unruh and Gregg Yost.

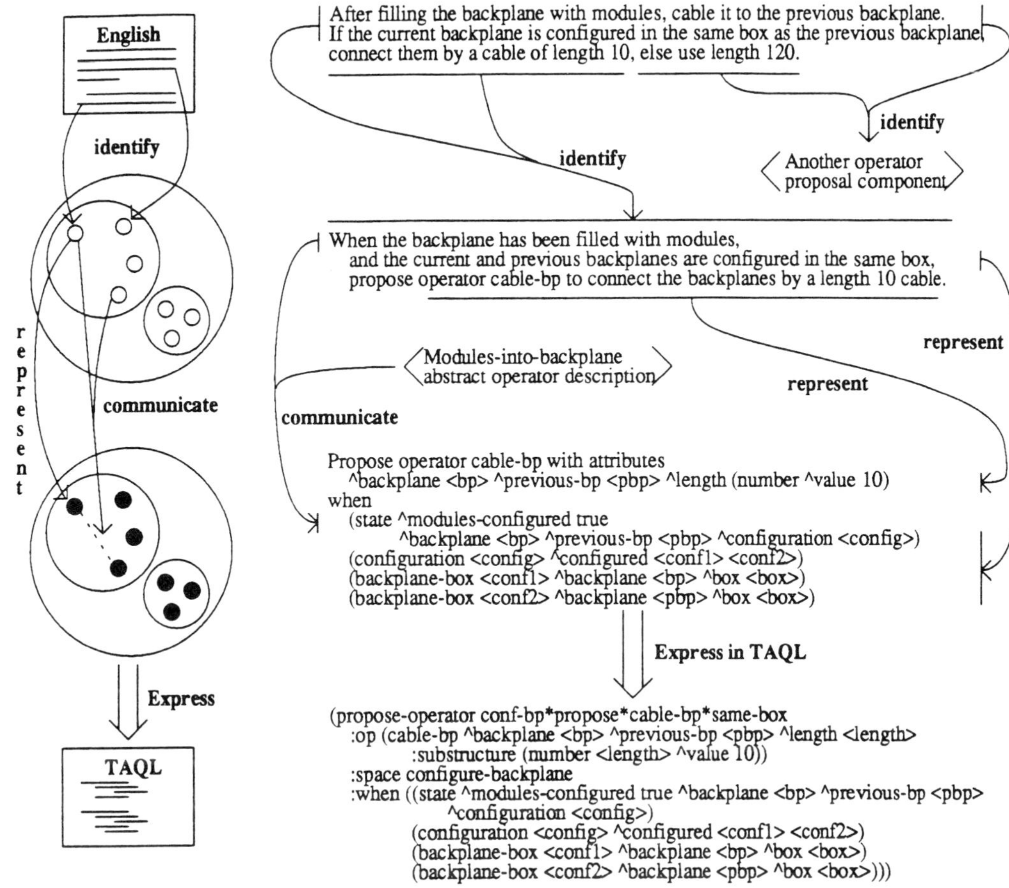

Figure 2: The operationalization of part of R1 in TAQL

organization into which local control knowledge can be placed without having to design any methods or higher-level organizations. In this respect, PSCM differs from RIME (Bachant, 1988), a programming methodology based on problem spaces and in some ways similar to PSCM. In RIME, each problem space is required to specify a single method that will determine the course of problem solving in that space. In PSCM (as in Soar), method-based behavior is an emergent phenomena of localized problem-solving decisions.

Of course, methods can be quite useful. Once coded, they can be reused in similar tasks by simply modifying a few bits of domain knowledge. Methods determine the behavior of an entire set of problem solving components, and they can provide very concise specifications in appropriate situations. However, if the desired task behavior does not very closely match the method's behavior, it can be quite difficult to force the task to fit the method. The key point here is that PSCM provides the flexibility to either use methods or not, depending on which is most appropriate in a given situation. TAQL does provide a set of methods, which can be used when appropriate. However, only one situation occurs in R1-TAQL where the use of a method (limited depth-first search) is more appropriate than a customized set of components. An important result of our work is that the nature of the PSCM operationalization processes facilitates the selection of appropriate sets of these customized components.

6. Conclusions

This paper has exhibited a computational model and associated formal language for which the processes of operationalizing naturally-expressed expert system task knowledge are quite simple, in particular avoiding method-design while having a quite general scope. Our explicit focus on the processes that transform from the task domain to the computation domain is a departure from much of the expert system specification literature. Many efforts are involved with the invention of new formal languages and the description of the processes, sometimes quite complex, by which those languages are reduced to some previously-known operational computing system (for example, GIST (London & Feather, 1982) and KEE (Filman, 1988)). While such work is both interesting and useful, it is often left to the reader's intuition to see why it might be easier to use the new language rather than some existing language. Our study of the processes that construct TAQL specifications from an informal English description of task knowledge is an attempt to articulate these intuitions for a particular computational model (PSCM).

Our future work will proceed along two paths. First, we plan to build a tool that helps a knowledge engineer carry out the PSCM operationalization processes. The knowledge engineer will bring natural English descriptions of task knowledge to the tool. The tool will help select and apply appropriate instances of the identification, representation, and communication processes, ultimately producing a TAQL implementation of the task. We will evaluate the effectiveness of our tool with respect to existing tools over a wide range of tasks.

We do not believe it will be possible in the near future to fully automate operationalization in a general-purpose expert system development tool, and we will not attempt this. The language skills required are well beyond the state of the art. Many research effort resolve this problem by limiting the generality of the tool. We take a different approach. Our tool will leave the language skills with a human knowledge engineer, who can perform them routinely. We focus instead on the aspect of operationalization people find most difficult: mapping knowledge from task domain terms to computational terms. The PSCM operationalization processes that have been the focus of this paper seem sufficiently limited that a computer can provide strong guidance in their application.

The second path we intend to explore is more theoretical. Now that we have some understanding of the operationalization processes for TAQL, we want to discover what aspects of the underlying computational model determine the simplicity of these processes. As discussed in Section 5, that PSCM does not require method-design is one such aspect. However, there are surely others we have not yet identified. We also want to explore whether the processes we have identified apply to tasks substantially larger than the unibus configuration task, and, if not, we want to explore what higher levels of organization might be required for large tasks.

Acknowledgments

We wish to thank Amy Unruh, for rewriting much of R1-Soar to correspond to our English description of the task; Erik Altmann, Thad Polk, and Milind Tambe, three TAQL users who have provided much valuable feedback; Paul Rosenbloom, for his comments on earlier drafts of this paper; and John McDermott for helping us understand the R1 task, for his insights into the nature of the expert systems development, and for his continued assistance.

References

Bachant, J. (1988). RIME: Preliminary work toward a knowledge-acquisition tool. In Marcus, S. (Ed.), *Automating Knowledge Acquisition for Expert Systems*. Boston, MA: Kluwer Academic Publishers.

Clancey, W. (1983). The advantages of abstract control knowledge in expert system design. *Proceedings of the Third National Conference on Artificial Intelligence*. Washington, D.C..

Filman, R. E. (1988). Reasoning with worlds and truth maintenance in a knowledge-based programming environment. *Communications of the ACM, 31*(4), 382-401.

Forgy, C. L. (July 1981). *OPS5 user's manual* (Tech. Rep. CMU-CS-81-135). Carnegie Mellon University, Computer Science Department.

Laird, J. E. (1986). *Soar User's Manual: Version 4.0*. Intelligent Systems Laboratory, Palo Alto Research Center, Xerox Corporation.

Laird, J. E., Newell, A., and Rosenbloom, P. S. (1987). Soar: An architecture for general intelligence. *Artificial Intelligence, 33*(1), 1-64.

London, P. and Feather, M. (1982). Implementing specification freedoms. *Science of Computer Programming, 2*(2), 91-131.

McDermott, J. (1982). R1: A rule-based configurer of computer systems. *Artificial Intelligence, 19*(1), 39-88.

McDermott, J. (1988). Preliminary steps toward a taxonomy of problem-solving methods. In Marcus, S. (Ed.), *Automating Knowledge Acquisition for Expert Systems*. Boston, MA: Kluwer Academic Publishers.

Rosenbloom, P. S., Laird, J. E., McDermott, J., Newell, A., and Orciuch, E. (1985). R1-Soar: An experiment in knowledge-intensive programming in a problem-solving architecture. *IEEE Transactions on Pattern Analysis and Machine Intelligence, 7*(5), 561-569.

Yost, G. R. (1988). TAQL 2.0: Soar Task Acquisition Language User Manual. Computer Science Department, Carnegie Mellon University, October, 1988.

The Soar Papers

1990

CHAPTER 47

Learning Control Knowledge in an Unsupervised Planning Domain*

C. B. Congdon, University of Michigan

Abstract

The LEGO-SOAR project is designed to investigate the interactions that arise when problem-solving and learning are combined. The system can select its own initial state and construct its own desired state, enabling it to explore the domain without human supervision. Without any initial domain-specific control knowledge, the system learns rules that enable it to perform well in the domain, and is even able to overcome the effects of overgeneral control rules. An analysis of the system indicates several abilities lacking in LEGO-SOAR but needed by a general problem-solver. These include recognizing duplicate states, giving up on a task after a period of time, and learning from failure. Though illustrated in the SOAR architecture, the issues are not confined to SOAR and indicate the need for further research in the field.

Primary Topic: Machine Learning
This paper is also relevant to Automated Reasoning (Planning).

*This research was sponsored by grant NCC2-517 from NASA Ames.

1 Introduction

LEGO-SOAR is a learning and planning system designed to examine how SOAR can learn to make control decisions in a domain with a large number of potential operators at each decision point. By slightly changing the constraints of the standard blocks world, the size of the search space increases considerably, and learning general control rules becomes particularly important.

Several capabilities of the SOAR architecture were demonstrated in the course of this research. Among these are "play mode", where LEGO-SOAR can construct its own desired state, and a "time-out" mechanism, where LEGO-SOAR is prevented from spending too much time investigating a path in a subgoal.

In addition, this research illustrates the need for further research in terms of remembering previous states and learning from failure. SOAR's performance here is compared to that of PRODIGY [7, 8], which has an architectural mechanism for recognizing previous states, and thus, has different results when learning from failure.

2 A Soar Synopsis

Although the decision procedure in SOAR involves manipulation of four types of objects — goals, problem spaces, states, and operators — we will be concerned primarily with the processes related to operator selection. In most production systems, the application of an operator is equated with the firing of a production, but in SOAR the semantics of operator application are different. Instead, operators are instantiated as working memory elements via the firing of productions. Multiple operators may be instantiated for a given state, but only one will be selected to apply; the particular operator chosen to be applied is determined by the decision procedure through the evaluation of *preferences*. One or more preferences will be associated with each operator instantiation; these preferences establish a partial ordering among the available operators, and assist in selecting between them. Operators must have an acceptable preference in order to be considered at all. They may also have require, best, better, indifferent, worse, worst, reject, or prohibit preferences. The semantics of these preferences is described fully in [5].

The architecture determines a maximal subset of operators not dominated by any others; if the preferences are not sufficient to select one best operator, the architecture creates a *tie impasse*; in response to the impasse, a new subgoal is created in order to gain additional knowledge about the operators. In the tie-impasse subgoal, SOAR does a lookahead search with each of the tied operators. One is selected, and subgoaling along that path continues until either a success or a failure is recognized. In the case of a success, the original operator being evaluated is determined to be best among the alternatives, and the subgoal terminates with the selection of that operator, which is then applied at the top level. In the case of a failure, the operator being evaluated is determined to be worst among the alternatives, and control returns to the level of the tie impasse, where another operator can be tried in the lookahead search. See Figure 1 for an illustration of the subgoaling involved in evaluating a tie impasse.

Whenever a subgoal terminates, SOAR's chunking mechanism caches the knowledge gained in the subgoal. Chunking is a form of automatic learning related to explanation-based learning; it backtraces through the conditions of the subgoal to determine those

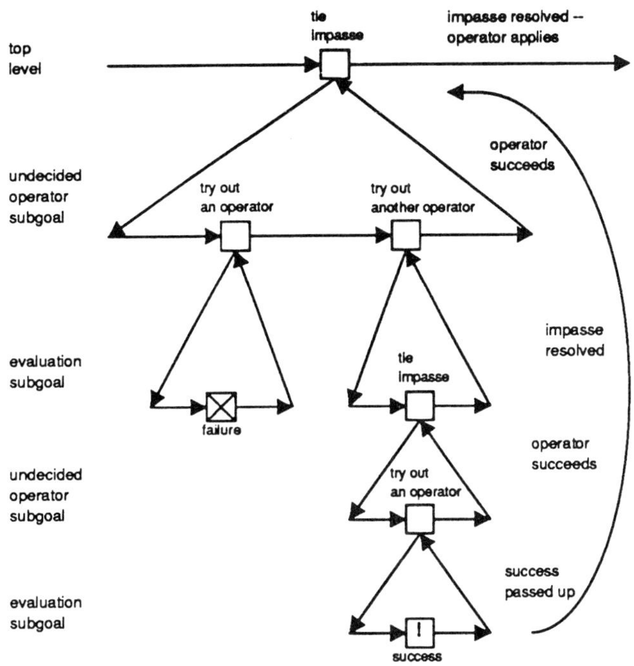

Figure 1: In the figure above, SOAR does not have enough knowledge to decide between operators at the top level, which leads to a tie impasse. The first operator is tried and found to lead to failure. The second operator is tried, and this leads to another tie impasse. Another subgoal is created to investigate the tied operators; the first of these leads to success. This terminates the entire subgoal stack, and the second operator investigated is chosen at the top level. (The subgoal stack will be terminated even if there are other operators that have not yet been evaluated.)

conditions responsible for the creation of the best or worse preference and creates a new production with these conditions (including the instantiated operator) and the preference as the action. This production is added to long-term memory and is equal in status to all other productions, i.e. it will fire whenever its conditions are met.

3 Background

3.1 Other Blocks Worlds; Other Architectures

A blocks world seemed to be a good domain for investigating the interactions between learning and planning in SOAR because the similarity between the block structures to be built creates many opportunities for chunks to be learned and used. However, the standard blocks world, with its identical blocks, and the restriction that only one block can be moved at a time, is quite constrained. We used Fahlman's BUILD [3] program for an inspiration in extending the domain. Fahlman used blocks of differing sizes and shapes and allowed the robot to pick up a stack of blocks; these ideas have been incorporated into the LEGO-SOAR domain. Unlike LEGO-SOAR, BUILD used a real robot arm to manipulate real blocks, and used sophisticated building techniques such as the use of temporary support blocks. However, BUILD used a heuristic control structure *specifically designed for the blocks world* to generate its plans. In contrast, LEGO-SOAR starts with no domain-specific control knowledge, and relies on problem-solving experience to gain the needed heuristics. The idea is not to see what SOAR can be programmed to do, but rather, what it can learn to do.

Due to the differences in the domain, LEGO-SOAR bears only a superficial resemblance to most blocks worlds described in the literature, and there is no need to discuss them here. However, PRODIGY [7, 8], a general-purpose problem-solving architecture with an Explanation-Based Learning (EBL) component provides an interesting contrast to SOAR. The simple blocks world that has been implemented in PRODIGY illustrates different solutions to some of the problems encountered by SOAR, and this will be discussed later. In analyzing SOAR's strengths and weaknesses, it is useful to have such an alternative to serve as a reference point.

3.2 The Lego-Soar Domain

The objects in the LEGO-SOAR world are two-dimensional blocks. All are the same height — call it one unit — but blocks can be one, two, or three units wide. (Since it seems strange to be manipulating two-dimensional blocks, we often imagine these blocks to be one-unit deep, but the blocks cannot be placed one behind the other, which is why the LEGO-SOAR world is two-dimensional.) Each unit of a block has a "pin" at the top and a "socket" at the bottom; when one block is stacked on top of another, the socket of the top block is thought to rest upon the pin of the supporting block. This representation is used only to limit the number of ways one block can be stacked upon another. The "pins" and "sockets" are not imagined to be literal physical characteristics of the blocks, but rather, reference points (real Lego blocks are more stable than the blocks we are using here). In most blocks worlds, the table is considered to be a magically infinite surface that always has room to hold another block, but in LEGO-SOAR, some fixed number of pins must be

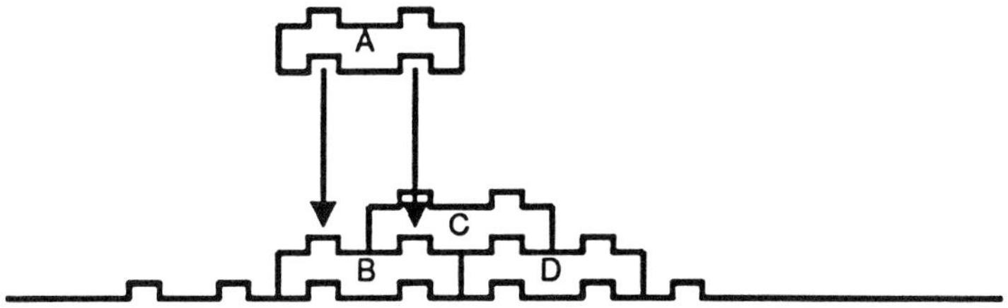

Figure 2: An example of a "knockdown": When socket A0 is PUTDOWN on pin B0, block C will be knocked down.

specified for the table. The LEGO-SOAR table may or may not have enough room to hold all the blocks.

Moving a block is considered to involve picking it up and placing one of its sockets onto some unoccupied pin of another block. Note that it is no longer sufficient to specify an operator as PUTON(A, B)). Instead, the operator must specify a particular socket of A and a particular pin of B. Two things can happen when a block is moved:

- The block is successfully and securely placed.
- The block is placed, but doing so leads to one of two types of failure:
  - The block is successfully placed, but not sufficiently supported. This results in a "collapse", for example, if one end of three-unit block is placed above a one-unit block, and the other end of the three-unit block is unsupported.
  - Placing the specified socket on the specified pin is not possible because some other socket of the block would have to rest on a pin that is already occupied. In this situation, the operator is said to "knock down" the structure. (See Figure 2 for an example of this type of failure).

Though it would be possible to interface LEGO-SOAR to a real-world environment (as has been done in the ROBO-SOAR project [6]), or even to a sophisticated modeling system (such as the World Modeler [2]), for the purposes of this research it is sufficient to maintain a restricted sense of stable structures. We are overly conservative in judging which structures collapse. A one-unit block will always be stable; a two-unit block will be stable only if supported at both sockets; and a three-unit block will be stable if both ends are supported, and under certain other conditions. Unstable structures are recognized by one of five general productions.

LEGO-SOAR quickly learns the chunks it needs to build constructions with one- and two-unit blocks; it can also learn the two chunks that will prevent failure in the form of collapse or knock-down. The specific number of training examples required to learn these chunks depends on the complexity of the sample tasks and the operators suggested by the tutor; for example, the tutor might suggest trying an operator that will lead to a COLLAPSE in order to allow LEGO-SOAR to learn about COLLAPSEs. If LEGO-SOAR's first task involves subconstructions, such as building a tower of one-unit blocks as well as a tower of two-unit blocks, it is possible to learn the chunks in one example. However, the training examples are typically simple (such as building a two-block tower, as described above), so more examples are used.

4 The Lego-Soar System

4.1 Unsupervised Building, a.k.a. Play Mode

One of the first features added to the system was what we call Play Mode. The idea was to give LEGO-SOAR the ability to create its own goals, and then go off to try to achieve them. This way, LEGO-SOAR could run with only minimal supervision for some extended period of time, to see what it could learn on its own.

To implement Play Mode, we added an operator that allows LEGO-SOAR to specify any one of several potential initial states (with different numbers of different sizes of blocks), leaving the desired state unspecified. The unspecified desired state leads the system to subgoal and select a new problem space that has operators to construct a desired state based on the objects in the initial state. In the new problem space, an operator called ADD-ABOVE is instantiated for each pair of blocks in the initial state; selection of an ADD-ABOVE instantiation with two blocks indicates that the one block should be above the other in the desired state. After the two blocks are chosen, a second operator, CHOOSE-PINS, is instantiated with all possible combinations of the top block's sockets and the base block's pins; selection of one of these operators specifies a pin and socket pair, and an ABOVE relation is added to the desired state.

After one or more ABOVE relations have been added to the desired state, an operator called BUILD-NOW is instantiated, and can be selected by the system as an alternative to the ADD-ABOVE operators. Selection of BUILD-NOW signals that the desired state has been specified. The desired state is then added to the goal, and control returns to the top-level state, where LEGO-SOAR can begin problem solving to try to achieve the desired state. [1]

Once Play-Mode was implemented, it was possible to let the system run through a series of tasks without supervision, choosing at random between operators when it did not have sufficient knowledge to select one of the alternatives. (When operating under a tutor's supervision, LEGO-SOAR will ask the user to select between the alternatives.) In running a task in Play-Mode, LEGO-SOAR would eventually stumble onto a correct operator sequence and achieve the goal, though it sometimes would spend a great deal of time pursuing an unpromising branch of the search tree. After running a series of tasks, the system would acquire similar chunks to those it learned when under the supervision of a tutor. The chunks learned in both cases preferred operators likely to lead to success and rejected operators likely to lead to failure.

4.2 Imposing a Time Limit on Subgoaling

In implementing Play Mode, it soon became apparent that the system could stumble onto an unfortunate sequence of operators that were leading far away from the path to the goal, and would not be able to realize this. (Recall that SOAR does a look-ahead search that can expand to an arbitrary depth if not terminated by the recognition of success or failure.)

To prevent such behavior, we implemented a series of productions to keep track of the time spent on a given task. Upon starting a task, and at returning to the top-level state

[1] Although it would be possible to have LEGO-SOAR learn about how to create goals for itself (e.g. one might want LEGO-SOAR to learn to include interestingness factors such as the height of the structure), this is a separate research issue that is not addressed in this work. Instead, no learning was done in this problem space.

after completion of subgoaling, LEGO-SOAR sets a "timer" for itself. When the time on the timer has elapsed, failure is recorded in the subgoal and control returns to the top level. At this point, the timer is reset. With chunks learned, SOAR may do a great deal of problem-solving at the top level, but not necessarily move straight to the goal. So the time limit may also expire when SOAR is in a top-level state; if this happens, the system will stop working on the current task, and can go on to another one.

The time-out mechanism prevents LEGO-SOAR from spending too much time on tasks that are too difficult for it, i.e., those which are possible, but which the system doesn't have enough knowledge to solve. At a later time, LEGO-SOAR may return to a task that it was once unable to complete; in the interval, the system might have learned something that will enable it to successfully achieve the goal. The time-out mechanism is also successful in allowing LEGO-SOAR to "give up" on an impossible task — one that would otherwise require an exhaustive search of a very large search tree.

4.3 The Effects of Overgeneral Knowledge

In moving from simple tasks to more complicated ones, LEGO-SOAR ran into an unexpected complication with learning. In early learning situations, LEGO-SOAR learns that if a socket of block A is above a pin of block B in the desired state, then it's a good thing to pick up block A. However, in more complex tasks, this is not always the best thing to do. For example, when building an arch, the two supporting blocks must first be in place before the cross block is placed.

Since LEGO-SOAR does its initial problem-solving in subgoals, this would not seem to cause difficulties; the chunks that fire will be tried and discovered to lead to failure, and another operator will be tried. However, the resulting operator sequence is not always what we would hope for, as an example will demonstrate.

The general behavior can be illustrated by a sample problem: building an arch with blocks A, B and C. The initial and desired states are illustrated in Figure 3. In this example, it is assumed that LEGO-SOAR has had some previous tasks, and has learned general chunks regarding the PICKUP and PUTDOWN operators.

First, LEGO-SOAR picks up block C. Next, it puts socket C0 on pin A0[2]. This results in a failure, so the operator that led to failure, the PUTDOWN, is rejected, and LEGO-SOAR puts the block down someplace else. The next operator to fire will be some instantiation of the PICKUP operator; again, block C will be chosen. This loop will continue ad infinitum. Two problems are illustrated by this simple task:

1. After just one loop through this PICKUP/PUTDOWN cycle, LEGO-SOAR will have two contradictory chunks for the PUTDOWN step. One will create a best preference for the operator that puts C0 on A0, since that leads to partial completion of the goal. The other will create a worst preference for this same operator, since it leads to a collapse. The semantics of SOAR preferences is such that an operator that is both best and worst is resolved to be best, and in effect, the knowledge of the collapse is lost.

2. In a domain such as this, SOAR has no means of recognizing that the operator that

[2]Equivalently, it may put socket C2 on pin B0. Best preferences will be created for both of these operators, and the specific one chosen has no bearing on this discussion.

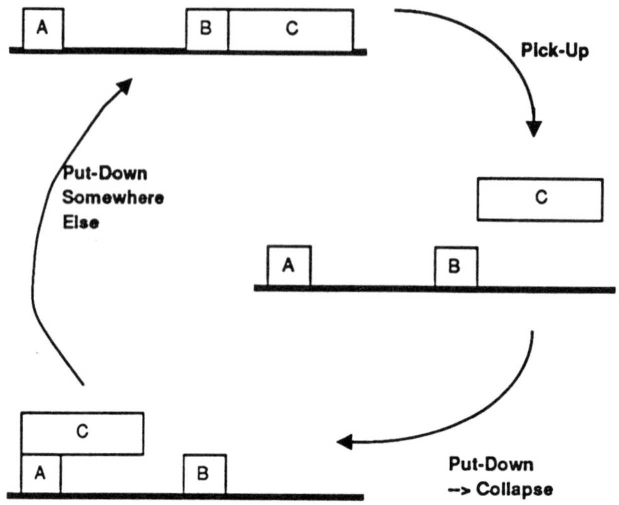

Figure 3: An example of the infinite looping that occured when trying to build an arch. If block C is PUTDOWN on block A, a collapse will result, so LEGO-SOAR must put block C down somewhere else. Block C will immediately be picked up again.

immediately preceded the failure was not the *cause* of the failure. In the sample problem, the cause of the failure was picking up block C prematurely.

A discussion of these two problems will be covered in following sections.

4.4 Default Productions

The default productions of SOAR [5] are responsible for the creation of a worst preference for an operator that leads to failure. The problem with this arrangement is that there is no distinction between a failure due to an operator that simply does not lead to the goal, and a failure due to an operator that makes it impossible to *ever* achieve the goal. The weakest type of failure is assumed (inconvenience, rather than disaster), and, therefore, a worst preferences is created when a failure is recognized. However, the second type of failure actually calls for a reject preference — the operator should *never* be chosen.

For the LEGO-SOAR system, this problem is overcome by adding a new production to the set of existing default productions. The new production causes a reject preference to be created for an operator that leads to disaster. This eliminates the conflict between best and worst preferences; the operator is now best and *rejected*, and so will not be chosen. However, this does not solve the infinite loop problem in LEGO-SOAR. With the new default production, the system will still pick up C; it just won't try to put C0 on A0. Instead, it will put C down someplace else, and immediately picks it up again. Thus, the infinite looping continues.

4.5 Remembering a State

The obvious next step in resolving the infinite looping behavior was to endow LEGO-SOAR with the ability to recognize that it has entered a state it's been to before, and therefore, to reject the state. (It may seem surprising that the SOAR architecture does not provide such a mechanism; this will be discussed in Section 5.) A solution to this problem had been examined previously in SOAR, resulting in a set of productions to "remember" states in a particular domain.

Use of the REMEMBER operator required adding a few domain-specific productions to establish the features that define a state for the purposes of remembering. Each time a new state is entered, the REMEMBER operator is selected. If the new state has a REMEMBER augmentation, it will be rejected; if not, the operator creates a subgoal that ultimately changes the state by adding a REMEMBER augmentation. When the subgoal is terminated its results are saved into a chunk. This chunk has as its conditions the bindings of the relevant state features, and as its actions, the REMEMBER augmentation. If a new state is entered with the same bindings, this chunk will fire, adding the REMEMBER augmentation to the state, and causing the state to be rejected as a duplicate.

Relevant features for Lego-Soar include the blocks in the state, and the locations of these blocks as specified by ABOVE relations. Also, a state encountered in a lookahead search should not be rejected if encountered later at the top level. Finally, a state encountered in a previous task should not cause a state in a future task to be rejected.

The REMEMBER operator gave LEGO-SOAR the ability to recognize what had been tried, and therefore broke the infinite loop, but the search required to achieve the goal could be fairly extensive. LEGO-SOAR picks up block C and tries to put C0 down in a number of places, eventually exhausting the possibilities. Then it tries to put C1 down, and must exhaust the possibilites for PUTDOWN with that socket. This repeats with the third socket of C. Having now exhausted these possibilities, LEGO-SOAR backs up in the subgoal stack, and tries to pick up another block.

Thus, the addition of the REMEMBER operator enabled LEGO-SOAR to complete its task of building an arch. However, since neither success nor failure is reported until the final stages of this extensive search (exhaustion does not constitute failure in SOAR), no chunks are learned that will make it easier for LEGO-SOAR to build an arch in the future. In this stage of development, LEGO-SOAR could build arches only by going through the lengthy search procedure.

4.6 Recovering from Incorrect Knowledge

The productions created by SOAR's chunking mechanism are never removed and are never altered by the system. But it is possible to add an additional chunk to the system that will override the effects of an overgeneral chunk. A solution is provided by Laird [4]. The first stage of the recovery process involves detecting that an incorrect decision has been made; in LEGO-SOAR, this is signaled by exhausting the available operators. Next, RECOVERY forces a reconsideration of the offending operator (one decision back in the goal stack), which allows other operators to be tried, and finally, the correction found is saved through chunking. For a detailed explanation of the RECOVERY process, see [4].

After one run trying to build an arch with RECOVERY, LEGO-SOAR builds a chunk that allows it to move straight to the goal on future arch-building problems.

5 Analysis

5.1 Learning by Playing

One result of the experiment with Play Mode was that LEGO-SOAR learned the same things about its world that it learned when guided by a tutor, although, of course, it took much longer to select the relevant operators. The chunks learned in both cases were of the same generality, and identified the same situations in which it was advisable or inadvisable to select PICKUP and PUTDOWN operators.

When the system was running without guidance, however, a pattern became apparent. The *order* that LEGO-SOAR tries particular operators has a long-lasting effect on the resulting performance. If there are two ways to accomplish the same task, LEGO-SOAR may learn one way and never try the other. For example, there are basically two ways for LEGO-SOAR to build a three-block tower; the middle block can be placed on the base block first, or the top block can be placed on the middle block first (recall that LEGO-SOAR is able to lift a stack of blocks). Once LEGO-SOAR tries one of these possibilities, it will tend to be "superstitious" about it, preferring that construction technique to the other one, even though there is no clear advantage of one technique over the other.

5.2 Issues of Cognitive Plausibility

Although SOAR has also been proposed as a theory of cognition [9], the time-out mechanism and the remembering mechanism are not intended to make any claims about cognition. Rather, they are tools to be used in the interim before relevant cognitive mechanisms can be developed. The time-out mechanism approaches cognitive plausibility, in that humans seem to give up on certain goals if they have not achieved them within a certain amount of time. However, the time-out mechanism lacks any model of LEGO-SOAR having a *goal* to watch the time (a goal that could be invoked or ignored at whim), nor does the specific time-limit adapt to suit a particular goal. (For example, the time allowed to do a construction with 9 blocks should probably be greater than that allowed for 3 blocks.)

The remembering mechanism is likewise a handy crutch, but has even less cognitive plausibility. Clearly, humans are able to recall similarities between their current situation and previous situations they've been in. However, it is also clear that human memory is not generally as perfect as that demonstrated by the REMEMBER operator. Humans would err in two directions: thinking they had tried an operator that in fact they had not, and thinking they had not tried an operator that in fact they had. Again, a question arises in terms of the *goals* of the agent; with a goal to pay attention to previous states, the performance of remembering should be greatly improved over "passive" remembering.

Another problem with the REMEMBER operator is that the "relevant" features of the state must be established ahead of time. Ideally, SOAR would have to *learn* to identify the relevant attributes of a state.

5.3 The Semantics of Failure

As has perhaps become apparent, the learning that SOAR does in response to success is not nearly as revealing as the learning it does (or doesn't do) in response to failure. SOAR is very proficient at learning from success, so proficient, in fact, that this tends to be taken for granted in the system. However, SOAR seems to lack a comprehensive model of learning from failure.

One problem with failure as handled by SOAR is that its determination is not as straightforward as that of success. There is one pre-defined, domain-independent, mechanism for establishing success — the comparison of the desired state to the current state. There is no equivalently simple mechanism for detection of failure. Instead, the user must provide productions that will add failure augmentations to the state in a domain-dependent fashion.

Since there is no means of distinguishing between a failure that does not lead to the goal and one that causes the goal to be unattainable, the system must assume the weakest type of failure, and merely create a worst preference for the relevant operator, rather than rejecting it outright. However, it is clear that the second type of failure should lead to a reject preference, i.e., such an operator should *never* be selected.

Furthermore, it seems that SOAR should have some means of recognizing the failure that occurs by exhausting the alternatives at a decision point. In general, it is not possible to recognize that the alternatives have been exhausted without making use of some process such as remembering, so a model of remembering (as discussed above) would first have to be introduced. This type of failure should undoubtedly result in reject preferences, to prevent the branch in the search tree from being explored again.

This indicates a topic for further research in SOAR, the creation of a set of productions with which SOAR could learn about different types of failure. With this in place, SOAR could develop a means of discrimination that would lead to different preferences for different types of failure.

5.4 Comparison to Prodigy's Failure Mechanisms

PRODIGY is a general-purpose learning system that takes a different approach to the problem of cycles in the search tree, and thus, is able to learn in this situation. PRODIGY provides an *architectural* mechanism for recognizing duplicate states. Due to this, cycles are detected without the need for the user to specify relevant state attributes. Instead, *all* attributes are considered relevant.

One implication of this structure is that PRODIGY would indeed have problems with looping if presented with an over-specified state in which attributes irrelevant to the task at hand were allowed to change. In this situation, PRODIGY would continue to subgoal, much in the way that SOAR does.

A second implication is that PRODIGY is unable to alter its performance in terms of recognizing duplicate states. In other words, PRODIGY is unable to *learn* about remembering where it's been. A mechanism that checks each new state against previous states is likely to slow down a system that is allowed to run over a period of time, since the number of previous states will continue to grow. Therefore, a system that could alter its remembering behavior in response to different situations would be preferable. To allow different remembering behaviors, this ability should not be built into the architecture.

5.5 Recognizing the Cause of a Failure

In learning from failure, an important consideration for the system is that the most recent operator is not necessarily what led to an error. When we look at the arch problem, we can quickly realize that the mistake was picking up block C, and not our choice of where to put it down. Through the use of RECOVERY, LEGO-SOAR is eventually able to back up in the operator sequence and discover the cause of the failure, and build a chunk that will prevent the same failure in the future. But LEGO-SOAR learns no general rules about failures in the domain: It does not learn that when picking up and stacking blocks it is *often* the case that a failure is due to picking up the wrong block.

The ability to reason about the assignment of credit and blame would seem to be a general problem-solving skill, aquired through experience across several domains. Like remembering, the specific performance of a credit-assignment ability should vary from domain to domain, and experience in a particular domain should lead to an improved performance in terms of recognizing the operators that contributed to successes or failures

The addition of such a capability would require that SOAR have some internal model of itself, i.e., that it be able to reason about its own reasoning process. When taken to an extreme, this behavior resembles the introspection advocated by Batali in [1], but Batali's form of self-knowledge appears to be too strong to be required of a cognitive agent. It is neither necessary that a successful architecture have direct access to the processes that control its behaviors nor that it have the abilities to directly modify its behavior at will. Rather, it is sufficient that an agent have a model of its own behavior and be able to influence this behavior by refering to the internal model of the processes that cause the behavior rather than the processes themselves.

6 Summary

Though illustrated in the SOAR architecture, the issues raised by LEGO-SOAR are not problems unique to SOAR and will have to be addressed by researchers in other architectures as well. The abilities to explore the world independently, give up on a problem after a period of time, recognize a duplicate state, learn from failed attempts, and assign credit and blame to operators seem to be necessary components of a general problem-solving architecture. The research in LEGO-SOAR investigates some of these capabilities, and illustrates the need for other capabilities.

Acknowledgements

The author would like to thank John Laird for his invaluable advice in developing LEGO-SOAR and for insightful comments on this paper. Thanks also to Eric Chown and Michael Hucka for their comments. Arie Covrigaru developed the original implementation of the REMEMBER code.

References

[1] J. Batali. Computational introspection. Technical report, Artificial Intelligence Laboratory, Massachusetts Institute of Technology, February 1983. AI Memo 701.

[2] J. G. Carbonell and G. Hood. The World Modelers project: Learning in a reactive environment. In *Machine Learning: A Guide to Current Research.* Kluwer Academic Press, 1986.

[3] S. E. Fahlman. A planning system for robot construction tasks. *Artificial Intelligence*, 5:1–49, 1974.

[4] J. E. Laird. Recovery from incorrect knowledge in Soar. In *Proceedings of the AAAI-88*, 1988.

[5] J. E. Laird, K. Swedlow, E. Altmann, C. B. Congdon, and M. Wiesmeyer. Soar 4.5 user's manual. Carnegie Mellon University and The University of Michigan, unpublished, 1989.

[6] J. E. Laird, E. S. Yager, C. M. Tuck, and M. Hucka. Learning in tele-autonomous systems using Soar. In *Proceedings of the 1989 NASA Conference on Space Telerobotics*, 1989.

[7] S. Minton. *Learning Effective Search Control Knowledge: An Explanation-Based Approach.* PhD thesis, Carnegie Mellon University, 1988.

[8] S. Minton, J. Carbonell, C. Knoblock, D. R. Kuokka, O. Etzioni, and Y. Gil. Explanation-based learning: A problem-solving perspective. 1989.

[9] A. Newell. *Unified Theories of Cognition.* Harvard University Press, Cambridge, MA, 1990. (in press).

CHAPTER 48

Task-Specific Architectures for Flexible Systems

T. R. Johnson, J. W. Smith, and B. Chandrasekaran, The Ohio State University

Abstract

This paper describes our research which is an attempt to retain as many of the advantages as possible of both task-specific architectures and more general problem-solving architectures like Soar. It investigates how task-specific architectures can be constructed in the Soar framework and integrated and used in a flexible manner. The results of our investigation are a preliminary step towards unification of general and task-specific problem-solving theories and architectures.

1 Introduction

Two trends can be discerned in research in problem-solving architectures in the last few years: On one hand, interest in *task-specific architectures* (Chandrasekaran, 1986; Clancey, 1985; Marcus, 1988) has grown, wherein types of problems of general utility are identified, and special architectures that support the development of problem-solving systems for those types of problems are proposed. These architectures help in the acquisition and specification of knowledge by providing inference methods that are appropriate for the type of problem. However, knowledge-based systems which use only one type of problem-solving method are very brittle, and adding more types of methods requires a principled approach to integrating them in a flexible way.

Contrasting with this trend is the proposal for a flexible, general architecture that is best exemplified by the work on Soar (Laird, et al., 1987). Soar has features which make it attractive because it allows flexible use of all potentially relevant knowledge or methods. But as a theory Soar does not make commitments to specific types of problem solvers or provide guidance for their construction.

In this paper we investigate how task-specific architectures (TSA's) can be constructed in Soar to retain as many of the advantages as possible of both approaches. We will be using examples from the Generic Task (GT) approach for building knowledge-based systems since this approach had its genesis at our Laboratory where it has been further developed and applied for a number of problems; however the ideas are applicable to other task-specific approaches as well.

2 Flexible Systems: A Definition

At a high level of abstraction, a flexible system is a system that can make reasonable progress on any problem instance it is given. If additional knowledge is required to make progress, then the system should work to acquire that knowledge. To be more specific we consider a flexible system to be a problem-solving system that:

1. Can engage in complex problem solving about the potential actions that can be used to solve a problem.

2. Can engage in complex problem solving about what action to take to solve a problem (given a set of potential actions).

3. Allows easy modification of its knowledge through incorporation of new knowledge or changes to existing knowledge.

Note that a flexible system, by this definition, is not necessarily robust. Without appropriate knowledge a flexible system can still be brittle; however, a flexible system has the potential to be robust and adaptive.

3 Limitations of Inflexible Systems

An inflexible system is forced to apply the same reasoning method, or sequence of operations, for every problem instance—the system cannot adapt its reasoning method to the problem being solved. This has several consequences. First, inflexibility can lead to a brittle system. A system is said to be brittle if it cannot behave appropriately when there are small variations in the task or task environment. There are several kinds of inappropriate behavior. First, the system might break, i.e., abnormally halt. For example, suppose that a diagnostic system has a subgoal to determine the confidence of hypotheses by returning *-1, 0,* or *1*. The subgoal could produce a value outside the prescribed range, such as *high*. Unless the system has a way of handling the unexpected value, the system could break when it attempts to use the value. In this case, *high* might cause an arithmetic function to fail.

Second, the system might get an incorrect answer. For instance, if the diagnostic system described above only considered hypotheses with a confidence of *1*, it would ignore any hypotheses that had nonstandard confidence values, like *high*. This could result in selecting an incorrect hypothesis for the final result.

The third consequence of an inflexible system is that the system might behave in a nonoptimal or unusual way. For example, the diagnostic system might be forced to pursue one hypothesis while holding off the exploration of a more likely hypothesis. Another example is when a system continues to pursue subgoals even though the topmost goal has already been met.

4 Why are Flexible Systems Needed?

Clearly, it is undesirable for a system to behave in the ways described above. However, you might still wonder why we should expect or want systems to work outside the narrow domain in which they were originally designed. After all, we use programs every day that are designed to work only in narrow domains or solve specific types of problems (e.g., word processors, spreadsheets, and databases). Why should we expect AI systems to be any different?

There are two reasons. First, general intelligence is not defined as the ability to solve a single, bounded problem. An intelligent agent must be ready to solve any problem thrown at it over the course of its existence. An important defining feature of an intelligent system is its ability to dynamically adapt to solve the problem at hand. If we want to build intelligent systems then we should expect no less of them.

Second, most problems being tackled by AI systems are so ill-defined that the input and output for a system cannot be precisely specified at design time. Even if it could be precisely specified, the specification might change because: (1) knowledge about the task or domain might grow or change; (2) the task that the system is designed to do might change (thus requiring a different specification); and (3) the knowledge available to solve the task may be different than what was assumed when the system was first built.

Thus, the ill-defined nature of most AI problems combined with the dynamic nature of task environments demand systems that can adapt to new situations. Whether the adaptation needs to be dynamic or through human intervention depends on the system. Dynamic or automatic adaptation is required when a system must be autonomous or if the task is always varying. Human intervention (i.e., modification of the system by reprogramming) is sufficient whenever little autonomy is required or the task is fairly well-defined. However, even if intervention is acceptable, the system must be capable of supporting change. Unfortunately, many AI systems cannot accommodate these changes. The redesigned tools described in this paper allow both kinds of adaptation.

5 The Generic Task Paradigm

Generic tasks (GT's) (Chandrasekaran, 1986) provide an implementation-independent vocabulary for describing problem-solving systems. They allow systems to be described in terms of goals and knowledge that directly relate to the task, instead of implementational formalisms such as rules, frames, or LISP. The paradigm has three main parts:

1. The problem solving of an intelligent agent can be characterized by generic types of goals. Many problems can be solved using some combination of these types.

2. For each type of goal there are one or more problem-solving methods, any one of which can potentially be used to achieve the goal.

3. Each problem-solving method requires certain kinds of knowledge of the task in order to execute. These are called the *operational demands* of the method after (Laird, et al., 1987).

A generic task refers to the combination of a *type of goal* with a *problem-solving method* and the *kinds of knowledge* needed to use the method. For example, the GT for hierarchical classification used in CSRL (Bylander and Mittal, 1986) is specified as:

Type of Goal: Classify a (possibly complex) description of a situation as a member of one or more categories. An instance of this goal is the classification of a medical case description as one or more diseases.

Problem-solving Method: This is a hierarchical classification method that works by evaluating and refining hypotheses about the situation. If a hypothesis can be established (i.e., it has a high likelihood of being true), then it is refined into hypotheses of greater detail. CSRL stops when it has run out of refinements to explore, or it has ruled-out every branch of the hierarchy. Here the method is described using a main procedure (*Classify*) which calls on a recursive sub-procedure (*E-R*).

```
Classify(root-hypothesis)
    E-R(root-hypothesis)
end Classify

E-R(hypothesis)
    Determine-certainty(hypothesis)
    If High-certainty(hypothesis) then
        H ← Refinements(hypothesis)
        for each hypothesis, h, in H do
            E-R(h)
        end for
    end if
end E-R
```

Kinds of Knowledge: These consist of a refinement hierarchy, hypotheses about the presence of classes, confirmation/rule-out knowledge for these hypotheses, and knowledge to determine when the goal of classification has been achieved.

Note that a GT is a theory about how to do a general task. It specifies the task, a method for doing the task, and the knowledge required by the method, but it does not specify any details of implementation. The GT specification mentions what knowledge is required, but doesn't say how the knowledge should be represented or computed. Likewise, the problem-solving method specifies subgoals and how the subgoals work together, but it does not specify how the subgoals should be achieved. Hence, a GT analysis of a task can be used to describe systems that are implemented in many different architectures or languages.

To build a system, we must specify how all the knowledge required by a GT's method is to be computed. Instead of moving directly to an implementation formalism, the generic task paradigm can be applied to the subgoals of a GT problem-solving method. For example, we can specify a GT for the task of testing a hypothesis. This recursive application of the GT paradigm leads to a hierarchical goal/subgoal decomposition of a system called the *task structure* (Chandrasekaran, 1989). The task structure shows how a task is solved in terms of other tasks. One possible task structure for a diagnostic system is shown in Figure 1. The task of diagnosis has been decomposed into two subtasks: *classify findings*

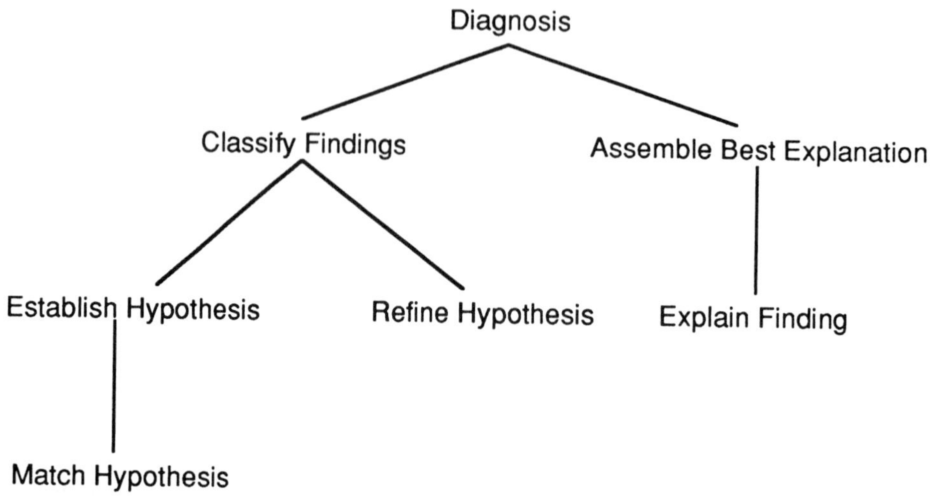

Figure 1: Task structure for a diagnostic system.

and *assemble best explanation*. *Classify findings*, in turn, has been further decomposed into two additional tasks: *establish hypothesis* and *refine hypothesis*.

6 Task-Specific Architectures

A TSA implements a GT by providing a task-specific inference engine and knowledge-base representation language. The inference engine implements a GT's problem-solving method. The knowledge base provides primitives for encoding the domain specific knowledge needed to instantiate the method. The combination of the encoding of the domain knowledge in the knowledge base and the method that can use it is called a *problem solver*. Thus, a system built using CSRL is called a *hierarchical classification problem solver* or simply a *classifier*.

In addition to CSRL, the GT paradigm has been used to design TSA's for object synthesis by plan selection and refinement (Brown and Chandrasekaran, 1989), assembly of explanatory hypotheses (abduction) (Josephson, et al., 1987), and pattern-directed hypothesis matching (Johnson, et al., 1989). Other researchers have used related approaches to design tools for these and other tasks. Some examples are Clancey's Heracles (Clancey, 1985), McDermott's role-limiting methods (McDermott, 1988), and Kingsland's criteria tables (Kingsland III and Lindberg, 1986).

A problem-solving system often consists of multiple problem solvers that work together, such as a diagnostic system with a classifier, several hypothesis matchers (one for each hypothesis in the classification hierarchy) and an abducer (a problem solver that finds a best explanation). Problem solvers are often related as goal/subgoal pairs. For example, *determine-certainty* is a subgoal of the *E-R* procedure, that can be achieved by using a hypothesis matcher.

Although the GT paradigm naturally leads to TSA's, it is important to realize that a GT analysis does not require the construction of a TSA. Once a GT specification is done for a system, the system can be implemented in whatever language or tools the system builder has available.

6.1 Advantages

TSA's offer a number of advantages over general architectures:

- They provide implementation-independent abstractions for describing and building systems. Thus, a system can be said to be doing classification regardless of whether it is written in a production system or in lisp.
- They provide a theory of how to solve a wide range of problems.
- Deciding when to use a tool is facilitated because the knowledge operationally demanded by the method is explicit in the definition of the tool.

- Knowledge-acquisition is facilitated because the representational primitives of the knowledge base directly correspond to the kinds of domain knowledge that must be gathered.

- Explanations based on a run-time trace can be couched in terms of the method and knowledge being used to apply it.

6.2 Inflexibility in TSA systems

Standard implementations of TSA systems tend to be inflexible for three reasons. First, each tool is usually based on a relatively fixed method. This leads to the following limitations:

- The sequence of operations (i.e., method subgoals) is largely predefined. (The systems do not engage in complex problem solving about the operations or about which to select.)

- Very few modifications can be made to change the operations or their sequence.

Second, a fixed knowledge-representation language makes it difficult to add knowledge that was not deemed necessary by the tool designer.

Third, complex operations are frequently done by directly calling on another problem solver. This has several implications:

- These calls are often "hard-wired" or fixed, thus the system cannot select, at run-time, from among a number of problem solvers.

- Problem solvers cannot easily access the knowledge encoded in other problem solvers. For example, a classification problem solver cannot easily access the knowledge in an abductive problem solver.

- A single problem solver always has control of the problem-solving system. For example, if a classification problem solver calls a hypothesis matching problem solver, the latter problem solver has complete control of the system. The classification problem solver cannot make any control decisions until the hypothesis matcher relinquishes control.

Of course, a TSA system can also contain incorrect domain knowledge that can lead to inflexibility. This, however, is true of any system, even a flexible one. The difference between a flexible system and an inflexible system is that the flexible system should be capable of correcting the incorrect knowledge once detected.

7 The Problem-Space Computational Model[1]

Soar is based on the problem-space computational model (PSCM) (Newell, et al., 1991), a methodology designed to support flexible problem solving. In the PSCM, all problem solving is defined as search for a goal state in a problem space. A problem space consists of an initial state, a goal state, and operators that modify the states. For example, Figure 2 illustrates part of the problem space for a simple blocks-world problem. The initial state is shown at the top of the diagram. The desired state is highlighted at the bottom of the diagram. The operators define the edges of the problem space. Each edge represents the application of an operator to a state.

A problem space has two kinds of knowledge: *task knowledge* and *search-control knowledge*. The task knowledge consists of the initial state, desired state, and operators. Task knowledge defines the problem space, i.e., the shape of the tree and which states in the tree are initial and desired states. Search-control knowledge is knowledge about which operator to take from a given state. Thus search-control knowledge affects the search

[1] This section has benefitted from discussions with attendees of the Ninth Soar Workshop held at The Ohio State University, May 10-12, 1991. The inclusion of preferences and learning as elements of the problem-space computational model is based on these discussions.

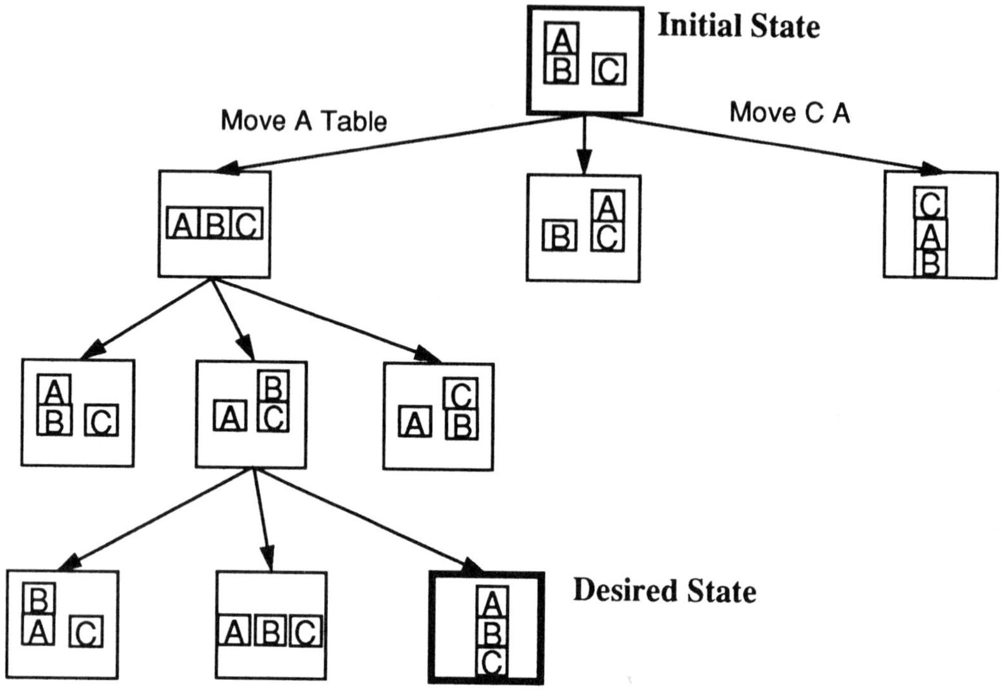

Figure 2: Part of a problem space for a simple blocks-world problem.

through the problem space for a desired state. Note that search-control knowledge affects the efficiency of problem solving, but not the correctness. The correctness of the solution is dependent on the task knowledge that defines the desired state.

Figure 3 shows the steps involved in solving a problem using a problem space. Each of the four boxes represents a PSCM function. The arrows show how the functions are related. To begin, *formulate-task* selects a problem space, the initial state, and the set of desired states. *Select-operator* then selects an operator to apply to the state and *apply-operator* applies it to produce a new state. *Terminate-task* checks to see if the new state is one of the desired states or if success is not possible. If either is true, *terminate-task* halts; otherwise, control loops back to *select-operator* so that an operator can be selected to apply to the new state.

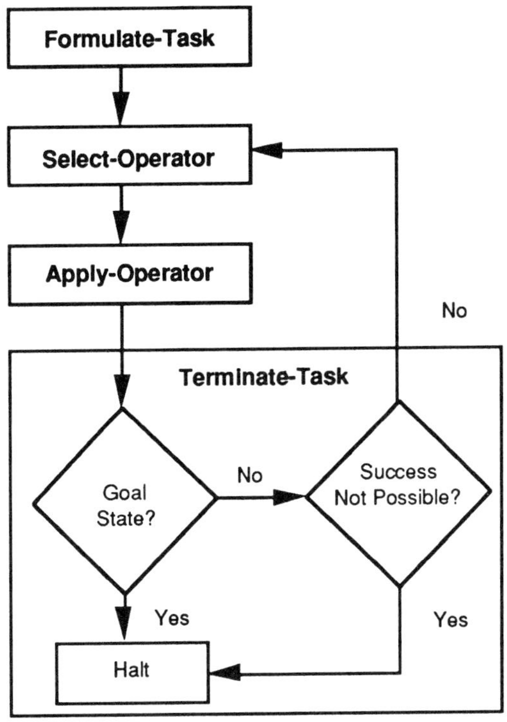

Figure 3: PSCM function flowchart.

To talk about and write down the search-control knowledge that a problem space has we need a way to represent this knowledge. At the PSCM search-control knowledge is described using preferences. A preference represents knowledge about the desirability of objects. There are several different kinds of preferences. Each kind is described below along with an example illustrating how it could be applied to the selection of an operator.

- *acceptable*—Good enough to be considered. If an operator has an acceptable preference, then it can be applied to the current state.

- *reject*—Not to be selected. If an operator has a reject preference, it will not be applied to the current state.

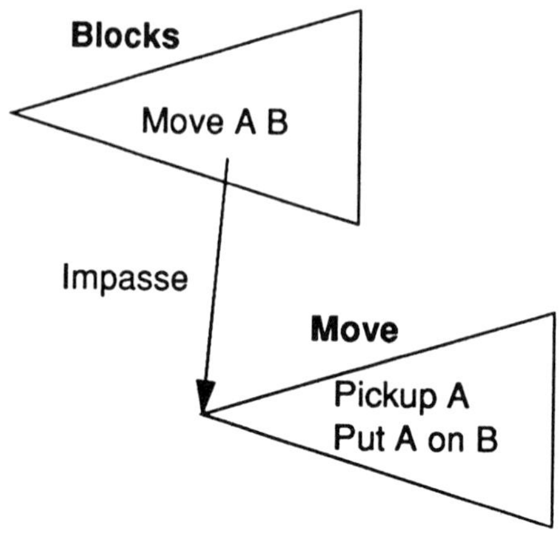

Figure 4: An impasse to acquire knowledge.

- *best*—The object is better than all other objects. If O_1 has a best preference, then it is better than all operators.
- *better*—O_1 is better than O_2.
- *indifferent*—O_1 is indifferent to O_2. This means that it does not matter which operator is selected.
- *worse*—O_1 is worse than O_2.
- *worst*—O_1 is worst (worse than all others).

A problem space must have knowledge to implement each of the PSCM functions. If a problem space does not have the knowledge to implement a function, then an impasse occurs—no further problem solving can be done until the impasse is resolved. Impasses are resolved by formulating a subgoal to acquire the missing knowledge. The subgoal is set up as a task to be solved by another problem space. For example, Figure 4 shows what happens when a problem space does not have the knowledge needed to apply an operator. The top problem space, *Blocks*, is attempting to apply *Move A B*, but lacks the knowledge needed to do it. A subgoal is automatically formulated to acquire this knowledge. A second problem space, *Move*, is selected to achieve the subgoal. *Move* has knowledge about how to apply the *move* operator. It does this by applying two operators in sequence: *Pickup A* and *Put A B*. This results in successful application of the operator (*Move A B*), and hence the impasse is resolved.

Several types of impasses can occur:

- **Tie:** Arrises when preferences do not distinguish between two or more objects with acceptable preferences. For example, if two operators have acceptable preferences and there are no other preferences, then a tie impasse occurs, because the knowledge encoded in the preferences is insufficient for selecting a single operator.

- **Conflict:** Arises when there are conflicting preferences. For example, if O_1 is better than O_2 and O_2 is better than O_1, a conflict impasse occurs.

- **No-change:** Arrises if a problem space, state, or operator cannot be selected, or if the current operator cannot be applied.

Whenever an impasse is resolved (such as that shown in Figure 4) learning takes place, resulting in a transfer of knowledge from the subspace to the superspace. For example, in Figure 4 the knowledge about how to move blocks is transferred from the *Move* space to the *Blocks* space. After learning, the *Blocks* space has acquired the following knowledge:

To *Move x to y*:

If *x* and *y* are clear then *Pickup x* and then *Put x on y*.

Note that inductive generalization has occurred. The system induces that all clear blocks can be moved in the same manner as *A* and *B*.

7.1 Advantages and Limitations

The main advantage of the PSCM is that it provides the potential for flexible behavior. Complex problem solving can be used to determine potential actions as well as to select an action from a list of potential actions. The separation of task and search-control knowledge makes it easy to modify the behavior of the system by adding new operators or new search-control knowledge.

Another advantage is the transfer of knowledge achieved through learning. This allows complex problem solving to be avoided. Without learning, a problem-space system would be forced to forever deliberate—impasses could not be avoided.

The main limitation of the PSCM (with respect to building knowledge systems) is that it does not supply a content theory for high-level tasks. For example, the PSCM says little about how to do classification, or solve diagnosis problems.

8 Task-Specific Architectures for Flexible Systems

To produce TSA's that can be used to build flexible systems, we have followed two main steps. First, the GT of interest is reformulated to be as flexible as possible. This means that any unnecessary constraints on the knowledge and method are removed. Second, the GT is implemented as a TSA in Soar. The ability of the TSA to produce flexible systems depends on both of these steps. The first step increases the flexibility of a single GT; the second step provides an implementation that retains this flexibility and allows multiple TSA's to work together.

8.1 A New Language for Describing GT's

We have found it useful to use the language of problem spaces to describe reformulated GT's. A problem space description allows us to specify the method in terms of potential subgoals and preferences on the order of the subgoals without forcing us to specify any unnecessary commitments. Once the GT is properly reformulated and described as a problem space, it can be implemented in Soar in a straightforward manner.

Note that the use of the problem-space language is useful regardless of the means used to implement a GT. The problem-space language implies only that a GT be viewed as having subgoals, knowledge about how to achieve the subgoals, and knowledge about how to order the subgoals. In order to specify flexible GT's, a language of this type must be used—a procedural language forces us to add too many constraints to the specification.

Originally, GT's were specified by giving the type of goal, the problem-solving method, and the kinds of knowledge. This is what we did earlier in the paper when we presented the GT used for CSRL. Using the problem-space language, we now specify a GT by describing knowledge of: the initial state schema; the desired state schema; the operators that apply to states; and how to select from a set of potential operators (*search-control knowledge*).

Initial State Schema: A description of the initial *knowledge state* for the task. A knowledge state is a description of state in terms of it's knowledge content, not it's representation. The schema characterizes all possible initial states (or inputs) for the task. The state can contain knowledge about a real world state, an agent's internal knowledge, or a combination of both.

Desired State Schema: A description of the desired knowledge state for the task. Just as with the initial state, the desired state schema characterizes all possible desired states for the task.

Operators: The operators specify the subgoals of the GT method. An operator modifies a knowledge state to produce a new knowledge state. The modification consists of any number of deletions and additions to the knowledge in the state. If knowledge is added, the operator description must include a specification for that knowledge. Operators can have preconditions and/or enabling conditions. The

Table 1: How elements of the standard GT language map into the PSCM language.

Standard GT Elements	GTPS Elements
Type of Goal	Initial State Schema Desired State Schema
Problem-Solving Method	Operators Search-Control Knowledge
Kinds of Knowledge	The other GTPS elements define the kinds of knowledge needed to use the GT.

preconditions must be satisfied before the operator can be used. The enabling conditions indicate when an operator is to be considered.

Search Control Knowledge: Knowledge about how to prefer operators based on the current state and competing operators. Search control along with operator preconditions and enabling conditions serve to sequence operators. Only search control that is absolutely essential needs to be specified for a GT. Thus, if a GT has nothing to say about how a particular set of subgoals (operators) should be ordered, then nothing needs to said about them. The search control language allows statements of the form: O_1 is better then O_2; O_2 is worse than O_3; O_4 is best; O_5 is worst; and O_6 and O_7 are equivalent.

There are three important points about this GT description language. First, every feature of the old GT specification language is present in the new one. Table 1 shows how each element of the old description maps into the new description. Second, the new description is given entirely in terms of knowledge. In the past, we were often forced to use symbol-level terms when describing the problem-solving method. Third, the new description of the problem-solving method (in terms of operators and search control) allows us to describe the method without giving an overconstrained procedural description of the steps needed to do the task.

To Illustrate these three points, consider the following reformulation of the hierarchical classification GT used in CSRL.

Initial State Schema: The initial state contains knowledge about the data being classified. Possibly knowledge of an initial hypothesis for the data.

Desired State Schema: The desired state contains knowledge about which category the data best describes.

Operators: The classify problem-space uses 3 operators:

suggest-initial-hypotheses: Add one or more initial hypotheses to the state. Hence, the system needs to know of a general class that the data falls into. This should only be used if the state has no hypotheses. Each hypothesis in the state must have an indication of whether it has been tested and refined.

establish *hyp*: Determine whether the hypothesis, *hyp*, should be confirmed or rejected. This is to be used for any hypothesis in the state that is not yet confirmed or rejected.

generate-refinements *hyp*: Generate (add to the state) those hypotheses that should be considered as a refinement of *hyp*. This is used for all of the confirmed hypotheses in the state.

Domain knowledge: To use the E-R (establish-refine) strategy in a particular domain, knowledge to perform the following functions must be added to the Soar implementation.

Search Control Knowledge: No search control is specified. The only sequencing of operators is that imposed by the preconditions of the operators. If *generate-refinements* and *establish* operators are applicable at the same time, additional knowledge must be used to select one; however, this knowledge is not an essential part of the GT so it is not specified. This allows the designer of a system to add system specific search control.

In a GT system, like the system shown in Figure 1, there might be alternative GT's

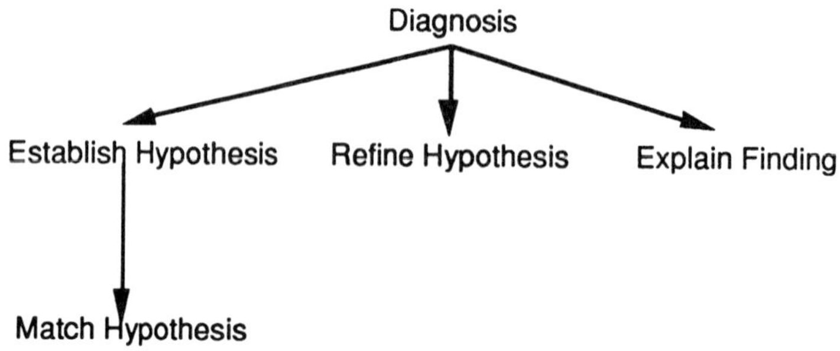

Figure 5: An integrated task-structure for diagnosis.

for implementing the same subgoal. For example, the *establish* subgoal might be done using the match GT or a simulation GT. In these cases, each of the GT's can be specified and we can describe the knowledge needed to select between the GT's. This knowledge is associated with the system, not the GT.

The new GT language also allows us to describe tightly integrated systems. For example, the diagnostic system in Figure 1 completely separates the classification GT from the best explanation GT. Figure 5 shows a new task structure for diagnosis. The new task structure mixes the goals of the classification GT and the best explanation GT. This means that the system can mix classification problem solving with best explanation problem solving.

8.2 Implementing TSA's in Soar

The implementation of TSA's in Soar follows directly from the GT specification. Each GT is implemented as a problem space with the specified operators. A representation for both the states and the operators must be selected. All of the knowledge to propose and select operators and alternative GT's is encoded in productions. Knowledge of the desired state is encoded as a production that tests the current state of the space to see if it is a member of the set of desired states.

So far we have implemented TSA's in Soar for classification, abduction (finding a best explanation), and hypothesis matching (Johnson, 1991; Johnson and Smith, 1991). To use a tool, the system builder must specify how all the operators are implemented, as well as, any additional preferences for the ordering of the operators. To assist tool users, we have provided several default techniques for implementing common GT subgoals.

We have also used these tools to implement an integrated system, RedSoar (Johnson, et al., 1991), which has a task-structure similar to the diagnostic system described in Figure 5. The flexibility of the Soar implementation allows us to easily experiment with different control strategies as well as strategies that mix subgoals from several GT's.

9 Discussion

It might seem strange to build task-specific architectures in a general architecture. After all, TSA's were motivated by the problems of general architectures. Actually, building TSA's in Soar is not so different: first, TSA's were a reaction against the single level view of problem-solving systems often provided by general architectures, not against the utility of a general architecture. The Soar versions of our TSA's retain the multilevel task-dependant view. Soar is not just a collection of rules or problem-spaces. A Soar program has specific goals, and representations. Second, TSA's have always been built on top of some kind of general architecture, be it Lisp, an object system, or some other kind of programming language. Soar is just as valid an implementation medium as these other languages are. Third, just as TSA's are good for building systems that solve a particular kind of task, Soar is good at building flexible systems. If TSA's are so useful because they provide special support for a task, then certainly we should not ignore general architectures that provide support for constructing flexible TSA's.

The new TSA's combine the advantages of the GT approach with the advantages of the Soar architecture. Knowledge acquisition, ease of use, and explanation are all facilitated because subgoals of the problem-solving method and the kinds of knowledge needed to use the method are explicitly represented in the GT description and in the implementation. The subgoals of the method are directly represented as problem-space operators. The kinds of knowledge needed to use the method are either encoded in productions or computed in a subgoal. The same advantages apply to the supplied methods for achieving subgoals. Finally, the implementation mirrors the GT specification quite closely making the TSA's easy to understand and use.

The new TSA-based systems overcome many of the limitations suffered by previous GT systems. Automatic subgoaling allows unanticipated situations to be detected and handled. If no specific method for handling the situation is available, an appropriate weak method can be used. Whenever a goal needs to be achieved it is done by first suggesting problem spaces and then selecting one to use. This allows new methods (i.e., GT's) in the form of problem spaces to be easily added to existing problem solvers. If no specific technique exists to determine which method to use, Soar will try to pick one using a weak method such as lookahead to see which is better. Automatic goal termination provides an integration functionality not available in previous GT architectures. In general, the integration capabilities of the new tools are greatly enhanced. Because of preferences and the additive nature of productions, new knowledge can be added to integrate multiple tools without modifying existing control knowledge.

10 Acknowledgments

We thank the members of the Division of Medical Informatics and the Soar Community for their comments and discussion on this paper. This research is supported by National Heart Lung and Blood Institute grant HL-38776, National Library of Medicine grant LM-04298, Defense Advanced Research Projects Agency grant F49620-89-C-0110, and Air Force Office of Scientific Research grant 89-0250.

Bibliography

Brown, D. C., and Chandrasekaran, B. (1989). *Design Problem Solving: Knowledge Structures and Control Strategies*. San Mateo, California: Morgan Kaufmann Publishers.

Bylander, T., and Mittal, S. (1986). CSRL: A language for classificatory problem solving. *AI Magazine*, *VII*(3), 66-77.

Chandrasekaran, B. (1986). Generic tasks in knowledge-based reasoning: High-level building blocks for expert system design. *IEEE Expert*, *1*(3), 23-30.

Chandrasekaran, B. (1989). Task-structures, knowledge acquisition, and learning. *Machine Learning*, *4*(339-345), 93-99.

Clancey, W. J. (1985). Heuristic classification. *Artificial Intelligence*, *27*(3), 289-350.

Johnson, K. A., Johnson, T. R., Smith, J. W., Jr., DeJongh, M., Fischer, O., Amra, N. K., and Bayazitoglu, A. (1991). RedSoar—A system for red blood cell antibody identification. In *Proceedings of SCAMC 91*. Washington D.C.

Johnson, T. R., Smith, J. W., and Bylander, T. (1989). HYPER—Hypothesis matching using compiled knowledge. In W. E. Hammond (Ed.), *Proceedings of the AAMSI Congress 1989*, (pp. 126-130). San Francisco, California: American Association for Medical Systems and Informatics.

Johnson, T. R., and Smith, J. W. (1991). A framework for opportunistic abductive strategies. In *Proceedings of the Thirteenth Annual Conference of the Cognitive Science Society*, (pp. 760-764). Chicago: Lawrence Erlbaum Associates.

Johnson, T. R. (1991) *Generic Tasks in the Problem-Space Paradigm: Building Flexible Knowledge Systems While Using Task-Level Constraints*. Ph.D. Dissertation, The Ohio State University.

Josephson, J., Chandrasekaran, B., Smith, J., and Tanner, M. (1987). A mechanism for forming composite explanatory hypotheses. *IEEE Transactions on Systems, Man, and Cybernetics*, *17*(3), 445-454.

Kingsland III, L. C., and Lindberg, D. A. B. (1986). The criteria form of knowledge representation in medical artificial intelligence. In *MEDINFO 86*

Laird, J., Congdon, C. B., Altmann, E., and Swedlow, K. (1990). *Soar User's Manual Version 5.2* (Technical Report No. CMU-CS-90-179). Carnegie Mellon.

Laird, J. E., Newell, A., and Rosenbloom, P. S. (1987). SOAR: An architecture for general intelligence. *Artificial Intelligence*, *33*, 1-64.

Marcus, S. (1988). Salt: A knowledge acquisition tool for propose-and-revise systems. In S. Marcus (Eds.), *Automating Knowledge Acquisition for Expert Systems* (pp. 81-123). Boston: Kluwer Academic Publishers.

McDermott, J. (1988). Preliminary steps toward a taxonomy of problem-solving methods. In S. Marcus (Eds.), *Automating Knowledge Acquisition for Expert Systems* (pp. 225-256). Kluwer Academic Publishers.

Newell, A., Yost, G., Laird, J. E., Rosenbloom, P. S., and Altmann, E. (1991). Formulating the problem space computational model. In R. F. Rashid (Eds.), *Carnegie-Mellon Computer Science: A 25-Year Commemorative* Reading, MA: ACM-Press: Addison-Wesley.

CHAPTER 49

Correcting and Extending Domain Knowledge Using Outside Guidance

J. E. Laird, M. Hucka, E. S. Yager, and C. M. Tuck, University of Michigan

Abstract

Analytic learning techniques, such as explanation-based learning (EBL), can be powerful methods for acquiring knowledge about a domain where there is a pre-existing theory of the domain. One application of EBL has been to learning apprentice systems where the solution to a problem generated by a human is used as input to the learning process. The learning system analyzes the example and is then able to solve similar problems without outside assistance. One limitation of EBL is that the domain theory must be complete and correct. In this paper we present a general technique for learning from outside guidance that can correct and extend a domain theory. In contrast to hybrid systems that use both analytic and empirical techniques, our approach is completely analytic, using the chunking learning mechanism in the Soar architecture. This technique is demonstrated for a block manipulation task that uses real blocks, a Puma robot arm and a camera vision system.

1 Introduction

Learning through interacting with a human is an efficient method to increase the knowledge of an intelligent agent. Initially, an intelligent agent may have only very general abilities and may require significant guidance from a human operator. Through its experiences, the agent can become more and more autonomous, making most decisions on its own and requiring guidance only for novel situations. It can increase its repertoire of methods for solving problems, improve its reaction time to events in the environment, learn to notice new properties of objects in the environment, as well as refine and extend its own model of the domain.

*This research was sponsored by grant NCC2-517 from NASA Ames and ONR grant N00014-88-K-0554.

Many approaches are possible for learning from experience and outside guidance. In the simplest case, the human solves a problem and the learning system must "watch over the shoulder" of the human as the problem is solved. This is the scheme used in robotic programming systems where a human leads the system through a fixed set of commands to achieve a goal. When the commands are stored, the system can perform only that one task and there is no conditionality in the learned plan. The robot will execute exactly the learned set of actions, independent of the state of the environment.

To avoid these problems, "learning apprentices" have been developed that create generalized plans, indexed by the appropriate goal. These systems, such as LEAP [Mitchell *et al.*, 1985] are based on a learning strategy called explanation-based learning (EBL) [DeJong & Mooney, 1986; Mitchell *et al.*, 1986]. In a learning apprentice system, the human provides a complete solution to a problem. An underlying "domain theory" is then used to "explain" the actions of the human expert. From the derived explanation, all of the dependencies between the actions are recovered and a general plan is created.

Two extensions to this basic model of external guidance have been previously made using the Soar architecture which uses an analytic learning mechanism similar to EBL, called *chunking* [Golding *et al.*, 1987; Laird *et al.*, 1987; Rosenbloom & Laird, 1986]:

1. The learning through guidance is integrated with general problem solving and autonomous learning. The system can learn from its own experiences with or without outside guidance.

2. The system actively seeks advice while solving its own problems as opposed to passively monitoring a human problem solver. In addition, the guidance occurs in the context of the system solving a problem and the guidance is at the level of individual decisions instead of complete plans.

In this paper we will demonstrate that this technique can be extended to learning new domain knowledge, not just control knowledge. The tasks we will use involve simple manipulations of blocks using a Puma robot arm and a single camera machine vision system. This a simplification of the manipulator control tasks performed by Segre's ARMS system [Segre, 1987]; however, ARMS worked only in a simulated environment. With the real robot, the domain theory is complicated by incomplete and time-dependent perception; the camera provides only two-dimensional information and is sometimes obscured by the robot arm, and the vision processing time is 4 seconds. The goal of the task is to line up a set of blocks that have been scattered over the work area. In one task, all of the blocks are simple cubes that the gripper can pick up in two different orientations. In the second task, one of the blocks is a triangular prism. The gripper is unable to pick up the prism when it closes over the inclined sides. Instead it must be oriented so that it closes over the vertical faces of the block.

One restriction on using analytic methods such as EBL and chunking is that they require a complete and correct domain theory. The domain theory is an internal model of all of the preconditions and effects of the operators used to perform the tasks. For the block manipulation task, the operators are commands to the robot controller such as open gripper, close gripper, and withdraw gripper from work area. If the internal model of these operators is in some way incorrect, then the control knowledge learned through guidance will also be incorrect. For example, if the domain knowledge is not sensitive to the special properties of a prism block, the control knowledge it learns will ignore the orientation of a prism block when attempting to pick it up. We will show how it is possible to correct control knowledge using outside guidance and a domain theory for determining the relevant features of the environment and relating them to robot actions.

Even if the learned control knowledge can be corrected, the original domain theory may still be incorrect. We show that our system can correct the original domain theory by replacing incorrect operator definitions with new, corrected definitions, and that it can extend the domain theory by creating completely new operators. In both cases, no modification is made to the underlying architecture; instead knowledge is added to correct and create operators. In the block manipulation task, we will demonstrate the acquisition of planning and execution knowledge for the `rotate-gripper` operator. These extensions are based on the creation of an underlying domain theory for the construction of new operators. In the limit, a complete domain theory can be acquire through ouside guidance, with only very limited predefined knowledge of the task.

Section 2 presents the system architecture. Section 3 gives an example of learning control knowledge through outside guidance. This reproduces the results of Golding, Rosenbloom and Laird (1987) but in a task requiring interaction with a real environment. In Section 4 we extend this work by demonstrating the correction of control knowledge using outside guidance.[1] Sections 5 and 6 present demonstrations of the correction and extension of domain knowledge through guidance. The final section discusses the contributions and limitations of the current approach.

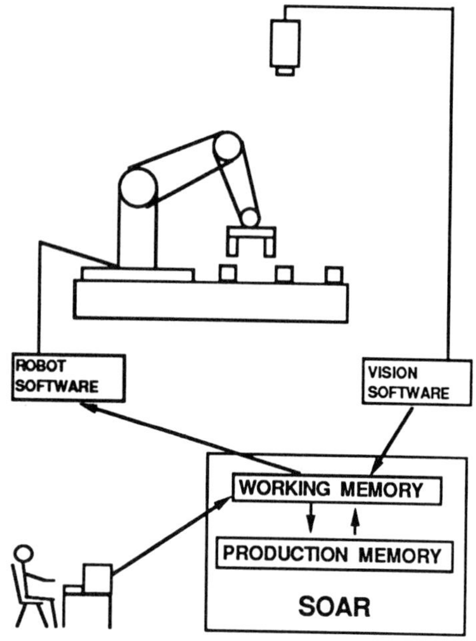

Figure 1: Robo-Soar system architecture.

2 System Architecture

The system we are developing is called Robo-Soar [Laird *et al.*, 1989].[2] Figure 1 shows its architecture. Visual input comes from a camera mounted directly above the work area. A separate computer processes the images, providing asynchronous input to Soar. The vision processing extracts the positions and orientations of the blocks in the work area as well as distinctive features of the blocks. The vision and robotic systems are sufficiently accurate so that there are no significant sensor or control errors for the block manipulation tasks.

In Soar, a task is solved by selecting and applying operators to transform an initial state to some desired state. Operators are grouped into *problem spaces* and Soar selects an appropriate problem space for each goal. For the block manipulation task, the states are different configurations of the blocks and gripper in the

[1] Some of the material in Sections 2, 3 and 4 has been previously presented in Laird *et al.*, (1989).

[2] Robo-Soar is implemented in Soar 5, a new version which supports interaction with external environments [Laird *et al.*, 1990].

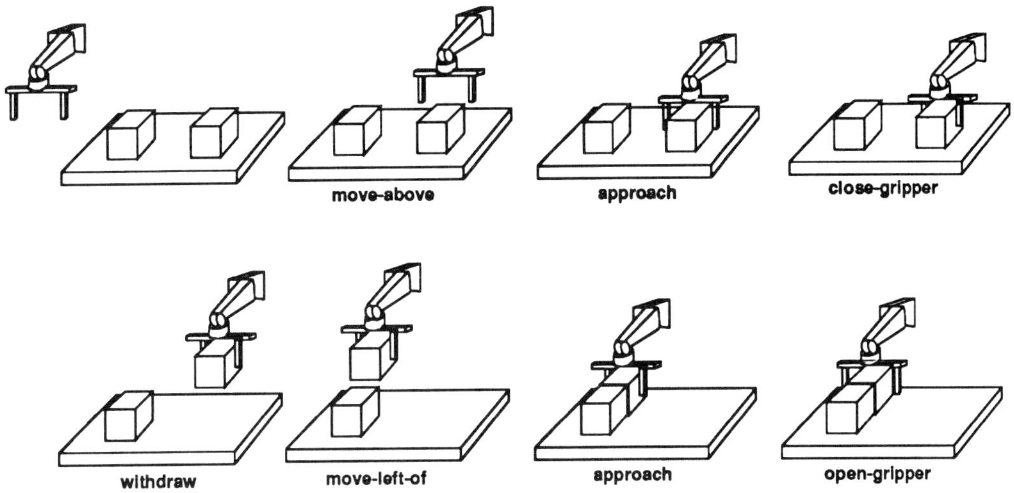

Figure 2: Moving a block using the primitive Robo-Soar operators.

external environment. Some basic operators are shown in the trace of Robo-Soar solving a simple block manipulation problem in Figure 2. These operators generate motor commands for the Puma.

One complication is that the camera is mounted directly above the work area so that the arm obscures the view of a block that is being picked up. Two operators, **snap-in** and **snap-out**, move the arm in and out of the work area so that a clear image can be obtained. These operators are necessary, but for simplicity, they will not be included in any of the examples.

This characterization of Robo-Soar does not distinguish it from any other robot controller. What is different is the way Soar makes the decisions to select an operator. Many AI or robotic systems create a plan that the robot must execute to select one operator after another. Instead of creating a plan, Soar makes each decision based on a consideration of its long-term knowledge, its perception of the environment, and its own internal state and goals. Soar's long-term knowledge is represented as productions that are continually matched against the working memory which includes all input from sensors, guidance from an advisor, and internal data structures and goals. Commands to the robot controller are issued by creating data structures in working memory.

In contrast to traditional production systems such as OPS5, Soar fires all successfully matched production instantiations in parallel, which in turn elaborate the current situation, or create *preferences* for the next operator to be taken. Soar's language of preferences allows productions to control the selection of operators by asserting that operators are acceptable, not acceptable, better than other operators, as good as others, and so on. Production firing continues until no additional productions match, at which point, Soar examines the preferences and selects the best operator for the current situation. Once an operator is selected, productions can fire to apply the operator. If the operator affects the external environment, the productions create commands to the motor system. If the operator is used for planning or internal processing, the productions directly modify the internal data structures in working memory. Additional productions test for operator completion and signal that a new operator can be selected.

In a familiar domain, Soar's knowledge may be adequate to select and apply an operator without difficulty. However, when the preferences do not determine a unique choice, or when the productions are unable to implement the selected operator, an *impasse* arises and Soar automatically generates a subgoal. In the subgoal, Soar uses the same approach; it selects and applies operators from an appropriate problem space to achieve the subgoal. The operators in the subgoal can modify or query the environment, or they may be completely internal, possibly simulating external operator applications on internal representations.

When Soar creates results in its subgoals, it learns productions, called *chunks*, that summarize the processing that occurred. The actions of a chunk are based on the results of the subgoal. The conditions are based on only those working-memory elements that were tested and found *necessary* to derive the results. Thus, knowledge used to control the selection of operators in the subgoal is not included in the derivation because it affects only the efficiency of producing the results, not their correctness.

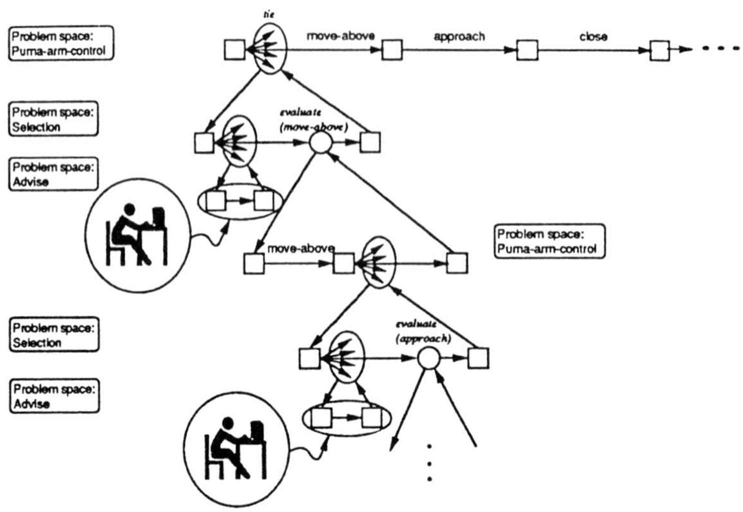

Figure 3: Trace of problem solving using external guidance to suggest appropriate task operators for evaluation. The problem solving goes left to right with squares representing states, while horizontal arcs represent operator applications. Downward pointing arcs are used to represent the creation of subgoals, and upward pointing arcs represent the termination of subgoals.

3 Learning Control Knowledge

To attempt the block manipulation task, knowledge about the operators must be encoded as productions. This knowledge includes productions that suggest operators whenever they can be applied legally, as well as productions that implement the operators by creating motor commands to move the arm. Because the feedback from the vision system is incomplete when the arm is being used to pick up a block, some productions must also create internal expectations of the position of blocks until feedback is received when the arm is moved out of the way.

With just this basic knowledge, Robo-Soar can attempt a task, but it will encounter impasses whenever it tries to select a task operator, as shown in Figure 3. To resolve these *tie* impasses, the tied task operators are evaluated in a subgoal and preferences are created to pick the best one. The evaluations are carried out by operators created in the subgoal of the tie impasse. Within this subgoal, a decision must be made as to which evaluation operator should be selected first, and thus, which task operator should be evaluated first. If the task operator that leads to the goal is evaluated first, the other task operators can be ignored because the 'best' operator has been found. As with the original decision to select between the task operators, the decision to select an operator to be evaluated will lead to a tie impasse.

Outside guidance can be used to select the best operator to evaluate. The guidance is used to determine which operator to evaluate first, not which operator to apply. The advantage of this approach is that the guidance acts only as a heuristic that is verified by internal problem solving. The problem solving calculates the internal evaluation and determines whether the chosen operator is really appropriate. The system can then learn the conditions under which the operator is appropriate. If advice directly selected a task operator that led to motor commands, there would be no internal analysis of the operator that could be used for learning.

To acquire the guidance within the subgoal, Robo-Soar uses its ***advise*** problem space which has operators that print out the acceptable task operators, ask for guidance, and wait for a response. If guidance is available, the appropriate operator is selected for evaluation. If no guidance arrives while the system is waiting, a random selection is made. All guidance in Soar takes this form where the advisor selects between competing operators. This restricts the guidance to be from predefined alternatives (the tied operators) and does not allow the input of arbitrary data structures.

Once an operator has been selected to be evaluated, an impasse arises because there are no productions that can directly compute the evaluation. The default response to this impasse is to simulate the task operator on an internal copy of the external environment. This requires an internal model of the preconditions and effects of the operators which correspond to the domain theory of an EBL system. The internal search continues through the recursive creation of tie-impasses, advice, and evaluation until a state is found that achieves the goal.

After the goal is achieved within the internal search, preferences are created to select those operators evaluated on the path to the goal. Each of these preferences is a result of a tie-impasse, and chunks are built to summarize the processing that led to their creation. This processing includes all the dependencies between the operator's actions and the preconditions and actions of the operators that were applied after it to finally achieve the goal, essentially the same as the goal regression techniques in EBL [Rosenbloom & Laird, 1986]. Figure 4 is an example of the production that is learned for the **approach** operator. Notice that the production not only tests aspects of the current situation, but also aspects of the goal. The productions learned from this search are quite general and do not include any tests of the exact positions or names of the blocks because these features were not tested in the subgoal. The internal search is based on relationships such as **left-of** or **above** instead of the exact x, y, and z locations of the blocks.

```
If the approach operator is applicable, and
   the gripper is holding nothing
       in the safe plane above a block,
   and that block must be moved
     to achieve the goal,
then create a best preference for
     the approach operator.
```

Figure 4: Example production learned by Robo-Soar.

Following the look-ahead search, Robo-Soar has learned which operator to apply at each decision point. Robo-Soar applies the operators by generating motor commands and moving the real robot arm. This is not, however, a blind application of a plan. Each of the learned productions will test aspects of the environment to insure that an operator is selected only when appropriate.

4 Correcting Control Knowledge

A problem with the analytic learning approaches such as EBL and chunking is that the learning is only as good as the underlying knowledge. If there is an error in the original domain theory, the learning will preserve the error. External guidance is of no help when restricted to suggesting task operators because the error can be in the underlying implementation of operators used by the learning procedure.

We consider a simple case of this problem by attempting the same task as before except with blocks shaped as triangular prisms. If the original operators were encoded with only cubes in mind, all of the control knowledge and underlying simulation would be insensitive to a feature in the input that must be attended to. To the Robo-Soar vision system, the prisms look just like cubes, except for a line down the middle at the apex of the triangle. In order to pick up these blocks, the gripper must be aligned with the vertical faces of the block, not just any two sides as with a cube. Figure 5 shows the operators Robo-Soar applies for this problem. If the gripper is not correctly aligned, the gripper will close but not grasp the block. Upon withdrawing the gripper, the block will not be picked up.

There are many possible machine learning approaches that could be used to correct the underlying knowledge. First, the system could have an underlying "subdomain" theory [Doyle, 1986] of inclined planes, grippers, and friction that it uses to understand why the block was not picked up. This requires knowing beforehand that this knowledge will be necessary, and for many tasks this additional domain knowledge may be difficult to obtain. A second approach is to gather examples of failure and use inductive learning techniques to hypothesize which feature in the environment was responsible for the problem. This may identify the feature, but it requires many failures and also gives no hint as to the appropriate action. A third approach is for the system to experiment with its available operators to see what actually works [Carbonell & Gil, 1987]. This approach can be quite effective, but it also can be quite time consuming and possibly dangerous. Our approach involves increasing the interaction between the advisor and the robot so that the advisor can point out relevant features in the environment and associate them with the potential success or failure of a given operator or set of operators.

This approach incorporates outside guidance with prior work in Soar on recovery from incorrect knowledge [Laird, 1988]. Instead of correcting the productions, our recovery scheme learns new productions whose actions correct the decision affected by the incorrect production. The advisor provides guidance in re-evaluating the operators being consider for a decision, leading to new productions that correct the error. This process of recovery is a domain-independent strategy encoded as productions.

The recovery method is invoked when the system notices that an error has been made. In Robo-Soar, the vision system detects that the prism block is still on the table following an attempt to pick it up. The decision that must be corrected is the choice of the **approach** operator when, in fact, the gripper should be rotated so that it is aligned with the vertical sides of the prism block. Figure 6 shows an abbreviated trace of the problem solving to correct this decision.

Once an error has been detected, the system tries to push forward to the goal, but more deliberately, so that the errant control knowledge does not select the wrong operator. Previously learned control knowledge is overridden by forcing impasses for every task operator decision. Within the context of each of these impasses, all of the available operators can be evaluated and new preferences can be created to modify a decision if it is incorrect.

The underlying internal domain knowledge that gen-

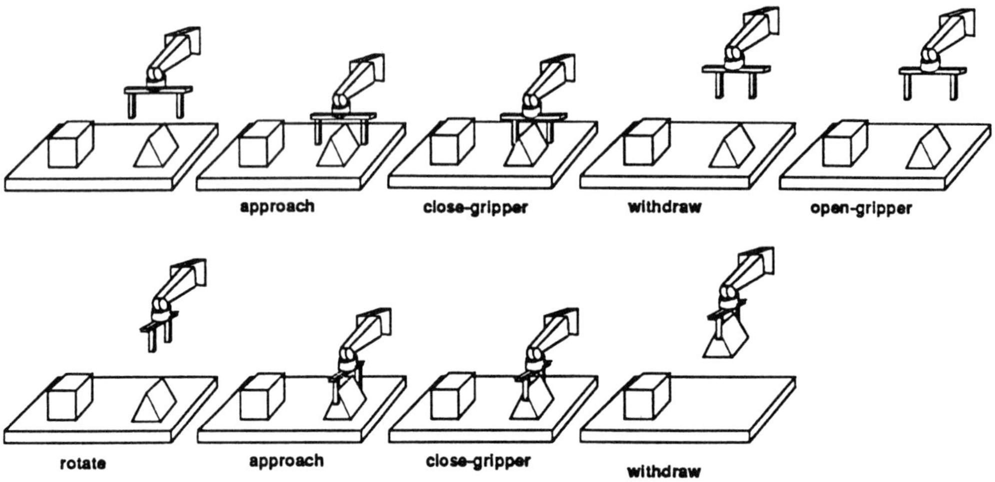

Figure 5: Trace of operator sequence using recovery.

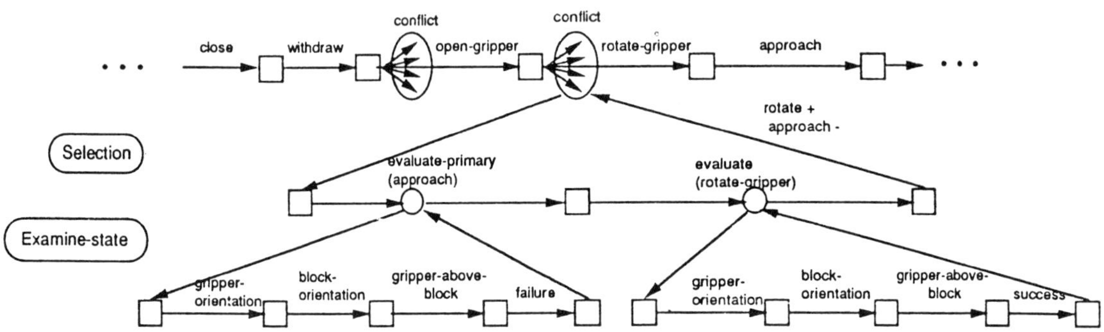

Figure 6: Trace of problem solving with recovery. The subgoals that allow outside guidance are omitted and would be used to select operators in both the selection and examine-state problem spaces.

erates the evaluation may also be incorrect. Therefore, the evaluation process is modified so that outside guidance can be used to evaluate an operator and associate that evaluation with relevant features of the environment. This modified evaluation is performed in the *examine-state* problem space.

The examine-state problem space is an underlying theory for determining the features of the environment that are relevant to the operator being evaluated and relating them to a specific evaluation. There are three classes of operators in the problem space. The first class, called `notice-feature`, explicitly tests the existence of a feature of the current task state or goal. This operator allows this system to explicitly search through the feature space of the task. In our example, this allows the system to test the line down the middle of the prism block, which was previously ignored by the task productions. For future reference in this paper we will call this feature *block-orientation*. The second class of operators, called `compare-features`, can perform simple comparisons between noticed features, such as detecting that two features have the same value. The third class of operators creates an evaluation, such as success or failure, for the task operator being evaluated. Together, these three classes of operators provide a complete domain theory for computing evaluations and relating these evaluations to relevant features of the environment. Although complete, it is underconstrained because any evaluation can be paired with any set of features.

External guidance can lead Robo-Soar to select the operators that notice only those features relevant to the current task state and associate them with the appropriate evaluation. If an operator is deemed to be on the path to success, a preference will be created to prefer it over an operator that leads to failure. In our example, the advisor first points out that the **approach** operator will fail when the gripper is above a block where the orientation of the operator is not aligned with the block-orientation. The advisor then suggests evaluating the **rotate-gripper** operator, and points out the relevant features that make its selection desirable. Figure 7 shows the productions that are learned to avoid the **approach** operator and select the **rotate-gripper** operator whenever the gripper is not aligned.

```
If the approach operator is applicable, and
   the gripper is above a block, and
   the gripper's orientation is different
       from a line in the middle of the block,
then create a preference to reject approach.

If the rotate operator is available, and
   the gripper is above a block, and
   the gripper's orientation is different
       from a line in the middle of the block,
then create a best preference for rotate-gripper.
```

Figure 7: Example correction productions learned by Robo-Soar.

Once these evaluations are made, the recovery knowledge detects that the previously preferred operator is now rejected, and therefore assumes that the error has been corrected. The error signal is removed so that future decisions are made without forced impasses. From this point, the chunks apply and take Robo-Soar to the solution, as shown in Figure 5. In future situations, Robo-Soar correctly aligns the gripper before approaching a prism. If errors still exist, the advisor can signal this by merely typing **error** to Robo-Soar. The advisor can also signal that an error has been fixed if Robo-Soar is unable to detect it automatically.

5 Correcting Domain Knowledge

Although the method described in the previous section corrects control knowledge, it does not correct the underlying domain knowledge; specifically, it does not add the precondition for the **approach** operator that the gripper be aligned with the block. Although the new control knowledge prevents the operator from being applied, the missing operator preconditions will lead to errors in learning when the operator is correctly applied. Learning will be incorrect because the missing preconditions will not be incorporated in future chunks that depend upon the application of the **approach** operator.

Instead of attempting to modify the productions that propose and implement the approach operator, Robo-Soar creates a new approach operator that replaces the original. The new operator will have the appropriate preconditions and will always be preferred to the original operator; the original is essentially forgotten. The general approach is to create a new operator, notice additional preconditions in the task state, then learn the implementation of the new operator using the original **approach** operator. Throughout this discussion, all guidance is through the advise problem space as described earlier.

To control the creation of the new operator, the selection problem space is augmented so that when there is an error, one alternative is to evaluate a completely new operator. If the advisor selects this alternative, a new operator is created and evaluated to be better than the original, thus replacing it. When the decision is made to evaluate the new operator, the examine-state problem space is used (along with outside guidance) and appropriate control productions are learned to propose and select this new operator.

At this point, the system does not have the knowledge to apply this operator; therefore, when the new operator is selected, another impasse arises. In response to this impasse, the examine-state problem space is again selected, but it has been augmented with an additional operator that can apply a task operator. To build the correct definition of the new operator, **notice-feature** operators are selected through outside guidance to incorporate the missing preconditions, which for our example are the orientation of the gripper and the block-orientation. Following the determination of the appropriate features, additional guidance can specify a task operator that should be used to implement the new operator in the subgoal. In this case, it would be the original **approach** operator. This operator is applied to the task state within the subgoal and the changes it makes to the state are results of the subgoal. These results lead to the creation of chunks that test for the new operator and its preconditions, and then apply the operator to the state. The new, corrected operator replaces the old operator, thus correcting the underlying domain theory.

6 Extending Domain Knowledge

The method we have described for creating a new operator using an existing operator definition can be extended so that a new operator can be learned from scratch through guidance. This is useful for building a new domain theory, as well as completing an existing domain theory. In Robo-Soar, we consider the situation in which the original programmer decided that it was not necessary to include a **rotate-gripper** operator.

We extend the previous approach by adding domain-independent knowledge that can generate the individual actions of an operator. This knowledge is encoded as additional operators in the examine-state problem space. These operators modify or remove existing structures on the state or new task operator, create new intermediate structures, or terminate the new operator. Once the new operator terminates, chunking creates productions that implement it without the need for further impasses or guidance.

To teach the system an internal simulation of **rotate-gripper**, the orientation of the gripper and the block are noticed, and then the gripper orientation is modified to be the orientation of the block. The exact values (and representations) of the orientations of the block and the gripper are irrelevant. All that is needed is copy a pointer of the orientation of the block on to the data structure representing the orientation of the gripper. From a single example the system learns a general production for implementing **rotate-gripper**.

These extensions are sufficient for creating operators that modify or remove existing structures or create new intermediate structures. They are insufficient for implementing operators that must create new structures with specific symbols that do not pre-exist in working memory. The problem is that there is no way to generate these symbols so that the can be selected by an advisor. This is the one case where guidance by selecting from a fixed set of alternatives breaks down. Fortunately, the only time that specific symbols are necessary is when issuing commands to the motor system. Therefore, we have included an operator that can generate all of the robot command symbols, such as **move**, **open**, and **rotate**. This is the only domain-dependent knowledge that must be pre-encoded in the system.

All of these extensions expand the examine-state problem space so that it has sufficient symbol manipulation capabilities for creating and implementing task operators through the composition of primitive domain-independent operators. However, outside guidance is necessary to control the composition of features and actions so that only legal operator implementations are generated.

In a previous version of Soar, the system was taught to play Tic-Tac-Toe from scratch. The system initially had no notion of two player games, three-in-a-row, winning, or losing. The system did have an initial representation of the board, the symbols X and O, and the command to make a move. Through outside guidance, operators were created to pick the side to move next, make a move of the chosen side, wait for the opponent to make a move, and detect winning and losing positions.

7 Discussion

There are two major contributions of this work. First, we have demonstrated that it is possible to extend analytic learning systems so that not only can they learn control knowledge using an existing domain theory, but through outside guidance they can also be used to correct and create new domain knowledge. The examine-state problem space is somewhat of a brute-force technique to learn new features and operators. It currently requires an outside agent to lead the system through a search of potentially relevant features and actions. Although it may not be considered the most elegant or complex machine learning technique, it allows the advisor to easily correct and extend the system.

This same approach could be used without an outside agent by having the system engage in experimentation. To experiment, the system can guess at relevant features and associated actions. It may pay attention to irrelevant features, and thus create overgeneral or incorrect chunks. But after many interactions with an environment where there is sufficient feedback, it could gradually learn those correct associations. Many powerful heuristics are available to avoid a blind search through this hypothesis space, such as concentrating on new, unknown features, as well as those features that are modified by the operators under consideration. For example, if the system has discovered that the rotate operator is necessary, it could concentrate its search for features relevant to avoiding **approach** to those features modified by **rotate-gripper**. This approach could also support hybrid methods that involve both outside guidance and experimentation, where the system experiments when on its own but uses guidance when it is available.

The second major contribution is to demonstrate the generality of guidance in knowledge acquisition. The form of guidance we allow is very restricted in that the advisor must pick from a set of available options. One advantage of this scheme is that the advice is given within the context of a specific problem and advice is asked only for those decisions for which the system has incomplete knowledge. A second advantage is that the advisor does not have to make explicit the reasons for the selection of an operator for which the system has a correct internal model; the learning mechanism performs the necessary analysis. A third advantage is that the guidance and learning occur while the system is running. There is no need to ever turn off the performance system to update or correct its knowledge base. Finally, by integrating the guidance, the problem solving and learning within a single architecture such as Soar, the guidance can be used to correct or extend any of the long term knowledge of the system.

The weakness of this approach is that the advisor sometimes must specify individual preconditions and effects of an operator. This can be quite tedious and it requires the human to identify which preconditions or effects that are missing when correcting a domain theory. These problems would be greatly reduced if our interface were improved so that the advisor could more directly observe the structure of the current state and operator. A more long-term solution is to provide the system with additional knowledge that allows it to perform more of the diagnosis and correction by itself.

The goal of our research was to demonstrate the practicality and generality of learning using only analytic techniques combined with outside guidance. Although the demonstrations were performed within the Soar architecture, the results should extend to similar systems such as Prodigy [Minton *et al.*, 1989] and Theo [Mitchell *et al.*, 1990] that combine problem solving and EBL. These systems may require some architectural extensions, for example, adding the ability to cast operator creation, selection, and implementation as subproblems.

The actual task performed by Robo-Soar was quite simple, and did not address many of the complexities of interacting with external environments, such as dealing with sensor and control errors. Our current goal is to extend Robo-Soar to more complex tasks and expand the spectrum of human interaction. At one end, we plan to investigate refining the guidance so that it is easier to correct and extend the domain theory, approaching the goals of the Instructable Production System where a system is never programmed, only given external guidance [Rychener, 1983]. On the other end of the spectrum, we plan to study experimentation techniques so that Robo-Soar will be able to learn much of the same information on its own, when human guidance is unavailable.

References

[Carbonell & Gil, 1987] J. C. Carbonell & Y. Gil. Learning by experimentation. In *Proceedings of the Fourth International Workshop on Machine Learning*, pages 256–266, 1987.

[DeJong & Mooney, 1986] G. DeJong & R. Mooney. Explanation-based learning: An alternative view. *Machine Learning*, 1(2):145–176, 1986.

[Doyle, 1986] R. Doyle. Constructing and refining causal explanations from an inconsistent domain theory. In *Proceedings of AAAI-86*. Morgan Kaufmann, 1986.

[Golding *et al.*, 1987] A. Golding, P. S. Rosenbloom, & J. E. Laird. Learning general search control from outside guidance. In *Proceedings of IJCAI-87*, Milano, Italy, August 1987.

[Laird *et al.*, 1987] J. E. Laird, A. Newell, & P. S. Rosenbloom. Soar: An architecture for general intelligence. *Artificial Intelligence*, 33(3), 1987.

[Laird *et al.*, 1989] J.E. Laird, E.S. Yager, C.M. Tuck, & M. Hucka. Learning in tele autonomous systems using Soar. In *Proceedings of the 1989 NASA Conference on Space Telerobotics*, 1989.

[Laird *et al.*, 1990] J. E. Laird, K. Swedlow, E. Altmann, & C. B. Congdon. *Soar 5 User's Manual.* The University of Michigan, 1990.

[Laird, 1988] J. E. Laird. Recovery from incorrect knowledge in Soar. In *Proceedings of the AAAI-88*, August 1988.

[Minton *et al.*, 1989] S. Minton, J. G. Carbonell, C.A. Knoblock, D.R. Kuokka, O. Etzioni, & Y. Gil. Explanation-based learning: A problem solving perspective. *Artificial Intelligence*, 40(1–3):163–118, 1989.

[Mitchell *et al.*, 1985] T. M. Mitchell, S. Mahadevan, & L. I. Steinberg. LEAP: A learning apprentice for VLSI design. In *Proceedings of IJCAI-85*, pages 616–623, Los Angeles, CA, August 1985.

[Mitchell *et al.*, 1986] T. M. Mitchell, R. M. Keller, & S. T. Kedar-Cabelli. Explanation-based generalization: A unifying view. *Machine Learning*, 1, 1986.

[Mitchell *et al.*, 1990] T Mitchell, J. Allen, P. Chalasani, J. Cheng, O. Etzionoi, M. Ringuette, & J. Schlimmer. Theo: A framework for self-improving systems. In K. VanLehn, editor, *Architectures for Intelligence*. Erlbaum, Hillsdale, NJ, 1990. In press.

[Rosenbloom & Laird, 1986] P. S. Rosenbloom & J. E. Laird. Mapping explanation-based generalization onto Soar. In *Proceedings of AAAI-86*, Philadelphia, PA, 1986. American Association for Artificial Intelligence.

[Rychener, 1983] M. D. Rychener. The instructable production system: A retrospective analysis. In *Machine Learning: An Artificial Intelligence Approach.* Tioga, Palo Alto, CA, 1983.

[Segre, 1987] A. M. Segre. *Explanation-Based Learning of Generalized Robot Assembly Plans.* PhD thesis, University of Illinois at Urbana-Champaign, 1987.

CHAPTER 50

Integrating Execution, Planning, and Learning in Soar for External Environments

J. E. Laird, University of Michigan, and P. S. Rosenbloom, USC–ISI

Abstract

Three key components of an autonomous intelligent system are planning, execution, and learning. This paper describes how the Soar architecture supports planning, execution, and learning in unpredictable and dynamic environments. The tight integration of these components provides reactive execution, hierarchical execution, interruption, on demand planning, and the conversion of deliberate planning to reaction. These capabilities are demonstrated on two robotic systems controlled by Soar, one using a Puma robot arm and an overhead camera, the second using a small mobile robot with an arm.

Introduction

The architecture of an intelligent agent that interacts with an external environment has often been decomposed into a set of cooperating processes including planning, execution and learning. Few AI systems since STRIPS [Fikes *et al.*, 1972] have included all of these processes. Instead, the emphasis has often been on individual components, or pairs of components, such as planning and execution, or planning and learning. Recently, a few systems have been implemented that incorporate planning, execution, and learning [Blythe & Mitchell, 1989; Hammond, 1989; Langley *et al.*, 1989].

Soar [Laird *et al.*, 1987] is one such system. It tightly couples problem solving and learning in every task it attempts to execute. Problem solving is used to find a solution path, which the learning mechanism generalizes and stores as a plan in long-term memory. The generalized plan can then be retrieved and used during execution of the task (or on later problems). This basic approach has been demonstrated in Soar on a large number of tasks [Rosenbloom *et al.*, 1990]; however, all of these demonstrations are essentially internal — both planning and execution occur completely within the scope of the system. Thus they do not involve direct execution in a real external environment and they safely ignore many of the issues inherent to such environments.

Recently, Soar has been extended so that it can interact with external environments [Laird *et al.*, 1990b]. What may be surprising is that Soar's basic structure already supports many of the capabilities necessary to interact with external environments — reactive execution, hierarchical execution, interruption, on demand planning, and the conversion of deliberate planning to reaction.

In this paper, we present the integrated approach to planning, execution, and learning embodied by the Soar architecture. We focus on the aspects of Soar that support effective performance in unpredictable environments in which perception can be uncertain and incomplete. Soar's approach to interaction with external environments is distinguished by the following three characteristics:

1. Planning and execution share the same architecture and knowledge bases. This provides strong constraints on the design of the architecture — the reactive capabilities required by execution must also be adequate for planning — and eliminates the need to explicitly transfer knowledge between planning and execution.
2. External actions can be controlled at three levels, from high-speed reflexes, to deliberate selection, to unrestricted planning and problem solving.
3. Learning automatically converts planning activity into control knowledge and reflexes for reactive execution.

Throughout this presentation we demonstrate these capabilities using two systems. The first is called *Robo-Soar* [Laird *et al.*, 1989; Laird *et al.*, 1990a]. Robo-Soar controls a Puma robot arm using a camera vision system as shown in Figure 1. The vision system provides the position and orientation of blocks in the robot's work area, as well as the status of a trouble light. Robo-Soar's task is to align blocks in its work area, unless the light goes on, in which case it must immedi-

*This research was sponsored by grant NCC2-517 from NASA Ames and ONR grant N00014-88-K-0554.

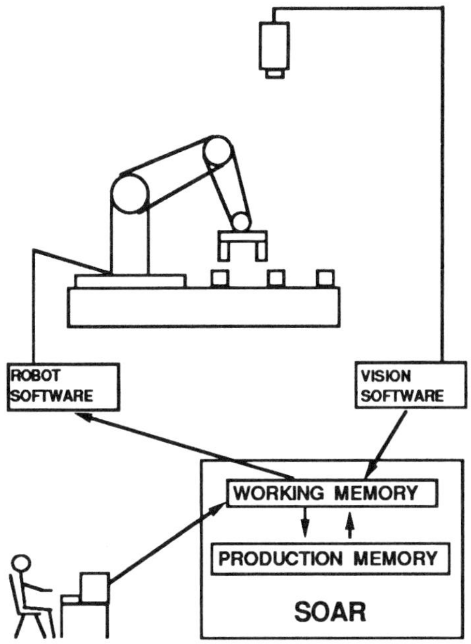

Figure 1: Robo-Soar system architecture.

ately push a button. The environment for Robo-Soar is unpredictable because the light can go on at any time, and an outside agent may intervene at any time by moving blocks in the work area, either helping or hindering Robo-Soar's efforts to align the blocks. In addition, Robo-Soar's perception of the environment is incomplete because the robot arm occludes the vision system while a block is being grasped. There is no feedback as to whether a block has been picked up until the arm is moved out of the work area.

The second system, called *Hero-Soar*, controls a Hero 2000 robot. The Hero 2000 is a mobile robot with an arm for picking up objects and sonar sensors for detecting objects in the environment. Hero-Soar's task is to pick up cups and deposit them in a waste basket. Our initial demonstrations of Soar will use Robo-Soar. At the end of the paper we will return to Hero-Soar and describe it more fully.

Execution

In Soar, all deliberate activity takes place within the context of goals or subgoals. A goal (or subgoal) is attempted by selecting and applying operators to transform an initial state into intermediate states until a desired state of the goal is reached. For Robo-Soar, one goal that arises is to align the blocks in the work area. A subgoal is to align a pair of blocks. Within a goal, the first decision is the selection of a problem space. The problem space determines the set of operators that are available in a goal. In Robo-Soar, the problem space for manipulating the arm consists of operators such as `open-gripper` and `move-gripper`.

The second decision selects the initial state of the problem space. For goals requiring interaction with an external environment, the states include data from the system sensors, as well as internally computed elaborations of this data. In Robo-Soar, the states include the position and orientation of all visible blocks and the gripper, their relative positions, and hypotheses about the positions of occluded blocks. Once the initial state is selected, decisions are made to select operators, one after another, until the goal is achieved.

Every decision made by Soar, be it to select a problem space, initial state, or operator for a goal, is based on *preferences* retrieved from Soar's long-term production memory. A preference is an absolute or relative statement of the worth of a specific object for a specific decision. The simplest preference, called *acceptable,* means that an object should be considered for a decision. Other preferences help distinguish between the acceptable objects. For example, a preference in Robo-Soar might be that it is better to select operator `move-gripper` than operator `close-gripper`.

A preference is only considered for a decision if it has been retrieved from the long-term production memory. Productions are continually matched against a working memory — which contains the active goals and their associated problem spaces, states, and operators — and when matched, create preferences for specific decisions. For example, a production in Robo-Soar that proposes the `close-gripper` operator might be:

```
If the problem space is robot-arm and
   the gripper is open and surrounds a block
then create an acceptable preference
   for the close gripper operator.
```

Once an operator is proposed with an acceptable preference, it becomes a candidate for selection. The selection of operators is controlled by productions that create preferences for candidate operators. For example, the following production prefers opening the gripper over moving a block that is in place.

```
If the goal is to move block A next to block B and
   the problem space is robot-arm and
   block A is next to block B and
   the gripper is closed and surrounds block A
then create a preference that opening the gripper
   is better than withdrawing the gripper.
```

Arbitrary control knowledge can be encoding as productions so that Soar is not constrained to any fixed method. The exact method is a result of a synthesis of all available control knowledge [Laird *et al.*, 1986].

Soar's production memory is unusual in that it fires all matched production instantiations in parallel, and it *retracts* the actions of production instantiations that no longer match, as in a JTMS [Doyle, 1979].[1] Thus,

[1] Retraction in Soar was introduced in version 5. Earlier versions of Soar did not retract the actions of productions.

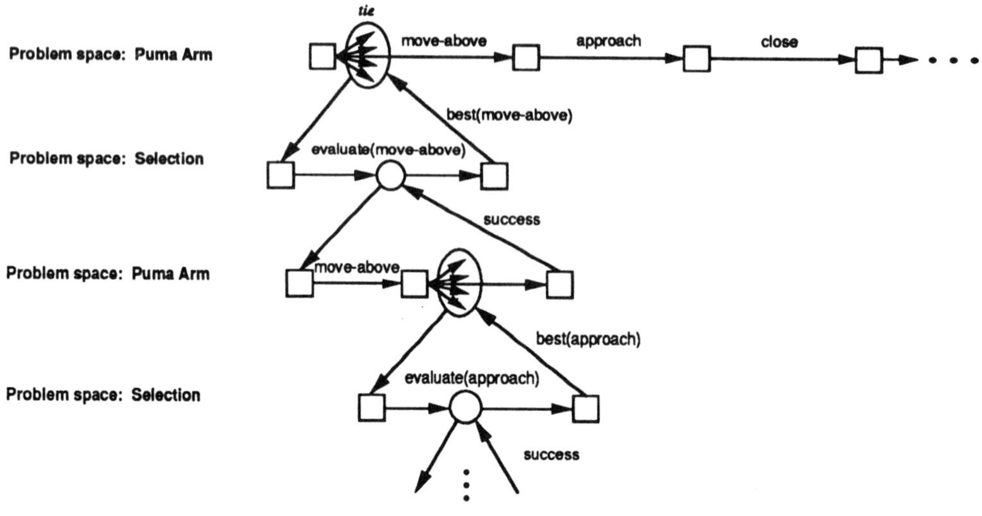

Figure 2: Example of planning in Robo-Soar to move a block. Squares represent states, while horizontal arcs represent operator applications. Downward pointing arcs are used to represent the creation of subgoals, and upward pointing arcs represent the termination of subgoals and the creation of results.

sufficient preferences have been created to allow the decision procedure to make a single choice, the subgoal is automatically terminated and the appropriate selection is made.

If there is more than a single point of indecision on the path to the goal, then it is necessary to create a longer term plan. If other decisions are underdetermined, then they will also lead to impasses and associated subgoals during the look-ahead search. The result is a recursive application of the planning strategy to each decision in the search where the current knowledge is insufficient.

Figure 2 shows a trace of the problem solving for Robo-Soar as it does look-ahead for moving a single block. At the left of the figure, the system is faced with an indecision as to which Puma command should used first. In the ensuing impasse, it performs a look-ahead search to find a sequence of Puma commands that pickup and move the block. Because of the size of the search space, Robo-Soar uses guidance from a human to determine which operators it should evaluate first [Laird *et al.*, 1989]. When a solution is found, preferences are created to make each of the decisions that required a subgoal, such as `best(approach)` and `best(move-above)` in the figure. Unfortunately, these preferences cannot directly serve as a plan because they are associated with specific planning subgoals that were created for the look-ahead search. These preferences are removed from working memory when their associated subgoals are terminated.

At this point, Soar's learning mechanism, called *chunking*, comes into play to preserve the control knowledge that was produced in the subgoals. Chunking is based on the observation that: (1) an impasse arises because of a lack of directly available knowledge, and (2) problem solving in the associated subgoal produces new information that is available to resolve the impasse. Chunking caches the processing of the subgoal by creating a production whose actions recreate the results of the subgoal. The conditions of the production are based on those working-memory elements in parent goals that were tested by productions in the subgoal and found necessary to produce the results. This is a process very similar to explanation-based learning [Rosenbloom & Laird, 1986].

When chunking is used in conjunction with the planning scheme described above, Robo-Soar learns new productions that create preferences for operators. Since the preferences were created by a search for a solution to the task, the new productions include all of the relevant tests of the current situation that are necessary to achieve the task. Chunking creates new productions not only for the original operator decision, but also for each decision that had an impasse in a subgoal. As a result, productions are learned that create sufficient preferences for making each decision along the path to the goal. Once the original impasse is resolved, the productions learned during planning will apply, creating sufficient preferences to select each operator on the path to the goal. This is shown in Figure 2 as the straight line of operator applications across the top of figure after the planning is complete.

In Robo-Soar, the productions learned for aligning blocks are very general. They ignore all of the details of the specific blocks because the planning was done using a abstract problem space. Similarly, the productions preferences and working memory elements exist only when they are relevant to the current situation as dictated by the conditions of the productions that created them. For example, there may be many productions that create preferences under different situations for a given operator.

Once the relevant preferences have been created by productions, a fixed decision procedure uses the preferences created by productions to select the current problem space, the initial state, and operators. The decision procedure is invoked when Soar's production memory reaches quiescence, that is, when there are no new changes to working memory.

Once an operator is selected, productions sensitive to that operator can fire to implement the operator's actions. Operator implementation productions do not retract their actions when they no longer match. By nature they make changes to the state that must persist until explicitly changed by other operators. For an internal operator, the productions modify the current state. For an operator involving interaction with an external environment, the productions augment the current state with appropriate motor commands. The Soar architecture detects these augmentations and sends them directly to the robot controller. For both internal and external operators, there is an additional production that tests that the operator was successfully applied and signals that the operator has terminated so that a new operator can be selected. The exact nature of the test is dependent on the operator and may involve testing both internal data structures and feedback from sensors.

At this point, the basic execution level of Soar has been defined. This differs from the execution level of most systems in that each control decision is made through the run-time integration of long-term knowledge. Most planning systems build a plan, and follow it step by step, never opening up the individual decisions to global long-term knowledge. Other "reactive" learning systems, such as Theo [Blythe & Mitchell, 1989; Mitchell *et al.*, 1990] and Schoppers' Universal plans [Schoppers, 1986] create stimulus-response rules that do not allow the integration at run-time of control knowledge. Soar extends this notion of run-time combination to its operator implementations as well, so that an operator is not defined declaratively as in STRIPS. This will be expanded later to include both more reflexive and more deliberate execution.

Planning

In Soar, operator selection is the basic control act for which planning can provide additional knowledge. For situations in which Soar has sufficient knowledge, the preferences created for each operator decision will lead to the selection of a single operator. Once the operator is selected, productions will apply it by making appropriate changes to the state. However, for many situations, the knowledge encoded as productions will be incomplete or inconsistent. We call such an underdetermined decision an *impasse*. For example, an impasse will arise when the preferences for selecting operators do not suggest a unique best choice. The Soar architecture detects impasses and automatically creates subgoals to determine the best choice. Within a subgoal, Soar once again casts the problem within a problem space, but this time the goal is to determine which operator to select. Within the subgoal, additional impasses may arise, leading to a goal stack. The impasse is resolved, and the subgoal terminated, when sufficient preferences have been added to working memory so that a decision can be made.

To determine the best operator, any number of methods can be used in the subgoal, such as drawing analogies to previous problems, asking an outside agent, or various planning strategies. In Soar, the selection of a problem space for the goal determines which approach will be taken, so that depending on the available knowledge, many different approaches are possible. This distinguishes Soar from many other systems that use only a single planning technique to generate control knowledge.

Robo-Soar uses an abstract look-ahead planning strategy. Look-ahead planning requires additional domain knowledge, specifically, the ability to simulate the actions of external operators on the internal model of the world. As expected, this knowledge is encoded as productions that directly modify the internal state when an operator is selected to apply to it.

The internal simulations of operators do not replicate the behavior of the environment exactly, but are abstractions. In Robo-Soar, these abstractions are predetermined by the productions that implement the operators, although in other work in Soar abstractions have been generated automatically based on ignoring impasses that arise during the look-ahead search [Unruh & Rosenbloom, 1989]. For Robo-Soar, an abstract plan is created to align a set of blocks by moving one block at a time. This level completely ignores moving the gripper and grasping blocks. This plan is later refined to movements of the gripper by further planning once the first block movement has been determined. Even this level is abstract in that it does not simulate exact sensor values (such as block A is at location 3.4, 5.5) but only relative positions of blocks and the gripper (block A is to the right of block B).

Planning in Robo-Soar is performed by creating an internal model of the environment and then evaluating the result of applying alternative operators using available domain knowledge. The exact nature of the search is dependent on the available knowledge. For some tasks, it may be possible to evaluate the result of a single operator, but for other tasks, such as Robo-Soar, evaluation may be possible only after applying many operators until a desired (of failed) state is achieved. Planning knowledge converts the evaluations computed in the search into preferences. When learned for moving the gripper ignore the exact names and positions of the blocks, but are sensitive to the final relative positions of the blocks.

The ramifications of this approach to planning are as follows:

1. **Planning without monolithic plans.**
In classical planning, the plan is a monolithic data structure that provides communication between the planner and the execution module. In Soar, a monolithic declarative plan is not created, but instead a set of control productions are learned that jointly direct execution. The plan consists of the preferences stored in these control rules, and the rule conditions which determine when the preferences are applicable.

2. **Expressive planning language.**
The expressibility of Soar's plan language is a function of: (1) the fine-grained conditionality provided by embedding the control knowledge in a set of rules; and (2) the preference language. The first factor makes it easy to encode such control structures as conditionals, loops, and recursion. The second factor makes it easy to not only directly suggest the appropriate operator to select, but also to suggest that an operator be avoided, or that a partial order holds among a set of operators. This differs from systems that use stimulus-response rules in which the actions are commands to the motor system [Mitchell *et al.*, 1990; Schoppers, 1986]. In Soar, the actions of the productions are preferences that contribute to the decision as to which operator to select. Thus Soar has a wider vocabulary for expressing control knowledge than these other systems.

3. **On-demand planning.**
Soar invokes planning whenever knowledge is insufficient for making a decision and it terminates planning as soon as sufficient knowledge is found. Because of this, planning is always in service of execution. Also because of this, planning and replanning are indistinguishable activities. Both are initiated because of indecision, and both provide knowledge that resolves the indecision.

4. **Learning improves future execution and planning.**
Once a control production is learned, it can be used for future problems that match its conditions. These productions improve both execution and planning by eliminating indecision in both external and internal problem solving. The effect is not unlike the utilization of previous cases in case-based reasoning [Hammond, 1989]. This is in contrast to other planning systems that build "situated control rules" for providing reactive execution of the current plan, but do not generalize or store them for future goals [Drummond, 1989].

5. **Run-time combination of multiple plans.**
When a new situation is encountered, all relevant productions will fire. It makes no difference in which previous problem the productions were learned. For a novel problem, it is possible to have productions from many different plans contribute to the selection of operators on the solution path (unlike case-based reasoning). For those aspects of the problem not covered by what has been learned from previous problems, on-demand planning is available to fill in the gaps.

It is this last observation that is probably most important for planning in uncertain and unpredictable environment. By not committing to a single plan, but instead allowing all cached planning knowledge to be combined at run-time, Soar can respond to unexpected changes in the environment, as long as it has previously encountered a similar situation. If it does not have sufficient knowledge for the current situation, it will plan, learn the appropriate knowledge, and in the future be able to respond directly without planning.

Interruption

The emphasis in our prior description of planning was on acquiring knowledge that could be responsive to changes in the environment during execution. This ignores the issue of how the system responds to changes in its environment during planning. Consider two scenarios from Robo-Soar. In the first scenario, one of the blocks is removed from the table while Robo-Soar is planning how to align the blocks. In the second, a trouble light goes on while Robo-Soar is planning how to align the blocks. This light signals that Robo-Soar must push a button *as soon as possible*. The key to both of these scenarios is that Soar's productions are continually matched against all of working memory, including incoming sensor data, and all goals and subgoals. When a change is detected, planning can be revised or abandoned if necessary.

In the first example, the removal of the block does not eliminate the necessity to plan, it just changes the current state, the desired state (fewer blocks need to be aligned) and the set of available operators (fewer blocks can be moved). The change in the set of available operators modifies the impasse but does not eliminate it. Within the subgoal, operators and data that were specific to the removed block will be automatically retracted from working memory. The exact effect will depend on the state of the planning and its dependence on the eliminated block. In the case where an outside agent suddenly aligned all but one of the blocks, and Robo-Soar had sufficient knowledge for that specific case, the impasse would be eliminated and the appropriate operator selected.

In the second example, we assume that there exists a production that will direct Robo-Soar to push a button when a light is turned on. This production will test for the light and create a preference that the `push-button` operator *must* be selected. When the next operator decision is made, there is no longer a tie, and the **push-button** operator is selected. Interruption of planning can be predicated on a variety of stimuli. For example, productions can keep track of the time spent planning and abort the planning if it is taking too much time. Planning would be aborted by creating a preference for the best action given the currently available information. One disadvantage of this scheme is that any partial planning that has not been captured in chunks will be lost.

Hierarchical Planning and Execution

In our previous Robo-Soar examples, the set of operators corresponded quite closely to the motor commands of the robot controller. However, Soar has no restriction that problem space operators must directly correspond to individual actions of the motor system. For many problems, planning is greatly simplified if it is performed with abstract operators far removed from the primitive actions of the hardware. For execution, the hierarchical decomposition provided by multiple levels of operators can provide important context for dealing with execution errors and unexpected changes in the environment.

Soar provides hierarchical decomposition by creating subgoals whenever there is insufficient knowledge encoded as productions to implement an operator directly. In the subgoal, the implementation of the abstract operator is carried out by selecting and applying less abstract operators, until the abstract operator is terminated.

To demonstrate Soar's capabilities in hierarchical planning and execution we will use our second system, Hero-Soar. Hero-Soar searches for cups using sonar sensors. The basic motor commands include positioning the various parts of the arm, opening and closing the gripper, orienting sonar sensors, and moving and turning the robot. A more useful set includes operators such as **search-for-object**, **center-object**, **pickup-cup**, and **drop-cup**. The execution of each of these operators involves a combination of more primitive operators that can only be determined at run-time. For example, **search-for-an-object** involves an exploration of the room until the sonar sensors detect an object.

In Hero-Soar, the problem space for the top-most goal consists of just these operators. Control knowledge selects the operators when they are appropriate. However, once one of these operators is selected, an impasse arises because there are no relevant implementation productions. For example, once the **search-for-object** operator is selected, a subgoal is generated and a problem space is selected that contains operators for moving the robot and analyzing sonar readings.

Operators such as **search-for-object** would be considered goals in most other systems. In contrast, goals in Soar arise only when knowledge is insufficient to make progress. One advantage of Soar's more uniform approach is that all the decision making and planning methods also apply to these "goals" (abstract operators like **search-for-object**). For example, if there is an abstract internal simulation of an operator such as **pickup-cup**, it can be used in planning for the top goal in the same way planning would be performed at more primitive levels.

A second advantage of treating incomplete operator applications as goals is that even seemingly primitive acts, such as **move-arm** can become goals, providing hierarchical execution. This is especially important when there is uncertainty as to whether a primitive action will complete successfully. Hero-Soar has exactly these characteristics because its sensors are imperfect and because it sometimes loses motor commands and sensor data when communicating with the Hero robot. Hero-Soar handles this uncertainty by selecting an operator, such as **move-arm**, and then waiting for feedback that the arm is in the correct position before terminating the operator. While the command is executing on the Hero hardware, a subgoal is created. In this subgoal, the **wait** operator is repeatedly applied, continually counting how long it is waiting. If appropriate feedback is received from the Hero, the **move-arm** operator terminates, a new operator is selected, and the subgoal is removed. However, if the motor command or feedback was lost, or there is some other problem, such as an obstruction preventing completion of the operator, the waiting continues. Productions sensitive to the selected operator and the current count detect when the operator has taken longer than expected. These productions propose operators that directly query the feedback sensors, retry the operator, or attempt some other recovery strategy. Because of the relative computational speed differences between the Hero and Soar on an Explorer II+, Hero-Soar spends approximately 30% of its time waiting for its external actions to complete.

Hierarchical execution is not unique to Soar. Georgeff and Lansky have used a similar approach in PRS for controlling a mobile robot [Georgeff & Lansky, 1987]. In PRS, declarative procedures, called *Knowledge Areas* (KAs) loosely correspond to abstract operators in Soar. Each KA has a body consisting of the steps of the procedure represented as a graphic network. Just as Soar can use additional abstract operators in the implementation of an operator, a KA can have goals as part of its procedure which lead to additional KAs being invoked. PRS maintains reactivity by continually comparing the conditions of its KAs against the current situation and goals, just as Soar is continually matching it productions. A significant difference between PRS and Soar is in the representation of control knowledge and operators. Within a KA, the control is a fixed declarative procedure. Soar's control knowledge is represented as preferences in productions that can be used for any relevant decision. Thus the knowledge is not constrained to a specific procedure, and will be used when the conditions of the production that generates the preference match the current situation. In addition, new productions can be added to Soar through learning, and the actions of these productions will be integrated with existing knowledge at run-time.

Reactive Execution

Hierarchical execution provides important context for complex activities. Unfortunately it also exacts a cost in terms of run-time efficiency. In order to perform a primitive act, impasses must be detected, goals created, problem spaces selected, and so on, until the motor command is generated. Execution can be performed more efficiently by directly selecting and applying primitive operators. However, operator application has its own overheads. The actions of an operator will only be executed after the operator has been selected following quiescence, thus forcing a delay. The advantage of these two approaches is that they allow knowledge to be integrated at run-time, so that a decision is not based on an isolated production.

Soar also supports direct reflex actions where a production creates motor commands without testing the current operator. These productions act as reflexes for low level responses, such as stopping the wheel motors when an object is directly in front of the robot. Along with the increase responsiveness comes a loss of control; no other knowledge will contribute to the decision to stop the robot.

The ultimate limits on reactivity rest with Soar's ability to match productions and process preferences. Unfortunately, there are currently no fixed time bounds on Soar's responsiveness. Given Soar's learning, an even greater concern is that extended planning and learning will actually reduce responsiveness as more and more productions must be matched [Tambe & Newell, 1988]. Recent results suggest that these problems can be avoided by restricting the expressiveness of the production conditions [Tambe & Rosenbloom, 1989].

Although there are no time bounds, Soar is well matched for both Hero-Soar and Robo-Soar. In neither case does Soar's processing provide the main bottleneck. However, as we move into domains with more limited time constraints, further research on bounding Soar's execution time will be necessary.

Discussion

Perhaps the key reason that Soar is able to exhibit effective execution, planning (extended, hierarchical, and reactive), and interruption, is that it has three distinct levels at which external actions can be controlled. These levels differ both in the speed with which they occur and the scope of knowledge that they can take into consideration in making a decision. At the lowest level, an external action can be selected directly by a production. This is the fastest level — Soar can fire 40 productions per second on a TI Explorer II+ while controlling the Hero using 300 productions — but the knowledge utilized is limited to what is expressed locally in a single production.[2] This level is appropriately described as reflexive behavior — it is fast, uncontrollable by other knowledge, and difficult to change.

At the middle level, an external action can be selected through selecting an operator. This is somewhat slower — in the comparable situation as above, only 10 decisions can be made per second — but it can take into account any knowledge about the current problem solving context that can be retrieved directly by firing productions (without changing the context). It allows for the consideration and comparisons of actions before a selection is made. This level is appropriately described as a dynamic mixture of top-down (plan-driven) and bottom-up (data-driven) behavior. It is based on previously-stored plan fragments (learned control rules) and the current situation, and can dynamically, at run-time, adjudicate among their various demands. This level can be changed simply by learning new plan fragments.

At the highest level, an external action can be selected as a result of extended problem solving in subgoals. This can be arbitrarily slow, but potentially allows any knowledge in the system — or outside of it, if external interaction is allowed — to be taken into consideration. This level is appropriately described as global planning behavior.

Soar's learning is closely tied into these three levels. Learning is invoked automatically whenever the knowledge available in the bottom two levels is insufficient. Learning moves knowledge from planning to the middle level of deliberate action and, also to the bottom level of reflexes. Without learning, one could attempt to combine the bottom and middle layers by precompiling their knowledge into a fixed decision network as in REX [Kaelbling, 1986; Rosenschein, 1985]. However, for an autonomous system that is continually learning new control knowledge and operators [Laird *et al.*, 1990a], the only chance to bring together all of the relevant knowledge for a decision is when the decision is to be made.

The integration of planning, execution, and learning in Soar is quite similar to that in Theo because of the mutual dependence upon impasse-driven planning and the caching of plans as productions or rules. Schoppers' Universal Plans also caches the results of planning; however, Schoppers' system plans during an initial design stage and exhaustively generates all possible plans through back-chaining. In contrast, Theo and Soar plan only when necessary, and do not generate all

[2]Hero-Soar is limited in absolute response time by delays in the communication link between the Hero and the Explorer, and the speed of the Hero central processor. The actual response time of Hero-Soar to a change in its environment is around .5 seconds.

possible plans; however, Theo as yet does not support interruption, nor can it maintain any history. All decisions must be based on its current sensors readings. Soar is further distinguished from Theo in that Soar supports not only reactive behavior and planning, but also deliberative execution in which multiple sources of knowledge are integrated at run-time. This middle level of deliberate execution is especially important in learning systems when planning knowledge is combined dynamically at run-time.

Acknowledgments

The authors would like to thank Michael Hucka, Eric Yager, Chris Tuck, Arie Covrigaru and Clare Congdon for help in developing Robo-Soar and Hero-Soar.

References

[Blythe & Mitchell, 1989] J. Blythe & T. M. Mitchell. On becoming reactive. In *Proceedings of the Sixth International Machine Learning Workshop*, pages 255–259, Cornell, NY, June 1989. Morgan Kaufmann.

[Doyle, 1979] J. Doyle. A truth maintenance system. *Artificial Intelligence*, 12:231–272, 1979.

[Drummond, 1989] M. Drummond. Situated control rules. In *Proceedings of the First International Conference on Principles of Knowledge Representation and Reasoning*, Toronto, May 1989. Morgan Kaufmann.

[Fikes *et al.*, 1972] R. E. Fikes, P. E. Hart, & N. J. Nilsson. Learning and executing generalized robot plans. *Artificial Intelligence*, 3:251–288, 1972.

[Georgeff & Lansky, 1987] M. P. Georgeff & A. L. Lansky. Reactive reasoning and planning. *Proceedings of AAAI-87*, 1987.

[Hammond, 1989] K. J. Hammond. *Case-Based Planning: Viewing Planning as a Memory Task*. Academic Press, Inc., Boston, 1989.

[Kaelbling, 1986] L. P. Kaelbling. An architecture for intelligent reactive systems. In M. P. Georgeff & A. L. Lansky, editors, *Reasoning about Actions and Plans: Proceedings of the 1986 Workshop*, 95 First Street, 1986. Morgan Kaufomann.

[Laird *et al.*, 1986] J. E. Laird, P. S. Rosenbloom, & A. Newell. *Universal Subgoaling and Chunking: The Automatic Generation and Learning of Goal Hierarchies*. Kluwer Academic Publishers, Hingham, MA, 1986.

[Laird *et al.*, 1987] J. E. Laird, A. Newell, & P. S. Rosenbloom. Soar: An architecture for general intelligence. *Artificial Intelligence*, 33(3), 1987.

[Laird *et al.*, 1989] J. E. Laird, E. S. Yager, C. M. Tuck, & M. Hucka. Learning in tele-autonomous systems using Soar. In *Proceedings of the 1989 NASA Conference on Space Telerobotics*, 1989.

[Laird *et al.*, 1990a] J. E. Laird, M. Hucka, E. S. Yager, & C. M. Tuck. Correcting and extending domain knowledge using outside guidance. In *Proceedings of the Seventh International Conference on Machine Learning*, June 1990.

[Laird *et al.*, 1990b] J. E. Laird, K. Swedlow, E. Altmann, & C. B. Congdon. *Soar 5 User's Manual.* University of Michigan, 1990. In preparation.

[Langley *et al.*, 1989] P. Langley, K. Thompson, W. Iba, J. H. Gennari, & J. A. Allen. An integrated cognitive architecture for autonomous agents. Technical Report 89-28, Department of Information & Computer Science, University of California, Irvine, September 1989.

[Mitchell *et al.*, 1990] T. M. Mitchell, J. Allen, P. Chalasani, J. Cheng, O. Etzionoi, M. Ringuette, & J. Schlimmer. Theo: A framework for self-improving systems. In K. VanLehn, editor, *Architectures for Intelligence*. Erlbaum, Hillsdale, NJ, 1990. In press.

[Rosenbloom & Laird, 1986] P. S. Rosenbloom & J. E. Laird. Mapping explanation-based generalization onto Soar. In *Proceedings of AAAI-86*, Philadelphia, PA, 1986. American Association for Artificial Intelligence.

[Rosenbloom *et al.*, 1990] P. S. Rosenbloom, J. E. Laird, A. Newell, & R. McCarl. A preliminary analysis of the foundations of the Soar architecture as a basis for general intelligence. In *Foundations of Artificial Intelligence*. MIT Press, Cambridge, MA, 1990. In press.

[Rosenschein, 1985] S. Rosenschein. Formal theories of knowledge in AI and robotics. *New Generation Computing*, 3:345–357, 1985.

[Schoppers, 1986] M. J. Schoppers. Universal plans for reactive robots in unpredictable environments. In M. P. Georgeff & A. L. Lansky, editors, *Reasoning about Actions and Plans: Proceedings of the 1986 Workshop*. Morgan Kaufmann, 1986.

[Tambe & Newell, 1988] M. Tambe & A. Newell. Some chunks are expensive. In *Proceedings of the Fifth International Conference on Machine Learning*, 1988.

[Tambe & Rosenbloom, 1989] M. Tambe & P. S. Rosenbloom. Eliminating expensive chunks by restricting expressiveness. In *Proceedings of IJCAI-89*, 1989.

[Unruh & Rosenbloom, 1989] A. Unruh & P. S. Rosenbloom. Abstraction in problem solving and learning. In *Proceedings of IJCAI-89*, 1989.

CHAPTER 51

Soar as a Unified Theory of Cognition: Spring 1990

R. L. Lewis, Carnegie Mellon University, S. B. Huffman, University of Michigan, B. E. John, Carnegie Mellon University, J. E. Laird, University of Michigan, J. F. Lehman, Carnegie Mellon University, A. Newell, Carnegie Mellon University, P. S. Rosenbloom, USC–ISI, T. Simon, Carnegie Mellon University, and S. G. Tessler, Carnegie Mellon University

Soar is a theory of cognition embodied in a computer system. In 1987 it was used as the central exemplar to make the case that cognitive science should attempt unified theories of cognition (UTC) [13][1]. Since then, much research has been done to move Soar toward being a real UTC, rather than just an exemplar. Figure 1 lists the relevant studies[2]. They have been done by a broad community of researchers in the pursuit of a multiplicity of interests. This symposium presents four of these studies to convey the current state of Soar as a UTC (their names are marked with asterisks in the figure). This short paper provides additional breadth and context.

THE SOAR ARCHITECTURE

We review here the basic structure of the Soar architecture, which has been described in detail elsewhere [8, 13, 20]. Soar formulates all tasks in *problem spaces*, in which *operators* are selectively applied to the *current state* to attain *desired states*. Problem spaces appear as triangles in Figure 2 (which describes a Soar system for comprehending natural language). Problem solving proceeds in a sequence of *decision cycles* that select problem spaces, states, and operators. Each decision cycle accumulates knowledge from a long term *recognition memory* (realized as a production system). This memory continually matches against *working memory*, elaborating the current state and retrieving preferences that encode knowledge about the next step to take. Access of recognition memory is involuntary, parallel, and rapid (assumed to take on the order of 10 milliseconds). The decision cycle accesses recognition memory repeatedly to quiescence, so each decision cycle takes on the order of 100 milliseconds.

If Soar does not know how to proceed in a problem space, an *impasse* occurs. Soar responds to an impasse by creating a subgoal in which a new problem space can be used to acquire the needed knowledge. If a lack of knowledge prevents progress in the new space, another subgoal is created and so on, creating a goal-subgoal hierarchy. Figure 2 shows how *multiple problem spaces* arise. Once an impasse is resolved by problem solving, the *chunking* mechanism adds new productions to recognition memory encoding the results of the problem solving, so the impasse is avoided in the future. All incoming perception and outgoing motor commands flow through the state in the top problem space (which occurs above the spaces in Figure 2).

FOUR EXAMPLES OF RECENT PROGRESS

NL-Soar (Huffman, Lehman, Lewis and Tessler)

The goal of the NL-Soar work is to develop a general natural language capability that satisfies the constraint of real-time comprehension. To achieve rates of 200-300 words per minute, NL-Soar must *recognitionally* bring to bear multiple sources of knowledge (e.g., syntactic, semantic, and task knowledge). In addition to

---

[1] Soar research encompasses artificial intelligence and human computer interaction (HCI) as well, which we will largely ignore here.

[2] We include several unpublished studies to better convey Soar's current state.

Time Scale	Name	Domain	Phenomena modelled	Notes	References
short ↑	Neuro-Soar	Neural net implementation of Soar	Implementation technology of the architecture	A	[17]
	Visual Attention	Attention within field of view	Conjunctive, disjunctive feature searches; illusory conjunction	A	[27]
	Immed. Behavior	Simple reaction tasks; typing	Performance times	Z	[13]
	ET-Soar	Intelligent tutor for electrostatics	Perception-action loop in problem-solving with external display	S	[26]
	Phone Operator	Operators assisting in collect calls	Performance time of task involving multiple modalities	Z	[4]
	* Browser-Soar	Computer browsers	Browsing an on-line reference manual	P	[5]
	* Robo-Soar	Puma robot arm in blocks world	On-demand flexible planning, interruptibility	S	[7,9]
	* Hero-Soar	Hero mobile robot picking up cups	Reactive execution; operating in noisy, uncertain environments	S	[9]
	* NL-Soar	Natural language comprehension	Real-time comprehension; integrates multiple knowledge sources	S	[11]
	IR-Soar	Immediate reasoning tasks (< 60s)	Regularities across multiple IR tasks (syllogisms, Wason, etc.)	Q	[15,16]
	IR-Soar(Syl)	Categorical syllogisms	Individual differences	I	[15,16]
	BI-Soar	Taking instructions for IR tasks	Acquisition of new tasks from natural language instructions	S	[11]
	* SC-Soar	Series completion	Relative difficulty of different series	Q	
	Subtraction	Multi-column subtraction	Learning new subtraction procedure; two common bugs	S, N	[20]
	Cryptarithmetic	Cryptarithmetic puzzles	Control of search in cryptarithmetic task space	P, N	[13]
	TOH-Soar	Tower of Hanoi	Strategy change, within-trial learning	P	[21]
	Verbal Learning	Paired-associate, cued recall, etc.	Learning new declarative knowledge (knowledge level learning)	S	[19]
	Inductive KLL	Concept learning	Inducing concepts from examples (knowledge level learning)	S	[18]
	Text Editor	Learning to use a text editor	Conceptual errors in using a new text editor	Q	[28]
	Data-Soar	Learning new data structures	Use of analogy in learning "stack" data type	P	[24]
	Generic Design	Architectural, instructional design	Design of instructional material for word processor	P	[14]
	Lexical Acquis.	Early lexical acquisition	Prototype effects; underextension; one-concept-one-word bias	Q	[12]
	ABC-Soar	Analysis-based concept acquisition	Acquisition of number conservation concepts	S	[23]
long ↓	Balance Beam	Balance beam task	Developmental transitions in balance beam task	Q, N	[13]

NOTES: A: work on the architecture itself I: accounts for individual differences N: work no longer in progress P: protocol simulation Q: qualitative coverage of phenomena S: sufficiency demonstration Z: zero parameter predictions

Figure 1: **Some efforts on Soar as a unified theory of cognition.**

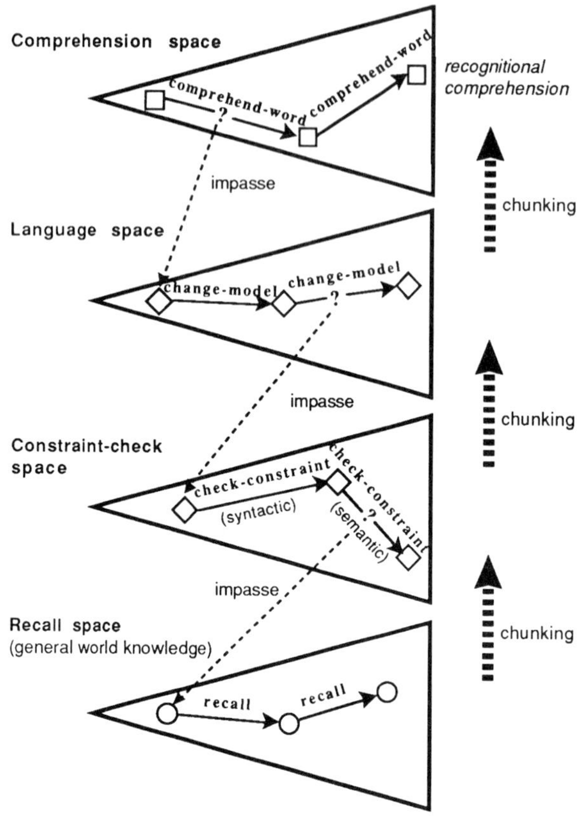

Figure 2: **Achieving recognitional comprehension from deliberate comprehension in NL-Soar.**

supporting this kind of processing, the system must integrate with the rest of Soar to work in any task that requires language understanding.

NL-Soar realizes real-time comprehension by applying a *single operator* to comprehend each word as it is read, dropping into lower problem spaces to complete the comprehension when the required knowledge is not directly available (i.e., an impasse is reached). Figure 2 shows this behavior. As in previous work [11], we assume that comprehension builds a *situation model* of what the utterance is about, and an *utterance model* that encodes the syntactic structure of the utterance. When Soar impasses on a **comprehend-word** operator, it drops into the **Language** space, which has operators that make changes to the two models. Any kind of knowledge can propose an operator (e.g., syntactic or semantic), but operators have constraints that must be satisfied before they can apply. These constraints can be arbitrarily complex syntactic, semantic, or pragmatic tests. The constraints are checked serially in the **Constraint-check** space, which consults the situation and utterance models. Checking semantic constraints may require accessing general world knowledge, which occurs in the **Recall** space. Other spaces may be involved in comprehension; for example, referent resolution happens in the **Resolve-referent** space (not shown in the figure). Once the deliberate problem solving produces the knowledge to resolve the **comprehend-word** operator's impasse at the top, chunking adds new elements to long term memory so comprehension can proceed by recognition for similar utterances and contexts in the future. These chunks do the constraint checking in parallel, integrating into a single recognition the disparate knowledge sources tapped in the deliberate problem solving.

NL-Soar is a functioning language system: its syntactic knowledge currently comprises about 75% of James Allen's outline of English in [1], and it can handle the semantics of simple instructions for the immediate reasoning [11] and Robo-Soar blocks-world tasks [7, 9]. The novel aspect of the recent work is using chunking to routinely move knowledge up the problem space hierarchy to create an integrated recognitional comprehension system. A preliminary analysis over a very small set of test sentences indicates that about half the chunks perform lexical access (i.e., the chunks are specific to lexical items). The remaining non-lexical chunks are also fairly specific, usually tied to particular syntactic forms and semantic categories. While there is transfer to new utterances, the transfer is limited by the specificity of the chunks. This implies a model of comprehension that depends on a large number of fairly specific chunks [13]. This does not mean there is no generality in NL-Soar's linguistic knowledge. Quite the opposite, the **Language** space comprises very general sources of knowledge. It simply means that the generality is limited at the recognitional level. Additional research is necessary to fully establish the sufficiency of this model.

SC-Soar (Simon)

The goal of the SC-Soar work is to develop a model of regularity detection as it occurs in series completion tasks (e.g., A, B, A, C, A, ?). Solving these puzzles requires the capability to hypothesize and test the underlying rule of the series. The series-completion task provides a microcosm for studying concept acquisition; it involves inducing a concept from examples and encoding the environment in terms of the new concept.

SC-Soar solves a series completion problem by casting it as a comprehension task: comprehension operators are applied to each item in the series, and subspaces encode the knowledge of how to hypothesize and test the underlying rule. The structure is that of NL-Soar, although the knowledge is not about language but about the relations that characterize the series, and the focus is on the deliberate phase of this specialized comprehension. Comprehending an item involves finding relationships between the item and other items in the series (relationships can be alphabetic or identity). To establish a relationship, attention must be focused on at least one other item; the *attention operators* posited for the work on immediate reasoning [16] provide this functionality. Attending to other items may also trigger knowledge to hypothesize a period size for the series. Once a period is hypothesized, SC-Soar *re-represents* the series by structuring it into groups of items. This is not accomplished in one massive step, but occurs by re-reading the series. Thus, SC-Soar exhibits a form of progressive deepening. Comprehension chunks learned during the first pass transfer to subsequent passes, so that some of the deliberate processing can be avoided. After this re-encoding, comprehension proceeds by establishing relationships between groups rather than single items. A relationship between groups, combined with the simpler relationships within groups, establishes a hypothesis for the underlying rule of the series. This hypothesis is tested by generating expectations and matching them against the rest of the series.

The novel features of SC-Soar are structuring the system into comprehension operators, modulating problem solving by attention, and learning during the task. The first two have independent support for their plausibility from other work [11, 13, 16]. The learning is important for modeling progressive deepening behavior and improvement across trials. Currently SC-Soar solves ten out of fifteen series in the original Simon and Kotovsky set [22]. The five series it cannot solve were among the most difficult. For the ten it solves, the number of decision cycles it takes to hypothesize the correct pattern provides a measure of duration that corresponds closely to the relative difficulty of these series for the subjects. The learning has not yet been compared with human data.

Robo-Soar and Hero-Soar (Laird)

The goal of the Robo-Soar and Hero-Soar work is to get Soar to interact with an external environment. The functional demands of working in a dynamic environment include *reactive execution, interruptibility, flexible on-demand planning*, and the *conversion of deliberate planning to reactive execution*. Robo-Soar and Hero-Soar are robotic systems developed to explore how Soar can support these capabilities [7, 9]. Robo-Soar controls a Puma arm and receives perceptual input through a camera; its task is to align blocks in a work area, unless interrupted by a flashing "trouble" light, in which case it should immediately push a button. Hero-Soar controls a mobile robot with grippers and sonar sensors; its task is to navigate around a room looking for cups to retrieve.

Robo-Soar and Hero-Soar cope with the demands of external interaction by taking advantage of the three different ways that Soar can intend actions: by recognition, by deliberate operator selection, and by unrestricted problem solving. At the lowest level, actions can be evoked by a single chunk in recognition memory. This supports high-speed response for automatic reflexes, such as stopping the wheel motors when Hero-Soar detects an object in its path. No deliberation is involved, hence the action cannot be modulated by additional knowledge. At the next level of control, Soar chooses an action by selecting an operator in a problem space. For example, in Robo-Soar operators exist for **close-gripper**, **open-gripper**, and **move-gripper**. At each decision cycle, recognition memory retrieves all the relevant preferences about what action to do next, and the decision procedure interprets these preferences to make a unique selection. Thus, the decision is based upon an integration of all immediately available knowledge, rather than an isolated stimulus. This makes Soar *interruptible,* as at each decision cycle any operator can be proposed and considered (e.g., the operator to push the button). The cost of bringing more knowledge to bear is time. However, the decision cycle is fast enough (about ten decisions per second) that the operator level effects reactive execution. When Soar lacks the knowledge to select the next action uniquely, an impasse arises. Soar responds by formulating this selection as a problem to be solved in a problem space. Planning is but one of a number of methods available. For example, Soar could ask an outside agent for help. Once the impasse is resolved, chunks are added to recognition memory that will allow the decision to be made in the future without problem solving. Thus, as in NL-Soar (Figure 2), chunking supports the conversion of deliberate processing to reactive execution.

Robo-Soar and Hero-Soar are not psychological models of perception and action. However, whether the goal is to build a mobile robot or model human behavior, the functional demands of working in a dynamic, uncertain environment are the same. From the UTC perspective, the Robo/Hero-Soar work establishes that Soar is sufficient to handle some of these demands and permits the exploration of how perception and motor behavior integrate with central cognition and learning. It paves the way for adopting psychologically realistic perceptual and motor systems.

Browser-Soar (John)

The goal of the Browser-Soar work is to model how humans interact with a reactive environment (a computer browser) in a rapid perception-action loop [5]. Browser-Soar is intended to be a detailed psychological model of the moment-by-moment interaction.[3] Browsers are application programs that allow multiple access paths to data bases via recognition of pointers (as opposed to retrieval by a query command language). The use of browsers is characterized by both deliberate search and opportunistic switches in search strategy. The specific browser studied is the on-line help system for cT, an interactive graphics programming language[4]. This browser consists of three windows: one provides access to topics via a hierarchical menu, another

---

[3]Browser-Soar does not yet interface with actual robotic effectors and perceptual devices.

[4]cT was developed at the Center for the Design of Educational Computing (CDEC), Carnegie Mellon University.

provides access via an alphabetic list, and the third displays the help text for a selected topic.

Browser-Soar consists of a set of problem spaces that provide the capability to search deliberately through the help windows, while allowing recognition of new items to trigger knowledge at any time that may change the search strategy. The top problem space in Browser-Soar (**Browse**) is entered when an impasse arises in the task space for programming in the cT language. A browsing episode involves bringing up the help window, finding the appropriate help, and applying the newly found information to the problem at hand. Each of these activities corresponds to an operator in the **Browse** space. Currently, Browser-Soar implements the **find-appropriate-help** operator. Applying this operator results in an impasse because the operator cannot be implemented by recognition. Soar responds by setting up another problem space, with operators that define the search criteria (e.g., what labels to look for in the help windows), define the evaluation criteria (how to decide that some piece of information will actually help resolve the impasse in the task space), carry out the search, and evaluate the search results. Each of these operators is also implemented in a problem space; for example, carrying out the search for the defined criteria is accomplished in a space with operators that select among search methods and execute them. At the bottom of the problem space hierarchy are motor operators that control mouse and keyboard actions, and cognitive operators that can be applied with directly available knowledge. The operators in Browser-Soar can be viewed as deliberate goals, and this organization is useful for modeling the goal-oriented component of browsing as well as the mechanics of manipulating the windows used for browsing. Data-driven, opportunistic behavior emerges because an additional operator, **evaluate-new-items**, is proposed whenever new information is brought within the scope of attention (**evaluate-new-items** is available in every Browser-Soar problem space). The current problem solving is thus *interrupted* (as in Robo/Hero-Soar) so the new items may be considered, possibly suggesting a more relevant path to pursue.

Browser-Soar simulates in detail a 67 second episode of a cT programmer using the on-line help to try to find a particular graphics command. The simulation shows the user's behavior to be largely GOMS-like [2], i.e. a *routine* cognitive skill, even though, because of the continuous rapid feedback, the behavior might seem more open and intelligently spontaneous. On the other hand, the episode contains three failed accesses of help text and two changes of search strategy. To handle these requires forms of control that lie outside of the GOMS-style procedural hierarchy (e.g., the interrupt). Thus, Browser-Soar not only shows that this browsing behavior is GOMS-like, but characterizes the ways in which it departs from that simple model.

MAKING PROGRESS TOWARD A UNIFIED THEORY OF COGNITION

We now step back from an examination of specific models to look at how Soar as a whole is developing. Breadth should be the hallmark of a UTC. In fact, a UTC effort that engages a large number of independent investigators will by nature proceed breadth-first. Soar certainly fits this model, and continues to cover a wide range of cognitive phenomena (Figure 1)[5]. The task variety exhibited in Figure 1 ranges from traditional problem solving tasks like Tower of Hanoi, to highly skilled tasks such as natural language, to planning and interacting in a dynamic external environment. The span of time-scales is also evident from Figure 1, ranging from immediate response tasks to developmental tasks. We are beginning to take advantage of *cross-domain integration*. By integrating different capabilities to model a whole task, we can bring more constraints to bear and reduce theoretical degrees of freedom. This kind of integration is evident in the close relation between NL-Soar and the series completion model (SC-Soar), and in work on taking

[5]We talk about individual attempts to use Soar as a cognitive theory as if they were separate systems, and give them unique names, such as XX-Soar. In fact, each such system is the same Soar, but with different knowledge. Such knowledge is often ad-hoc, which poses a problem of identifying the contributions of the theory, but this is a problem for all of psychology. See [11] for an approach to this problem with Soar.

instructions (NL-Soar, BI-Soar, and IR-Soar [11]).

In addition to achieving wide coverage, Soar must ultimately provide theories that press the scientific frontiers of specific domains. Soar is beginning to achieve such depth in diverse ways. The immediate behavior models provide *zero-parameter predictions* of performance times for simple reaction, choice reaction, transcription typing, and stimulus-response compatibility tasks [4, 13]. IR-Soar(Syl), the syllogistic reasoning model [15, 16], has recently been extended to give a detailed account of *individual differences*. The Browser-Soar, Data-Soar [24], Generic Design [14], and TOH-Soar [21] models provide *simulations of thinking aloud protocols* for their respective tasks. The Tower of Hanoi simulation is particularly interesting as it uses chunking to model strategy change. Figure 1 notes some of the different ways that Soar theories model behavior: accounting for individual differences (I), simulating protocols (P), providing qualitative coverage of phenomena (Q), demonstrating the sufficiency of Soar to accomplish the task (S), and making zero parameter predictions (Z).

Soar theories can be novel in their predictions and explanations, and/or synthetic, by incorporating existing theories and well understood mechanisms. For example, besides providing a new theory of individual differences, IR-Soar(Syl) is synthetic in its incorporation of the theory of mental models [6]. Browser-Soar is essentially a GOMS-like model, but introduces new control mechanisms. NL-Soar is synthetic in its assimilation of existing linguistic knowledge, but is novel in its method for automatically becoming recognitional. In contrast, the immediate behavior theory builds mostly on previous work in HCI [2, 3], while the model of the balance beam task [13] is completely unique to Soar.

FUTURE DIRECTIONS

We believe it is now fair to assess Soar as a genuine candidate for becoming a generally useful UTC. Soar's breadth is impressive and there are beginning to be places where it makes specific contributions at the frontier. However, the coverage remains quite patchy, which substantially diminishes the assessment of Soar as a coherent theory. Also, Soar efforts often evolve along idiosyncratic paths, viewed against the standard ways theory and data develop in psychology. For instance, NL-Soar's mechanism for the transition from deliberate to recognitional comprehension emerges well before NL-Soar confronts any standard linguistic or psycholinguistic phenomena. There are reasons for this priority, namely, the functional necessity of creating and growing the mass of **comprehend-word** operators. But it leaves NL-Soar deficient when evaluated by current criteria in either linguistics or psycholinguistics. More examples can be easily found. Thus, our net assessment is that Soar must still be viewed as nascent, and a substantial wait-and-see attitude is still justified.

Yet if one looks for encouraging results, they are also easily discerned. Integration of perception, cognition, and motor behavior is proceeding, although much still needs to be done. The little cluster of integration of language comprehension (NL-Soar), immediate reasoning (IR-Soar), instruction-taking (BI-Soar), and concept formation (SC-Soar) is an important harbinger.

Important changes are occurring that involve evolution of the Soar architecture itself. We have shifted to an underlying processing of states by continuous modification rather than discrete copying [10]. We continue to move toward using an *annotated models* representation [16] in all of our systems. The effort is already underway to extend Soar perception to model visual attention [27]. We have become convinced that the existing recognition memory is computationally unrealistic, so work is in progress to examine alternative formulations [25]. We are also exploring the possibility of implementing the Soar architecture using a neural network [17].

Acknowledgements

Many thanks to Thad Polk and Kathryn Swedlow for useful comments. This work was supported by the Information Sciences Division, Office of Naval Research, under contract N00014-86-K-0678, and by the National Science Foundation fellowship program in which Richard Lewis participates. The views expressed in this paper are those of the authors and do not necessarily reflect those of the supporting agencies. Reproduction in whole or in part is permitted for any purpose of the United States government. Approved for public release; distribution unlimited.

References

[1] Allen, J. **Natural Language Understanding**. Benjamin/Cummings, Menlo Park, CA, 1987.

[2] Card, S., Moran, T. P., and Newell, A. **The Psychology of Human-Computer Interaction**. Erlbaum, Hillsdale, NJ, 1983.

[3] John, B. E. *Contributions to Engineering Models of Human-Computer Engineering*. Department of Psychology, Carnegie Mellon University, May 1988. *Ph.D. Thesis*.

[4] John, B. E. *Extensions of GOMS analyses to expert performance requiring perception of dynamic visual and auditory information*. To appear in the *Proceedings of the Conference on Human Factors and Computing Systems*, April, 1990.

[5] John, B. E., Newell, A., and Card, S. *Browser-Soar: A GOMS-like model of a highly interactive task. Talk presented as the Human Computer Interaction Consortium Winter Workshop, San Diego, CA, February 12, 1990.*

[6] Johnson-Laird, P. **Mental Models**. Harvard, Cambridge, MA, 1983.

[7] Laird, J. E., Hucka, M., Yager, E. S., and Tuck, C. M. *Correcting and extending domain knowledge using outside guidance*. in: **Proceedings of the Seventh International Conference on Machine Learning**. 1990.

[8] Laird, J. E., Newell, A., and Rosenbloom, P. S. *Soar: An architecture for general intelligence*. **Artificial Intelligence**, vol. 33 (1987), pp. 1–64.

[9] Laird, J. E. and Rosenbloom, P. S. *Integrating planning, execution, and learning in Soar for external environments*. February 1990. *Artificial Intelligence Laboratory, The University of Michigan. An earlier version of this paper will appear in the 1990 AAAI Spring Symposium Workshop on Planning in Uncertain, Unpredictable, and Changing Environments.*

[10] Laird, J. E., Swedlow, K., Altmann, E., and Congdon, C. B. *Soar 5 User's Manual*. 1990. *In preparation.*

[11] Lewis, R. L., Newell, A., and Polk, T. A. *Toward a Soar theory of taking instructions for immediate reasoning tasks*. in: **Proceedings of the Eleventh Annual Conference of the Cognitive Science Society**. 1989, pp. 514–521.

[12] Miller, C. S. and Laird, J. E. *A Simple, Symbolic Model for Associative Learning and Retrieval*. March 1990. *Artificial Intelligence Laboratory, The University of Michigan. Unpublished.*

[13] Newell, A. **Unified Theories of Cognition**. Harvard University Press, Cambridge, Massachusetts, 1990. *In press.*

[14] Pirolli, P. *Generic design. Talk presented at the Seventh Soar Workshop, Carnegie Mellon University, Pittsburgh, PA, February 23-25, 1990.*

[15] Polk, T. A. and Newell, A. *Modeling human syllogistic reasoning in Soar*. in: **Proceedings of the Tenth Annual Conference of the Cognitive Science Society**. 1988, pp. 181–187.

[16] Polk, T. A., Newell, A., and Lewis, R. L. *Toward a unified theory of immediate reasoning in Soar*. in: **Proceedings of the Eleventh Annual Conference of the Cognitive Science Society**. 1989, pp. 506–513.

[17] Rosenbloom, P. S. *A symbolic goal-oriented perspective on connectionism and Soar*. in: **Connectionism in Perspective**, edited by R. Pfeifer, Z. Schreter, F. Fogelman-Soulie, and L. Steels. Elsevier (North-Holland), Amsterdam, The Netherlands, 1989, pp. 245–263.

[18] Rosenbloom, P. S. and Aasman, J. *Knowledge Level and Inductive Uses of Chunking (EBL)*. February 1990. *Information Sciences Institute, University of Southern California. Unpublished.*

[19] Rosenbloom, P. S., Laird, J. E., and Newell, A. *The chunking of skill and knowledge*. in: **Working Models of Human Perception**, edited by H. Bouma and A. Elsendoorn. Academic Press, London, England, 1988, pp. 391–410.

[20] Rosenbloom, P. S., Laird, J. E., Newell, A., and McCarl, R. *A preliminary analysis of the Soar architecture as a basis for general intelligence*. in: **Proceedings of the Workshop on Foundations of Artificial Intelligence**, edited by D. Kirsh and C. Hewitt. MIT Press, Cambridge, Massachusetts, 1989.

[21] Ruiz, D. and Newell, A. *Tower-noticing triggers strategy-change in the Tower of Hanoi: A Soar model*. in: **Proceedings of the Eleventh Annual Conference of the Cognitive Science Society**. 1989, pp. 522–529.

[22] Simon, H. A. and Kotovsky, K. *Human acquisition of concepts for sequential patterns*. **Psychological Review**, vol. 70 (1963), pp. 534–546.

[23] Simon, T. *Modeling conceptual development: A computational account of conservation learning*. in: **Computational Approaches to Concept Formation**, edited by D. Fisher and M. Pazanni. Morgan Kaufmann Publishers, Inc., Los Altos, California, 1990. *In press.*

[24] Steier, D. and Adelson, B. *Data-Soar: Simulating a student learning about data structures. Talk presented at the Seventh Soar Workshop, Carnegie Mellon University, Pittsburgh, PA, February 23-25, 1990.*

[25] Tambe, M. and Rosenbloom, P. S. *Eliminating expensive chunks by restricting expressiveness*. in: **Proceedings of the Eleventh International Joint Conference on Artificial Intelligence**. 1989, pp. 731–737.

[26] Ward, B. *A Soar-Based Intelligent Tutor for Electrostatics*. May 1988. *Thesis proposal, Computer Science Department, Carnegie Mellon University.*

[27] Wiesmeyer, M. and Laird, J. E. *A Computer Model of 2D Visual Attention*. March 1990. *Artificial Intelligence Laboratory, The University of Michigan. Unpublished.*

[28] Young, R. M. and Whittington, J. *Using a knowledge analysis to predict conceptual errors in text-editor usage*. To appear in the *Proceedings of the Conference on Human Factors and Computing Systems*, April, 1990.

CHAPTER 52

Applying an Architecture for General Intelligence to Reduce Scheduling Effort

M. J. Prietula, W. Hsu, D. M. Steier, and A. Newell, Carnegie Mellon University

Abstract

A system called *Merle-Soar* is described which demonstrates how a specific architecture for general intelligence and learning (Soar) can be used to reduce scheduling effort when solving simple scheduling problems. In particular, we describe how Merle-Soar schedules sequences of jobs on a single bottleneck machine in a job shop. The knowledge of dispatching, acquired from examining how a human expert performs the task, is cast as search rules. A study was conducted which examined the extent to which learning could contribute to decreases in scheduling effort; specifically, the contribution of learning *within-tasks* was explored — the change in reasoning effort while solving a particular scheduling problem as knowledge is accumulated from successive trials. The results indicated that dramatic reductions in scheduling effort (in terms of the Soar architecture) were obtained. Knowledge gained early in the scheduling task was subsequently applied later in the task to reduce deliberation, and knowledge gained from one trial successfully reduced deliberation effort in subsequent trials. Additionally, the reduction exhibited the general power law of learning documented in psychological studies of skill acquisition.

1. Introduction

Experts argue effectively that to compete in the global marketplace, it is essential to build a strong manufacturing base [Cohen and Zysman, 1987]. Within manufacturing, production scheduling is one of the most important, yet one of the most difficult, tasks that must be performed. Decisions regarding what job to run on which machine at what time must be made continually. This is quite problematic, as scheduling problems are often dominated by many constraints that may be quite difficult to quantify and even simple versions, or even sub-components, of the task quickly become NP-hard, requiring approximate, rather than exact, techniques [Bitran and Yanasse, 1982; Florian, Lenstra and Rinnooy Kan, 1980; Hax and Candea, 1984]. Furthermore, investigations of production environments that are competitive, such as the just-in-time systems, have shown they are extremely sensitive to scheduling effects [Krajewski, King, Ritzman and Wong, 1983; Ritzman and Krajewski, 1983].

Over the past decades, insights and advances have been made in scheduling theory [e.g., Graves, 1981]. For the most part, this success has been the direct result of efforts arising from the "traditional" areas of operations research. Complaints, however, are occasionally registered on the (sometimes dramatic) difference between scheduling theory and practice [McKay, Safayeni and Buzacott, 1988]. When the nature of an actual scheduling situation diverges from the highly constrained artifacts of scheduling theory, the fragility of the theoretical solutions are quickly evidenced.

Attempts at avoiding the combinatorics of the scheduling problem have been addressed in somewhat different (though not necessarily mutually exclusive) perspectives by various researchers. One perspective has been to decompose the scheduling problem in order to provide the human scheduler with specific decision support tools for the more complex components [e.g., Morton, Lawrence, Rajagopolan and Kekre, 1988], which necessitates a detailed and critical investigation into the nature of how human capabilities and scheduling tasks can be integrated [see Sanderson, 1988].

A second stream of research, and the one to which this paper is addressed, attempts to apply artificial intelligence (AI) techniques to the scheduling process.

AI approaches to scheduling as of 1986 are surveyed in Steffen [1986], with several systems emerging since that review, such as SONIA [Collinot, LePape and Pinoteau, 1988], OPAL [Bensana, Bel and Dubois, 1988], CALLISTO [Sathi, Morton and Roth, 1988], DEVISER [Vere, 1983], Micro-Boss [Sadeh, 1991], PLANEX [Zozaya-Gorostiza, Hendrickson and Rehak, 1989], ALPLAN [Arff and Hasle, 1989], Dynamic Rescheduler [Brown, 1988], IPPS [Lee and Kang, 1988], INCS [Matsuo, Shang and Sullivan, 1989], PAMS [Lee and Suh, 1988], an FMS system described by Bruno, Elia and Laface [1986], and a semiconductor manufacturing application described by Savell, Perez and Koh [1989]. Furthermore, additional approaches are described in recent special issues of the *Journal of the Operational Research Society* edited by Doukidis and Paul [1990a,b]. The most extensive efforts have emerged from the ISIS experimental job-shop scheduling systems [Fox and Smith, 1984], which incorporate multiple levels of abstraction and a progressive constraint relaxation approach within a frame-based system. The concepts of ISIS have been extended into a series of OPIS systems [Ow and Smith, 1987, 1988; Ow, Smith and Thirez, 1988; Smith, Fox and Ow, 1986; Smith, Ow, Potvin, Muscettola and Matthys, 1990] which use what they call "multi-perspective scheduling" that relies on a blackboard architecture (see Englemore and Morgan [1988]) implementing constraint-based techniques in an opportunistic fashion to focus the scheduling effort. Recent efforts by that group have focused on distributed approaches [Sycara, Roth, Sadeh and Fox, 1991].

Both approaches (if a distinct dichotomy is allowed) bring different perspectives to the problem and, consequently, succeed and fail in different ways. In fact, Glover and McMillan [1986] convincingly demonstrate the success of integrating search methods from AI with traditional operations research techniques by solving versions of a real-world scheduling problem exceeding four million variables (with several thousand contraints) on a personal computer in thirty minutes within a few percent of optimal.

It is the purpose of this paper to provide another perspective which is a variation on the theme afforded by the current AI approaches to scheduling. Specifically, none of the AI systems discussed effectively modify the results of their scheduling tactics in a manner that can reduce effort on subsequent encounters — that is, none can *learn* from experience. Recently, however, researchers have begun to examine the role that machine learning can play in scheduling and much of this interest is focused around the application of *genetic algorithms* to the task.[1] For example, Hilliard and Liepins [1988] describe their experiences in configuring a system to discover the rule

[1] Genetic algorithms require that the optimization parameter set be configured as a finite-length string of symbols defined over a finite and well-defined alphabet. Subsequent search is implemented through the invocation of operators which evaluate, propagate and eliminate collections

which minimizes tardiness in a simple, single machine case. Whitley, Starkwearther and Fuquay [1989] present interesting work on addressing the Traveling Salesman Problem and have adapted it for scheduling. Davis [1985] presents an approach to solving a simple, but classic form, of a job-shop scheduling problem with a genetic algorithm. Subsequently, Cleveland and Smith [1989] provide a series of experiments in an investigation of alternative configurations of genetic algorithms for scheduling flow-shop release times. Finally, Shaw and Whinston [1989] focuses on scheduling a flexible manufacturing system at the operations level which involves assignment of jobs to machine sequences. The approach taken in this system is basically a non-linear planning system which, however, is augmented with an inductive capability to guide the selection of alternative scheduling rules based on an appropriate training set of manufacturing patterns.

Although this path of research is both interesting and promising, a few comments can be made regarding how some of the characteristics of the genetic algorithm approaches to scheduling constrain certain types of applications or the type of specific research questions which can be asked. First, learned rules are not incorporated into scheduling in real-time. Representative data must be accumulated and presented to the algorithm as a training set from which the set of rules may be induced. Second, the type of knowledge that can be gained is limited in a particular system to what can be anticipated at system-design time. What is required is a specific characterization of the parameters of interest and the objective function to determine acceptable configurations for selection. Third, as rules evolve, the ancestors are disgarded and rendered inapplicable to the problem at hand or any subsequent problems. In the parlance of genetic algorithms, they have "lost" the battle for survival. Fourth, the movement from one rule to another is random. In fact, an element of randomness is fundamental to (the success of) the approach. An explanation of why one rule evolved from another centers around jointly considering the random events of a reformulation algorithm (that configure the new versions of rules) and the specified objective function (to choose the best one). Finally, a deliberate reformulation of the task that would involve symbolic representations is not possible with genetic algorithms. For example, much of the power of the symbolic approaches resides in the ability to exploit a strong domain theory (if one exits). These observations are not offered as criticisms, but serve to define, in part, the distinction between the genetic algorithm approach and other syntactic inductive methods to learning and

of those symbols in a manner which can effectively find optimal, or near-optimal, solutions in domains which are discontinuous, noisy, and multimodal [Goldberg, 1989]. Some authors characterize the approach as a "modified Monte Carlo" technique [Forsyth and Rada, 1986].

the approach we present in this paper. Our approach focuses on the resuability of the "learned skills" for problem solving and may be categorized as a type of computational method for speedup and skill acquisition.

We propose that the scheduling task is also amenable to more *symbolic* learning methods which apply domain-independent methods to acquire new knowledge about the domain. Such approaches to machine learning are also generally emerging. Some of these systems learn control rules to assist its brute-force search method, such as SAGE [Langley, 1985], while others learn macro-operators to assist their heuristic search algorithm [Iba, 1985].[2] The explanation-based learning component of the PRODIGY system [Minton, 1988, 1990] learns search control rules that improve the performance of its backwards-chaining problem-solver.[3] SteppingStone [Ruby and Kibler, 1989] learns new subgoal sequences to resolve impasses based on the results of means-ends-analysis and forward search. PRODIGY and its variants [Carbonell, Knoblock and Minton, 1990; Etzioni, 1990; Knoblock 1991; Minton, 1988] has been applied to several tasks, including a simple scheduling task. Finally, the goal-directed conceptual aggregation system of Chaturvedi [Chaturvedi, 1989; Chaturvedi, Hutchinson and Nazareth, in press] employs a conceptual clustering algorithm which interacts with a simulation and a database in order to generate schedules.

There are fundamental disparities in underlying architectures and assumptions that would make direct comparisons of different systems difficult [cf. Minton, 1990]. However, despite the differences, there is a similarity in that these symbolic systems propose that significant improvements in problem solving performance are to be gained, in the long run, by understanding how a general learning mechanism can adapt to the specificities of a task over time. That is, if a machine can be configured to adapt to the demands of the task *automatically* and learn to improve its performance in response to those demands, then that machine will discover the best ways to solve problems (i.e., what knowledge is to be brought to bear) in the service of the goals presented. In fact, such systems serve as models of skill development; that is,

---

2 Macro-operators may be viewed as the composed sequence of simpler operators for solving a problem. The value of this approach lies with its ability to handle what are called *non-serializable* subgoals — subgoals that once satisfied, must be subsequently violated to achieve progress toward the solution [Korf, 1985].

3 *Explanation-based learning* methods focus on analyzing and generalizing from a training example the features/components that comprise the sufficient conditions for concept description. This is generally in contrast to the more statistically-driven inductive methods which require many instances to formulate concept hypotheses. Mitchell, Keller and Kedar-Cabelli [1986] propose a unified approach called *explanation-based generalization* which presents explanations which can serve as a form of "proof," if the domain theory is complete and consistent.

mechanisms affording the development of machine expertise.

In this paper we describe a symbolic system that incorporates such a general learning mechanism and applies it to a scheduling task with the objective of reducing the amount of effort requiring to produce a schedule. The mechanism is embodied in a software system, called Soar, that characterizes all symbolic goal-oriented behavior as search in problem spaces (see below) and serves as an architecture for general intelligent behavior [Laird, Newell and Rosenbloom, 1987]. Therefore, it greatly facilitates the integration of various types of knowledge, such as heuristics, control strategies, macro-operators, intermediate subgoals, and declarative knowledge, which can (and often must) be brought to bear in solving (and learning how to solve) difficult problems. The scheduling task itself is small, but is derived from a real scheduling task we have investigated elsewhere [Hsu, Prietula, Thompson and Ow, in press; Prietula, Hsu and Ow, 1991] and serves to illustrate how scheduling problems may be cast and investigated with this approach. We do not describe HOW the solution to the scheduling problem itself was crafted. The particular solution strategy was extracted from detailed analyses of an expert's methods conducted over several months. The production rules in Merle-Soar represent a subset of the documented method of the expert. Here we wish to investigate learning in the context of a simple scheduling problem rather than solving the particular scheduling problem itself.

We first summarize the Soar architecture and explain the assumptions and evidence supporting the general validity of the approach. We then explain the specific task environment within which the scheduling problems reside and discuss the configuration of the Soar system we have developed to solve this problem — Merle-Soar. Following this, we describe the study in which we examined how Merle-Soar's capacity to learn could reduce scheduling effort when applied to tasks that did not vary from trial to trial — *within-task transfer* of knowledge.

2. The Soar Architecture

Soar is a system which characterizes all symbolic goal-oriented behavior as search in problem spaces and serves as an architecture for general intelligent behavior [Laird, Newell and Rosenbloom, 1987; Newell, 1980][4] A *problem space* defines a set of states (i.e., specific situations in some aspect of the problem domain) that can be reached within that problem space, and an associated collection of *operators*. Operator applications move Soar from state to state and, hence, search in the problem space.

4 The form of the architecture described in this section (and the experiments conducted in this paper) refer to Soar 4.5. Subsequent versions of Soar differ in some details, but the overall characterizations do not.

On entering the problem space, Soar defines an initial state and a desired state (or states), articulating the goal condition for search termination.

Decisions are the primitive acts of the system used for the search (i.e., generation and selection) of appropriate problem spaces, states and operators as well as the application of operators for new state configuration, in the pursuit of goals specified in a *goal hierarchy*. To make decisions, Soar operates in terms of a two-phase *decision cycle*. Each cycle starts with an *elaboration phase*. During this phase, the description of the current situation is elaborated with relevant information from Soar's long-term memory. All long-term memory knowledge in Soar is realized as productions; when the antecedent conditions of a production are met, it adds results to a globally accessible working memory, which describes the problem solving situation.[5] All productions are "fired" in parallel and no conflict resolution is performed to restrict the application of productions during this phase. When no more productions can fire, the second phase of the decision cycle, the *decision procedure*, is entered. The decision procedure interprets the preferences in the working memory. In the Soar architecture, *preferences* are used to describe the desirability and acceptability of the alternatives being considered for selection. If the preferences uniquely identify an object to be selected, such as a particular problem space, state or operator, the decision is made and the decision cycle repeats, starting with another elaboration phase. However, when the preferences are incomplete or inconsistent, an impasse occurs, and the Soar architecture automatically sets up a subgoal to resolve the impasse. Given a subgoal, Soar applies its full problem solving capability and knowledge (as it did for the higher-level goals) to resolve the impasse that caused the subgoal. There are four types of impasses in the Soar architecture:

- **Tie**, when multiple objects are considered as acceptable for a given goal;
- **Conflict**, when two or more objects have mutually conflicting preferences (e.g, both $object_a > object_b$ and $object_b > object_a$ hold at the same time, where $>$ indicates a strict preference ordering);
- **No-change**, when the elaboration phase runs to quiescence without distinquishing preferences for any objects; and,
- **Rejection**, when some object is explicitly determined to be not considered.[6]

---

5 *Productions* are if-then rules that consist of "conditions" (the if-part of the rule) and "actions" (the then-part of the rule) that occur when the conditions are satisfied [see Brownston, Farrell, Kant and Martin, 1985].

6 Note that there is a difference between a lack of knowledge to suggest an object, which is a form of indifference that must be resolved via subgoal activity, and *rejection* which reflects the result of knowledge that inhibits consideration for a particular alternative.

Subgoals are satisfied in Soar by finding knowledge that terminates an impasse in a higher level space, and thus allows the problem-solving to proceed. The type of knowledge required depends on the type of impasse. For a tie, it will be the knowledge about relative desirability of the tied candidates that allows Soar to conclude that one candidate is better than the rest. For a conflict, the knowledge should say that it is in fact necessary to reject or select one of the candidates. For rejection impasses, problem solving in the subgoal needs to discover a new acceptable candidate. What Soar's subgoaling mechanisms provides, then, is a framework for resolving all possible impasses that could be encountered, and an efficient method for detecting that they have been resolved (i.e when the decision procedure for a higher level goal produces a change). Soar does not address the specifics of what domain specific knowledge is to be used in impasse resolution, or to evaluate quality of solutions; Soar must still be provided with that, and we discuss these issues in the context of our scheduling system later in the paper.

A key component of this architecture is the learning capability which relies on a common universal mechanism — chunking [Laird, Rosenbloom and Newell, 1986]. Soar learns by producing chunks of knowledge (productions) as a result of resolving impasses, that is, as a result of achieving a (sub)goal. The chunks produced by Soar within the impasse resolution process reflect the relevant objects in working memory that caused the impasse (crafted in the antecedent portion of the generated production) and the subsequent results obtained by the subgoaling search effort (crafted in the consequent portion of the generated production). Thus the results of subgoaling are chunks that embody knowledge to reduce the search effort by permitting decisions to be made. To the extent that subsequent encounters generate similar impasses, these decisions will be made directly and without further deliberation via subgoaling allowing more direct (and efficient) problem solving. As this process is recursive, it is quite possible to generate impasses (and subgoaling) while attempting to resolve an impasse through subgoaling. However, as the approach to impasse resolution is consistent throughout Soar, the system is not only coherent, but can result in dramatic reductions in problem solving effort through the exploitation of the chunking mechanism in service of the goals it is attempting to achieve. Soar, then, is unique in that goals are created, deliberated upon, and resolved (i.e., terminated) solely by the underlying architecture. The chunks (i.e., knowledge) created by Soar during deliberation are subsequently always available for activation, if appropriate.[7]

[7] This, in effect, reflects the non-destructive nature of the long-term memory component of Soar. Whether or not productions are subsequently activated depends on the specificity of the

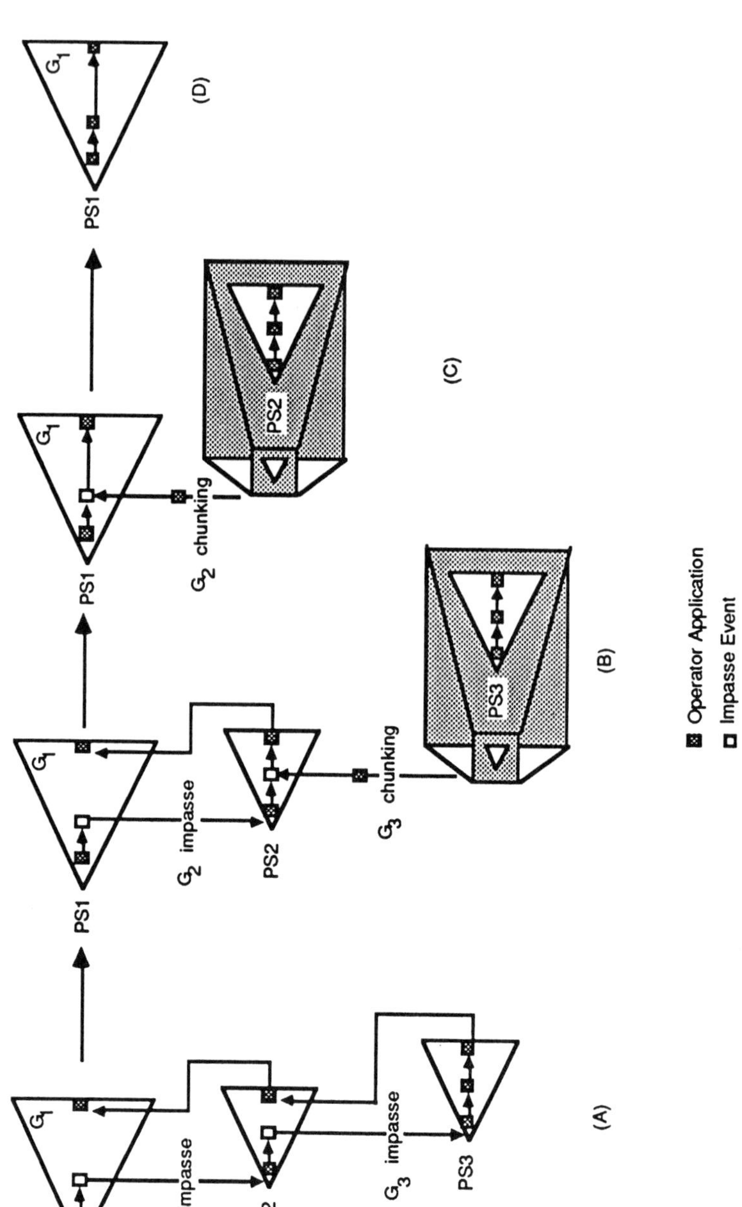

Figure 1. Problem spaces and impasse-driven subgoaling in Soar

Soar offers three modes of learning (chunk formation) during problem solving that determine when chunks are built during the problem solving process. Chunking in *no-learning* mode inhibits the formation of any chunks during problem solving. If the same problem is given to Soar twice in a row, the same amount of effort will be required to produce an answer both times. It functions as an essentially memoryless system where recurring and familiar goals must be repeatedly deliberated upon and resolved. On the other hand, chunking *all-goals* learning mode causes chunks to be formed whenever any subgoal terminates. Given the same problem, Soar will immediately solve it with minimal effort as it is essentially engaging in total task recognition — it recalls all critical aspects of the problem, including its solution. Finally, chunking in *bottom-up* learning mode causes Soar to form chunks only for terminal subgoals (subgoals that have no other subgoals). Subsequent encounters with the same problem will result in additional chunking and, consequently, increasingly better performance. Theoretically, repeated applications of bottom-up learning in this context should demonstrate convergence to all-goals learning with the rate of convergence is predicted by the power law of practice [Newell and Rosenbloom, 1981]. This reflects a quite robust finding in psychology that skill acquisition (cognitive and perceptual-motor), reflected in the improvement in time to perform a task error-free, is often proportional to a power of the amount of practice with the task. The general form can be given relating the time to perform a task, T_n, on the nth trial as: $T_n = T_1 n^{-\alpha}$ where α is a task-dependent constant [Newell and Rosenbloom, 1981]. In the resolution of a goal, several chunks are formed addressing various aspects of the particular goal. The formation of a given chunk within pursuit of that goal occurs as soon as it is possible, rather than waiting for the termination of the goal. This permits intermediately developed knowledge to be available if any further subgoaling (impasses) occur in the attempt to achieve the original subgoal. It is important to note that Soar does not impose a strict ordering on goal attainment. A goal terminates when there is sufficient knowledge to resolve an impasse, regardless of the goal's location on the stack.

Figure 1 illustrates the fundamental concepts in Soar. In Part A of the figure, problem solving begins with an attempt to achieve goal G_1 in the triangular-shaped problem space labelled "PS1." The small boxes within the problem space represent applications of operators to alter the state configuration and achieve progress (hopefully) toward the goal configuration. In PS1, one operator has been successfully applied (hence the shaded box) but an attempt to apply the second operator has

---

context in which the chunks are considered.

generated some sort of impasse event. At this time, Soar generates a subgoal to be resolved, G_2 (representing the resolution of the impasse), invokes a second problem space, PS2, and proceeds to apply operators to achieve G_2. Again, difficulties emerge and a new subgoal, G_3, is defined as an impasse within the PS2 problem space occurs. In Part B of Figure 1, the resolution of the G_3 subgoal within the PS3 problem space is successful and problem solving proceeds in PS2. Assuming no more difficulties in PS2, the goal G_2 is also resolved (Part C of Figure 1) and problem solving in the original problem space, PS1, can continue (Part D).

Note with this figure we can also describe the effects of learning and chunk formation. If no learning was permitted in the prior sequence of events in pursing goal G_1, the entire process would be duplicated (Parts A through D). On the other hand, if bottom-up chunking was enabled, chunks would be formed and retained only in the subgoal hierarchy where no subsequent subgoals where encountered. In Figure 1, this means that chunks are formed while deliberating about G_3 in PS3 (Part B) only. The impasse resulting in goal G_3 and the invocation of PS3 would not occur; however, the impasse generating G_2 (an intermediate subgoal) would occur. With all-goals chunking, all intermediate goals result in chunks, so the resolution of G_2 in PS2 would add to the chunk formation and the impasse generating G_2 would be avoided and the original goal, G_1 would be solved immediately.

Summarizing, Soar is a symbolic system that casts all tasks as a collection of interacting *problem spaces*, where each problem space is associated with *goals* situated within a goal hierarchy. Within a problem space, the symbolic components representing *states* of the problem space are changed by the application of appropriate *operators*. *Subgoals* (and hence new problem spaces) are invoked when problem solving cannot proceed in the current problem space as a result of *impasses*. The resolution of impasses (subgoal success) permit problem solving to continue and forms the basis for learning. One learning mechanism is used universally in Soar, called *chunking*. Control over when chunking occurs defines three forms of learning (including no learning) to ensue. In the next section we describe the scheduling task and the Merle-Soar system.

3. The Task Environment: Producing Windshields

For the experiments described in this paper, we incorporated a simplified version of an actual scheduling problem to demonstrate how such a task may be characterized and investigated within the Soar architecture.[8] The particular scheduling task we

[8] The full version of the scheduling problem has been addressed through the use of a combi-

describe concerns the production of replacement windshields for automobiles. The primary raw materials for producing windshields are glass and vinyl, where each windshield consists of two pieces of glass and one piece of vinyl. The glass needs to be cut and bent, and the vinyl needs to be stretched, screened, and cut before the two can be put together. Further operations such as laminating, vacuuming, and attaching the ancillary parts (e.g., rear-view mirror attachments) are applied before the finished products can be added to the inventory. Figure 2 summarizes this process.

The most critical phase of production is the bending process. In the bending process, two pieces of matched automotive glass are placed on a special rack-holder, called an *iron*, and moved through a large oven, called a *lehr*. As the glass is heated, it softens and bends in a certain shape determined by the interaction of gravity, counterweights on the iron, the particular heating pattern imposed on it, the speed of its route through the lehr, and attributes of the glass itself (e.g., thickness, composition). It continues on the conveyer out of the oven and around the plant to cool before any further assembly can be done. In the plant, the lehr for bending the raw glass is the bottleneck resource. This particular scheduling task includes deciding which windshield glass should be bent at what time and for how long (the length of the time usually determines the quantity of glass to be bent as well). At times, different types of windshield glass can be bent in the same lehr setting (e.g., temperature, humidity, pressure) and therefore can be scheduled to run through the lehr at the same time period without a new setup. However, no more than two different type of windshields will be scheduled in the same time. Setups in this process are generally expensive and require on the average of 45 minutes of down-time for the ovens due to the exchange of iron racks and manipulations to oven settings. On the other hand, if two different, but *compatible*, windshields can be scheduled for the lehr at the same time, only one setup is required for both jobs. Such setup-collapsing schemes are commonly practiced in job-shop scheduling.

The solution to one of these scheduling problems is the generation of a schedule based on a set of supplied orders of the form $\{m_1G_1, m_2G_2, ..., m_nG_n\}$, where m_i is the number of unit-orders for windshield type G_i. Associated with each type is a set of four properties which determine the cross-type compatibility: bend-category (reflect lehr settings for bending), transparency (type of glass), blocksize-length, and block-size width (both reflecting dimensions of the glass to be bent). A schedule is comprised of a set of 3-tuples of the form $[s_1, s_2, t_i]$ where s_1 and s_2 are schedule-

nation of non-learning, artificial intelligence and operations research techniques functioning collaboratively as a "scheduler's workbench" offering an interactive, *mixed-initiative* approach to scheduling complex production environments [Hsu, Prietula, Thompson and Ow, in press].

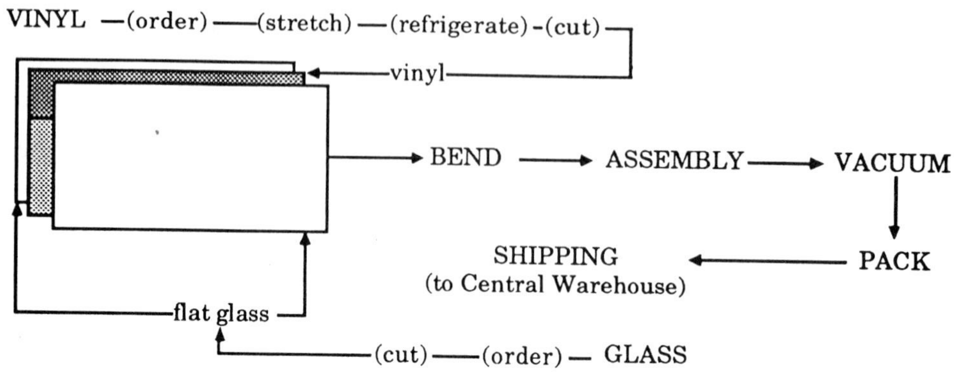

Figure 2. Overview of the windshield production process

reservation slots (reflecting machine capacity) to which unit-orders are bound at time, t_i. For example, a set of orders $\{3A, 2B, 2C\}$ defines three unit-orders of type A and two unit orders each of types B and C. If none of these types are compatible, then a setup is required between each schedule-reservation slot resulting in a schedule that might look like the following:

$$[A, A, t_1], [A, idle, t_2], [setup, t_3], [B, B, t_4], [setup, t_5], [C, C, t_6]$$

Each schedule-reservation slot may contain either (a) an *order* — for the production of a unit-order of a particular windshield type, (b) an *idle time* — indicating that only a portion of a full load is to be run (and that the machine is being underutilized), or (c) a *machine setup-time* — when production on a machine is halted as it is being prepared for another type of job. Given that two schedule-reservation slots are available per time unit, two unit-orders are scheduled together at the same time to bring the lehr up to capacity.

The objectives of the scheduling process are the minimization of finished goods inventory, stock outage, and setup time. In the real-life application, scheduling of the lehrs are done by two employees who have over thirty years of experience between them. Throughout those years, they have developed and relied on effective heuristic methods to schedule lehr production runs. Many of the heuristics they use concern the working conditions of the employees. For example, large jobs tend to exhaust the workers and hence interweaving large and small jobs is desirable. This kind of knowledge is very difficult to factor into traditional scheduling problem solving, yet is fundamental to the formation, diagnosis and repair of schedules, and, consequently, essential to the adoption of scheduling techniques [McKay, Safayeni and Buzacott, 1988]. In this paper we do not address the generation of "optimal" schedules nor do we employ an examination of explicit objective functions; rather, our purpose is to examine a simple version of the task, and employ rudimentary examinations of that version, to begin to understand the methods and implications of crafting scheduling systems that can learn. Thus, it is less a study of scheduling and more of an exploratory study of a learning system that can solve a simple scheduling problem.

4. The Structure of Merle-Soar

Merle-Soar is comprised of 589 productions. Mathematical reasoning (393 productions, 66.7%) is not done via calls to system routines, but through symbolic representation and deliberation as any other problem through a collection of problem spaces and operators. Ancillary productions (69 productions, 11.7%) function as "default" knowledge to facilitate certain aspects of deliberation and representation. The mathematical reasoning and default productions are available for all Soar applications.

The primary scheduling knowledge in Merle-Soar is represented by 131 productions (22%). The productions implement seven basic problem spaces for the scheduling task (Figure 3). Contained within each of the seven problem spaces are various productions which play specific task-independent roles in problem solving. There are six such roles in Soar: problem space proposal, initial state proposal, desired state detection, operator proposal, operator selection, and operator implementation.

Problem space proposal productions detect situations where it is necessary to propose specific problem spaces. *Initial state proposal* propose a specific configuration of structures which represents the objects of interest comprising the problem state. Such state structures may be arbitrarily complex. *Desired state detection* productions monitor the state structure to detect when a goal is achieved. *Operator proposal* productions watch for specific state conditions and suggest operators to try to apply. *Operator selection* productions indicate relative preferences for candidate operators under particular problem-solving conditions. This knowledge is explicitly distinct from the knowledge which proposes operators. Finally, *Operator implementation* productions specify the state changes necessary to apply a selected operator. Examples of each of these are shown in Table 1 along with their English interpretation. The distribution of production types across problem spaces is presented in Table 2.

In order to understand the basics components of Table 1, it is necessary to provide a brief description of Soar productions. The general syntax of the productions resemble those of more traditional forward-chaining production systems, like OPS5 [Brownston at al., 1985].[9] Essentially, the left-hand side of a Soar production (i.e., the conditions which determine if the production is relevant) forms a distinct pattern which is matched to the elements of working memory. If this pattern matches, then one (or possibly more) instantiations of the production are generated. One difference between Soar and other production systems is that most production systems incorporate a form of conflict resolution in which multiple instantiations of productions yield only a single candidate to be applied. Thus the locus of control is the individual *production*. However, in Soar, the focus is on the selection of an appropriate *operator* (defined by several productions).[10] For the most part, the right-hand side (i.e,

[9] Details of the syntax and semantics of Soar can be found in [Laird, Congdon, Altmann and Swedlow, 1990]. For a comparison, see Bruno, Elia and Laface's [1986] description of a scheduling system written in OPS5.

[10] Other significant differences exist and are articulated in the Soar manual [Laird et al., 1990].

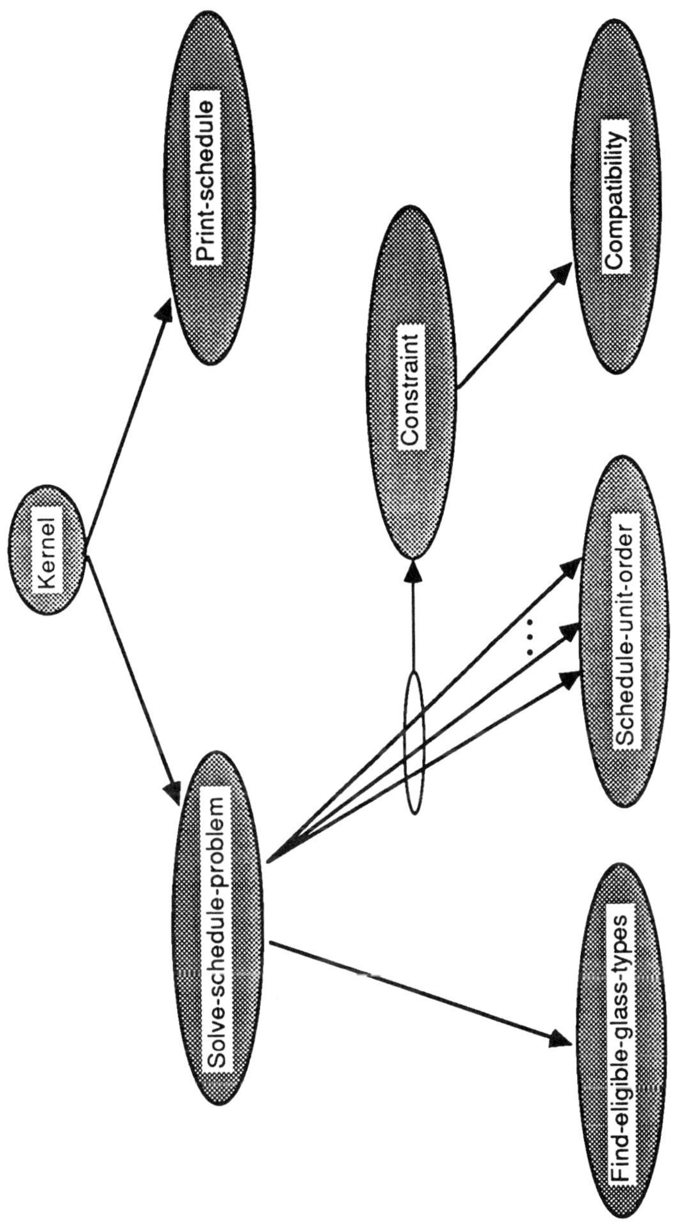

Figure 3. Task-specific problem spaces in Merle-Soar

Table 1. Examples of Primary Merle-Soar Productions

Production Type	Merle-Soar Example	English Interpretation of Production
Problem space proposal	(sp fegt*propose-fegt-problem-space*implement-fegt-op (goal <g> ^object <sq>) (goal <sg> ^operator <sq>) (operator <sq> ^name find-eligible-glass-types) --> (goal <g> ^desired <d>) (preference <p> ^role problem-space ^value acceptable ^goal <g>) (desired <d> ^name find-eligible-glass-types) (problem-space <p> ^name fegt))	If there is an operator no-change impasse while applying the find-eligible-glass-types operator, then propose the fegt problem space in which to resolve the impasse.
Initial state proposal	(sp fegt*propose-initial-state*create-state-object-and-preference (goal <g> ^problem-space <p> ^object <sg>) (problem-space <p> ^name fegt) (goal <sg> ^state <ss>) (state <ss> ^glass-type-list <list>) --> (preference <s> ^role state ^value acceptable ^goal <g> ^state undecided) (state <s> ^glass-type-list <list> ^current-type <list> ^eligible-glass-types <egt>))	If the fegt space has been selected, and the superstate (state in the context immediately above this goal) has a list of known glass types, then propose an initial state with attributes of the list of glass types, a pointer to the current glass type initialized to the head of the complete list, and a new variable to hold the pointer to the eligible glass types.
Desired state detection	(sp fegt*detect-find-eligible-glass-types-done*note-none-eligible (goal <g> ^problem-space <p> ^state <s>) (problem-space <p> ^name fegt) (state <s> ^eligible-glass-types <list> ^done -^eligible-found) --> (eligible-glass-types <list> ^none-eligible true))	If the state in the fegt space has a ^done attribute, indicating all the known glass types have been checked, and no eligible glass types have been found, then mark the eligible glass types list with an attribute saying no eligible types have been found. (Another production will pass this list back up to the supergoal)
Operator proposal	(sp constraint*propose-compatibility-constraint-operator (goal <g> ^problem-space <p> ^state <s>) (problem-space <p> ^name constraint) (state <s> -^compatibility-constraint-applied) --> (preference <q> ^role operator^value acceptable ^goal <g> ^state <s> ^problem-space <p>) (operator <q> ^name compatibility-constraint))	If the constraint space has been selected, and there is no indication on the state that the compatibility-constraint has been checked, then propose as acceptable an operator to apply the compatibility constraint.

Table 1 (continued). Examples of Primary Merle-Soar Productions

Production Type	Merle-Soar Example	English Interpretation of Production
Operator selection	(sp constraint*detect-operator-chosen*create-reject-preference-for-superoperator (goal <g> ^problem-space <p> ^state <s> ^object <sg>) (problem-space <p> ^name constraint) (state <s> ^op-status <os> ^ready-to-select-operator true) (op-status <os> ^operator <sq> ^status <reject>) (status <reject> ^name reject) (goal <sg> ^problem-space <sp> ^state <ss>) (preference <sq> ^role operator^value acceptable ^goal <sg> ^state <ss> ^problem-space <sp>) --> (preference <sq> ^role operator^value reject ^goal <sg> ^state <ss> ^problem-space <sp>))	If in the constraint problem space, and the state indicates that all operators have been evaluated, and one of the operators has been marked for rejection, then create a reject preference for that operator in the supergoal.
Operator application	(sp suo*apply-add-slot-binding (goal <g> ^problem-space <p> ^operator <q> ^state <s>) (problem-space <p> ^name suo) (state <s> -^slot-binding-added <interval>) (operator <q> ^name add-slot-binding ^binding <b> ^interval <interval>) (time-binding <interval> -^slot-binding <b>) --> (operator <q> ^newstateneeded true ^change <a>) (add ^slot-binding-added <interval>) (time-binding <interval> ^slot-binding <b>))	If in the suo (schedule unit order) space, and applying the add-slot-binding operator, augment the operatorto specify that the state should be marked that the operator was applied and add a slot binding to the time binding representing the interval.

Table 2. Distribution of primary productions by type and problem space
(does not include mathematical and default reasoning productions)

Problem Space (PS)	Production Type						TOTAL (by PS)
	PSP	SP	DSD	OP	OI	OS	
1. Kernel	1	1	1	2	2		7
2. Solve-schedule-problem	1	4	3	4	9		21
3. Find-eligible-glass-types	1	1	2	1	4		9
4. Schedule-unit-order	1	1	5	23	7		37
5. Constraint	1	3	5	1	1		11
6. Compatibility	1	4	6	4	16	2	33
7. Print-schedule	1	2	1	1	8		13
TOTAL (by Type:1-7)	7	16	23	36	47	2	131

PSP = Problem Space Proposal, SP = State Proposal, DSD = Desired State Detection
OP = Operator Proposal, OI = Operator Implementation, OS = Operator Selection

condition) of the production involves manipulting preferences for objects and altering objects in the particular state. The pattern elements, referred to as *augmentations* of working memory, are of the form: (class identifier ^attribute value). There can be more than one ^attribute:value pair in an augmentation and variables (expressed as symbols with brackets: <ob1>) can be (and generally are) incorporated. Soar productions must have, via elements in their left-hand side, explicit links to goals which determine the context in which they are to be considered. This is expressed as including a specific augmentation with the class "goal." Other constraints on their specification can be given by providing additional class types (e.g., problem spaces, operators, or objects existing in the state), attributes and variables.

It is important to emphasize several elements of the encoding of scheduling knowledge. First, the granularity of encoding is such that knowledge is spread across many productions, rather than encoded in a singular production representing a particular aspect of an operator (e.g., detection, implementation, selection). Second, there is no *a priori* sequencing imposed upon the productions. Although there are classes of orderings implicit in the architecture (e.g., an operator must be proposed before it can be selected), the exact firings of the productions are a consequence of their relevance to the task at hand (i.e, data-driven) and are augmented by the knowledge accumulating from learning. Third, no production may explicitly invoke another production. This, in effect, is a tacit assumption in most production systems, but rigorously enforced within this architecture. Fourth, all aspects of the scheduling task are encoded in a similar and coherent framework. This permits the application of the learning mechanism to exploit *any* aspect of the problem to its advantage. Finally, we referred to the inital set of Merle-Soar productions as the primary scheduling knowledge. As Merle-Soar learns from experience, the set of productions which comprise it grows accordingly.

The seven problem spaces reflect a specific decomposition of the scheduling problem (see prior Figure 3). The *Kernel* problem space is the top-level space that initiates problem solving and directs the high-level goals in the form of desired-state conditions that are to be achieved by Merle-Soar: solve the scheduling problem and print the results. Initial entry into the Kernel problem space results in an impasse, as the scheduling problem has not been solved and the proposed operator (called "solve-scheduling-problem") cannot be effectively applied. This results in the invocation of the *Solve-scheduling-problem* problem space. When initially selected, the productions in this problem space create a state which is composed of structures representing an empty schedule, the glass orders to be processed, and ancillary components to facilitate processing (e.g., counters). Productions in this space repeatedly monitor the status of the list of glass orders and attempt to propose operators that (a) determine the candidate glass types to schedule, and (b) determines the order to be assigned at a specific time slot. The first type of operator proposal results in the activation of the *Find-eligible-glass-type* problem space which the second invokes the *Schedule-unit-order* problem space. Deliberation in the *Find-eligible-glass-type* problem space is generally concerned with monitoring what orders are available in terms of type and amount. On the other hand, the *Schedule-unit-order* problem space determines what type of glass is to be assigned to the next available slot in the schedule. To accomplish this, explicit considerations of various types of constraints must be considered; therefore, a *Constraint* space exists which is invoked when multiple options (i.e., scheduling alternatives) result in tie impasses.[11] The knowledge of a given class of constraints is grouped within its own problem space. In the Merle-Soar example for this paper, there is one class of constraint programmed and, therefore, one invocable type of constraint problem space, the *Compatibility* problem space which examines certain properties of the possible alternatives for incompatibility (e.g., size, color). Therefore, the configurable schedule alternatives are based on the particular "compatibility mix" of orders presented.

In reviewing Table 2 and the prior discussion, it is important to note that little search-control knowledge has been encoded as productions; rather, search control is cast as operators (a more abstract concept) in problem spaces. The bulk of the knowledge is used to assign an order and a setup, if necessary (i.e., crafting the state), implementing the *Schedule-unit-order* operator (within its own problem space), and computing the results of the compatibility constraint operators contained in the *Compatibility* problem space. In this incarnation of Merle-Soar, the first feasible schedule (i.e., one which does not violate any hard constraints) is accepted. An extension of Merle-Soar can be envisioned in which objective functions were incorporated by using other problem spaces to evaluate the quality of candidate feasible solutions, but this has not been implemented. For now, the search is for a feasible solution with backtracking if it is found that a partial solution cannot be extended to satisfy all constraints.

---

[11] A violation of a *constraint* reflects intolerance with an important assumption, such as, non-compliance with a physical reality that inhibits the production of a feasible solution.

5. The Effects of Learning

To investigate the reduction of scheduling effort by characterizing a scheduling problem in this framework we examined Merl-Soar's performance on a set of small scheduling problems. Eighteen different scheduling problems were run reflecting two independent variables: volume and compatibility. *Volume* reflects the total number of windshield unit-orders (across types) in the set of orders. *Compatibility* refers to whether all (or only some) of the order types can be run contiguously without incurring a setup, as defined by the property values. Each task contained three different job types (A, B, and C) with n unit-orders requested for each type, where $1 \leq n \leq 9$, thus defining nine separate cases specifying nine levels of order volume (3 to 27). One type of compatibility was manipulated in which bend-categories of glass type A was incompatible with types B and C, thus defining two levels of compatibility: all or some.

Three (previously described) learning modes controlling the timing and extent of chunk formation available to Merle-Soar under each condition were investigated: no-learning, all-goals learning, and bottom-up learning. All eighteen problems were run on all three learning conditions with the trace and summary statistics saved for analysis. *no learning* inhibits chunks from being formed, though the problem spaces are still created and explored and subgoals (and the problem) are still resolved. It is an essentially memoryless system. This served as a baseline control condition.[12]

The primary dependent variable for the study is a metric reflecting the amount of deliberation required to solve each problem. The basic units of "reasoning effort" for Soar is called a decision cycle (D_c). A *decision cycle* reflects the combined tasks of examining all of the long-term memory productions that are directly relevant for a particular state and then reviewing the associated preferences to produce a specific decision regarding problem spaces, states and operators. Therefore, the more search required for problem solving, the higher the number of decision cycles — the less search required, the lower the number of resulting decision cycles. Learning is reflected by a reduction in required decision cycles.[13] In addition, information was

12 Recall that *all-goals learning* can result in chunks being created whenever a subgoal is explored. It reflects a one-trial learning capability for a particular task and, when that exact task is again encountered, Soar solves it directly by recognition. In *bottom-up learning*, chunks are created only for the bottom-most, terminal subgoals (i.e., the subgoals which have no subgoals). Except for the smallest of tasks, it takes multiple trials to accumulated the chunks required to solve a particular task by recognition.

13 There are, of course, task-specific limits on the lower limit of decision cycles. If a particular problem (or sub-goal) required a specific sequence of distinct, deterministically chosen

also gathered on the deliberation process (i.e., a trace of the problem solving activity) and the byproduct of deliberation (i.e., the chunks formed).

The first analysis examined the effect of volume levels (v) on scheduling effort as measured by decision cycles (D_c) without learning. The effect is decidedly non-linear and both curves are well-described by logarithmic functions. Figure 4 presents a log-log graph of decision cycles by volume (v) for both sets of schedules. For the All-compatible tasks, the fit reveals an r^2 of .98 with $D_c = 306.8v^{1.41}$. The Some-compatible tasks had a slightly better fit ($r^2 = .99$) with $D_c = 192.5v^{1.47}$. It is clear, then, that increasing the volume of cases to Merle-Soar quickly acrues a penalty in decision cycle costs — scheduling three compatible windshield orders can be accomplished in 1,815 decision cycles, but scheduling twenty-seven compatible orders requires 32,327 decision cycles.

The next step in the analysis was to determine the effect of all-goals learning (occuring within a problem solving trial) on scheduling effort across compatibility types. In effect, this examines the extent to which learning can contribute to the reduction of deliberation effort within a particular trial. The effects were dramatic, with the larger order volumes displaying the larger (proportional) benefits — the effort required for scheduling twenty-seven compatible orders was reduced from 32,327 to 1,156 decision cycles. Figure 5 overlays the plot of decision cycles required when all-goals learning is engaged with Figure 4 (when it was not). In Figure 5 the new curves are plotted non-logarithmically to indicate their relative shape and scale. Higher fit coefficients were obtained with linear (rather than logarithmic) curves with the All-compatible tasks being described with $D_c = 102.4 + 38.2v$ ($r^2 = .99$) and the Some-compatible tasks as $D_c = 163 + 37v$ ($r^2 = .99$). From the data, it cannot be unequivocally determined whether the problem has been "linearized" through the effects of learning or whether the curve growth has been curtailed (through the adjustment of the volume exponents) to approach linearity over the order volumes tested. Further analysis on larger volumes are to be examined. Regardless, all-goals learning does indeed reduce scheduling effort as measured by the decision cycle metric.

The third step in the analysis was to further investigate the nature of learning as revealed by the data from the *bottom-up learning* condition. We iteratively ran Merle-Soar for multiple trials on each of the eighteen scheduling problems until a trial occured where no chunks were further formed, that is, until it solved each

---

operators whose granularity and/or precedence must be retained (e.g., a sequence of robotic movements), these operators would not be "chunked." Rather, learning would involve (if correctly programmed) the acquisition of search control knowledge that would impose operator precedence through explicit preferences.

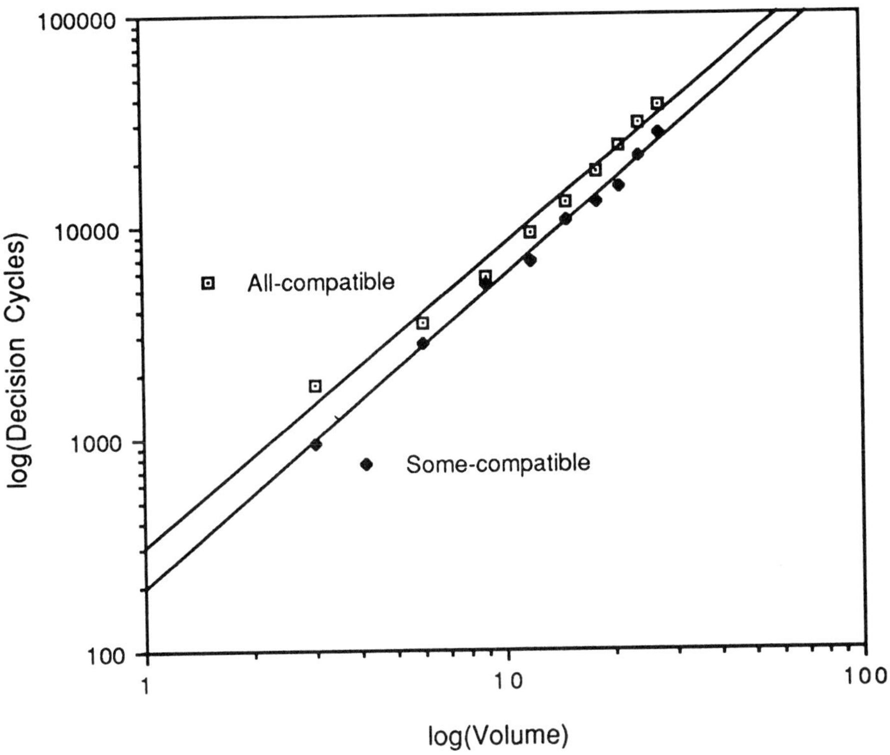

Figure 4. Decision cycle by order volume: no learning

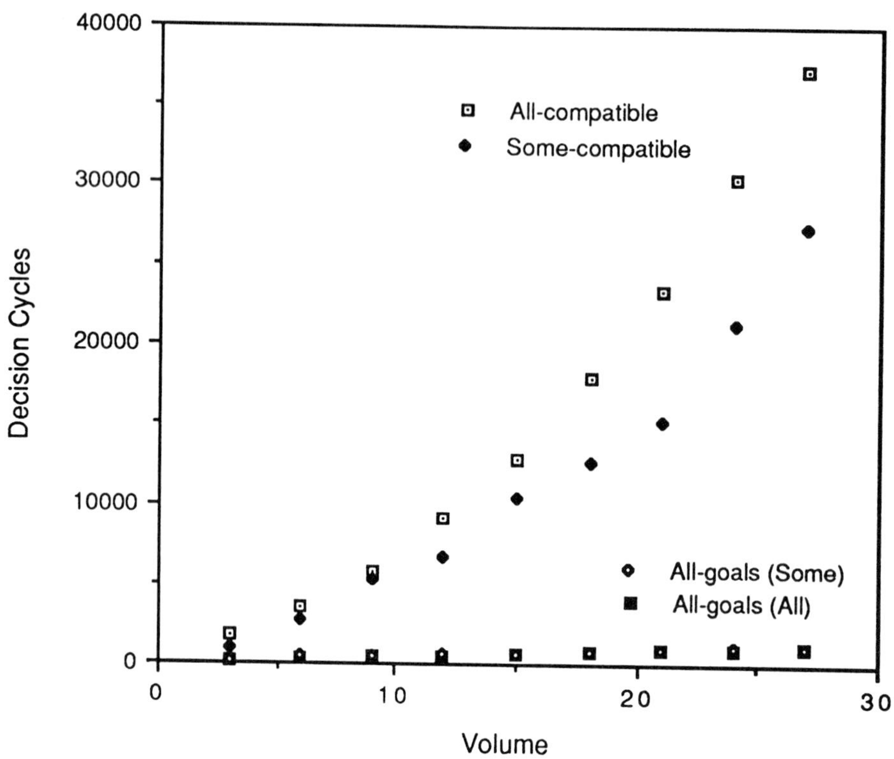

Figure 5. Decision cycle by order volume: all-goals and no learning

particular problem by recognition and did not generate subgoals. All tasks achieved the asymptotic minimum limit of $D_c = 6$ (the minimum number of decision cycles needed to select the problem space, initial state, apply two operators, and obtain their resulting state). What is of interest is the form of the function *describing* the convergence. For example, if the revealed form is linear over the number of trials it takes for convergence to the limit (of $D_c = 6$), then the contribution of knowledge to the solution on each trial is constant; that is, the decrement in deliberation effort between any two trials is a constant. On the other hand, if the convergence is distinctly non-linear, than the amount of contribution of the chunks formed in a trial is a function of when that trial occured.

The results of this analysis indicate that the effects of bottom-up learning are indeed non-linear and, in fact, contribute early in the task to reduce deliberation effort. In Figure 6, we have plotted D_c by $Trial$ for the lowest and highest order volume problems in the Some-compatibile (Some) and All-compatible (All) conditions. These are plotted in log-log format as all curves were well-described by power laws of the form: $D_{cn} = D_{c1}n^{-\alpha}$, where D_{c1} is the number of decision cycles required to solve the problem on the first trial and D_{cn} is the number of decision cycles required on the nth trial. Visually, it can be seen that there is a linear decline in plot, indicating the non-linearity of deliberation effort (D_c) over trials, and that the curves are close to parallel, indicating that the exponent, $-\alpha$, seems to indeed serve as a task-dependent constant showing little variance as volume changes, exhibiting little correlation with the order volume for either the Some-compatible ($r^2 = .19$) or the All-compatible ($r^2 = .43$) conditions. Table 3 summarizes the derived equations for the tasks and presents the associated r^2 of the fit for each. Note that there appears to be a distinctly linear increase in the D_c required for the first trial across conditions. In fact, a linear fit explains the growth in both the Some-compatible ($r^2 = .98$) and the All-compatible ($r^2 = .94$) conditions.

Thus, learning can greatly facilitate deliberation as measured by D_c, and that learning is manifest by the production of chunks, therefore, an analysis of chunk production was performed based on all-goals learning. Given the initial set of Merle-Soar productions (589), the amount of accumulated productions ranged from 38 (Volume = 3, All-compatible condition) to 161 (Volume = 27, Some-compatible condition). Accordingly, we examined the extent to which order volume predicted the number of chunks learned. Figure 7 plots the number of chunks produced from all-goals learning by the order volume. Essentially, this suggests that the increase in chunks produced, C_h, is a *linear* function of order volume (v). For the All-compatible

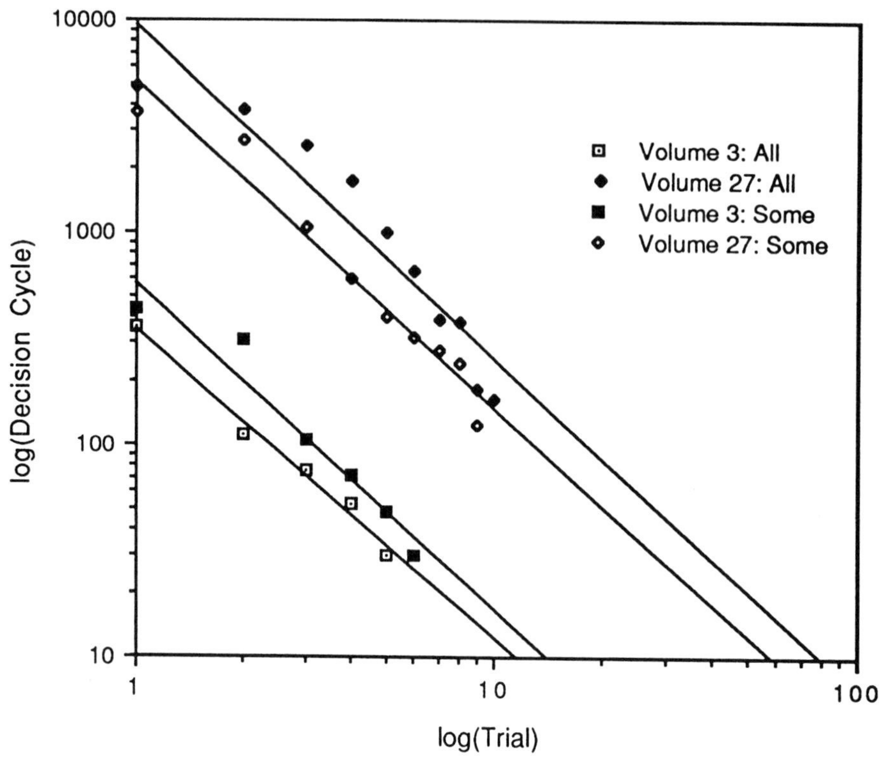

Figure 6. Decision cycles for lowest and highest order volume problems for compatibility conditions (All, Some)

Table 3. Learning curve parameters and correlations for bottom-up learning mode

Case (Volume)	D_{C1}	α	r^2
Some Compatible:			
3	575.8	-1.53	.937
6	1088.5	-1.49	.935
9	730.85	-1.32	.976
12	1588.5	-1.38	.972
15	2392.5	-1.46	.923
18	2614.2	-1.49	.971
21	3625.0	-1.47	.952
24	3974.9	-1.56	.960
27	5153.3	-1.54	.956
All Compatible:			
3	346.0	-1.45	.985
6	703.8	-1.43	.942
9	1288.3	-1.44	.940
12	2018.7	-1.53	.884
15	2668.4	-1.52	.944
18	3567.6	-1.95	.904
21	4676.9	-2.04	.914
24	5225.2	-1.91	.926
27	9360	-1.57	.892

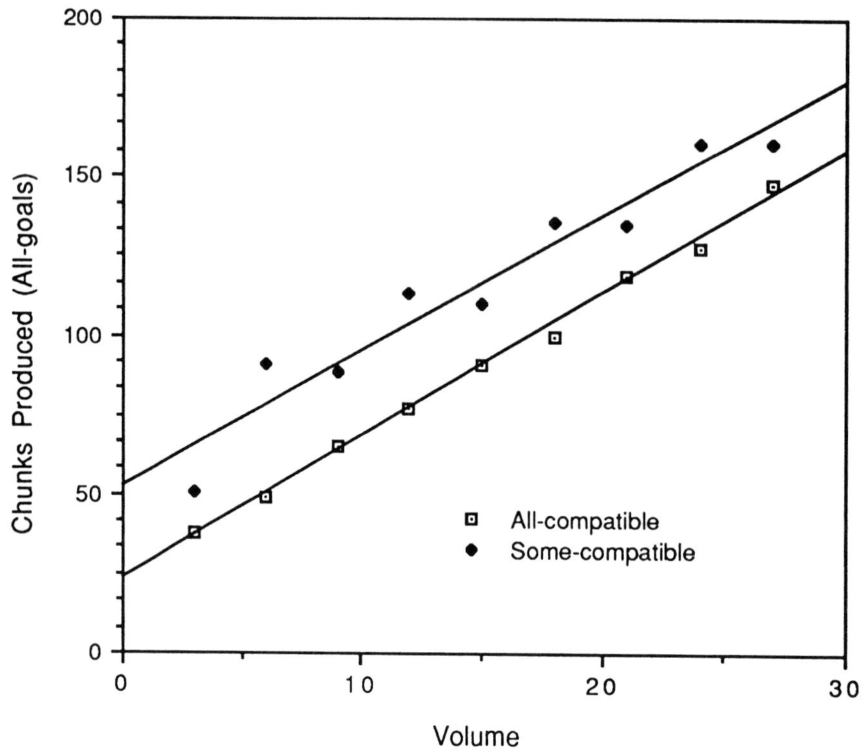

Figure 7. Number of chunks produced by order volume

condition, the equation derived is: $C_h = 23.2 + 4.48v$ with an $r^2 = .99$. For the Some-compatible condition, the equation is: $C_h = 52.3 + 4.26v$ with an $r^2 = .93$. Thus the fit of the linear model is slightly better for the All-compatible condition data.

The final step in this analysis consisted of examining how learning contributed to the overall reduction in scheduling effort. To accomplish this, we show (1) *where* learning occurred in the process by noting the problem spaces in which chunks were formed, and (2) *what* learning occurred by noting where the formed chunks were subsequently applied in the process to reduce scheduling effort. As problem spaces are invoked to realize goals, one approach to explicating sources of performance improvement is to examine how the invocation of specific problem spaces differed across learning and order volume conditions. Table 4 summarizes the number of times specific problem spaces were engaged for the two extreme volume levels in the All-compatible problem sets, with and without (all-goals) learning.[14] As the table indicates, Low order volume improvements vary across problem space as well as differing in the relative improvements (i.e., reduction in problem space invocations). The High order volume case shows that differences in relative improvements are disappearing and significant reductions in problem space invocations occured across types. What this means is that specific goals that were achieved earlier in the problem solving process did not have to be subsequently re-deliberated.

The mechanisms for the specific improvments are realized in the form of the generation of task-specific chunks arising from encounters with those earlier goals and problem spaces. Figure 8 displays the number of chunks produced (under the all-goals learning condition) by problems space for the two extreme order volumes. Two observations can be made. First, there is a differential contribution to total chunk production across problem spaces — "more learning" (as measured by the absolute number of chunks produced) is occurring in some problems spaces than in others. Second, this differential contribution varies across the two volume levels — there is an interaction between problem space type and volume level. Two problem spaces produce chunks at (absolute) levels that were relatively insensitive to changes in order volume: *Math* and *Constraint*. However, the remaining spaces are sensitive to volume level and the total number of chunks produced in those problem spaces increases.

[14] As most of the variance in effort was accounted for by order volume, the remaining analyses focused on the All-compatible problem set solved by Merle-Soar.

Table 4. Problem spaces engaged with no learning and all-goals learning
(All-compatible problem set)

PROBLEM SPACE (PS) Engaged When Scheduling	Entries into PS with No Learning		Entries into PS with Learning (and % decrease)	
	Vol: 3	Vol: 27	Vol: 3 (%)	Vol: 27 (%)
Solve-scheduling-problem	14	493	5 (64.2%)	25 (94.9%)
Find-eligible-glass-type	20	809	4 (80%)	28 (96/5%)
Schedule-unit-order	26	825	3 (88.4%)	23 (97.2%)
Constraint	24	433	3 (87.5%)	12 (97.2%)
Math	144	1828	6 (95.8%)	11 (99.3%)
TOTALS	228	4388	21 (90.7%)	99 (97.7%)

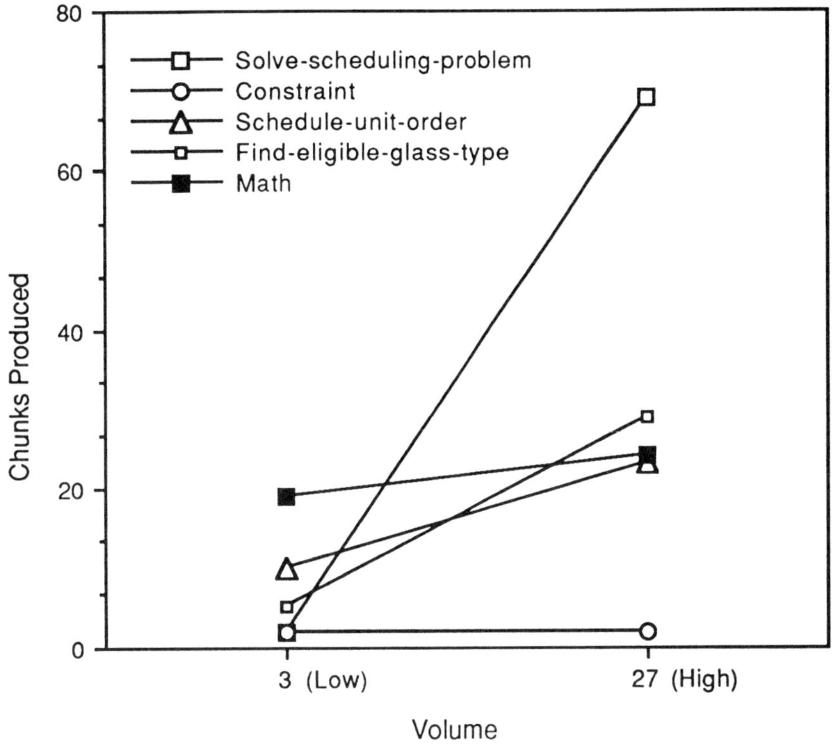

Figure 8. Chunks produced with all-goals learning by problem space for low and high order volume problem sets

Given the chunks that are produced, what is the nature of their contribution to learning as revealed by reduction in scheduling effort? An example (Operator Selection) chunk is shown in Figure 9. The chunk states that if Merle-Soar is in the ssp (Solve-scheduling-problem) space, and an operator is being considered to schedule a windshield of ss (colored) glass alongside a windshield of cl (clear) glass with width 1 and a length of 3, and another operator is being considered to schedule as a companion to the same clear windshield, a windshield of width 6 and length 3, then reject the operator for scheduling the windshield of width 6 — indicated by the negative sign in the resulting right hand side goal augmentation: (goal <g1> ^operator <q2> -). The chunk is the result of compiling problem solving that detects that windshields of width 1 and width 6 are incompatible because the difference between the widths is greater than 3 (the numbers have been changed from the original proprietary ones and are not intended to indicate realistic values).[15]

Prior Table 4 presented an overall indication of problem space activity; however, a more detailed analysis is required to understand the generation and use of the chunks produced via engaging those problem spaces. Table 5 presents a comparative analysis of where chunks were produced and where chunks were applied. The application of a chunk indicates a specific reduction in scheduling effort. The problem space in which a chunk was applied indicates where a reduction in scheduling effort occurred. In the Low order volume case, most of the chunks were produced in the *Math* space and applied in the *Math* space. However, in the High order volume case, most of the chunks are produced in the *Solve-scheduling-problem* and space and applied in the same space. The reason for this difference is that there is a relatively stable set-up cost for learning the basic *Math* chunks that, once learned, generalize throughout increases in order volume levels. However, as the order volume level increases, decisions regarding selection and evaluation of potential parts must be made "above and beyond" the *Math* space. These decisions result in more chunks made, as well as applied, at higher-level (task-specific) problem spaces.

We developed three metrics for an additional comparative analysis of the relative efficiency and effectiveness of the produced knowledge. The first metric measures the chunk *production efficiency* (η_{prod}) and is the proportion of produced chunks that were eventually applied in the same trial (using all-goals learning). Let us define a constraint on the summand as follows:

---

15 The augmentations (i.e., conditions described within a set of parentheses) that begin with the class "integer", "column", or "digit" reflect how Merle-Soar represents integers as lists of symbols. Operations on integers (addition, subtraction) are handled by productions that manipulate these symbolic representations.

Figure 9. An Operator Selection chunk produced during All-goals learning

```
(sp p277 elaborate
  (goal <g1> ^problem-space <p1> ^state <d4>
        ^operator <q2> + { <> <q2> <q1> } +)
  (problem-space <p1> ^name ssp)
  (operator <q2> ^glass-type <a1> -^glass-type <c5>)
  (glass-type <a1> ^transparency <s2>)
  (transparency <s2> ^name ss)
  (state <d4> ^unassigned-binding <n1>)
  (slot-binding <n1> ^glass-type <c5>)
  (operator <q1> ^glass-type { <> <a1> <b1> } -^glass-type <c5>)
  (glass-type <c5> ^transparency { <> <s2> <c4> } ^blocksize-width <o1>
        ^blocksize-length <t1>)
  (transparency <c4> ^name cl)
  (integer <o1> ^head <c2> ^tail <c2>)
  (column <c2> ^anchor head tail ^digit <d2>)
  (digit <d2> ^name 1)
  (integer <t1> ^head { <> <c2> <c1> } ^tail <c1>)
  (column <c1> ^anchor head tail ^digit { <> <d2> <d1> })
  (digit <d1> ^name 3)
  (glass-type <b1> ^blocksize-length <t1>
        ^blocksize-width { <> <o1> <s1> })
  (integer <s1> ^head { <> <c1> <> <c2> <c3> } ^tail <c3>)
  (column <c3> ^anchor head tail ^digit { <> <d1> <> <d2> <d3> })
  (digit <d3> ^name 6)
  -->
  (goal <g1> ^operator <q2> ))
```

Table 5. Analysis of chunks produced with all-goals learning by problem space
(All-compatible problem set)

PROBLEM SPACE (PS)	Number of Chunks Created in PS		Per Cent of Total Chunks Created in PS		Per Cent of Chunks Applied in PS	
	Vol: 3	Vol: 27	Vol: 3	Vol: 27	Vol: 3	Vol: 27
Solve-scheduling-problem	2	69	5 %	46 %	17 %	34 %
Find-eligible-glass-type	5	29	13 %	19 %	12 %	31 %
Schedule-unit-order	10	23	26 %	15 %	0 %	0 %
Constraint	2	2	5 %	1 %	29 %	21 %
Math	19	25	50 %	16 %	40 %	12 %
TOTALS	38	148	100 %	100 %	100 %	100 %

$$[A(k)] = \begin{cases} 1, & \text{if chunk } k \text{ is applied at least once within the trial} \\ 0, & \text{if chunk } k \text{ is is not applied within the trial.} \end{cases}$$

Then the metric η_{prod} can be defined (for N chunks produced on a trial) as:

$$\eta_{prod} = \frac{\sum_{1 \leq k \leq N} [A(k)]}{N}$$

Therefore, η_{prod} ranges from 0.0 (none of the produced chunks were applied in the trial) to an upper limit of 1.0 (achieved when every chunk produced is applied at least once in the trial). The values for η_{prod} on the Low and High order volume problems are .71 and .60 respectively. A higher proportion of the total chunks produced were subsequently used within the same trial for the Low order volume problem than the High order volume problem.

The second metric, η_{util}, estimates the *utility* of the produced chunks as reflected in the number of times the chunks are applied within the same trial. η_{util} is calculated by dividing the total number of times the chunk instantiations were applied within the trial, $N_{applied}$, by the number of chunks produced that were eventually applied:

$$\eta_{util} = \frac{N_{applied}}{\sum_{1 \leq k \leq N} [A(k)]}$$

η_{util} can (theoretically) range from 0.0 (when none of the produced chunks were applied in the same trial) to an arbitraty upper bound of multiple instantiations of produced chunks. The values for η_{util} obtained from the Low and High order volume problems were 2.62 and 2.67 respectively. Therefore, while there is a distinct drop in the production efficiency (as measure by η_{prod}), there *appears* to be a consistency in the chunk utility across order volumes.

The final metric, η_{eff}, measures the relative *effectiveness* of the applied chunks and is calculated by dividing the effort saved (expressed in decision cycles, D_c) by the number of unique chunks that were produced and eventually applied in the same trial (as defined in the denominator of η_{prod}). η_{eff}, then, yields a "D_c per chunk" number which reflects the average within-trial contribution for the applied chunks. Letting D_c^l represent the number of decision cycles taken to solve the problem when all-goals learning is applied and D_c^n represent the required decision cycles when no learning is applied, then

$$\eta_{eff} = \frac{D_c^n - D_c^l}{\sum_{1 \leq k \leq N} [A(k)]}$$

η_{eff} can theoretically range from 0.0 (when there is no reduction in D_c through learning) to an arbitrary number reflecting the "work" done per unit (i.e., chunk) produced. The Low and High order volume problems produced η_{eff} values of 58.88 D_c/chunk and 346.34 D_c/chunk respectively. Thus there were extremely large differences in the absolute effectiveness of the chunks produced (as measured in the raw reduction of D_c). However, note that a D_c reduction of 58.88 is equivalent to about a 3.7% change in the Low order volume effort and a 346.43 reduction accounts for about a 1.1% change in High order volume effort.

These metrics are, to a certain extent, Soar-specific and their usefulness has not been fully explored. We can make an intuitive argument that they do provide a basis for comparing aspects of chunk generation and use. This could be beneficial when exploring alternative representational schemes in Merle-Soar. Ideally, one would look for schemes that were high in production efficiency (η_{prod}), chunk utility (η_{util}), and chunk effectiveness (η_{eff}). Though this may be a goal in restricted and stable task environment, there may be important tradeoffs to be made concerning the generality of the chunks produced over variations in task parameters. This type of analysis has not been conducted before and the implications are yet to be fully appreciated; however, we believe that these (or similar) metrics are important to fully understand the behavior of the systems we are building. It is important to realize that these are descriptive, not evaluative, metrics that may eventually prove useful in guiding subsequent design and analysis of Soar (and Soar-like) systems.

If we view this scheduling problem as a task involving many recurring subgoals, it becomes apparent that many components of scheduling problems are solved repeatedly. Encounters with impasses result in new goal specification and problem space exploration while the resolution of impasses results in knowledge which can be applied when the conditions of the impasse are again encountered. We found significant *within-trial* (as demonstrated by all-goals learning) and *within-task* (as demonstrated by bottom-up learning).

6. Conclusion

In this paper we have demonstrated how a mechanism for general intelligence and learning can solve a simple production scheduling problem. Our goal was not to demonstrate the ability of Merle-Soar to *solve* a scheduling problem, for the problem itself is trivial; rather, our goal was to represent the scheduling task in a general way and examine how *learning* contributed to the reduction in effort to solve the task. We have seen that Merle-Soar is capable of significant deliberation effort reduction through learning; furthermore, the reduction in effort is described by a power law.

Crafting systems that learn (in a general manner) is a new field in manufacturing and much research must proceed before we can explore how to apply this powerful technology. For example, it is not clear how to anticipate the interaction between the formulation of the task representations and the subsequently encountered task variations. A system that performs adequately under one set of task assumptions may fail when certain assumptions are removed. But how do you design sufficient generality and resilience into an intelligent machine that can monitor and adapt to the changing aspects of the task? Intelligent systems should be able to learn from their experience and demonstrate a reduction in deliberation effort when addressing familiar ground. But what is considered familiar ground? In one sense, we cannot "step into the same river twice" because aspects of the scheduling problem are continually shifting. Yet scheduling does get done and people do demonstrate mastery over aspects of the task. Discovering how to produce an intelligent agent that can discern and exploit task invariants is a central research issue.

We also explored methods of analyzing the performance of Merle-Soar in a variety of ways. This is related to the prior discussion. Given that there are many ways of building a Soar system to solve a scheduling problem, how can we evaluate the sufficiency of the mechanisms we have crafted? One method is to analyze the performance in terms of problem space behavior and chunk production. What problem spaces are being invoked? How valuable are the chunks being produced? We offered three simple metrics to provide gross measures in this direction: production efficiency (η_{prod}), chunk utility (η_{util}), and chunk effectiveness (η_{eff}).

Finally, the transfer of learning is an important issue in any system which has the capacity to learn and efforts are now focusing on explicating the phenomena underlying that topic [e.g., Singley and Anderson, 1989]. In this paper we have not yet explored the issue of transfer for Merle-Soar tasks; however, preliminary findings suggest that there is a subtle interaction between task parameters and the transfer of chunks [Prietula, Hsu, Steier and Newell, 1989]. Future research should focus on the complex interplay between knowledge gained in one task setting and the demands of alternative settings.

In conclusion, learning has not been extensively applied to complex manufacturing problems; however, we believe that the next generation of AI tools to contribute substantially to, and even alter the face of, manufacturing will be those with the capacity to learn from their behavior. In many scheduling environments, the formulation and adjustment of schedules is much more than "number crunching" and involves considerations that go well beyond the factory floor [McKay, Buzacott,

Charness and Safayeni, 1991]. Our efforts at this time are modest and necessarily incomplete, but may well serve us to consider the implications of truly intelligent manufacturing systems.

7. References

Arff, S. and Hasle, G. [1989]. ALPLAN: A knowledge-based system for production planning in aluminum foundaries. In K. Karwan and J. Sweigart (Eds.), *Proceedings of the Third International Conference: Expert Systems and the Leading Edge in Production and Operations Management*, Hilton Head, SC.

Bensana, E., Bel, G. and Dubois, D. [1988]. OPAL: A multi-knowedgedbased system for industrial job-shop scheduling, *International Journal of Production Research*, 25, 795-819.

Bitran, G., and Yanasse, H. [1982]. Computational complexity of the capacitated lot size problem, *Management Science*, 28, 1174-1186.

Brown, M. [1988]. The dynamic rescheduler: Conquering the changing production environment. *Proceedings of the Fourth Conference on Artificial Intelligence Applications.* San Diego, CA: IEEE Press.

Brownston, L., Farrell, R., Kant, E. and Martin, N. [1985]. *Programming expert systems in OPS5: An introduction to rule-based programming.* Reading, MA: Addison-Wesley.

Bruno, G., Elia, A. and Laface, P. [1986]. A rule-based system to schedule production, *IEEE Computer*, July, 32-40.

Carbonell, J., Knoblock, C. and Minton, S. [1990]. Prodigy: An integrated architecture for planning and learning. In K. VanLehn (Ed.), *Architectures for Intelligence.* Hillsdale, NJ: Erlbaum.

Chaturvedi, A. [1989]. *Goal-directed conceptual aggregation: An artificial intelligence technique to support management decision-making.* Unpublished doctoral dissertation, University of Wisconsin-Milwaukee.

Chaturvedi, A., Hutchinson, G. and Nazareth, D. [in press]. A synergistic approach to manufacturing systems control using machine learning and simulation, *Journal of Intelligent Manufacturing.*

Cleveland, G. and Smith, S. [1989]. Using genetic algorithms to schedule flow shop releases. *Proceedings of the 3rd International Conference on Genetic Algorithms.* San Mateo, CA: Morgan Kaufmann.

Cohen, S. and Zysman, J. [1987]. *Manufacturing Matters. The Myth of the Post-Industrial Economy.* New York, NY: Basic Books.

Collinot, A., LePape, C. and Pinoteau, G. [1988]. SONIA: A knowledge-based scheduling system, *Artificial Intelligence in Engineering*, 3, 86-94.

Davis, L. [1985]. Job shop scheduling with genetic algorithms. *Proceedings of an International Conference on Genetic Algorithms.* Carnegie Mellon University, Pittsburgh, PA.

Doukidis, G. and Paul, R. (Eds.). [1990a]. Artificial intelligence and expert systems, Part I: Production planning, applications and methodogy [Special issue]. *Journal of the Operational Research Society*, 41(5).

Doukidis, G. and Paul, R. (Eds.). [1990b]. Artificial intelligence and expert systems, Part II: Simulation and scheduling [Special issue]. *Journal of the Operational Research Society*, 41(6).

Englemore, R. and Morgan, T. (Eds.). [1988]. *Blackboard Systems.* Reading, MA: Addison-Wesley.

Etzioni, O. [1990]. *A structural theory of explanation-based learning.* Technical Report CMU-CS-90-185, School of Computer Science, Carnegie Mellon University, Pittsburgh, PA.

Florian, M., Lenstra, J. and Rinnooy Kan, K. [1980]. Deterministic prodution planning: Algorithms and complexity, *Management Science*, 26, 12-20.

Forsyth, R. and Rada, R. [1986]. *Machine Learning: Applications in Expert Systems and Information Retrieval.* West Sussex, England: Ellis Horwood.

Fox, M. and Smith, S. [1984]. ISIS: A knowledge-based system for factory scheduling, *Expert Systems*, 1(1), 25-49.

Glover, F. and McMillan, C. [1986]. The general employee scheduling problem: An integration of MS and AI, *Computers and Operations Research*, 13, 563-573.

Goldberg, D. [1989]. *Genetic Algorithms in Search, Optimization and Machine Learning.* Reading, MA: Addison-Wesley.

Graves, S. [1981]. A review of production scheduling, *Operations Research*, 29(4), 646-675.

Hax, A. and Candea, D. [1984]. *Production and Inventory Management.* Englewood Cliffs, NJ: Prentice Hall.

Hilliard, M. and Liepens, G. [1988]. Machine learning applications to job shop scheduling. *Proceedings of the First International Conference on Industrial and Engineering Applications of Artificial Intelligence and Expert Systems – Volume II.* ACM Press.

Hsu, W-L.,Prietula, M., Thompson, G. and Ow, P.S. [in press]. A Mixed-initiative scheduling workbench: Integrating AI, OR and HCI, *Decision Support Systems.*

Iba, G. [1985]. Learning by discovering macros in puzzle solving. *Proceedings of the Ninth International Joint Conference on Artificial Intelligence.*

Knoblock, C. (1991). *Automatically Generating Abstractions for Problem Solving.* Unpublished doctoral dissertation, Carnegie Mellon University, Pittsburgh, PA. Available as Technical Report CMU-CS-91-120, School of Computer Science, Carnegie Mellon University.

Korf, R. [1985]. *Learning to solve problems by searching for macro-operators.* Boston, MA: Pitman.

Krajewski, L., Ritzman, B., King, B. and Wong, D. [1983]. Kanban, MRP and shaping the production environment, *Management Science*, 33, 39-57.

Laird, J., Congdon, C.B., Altmann, E. and Swedlow, K. [1990]. *Soar User's Manual: Version 5.2.* CMU-CS-90-179, School of Computer Science, Carnegie Mellon University, Pittsburgh, PA.

Laird, J., Newell, A. and Rosenbloom, P. [1987]. Soar: An architecture for general intelligence, *Artificial Intelligence*, 33(1), 1-64.

Laird, J., Rosenbloom, P. and Newell, A. [1986]. Chunking in Soar: The anatomy of a general learning mechanism, *Machine Learning*, 1(1), 11-46.

Langley, P. [1985].Learning effective search heuristics. *Proceedings of the Eighth International Joint Conference on Artificial Intelligence.*

Lee, J. and Kang, B. [1988]. Intelligent production planning system using the post-model analysis approach. In E. Turban and P. Watkins (Eds.), *Applied Expert Systems.* Elsevier Science.

Lee, J. and Suh, M. S. [1988]. PAMS: A domain-specific knowledge-based parallel machine scheduling system, *Expert Systems*, 5(3), 198-213.

Matsuo, H., Shang, J. and Sullivan, R. [1989]. A knowledge-based system for stacker crane control in a manufacturing environment, *IEEE Transactions on Systems, Man, and Cybernetics*, 19(5), 932-945.

McKay, K., Buzacott, N., Charness, N. and Safayeni, F. [1991]. The scheduler's predictive expertise: An interdisciplinary perspective. In R. Paul (Ed.), *Artificial Intelligence in Operations Research*. MacMillan.

McKay, K., Safayeni, F. and Buzacott, J. [1988]. Job-shop scheduling theory: What is relevant? *Interfaces*, 18(4), 84-90.

Minton, S. [1988]. *Learning effective search control knowledge: An explanation-based approach*. Unpublished doctoral dissertation, Carnegie Mellon University, Pittsburgh, PA.

Minton, S. [1990]. Quantitative results concerning the utility of explanation-based learning. *Artificial Intelligence*, 42(2-3), 363-391.

Mitchell, T., Keller, R. and Kedar-Cabelli, S. [1986]. Explanation-based generalization: A unifying view, *Machine Learning*, 1, 47-80.

Morton, T., Lawrence, S., Rajagopolan, S. and Kekre, S. [1988]. SCHED-STAR: A price-based shop scheduling module, *Journal of Manufacturing and Operations Management*, 1, 131-181.

Newell, A. [1980]. Reasoning, problem solving and decision processes: The problem space as a fundamental category. In R. Nickerson (Ed.), *Attention and Performance VIII*. Hillsdale, NJ: Lawrence Erlbaum.

Newell, A. and Rosenbloom, P. [1981]. Mechanisms of skill acquistion and the law of practice. In J. Anderson (Ed.), *Cognitive Skills and Their Acquisition*. Hillsdale, NJ: Lawrence Erlbaum.

Ow, P.S. and Smith, S. [1987]. Two design principles for knowledge-based systems, *Decision Sciences*, 18(3), 430-447.

Ow, P.S. and Smith, S. [1988]. Viewing scheduling as an opportunistic problem-solving process, *Annals of Operations Research*, 12, 85-108.

Ow, P.S., Smith, S. and Thirez, A. [1988]. Reactive plan revision. In *Proceedings of the 7th National Conference on Artificial Intelligence*, St. Paul, MN.

Prietula, M., Hsu, W.L. and Ow, P.S. [1991]. A coincident problem space perspective to scheduling support. *Proceedings of the Fourth International Symposium on Artificial Intelligence*, Cancun, Mexico.

Prietula, M., Hsu, W-L, Steier, D. and Newell, A. [1989]. Sharing Scheduling Knowledge Between Distributed Intelligent Architectures. Paper presented at the *Workshop on AI and Manufacturing*, 11th International Joint Conference on Artificial Intelligence, Detroit, MI.

Ritzman, L. and Krajewski, L. [1983]. Comparison of material requirements planning and reorder point systems. In H. Bekiroglu (Ed.), *Simulation in Inventory and Production Control*. La Jolla, CA: Society for Computer Simulation.

Ruby, D. and Kibler, D. [1989]. Learning to Plan in Scheduling Domains. Working notes for the Workshop on Manufacturing Production Scheduling. *Eleventh International Joint Conference on Artificial Intelligence*.

Sadeh, N. [1991]. *Look-ahead techniques for micro-opportunistic job shop scheduling.* Doctoral dissertation, Carnegie Mellon University, Pittsburgh, PA. Available as CMU-CS-91-102 Technical Report, School of Computer Science, Carnegie Mellon University.

Sanderson, P. [1988]. The human planning and scheduling role in advanced manufacturing sytsems: A critical review of field and laboratory research, *Human Factors*, 31(6), 635-666.

Sathi, A., Morton, T. and Roth, S. [1988]. CALLISTO: An intelligent project management system, *AI Magazine*, 7(5), 34-52.

Savell, D., Perez, R. and Koh, S. [1989]. Scheduling semiconductor wafer production: An expert system implementation, *IEEE Expert*, Fall, 9-15.

Shaw, M. and Whinston, A. [1989]. An artificial intelligence approach to the scheduling of flexible manufacturing systems, *IIE Transactions*, 21(2), 170-183.

Singley, M. and Anderson, J. [1989]. *The transfer of cognitive skill.* Hillsdale, NJ: Lawrence Erlbaum.

Smith, S., Fox, M. and Ow, P.S. [1986]. Constructing and maintaining detailed production plans: Investigations into the development of knowledge-based factory scheduling systems, *AI Magazine*, 4, 45-61.

Smith, S., Ow, P.S., Potvin, J., Muscettola, N. and Matthys, D. [1990]. An integrated framework for generating and revising factory schedules, *Journal of the Operations Research Society*, 41(6), 539-552.

Steffen, M. [1986]. A survey of artificial intelligence-based scheduling systems. *Proceedings of the IIE Fall Industrial Engineering Conference*, Atlanta, GA.

Sycara, K., Roth, S., Sadeh, N. and Fox, M. [1991]. Resource allocation in distributed factory scheduling, *IEEE Expert*, February, 29-40.

Vere, S. [1983]. Planning in time, windows and durations for activities and goals, *IEEE Transactions on Pattern Analysis and Machine Intelligence*, 5, 246-266.

Whitley, D., Starkweather, T. and Fuquay, D. [1989]. Scheduling problems and traveling salesmen: The genetic edge recombination operator. In *Proceedings of the 3rd International Conference on Genetic Algorithms.* San Mateo, CA: Morgan Kaufmann.

Zozaya-Gorostiza, C., Hendrickson, C. and Rehak, D. [1989]. *Knowledge-based Process Planning for Construction and Manufacturing.* New York, NY: Academic Press.

This work was supported, in part, by a Faculty Development Grant from Carnegie Mellon University, by the Engineering Design Research Center at Carnegie Mellon University (an NSF Engineering Research Center), the Center for the Management of Technology at GSIA/CMU, and by the Defense Advanced Research Projects Agency (DOD) and monitored by the Avionics Laboratory, Air Force Wright Aeronautical Laboratories, Aeronautical Systems Division (AFSC), Wright-Patterson AFB, OH 45433-6543 under Contract F33615-87-C-1499, ARPA Order No. 4976, Amendment 20. The views and conclusions contained in this document are those of the authors and should not be interpreted as representing the official policies, either expressed or implied, of the Defense Advanced Research Projects Agency, the National Science Foundation or of the U.S. Government.

ACKNOWLEDGEMENTS: We gratefully acknowledge the insightful and detailed comments from the reviewers.

CHAPTER 53

Knowledge Level and Inductive Uses of Chunking (EBL)

P. S. Rosenbloom, USC–ISI, and J. Aasman, Rijksuniversiteit Groningen

Abstract

When explanation-based learning (EBL) is used for knowledge level learning (KLL), training examples are essential, and EBL is not simply reducible to partial evaluation. A key enabling factor in this behavior is the use of domain theories in which not every element is believed a priori. When used with such domain theories EBL provides a basis for rote learning (deductive KLL) and induction from multiple examples (nondeductive KLL). This article lays the groundwork for using EBL in KLL, by describing how EBL can lead to increased belief, and describes new results from using Soar's chunking mechanism – a variation on EBL – as the basis for a task-independent rote learning capability and a version-space-based inductive capability. This latter provides a compelling demonstration of nondeductive KLL in Soar, and provides the basis for an integration of conventional EBL with induction. However, it also reveals how one of Soar's key assumptions – the *non-penetrable memory assumption* – makes this more complicated than it would otherwise be. This complexity may turn out to be appropriate, or it may point to where modifications of Soar are needed.

Introduction[1]

Recent analytical papers on explanation-based learning (EBL) (DeJong & Mooney, 1986; Mitchell, Keller, & Kedar-Cabelli, 1986) comment on how training examples are not logically necessary for EBL (Prieditis, 1988; van Harmelen & Bundy, 1988). Their point is that a training example may serve a useful search control function in EBL – guiding the learner to regions of performance which it would be useful to operationalize – but that the resulting operationalized rule is just a specialization, in the general case, of what a partial evaluation (PE) mechanism could achieve without the training example. This is an important point which reveals a previously submerged connection between learning and program transformation. However, it is flawed by its neglect of the use of EBL in knowledge level learning (KLL) (Flann & Dietterich, 1989; Rosenbloom, Laird, & Newell, 1987); that is, for the acquisition of knowledge not implied by what is already known (Dietterich, 1986). In such situations, the combination of the training example and goal concept – an *instance* – plays an essential role; one that is quite comparable to the role of instances in classic inductive concept learning systems.

The first task of this article is to lay necessary groundwork for the use of EBL in KLL. The key idea is to explain – actually, to *rationalize* – instances via a low-belief domain theory, and then to use EBL to acquire a high-belief rule from the rationalization. Unlike in PE, the instances play a crucial role here in determining what is rationalized, and thus what becomes believed. We then build on this foundation in the context of Soar (Laird, Newell, & Rosenbloom, 1987; Rosenbloom *et al.*, 1990) – whose learning mechanism, chunking, is a variation on EBL (Rosenbloom & Laird, 1986) in which new rules are acquired from a dependency analysis of the traces of rules that fire during subgoal-based problem solving – to take several steps towards the realization of the *integrated-learning hypothesis* (Rosenbloom, 1988). This hypothesis states that "Rote learning, empirical generalization, and explanation-based learning arise as variations in the knowledge-reconstruction process", where "knowledge-reconstruction" should be read as "rationalization". Traditional explanation-based learning differs from rote memorization and induction in that the former uses only high-belief rationalizations while the latter two necessitate aspects that are initially low in belief. Rote memorization differs from induction in that the latter utilizes additional knowledge to affect rationalization.

The subsequent sections introduce a new task-independent, rote-memorization capability in Soar;

[1]This research was sponsored by the National Aeronautics and Space Administration under cooperative agreement number NCC 2-538, and by the Defense Advanced Research Projects Agency (DOD) under contract number N00039-86C-0033 (via subcontract from the Knowledge Systems Laboratory, Stanford University). We would like to thank Yoram Reich, Haym Hirsh, Craig Miller, Peter Pirolli, and John Laird for their helpful comments.

extend this to induction from multiple examples, providing a compelling example of nondeductive knowledge level learning (NKLL) (Dietterich, 1986) in Soar, and introducing a complication caused by Soar's inability to directly examine its own rules; cover the third leg of the integrated-learning hypothesis, explanation-based learning, and its use in induction; and conclude.

EBL and KLL

EBL can be applied over many types of domain theories – the only requirement being the provision by the domain theory of a way to generate a (possibly generalized) dependency structure for the instance that relates the training example to the goal concept. In a classical EBL domain theory, all of the elements – e.g., facts and rules – are ascribed a uniform high level of belief. In such a domain theory, EBL performs symbol level learning by explicitly storing knowledge that is already implicit in this domain theory. However, it does not alter levels of belief – they are all already as high as they can get. For knowledge level learning, the domain theory needs to include low-belief elements. With such a theory, EBL can lead to knowledge level learning by increasing the level of belief in selected elements of the theory.

Consider the example of a system with a domain theory that allows it to abductively generate rationalizations – that is, plausible explanations – for what it sees (or hears). One of the key ways in which a rationalization differs from a simple deductive proof – as used in EBG (Mitchell, Keller, & Kedar-Cabelli, 1986), for example – is that the facts and rules utilized in a rationalization need not be completely believed in order to be used. It is in fact essential to the rationalization process that the system be able to derive from its domain theory not just facts that are known to be true, but also ones which are not yet believed. For example, suppose the instance consists of telling the system that "Fred, a dolphin, is warm blooded" – "Fred is a dolphin" is the training example, and "Fred is warm blooded" is the goal concept. To rationalize this knowledge it might use that "dolphins are mammals" and "mammals are warm blooded", even if its a priori belief is that dolphins are fish rather than mammals. This explanation could have been created in the absence of the instance, but it would have little a priori believability. It is the existence of the instance that provides grounds for increasing the believability of the explanation.

When this example is extended to the EBL/PE situation, it becomes clear that arbitrary rules created by partially evaluating this domain theory would have low believability, while comparable rules created by EBL for specific instances could have much higher believability. The instances allow EBL to increase the scope of what is believed, thus enabling knowledge level learning. In the extreme it is possible to start with a theory consisting of a generator able to produce data structures representing all possible pieces of knowledge, all with zero belief. Such a theory has all possible knowledge implicit in it, but none of it initially believed. EBL, in conjunction with appropriate instances, can then be used selectively to learn anything, by increasing the level of belief in the appropriate, possibly implicit, knowledge structures.

One way to view this process is as explicit belief propagation, where there are belief-propagation rules that are used to compute a level of belief for an explanation – and thus for the rules learned via EBL from the explanation – as a function of the believability of the individual domain theory elements and the instance. An alternative view of this process, and the one that guides the research reported here, is that the instance acts as a filter, letting through only those explanations which should be believed. Learning then only occurs for these believed explanations.

To support this type of processing, ***plausible*** domain theories – that is, theories in which only plausible explanations can be generated for conclusions – are required. Such a theory can potentially explain things that aren't true – necessitating the use of instances as filters – but what is true is explained in a plausible manner. As long as a domain theory meets this condition, the a priori believability of the individual elements of the theory can be zero without affecting the believability of what is learned. At the extreme end, the domain theory could contain elements which are not representational in the domain, such as the letter "d" – or which are representational but do not have belief values, such as "dolphin" – but which can be combined syntactically to generate elements which do have belief values.

Given EBL and plausible low-belief domain theories, the one missing component is what makes the newly learned rule believed. A variety of approaches are possible, including ones that augment the EBL mechanism to generate explicit belief values, and ones that partition learned rules – which automatically receive high belief – from domain theory rules. In Soar a variation on this latter approach is used. The domain theory corresponds to the problem space used in a subgoal (Rosenbloom & Laird, 1986) – in our case, this might be a *generation* problem space, where all possible structures are generatable, but none are believed. However, the learned rule is always created for the problem space in the parent goal; perhaps a *fact* problem space, in which all retrievable structures are believed. If restrictions are then placed on which problem spaces are utilized at any point in time, it is possible to know what level of belief – 0 or 1 – to assign to the retrieved knowledge. This point is related to the one recently made in (Flann & Dietterich, 1989). They focus on how EBL can perform KLL if an explanation that is generated for one concept is used to define a second concept that is a specialization of the first one. In our work, EBL performs KLL by transferring (possibly implicit) structures from an unbelieved domain theory to a believed domain theory that contains a subset of the structures in the original theory. Despite the differences, what both have in common — in fact, what every use of EBL for KLL must have in common — is that the learned knowledge is used differently than would be the domain theory from which it is learned. It can be used at a different belief level (as here), for a different goal concept (Flann & Dietterich, 1989), or even as evidence that a particular episode occurred (in which the rule was learned) (Rosenbloom, Newell, & Laird, 1990).

Rote Memorization

In previous work this general approach to knowledge level learning has been employed to perform several simple rote memorization tasks — recognition, recall, cued recall, and paired-associate recall — for hierarchical letter strings and for objects that are described by attributes with values (Rosenbloom, Laird, & Newell, 1987; Rosenbloom, Laird, & Newell, 1988; Rosenbloom, Newell, & Laird, 1990). This work also provided solutions for two additional problems that arise when rules are to be learned that recall new structure: (1) the *data chunking problem* — how to enable the retrieval of new information without its already being present — and (2) the *selective retrieval problem* — how to avoid retrieving everything ever learned. The data chunking problem is solved by reconstructing new knowledge from what is already known — that is, the domain theory — rather than directly rationalizing the input structures representing the new knowledge. Since this reconstruction process is not dependent on the input structures, tests of the input do not appear in the conditions of the learned rules. The selective retrieval problem is solved by selectively acquiring retrieval cues as conditions of learned rules.

Recently, this earlier work has been extended with the development of a general, task-independent rote-memorization operator. This is a normal Soar operator that uses problem solving in a subgoal to implement solutions to the data chunking and selective retrieval problems. The operator takes two arbitrary graphs of Soar working memory elements as inputs — the first is the training example, and the second is the goal concept. The result of memorizing the pair is the acquisition of a rule that tests for the existence of the first graph (the *cue graph*) and if the test succeeds, retrieves the second graph (the *recalled graph*) into working memory. To do this, the memorization operator reconstructs the recalled graph by assembling primitive domain-theory elements into a copy of the graph (solving the data chunking problem), and then makes this copy dependent on the structure of the cue graph (solving the selective retrieval problem). Figure 1 shows such a chunk, schematized as a pair of graph structures. The cue and recalled graphs are attached to operator <O1> in the rule's conditions and actions, respectively.

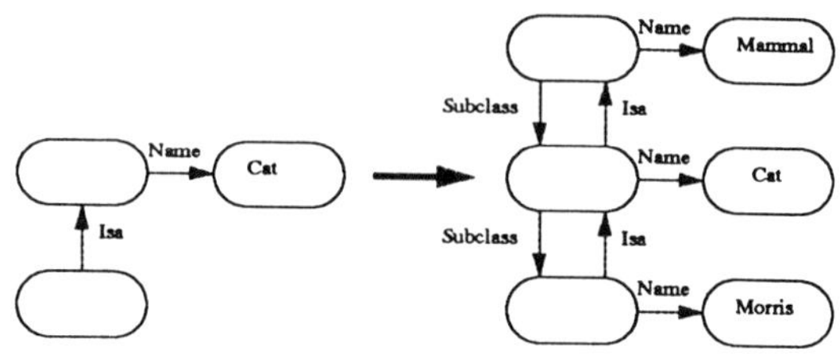

Figure 1: Chunk learned from memorizing a pair of graph structures.

Multi-Example Induction

When the contents of the initial domain theory are restricted to only elements that are completely believed, it is not possible for the domain theory itself to perform inductive leaps. If a system containing such a domain theory is to perform inductive generalization, it must be done outside the domain theory — in the EBL mechanism, for example. The most common approach is to augment EBL's standard explanation processing with some form of inductive postprocessing of either the entire explanation, or just its operational components (Flann & Dietterich, 1989; Hirsh, 1989; Sarrett & Pazzani, 1989).

If, on the other hand, the contents of the initial domain theory can include unbelieved elements, the option opens up of doing induction directly in the domain theory, and leaving explanation processing unaltered. This was proposed in (Rosenbloom, 1988) as part of the integrated-learning hypothesis, and is the approach taken here.[2] The domain theory includes knowledge about how to reconstruct presented objects (a stripped-down version of the task-independent memorization operator), generalization hierarchies (the basis of the concept language), rules which perform inductive leaps, and rules learned from prior instances. When a new instance is perceived, this domain theory is used to determine what is to be rationalized — it may be a generalization of the instance, rather than the instance itself — as well as how it should be rationalized.

---

[2]Widmer recently proposed a similar "Explain and Compile" approach to using EBL over an expanded range of domain theories (Widmer, 1989). Anderson has also used knowledge compilation, a form of EBL, over analogical and discriminative theories (Anderson, 1986).

One decision that must be made at this point is the orientation of the rule to be learned — whether the concept's name should be in the actions and its definition in the conditions, or vice versa. In EBL (and chunking), the concept definition appears in the conditions because that is where EBL has its primary generalization effect, and also where the definition can act as a recognizer of instances of the concept. However, to go beyond simple concept recognition — to retrieval and modification of the concept definition as further instances are processed — requires a fuller declarative access to the definition. Such access is not available in Soar if the definition is stored in the conditions because Soar's rule memory is *non-penetrable* — rules can be executed (forward), but can not be directly examined. Non-penetrability arises because the rules are compiled procedures that can be executed but not examined. In psychological terms, they represent *automatized* behavior (for example, (Shiffrin & Schneider, 1977)). A consequence of non-penetrability is that, to access the concept definition explicitly, it must be stored in the rule's actions, where it can be retrieved by rule execution. Once retrieved, the concept definition can be used to influence what is learned for new instances, and to interpretively recognize instances of the concept (concept recognition rules, in which the definition is in the conditions, can be learned by chunking this interpretation process). As discussed later, the downside of this decision is that the generality of the concept definition is affected only by the decision of what to rationalize, and not by the rationalization process or the chunking/EBL mechanism.

The domain theory that has been implemented within Soar utilizes a variant of the Focussing algorithm (Young, Plotkin, & Linz, 1977; Bundy, Silver, & Plummer, 1985). This is a version space algorithm that works for spaces describable by a conjunction of attributes, where each attribute is defined by a tree-structured generalization hierarchy. The key ideas underlying the implemented algorithm are that: (1) the version space is kept factored — bounds are maintained independently for each attribute (Subramanian & Feigenbaum, 1986); (2) only near-miss negatives (Winston, 1975) are processed (the *zero option*)[3] to guarantee that the boundary sets will not fragment; and (3) once the first positive example is processed, the entire factored version space is explicitly represented, rather than just the boundary sets (at worst this requires space proportional to the number of attributes times the maximum depth of the generalization hierarchies).

Suppose that the task is to learn that the definition of (GOOD=TRUE) is (MOBILITY=MOBILE, SHAPE=ANY, SIZE=ANY). The algorithm starts with the goal concept, (GOOD=TRUE), and a positive example, such as (MOBILITY=WHEELED, SHAPE=SQUARE, SIZE=LARGE).[4] It then uses the generalization hierarchies in the domain theory to elaborate the example with all of the superclasses of its attributes' values, yielding for this case (MOBILITY={ANY, MOBILE, WHEELED}, SHAPE={ANY, POLYGON, REGULAR, SQUARE}, SIZE={ANY, LARGE}). This elaborated example is then memorized as the initial version space, with the retrieval cue being the goal concept:

```
(GOOD=TRUE) -->
         (MOBILITY={ANY, MOBILE, WHEELED},
          SHAPE={ANY, POLYGON, REGULAR, SQUARE},
          SIZE={ANY, LARGE})
```

The memorization operator succeeds here only because the initial domain theory implicitly contains within itself every possible version space that could be generated for (GOOD=TRUE), all initially unbelieved. The example then determines which of these version spaces is explicitly stored, and thus believed.

When a succeeding positive example of this same goal concept is encountered, processing again begins by elaborating it with its values' superclasses. The current version space for the concept is then retrieved and compared to the elaborated example. All value classes in the concept version space that are not also in the elaborated example are then rejected from the version space (a form of incremental version space merging (Hirsh, 1989)). Chunking over this rejection process yields rules which, in the future, reject the inappropriate segments of the old version space. This rejection process is itself reconstructive so that the updated version space can later be retrieved without the presence of the positive example.

As an example, suppose that the next example for this goal concept is (MOBILITY=TRACKED, SHAPE=ELLIPSE, SIZE=LARGE), which when elaborated becomes (MOBILITY={ANY, MOBILE, TRACKED}, SHAPE={ANY, CONIC, ELLIPSE}, SIZE={ANY, LARGE}). From this example, the following rejection rules are learned:

```
(GOOD=TRUE, MOBILITY=WHEELED) -->
                            (MOBILITY=WHEELED)-
(GOOD=TRUE, SHAPE=POLYGON) --> (SHAPE=POLYGON)-
(GOOD=TRUE, SHAPE=REGULAR) --> (SHAPE=REGULAR)-
(GOOD=TRUE, SHAPE=SQUARE) --> (SHAPE=SQUARE)-
```

The next time the same goal concept is seen, all five learned rules fire, yielding the following updated version space: (MOBILITY={ANY, MOBILE}, SHAPE=ANY, SIZE={ANY, LARGE}).

Learning from negative examples introduces an additional issue: because all of the knowledge learned from positive examples is cued off of

[3] With a suitable training order, far misses are not needed for convergence (Bundy, Silver, & Plummer, 1985).

[4] This example, and all later ones have been implemented in Soar (Version 5.0.2), and verified to run correctly.

(GOOD=TRUE), it will not be retrieved automatically for a negative example, where (GOOD=FALSE) (the converse is also true). The solution to this is to transiently cue with both TRUE and FALSE, thus retrieving all of the knowledge so far learned about the concept, and then to proceed to process the example while maintaining only the correct value (FALSE, in this case). Then, if the example is a near-miss — that is, if it mismatches in at most one attribute — those classes of the mismatched attribute that match are rejected from the version space. If the example is a far miss, it is ignored.

As an illustration, suppose the third example is the negative example (MOBILITY=STATIONARY, SHAPE=RECTANGLE, SIZE=LARGE). This example is elaborated with superclass information to become (MOBILITY={ANY, STATIONARY}, SHAPE={ANY, POLYGON, IRREGULAR, RECTANGLE}, SIZE={ANY, LARGE}), and then the existing information about the concept definition is retrieved. The mismatched attribute is MOBILITY, and the class that matches for that attribute is ANY. The rule learned for rejecting this class is:

```
(GOOD=FALSE, MOBILITY=ANY) --> (MOBILITY=ANY)-
```

The resulting concept version space is (MOBILITY=MOBILE, SHAPE=ANY, SIZE={ANY, LARGE}).

These examples demonstrate that Soar can be used not only as the basis for rote memorization (deductive KLL), but also for induction (nondeductive KLL). Inductive augmentations of the EBL mechanism are not required, because the induction occurs directly in using the domain theory. As suggested by the integrated-learning hypothesis, rote learning and induction are distinguished by differences in the rationalization process. However, contrary to the intent of the hypothesis, the difference is in terms of what is rationalized rather than how it is rationalized (forced by the decision to store the concept definition in actions rather than conditions). In the induction case, rather than directly rationalizing the concept name in terms of the training example, it is rationalized in terms of the version space (or changes to it). This choice of what to rationalize is essentially a choice of what to learn. Here, this choice was based on the instance, the generalization hierarchies, the previous version space, and knowledge about how to induce. Bringing other knowledge to bear should allow additional useful variations on this choice.

Explanation-Based Learning

Using the chunking/EBL mechanism to perform explanation-based learning — that is, the standard form of symbol level learning — supports the third, and final leg of the integrated learning hypothesis. However, this needs no explicit demonstration here, as it is the foundational result of EBL. Instead, what is of interest here is the extent to which, in practice, this use of EBL can be integrated with the induction process described in the previous section. In this section we examine three successively weaker versions of this question. The first version is whether the direct use of EBL in induction, as described in the previous section, provides the requisite form of symbol level learning — that is, is EBL itself performing significant acts of "justifiable" generalization during induction? The answer, upon inspection, is "no". EBL is storing the results of inductive processing, but it is not itself contributing to their level of generalization. This is forced by the decision to store the concept definition in rule actions.

The second version is whether the standard use of EBL to perform symbol level learning — that is, with a classical believed domain theory — can help the inductive process described in the previous section (which is independently using EBL). The answer to this version of the question is once again "no". To see this, consider a domain theory with the following two believed rules.

```
(MOBILITY=WHEELED) --> (FAST=TRUE)
(FAST=TRUE, SHAPE=CONIC) --> (GOOD=TRUE)
```

If these rules are used to relate the training example to the goal concept, the following rule is learned.

```
(MOBILITY=WHEELED, SHAPE=CONIC) --> (GOOD=TRUE)
```

This is exactly what EBL should learn. However, it is difficult to use in the induction process described in the previous section because the generalized example is in the conditions of the rule — thus the rule retrieves the goal concept when a matched training example is present, rather than retrieving the generalized example when the goal concept is present. This failure is disturbing because this is the type of gain achieved by other hybrid approaches, such as (Flann & Dietterich, 1989; Hirsh, 1989; Sarrett & Pazzani, 1989). In these other approaches, this problem is solved by enabling the induction process to directly access the explanation, its operational fringe, or the resulting rule. In the present approach, the rule can be fired, but neither it nor any part of the explanation can be directly examined.

The third version is whether some form of explanation-based learning can lead to generalizations that are useful in the induction process described in the previous section. The answer here is finally "yes". However, it requires augmenting the domain theory itself with the ability to interpret rules and to generate and process explanations. These rules are not Soar's native rules, but declarative structures of limited expressibility that are stored in the actions of Soar's rules. These rules are retrieved as needed to support a backward-chaining process that starts with the goal concept and ends when it grounds out in attribute-value pairs contained in the elaborated example (the operational predicates). The operational fringe of the explanation derived from this process is a generalization of the example. Based on the approach in (Hirsh, 1989), this generalized example is used in induction by converting it into an explicit, factored version space – by assigning values to unmentioned attributes ({ANY} for positive examples, and the values in the concept version space for negative examples) and then elaborating it with superclasses – and then merging it with the current concept version space.

As illustration, consider the positive example (MOBILITY=WHEELED, SHAPE=CIRCLE, SIZE=SMALL), which becomes upon elaboration (MOBILITY={ANY, MOBILE, WHEELED}, SHAPE={ANY, CONIC, CIRCLE}, SIZE={ANY, SMALL}). If the domain theory consists of the two rules above, backward chaining yields an operational fringe of (MOBILITY=WHEELED, SHAPE=CONIC), which is more general than the original example because it ignores SIZE, and generalizes SHAPE from CIRCLE to CONIC. When this generalized example is extended to cover the unmentioned attributes, and elaborated, it becomes (MOBILITY={ANY, MOBILE, WHEELED}, SHAPE={ANY, CONIC}, SIZE=ANY). When this description is then merged with the concept version space, the result is (MOBILITY=MOBILE, SHAPE=ANY, SIZE=ANY). The rule learned from this processing is:

```
(GOOD=TRUE) --> (SIZE=LARGE)-
```

This same general approach can be used to incorporate other forms of knowledge into the induction process. So far, we have partial implementations of the use of irrelevance knowledge (Subramanian & Genesereth, 1987) and determinations (Davies & Russell, 1987; Mahadevan, 1989; Russell, 1988; Widmer, 1989) in the induction process.

When taken together, the answers to the three versions of the question reveal that explanations can be effectively combined with induction in this approach, but that this is achieved only by building additional declarative rule interpretation and EBL mechanisms into the domain theory. The native mechanisms are not usable because there is no way to access the rules (or explanations) they create as declarative structures, as required by the induction process.

The question this raises is whether this is evidence that the Soar architecture needs to be changed or is evidence that some of our preconceived notions about induction, and its interaction with chunking/EBL, need to be changed. While the former is a distinct possibility, the utility of architectures as theories of intelligence stems in large part from their ability to predict unexpected but important phenomena. If the architecture is changed whenever one of its consequences violates preconceived notions, this benefit is lost. Also potentially lost are the positive consequences of the way the changed component currently works. The component is usually the way it is for good reason, which in this case is the ability to model basic aspects of human memory. Thus it is useful, before jumping in and changing the architecture, to first consider the possibility that Soar is revealing something important here. When this is done, at least one intriguing speculation arises – that chunking and EBL, though quite similar in mechanism (both compile dependency structures), are really distinct capabilities. Chunking is an automatic architectural process (it learns for every result of every subgoal, and does not compete for cognitive resources with performance), of fixed capability (how it works is not affected by what the system knows), which compiles recognition-driven procedures (productions) from experience. It is an appropriate, and effective, generalized long-term caching mechanism; but it really is a low-level mechanism that is in some ways more analogous to neural-network learning algorithms than to EBL. However, an intelligent system also needs to be able to deliberately create and utilize declarative explanations of new phenomena. This is where EBL, as used here in concept learning, comes in. It is a deliberate cognitive process, of open capability, which processes and creates declarative structures that can be used in induction, and which can also yield behavior, but only indirectly, through interpretation.

Conclusions

By making a distinction between what is in the domain theory (either implicitly or explicitly) and what is believed, it is possible to distinguish the symbol level and knowledge level uses of EBL – symbol level uses make implicit knowledge explicit, while knowledge level uses make unbelieved knowledge believed. This idea has been explored here as the foundation for chunking(EBL)-based rote memorization (deductive KLL) and induction (nondeductive KLL) capabilities. Utilizing unbelieved knowledge enables induction to be performed in the domain theory itself, rather than as a post hoc process. Chunking is used in this induction process to store the initial version space, and to record modifications to it that are required by new instances of the concept. These capabilities demonstrate why EBL is not simply reducible to partial evaluation – the training examples are essential.

When combined with the standard use of EBL for symbol level learning, these capabilities provide the three legs of support required by the integrated learning hypothesis. However, the support is weakened by the difference between rote learning and induction arising from differences in what is rationalized rather than how it is rationalized. Further weakening is engendered by the difficulty in using EBL to generalize instances for use by induction. This has been accomplished, but only by implementing an additional declarative EBL mechanism in the domain theory. Both of these weaknesses occur because of the choice to store the inductive concept definition in the actions of learned rules (rather than in the conditions), which is itself forced by the non-penetrability of Soar's rules, and the resulting difficulty in determining the contents of rule conditions. As discussed in the previous section, this may actually turn out to be appropriate, or it may reveal an aspect of Soar that should be altered.

References

Anderson, J. R. 1986. Knowledge compilation: The general learning mechanism. In R. S. Michalski, J. G. Carbonell, & T. M. Mitchell (Eds.), *Machine Learning: An Artificial Intelligence Approach, Volume II*. Los Altos, CA: Morgan Kaufmann Publishers, Inc.

Bundy, A., Silver, B., & Plummer, D. 1985. An analytical comparison of some rule-learning programs. *Artificial Intelligence, 27*, 137-181.

Davies, T. R., & Russell, S. J. 1987. A logical approach to reasoning by analogy. *Proceedings of IJCAI-87*. Milan.

DeJong, G., & Mooney, R. J. 1986. Explanation-based learning: An alternative view. *Machine Learning, 1*, 145-176.

Dietterich, T. G. 1986. Learning at the knowledge level. *Machine Learning, 1*, 287-315.

Flann, N. S., & Dietterich, T. G. 1989. A study of explanation-based methods for inductive learning. *Machine Learning, 4*, 187-226.

Hirsh, H. 1989. Combining empirical and analytical learning with version spaces. *Proceedings of the Sixth International Workshop on Machine Learning*. Cornell.

Laird, J. E., Newell, A., & Rosenbloom, P. S. 1987. Soar: An architecture for general intelligence. *Artificial Intelligence, 33*, 1-64.

Mahadevan, S. 1989. Using determinations in EBL: A solution to the incomplete theory problem. *Proceedings of the Sixth International Workshop on Machine Learning*. Cornell.

Mitchell, T. M., Keller, R. M., & Kedar-Cabelli, S. T. 1986. Explanation-based generalization: A unifying view. *Machine Learning, 1*, 47-80.

Prieditis, A. E. 1988. Environment-guided program transformation. G. F. DeJong (Ed.), *Proceedings of the AAAI Symposium on Explanation-Based Learning*. Stanford, CA: AAAI.

Rosenbloom, P. S. 1988. Beyond generalization as search: Towards a unified framework for the acquisition of new knowledge. G. F. DeJong (Ed.), *Proceedings of the AAAI Symposium on Explanation-Based Learning*. Stanford, CA: AAAI.

Rosenbloom, P. S., & Laird, J. E. 1986. Mapping explanation-based generalization onto Soar. *Proceedings of AAAI-86*. Philadelphia.

Rosenbloom, P. S., Laird, J. E., Newell, A., & McCarl, R. 1990. A preliminary analysis of the Soar architecture as a basis for general intelligence. *Artificial Intelligence*, . In press.

Rosenbloom, P. S., Laird, J. E., & Newell, A. 1987. Knowledge level learning in Soar. *Proceedings of AAAI-87*. Seattle.

Rosenbloom, P. S., Laird, J. E., & Newell, A. 1988. The chunking of skill and knowledge. In B. A. G. Elsendoorn & H. Bouma (Eds.), *Working Models of Human Perception*. London: Academic Press.

Rosenbloom, P. S., Newell, A., & Laird, J. E. 1990. Towards the knowledge level in Soar: The role of the architecture in the use of knowledge. In K. VanLehn (Ed.), *Architectures for Intelligence*. Hillsdale, NJ: Erlbaum. In press.

Russell, S. J. 1988. Tree-structured bias. *Proceedings of AAAI-88*. St. Paul, MN.

Sarrett, W. E. & Pazzani, M. J. 1989. One-sided algorithms for integrating empirical and explanation-based learning. *Proceedings of the Sixth International Workshop on Machine Learning*. Cornell.

Shiffrin, R. M. & Schneider, W. 1977. Controlled and automatic human information processing: II. Perceptual learning, automatic attending, and a general theory. *Psychological Review, 84*, 127-190.

Subramanian, D., & Feigenbaum, J. 1986. Factorization in experiment generation. *Proceedings of AAAI-86*. Philadephia.

Subramanian, D., & Genesereth, M. R. 1987. The relevance of irrelevance. *Proceedings of IJCAI-87*. Milan.

van Harmelen, F. & Bundy, A. 1988. Explanation-based generalization = partial evaluation. *Artificial Intelligence, 36*, 401-412.

Widmer, G. 1989. A tight integration of deductive and inductive learning. *Proceedings of the Sixth International Workshop on Machine Learning*. Cornell.

Winston, P. H. 1975. Learning structural descriptions from examples. In Winston, P. H. (Ed.), *The Psychology of Computer Vision*. New York: McGraw Hill.

Young, R. M., Plotkin, G. D., & Linz, R. F. 1977. Analysis of an extended concept-learning task. *Proceedings of IJCAI-77*. Cambridge.

CHAPTER 54

Responding to Impasses in Memory-Driven Behavior: A Framework for Planning

P. S. Rosenbloom, USC–ISI, S. Lee, USC–ISI, and A. Unruh, Stanford University

Abstract

One approach to bringing coherence to the area of planning is to develop a framework that covers the set of requisite planning behaviors, enables comparisons among them by decomposing the behaviors into common primitives, and forms the basis for an integrated planning system. In this article we report on an on-going effort to build such a framework from the combination of a basic memory-driven agent, behavioral impasses, and generic responses to these impasses. This framework is loosely based on the planning strategy embodied within the Soar architecture, and is illustrated with examples from Soar. Though the framework's current level of development still falls far short of an integration of all of planning, progress has been made.

1. Introduction[1]

What is the range of planning behaviors necessary in an intelligent agent, and how do (or should) they arise during performance? Though this is a key question in the design and construction of intelligent agents, we – the AI community – are still rather far from answering it. What we have are partial answers to both parts of this question. For the first part, we have identified a grab bag of planning methods and behaviors – such as linear planning, nonlinear planning, opportunistic planning, wait-and-see planning, hierarchical planning, abstraction planning, goal decomposition, least-commitment planning, constraint posting, case-based reasoning, tweaking, schema-based planning, skeletal planning, reaction planning, reactive planning, backward chaining, operator subgoaling, means-ends planning, simulation, envisionment, projection, lookahead search, state-space search, and temporal planning – and have a few attempts to build planners capable of multiple behaviors, such as NOAH [Sacerdoti, 1977], MOLGEN [Stefik, 1981a; Stefik, 1981b], SIPE [Wilkins, 1984], and TWEAK [Chapman, 1987]). For the second part, we have proposed three general classes of answers. (1) The traditional answer is that these behaviors are preprogrammed into a general planning method that is run prior to performing each task and (possibly) when the application of the plan to the task goes awry. (2) The reactive answer is that the agent is already structured in such a way as to obviate the need for planning at run time, so no planning behaviors occur either just prior to, or during task performance. (3) The hybrid answer is to avoid the initial planning phase by utilizing the agent's existing structure, but to fall back on more general planning methods when this structure proves to be inadequate (and possibly to acquire more structure as a result).

The purpose of this article is to report on an on-going effort at taking a next step towards answering the above question. The approach underlying this effort is to construct, and implement, a generic framework for planning by combining a particular instantiation of the hybrid approach – a recursive memory-driven agent roughly based on the approach to planning embodied in the Soar system [Laird, Newell, & Rosenbloom, 1987; Laird & Rosenbloom, 1990] – with a set of generic responses to behavioral impasses. What this yields is a space of planning behaviors that overlaps with the set of behaviors listed above. The intent in so doing is to provide an organization over this space of behaviors, characterize when the individual behaviors can arise, provide a decomposition of the behaviors that allows comparisons in terms of common primitives, and to provide the foundation for the construction of a powerful and flexible planner. Though this still leaves several important things partially or

[1]This research was sponsored jointly by the Defense Advanced Research Projects Agency (DOD) and the Office of Naval Research under contract number N00014-89-K-0155.

completely undone — the framework does not include all known planning behaviors, nor does it characterize which behaviors are necessary in an intelligent agent or precisely when the individual behaviors are desirable — the hope is that this is a step in a useful direction.

Section 2 describes the hybrid approach, with short digressions to ground the abstract characterization in Soar. Section 3 catalogues the behavioral impasses and a set of generic responses to them. This does not yet provide a complete set of response types, but is a start towards such a set. A sampling of the planning behaviors resulting from these impasses and responses are also provided from research on this framework in Soar. Section 4 relates this overall approach to other work in the field. Section 5 concludes and discusses future directions.

2. A Hybrid Planning Framework

Start with an agent capable of performing *operations* to achieve some end, where "operation" is used in a generic sense, referring to any specification of something to be accomplished. The operation can be external (a motor act) or internal (in a simulated world, for example), and either primitive (closing a gripper) or high-level (picking up a block). The specification can be procedural (directly executable) or declarative (interpretable), and specified in terms of what is to be accomplished (a goal) or how it is to be accomplished (an operator). The agent proceeds by cycling through four *steps*:

1. *Generation:* Generate a set of candidate operations.
2. *Selection:* Select an operation from the set of candidates.
3. *Applicability:* Determine if the selected operation is applicable in the current situation (or make it applicable).
4. *Execution:* Execute the selected operation.

In Soar, this corresponds to the process of selecting and applying operators in problem spaces.

So far, this describes a generic, serial, agent[2] — though one with a particularly local drive, as it is always attempting to take the next step towards some end. What is missing, and what distinguishes the various planning behaviors, is how the four steps come to be performed. In our hybrid agent, precedence is given to a context-dependent, *memory-driven* performance strategy. In a memory-driven strategy, the information required for the performance of each step is directly accessed from the agent's memory — no involved chains of reasoning are involved. In a context-dependent, memory-driven strategy, the current context — provided by perception, goals, etc. — determines what is accessed. For example, in a robot manipulation domain, the problem leads to accessing the available manipulation operations (for example, `pickup`, `putdown`, `translate`, `open`, and `close`). Based on the goal and situation, memory is then accessed about which operation to select (`close`, for example). Memory is then accessed about whether the preconditions of `close` are met in this type of situation. If the preconditions are met, then the final memory access either determines how the situation is changed by the operation (if this is an internal, or simulated, operation), or which motor actions are to be performed (if this is an external operation).

The exact form of the memory is not critical for this behavior — it could be declarative or procedural; contain information that is generalized (plans) or instantiated (cases); and be structured as boolean circuits, rules, or frames. However, what does matter is that access to the memory be computationally limited. Without this restriction, arbitrary amounts and kinds of processing — such as full first-order theorem proving — can be surreptitiously imported under the heading of "memory access". The resulting agent — the *basic* agent — is a generic, computationally-bounded, memory-driven agent. While this is a fairly simple sort of agent, it forms the core out of which more complex planning behaviors can emerge. It also serves as a useful abstraction over a set of common agent types — depending on the exact details of the memory, the basic agent can be a *reactive* agent (if the memory is sufficiently limited computationally), a *rule-based* agent (if the memory contains computationally-limited rules about step performance), a tweak-free *case-based* agent (if the memory contains previous problem instances), or a non-hierarchical *schema-based* agent (if the memory contains generalized plans).

In Soar, the memory is structured as a parallel production system. Knowledge about step peformance is stored predominantly in procedural form, as productions that generate preferences about changes to working memory; however, it can also be stored in more episodic or declarative forms [Rosenbloom, Newell, & Laird, 1990]. Likewise, what predominantly corresponds to a plan is a set of preference-generating productions that jointly determine the agent's behavior, rather than more declarative specifications that yield behavior through interpretation. The latter is possible — see [Reich, 1988], for example — but is not the predominant approach.

More complex — planning — behaviors arise when the basic agent hits *impasses*. Impasses occur whenever the memory is inadequate for the

[2] For simplicity we will stick to serial agents in this article. However, it should be possible to extend the framework to agents capable of performing operations in parallel.

performance of one of the four basic steps – for example, when the memory proves insufficient for generating a set of candidate operations. When such an impasse occurs, the agent is applied recursively to the problem of resolving the impasse. The hybrid agent consists of the basic agent – a generic, computationally-limited, memory-driven agent – plus this ability to recur on impasses. In its most flexible form, this recursion allows full meta-level – or, equivalently, reflective – processing. In Soar, this recursion occurs via the automatic generation of subgoals within which flexible meta-level processing is possible via the selection and use of further problem spaces [Laird, 1983; Rosenbloom, Laird, & Newell, 1988].

The range of responses available during the recursive processing determines the range of planning behaviors exhibited by the hybrid agent. Consider two illustrative examples. In the first example, the agent is performing operations in the external world – it is in "execution mode" – and an impasse occurs because of an inability to select the next operation from the set of candidates. This drops the agent into "planning mode" where it can, for example, perform a lookahead search; that is, execute the candidates in a simulated world to determine which ones are likely to achieve its end. The resulting behavior corresponds to a classical case of execution monitoring – detecting that the agent has reached a situation for which it does not have a preprogrammed response – and dynamic replanning. In the second example, the agent reaches an impasse because the selected operation is not applicable to the current situation. If it responds to this impasse by selecting a second operation in the recursive space that can modify the situation so that the first operation is applicable, the resulting behavior is appropriately characterized as backward chaining or operator subgoaling.

Because impasses are tackled via a recursive process, further impasses can occur within this processing, leading to yet further levels of recursion. One implication of this recursion is that many of the same phenomena will occur for both execution and planning – both involve applying sequences of operations, and both can run into impasses on the same performance steps. This uniformity not only simplifies the structure of the planner – for example, making particularly simple the transfer of information from planning to execution – it also simplifies the subsequent analyses of planning behaviors. A second implication of this recursion is that many planning behaviors may arise from a cascade of impasses and responses, rather than from just single ones. Consider the first illustrative example above, which is described in a simple two-level fashion. This example actually occurs in Soar over three levels of behavior (two levels of impasses). As above, the first level consists of task execution. However, at the second level the operations are ones that evaluate the first-level candidates. If an impasse occurs during execution of one of these second-level operations – because of a lack of memory structures about the value of the first-level operation – a lookahead search is performed, beginning with the simulated execution of the first-level candidate.

One important consequence of this overall hybrid framework is that planning occurs on an as-needed basis. Performance is predominantly memory-driven, but when memory is insufficient, planning is possible. Such a strategy can be quite effective in many situations, as it avoids expensive deliberation until it is needed, and can potentially be improved by simple learning strategies. However, in hazardous and/or time-limited domains it can get into trouble if the memory contains incorrect information, or if the memory turns out to be incomplete when attempting to perform a time-critical step (for which there is insufficient time to perform on-the-fly planning). Under such circumstances a prudent agent would be sensitive to its context, and deliberately do contingency planning prior to performing in the real domain. The results of this contingency planning could be used to alter the agent's memory structures so that when the real problems are faced, issues of incorrectness and incompleteness do not arise. If these memory alterations are persistent, this amounts to a form of learning. If the architecture is sufficiently uniform, the same approach can also be used to learn new memory structures from all planning episodes – whether it be deliberate contingency planning or as-needed planning (or replanning). If enough learning occurs in a domain, it may be possible to eliminate all impasses, and thus all planning, converting the agent into a completely memory-driven agent (for that domain). In Soar, this form of learning occurs via a chunking process that adds new productions to memory from the results of subgoal-based processing.

3. Generic Responses to Impasses

The hybrid framework presented in Section 2 implicitly defines four distinct impasse types, one for each type of step:

1. *Generation:* Failure to generate a set of candidate operations.
2. *Selection:* Failure to select an operation from the set of candidates.
3. *Applicability:* Failure to determine if the selected operation is applicable (or to make it applicable).
4. *Execution:* Failure to execute the selected operation.

The principal thesis underlying this article is that if

these impasse types are crossed with a set of generic response types, then a framework is generated which covers a significant fraction of the important planning behaviors. A complete rendering of such a framework is currently beyond our means. However, what has been accomplished so far is the isolation of four generic response types, an understanding of some of the planning behaviors that fall within their scope, and implementations of some of these behaviors within Soar.

In the remainder of this section we characterize these four generic response types:

1. *Pursuit:* Pursue resolution of the impasse.
2. *Termination:* Terminate the line of development.
3. *Suspension:* Suspend the line of development.
4. *Obviation:* Alter context to make impasse irrelevant.

A sampling of the planning behaviors generated in the context of Soar will be presented as illustrations.

3.1. Pursuit

Pursuit is the classical response to an impasse. It covers strategies that manipulate either the agent's knowledge, or the world itself, to resolve the impasse. For example, simulated lookahead is a typical pursuit strategy for selection impasses – it is a potentially unbounded method for squeezing out more information from what the agent already knows. Pursuit methods are widespread in planning. They include linear and nonlinear planning, the simulation methods (simulation, envisionment, projection, lookahead search, state-space search, operator subgoaling, and backward chaining), the decomposition methods (AND hierarchies, skeletal planning, schema-based planning, macro expansion), the deductive methods (theorem proving)[3], the inductive methods (case tweaking, analogical transfer), the attentional methods (shift of attention, extended memory search), the experimentation methods, and the advice-taking methods. Such a large and diverse list reveals that pursuit is rather a large grab bag itself, and implies that further levels of structure will eventually be needed in a complete framework. However, part of this diversity is only apparent, as it arises from the use of different terms for essentially the same behavior – such as simulation, projection, envisionment, lookahead search, and state-space search – while part of the remaining diversity arises from the development of different classes of responses for different impasse types: the just-mentioned simulation behaviors for selection impasses; the backward chaining (operator subgoaling) method for applicability impasses; the decomposition methods for execution impasses; and the attentional methods for generation impasses. So the picture isn't quite as bleak as it might at first appear.

Previous articles on Soar have already detailed the implementation of a number of these behaviors. Decomposition occurs when a problem space containing more primitive operators is used in response to an impasse. Examples of decomposition for both selection impasses – where the `selection` problem space is used to decompose the problem into one of computing evaluations for each of the candidate operations – and execution impasses – where high-level operations, such as configuring a computer backplane, are decomposed into a conjunction of more primitive operations, such as configuring a module into a slot of the backplane – can be found in [Laird, Newell, & Rosenbloom, 1987]. The use of simulation for execution impasses – for the operations in the selection problem space – can also be found in [Laird, Newell, & Rosenbloom, 1987]. The use of advice taking for selection is described in [Golding, Rosenbloom, & Laird, 1987], and for more general impasses, in [Laird *et al*, 1990].

Rather than reprise this existing material in any detail, we will make do with a brief return to the issue of lookahead search – which nicely illustrates how planning behaviors can arise out of combinations of impasses and responses – and then look at recent implementations of ***linear*** and ***nonlinear*** planning. When lookahead was first introduced in Section 2, it was described as a response to a selection impasse. Later, this was refined to two levels of impasses: a selection impasse and an execution impasse. Now it can be further refined to a decomposition response to a selection impasse, plus a simulation response to an execution impasse. In fact, under many circumstances, this pair of impasses only yields one step of lookahead – once the simulated candidate has been executed, a new selection impasse may occur because of a lack of memory about what operation to select next. Thus, each such additional level of lookahead can correspond to two new levels of impasses.

Both linear and nonlinear planning are quite familiar to the community by now. What makes them interesting here is not their novelty, but that they both turn out to be complex combinations of multiple impasses with varying pursuit responses. They thus turn out to be good examples for illustrating the framework. In addition, by decomposing each method into a set of impasses and responses, the framework makes explicit their normally implicit, fine-grained structure, and reveals their similarities and differences.

---

[3] Many of the other methods are also technically deductive, but it seems useful to separate them out from the pure theorem proving methods.

Both linear and nonlinear planning start with an operation that represents a conjunctive goal, and reach an execution impasse on this operation. They both then pursue this impasse, but in different fashions. In linear planning – as shown for the blocks world in Figure 1 – the agent responds to this execution impasse by decomposing the original operation into a set of operations, one for each conjunct. A selection impasse then occurs, unless there is memory about how to pick among them, or there is only one conjunct (in which case the decomposition also need not occur). In this selection impasse, a simulation begins by selecting one of the candidates.[4] Execution of the operation then consists of achieving the corresponding conjunct. If the conjunct is not already met, it cannot be achieved by simple memory access, so an execution impasse occurs ("goals" as operations have the property that they are always applicable, so no applicability impasse will occur). This execution impasse is responded to by a simulation in which means-ends analysis is used to generate a set of candidate operations from the operators in the domain. If there are multiple candidates, another selection impasse occurs. However, in this example there is only one candidate, so it is just selected. Its applicability is then tested, and if it is known to be applicable it is executed; otherwise, as is the case here, an applicability impasse occurs. The whole process then recurs, with the achievement of the operation's preconditions as the new goal, which in this case is non-conjunctive.

In nonlinear planning[5] – Figure 2 – the original operation is not decomposed. The agent instead responds immediately with a simulation in which the candidate operations are generated via means-ends analysis from the entire set of conjuncts. An operation is then selected, and if it is applicable, it is executed. If an applicability impasse occurs, the whole process then recurs, with a set of goal conjuncts corresponding to the original set, except that the conjunct responsible for generating the selected operation is replaced by the operation's preconditions.

From these descriptions it can be determined that the key differences between these methods are: (1) at any point in time, linear planning generates a candidate set of operations by looking at only one goal conjunct – the *current* one – while nonlinear planning looks at all active goal conjuncts (irrespective of their level of generation); (2) linear planning must achieve a goal conjunct before moving on to a sibling (or higher level) conjunct, while nonlinear planning can intermingle operations generated from any of the active conjuncts; and (3) when linear planning finishes with a goal conjunct, it proceeds to one of the conjunct's siblings, while nonlinear planning has no locus of control (all active conjuncts are considered at all times). The bottom line is that linear planning obeys a strict depth-first progression. It looks at only one goal conjunct at a time, continues looking at that conjunct until it is resolved, and moves on to one of the conjunct's siblings when it is resolved. Nonlinear planning, on the other hand, is free to move around at will.

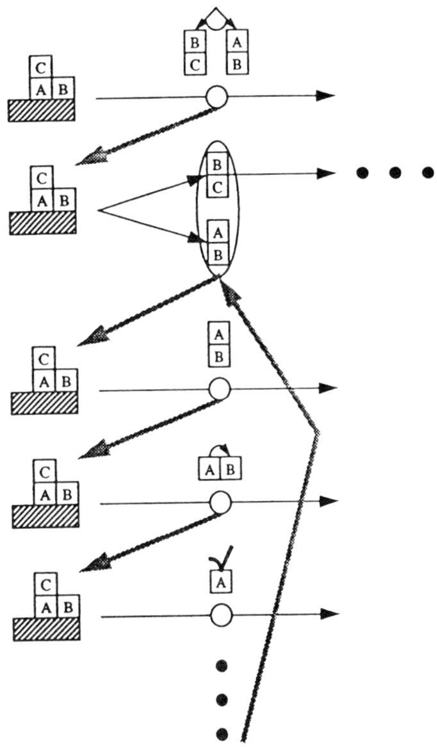

Figure 1: Trace of linear planning in the blocks world.

Given this breakdown of the differences between the two methods, it can be used to generate methods intermediate between the two extremes. One such intermediate method is like linear planning, except that no decomposition occurs before operation

[4] For simplicity of presentation, and since we have already gone over the structure of lookahead, this and later figures show simulation directly arising from a selection impasse.

[5] There is some confusion in the use of the term "nonlinear planning" in the field. Here we take it to mean the construction of plans whose ordering of operations does not respect subgoal boundaries. In other words, operations for different goals can be interleaved. Least commitment is one technique for generating nonlinear plans, but it is not what is meant by "nonlinear planning". Likewise, nonlinear plans can be built from partially ordered plans, but they need not be (see [Veloso, 1989], for example).

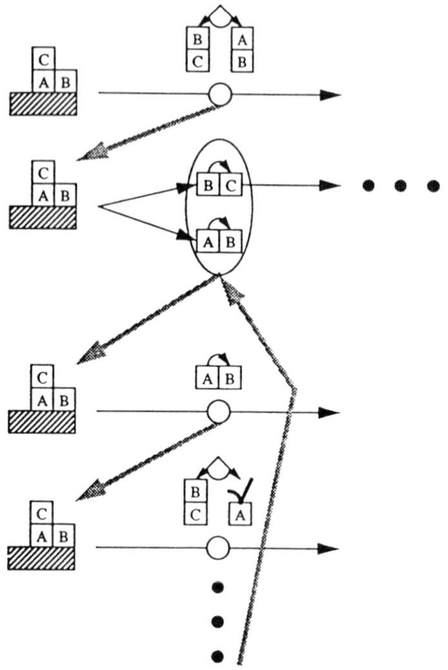

Figure 2: Trace of nonlinear planning in the blocks world.

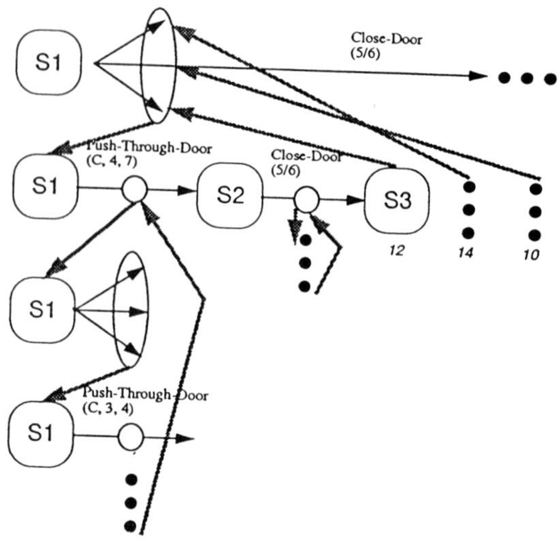

Figure 3: Trace of intermediate planning in the robot domain, starting from the pursuit of the conjunctive goal. The task is to find the shortest path for achieving the problem in Figure 4, so evaluations correspond to minimal path lengths.

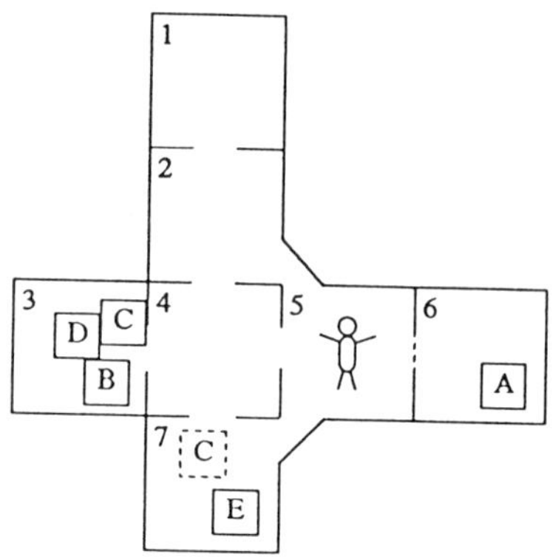

Figure 4: Initial state and goal for the robot-domain problem. The goal conjuncts are dashed (move block C into room 7 and close the door between rooms 5 and 6.)

generation; or equivalently, it is like nonlinear planning, except that the conjunctive goal in the recursive step consists of only the selected operation's preconditions. Figure 3 shows a trace of such a method in a simple robot domain. This trace also contains two simplifications with respect to the traces we have seen so far. The first simplification is that the original conjunctive goal is not represented as an operation. Instead it is represented directly as the (only) end the agent is to achieve. The second simplification is that when an applicability impasse occurs, it is pursued directly by a simulation using operations generated via means-ends analysis from the impassed operation's preconditions. This contrasts with the more involved approach used in the previous traces, where there is an intermediate step of creating a new operation for the new conjunctive goal, and simulation isn't used until an execution impasse occurs on this new operation. Other such simplifications – eliminations of impasse levels – are also possible under the appropriate circumstances.

The trace begins with the pursuit of the conjunctive goal via a simulation. When applicability impasses occur during the simulation, further simulation is performed to pursue them. This method can violate the strict depth-first progression used by linear planning, but only during operation selection for sibling conjuncts.

In addition to using simplifications such as those in this last trace, another way to eliminate impasse levels, and thus to simplify performance, is to augment the agent's memory so that the impasses don't occur. This can occur by deliberate prestructuring of the agent's memory, or it can happen dynamically via learning. As an example, Figure 5 shows a control production learned for the initial selection impasse in the intermediate trace from Figure 3. This production, in conjunction with others that are also learned, forms a control plan that allows selection to proceed for this task in a totally memory-driven fashion. Learned productions can also potentially transfer to other situations, thus allowing other selections to be performed in a memory-driven fashion.

```
In the robot problem space,
want door <d1> closed
     and box <b> in room <r2>,

the robot is in room <r1>,
door <d1> is to room <r1>,
door <d2> is to rooms <r2> and <r3>,
door <d3> is to rooms <r1> and <r2>,
door <d4> is to rooms <r1> and <r3>,
door <d5> is to rooms <r3> and <r4>,
doors <d1> through <d5> are open,
box <b> is in room <r4>,
box <b> is next to door <d5>,
box <b> is pushable,

operators <o1> and <o2> are candidates,
operator <o1> is Close-Door(<d1>),
operator <o2> is
     Push-Through-Door(<b>, <r3>, <r2>)

  -->

prefer <o1> to <o2>.
```

Figure 5: Control production learned for the initial selection impasse in the intermediate robot trace of Figure 3. Angle brackets denote variables, and different variables bind to different objects.

3.2. Termination

Termination covers strategies that abort lines of development (that is, sequences of operation executions) that result in impasses. It leads to a class of what can be called *completeness* methods, because they assume that memory can be complete enough for successful step performance. In *applicability completeness*, lines of development are terminated if they lead to applicability impasses. When this response is used for execution-time applicability impasses, it aborts any problem in which a selected operation is not applicable. When this response is used during planning-time applicability impasses, it focuses effort on lines containing operations known to be applicable. As an example, consider the blocks-world problem presented in the previous subsection. If this is initially pursued as with linear planning, but applicability impasses are responded to with termination, the behavior shown in Figure 6 arises. This behavior can be described as a search through the permutations of (subsets of) the operations generated for the original goal conjuncts. The planning methods described in the previous section also searched through sets of permutations, but they were different sets. Those methods had the additional ability to introduce new goal conjuncts – from the preconditions of selected operations – and thus to introduce new permutations based on the operations generated from these conjuncts. To counterbalance this increased flexibility, the linear and intermediate methods then use goal boundaries to restrict the set of permutations that are considered.

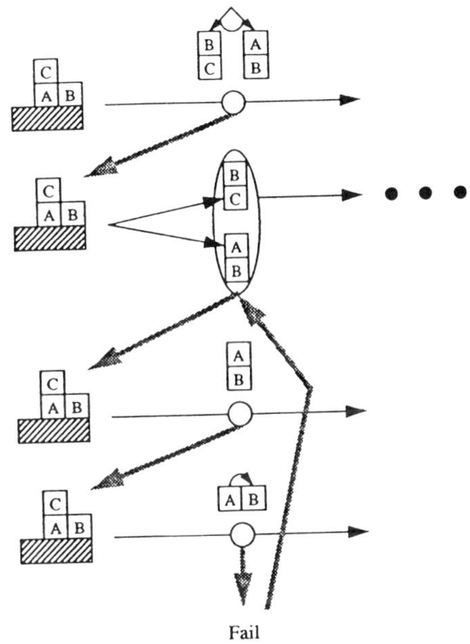

Figure 6: Trace of applicability completeness in the blocks world.

Other (not yet implemented) completeness methods yield variations on this behavior. For example, with *selection completeness*, lines of development that yield selection impasses are terminated; essentially giving up whenever an ambiguous choice is reached. If termination is used for all impasses, pure memory-driven behavior – reactive behavior(?) – is forced.

3.3. Suspension

Suspension covers strategies that delay the development of lines that lead to impasses. An example is execution suspension, where lines that lead to operations with nonobvious execution methods are delayed. It is like termination, except that it is possible to return to the aborted lines at a later point. It also corresponds to a form of least-commitment behavior, in which there is a preference to investigate "understood" lines first. No suspension methods have been implemented so far in Soar, and it is still to be determined whether Soar provides the primitive functionality to implement such responses in a straightforward fashion.

3.4. Obviation

Obviation consists of changing the performance context so that the impasse no longer matters. It covers strategies that reformulate either the ends (the goal to be achieved) or the means (the operations) in such a way that the impasse becomes irrelevant. The difference between this and pursuit is that, in pursuit the impasse is resolved, while in obviation changes are made so that the impasse can be avoided without being resolved. One classical example of an obviation strategy is *precondition abstraction*, where applicability impasses are obviated by deleting those operation preconditions that lead to the impasses. When this is done during planning, it can yield an abstract plan which may be refined later. When this is done during execution, it corresponds to an attempt to bull through the constraints imposed by the world.

Figure 7 shows what happens when obviation (precondition abstraction) is used in response to the applicability impasses that occur during planning for the robot-domain problem of Figure 4.[6] As before, the original conjunctive goal is responded to via pursuit (simulation), but now applicability impasses are glossed over by assuming that unmet preconditions are actually met — this is a local way of deleting a precondition, without its affecting other uses of the same operation — and the operation is executed to the extent possible. Because the abstraction of a precondition can lead to partial execution of the corresponding operation, and thus to the generation of an abstract state, the abstraction propagates dynamically through the simulation (not shown).

When the abstract simulations have successfully completed, they yield an abstract plan that determines what operations to perform during execution. Figure 8 shows a control production learned for the initial selection impasse in this trace. This production is quite similar to the one learned in the corresponding non-abstract trace (Figure 5), except that many of the situational conditions are missing. This occurs because successful completion of the abstract simulation depends on fewer aspects of the situation. The result is a more general production, which can be used in more situations, though not necessarily always correctly.

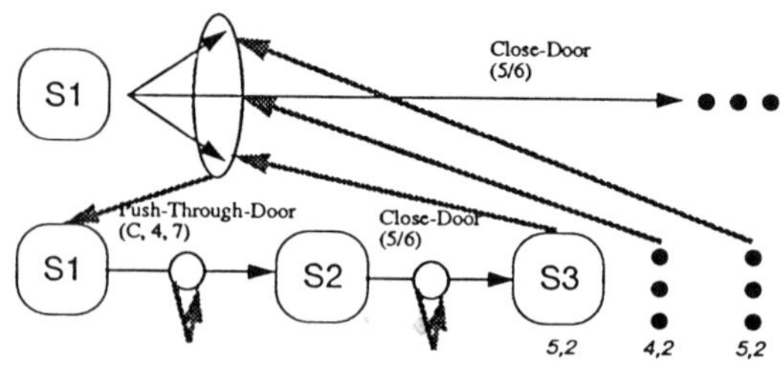

Figure 7: Trace of precondition abstraction in the robot domain, starting from the pursuit of the conjunctive goal. The task is to find the shortest path for achieving the problem in Figure 4. A lexicographic evaluation function is used whose first component is the number of preconditions that have been deleted, and whose second component is the minimal path length.

```
In the robot problem space,
want door <d1> closed
     and box <b> in room <r2>,

the robot is in room <r1>,
door <d1> is to room <r1>,
door <d2> is to rooms <r2> and <r3>,
doors <d1> and <d2> are open,
box <b> is pushable,

operators <o1> and <o2> are candidates,
operator <o1> is Close-Door(<d1>),
operator <o2> is
     Push-Through-Door(<b>, <r3>, <r2>)

 -->

prefer <o1> to <o2>.
```

Figure 8: Control production learned for the initial selection impasse in the abstract robot trace of Figure 7. Angle brackets denote variables, and different variables bind to different objects.

Refinement of the abstract plan occurs when the operations that were abstracted during simulation are reselected during execution. When applicability impasses occur during execution, they are not obviated, since this is quite difficult in the real world; instead, they are responded to via pursuit methods. If further applicability impasses occur during the planning of this pursuit, then further abstraction

---

[6] See [Unruh, Rosenbloom, & Laird, 1987; Unruh & Rosenbloom, 1989; Unruh & Rosenbloom, 1990] for more details about, and results from, *impasse-driven abstraction* in Soar; including the presentation of more sophisticated methods, such as *iterative abstraction* [Unruh & Rosenbloom, 1990].

occurs (and so on). Figure 9 shows a fragment of the refinement process for the trace in Figure 7. This processing is just a continuation of the earlier trace from the point where `Close-Door(5/6)` is selected for execution. Once this is done, the operation is executed without further impasses (the robot is already in the room containing the door to be closed). A random selection is then made between the other two options, because their abstract evaluations are equal,[7] and an applicability impasse occurs. This impasse is obviated, and processing continues. The resulting behavior corresponds to multi-level refinement, where the original plan is as abstract as possible, and each level of refinement adds one more level of detail. It arises here not because of the deliberate construction of a multi-level agent, but because: (1) obviation is used for applicability impasses that occur during simulation, while pursuit is used for applicability impasses that occur during execution; and (2) the same processes occur during planning and replanning.

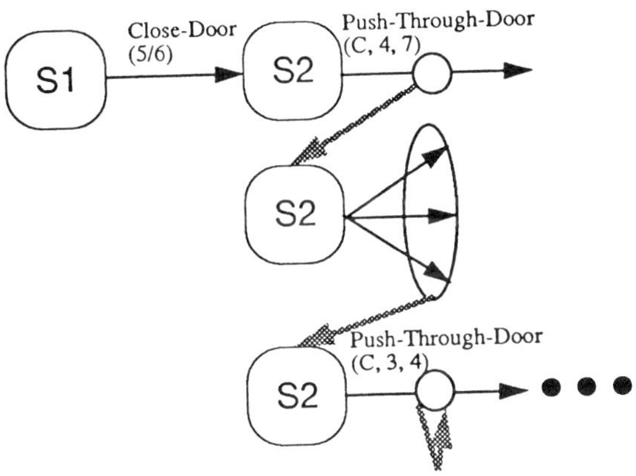

Figure 9: Refinement of the abstract plan in the robot domain.

As with as-needed planning in general, impasse-driven abstraction engages in some trade-offs with respect to the more traditional, preprocessing approaches to abstraction, such as ABSTRIPS [Sacerdoti, 1974] and ALPINE [Knoblock, 1990]. The principal advantage is that the determination of what to abstract when can be driven by the dynamic needs of the agent in the context of the problem to be solved. The principal disadvantage is that, because abstraction is focused on obviating the local impasse, rather than on optimizing global performance, potentially powerful abstractions may be missed.

In addition to obviating (abstracting) applicability impasses, research in Soar on obviating (abstracting) execution impasses in a computer-configuration domain is reported in [Unruh, Rosenbloom, & Laird, 1987; Unruh & Rosenbloom, 1989]. This leads to successive-refinement behavior for the execution of operations. More general impasse-driven goal and/or problem space reformulations are also conceivable, but have not yet been investigated in any great depth.

4. Relationship to Other Work

This work does not stand alone. Because the flexibility of the framework comes from reflective processing in response to impasses, there is a close relationship to other work on meta-level architectures and reflection [Maes & Nardi, 1988]. In focusing on a set of standardized responses to behavioral impasses, this work is very much in the spirit of repair theory [Brown & VanLehn, 1980]. Veloso has developed a nonlinear planner for the PRODIGY architecture [Veloso, 1989], has proposed to use a memory-driven (case-based) strategy to drive the planning, and has identified a set of three general responses to be made when a justification from a case fails to apply [Veloso & Carbonell, 1990]. The BUILD system employed the notion of "gripes" and of "gripe handlers" that had flexible meta-level access to the situation [Fahlman, 1974]. In TWEAK, Chapman developed an integrative framework for partial-order planning [Chapman, 1987].

5. Conclusions

Planning is an important, but still rather disorganized, subdomain of artificial intelligence. One route towards ameliorating this is to develop a framework for planning behaviors. Not only might it help bring organization to the field, but it might also provide the basis for constructing flexible and powerful planning agents.

In this article, we have described one on-going research effort aimed at doing just this. The framework is based on the combination of a basic memory-driven agent, behavioral impasses, and generic responses to these impasses. Learning is also discussed as a way to compile impasse responses into bounded memory structures, thus allowing future behavior to be more memory-driven. Though the framework is still quite a ways from completion, several methods have already been covered, and decomposed into combinations of more primitive elements.

A number of things remain to be done. First, the existing framework needs to be refined, especially in areas like pursuit, where it casts too coarse a net. Second, the scope of the framework must be expanded to cover a wider range of planning

[7] This assumption is relaxed in the iterative abstraction method.

behaviors, such as temporal planning. Covering these may only require extending our understanding of the existing framework, but it is likely that actual extensions of the framework will also be required. Third, a more systematic investigation is required in which all of the generic responses are crossed with all of the impasse types. This should reveal how additional known planning methods are covered, and, more importantly, may yield new interesting methods. Fourth, investigations are needed into how to intelligently mix the generic responses across different types of impasses, and across different impasses of the same type. We have already seen some of this sort of mixing – of different forms of pursuit, of pursuit with termination, and of pursuit with obviation – but much more is possible. This has the potential to generate both novel methods, and more sophisticated versions of existing methods. For example, more sophisticated abstraction methods could be enabled by making decisions on an impasse-by-impasse basis about whether to obviate or pursue applicability impasses. This fits well within the framework, but it is not yet clear what knowledge is needed to make such decisions in an intelligent fashion. Fifth, and finally, this framework needs to be tied in with work on weak problem solving methods and on skill acquisition. On the former, the weak problem solving methods – such as depth-first search and hill climbing – cover a large segment of the generic pursuit methods, so efforts at developing integrative frameworks for the weak methods [Laird & Newell, 1983; Bennett & Dietterich, 1986; Nau, Kumar and Kanal, 1982] are particularly relevant. On the latter, augmenting memory with new plan information is a form of skill acquisition, so work on such topics as control-rule and macro-operator acquisition [Fikes, Hart, & Nilsson, 1972; Korf, 1985; Laird, Rosenbloom, & Newell, 1986; Langley, 1985; Mitchell, Utgoff, & Banerji, 1983] is particularly relevant.

Acknowledgements

We would like to thank John Laird and Bill Swartout for helpful discussions on this topic.

References

Bennett, J. S., & Dietterich, T. G. (1986). *The test incorporation hypothesis and the weak methods* (Tech. Rep. 86-30-4). Department of Computer Science, Oregon State University.

Brown, J. S. & VanLehn, K. (1980). Repair theory: A generative theory of bugs in procedural skills. *Cognitive Science, 4*, 379-426.

Chapman, D. (1987). Planning for conjunctive goals. *Artificial Intelligence, 32*, 333-377.

Fahlman, S. (1974). A planning system for robot construction tasks. *Artificial Intelligence, 5*, 1-49.

Fikes, R. E., Hart, P. E., & Nilsson, N. J. (1972). Learning and executing generalized robot plans. *Artificial Intelligence, 3*, 251-288.

Golding, A. R., Rosenbloom, P. S., & Laird, J. E. (1987). Learning general search control from outside guidance. *Proceedings of the Tenth International Joint Conference on Artificial Intelligence*. Milan: IJCAII.

Knoblock, C. A. (1990). Learning abstraction hierarchies for problem solving. *Proceedings of the Eighth National Conference on Artificial Intelligence*. Boston: AAAI, In press.

Korf, R. E. (1985). Macro-operators: A weak method for learning. *Artificial Intelligence, 26*, 35-77.

Laird, J. E. (1983). *Universal Subgoaling*. Doctoral dissertation, Carnegie-Mellon University, (Available in Laird, J. E., Rosenbloom, P. S., & Newell, A. *Universal Subgoaling and Chunking: The Automatic Generation and Learning of Goal Hierarchies*, Hingham, MA: Kluwer, 1986).

Laird, J. E. & Newell, A. (1983). A universal weak method: Summary of results. *Proceedings of the Eighth International Joint Conference on Artificial Intelligence*. Karlsruhe: IJCAII.

Laird, J. E., & Rosenbloom, P. S. (1990). Integrating execution, planning, and learning in Soar for external environments. *Proceedings of the Eighth National Conference on Artificial Intelligence*. Boston: AAAI, In press.

Laird, J.E., Hucka, M., Yager, E.S., and Tuck, C.M. (1990). Correcting and extending domain knowledge using outside guidance. *Proceedings of the Seventh International Conference on Machine Learning*. Austin.

Laird, J. E., Newell, A., & Rosenbloom, P. S. (1987). Soar: An architecture for general intelligence. *Artificial Intelligence, 33*, 1-64.

Laird, J. E., Rosenbloom, P. S., & Newell, A. (1986). Chunking in Soar: The anatomy of a general learning mechanism. *Machine Learning, 1*, 11-46.

Langley, P. (1985). Learning to Search: From weak

methods to domain-specific heuristics. *Cognitive Science, 9,* 217-260.

Maes, P., & Nardi, D. (Eds.). (1988). *Meta-Level Architectures and Reflection.* Amsterdam: North Holland.

Mitchell, T. M., Utgoff, P. E., & Banerji, R. (1983). Learning by experimentation: Acquiring and refining problem-solving heuristics. In R. S. Michalski, J. G. Carbonell, T. M. Mitchell (Eds.), *Machine Learning: An Artificial Intelligence Approach.* Palo Alto, CA: Tioga Publishing Co.

Nau, D. S., Kumar, V. and Kanal, L. (1982). A general paradigm for A.I. search procedures. *Proceedings of the National Conference on Artificial Intelligence.* Pittsburgh: AAAI.

Reich, Y. (1988). Learning Plans as a Weak Method for Design. Department of Civil Engineering, Carnegie Mellon University, March, 1988, Unpublished.

Rosenbloom, P. S., Laird, J. E., & Newell, A. (1988). Meta-levels in Soar. In P. Maes & D. Nardi (Eds.), *Meta-Level Architectures and Reflection.* Amsterdam: North Holland.

Rosenbloom, P. S., Newell, A., & Laird, J. E. (1990). Towards the knowledge level in Soar: The role of the architecture in the use of knowledge. In K. VanLehn (Ed.), *Architectures for Intelligence.* Hillsdale, NJ: Erlbaum. In press.

Sacerdoti, E. D. (1974). Planning in a hierarchy of abstraction spaces. *Artificial Intelligence, 5,* 115-135.

Sacerdoti, E. D. (1977). *A Structure for Plans and Behavior.* New York: Elsevier.

Stefik, M.J. (1981) Planning with constraints (MOLGEN: Part 1). *Artificial Intelligence, 16,* 111-139.

Stefik, M.J. (1981). Planning and meta-planning (MOLGEN: Part 2). *Artificial Intelligence, 16,* 141-169.

Unruh, A. & Rosenbloom, P. S. (1989). Abstraction in Problem Solving and Learning. *Proceedings of the Eleventh International Joint Conference on Artificial Intelligence.* Detroit: IJCAII.

Unruh, A., & Rosenbloom, P. S. (1990). Two new weak method increments for abstraction. T. Ellman (Ed.), *Working Notes of the AAAI-90 Workshop on Automatic Generation of Approximations and Abstractions.* Boston: AAAI, In press.

Unruh, A., Rosenbloom, P. S., & Laird, J. E. (1987). Dynamic abstraction problem solving in Soar. *Proceedings of the Third Annual Aerospace Applications of Artificial Intelligence Conference.* Dayton, OH.

Veloso, M. M. (December 1989). *Nonlinear problem solving using intelligent casual-committment* (Tech. Rep. 89-210). School of Computer Science, Carnegie Mellon University.

Veloso, M. M. & Carbonell, J. G. (1990). Integrating analogy into a general problem-solving architecture. M. Zemankova and Z. Ras (Eds.), *Intelligent Systems.*

Wilkins, D.E. (1984). Domain-independent planning: representation and plan generation. *Artificial Intelligence, 22,* 269-301.

CHAPTER 55

Intelligent Architectures for Integration

D. M. Steier, Carnegie Mellon University

Abstract

As the number and complexity of design tools grows, the problem of selecting the proper tools for a given application will become a significant obstacle to further increases in design productivity. Environments such as the FORS tool integration system provide uniform methods and interfaces for interconnecting and invoking tools, but do not provide support for tool selection. A knowledge-based system could observe the user and learn to assist in many of the necessary control functions for FORS. Building such system is facilitated by embedding it within an architecture for intelligence, such as Soar, which supports integrated planning, execution, and learning. A system, Soar-FORS, has been built allowing Soar to function as an intelligent controller for FORS. This paper describes Soar-FORS, illustrates its behavior using the IBDE collection of building design tools as an example, and outlines some directions for incorporating further knowledge into Soar-FORS.

1. INTRODUCTION

When apes were first reported to have been seen using twigs as tools for retrieving food, there was considerable controversy in anthropological circles; many researchers were skeptical about the reality of such intelligent behavior in non-humans. This underlying strong connection between tool use and intelligence seems noteworthy to us as we begin to build software environments for tool integration: if we want our systems to be able to use a variety of tools, perhaps those systems could benefit from incorporating computational mechanisms for intelligent behavior. This paper explores one method of applying these methods within tool integration systems, the use of a problem-solving and learning architecture as an intelligent controller for integration environments.

In engineering design, where our research is focused, the problem of tool selection and use is particularly acute. A VLSI designer, for instance, may have access to a hundred or more tools, many of which were created independently, assuming different invocation conventions and data formats. It is possible to build an integration environment tailored to a specific application, in which the particular collection of tools is known in advance. But building such an environment for each application is a laborious process, and such environments are notoriously difficult to modify when the task requirements or the set of available tools changes.

Human designers, in contrast, are remarkably adaptive. They solve the tool integration problem by learning enough about a new tool to use it in the appropriate circumstances. They may do some problem-solving to acquire this information. With sufficient experience, they learn the approximate functionality, tool compatibilities and common invocation sequences for the tools at their dispoṡal. The human approach to tool integration suggests one possibility for integrating tool use into artificial systems: use a framework sufficiently general to serve as a base representation for all possible design processes and tools. A system could then acquire new tools by building models of their behavior within the framework, and test and refine those models. With feedback from experience, the system's design process could evolve from a slow, deliberate interpretation and experimentation to fast recognition and response.

Such a framework would require very general and powerful mechanisms for acquiring, retrieving and applying knowledge. We believe that the necessary capabilities, which are at the heart of intelligent behavior, are present in the Soar architecture [6]. This paper describes research in progress on how ***Soar*** might learn to use tools effectively. It discusses the need for such intelligent integration and illustrates the problem using a collection of building design tools embedded within the FORS integration environment [9]. A system built to integrate Soar and FORS, known as Soar-FORS, is described, and a simple example of its behavior presented. The paper concludes by outlining our plans for integrating more knowledge into Soar-FORS.

2. THE NEED FOR INTELLIGENT INTEGRATION

This paper will illustrate the ideas behind Soar-FORS using the collection of building design tools created by the IBDE (Integrated Building Design Environment) project [1], which is further described in the paper by Fenves and Terk at this panel session. IBDE contains seven knowledge-based tools, which, used together, can generate a complete high-rise office building design, down to the construction plan, from a set of owner requirements for area and cost. While some of the programs only solve simplified versions of the design problems they cover, they encompass the diversity of representations and activities involved in the design of a building. The seven tools in IBDE are:

ARCHPLAN	Input: owner requirements for area and cost Output: Space allocation, 3D structural grid, architectural layout
CORE	Input: Owner requirements, space allocation Output: Building core design
STRYPES	Input: Structural grid Output: Structural system selection
STANLAY	Input: Structural system selection Output: Approximate forces on design, structural layout
SPEX	Input: Approximate forces on design Output: Structural component design
FOOTER	Input: Structural layout, structural design Output: Foundation component design
PLANEX	Input: Structural layout, structural design, foundation component design Output: Construction plan

The tools in IBDE are currently being ported to the FORS (Flexible ORganizationS) integration environment [9]. In FORS, each type of view or partial description of the designed artifact is an *aspect-class*, and each tool is an *operator* that maps aspect-classes to other aspect-classes. So in FORS-based IBDE, FOOTER is an operator that maps two input aspect-classes, structural component design and approximate forces, to an output aspect-class, foundation component design. A particular view or model of an artifact of a type defined by an aspect-class, e.g. the foundation design for a particular building, is an *aspect*. The advantage of using FORS as a basis for design systems is that it offers flexible mechanisms for interconnecting diverse operators and aspects. These tools and aspects can be stored anywhere on a network of UNIX-based machines and can be written in languages as diverse as Lisp, Fortran, C, and Ops5. A graphical, icon-based interface allows FORS users to arrange aspects and operators to form arbitrary computational paths.

Where FORS does not yet provide a high degree of support is in the area of planning and control. Each operator must be applied so that inputs and outputs are available when needed to build a consistent design. FORS currently provides a simple planner that finds all paths through the graph (known in FORS terminology as a *TAO-graph*) formed by linking the set of aspects through the available tools. Alternatively, a user can manually direct FORS to execute a known sequence of operators. Both of these approaches will become severe performance bottlenecks as the number of operators and aspects in the system grows. One would like to give the system a capacity for experimentation, for learning from observation, and for applying sophisticated control schemes, particularly when the availability, accuracy, or reliability of tools cannot be guaranteed in advance of their execution. Soar-FORS is intended to address these issues, since any planning and control that the environment can take care of by itself will free the user to perform more creative and satisfying design tasks.

3. SOAR AS AN INTELLIGENT ARCHITECTURE FOR TOOL INTEGRATION

Soar is the current product of a large-scale (hundreds of person-years) investigation into what is required for an architecture for general intelligence. By an architecture for general intelligence, we mean a fixed structure (realized in hardware and software) that will produce behavior such as problem-solving and learning, given the appropriate knowledge for any cognitive goal-directed task. Underlying Soar is the hypothesis that all such tasks can be cast as search of *problem spaces*. A problem space for a particular task is a set of states and a set of operators to move from state to state, combined with the knowledge that any path from a given initial state to a desired state will be accepted as a solution to the task. The problem space framework meshes well with the philosophy behind FORS. For example, the IBDE tools listed above form the set of operators in a building-design problem space. An input aspect of owner requirements characterizes the initial state, and appropriate tools are selected to reach a final state containing a construction plan aspect. Given perfect knowledge of how to perform a task, Soar would be able to make a series of decisions to proceed directly from initial to desired state. These decisions relate to generation and selection of problem spaces, states, and operators, and implementation of operators to produce new states. An example of an operator selection decision would be one to invoke the operator that executes the ARCHPLAN tool first, given a set of owner requirements.

The knowledge Soar uses to make decisions is stored in a recognitional memory, currently implemented as a production system. The patterns used for retrieval from recognition memory are simple conditions on the problem-solving situation, such as what problem space or operator is selected, or for the presence or absence of specific features of the state. The problem-solving situation is described by a collection of objects, attributes, and values stored in a short-term working memory. When the conditions tested by a particular pattern are satisfied, support is produced for changes to working memory. These changes can take the form of preferences for particular problem space actions such as operator selection, or for other additions or deletions to the objects in working memory.

Soar-FORS is a collection of knowledge that allows Soar to be used as an intelligent controller for FORS. Soar-FORS' knowledge is specified in terms of task constructs in TAQL [11], a language that allows users to specify task information directly in terms of problem space actions. For example, the task construct in Figure 3-1 specifies that a desired state had been reached in the **bd** (building-design) space when a construction plan exists, as indicated by presence of a `padescription` aspect. Soar-FORS now contains 48 task constructs. A compiler automatically converts TAQL task constructs into Soar productions, which are then dynamically tested against the contents of working memory by a highly optimized Rete-based [2] matcher. Soar-FORS, which contains 183 productions at the start of a run, is able to fire about 20 productions per second on a DECstation 3100, and it achieves this performance at the same time as it is acquiring another 97 productions due to learning (described later in this section).

```
(goal-test-group bd*goal-test
  :group-name bd
  :group-type success
  :space bd
  :test
   (construction-plan-exists
   :when ((state ^aspect-list <list>)
          (aspect <list> ^aspect-class <padescription>)
          (aspect-class <padescription> ^name padescription))))
```

Figure 3-1: Goal-test task construct from Soar-FORS.

In Soar systems, the production match and changes to working memory cycle until *quiescence* (equilibrium) is reached, at which time the accumulated preferences are examined to select the next problem space action. A domain-independent *decision procedure* sorts the acceptable actions (which would select a problem space, state or operator) according to relative desirability, and attempts to determine the best candidate. If there is sufficient knowledge to pick a best candidate, then the appropriate change is made to the problem-solving context, and the cycle, known as a decision cycle, repeats. Sometimes, however, the available knowledge is insufficient to make such decisions, and Soar finds itself in an *impasse*, something which occurs about once every five or six decision cycles in Soar-FORS. Impasses arise directly from difficulties in proceeding through a problem space, and there are only four types of impasses in Soar: *no-changes*, when there are no candidates for changes, *ties*, when there are multiple candidates but insufficient knowledge to choose among them, *conflicts*, when there is conflicting information on the relative desirability of multiple candidates, and *constraint-failure*, resulting from conflicting preferences that require or prohibit selecting a candidate. Each impasse causes the creation of a subgoal to acquire the information to resolve the impasse; in a tie, for example, the subgoal would be to find the information that allows the selection of a best candidate. All subgoals are treated uniformly by Soar: a problem space, initial state, and operators are chosen until the impasse is resolved and the subgoal terminated. Impasses can arise in the process of resolving a subgoal, leading to a stack of goals and associated problem-solving contexts, known as a *context stack*.

The trace in Figure 3-2 illustrates several impasses and the resulting generation of a goal stack during the first 25 decision cycles of a run of Soar-FORS on the building design example. The decision cycle number begins each line in the trace, and G, P, S, O stand for goal, problem space, state and operator, respectively. Soar-FORS always runs in the **top-space** problem space . It attempts to apply the `use-fors` operator in decision cycle 3. The first impasse occurs in the next decision cycle (each impasse is indicated by "==>" and causes the trace to be indented an additional level). The impasse, an operator no-change, occurs because insufficient knowledge can be retrieved from recognition memory to apply the operator. The **fors** space is selected for the resulting subgoal, and the solve-building-design-problem operator is chosen because an aspect of class "owner-requirements for a building" (not shown here) exists in the state. Another operator no-change impasse arises (in decision cycle 8) and a subgoal is generated to implement the solve-building-design-problem operator. The problem space selected for this subgoal is **bd** (short for building design), and after an initial state with a list of tools is selected for this space, another impasse arises in decision cycle 11. This impasse, a state no-change, occurs because no operators can be proposed for the state; the operators must be generated by examining the list of tools, which is done in the **bdops** space. Operators in this space generate operators that will execute each of the seven tools, and when the end of the list is reached (in decision cycle 20), those operators are proposed for consideration in the higher-level space **bd**. But a choice can not be made among these candidates, so yet another impasse occurs, this time an operator tie. The **selection** space is then chosen in response to that subgoal for that impasse. Evaluation of each candidate occurs in the **selection** space with a succession of evaluate-object operators, beginning with the an evaluation of the possibility of executing the STRYPES tool in decision cycle 24.

```
0    G: g1
1    P: p3 (top-space)
2    S: s15
3    O: o13 (use-fors)
4    ==>G: g18 (operator no-change)
5       P: p23 (fors)
6       S: s30
7       O: o32 (solve-building-design-problem)
8       ==>G: g33 (operator no-change)
9          P: p38 (bd)
10         S: s51
11         ==>G: g53 (state no-change)
12            P: p58 (bdops)
13            S: s63
14            O: o65 ((archplan) add-op)
15            O: o71 ((core) add-op)
16            O: o77 ((footer) add-op)
17            O: o83 ((planex) add-op)
18            O: o89 ((spex) add-op)
19            O: o95 ((stanlay) add-op)
20            O: o101 ((strypes) add-op)
              Space bdops succeeded in goal g53.
21         ==>G: g115 (operator tie)
22            P: p116 (selection)
23            S: s121
24            O: o124 (((strypes) execute) evaluate-object)
25            ==>G: g139 (operator no-change)
```

Figure 3-2: Trace of beginning of Soar-FORS execution.

Without any additional knowledge (and this very early version of Soar-FORS does not contain any), Soar evaluates candidates by trying them out to see where they will lead. This type of exhaustive search usually does a lot of redundant work, and one way to increase the efficiency of the search to take advantage of early results to prune the tree. Soar incorporates a learning mechanism, *chunking*, that provides such a capability. Whenever problem-solving in a subgoal generates a result that is used at a higher level, such as the evaluation of an operator used to make a selection, a new production, known as a *chunk*, is created and added to production memory. The patterns tested by the chunk include all aspects of the problem-solving situation that existed prior to the subgoal and were tested in the chain of productions that fired to create the result. If a future situation is encountered that is sufficiently similar to the one leading to the chunk's creation, the chunk's conditions will be satisfied again, and the result will be generated immediately, without the need for a new subgoal. Since the chunk only includes conditions tested in creating the result, chunking can abstract from irrelevant attributes of the original situation. This leads to transfer that has been shown to produce a wide variety of types of learning, including analogy and explanation-based learning [10].

In Soar-FORS, chunking reduces the number of decision cycles needed to search the building design space described above from 919 to 270 (reducing the elapsed time on a DEC 3100 from 410 to 130 seconds). In the process of solving the problem, Soar-FORS acquires 97 chunks. Of these, 7 propose the operators for the **building-design** space, 7 select operators in that space, and the remaining 83 implement operators, mostly the `execute` operator implementation. The English equivalent of an operator selection chunk is:

```
If in the building-design problem space and
   execute is a candidate operator
   the tool to be executed requires
     an input aspect of a given class, and
   the current aspect list contains only
     one aspect, not of that class
then
   reject the operator as a candidate.
```

Over two-thirds of the chunks are used to save additional effort within the same design in which they are built. The effects of the chunks are seen in Figure 3-3, which shows the behavior of Soar-FORS with chunking on. The arcs are labeled with the tool executed, and the nodes with the decision cycle numbers at which the node was visited. By the last few decision cycles, there is no search, because chunks specify the path completely. The chunks form a collection of rules at encodes, at a very fine grain, the TAO graph represented by a successful path through the space. Paths through the TAO graph, if represented as a single monolithic data structure, would be similar to the output of conventional AI planners. The advantages of Soar-FORS' representation of plans, based on Soar's chunks, are that knowledge from the plan automatically applies when it is relevant to a given decision, and fragments of multiple plans can be integrated naturally. Also, it is not difficult to interleave planning with execution, leading to a robust problem solver that can react to unpredictable situations. These properties were also used to great advantage in building the Robo-Soar system [4] at the University of Michigan. Robo-Soar integrates planning, execution, and learning in a Soar-based robot controller, and while robotic control may at first seem unrelated to engineering design tool integration, the commitment to working within the same intelligent architecture allows us to discover such connections with some frequency.

4. INTEGRATING MORE KNOWLEDGE INTO SOAR-FORS

The current implementation of Soar-FORS barely begins to tap the potential for the use of Soar in this context. To understand the plans for expanding Soar-FORS, it is helpful to begin by asking what does Soar-FORS know and learn, and how could it know and learn more.

With respect to the problem space computational model at the heart of Soar, knowledge can be described in terms of the role played in proposing, selecting, or implementing candidates of a problem

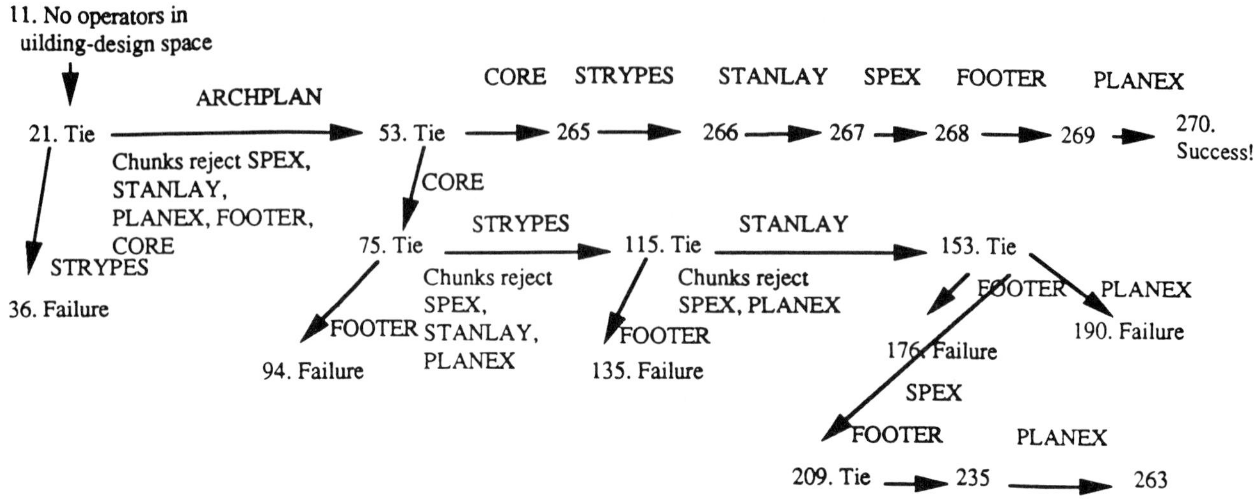

Figure 3-3: Behavior of Soar-FORS on IBDE example.

space. Although some knowledge in Soar-FORS is used to propose and select spaces or to propose initial states, most of the system's knowledge relates to operators. For example, the system begins with no operator proposal knowledge for the building-design space, but soon acquires it by chunking over a space **(bdops)** that generates operators by examining the list of available tools. Operator selection knowledge is acquired by examining the prerequisite aspect classes for each tool, and trying out operators with satisfied prerequisites that haven't been applied before to see if they lead to a final state. Operators are implemented by modifying the list of aspects to include those on the output aspect list of the operator being applied in a simulation of the execution of the tool.

For each of these roles in the problem space framework, more knowledge could be added to Soar-FORS. Operator proposal could be performed on the basis of more sophisticated operator applicability tests. For operator selection, the current depth-first search method could be supplemented by other general selection methods. These could include backwards-chaining, or analysis techniques that would weigh the benefits of applying a tool in terms of accuracy or quality of results against the cost of its application. Operator implementation knowledge could be gained by observing the actual operator effects on the FORS workspace.

Since the goal of Soar-FORS is to augment rather than supplant the FORS user, one way to acquire some of this knowledge is to allow Soar-FORS to make greater use of external guidance, as a *learning apprentice* [8]. The plans for accomplishing this draw heavily on previous research in Soar's use of external guidance, in learning to solve algebra problems [3] and again on the more recent work in robot control [5]. A scenario is envisioned in which Soar-FORS would try to make selections at the same time as the user, but use the actual decision by the user as guidance on what alternatives to evaluate. In this way, it would act as a skeptical but motivated student would, observing the tutor and trying to explain why the tutor action is correct. From the explanation, generalized guidance could be extracted to guide similar decisions in the future (this is the idea behind *explanation-based generalization* [7]). At first, there would be many instances in which Soar-FORS would be unable to construct the explanation, so it could present the user with a list of features it thinks are relevant, and ask which one was used in making the decision. These features might pertain to the domain, the aspect class, or a specific attribute of an aspect. If the feature is known, it could be incorporated into the explanation and its generalization as a discriminator. If the user suggests a feature not on the list, it could be added as a new discriminator, and if necessary, to the list of known effects of a previous operator. In this way, Soar-FORS' understanding of the tools (its domain theory) and when to use them (its control knowledge) could be revised and extended as the need arises.

5. DISCUSSION

This paper has described an approach to tool integration that depends on mechanisms for intelligence available in the Soar architecture. Tool use itself is fundamental to intelligent design, since tools are important sources of knowledge to be used in the design process. This suggests a role for knowledge-intensive systems that is just beginning to be explored in AI research (and indeed within the Soar project itself), that of intelligently coordination of existing software systems. We may well discover that making the use of tools routine is as important for the progress of artificial intelligence in the future as it was for the progress of natural intelligence in the past.

ACKNOWLEDGEMENTS

This research is sponsored by the Engineering Design Research Center, a National Science Foundation Research Center under grant CDR-8522616. The author is indebted to the members of the Soar (especially Allen Newell), FORS, and IBDE projects, for the foundations of the systems that made this research possible.

References

[1] Fenves, S. J., Hendrickson, C., Maher, M. L., Flemming, U, & Schmitt, G.
An integrated software environment for building design and construction.
Computer-Aided Design 22(1):27-36, 1990.

[2] Forgy, C. L.
On the Efficient Implementation of Production Systems.
PhD thesis, Computer Science Department, Carnegie Mellon University, February, 1979.

[3] Golding, A., Rosenbloom, P. S. & Laird, J. E.
Learning general search control from outside guidance.
In *Proceedings of the Tenth International Joint Conference on Artificial Intelligence*, pages 334-337. August, 1987.

[4] Laird, J. E., Hucka, M., Yager, E. S. & Tuck, C.M.
Robo-Soar: An integration of external interaction, planning and learning using Soar.
Machine Learning for Autonomous Agents.
, 1990.
(tentative title).

[5] Laird, J. E., Hucka, M., Yager, E. S. & Tuck, C.M.
Correcting and extending domain knowledge using outside guidance.
In *Proceedings of the Seventh International Conference on Machine Learning*. June, 1990.

[6] Laird, J. E., Newell, A., & Rosenbloom, P. S.
Soar: An architecture for general intelligence.
Artificial Intelligence 33(1):1-64, 1987.

[7] Mitchell, T. M., Keller, R. M., & Kedar-Cabelli, S. T. .
Explanation-based generalization: A unifying view.
Machine Learning 1(1):47-80, 1986.

[8] Mitchell, T., Mahadevan, S. & Steinberg, L.
LEAP: A Learning Apprentice for VLSI Design.
In *Proceedings of the Ninth International Joint Conference on Artificial Intelligence*, pages 573-580. August, 1985.

[9] Papanikolopolous, N.
FORS: Flexible Organizations.
Master's thesis, Carnegie Mellon, 1989.

[10] Steier, D. M., Laird, J. E., Newell, A., Rosenbloom, P. S., Flynn, R. A., Golding, A., Polk, T. A., Shivers, O. G., Unruh, A., & Yost, G. R.
Varieties of learning in Soar: 1987.
In *Proceedings of the Fourth International Workshop on Machine Learning*, pages 300-311. June, 1987.

[11] Yost, G. R. & Altmann, A.
TAQL 3.0 Soar Task Acquisition Language User Manual.
December, 1989.
Unpublished.

CHAPTER 56

The Problem of Expensive Chunks and its Solution by Restricting Expressiveness

M. Tambe, Carnegie Mellon University, A. Newell, Carnegie Mellon University, and P. S. Rosenbloom, USC–ISI

Abstract. Soar is an architecture for a system that is intended to be capable of general intelligence. Chunking, a simple experience-based learning mechanism, is Soar's only learning mechanism. Chunking creates new items of information, called chunks, based on the results of problem-solving and stores them in the knowledge base. These chunks are accessed and used in appropriate later situations to avoid the problem-solving required to determine them. It is already well-established that chunking improves performance in Soar when viewed in terms of the subproblems required and the number of steps within a subproblem. However, despite the reduction in number of steps, sometimes there may be a severe degradation in the total run time. This problem arises due to *expensive chunks*, i.e., chunks that require a large amount of effort in accessing them from the knowledge base. They pose a major problem for Soar, since in their presence, no guarantees can be given about Soar's performance.

In this article, we establish that expensive chunks exist and analyze their causes. We use this analysis to propose a solution for expensive chunks. The solution is based on the notion of restricting the expressiveness of the representational language to guarantee that the chunks formed will require only a limited amount of accessing effort. We analyze the tradeoffs involved in restricting expressiveness and present some empirical evidence to support our analysis.

Keywords. Soar, chunking, explanation-based learning, expensive chunks, restricting expressiveness, utility of learning

1. Introduction

The goal of the Soar project is to build a system capable of general intelligent behavior and autonomous existence (Laird, Newell, and Rosenbloom, 1987). One central hypothesis is that chunking (Laird, Rosenbloom, and Newell, 1986), an elementary experience-based learning mechanism, can form the basis of a general learning mechanism. Soar uses a production system (rule-based system) to encode its knowledge base. Chunking creates new productions (chunks), based on the results of problem-solving, and adds them to the production system. These chunks then fire in appropriate later situations, directly producing a result in situations which once required problem-solving to determine. This chunking process is a form of explanation-based learning (EBL) (DeJong and Mooney, 1986; Mitchell, Keller, and Kedar-Cabelli, 1986; Rosenbloom and Laird, 1986).

It is already well-established that chunking improves performance in Soar when viewed in terms of the subproblems required and the number of steps within a subproblem (Steier, et al., 1987). However, despite the reduction in number of steps, there may sometimes be a severe degradation in the total run time. This problem arises due to *expensive chunks*, i.e., learned productions that consume large amounts of processing in the match. In the worst case, matching expensive chunks is NP-hard (Tambe and Newell, 1988). Expensive chunks pose a major problem for Soar, since in their presence, no guarantees can be given about Soar's performance.

This article is an investigation into expensive chunks.[1] We establish that expensive chunks exist and analyze their causes. This analysis reveals that expensive chunks are formed due to particular representations of tasks in Soar. We then present a solution to the problem of expensive chunks. The solution guarantees that chunking will create only *cheap*, i.e., inexpensive chunks, with a linear bound on the match. The central notion in the solution is to restrict the expressiveness of Soar's production system, so as to prohibit those task representations that lead to expensive chunks. As a result, tasks have to be encoded with a less expressive production system language. Thus, we trade off some amount of expressiveness for a guarantee of inexpensive chunks.[2]

Concern about degradation in performance due to learning has appeared widely in the EBL literature (Iba, 1989; Keller, 1987; Markovitch and Scott, 1988; Minton, 1985; Minton, 1988a). Various approaches have been used to deal with this degradation, most focusing on some form of a cost–benefit analysis of the learned material. In contrast, the overall goal of this work is to achieve the safety of chunking, where safety of chunking is defined as a guarantee that chunking will not degrade Soar's performance. To do this, our solution for expensive chunks focuses on reducing the cost of chunks to a negligible level. Though the solution provides no explicit guarantees about the benefits of chunking, empirical and analytical case studies of several tasks suggest that the solution does help Soar obtain performance benefits via chunking.

This article is organized as follows: Section 2 establishes that expensive chunks exist. Section 3 provides background information about Soar and its production matcher. Section 4 uses the background material to decompose the causes of expensive chunks into two components. Section 5 presents the solution for expensive chunks based on restricting expressiveness. Section 6 analyzes the tradeoffs involved in adopting the solution. Section 7 provides detailed experimental results bearing on expensive chunks. Section 8 presents a discussion of some issues related to expensive chunks. Section 9 discusses the relevance of this research to other research efforts. Finally, Section 10 summarizes the results and discusses the open issues remaining for future work.

2. The problem of expensive chunks

The problem of expensive chunks is Soar's particular version of a more general problem: the high cost of accessing learned knowledge in problem-solving systems (Minton, 1988a). This accessing cost arises from testing the applicability of the learned knowledge in a problem-solving situation. In the extreme, testing the applicability of a piece of learned knowledge can be so expensive that a problem-solver may slow down with learning, a clearly undesirable effect.

To analyze this problem in the context of Soar, we need to separate out various aspects of what happens to Soar's performance with learning. Intelligent systems such as Soar, that are based on symbolic architectures (Newell, Rosenbloom, and Laird, 1990), partition the complete system into two domains. Above the architecture is the cognitive domain of flexible symbol processing. Below the architecture is the implementation domain of fixed computational processes. In Soar, the cognitive domain consists of problem space search. It is a symbolic process that can itself be controlled by further symbol processing, i.e., the problem space search can be controlled using search control knowledge. The implementation domain, on the other hand, performs production match, i.e., it tests applicability of the productions in the knowledge base. Production match is a fixed process that runs to completion unaffected by the knowledge in the cognitive domain, i.e., search control is unavailable in the implementation domain.

Thus, the computations in the cognitive and implementation domains are quite distinct. Analogously, the phenomena in these domains that arise out of chunking are also qualitatively different in nature. Therefore, it is useful to partition the effects of learning on task performance in the two domains into two different effects: the *cognitive effect* (in the cognitive domain) and the *computational effect* (in the implementation domain). The cognitive effect is the change in the number of cognitive operations required to perform the task. The computational effect is the change in the amount of time required to perform the individual cognitive steps. For Soar, the cognitive effect of chunking is the change in the number of (right-hand-side) actions of productions that are executed, since actions are the smallest cognitive operations. The computational effect of chunking is the change in the time required per action that is executed. The implementation domain performs production match for each action in the cognitive domain. This match computation per action in the implementation domain cannot be terminated or altered by the addition of any amount of knowledge in the cognitive domain. Therefore, it is important to bound the match computation per action to guarantee the performance of the system. This constraint gives rise to the notion of an *ideal computational model*, which says that the time per action should be constant. This ideal computational model relates back to our goal of safety of chunking—achieving a constant time per action implies that chunking has not added any match cost. The computational effect is then a measure of the amount of distortion in the ideal computational model due to chunking.

Table 1 shows the effects of chunking for eight tasks implemented in Soar (a description of these tasks and the representations used in solving them appears in Appendix I). Column 1 gives the cognitive effect for the eight tasks. It is defined as the number of actions before chunking divided by the number of actions after chunking, i.e., the speedup, in number of actions, achieved due to chunking. Column 2 gives the computational effect, defined as the time-per-action before chunking divided by the time-per-action after chunking. Ideally the computational effect should be unity. Note that in calculating both the computational and cognitive effects, the before-chunking quantity is in the numerator and the after-chunking quantity is in the denominator. Thus, if the cognitive effect and the computational effects are multiplied, they provide the speedup in total match time. Column 3 gives this speedup in total match time. Column 4 gives the number of chunks added to the system in the course of the run. These measurements were done on Soar/PSM-E (Tambe, et al., 1988), a system that uses a highly optimized implementation of the Rete matcher, based on OPS83 software technology (Forgy, 1984).[3]

Table 1. Effects of chunking on performance.

Task	Cognitive Effect	Computational Effect	Total Speedup	Number of Chunks
Eight-puzzle	6.53	0.15	0.99	11
2-Queens	5.21	0.06	0.32	3
Grid	13.54	0.06	0.85	14
Magic-square	6.59	0.04	0.25	5
Syllogisms	11.59	0.89	10.27	10
Monkey and Bananas	6.20	0.83	5.16	4
Waterjug	9.13	0.57	5.22	11
Farmer	11.09	0.45	5.04	14

In all the tasks, chunking causes a large cognitive effect, i.e., it provides a big speedup in the number of actions. However, for the tasks in the upper half of the table, i.e., the Eight-puzzle, 2-Queens, Grid, and Magic-square, the speedup in terms of total match time is less than 1—the match time has actually *increased* after chunking. For instance, the Magic-square task shows a total speedup of 0.25, i.e., a four-fold slowdown after chunking. This anomaly occurs because of the computational effect, which shows that the time per action for these four tasks has increased by as much as a factor of 25 (for the Magic-square). For other tasks, e.g., Syllogisms, Monkeys and Bananas, Waterjug, and Farmer, the speedup in terms of the number of actions due to chunking is followed by a concomitant speedup in the total match time.

Thus, despite the optimized implementation, matching a few chunks causes a very large increase in time per action in some tasks, causing a gross violation of Soar's ideal computation model. These chunks are called *expensive chunks*.[4] The slowdowns caused by expensive chunks come from the large (combinatorial) match effort for individual chunks, rather than the number of chunks, or combinatoric firings of chunks. As shown later in this paper, in the set of tasks examined, this large match effort in the expensive chunks is due to the complexity of the match process rather than the total number of conditions in the chunks. Expensive chunks occur in the Eight-puzzle, 2-Queens, Grid, and Magic-square tasks, while the chunks in the other tasks are relatively cheap.

In Table 1, the four tasks containing cheap chunks are typical of cheap-chunks tasks. The four expensive-chunks tasks in Table 1 were the only ones found that exhibit expensive chunks, out of several dozen tasks in the history of the Soar project (Steier, et al., 1987). Thus, expensive chunks do not occur often.[5] But when they do occur, they clearly pose a big performance penalty for the system.

Problems similar to expensive chunks can also arise in hand-coding of productions (recall that chunks are not hand-coded, they are learned productions). The analysis presented here applies to such hand-coded productions as well. However, hand-coding allows the flexibility of a detailed analysis of the problem; the programmer involved may then restructure the task or rewrite the productions to remove inefficiencies (Brownston, Farrell, Kant, and Martin, 1985; Steier, 1986). Therefore the issues of expensive productions are not (and have not been) as imperative in hand-coding as they are in an automated process like chunking.

3. Background

The first subsection below presents a brief overview of Soar. This overview helps to ground the discussion of expensive chunks in the following sections. The overview is divided into three portions describing the performance system, the *non-penetrability of memory* assumption, and the chunking mechanism. Readers familiar with these issues may wish to skip this overview. The second subsection presents a simple model of Soar's production matcher—*the k-search model*—to free the analysis of expensive chunks from the complexities of the implementation.

3.1. Soar[6]

Soar is based on formulating all symbolic goal-oriented processing as search in problem spaces. The problem space determines the set of states and operators that can be used during the processing to attain a goal. The states represent situations. There is an initial state, representing the initial situation, and a set of desired states that represent the goal. An operator, when applied to a state in the problem space, yields another state in the problem space. The goal is achieved when a desired state is reached as a result of a sequence of operator applications starting from the initial state.

Each goal defines a problem-solving context. A context is a data structure in Soar's working memory—a short-term declarative memory—that contains, in addition to a goal, roles for a problem space, a state, and an operator. Problem solving for a goal is driven by the acts of selecting problem space, states, and operators for the appropriate roles in the context. Each such deliberate act of the Soar architecture is accomplished by a decision cycle that consists of two phases: an elaboration phase and a decision phase.

The elaboration phase proceeds in synchronous cycles. During each cycle of the elaboration phase, all of the productions in the production memory—a long-term procedural memory—are matched against working memory, and then all of the resulting production instantiations are fired. The net effect of these production firings is to add information to working memory. New objects are created, new knowledge is added about existing objects, and *preferences* are generated.

There is a fixed language of preferences, which is used to describe the acceptability and desirability of the alternatives being considered for selection. By using different preferences, it is possible to assert that a particular problem space, state or operator is acceptable (i.e., should be considered for selection), rejected (i.e., should not be considered for selection), better than another alternative, etc. When the elaboration phase reaches quiescence—that is, no more productions can fire—the second phase of the decision cycle, the decision procedure, is entered. The decision procedure is a fixed body of code that interprets the preferences in working memory according to their fixed semantics. If the preferences uniquely specify an object to be selected for a role in a context, then a decision can be made, and the specified object becomes the current value of the role. The decision cycle then repeats, starting with another elaboration phase.

If, when the elaboration phase reaches quiescence, the preferences in working memory are either incomplete or inconsistent, an impasse occurs in problem solving because the system does not know how to proceed. When an impasse occurs, a subgoal with an associated problem-solving context is automatically generated for the task of resolving the impasse. The impasses, and thus their subgoals, vary from problems of selection (of problem spaces, states, and operators) to problems of generation (e.g., operator application). Given a subgoal, Soar can bring its full problem-solving capability and knowledge to bear on resolving the impasse that caused the subgoal. In this reflective process, Soar can access all of the structures in working memory and fire all of the productions which match this working memory. However, it cannot directly examine the production memory. Productions are compiled code, which is inaccessible, i.e., the production memory is *non-penetrable*. (This constraint has a major impact on the solution to the expensive chunks problem.) When impasses occur in the course of resolving other impasses, then subgoals occur within subgoals, and a goal hierarchy results.

Chunking is Soar's sole learning mechanism. It acquires new productions, called chunks, that summarize the processing that leads to results of subgoals. Chunking only creates new productions; it does not delete, modify, or replace productions. The actions of the chunk are based on the results of the subgoal. The conditions of the chunk are based on those aspects of the goals above the subgoal (the supergoals) that are relevant to the determination of the results. Relevance is determined by using the traces of the productions that fired during the subgoal. Starting from the production trace that generated the subgoal's result, those production traces that generated the working-memory elements in the condition elements are found, and so on, until elements are reached that exist in the supergoals.

An example of this chunking process is shown schematically in Figure 1. (This is a highly simplified example of chunking. See (Laird, Rosenbloom, and Newell, 1986) for more details.) The circled letters are objects in working memory. The two vertical bars mark the beginning and ending of the subgoal. The objects to the left of the first bar (A, B, C, D, E, and F) exist in the supergoals. The objects between the two bars (G, H, and I) are internal to the subgoal. P1, P2, P3 and P4 are production traces; for example, production trace P1 records that a production fired which examined objects A and B and generated object G. The highlighted production traces are those that are involved in the backtracing process.

Chunking in this figure begins by making the result object (J) the basis for the action of the chunk. The condition finding process then begins with object J, and determines which production trace produced it—trace P4. It then determines that the conditions of trace P4 (objects H and I) are generated by traces P2 and P3, respectively. The condition elements of traces P2 and P3 (objects C, D, E and F) existed in the supergoals, so they form the basis for the conditions of the chunk. The resulting chunk is:

C & D & E & F → J

(In the actual chunking process, the objects C, D, E and F would be included in the conditions of the chunk after some variabilization.) Once a chunk has been learned, the

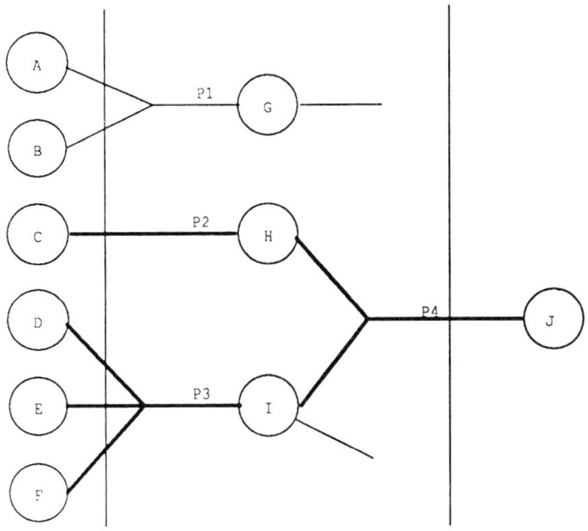

Figure 1. Schematic view of the chunking process in Soar.

new production will fire during the elaboration phase in relevant situations, directly producing the required information. No impasse will occur, and problem solving will proceed smoothly. Chunking is thus a form of goal-based caching that avoids redundant efforts by directly producing a result that once required problem-solving to determine.

3.2. Modeling Soar's production match

The k-search model of production system match algorithms is based on the notion of tokens, i.e., partial instantiations of productions. Tokens indicate what conditions have matched and under what variable bindings. They allow analysis of expensive chunks independent of the complexities of the physical machine or match algorithms typically used in production systems.

Consider the production shown in Figure 2(a). (This is not a real Soar production. See Figure 6 for an example of a real Soar production.) The production contains three condition elements (CEs or conditions) and one action. In the figure, up-arrows (^) indicate attribute names and angled brackets (< >) indicate variables. Figure 2(b) shows the working memory in the production system. The working memory describes the directed graph shown in Figure 2(c). Note that the conditions in the production contain variables (<x>, <y>, etc.) or constants, while working memory elements (or WMEs) can only contain constants (B, C, etc.). The production in Figure 2(a) cannot be instantiated for the working memory in Figure 2(b), since there is no match for the first CE.

Now, suppose the WME (current-position B) is added to the system. The production will now match the working memory. While matching the production, tokens will be generated, some of which are: (2; <x> = B, <z> = C), (2; <x> = B, <z> = D), etc. The first number in the token indicates the number of CEs matched and the other elements indicate the

```
(Production::Length-2
      (current-position <x>)
      (point <x>  ^connected-to <z>)
      (point <z>  ^connected-to <y>)
  -->
      (write exists-path of length 2 from <x> to <y>))
```

(a)

```
/** The working memory **/
 (point B  ^connected-to C)
 (point B  ^connected-to D)
 (point B  ^connected-to E)
 (point C  ^connected-to A)
 (point D  ^connected-to A)
```

(b)

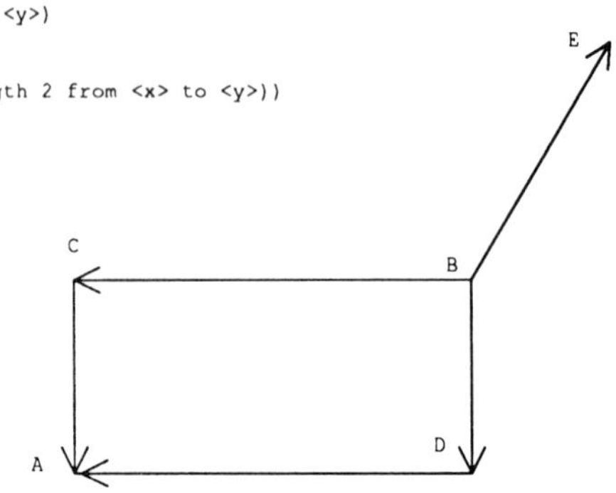

(c)

Figure 2. An example production system: (a) a production, (b) working memory, (c) the directed graph described by the working memory.

bindings for the variables. Thus, the first token shows that the first two condition elements were matched with the bindings B for variable <x>, and C for variable <z>.

The tokens generated in the match can be represented in the form of a *match* tree, as shown in Figure 3 (at every stage only the additional variable bindings are shown). This match tree represents the search conducted, using tokens, by the matcher in order to match the production. Since this search is done in the production system, i.e., in the knowledge base, it is called *k-search*, in order to distinguish it from problem space search.

Measurements on Soar/PSM-E (Tambe, et al., 1988) indicate that the time spent in match per token is approximately constant.[7] Therefore, for Soar productions, the *number of tokens* in the k-search tree is a reasonable estimate of the work done in performing match.

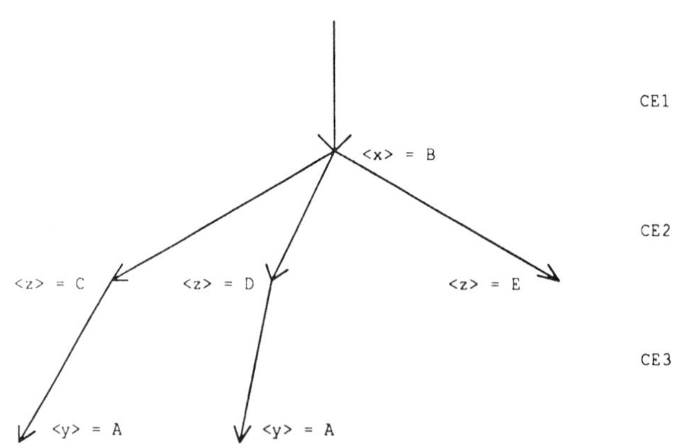

Figure 3. The match tree of tokens generated when the production in Figure 2(a) matches the working memory in Figure 2(b).

The k-search model extends to various match algorithms such as Rete (Forgy, 1982), Treat (Miranker, 1987; Nayak, Gupta, and Rosenbloom, 1988), and Oflazer's algorithm (Oflazer, 1987). There are two important optimizations done in these matching algorithms—*sharing* and *state saving*. Sharing common parts of CEs in a single production or across different productions reduces the number of tests required to do match. We do not do model sharing, since in practice, the effect of sharing has turned out to be quite limited (a factor of 1.1 to 1.6) both for hand-coded productions (Gupta, 1986; Miranker, 1987), and for learned productions (Tambe, et al., 1988). State saving accumulates partially completed k-search from previous decision/elaboration cycles for use in future cycles. Even if the WMEs generated in a cycle fail to match a production, the resulting k-search is saved. Thus, if a new WME is added in a new cycle, only the new WME has to be matched; the k-search from the previous cycles is not repeated. Typically, once the production fires, the state accumulated from previous cycles gets removed. The next firing requires a different k-search.[8] Therefore, performing k-search on each production in isolation, for every firing of a production, appears to be a reasonable way of modeling the activity of matching a production.

As shown in (Tambe and Newell, 1988), there are two key characteristics of k-search (as performed in Rete, Treat, and Oflazer's algorithm):

1. K-search does not allow heuristics.
2. K-search finds all possible solutions.

Thus, the matcher performs an exhaustive search to find all possible ways in which a production can match working memory. The number of tokens in the k-search tree generated in this process determines the cost of a production (chunk). Consider a k-search tree of depth D and a constant branching factor of B. The cost of this k-search tree in tokens is:

$$\text{Cost} = \sum_{k=1}^{D} B^k > B^D \text{ tokens}$$

Thus, the cost of this k-search tree is exponential in the depth D. A chunk with such a k-search tree is clearly an expensive chunk, since it consumes a large match effort (for large B and D).

4. Expensive chunks: The contributing factors

The previous section showed that the cost of matching a chunk is determined by the number of tokens in the k-search tree generated during the match. An expensive chunk generates a large number of tokens in the k-search tree. Two factors determine the number of tokens in the k-search tree—the height of the k-search tree and the branching of the k-search tree. An expensive chunk has a tall, branchy k-search tree. In this section, we look at these factors in detail.

4.1. Height of k-search tree

The height of the k-search tree is determined by the size of the *footprint*, where a footprint is defined as the set of WMEs in the supergoals examined during processing in a subgoal. These WMEs (after variabilization) form the conditions of the chunk that results from solving the subgoal. Thus, the size of the footprint determines the number of conditions in a chunk, which in turn determines the height of the k-search tree. Although the footprint size can have a big impact on the cost of a chunk (as shown in the example below), overall, the footprint size explains only a minor part of the expensive chunks phenomenon.

An example demonstrating the effect of the footprint can be found in the Eight-puzzle task. The representation used for this task is described in Appendix I. It has eight numbered tiles in a 3×3 frame with one blank cell. There is a single general operator to move adjacent tiles into the blank cell. For a given state, an instance of this operator is created for each of the cells adjacent to the blank cell. This gives rise to an impasse to select the appropriate instantiated operator to apply next. To resolve the impasse, the instantiated operators are evaluated in a subgoal using comparison of the tiles in the current state and the desired state. This evaluation is used in selecting the operator to apply next. (The evaluation scheme used is that if an operator moves a tile into its location in the desired state, it is given a positive evaluation; if it moves a tile out of its location in the desired state, it is given a negative evaluation; otherwise it is evaluated as zero.) Thus, to decide the better of two instantiated operators, the problem-solver examines the tiles in the current and desired states for both the operators. This creates a big footprint, given the representation used, since the current state and desired state form part of the supergoal. Figure 4(a) shows the evaluation of one of the instantiated operators. The operator is indicated by an arrow (→). The figure shows how the tile to be moved (tile 2) is compared in the current and desired state. A similar comparison and evaluation is performed for the second instantiated operator. The big footprint generated via the two evaluations leads to a large number of CEs in the chunk (34), causing the chunk to be expensive, with a computational effect of 0.15 (recall from Section 2 that a low computational effect implies a big increase in time per action with chunking).

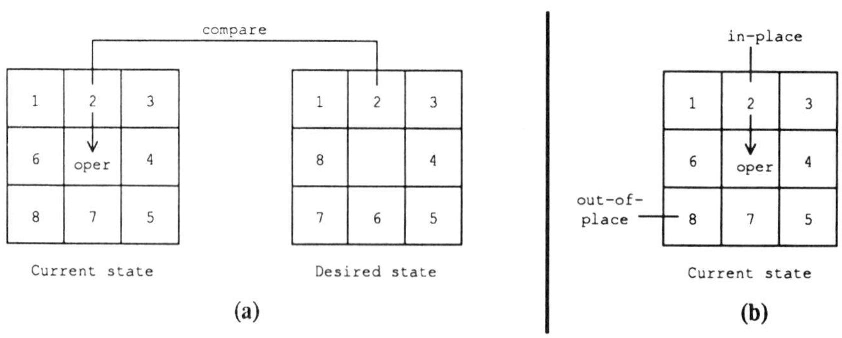

Figure 4. The footprint for the Eight-puzzle (a) when comparison of tiles in the current and desired state for evaluating an operator is required and (b) when a comparison of the tiles with the desired state is not required (in-place and out-of-place augmentations for only two of the tiles shown).

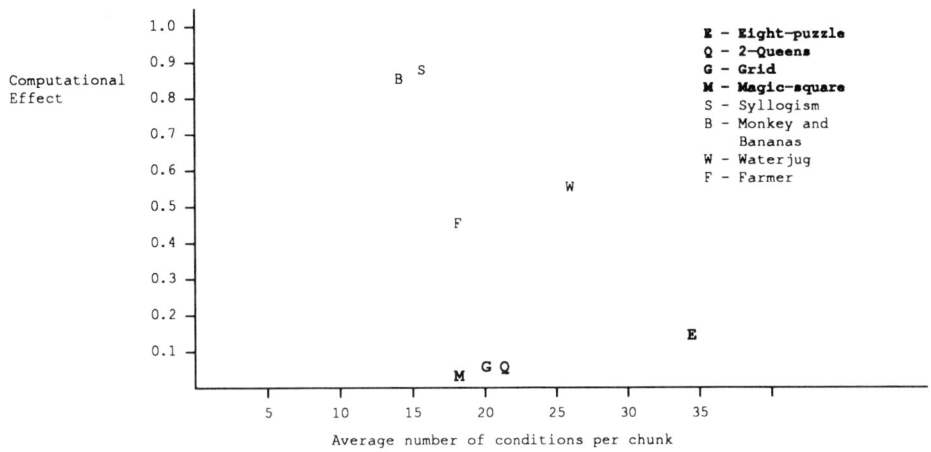

Figure 5. Average number of conditions in the chunks formed in various tasks (on the x-axis) and their corresponding computational effects (on the y-axis). The expensive-chunks tasks are highlighted.

The representation of the Eight-puzzle can be changed, such that explicit in-place and out-of-place augmentations (attributes) are used to describe the position of each tile relative to the desired state.[9] Thus for any given state, the in-place or out-of-place status of each tile is known; and it is updated after every move by an explicit comparison with the desired state. Therefore, the operator selection does not always require an examination of the desired state. For instance, as shown in Figure 4(b), evaluation of the operator moving tile 2 does not require a comparison with the desired state—the operator is moving tile 2 out of its location in the desired state. For evaluating this operator, the chunk formed includes only the in-place augmentation of the current-state tile in its conditions; it does not include the conditions for the corresponding tiles from the desired state. This reduction in the size of the footprint reduces the cost of the chunks. With this changed representtion, the same number of chunks are added, but the average number of CEs in the chunks reduces from 34 to 22 and the computational effect increases from 0.15 to 0.25, i.e., the slowdown is lessened.

Figure 5 graphically depicts the relation between the number of conditions in the chunks and the computational effects for the tasks from Table 1. It shows that tasks with larger footprint size (more conditions per chunk) tend to be the expensive-chunks tasks (with low computational effects), but not always. On average, expensive chunks have a somewhat larger footprint size (23.2 CEs) than cheap chunks (18.2 CEs). However, this separation in the average footprint size is quite small (this small separation is also reflected in Figure 5) indicating that the footprint explains only a minor part of the expensive-chunks phenomenon.

4.2. Branching of the k-search tree

The branching of a production's k-search tree is a function of the number of WMEs that match each condition and the amount of constraint provided by the variable tests. All the WMEs in Soar's production system are *a priori* candidates to match a condition. This match would lead to a k-search tree with a number of tokens greater than $\#\text{WMEs}^{\text{conditions}}$. However, constants and variables bound in the conditions prior to the current condition can provide a strong filter on the set of WMEs that can possibly be bound. Most Soar conditions, referred to as object-conditions, have four fields: (*class identifier attribute value*). The condition (`point <x> ^connected-to <z>`) from Figure 2(a) is an example of an object-condition. Two of the fields in object-conditions are constant [class and attribute] (almost always), one of the fields is a prebound variable [identifier] (almost always), and the remaining field can be a constant, a prebound variable, or an unbound variable [value]. Here, a prebound variable is a variable bound in a previous condition. Thus, *an unbound varaible should only occur in the value field*, and branching only occurs in matching a Soar condition if there are multiple possible values corresponding to the three already fixed fields; or, in more semantic terms, if there is more than one value for an attribute.[10]

The other type of Soar conditions match preferences and are called preference-conditions. For the purposes of this article, it is not necessary to understand the details of these conditions, except that their identifier field is the only possible field which can be unbound. Thus, these conditions can give rise to multiplicity if similar preferences with distinct identifiers are present in the system.

Figure 6 presents a Soar production that demonstrates the restrictions described in the previous paragraphs. The conditions of the production test whether a block with an identifier matching <b1> is on top of a block with an identifier matching <b2>, and there is a preference for an operator called *put-down*. The single action of the production gives a best preference to the put-down operator. Conditions one through four, and six are object-conditions. Their class and attribute fields contain constants, their identifier fields contain prebound variables (except for the first condition) and their value fields contain unbound variables or constants. The fifth condition is a preference-condition. Its identifier field—the second field in the condition—is unbound.

```
        (Production::PUT-DOWN-is-best
CE1        (goal <g>  ^problem-space <p>)
CE2        (goal <g>  ^state <s>)
CE3        (state <s>   ^block <b1>)
CE4        (block <b1>  ^on-top-of <b2>)
CE5        (preference <o1>  ^role OPERATOR  ^value ACCEPTABLE
                       ^goal <g>  ^problem-space <p>  ^state <s>)
CE6        (operator <o1>  ^name PUT-DOWN)
        -->
           (preference <o1>  ^role OPERATOR  ^value BEST
                       ^goal <g>  ^problem-space <p>  ^state <s>)
```

Figure 6. A production from the blocks world domain.

Given these restrictions on matching Soar's conditions, there remain only two sources of branching in the k-search tree: multi-objects (multi-attributes and preferences) and poor condition ordering. We discuss these two factors in detail below.

4.2.1. *Multi-objects: Multi-attributes and preferences*

Multi-objects refer to a combination of multi-attributes and preferences. A multi-attribute refers to a set of WMEs with multiple values for a fixed class, identifier, and attribute.[11] For instance, if there are three blocks in the blocks world, they can be represented as a multi-attribute of the state (this is also referred to as the state pointing to the three blocks):

```
(state S1 ^block B1), (state S1 ^block B2), (state S1 ^block B3)
```

Figure 7 shows how multi-objects are a source of branching in the k-search tree. Figure 7(a) shows the working memory, to be matched by the production in Figure 6. In Figure 7(a), `block` is a multi-attribute of the state, with the values `B1`, `B2`, and `B3`. The figure

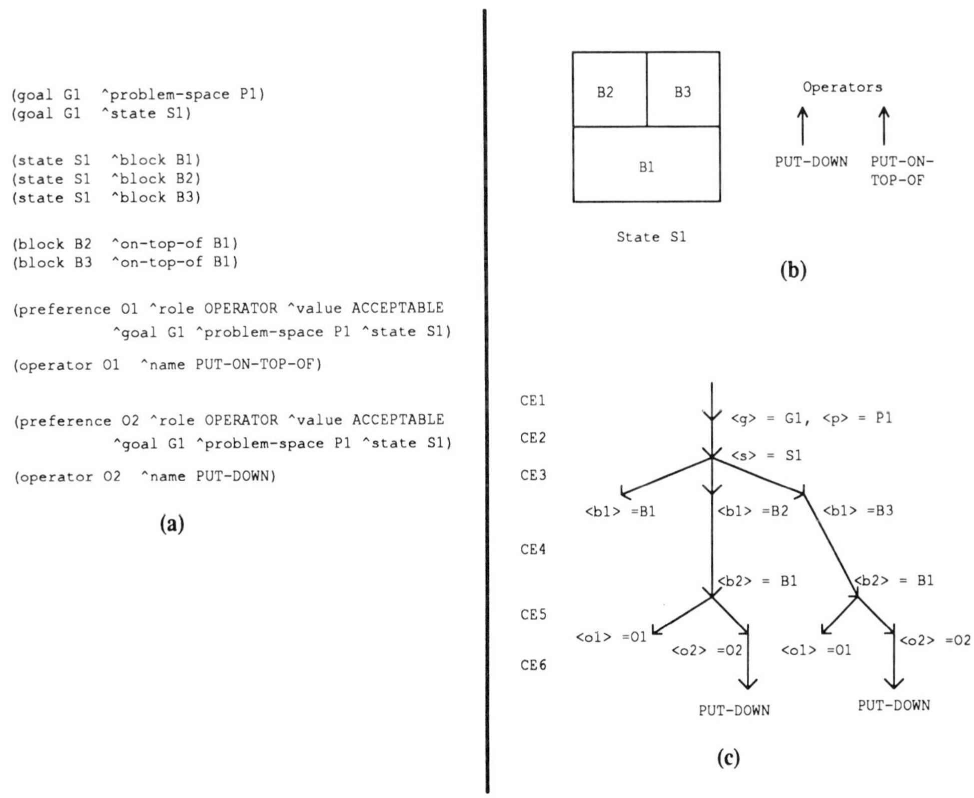

Figure 7. Blocks-world demonstration of branching in the k-search tree—(a) working memory, (b) situation represented by the working memory, (c) k-search tree for production PUT-DOWN-is-best.

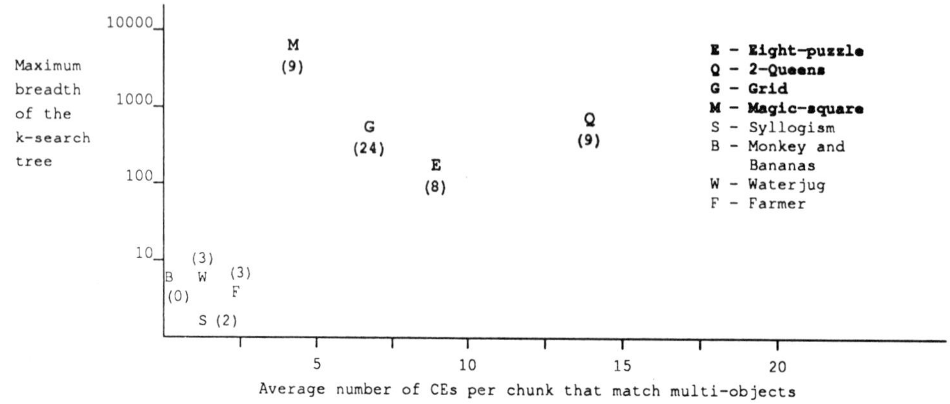

Figure 8. The impact of multi-objects on branching in the k-search tree for the eight tasks. The maximum breadth of the k-search tree is an indicator of the amount of branching in the k-search tree. The numbers in parentheses indicate the maximum number of elements per multi-object in that task representation. The expensive-chunks tasks are highlighted.

also shows two preference WMEs for the operators O1 (put-on-top-of) and O2 (put-down). Figure 7(b) shows the situation in the blocks world described by the working memory. Figure 7(c) shows the k-search tree generated in the match of the production in Figure 6. Since block is a multi-attribute of the state, the k-search tree branches at the third condition to match the blocks B1, B2, and B3. Similarly, since more than two matching preferences are presnt, the k-search tree branches in the fifth conditon. At every other point, the matcher is able to make a *unique* choice of what to match using the name of the attribute.

Thus, multi-objects are the only WMEs that can cause branching in the k-search tree. This conclusion suggests that expensive chunks, i.e., chunks with a large branching of the k-search tree, can only be formed in the presence of multi-objects. Figure 8 presents data on the eight tasks that supports the above analysis. The x-axis plots the average number of CEs per chunk that match multi-objects. The numbers in parentheses associated with each task are the maximum number of elements in any single multi-object used in the representation. The y-axis gives the maximum breadth of the k-search tree during the course of the run; i.e., the maximum number of tokens generated during the course of the run, for matching a single condition element in the chunk. The breadth of the k-search corresponds to the number of nodes at a particular height in the k-search tree, and maximum breadth is an indicator of the amount of branching in the k-search tree. The y-axis is actually plotted on a log scale. Figure 8 does not indicate any precise relation between branching and multi-objects. However, the figure shows that expensive chunks, i.e., chunks with a large amount of branching in their k-search trees, have a larger number of CEs matching multi-objects and a larger number of elements per multi-object.

This analysis shows why in the presence of multi-attributes it is possible for the matcher to generate an exponential (in the depth of the k-search tree) number of tokens. With multi-attributes, it is possible to encode a general graph structure in both working memory and productions, thus implementing a subgraph isomorphism problem, which is a well-known

NP-complete problem (Garey and Johnson, 1978). It is quite possible for chunks encoding such graph structures to be generated in Soar (Tambe and Newell, 1988). Thus, matching expensive chunks is NP-hard.

4.2.2. Condition element ordering

The second source of branching in the k-search tree is the poor ordering of condition elements. Recall that the intercondition variable tests in productions provide a constraint on the values of attributes. A poor condition ordering can reduce this constraint and thus generate a large number of tokens in the k-search.

As matching expensive chunks is NP-hard, in the extreme, the condition ordering mechanism cannot eliminate the exponential k-search. However, in practice, a good condition ordering can provide big speedups in production systems (Ishida, 1988). To investigate the impact of the ordering of CEs in the expensive chunks, an optimal ordering of CEs is helpful. The problem of generating an optimal ordering is, however, itself NP-complete (Ullman, 1982). Currently, Soar has a simple ordering algorithm (Scales, 1986), that orders the CEs of the original productions and the chunks (the analysis of the prior section depended on this simple algorithm). Since Soar productions can have a large number of CEs (e.g., Cypress-Soar (Steier, 1987) has over 100 condition elements in some chunks), guaranteeing optimality could be very expensive. Hence the present ordering algorithm cuts down the number of orderings it has to search through, by using heuristics that sacrifice guaranteed optimality.

We therefore created another ordering algorithm that inputs estimates of the number of WMEs matching the CEs and some data about the generation of tokens. It then performs a complete search and outputs an optimal ordering (Tambe and Newell, 1988). The new algorithm performs branch and bound search and uses heuristics from (Smith and Genesereth, 1986), which are guaranteed to preserve optimality. (Despite these heuristics, it may take up to an hour to order a production.[12] Therefore the new algorithm cannot replace the old one in running Soar tasks.)

Figure 9 shows the result of the new ordering algorithm across the eight tasks. The figure shows a graph identical to Figure 5, except for the arrows. In Figure 9, the x-axis depicts the average number of conditions in the chunks formed in various tasks and the y-axis depicts the corresponding computational effect. The arrows indicate the change in the computational effect with the new ordering algorithm. Thus, in the Eight-puzzle task, the computational effect has increased from 0.15 to 0.35 with the new ordering algorithm. However, there are no arrows associated with the cheap-chunks tasks. This is because the cheap-chunks tasks show no difference in the computational effect with the new ordering algorithm. The branching of the k-search tree in the cheap chunks is very low. Thus, ordering cannot make a measurable difference in these tasks. In the expensive-chunks tasks, about 50% to 75% of the cost is attributable to a bad ordering by the old Soar ordering scheme—the computational effect in these tasks has increased by a factor of two to three.[13] This is because multi-objects and a large number of CEs exact a heavy price if the ordering heuristics do not work. The figure shows that the computational effect in the expensive-chunks tasks is still quite pronounced compared to the cheap-chunks tasks—although it is now closer to the computational effect of the Waterjug and Farmer tasks.

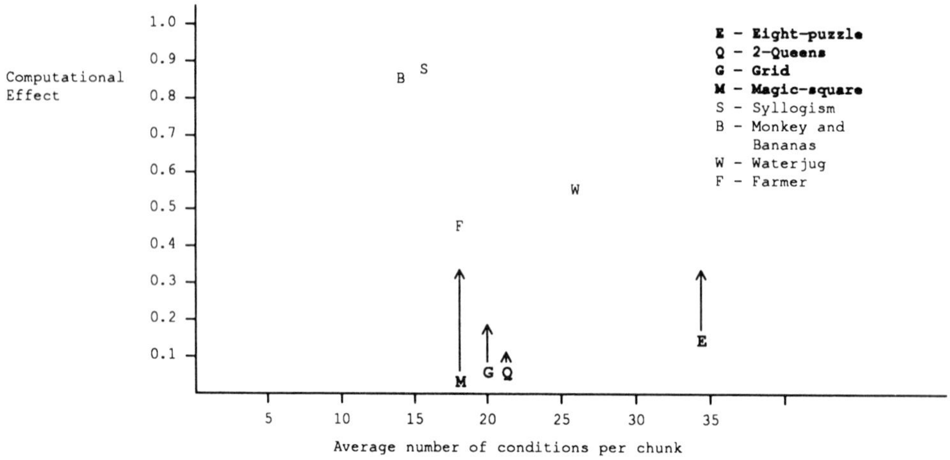

Figure 9. Average number of conditions in the chunks formed in various tasks (on the x-axis) and their corresponding computational effects (on the y-axis). The arrows indicate the effect of using the new ordering algorithm on the computational effect. The expensive-chunks tasks are highlighted.

At this point, we summarize the main points of this section: expensive chunks are caused by big footprints, multi-objects, and bad condition orderings. A big footprint causes a tall k-search tree to be generated in matching an expensive chunk, while multi-objects and bad condition ordering cause branching in the k-search tree. Out of these three factors, big footprints explain a relatively minor portion of the expensive chunks phenomenon.

5. Eliminating expensive chunks

Before discussing the strategies to eliminate expensive chunks, we need to consider the following question: What does it mean to solve the expensive chunks problem? An ideal solution to this problem would impose a fixed upper bound on the cost of each chunk, allowing the system to bound its time per action (there is still an issue if the number of chunks is unbounded, but we will deal with that issue later). Currently, this cost can be unbounded, since the cost of a chunk can be exponential in the number of conditions, and there is no bound on the number of conditions in a chunk. Even if a fixed bound cannot be imposed, it would be prefereable to let the cost of the chunks be a small polynomial function rather than the existing exponential function. Such chunks will require only a few additional tokens to match them (when compared to the original system) and hence will only minimally distort the constant time per action model.

5.1. Strategies for eliminating expensive chunks

Among the various strategies for eliminating expensive chunks, two that initially look like potential solutions can immediately be ruled out by the inherently exponential nature of the production match. One technique is the use of smarter match algorithms. This could involve either better automated condition orderings, or other techniques such as selective backtracking (Pereira and Porto, 1982). A better conditon ordering can definitely reduce the amount of k-search, as shown in the previous section, but cannot completely eliminate it, or even make it non-exponential in general. Unfortunately, other smart match algorithms suffer from a similar problem—they cannot make the k-search non-exponential in general. In fact, smart match algorithms may adversely affect optimizations like state-saving and thus introduce additional overheads. The other technique that looks like a potential solution is the use of massive parallelism. However, given any amount of parallelism it is always possible to have an exponential match that will exceed the capacity of the machine.

After eliminating the above approaches, the remaining known strategies addressing the problem of expensive chunks (or more generally, expensive learned rules) can be divided into two major categories:

1. *Selective solutions:* These approaches depend on selectively avoiding the accessing of expensive learned rules from the knowledge base. They can be further divided into three subcategories:
   a. *Selective learning and forgetting:* The learning system goes through the process of creating the rule to be learned after solving a problem. It then determines if the rule is expensive or cheap. If the rule is expensive, the system does not add it to its knowledge base. The system may have an additional capability of selective forgetting. With selective forgetting, the system adds the rule to its knowledge base, but if it finds out that the rule becomes expensive while in use, it throws the rule away.

      Typically selective learning/forgetting systems adopt the following criterion for determining the expense of a rule: a rule is expensive if its estimated processing cost exceeds its estimated benefits (Keller, 1987; Markovitch and Scott, 1988; Minton, 1985; Minton, 1988b).
   b. *Selective Matching:* The learning system creates the rule to be learned and adds it to the knowledge base. The matcher reasons about the expense of the learned rules and other rules that may be applicable and decides the best rule to apply at that point in time. Thus, the compiled rule always remains in the knowledge base (Markovitch and Scott, 1989a); it is not thrown away.
   c. *User Intervention:* In this approach, the user of the system monitors its performance. If he/she notices a performance problem during learning, then he/she intervenes and removes the efficiency bugs in the system.
2. *Transforming the pattern to be matched:* These approaches depend on uniformly reducing the cost of the learned rule by transforming it, so that expensive rules are not added to the knowledge base in the first place. They can be further divided into two subcategories:
   a. *Modifying learned rules:* This approach requires the system to modify learned rules. After learning a rule, its left-hand side is simplified to reduce its match cost. This reduction may be accomplished by processes such as compression (Minton, 1988b) and removing applicability conditions (Chase, et al., 1989).
   b. *Restricting expressiveness:* This approach requires the system to give up some expressiveness of its language to guarantee that all learned rules are cheap. Thus, no evaluation need be done to guarantee that the system will not degrade in performance.

Furthermore, the system is not required to modify learned rules. This tradeoff is similar to the tradeoff between the expressiveness of a representational language and its computational tractability (Levesque and Brachman, 1985).

Two important criteria for adopting a particular approach from the above list are: (1) the effectiveness of the approach in addressing expensive chunks and (2) how well the approach integrates with the rest of the system, given the assumptions underlying the system. The approach adopted in this article is one of restricting expressiveness. Meeting the first criterion above, i.e., demonstrating the effectiveness of this approach, is the focus of the rest of this article. Meeting the second criterion, i.e., establishing that this approach best conforms with the assumptions in Soar, compared to the other approaches presented, is the focus of the following four paragraphs.

Among the approaches presented, the user intervention approach is ruled out immediately, since the goal of the Soar project is to build a system capable of autonomous existence, i.e., a system that is not dependent on the user. In fact, the requirement for autonomy is one key way in which the problem of expensive chunks differs from the more general problem of expensive productions.

The selective learning/matching approaches depend on analyzing the cost and/or benefits of individual productions. This can be achieved by two different methods:

1. Using a fixed piece of code as part of the architecture, i.e., using a mechanism in the implementation domain.
2. By problem-solving, i.e., using a mechanism in the cognitive domain.

Including a mechanism for cost/benefit analysis in the architecture is against one of Soar's major design principles—no fixed *trap-state* mechanisms (Newell, 1990). A trap-state mechanism is one whose commands the system has to accept, but which has insufficient knowledge to cover all potential situations. The conflict-resolution phase in OPS5 is an example of a trap-state mechanism. When the knowledge encoded in the trap-state mechanism fails, as it necessarily has to if the enountered situations are diverse enough, the system can be led into problems from which it cannot recover—in this case matching a very expensive chunk. Resource bounds may help the system recover from such problems, e.g., they may impose some time-outs on the match. But these resource bounds are trap-state mechanisms in themselves. Consider the example of imposing time-outs on the match. Suppose there is a production that controls some important external device. The time-out may prevent the production from controlling the external device in a critical real-time situation, leading to a disaster. Thus, a time-out mechanism is a trap-state mechanism that could interfere in getting Soar to do real-time tasks sometime in the future.

The cognitive domain approach for cost-benefit analysis does not suffer from the trap-state problem. However, this approach cannot be used, since it would require keeping track of the costs and benefits of the productions in the cognitive domain, which violates the non-penetrable memory assumption mentioned in Section 3.1. A similar argument eliminates the possibility of modifying learned rules—it would be a trap-state mechanism in the implementation domain and would violate the non-penetrable memory assumption in the cognitive domain.

The approach based on restricting expressiveness is not dependent on any mechanism, in either the cognitive or the implementation domain. Thus, it entirely avoids the issues of non-penetrability or trap-states faced by the other approaches and is in fact, the only approach that conforms with the assumptions underlying Soar. But how should schemes for restricting expressiveness be selected or even devised? An important constraint that will be used for selection is the guarantee of *closure under chunking*, i.e., if the productions and working memory meet the restrictions imposed by a scheme before chunking, then the chunks should also meet the restrictions. If chunking violates the restrictions and creates expensive chunks, then that would clearly defeat the purpose of this exercise.

In devising schemes for restricting expressiveness, two obvious candidates are: restricting the size of the footprint, and restricting the use of multi-objects. A restriction on the size of the footprint will bound the depth of the k-search tree. This will make the cost of the chunk a polynomial in the branching factor fo the k-search tree. However, unless this bound is small, it will not be useful. But a small bound on the number of CEs will require extensive modifications to the current methods of task representations in Soar. It would also be difficult to guarantee closure under chunking since chunks usually have a higher number of CEs than hand-written productions (Tambe, et al., 1988). Providing such guarantees may require modifications to chunking, and perhaps also to the rest of Soar. Thus, it would be preferable no to impose an arbitrary bound on the size of the footprint.

The other alternative of restricting multi-objects seems more promising. One category of restrictions in this mode would be to impose a partial restriction on the use of multi-objects—for instance, to limit the number of conditions per production that can match multi-objects. However, it is difficult to guarantee closure under chunking for such partial restrictions. In the previous example, the chunks formed can easily exceed the limit on conditions per production that match multi-objects. A better approach is to eliminate multi-objects altogether, which clearly guarantees closure under chunking. Multi-objects control the branching of the k-search tree. Therefore, eliminating multi-objects eliminates the exponential from the cost (B^D) of the k-search tree—it reduces the branching factor of the k-search tree ot one. This limits the number of tokens in the k-search tree to the size of the footprint. Thus,

The cost of matching a chunk will be linear in the number of conditions.

As stated earlier in this section, this is a very agreeable bound on the cost of the chunks. The size of the footprint grows at most linearly with the amount of time spent in the subgoal. Thus, eliminating multi-objects imposes a very reasonable limit on the cost of a chunk—these chunks are cheap chunks. However, it is still possible for a chunk with a very large footprint to distort the constant time per action model. Dealing with such footprints will be the subject of future work.

5.2. Eliminating multi-objects

Recall that multi-objects refer to a combination of multi-attributes and preferences. The elimination of multi-attributes implies that the system is not allowed to assign two or more values to any attribute. The new restricted representation without the multi-attributes is

```
(state S1   ^block B1)    ┐
(block B1   ^next B2)     │   A linked list of blocks
(block B2   ^next B3)     ┘   is introduced
(block B2   ^on-top-of B1)
(block B3   ^on-top-of B1)
```

Figure 10. Unique-attribute encoding of the blocks world from Figure 7.

referred to as the *unique-attribute* representation. Figure 10 shows how the blocks in the blocks world, represented originally as multi-attributes in Figure 7(a), are represented as unique-attributes. Note that the blocks are no longer a multi-attribute of the state. Instead, a linked list is introduced, with the state pointing the head of the list. The issues in adopting such unique-attribute representations will be discussed in detail in Section 8.1.

Preferences are dealt with somewhat differently. Recall that preferences cause branching in the k-search tree due to their unbound identifiers. Therefore, a restriction is imposed to require that all preference identifiers be prebound. However, chunking may violate this restriction, and create chunks which include preferences with unbound identifiers. Soar's chunking algorithm has therefore been modified (on an experimental basis) so that preferences with unbound identifiers are not included in the chunks. This modification prevents the preferences from causing branching in the k-search tree.

The restrictions for the cheap chunks are summarized below.[14]

1. Multi-attributes are not allowed; only unique-attributes may be used.
2. Preference identifiers must be prebound.

One of the flexibilities not restricted is the ability to match multiple goals in the hierarchy. The number of goals in the goal-hierarchy can grow only linearly with time, as measured by the number of decision cycles. In fact, typically there are only about three to four goals in the goal-hierarchy. This causes a maximum k-search breadth of three to four tokens in the first one or two CEs of a chunk. This low cost appears to be worth the flexibility of matching multiple goals in the goal hierarchy, which allows a chunk to transfer to any of the goal-contexts in the context hierarchy. However, if matching multiple goals turns out to be a problem, then this capability can also be restricted.

Except for the experimental modification to chunking, the other restrictions can be adopted in the current version of Soar using a set of conventions. We have used this version for the empirical analysis presented in this paper. In the actual implementation, assigning multiple values to a single attribute should lead to the creation of an impasse, allowing the architecture to enforce a representation without multi-attributes. The new version of Soar (Soar 5) will allow a very straightforward incorporation of this mechanism (interestingly, unique-attributes did not influence the design of Soar 5).

Table 2 presents data from nine different Soar tasks.[15] Except for the Tree task to be introduced in Section 6.2, these tasks are from Table 1. The main message of this table is that the unique-attributes eliminate expensive chunks. The first column gives the total run time before chunking, using the multi-attribute representation. The second column gives

Table 2. The total run time after chunking with two different representations.

Task	Total run time multi-attr. before chunking (sec.)	Total run time multi-attr. after chunking (sec.)	Total number of chunks multi-attr.	Total run time unique-attr. before chunking (sec.)	Total run time unique-attr. after chunking (sec.)	Total number of chunks unique-attr.
Eight-puzzle	28.69	34.56	11	26.67	8.88	86
2-Queens	4.48	13.52	3	3.55	0.40	3
Grid	23.44	12.65	17	19.81	3.09	142
Magic-square	13.92	18.72	5	12.62	2.72	5
Tree	10.28	1.55	11	9.94	1.39	72
Syllogisms	8.46	0.82	11	7.92	0.82	11
Monkey	7.13	1.73	5	8.21	1.83	5
Waterjug	21.43	3.56	11	19.84	2.25	11
Farmer	26.94	4.39	14	20.25	2.07	14

the total run time after chunking, using the multi-attribute representation. The third column gives the number of chunks formed in the multi-attribute representation. The last three columns give comparable data for the unique-attribute representation.

The table shows that the time to complete the task without chunking in both representations is comparable. However, in the four expensive-chunks tasks, the multi-attribute representation goes on to form expensive chunks. Chunks formed in the unique-attribute representation are cheap and the total run time after chunking is much lower than the total run time before chunking. The two cheap-chunks tasks (Waterjug and Farmer) that had a significant computational effect also show a speedup with the unique-attributes.

Note that, in some tasks, a significantly larger number of unique-attribute chunks are learned. This effect is due to a secondary impact of unique-attributes—the chunks that are learned may be less general. This reduction in generality occurs because a multi-attribute condition can match any element of a set, while a unique-attribute conditon can match only one possible element. When the unique-attribute chunks were less general than the multi-attribute ones, additional trials were run on the same task until enough chunks had been learned to cover the same scope as the multi-attribute chunks. For this experiment, these trials were selected by hand so as to cover chunks not yet learned. (This issue is picked up in more detail in the following sections.) However, the table shows that even after learning the larger number of chunks, the unique-attribute run times are much lower than the multi-attribute run times.

6. Complexity analyses of two illustrative tasks

The previous section presented the unique-attributes restriction on the expressiveness of Soar's production system language. Unique-attributes allow us to guarantee that only cheap chunks will be produced by the system. This section presents complexity analyses of two simple tasks to demonstrate the expressiveness-efficiency tradeoff involved in unique-

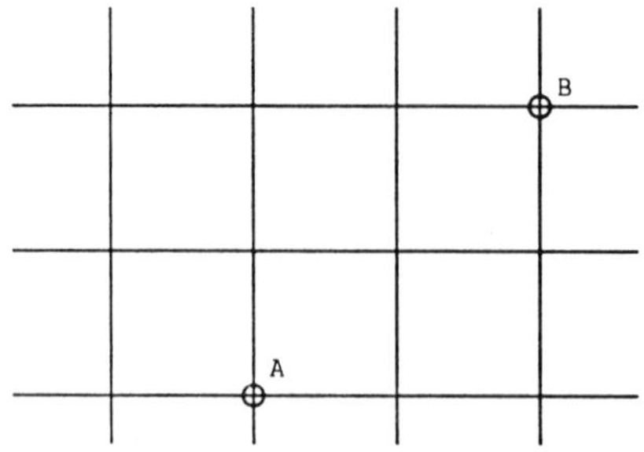

Figure 11. The Grid task.

attributes. The first subsection use the Grid task to illustrate this tradeoff. The second subsection uses the Tree task to present a best- and worst-case analysis of the expressiveness-efficiency tradeoff.

6.1. The Grid task: An illustration of the expressiveness-efficiency tradeoff

Consider an example from the Grid task, shown in Figure 11. To simplify some of the following analysis, assume that this grid is infinite. The problem is to go from point A to point B, a path of length four. This problem is solved first using multi-attributes and then using unique-attributes.

In the multi-attribute version, the grid is represented using *connected* as a multi-attribute of a *point* on the grid. Any point Y adjacent to a point X on the grid is represented as: (`point X ^connected Y`). Thus, the multi-attribute *connected* represents an unstructured set of connections between a point and all of its immediate neighbors. The problem space has only one operator: *move*. The state contains a pointer to the current position on the grid. If the current position is at point *x*, then for each point *y* connected to point *x*, the operator *move* will be instantiated. The problem-solver will solve the problem using some heuristics, or outside guidance, generating a k-search tree of tokens as shown in Figure 12(a). This process generates 16 tokens, with four tokens per each step generated from the four options available to the problem-solver at each point on the grid. Even if the heuristics do not directly lead the problem-solver to the solution, the matcher will generate only 4 tokens per step. Note that this is a highly simplified version of the real Soar production system. For instance, we have not accounted for the cost of subgoaling, or for the cost of the heuristics. However, since the purpose here is to analyze the cost of multi- and unique-attribute chunks, we will use this simple model.

The chunk formed in solving the task is shown in Figure 12(b). The chunk says that if the goal is to reach a point <d>, and if the current position is point <x>, and if there is a path of length four between them, then prefer the instantiated *move* operator along that path. (The prefer action indicates a preference for a path from <x> to <y> over all other paths; recall from Section 3.2 that < > indicates variables.) This chunk does not consider the points along which the path goes or the direction the path takes. The chunk will therefore transfer to all pairs of points with a path length of four between them.

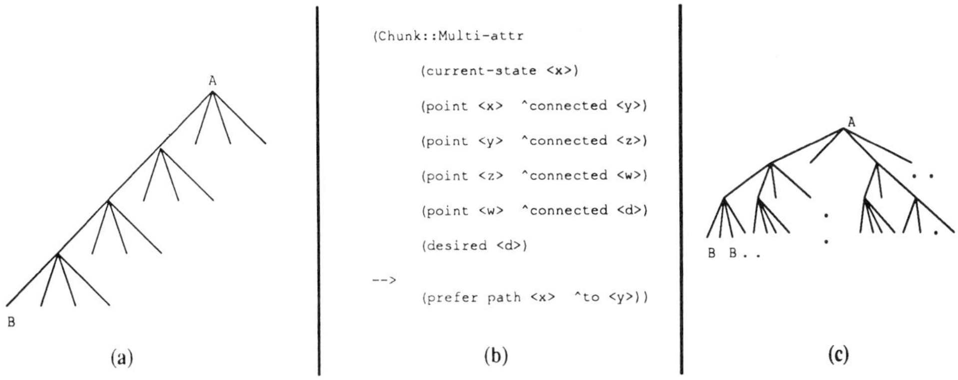

Figure 12. The Grid task with multi-attributes: (a) the k-search tree for the entire task consisting of four problem solving steps; (b) the chunk formed (prefer action indicates a preference for a path from <x> to <y> over all other paths); and (c) the k-search tree formed in matching the chunk (generated for one problem-solving step).

Figure 12(c) shows the k-search tree formed in matching the chunk. For the sake of simplicity in the analysis, only the conditions of class-name *point* in the chunk are considered. (Considering other conditions does not change the results.) Here, each condition has multiplied the number of tokens by four, which is the number of points connected to any given point. Since there are four conditons in the chunk (for a path of length four), the total number of tokens (4 + 16 + 64 + 256 =) 340 tokens. These 340 tokens are generated in one step. Comparing this with the four tokens per step in the original problem-solving, we see that the chunk is *expensive*. The 340 tokens correspond to all possible paths originating from point A that have a length of four.

In the unique-attribute version, the state points to the current location on the grid, similar to the multi-attribute version. However, each location points to its four adjacent locations using specific unique-attributes; *up*, *down*, *left*, and *right*. Instead of one *move* operator, there are four different operators, *move-up*, *move-left*, *move-right*, and *move-down*. Again, the problem-solver moves from A to B using heuristics or outside guidance, generating the tree of tokens shown in Figure 13(a).

However, the chunk formed in this process is different. The chunk is shown in Figure 13(b). It says that if the goal is to move to point <d> from point <x> and if the connection between the two points is through the specific relation (*up-right-up-right*) described, then choose the appropriate operator: *move-up*. The k-search tree formed is shown in Figure 13(c). There are only four tokens per step formed in this case. The chunk formed is much cheaper than the chunk in the multi-attribute case. However, the chunk will transfer only if the two points are connected in a specific manner—*up-right-up-right* in this case, as opposed to any arbitrary connection of length four in the earlier case.[16]

Table 3 summarizes the cost and generality of the two representations. The generality is measured in terms of the number of transfers in an *nxn* grid, i.e., the number of source destination pairs that the chunk can transfer (or apply) to. The length of the path traversed in the grid is assumed to be *p*. However, boundary effects are ignored for simplicity. (See Appendix II for the derivations.)

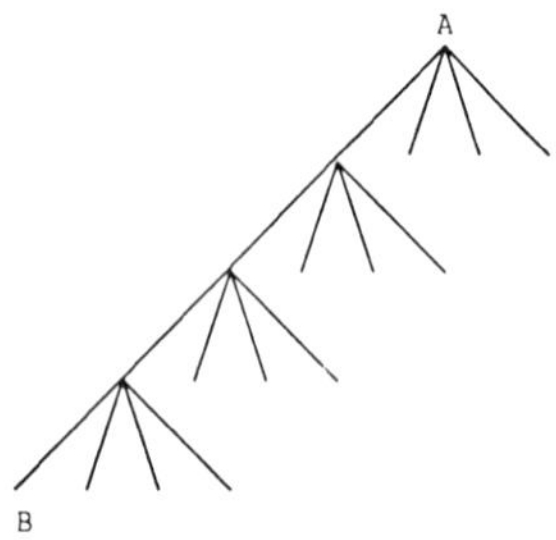

(a)

```
(Chunk::Unique-attr
    (current-state <x>)
    (point <x>  ^up-connected <y>)
    (point <y>  ^right-connected <z>)
    (point <z>  ^up-connected <w>)
    (point <w>  ^right-connected <d>)
    (desired <d>)
-->
    (prefer path <x>  ^to <y>))
```

(b)

(c)

Figure 13. The Grid task with unique-attributes: (a) the k-search tree for the entire task consisting of four problem-solving steps; (b) the chunk formed (prefer action indicates a preference for a path from <x> to <y> over all other paths); and (c) the k-search tree formed in matching the chunk (generated for one problem-solving step).

Table 3. The cost and generality of the multi- and unique-attribute representations for the Grid task. Here n is the number of nodes in the grid and p is the path length.

Representation used	Cost in tokens per chunk	Generality in number of transfers per chunk	Number of chunks required for same level of generality as multi-attr.	Cost in tokens after achieving the same level of generality
Multi-attributes	$(4^{p+1} - 4)/3$	$n^2*(p+1)^2$	1	$(4^{p+1} - 4)/3$
Unique-attributes	p	n^2	$(p+1)^2$	$(p+1)^2*p$

Comparing the multi-attributes and unique-attributes, we see that the multi-attributes allow generality that is $(p + 1)^2$ times more than the generality achieved by a single unique-attribute chunk. Thus to achieve the same generality, the unique-attribute system has to learn $(p + 1)^2$ chunks. However, even after learning all those chunks, the cost of matching all of the productions is only a polynomial number of tokens in the unique-attribute system. It is exponential (in p) in the multi-attribute system.

Thus, the unique-attribute system has paid polynomial space to eliminate exponential time—which may, at first, appear counterintuitive. This apparent anomaly can be explained as follows. Figure 14 shows the number of positions tht can be reached in the Grid task by the chunk shown in Figure 12(b) (a path length of four). The node marked *x* indicates the source location. The nodes marked with small circles indicate the positions that can be reached. The chunk shown in Figure 12(b) is an expensive chunk, based on multi-attributes. This single expensive chunk can generalize to all the situations shown, with the source fixed at the location marked *x*. There are only a polynomial number of positions that can be reached from *x*: $(p + 1)^2 = 25$; however, there are an exponential number of paths of length four, to these positions: $4^p = 256$. When given the goal of reaching one particular position, the chunk from Figure 12(b) finds all possible paths of length four, discovering all 256 paths to all 25 positions—an excessive amount of k-search, since only

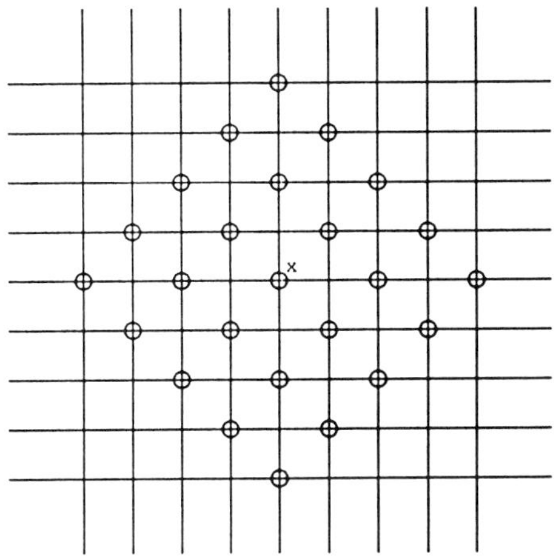

Figure 14. Locations reached by a path of length four in the Grid task.

a single path to any particular position is required. This k-search of all paths to each of the positions gives rise to the exponential factor.

In contrast, a chunk learned by the unique-attribute representation performs the minimal k-search of finding a single path to a single position, as shown in Figure 13(c). Even after learning all $(p + 1)^2$ chunks in this representation, the total amount of k-search done is proportional to the number of destinations (25), and not to the total number of paths to each of the destinations (256). The unique-attribute system avoids the useless computation of finding all paths to each position.[17] Thus, it is able to trade off polynomial space for exponential time.

This example also illustrates the relation between k-search and generality. Consider a single unique-attribute chunk. It can perform a limited amount of k-search. In the Grid task, it can find a single path to a single position. The multi-attribute chunk performs more k-search. In the Grid task, it uses k-search to reach all the locations marked with small circles in Figure 14. Thus, the difference in the two representations is the amount of k-search that can be performed to find situations in which the conditions of a chunk match. The inability of unique-attributes to perform k-search manifests itself as an effective loss of generality. To make up for this, the unique-attribute system learns more chunks, where each chunk performs a limited amount of k-search.

Thus, the multi-attribute representation uses k-search to gain generality. Comparing the k-search performed by the multi- and unique-attributes in the Grid example, we see that the amount of k-search done (and the generality obtained thereby) by the multi-attributes is composed of two portions: (1) an essential portion, (2) an excessive portion. The essential portion of the k-search consists of a single k-search path to each of the destinations on the grid. The excessive portion of the k-search, a typical characteristic of the multi-attribute representation (Tambe and Newell, 1988), consists of everything except the essential portion. This excessive portion does not provide any useful generality. The unique-attribute system only performs the essential portion of the k-search; it entirely avoids the excessive portions.

In summary, more expressiveness provides greater generality in chunking. However, the price paid for the higher level of generality is an increase in the amount of k-search at performance time. The k-search for a chunk in the two representations can be characterized as follows:

1. *Multi-attributes:* The number of tokens in the k-search tree can be exponential in the number of CEs. However, the depth of the k-search is bounded by the number of CEs.
2. *Unique-attributes:* The number of tokens in the k-search tree is bounded by the number of CEs in the chunk.

The restriction on multi-attributes does not imply that a Soar system has lost all of its sources of generality. Other sources of generality, which are independent of the amount of k-search done, can still be exploited. For example:

1. *Implicit generalization:* Chunks are based only on those aspects of the situation that were referenced during problem-solving in the subgoal to produce results (Laird, Rosenbloom, and Newell, 1986). For example, in subsection 3.1, the CEs of the chunk are based on only a fraction of the existing working memory.
2. *Focus:* The notion of focus is based on the notion of relative representation, i.e., representing objects or positions relative to a particular object or a position called focus. For example, positions on the grid are *up-down-left-right* relative to the current focus, i.e., the current position. Chunks learned reflect the representation relative to the current focus, allowing transfer if the focus shifts.
3. *Decomposition:* If a task is decomposed into smaller subtasks, then chunking the smaller subtasks independently provides another source of generality. For instance the Seibel task requires reacting to the on-off conditions of ten lights (Rosenbloon and Newell, 1986). Instead of considering all the lights at once, if small subgroups (of 2–4 lights) are considered independently, then chunking on those provides an alternative source of generality. The smaller subgroups will transfer to subparts of some other combination of lights.

The unique-attribute representation for the Grid task exploits all three sources of generality listed above:

1. *Implicit generalization:* Chunks are based only on the path traversed. The rest of the grid does not appear in the chunks. The chunks can therefore transfer irrespective of the grid formation, as long as the given path exists.
2. *Focus:* The chunk uses a path relative to the current focus, i.e., the current position on the grid. This allows a *translational* transfer, if the focus is moved to a different source.
3. *Decomposition:* The process of solving a particular problem for a path length of four generates subgoals for all intermediate path lengths, and hence generates chunks for all intermediate path lengths.

6.2. The best and the worst case for the expressiveness-efficiency tradeoff

The previous subsection illustrated the expressiveness-efficiency tradeoff involved in the Grid task. This subsection presents a best and worst case analysis for the tradeoff. In the best case of the expressiveness-efficiency tradeoff, a single unique-attribute chunk is just

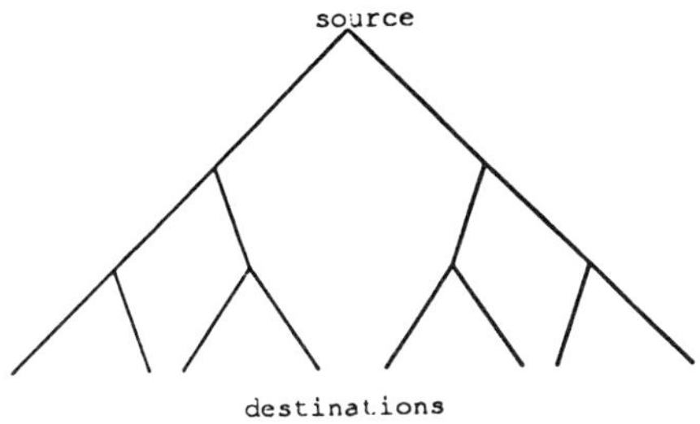

Figure 15. The Tree task.

as general as the corresponding multi-attribute chunk, but a lot cheaper (the unique-attribute chunk saves time). In the worst case for the expressiveness-efficiency tradeoff, a single unique-attribute chunk is quite specific and a large number of unique-attribute chunks are required to reach the same level of generality as a multi-attribute chunk. However, the large number of unique-attribute chunks are just as expensive as the multi-attribute chunk. A good example for demonstration of these cases is the Tree task shown in Figure 15. The Tree task is just like the Grid task except that the structure to be searched is a binary tree of uniform depth, and the path to be found is always from the root to one of the leaves.

The multi-attribute and unique-attribute representations in this task are similar to those in the Grid task, except for the use of *left-connected* and *right-connected* rather than *up*, *down*, *left*, and *right* for the unique-attributes. The most general chunk (with multi-attributes) is shown in Figure 16(a). It covers all the destinations (the leaves), given the root of the tree as the source. One particular unique-attribute chunk is shown in Figure 16(b). The unique-attribute chunk will cover *only one* particular leaf of the tree. This observation reveals an important characteristic of the Tree task—the only source of generality available is k-search. The unique-attribute system does not benefit from any other sources of generality. It does not benefit from using a focus, implicit generalization, or decomposition, since (1) the source for this task is always the root, (2) the destination is always one of the leaves, (3) the path length is fixed, and (4) the path to each destination is unique.

```
(Chunk::Multi-attr
      (current-state <x>)
      (point <x>  ^connected <y>)
      (point <y>  ^connected <z>)
      (point <z>  ^connected <d>)
      (desired <d>)
-->
      (prefer path <x>  ^to <y>))
```

(a)

```
(Chunk::Unique-attr
      (current-state <x>)
      (point <x>  ^left-connected <y>)
      (point <y>  ^right-connected <z>)
      (point <z>  ^left-connected <d>)
      (desired <d>)
-->
      (prefer path <x>  ^to <y>))
```

(b)

Figure 16. Chunk formed in the Tree task with the two representations.

Table 4. The cost and generality of the multi-attribute and unique-attribute representations for the Tree task, assuming a branching factor of B and a depth of D. In deriving the cost for unique-attributes worst case, sharing (Section 3.2) is assumed for conditions in the chunks. The best and worst case refers to the best and worst case of the expressiveness-efficiency tradeoff.

Representation used	Cost in tokens per chunk	Generality in number of Transfers	Number of chunks required for same level of generality as Multi-attr.	Cost in tokens after learning all chunks
Multi-attributes	$B*(B^d-1)/(B-1)$	B^d	1	$B*(B^d-1)/(B-1)$
Unique-attributes best case	d	1	1	d
Unique-attributes worst case	d	1	B^d	$B*(B^d-1)/(B-1)$

Since k-search is the only source of generality in this task, it exhibits the expressiveness-efficiency tradeoff in its clearest form. Table 4 presents data on the cost and the generality of the chunks for the multi- and unique-attributes (for both the best and worst cases) assuming a Tree task with a branching factor of B and a depth of D. In the best case for the unique-attributes, the task is to reach only one of the leaves, i.e., only a single destination has to be chunked. This task is accomplished by learning a single chunk, with a cost proportional to the depth of the tree. In this case, almost all of the exponential k-search of the multi-attributes—except for the one required k-search path—is excessive. Thus, the unique-attribute system exhibits a big efficiency gain, without any losses in terms of generality.

In the worst case for the unique-attributes, all of the destinations (or leaves) of the tree have to be chunked. In this case, the cost of matching all unique-attribute chunks (one chunk per path) is equal to the cost of matching one multi-attribute chunk. There is no excessive k-search involved in matching the multi-attribute chunk. Since there is no excessive k-search, this task demonstrates the worst-case for the expressiveness-efficiency tradeoff. Furthermore, the lower generality of the unique-attribute chunks demands an exponential number of chunks (exponential in the depth D) to cover the level of generality of one multi-attribute chunk.

An obvious question that the worst case analysis raises is: If the unique-attribute version is going to have to acquire an exponential match anyway (to match the exponential number of productions), why not acquire it all at once via the multi-attribute chunk? The answer to this question lies in the issue of the safety of chunking, i.e., the issue that chunking should not hurt Soar's performance. The multi-attribute chunk can add an arbitrarily large exponential cost in a single learning trial. In contrast, the unique-attribute version learns about the individual branches as they are encountered. The match cost always increases gradually (at worst), and remains bounded by the number of branches that have been encountered. At worst the number of branches that have been encountered is equal to the number in the tree, but in many domains only a small portion of the entire exponential space is ever encountered. A related point is that the system is also protected from learning an exponential number of chunks by its finite lifetime. If the chunking rate is approximately constant over time (see Section 8.2), then there is a finite number of chunks that the system will ever be able to acquire. Under these circumstances the system can work in arbitrarily large exponential domains, but it will never have enough time to learn everything about the domain (as opposed to learning everything about the domain quickly, but never having enough time to use it). Of course, not having enough time to learn everything about a domain also implies that Soar may not actually benefit from chunking.

In the interest of clarity of exposition, this section analyzed a simple tree-structure (with uniform branching factor B) to demonstrate the best and worst cases of the expressiveness-efficiency tradeoff. The actual complexity expressions for the best and the worst cases can vary according to the individual problem being solved e.g., instead of the simple tree-structure, it is possible to consider a complex tree-structure where the branching factor grows exponentially with depth.

It is useful to analyze how unfavorable the expressiveness-efficiency tradeoff can get in performing the Tree task. Note that for performing this task, the tree-structure must be present in working memory. If this tradeoff is to be heavily set against the unique-attribute system, the tree-structure present in working memory must be very large. However, the tree-structure is exponential in the depth of the tree. An exponential amount of time must be spent in generating such an exponential structure. (In this respect, the Tree task is to be contrasted with the Grid task, where the size of the structure is limited, but matching the structure requires exponential time due to connectivity.) The unique-attribute system is thus protected by its finite lifetime—it is unlikely that the problem-solver will be able to generate such large tree-structures in its lifetime. If the tree-structure is not large, the expressiveness-efficiency tradeoff is not very unfavorable to begin with; the unique-attribute system will be able to obtain the required coverage fairly quickly. Thus, this tradeoff is expected to not be set heavily against unique-attributes. Interestingly, none of the tasks from Table 2 have exhibited the worst case of the expressiveness-efficiency tradeoff in the unique-attribute representation.

In conclusion, in the worst case (the tree search) of the expressiveness-efficiency tradeoff, there is no excessive k-search involved. However, from the example of the best case in this section, the Grid task in the previous subsection, and the analysis of the expensive-chunks tasks (Tambe and Newell, 1988), we expect that in the general case, multi-attribute chunks will generate excessive k-search. There is no tradeoff involved in this excessive k-search; the unique-attribute representation simply gets rid of it.

7. Experimental analysis

This section provides a detailed comparative performance analysis of the multi- and unique-attribute based systems. It first compares the computational effects of multi- and unique-attribute representations for the four expensive chunks tasks from Table 1: Grid, Eight-puzzle, 2-Queens, and Magic-square. It then presents a finer grained analysis of the impact of chunking on the overall performance of the multi- and unique-attribute systems.

For each representation and task, the system was run without chunking. The tokens per action and the time per action in performing the task were noted. The system was then allowed to chunk on the problem. It was then run on the same problem, i.e., after having chunked on the problem, and the tokens per action and the time per action in performing the task were noted. A sequence of such experiments was performed with the unique-attribute representation to accumulate a set of chunks yielding the same level of generality as the multi-attribute system. (See Sections 6.1 and 6.2 for examples of how this same level of generality is determined.)

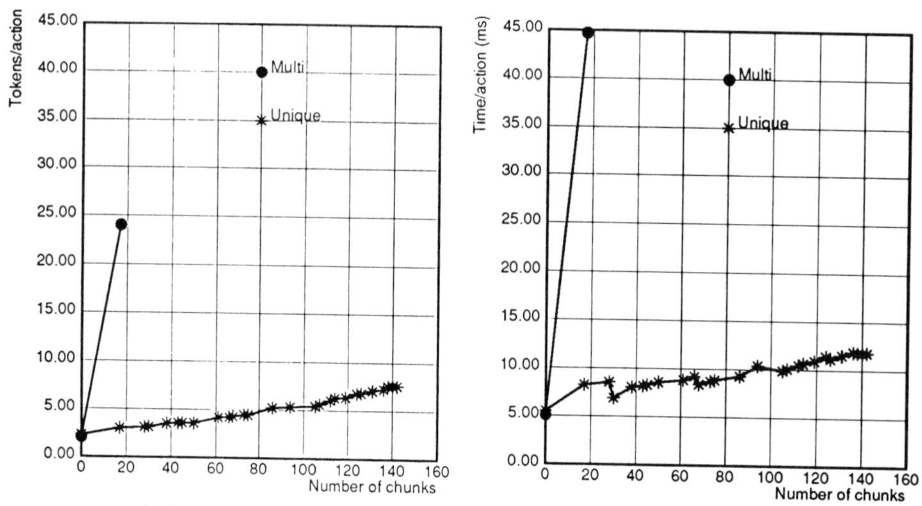

(a) Tokens per action

(b) Time per action

Figure 17. Computational effects in the Grid task.

In the Grid task, a 5 × 5 grid was chosen, with *p*, the length of the path, set at six. Recall that we had assumed an unbounded grid in obtaining the results in Table 3. The results of our experiments will be somewhat different from those results, since these experiments are run with a bounded grid. However, a large grid size would make the chunks in the multi-attribute representation too expensive to allow running the experiments. The multi-attribute and unique-attribute representations used for this task were the ones introduced in the previous section. Figure 17 shows the change in tokens per action and time per action with the addition of chunks for the two representations. The time is measured in milliseconds. The multi-attribute representation learns 17 chunks and causes an increase in tokens per action from about 3 tokens per action to 24 tokens per action[18] and causes a computational effect of about 0.11; i.e., the time per action has gone up by about a factor of 9. The unique-attribute representation requires learning on more problems to reach the same level of generality (each asterisk (*) represents one problem). It accumulates 142 chunks in this process, but its tokens per action and time per action are seen not to increase as much. Even after achieving the same level of generality as the multi-attribute system, the computational effect here is much more limited (about 0.46). These graphs thus support the analysis of the Grid task presented in the previous section—the unique-attribute system is able to avoid large portions of the k-search performed by the multi-attribute system.

Although the computational effect of the unique-attribute system in the Grid task is limited to 0.46, it is not unity, as required for the ideal computational model. This deviation from the ideal computational model occurs because, even though the chunks in the unique-attribute system are individually cheap, each chunk does add something to the match cost. This issue is picked up in more detail in Section 8.2.

The Eight-puzzle task requires arranging eight numbered tiles in a 3×3 frame in a specific order. One of the cells in the 3×3 frame is always blank and adjacent tiles can be moved into the blank cell. In the multi-attribute representation, a state points to nine bindings, each of which connects a cell from the static 3×3 structure of cells to a tile. For example, *(binding B1 ^cell C1)* *(binding B1 ^tile T1)* connects cell C1 to tile T1. A cell points to all

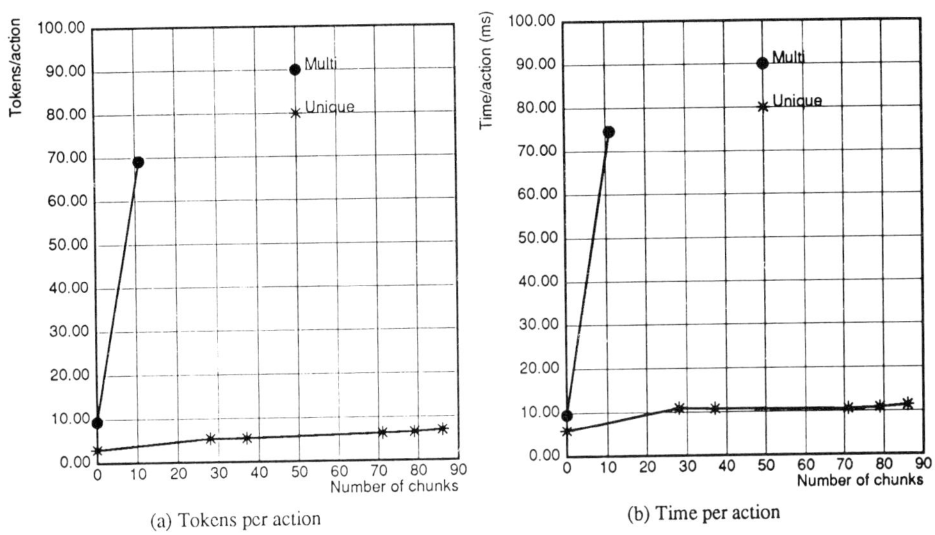

Figure 18. Computational effects in the Eight-puzzle task.

its neighboring cells. For example, (*cell C1 ^next C2*), (*cell C1 ^next C3*), etc. In the unique-attribute representation, bindings are not used. The state points to the blank cell. The blank cell points to its neighbors, which in turn point to their neighbors, using attributes *up, down, right* and *left*. For example, (*cell C1 ^up C2*), (*cell C1 ^down C3*), etc. The cells directly point to tiles. For example, (*cell C1 ^tile T1*). Figure 18 shows data from runs with both representations. The analysis of these graphs is very similar to the analysis of the graphs in Figure 17 for the Grid task. There is only a limited (less than a factor of 2) increase in time per action in the unique-attribute system.

It is important to analyze the sources of generality available in the Eight-puzzle task, in a manner analogous to the Grid task. The chunks learned in the Eight-puzzle are search control rules that give a preference to one operator over the other. For instance, in Figure 19, it is possible to move the blank in two directions: right and up. Depending on the tiles in the current state and their situation in the desired state, the search control chunk formed will prefer one operator over the other. There are three sources of generality available to the multi-attribute version:

- *Implicit Generalization:* The chunk does not take into account the position of the other tiles and cells, except the ones affected by the move operator. It also does not take into account what numbers are on the tiles.
- *Focus*: The chunk is relative to the position of the blank cell. The chunk will transfer to other situations based on the position of the blank cell.
- *K-search*: The chunk will transfer to any other configuration of two operators; it is not sensitive to directions, such as right and up.

Of the three sources listed above, the unique-attribute version cannot use k-search for generalization. The chunks learned will be specific to the direction of the operators. For instance, in Figure 19 the operators under consideration have to move the blank right and up. However the important point is not how much generality is lost. Rather it is how much has remained, in comparison to a no-transfer situation (no-transfer chunks refer to chunks

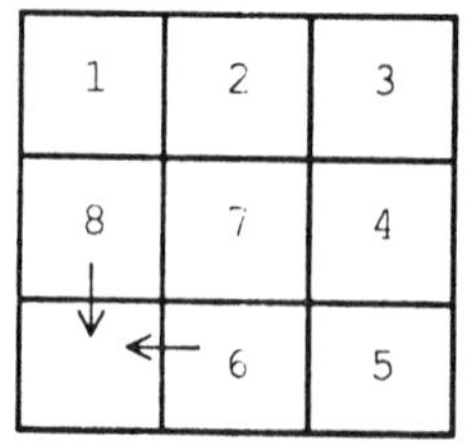

Figure 19. Move operators in the Eight-puzzle task.

Table 5. Number of chunks required in three representations to achieve the same generality for the Eight-puzzle.

Eight-puzzle Representations	Multi-attributes	Unique-attributes	No-transfer
Number of Chunks	5	60	8 million

which have absolutely no source of generality available. Calculations using a somewhat simplified version of the chunks learned in this task show the ratio in Table 5 (see Appendix III for the derivations).

Thus, a substantial amount of transfer is still available to the unique-attribute representation. Although the unique-attribute system forms chunks of lower generality, it obtains a big reduction in the match effort by avoiding excessive k-search.

The results for the 2-Queens and Magic-square tasks are presented in Figure 20. The tokens-per-action graphs in these two cases are similar. Both graphs show the advantage of going with unique-attributes. (For details of the representations employed see (Tambe and Rosenbloom, 1988).) An important point here is that these two tasks are such that

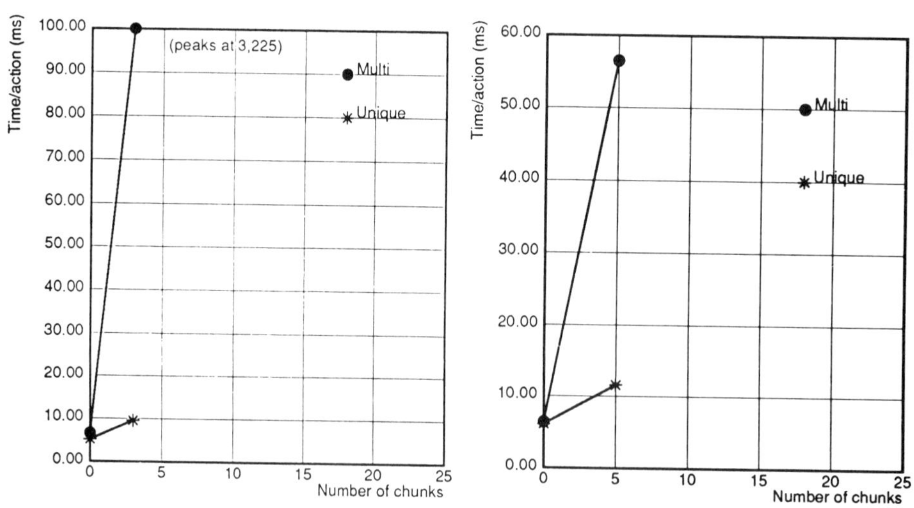

(a) Time per action in the 2-Queens task

(b) Time per action in the Magic-square task

Figure 20. Computational effects in the 2-Queens and Magic-square tasks.

the unique-attribute system *does not have to learn any extra chunks* to achieve the same level of generality as the multi-attribute system.

The results presented in this section so far, along with those in Table 2, show that the unique-attribute version is more efficient after reaching the same level of generality as the multi-attribute version, but they don't show the finer-grained behavior of what happens during the learning process. Specifically, they don't address the issue of the extra time spent by the unique-attributes version in acquiring the extra chunks. To understand this issue, a set of randomly generated problems in the Eight-puzzle domain were run with both versions. Both versions started off with no chunks, and solved the set of problems with chunking turned on, i.e., chunking continuously across the set of problems. Thus, the systems used the chunks learned in one problem to solve the subsequent problems, simultaneously learning more chunks in situations where the earlier chunks did not apply.[19]

Figure 21(a) shows the cumulative times for the two systems on the 20 problems. The unique-attribute system consistently outperforms the multi-attribute system. Figure 21(b) compares the time required by the two versions for the individual problems. This graph shows that even in each individual problem, the performance of the unique-attribute version dominates the performance of the multi-attribute version. Figure 21(c) shows the time per decision for the two systems. Decisions are typically used in Soar to measure the amount of problem-solving effort. The point corresponding to the zeroth problem shows the time per decision prior to learning. The main message of this graph is that time per decision remains fairly constant in the unique-attribute version, while it takes some fairly large jumps in the multi-attribute version. Thus, the number of decisions does not accurately reflect the problem-solving time in the multi-attribute system, but it does so in a unique-attribute system. Finally, Figure 21(d) compares the number of decisions required for solving the problems in the two systems. This graph shows that unique-attributes require more decision cycles than multi-attributes in achieving the goal. The chunks learned by the multi-attribute system are more general, and hence the reduction in the number of decisions per problem happens more quickly than with unique-attributes. However, as more problems are solved, and more unique-attribute chunks are acquired, the difference in number of decisions decreases. Similar results were obtained for the Grid task (Tambe and Rosenbloom, 1988).

8. Discussion

A detailed comparative analysis of the efficiency (and efficiency-related tradeoffs) of the more expressive multi-attributes and the less expressive unique-attributes was presented in Sections 5, 6, and 7. This section focuses on various issues related to unique-attributes: the difficulty of encoding tasks in unique-attributes, the average growth effect, the bounded elaboration phases, and others.

8.1. Difficulty of encoding tasks with unique-attributes

The approach adopted in this article to deal with expensive chunks is to restrict the expressiveness of the production system language. Such restrictions are to be contrasted with the trends in some EBL systems to make the language more expressive (Cohen, Mostow,

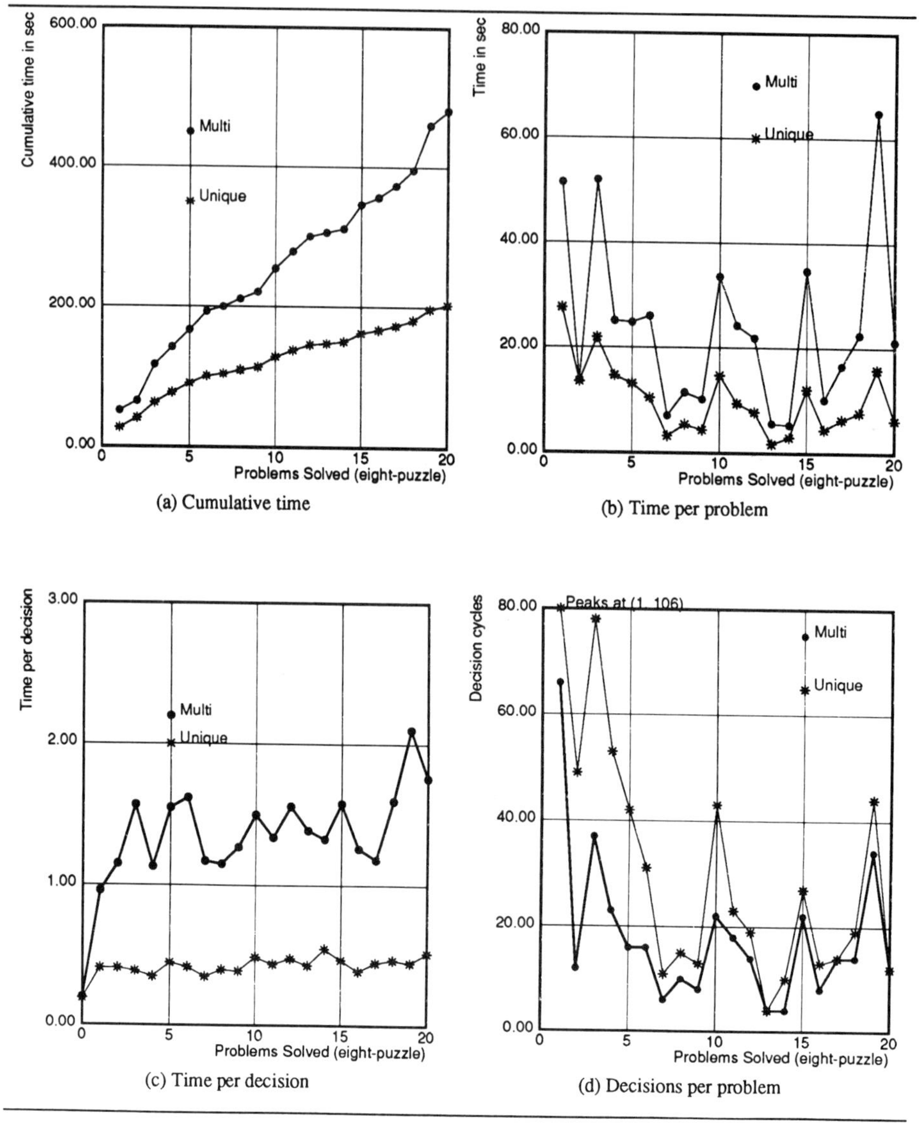

Figure 21. Results for the set of random problems from the Eight-Puzzle task.

and Borgida, 1988; Shavlik and DeJong, 1987). This contrast raises an important question: with the elimination of multi-attributes, would it be considerably more difficult to encode tasks in Soar?

Multi-attributes are used for representing unstructured sets in working memory. In the blocks-world example (see Figure 7(a)), it is possible to keep all the blocks as a structureless collection of items. A single production accesses all three of the blocks via match (see Figure 6). Thus, from a task-encoding perspective, the following features of a multi-attribute based set representation emerge:

1. The elements of the set are accessed using production match, i.e., using k-search in the implementation domain.
2. Since the elements of the set are accessed using production match, they are accessed in parallel, i.e., the matcher returns the set of all matching elements simultaneously.
3. Some set operations, such as search, add, delete, etc., are facilitated.

The elimination of multi-attributes implies that unstructured sets cannot be represented directly in working memory. All sets in working memory have to be structured as lists, trees, or some other task-specific structures. Figure 10 showed how the set of blocks can be structured as a list. (Note that the list structure is chosen in the interests of clarity. This might not be the most suitable encoding for performing this task.) To access individual elements of such structures via production match, multiple productions would have to be written, one for each element in the structure. This requirement poses a problem—a large number of productions would have to be written—especially if the structure contains a large number of elements. This problem can be avoided by accessing the structure in the cognitive domain, i.e., using states and operators.[20] In the example from Figure 10, the execution of an operator can examine one block from the list of blocks (the current focus), and advance the focus to the next block in the list. Thus, from a task-encoding perspective, the following features of a unique-attribute representation for sets emerge:

1. The elements of a set are accessed using problem space search, i.e., using search in the cognitive domain.
2. Since the elements of the set are accessed using problem space search, they are accessed in a serial fashion. (Problem space search is serial because it requires moving from state to state in a serial fashion.)
3. Set operations such as search, add, delete, etc. are performed using operators in the problem space.

As revealed by the features listed above, the principal impact of encoding tasks with unique-attributes is the removal of the combinatorial k-search from the implementation domain. Some of the combinatorics is transferred to the cognitive domain in the form of problem space search, while some, like the excessive portion of the k-search in the Grid task, just disappears. A task encoded with unique-attributes must bear the overheads associated with problem space search (selection of states, operators, etc.). These overheads can cause the system to slow down by a constant factor. The advantage of carrying out the search in the problem space lies in the ability to use search-control knowledge to terminate or control it. This ability can avoid the possibility of exponential slowdowns, which can occur in the implementation domain if multi-attributes are used. Moreover, chunking in a space encoded using unique-attributes will gradually reduce and ultimately eliminate the overheads associated with the problem space search (selection of states, operators, etc.). In the process of eliminating the overheads of problem-space search, chunking will increase the match effort in the implementation domain; however, this increase will always be gradual at worst (the next subsection discusses this issue in more detail). Chunking will also return to the implementation domain the capability of retrieving all elements of a (structured) set in parallel. Consider the structured set shown in Figure 10. If chunks are formed in that domain,

```
(chunk::access-block-B1
   (goal <g>  ^problem-space <p>)
   (goal <g>  ^state <s>)
   (state <s>  ^block <b1>)
             .
             .
             .
             .
```

```
(chunk::access-block-B2
   (goal <g>  ^problem-space <p>)
   (goal <g>  ^state <s>)
   (state <s>  ^block <b1>)
   (block <b1>  ^next <b2>)
             .
             .
             .
```

```
(chunk::access-block-B3
   (goal <g>  ^problem-space <p>)
   (goal <g>  ^state <s>)
   (state <s>  ^block <b1>)
   (block <b1>  ^next <b2>)
   (block <b2>  ^next <b3>)
             .
             .
```

Figure 22. Access with unique-attributes.

they will access the three blocks as shown in Figure 22, without any problem space search to access the three blocks. Furthermore, by matching the three chunks, the matcher can access the blocks B1, B2, and B3 in parallel. But now, the structure of the set represented by the unique-attributes is reflected in the chunks formed; the chunks encode the *next* relation. The structure of the set is used by the matcher to restrict the k-search branching factor to one, e.g., only one block is next to the current block, guaranteeing the chunks to be cheap.

To further facilitate the encoding of common set operations like search, add, delete, etc., a set of operators which can perform many common set operations has been implemented. These operators are expected to effectively replace the functionality provided by multi-attributes.

To gain a better understanding of the difficulties in encoding tasks, some complex task domains need to be converted to unique-attributes. Toward this end, R1-Soar (Rosenbloom, et al., 1985), a large Soar task with about 450 productions, which forms part of an expert system task for computer configuration, was converted into the unique-attribute representation. This conversion was expected to take about a week or two. However, the conversion took only about two person days. This was mainly because R1-Soar uses only four different multi-attribute-based unstructured sets. Furthermore, R1-Soar does not form expensive chunks; thus, there was only about a 5–10% change in decisions and run time due to the conversion. Conversions of other Soar tasks are not always expected to be as easy—especially if a particular Soar task makes more extensive use of multi-attributes. In any event, it would obviously be preferable to automate such conversions. We are currently working on this automatic conversion problem in collaboration with an independent research effort in Soar called RTAQ (Yost and Newell, 1989; Yost and Altmann, 1989), which aims at acquiring new tasks (or problem spaces) from external descriptions.

8.2. *Average growth effect*

This article has considered techniques whereby, instead of learning a single expensive chunk, the system may learn a number of individually cheap chunks. For the cheap chunks, the growth of tokens is at worst linear in the number of chunks. However, learning a large number of cheap chunks could clearly overwhelm the system after some time. This effect is called the *average growth effect*—the distortion in Soar's computational model due to the addition of a large number of cheap chunks. The average growth effect is seen in all of the unique-attribute tasks examined in Section 7. For instance, in Figure 17, the accumulation of 142 chunks causes a computational effect of 0.46.

The point to be noted here is that the average growth effect increases the intrinsic or available parallelism in the system (Tambe, et al., 1988). Therefore, we speculate that this problem could be solved by parallelism (Tambe, 1988). More specifically, we expect that with future research in parallel production systems (Gupta, 1986; Gupta and Tambe, 1988; Tambe, et al., 1988), it will be possible to convert the increase in concurrency into real parallelism, allowing Soar to preserve its ideal computational model (modulo the footprint size issue mentioned in Section 5.1).

However, even at this level of speculation about parallelism, some important issues need to be addressed. The first issue is bounding the number of chunks in the system. As in Section 6.2, if we assume a finite lifetime for the problem-solver, then the number of chunks that the system will be able to acquire is bounded. Given the finite lifetime, if the rate of chunking is known, it is possible to estimate the increase in concurrency with chunking over the lifetime. It is then possible to estimate the quantity of processor and memory resources that will be required for converting that increase in concurrency into real parallelism and provide those processor and memory resources ahead of time. Note that the discussion here is only regarding cheap chunks, hence the argument about exponential matches for individual chunks raised in Section 5.1 does not apply.

The previous paragraph raises a second important issue: establishing a polynomial bound on the rate of growth of cheap chunks. An exponential growth in the number of chunks, even with a finite lifetime, would be highly problematical in terms of processor and memory resources. In Soar, the growth of chunks is assumed to be linear in the number of decision cycles—the constant rate of chunking is one of the bases of the chunking theory of learning (Newell and Rosenbloom, 1981). This article is not focused on establishing the validity of this assumption. However, some evidence for the assumption is provided in Figure 23.

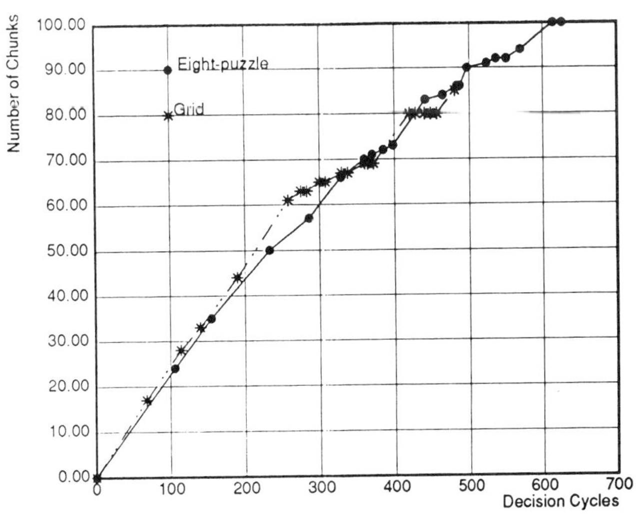

Figure 23. The rate of growth of chunks for the Eight-puzzle and Grid tasks.

It shows the growth in the number of chunks in the two unique-attribute tasks that learn a large number of chunks. For both tasks, the increase in number of chunks plotted against the number of decision cycles for learning on 20 different random problems presented to the system. For the Eight-puzzle these problems are the same as those shown in Figure 21; for the Grid task, the problems are from (Tambe and Rosenbloom, 1988). In both these tasks, the growth of chunks is seen to be linear (or sublinear) in the number of decision cycles. Since these chunks are cheap, the graph indicates that the average growth effect will cause the time per action to grow linearly with the number of decision cycles.

In fact, the following two effects would further reduce the impact of the average growth effect:

1. *Sharing*: As mentioned in Section 3.2, the effect of sharing in general is quite limited in the multi-object based matcher. However, for cheap chunks, this property could become important. For example, in (Prieditis and Mostow, 1987) a problem about learning *membership* of an item in a list is presented. This task leads to learning a large number of chunks, one for each position of the item in the list. However, the chunks have a large number of conditions that are common. All these common conditions get shared if the Rete algorithm is used. Thus, with matching algorithms like Rete, the addition of large numbers of similar chunks requires very little additional processing.
2. *Problem-space decomposition*: Large Soar tasks are composed of many distinct search spaces (called problem spaces). It is unlikely that all the chunks learned will belong to a single one of these problem spaces. Thus, only a fraction of the chunks learned, i.e., those belonging to the current problem space, will be actively matched at a time. The rest will require only one comparison (of their problem space) to determine that they do not belong to the current problem space and will not participate in the match. Furthermore, the total number of problem spaces itself is not fixed—new problem spaces can be constructed at run time (Newell, 1990, Chapter 8), thus reducing the match effort.

Thus, the growth in the processing requirement with chunking is at worst linear, making an effective elimination of the average growth effect with parallelism seem plausible.

8.3. Unique-attributes bound the elaboration phase

Recall from Section 3.1 that a decision cycle in Soar consists of an elaboration phase followed by a decision phase. An elaboration phase consists of multiple elaboration cycles, where multiple productions are fired in each elaboration cycle. With a multi-attribute representation, these elaboration phases are not bounded, i.e., it is possible for elaboration cycles to follow each other in an unbounded fashion in a single elaboration phase. For instance, it is possible to start counting the natural numbers in a single elaboration phase. Figure 24 presents a single production for counting the natural numbers in a single elaboration phase. This production will repeatedly add 1 to the existing value of the attribute *count* and fire with the new value. Note that count is a multi-attribute, which increases in size with each firing of the production.

```
(Production::Count-natural-numbers
      (current-state <x>)
      (state <x> ^count <y>)
-->
      (state <x> ^count (add 1 <y>) ))
```

Figure 24. Counting the natural numbers in a single elaboration phase.

Here, unique-attributes provide another useful bound—they bound the elaboration phase. This bound follows from the following argument. Since the k-search tree of a unique-attribute production has a branching factor of unity, it is clear that a unique-attribute production can generate only a single instantiation at a time (assuming a single goal). Furthermore, the WMEs (and the values) that instantiate the production cannot change within a single elaboration phase, so that new instantiations for this already instantiated production cannot be generated within a single elaboration phase. Since only a single instantiation is generated, a unique-attribute production can fire only once in a single elaboration phase. For instance, with unique-attributes, the production in Figure 24 can fire only once in a single elaboration phase, since only a unique value of count is possible in a single decision cycle. (In reality, this production's action would have to be changed with unique-attributes, since firing the production introduces a multi-attribute.) Thus, the number of productions that can fire in an elaboration phase is bounded by the number of productions in the production system.[21] However, bounding the elaboration phase also implies that arbitrarily large working memory structures cannot be processed in a single decision. These structures require multiple decisions for processing. Again, if these large structures are fixed, then with chunking, the system can learn more productions to deal with them.

8.4. Effect of macro-operator learning on branching factor

A problem related to expensive chunks is that of the increase in the branching factor of a search space with macro-operator learning. This increase in the branching factor can potentially cause a slowdown in a system, as it tries to apply the macro-operators in situations where they are incapable of efficiently solving the problem at hand. In (Mooney, 1989; Iba, 1989; Markovitch and Scott, 1989b; Greiner and Likuski, 1989), various strategies are described to deal with this branching-factor problem, to avoid the slowdown with learning.

The branching-factor problem is related to expensive chunks in that both can cause a slowdown with learning. However, the problem of expensive chunks is not concerned with the branching factor of the search space—it is only concerned with the match for individual productions/chunks. The branching factor problem could arise in Soar, if Soar learns new operators for a problem space, without learning the appropriate search control knowledge for that space. The research in (Mooney, 1989; Iba, 1989; Markovitch and Scott, 1989b; Greiner and Likuski, 1989) could potentially be relevant to Soar in that situation. However, the chunks learned in the various tasks (especially the expensive-chunks tasks) in this paper are search control chunks that select among various existing operators; these tasks do not learn new operators.

8.5. Restricting expressiveness versus enriching expressiveness

In sharp contrast to the research reported in this article, some research efforts have focused on enriching the expressiveness of the rule language. These efforts are aimed at learning iterative concepts, especially by allowing looping constructs in the rule language (Shavlik and DeJong, 1987; Cohen, 1988; Shavlik, 1989). Iterative rules will reduce the average growth effect, since they avoid the necessity of learning multiple rules, one for each value of the loop variable. However, iterative constructs raise difficulties in guaranteeing boundedness of the match process.

In (Shell and Carbonell, 1989), the problem of expensive chunks is explicitly addressed. They are also exploring ways of enriching the operator language to allow iterative and disjunctive macro-operators. As we noted in footnote 2 (on page 1), there are a number of paths that need to be explored to fully understand how to deal with expensive chunks. Furthermore, the advantages and disadvantages of going along different paths remain ill-understood. Thus, the issue of restricting expressiveness versus enriching expressiveness remains an interesting open research issue.

9. Relevance to other research efforts

An important question is the relevance of this research for the non-Soar community. The representation in Soar and the unique-attribute restriction presented in this paper are both based on attribute-value representations. Rule-based systems with attribute-values and a combinatorial match are fairly widespread in AI, e.g., OPS5 (Brownston, Farrell, Kant, and Martin, 1985) and Prodigy (Minton, 1988a; Minton et al., 1989). The unique-attribute representation should map over to some of those systems and help in eliminating combinatorics from the match. Even if the unique-attribute representation does not map over directly, it is possible to look at the idea of restricting k-search in the production match and map that over. Given the tradeoffs involved in the unique-attribute representation, it is not clear exactly when such mappings would be helpful. However, it appears that the mappings might at least be helpful in those situations where excessive k-search is involved.

Unique-attributes appear to be relevant to frame-based systems as well. Recently, Chalasani and Altmann (Chalasani and Altmann, 1989) pointed out that the knowledge representation scheme adopted by Theo, a frame-based architecture for problem-solving and learning (Mitchell et al., 1989), corresponds to the unique-attribute representation. This correspondence makes a plausibility argument for unique-attributes, since it shows that an entire symbolic architecture, considerably different from Soar, is based on the unique-attribute representation. Theo's knowledge-access language is restricted so that it works within the unique-attributes framework. Sets in the knowledge base are represented in Theo in the form of linked lists. Such lists are then processed by user-written Lisp routines (rather than by constructs in the query language).

10. Summary and future work

Expensive chunks are caused by three factors: multi-objects (multi-attributes and preferences), big footprints, and bad condition ordering. Multi-objects allow combinatorial searches to occur in the match. These searches can result in exponential slowdowns. Eliminating multi-objects from the representation bounds the cost of a chunk to be linear in the number of its condition elements. The new restricted representation is referred to as the unique-attribute representation. The principal impact of the unique-attribute representation is the removal of the combinatorics from the matcher. The combinatorics can still occur in the problem space, where they can (in principle) be controlled or terminated using search control knowledge. Analytical and empirical evidence was presented to show that the unique-attribute representation not only guarantees cheap chunks, but it actually eliminates some excessive (and expensive) match. Two issues arise with the representational restrictions in unique-attributes: (1) all sets in working memory have to be structured as lists, trees, or some other task specific structures, (2) the chunks formed are less general. The paper addressed both these issues in some detail.

However, the issue of big footprints remains to be addressed. A chunk can still have an arbitrary number of condition elements. This issue will be one of the subjects of investigation in the near future. The space of match algorithms that would be better suited for the unique-attribute system also needs to be explored. The issue of match algorithms has been addressed in the context of the Soar system with multi-objects (Nayak, Gupta, and Rosenbloom, 1988), with the conclusion that the state-saving Rete algorithm is better suited for Soar than the Treat algorithm, which saves less state. However, the conclusions in the absence of multi-objects are not clear.

The results presented in this paper are based on a variety of toy tasks, such as the Eight-puzzle, Waterjug, and others. To complete the analysis of the impact of unique-attributes, some of the larger Soar tasks need to be converted to the unique-attribute representation. Toward this end, Rl-Soar (Rosenbloom, et al., 1985), a large Soar task with about 450 productions was converted into the unique-attribute representation. The possibility of converting other large Soar tasks, such as Neomycin-Soar (Washington and Rosenbloom, 1988) and Merl-Soar (Hsu, Prietula, and Steier, 1989) to unique-attributes is being investigated.

Another interesting topic for future work is automating the conversion of tasks in Soar from the current representation to the unique-attribute representation. This work will be in collaboration with an independent research effort called RTAQ (Yost and Newell, 1989; Yost and Altmann, 1989), which aims at acquiring new tasks (or problem spaces) from external descriptions. We are currently also investigating other schemes besides unique-attributes for restricting expressiveness (Tambe and Rosenbloom, 1990). We hope that these investigations will allow us to gain a better understanding of the interaction between learning, representation, and efficiency.

Appendix I. Descriptions of the nine tasks

Eight-Puzzle

Problem-statement: There are eight numbered movable tiles in a 3×3 frame. One cell of the frame is always blank, making it possible to move an adjacent tile into the blank cell. The problem is to transform one configuration to a second by moving the tiles.

States: The state is described in terms of nine bindings each of which connects a cell from a static 3×3 structure of cells to a tile from a dynamic structure of individual tiles.

Operators: There is only one operator: move-tile. The instances of this operator are the only instantiated operators and there can be up to four of them at a time. These instantiated operators move the dynamic structure around until the desired configuration is reached.

2-Queens

Problem-statement: Placing 2 queens on a 3×3 chessboard such that no queen takes another.

States: The states are represented as a 3×3 array of positions. Each position has one horizontal, one vertical and two diagonal attributes.

Operators: There is only one operator: place-queen. Up to nine instantiations of this operator may be created at a time.

Grid

Problem-statement: Finding a path between two points on a 4×4 grid.

States: The grid-structure with nodes and the paths that connect nodes. The destination node is marked with a desired flag.

Operators: There is only one operator: goto. There can be up to four instantiated goto operators at one time, for moving to the points adjacent to the current position on the grid.

Magic-Square

Problem statement: Completing a 3×3 magic-square. In a magic-square, the sums of the numbers along each of the columns, rows and diagonals equal one another.

States: A state has nine bindings that associate a number with a square.

Operators: There is only one operator for placing a number in a square and it can create up to nine instantiations.

Tree

Problem-statement: Finding a path between the root and a destination point in a tree of height 4 and branching factor of 2.

States: The tree-structure with nodes and the paths that connect nodes. The destination node is marked with a desired flag.

Operators: There is only one operator: goto. There can be up to two instantiated goto operators at one time, for moving to the points adjacent to the current position on the tree.

Syllogisms

Problem-statement: A syllogism is a logic puzzle where two assertions involving pairs of terms (e.g., All P are Q; All Q are R) are given. From these given assertions some conclusion (in this example: All P are R) is to be drawn.

States: Each state is made up of two premises or statements, one model built out of two to three objects, and the focus (on one object in the model). See (Polk and Newell, 1988) for details.

Operators: There are four different operators that can add an object, focus on a premise, focus on an object, and augment an object.

Monkeys and Bananas

Problem-statement: A monkey has to get the bananas hung from the ceiling in a room. A ladder is placed under the bananas. The task for the monkey is to climb the ladder and get the bananas.

States: The position of the Monkey in terms of its position on the ground and its height, and the position of the bananas.

Operators: There are five different operators available to the Monkey: climb the ladder, eat the bananas, get the bananas, climb down the ladder, and move.

Waterjug

Problem-statement: Given a five gallon jug and a three gallon jug, how can precisely one gallon of water be put into the three gallon jug? There is a well nearby, but no measuring devices are available, other than the jugs themselves.

States: The amounts of water in the five gallon and three gallon jugs.

Operators: Six operators are available, one for each combination of pouring water between the well and the two jugs. Each operator specifies what container it is pouring water to and what it is pouring water from. Each operator must empty the source or fill the destination container.

Farmer

Problem-statement: A farmer has to cross a river with a wolf, a sheep and some cabbage. There is a boat that can carry him and one more load at a time. The farmer cannot leave the sheep and the wolf together unattended and cross the river with the cabbage, since the wolf may eat the sheep. Similarly, he cannot leave the sheep and the cabbage together.

States: The status of four different objects: The farmer, the sheep, the wolf, and the cabbage.

Operators: Two operators are available: one for the farmer to cross the river alone and one for the farmer to cross the river with one load. Three or four instantiations of the two operators combined are available in any one state.

Appendix II. Cost and generality of chunks in the grid world

A grid of size $n \times n$ is assumed. In the interests of simplicity, boundary effects are ignored.

Multi-attribute representation

- *Cost*: As shown in Figure 12, each condition element multiplies the number of tokens in the chunk by four, the number of connections emerging from any given point. The cost of the chunk is the total number of tokens generated by the match. If the path length is p, and the cost of the chunk is C_m, then:

$$C_m = 4 + 4^2 + 4^3 + \ldots + 4^p$$
$$= \Sigma_{k=1}^{p} 4^k = (4^{p+1} - 4)/(4 - 1)$$
$$= (4^{p+1} - 4)/3$$

- *Generality*: The chunk transfers to any two points on the grid connected by a path of length p. There are n^2 points on the grid that can act as a source. To calculate the number of destinations possible from a given source, consider Figure 14. The points reached from the source form squares (or euclidean circles), around the source. If the path length is p, then the squares are at a distance of 2, 4, 6, . . . , p (for an even p), and at a distance of 1, 3, 5, . . . , p (for an odd p). Let us call this distance the radius of the square.
  Let k be the radius of a square. Let x and y be the cartesian coordinates of a destination point on the square with the source as the origin. Then the number of possible destinations is obtained by enumerating the solutions of the following equation for integer values of x and y.

$$|x| + |y| = k$$

There are $4*k$ solutions to this equation, since both x and y can vary between $-k$, . . . 0, . . . , k. Thus there are $4*k$ destinations on a square of radius k.
  If M is the total number of points that can be reached from a given source, then for an even p (the analysis is very similar for an odd p):

$$M = 1 + 4 * 2 + 4 * 4 + \ldots. + 4 * p \text{ [1 is for the source]}$$
$$= 1 + 8\,(1 + 2 + \ldots + p/2) = 1 + p^2 + 2p$$
$$= (p + 1)^2$$

The total number of transfers

$$= \text{sources} * \text{destinations per source}$$
$$= n^2 * (p + 1)^2$$

- *Total cost*: The total cost is the product of the cost per chunk and the number of chunks. Since only one chunk is learned, the total cost is equal to the cost of that one chunk.

Unique-attribute representation

- *Cost*: As shown in Figure 13, the number of tokens in the chunk is linear in the length of the path (p).

- *Generality*: The chunk can transfer to any two points connected in a specific manner, e.g., up-right-up-right. Thus, for one given source, the chunk will transfer to one destination. There are n^2 points on the grid. Therefore the generality is n^2.
- *Total cost*: The total cost (without sharing) is the product of the cost (p) of one chunk and the total number ($(p + 1)^2$) of chunks learned. The total number of chunks learned in this representation is obtained from the discussion in Section 6.1.

Appendix III. Generality of chunks in the Eight-puzzle task

This analysis compares the generality of chunks in three different representations: no-transfer, multi-attributes, and unique-attributes. We assume that some simple search-control chunks are to be learned. Given two possible operators (see Figure 19 for examples of operators in the Eight-puzzle domain), the chunks give a preference to one operator over the other. The operators are evaluated as follows:

- If an operator moves a tile from out-of-place to in-place: + 1
- If an operator moves a tile from in-place to out-of-place: − 1
- If an operator moves a tile from out-of-place to out-of-place: 0

In-place and out-of-place are determined by explicit comparison of the positions of the tiles in the present state and the desired state. If the two operator evaluations result in the same value, then an *indifferent* preference is generated, i.e., the two operators are equally preferable (or unpreferable).

No-transfer chunks. A no-transfer chunk has the format shown in Figure 25. Note that this chunk does not have any variables. It first matches the entire present state, then the entire desired state, then the two operators, and then prefers one operator over the other.

```
(Production::No-transfer-case-78200

    (Desired-state-position 11  ^tile  1)
    (Desired-state-position 12  ^tile  2)
    (Desired-state-position 13  ^tile  3)
                    .
                    .

    (Present-state-position 11  ^tile  1)
    (Present-state-position 12  ^tile  0)
    (Present-state-position 13  ^tile  2)
                    .
                    .

    (Operator-move-tile  OP1  ^tile  1)
    (Operator-move-tile  OP2  ^tile  2)
-->
    (Preference  Operator-move-tile  OP1  worse-than  Operator-move-tile OP2))
```

Figure 25. A no-transfer chunk in the Eight-puzzle domain.

For each possible present and desired state, we require one such chunk. There are 9! possible desired states in the Eight-puzzle. There are 9! possible present states. The total number of configurations of the present and desired states cannot be simply multiplied together, since depending on the position of the blank-tile, the number of two-operator combinations in each state is different. There are nine possible positions of the blank-tile. For each, the number of present-state and operator combinations need to be computed.

- If the blank-tile is in the center, four operators are available. The four operators can be combined in (4 choose 2 =) 6 ways. The rest of the tiles can be permuted in 8! ways—a total of 6*(8!) ways.
- If the blank-tile is in a corner, only two operators are available. There are four corner-positions for the blank-tile. For each of those, there are 8! permutations of the other tiles—a total of 4*(8!) ways.
- For the other positions of the blank-tile, three operators are available. We can combine them in three (3 choose 2) ways. There are four such positions of the blank-tile, and for each of those, there are 8! permutations of the other tiles—a total of 4*3*(8!) ways.

Combining all the above numbers, we get 9! (for the desired-state) * 8!*(4*3 + 4 + 6) (for the present state) = *7983360* (≈ 8 million) no-transfer chunks to cover the entire space.

Multi-attributes. Consider a multi-attribute equivalent of the chunk in Figure 25. This chunk has the following features: it includes variables and uses the representation presented in Appendix I. Instead of matching the entire present state and desired state, it matches only the relevant tiles. Since it performs the match using multi-attributes and variables, it is completely general in terms of the operators being considered, the present state and the desired state. This implies that only a single chunk should be able to cover the entire space. However, since the two operators being considered in one search control chunk may still evaluate to different values, five different chunks would be required:

- One chunk each would be required for the following combinations of operator evaluations: (−1, −1), (−1, 0), (0, 0), (−1, 1), (0, 1)
- The combination of (1, 1) is not possible, as that would mean two tiles from the present state occupy the same cell in the desired state.

Therefore, five multi-attribute chunks suffice to cover the entire space covered by the ≈ 8 million no-transfer chunks.

Unique attributes. Consider a unique-attribute equivalent of the chunk in Figure 25. The analysis is similar to the analysis for the multi-attribute chunks. However, the operators in unique-attribute chunks have to be in specific directions *up*, *down*, *right*, *left*. There are six (4 choose 2) possible combinations of the four directions. Furthermore, for each possible combination of directions, there are 10 possible combinations of evaluations. For instance, one unique-attribute chunk will compare an operator for moving a tile *up* with an evaluation of −1, to an operator moving a tile *down* with an evaluation of 0. Therefore, (6*10 =) 60 unique-attribute chunks are needed to cover the entire space.

Acknowledgments

We thank John Laird, Steve Minton, David Steier, Don Cohen, Bob MacGregor, and members of the Soar group for many interesting discussions on expensive chunks. Jack Mostow and the three anonymous reviewers provided valuable feedback for improving the quality of this paper. We also thank Kathy Swedlow for technical editing.

This research was sponsored by the Defense Advanced Research Projects Agency (DoD) under contract numbers F33615-87-C-1499 and N00039-86C-0033 (via subcontract from the Knowledge Systems Laboratory, Stanford University), by the National Aeronautics and Space Administration under cooperative agreement number NCC 2-538, and by Encore Computer Corporation.

Notes

1. This article is an expanded version of the following two conference papers: (Tambe and Newell, 1988) and (Tambe and Rosenbloom, 1989).
2. The particular scheme for restricting expressiveness presented here is not the only one possible. Various other schemes are also possible (Tambe and Rosenbloom, 1990). However, this scheme remains one of the most interesting ones and deserves extended treatment.
3. Soar/PSM-E is implemented on the Encore multi-processor. For these measurements, the system was run in a uniprocessor mode.
4. Note that in all of the tasks above, where expensive chunks occurred, problem size was reduced to reduce the cost of the chunks. Without such a reduction, the problems would have been intractable after chunking. For instance, the N-queens task was converted to a 2-Queens task.
5. Since the completion of this investigation three other cases of expensive chunks were detected in (Washington and Rosenbloom, 1988), (Hsu, Prietula, and Steier, 1989), and (Reich, 1988). The analysis in this paper applies to those systems as well.
6. The Soar version decribed here and used in the experiments in this article is Soar 4.5 (Laird, et al., 1989).
7. Variations of about a factor of 2 have been seen in time/token. Therefore, a model built on tokens will not be extremely precise. However, the purpose here is to allow us to compare expensive and cheap chunks, independent of the machine implementation. Given the order of magnitude difference in the costs of those chunks, a token-based model seems to serve the purpose.
8. This assertion follows from a detailed analysis of the chunks learned in the tasks from Table 1 and an informal analysis of the productions and chunks in various other Soar tasks. This particular effect usually occurs because these productions/chunks test the current state in the problem space. After a single firing of the production, this state typically changes, removing previously accumulated k-search. Actually, even if the production does not fire, the k-search model manages to estimate the production's match cost. However, the k-search model may not work well if the production fires many different times without requiring any additional k-search.
9. We thank John Laird for this representation.
10. Having variables in the class and attribute fields is very rare in Soar. None of the tasks in this paper use such variabilized class and attribute fields. In fact, variabilization in these two fields is on the verge of elimination from Soar. The only consistent exception to the prebound variable in the identifier field is, obviously, the first condition in the production. This condition is the one that matches the current goal, and hence usually only a single WME—thus it does not change the main conclusion here about multiplicity in matching.
11. These multi-attributes should not be confused with the multi-attributes used in file indexing (Wiederhold, 1987).
12. Written in C, and running on a Vax 8800, which is about 6 MIPs.
13. The large speedup in Magic-square is partly because the original ordering required a large number of tokens, which cluttered up some of the hash tables used in this implementation, increasing the time per token.
14. Some other minor restrictions are also required: (1) Variable attributes must be prebound. (2) Soar's Rete match algorithm needs a small modification to handle conjunctive negations in Soar. The impact of these restrictions is expected to be very limited. See (Tambe and Rosenbloom, 1988) for details.

15. These and other subsequent measurements were done using a Common Lisp version of Soar running on a Vax 8800. Due to the differences in the implementation, and some small change in the Grid and Magic-square task sizes, the execution times of the multi-attributes presented here do not completely correspond with the numbers in Table 1. Also, the measurements here present the total run time as opposed to the match time in Table 1.
16. In addition to the unique- and multi-attributes, a representation that allows no generality whatsoever is also possible. For a comparative analysis of such a representation, see (Tambe and Rosenbloom, 1988).
17. Note that once Soar learns a chunk to solve a problem, it will not create more chunks to solve the same problem. In this particular case, once the unique-attribute system has learned a chunk covering a single path to a destination, it will not learn more chunks covering different paths for the same destination.
18. The large number of chunks (17) result from a variety of subgoals being chunked.
19. For this experiment, problems were generated by randomly walking back (a maximum of 12 steps) from a fixed goal-state. Both the number of steps and the move at each step were randomly generated using the microsecond clock of the Vax 8800.
20. Macros for writing productions may be another way to address this problem.
21. The result of the unique-attribute representation bounding the elaboration phase holds even if multiple goals are present in the goal hierarchy. However, the argument becomes somewhat more complex.

References

Brownston, L., Farrell, R., Kant, E. and Martin, N. (1985). *Programming expert systems in OPS5: An introduction to rule-based programming*. Reading, MA: Addison-Wesley.

Chalasani, P. and Altmann, E. (1989). Comparing the representations in Soar and Theo. Unpublished, School of Computer Science, Carnegie Mellon University.

Chase, M.P., Zweben, M., Piazza, R.L., Burger, J.D., Maglio P.P. and Hirsh, H. (1989). Approximating learned search control knowledge. *Proceedings of International Workshop on Machine Learning* (pp. 218–220).

Cohen, W. (1988). Generalizing number and learning from multiple examples in explanation-based learning. *Proceedings of the Fifth International Conference on Machine Learning* (pp. 256–269).

Cohen, W., Mostow, J. and Borgida, A. (1988). Generalizing number in explanation-based learning. *Proceedings of the Spring Symposium on Explanation-Based Learning* (pp. 68–72).

DeJong, G.F. and Mooney, R. (1986). Explanation-based learning: An alternative view. *Machine Learning, 1*, 145–176.

Forgy, C.L. (1982). Rete: A fast algorithm for the many pattern/many object pattern match problem. *Artificial Intelligence, 19*, 17–37.

Forgy, C.L. (1984). *The OPS83 Report* (Technical Report CMU-CS-84-133) Pittsburgh, PA: Carnegie Mellon University, Computer Science Department.

Garey, M.R. and Johnson, D.S. (1978). *Computers and intractability: A guide to the theory of NP-completeness*. San Francisco, CA: W.H. Freeman and Company.

Greiner, R. and Likuski, J. (1989). Incorporating redundant learned rules: A preliminary formal analysis of EBL. *Proceedings of the Eleventh International Joint Conference on Artificial Intelligence* (pp. 744–749).

Gupta, A. (1986). *Parallelism in production systems*. Doctoral dissertation, Computer Science Department, Carnegie Mellon University. Also a book, Morgan Kaufmann, (1987).

Gupta, A. and Tambe, M. (1988). Suitability of message passing computers for implementing production systems. *Proceedings of the Seventh Conference on Artificial Intelligence* (pp. 687–692).

Hsu, W., Prietula, M. and Steier, D. (1989). Merl-Soar: Scheduling within a general architecture for intelligence. *Proceedings of the Third International Conference on Expert Systems and the Leading Edge in Production and Operations Management* (pp. 467–481).

Iba, G.A. (1989). A heuristic approach to the discovery of macro-operators. *Machine Learning, 3*, 285–318.

Ishida, T. (1988). Optimizing rules in production system programs. *Proceedings of the Seventh National Conference on Artificial Intelligence* (pp. 699–704).

Keller, R. (1987). Defining operationality for explanation-based learning. *Proceedings of the Sixth National Conference on Artificial Intelligence* (pp. 482–487).

Laird, J.E., Swedlow, K.R., Altmann, E.M., Congdon, C.B. and Wiesmeyer, M. (1989). *Soar 4.5 user's manual.* School of Computer Science, Carnegie Mellon University and Department of Electrical Engineering and Computer Science, University of Michigan, June, 1989.

Laird, J.E., Newell, A. and Rosenbloom, P.S. (1987). Soar: An architecture for general intelligence. *Artificial Intelligence, 33* 1-64.

Laird, J.E., Rosenbloom, P.S. and Newell, A. (1986). Chunking in Soar: The anatomy of a general learning mechanism: *Machine Learning, 1,* 11-46.

Levesque, H.J. and Brachman, R. J. (1985). A fundamental tradeoff in knowledge representation and reasoning. In Brachman, R.J. and Levesque, H.J. (Eds.), *Readings in Knowledge Representation.* Los Altos, CA: Morgan Kaufmann Publishers, Inc.

Markovitch, S. and Scott, P.D. (1988). The role of forgetting in learning. *Proceedings of the Fifth International Conference on Machine Learning* (pp. 459–465).

Markovitch, S. and Scott, P.D. (1989). Information filters and their implementation in the SYLLOG system. *Proceedings of the Sixth International Workshop on Machine Learning* (pp. 404–407).

Markovitch, S. and Scott, P.D. (1989). Utilization filtering: a method for reducing the inherent harmfulness of deductively learned knowledge. *Proceedings of the Eleventh International Joint Conference on Artificial Intelligence* (pp. 738–743).

Minton, S. (1985). Selectively generalizing plans for problem-solving. *Proceedings of the Ninth International Joint Conference on Artificial Intelligence* (pp. 596–599).

Minton, S. (1988). Quantitative results concerning the utility of explanation-based learning. *Proceedings of the Seventh National Conference on Artificial Intelligence* (pp. 564–569).

Minton, S. (1988). *Learning Effective Search Control Knowledge: An explanation-based approach.* Doctoral dissertation, Computer Science Department, Carnegie Mellon University.

Minton, S., Carbonell, J.G., Knoblock, C.A., Kuokka, D.R., Etzioni, O. and Gil, Y. (1989). Explanation-based learning: A problem solving perspective. *Machine Learning,* Vol. *40* (pp. 63–118).

Miranker, D.P. (1987). Treat: A better match algorithm for AI production systems. *Proceedings of the Sixth National Conference on Artificial Intelligence* (pp. 42–47).

Mitchell, T.M., Allen, J., Chalasani, P., Cheng, J., Etzioni, O., Ringuette, M. and Schlimmer, J.C. (1989). Theo: A framework for self-improving systems. In VanLehn, K. (Ed.), *Architectures for Intelligence.* Hillsdale, NJ: Lawrence Erlbaum Associates.

Mitchell, T.M., Keller, R.M. and Kedar-Cabelli, S.T. (1986). Explanation-based generalization: A unifying view. *Machine Learning, 1,* 47-80.

Mooney, R. (1989). The effect of rule use on the utility of explanation-based learning. *Proceedings of the Eleventh International Joint Conference on Artificial Intelligence* (pp. 725–730).

Nayak, P., Gupta, A. and Rosenbloom, P. (1988). Comparison of the Rete and Treat production matchers for Soar (A summary). *Proceedings of the Seventh National Conference on Artificial Intelligence* (pp. 693–698).

Newell, A. (1990). *Unified theories of cognition.* Cambridge, MA: Harvard University Press. In press.

Newell, A. and Rosenbloom, P.S. (1981). Mechanisms of skill acquisition and the law of practice. In Anderson, J.R. (Ed.), *Cognitive Skills and Their Acquisition.* Hillsdale, NJ: Lawrence Erlbaum Associates.

Newell, A., Rosenbloom, P.S. and Laird, J.E. (1990). Symbolic architectures for cognition. In M.I. Posner (Ed.), *Foundations of Cognitive Science.* Cambridge, MA: Bradford Books/MIT Press. In press.

Oflazer, K. (1987). *Partitioning in Parallel Processing of Production Systems.* Doctoral dissertation, Computer Science Department, Carnegie Mellon University.

Pereira, L.M. and Porto, A. (1982). Selective backtracking. In Clark, K.L. and Tarnlund, S.A. (Eds.), *Logic Programming.* NY: Academic Press.

Polk, T.A. and Newell, A. (1988). Modeling human syllogistic reasoning in Soar. *Proceedings of the Annual Conference of the Cognitive Science Society* (pp. 181–187).

Preiditis, A. and Mostow, J. (1987). PROLEARN: Towards a Prolog interpreter that learns. *Proceedings of the Sixth National Conference on Artificial Intelligence* (pp. 494–498).

Reich, Y. (1988). Learning plans as a weak method for design. Department of Civil Engineering, Carnegie Mellon University, Unpublished.

Rosenbloom, P.S. and Laird, J.E. (1986). Mapping explanation-based generalization onto Soar. *Proceedings of the Fifth National Conference on Artificial Intelligence* (pp. 561–567).

Rosenbloom, P.S. and Newell, A. (1986). The chunking of goal hierarchies: A generalized model of practice. In Laird, J.E., Rosenbloom, P.S., and Newell, A. (Eds.), *Universal Subgoaling and Chunking: The Automatic Generation and Learning of Goal Hierarchies.* Boston, MA: Kluwer Academic Publishers.

Rosenbloom, P.S., Laird, J.E., McDermott, J., Newell, A. and Orciuch, E. (1985). Rl-Soar: An experiment in knowledge-intensive programming in a problem-solving architecture. *IEEE Transactions on Pattern Analysis and Machine Intelligence, 7,* 561–569.

Scales, D.J. (1986). *Efficient matching algorithms for the Soar/Ops5 production system* (Technical Report KSL-86-47). Palo Alto, CA: Stanford University, Knowledge Systems Laboratory, Department of Computer Science.

Shavlik, J. (1989). Acquiring recursive concepts with explanation-based learning. *Proceedings of the Eleventh International Joint Conference on Artificial Intelligence* (pp. 688–693).

Shavlik, J.W. and DeJong, G.F. (1987). An explanation-based approach to generalizing number. *Proceedings of the Tenth International Joint Conference on Artificial Intelligence* (pp. 236–238).

Shell, P. and Carbonell, J. (1989). Towards a general framework for composing disjunctive and iternative macro-operators. *Proceedings of the Eleventh International Joint Conference on Artificial Intelligence* (pp. 596–602).

Smith, D.E. and Genesereth, M.R. (1986). Ordering conjunctive queries. *Artificial Intelligence, 26,* 171–215.

Steier, D.M. (1986). Speeding up Soarware. School of Compuer Science, Carnegie Mellon University, Unpublished.

Steier, D.M. (1987). Cypress-Soar: A case study in search and learning in algorithm design. *Proceedings of the Tenth International Joint Conference on Artificial Intelligence* (pp. 327–330).

Steier, D.M., Laird, J.E., Newell, A., Rosenbloom, P.S, Flynn, R.A., Golding, A., Polk, T.A., Shivers, O.G., Unruh, A. and Yost, G.R. (1987). Varieties of learning in Soar: 1987. *Proceedings of the Fourth International Workshop on Machine Learning* (pp. 300–311).

Tambe, M. (1988). Speculations on the computational effects of chunking. Computer Science Department, Carnegie Mellon University, Unpublished.

Tambe, M. and Newell, A. (1988). Some chunks are expensive. *Proceedings of the Fifth International Conference on Machine Learning* (pp. 451–458).

Tambe, M. and Rosenbloom, P. (1988). *Eliminating expensive chunks* (Technical Report CMU-CS-88-189). Pittsburgh, PA: Carnegie Mellon University, Computer Science Department.

Tambe, M. and Rosenbloom, P. (1989). Eliminating expensive chunks by restricting expressiveness. *Proceedings of the Eleventh International Joint Conference on Artificial Intelligence* (pp. 731–737).

Tambe, M. and Rosenbloom, P. (1990). A framework for investigating production system formulations with polynomially bounded match. *Proceedings of the Eighth National Conference on Artificial Intelligence.* (To appear.)

Tambe, M., Kalp, D., Gupta, A., Forgy, C.L., Milnes, B.G. and Newell, A. (1988). Soar/PSM-E: Investigating match parallelism in a learning production system. *Proceedings of the ACM/SIGPLAN Symposium on Parallel Programming: Experience with applications, languages, and systems* (pp. 146–160).

Ullman, J.D. (1982). *Principles of database systems.* Rockville, MD: Computer Science Press.

Washington, R. and Rosenbloom, P.S. (1988). Applying problem solving and learning to diagnosis. Knowledge Systems Laboratory, Stanford University, December, 1988, Unpublished.

Wiederhold, G. (1987). *File organization for database design.* NY: McGraw-Hill.

Yost, G.R. and Altmann, E.M. (1989). TAQL 3.0: Soar task acquisition system user's manual. School of Computer Science, Carnegie Mellon University, December, 1989, Unpublished.

Yost, G.R. and Newell, A. (1989). A problem space approach to expert system specification. *Proceedings of the Eleventh International Joint Conference on Artificial Intelligence* (pp. 621–627).

CHAPTER 57

A Framework for Investigating Production System Formulations with Polynomially Bounded Match

M. Tambe, Carnegie Mellon University and P. S. Rosenbloom, USC–ISI

Abstract

Real time constraints on AI systems require guaranteeing bounds on these systems' performance. However, in the presence of sources of uncontrolled combinatorics, it is extremely difficult to guarantee such bounds on their performance. In production systems, the primary source of uncontrolled combinatorics is the production match. To eliminate these combinatorics, the unique-attribute formulation was introduced in (Tambe and Rosenbloom, 1989), which achieved a linear bound on the production match. This formulation leads to several questions: is this unique-attributes formulation the best conceivable production system formulation? In fact, are there other alternative production system formulations? If there are other formulations, how should these alternatives be compared with the unique-attribute formulation?

This paper attempts to address these questions in the context of Soar. It identifies independent dimensions along which alternative production system formulations can be specified. These dimensions are based on the fixed class of match algorithms currently employed in production systems. These dimensions create a framework for systematically generating alternative formulations. Using this framework we show that the unique-attribute formulation is the best one within the dimensions investigated. However, if a new class of match algorithms is admitted, by relaxing certain constraints, other competitor formulations emerge. The paper indicates which competitor formulations are promising and why. Although some of the concepts, such as unique-attributes, are introduced in the context of Soar, they should also be relevant to other rule-based systems.[1]

1. Introduction

Soar is an architecture for a system that is intended to be capable of general intelligence. It is based on formulating all symbolic goal-oriented behavior as search in problem spaces (Laird, Newell, and Rosenbloom, 1987). The primitive acts of the system, called *decisions*, are those required to pursue this search: the selection of problem spaces, states, and operators, plus the application of operators to states to generate new states. The information necessary for the performance of these primitive acts can be provided in one of two ways: from Soar's knowledge base, which is implemented as a production system, or by the recursive use of problem space search in subgoals. Both can result in adding new working memory elements (wmes) to the system's existing working memory. Soar learns by converting subgoal-based search into productions that generate comparable results under similar conditions (Laird, Rosenbloom, and Newell, 1986). The actions of the new productions are based on the results of the subgoals. The conditions are based on those wmes in parent goals upon which the results depended. This *chunking* process is a form of explanation-based learning (Rosenbloom and Laird, 1986).

This paper is focused on providing Soar with an efficient and non-combinatorial (polynomially bounded) production match, particularly in the presence of continuous chunking. Production match in Soar is a key performance bottleneck. Soar's current production match is OPS5-based (Forgy, 1981), i.e., it is NP-hard (Tambe and Newell, 1988). Production match occurs at every decision in problem solving in Soar, and unpredictable combinatorial processing can occur in the match at any such decision.

This combinatorial match leads to various problems in Soar: (1) It prevents Soar from operating in real time (Newell, 1989). (2) It leads to the problem of *expensive chunks*, i.e., productions learned in the course of problem solving that can cause a severe degradation in Soar's performance (Tambe and Newell, 1988). (3) It is problematical for Soar's quest of modeling human cognition (Newell, 1990). (4) It leads to load-balancing problems in parallelization (Acharya and Tambe, 1989, Gupta, et. al., 1989, Tambe and Acharya, 1989). An efficient and bounded production match could alleviate all these problems.

In (Tambe and Rosenbloom, 1989), the ***unique-attribute*** formulation was introduced to guarantee an efficient and bounded production match. This formulation eliminated combinatorics from the match by trading off some expressive power. This formulation leads to several questions: is this unique-attributes formulation the best conceivable alternative to the current production system formulation? Are there any other alternative production system formulations? If there are, how should they be compared with the unique-attribute formulation?

This paper attempts to address these questions in the context of Soar. The paper identifies different dimensions along which alternative production system formulations can be specified. These dimensions are based on the fixed class of match algorithms currently employed in production systems. These dimensions create a framework for systematically identifying the different production system formulations. This paper shows how the unique-attribute formulation fits into the framework presented. Using this framework the paper shows that unique-attributes are the best possible formulation within the dimensions investigated. However, if a new class of match algorithms is admitted, other competitor formulations emerge. The paper indicates which competitor formulations are promising and why. Although these results are introduced in the context of Soar, Section 9 discusses their relevance to other systems.

All alternative formulations investigated in this paper tradeoff expressive power for production match complexity, thus providing some additional data points in understanding the general tradeoff in knowledge representation and reasoning (Levesque and Brachman, 1985, Patel-Schneider, 1989). Additionally, Soar's chunking provides a unique opportunity to

[1]This research was sponsored by the Defense Advanced Research Projects Agency (DOD) under contract numbers F33615-87-C-1499 and N00039-86C-0033 (via subcontract from the Knowledge Systems Laboratory, Stanford University), by the National Aeronautics and Space Administration under cooperative agreement number NCC 2-538.

gain a better understanding of how learning interacts with this tradeoff.

The paper is organized as follows: Section 2 provides an implementation-independent model of the production match, since this paper depends on a deeper understanding of production match. Section 3 presents the unique-attribute formulation. Section 4 discusses issues in evaluating alternative production system formulations. Section 5 introduces the framework for generating alternative formulations and shows how unique-attributes fit in the framework. Section 6 introduces tokenless match, the basis for the new class of match algorithms. Section 7 shows how promising new alternative formulations emerge with the introduction of tokenless match. Section 8 provides some evidence about the generality of the formulations presented here, by showing how marker passing — a formulation quite different from the standard production match — maps onto it. Section 9 outlines the contributions of this paper and its relevance to other research.

2. Modeling Soar's Production Match

The *k-search model* (Tambe and Newell, 1988) of production match covers match algorithms that find all possible solutions, without the aid of heuristics. This includes widely used match algorithms such as Rete (Forgy, 1982) and Treat (Miranker, 1987). The k-search model is based on the notion of tokens, or partial instantiations. Consider the (simplified) production **Length-3** shown in Figure 2-1-a. In the figure, up-arrow (^) indicates an attribute, and angeled bracket (<>) indicates a variable. Figure 2-1-b shows the working memory of the production system, which describes the graph in Figure 2-1-c. On the creation of the wme **(current-position A)**, the production **Length-3** will match the working memory, generating tokens, e.g., **(2; <x> = A, <z> = B)**. The first number in the token indicates the number of conditions matched and the other elements indicate the bindings for the variables. Thus, tokens indicate what conditions have matched and under what variable bindings. These tokens can be represented in the form of a *k-search* tree, as shown in Figure 2-1-d. This k-search tree represents the search conducted by the matcher, using tokens, to match the production. The result of the k-search is the four tokens (instantiations) shown at the leaves of the k-search tree. The time/token is approximately constant (Tambe and Newell, 1988). Therefore, for Soar productions, the *number of tokens* in the k-search tree is a reasonable estimate of the time spent in match.

The causes of Soar's combinatorial production match can now be explained. All the wmes in Soar's production system are *a priori* candidates to match a condition, leading to a k-search tree with a number of tokens greater than $\text{wmes}^{\text{conditions}}$. However, variables bound in the conditions prior to the current condition, and constants, can provide a strong filter on the match. Soar conditions have four fields: *(class identifier attribute value)*. The class and attribute fields are constant (almost always), the identifier field is prebound (almost always) and the value field can be a constant, a prebound variable, or an unbound variable. Thus, *an unbound variable should only occur in the value field*, and multiplicity only occurs in matching a Soar condition if there are multiple possible values corresponding to the three already fixed fields, i.e., there is more than one value for an attribute. This is referred to as a *multi-attribute*. For instance, in Figure 2-1-b, **connected-to** is a multi-attribute of the objects A and D — point A is **connected-to** both B and C, while D is **connected-to** to both E and F. As shown in Figure 2-1-d, the k-search tree branches out

```
(Production Length-3
  (current-position <x>)
  (point <x>  ^connected-to <z>)
  (point <z>  ^connected-to <y>)
  (point <y>  ^connected-to <w>)
-->
  (write path of length 3 from
              <x> to <w>))
```

(a)

```
/** The working memory **/
(point A  ^connected-to B)
(point B  ^connected-to D)
(point A  ^connected-to C)
(point C  ^connected-to D)
(point D  ^connected-to E)
(point D  ^connected-to F)
```

(b)

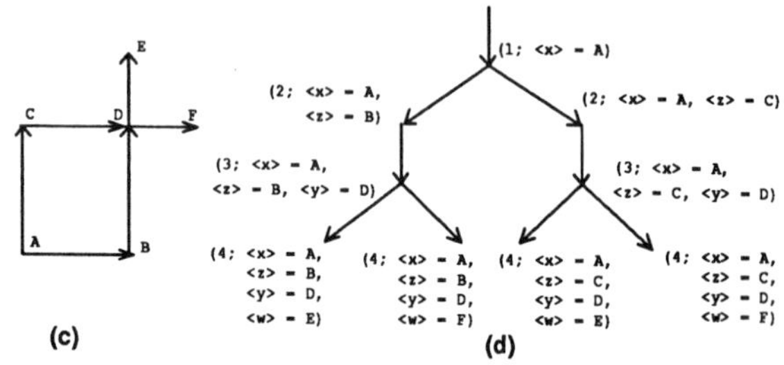

Figure 2-1: An example production system.

in matching the multi-attributes with conditions 2 and 4. Thus, combinatorics can occur in Soar's production match only in the presence of multi-attributes. (Preferences — special control elements in Soar — can also contribute to the combinatorics. However, their impact is much smaller than multi-attributes, and they are ignored here. See (Tambe, Newell and Rosenbloom, 1990) for details.)

3. Unique-attributes

If multi-attributes are eliminated completely, the branching of the k-search tree is also eliminated. This will then limit the number of tokens in the k-search tree to the number of conditions in the production. Thus, *the cost of a production will be linear in the number of conditions*, i.e., the match cost will be bounded linearly rather than being NP-hard. For productions containing variables, this O(conditions) match bound is optimal, since all the conditions of a production must be examined for the match in any event. The new formulation is referred to as the *unique-attribute* formulation (Tambe and Rosenbloom, 1989). In contrast, Soar's current production system formulation will be henceforth referred to as the *unrestricted* formulation, i.e., a formulation with no representational restrictions. (This unrestricted formulation was referred to as the multi-attribute formulation in (Tambe and Rosenbloom, 1989, Tambe, Newell and Rosenbloom, 1990)).

The principle computational impact of going with unique-attributes is the removal of the combinatorial k-search from the match — all combinatorics will now occur as search in problem spaces. In (Tambe and Rosenbloom, 1989), detailed experiments on unique-attributes demonstrated the ability of the unique-attributes to eliminate the combinatorics from the production match, and to outperform the unrestricted Soar formulation in various tasks.

Basically, the unique-attribute formulation trades off some expressive power to gain efficiency in the production match. This loss in expressive power is not inconsequential. It manifests itself in three issues. First, multi-attributes are used in encoding unstructured sets in working memory. For instance, in Figure 2-1-b, points **B** and **C** are an unstructured set of points connected to point **A**. With unique-attributes, all sets in working memory have to be structured (e.g., lists), which may not always be easy (Tambe and Rosenbloom, 1989). Second, the loss of multi-attributes causes a loss in chunk generality. A much larger number of unique-attribute chunks may be required to gain the same amount of coverage as an unrestricted chunk. Until such coverage is obtained, the unique-attributes have to perform potentially expensive problem-space search. So far, in the tasks encoded in the unique-attribute formulation, these two issues have not been a major problem (Tambe and Rosenbloom, 1989).

The third implication of the unique-attributes is the inability to process arbitrary sets in a single decision, which is important in cognitive modeling tasks such as syllogisms (Polk, Newell, and Lewis, 1989). The unrestricted formulation allows this type of processing. With unique-attributes, sets are structured and have to be processed in multiple decisions (or a large number of chunks have to be learned to allow the processing to occur in a single decision) (Tambe and Rosenbloom, 1989). These three issues imply that the unique-attribute formulation is ***not the best conceivable*** alternative to the current formulation — its expressive power can potentially be improved.

4. Evaluating Alternative Formulations

The unique-attribute formulation is not the best conceivable formulation. But, in practice, *is it the best possible?*, i.e., is the tradeoff in unique-attributes the *best tradeoff*? This is a difficult question. As shown later, different formulations, which polynomially bound the match, restrict the production system in different ways and engage in different tradeoffs. The concept of *the best tradeoff* is imprecise.

Thus, it is impossible to devise an independent test to determine if the unique-attribute, or any other formulation is the best possible in practice, without a comparison with other formulations. That is, to determine the best, different formulations have to be compared and ranked. Even this comparison is quite difficult. However, we can enumerate a set of requirements, which will help in comparing different formulations. These requirements can be divided into *absolute* and *relative*. Absolute requirements allow formulations to be evaluated independent of each other, while relative requirements only enable comparative evaluations. The absolute requirements are:

1. *Polynomial bound on match complexity:* The match complexity of the desired representation should be polynomially bounded (in number of conditions in a production and wmes in the system).
2. *Closure under chunking:* If the productions and the working memory meet the restrictions imposed by a particular representation scheme before chunking, the chunks should also meet the restriction. If chunking violates the restrictions and creates expensive chunks, clearly that defeats the purpose of this exercise.
3. *Correctness of match:* The match should provide correct results.

The relative requirements are:

1. *Expressive adequacy:* How easy/difficult is it to encode various existing Soar tasks in a given representation? The previous section discussed this issue with respect to unique-attributes. Schemes that allow easier encoding of various Soar tasks are preferred.
2. *Relative efficiency:* Within the space of polynomially bounded formulations, schemes with smaller polynomial bounds are preferred.
3. *Chunking generality:* This refers to the number of chunks required in a particular representation to cover a given concept. A formulation providing higher chunking generality is preferred.
4. *Principle of uniformity:* Formulations that do not introduce arbitrary divisions in productions or working memory are preferred. Soar strongly adheres to the principle of uniformity in various architectural mechanisms (Newell, 1990). This requirement extends that principle to the production system formulation.

These are diverse requirements, possibly conflicting with each other. Hence these requirements have to be prioritized: the requirements are listed above in their order of priority. Given the goals of the current research, we adopt the position that the absolute requirements must be met by any candidate formulation. Even with this, the candidate formulations are not well ordered. First, the relative requirements are quite subjective. Second, there are interesting tradeoffs/interactions among these requirements, e.g., it may be possible that a formulation with an $O(n^2)$ match bound may provide better chunking generality than a formulation with a $O(n)$ match bound. Even with these shortcomings, the requirements and priorities outlined above are of great help in the search for alternative formulations.

As an example of the use of these requirements, consider a combination of unique- and multi-attributes that attempts to introduce limited amounts of multi-attributes to gain expressibility without sacrificing efficiency. First, suppose this formulation adheres to the principle of uniformity and does not explicitly separate out multi- and unique-attributes from each other. Then, it has no way of controlling the number of multi-attributes matching a production — it is exactly like the unrestricted Soar system. The match cost of productions becomes unpredictable and the polynomial match bound requirement is violated.

Now, suppose the violation of the principle of uniformity is accepted: the system explicitly labels and separates unique- and multi-attributes. It can then bound the number of multi-attribute-matching conditions in any single production — thus controlling the match cost. However, it is possible for such a system to create chunks where the number of multi-attribute-matching conditions in the production exceeds the specified bound — generating expensive chunks. This violates the requirement of closure under chunking. Thus, this unique- and multi-attribute combination does not work.

Note that in this paper, schemes that impose arbitrary time-based cutoffs on the match or those that require Soar to chunk selectively, are rejected as possibilities. Such schemes do not integrate well with the rest of the Soar architecture, i.e., they do not conform with the assumptions underlying the Soar architecture (Tambe, Newell and Rosenbloom, 1990).

5. Formulations Based on Existing Match Algorithms

The previous section showed that the combination of unique-plus multi-attributes does not meet all the absolute and relative requirements. Generating a formulation that satisfies all the requirements is difficult — there is no method that, given the requirements, will directly provide a formulation satisfying them. Combined with the need for comparing different formulations to determine the best among them, this situation dictates a strategy for ***exhaustively*** searching the space of alternative formulations; then for each formulation, testing if it meets the requirements, and then comparing its properties with other formulations to test if it is better.

Although part of the search has already been conducted (Section 3 and 4), how should the exhaustive search proceed further? The problem here is the absence of a device to systematically generate required alternatives. Without such a device, we cannot understand and usefully exploit the structure of the space of alternative formulations. Therefore, this paper introduces a framework for systematically generating alternative production system formulations. To specify the framework, it is necessary to first identify the independent dimensions of this framework. Roughly, these dimensions can be divided into two categories: (1) those that do not require any modification to the current set of token-based match algorithms (introduced in Section 2) (2) those that require some modification. Section 6 introduces dimensions from the second category. This section introduces dimensions only from the first category. These dimensions are based on restrictions on Soar's working memory format: **(class identifier attribute value)**. They are:

1. *Forward-attribute*: Given a fixed identifier, this dimension imposes restrictions on the number of attributes for that identifier. For example, suppose the number of attributes is restricted to one. If **B1** is an identifier, then **(class1 B1 attribute-1 val1)** and **(class1 B1 attribute-2 val2)** are not allowed simultaneously to exist in working memory.
2. *Values-per-attribute*: Given a fixed identifier, this dimension imposes restrictions on the number of values-per-attribute for that identifier. If the number of values-per-attribute is restricted to one, the unique-attributes formulation is obtained. Multi-attributes refer to multiple values-per-attribute.
3. *Reverse-attribute*: Given a fixed value, this dimension imposes restrictions on the number of attributes for that value. This is symmetrical to the forward-attribute dimension. Thus, if **val1** is a value, then **(class1 B1 attribute-1 val1)** and **(class1 B2 attribute-2 val1)** are not allowed simultaneously to exist in working memory, as **attribute-1** and **attribute-2** are two different attributes with the same value **val1**.
4. *Identifiers-per-attribute*: Given a fixed value, what are the restrictions on the number of identifiers-per-attribute for that value. This is symmetrical to the values-per-attribute dimension.

(The class slot in Soar's wmes does not serve any semantic role. Hence the paper does not refer to the class slot.) Figure 5-1 shows the four dimensions in a tabular format. There are two co-ordinates along each of the four dimensions — 1 and *. Here, an asterisk (*) refers to an arbitrary number of values, i.e., no restrictions on the values. In the figure, to lay out these four dimensions in two dimensions, the forward-attribute and values-per-attribute dimensions are paired. Similarly, the reverse-attribute and identifiers-per-attribute dimensions are paired. The figure shows that different combinations of co-ordinates along these dimensions identify different working memory representations.

The choice of 1 and * for the co-ordinates is an interesting issue. This choice of co-ordinates covers both the unique-attribute and the unrestricted working memory and yields semantically meaningful representations like the *Tree* representation (introduced below). Furthermore, if the number of values-per-attribute are increased to two or more, match becomes combinatoric and does not admit the linear bound of unique-attributes. However, whether no other co-ordinates besides 1 and * are useful, remains unclear.

In the unrestricted working memory representation, with a fixed identifier, it is possible to have an arbitrary number of forward-attributes and values-per-attribute. Similarly, with a fixed value, it is possible to have an arbitrary number of reverse-attributes and identifiers-per-attribute. Therefore, the unrestricted working memory occupies the square in the center of the table, where all four dimensions have a value of *. For unique-attributes, the restriction is only on the values-per-attribute — for a fixed identifier, there can be only one value-per-attribute. Its other dimensions are unrestricted and take the value of *.

<ua Indicates more restrictive than unique-attributes

<ui Indicates more restrictive than unique-identifiers

* Indicates an arbitrary number

<ts Indicates more restrictive than the tree-structures

→ Indicates increasing restrictiveness

(reverse-attribute, identifiers-per-attribute) \ (forward-attribute, values-per-attribute)	(1, 1)	(*, 1)	(*, *) [Multi-Attr]	(1, *) [Multi-Attr]	(1, 1)
(1, 1)	<ua <ui <ts	<ua <ui <ts	Tree <ui	<ui <ts	<ua <ui <ts
(*, 1)	<ua <ui	<ua <ui	Unique-ident	<ui	<ua <ui
(*, *)	<ua	Unique-Attr	Current Unrestr Represnt		<ua
(1, *)	<ua	<ua			<ua
(1, 1)	<ua <ui <ts	<ua <ui <ts	<ui Tree	<ui <ts	<ua <ui <ts

Figure 5-1: Dimensions of alternative representations.

In Figure 5-1, the square marked as *Tree* restricts the reverse-attributes and identifiers-per-attributes to one and leaves the other dimensions unrestricted. This representation implies that two different working memory elements cannot have the same value in their value fields. More semantically, this representation corresponds to a tree-structured organization of the working memory. The square marked as *unique-identifiers* restricts the identifiers-per-attribute to one, but does not restrict any other dimension. The table shows that the Tree and unique-identifiers allow an arbitrary number of values-per-attribute, i.e., they allow multi-attributes. In fact, all the working memory representations in two of the columns allow multi-attributes; these columns are labeled with **[Multi-attr]**.

The table shows the unrestricted working memory as the least restrictive form of representation. It occupies the center square in the table. The other representations form a restriction lattice. The first column and the first row are repeated to show the symmetry in this lattice. The most restrictive working memory representation is the one where all the dimensions have the value 1. The table also shows that the Tree structures are more restrictive than the unique-identifiers; but unique-attributes are unrelated in terms of restrictions to either one of these.

The important conclusion that can be made from the table is: *unique-attributes provide the best possible formulation within the four dimensions investigated.* That is, the unique-attributes provide the best fit to all the absolute and relative requirements. All other formulations are either combinatoric, so that they violate the absolute requirement of a polynomial match bound; or they are more restrictive than the unique-attributes, so that unique-attributes fit the relative requirements better. First, consider the formulations in the third and fourth columns of the table. They include the Tree and unique-identifiers, which restrict the identifiers-per-attribute. These representations allow multi-attributes. As described in Section 2, the match in the presence of multi-attributes is combinatoric: thus, all these formulations violate the polynomial match bound requirement.

Second, consider the formulations in the first and second columns of the table. This includes the unique-attributes and the formulations more restrictive than the unique-attributes. The formulations that are more restrictive than the unique-attributes do not reduce the match bound: it is optimal to begin with. Furthermore, these formulations are guaranteed to not be better than unique-attributes along the expressive adequacy or chunking generality requirements, since they are more restrictive.

More generally, we can also conclude that if a given formulation meets all the absolute requirements, *then more restrictive formulations, which do not reduce the match bound, need not be investigated.* If the more restrictive formulations possess the same match bound as the given formulation, only the remaining relative requirements like expressive adequacy, choose the better among them. However, the more restrictive formulations are guaranteed to *not* meet these remaining relative requirements better than the given formulation.

Thus, the unique-attribute formulation is the best possible one in practice, within the four dimensions investigated. The general conclusions drawn here illustrate the power of the framework: the conclusions exploit the structure of the search space made explicit by the framework. Thus, the need for detailed evaluation of each formulation is eliminated.

6. Tokenless Match: A New Match Scheme

The formulations introduced in the previous section were based on the the token-based match scheme (henceforth called token match). The conclusion about unique-attributes being the best among these formulations is based on this token match. In a token match, a single token indicates what variable bindings go together. For example, the token **(2; <x> = A, <z> = C)** from Figure 2-1-d indicates that the binding **A** for **<x>** and **C** for **<z>** go together. The outcome of the match is a set of instantiations, indicating which bindings go together.

If a *tokenless match* is allowed, then new formulations emerge: the unique-attribute formulation is no longer guaranteed to be the best. In *a tokenless match*, each variable obtains a list of bindings, *independent* of the bindings of other variables. The outcome of this match is a set of bindings for each variable, rather than the separate instantiations. If the production **Length-3** in Figure 2-1-a is matched with the working memory from Figure 2-1-b, the result is a set of bindings for the variables as follows:**<x> = A; <z> = B, C; <y> = D; <w> = E, F**. The matcher guarantees that these bindings are consistent with each other; however, it does not explicitly create tokens and instantiations. This consistency requirement is explained in the subsection below with the help of a mapping. This mapping also provides ready-made algorithms to perform tokenless match.

6.1. Tokenless Match and Constraint Satisfaction

A constraint-satisfaction problem is defined as follows: given a set of N variables each with an associated domain and a set of binary constraining relations between the variables, find all possible N-tuples such that each N-tuple is an instantiation of the N variables satisfying the constraining relations (Mackworth and Freuder, 1985). This problem can be represented as a *constraint-graph* where the variables are represented by nodes and the constraints by arcs. Each constraint specifies the set of permitted pairs of values for the two variables involved. Thus, if X_i and X_j are two variables with domains D_i and D_j respectively, then the constraint R_{ij} between X_i and X_j is a subset of the cartesian product of their domains, i.e., $R_{ij} \subseteq D_i \times D_j$

The match for a single Soar production maps on to the constraint satisfaction problem as follows. The variables in the conditions form the variables in the constraint satisfaction problem. For example, the production in Figure 2-1-a can be represented as the constraint network in Figure 6-1. The symbols in working memory, i.e., symbols occupying the identifier and value fields of working memory elements, form the domains of the variables. A condition containing two variables is a constraint between the two variables. The condition specifies (or selects) the wmes with its attribute, so that each wme represents a permitted pair of values for the variables linked by the condition. If a condition contains **A1** as an attribute, it specifies all the wmes with the attribute A1. Thus, the conditions from Figure 6-1 with the attribute **connected-to** specify all the wmes from Figure 2-1-b. Finding all possible solutions of the constraint satisfaction problem formed by a production will result in finding all possible instantiations of the production.

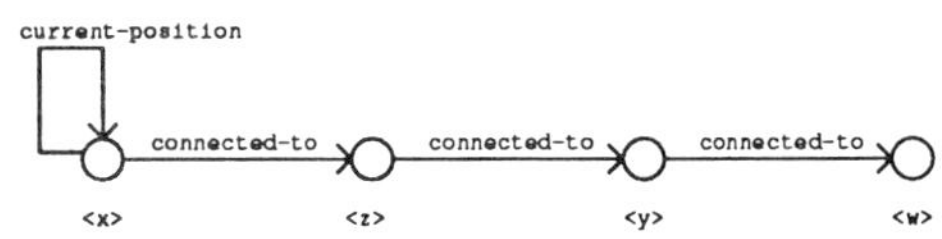

Figure 6-1: Mapping tokenless match to constraint satisfaction.

The constraint satisfaction literature distinguishes between obtaining consistent bindings and forming an instantiation (Dechter and Pearl, 1988). Once consistent bindings are obtained, individual instantiations from the bindings are obtained separately. The tokenless match achieves a similar consistent set of bindings, without forming any instantiations. Thus, there is a mapping between the tokenless match and obtaining consistent bindings in constraint satisfaction problems.

6.2. Implications of the Mapping

The mapping between the tokenless match and constraint satisfaction problems provides an important notion: the relation between the structure of a production and the effort required in obtaining consistent bindings for that production. The structure of the production refers to the equality tests across the value fields of the production's conditions. For instance, if a Soar production admits no equality tests between two variables in the value fields of its conditions, then the production has a tree structure. (To understand why such productions are tree-structured, consider a graph where the variables in the identifier and value fields of the production's conditions are nodes; and the attributes in the conditions are links between the nodes. This graph is tree-structured.) Figure 2-1-a presents one such production without any equality tests across its value fields. To demonstrate how the production structure can be exploited, we need the concept of *arc consistency* in constraint-satisfaction problems.

In constraint-satisfaction problems, arc-consistency is a form of local consistency. Arc-consistency does not solve the general constraint-satisfaction problem. A constraint graph is arc-consistent if each of its arcs is arc-consistent. An arc between variables X_i and X_j is arc-consistent iff for any value $x \in D_i$

there is a value $y \in D_j$ such that $R_{ij}(x, y)$ (Mackworth, 1977). Here $R_{ij}(x, y)$ stands for the assertion that (x, y) is permitted by the explicit constraint R_{ij}. We add the following small symmetric requirement to the situation above: if there is a value $y \in D_j$ then there is a value $x \in D_i$ such that $R_{ij}(x, y)$.

In terms of the production match mapping, the following has to be satisfied for a condition with an attribute A1 to be arc consistent: If there is a binding x for the variable <x> in its identifier field, then there is a binding y for its variable <y> in its value field, such that there exists a wme with attribute A1, identifier x and value y. Symmetrically, if there is a binding y for its variable <y> in the condition's value field, then there exists a binding x for the variable <x> in its identifier field such that there exists a wme with attribute A1, identifier x and value y.

Arc consistency is used along with the production structure in the following result based on an important result from (Dechter and Pearl, 1988):

*If a production is tree structured, and it is made arc-consistent, then the bindings obtained for its variables are consistent. Furthermore, this arc-consistency can be achieved in O(wmes*conditions).*

Here, wmes refers to the number of working memory elements. Thus, if productions are tree-structured, then a tokenless match can be obtained in polynomial time, i.e., the match guarantees consistent bindings for the variables in the production using arc consistency. Note that the tokenless match is important in achieving this bound. A token match, despite tree structured productions, is still exponential — $O(\text{wmes}^{\text{conditions}})$ (see section 4 of (Tambe and Rosenbloom, 1989) for a demonstration of this effect).

Note, however, that if a production is not tree structured, i.e., it has an equality test across the value fields of its conditions, arc consistency may provide a wrong result. That is, it might provide a binding for a variable, when a token match for the same production would have provided none (Tambe and Rosenbloom, 1990). Thus, there is a tradeoff in the complexity of the tokenless match and the restrictions on the equality tests. By restricting the structure of the production in specific ways, different (and increasingly complex) bounds on the tokenless match can be obtained (Dechter and Pearl, 1988). With this result, the structure of the productions emerges as an important dimension. *Thus, two new dimensions are now available in the framework: tokenless match and production structure.*

7. Tokenless Match: New Formulations Emerge

The token/tokenless match and production structure dimensions, along with the four dimensions introduced previously (see Figure 5-1), provide us with a total of six dimensions. From this expanded space, new formulations emerge, and unique-attributes are no longer guaranteed to be the best fit to the absolute and relative requirements. To illustrate this, consider a specific formulation, called the *unrestricted-tree formulation*, that works with an unrestricted working memory representation (from Figure 5-1) and a tokenless match, but restricts productions to be tree-structured. This formulation satisfies all of the absolute requirements. First, polynomial match bound is guaranteed because of the use of a tokenless match and tree-structured productions. As noted in Section 6.2, this combination yields polynomial match bound — O(wmes*conditions) — irrespective of the representation used in working memory. Second, with a small modification to chunking — disallowing introduction of new equality tests across value fields of conditions — this formulation provides closure under chunking. That is, only tree-structured productions will be chunked. Third, due to the consistency requirements imposed, this formulation provides correct results. Therefore, all the absolute requirements are satisfied.

When the relative requirements are compared for the unrestricted-tree and unique-attribute formulations, it becomes clear that neither formulation dominates the other, and hence neither can be pruned *a priori*. In particular, in terms of expressive adequacy, in the unrestricted-tree formulation, working memory restrictions are absent (compared to unique-attributes); however, since equality tests across value fields of conditions are not available, productions have to be written in a fairly different manner. (If such tests become absolutely necessary, productions can directly test constants.) Therefore, we need to implement a set of tasks with this new formulation, and compare its performance with unique-attributes. Initial analysis seems to indicate some promising results for the unrestricted-tree formulation. For example, in the grid task (Tambe and Rosenbloom, 1989), the unrestricted-tree formulation should be able to outperform the unique-attribute and unrestricted formulations. The unrestricted-tree formulation would provide chunks with polynomial match cost, where similar chunks in the unrestricted formulation require an exponential match cost (see Section 4 of (Tambe and Rosenbloom, 1989)); but simultaneously it would avoid the loss in chunk generality that afflicts the unique-attributes (Tambe and Rosenbloom, 1990). The work of implementing tasks in this new formulation is currently in progress and remains a key issue for future work.

Besides the unrestricted-tree formulation, other formulations based on tokenless match are also possible (Tambe and Rosenbloom, 1990). For instance, by adopting consistency algorithms more constraining than arc consistency (Dechter and Pearl, 1988), it is possible to introduce limited equality tests across value fields of conditions of productions. Such new formulations may perform better along the expressive adequacy dimension than the unrestricted-tree formulation, but require a higher polynomial bound. Other formulations that are based on the tree and unique-identifier working memory representations from Figure 5-1 are also possible (Tambe and Rosenbloom, 1990). All these formulations are competitors for the unique-attribute formulation. Further investigations of these new formulations is another key issue for future work.

8. Relationship to Marker Passing Systems

This section develops a mapping between the unrestricted-tree formulation and marker passing systems. This mapping illustrates the generality of the framework presented in this paper for alternative production system formulations — it manages to capture a fairly different production system formulation. This mapping is illustrated using the NETL parallel marker passing system (Fahlman, 1979).

Conceptually, NETL is composed of a large collection of object nodes, like semantic nets, and a large collection of bi-directional links or arcs organized so that each object node can be linked arbitrarily to any number of other nodes in the system. Markers (signals) may be propagated along different links in parallel. Queries are posed to the NETL system, and answers are retrieved by passing markers between nodes. (No cancellation links are assumed, hence the problems from (Touretzky, 1986) associated with marker passing systems are not relevant here.)

The mapping onto NETL relies on describing each symbol in the working memory as an object node of NETL. The attributes in working memory are links between nodes. The production to be matched is the query to the NETL system. Match is performed by passing markers between symbols. Matching a single condition is equivalent to sending a marker from a symbol bound to the identifier field of the condition (since the identifier of a condition is bound before matching the condition) to the symbols linked via the attribute in the condition. The result of passing this marker is a set of bindings in the value field of the condition. This allows bindings to be obtained for the next condition via marker passing. Again, the result of the match is a set of variable bindings, without the token information.

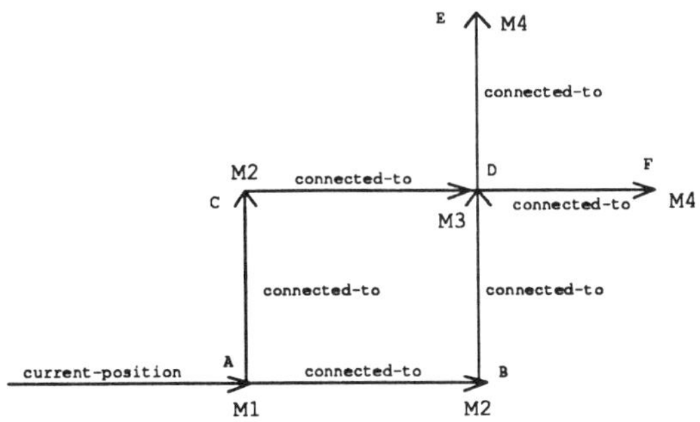

Figure 8-1: Mapping onto marker passing.

Figure 8-1 shows this mapping with the help of the simple example from Figure 2-1. The figure shows the structure described by the working memory in Figure 2-1-b, with the addition of the wme **(current-position A)**. This working memory is to be matched with the production in Figure 2-1-a. Matching the first condition results in the marker **M1** being sent to the symbol A. This binds the variable <x> to A. Matching the second condition results in marker **M2** being sent to the symbols **B** and **C**, which become the bindings for the variable <z> in the value field of the second condition. Matching the third condition results in passing marker **M3** and obtaining binding **D** for the variable <y>. Note that when two **M3** markers from **B** and **C** reach **D**, they are ORed together. Finally, passing marker **M4** obtains bindings for variable <w>. The result of the match is the same as the result of the arc consistency match:<x> = **A**; <z> = **B**, **C**; <y> = **D**; <w> = **E**, **F**.

As in the previous modification to the definition of arc consistency, markers actually have to be passed in a bidirectional manner to achieve complete consistency in tree-structured productions. That is, once the markers have reached the leaves of the production, they are transmitted back toward the root. In this example, the backward marker propagation phase would begin by sending marker **M4** back and then continuing onwards with **M3**, **M2** and **M1**. (In an actual implementation, correctness requires that the backward marker propagation be done first. However, for expository purposes, we have reversed the order of marker propagation.)

The bidirectional marker passing results in the following: suppose there is a binding x for a variable <x> in the identifier field of a condition with attribute A1. Now, with marker passing in the forward direction along the A1 link, bindings from the value fields of wmes with attribute A1 are obtained for the variable <y> in the value field of the condition. Symmetrically, if there is a binding y for its variable <y> in the condition's value field, then with marker passing in the reverse direction along the A1 link, bindings from the identifier fields of the wmes with attribute A1 are obtained for the variable <x> in the identifier field of the condition. This is exactly what the arc consistency match achieves.

Why are tree-structured productions (queries) needed in this mapping? In parallel marker passing systems, the particular equality test issues are well known as the *copy confusion* problems. That is, only tree-structured productions can be matched accurately.

9. Summary and Relevance to Other Work

A combinatorial production match is problematical for Soar for several reasons. This paper was focused on eliminating these combinatorics by introducing alternative production system formulations. The contributions of this paper can be summarized as follows: (1) it introduces absolute and relative requirements for evaluating alternative formulations; (2) it introduces a framework for generating alternative formulations; (3) using the framework it shows that the unique-attribute formulation is the best ***within*** the dimensions investigated, assuming a token match; (4) it introduces the tokenless match and maps it onto constraint satisfaction; (5) it shows that with tokenless match, other formulations may fit the absolute and relative requirements better than the unique-attributes; (6) it shows how an entirely different formulation — the marker-passing formulation — maps onto a formulation generated via the dimensions introduced in this paper, providing some evidence for the generality of the formulations considered here.

An important question is the relevance of this research for the non-Soar community. The combinatorial production match is not a Soar speciality. It is observed in various other systems — OPS5-based systems (Brownston, Farrell, Kant, and Martin, 1985) and rule-based systems like Prodigy (Minton, 1988a). In all these systems, there is continuing research on achieving real time performance (Barachini and Theuretzbacher, 1988, Parson and Blank, 1989), on eliminating expensive learned rules (Chase et al., 1989, Minton, 1988b) and load balancing schemes for attaining high parallelism (Acharya and Tambe, 1989, Miranker, 1987, Tambe and Acharya, 1989) However, in general, the area of alternative production system formulations for solving the problems facing these systems has not been investigated. The representations in these systems are based on attribute-values, very similar to Soar's representation — allowing a mapping between the results based on Soar's representation to those systems. For instance, the utility of the distinction between unique- and multi attributes for Prodigy is shown in (Etzioni, 1990). Furthermore, representations in frame-based systems like Theo (Mitchell et. al., 1989) map quite well into attribute-values, in fact, the version used by Theo already corresponds to the unique-attributes (Tambe and Rosenbloom, 1989). Thus, the results derived in this paper would appear to be relevant to all these systems. In particular, the idea of a tokenless match, that would eliminate a significant amount of combinatorics, appears to be very relevant to these systems. We hope that our research in Soar and related research in these other systems will allow us to gain a better understanding of the tradeoffs in knowledge representation, efficiency and learning.

Acknowledgements

We thank Allen Newell, Brian Milnes, Anurag Acharya, Dirk Kalp and Gary Pelton for useful comments on earlier drafts of this paper. We also thank Kathy Swedlow for technical editing.

References

Acharya, A. and Tambe, M. (1989). Production systems on message passing computers: Simulation results and analysis. *Proceedings of the International Conference on Parallel Processing*. pp. 246-254.

Barachini, F. and Theuretzbacher N. (1988). The challenge of real-time process control for production systems. *Proceedings of the National Conference on Artificial Intelligence*. pp. 705-709.

Brownston, L., Farrell, R., Kant, E. and Martin, N. (1985). *Programming expert systems in OPS5: An introduction to rule-based programming*. Reading, Massachusetts: Addison-Wesley.

Chase, M. P., Zweben, M., Piazza, R. L., Burger, J. D., Maglio, P. P. and Hirsh, H. (1989). Approximating learned search control knowledge. *Proceedings of International Workshop on Machine Learning*. pp. 218-220.

Dechter, R., and Pearl., J. (1988). Network-Based Heuristics for Constraint-Satisfaction Problems. *Artificial Intelligence*, *34*(1), 1-38.

Etzioni, O. (1990). *A structural theory of search control*. Ph.D. diss., School of Computer Science, Carnegie Mellon University. In preparation.

Fahlman, S. E. (1979). Representing and using real-world knowledge. In Winston, P. H. and Brown, R. H. (Eds.), *Artifical Intelligence, An MIT perspective*. Cambridge, Massachusetts: MIT Press.

Forgy, C. L. (1981). *OPS5 User's Manual* (Tech. Rep. CMU-CS-81-135) Computer Science Department, Carnegie Mellon University.

Forgy, C. L. (1982). Rete: A fast algorithm for the many pattern/many object pattern match problem. *Artificial Intelligence*, *19*(1), 17-37.

Gupta, A., Tambe, M., Kalp, D., Forgy, C. L., and Newell, A. (1989). Parallel implementation of OPS5 on the Encore Multiprocessor: Results and analysis. *International Journal of Parallel Programming*, Vol. *17*(2).

Laird, J. E., Newell, A. and Rosenbloom, P. S. (1987). Soar: An architecture for general intelligence. *Artificial Intelligence*, *33*(1), 1-64.

Laird, J. E., Rosenbloom, P. S. and Newell, A. (1986). Chunking in Soar: The anatomy of a general learning mechanism. *Machine Learning*, *1*(1), 11-46.

Levesque, H. J., and Brachman, R. J. (1985). A fundamental tradeoff in knowledge representation and reasoning. In Brachman, R. J., and Levesque, H. J. (Eds.), *Readings in knowledge representation and reasoning*. Morgan Kaufmann Publishers, Inc.

Mackworth, A. K. (1977). Consistency in Networks of Relations. *Artificial Intelligence*, *8*(1), 99-118.

Mackworth, A. K., and Freuder, E. C. (1985). The Complexity of Some Polynomial Network Consistency Algorithms for Constraint Satisfaction Problems. *Artificial Intelligence*, *25*(1), 65-74.

Minton, S. (1988). *Learning Effective Search Control Knowledge: An explanation-based approach*. Ph.D. diss., Computer Science Department, Carnegie Mellon University.

Minton, S. (1988). Quantitative results concerning the utility of explanation-based learning. *Proceedings of the Seventh National Conference on Artifical Intelligence*. pp. 564-569.

Miranker, D. P. (1987). *Treat: A New and Efficient Match Algorithm for AI Production Systems*. Ph.D. diss., Computer Science Department, Columbia University.

Mitchell, T.M., Allen, J., Chalasani, P., Cheng, J., Etzioni, O., Ringuette, M., and Schlimmer, J.C. (1989). Theo: A framework for self-improving systems. In VanLehn, K. (Ed.), *Architectures for Intelligence*. Hillsdale, New Jersey: Lawrence Erlbaum Associates.

Newell, A. (1989). The Quest for Architectures for Integrated Intelligent Systems. Talk at IJCAI 89 on Recieving the Research Excellence Award.

Newell, A. (1990). *Unified theories of cognition*. Cambridge, Massachusetts: Harvard University Press. In press.

Parson, D. E., and Blank, G. D. (1989). Constant-time pattern matching for real-time production systems. *SPIE Vol. 1095 Applications of Artificial Intelligence VII*. pp. 971-982.

Patel-Schneider, P. F. (1989). A four-valued semantics for terminological logics. *Artificial Intelligence*, *38*(3), 319-351.

Polk, T.A., Newell, A., and Lewis, R.L. (1989). Toward a unified theory of immediate reasoning in Soar. *Proceedings of the Annual Conference of the Cognitive Science Society*. pp. 506-513.

Rosenbloom, P. S. and Laird, J. E. (1986). Mapping explanation-based generalization onto Soar. *Proceedings of the Fifth National Conference on Artificial Intelligence*. pp. 561-567.

Tambe, M. and Acharya, A. (1989). Parallel implementations of production systems. *VIVEK: A quarterly in artificial intelligence*, *2*(2), 3-22.

Tambe, M. and Newell, A. (1988). Some chunks are expensive. *Proceedings of the Fifth International Conference on Machine Learning*. pp. 451-458.

Tambe, M. and Rosenbloom, P. (1989). Eliminating expensive chunks by restricting expressiveness. *Proceedings of the Eleventh International Joint Conference on Artificial Intelligence*. pp. 731-737.

Tambe, M. and Rosenbloom, P. (1990). Investigating alternative production system formulations. School of Computer Science, Carnegie Mellon University, In preparation.

Tambe, M., Newell, A., and Rosenbloom, P. S. (1990). The problem of expensive chunks and its solution by restricting expressiveness. *Machine Learning*, Vol. *5*. (To appear).

Touretzky, D. S. (1986). *The mathematics of inheritence systems*. Los Altos, California: Morgan Kaufmann Publishers, Inc.

CHAPTER 58

Two New Weak Method Increments for Abstraction

A. Unruh, Stanford University, and P. S. Rosenbloom, USC–ISI

Abstract

Two method increments for an automatic weak abstraction method are presented, and evaluated experimentally. With this abstraction method, abstraction is driven by difficulties encountered during the problem-solving process. Abstract problem-spaces are created dynamically in response to the problem-solving characteristics of the task at hand, and abstract plans are learned as a result. When the method increments, called *iterative abstraction* and *assumption counting*, are added to this basic abstraction method, they produce new, more useful, weak methods. The two new methods make better use of a task's global problem state to estimate the utility of abstractions, while remaining domain-independent. The new weak methods combine synergistically with each other, and work well in a broader range of domains than does the basic abstraction method.

1 Introduction

The utility of abstraction for increasing the tractability of problem-solving search is widely acknowledged. In [UR89] we described an automatic weak method for abstraction. A *weak method* is one which places few demands on the knowledge available about the problem-solving domain, and can thereby be used in many domains. The abstraction method demonstrated the following qualities:

- It reduced problem-solving time while producing solutions of acceptable quality. That is, on average, the time to solve a problem using abstraction was less than the time without.
- It reduced learning time. That is, it took less time, using abstraction, to begin to learn about a task.
- It increased the transfer of learned rules. That is, the learning that took place during abstract problem-solving produced more generalized rules than those from non-abstract problem solving.

However, when the automatic abstraction method was applied in new domains, it was often too weak—the abstraction method sometimes abstracted away too much information about the task, making the use of abstraction unhelpful. Two new increments to the automatic abstraction method have been developed, called *iterative abstraction* and *assumption counting*, to deal with this problem. The method increments, when

*This research was sponsored by the Hughes Aircraft Company Artificial Intelligence Center, and by the Defense Advanced Research Projects Agency (DOD) and the Office of Naval Research under contract number N00014-89-K-0155. The views and conclusions contained in this document are those of the authors and should not be interpreted as representing the official policies, either expressed or implied, of the Hughes Aircraft Company, the Defense Advanced Research Projects Agency, the Office of Naval Research, or the US Government.

added to the original abstraction method, produce new abstraction methods which use more information about the global problem-solving state, though still making limited demands on knowledge about the problem domain. These two new abstraction methods combine synergistically with each other, and while remaining domain-independent, are stronger and work well in a broader range of domains.

This paper reviews the abstraction method presented in [UR89], describes the two new augmentations of the method, then presents results from experiments with an implementation of the method in the Soar problem-solving architecture [LNR87]. The remainder of this section presents a brief overview of some of the motivating issues for the development of the abstraction techniques.

- **The abstraction technique should be a weak problem-solving method.** The abstraction method should be applicable in any problem domain in the absence of (or in conjunction with) domain-specific knowledge about how to abstract[1].
- **The abstraction method should only abstract when necessary.** The problem solver will use abstraction only when existing search control is not sufficient; there is no need for it to abstract when it already knows what it will do next.
- **The abstraction method will use problems in performance to determine what to abstract.** Other automatic abstraction methods, such as [Chr90, Ben89, Ell88, Kno89, Ten88], derive abstractions before problem solving for a task begins, based on a description of the domain and task. The abstraction method described here draws on a different source of knowledge, that of difficulties encountered during problem solving, and enables dynamically generated abstract problem spaces and abstraction levels. Thus, this source of knowledge may be available when more declarative descriptions of the domain problem spaces are not— and may perhaps be used in conjunction with other abstraction methods to produce even more effective behavior.

2 Description of Automatic Weak Abstraction Method

This section will first describe the problem-solving context in which a problem solver makes use of the abstraction techniques, then present the way in which a problem space may be dynamically abstracted. Given this background information, the two new increments to the abstraction method, and the way in which they increase the utility of the abstractions that are created, will be discussed.

In Soar, problems are solved by search in *problem spaces*, in which operators are applied to yield new states. Inadequate knowledge about how to proceed will produce an *impasse*, which the system tries to resolve by problem solving in a subgoal generated to resolve the impasse. Further subgoals may be recursively generated. *Control impasses* occur whenever the problem solver is in a situation where more than one option exists for its next action, and it does not know what to do next. Learning occurs by converting subgoal-based search into rules that generate comparable results under similar conditions (a form of explanation-based learning). The abstraction method is presented using this general Soar problem-solving framework, but the ideas behind the method are not Soar-specific, and should be applicable to other problem solvers which perform search in problem spaces and apply explanation-based learning techniques.

2.1 The context in which abstraction occurs

Abstraction is used to reduce the amount of effort required to perform *look-ahead* searches, which are searches performed towards the resolution of a control impasse, during which the available options are each explored and evaluated in turn. Without specifying yet how this occurs, the look-ahead searches are performed abstractly; the abstract problem spaces are created as the search proceeds. These abstract searches usually take less time than non-abstract searches.

[1] It is important to note that the limited operational demands of a weak method sometimes translate into poor performance; it is not guaranteed to work well in every domain in which it is applicable.

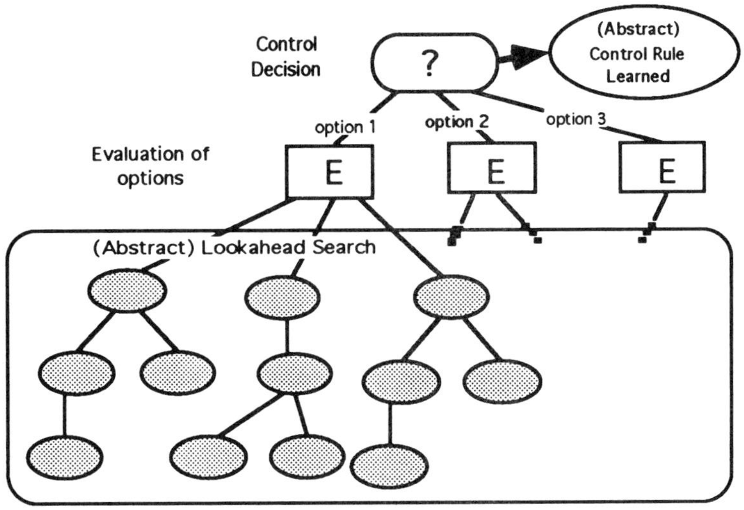

Figure 1: The Abstraction Context

A decision about the control impasse will be reached based on the evaluations, thus resolving the impasse. Search control rules are learned as a product of this resolution. Abstract look-ahead search will result in abstract, or generalized, search control rules. This is because the "explanation" of the decision, used to construct the new rules, includes fewer problem details. The accumulation of new search control rules may be thought of as the incremental construction of a plan (an abstract one); in relevantly similar future situations, the search control rules will apply to guide the problem solver and avoid another control impasse. Figure 1 shows the control decision process.

Once the control decision is made, execution continues. The problem-solver interleaves planning and execution in this manner — it does not need to have a full plan for the current task before executing a move. If the abstract lookahead search requires less time than non-abstract search, decisions are reached more quickly. In addition, if the environment is not static, it may be pointless to spend time developing a full, non-abstract plan[2]. At further control impasses, abstract search can occur again.

2.2 Basic automatic problem-space abstraction technique: precondition abstraction

If the problem-solver is searching in a context in which it wishes to abstract, then it does so by abstracting any unmet precondition impasses (impasses generated because a precondition is not achieved) of the operators that it applies. The unmet precondition impasses are abstracted by having the problem solver "assume" that the preconditions have been met, and ignore the impasse. (Another way of looking at this is that some nodes in the proof tree for the lookahead search are effectively replaced with the value *TRUE*. Alteration of a proof tree in this manner has been proposed by [Elk90, Kel88] as a method of forming approximate concepts.) The operator is then applied as completely as possible given the current state; partial application may occur.

Abstract problem spaces are dynamically created from the original problem spaces when operators apply abstractly in this fashion; no special "abstract" problem spaces need to be supplied. It is possible for the abstraction process to result in an abstract space containing incomplete or incorrect state information, and

[2] One advantage of this incremental approach to plan construction is that there is no need to assume that the environment or operator set stays static to benefit from the plans; if the situation changes, portions of the plan may still apply. The more general the plan, the better chance that it will indeed apply in new situations.

the problem solver must be able to continue in spite of it. This ability is achieved by a domain-independent process called *factorization*, which is described in [UR89]. The abstraction method falls under the general class of *approximating* abstractions.

2.3 Finding a useful level of abstraction: new method increments

A problem with the abstraction technique as presented thus far is that abstracting away all unmet precondition impasses during look-ahead search is often too extreme; too much information is lost. However, recall that this weak abstraction method does not utilize domain information about what to abstract, or access declarative representations of the domain operators.

2.3.1 Iterative Abstract Evaluation

To address the problem of making more discriminate abstractions without domain-specific knowledge, the technique of *iterative abstraction* is used.

Iterative abstraction is based on the hypothesis that if the problem-solver can't distinguish between the results of evaluating two options at a control impasse, it's operating at too high a level of abstraction. The iterative abstraction technique uses the following general algorithm: first try to make the control decision while evaluating the options at the problem-solver's highest level of abstraction. If this provides insufficient information to completely discriminate between options, then rather than making a random choice, re-evaluate those options which looked the best at an increased level of detail (don't reconsider the options which looked worse). Continue the iteration cycle until the problem solver is able to distinguish between the remaining options (or ascertain that they are equivalent for its purposes).

The concept of "increased level of detail" is operationalized with respect to domain-independent precondition abstraction in the following way: At each iteration, perform the abstract look-ahead searches in more detail by requiring the problem solver to achieve those operator preconditions (call them "set A") which it abstracted away before. The result is a more detailed consideration of the task than occurred in the previous iteration. However, in this new iteration the problem-solver will still abstract away the preconditions of the operators which achieve set A. Call these newly ignored preconditions "set B". (Because set A was abstracted in the previous iteration, there was no need to even consider set B previously). The process continues; in the next iteration, set B as well as A must now be considered. However, any preconditions of the operators which achieve the preconditions in set B will still be abstracted.

As an example, consider a set of operators in an ABStrips-like robot domain [Sac74]. Suppose that among the operators being evaluated abstractly at a control impasse is the operator GO-THROUGH-DOOR. A precondition of this operator is that the door in question must be **open**. During the first iteration for this control impasse, the problem-solver will abstract away the **open** precondition of the operator. However, suppose that the first iteration does not provide enough information to resolve the control impasse. During the next iteration, the problem solver will no longer ignore the **open** precondition. It will try to achieve the precondition, perhaps by applying the OPEN-DOOR operator. However, any preconditions of the OPEN-DOOR operator (e.g., **robot-next-to-door**) will themselves be abstracted. The iteration process continues in this manner. The sets of preconditions generated in this way can be thought of as describing the abstraction levels explored during the iteration process. However, the levels are generated dynamically– there is no predetermined precondition ordering.

As discussed above, the problem solver learns search control rules as a result of the abstract evaluations. A search control rule is learned each time the problem solver is able to distinguish between a pair of options. This can happen at any iteration cycle— at each iteration, some options may be ruled out. Therefore, during the process of making a single control decision, search control rules may be learned at varying levels of abstraction. Some options may have been distinguishable at a high level of abstraction, while others needed to be compared in more detail.

With this iteration process, more effort than before is being spent searching for an initial abstract plan, so as to increase the chances of being able to effectively and efficiently implement it. The process is related to traditional multi-level planning, but the multiple levels occur here in service of creating the abstract plan, whereas traditionally they occur in instantiating the abstract plan[3]. Iterative abstraction is similar in spirit to the technique of iterative deepening, although here the iteration is on abstraction level (subgoal expansion depth) rather than search depth.

2.3.2 Assumption Counting

In addition to iterative abstraction, a second increment to the abstraction method has been developed. It makes use of another technique for estimating the utility of an abstract search, called *assumption counting.* This technique is orthogonal to the use of iterative abstraction, and may be used in conjunction with it.

Existing domain evaluation criteria are combined with a meta-evaluation based on the number of assumptions, or abstracted preconditions, required to complete an abstract search. The new combined evaluation criteria is used instead of the domain function at each iteration to compare the results of the abstract lookahead searches for each option. Currently the two evaluation criteria are combined lexicographically; to compare two options, the problem-solver looks first at the number of assumptions made and compares the domain evaluations only if these are equal. This provides a measure (though not an exact one) of the difficulty of instantiating the abstract plan discovered during the search[4].

3 Experimental Results

3.1 Eight-Puzzle Domain

Experimental results for the abstraction method, using iterative abstraction and assumption counting, have been obtained with Soar in two domains thus far. One is the Eight-Puzzle domain. In this domain, the use of assumption counting is effective in discriminating between options at a control decision; in fact, the problem-solver does not need to make much use of the iteration process to help discriminate. (That is, at a control decision, the problem-solver only needs to perform abstract look-ahead search at the highest level of abstraction to make a decision). Using abstraction, the problem-solver is able to solve problems which are intractable without abstraction (given its existing search control knowledge and problem-solving method). The intractability stems in part from the fact that if the problem-solver gets very far from an "optimal" solution path, the interactions among the subgoals make it hard for it to recover from its mistake. Assumption-counting proves to be quite effective in estimating the relative difficulty of achieving different abstract plans, and keeping the problem-solver on a good solution path.

Figure 2 shows the relative tractability of ten Eight-Puzzle tasks, solved both with abstraction and without, where in both cases the problem solver is attempting to make the best choice at a control impasse. For each task, the number of problem-solving steps required to discover and execute a solution is shown. Any task which took more than 4000 steps was cut off[5].

3.2 Robot Domain

The other domain is a robot planning domain, the one used in the ABStrips work [Sac74], with means-end search control knowledge. In this domain a robot moves itself and manipulates boxes within a set of interconnected rooms, with connecting doors that can be opened and closed by the robot. Here, both the iterative abstraction process and assumption counting play large parts in the abstract search and evaluation.

In the robot domain, 32 tasks of varying difficulty were given to the problem solver[6], where difficulty

[3]The more traditional notion of multi-level planning also occurs naturally with this abstraction method — after an abstract plan is selected, it will then be refined.

[4]Lexicographic ordering may not be the best way to combine the two evaluation metrics in general, but this is a topic for future research.

[5]The problem-solving steps are Soar decision cycles— they are related to operator applications, but not identical to them. Also included are the generation of subgoals and the selection of problem-spaces, states, and operators.

[6]We would like to thank Craig Knoblock for providing these benchmark tasks.

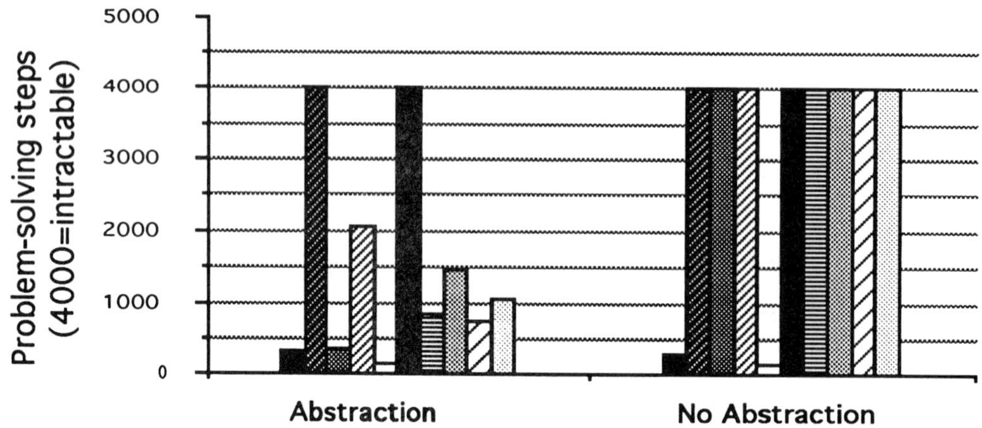

Figure 2: Eight-Puzzle Domain

	Method Abstract/Best	Method NonAbstract/Best	Method NonAbstract/First
Average Solution Length:			
Group 1	12.84	11.63	20.15
Group 2	20.3	16.4	27.7
Group 3	21.5	19	25.25
Avg. No. of Problem-solving steps:			
Group 1	505	1681 (est.)	358
Group 2	979	intractable	518
Group 3	1569	intractable	527

Table 1: Robot Task Results

is measured by the number of conjuncts in the task's goal statement. Each task was attempted three different ways; using abstraction to try to find the shortest-path solution (Method Abstract/Best), finding the shortest solution without abstraction (Method NonAbstract/Best), and taking the "first" solution path explored, without abstraction (Method NonAbstract/First). For this last method, the problem solver would settle for any solution it was able to find using its means-end knowledge rather than trying to discover the best solution.

The 32 tasks are divided into three groups according to task difficulty. Group 1 contained tasks with two goal conjuncts; Group 2 contained tasks with three goal conjuncts, and Group 3, four goal conjuncts. Table 1 shows, for each group, and for each problem-solving method, the average solution length and the average number of problem-solving steps required to come up with that solution and execute it. Note that information about the average number of problem-solving steps using Method NonAbstract/Best is available only for Group 1, which was the easiest set of tasks. For the other tasks, this problem-solving method was intractable. (It was intractable even for some of the Group 1 tasks, but a threshold was set, and this was used in the averaging.) Method NonAbstract/Best produces optimal solutions if it manages to finish. For the purposes of comparison with the other methods, optimal solution lengths were figured by hand when necessary.

The solutions produced using abstraction (Method Abstract/Best) are consistently better than those solutions obtained by having the problem solver settle for the first solution path it could find (Method

NonAbstract/First). In addition, the total time required to come up with a solution using abstraction is significantly less than the time the problem solver takes to find the best solution without abstraction (Method NonAbstract/Best). Even for the easiest group of tasks, the problem-solving time for this latter method is an underestimate.

In the majority of the tasks, the number of steps required to find any solution path is less than the time to find a more optimal path using abstraction. A speed-accuracy tradeoff is occurring in this domain— the more effort spent in lookahead search, the more optimal the solution. This is not surprising, since the problem-solver does not need to use much effort to find some solution; with this domain and task set, the penalties for making mistakes are fairly low.

It is expected that in domains with a higher penalty for non-optimal search paths, the effort invested to find a good solution will pay off more noticeably in terms of total problem-solving time. Early results indicate that this in fact will be true for the Eight-Puzzle domain. In addition, this effect has been observed for a new version of the robot domain in which state complexity is increased.

3.2.1 Increasing Robot Domain Complexity

In this new robot domain the set of rooms in which the robot can maneuver, and the doors connecting them, are extended. The new domain contains 19 rooms (increased from 7) and 22 doors (increased from 8). All other aspects of the domain remain the same. In this modified domain, the penalties for pursuing a bad path can be higher, since more work is required to get back to a room in which a useful action may occur.

Tests were run in this domain on a subset of 18 of the tasks above— 13 from Group 1 and 5 from Group 2 (randomly selected from each group). The tests were run for methods Abstract/Best and NonAbstract/First only; method NonAbstract/Best would have been intractable for most of the tasks. The original components of the initial state– the initial placements of the robot and boxes, the original door configurations, etc., all remained the same for each task, as did the goal states. The new doors in the layout were kept in the same state (either open or closed) for all of the tasks. The additional rooms in the new layout do not add shortcuts, so the optimal solutions for the tasks remained the same as well.

The more complex room configuration made the tasks significantly more difficult for method NonAbstract/First to solve. For all 5 tasks from Group 2, and for 7 tasks from Group 1, the tasks proved intractable. Here the intractability stemmed primarily from space allocation problems resulting from the combinatorics of matching rules against very deep subgoal stacks. These deep stacks can be generated when the problem solver attempts to search by performing entirely non-abstract backchaining from a distant goal.

In contrast, with method Abstract/Best, the tasks remained tractable for all but one task from each group. As with the original room configuration, the abstract lookahead enables the problem solver to discover better solution paths than those produced by NonAbstract/First, but here this ability is more critical. In addition, shorter subgoal stacks are generated during abstract lookahead search.

Because so many of the tasks attempted with method NonAbstract/First were intractable, numerical comparison between problem-solving methods is more difficult for this extended robot domain. For the 6 tasks from Group 1 which the problem-solver *was* able to finish using both problem-solving methods, Table 2 compares the average performance of methods Abstract/Best and NonAbstract/First with both the original and extended room layouts. (Since the extended domain increases problem difficulty, but does not increase optimal solution length, the original tasks are included for comparison.) In the extended domain, in contrast to results observed in the original domain, searching abstractly for the best solution leads the problem to a solution more quickly than does searching non-abstractly for any solution.

As in the original domain, the solutions produced in the extended domain using abstraction are better than the solutions produced using method NonAbstract/First. (Because mistakes are more costly, the solution quality in the extended domain tends to degrade with both methods). Though not shown in the table, the results of using method Abstract/Best for the Group 2 tasks are consistent with these results; in fact solution quality did *not* degrade for the five Group 2 tasks tested, though problem-solving time did increase.

Although results in the extended robot domain are still preliminary, they reinforce the hypothesis

	Original Abstract/Best	Extended Abstract/Best	Original NonAbstract/First	Extended NonAbstract/First
Average Solution Length:	8.2	12.3	15	20
Avg. No. of Problem-solving steps:	233.7	268.2	203.2	396.5

Table 2: Robot Task Results– Six Tasks in Extended Domain

that the more difficult the problem-solving domain, the higher the payoff in searching for a *good* solution inexpensively (rather than settling for any solution).

3.2.2 Learning and Rule Transfer

Experiments were also run with the original room layout on a random subset of eight of the robot tasks in Group 1, to test the *transfer* of the rules learned during problem-solving. Each test was run using Method Abstract/Best, and was tested with rules learned from solving the other seven tasks both abstractly and non-abstractly. That is, for each of the eight tasks two tests were done; one using all seven other sets of abstract rules and one using all seven other sets of non-abstract rules. (As always, learning was also enabled during the tests).

For all eight tasks, *no* non-abstract rules (rules learned during problem-solving without abstraction) transferred to other tasks. The explanations constructed from the non-abstract problem-solving were too task-specific to transfer except in very similar situations. (The fact that all tests were run using the abstract search method has no bearing on the amount of transfer achieved by the added non-abstract rules; these rules do not test whether or not abstraction is occurring.)

However, for all eight of the tasks, there did occur transfer of abstract, or generalized information learned from other tasks. For seven of these tasks, the usage of this new abstract information decreased the number of problem-solving steps, sometimes considerably, without affecting solution length. In one of the tasks, the new abstract rules turned out to be too general, and both problem-solving time and solution quality suffered. For the eight tasks, the average number of problem-solving steps without the additional abstract rules was 445; using the abstract rules, the average was 344 (a 23% reduction).

4 Discussion

Results so far for this automatic weak abstraction method have been encouraging, and suggest that it can be a viable abstraction method when domain knowledge about abstractions is not available (or there is not time to derive the domain-specific knowledge mid-task).

The effectiveness of this automatic abstraction method depends in part upon the characteristics of the tasks to which it is applied. The following are some of the issues which can affect abstraction efficiency and content.

- How often options at a control impasse are very similar: very similar options can result in many iterations on the abstraction level before a decision is made. It is possible that for large tasks, as is the case with traditional iterative deepening, all but the last iteration may be considered of negligible expense. However, this has not yet been ascertained.

- The branching factor of the domain search: how many options must be explored at each control decision?

- How operators are conceptualized: The operator preconditions define the set of possible abstractions that may occur, and the interactions that the abstraction method will detect.

Future work will include obtaining empirical results for the abstraction technique in other domains, as well as studying variances of the technique. For example, in a real-time planning environment, it may be useful to allow the problem-solver to pick randomly from its current choice set if it is interrupted mid-decision, and to use the plan from its current iteration level even if the iteration process isn't finished. In addition, it may be possible to develop a means of limiting the iteration process if it seems likely that the options being compared are very similar, and that extensive iteration is not cost-effective.

We also hope to investigate ways to notice and learn from unexpected goal interactions while using the abstract plans; these interactions indicate situations where too much information was abstracted away. Lastly, it is hoped that the abstraction method described here will interact in synergistic ways with other automatic abstraction methods utilizing domain descriptions; this also is a topic for future research.

References

[Ben89] D. P. Benjamin. Learning problem-solving abstractions via enablement. In *AAAI Spring Symposium Series: Planning and Search*, 1989.

[Chr90] J. Christensen. A hierarchical planner that generates its own hierarchies. In *Proceedings of AAAI-90*, 1990. In Press.

[Elk90] C. Elkan. Incremental, approximate planning: abductive default reasoning. In *Proceedings of the AAAI Spring Symposium Series on Planning in Uncertain, Unpredictable, or Changing Environments*, 1990.

[Ell88] T. Ellman. Approximate theory formation: An explanation-based approach. In *Proceedings of the Seventh National Conference on Artifical Intelligence*, 1988.

[Kel88] R. Keller. Learning approximate concept descriptions. Technical Report KSL-88-57, Stanford University, Knowledge Systems Lab, 1988.

[Kno89] Craig A. Knoblock. Learning hierarchies of abstraction spaces. In *Proceedings of the Sixth International Workshop on Machine Learning*. Morgan Kaufmann, 1989.

[LNR87] J. E. Laird, A. Newell, , and P. S. Rosenbloom. Soar: An architecture for general intelligence. *Artificial Intelligence*, 33:1–64, 1987.

[Sac74] E. D. Sacerdoti. Planning in a hierarchy of abstraction spaces. *Artificial Intelligence*, 5:115–135, 1974.

[Ten88] J. Tenenberg. *Abstraction in Planning*. PhD thesis, University of Rochester, 1988.

[UR89] A. Unruh and P. S. Rosenbloom. Abstraction in problem solving and learning. In *Proceedings of IJCAI-89, Eleventh International Joint Conference on Artificial Intelligence*. Morgan Kaufmann, 1989.

CHAPTER 59

Using a Knowledge Analysis to Predict Conceptual Errors in Text-Editor Usage

R. M. Young and J. Whittington, MRC Applied Psychology Unit

ABSTRACT

The knowledge analysis of a device and a task, when written in an external Instruction Language and translated into rules for a programmable cognitive architecture, enables a designer to predict conceptual errors in device usage. This kind of prediction lies outside the scope of GOMS-based models. The cognitive architecture, which is referred to as a "Programmable User Model" (PUM), incorporates a limited problem-solving capability based upon means-ends analysis and multiple problem spaces. The example presented, concerning a simple text editor, illustrates the application of a PUM and demonstrates that a correct description of local knowledge does not necessarily lead to correct behaviour. This can serve to alert the designer to difficulties with the usability of a proposed interface.

KEYWORDS: User models, errors, GOMS, PUMs.

BACKGROUND

The prediction of errors is one of the harder challenges facing researchers attempting to build models of the user. So far, the most influential family of user models, derived from the "Model Human Processor" of Card, Moran & Newell (1983), has been developed to the point where analyses in terms of the "GOMS" model can predict the performance time for a variety of computer-based tasks (e.g. Olson & Nilsen, 1988), and can provide approximate, engineering-style accounts for quantitative and qualitative aspects of related laboratory-based tasks (e.g. John & Newell, 1989). "Cognitive Complexity Theory" (Kieras & Polson, 1985) — which is essentially a realisation of GOMS as a production system — can explain effects such as the relative speed of learning of different designs, or the transfer of training between them (Polson, 1988; Polson, Bovair & Kieras, 1987). Predicting errors, however, has proved more difficult. One recent approach (Lerch, Mantei & Olson, 1989) uses a GOMS analysis to track the number of items a user needs to hold in memory at each step of the procedure, and demonstrates that more errors occur for designs which impose higher peak memory loads. Although ingenious, such an approach is inherently correlational (the higher the peak load, the more likely the errors) and is restricted to a particular class of errors, namely those due to loss of items from working memory (*overload* errors, which Lerch *et al* distinguish from *conceptual* errors).

More generally, one can argue that all analyses based upon the Model Human Processor require the analyst to specify beforehand, in detail, the procedure to be followed by the user. In other words, the 'Method' component of GOMS has to be *given* before the analysis can apply. Such analyses are therefore barred, in principle, from being able to predict errors that result in users *doing the wrong thing*. Errors of procedure, resulting say from the user's misunderstanding of the device or from a mismatch between the user's conceptualisation of the task and that built into the device, are inherently beyond their scope.

More recently, a new approach to user modelling has been proposed which, while sharing many of the commitments and aspirations of the GOMS family, overcomes this limitation. With "Programmable User Models", or PUMs (Young, Green & Simon, 1989), the analyst is assumed to be an interface designer, who is presented with a programmable cognitive architecture embodying psychological principles and constraints. The designer is invited to 'instruct' the architecture to perform a range of representative tasks with a proposed interface, by describing the tasks and the interface in an external "Instruction Language" which is then converted into rules for the architecture. Given that description, the simulated cognitive architecture does its best to figure out how to perform the tasks. Both the activity of instructing the architecture and the running of the resulting model serve to draw the designer's attention to aspects of the proposed design that affect its usability.

One of the key properties of the PUM approach for present purposes is that the detailed procedure to be followed by the user is *not* specified by the analyst beforehand. Rather, the analyst provides knowledge about the local behaviour and properties of the task and the interface. The implications of this knowledge for the resulting behaviour emerge only dynamically during the course of the simulated performance. This enables a PUM, in principle, to predict cases of conceptual error which result in the user's following a faulty course of action, something which we have seen is outside the scope of GOMS models.

This paper presents an illustrative example of a PUM-style analysis for a simple interface. Since we are still in the midst of a long-term research programme, there does not yet exist a fully-designed PUM or Instruction Language. What we do in the paper is therefore to employ an informal Instruction Language in which we lay out the relevant conceptual objects, the conceptual operations on them, and hints about the usage of the available operations. This description we then translate by hand into rules for a simulated cognitive architecture built upon SOAR, after which the model can be run. SOAR (Newell, 1989; Laird, Newell & Rosenbloom, 1987; Waldrop, 1988) is a problem-solving architecture built round a nested series of problem spaces constructed from states and operators. The structural correspondence between the Instruction Language and the architecture is straightforward, with different task domains mapping into different SOAR problem spaces, conceptual objects mapping into entities attached to SOAR states, and conceptual operations into SOAR operators.

ANALYSIS OF THE TEXT-EDITOR EXAMPLE

The Domain and the Task

Our example concerns the use of a simplified text editor to accomplish specified changes to a pre-existing document. The document is assumed to contain, in part, some text we will call TextA at a location in the document called LocA: this assumption is written *Text(TextA,LocA)*. Similarly, we assume there is another piece of text of interest, *Text(TextB,LocB)*. The specified changes are to delete TextB and replace it by a copy of TextA, i.e. to replace *Text(TextB,LocB)* by *Text(TextA,LocB)*.

The text editor, for present purposes, can be regarded as offering just three relevant editing actions: *Mark(T,L)*, which marks the text T at location L; *Wipe(T,L)*, which deletes the marked text and stores a copy of T in an internal buffer; and *Yank(T,L)*, which inserts at location L a copy of the text T held in the buffer. (For Macintosh users, these three actions correspond to *Select*, *Cut*, and *Paste*, with the internal buffer corresponding to the *Clipboard*.) Viewed in problem-solving terms, the challenge is to construct a sequence of these actions, suitably instantiated, to accomplish the required changes. It is known empirically that text editors that rely upon the the use of this kind of internal buffer pose difficulties for their users. We assume that the designer intends that users should perform the part of the task requiring the copying of TextA to LocA by first *Wiping* TextA from LocA to get a copy in the buffer, and then immediately restoring the text at LocA with a *Yank* before doing another *Yank* to copy it to LocB. As we shall see, this is not always the behaviour that the model predicts.

Introduction to the Knowledge Analysis

In approaching the knowledge analysis, we need to bear in mind the nature of the game being played. It is not the case that the analysis should be regarded as the input to a powerful problem solver, for example one embodying advanced AI planning techniques capable of foreseeing and handling all the detailed interactions that might arise between subgoals of the problem solution (Young & Simon, 1987). Instead, the cognitive architecture should be assumed to provide a *minimal* problem solving capability, responsive to a possibly wide variety and range of relevant knowledge but able to undertake only the obvious steps in the light of that knowledge. The reason for this is related to the overall purpose of the PUM analysis. The idea is that a failure by the PUM should alert the designer to a possibly troublesome aspect of the interface, not that it should be treated as a prediction that users will always make a particular mistake. Being deliberately conservative about the problem solving power of the architecture contributes to this objective, whereas assuming super-human problem solving abilities would undermine it.

The limited problem-solving ability that we need is referred to as "mini-planning" (Young *et al*, 1989), which we currently regard as resting on two components,

(1) the use of multiple problem spaces for problem solving, e.g. by exploiting the different representations available in the different spaces; and

(2) simple means-ends analysis, i.e. the ability to choose actions with regard to their effectiveness at reducing the difference between the current and desired situations (Newell & Simon, 1972).

For the present analysis, we employ two problem spaces. One is the *Task Space*, which treats the document and the task as forming a small problem domain in its own right, more-or-less independent of any particular text editor. In other words, this is a simple world of documents and document changes. The other is the *Editor Space*, in which the internal buffer and the specific editing actions are represented, and in which the serious problem solving has to take place. Clearly, the contents of this space reflect the particular text editor we have chosen to analyse.

The relationship between these two spaces is consonant with the "external and internal task" analysis of ETIT (Moran, 1983), as it is also with the later and related "yoked space hypothesis" of Payne (1987, 1989). Payne argues that users of an interactive device need to construct two different spaces — one for the task domain and one for the device — and the semantic mapping between them. Our two spaces — and for that matter, Payne's also — can be regarded as instantiating two of the levels of the Command Language Grammar (CLG: Moran, 1981), the *task* level and the *semantic* level. (And indeed our full analysis of this example includes a third space, the *Keystroke* space, which corresponds to the *syntactic* level of CLG. But that third space is not relevant to the purposes of this paper.)

TASK SPACE:	*Conceptual objects:*	TextA, TextB, LocA, LocB
	Conceptual operations:	Add(T,L), Remove(T,L)
	Semantics of operations:	... ...
EDITOR SPACE:	*Conceptual objects:*	TextA, TextB, LocA, LocB, BufferContents, MarkedText
	Differences:	Text+, Text-, BufferContents, MarkedText
	Ordering of importance:	{Text+, Text-} > BufferContents > MarkedText

Conceptual operations

Operator	Preconditions	Effects	Relevant to
Mark(T,L)	Text(T,L)	Marked(T,L)	MarkedText
Wipe(T,L)	Marked(T,L)	- Text(T,L) Buffer(T) - Marked(T,L)	Text- BufferContents
Yank(T,L)	Buffer(T)	+ Text(T,L)	Text+

Figure 1. Summary of the Knowledge Analysis

Task Space

The core of a knowledge analysis consists of laying out the relevant conceptual objects and operations, as shown in Figure 1. In the case of the Task Space this is very simple. The conceptual objects are the pieces of text and the locations implicated in the task, namely *TextA, TextB, LocA* and *LocB*. In addition, we need a small repertoire of operations for acting on those objects. For this example we use just two operations. One is *Add(T,L)*, which is used for putting text at a location where it is wanted but does not currently exist. The other is *Remove(T,L)*, used for deleting text from a location where it currently exists but is not wanted.

Looking ahead a little, we can see that this space will allow a simple two-step solution to the problem, involving the actions *Add(TextA,LocB)* and *Remove(TextB,LocB)*, performed in either order. The implications of that solution are discussed below.

Editor Space

The Editor Space is a little richer, and we will analyse it in more detail (see Figure 1). The conceptual objects, as for the Task Space, include the relevant locations and pieces of text, but for the Editor Space these have to be supplemented by two further objects which belong to the editor itself rather than to the document: the current contents of the buffer (if known), and the currently marked text (if any).

The conceptual operations correspond to the three editing actions mentioned earlier. The table in Figure 1 describes them in classical AI style, by specifying for each action (a) the preconditions which have to hold for the action to be applied, and (b) its effects, i.e. the changes that result from applying it.

To be able to use means-ends analysis in a domain, we have to specify four kinds of information. For the editor space, these are:

- The *kinds of differences* between the current and desired situations. These are: *Text+*, when some wanted text does not currently exist; *Text-*, when some text exists but is not wanted; *BufferContents*, when the contents of the buffer is not what is wanted; and *MarkedText*, when the text currently marked is not what is wanted.
- An *importance ordering* of differences. Both *Text* differences are more important than a *BufferContents* difference, which in turn is more important than a difference of *MarkedText*.
- Which actions are *relevant* to which differences. This information can be derived from the effects of the actions, and is shown in the rightmost column of the table in Figure 1.
- The *preconditions* for each action. This information is already given in the table.

BEHAVIOUR OF THE MODEL

If we take the analysis of the Task and Editor spaces just given, translate it into SOAR rules, and then feed it into a simulated cognitive architecture incorporating an appropriate capability for mini-planning, what is the behaviour of the resulting model? We will answer the question in stages, dealing first with the problem-solving in the Task Space, next with the deletion of TextB in the Editor Space, and then with several versions of the copying of TextA.

Solution in the Task Space

As we have already noted, the Task Space allows a solution to the problem consisting of the actions *Add(TextA,LocB)* and *Remove(TextB,LocB)*, performed in either order. This two-step solution is found easily by problem solving in the space, using either means-ends analysis or lookahead search. Finding this solution, however, does not mean that problem-solving is finished, because the solution is in the "wrong" space. The job does not get accomplished merely by wishful thinking, as it were. The work of finding and executing a series of actions on the text editor has still to be done.

What happens is that once the two-step solution has been discovered in the Task Space, the first step — say *Remove(TextB,LocB)* — is taken and an attempt made to execute it by spelling it out in the Editor Space. Doing this requires problem solving in the Editor Space, of course: What sequence of editor actions is needed to realise *Remove(TextB,LocB)*? Once the Editor Space finishes with that problem, problem-solving resumes in the Task Space to complete the given task. If everything has gone well in the Editor Space, all that will be left to do is to realise the *Add* step in a similar way. In general, however, the result after working in the Editor Space may not be exactly as anticipated by the earlier work in the Task Space, and further (but still simple) problem solving will be required.

Despite the near-triviality of the problem solving in the Task Space, the emerging solution provides two beneficial results:

(1) It breaks apart the original overall goal into two simpler subgoals. This kind of goal decomposition constitutes an important problem-solving mechanism. In the Editor Space, where the hard problem solving gets done, it is much easier to solve these two sub-problems one after another, than to have to deal with the original problem in one go.

(2) It imposes a Unit Task structure on the behaviour (see Card *et al*, 1983). The Task Space can be regarded as a generator of Unit Tasks, each of which gets carried out in the Editor Space.

In Editor Space: Delete Text at B

The realisation of *Remove(TextB,LocB)* in the Editor Space provides a straightforward illustration of means-ends analysis in operation. The behaviour is summarised in Figure 2, with the lines numbered for ease of reference. Initially, the difference between the current situation and the target is one of *Text-* [line 2], to reduce which a relevant action is *Wipe* [line 3]. But *Wipe* cannot be applied in the current situation, so a subgoal is created to achieve its precondition [4,5]. The difference between the situation and the precondition is one of *MarkedText*, for which a relevant action is *Mark* [6]. That action applies, and in the resulting situation the subgoal is achieved [7], so that the *Wipe* action can now apply [8]. The resulting situation satisfies the given goal [9].

S:	Text(TextB,LocB)	[1]
G:	-Text(TextB,LocB)	[2]
	⟶ D: Text- ⟶ A: Wipe	[3]
	subgoal: achieve precondition for Wipe	[4]
	G: Marked	[5]
	⟶ D: MarkedText ⟶ A: Mark	[6]
	R: Marked	[7]
	can now apply Wipe	[8]
R:	-Text(TextB,LocB)	[9]

Figure 2. Means-ends analysis realisation of *Remove(TextB,LocB)*. (S = initial situation, G = goal, D = difference, A = relevant action, R= result of action)

In Editor Space: Add Text A at B

The attempt to realise *Add(TextA,LocB)* in the Editor Space, shown in Figure 3, is less straightforward. In outline, the behaviour is analogous to that for *Remove*, except that it requires two levels of subgoaling instead of one. Initially the difference between the current and desired situations is one of *Text+*, for which a relevant action is *Yank* [3]. But *Yank* cannot be applied until the right text exists in the buffer, so a subgoal is created to achieve this precondition [4,5]. The difference between the current situation and the precondition is one of *BufferContents* [6], for which the relevant action is *Wipe* [7]. As before, *Wipe* cannot apply immediately, so that another subgoal is created [8,9]. Again as before, the *Mark* action applies [11], then *Wipe* [13], and then *Yank* [15] as the subgoals unwind themselves. As a result of the *Yank*, the given goal of having TextA at LocB has been achieved [16].

However, the application of *Wipe* also has a side effect, that of deleting the text from LocA [14]. In consequence, the net effect of this behaviour has been to *move* text A to B, instead of *copying* it there.

Exactly what happens next depends upon the details of how the model is built, and in particular upon the point at

```
S: ...                                              [1]
G: Text(TextA,LocB)                                 [2]
   ⟶ D: Text+ ⟶ A: Yank(TextA,LocB)                 [3]
      subgoal: achieve precondition for Yank        [4]
      G: Buffer(TextA)                              [5]
         ⟶ D: BufferContents                        [6]
         ⟶ A: Wipe(TextA,LocA)                      [7]
            subgoal: precondition for Wipe          [8]
            G: Marked                               [9]
               ⟶ D: MarkedText                      [10]
               ⟶ A: Mark                            [11]
            R: Marked                               [12]
            can now apply Wipe                      [13]
      R: Buffer(TextA) & -Text(TextA,LocA)          [14]
      can now apply Yank                            [15]
R: Text(TextA,LocB)                                 [16]
```

Figure 3. Means-ends analysis realisation of *Add(TextA,LocB)*. (S = initial situation, G = goal, D = difference, A = relevant action, R= result of action)

which the deletion of TextA from LocA gets "noticed". As we have specified it, what happens is that the Editor Space finishes working, confident that it has successfully solved the sub-problem of realising *Add(TextA,LocB)* — as indeed it has. Back in the Task Space, the problem solver discovers a new difference between the current situation and the goal (i.e. that *Text(TextA,LocA)* is missing), and it solves that subproblem by means of an *Add(TextA,LocA)*. It then calls upon the Editor Space for a third time, to realise that *Add*. Fortunately, because TextA is still sitting in the buffer, that goal can be accomplished with a single *Yank*. The end result is that the problem solver accomplishes the given task, but only with a last-minute "correction" to an earlier "mistake".

Numerous variants of this behaviour are possible. If, for example, the *Add* were applied in the Task Space before the *Remove* instead of after, then it would be possible for the *Remove* to intervene between the initial *Add(TextA,LocB)* and the later *Add(TextA,LocA)* needed to correct the unintended deletion. The outcome is a messy piece of behaviour (the details of which are left as an exercise for the reader), requiring yet a fourth call on the Editor Space before the job is finished. If the Editor Space is provided with a fuller characterisation of its target, it is possible for the deletion to be corrected before leaving the Editor Space, but still only as an "afterthought". And if the implementation of the task-level action were handled slightly differently by the Task Space, it would be possible to have a model which finishes work believing it has done the job it was asked, without noticing the missing text at all.

An important lesson from these variant behaviours is that in none of the cases does the model exhibit the behaviour which the designer presumably intended, namely that it should *Yank* TextA back to A immediately after *Wiping* it, and only then proceed to *Yank* a copy of the text elsewhere. The nature of the problem-solving in fact precludes such behaviour. The fact that a subgoal serves to focus the immediate problem solving, in this case on the satisfaction of the preconditions for a *Yank* action, is also what prevents it from "seeing" secondary differences created during the course of the subgoal. In other words, the problem solver deals with a goal or subgoal before noticing any side-effects.

```
... ... ... ... ... ... ... ... ... ... ...
subgoal: achieve precondition for Yank                   [4]
G: Buffer(TextA)                                         [5]
   ⟶ D: BufferContents                                   [6]
   ⟶ A: Copy-to-Buffer(TextA,LocA)                       [7]
      subgoal: precondition for Copy-to-Buffer           [8]
      G: Marked                                          [9]
         ⟶ D: MarkedText ⟶ A: Mark                       [10]
      R: Marked                                          [12]
      can now apply Copy-to-Buffer                       [13]
      subgoal: realise Copy-to-Buffer                    [13.1]
      G: Buffer(TextA) & Text(TextA,LocA)                [13.2]
         ⟶ D: BufferContents                             [13.3]
         ⟶ A: Wipe                                       [13.4]
      R: Buffer(TextA) & -Text(TextA,LocA)               [13.5]
         ⟶ D: Text+ ⟶ A: Yank                            [13.6]
      R: Buffer(TextA) & Text(TextA,LocA)                [14]
      have now realised Copy-to-Buffer                   [14.1]
can now apply Yank(TextA,LocB)                           [15]
... ... ... ... ... ... ... ... ... ... ...
```

Figure 4. Means-ends analysis realisation of *Add(TextA,LocB)* with *Copy-to-Buffer*. (S = initial situation, G = goal, D = difference, A = relevant action, R = result of action. The line numbers correspond to those of Figure 3.)

Effect of Including a Copy-to-Buffer Action

The behaviour of the model in regard to this difficulty can be changed radically merely by offering a "hint" to the mini-planner. We can extend the knowledge analysis by telling the architecture of the existence of a further, compound action called *Copy-to-Buffer*, which has the effect of copying the marked text to the buffer instead of deleting it as *Wipe* does. The result of including this further conceptual operation is shown in Figure 4, which is numbered to correspond to Figure 3. Assume that the *Copy-to-Buffer* gets chosen instead of *Wipe* [7]. As with *Wipe*, it requires the *Mark* action [10] to satisfy its precondition before it can be applied [13]. The mini-planner then has to figure out how to carry out that compound action [13.1]. Means-ends analysis recommends *Wipe* to remove the difference of *BufferContents* [13.3,13.4], and after that has been done recommends *Yank* to remove the new difference of *Text+* at A [13.6]. The net result of carrying out the *Copy-to-Buffer* [14] is that TextA has been *Yanked* back to its original position immediately after having been *Wiped* to the buffer, thereby avoiding the previous difficulty.

It should be noted that the success of this additional operation reveals that the original difficulty was due to a *conceptual* shortcoming, not one of problem solving. It is not necessary to tell the mini-planner how to carry out the compound action. Means-ends analysis proves perfectly adequate to working out the sequence of editing actions for itself. The addition of *Copy-to-Buffer* to the knowledge analysis merely provides the *idea* of constructing a sequence of behaviour in terms of such an action. This is roughly equivalent to whispering in the user's ear, "Why not imagine that the editor provides another action which copies the marked text to the buffer?" Nothing more is needed.

DISCUSSION

The knowledge analysis presented here has shown how a description of the editor and the task, expressed in an Instruction Language and combined with a simulated cognitive architecture incorporating a limited capability for problem-solving, can predict that users will have difficulty with a particular aspect of the editor. The resulting model, when run, generates a sequence of actions which indicates that users are liable to make conceptual errors leading them to execute a faulty procedure. We noted that this kind of prediction is inherently beyond the scope of GOMS-like analyses, which demand that the "Method" be specified by the analyst.

It should be understood that the faulty behaviour does not arise from mistakes in the knowledge analysis. An important conclusion from this exercise has been that correct *local* knowledge of the device and the task does not guarantee the intended behaviour. The interaction of the knowledge with the cognitive architecture, embodying psychological constraints, can lead to behaviour different to what the designer expected. In the present case, the designer would presumably have intended users trying to copy text from one place to another to restore the original text with a *Yank* immediately after moving it to the buffer with a *Wipe*. Our analysis has shown that this behaviour depends crucially upon users' having the concept of copying-to-the-buffer. Without it, certain aspects of the structure of the cognitive architecture actually prevent the intended behaviour from occurring.

The analysis does also enable us to explore what happens if the user has a faulty mental model, reflecting a misconception about how the editor operates. Our analysis predicts that such shortcomings typically give rise to characteristic patterns of sub-optimal or erroneous behaviour. If, for example, users mistakenly believe that the *Yank* operator is the exact converse of *Wipe*, in that it deletes the contents of the Buffer as well as inserting those contents into the document, then although they would still be able to perform a task requiring them to *move* text (i.e. by a *Wipe* followed by a *Yank* to the target location), they would be unable to devise a sequence of operations to *copy* text from one location to another.

Our approach in this paper has been not to attempt the accurately detailed modelling of any one specific sample of user behaviour, but rather to treat an "error" by the model as a warning that users are likely to encounter difficulty at that point. For that reason, we take most seriously those phenomena which display a degree of robustness, by persisting across small variations of the model. In fact one of the clear lessons of this exercise has been to dispel any notion that the application of a PUM could consist of a single once-off analysis followed by the running of a single model. Even this small example makes clear that the payoff emerges from the exploration involved in "playing around" with variants of the initial analysis. The sensitivity to the inclusion of the concept of Copy-to-Buffer, for example, emerges only when we run two versions of the analysis, one with and one without that conceptual operation, and then consider still further versions to establish that it is indeed the crucial factor. This is something entirely consonant with our claim (Young *et al*, 1989) that information for the designer emerges at least as much from the process of "instructing" the PUM as from running the resulting models.

Finally, from this exercise we draw encouragement for the future of PUM-based modelling. It has demonstrated the feasibility and value of the analysis, and its ability to predict conceptual errors. It has illustrated the central argument of PUMs, that a knowledge analysis, combined with a simulated cognitive architecture, can serve to draw attention to potential difficulties with the usability of a proposed design.

ACKNOWLEDGEMENTS.

We are grateful to Judith Olson and Phil Barnard for helpful comments. The work reported here was done in part under Alvey Project MMI/112 on "Programmable User Models", and in part under AMODEUS, ESPRIT Basic Research Action 3066.

REFERENCES

Card, S. K., Moran, T. P. & Newell, A. (1983) *The Psychology of Human Computer Interaction.* Erlbaum.

John, B. E. & Newell, A. (1989) Cumulating the science of HCI: From S-R compatibility to transcription typing. In K. Bice & C. Lewis (Eds.) *Proceedings CHI'89 Human Factors in Computing Systems,* 109-114. New York: ACM Press.

Kieras, D. E. & Polson, P. G. (1985) An approach to the formal analysis of user complexity. *International Journal of Man-Machine Studies, 22,* 365-394.

Laird, J. E., Newell, A. & Rosenbloom, P. S. (1987) SOAR: An architecture for general intelligence. *Artificial Intelligence, 33,* 1-64.

Lerch, F. J., Mantei, M. M. & Olson, J. R. (1989) Skilled financial planning: The cost of translating ideas into action. In K. Bice & C. Lewis (Eds.) *Proceedings CHI'89 Human Factors in Computing Systems,* 121-126. New York: ACM Press.

Moran, T. P. (1981) The Command Language Grammar: A representation for the user interface of interactive computer systems. *International Journal of Man-Machine Studies, 15,* 3-50.

Moran, T. P. (1983) Getting into a system: External-internal task mapping analysis. In A. Janda (Ed.) *Proceedings CHI'83 Human Factors in Computing Systems,* 45-49. New York: ACM Press.

Newell, A. (1989) *Unified Theories of Cognition: The 1987 William James Lectures.* Harvard University Press (in press).

Newell, A. & Simon, H. A. (1972) *Human Problem Solving.* Englewood Cliffs, NJ: Prentice-Hall.

Olson, J. R. & Nilsen, E. (1988) Analysis of the cognition involved in spreadsheet software interaction. *Human Computer Interaction, 3,* 309-349.

Payne, S. J. (1987) Complex problem spaces: Modelling the knowledge needed to use interactive devices. In H.-J. Bullinger & B. Shackel (Eds.) *Human-Computer Interaction — INTERACT'87.* Elsevier.

Payne, S. J. (1989) A notation for reasoning about learning. In J. Long & A. Whitefield (Eds.) *Cognitive Ergonomics and Human-Computer Interaction,* 134-165. Cambridge University Press.

Polson, P. G. (1988) The consequences of consistent and inconsistent interfaces. In R. Guindon (Ed.) *Cognitive Science and its Applications for Human Computer Interaction.* Hillsdale, NJ: Erlbaum.

Polson, P. G., Bovair, S. & Kieras, D. E. (1987) Transfer between text editors. In J. M. Carroll & P. P. Tanner (Eds.) *CHI + GI Conference Proceedings: Human Factors in Computing Systems and Graphics Interface,* 27-32. New York: ACM Press.

Waldrop, M. M. (1988) Toward a unified theory of cognition. *Science, 241,* 27-29; Soar: A unified theory of cognition? *Science, 241,* 296-298.

Young, R. M. & Simon, T. (1987) Planning in the context of human-computer interaction. In D. Diaper & R. Winder (Eds.) *People and Computers III,* 363-370. Cambridge University Press.

Young, R. M., Green, T. R. G. & Simon, T. (1989) Programmable user models for predictive evaluation of interface designs. In K. Bice & C. Lewis (Eds.) *Proceedings CHI'89 Human Factors in Computing Systems,* 15-19. New York: ACM Press.

The Soar Papers

1991

CHAPTER 60

Neuro-Soar: A Neural-Network Architecture for Goal-Oriented Behavior

B. Cho, USC–ISI, P. S. Rosenbloom, USC–ISI, and C. P. Dolan, Hughes Research Labs

Abstract

The ability to set and achieve a wide range of goals is one of the principal hallmarks of intelligence. The issue of goals, and of how they can be achieved, has been one of the major foci of Artificial Intelligence (AI), and the understanding of how to construct systems that can accomplish a wide range of goals has been one of the major breakthroughs provided by the study of symbolic processing systems in AI. Neural networks, however, have not shared this focus on the issue of goals to any significant extent. This article provides a progress report on an effort to incorporate such an ability into neural networks. The approach we have taken here is to implement a symbolic problem solver within a neural network; specifically we are creating Neuro-Soar, a neural-network reimplementation of the Soar architecture. Soar is particularly appropriate for this purpose because of its well-established goal-oriented abilities, and its mapping onto levels of human cognition — in particular, the ways in which it already either shares, or is compatible with, a number of key characteristics of neural networks.

Introduction

An ability to set and achieve a wide range of goals is one of the principal hallmarks of intelligence. The issue of goals, and of how they can be achieved, has been one of the major foci of Artificial Intelligence (AI), and the understanding of how to construct systems that can accomplish a wide range of goals has been one of the major breakthroughs provided by the study of symbolic processing system in AI. Neural networks have not shared this focus on the issue of goals to any significant extent. However, if neural networks are to be serious contenders as the basis for a complete intelligent system, they must eventually incorporate the ability to set and achieve the full range of goals faced by such systems.

This article provides a progress report on an effort to incorporate such an ability into neural networks. The approach we have taken here is to implement a symbolic problem solver within a neural network; specifically we are creating Neuro-Soar, a neural-network reimplementation of Soar — a symbolic architecture for intelligence that integrates basic mechanisms for problem solving, use of knowledge, learning, and perceptual-motor behavior [Laird *et al.*, 1987]. Soar[1] is particularly appropriate for this purpose because of its well-established goal-oriented abilities, and its mapping onto levels of human cognition [Newell, 1990] — in particular, the ways in which it already either shares, or is compatible with, a number of key characteristics of neural networks [Rosenbloom, 1989]. Work to date on Neuro-Soar covers the lowest three levels of Soar — memory accessing, decision making, and (problem space) operations. Together these capabilities are sufficient to enable goal-oriented behavior in a single problem space, but are not yet sufficient to enable higher-level search and learning behaviors. One of the key developments in accomplishing this is the implementation of a novel neural-network-based production system that allows multiple variables per production, and parallel matching and firing of multiple productions.

From Soar to Neuro-Soar

In Soar, all symbolic goal-oriented behavior is formulated as steps in problem spaces. A problem space is a uniform task representation that allows Soar to be applied to a wide range of goals. The problem space determines the set of states and operators that can be used during the processing to attain a goal. Goals, problem spaces, states, and operators exist as data structures in Soar's working memory — a transient declarative memory. Each goal defines a problem solving context which contains roles for a problem space, a state, and an operator.

Problem solving is driven by the acts of selecting problem spaces, states, and operators for the appropriate roles in the context; where each selection is accomplished via a two-phase decision cycle. First, during the *elaboration phase*, the description of the current situation (that is, the content of working memory) is elaborated with relevant information from long-term memory — an associative memory, constructed as a parallel production system. The rules contain variabilized conditions that are matched against the contents of working memory, and actions that add elements to working memory when all of the conditions are met. One important type of knowledge that may be added during the elaboration phase is *preferences*. There is a fixed

*This research was partially supported by a gift from the Artificial Intelligence Center of the Hughes Aircraft Company.

[1] In this article, we focus on Soar version 4.

language of preferences which is used to describe the acceptability and desirability of the alternatives being considered for the selection. There are two types of preferences, unary and binary. The former states an absolute preference to all others (e.g., "best"), while the latter states a preference between two objects (e.g., "better"). In the second phase, the *decision phase*, the preferences in working memory are interpreted by a fixed decision procedure. If the preferences uniquely specify an object to be selected for a role in a context, then a decision can be made, and the specified object becomes the current value of the role. However, if the preferences for a decision are either incomplete or inconsistent, then an impasse occurs. Soar automatically generates a subgoal for the task of resolving the impasse and creates a new problem solving context within which it can be resolved. Soar learns by acquiring new productions which summarize the processing that leads to results of subgoals, a process called chunking.

Soar has been used to implement goal-oriented systems in a wide variety of domains: immediate reasoning tasks, simple puzzles and games, classical expert system domains, robotic control tasks, and natural language understanding. It has also demonstrated the ability to utilize a wide variety of problem solving methods. However, despite all of this high-level symbolic capability, much of the architectural functionality described above can be mapped to corresponding neural network concepts (at least at a gross level). In particular, Soar's production memory is just a fine-grained parallel associative memory — though it does work with graph-structured objects and does allow multiple variables — and its decision procedure is just a method for locally integrating together multiple constraints on selection, as is generally done via activation combination in neural networks. The need to allow parallel matching and firing of productions over graph-structured objects with multiple variables adds some complexity to this mapping; however, in contrast to traditional production systems, a novel formulation — that restricts attributes to having at most one value at a time (referred to as the *unique-attribute* formulation) — has been developed for Soar that greatly simplifies implementation in neural networks by guaranteeing both linear-time match complexity and a maximum of one binding per variable [Tambe *et al.*, 1990].

In the remainder of this article we focus on how Soar's production system and decision procedure can be implemented in a neural network, and how these two capabilities can be combined to enable the selection and application of sequences of problem-space operators that solve simple blocks world problems. Impasse detection, subgoal generation (with the concomitant abilities of using multiple problem spaces and searching), and learning are left for another day.

Representing Problem Solving Knowledge

In problem solving behavior in a simple blocks world problem (Sussman's anomaly), three blocks are arranged on a table, and there are operators that allow blocks to be moved onto either other blocks or the table. In the first situation, three operators are suggested, and sufficient preferences are retrieved from long-term memory to allow the correct operator to be selected. Once it is selected, further memory retrieval effectively applies the operator

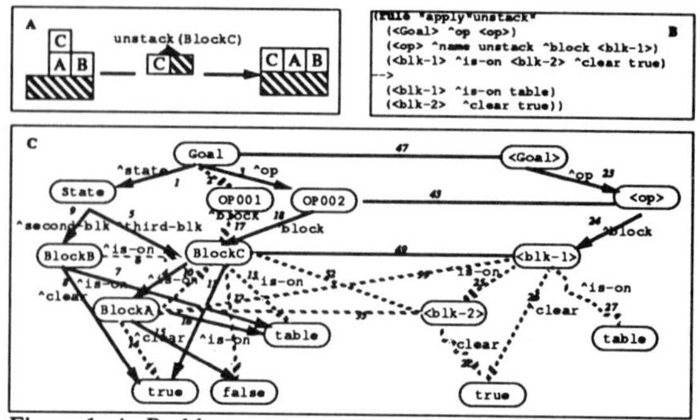

Figure 1. A. Problem space representation for operator application. B. Corresponding production rule. C. The graph view. One unit will be assigned to each number. Some edges for the working memory and bindings are not shown for clarity.

by modifying the problem solving state. Problem solving then continues by repeating the entire process.

Figure 1A focuses on a fragment of this overall behavior — the application of the selected operator to modify the state. In the remainder of this section we focus on how the knowledge is represented in Soar and the transformations that lead from this representation to the one used in Neuro-Soar. Figure 1B provides a *text view* of how this is represented in Soar (in a slightly simplified form) as a production. The conditions are prior to the arrow and the actions after. Symbols preceded by " ^ " and bounded by " <> " are attributes and variables, respectively.

To get from this text view of the information to the *neural view*, it is useful to go through an intermediary *graph view*, as shown in Figure 1C. In the graph view, each individual triple of an object, attribute, and value is represented by a labeled directed edge from the object to the value. In the working memory, a solid edge indicates a working memory element and a dashed edge indicates an element that potentially could be in working memory, but currently isn't. This distinction is not needed in the text view, but is crucial for the neural view. In production memory, there are two types of edges, one for the conditions (denoted with straight edges), and the other for actions (denoted with jagged edges). Solid and dashed edges denote matched and unmatched triples, respectively. The bindings are represented by undirected edges between the vertices of the working memory graph and the production memory graph. A solid edge indicates a binding of a production variable to an object in working memory, and a dashed edge indicates a potential binding.

A match between the working memory and a production occurs when there is an exact match between a subgraph of working memory and the production graph through a set of bindings[2]. For a successful match, there will be exactly one solid edge from each vertex in the production to some vertex in the working memory.

Production systems in the neural view are composed of relatively simple, neuron-like processing units ("units" for short) and weighted connections between them. In the neu-

[2]In contrast to Soar 4, preferences are not in working memory, instead they exist in preference memory, which cannot be matched by productions.

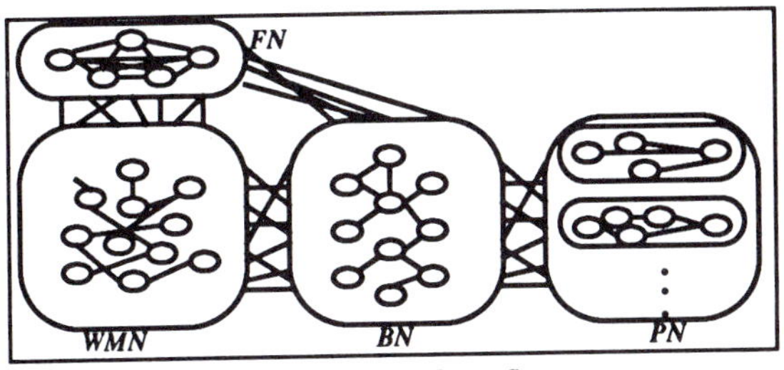

Figure 2. Network Architecture of Neuro-Soar.

ral view, there is one unit for each edge in the graph view. The details are provided in the following section.

Representation in Neuro-Soar

Neuro-Soar is composed of four sub-networks and connections between them (see Figure 2). Three of the sub-networks correspond to the three components described in the previous section: the working memory network, the production network, and the binding network. The fourth sub-network is the preference network, which did not appear in the previous section because it is used in the selection of operators, but not in their application.

The role of the working memory network (WMN) is to represent the contents working memory as a combination of unit activations. In the neural view, each WMN unit corresponds to an edge in the graph view. WMN units are activated by production actions, and deactivated when there is no longer an activated path between them and the goal node. This deactivation process corresponds to a garbage collection process in the symbolic implementation of Soar.

The production network (PN) is actually a set of networks, one for each production. Each network can be activated individually, in parallel, by the active segments of WMN via the binding network. To create a PN for a particular production, condition and action units are created for the condition and action edges in the graph view (one unit per edge). Each production also needs a rule unit to detect the joint activations of all the condition units. Each condition unit is connected to the rule unit, and the threshold of the rule unit is simply the number of condition units. The rule unit activates the action units, which in turn activate working memory units.

The binding network (BN) is the vehicle by which conditions are matched to working memory, and by which actions have their effects on working memory. In so doing, it computes variable bindings between the PN and WMN, and ensures their consistency — each instance of the same variable in a production must bind to the same object, each object must bind to no more than one variable[3], and no more than one object can be bound to any variable at the same time. The basic binding units are obtained from edges in the graph view of binding. Each binding unit represents a particular instantiation of a variable of a production to a (potential) object in working memory.

Figure 3 shows how consistent bindings are computed. The binding of at most one object to a variable is en-

[3] Soar actually enforces this restriction in learned rules, but not in programmed rules. In Neuro-Soar it is enforced for all rules.

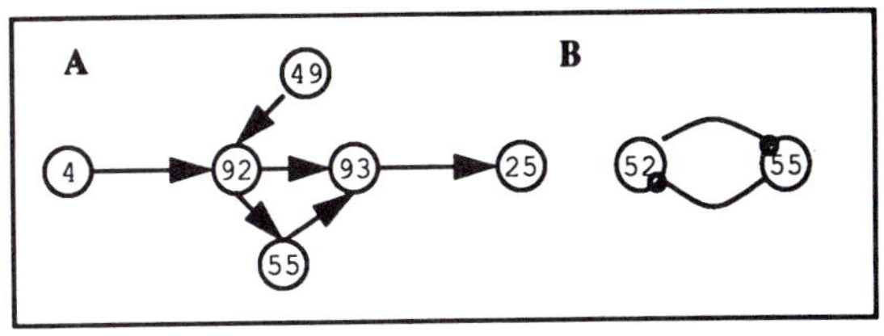

Figure 3. A. Matching mechanism in Neuro-Soar. Units 4 and 25 are WMN and PN units, respectively. Units 49 and 55 are binding units. Units 92 and 93 are instantiation units. B. Mutual inhibition among units whose bindings are contradictory to each other, through which consistent variable bindings are computed.

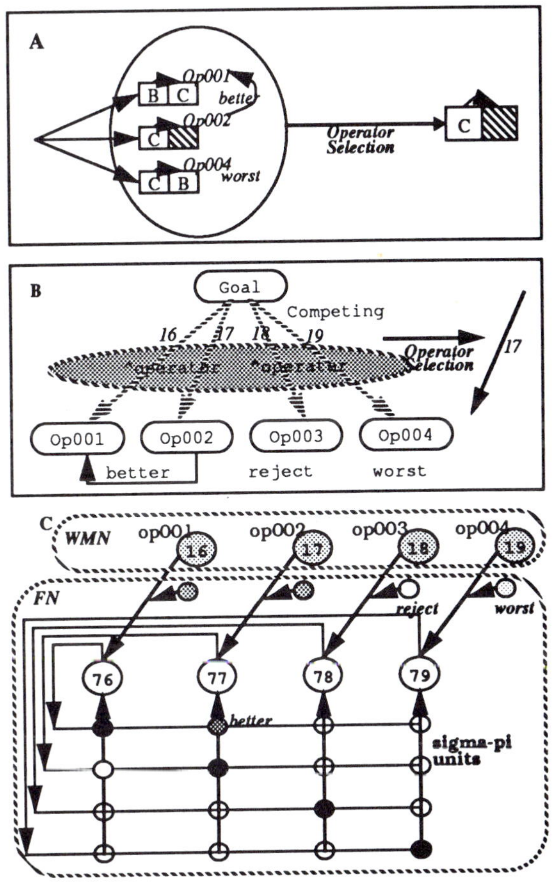

Figure 4. Neuro-Soar decision procedure. *A*. Problem space representation for operator selection. B. Corresponding graph view. C. Neural network implementation of corresponding preference information. A new layer of units (76,77,78,79) is introduced where mutual inhibitory connections exist by default. Preferences are stored in sigma-pi units (small units). A selection of unit 77 by the neural decision procedure will feed back to unit 17 in the WMN.

forced by mutually inhibitory connections among the binding units for the variable (Figure 3B). Likewise, the binding of an object to at most one variable is enforced by mutual inhibition among the binding units for the object. Consistent bindings across multiple occurences of the same variable are enforced as shown in Figure 3A. This fragment of the binding network exists to match the working memory triple (BlockA ^ on BlockB) to the condition (<blk-1> ^ on <blk-2>). As before the units in the figure are identified by their numbers: 4 is the working memory unit, 25 is the condition unit (in PN), 49 and 55 are binding units, and 92 and 93 are (partial) instantiation units. In the current situation, both unit 4 (representing that BlockA is on BlockB) and unit 49 (representing the binding of BlockA to <blk-1>) are active. This combination then activates unit 92, which represents a partial instantiation of condition unit 25; that is, that the appropriate element is in working memory, and its first symbol is bound to the first variable in the condition. To pursue the match further, unit 55 (representing the binding of BlockB to <blk-2>) needs to be activated. This unit receives activation from unit 92, so if there is no competition from other binding units for <blk-2> — or if unit 55 simply wins the competition — unit 55 will become activated. Unit 93 is analogous to unit 92, but it represents a complete instantiation of condition unit 25 — there would be one unit like 93 for each possible instantiation of condition unit 25. This then activates condition unit 25, thus successfully completing this segment of the match.

The overall match starts with an initial binding between the goal object in working memory and the first condition in each production. From there, the match ripples down the networks, with each new binding that is established enabling further matches to proceed (or be inhibited). When all of the conditions of a production are matched, the production unit becomes active, and in turn activates the action units. The action units then modify working memory activations through an inverted binding network.

In addition to the straightforward effect of action units on working memory, action units can also modify working memory indirectly by asserting preferences among units in WMN — this is how problem solving operators are selected. The role of the preference network (FN) is to reflect these current preferences (during the elaboration phase) and to select a unit out of the competing candidate units, based on their preferences (during the decision phase).

Figure 4A shows the operator selection episode, elaborated with the preferences that lead to the selection of Op002 (put Block C on the table). This operator is selected because it is *better* than Op001, and the other candidate (Op004) is *worst*. Figure 4C shows how this behavior is implemented as a neural decision procedure in the preference network. The FN is built on top of the WMN as an additional layer that stores and processes preferences (see units 76, 77, 78, 79 in Figure 4C)[4]. The FN is basically formed as winner-take-all network with a guide of preferences. Unary preferences are encoded as wieghts between the WMN units and the FN units, while binary preferences are encoded as weights between the competing units in FN. The use of Sigma-Pi units[Rumelhart *et al.*, 1986] is required for this (see small units in Figure 4C).

[4] In reality, there is also one additional layer that handles *indifferent* preference.

At first, each competing unit in FN receives a level of activation from the correponding unit in WMN that is a function of its unary preferences. Prodded by these activations, competition then occurs in the binary preference layer, which then feeds back to the WMN units. If a selection can be made, processing continues with another elaboration phase. Otherwise, the resulting impasse leads to termination (though ultimately Neuro-Soar must be extended perform subgoal generation instead).

The Neuro-Soar approach of encoding preferences as constraints on activation combination is not guaranteed to yield the same outcome as would be achieved through Soar's decision procedure, but it does capture the spirit of their meaning. The extent to which the Neuro-Soar scheme is actually better or worse than the symbolic approach is still to be determined.

Experiments and Analysis

So far, Neuro-Soar has been applied in two domains: the blocks world and the tower of Hanoi. In this section, we focus on results from the blocks world. The implementation consists of 8 productions. Two test problems have been run — Sussman's anomaly and a simpler problem of unstacking a tower of three blocks. In both cases Neuro-Soar solved the problem by replicating the sequence of operator selections and applications that were produced by Soar when it was given the same knowledge.

Since Neuro-Soar employs a local representation scheme, a sufficient number of units in working memory must be preallocated. This number is dependent on the number of objects in working memory and their attributes. The number of units in PN is dependent on the number of conditions and actions in the productions. Likewise, the number of units in the binding network is related to the number of objects in working memory and the productions. Only a small number of units are required in FN since they are built on top of a small part of working memory. The blocks world implementation requires 135 WMN units, 119 PN units (of which there are 8 production units, 48 condition units, and 63 action units), 2148 BN units (of which there are 185 binding units and 1963 instantiation units), and 10 FN units. More generally, the worst space complexity of a task implemented in Neuro-Soar is as follows. Let $nUNIT_{netwrok}$ be the number of units in network *network*.

$$nUNIT_{PN} = O(nTrp)$$

$$nUNIT_{WMN} = O(\sum_{attr} nObjHas_{attr} * nObjOf_{attr})$$

$$nUNIT_{BN} = O(nOBJ_{WMN} * nOBJ_{PN} + \sum_{attr} nWMN_{attr} * nPN_{attr})$$

$$nUNIT_{FN} = O(nOBJ_{WMN})$$

where $nTrp$ is the number of triples in productions; $nObjHas_{attr}$ and $nObjOf$ are the number of objects of working memory that can have attribute $attr$ and can be the value of $attr$, respectively; $nOBJ_{network}$ is the number of objects in *network*; and $nWMN_{attr}$ and nPN_{attr} are the number of units which have attribute $attr$.

The time complexity for matching a production in Neuro-Soar is on the order of the maximum depth of the graph representation of the production. The depth of the graph representation is approximately $log(nTrp)$. The matching process is relatively fast and efficient in terms of neurosimulation cycles, not only because the rules are fired in parallel, but also because the valid partial matches are kept (analogous to state saving in the Rete algorithm

[Forgy, 1982]).

Related Work

The two classes of related work to which it is most important to compare Neuro-Soar (other than Soar itself) are: other attempts at constructing neural production systems, and other attempts at constructing neural problem solvers. On the former, two previous systems have implemented production systems using neural networks, the Distributed Connectionist Production System by Touretzky and Hinton[Touretzky and Hinton, 1988] and the Tensor Product Production System by Dolan and Smolensky[Dolan and Smolensky, 1988], both of which used distributed representations. Neuro-Soar, though simpler in that it uses a local representation, goes significantly beyond these two systems in allowing parallel matching and execution of productions, (unique-attribute) graph-structured representations, and multiple variables per production.

Ajjanagadde and Shastri[Ajjanagadde and Shastri, 1990] have developed a connectionist system that represents knowledge as rules and facts with multi-place predicates. A multi-phased clock is proposed as a solution to the variable binding problem. The system produces answers, when given 'yes/no' questions, based on the knowledge. However, the system lacks a capability to create and alter the content of its temporary knowledge so that situation dependent firing of rules (or planning) is not possible.

This is by no means the first effort to construct a neural-network-based problem solver (see, for example, [Sutton and Barto, 1981, Anderson, 1989]). However, the current effort differs from most of the earlier approaches in adding representational and structural complexity — specifically, graph-structured objects and the decomposition of the overall memory into four specialized subnetworks — in service of domain generality. The hope is that this will allow Neuro-Soar to be extended up to Soar's full level of capability, without ultimately sacrificing learnability or neural plausibility.

Conclusions and Future Work

Work to date on Neuro-Soar has demonstrated that it is possible to reproduce key aspects of Soar's general goal-oriented ability even when the implementation technology is shifted from "symbolic" to "neural network". In particular, we have demonstrated a domain-independent approach to knowledge-driven operator selection and application. To accomplish this, we have developed a preference-based neural-network decision procedure, and a novel neural network production system that allows parallel matching and firing of rules, graph structured objects, and multiple variables per rule.

However, much remains to be done in three general areas. The first area is the completion of Neuro-Soar with respect to Soar's functionality. This primarily involves the incorporation of impasse detection and subgoaling, use of multiple problem spaces, and learning. The second area is the loosening up of the design so that it less slavishly follows how things are currently done in Soar, and more takes advantage of the strengths of neural networks. We have begun with the conservative approach of trying to model the existing Soar architecture as closely as possible; however, we eventually want to get to where we can ask whether the specification of Soar ought to be altered because of the advantages accruable from using neural networks. For example, what would happen if we were to shift to a distributed representation for memory, based perhaps on a tensor-product formulation [Smolensky, 1990], or if we were to shift from a neural-network analogue of chunking to a more typically neural learning algorithm. Would such changes result in a more robust system that can learn more effectively? The third area is to see whether Neuro-Soar provides leverage in interfacing Soar to external environments. Would encoding the required signal-to-symbol transducers in neural-networks that are directly connected to Neuro-Soar provide a more seamless interface than is now provided by the use of Lisp code for the transducers?

References

[Ajjanagadde and Shastri, 1990] V. Ajjanagadde and L. Shastri. An optimally efficient limited inference system. In *Proceedings of AAAI 90*, pages 563–570, 1990.

[Anderson, 1989] C. W. Anderson. Tower of hanoi with connectionist networks: Learning new features. In *Proceedings of the Sixth International Workshop on Machine Learning*, pages 345–349, 1989.

[Dolan and Smolensky, 1988] C. P. Dolan and P. Smolensky. Implementing a connectionist production system using tensor products. Technical Report UCLA-AI-88-15, University of California, Los Angeles, 1988.

[Forgy, 1982] C. L. Forgy. Rete: A fast algorithm for the many pattern/many object pattern match problem. *Artificial Intelligence*, 19:17–37, 1982.

[Laird *et al.*, 1987] J. E. Laird, A. Newell, and P. S. Rosenbloom. Soar: An architecture for general intelligence. *Artificial Intelligence*, 33:1–64, 1987.

[Newell, 1990] A. Newell. *Unified Theories of Cognition*. Harvard University Press, Cambridge, MA, 1990.

[Rosenbloom, 1989] P. S. Rosenbloom. A symbolic goal-oriented perspective on connectionism and soar. In R. Pfeifer, editor, *Connectionism in Perspective*. North-Holland, 1989.

[Rumelhart *et al.*, 1986] D. E. Rumelhart, G. E. Hinton, and J. L. McClelland. A general framework for parallel distirbuted processing. In D. E. Rumelhart, J. L. McClelland, and the PDP Research Group, editors, *Parallel Distributed Processing, Volume 1: Foundations*, pages 45–76. Bradford Books/MIT Press, 1986.

[Smolensky, 1990] P. Smolensky. Tensor product variable binding and the representation of symbolic strucutre in connectionist systems. *Artificial Intelligence*, 46:159–216, 1990.

[Sutton and Barto, 1981] R. S. Sutton and A. G. Barto. An adaptive network that constructs and uses an internal model of its world. *Cognition and Brain Theory*, 4:217–246, 1981.

[Tambe *et al.*, 1990] M. Tambe, A. Newell, and P. S. Rosenbloom. The problem of expensive chunks and its solution by restricting expressiveness. *Machine Learning*, 5:299–348, 1990.

[Touretzky and Hinton, 1988] D. Touretzky and G. E. Hinton. A distributed connectionist production system. *Cognitive Science*, 12:423–466, 1988.

CHAPTER 61

Predicting the Learnability of Task-Action Mappings

A. Howes and R. M. Young, MRC Applied Psychology Unit

ABSTRACT

Programmable User Models (PUMs) are tools based on psychological theory that enable interface designers to predict the usability of a proposed design. This paper presents a variant in which the PUM, implemented in Soar and incorporating the constraints of Display-based Task-Action Grammars, learns the task-action mapping by being guided by the designer during performance. We show that the more consistent and interactive the interface, the easier it is for the designer to teach the PUM the necessary task-action mapping.

PREDICTING INTERFACE LEARNABILITY

A Programmable User Model (PUM, [14]) is a psychologically constrained architecture in which the interface designer is invited to program a simulation of a user. By making the user's knowledge explicit, PUMs enable the designer to consider usability early in design. PUMs can help the designer in two ways. Firstly, the constraints in the architecture make it easier to program for some interfaces than others. The claim is that if the designer finds it hard to program the PUM for an interface then a user will find it hard to use that interface. Secondly, the simulation, when run, predicts the user's behaviour.

Young et al. [14] describe a PUM as having two components, an instruction language and an underlying cognitive architecture. The architecture is used to interpret the knowledge specified in the instruction language. The model reported here explores a novel variation on this theme in which rather than specifying the user program in an instruction language, the designer acts as an advisor to the PUM as it tries to learn about the device by using it. Whenever the PUM is unsure about what to do next it consults its advisor.

The paper reports work on the task-action mapping component of a PUM. It draws on previous work on Task-action Grammars, TAG [12, 13]. TAGs model users' representation of the interface language of computer systems. They have two weaknesses which are addressed in this work. Firstly, writing a TAG is like writing a computer program but without the benefits of an interpreter to check that the program is correct. Secondly, despite extensions reported by Howes & Payne [4] TAGs fail to reflect many aspects of the role of the device in guiding users' behaviour.

The aim of this paper is to give a flavour of the underlying cognitive architecture of a task-action mapping PUM and illustrations of how the PUM can help a designer. The following sections describe the knowledge constraints on this model in terms of Display-based Task-action Grammars D-TAG [4] and the architectural constraints in terms of Soar [6], and then give examples of how the PUM can alert the designer to issues of learnability. As is the case with people, the PUM finds a more consistent and interactive device easier to learn.

DISPLAY-BASED TASK-ACTION GRAMMARS

Task-action grammars [12] define mappings between simple-tasks and the actions required to carry out the tasks on a particular device. A simple-task is any task that can be performed routinely with no demand for a control structure, such as iteration. The aim of TAG is to expose the relative consistency of interface languages. However it assumes that the display plays no role in mapping tasks into actions. In contrast the theoretical work of Draper [1] and the empirical results of Mayes, Draper, McGregor & Oatley [8] suggest that becoming skilled with a system does not necessitate learning a set of packaged methods. Rather, in the service of performance, skilled users become good at getting the right information from the display. In response Howes & Payne [4] have described Display-based Task-action Grammars (D-TAG) which provide a mechanism for modelling precisely this aspect of skill.

A fragment of a D-TAG is shown in Figure 1. This grammar is for performing operations on files from within the Microsoft Word (MS-Word) application on the Apple Macintosh computer. The rules map tasks, described in terms of semantic features, into actions. In Figure 1, the Effect feature may, for example, take the values: open and save. The Object-id feature identifies the particular file to which it is desired that the Effect is applied.

Rule 1 captures the syntax for using a pull-down-menu: first select the class of the operation from the menu-bar and

```
1.  Task[Class, Effect]
    display-item([Class],[frame=menu-bar]
    ->  action(press,value-from-display-item)
        action(release, display-item([Effect],
                                [frame=pull-down]))

2.  Task[Object-id]
    display-item([Object-id],[frame=file-list])
    ->  action(double-click, value-from-display-item)

3.  Task[Object-id, Effect=save-new-name]
    display-item([],[frame=command-line]
    ->  action(type, known-item(Object-id))
        action(click, return)
```

Figure 1: A D-TAG for MS-Word file operations.

then select the operation from the pull-down. Rule 2 will fire only if there is a file name visible in a file-list which matches to Object-id. Rule 3 fires when the task is to save a file with a new name and a command-line is available on the display. Rules 2 and 3 illustrate one aspect of the way that D-TAG can use the display in task-action mapping. In the context of the specified task it is the device that interactively determines which and when one of these rules will fire.

Note that there are many possible variations on this grammar to capture many levels of expertise. For example the grammar may, instead of having a rule that captures the syntax for using a menu-bar and pull-down (rule 1), have two rules, one for selecting from the menu-bar and the other for selecting from the pull-down. The grammar will then be totally dependent on the display to determine the order in which these rules should fire.

A SOAR ANALYSIS OF TASK-ACTION MAPPING

The PUM of display-based task-action mapping, called TAG-PUM, is a Soar model [6]. It is the result of the integration of the complementary constraints of Soar and D-TAG. The model is deliberately conservative, the aim being not that it should learn all D-TAGs but simply that it should learn those which people find easy to learn.

Soar: A cognitive architecture

Soar captures the hypotheses that the problem-space is the fundamental category of cognition and that learning is tightly intertwined with performance.

Given a goal, Soar proceeds by choosing the initial state and then repeatedly applying operators until the goal is achieved. When problem solving cannot proceed, perhaps because the system has the option of two operators to apply, an impasse occurs and Soar sets up a subgoal to resolve the impasse. The subgoal may be solved in many ways depending on the knowledge that the system possesses, for example by analogy with an isomorphic problem or by lookahead (i.e. try one of the operators and see where it leads) or by asking an advisor. The important point is that whenever Soar can no longer proceed in one problem space, that is it runs into an impasse, it can bring the full power of the architecture to bear to find a solution to the impasse.

When an impasse is resolved a rule is learnt which connects the relevant part of the pre-impasse situation to the results produced by the subgoal, so that next time Soar meets a similar situation the impasse is avoided. This is known as chunking.

Task-action mapping in Soar

TAG-PUM is given a task described in terms of TAG-like semantic features. It attempts to find a solution to this task by interacting with a simulation of the proposed interface. Initially the only knowledge that it has is a set of actions with which to manipulate the device, knowledge about how to parse the display and a semantic dictionary relating display items to task features. It repeatedly applies actions to the device simulation and reparses the display until the task is achieved. Whenever it has multiple choices of what to do next it asks for guidance.

The learning mechanism can be described in terms of three activities. The first activity consists of *generating candidate subtasks*, the second is *taking advice* as to which candidate is correct and the third is *remembering a rule* which obviates the need to take advice in future.

Each of these activities is carried out in three nested mapping spaces: the communicate-space, the display-space and the action-space. Each space is desribed in the following paragraphs with reference to a trace of the model learning to open a file containing an invitation to a party, from within MS-Word (Figure 2). The semantic features for the task are Effect=open, Oject-id=party-invitation and Class=file-op.

The goal of the *communicate-space* is the overall task to be achieved (in this case opening a file). Candidate subtasks are automatically generated by decomposing this task into a subtask for each of its semantic features. In our example TAG-PUM generates a subtask to communicate the Effect, a subtask to communicate the Object-id and a subtask to communicate the Class. Initially the model does not have the knowledge to decide which one of these candidates to do first. The result is an impasse (Figure 2, line (a)) and the model asks the advisor to select between the candidates. The advisor responds by instructing the model to communicate the Class feature first (line (b), Figure 2). TAG-PUM then learns a rule in which the value of the Class feature is generalized:

> **IF** there is a Class feature in the task and no subtasks have been done yet **THEN** communicate the Class.

Now with the goal to communicate the Class, the *display-space* is invoked. It maps communicate operators into a sequence of display-frame operators. Display-frame operators are cued by the display of the device. Thus in this space the generation of candidate subtasks is

```
Goal: Effect=open, Object-id=party-invitation,
    Class=file-op
Problem-space: communicate
=> Impasse: Which of the following should I do?....... (a)
    1. communicate [Class=file-op]
    2. communicate [Effect=open]
    3. communicate [Object-id=party-invitation]
    4. finish
Advisor: 1 ..................................................... (b)

Goal: Subtask=communicate, Class=file-op
Problem-space: display
=> Impasse: Which of the following should I do? ...... (c)
    1. use-display-frame [Frame=menu-bar]
    2. use-display-frame [Frame=workspace]
    3. finish
Advisor: 1 ..................................................... (d)

Goal: Subtask=use-display-frame, Frame=menu-bar
Problem-space: action
Action: focus-first
Action: read <- Apple
Action: focus-next
Action: read <- File
Match to task description
=> Impasse: Which of the following should I do?....... (e)
    1. action [click, mouse-button]
    2. action [press, mouse-button]
    3. action [double-click, mouse-button]
    4. finish
Advisor: 2
```

Figure 2: Part of a simplified trace of a TAG-PUM without mapping knowledge.

determined by the current state of the display. Again in our example more than one candidate is generated and an impasse occurs (line (c), Figure 2). The advisor responds with option 1 which is to use the menu-bar (line (d)). The following rule is learnt:

> **IF** the subtask is to communicate a Class and there is a menu-bar on the display **THEN** use the menu-bar.

The goal is now to use the menu-bar and to do so the *action-space* is used. This maps a display-frame subtask into a sequence of actions that are subsequently performed on the device. The action-space contains a range of actions some of which are always available to the model and some of which are generated by examining the current display state. Example actions include click-mouse-button, scan-display-frame and match-display-items. In Figure 2 the goal is solved by examining each successive item on the menu-bar until a semantic match is found to the task (using the semantic dictionary specified before hand by the designer). Then after the last impasse in Figure 2, line (e), the model asks for advice as to which action to do to select a menu-bar option.

These activities continue until the task is complete, by which time TAG-PUM will have learnt a display-based task-action grammar for manipulating files from within MS-Word. For a more detailed description of the mechanism and its implications see [3].

As with TAG the hierarchy of mapping knowledge is used to capture regularities between tasks. A mapping learnt for a particular semantic feature and value in the context of one task will reapply to all values of the feature found in the context of any other task. For example once the model has learnt to use a pull-down menu for opening a file it will know how to use a pull-down menu for changing the font.

In general the communicate-space provides a level of organisation in which it is assumed that the interface will be consistent with respect to the task semantics. The display-space provides a level of organisation in which it is assumed that mappings will be consistent with respect to the display (eg that all options on a menu-bar will be selected using the same actions).

Guiding TAG-PUM through the space of possible candidate mappings is a sufficient strategy for learning consistent mappings. Learning inconsistent mappings is more problematic. To do so rules must be pre-programmed into the model that propose subtask candidates which are sensitive to the values of the features affected by the inconsistency. These 'exception' rules over-ride the default mechanisms for generating candidates.

In summary the PUM, except where it is programmed otherwise, assumes that the device is consistent with respect to the task semantics. If the interface is inconsistent then either knowledge must be added to the model to handle the exceptions or the model will over-generalize and make errors. As we shall see in the next section this is where it derives its strength for predicting learnability.

PREDICTING LEARNABILITY

To use TAG-PUM, it is up to the designer to build a prototype of the device, specify the meaning of device labels and specify the actions for manipulating the device. When the model is given a task to perform the designer must advise it whenever it has a multiple choice of actions or subtasks.

There are many ways in which the model can help the designer to spot learnability problems. Here we have space to illustrate only two. The first concerns the consistency of a mapping and the second the physical constraints inherent in interacting with a device.

The examples used in the following sections continue to use a D-TAG-like notation to describe grammars even though a notation that more accurately reflected the TAG-PUM structure might be more appropriate. We use D-TAG because it is sufficient to illustrate the points that we want to make and because it avoids encumbering the reader with a new notation.

Consistency

Recall the grammar in Figure 1, which describes the knowledge necessary to manipulate files from within MS-Word. Rule 1 of the grammar specifies how to use a pull-down-menu. To learn it TAG-PUM need only do one guided example. In contrast consider Figure 3 which illustrates rules for using the MS-Word accelerators. Accelerators are keyboard commands which may be used as a faster way of performing tasks than using menus. Rules 1a, 1b and 1c in Figure 3 capture some of the knowledge required to use MS-Word accelerators.

Whilst accelerators have undoubted usability advantages their learnability is patchy. The designers have attempted to follow a consistent schema of using the first letter of the desired operation in the command (rule 1a). However there are inevitably name clashes where two or more commands have the same first letter, and in these situations the designers have made a decision to arbitrarily rename one of the commands with a letter that bears no semantic relation to its operation (eg. the accelerator for Close-a-file is "w" - rule 1b in Figure 3).

If the designer wants to teach the model how to use accelerators then before an example can be tried the model must be programmed with the concept of "first-letter-of". With this in hand the model can learn rules 1a and 2 in just one example. With this knowledge it can generate correct action sequences for any task that has a mapping which uses the "first-letter-of" rule. However if the model is given an irregular example, such as close-file, then it will over-generalize. In fact it will assume that the correct action sequence is: action(type, clover-key + "c"). This is wrong, in MS-Word it will cause a copy operation instead of the desired close operation.

For the PUM to learn how to use the irregular accelerators on the file menu the designer must program it to tell it which Effects are to be treated as special cases and then guide it through examples for each case. To learn the accelerators in Figure 3, three examples are required: one for the general rule of taking the first letter and two more for the exceptions which do not follow this rule. This compares to the one example required to use the menu itself (Figure 1). And of course there are far more exceptions than we have illustrated here.

These alternative design scenarios illustrate the two ways in which PUMs can give the designer feedback: (1) running the architecture will highlight errors in what the designer believes to be the required knowledge, and (2) the constraints of the architecture, in this case the way the architecture learns, make it harder to program for less learnable interfaces.

Learnability metrics are taken from TAGs by counting the number of top level rules [12]. If two interfaces are being compared then the one that has fewer rules in its Task-Action Grammar is predicted to be more learnable. Similarly metrics can be taken from TAG-PUM, by counting the number of exception rules that have to programmed in. A highly consistent and therefore learnable interface will not require any exception rules and the rule count will be zero. However 'counting' the exception rules may not be the most adroit use for them. TAG-PUM's exception rules give explicit pointers to trouble-spots in the interface and can therefore be used to direct redesign.

```
1a. Task[Effect]
      -> action(type, clover-key + first-letter-of[Effect])

1b. Task[Effect=close-file]
      -> action(type, clover-key + "w")

1c. Task[Effect=preview]
      -> action(type, clover-key + "i")

2.  Task[Object-id]
    display-item([Object-id],[frame=file-list])
      -> action(double-click, value-from-display-item)

3.  Task[Object-id, Effect=save-new-name]
    display-item([],[frame=command-line]
      -> action(type, known-item(Object-id))
         action(click, return)
```

Figure 3: A D-TAG for MS-Word operations using the accelerators. NB. to avoid conflict between the exception rules (1b and 1c) and the general rule (1a), exception rules are prefered.

The previous example illustrates how the model can help predict the relative learnability of interfaces that provide different degrees of support for inferring command names from the task semantics. In the same way it can alert the designer to syntactic inconsistencies. Examples of such interfaces have been described in terms of TAG [12] and D-TAG [4].

Physical Constraint

Interactive devices can restrict the possible action sequences that a user can generate by using physical constraints. In essence the display can be used to constrain the syntax of a mapping. Recall the example of file tasks in MS-Word. The syntax of these tasks is constrained by the use of a selection box to specify the file name. The required operation (e.g. open or save or new) must be selected on the pull-down menu before the selection box appears on the display, hence it is impossible to get the order of the two subtasks (select-operation and select-file) muddled.

In TAG-PUM, as in D-TAG, the device display can cue the next subtask. In the example of the MS-Word file tasks, the subtask to select from a file list is cued by the appearance of the file selection box, hence the PUM only considers selecting from a file list at the correct time. However in contrast to D-TAG the PUM can expose learnability problems that are due to a lack of physical constraint in the interface.

Grammar notations such as D-TAG only capture one mapping. Learnability can be assessed by measuring the simplicity of this mapping. However learning to use a device is as much about what shouldn't be done as what should. Unlike D-TAG the novice PUM considers all of the plausible courses of action, hence when it impasses, it reveals to the designer whether the display is misleadingly cueing actions.

Consider an example of where an interface does not take advantage of physical constraints. The MS-Word menu-bar, even when options cannot be selected from it, remains visible on the Macintosh screen. Novice, and even moderately skilled users can often be seen attempting to select options from the menu-bar when it is visible but otherwise deactivated, for example when there is a control panel on the screen. In this situation the menu-bar serves no function and should be removed from the screen (or dimmed), hence reducing the number of actions that the PUM and the novice user will consider.

There are many examples of physical constraint in task-action mapping. One of the simplest examples is the use of the press, drag and release actions on a mouse button to constrain the action sequence required to select from a pull-down menu. The point is that as long as the mouse button is pressed it cannot be re-pressed or clicked or double-clicked. The only available action to select an option from the pull-down menu is release. This simple and elegant design helps ensure that the knowledge of how to use a menu is rapidly and intuitively acquired by novice Macintosh users. As with higher-order tasks the press/release constraint is captured in the TAG-PUM. Actions are cued by the environment, hence the actions that are made available to the advisor are limited to those that can actually be done.

In general the designer can assess this aspect of learnability by examining the contents of the the list of alternatives presented by the TAG-PUM when it impasses. If there are items in the list which, if selected, would cause an error then the designer should consider redesigning this aspect of the interface.

COGNITIVE VALIDITY

The learnability predictions made by TAG are well supported in the literature. The relevant empirical findings are reviewed and extended in [12, 10]. In one of these experiments, carried out by Payne [10], subjects learned to operate a toy "lost property office" computer system. Subjects could perform three categories of task: request information from a database, send messages to colleagues in other locations, and play games. There were three experimental languages for the toy system. Language 1 exhibited syntactic consistencies within and across entire semantic categories. A TAG of this language contained just one top level rule. Language 2 was consistent within semantic categories but not across them. Its TAG consisted of three top level rules. Language 3 was consistent across groupings of task that were orthogonal to the semantic organization of the interface. Its TAG consisted of eight top level rules. Thus TAG predicted that Language 1 would be more learnable than Language 2 which in turn would be more learnable than Language 3. This prediction was confirmed by the experimental results.

TAG-PUM shares with TAG its central theoretical assumption: that task-action mappings are organised according to their semantic similarities and differences. Unsurprisingly on the examples that the authors have examined the two formalisms make identical predictions of relative consistency. In the case of the "lost property office" experiment TAG-PUM learns Language 1, without any extra top level rules having to be programmed, taking 4 impasses in just one example. To learn Language 2 requires the addition of one extra communicate operator and takes 10 advice impasses over 3 examples. Lastly to learn language 3 requires the addition of one extra communicate operator and takes 28 advice impasses over 8 examples. Hence TAG-PUM makes the same prediction as TAG, that Language 1 will be better than Language 2 which will be better than Language 3.

TAG-PUM also makes learnability predictions due to physical constraints and due to the advantage of being able to choose command names by recognition rather than recall. The learnability advantage of physical constraint can be demonstrated by pointing out that when there is no physical constraint on the syntax of a command there is evidence that learners make order errors [2]. It is simply impossible to make these errors on a device with physically constrained mappings. Also see Norman [9] for many entertaining and persuasive examples. The learnability advantage of recognition is supported by evidence that experts do use recognition oriented methods [8, 11].

In addition to empirical validation the model is supported by coherence validity. That is TAG-PUM is grounded in two separate lines of theoretical work, TAG and Soar. Bringing the models together did not require the invention of any new computational machinery. Indeed many of the apparently unrelated aspects of the TAG and Soar models have been shown to work well together in TAG-PUM. From TAG comes the organisation of tasks according to their semantic similarities and differences and from Soar comes the impasse-driven performance and integrated learning mechanisms.

DISCUSSION

We have described a model that learns consistent interfaces from guidance rather than being programmed. The designer has to describe the task descriptions and semantic relations, but does not have to specify the methods. The PUM learns these by generalizing from the examples through which the designer guides it.

TAG-PUM is related to work on the induction of task-action mapping knowledge from demonstration (EXPL: [7], Explor: [5]). The models differ in two significant ways. First, rather than learning from passive observation (EXPL and Explor), the Soar model learns from experience and guidance during goal-directed behaviour. Both educational theory and the Soar architecture argue that this is a more effective way to learn. Second, Explor is a detailed account of how a user employs the semantics of the task to justify the role of actions in a procedure. It suggests that learning meaningful procedures is easier than learning arbitrary sequences of actions. The PUM in contrast, simply remembers all actions specified by the advisor. In this case it is Explor that is aligned with educational theory. Integration of these complementary models is the subject of further research.

There is also further work to do on the interactive constraints of task-action mapping. As it stands, the TAG-PUM must decide which task feature to communicate *before* it looks at the screen. However human performance may be more dependent on the content of the display. For example, in the case of MS-Word file manipulation, it is likely that novices decide to specify that the task involves a file operation *after* they have seen the word "File" on the menu-bar. Our model does not, in its present form, account for this use of the display to choose which feature to communicate. But the current mechanism is consistent with the use of interatction to resolve such higher level decisions. Our initial investiagations imply that the use of the display could be integrated into the model by replacing the advice problem space by a problem space that examines the display for clues as to what to do. This would decrease the reliance of the model on external advice and increase its responsiveness to the display.

We have illustrated a model of the acquisition of task-action mappings that is able to take advantage of two sources of implicit support provided by the interface: (a) consistency, in the sense captured by task-action mapping rules, means that a rule learned from one example applies to all "similar" examples, where similarity is defined by the semantic features of the tasks, and (b) interactivity, that is aspects of the interface design which serve to constrain the variety of choices available to the user. We have shown how the PUM can expose aspects of consistency and interactivity, thereby helping the designer to assess the learnability of the device.

ACKNOWLEDGMENT

This work was supported by the UK Joint Research Council Initiative in Cognitive Science and HCI.

REFERENCES

1. Draper, S.W. (1986) Display managers as the basis for user machine communication. In D.A. Norman & S.W. Draper, (Eds.) *User Centred System Design.* Hillsdale, NJ: Lawrence Erlbaum.

2. Duff, S.C. (1989) Reduction of action uncertainty in process control systems: The role of device knowledge. In Megaw, E. (ed) *Contemporary Ergonomics*, 213-219. Taylor & Frances.

3. Howes, A. (1991) A performance model of the acquisition of task-action mapping knowledge. Manuscript in Preparation.

4. Howes, A. & Payne, S.J. (1990a) Display-based competence: Towards user models for menu-driven interfaces. *International Journal of Man-Machine Studies, 33* (6), 637-655.

5. Howes, A. & Payne, S.J. (1990b) Semantic analysis during exploratory learning. In J.C. Chew & J. Whiteside (Eds.) *Empowering People - CHI'90 Conference Proceedings: Human Factors in Computing Systems* (Special Issue of the SIGCHI ulletin). Seattle, Washington: ACM Press, 399-406, 1990.

6. Laird, J.E., Rosenbloom, P.S., Newell, A. (1987) SOAR: An architecture for general intelligence. *Artificial Intelligence 33*, 1-64.

7. Lewis, C.H. (1988) Why and how to learn why: Analysis-based generalization of procedures. *Cognitive Science ,12,* 211-256.

8. Mayes, J.T., Draper, S.W., McGregor, M.A. & Oatley, K. (1988) Information flow in a user interface: the effect of experience and context on the recall of MacWrite screens. In D.M. Jones & R. Winder *People and Computers IV.* Cambridge University Press.

9. Norman, D.A. (1988) *The Psychology of Everyday Things.* Basic Books. New York.

10. Payne, S.J. (1985) *Task-action grammars. The mental representation of task languages in human-computer interaction.* Unpublished doctoral dissertation, University of Sheffield.

11. Payne, S.J. (1991) Display-based action at the user interface. *International Journal of Man Machine Studies, 35*, 275-289.

12. Payne, S.J. & Green, T.R.G. (1986) Task-action grammars: A model of the mental representation of task languages. *Human-Computer Interaction, 2,* 93-133.

13. Schiele, F & Green, T.R.G. (1990) HCI formalisms and cognitive psychology: the case of task-action grammar. In Harrison and Thimbleby (Eds.) *Formal methods in HCI.* Cambridge University Press.

14. Young, R.M., Green, T.R.G. & Simon, T. (1989) Programmable user models for predictive evaluation of interface designs. In K.Bice & C.Lewis (Eds.) *Proceedings of CHI'89 Human Factors in Computing Systems,* 15-19. New York: ACM Press.

CHAPTER 62

Towards Real-Time GOMS

B. E. John[1], A. H. Vera[2], and A. Newell, Carnegie Mellon University

Abstract

We present an analysis of an expert performing a highly interactive computer task. The analysis uses GOMS models, specifying the ***G***oals, ***O***perators, ***M***ethods, and ***S***election rules used by the expert; the GOMS models are implemented within an unified theory of cognition called Soar. Two models are presented, one with *function-level* operators which perform high-level functions in the domain, and one with *keystroke-level* operators which describe hand movements. For a segment of behavior in which the expert accomplished about 30 functions in about 30 seconds, the function-level model predicted the observed behavior well, while the keystroke-level model predicted only about half of the observed hand movements. These results, including the discrepancy between the models, are discussed.

This research was supported by the Office of Naval Research, Cognitive Science Program, Contract Number N00014-89-J-1975N158. The views and conclusions contained in this document are those of the authors and should not be interpreted as representing the official policies, either expressed or implied, of the Office of Naval Research or the U. S. Government.

[1]School of Computer Science and Department of Psychology
[2]Department of Psychology

MOTIVATION

This research was done in preparation for a panel at the Human Factors Society (HFS) Meeting in Orlando, Oct. 5-12, 1990, organized by Wayne Gray and Mike Atwood of the Intelligent Interfaces Group at the NYNEX Science and Technology Center. The purpose of the panel was to demonstrate GOMS analyses to the human factors (HF) community in an exciting manner so that HF practitioners would be motivated to learn more about GOMS and use it in their work.

Three applied psychology researchers (Judy Olson of the University of Michigan, Jay Elkerton, of Philips Laboratories, and Bonnie John of Carnegie Mellon University) agreed to analyze a task selected by Wayne Gray. Gray selected a human-computer interaction domain, made a videotape of an expert interacting in that domain, and gave the videotape and an associated transcription to each researcher (Appendix I). In the interest of enticing HFS conference participants to the panel, and stretching the GOMS methodology to include real-time, interactive domains, Gray selected a domain hitherto unanalyzed with GOMS: video game play (in particular, Nintendo's Super Mario Bros. 3[1] adventure game). The four panelists (the three previously named researchers and Wayne Gray, himself) each did a GOMS analysis of the interaction independently, and presented the results to each other, and to the HFS audience, for the first time during the panel session. Because of limited presentation time, the panelists restricted their analyses to the first 27 seconds of the expert's interaction (a natural break in the play, where the expert flies the game's main character, Mario, off the screen and to a different part of the game's world). The panel continued with a discussion of the similarities, differences, and uses of the analyses. Informal comments to the panelists indicate that the attendees were indeed excited by the presentations and were motivated to learn more about GOMS, with the hope of using it in their work.

Our own research interests lie in the creation of *engineering models* of computer users that allow quantitative prediction of hard measures (performance time, learning time, the commission, detection , and repair of errors, etc.) in the specification stage of system design (see Newell & Card, 1985, 1986; John, 1988 for detailed discussions of this position). We are currently extending GOMS to highly interactive task domains. By highly interactive tasks, we mean tasks in which a user perceives a display, comprehends and responds to that display on the order of once every second, for several seconds at a time. We call this rapid interaction the *immediate interaction cycle*. Tasks displaying the immediate interaction cycle are common in human-computer interaction (HCI): searching for information with computer browsers, constructing a new diagram with an interactive graphics package, playing "what-if" with a spreadsheet, creating a schedule with PERT charts, exploring mathematical relationships with graphical statistics programs, creating real-time, multi-media presentations. The list seems endless. Video games are extreme examples of such tasks. The interaction in many video games seems almost manically driven by the game rather than by the player. Goals seem to be interrupted, suspended and returned to. Yet, similar to other domains successfully modelled by GOMS, an expert's behavior looks to be highly knowledge intensive and eventually seems to become routine. We welcomed the opportunity to stretch our analysis techniques to the challenge of Super Mario Bros. 3.

---

[1] Super Mario Bros. 3, Nintendo, and the games and characters discussed in this paper are trademarks of, and under copyright to, Nintendo of America, Inc.

This technical report provides documentation of the analyses presented by Bonnie John at that HFS panel. The content of the analyses remains essentially the same. At the time of the presentation, many assumptions and decisions made were made from intuitions born of intimate knowledge of GOMS analyses. Here, we present the logic underlying those initial intuitions. We hope this report will further encourage the panel's attendees, and others in the fields of applied psychology and cognitive modeling, to learn more about the GOMS methodology, and the extensions to it made with the Soar unified theory of cognition described herein.

GOMS MODELS

GOMS is a formalism for representing routine cognitive skill. The original concept appeared in *The Psychology of Human-Computer Interaction*, by Card, Moran, and Newell (1983, and also in an earlier article, Card, Moran, & Newell, 1980) as a model of the performance of computer users. GOMS stands for *G*oals, *O*perators, *M*ethods, and *S*election rules. A *goal* is a symbolic structure that defines a state to be achieved, and determines a set of methods by which it may be accomplished. *Operators* are elementary perceptual, cognitive, or motor acts, whose execution is necessary to change any aspect of the user's mental state or to affect the task environment. An operator is defined by a specific effect (output) and by a specific duration. An operator may take inputs, and its outputs and duration may be a function of its inputs. The selection of operators for any specific GOMS model defines its grain of analysis.[2] *Methods* are procedures for accomplishing a goal. A method is a sequence of goals and operators, with conditional tests on the contents of the user's immediate memory and on the state of the task environment. In routine cognitive tasks, methods are assured of success (up to the possibility of having been mis-selected, errors in implementation, and the reliability of the equipment). By contrast, in problem-solving tasks, methods may or may not lead to success depending on the user's lack of knowledge or understanding of the task environment. Also, GOMS methods are procedures that the user already has at performance time, as opposed to plans created during task performance. If more than one method can be used to accomplish a goal, a selection must be made. The essence of skilled behavior is that these selections are not problematic, that they proceed quickly and smoothly. Although the original description of GOMS acknowledges that extended (but still unproblematic) decision processes may be necessary in some situations, *selection rules*, which are if-then rules that recognize the method appropriate for the specific task situation, are a signature of routine cognitive skill and GOMS.

This original specification of GOMS had many limitations. Among them, GOMS predicted only error-free behavior with no mechanisms for predicting the occurrence of errors, neither frequency, type, nor when they might occur. There was no mechanism for learning. The goal-stack control structure was inadequate for handling interruptions. Operators in the original GOMS model were on the order of one half second, at their smallest grain of analysis, and many contained mixtures of perceptual, cognitive and motor acts. This confounding of processes dictated that operators be sequential, whereas many skilled tasks exhibit concurrent perceptual, cognitive, and motor acts.

Although not limited by the architecture of GOMS, the example tasks in the 1983 volume implicitly defined boundaries of GOMS analyses. These early tasks had a static visual

---

[2] Card et. al. (1983, Chapter 5) demonstrate GOMS models of text-editing at four levels of analysis, from the unit task level where each editing modification (e.g., delete a paragraph) is accomplished in a single EDIT-UNIT-TASK operator, down to the keystroke level where the operators were keystrokes and mouse-movements.

display for the inputting information to the user (e.g., marked-up manuscript for text editing, sketch of a circuit for VLSI layout). They allowed the user to work at her or his own pace; the user did not have to wait for critical information to appear, and critical information did not disappear. Subtasks were not thrust upon the user by a changing environment. Thus, these early studies did not demonstrate the appropriateness of the GOMS models for interactive tasks.

Since its introduction, GOMS analyses have been used to model many tasks in a diversity of domains and several extensions have been made to the original formulation (Olson & Olson, 1990). GOMS models have been demonstrated within a production system architecture to model performance and learning (Kieras & Polson, 1985; Polson & Kieras, 1985; Kieras & Bovair, 1986; Singley & Anderson, 1989). The operators have been brought down to the level of elementary perceptual, cognitive, and motor operations (Rosenbloom, 1983; John, Rosenbloom, & Newell, 1985). This allows perceptual, cognitive, and motor processes to be expressed as occurring in parallel when the task environment allows look-ahead or anticipation of operations (John & Newell, 1989). Errors attributed to working-memory limitations have been predicted (Lerch, Mantei, & Olson, 1989). Verbal input and output and tasks driven by the environment have extended the characteristics of GOMS tasks (John, 1990). Task domains modelled in GOMS now include graphic editors (Ziegler, Hoppe, & Fahnrich, 1986), spreadsheets (Olson & Nilsen, 1988), computer command abbreviations (John, et al., 1985; John & Newell, 1987) oscilloscopes (Lee, Polson, & Bailey, 1989), touch typing (John, 1988; John & Newell, 1989), and telephone operator call handling (John, 1990; Gray, John, Stuart, Lawrence, & Atwood, 1990).

GOMS, THE MODEL HUMAN PROCESSOR, AND SOAR

Since GOMS provides a formalism within which to describe and predict a range of user behaviors, it could be considered a closed model, sufficient in itself. In actuality, GOMS presupposes an underlying general theory of human cognition, for which it is the specialization and instantiation of that theory to specific task environments and types of humans. GOMS was initially presented exactly this way (Card, et. al., 1983). The underlying cognitive theory was the Model Human Processor (MHP). It comprised an architectural structure, composed of memories (long-term memory, working memory and sensory buffers) and processors (perceptual, cognitive and motor). The operation of this structure was not given in full detail (as in a computer architecture). Instead a series of operating principles were given, such as decreasing speed of the cognitive processor with uncertainty, and the use of problem spaces as an overall way of organizing performance. The MHP was meant to summarize, circa the early 1980's, what had been learned in cognitive science about the operation of basic information processing. The version of GOMS originally presented was entirely consistent with the MHP. In turn, the MHP was meant to do more than simply justify GOMS. It was to provide a basis for reasoning more generally about users interacting with computers. (Indeed, it made no pretense to be a general model of all human cognition, but was itself a specialization to the situations of interest to HCI.)

The MHP was far from a complete cognitive theory, even in the HCI domain to which it was specialized. The state of the art of cognitive science was simply not sufficient to provide such a theory. Nevertheless, the MHP has proved sufficient to conceptually support all of the extensions that have been made to GOMS. The MHP was cast in terms of productions and recognition-act cycles; this provided an alternative formalism to the procedural-language formalism of the original GOMS, permitting the extension to skill learning. The MHP defined enough internal memory structure for the cognitive processor to support the refinement of GOMS operators from the half second level down to the 50 msec level. This memory structure was also sufficient to support the extension of GOMS to account for some working memory errors. And, finally, the three-processor structure of the MHP (perceptual, cognitive and motor) was sufficient to extend GOMS to continuous interaction tasks, such as typing and talking-while-keying tasks, where the human operates in a pipelined, overlapped mode.

Although it is impressive that the MHP has been conceptually rich enough to support all these extensions, the MHP remains a highly sketchy theory. The memories are characterized only by a few descriptive parameters (such as half-life) and the principles of operation are not computationally described (for example, it is simply stated that the power law of practice is obeyed). It is not literally possible to derive GOMS (in any of its variants) from the MHP. Additional detail is always required, for example, the particular procedural language structure of the original GOMS. What remains true is that detailed GOMS systems are further specifications of the structure and principles of the MHP. Finally, unlike GOMS itself, which has been continuously tested and extended since it was initially introduced, no such activity of updating, exercising or refinement has occurred for the MHP. Thus, good reasons exist to adopt a better base for GOMS analyses than the MHP, if a suitable one can be found. There are some minimal conditions for any basic psychological theory to support GOMS, namely, that it support the particular control structure of goals, operators, methods and selections rules. Many cognitive architectures can do this, but certainly not all, e.g., Act* (Anderson, 1983) can, but in general connectionist architectures cannot (Rumelhart, et. al., 1986). Furthermore, the real leverage in a new base should be the ability to support further extensions of GOMS and its integration with the many other cognitive and perceptual processes that are relevant to interacting with computers.

Soar is a recent attempt to provide an architecture for human cognition (Laird, Newell & Rosenbloom, 1987; Newell,1990). It is generally consonant with the MHP, and hence supports the basic control mechanisms of GOMS. But, unlike the MHP, Soar is a completely specified architecture. That is, rather than being given as an abstract memory/process structure plus an set of abstract principles of operation, Soar is given in the fashion of a programmed computer, with data structures, memory accessing organization, and full details of the operation of the processors. Thus, one can specify the contents of Soar memory structures for particular users in particular task situations. These contents, in effect, program Soar so that it produces simulations of the behavior of the user in the task.

As succinctly described in (Lewis, et al., 1990) and in more detail elsewhere (Laird, et. al., 1987; Newell,1990), the Soar architecture formulates all tasks in *problem spaces*, in which *operators* are selectively applied to the *current state* to attain *desired states*. Problem solving proceeds in a sequence of *decision cycles* that select problem spaces, states and operators, resulting in the application of the operator to move to a new state in the space. Each decision cycle accumulates knowledge from a long-term *recognition memory* (realized as a production system). This memory continually matches against *working memory*, elaborating the current state and retrieving preferences that encode knowledge about the next step to take. Access of recognition memory is involuntary, parallel, and rapid (on the order of 10 msec). The decision cycle accesses recognition memory repeatedly until quiescence, when no more knowledge can be brought to bear; then the decision is made about which step to take next. Each decision cycle takes on the order of 100 msec.

If, at quiescence, the accumulated coded knowledge in working memory is insufficient (or conflicting), so that Soar's next step cannot be determined, then an *impasse* occurs. Soar responds to an impasse by creating a subgoal in which a new problem space can be used to acquire the needed knowledge (or resolve the conflict). If, similarly, lack of knowledge prevents progress in this new space, another impasse occurs and another subgoal is created -- and so on, leading to an entire goal-subgoal hierarchy. Once an impasse is resolved by problem solving, the *chunking* mechanism adds new productions to the recognition memory that encode the results of the problem solving. Thus, the impasse is avoided in the future, because these productions provide the appropriate knowledge immediately.

Soar interacts with the external environment through perceptual and motor processes, which operate through the working memory. Incoming perceptions are added to the current state in the top problem space and motor commands are made part of this current state. The interactions occur asynchronously with the operation of the cognitive decision cycle.

Soar basically subsumes the MHP and provides a much better basis on which to construct GOMS models. However, the situation is not perfect. It remains an open issue to show that some of the MHP operating principles expressing global psychological laws (such as Fitts' law and Hick's law) follow from the Soar architecture. (Some global laws, such as the power law of practice, have already been shown to be characteristic of the architecture.) Some of the ways in which Soar does not yet adequately subsume the MHP relate to the perceptual and motor processors, which remain underspecified aspects of the Soar architecture. These difficulties do not substantially affect taking GOMS models as specializations of the Soar architecture for appropriate users doing appropriate tasks. In fact, the basic GOMS model refined for 50 msec operators has been derived from Soar (Newell, 1990, Chapter 5). This extends easily to longer duration GOMS operators, to the learning effects (in terms of Soar chunking), and to the three-processor GOMS models of continuous behavior, although all the details have not yet been fully worked out.

Soar is a better basis than the MHP on which to construct GOMS models for reasons that go beyond just reproducing the current GOMS, even if that can be done more elegantly. The most important is that Soar is complete enough and cognitively adequate enough so it is being used to model and explain many diverse cognitive phenomena (Lewis, et. al. 1990; Newell, 1990). Examples include natural language comprehension, problem solving, immediate reasoning, perceptual search, strategy discovery and change, and the taking of instructions. These tasks encompass the major dependent variables of interest in HCI -- time, errors, and learning rates. Thus GOMS automatically is subsumed within a theory which is being extended to many other areas of cognition relevant to HCI. These extensions, even when good psychology, do not always automatically extend GOMS in ways that preserve its property of permitting engineering calculations and making parameter-free predictions. But they provide excellent starting points for such extensions. The second reason is the universal availability of simulations using Soar, so that even when analytic calculations cannot be made, it is possible to put all the various parts of a user model together and simulate what should happen (John, Newell & Card, 1990, is an example in the domain of user's behavior with a browsing system).

Thus, from now on in this paper we will work within the Soar architecture, taking it as the architectural foundation upon which to build GOMS models.

THE TASK

Nintendo's Super Mario Bros. 3 was chosen for the HFS panel by Wayne Gray because it is a highly interactive task domain, its popularity as a video game was likely to draw a large audience to the panel, and an expert, KP, was readily available and willing to participate.

Super Mario Bros. 3 is a typical adventure game with treasure to collect, enemies to avoid or kill, and super powers to acquire and use. The user manipulates the hero, Mario, through the world by pressing buttons on a hand-held controller (Figure 1). The game has eight different worlds to traverse, and each world has several levels, with the difficulty of play increasing with the world and level number.

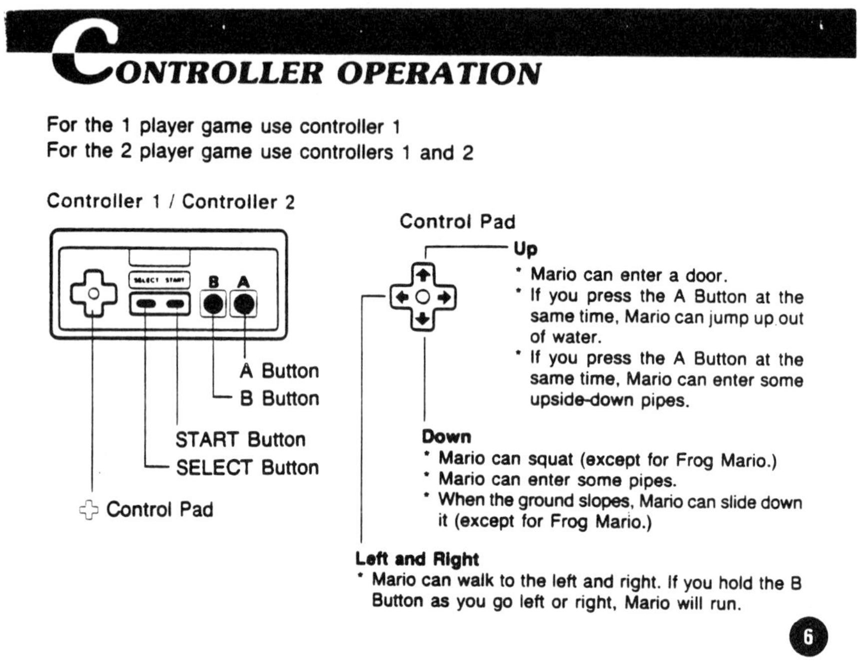

Figure 1. The hand-held controller for Super Mario Bros. 3. (from p. 6, *Super Mario Bros. 3. instruction booklet*, reprinted by permission of Nintendo of America, Inc.)

Several enemies populate these worlds, among them are *Goombas*, who can kill Mario by running into him but can be killed by Mario, *ParaGoombas* (flying Goombas with wings), *Venus Fire Traps*, invincible plants who live in pipes and throw deadly *fireballs*, and *Koopa Troopers (Koopas)*, turtle-like creatures who retreat into their shells, which can then be kicked or thrown by Mario to defeat other enemies or break open treasure blocks.

Treasures in these worlds include coins that allow Mario to buy additional lives, and mushrooms and leaves that give Mario super powers when he runs into them. Treasures can appear directly on the screen, or they can be hidden in blocks and only appear when the blocks are broken by Mario. Both killing enemies and collecting treasures give Mario points.

The display that appears to the user at the beginning of each game is shown in Figure 2. This display shows Mario, four question blocks, a type of block guaranteed to contain a treasure (QB.1 through QB.4), a Goomba (G.1), the level ground that Mario walks on (Ground1.1), and a scaffold he can climb on to reach treasures or avoid enemies (Scaff2.1).

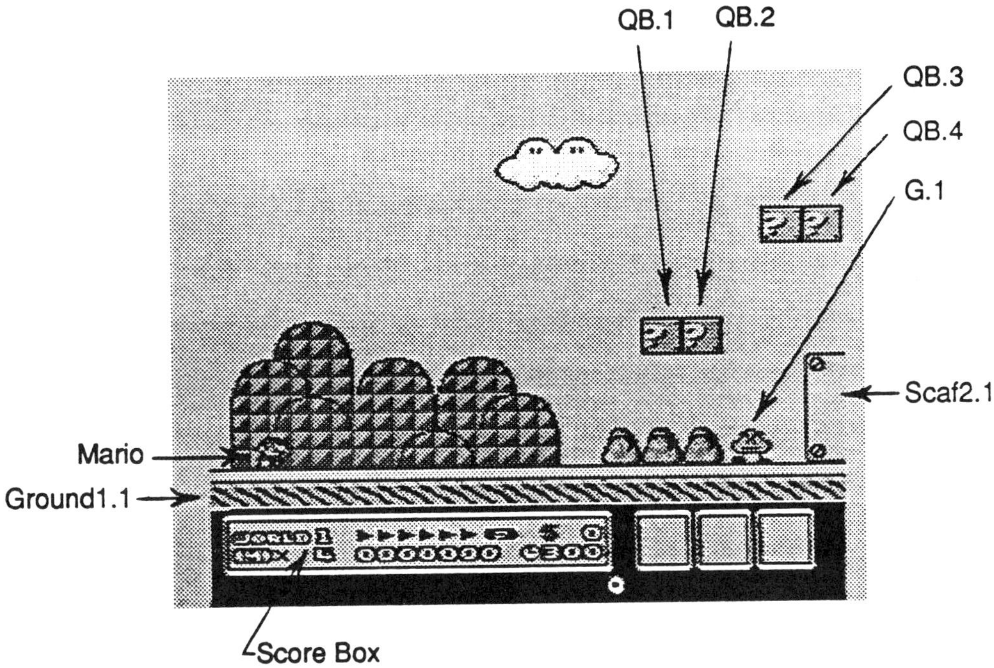

Figure 2. Start-up display for Super Mario Bros. 3 World 1 Level 1.

For simplicity sake (for both the Nintendo-naive panelists and the ease of generating data) Gray chose the task to be the lowest level of difficulty, World 1 Level 1. He asked the nine-year-old KP to traverse World 1 Level 1, collecting as many points as possible, thinking aloud as he played. Gray videotaped KP performing this task to provide observed behavior against which to measure the predictions of the GOMS analyses. The panelists were asked to analyze the first 27 seconds of play, in which time KP collected nine treasures, killed five enemies, avoided three dangers, added two super powers, and flew off the screen to another part of World 1 Level 1. The completion of World 1 Level 1 took KP and additional 43 seconds. Appendix I contains the transcription of KP's behavior for the analyzed segment.

TWO GOMS ANALYSES

GOMS suggests that the goals, operators, and methods can be defined from an objective analysis of the task. Optimal selection rules can often also be specified from a task analysis, but experience with human behavior indicates that selection rules in actual use are specific to an individual user and must be inferred from his or her behavior. We conducted the GOMS analyses with as little reference to the expert's behavior as possible, opting instead, for taking the knowledge explicit in the instruction booklet and reasoning about the task itself. We found that the goals, operators, and methods sufficient to play the game could be inferred from the instruction booklet and task analysis. Selection rules were determined through reference to the expert's behavior.

The analyses were carried out at two levels: the *function-level* where operators are at the level of gathering an item that gives points or killing an enemy, and the *keystroke-level*, where operators are at the level of individual finger movements on the game's control panel. Each level is considered a separate GOMS analysis, as in Chapter 5 of *The Psychology of Human-Computer Interaction* (Card, et. al. 1983) where nine models at four different levels were compared. We will present these analyses in parallel, first describing the goals, operators, methods and selection rules for each, then describing the process of applying this information to the task of playing Super Mario Bros. 3.

Goals, operators, methods, and selection rules of the task domain

The instruction booklet is the primary source of knowledge for this GOMS analysis. It provides the overall *goals* of the game: clear the level (in order to go on to the next level), increase your standing by accumulating points, coins, cards, and extra lives (these are the things measured in the score box at the bottom of the screen), and avoid death due to being touched by an enemy, falling into a hole or fire, or running out of time.

These goals can be accomplished by performing *function-level operators* (FLOs), also inferred from the instruction booklet. Figure 3 lists the goals of the game, the FLOs that act to fulfill those goals in the segment of behavior analyzed, and the passages in the instruction booklet from which the FLOs were inferred. In service of clearing the level, the FLOs are move-towards-end (in effect, moving to the right) and touch-goal, where the goal is a white box in the middle of a black screen at the end of the level (Mario must jump up to touch it). To increase standing, the FLOs are gather-item, search-in-block, and attack-enemy. Gather-item collects items on the screen that give points or money. Search-in-block hits blocks to see if something valuable comes out, which could then be gathered. Points can also be gotten with the attack-enemy FLO, although there is some risk involved; an attack could fail and the enemy could kill Mario, violating the goal to avoid death. To fulfill the goal to avoid death, the FLO is avoid-danger, where a danger can be an enemy, a hole in the ground (if Mario falls in, he dies), or fire. There is no FLO that prevents Mario from running out of time. However, a consideration of time is inherent in the selection among the other FLOs.

FLOs are realized through *keystroke-level operators* (KLOs).[3] The KLOs are the hand movements necessary to manipulate Mario, and involve hitting the six buttons on the controller (Figure 1). The four buttons in a cross configuration move Mario to the right, left, up, and down[4] and we call the KLOs press-right, press-left, press-up, and press-down, respectively. The A-button makes Mario jump, and when he has a tail, pressing the A-button repeatedly makes Mario fly. Holding the B-button down allows Mario to pick up things that lie next to him, and to accelerate when used in conjunction with the right- or left-buttons. Releasing the B-button causes Mario to drop whatever he is carrying.

These two levels of operators have a relationship described by Card, et al. (1983, Chapter 5) as being formed by *splitting operators*. That is, the FLOs are *split* into the hand

---

[3] I use the terms *goals*, *function-level operators* and *keystroke-level operators* to distinguish between three different levels in the typical GOMS goal hierarchy. This distinction is drawn to make the different levels easy to write about; it does not reflect a theoretical distinction between goals and operators. As Kieras (1988) observes for GOMS analyses in general, "this distinction is intuitively-based, and it is also relative; it depends on the level of analysis."

[4] Note that pressing the up button does not make Mario jump up, rather it allows him to move up in certain situations: to go up a pipe with its opening over his head (together with the A-button) or pop out of water (together with the A button) or to go through a door. None of these maneuvers are necessary in segment of behavior analyzed here. Likewise, the down button makes Mario squat, go down a pipe when he is standing on its opening, or to slide down a hill. Again, none of these maneuvers are used in this segment of behavior.

GOAL: FUNCTION-LEVEL OPERATOR	PARAMETERS	INSTRUCTION BOOKLET SOURCE	PAGE
Clear-level:		"...touch the goal to...clear the level"	19
Move-towards-end		"At the end of each action scene..."	19
Touch-goal		"...touch the goal to...clear the level"	19
Increase-standing:	no.of Marios remaining score,number of coins, cards taken	Score box at bottom of screen	16
Search-in-block	Question blocks, other blocks	"Hit blocks...A useful item might pop out!"	11
Gather-item	Coin, Starman, Super Leaf, 1-Up Mushroom, Super Mushroom, Fire Flower	"Gain more power by gathering items"	18
Attack-enemy		Points are given for attacking enemies	14
	Goomba	Attacks pictured	12,14
	Koopa	"After you have jumped on a Koopa..."	8
	Para-Goomba	"Once you jump on it..."	35
Avoid-death:	enemy, hole, fire, time-out	"BEWARE! THE FOLLOWING ARE DEADLY"	20
Avoid-danger	enemy, hole, fire	mentioned in deadly category	20

Figure 3. Goals and FLOs of the anlayzed segment of Super Mario Bros. 3 World 1 Level 1

movements necessary to accomplish them, defining the KLOs. KLOs are at a lower grain-size, and can be combined in different ways to accomplish many different FLOs. As in Card, et al., determining the sequence of operators at either of these levels constitutes a single GOMS analysis. Thus, determining both the sequence of FLOs and the sequence of KLOs is considered to be two GOMS analyses. However, since KLOs are simply split FLOs, the analysis process is to determine the appropriate FLO and then determine the KLOs that accomplish it; the analyses thus proceed in parallel.

The instruction booklet provides *methods*,[5] or sequences of KLOs, for accomplishing some FLOs (examples of methods from the instruction booklet are shown in Figure 4). Figure 5 lists the functional operators necessary to produce the observed behavior, the name of the methods provided by the instruction manual for accomplishing those FLOs, and the moves that make up the methods, and the KLOs that produce those moves. The exact KLOs making up a method depend on the relative position of Mario and the objects on the screen, so the keystrokes given are illustrative (e.g., a block may be to the right or left of Mario, so the KLO producing appropriate movement would be press-right-button or press-left-button, respectively).

---

[5] The instruction booklet uses the term *techniques* to describe what GOMS calls *methods*.

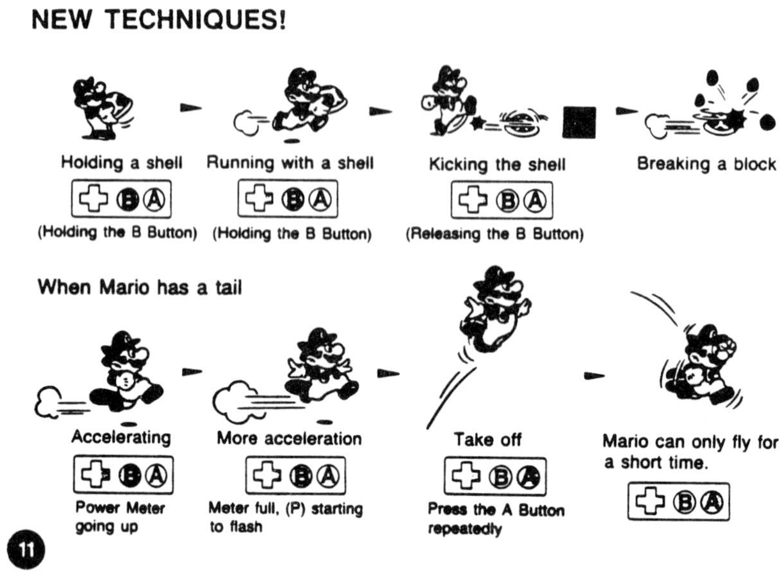

Figure 4. Methods suggested by the instruction booklet (from p. 11, *Super Mario Bros. 3. instruction booklet*, reprinted by permission of Nintendo of America, Inc.)

More than one method exists to accomplish each FLO used in the segment of the game studied (except for gather-item). We determined selection rules for these methods by analyzing two sources of information: the mechanics of the game itself (the necessary conditions for the methods to be applied), and the expert behavior observed in the videotape.

For the search-in-block FLO, the necessary conditions for the hit-from-bottom method are that the block be above Mario and that there be a clear path for him to jump up and hit it. For the hit-with-shell method, the necessary conditions are that there be a Koopa Trooper available to supply a shell and that there be a vantage point from which the shell can be thrown to hit the block. For the hit-with-tail method, Mario must possess a tail and the block must be vulnerable to tail-attack. In this segment of the game, none of the blocks are vulnerable to tail-attack, so this method is never observed. Because the hit-from-bottom-method has fewer steps it takes less time than the hit-with-shell methods; because it does not involve an enemy, it has less risk associated with it. Therefore, the selection rule we inferred is that, if the necessary conditions for the hit-from-bottom method exist, then the hit-from-bottom method will be selected. If not, then the hit-with-shell method will be selected. In this segment of behavior it is the case that if the necessary conditions for the hit-from-bottom method do not exist, the necessary conditions for the hit-with-shell method do exist, so this selection rule works. Reference to the expert's behavior did not contradict this inferred selection rule.

FLOs USED IN OBSERVED SEGMENT	POSSIBLE METHODS	CONDITIONS OF SELECTION RULES	MOVES IN METHOD	ILLUSTRATIVE KLOs TO ACCOMPLISH MOVES
search-in-block	hit from bottom	block is above Mario	move until under block	press-right-button
		path below block is clear	jump	press-A-button
	hit with shell	Koopa Trooper available	move to Kooppa	press-right-button
		vantage point available	immobilize Koopa	press-A-button
			pick up shell	hold-B-button
			move to block	press-right-button
			throw shell at block	release-B-button
	hit with tail	Mario has a tail	move to block	press-right-button
		block breakable via tail	hit block with tail	press-B-button
gather-item	move into		move to item	press-right-button
attack-enemy	stomp on	always applicable	move to enemy	press-right-button
		always selected	jump on enemy	press-A-button
	tail attack	Mario has a tail	move to enemy	press-right-button
		(not used by this expert)	hit with tail	press-B-button
avoid-danger	get out of way	a clear escape route exists	move away	press-right-button
		does not impede progress toward end of level		
	jump over	clear area above Mario's head	jump over	press-right-button
				press-A-button
		clear spot to jump to		
		"get out of way" impedes progress toward end		
	fly over	Mario has a tail	walk back	press-left-button
		clear runway	turn around	press-right-button
		clear take off airspace	accelerate	press-right-button
		only when there		hold-B-button
		are no other options	take-off and fly	release-B-button
				press-A-button (repeatedly)
move-toward-end	walk	always selected	walk to the right	press-right-button
	run	not used	run to the right	press-right-button
				hold-B-button

Figure 5 - FLOs, methods, selection rules, and illustrative KLOs for the analyzed segment of the experts behavior.

For the attack-enemy FLO, the necessary condition for the tail-attack method is that Mario have a tail. When Mario does not have a tail, then there is no selection rule because only the stomp-on method is applicable, and this is the situation for the first enemy attacked. When Mario has a tail, the selection rule may be determined by analyzing the rewards and penalties associated with each method. For instance, the stomp-on method seems to require more precise timing of action and has more risk of dying for a novice than the tail attack. It is assumed that an expert can execute whichever maneuver he or she intends, so the risk component probably does not enter into the determination of the expert's selection rule. In the case of killing a ParaGoomba, a tail attack gets only 100 points whereas the two successive jumps required to kill the enemy using the stomp-on method get 100 and 200 points respectively, giving 200 more points than the tail-attack method. This must be traded-off against the extra time it takes to kill a ParaGoomba with two jumps, about 800 msec. For World-1 Level-1, the average rate of point collection is 150 points per second, so the extra 800 msec to kill the ParaGoomba by jumping is well worth the 200 extra points that method produces. Therefore, the selection rule for attack-enemy, when the enemy is a ParaGoomba is to use the stomp-on method exclusively. In the case of killing a Goomba, the selection rule is not so clear; the tail-attack and stomp-on method seem to have the same risk (small) and the same reward (100 points). However, the tail-attack method is described in the instruction manual as being a new technique for Super Mario Bros. 3. Since our expert was an expert in Super Mario Bros. 1 and 2 before this game, it is reasonable to assume a bias towards familiar methods, again giving a selection rule that uses stomp-on exclusively.[6] These selection rules were not contradicted by the expert's behavior in this segment.

For the avoid-danger FLO, the necessary condition for the get-out-of-the-way method is that there be a direction of escape, right, left, up or down. The necessary condition for the jump-over method is that there be clear space over Mario's head so he can jump. The necessary conditions for the fly-over method are that Mario has a tail, there is a clear run-way to get up to speed and nothing overhead to block the take-off. The fly-over method takes so many more KLOs (to back up, accelerate and flap), that it should only be selected when there are no other options; this situation does not occur in the observed segment. The jump-over method takes one more KLO than the get-out-of-way method. However, if the get-out-of-way method is always taken when a danger is present, it may prevent forward progress in the game. For example, a pipe with a plant in it throwing fireballs at Mario may be to the right of Mario. The get-out-of-way method may send Mario running to the left until he is out of range of the fireballs. However, Mario would never progress beyond the fire-throwing plant with this selection rule in force, violating the clear-level goal and making Mario run out of time, thereby violating its own avoid-death goal. Therefore, the selection rule we infer is if the get-out-of-way method does not impede forward progress toward the end of the level, then use it, otherwise use the jump-over method for avoiding danger. The expert's behavior does not contradict this selection rule.

For the move-towards-end FLO, the methods are walk and run. The videotape did not to show clearly when the B-button was held down and when it was not. Also, the movement of Mario on the screen does not necessarily distinguish between these two methods without deeper knowledge of the mechanics of Mario's world (i.e. momentum). Therefore, we will not distinguish between these methods in our analyses, and just assume that move-towards-end is implemented by a press-right-button KLO.

---

[6] In the case of immobilizing a Koopa Trooper, the tail-attack method knocks the Koopa of the screen, so its shell is not available for use. Thus the attack of a Koopa Trooper embedded in the hit-with-shell method of the search-in-block FLO never uses the tail-attack method. This is one of the reasons why the attack of the Koopa Trooper embedded in the search-in-block FLO is not treated as a attack-enemy FLO.

The GOMS analysis process

Given these goals, FLOs, KLOs, methods and selection rules, analyzing the game involves perceiving the elements on the display and selecting the appropriate operators. First, a FLO is selected, then it is implemented by a series of KLOs, as described in Figure 6. The particular sequence of KLOs depend on the method used to implement the FLO and the relative position of Mario and the elements on the screen. The selection rules used to choose the appropriate method were described in the previous section and also appear in Figure 6. In the segment of behavior analyzed, these selection rules always result in a unique method, so there is no conflict resolution necessary for method selection. Therefore, at this stage in the analysis, we can uniquely determine the sequence of KLOs necessary to accomplish each FLO. This process of selecting FLOs constitutes the function-level GOMS analysis; that of selecting KLOs constitutes the keystroke-level GOMS analysis.

search-in-block(x)
is acceptable when block(x) is on the screen;
has preference over any other operator (best);
if there is no selected search-in-block(x) operator whose application is incomplete,
  and block(x) is closer to Mario than block(y),
  then search-in-block(x) is better than search-in-block(y).

gather-item(x):
is acceptable when item(x) is on the screen;
has preference over any other operator (best);
if there is no selected gather-item(x) operator whose application is incomplete,
  and item(x) is closer to Mario than item(y),
  then gather-item(x) is better than gather-item(y);
if item(x) is moving and item(y) is not moving,
  then gather-item(x) is better than gather-item(y);
if item(x) is moving and block(x) is on the screen,
  then gather-item(x) is better than search-in-block(x).

attack-enemy(x):
is acceptable when enemy(x) is on the screen and enemy(x) is killable;
if enemy(x) is an immediate threat,
  then attack-enemy(x) is better than search-in-block, gather item, avoid-danger, or move-towards-end;
if enemy(x) is not an immediate threat,
  then attack-enemy(x) is worse than move-towards-end.

avoid-danger(x):
is acceptable when danger(x) is on the screen and danger(x) is invincible;
if danger(x) is an immediate threat,
  then avoid-danger(x) is better than search-in-block, gather-item, attack-enemy, or move-towards-end;
if danger(x) is not an immediate threat,
  then avoid-danger(x) is worse than move-towards-end.

move-towards-end:
is always acceptable;
every other operator has preference over move-towards-end (worst).

Figure 6. Preferences for the proposal and selection of FLOs.

These analyses use a hand-simulation of what would happen if the GOMS models could interface directly with the game. That is, the analyst looks at the display, notes the elements visible, and uses the information in the preceding section to select an FLO and appropriate KLOs. Then the analyst presses the button corresponding to the next KLO to be performed. The button is only pressed until it has accomplished its function or until a display change occurs that creates the opportunity for a new FLO to be selected. For example, the hit-from-bottom method for the search-in-block FLO requires the analyst to move Mario horizontally until he is under the block to be searched. If the block is to the right of Mario, the analyst presses the A button until either Mario is under the block or another element appears on the display. This would be counted as one press-right-button KLO in the analysis. If no additional elements appear on the display before Mario reaches the block, the analyst releases the right-button (stopping Mario) then presses the A-button momentarily to make him jump straight up to break the block and land back below the block. The new display (now without the block just searched) is then analyzed to determine the next FLO and KLO, and the analysis cycle repeats.

In a Soar/GOMS model each FLO is *proposed* when certain elements are visible on the display. Each FLO has a set of *preferences* associated with it; proposing an operator is equivalent to making the preference for that operator *acceptable*. Other preferences may serve to resolve conflicts between competing FLOs. The conditions for proposal and the associated preferences are an integral part of the GOMS analyses, and, in this analysis, have been determined through a series of common-sense judgments about the task, described below.

Rules for proposing FLOs and preferences between competing operators are shown in Figure 6; a detailed explanation of the meaning of the preferences for the search-in-block FLO follows to help interpret that figure.

The search-in-block FLO is proposed (has an *acceptable* preference) any time there is an unexplored block on the display. In general, a search-in-block FLO is the best thing to do because it will often result in finding valuable items which give super powers, points, or money; this is stated in the instruction booklet, "Hit blocks...A useful item might pop out!". Thus, search-in-block is always given a *best* preference.[7] More than one unexplored block may be on the display at one time, so several search-in-block FLOs may be proposed, each evoked by one of the unexplored blocks, and each with a best preference. To resolve the conflict that arises from the existence of several best operators, other preferences are added to the operators, again based on task analysis, as follows.

The overall goal of attaining the most points possible dictates that the player be efficient in his or her actions, not only because running out of time kills Mario, but because any remaining time is converted into points at the end of the level. Thus, the block closest to Mario should be searched first. This is produced by making the search-in-block FLO for the closest block *better* than any of the other proposed search-in-block FLOs (L4 & L5 in Figure 6).

Occasionally, in the course of implementing a search-in-block FLO, Mario must move closer to an unexplored block (call it B) other than the current target (A). As they stand in the preceding paragraph, the preferences for search-in-block FLOs would change so that

---

[7] A *best* preference means that this operator is best if there are no other preferences that supersede best. However, other preferences can be in place that would make another operator *better* than the operator that is best, or *reject* the best operator, or create a tie with other best operators. For more details on the semantics of Soar preferences, see Soar 5 Manual.

search-in-block(B) would be better than search-in-block(A) as soon as Mario moves closer to block-B. This might be a reasonable strategy in many cases, exploring the closest block and going back to missed blocks later. However, it is easy to imagine arrangements of blocks that would cause the player to skip blocks and never get back to them because the presence of other blocks would continue to direct the preferences away from the skipped blocks. Thus, to get as many points as possible, the preferences must be adapted to prevent such target-switching when searching blocks. So the closer block can be better only when there is no existing search-in-block FLO that has not yet been accomplished (L3 in Figure 6). Reasoning similar to that presented here for the search-in-block FLO is used to construct the complete list of preferences shown in Figure 6.

To illustrate the course of an analysis, refer to Figure 2, the first display of the game, and Figure 7, a chart describing the performance of the model. (Complete charts for the analyzed segment appear in Appendix II.) In the display, Mario is on the extreme left, on the ground. There are four unexplored question blocks visible (QB.1 through QB.4) and an enemy (called a Goomba and labeled G.1). QB.1 and QB.2 are within reach of a jump, whereas QB.3 and QB.4 are too high and Mario must jump onto the scaffold below QB.4 to be able to reach them. This information is appears in Figure 7, in the boxes labelled OBJECTS SEEN and POSITION.

Each QB and the Goomba cause an FLO to be proposed, according to the preferences in Figure 6, and recorded in Figure 7's box PROPOSED FLO. The position of the QBs and Goomba cause preferences to be installed, shown in Figure 7's PREFERENCES box. In this case, search-in-block(QB.1) has a best preference and is better than search-in-block(QB.2), search-in-block(QB.3), and search-in-block(QB.4) because it is closest to Mario. Since the Goomba is on the far right of the screen, it is not an immediate threat to Mario and the preferences make attack-enemy(G.1) worse than the default FLO, move-towards-end (always acceptable, but worst). Given the semantics of Soar preferences, search-for-block(QB.1) is selected as the FLO to implement; this appears in the FLO SELECTED box.

The selected FLO is then implemented with a method comprised of several KLOs. The appropriate method is determined with the selection rules of Figure 5 and appears in the METHOD box in Figure 7. The moves that Mario has to make to accomplish that method are listed in the NECESSARY MOVES box. These moves are achieved by specific KLOs listed in the KLO box. As previously described, these KLOs are performed by hand by the analyst to determine their effects on the game's display.

Since this game is highly interactive, the situation may change before all the KLOs necessary to implement a specific FLO can be performed. This happens at the very beginning of the game; as the player presses the right-button to move Mario under QB.1, the Goomba runs to the left and becomes an immediate threat before Mario reaches QB.1. When the Goomba becomes an immediate threat, the preferences for FLOs change and must be reassessed. Thus, the press-right-button KLO is performed, but the press-A-button KLO (which would make Mario jump into the QB) is not performed before the situation changes sufficiently to interrupt the implementation of search-in-block(QB.1). Figure 7 records this information in the KLO PERFORMED box and indicates which KLO triggers the next display that causes a change in preferences to occur.

Appendix II contains charts like the one in Figure 7 that follow from the FLOs, methods, selection rules, preferences, and KLOs described above. To create those charts, we started with the initial display of the game, and moved Mario one KLO at a time until the elements on the screen changed sufficiently to require reassessment of preferences. That is, at the initial display, we pressed the right-button until either Mario was under QB.1 (where the

Display. 0 (Start-up screen) Mario starts at far left and Goomba is at far right moving left.
Mario is trying to get the first question block.

State of Mario: Small Mario

Selection of F.L.O

OBJECTS SEEN	POSITION	EVOKES	PROPOSED F.L.O.	PREFERENCES	F.L.O. SELECTED
Mario	far left, facing right				
Ground1.1	all				
QB.1	center, within reach	→	search-in-block(QB.1)	best	search-in-block(QB.1)
				better than search-in-block(QB.2)	
				better than search-in-block(QB.3)	
				better than search-in-block(QB.4)	
QB.2	just right of QB.1, within reach	→	search-in-block(QB.2)	best	
QB.3	right of QB.2 too high	→	search-in-block(QB.3)	best	
QB.4	just right of QB.3, too high	→	search-in-block(QB.4)	best	
G.1	far right (moving left)	→	attack-enemy(G.1)	worse than move-toward-end	
Scaf2.1	under QB.4				
			move-toward-end	worst	

Application of Selected F.L.O.

METHOD	NECESSARY MOVES	ACHIEVED BY	K.L.O.	K.L.O. PERFORMED	
hit-from-bottom	move-horizontal (until under)	→	press-right-button	performed	<--- Triggers Next Display
	jump	→	press-A-button	not performed	

Figure 7. Example of the charts in Appendix II explaining the predictions of the models

method for implementing search-in-block(QB.1) would require a press-A-button KLO) or something else happened to change the preferences. In this case, the Goomba became an immediate threat before Mario was under QB.1, so another chart was created (Display.1 in Appendix II).

To see the sequence of FLOs predicted by the model, read the entry in each chart's FLO SELECTED box. To see the sequence of KLOs predicted by the model, read the entries in each chart's KLO box that are marked *performed* in the KLO PERFORMED box.

RESULTS OF GOMS ANALYSIS

We compared the model's predictions to the observed performance of the expert, KP, using the charts in Appendix II and the transcription of KP's performance in Appendix I. KP's verbal protocol lagged his performance and in some cases later in the game he had to stop speaking altogether to continue to play the game. We believe this indicates that the verbal report of his goals was treated as a secondary task, dropping out when the primary task of playing the game was too difficult, and may not be complete. Therefore, our comparison uses only what KP makes Mario *do* rather than what KP *says* he is making Mario do.

Appendix III contains charts that record the comparison; an example for the first screen display appears in Figure 8. At the top of the chart, Display.x corresponds to the Display.x in the model charts (Appendix II).[8]

In the comparison charts, the top row of boxes, OBJECTS SEEN and POSITION, contains the information about what is on the screen at this point in the videotaped game and correspond closely to the same boxes in model charts. The correspondence between expert and model is not exact, because the model and the expert may not be in exactly the same position at every display change. The second row of boxes list the OBSERVED BEHAVIOR, the INFERED FUNCTION of that behavior, and INFERED FINGER ACTION. The inferred function is *ambiguous* if more than one function could be served by that behavior (e.g. moving to the right could move Mario towards the end of the level, or it could bring him under a block so he can search it), and listed as a particular function if only one function is obviously served (e.g. jumping into a QB unambiguously serves to search that QB). The finger action was inferred from the behavior because it was not directly observable from the videotape, but most movements of Mario can only be produced by specific button presses, so the inference is uncontroversial. The third row of boxes lists the FLOs that would be consistent with the observed behavior, the specific FLO predicted by the model, and the KLO that is predicted by the model. The FLO predicted by the model can be compared directly to the inferred function of the observed behavior in the box above it. The KLOs can be compared directly to the inferred finger actions in the box above it.

Figures 9 and 10 graphically present the comparisons between the observed expert behavior and the model's predictions. Figure 9 shows the comparison at the function-level and Figure 10 shows the comparison at the keystroke-level. In both figures, the operator names are listed along the vertical axis. The horizontal axis is labelled with the display number

---

[8] There are more charts for the model predictions than for the expert comparisons because the expert moves in a fluid, continuous motion while the model simulates Mario walking one step at a time, stopping before and after jumps. Some of the display changes occur only when Mario is moved beyond a specific place in the world. The model's incremental movement produces some displays where the next elements has not yet appeared and the only applicable FLO is move-toward-end. In contrast, the expert's fluid movement moves Mario beyond the triggering point in service of the previous function, so the displays where nothing new presents itself never occur.

Display. 0 (Start-up screen)

Mario starts at far left.
Goomba is at far right moving left.
Mario is trying to get the first question block.

State of Mario: Small Mario

On Screen

OBJECTS SEEN	POSITION
Mario	far left, facing right
Ground1.1	all
QB.1	center, within reach
QB.2	just right of QB.1, within reach
QB.3	right of QB.2 too high
QB.4	just right of QB.3, too high
G.1	far right (moving left)
Scaf2.1	under QB.4

Expert's Behavior

OBSERVED BEHAVIOR	INFERRED FUNCTION	INFERRED FINGER ACTION
Mario moves right	ambiguous	press-right-button

Comparison to Model

F.L.O. CONSISTENT WITH OBSERVED BEHAVIOR	F.L.O. PREDICTED BY MODEL	K.L.O. PREDICTED BY MODEL
search-in-block(QB.1)	search-in-block(QB.1)	press-right-button
search-in-block(QB.2)		
search-in-block(QB.3)		
search-in-block(QB.4)		
attack-enemy(G.1)		
move-to-end		

Figure 8. Example of the charts in Appendix III comparing the expert's observed behavior with the predictions of the models.

corresponding to the Display.x label on each of the model charts in Appendix II. This designation corresponds roughly to time, where each display represents about a second's worth of activity.

In Figure 9, for each display, a black dot marks the inferred function of the observed behavior (from the INFERED FUNCTION box of Figure 8). If no unique function can be inferred from the observed behavior, no black dot appears in that display column. A gray dot marks the FLO predicted by the model (from Figures 7 & 8). Thin black circles indicate the FLOs consistent with the observed behavior (from Figure 8). To highlight the predicted sequence of FLOs, the predicted FLOs (gray dots) are joined by gray lines; to highlight the

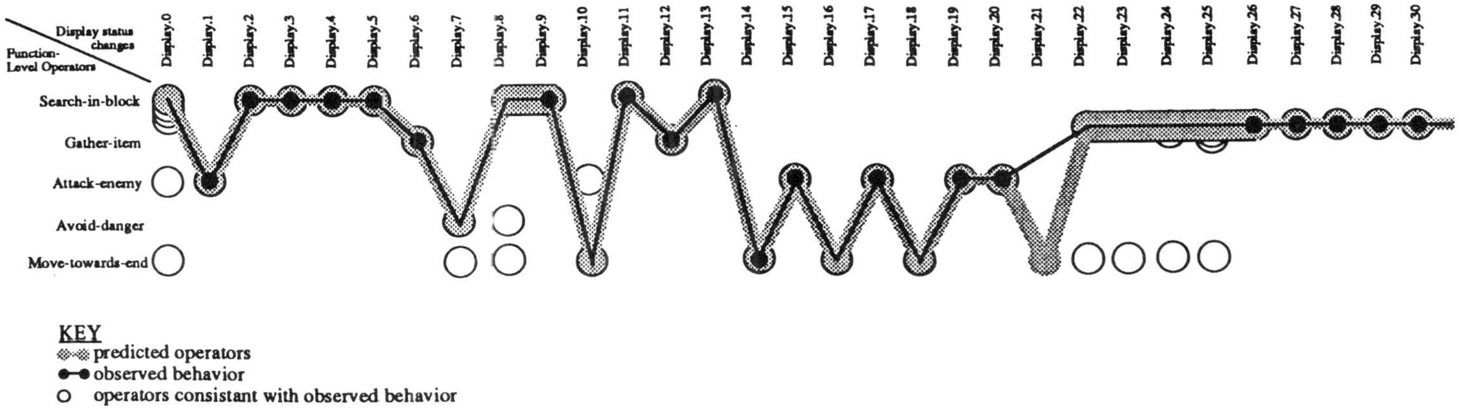

Figure 9. Comparison of the function-level model predictions with the observed behavior.

Black dots indicate functions inferred from the observed behavior. For instance, when Mario hits a block, we inferred that the intended function was to search in that block. Gray dots indicted the predicted FLOs. When an FLO is predicted but a corresonding function cannot be unambiguously inferred from the observed behavior, a gray dot appears, but no black dot is drawn in the same Display column. In that case, all the FLOs consistant with the observed behavior are indicated with thin black circles. Gray lines connect the predicted FLOs and black lines connect the inferred functions. When no function can be unambiguously inferred, the black line passes through the predicted FLO if that FLO is consistant with the behavior, and does not pass through the predicted FLO if that FLO is contradictory to the observed behavior. Elongated gray circles represent consecutive displays in which the same FLO, with the same argument, is selected. Elongated black circle indicate that the behavior observed throughout those displays is inferred to be in the service of the same function.

the redundant FLOs making it look like one elongated circle of an FLO (Displays.8 & .9, and Displays.23 to .27). When a function cannot be inferred from the observed behavior and no black dot appears in the display column, the black line is passed through the gray dot if the observed behavior is consistent with the predicted FLO; if they are inconsistent, the black line does not pass through the gray dot in that display column, but goes straight to the next inferred function.

The sense of this graphic display is that when the black and gray lines track each other, the model is making good predictions of observed behavior. Where the black and gray lines do not track, the model is not predicting the observed behavior. Where there is a haze of thin black circles above and below the black dots, the behavior is consistent with many possible functions and it is likely that any model prediction will track behavior; where black circles are few, the observed behavior is consistent with only a few functions and the model must be accurate to track behavior.

Figure 10 uses the same graphic conventions as Figure 9, but for the keystroke-level behavior and predictions. Each horizontal unit, delineated by dotted lines, corresponds to the FLO implemented by the KLOs shown in that unit and also to the display that caused the selection of that FLO. Therefore, each horizontal unit is labelled at the top with its corresponding Display.x and at the bottom with its associated FLO.

DISCUSSION OF THE GOMS ANALYSIS

Some caveats

Before discussing the implications of this analysis, three strong cautions must be presented. First, this analysis explores a short segment of behavior. Although a qualitative look at an additional segment twice as long as the current analysis, representing traversal of the rest of World 1 Level 1, indicates that much of that behavior is also predictable, the detailed analyses and comparisons must be done before any conclusions can be drawn with confidence.

Second, World 1 Level 1 is the simplest level in the game. Although it is not evident in the expert videotape, if Mario stops moving, nothing will happen most of the time at this level of play. Thus, the interaction is primarily user-driven, not system-driven. This feature is not common in many other types of video games and it does not even persist in Super Mario Bros. 3, as the higher worlds have many more enemies actively seeking to kill Mario.

Last, in this part of World 1 Level 1 the objective of the next cycle is almost always visible in the display. Although a FLO that searches through the world for blocks to break or items to gather can be deduced from the instruction booklet, it was not invoked in this segment of behavior because the next block to break, item to gather, or enemy to attack, was visible in 26 of the 31 displays. Other games, and other levels even within this game, are not as perceptually driven. Without constant triggering of operators by the elements in the display, the behavior would take on a more searching aspect (in the case of no knowledge), or a more planful aspect (in the case of additional knowledge of hidden items).

The nature of expertise in these analyses

Before examining the specifics results of these analyses, it is useful to locate the use of expertise in both the models and the expert's behavior. The GOMS models have no knowledge of Mario's world; they do not know anything except what is on the screen.

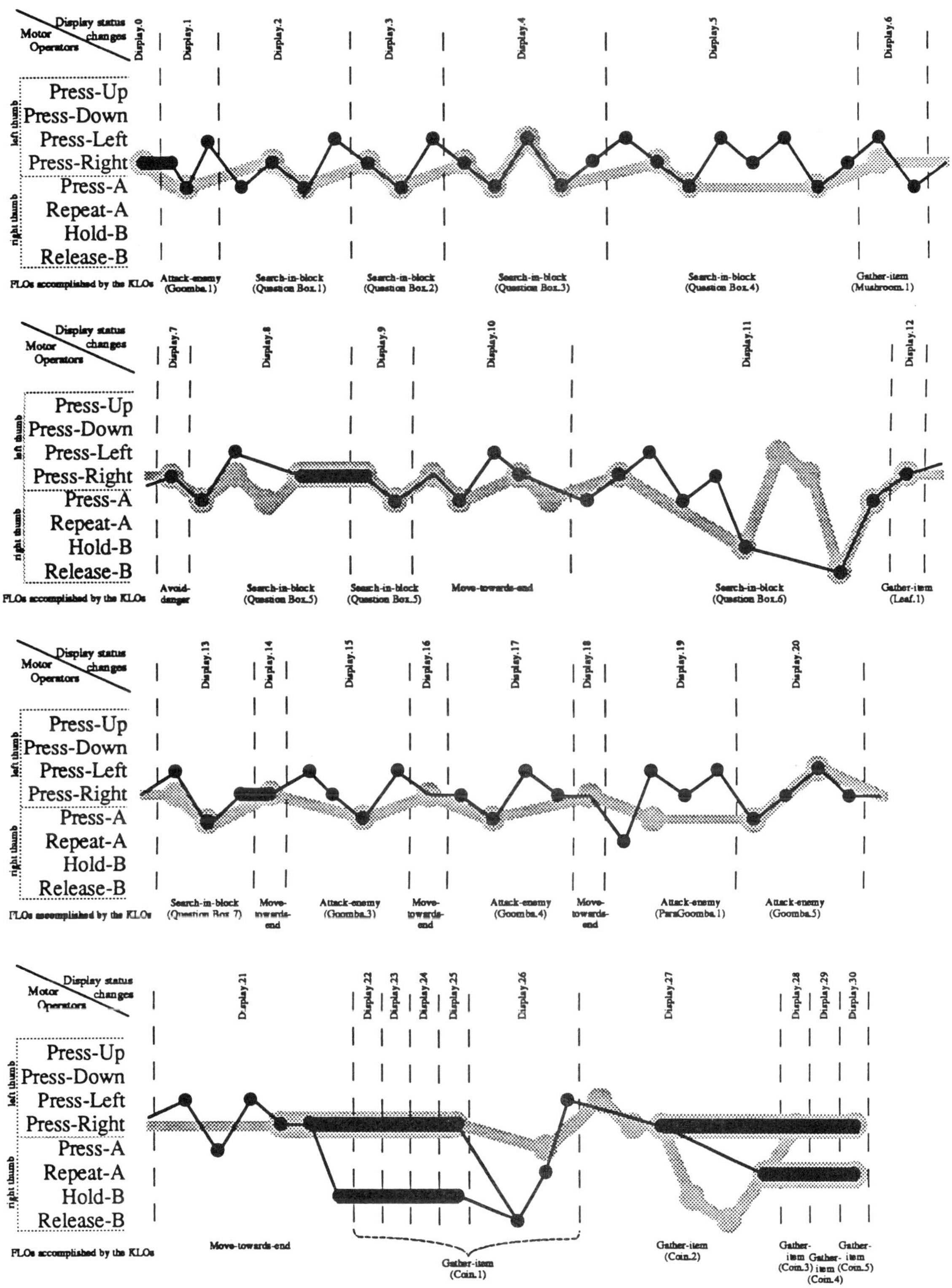

Figure 10. Comparison of keystroke-level predictions to observed behavior
(description same as that of Figure 9.)

Therefore, they cannot anticipate either functions or keystrokes. This is not true of the expert. A post-trial interview with KP, as well as observation of several trials of play, clearly showed that he knows every detail of World 1 Level 1. He knows where the treasures are hidden and what super powers they bestow. He knows when and where enemies will appear and whether each enemy should be killed or whether it can be ignored. His actions in two situations indicate that he anticipates functions to perform with elements not yet on the display. These situations are when he jumps to catch the mushroom before it emerges from QB.4 and when he starts his take-off to fly along a path of coins leading into the sky, before that path appears on the display. It is not surprising that an expert has such knowledge, only that this world requires him to use it so infrequently. The models make predictions without reference to it at all.

One the other hand, the GOMS models are expert in their execution of operators. KLOs are always assumed to accomplish their intended movement. For example, if a press-A-button KLO is used to jump on the back of an approaching enemy, it succeeds, never missing and allowing the enemy to kill Mario. This is clearly not the case with a human novice who has never used the Nintendo hand-held controller before. Informal observation of novice players shows many errors in execution: jumps are not timed correctly or are not initiated in the correct place so Mario doesn't kill an enemy or misses a block, buttons are not released in time so Mario runs off the cliff, etc. In addition, the selection rules in these models embody expert knowledge: the models always select the same method for accomplishing an FLO the expert selects. Since KLOs are always successful, and the method always reflect an expert selection, a sequence of KLOs in service of an FLO is always successful if it completed before another FLO is selected.

Thus, these GOMS models represent the behavior of a player with expert motor movements, expert knowledge of methods for collecting treasures and killing enemies, but no knowledge of what they will encounter in this world. This description coincidentally fits a human player who has played Super Mario Bros. and Super Mario Bros. 2., but never Super Mario Bros. 3. Such a person would have be expert in most methods and all keystrokes, but would not know the world at all. Further test of these models would benefit from observation and analysis of such a player.

Highlights of these analyses

The results of this analysis indicate that GOMS can capture the knowledge necessary to predict the course of this behavior. The FLOs in this segment of behavior are virtually dictated by some simple heuristics derived from the overriding goals of the game, the operators and methods described in the instruction booklet, and the elements visible on the display. Of the 31 FLOs predicted, 21 can be unambiguous inferred from the observed behavior, 9 are consistent with observed behavior, only 1 is inconsistent with observed behavior, and no behavior indicates any functions not predicted by the model. At the keystroke-level, of the 62 KLOs predicted, 46 are observed, 3 are consistent with observed behavior, 12 are inconsistent with observed behavior, and 35 keystrokes are observed but not predicted.

Figure 9, the comparison of the observed behavior to the predicted FLOs show some interesting features of the analysis. Most striking is the excellent agreement between the predicted FLOs and the observed behavior. Only once in 31 opportunities is an FLO selected that is inconsistent with observed behavior (Display.21). This instance is at a point in the game where the expert seems to anticipate gathering some coins that are not yet visible on the screen and for which he must attain flying speed. He moves left to get a running start for take-off. The model does not have the prior knowledge that coins will eventually appear to the right, and moves towards the end of the level (to the right) until it sees the coins, and then gathers them. Thus, the expert moves to the left in anticipation of flying, while the model moves to the right until it sees something to gather. As soon as the model sees the coins, the model and the expert have the same knowledge and they come back into synch.

A second interesting feature is that in 4 of the 11 displays in which the expert behavior does not match the predicted behavior (Displays.10, 16, 18, and 21), the predicted FLO is move-towards-end. This is the default FLO used when there are no elements on the display to trigger the proposal of other FLOs. In effect, the model is exploring the world when it selects this FLO. The expert, unlike the model, knows this part of the world quite well and anticipates the upcoming elements. The expert does not display this exploring behavior, but anticipates the next function and starts to perform it immediately. Thus, if the expert's cognitive processes were more clear from the verbal protocol, we expect more goal-directed behavior to emerge than is predicted by the model. However, if a novice were to play the game, with no knowledge of what comes next (like the model), the model predicts that this exploring behavior would be evident.

A third interesting feature is that only 8 of the 31 displays had observed behaviors consistent with several FLOs simultaneously (Displays 0, 7, 8, 10, 23, 24, 25, and 26). This means that the predicted FLOs must be exactly in line with the expert's goals to make a correct prediction. The behavior can be interpreted only as belonging to a single function most of the time, so picking an FLO with incorrect preferences, or at random, would rarely result in a match to observed behavior. This indicates that the function-level model is quite good at predicting the sequence of functions an expert will perform in this phase of the game.

The comparison of keystrokes inferred from the observed behavior and the KLOs predicted by the keystroke-level model, Figure 10, also has several interesting features. The most striking is the dramatic difference in predictive power between the function-level and KLO levels; the function-level predictions are almost perfect while the keystroke-level model predicts only about half of the observed behavior (46 of the 96 observed keystrokes). This is the same pattern of results obtained in Card, Moran, and Newell's analyses of text editing (1983), with FLOs predicting close to 100% of text-editing behavior and KLOs predicting about 60%.

Such a large drop in predictive power indicates that the keystroke-level models, both for the text-editing task and the game-playing task, may be missing important features that correspond to the unexplained behavior. For the text-editing task, Card, Moran, and Newell state that much of the unexplained behavior involved hand movements outside the model, e.g. the user licked her fingers before turning each page, an act not included in their model. In this analysis, there seems to be a similar type of unexplained behavior, twisting while jumping.

Twenty-four of the 37 observed keystrokes not predicted involve turning Mario left or right while jumping or floating. This twisting motion may be in service of a goal not represented in this model, e.g. displaying flashy behavior to impress other players. This hypothesis directs research attention to the social aspects of video game play to discover goals not evident from the instruction booklet. Alternatively this behavior may serves to slow Mario's horizontal motion while in the air. The second hypothesis, which we have recently been assured by other experts is the correct explanation, indicates that the motor model used in this analysis is too simple to capture the interaction of forces (e.g. the equivalents of gravity, friction, and air resistance) in Mario's world. A more detailed perceptual-motor model should include duration of button presses, perceptual monitoring, and the player's prediction of effects.

Questions of learning

Production-system formulations of GOMS have been used successfully to predict learning of several domains (e.g., Kieras & Bovair, 1986; Ziegler, et al, 1986; Lee, et al., 1989; Singley & Anderson, 1989), and may be useful for understanding learning in this domain as well. The learning predicted in the previous studies involved reading instructions and internalizing performance rules based on those instructions, plus practice with error feedback. That process describes the learning necessary to perform the actions and methods described in the instruction booklet. However, several other types of learning are evident in this interaction.

There is a strong component of motor learning; a novice continuously overshoots or undershoots runs and jumps, while an expert manipulates Mario more precisely. GOMS is not currently capable of predicting motor learning.

The other obvious learning behavior is "learning-by-dying", that is, Mario dies because of strategic mistakes and the player learns to avoid those mistakes in the future. For instance, the method of kicking a Koopa shell into a block on the ground to break it open is described in the instruction manual. When a novice performs this action on QB.6, the Koopa shell bounces off the block, right into Mario. This event happens too quickly for the immediate interaction cycle to produce adaptive behavior, and Mario dies. The novice then learns to modify the method to include jumping out of the way as soon as Mario kicks the shell. If the conditions surrounding each death are added to the condition of a production rule, and are combined with the appropriate avoidance tactic as the action of that production rule, new rules could be added to the knowledge in the GOMS analysis. Previous work with Soar, modeling strategy change in a developmental task (Newell, 1990) and modeling recovery from errors (Laird, 1988) indicates that the architectural mechanisms are sufficient to learn such knowledge when the learner can set the pace of learning. This situation raises the question as to whether those same mechanisms will be able to learn when the feedback occurs within the immediate interaction cycle. Another question is whether a regularity similar to the 30 seconds per operation[9] found in previous studies of learning and transfer would emerge from this interactive style of learning.

Other forms of learning produce behavior in the service of elements not yet visible on the display (discussed in the comparison between observed functions and predicted FLOs). At least two types of learning might occur to produce this behavior. The expert seems to anticipate elements before they are visible, so he might have learned cues that are visible prior to the elements of interest. Alternatively, KP says "get the ... mushrooms so you can turn into Super Mario", an indication of a goal above the FLO gather-item(mushroom); such higher level goals might serve to combine FLOs into methods themselves. These conjectures raise many questions. What knowledge structure is necessary to store and access goals in advance of directly relevant elements on the display? What role might a hierarchy of goals above the FLOs play in anticipatory behavior. How can the rapid interaction observed here, with a new FLO occurring every second and behavior being so time-critical and difficult that a verbal protocol cannot keep up, allow processing of the behavior to create these higher level goals, or store cues for anticipation of goals? Does such processing happen in the course of the game, or is there only learning-by-dying

---

[9] Soar *operators* are equivalent to the *productions* used in other research. Soar *productions* are at a lower grain-size and would not be expected to correspond to the learning times found previously.

(where the user reflects on what happened only when the immediate interaction cycle is broken by Mario's death), or perhaps learning occurs only even further outside the confines of the game in discussion with other players or while reading "Nintendo Power"[10] (a magazine containing game hints)? How can Soar's chunking mechanism produce this anticipatory behavior?

An interesting prediction about what is and is not learned arises from the environmentally driven characteristic of this portion of the game. Since expert knowledge about upcoming elements in the world is not used in the selection of FLOs,, different experts would follow the same FLO sequence, and even novices would produce the same function-level behavior. The motor operations would differ, especially for novices who are not able to manipulate Mario reliably, but the functions they try to accomplish (e.g. search-in-block(QB.1) then search-in-block(QB.2)) would not be a learned sequence, rather they would arise at all levels of skill from the elements on the display. Although verification of this prediction remains an open issue, informal observation of an additional expert and several novices do not contradict this prediction.

Speculation about motivation

Perhaps the most striking feature of video games is that people play them for hours on end. Empirical studies of computer games have produced speculation about the factors contributing to motivation (Malone, 1980), but as yet GOMS has not been used to explore this aspect of user-computer interaction. Based on the form and process of this GOMS analysis, we present some purely speculative words about why this game is so absorbing. First, the perceptually-based production system form of this model allows for the notion of *capture*. That is, since cues in the environment trigger operator proposal and selection, whenever those cues are present, those operators will be selected and executed. Thus, the environment captures the player and sends him or her looping through the immediate interaction cycle. Second, the rate of goal satisfaction (i.e., FLO accomplishment) may be related to this game's ability to absorb its players. If the rate is too high, the game is too easy and boring (e.g., KP yearned to go on to a higher level); if the rate is too low, the game becomes frustrating; if it is just right, the game captures players for hours on end. Thus, other open research questions are whether these concepts of capture and rate of goal satisfaction have any relation to what we know as fascination, or motivation, and, if so, whether the parameters of these concepts can be discovered and eventually manipulated to predict the fascination level of new games, educational programs, and other application interfaces.

Directions for future research

The stated purpose of the original panel, and this report, is to demonstrate GOMS analyses in the area of highly interactive tasks and encourage researchers and practitioners to use GOMS in their work. We see three directions in which future work may spring from our analyses.

The first direction is the extension of this particular analysis. The panel presentations represented a first pass GOMS analysis for each of the participants. This paper represents a "pass and a half" for our analyses, i.e., cleaned up but not substantially changed from the first pass. A second pass would tackle issues raised by the panel participants: perceptual monitoring of the effects of motor operations, a more detailed model of motor operators and their interactions with the forces designed into Mario's world, examination of the operator

---

[10] Nintendo Power is a trademark of, and is under copyright to, Nintendo of America.

durations and comparison to the human time course of behavior. A second pass would also include consideration of other research in the domain, notably the AI programs that play the video games Pengo and Amazon (Pengi in Agre & Chapman, 1987, and Sonja in Chapman, 1990, respectively). Although these programs were never intended to be cognitive models of human behavior, and were never formally compared to human behavior, they provide insight into a simple architecture that uses relatively little game knowledge but is sufficient for performing the immediate interaction necessary to play the game.

A second direction is for HF practitioners to use GOMS to make predictions of human behavior with the systems they help to design. At first, these analyses may be done in parallel with other HF methods, e.g. user trials, to validate the analytic predictions (see Gray, et. al. 1990 for an example). In time, we expect that confidence in GOMS analyses will grow and allow design decisions to be made in advance of the working prototypes (or Wizard-of-Oz mock-ups) and extensive user testing.

The third direction is to tackle the limitations of GOMS and extend the analysis technique itself. As presented above, GOMS is an evolving analytic technique. Its original formulation presented by Card, Moran and Newell (1980, 1983) has undergone several changes to extend the original scope, most recently this includes a change in the underlying architecture to the Soar unified theory of cognition. The change to Soar has allowed GOMS to encompass the interruption of tasks and responsiveness to the environment (as begun in this analysis and in John, et. al., 1990). We expect this change will lead to increased understanding and prediction of learning, errors, knowledge representations, and other issues of interest to the HF and HCI community, as well as to the cognitive science and cognitive psychology communities.

CONCLUSIONS

This analysis demonstrates GOMS's power to predict behavior in a highly interactive domain. It shows that GOMS is especially useful for making predictions of human behavior at the function level. It demonstrates how even an initial GOMs analysis can help direct research effort by focusing on areas of the model that do not predict human performance well. Further, it can make predictions about the general character of a task, e.g., that novices and experts alike will have the same function-level goal structure in this environmentally driven interaction.

This preliminary investigation also poses many questions. In pursuit of answers to those questions, this domain seems rich in behavioral phenomena, affording opportunities to explore the immediate interaction cycle with its rapid perception, cognition and motor actions, several aspects of learning, and perhaps even the elusive concept of fascination. In addition, research into the validation of GOMS analysis in real-world settings and the extension of the GOMS analytic technique would be valuable contributions to HF and HCI methodologies.

ACKNOWLEDGEMENTS

We would like to thank Kyle Gray, Jay Anderson, and Billy Esch for their expert advice about playing Super Mario Bros. 3, and Gin Peck and Carolanne Fisher for their comments on drafts of this paper.

REFERENCES

Agre, P. E. & Chapman, D. (1987) Pengi: An implementation of a theory of activity. *Proceedings of the AAAI'87: National Conference on Artificial Intelligence.* Menlo Park, Calif.: American Association for Artificial Intelligence.

Anderson, J. R. (1983). *The architecture of cognition.* Cambridge, Mass: Harvard University Press.

Card, S. K., Moran, T. P., & Newell, A. (1980) Computer text-editing: An inforamtion-processing analysis of a routine cognitive skill. *Cognitive Psychology, 12,* 32-74.

Card, S. K., Moran, T. P., & Newell, A. (1983) *The psychology of human-computer interaction.* Lawrence Erlbaum, Associates, Hillsdale, NJ.

Chapman, D. (1990) *Vision, Instruction, and Action.* (Tech. Rep. No. AI-TR 1204). Cambridge: MIT, Artificial Intelligence Laboratory.

Gray, W. D., John, B. E., Stuart, R., Lawrence, D., Atwood. M. E. (1990) GOMS meets the phone company: Analytic modelling applied to real-world problems. *Proceedings of Intertact '90 Third IFP Conference on Human-Computer Interaction.* Cambridge, England.

John, B. E. (1988) *Contributions to engineering models of human-computer interaction.* Doctoral dissertation, Carnegie Mellon University.

John, B. E. (1990) Extensions of GOMS analyses to expert performance requiring perception of dynamic visual and auditory information. In proceedings of *CHI, 1990* (Seattle, Washington, April 30-May 4, 1990) ACM, New York, 107-115.

John, B. E. & Newell, A. (1987) Predicting the time to recall computer command abbreviations. In proceedings of *CHI+GI, 1987* (Toronto, April 5-9, 1987) ACM, New York, 33-40.

John, B. E. & Newell, A. (1989) Culmulating the science of HCI: From S-R compatibility to transcription typing. In proceedings of *CHI, 1989* (Austin, Texas, April 30-May 4, 1989) ACM, New York, 109-114.

John, B. E., Newell, A., Card, S. K. (1990, February) *Browser-Soar: A GOMS-like model of a highly interactive task.* Talk presented at the Human Computer Interaction Winter Workshop, San Diego, California.

John, B. E., Rosenbloom, P. S., & Newell, A. (1985). A theory of stimulus-response compatibility applied to human-computer interaction. In proceedings of *CHI, 1985* (San Francisco, California, April 14-18, 1985) ACM, New York, 212-219.

Kieras, D. E. (1988) Towards a practical GOMS model methodology for user interface design in M. Helander (ed.) *Handbook of Human-Computer Interaction.* Elsevier Science Publishers B. V. (North-Holland).

Kieras, D. E., & Bovair, S. (1986) The acquisition of procedures from text: A production-system analysis of transfer of traning. *Journal of Memory and Learning,* 25, 507-524.

Kieras, D. E. & Polson, P. G. (1985) An approach to the formal analysis of user complexity. *International Journal of Man-Machine Studies, 22*, 365-394.

Laird, J. E. (1988) Recovery from incorrect knowledge in Soar. *Proceedings of the AAAI'88 National Conference on Artificial Intelligence*. Menlo Park, Calif.: American Association for Artificial Intelligence.

Laird, J. E., Newell, A., & Rosenblom, P. S. (1987) Soar: An architecture for general intelligence. *Artificial Intelligence, 33*, 1-64.

Laird, J. E., Swedlow, K., Altmann, E., & Congdon, C. B. (1990) *Soar 5 User's Manual*. Carnegie Mellon University.

Lee, A. Y., Polson, P. G. & Bailey, W. A. (1989) Learning and transfer of measurement tasks. In proceedings of *CHI, 1989* (Austin, Texas, April 30-May 4, 1989) ACM, New York, 115-120.

Lerch, F. J., Mantei, M. M., and Olson, J. R. (1989) Skilled financial planning: The cost of translating ideas into action. In proceedings of *CHI, 1989* (Austin, Texas, April 30-May 4, 1989) ACM, New York, 121-126.

Lewis, R. L., Huffman, S. B., John, B. E., Laird, J. E., Lehman, J. F., Newell, A., Rosenblom, P. S., Simon, T., & Tessler, S. G. "Soar as a Unified Theory of Cognition: Spring 1990. in the *Proceedings of the Twelfth Annual Conference of the Cognitive Science Society*, July, 1990.

Malone, T. W. (1980, August) *What makes things fun to learn? A study of intrinsically motivating computer games*. (Res. Rep. SSL-80-11). Xerox, Palo Alto Reasearch Center.

Newell, A. (1990) *Unified theories of cognition*. Cambridge, Mass: Harvard University Press.

Newell, A. & Card, S. K. (1986) Straightening out softening up: Response to Carroll and Campbell. *Human Computer Interaction, 2*, 251-267.

Newell, A. & Card, S. K. (1985) The prospects for psychological science in human-computer interaction. *Human Computer Interaction, 1*, 209-242.

Nintendo of America, *Super Mario Bros. 3 Instruction Booklet*.

Olson, J. R. & Nilsen, E. (1988) Analysis of the cognition involved in spreadsheet software interaction. *Human Computer Interaction, 3*, 309-350.

Olson, J. R. & Olson, G. M. (1990) The growth of cognitive modeling in human computer interaction since GOMS. *Human Computer Interaction, 5*, 221-266.

Polson, P. G., & Kieras, D. E. (1985). A quantitative model of learning and performance of text editing knowledge. In proceedings of *CHI, 1985* (San Francisco, California, April 14-18, 1985) ACM, New York, 207-212.

Rosenbloom, P. S. (1983) *The Chunking of Goal Hierarchies: A Model of Practice And Stimulus-Response Compatibilty*. Ph.D. diss., Computer Science Department, Carnegie Mellon University, Pittsbugh, PA.

Rumelhart, D. E., McClelland, J. L., & the PDP Research Group. 1986. *Parallel Distributed Processing: Explorations in the microstructures of cognition. Vol 1: Foundations*. Cambridge, Mass. MIT Press.

Singley, M. K. & Anderson, J. R. (1989) *The transfer of cognitive skill.* Cambridge, Mass: Harvard Univeristy Press.

Ziegler, J. E., Hoppe, H. U., & Fahnrich, K. P. (1986) Learning ans transfer for text and graphics with a direct manipulation interface. In Mantei and P. Orbeton (eds.), *CHI'86 Human Factors in Computing Systems* (Boston, April 13-17). New York: ACM.

Appendix I - Transcription of Observed Behavior

Transcribed by Wayne Gray, 7/31/90
Tape of S#1-KP
Take 5 WITHOUT eye scan, with keypad.
Tape sequence begins at 10:15:73, note that this refers to the large numbers at the bottom right (you may need to adjust the overscan on your monitor to see these clearly).

Auditory stuff done with the help of the Speech Lab, Sara Basson, et al.

Transcript supplied by Wayne Gray				*Inferences made during our analysis*	
TIME (SEC.) START	END	VOICE	SUPER MARIO'S MOVEMENTS	INFERRED FINGER ACTION	CORRESPONDING DISPLAY
16.23	17.23	**OK, Anders ready**			
19.12	20.02	**I'm going to the first**			
20.07	20.34	**level**			
20.42	21.54	**because you can't start anywheres else.**			
21.05			begin lateral movement	press-right-button	Display 0
21.70	22.34		SM begins jump/goal: stomp on goomba	press-A-button	
22.12			turns to face left in mid-flight at apogee	press-left-button	Display 1
22.06	23.53	**Stomp on the GOOMBA and get**			
	22.34		Stomp on goomba &		
22.34	23.51		begins second jump	press-A-button	
22.99			at apogee of second jump		
23.17			turns SM to face right	press-right-button	
	23.51		lands on ground &		Display 2
23.51	23.92		begins jump to CB1	press-A-button	
23.54	24.54	**the coins.**			
23.56			turns to face left	press-left-button	
23.67			hits CB1/begins to fall		

Transcript supplied by Wayne Gray				*Inferences made during our analysis*	
TIME (SEC.) START	END	VOICE	SUPER MARIO'S MOVEMENTS	INFERRED FINGER ACTION	CORRESPONDING DISPLAY
23.71			turns to right	press-right-button	
	23.92		on ground &		Display 3
23.92	24.32		begins jump to CB2	press-A-button	
24.01			turns to left	press-left-button	
24.11			hits CB2/turns to right	press-right-button	
	24.32		on ground &		
24.32	24.79		begins jump	press-A-button	
24.64			turns to left	press-left-button	
	24.79		lands on pink block		Display 4
24.94	25.19		moves to left		
25.16	25.57	**After you get**			
25.19	25.76		at left edge of pink block, jumps	press-A-button	
25.27			turns to right	press-right-button	
25.39			hits CB3		
25.64	26.16	**the coins**			
25.71			turns to left	press-left-button	
	25.76		lands on ground (error?)		
25.91			turns to right	press-right-button	
25.99	26.54		jumps	press-A-button	
26.07			turns left	press-left-button	
26.18	26.65	**in the fourth**			Display 5
26.23			turns right	press-right-button	
26.51			turns left	press-left-button	
	26.54		lands on pink block (recovery?) &		
26.54	0.00		jumps	press-A-button	
26.65	27.05	**block**			
26.66			turns right	press-right-button	
26.73			hits Q-block		

Transcript supplied by Wayne Gray				*Inferences made during our analysis*	
TIME (SEC.) START	END	VOICE	SUPER MARIO'S MOVEMENTS	INFERRED FINGER ACTION	CORRESPONDING DISPLAY
	26.93		lands on pink block		
26.99			turns left	press-left-button	Display 6
26.99	28.43		jumps (note that mushroom has not yet started to emerge from Q-block. This is an anticipation.)	press-A-button	Display 6
27.05	27.26	**get**			
27.53			gets mushroom @top of jump, becomes Super-Mario (shrinks & expands several times)		
28.12	28.78	**the aahh**			
28.28			turns right	press-right-button	Display 7
	28.43		lands on top of Q-block that mushroom emerged from.		
28.53	28.83		moves forward, off of Q-blk, begins fall down & to right		
28.78	29.35	**mushrooms**			
	28.83		lands on blue-block		
28.90	29.81		jumps	press-A-button	Display 8
29.35	31.31	**so you can turn into Super Mario**			Display 8
29.70			turns left	press-left-button	Display 8
	29.81		lands on green blk, beneath coin-blk, & to right of parana plant.		
29.85			turns right	press-right-button	Display 9
29.88	29.98		jumps	press-A-button	Display 9
29.93			hits coin-block		
	29.98		lands on green block (high green)		
30.20	31.13		jumps	press-A-button	Display 10
30.70			turns left -- floats while moving right	press-left-button	Display 10
31.06			turns right	press-right-button	Display 10
	31.13		lands on long green block, with KT on it.		

Transcript supplied by Wayne Gray				*Inferences made during our analysis*	
TIME (SEC.)				INFERRED	CORRESPONDING
START	END	VOICE	SUPER MARIO'S MOVEMENTS	FINGER ACTION	DISPLAY
31.14			jumps -- straight up	press-A-button	
31.38			at apogee begins to float to right	press-right-button	
31.56			turns left	press-left-button	
	31.70		stomps on KT (causing KT to retreat into its shell) &		
31.70	32.21		jumps towards the left	press-A-button	
31.73	31.98	**And**			
31.98	32.35	**kick the**			
	32.21		lands on long green blk &		Display 11
32.21			turns right	press-right-button	
32.35	32.85	**koopa**			
32.48			begins moving towards right (in the direction of the stomped upon KT)		
32.78			picks up KT	hold-B-button	
32.83			throws KT to right	release-B-button	
32.97	34.08		jumps towards right	press-A-button & press-right-button	Display 12
33.08	34.31	**so you can get the leaf**			
33.12			thrown KT hits Q-blk, blk vanishes & returns		
33.20			leaf emerges from Q-blk & floats up.		
33.50			SM contacts leaf in mid-air, both vanish momentarily		
33.88			SM reappears as "Raccoon Mario" (R-M)		
	34.08		R-M lands on small blocks &		
34.08			turns left (sliding towards right)	press-left-button	Display 13
34.25	34.35		jump	press-A-button	
34.28			turns right	press-right-button	Display 14
34.28			hits coins box		
	34.35		lands		

Transcript supplied by Wayne Gray				*Inferences made during our analysis*	
TIME (SEC.) START	END	VOICE	SUPER MARIO'S MOVEMENTS	INFERRED FINGER ACTION	CORRESPONDING DISPLAY
34.45			turns to face player (turns to front)		
34.52			turns left	press-left-button	Display 15 (34.52–34.97)
34.58			turns towards rear (with back towards player)		
34.65			turns to right	press-right-button	
34.73	35.28		jumps (goomba is coming)	press-A-button	
34.97			turns left	press-left-button	
35.02	36.04	**from getting the leaf**			
	35.28		stomps goomba &		
35.28			turns right	press-right-button	Display 17 (35.28–35.95)
35.28	36.10		jump	press-A-button	
35.75			turns left at apogee	press-left-button	
35.95			turns right	press-right-button	
	36.10		stomps another goomba &		
36.10			jumps	press-A-button (repeatedly)	Display 19 (36.10–36.80)
36.22	36.84	**go get**			
36.37			turns left (NOTE: flying KT is coming towards him) R-T flies higher and to the left	press-left-button	
36.50	37.02		turns right (floats in air)	press-right-button	
36.80			turns left (now over the flying KT who has now landed)	press-left-button	
36.89	38.43	**the other goomba so you can get**			
	37.02		stomps on flying KT (who loses his wings)		
37.02	37.85		jumps	press-A-button	Display 20 (37.02–37.75)
37.40			turns right at apogee	press-right-button	
37.51			turns left	press-left-button	
37.75			turns right (making many adjustments in order to land on the KT)	press-right-button	
	37.85		stomps KT		

Transcript supplied by Wayne Gray				*Inferences made during our analysis*	
TIME (SEC.) START	END	VOICE	SUPER MARIO'S MOVEMENTS	INFERRED FINGER ACTION	CORRESPONDING DISPLAY
37.85			turns left	press-left-button	Display 21
37.85	38.84		jumps	press-A-button	
38.43	38.63	**more**			
38.60			turns to rear		
38.65			turns left	press-left-button	
38.69	39.31	**points**			
	38.84		lands		
38.84			runs to left	press-left-button	
	39.52		stops (has gone to leaf blk, would have to jump to get by this)		
39.52			turns right	press-right-button	
39.52	41.87		runs to right, increasing speed	press-right-button &	Display 22 to
39.95	40.31	**And then you**		hold-B-button	Display 25
40.36	40.61	**pick up**			
40.61	40.88	**enough**			
41.03	42.46	**running speed and fly**		release-B-button &	
41.87	45.40		jumps -- flies	press-A-button (repeatedly)	Display 26
41.96			turns left	press-left-button	
42.11			gets first coin (in air)		
42.19			turns right (moving towards right)	press-right-button &	Display 27 to
42.46			gets coin	press-A-button (repeatedly)	Display 30
42.80			gets coin		
42.82			gets coin		
42.83	43.81	**to get the coins**			
43.19			gets coin		
43.56			gets coin		

Appendix II - Predictions of the GOMS Models

Display. 0 (Start-up screen) Mario starts at far left and Goomba is at far right moving left.
Mario is trying to get the first question block.

State of Mario: Small Mario

Selection of F.L.O

OBJECTS SEEN	POSITION	EVOKES	PROPOSED F.L.O.	PREFERENCES	F.L.O. SELECTED
Mario	far left, facing right				
Ground1.1	all				
QB.1	center, within reach	→	search-in-block(QB.1)	best	search-in-block(QB.1)
				better than search-in-block(QB.2)	
				better than search-in-block(QB.3)	
				better than search-in-block(QB.4)	
QB.2	just right of QB.1, within reach	→	search-in-block(QB.2)	best	
QB.3	right of QB.2 too high	→	search-in-block(QB.3)	best	
QB.4	just right of QB.3, too high	→	search-in-block(QB.4)	best	
G.1	far right (moving left)	→	attack-enemy(G.1)	worse than move-toward-end	
Scaf2.1	under QB.4				
			move-toward-end	worst	

Application of Selected F.L.O.

METHOD	NECESSARY MOVES	ACHIEVED BY	K.L.O.	K.L.O. PERFORMED	
hit-from-bottom	move-horizontal (until under)	→	press-right-button	performed	<--- Triggers Next Display
	jump	→	press-A-button	not performed	

Display. 1 Goomba gets threateningly close to Mario, so Mario attacks it.

State of Mario: Small Mario

Selection of F.L.O

OBJECTS SEEN	POSITION	EVOKES	PROPOSED F.L.O.	PREFERENCES	F.L.O. SELECTED
Mario	center, facing right				
Ground1.1	all				
G.1	moving left, close to Mario	→	attack-enemy(G.1)	best	attack-enemy(G.1)
				better than search-in-block(QB.1)	
				better than search-in-block(QB.2)	
				better than search-in-block(QB.3)	
				better than search-in-block(QB.4)	
QB.1	center, within reach	→	search-in-block(QB.1)	best	
QB.2	just right of QB 1, within reach	→	search-in-block(QB.2)	best	
QB.3	right of QB.2, too high	→	search-in-block(QB.3)	best	
QB.4	just right of QB.3, too high	→	search-in-block(QB.4)	best	
Scaf2.1			move-toward-end	worst	

Application of Selected F.L.O.

METHOD	NECESSARY MOVES	ACHIEVED BY	K.L.O.	K.L.O. PERFORMED	
stomp-on	jump	→	press-A-button	performed	<--- Triggers Next Display

Display. 2 Mario goes on to get the closest question block (QB.1).

State of Mario: Small Mario

Selection of F.L.O

OBJECTS SEEN	POSITION	EVOKES	PROPOSED F.L.O.	PREFERENCES	F.L.O. SELECTED
Mario	center, facing right				
Ground1.1	all				
QB.1	center, within reach	→	search-in-block(QB.1)	best better than search-in-block(QB.2) better than search-in-block(QB.3) better than search-in-block(QB.4)	search-in-block(QB.1)
QB.2	just right of QB.1, within reach	→	search-in-block(QB.2)	best	
QB.3	right of QB.2 too high	→	search-in-block(QB.3)	best	
QB.4	just right of QB.3, too high	→	search-in-block(QB.4)	best	
Scaf2.1	under QB.4				
Scaf3.2	just to the right of Scaf2.1				
			move-toward-end	worst	

Application of Selected F.L.O.

METHOD	NECESSARY MOVES	ACHIEVED BY	K.L.O.	K.L.O. PERFORMED
hit-from-bottom	move-horizontal (until under)	→	press-right-button	performed
	jump	→	press-A-button	performed

<--- Triggers Next Display

Display. 3 Mario goes on to get the next question block (QB.2).

State of Mario: Small Mario

Selection of F.L.O

OBJECTS SEEN	POSITION	EVOKES	PROPOSED F.L.O.	PREFERENCES	F.L.O. SELECTED
Mario	center, facing right				
Ground1.1	all				
QB.2	just right of QB.1, within reach	→	search-in-block(QB.2)	best better than search-in-block(QB.3) better than search-in-block(QB.4)	search-in-block(QB.2)
QB.3	right of QB.2 too high	→	search-in-block(QB.3)	best	
QB.4	just right of QB.3, too high	→	search-in-block(QB.4)	best	
Scaf2.1	under QB.4				
Scaf3.2	just to the right of Scaf2.1				
			move-toward-end	worst	

Application of Selected F.L.O.

METHOD	NECESSARY MOVES	ACHIEVED BY	K.L.O.	K.L.O. PERFORMED
hit-from-bottom	move-horizontal (until under)	→	press-right-button	performed
	jump	→	press-A-button	performed

<--- Triggers Next Display

Display. 4 Mario goes on to get QB.3 but it is too high so he jumps onto a scafold to reach it.

State of Mario: Small Mario

Selection of F.L.O

OBJECTS SEEN	POSITION	EVOKES	PROPOSED F.L.O.	PREFERENCES	F.L.O. SELECTED
Mario	center				
Ground1.1	all				
QB.3	right of QB.2 too high	→	search-in-block(QB.3)	best	search-in-block(QB.3)
				better than search-in-block(QB.4)	
QB.4	just right of QB.3, too high	→	search-in-block(QB.4)	best	
Scaf2.1	under QB.4				
Scaf3.2	just to the right of Scaf2.1				
			move-toward-end	worst	

Application of Selected F.L.O.

METHOD	NECESSARY MOVES	ACHIEVED BY	K.L.O.	K.L.O. PERFORMED
hit-from-bottom	move-horizontal (until next to Scaf2.1)	→	press-right-button	performed
	jump (onto Scaf2.1)	→	press-A-button	performed
	move-horizontal (until under QB.3)	→	press-left-button	performed
	jump	→	press-A-button	performed

<--- Triggers Next Display

Display. 5 Mario jumps back onto the scafold to reach QB.4.

State of Mario: Small Mario

Selection of F.L.O

OBJECTS SEEN	POSITION	EVOKES	PROPOSED F.L.O.	PREFERENCES	F.L.O. SELECTED
Mario	on ground under QB.3, facing right				
Ground1.1	all				
QB.4	just right of QB.3, too high	→	search-in-block(QB.4)	best	search-in-block(QB.4)
Scaf2.1	under QB.4				
Scaf3.2	just to the right of Scaf2.1				
Plant.1	far right	→	avoid-danger (Plant.1)	worse than move-toward-end	
			move-toward-end	worst	

Application of Selected F.L.O.

METHOD	NECESSARY MOVES	ACHIEVED BY	K.L.O.	K.L.O. PERFORMED
hit-from-bottom	move-horizontal (until under)	→	press-A-button	performed
	jump (onto Scaf2.1)	→	press-right-button	performed
	jump (to QB.4)	→	press-A-button	performed

<--- Triggers Next Display

Display. 6 A Mushroom pops out of QB.4 so Mario chases it in order to become Super Mario.

State of Mario: Small Mario

Selection of F.L.O

OBJECTS SEEN	POSITION
Mario	on Scaf2.1, facing right
Ground1.1	all
Mush.1	above QB.4
Scaf2.1	under QB.4
Scaf3.2	just to the right of Scaf2.1
Plant.1	far right

EVOKES	PROPOSED F.L.O.	PREFERENCES	F.L.O. SELECTED
→	gather-item(Mush.1)	best	gather-item(Mush.1)
→	avoid-danger (Plant.1)	worse than move-toward-end	
	move-toward-end	worst	

Application of Selected F.L.O.

METHOD	NECESSARY MOVES	ACHIEVED BY	K.L.O.	K.L.O. PERFORMED	
run-into	move-horizontal (until at)	→	press-right-button	performed	<--- Triggers Next Display

***Note:* the Mushroom moves randomly to the left or right of the screen after popping out of QB.4. The situation in which it moves to the right was selected for this model.**

Display. 7 A plant is shooting Fireballs at Mario; he avoids them by running right up next to the plant.

State of Mario: Super Mario

Selection of F.L.O

OBJECTS SEEN	POSITION
Mario	on Ground1.1, left of Plant.1
Ground1.1	all
Scaf2.1	under QB.4
Scaf3.2	just to the right of Scaf2.1
Plant.1	right
Fireball	coming toward Mario
Scaf2.3	to the right of Plant.1

EVOKES	PROPOSED F.L.O.	PREFERENCES	F.L.O. SELECTED
→	avoid-danger (Plant.1)	worse than move-toward-end	
→	avoid-danger(Fireball)	better than move-toward-end	avoid-danger (Fireball)
	move-toward-end	worst	

Application of Selected F.L.O.

METHOD	NECESSARY MOVES	ACHIEVED BY	K.L.O.	K.L.O. PERFORMED	
get-out-of-the-way	move-horizontal (until out of range)	→	press-right-button	performed	<--- Triggers Next Display

Display. 8 Mario goes after the next question block by jumping over the plant and onto Scaf2.3.

State of Mario: Super Mario

Selection of F.L.O

OBJECTS SEEN	POSITION	EVOKES	PROPOSED F.L.O.	PREFERENCES	F.L.O. SELECTED
Mario	on Ground1.1, next to Plant.1				
Ground1.1	all				
Plant.1	right (next to Mario)				
Scaf2.3	right of Plant.1		avoid-danger (Plant.1)	worse than move-toward-end	
QB.5	above Scaf2.3	→	search-in-block(QB.5)	best	search-in-block(QB.5)
			move-toward-end	worst	

Application of Selected F.L.O.

METHOD	NECESSARY MOVES	ACHIEVED BY	K.L.O.	K.L.O. PERFORMED	
hit-from-bottom	jump-horizontal (over Pipe.1)	→	press-A-button	performed	
		→	press-right-button	performed	
	jump-onto-Scaf2.3	→	press-A-button	performed	
		→	press-right-button	performed	
	move-horizontal-until-under	→	press-right-button	begun but not completed	<--- Triggers Next Display
	jump	→	press-A-button	not performed	

Display. 9 Goomba appears before Mario has reached QB.5 but it is not an immediate threat so Mario continues toward QB.5.

State of Mario: Super Mario

Selection of F.L.O

OBJECTS SEEN	POSITION	EVOKES	PROPOSED F.L.O.	PREFERENCES	F.L.O. SELECTED
Mario	on Scaf2.3 under QB.5, facing right				
Ground1.1	all				
Plant.1	far left	→	avoid-danger (Plant.1)	worse than move-toward-end	
Scaf2.3	right of Plant.1				
QB.5	above Scaf2.3	→	search-in-block(QB.5)	best	search-in-block(QB.5)
G.5	on Ground1.1 in front of Scaf2.3	→	attack-enemy(G.5)	worse than move-toward-end	
			move-toward-end	worst	

Application of Selected F.L.O.

METHOD	NECESSARY MOVES	ACHIEVED BY	K.L.O.	K.L.O. PERFORMED	
hit-from-bottom	move-horizontal-until-under	→	press-right-button	performed	
	jump	→	press-A-button	performed	<--- Triggers Next Display

Display. 10 Neither Goomba nor Koopa are an immediate threat. Mario moves forward by jumping onto the scafolds.

State of Mario: Super Mario

Selection of F.L.O

OBJECTS SEEN	POSITION	EVOKES	PROPOSED F.L.O.	PREFERENCES	F.L.O. SELECTED
Mario	on Scaf2.3, facing right				
Ground1.1	all				
Scaf2.3	far left				
Scaf3.4	center				
Scaf4.5	right				
Scaf1.6	below Scaf4.5				
G.5	on Ground1.1 in front of scafolds	→	attack-enemy(G.5)	worse than move-toward-end	
K.1	on Scaf1.6	→	attack enemy(K.1)	worse than move-toward-end	
			move-toward-end	worst	move-toward-end

Application of Selected F.L.O.

METHOD	NECESSARY MOVES	ACHIEVED BY	K.L.O.	K.L.O. PERFORMED
move-right-and -jump	move-horizontal	→	press-right-button	performed
	jump-onto-Scaf3.4	→	press-A-button	performed
	move-horizontal	→	press-right-button	performed
	jump-onto-Scaf4.5	→	press-A-button	performed

<--- Triggers Next Display

Display. 11 Mario sees block on the ground which can only be opened by thowing a shell at it.
So Mario stomps on the Koopa Trooper in order to get a shell to throw at the block.
Then Mario throws the shell at QB.6 and breaks it.

State of Mario: Super Mario

Selection of F.L.O

OBJECTS SEEN	POSITION	EVOKES	PROPOSED F.L.O.	PREFERENCES	F.L.O. SELECTED
Mario	on Scaf4.5, facing right				
Ground1.1	all				
Scaf2.3	far left				
Scaf3.4	center				
Scaf4.5	right				
Scaf1.6	below Scaf4.5				
G.5	on Ground1.1 in front of scafolds	→	attack-enemy(G.5)	worse than move-toward-end	
K.1	on Scaf1.6	→	attack enemy(K-1)	worse than move-toward-end	
Ground2.2	far right				
QB.6	far right on Ground2.2	→	search-in-block(QB.6)	best	search-in-block(QB.6)
			move-toward-end	worst	

Application of Selected F.L.O.

METHOD	NECESSARY MOVES	ACHIEVED BY	K.L.O.	K.L.O. PERFORMED
hit-with-shell	move-horizontal	→	press-right-button	performed
	(drops onto Koopa to immobilize it)			
	prepare-to-pick-up	→	hold-B-button	performed
	move-to-shell-and-pick-up	→	press-left-button	performed
	move-to-block	→	press-right-button	performed
	kick-shell	→	release-B-button	performed
	jump (out of the way)	→	release-A-button	performed <--- Triggers Next Display

Note:* *The last press-A-button is to jump out of the way of the richocheting Koopa shell. This KLO is added to the hit-with-shell method based on prior experience with being killed by the bouncing Koopa shell. See the text for more explanation of this learning process.

Display. 12 Mario goes to get the leaf that popped out of the question block (QB.6) so that he can turn into Racoon Mario.

State of Mario: Super Mario

Selection of Operator

OBJECTS SEEN	POSITION
Mario	in air, facing right
Ground1.1	left
Scaf3.4	far left
Scaf4.5	center
Scaf1.6	below Scaf4.5
G.5	on Ground1.1 in front of scafolds
Ground2.2	right
QB.6 (empty)	right, on Ground2.2
Leaf.1	over QB.6

EVOKES →

PROPOSED F.L.O.	PREFERENCES	F.L.O. SELECTED
attack-enemy(G.5)	worse than move-toward-end	
gather-item(Leaf.1)	best	gather-item(Leaf.1)
move-toward-end	worst	

Application of Selected F.L.O.

METHOD	NECESSARY MOVES
run-into	move-horizontal (until at)

ACHIEVED BY →

K.L.O.	K.L.O. PERFORMED
press-right-button	performed

<--- Triggers Next Display

Display. 13 Mario goes to get the next question block (QB.7).

State of Mario: Racoon Mario

Selection of F.L.O

OBJECTS SEEN	POSITION
Mario	between QB.6 and QB.7, facing right
Ground1.1	left
Scaf1.6	far left
Ground2.2	right
QB.6 (empty)	center, on Ground2.2
QB.7	in air to the right of QB.6

EVOKES →

PROPOSED F.L.O.	PREFERENCES	F.L.O. SELECTED
search-in-block(QB.7)	best	search-in-block(QB.7)
move-toward-end	worst	

Application of Selected F.L.O.

METHOD	NECESSARY MOVES
hit-from-bottom	move-horizontal (until under)
	jump

ACHIEVED BY →

K.L.O.	K.L.O. PERFORMED
press-right-button	performed
press-A-button	performed

<--- Triggers Next Display

Display. 14 There are no items or enemies on the screen so Mario just moves toward the end of the level.

State of Mario: Racoon Mario

Selection of F.L.O

OBJECTS SEEN	POSITION
Mario	to the right of QB.7, facing right
Ground2.2	all
QB.6 (empty)	far left
QB.7 (empty)	left

EVOKES →

PROPOSED F.L.O.	PREFERENCES	F.L.O. SELECTED
move-toward-end	worst	move-toward-end

Application of Selected F.L.O.

METHOD	NECESSARY MOVES
walk	move-horizontal

ACHIEVED BY →

K.L.O.	K.L.O. PERFORMED
press-right-button	performed

<--- Triggers Next Display

Display. 15 A goomba (G.3) moves toward Mario from the right (becoming an immediate threat), so Mario attacks him.

State of Mario: Racoon Mario

Selection of F.L.O

OBJECTS SEEN	POSITION
Mario	to the right of QB.7, facing right
Ground2.2	all
QB.7 (empty)	far left
G.3	moving toward Mario from the right

EVOKES →

PROPOSED F.L.O.	PREFERENCES	F.L.O. SELECTED
attack-enemy(G.3)	better than move-toward-end	attack-enemy(G.3)
move-toward-end	worst	

Application of Selected F.L.O.

METHOD	NECESSARY MOVES
stomp-on	jump (until land-on-back)

ACHIEVED BY →

K.L.O.	K.L.O. PERFORMED
press-A-button	performed

<--- Triggers Next Display

Display. 16 Again, there are no items or enemies on the screen so Mario just moves toward the end of the level.

State of Mario: Racoon Mario

Selection of F.L.O

OBJECTS SEEN	POSITION
Mario	to the right of QB.7, facing right
Ground2.2	all

EVOKES →

PROPOSED F.L.O.	PREFERENCES	F.L.O. SELECTED
move-toward-end	worst	move-toward-end

Application of Selected F.L.O.

METHOD	NECESSARY MOVES
walk	move-horizontal

ACHIEVED BY →

K.L.O.	K.L.O. PERFORMED
press-right-button	performed

<--- Triggers Next Display

Display. 17 Another goomba (G.4) moves toward Mario from the right (becoming an immediate threat), so Mario attacks him.

State of Mario: Racoon Mario

Selection of F.L.O

OBJECTS SEEN	POSITION
Mario	to the right of QB.7, facing right
Ground2.2	all
G.4	moving toward Mario from the right

EVOKES →

PROPOSED F.L.O.	PREFERENCES	F.L.O. SELECTED
attack-enemy(G.4)	better than move-toward-end	attack-enemy(G.4)
move-toward-end	worst	

Application of Selected F.L.O.

METHOD	NECESSARY MOVES
stomp-on	jump (until land-on-back)

ACHIEVED BY →

K.L.O.	K.L.O. PERFORMED
press-A-button	performed

<--- Triggers Next Display

Display. 18 Again, there are no items or enemies on the screen so Mario just moves toward the end of the level.

State of Mario: Racoon Mario

Selection of F.L.O

OBJECTS SEEN	POSITION
Mario	to the right of QB.7, facing right
Ground2.2	all

EVOKES

PROPOSED F.L.O.	PREFERENCES	F.L.O. SELECTED
move-toward-end	worst	move-toward-end

Application of Selected F.L.O.

METHOD	NECESSARY MOVES
walk	move-horizontal

ACHIEVED BY ⟶

K.L.O.	K.L.O. PERFORMED
press-right-button	performed

<--- Triggers Next Display

Display. 19 A para-goomba (PG.1) moves toward Mario from the right (becoming an immediate threat), so Mario attacks him.

State of Mario: Racoon Mario

Selection of F.L.O

OBJECTS SEEN	POSITION
Mario	to the right of QB.7, facing right
Ground2.2	all
PG.1	moving toward Mario from the right

EVOKES ⟶

PROPOSED F.L.O.	PREFERENCES	F.L.O. SELECTED
attack-enemy(PG.1)	better than move-toward-end	attack-enemy(PG.1)
move-toward-end	worst	

Application of Selected F.L.O.

METHOD	NECESSARY MOVES
stomp-on	jump (until land-on-back)

ACHIEVED BY ⟶

K.L.O.	K.L.O. PERFORMED
press-A-button	performed

<--- Triggers Next Display

Display. 20 **The para-goomba turns into a goomba (G.5) after Mario stomps on it, so he has to attack it again.**

State of Mario: Racoon Mario

Selection of F.L.O

OBJECTS SEEN	POSITION	EVOKES	PROPOSED F.L.O.	PREFERENCES	F.L.O. SELECTED
Mario	to the right of QB.7, facing right				
Ground2.2	all				
G.5	on Mario's left	⟶	attack-enemy(G.5)	better than move-toward-end	attack-enemy(G.5)
			move-toward-end	worst	

Application of Selected F.L.O.

METHOD	NECESSARY MOVES	ACHIEVED BY	K.L.O.	K.L.O. PERFORMED	
stomp-on	jump	⟶	press-A-button	performed	
	move-horizontal (until land-on-back)	⟶	press-left-button	performed	<--- Triggers Next Display

---

Display. 21 Again, there are no items or enemies on the screen so Mario just moves toward the end of the level.

State of Mario: Racoon Mario

Selection of F.L.O

OBJECTS SEEN	POSITION	EVOKES	PROPOSED F.L.O.	PREFERENCES	F.L.O. SELECTED
Mario	to the right of QB.7, facing right				
Ground2.2	all		move-toward-end	worst	move-toward-end

Application of Selected F.L.O.

METHOD	NECESSARY MOVES	ACHIEVED BY	K.L.O.	K.L.O. PERFORMED	
walk	move-horizontal	⟶	press-right-button	performed	<--- Triggers Next Display

Display. 22 A coin comes into view in mid-air at the far right; it is low enough for Mario to reach it by jumping.

State of Mario: Racoon Mario

Selection of F.L.O

OBJECTS SEEN	POSITION	EVOKES	PROPOSED F.L.O.	PREFERENCES	F.L.O. SELECTED
Mario	to the right of QB.7, facing right				
Ground2.2	all				
Coin.1	far right	→	gather-item(Coin.1)	best	gather-item(Coin.1)
			move-toward-end	worst	

Application of Selected F.L.O.

METHOD	NECESSARY MOVES	ACHIEVED BY	K.L.O.	K.L.O. PERFORMED	
hit-from-bottom	move-horizontal	→	press-right-button	performed	<--- Triggers Next Display
	jump (when under)	→	press-A-button	not performed	

Display. 23 A cliff apears at the far right as Mario moves toward the coin.

State of Mario: Racoon Mario

Selection of F.L.O

OBJECTS SEEN	POSITION	EVOKES	PROPOSED F.L.O.	PREFERENCES	F.L.O. SELECTED
Mario	to the right of QB.7, facing right				
Ground2.2	all				
Coin.1	right, before Cliff.1	→	gather-item(Coin.1)	best	gather-item(Coin.1)
Cliff.1	far right	→	avoid-danger(Cliff.1)	worse than move-toward-end	
			move-toward-end	worst	

Application of Selected F.L.O.

METHOD	NECESSARY MOVES	ACHIEVED BY	K.L.O.	K.L.O. PERFORMED	
hit-from-bottom	move-horizontal	→	press-right-button	performed	<--- Triggers Next Display
	jump (when under)	→	press-A-button	not performed	

Display. 24 A second coin comes into view; this one is over the cliff and too high for Mario to jump.

State of Mario: Racoon Mario

Selection of F.L.O

OBJECTS SEEN	POSITION	EVOKES	PROPOSED F.L.O.	PREFERENCES	F.L.O. SELECTED
Mario	to the right of QB.7, facing right				
Ground2.2	all				
Coin.1	right, before Cliff.1	→	gather-item(Coin.1)	best better than gather-item(Coin.2) worse than move-toward-end	gather-item(Coin.1)
Cliff.1	right	→	avoid-danger(Cliff.1)	best	
Coin.2	far right over Cliff.1	→	gather-item(Coin.2)		
			move-toward-end	worst	

Application of Selected F.L.O.

METHOD	NECESSARY MOVES	ACHIEVED BY	K.L.O.	K.L.O. PERFORMED	
hit-from-bottom	move-horizontal	→	press-right-button	performed	<--- Triggers Next Display
	jump (when under)	→	press-A-button	not performed	

Display. 25 A third coin comes into view; this one is also over the cliff and too high for Mario to jump.

State of Mario: Racoon Mario

Selection of F.L.O

OBJECTS SEEN	POSITION	EVOKES	PROPOSED F.L.O.	PREFERENCES	F.L.O. SELECTED
Mario	to the left of Coin.1, facing right				
Ground2.2	all				
Coin.1	right, before Cliff.1	→	gather-item(Coin.1)	best better than gather-item(Coin.2) better than gather-item(Coin.3) worse than move-toward-end	gather-item(Coin.1)
Cliff.1	right	→	avoid-danger(Cliff.1)	best	
Coin.2	far right over Cliff.1	→	gather-item(Coin.2)	best	
Coin.3	to the right and higher than Coin.2	→	gather-item(Coin.3)		
			move-toward-end	worst	

Application of Selected F.L.O.

METHOD	NECESSARY MOVES	ACHIEVED BY	K.L.O.	K.L.O. PERFORMED	
hit-from-bottom	move-horizontal	→	press-right-button	performed	<--- Triggers Next Display
	jump (when under)	→	press-A-button	not performed	

Display. 26 Mario arrives under Coin.1 and jumps to get it.

State of Mario: Racoon Mario

Selection of F.L.O

OBJECTS SEEN	POSITION	EVOKES	PROPOSED F.L.O.	PREFERENCES	F.L.O. SELECTED
Mario	to the left of Coin.1, facing right				
Ground2.2	all				
Coin.1	right, before Cliff.1	→	gather-item(Coin.1)	best	gather-item(Coin.1)
				better than gather-item(Coin.2)	
				better than gather-item(Coin.3)	
				worse than move-toward-end	
Cliff.1	right	→	avoid-danger(Cliff.1)	best	
Coin.2	far right over Cliff 1	→	gather-item(Coin.2)	best	
Coin.3	to the right and higher than Coin.2	→	gather-item(Coin.3)	best	
			move-toward-end	worst	

Application of Selected F.L.O.

METHOD	NECESSARY MOVES	ACHIEVED BY	K.L.O.	K.L.O. PERFORMED	
hit-from-bottom	move-horizontal (until-under)	→	press-right-button	performed	
	jump	→	press-A-button	performed	<--- Triggers Next Display

Display. 27 Mario cannot get the second coin by jumping to it so he has to back-up and fly to it.

State of Mario: Racoon Mario

Selection of F.L.O

OBJECTS SEEN	POSITION	EVOKES	PROPOSED F.L.O.	PREFERENCES	F.L.O. SELECTED
Mario	next to Cliff.1, facing right				
Ground2.2	all				
Cliff.1	right	→	avoid-danger(Cliff.1)	worse than move-toward-end	
Coin.2	over Cliff.1	→	gather-item(Coin.2)	best	gather-item(Coin.2)
				better than gather-item(Coin.3)	
Coin.3	to the right and higher than Coin.2	→	gather-item(Coin.3)	best	
			move-toward-end	worst	

Application of Selected F.L.O.

METHOD	NECESSARY MOVES	ACHIEVED BY	K.L.O.	K.L.O. PERFORMED
fly-to-it	walk back	→	press-left-button	performed
	turn around	→	press-right-button	performed
	accelerate	→	press-right-button	performed
		→	hold-B-button	performed
	take off and fly	→	release-B-button	performed
		→	press-A-button (repeatedly)	performed

<--- Triggers Next Display

Display. 28 After getting the second coin, Mario continues flying to the third coin, and a fourth and fifth coin come into view which he can also fly to.

State of Mario: Racoon Mario

Selection of F.L.O

OBJECTS SEEN	POSITION	EVOKES	PROPOSED F.L.O.	PREFERENCES	F.L.O. SELECTED
Mario	flying, facing right				
Coin.3	in the air	→	gather-item(Coin.3)	best better than gather-item(Coin.4) better than gather-item(Coin.5)	gather-item(Coin.3)
Coin.4	to the right and higher than Coin.3	→	gather-item(Coin.4)	best	
Coin.5	to the right and higher than Coin.4	→	gather-item(Coin.4)	best	
			move-toward-end	worst	

Application of Selected F.L.O.

METHOD	NECESSARY MOVES	ACHIEVED BY	K.L.O.	K.L.O. PERFORMED	
fly-to-it	fly	→	press-right-button	performed	
		→	press-A-button (repeatedly)	performed	<--- Triggers Next Display

Display. 29 After getting the third coin, Mario continues flying to the fourth coin.

State of Mario: Racoon Mario

Selection of F.L.O

OBJECTS SEEN	POSITION	EVOKES	PROPOSED F.L.O.	PREFERENCES	F.L.O. SELECTED
Mario	flying, facing right				
Coin.4	in the air	→	gather-item(Coin.4)	best better than gather-item(Coin.5)	gather-item(Coin.4)
Coin.5	to the right and higher than Coin.4	→	gather-item(Coin.4)	best	
			move-toward-end	worst	

Application of Selected F.L.O.

METHOD	NECESSARY MOVES	ACHIEVED BY	K.L.O.	K.L.O. PERFORMED	
fly-to-it	fly	→	press-right-button	performed	
		→	press-A-button (repeatedly)	performed	<--- Triggers Next Display

Display. 30 After getting the fourth coin, Mario continues flying to the fifth coin, and a scafold appears with more coins above it.

State of Mario: Racoon Mario

Selection of F.L.O

OBJECTS SEEN	POSITION	EVOKES	PROPOSED F.L.O.	PREFERENCES	F.L.O. SELECTED
Mario Coin.5	flying, facing right in the air	⟶	gather-item(Coin.5)	best	gather-item(Coin.5)
			move-toward-end	worst	

Application of Selected F.L.O.

METHOD	NECESSARY MOVES	ACHIEVED BY	K.L.O.	K.L.O. PERFORMED	
fly-to-it	fly	⟶	press-right-button	performed	
		⟶	press-A-button (repeatedly)	performed	<--- Triggers Next Display

Appendix III - Comparison between Observed Expert Behavior and Predictions of the GOMS Models

Display. 0 (Start-up screen)

Mario starts at far left.
Goomba is at far right moving left.
Mario is trying to get the first question block.

State of Mario: Small Mario

On Screen

OBJECTS SEEN	POSITION
Mario	far left, facing right
Ground1.1	all
QB.1	center, within reach
QB.2	just right of QB.1, within reach
QB.3	right of QB.2 too high
QB.4	just right of QB.3, too high
G.1	far right (moving left)
Scaf2.1	under QB.4

Expert's Behavior

OBSERVED BEHAVIOR	INFERRED FUNCTION	INFERRED FINGER ACTION
Mario moves right	ambiguous	press-right-button

Comparison to Model

F.L.O. CONSISTENT WITH OBSERVED BEHAVIOR	F.L.O. PREDICTED BY MODEL	K.L.O. PREDICTED BY MODEL
search-in-block(QB.1)	search-in-block(QB.1)	press-right-button
search-in-block(QB.2)		
search-in-block(QB.3)		
search-in-block(QB.4)		
attack-enemy(G.1)		
move-to-end		

Display. 1 Goomba gets threateningly close to Mario, so Mario attacks it.

State of Mario: Small Mario

On Screen

OBJECTS SEEN	POSITION
Mario	center, facing right
Ground1.1	all
G.1	moving left, close to Mario
QB.1	center, within reach
QB.2	just right of QB.1, within reach
QB.3	right of QB.2, too high
QB.4	just right of QB.3, too high
Scaf2.1	

Expert's Behavior

OBSERVED BEHAVIOR	INFERRED FUNCTION	INFERRED FINGER ACTION
Mario jumps to the right		press-right-button press-A-button
turns left at apogee		press-left-button
lands on G.1	attack-enemy(G.1)	

Comparison to Model

F.L.O. CONSISTENT WITH OBSERVED BEHAVIOR	F.L.O. PREDICTED BY MODEL	K.L.O. PREDICTED BY MODEL
attack-enemy(G.1)	attack-enemy(G.1)	press-A-button

Display. 2 Mario goes on to get the closest question block (QB.1).

State of Mario: Small Mario

On Screen

OBJECTS SEEN	POSITION
Mario	center, facing left
Ground1.1	all
QB.1	center, within reach
QB.2	just right of QB.1, within reach
QB.3	right of QB.2 too high
QB.4	just right of QB.3, too high
Scaf2.1	under QB.4
Scaf3.2	just to the right of Scaf2.1

Expert's Behavior

OBSERVED BEHAVIOR	INFERRED FUNCTION	INFERRED FINGER ACTION
Mario jumps off G.1		press-A-button
turns to the right at apogee		press-right-button
jumps again		press-A-button
turns to left and hits QB.1	search-in-block(QB.1)	press-left-button

Comparison to Model

F.L.O. CONSISTENT WITH OBSERVED BEHAVIOR	F.L.O. PREDICTED BY MODEL	K.L.O. PREDICTED BY MODEL
search-in-block(QB.1)	search-in-block(QB.1)	press-right-button
		press-A-button

Display. 3 Mario goes on to get the next question block (QB.2)

State of Mario: Small Mario

On Screen

OBJECTS SEEN	POSITION
Mario	center, facing left
Ground1.1	all
QB.2	just right of QB.1, within reach
QB.3	right of QB.2 too high
QB.4	just right of QB.3, too high
Scaf2.1	under QB.4
Scaf3.2	just to the right of Scaf2.1

Expert's Behavior

OBSERVED BEHAVIOR	INFERRED FUNCTION	INFERRED FINGER ACTION
Mario turns to right on ground		press-right-button
jumps		press-A-button
turns to left and hits QB.2	search-in-block(QB.2)	press-left-button

Comparison to Model

F.L.O. CONSISTENT WITH OBSERVED BEHAVIOR	F.L.O. PREDICTED BY MODEL	K.L.O. PREDICTED BY MODEL
search-in-block(QB.2)	search-in-block(QB.2)	press-right-button
		press-A-button

Display. 4 Mario goes on to get QB.3 but it is too high so he jumps onto a scafold to reach it.

State of Mario: Small Mario

On Screen

OBJECTS SEEN	POSITION
Mario	center, facing left
Ground1.1	all
QB.3	right of QB.2 too high
QB.4	just right of QB.3, too high
Scaf2.1	under QB.4
Scaf3.2	just to the right of Scaf2.1

Expert's Behavior

OBSERVED BEHAVIOR	INFERRED FUNCTION	INFERRED FINGER ACTION
Mario turns to right on ground		press-right-button
jumps		press-A-button
turns left and lands on Scaf2.1		press-left-button
jumps		press-A-button
turns to right and hits QB.3	search-in-block(QB.3)	press-right-button

Comparison to Model

F.L.O. CONSISTENT WITH OBSERVED BEHAVIOR	F.L.O. PREDICTED BY MODEL	K.L.O. PREDICTED BY MODEL
search-in-block(QB.3)	search-in-block(QB.3)	press-right-button
		press-A-button
		press-left-button
		press-A-button

Display. 5 From the scafold he can also reach QB.4.

State of Mario: Small Mario

On Screen

OBJECTS SEEN	POSITION
Mario	on ground under QB.3, facing right
Ground1.1	all
QB.4	just right of QB.3, too high
Scaf2.1	under QB.4
Scaf3.2	just to the right of Scaf2.1
Plant.1	far right

Expert's Behavior

OBSERVED BEHAVIOR	INFERRED FUNCTION	INFERRED FINGER ACTION
turns to left and lands on ground		press-left-button
turns to right		press-right-button
jumps		press-A-button
turns left in air		press-left-button
turns right in air		press-right-button
turns left and lands on Scaf2.1		press-left-button
jumps		press-A-button
turns to right and hits QB.4	search-in-block(QB.4)	press-right-button

Comparison to Model

F.L.O. CONSISTENT WITH OBSERVED BEHAVIOR	F.L.O. PREDICTED BY MODEL	K.L.O. PREDICTED BY MODEL
search-in-block(QB.4)	search-in-block(QB.4)	press-right-button
		press-A-button (to Scaf2.1)
		press-A-button (hit QB.4)

Display. 6 Mario jumps up to get the mushroom which pops out from QB.6 before it even starts emerging from the question block.

State of Mario: Small Mario

On Screen

OBJECTS SEEN	POSITION
Mario	on Scaf2.1, facing right
Ground1.1	all
Mush.1	above QB.4
Scaf2.1	under QB.4
Scaf3.2	just to the right of Scaf2.1
Plant.1	far right

Expert's Behavior

OBSERVED BEHAVIOR	INFERRED FUNCTION	INFERRED FINGER ACTION
turns left and lands on Scaf2.1		press-left-button
jumps to Mush.1	gather-item(Mush.1)	press-A-button

Comparison to Model

F.L.O. CONSISTENT WITH OBSERVED BEHAVIOR	F.L.O. PREDICTED BY MODEL	K.L.O. PREDICTED BY MODEL
gather-item(Mush.1)	gather-item(Mush.1)	press-right-button (run into Mush.1)

Display. 7 Mario jumps from QB.4 onto Scaf3.2, avoiding the fireball.

State of Mario: Small Mario

On Screen

OBJECTS SEEN	POSITION
Mario	on QB.4, facing left
Ground1.1	all
Scaf2.1	under QB.4
Scaf3.2	just to the right of Scaf2.1
Plant.1	right
Fireball	coming toward Mario
Scaf2.3	to the right of Plant.1

Expert's Behavior

OBSERVED BEHAVIOR	INFERRED FUNCTION	INFERRED FINGER ACTION
moves right landing on Scaf3.2	avoid-danger(Fireball)	press-right-button

Comparison to Model

F.L.O. CONSISTENT WITH OBSERVED BEHAVIOR	F.L.O. PREDICTED BY MODEL	K.L.O. PREDICTED BY MODEL
avoid-danger(Fireball) move-toward-end	avoid-danger(Fireball)	press-right-button

Display. 8 Mario goes after the next question block by jumping over the plant and onto Scaf2.3.

State of Mario: Super Mario

On Screen

OBJECTS SEEN	POSITION
Mario	on Scaf3.2, facing right
Ground1.1	all
Plant.1	right
Scaf2.3	right of Plant.1
QB.5	above Scaf2.3

Expert's Behavior

OBSERVED BEHAVIOR	INFERRED FUNCTION	INFERRED FINGER ACTION
Mario jumps over plant		press-A-button
turns left and lands on Scaf2.3	ambiguous	press-left-button

Comparison to Model

F.L.O. CONSISTENT WITH OBSERVED BEHAVIOR	F.L.O. PREDICTED BY MODEL	K.L.O. PREDICTED BY MODEL
search-in-block(QB.5)	search-in-block(QB.5)	press-A-button
avoid-danger(Plant.1)		press-right-button
move-toward-end		press-A-button
		press-right-button
		press-right-button

Display. 9 Goomba appears before Mario has reached QB.5.
It is not an immediate threat so Mario continues toward QB.5.

State of Mario: Super Mario

On Screen

OBJECTS SEEN	POSITION
Mario	on Scaf2.3 under QB.5, facing left
Ground1.1	all
Plant.1	far left
Scaf2.3	right of Plant.1
QB.5	above Scaf2.3
G.5	on Ground1.1 in front of Scaf2.3

Expert's Behavior

OBSERVED BEHAVIOR	INFERRED FUNCTION	INFERRED FINGER ACTION
turns to the right		press-right-button
jumps to QB.5	search-in-block(QB.5)	press-A-button

Comparison to Model

F.L.O. CONSISTENT WITH OBSERVED BEHAVIOR	F.L.O. PREDICTED BY MODEL	K.L.O. PREDICTED BY MODEL
search-in-block(QB.5)	search-in-block(QB.5)	press-right-button
		press-A-button

Display. 10 Neither Goomba nor Koopa are an immediate threat and Mario drops down onto Scaf1.6.

State of Mario: Super Mario

On Screen

OBJECTS SEEN	POSITION
Mario	on Scaf2.3, facing right
Ground1.1	all
Scaf2.3	far left
Scaf3.4	center
Scaf4.5	right
Scaf1.6	below Scaf4.5
G.5	on Ground1.1 in front of scafolds
K.1	on Scaf1.6

Expert's Behavior

OBSERVED BEHAVIOR	INFERRED FUNCTION	INFERRED FINGER ACTION
jumps		press-A-button
turns left		press-left-button
turns right and lands on Scaf1.6	ambiguous	press-right-button

Comparison to Model

F.L.O. CONSISTENT WITH OBSERVED BEHAVIOR	F.L.O. PREDICTED BY MODEL	K.L.O. PREDICTED BY MODEL
attack-enemy(K.1)	move-toward-end	press-right-button
move-toward-end		press-A-button
		press-right-button
		press-A-button

Display. 11 Mario sees QB.6 on the ground which can only be opened by thowing a shell at it. So Mario stomps on the Koopa Trooper in order to get a shell to throw at the block. Then Mario throws the shell at QB.6 and breaks it.

State of Mario: Super Mario

On Screen

OBJECTS SEEN	POSITION
Mario	on Scaf1.6, facing right
Ground1.1	all
Scaf2.3	far left
Scaf3.4	center
Scaf4.5	right
Scaf1.6	below Scaf4.5
G.5	on Ground1.1 in front of scafolds
K.1	on Scaf1.6
QB.6	far right on Ground2.2

Expert's Behavior

OBSERVED BEHAVIOR	INFERRED FUNCTION	INFERRED FINGER ACTION
jumps straight up		press-A-button
moves right in air		press-right-button
turns left and lands on K.1		press-left-button
jumps, landing left of the shell		press-A-button
turns right		press-right-button
picks up Koopa shell		hold-B-button
kicks Shell at QB.6		release-B-button
jumps out of way of Koopa shell	search-in-block(QB.6)	release-A-button

Comparison to Model

F.L.O. CONSISTENT WITH OBSERVED BEHAVIOR	F.L.O. PREDICTED BY MODEL	K.L.O. PREDICTED BY MODEL
search-in-block(QB.6)	search-in-block(QB.6)	press-right-button
		hold-B-button
		press-left-button
		press-right-button
		release-B-button
		press-A-button

***Note:** The last press-A-button is to jump out of the way of the richocheting Koopa shell. This KLO is added to the hit-with-shell method based on prior experience with being killed by the bouncing Koopa shell. See the text for more explanation of this learning process.*

Display. 12 A leaf pops out of the QB.6.
Mario goes to get it so he can turn into Racoon Mario.

State of Mario: Super Mario

On Screen

OBJECTS SEEN	POSITION
Mario	in air, facing right
Ground1.1	left
Scaf3.4	far left
Scaf4.5	center
Scaf1.6	below Scaf4.5
G.5	on Ground1.1 in front of scafolds
Ground2.2	right
QB.6 (empty)	right, on Ground2.2
Leaf.1	over QB.6

Expert's Behavior

OBSERVED BEHAVIOR	INFERRED FUNCTION	INFERRED FINGER ACTION
Mario moves to the right	gather-item(Leaf.1)	press-right-button

Comparison to Model

F.L.O. CONSISTENT WITH OBSERVED BEHAVIOR	F.L.O. PREDICTED BY MODEL	K.L.O. PREDICTED BY MODEL
gather-item(Leaf.1)	gather-item(Leaf.1)	press-right-button

Display. 13 Mario goes to get the next question block (QB.7)

State of Mario: Racoon Mario

On Screen

OBJECTS SEEN	POSITION
Mario	between QB.6 and QB.7, facing right
Ground1.1	left
Scaf1.6	far left
Ground2.2	right
QB.6 (empty)	center, on Ground2.2
QB.7	in air to the right of QB.6

Expert's Behavior

OBSERVED BEHAVIOR	INFERRED FUNCTION	INFERRED FINGER ACTION
moves right to QB.7		press-right-button
jumps		press-A-button
turns left and hits QB.7	search-in-block(QB.7)	press-left-button

Comparison to Model

F.L.O. CONSISTENT WITH OBSERVED BEHAVIOR	F.L.O. PREDICTED BY MODEL	K.L.O. PREDICTED BY MODEL
search-in-block(QB.7)	search-in-block(QB.7)	press-right-button
		press-A-button

Display. 14 There are no items or enemies on the screen so Mario just moves toward the end of the level.

State of Mario: Racoon Mario

On Screen

OBJECTS SEEN	POSITION
Mario	to the right of QB.7, facing left
Ground2.2	all
QB.6 (empty)	far left
QB.7 (empty)	left

Expert's Behavior

OBSERVED BEHAVIOR	INFERRED FUNCTION	INFERRED FINGER ACTION
moves right	move-toward-end	press-right-button

Comparison to Model

F.L.O. CONSISTENT WITH OBSERVED BEHAVIOR	F.L.O. PREDICTED BY MODEL	K.L.O. PREDICTED BY MODEL
move-toward-end	move-toward-end	press-right-button

Display. 15 A goomba (G.3) moves toward Mario from the right (becoming an immediate threat), so Mario attacks him.

State of Mario: Racoon Mario

On Screen

OBJECTS SEEN	POSITION
Mario	to the right of QB.7, facing right
Ground2.2	all
QB.7 (empty)	far left
G.3	moving toward Mario from the right

Expert's Behavior

OBSERVED BEHAVIOR	INFERRED FUNCTION	INFERRED FINGER ACTION
turns left		press-left-button
turns right		press-right-button
jumps		press-A-button
turns left and lands on G.3	attack-enemy(G.3)	press-left-button

Comparison to Model

F.L.O. CONSISTENT WITH OBSERVED BEHAVIOR	F.L.O. PREDICTED BY MODEL	K.L.O. PREDICTED BY MODEL
attack-enemy(G.3)	attack-enemy(G.3)	press-A-button

Display. 16 This is not a distinct display in the expert's protocol.
Since the expert has moved away from QB.7 instead of waiting for G.3 to approach (as the model does), G.4 appears on the screen before the expert has stomped G.3.

Display. 17 Another goomba (G.4) moves toward Mario from the right (becoming an immediate threat), so Mario attacks him.

State of Mario: Racoon Mario

On Screen

OBJECTS SEEN	POSITION
Mario	to the right of QB.7, facing left
Ground2.2	all
G.4	moving toward Mario from the right

Expert's Behavior

OBSERVED BEHAVIOR	INFERRED FUNCTION	INFERRED FINGER ACTION
turns right		press-right-button
jumps		press-A-button
turns left at apogee		press-left-button
turns right and lands on G.4	attack-enemy(G.4)	press-right-button

Comparison to Model

F.L.O. CONSISTENT WITH OBSERVED BEHAVIOR	F.L.O. PREDICTED BY MODEL	K.L.O. PREDICTED BY MODEL
attack-enemy(G.4)	attack-enemy(G.4)	press-A-button

Display. 18 This is not a distinct display in the expert's protocol.
Since the expert has continued to move right instead of waiting for enemies to approach (as the model does), PG.1 appears on the screen before the expert has stomped G.4.

Display. 19 A para-goomba (PG.1) moves toward Mario from the right (becoming an immediate threat), so Mario attacks him.

State of Mario: Racoon Mario

On Screen

OBJECTS SEEN	POSITION
Mario	to the right of QB.7, facing right
Ground2.2	all
PG.1	moving toward Mario from the right

Expert's Behavior

OBSERVED BEHAVIOR	INFERRED FUNCTION	INFERRED FINGER ACTION
turns left		press-left-button
jumps (higher than flying PG.1)		press-A-button (repeatedly)
turns right		press-right-button
turns left and lands on PG.1	attack-enemy(PG.1)	press-left-button

Comparison to Model

F.L.O. CONSISTENT WITH OBSERVED BEHAVIOR	F.L.O. PREDICTED BY MODEL	K.L.O. PREDICTED BY MODEL
attack-enemy(PG.1)	attack-enemy(PG.1)	press-A-button

Display. 20 The paragoomba turns into a goomba (G.5) after Mario stomps on it, so he attacks it again.

State of Mario: Racoon Mario

On Screen

OBJECTS SEEN	POSITION
Mario	to the right of QB.7, facing left
Ground2.2	all
G.5	on Mario's left

Expert's Behavior

OBSERVED BEHAVIOR	INFERRED FUNCTION	INFERRED FINGER ACTION
jumps		press-A-button
turns right at apogee		press-right-button
turns left		press-left-button
turns right and lands on G.5	attack-enemy(G.5)	press-right-button

Comparison to Model

F.L.O. CONSISTENT WITH OBSERVED BEHAVIOR	F.L.O. PREDICTED BY MODEL	K.L.O. PREDICTED BY MODEL
attack-enemy(G.5)	attack-enemy(G.5)	press-A-button
		press-left-button

Display. 21 Mario runs back to QB.6(empty) and then runs to the right accelerating to fly.

State of Mario: Racoon Mario

On Screen

OBJECTS SEEN	POSITION
Mario	in center on Ground2.2, facing right
Ground2.2	all

Expert's Behavior

OBSERVED BEHAVIOR	INFERRED FUNCTION	INFERRED FINGER ACTION
turns left		press-left-button
jumps		press-A-button
lands and runs to left		press-left-button
turns right		press-right-button
runs to right		press-right-button
accelerating	ambiguous	hold-B-button

Comparison to Model

F.L.O. CONSISTENT WITH OBSERVED BEHAVIOR	F.L.O. PREDICTED BY MODEL	K.L.O. PREDICTED BY MODEL
move-toward-end	move-toward-end	press-right-button

***Note:* The first three observed behaviors (where Mario turns left, jumps, and then runs to the left) are not consistent with any proposed F.L.O.s. The other three behaviors (where Mario turns right and then runs to the right while accelerating) are consistent with move-toward-end. The whole sequence of behavior is both ambiguous and consistent with move-toward-end.**

Display. 22 The first coin comes into view as Mario is picking up speed to fly.

State of Mario: Racoon Mario

On Screen

OBJECTS SEEN	POSITION
Mario	in center on Ground2.2, facing right
Ground2.2	all
Coin.1	next to Cliff.1

Expert's Behavior

OBSERVED BEHAVIOR	INFERRED FUNCTION	INFERRED FINGER ACTION
runs to right		press-right-button
accelerating	ambiguous	hold-B-button

Comparison to Model

F.L.O. CONSISTENT WITH OBSERVED BEHAVIOR	F.L.O. PREDICTED BY MODEL	K.L.O. PREDICTED BY MODEL
gather-item (Coin.1)	gather-item (Coin.1)	press-right-button
move-toward-end		

Display. 23 A cliff apears at the far right as Mario moves toward the coin.

State of Mario: Racoon Mario

On Screen

OBJECTS SEEN	POSITION
Mario	in center on Ground2.2, facing right
Ground2.2	all
Coin.1	next to Cliff.1
Cliff.1	far right

Expert's Behavior

OBSERVED BEHAVIOR	INFERRED FUNCTION	INFERRED FINGER ACTION
runs to right		press-right-button
accelerating	ambiguous	hold-B-button

Comparison to Model

F.L.O. CONSISTENT WITH OBSERVED BEHAVIOR	F.L.O. PREDICTED BY MODEL	K.L.O. PREDICTED BY MODEL
gather-item (Coin.1)	gather-item (Coin.1)	press-right-button
move-toward-end		

Display. 24 A second coin comes into view; this one is over the cliff and too high for Mario to jump.

State of Mario: Racoon Mario

On Screen

OBJECTS SEEN	POSITION
Mario	in center on Ground2.2, facing right
Ground2.2	all
Coin.1	next to Cliff.1
Cliff.1	right
Coin.2	far right and above Coin.1

Expert's Behavior

OBSERVED BEHAVIOR	INFERRED FUNCTION	INFERRED FINGER ACTION
runs to right		press-right-button
accelerating	ambiguous	hold-B-button

Comparison to Model

F.L.O. CONSISTENT WITH OBSERVED BEHAVIOR	F.L.O. PREDICTED BY MODEL	K.L.O. PREDICTED BY MODEL
gather-item (Coin.1)	gather-item (Coin.1)	press-right-button
gather-item (Coin.2)		
move-toward-end		

Display. 25 A third coin comes into view; this one is also over the cliff and too high for Mario to jump.

State of Mario: Racoon Mario

On Screen

OBJECTS SEEN	POSITION
Mario	in center on Ground2.2, facing right
Ground2.2	all
Coin.1	next to Cliff.1
Cliff.1	right
Coin.2	right and above Coin.1
Coin.3	far right and above Coin.2

Expert's Behavior

OBSERVED BEHAVIOR	INFERRED FUNCTION	INFERRED FINGER ACTION
runs to right		press-right-button
accelerating	ambiguous	hold-B-button

Comparison to Model

F.L.O. CONSISTENT WITH OBSERVED BEHAVIOR	F.L.O. PREDICTED BY MODEL	K.L.O. PREDICTED BY MODEL
gather-item (Coin.1)	gather-item (Coin.1)	press-right-button
gather-item (Coin.2)		
gather-item (Coin.3)		
move-toward-end		

Display. 26 Mario begins flying up to Coin.1.

State of Mario: Racoon Mario

On Screen

OBJECTS SEEN	POSITION
Mario	in center on Ground2.2, facing right
Ground2.2	all
Coin.1	next to Cliff.1
Cliff.1	right
Coin.2	over Cliff.1
Coin.3	to the right and above Coin.2

Expert's Behavior

OBSERVED BEHAVIOR	INFERRED FUNCTION	INFERRED FINGER ACTION
has enough speed to fly		release-B-button
jumps and flies		press-A-button (repeatedly)
turns left and gets first coin	gather-item (Coin.1)	press-left-button

Comparison to Model

F.L.O. CONSISTENT WITH OBSERVED BEHAVIOR	F.L.O. PREDICTED BY MODEL	K.L.O. PREDICTED BY MODEL
gather-item (Coin.1)	gather-item (Coin.1)	press-right-button
		press-A-button

Display. 27 Mario continues flying to the second coin.

State of Mario: Racoon Mario

On Screen

OBJECTS SEEN	POSITION
Mario	in center on Ground2.2, facing left
Ground2.2	all
Cliff.1	right
Coin.2	over Cliff.1
Coin.3	to the right and above Coin.2

Expert's Behavior

OBSERVED BEHAVIOR	INFERRED FUNCTION	INFERRED FINGER ACTION
turns right and flies to next coin	gather-item (Coin.2)	press-right-button press-A-button (repeatedly)

Comparison to Model

F.L.O. CONSISTENT WITH OBSERVED BEHAVIOR	F.L.O. PREDICTED BY MODEL	K.L.O. PREDICTED BY MODEL
gather-item (Coin.2)	gather-item (Coin.2)	press-left-button press-right-button press-right-button hold-B-button release-B-button press-A-button (repeatedly)

Display. 28 After getting the second coin, Mario continues flying to the third coin. Two more coins appear above and to the right of the third one.

State of Mario: Racoon Mario

On Screen

OBJECTS SEEN	POSITION
Mario	flying, facing right
Coin.3	in the air
Coin.4	to the right and above Coin.3
Coin.5	to the right and above Coin.4

Expert's Behavior

OBSERVED BEHAVIOR	INFERRED FUNCTION	INFERRED FINGER ACTION
flies to next coin	gather-item (Coin.3)	press-right-button press-A-button (repeatedly)

Comparison to Model

F.L.O. CONSISTENT WITH OBSERVED BEHAVIOR	F.L.O. PREDICTED BY MODEL	K.L.O. PREDICTED BY MODEL
gather-item (Coin.3)	gather-item (Coin.3)	press-right-button press-A-button (repeatedly)

Display. 29 After getting the third coin, Mario continues flying to the fourth coin.

State of Mario: Racoon Mario

On Screen

OBJECTS SEEN	POSITION
Mario	flying, facing right
Coin.4	in the air
Coin.5	to the right and above Coin.4

Expert's Behavior

OBSERVED BEHAVIOR	INFERRED FUNCTION	INFERRED FINGER ACTION
flies to next coin	gather-item (Coin.4)	press-right-button press-A-button (repeatedly)

Comparison to Model

F.L.O. CONSISTENT WITH OBSERVED BEHAVIOR	F.L.O. PREDICTED BY MODEL	K.L.O. PREDICTED BY MODEL
gather-item (Coin.4)	gather-item (Coin.4)	press-right-button press-A-button (repeatedly)

Display. 30 After getting the fourth coin, Mario continues flying to the fifth coin.

State of Mario: Racoon Mario

On Screen

OBJECTS SEEN	POSITION
Mario	flying, facing right
Coin.5	to the right and above Coin.4

Expert's Behavior

OBSERVED BEHAVIOR	INFERRED FUNCTION	INFERRED FINGER ACTION
flies to next coin	gather-item (Coin.5)	press-right-button press-A-button (repeatedly)

Comparison to Model

F.L.O. CONSISTENT WITH OBSERVED BEHAVIOR	F.L.O. PREDICTED BY MODEL	K.L.O. PREDICTED BY MODEL
gather-item (Coin.5)	gather-item (Coin.5)	press-right-button press-A-button (repeatedly)

CHAPTER 63

Extending Problem Spaces to External Environments*

J. E. Laird, University of Michigan

Abstract

Problem spaces have played a central role in artificial intelligence since its inception. For the most part they have been used as a theory of internal problem solving and have often been criticized as unextensible to tasks requiring interaction with an external dynamic environment. In this paper we examine the constraints of external environments and propose a model of problem spaces that supports both internal and external tasks. This model has been operationalized within the Soar 5 architecture. We consider the series of design decisions that led to Soar 5 from the previously reported versions of Soar. The most important of these is the "single state principle" in which only a single state is accessible within a goal.

Primary Topic: Planning, Scheduling and Reasoning about Action
Secondary Topic: Agent Architectures

---

*This research was sponsored in part by grant NCC2-517 from NASA Ames.

1 Introduction

The problem space model of goal-oriented behavior has had a strong influence on AI over the last 35 years [Newell *et al.*, 1957; Nilsson, 1971; Newell and Simon, 1972; Newell, 1980], with symbolic operators continuing to be a fundamental component of AI planning and problem solving systems [Hendler *et al.*, 1990]. The problem space model has been challenged for tasks in which an agent directly interacts with external "real world" environments [Brooks, 1987; Suchman, 1987]. In response, many systems have been developed with separate "customized" formulations for internal and external tasks [Fikes *et al.*, 1972].

The thesis of this paper is that a uniform problem space framework is sufficient for both internal and external tasks without sacrificing the generality and power of traditional AI systems or the responsiveness of execution-oriented systems. This avoids separate formulations for internal and external behavior, as well as the requisite transfers of control and translations of knowledge between modules. Instead, all knowledge is available for both planning and execution, and the switching between planning and execution is based on knowledge sensitive to the total situation.

As proof of this thesis, we present the Soar 5 architecture [Laird *et al.*, 1990a] which embodies a problem space model of both internal and external tasks. Soar5 is a revision of Soar 4 [Laird *et al.*, 1990b]. Soar 4 uses problem spaces as an organizational framework for all of its goal-oriented behavior [Laird *et al.*, 1987; Rosenbloom *et al.*, 1990] and was used by the Soar research group from 1986 until 1989. Soar 5 has demonstrated its capabilities on external tasks [Laird and Rosenbloom, 1990] and has been in use since early 1989. This paper provides the rationale for the design decisions used to extend Soar 4 to Soar 5, examining the connections between the underlying behavior constraints, and the architectural mechanisms.

2 Problem Spaces and Task Characteristics

We assume the standard formulation of problem spaces where a goal is achieved by applying operators to search through the space of potential states until a desired state of the goal is found. An operator transforms a state into a new state and the set of available operators determine the space that will be searched. The basic functions that must be performed within a problem space are: generating and selecting an operator to apply to the state; applying an operator to a state; and determining if the state achieves the goal.

In the development of Soar, we have extended the problem space formulation to include the following constraints about intelligent behavior in problem spaces.

Constraint 1 *All problem space functions can be influenced by directly available domain-specific long-term knowledge.*

Constraint 2 *Arbitrary problem solving, including search at multiple levels of abstraction, is available whenever direct knowledge is insufficient or contradictory.*

Constraint 3 *Learning is possible for all problem space functions.*

Soar's architecture supports the basic problem space functions by representing the selections of the current goal, problem space, state and operator in its short-term working memory. This working memory also contains proposed operators and the substructure of all of the proposed and current objects (goals, problem spaces, states, and operators). It encodes its long-term memory as a production system that is cued off of the contents of working memory. The problem space functions are performed by firing all relevant productions in parallel to modify working memory. For selections, the productions produce *preferences* for the candidate objects. A fixed decision procedure interprets the preferences retrieved from long-term memory and selects the preferred candidate object thereby meeting the demands of Constraint 1.

When the long-term memory has insufficient or conflicting knowledge for a problem space function, Soar automatically generates a subgoal in which the lack of knowledge is cast as a new problem to be solved in another problem space, thus satisfying Constraint 2. The activity in this subgoal may include search, or if control knowledge is sufficient, it may be a direct computation accomplished by applying a string of operators, one after the other. A subgoal is automatically terminated when the results it creates are sufficient to perform the problem space function that led to the subgoal. Constraint 3 is achieved through Soar's learning mechanism, called *chunking,* which summarizes the processing in subgoals by creating new productions whose actions are the results of the subgoal and whose conditions are based on those working memory elements that existed before that subgoal and that were necessary for creating the result.

To extend the problem space formulation to external tasks, we assume that the external task is cast as a problem space whose states contain perceptions from its sensors, as well as relevant information retrieved from long-term memory. The operators of a problem space can modify internal data structures directly, or can signal the motor system to perform primitive acts in the external environment, and through perception, receive information relevant to the results of these acts.

Extending problem spaces to external tasks adds the following constraints.

Constraint 4 *Operators can be composed of multiple external actions that are be performed in sequence or in parallel over extended periods of time.*

For example, in picking up a cup a robot must extend its arm, open its gripper, move the gripper into the cup (but only after the gripper is open), close the gripper until it has appropriate tactile feedback, raise the arm, possibly verifying that it actually has the cup through other sensors. Some problem solving and planning systems simulate external operators; however, these are internal simulations that are themselves atomic, predictable and instantaneous.

Constraint 5 *The state of an external problem space can change independently of the agent.*

The state of an internal task will change only when an operator is applied. In contrast, the environment of an external task can have its own dynamics that are not be controlled by the problem solver.

Constraint 6 *There is no selection of a current state.*

Within a internal problem space, control can return to a previous state merely by selecting it when the current state becomes unpromising. For external tasks, progress can be made only by going forward from the current state.

3 Problem Spaces for External Tasks

The constraints from external tasks challenge the standard formulation of problem spaces. In this section, we extend our earlier formulation of problem spaces in light of those constraints and we develop a set of architectural mechanisms to support this formulation. Throughout this section we will identify the new design decisions that have been made for Soar 5.

3.1 How Are Operators Represented?

Constraints 2 and 4 have direct consequences for the representation of operators. Essentially, an arbitrary amount of computation may be required to carry out the actions of an operator. STRIPS-like representations clearly are inadequate because they assume that all actions happen at once. Some expanded set of the action semantics is required for external tasks. One obvious ramification of Constraints 2 and 4 is that external operators will often have multiple implementations, one for internal temporal projection at an abstract level, and a second for actual execution in the environment.

Constraint 1 states that long-term knowledge must be able to influence the selection of operators. In order for that to be possible, some representation of the operator's actions must be available so that control knowledge can select between alternative operators. In STRIPS, the complete description of the operator is available, while in pure procedurally defined operators, the effects of an operator are unavailable. This constraint does not demand that all details of every operator must be available, only that sufficient information is available so that appropriate discrimination between operators is possible.

Constraint 3 demands that operators can be learned and can be modified by learning. This suggests modular representations of knowledge.

Soar 4 meets these constraints by representing operators with both declarative and procedural components. The declarative component is a description created in working memory that can be a cue for retrieving additional information about the operator, for controlling the selection, or for controlling the application of the operator. In practice, the declarative description consists of the operator's name and parameters to specialize the execution of the operator to the current state.

Soar's procedural component is its production memory. Productions test for the selection of an operator and the contents of the current state and then modify the state accordingly. The state has distinguished data structures corresponding to the motor system, and by creating appropriate structure, productions can send commands to the motor system. Productions can also be sensitive to whether the operator is being applied internally or externally, so that different operator implementations can be used for execution or planning. If there is sufficient declarative information about an operator, general purpose productions can interpret the declarative information. If a declarative specification is unavailable, operator-specific productions perform the appropriate actions. The inherent modularity of production systems makes it easy to modify the execution of an operator through learning.

Productions provide conditional execution based on intermediate results of the execution, but productions alone do not allow for the arbitrary problem solving required of some operators. Thus, an additional control scheme is required. However, our original thesis was that problem spaces are sufficient for intelligent action. The productions that apply operators do not violate this constraint because they are fired in parallel whenever their conditions matched, without any conflict resolution or selection mechanism. They perform a recognition-based computation that is not subject to intelligent control. If arbitrary computation is required, Soar's subgoaling mechanism automatically casts the problem of applying the operator as a subgoal to be achieved within the problem space framework. Thus, once the subgoal has been created, Soar will apply the operator by repeatedly selecting and applying operators from a more primitive implementation problem space. This provides a second type of procedural representation of an operator. An added feature of Soar is that chunking will compile the activity in the subgoal into productions, so that in the future, the operator will be applied directly by productions, without the need to repeat the subgoaling.

3.2 Does an operator create a new state?

The issue as to whether the application of an operator creates a new state or destructively modifies the existing state is the point of departure of Soar 5 from Soar 4. One approach is to create a new state that incorporates all of the changes required by the operator as well as all unmodified substructures. The advantage of this approach in internal problem solving is that all of the previously generated states of the problem space can maintained so that it is possible to backup to a previous state if the current state must be abandoned.

In Soar 4, productions create a new state with the changes required by the operator and additional "frame axiom" productions copy over those aspects of the previous state that were not changed by the actions of the operator. In contrast, systems such as STRIPS and PRODIGY [Minton *et al.*, 1989] specify the changes to the state. The underlying architecture interprets these actions and automatically copies all unmodified structures.

These approaches assume that a completely new state structure is created whenever there is a state transition in the problem space. However, for external tasks, part of the internal state is determined by the environment, which can change independent of the agent (Constraint 5). Thus, the internal state must reflect state transitions that are made by the external environment. Should a new internal state be created whenever a state transition is caused by the environment, or should the part of the state determined by perception be updated without the creation of a new state? If a new state is created, it is difficult to imagine how an operator with any significant duration can be applied. If a new state is not created, there is a significant inconsistency in the meaning of a state change.

A second problem is that these approaches either require space linear in the number of states visited during the search, or some additional mechanism to manage the number of states saved. These states may be useful for internal problems where backtracking is possible, but in external environments, it is not possible to backup to a previous state merely by selecting it (Constraint 6). In response to these problems, we have adopted the "single state principle" in Soar 5.

Design Decision 1 *There is only a single state available within a goal at any time. All operators are applied by modifying the current state.*

This requires changing the semantics of production actions so that they destructively modify the structure of the state. Thus, once the initial state is selected for a problem space, no additional state symbols are generated and all operators are applied by modifying the current state in place. Perception directly modifies the relevant parts of the state. This eliminates the need for copying, either explicitly with frame axioms, or implicitly by the architecture. It also eliminates the memory cost of representing each visited state in the problem space.

The obvious disadvantage of this scheme is that it eliminates the ability to backtrack during an internal search. The resolution of this problem in Soar 5 is a bit complicated because it is dependent on Soar's approach to internal search, but the basic idea is that the search occurs within the problem space, but across multiple subgoals. Recall that an impasse arises because there is insufficient knowledge to select an operator. These are the potential backtracking points of a search. In response to the impasse, the system can perform a search using a *copy* of the original state. Within the search, additional impasses can arise, leading to a recursive goal stack. Since the search is performed on copies, the original state is not disturbed by the search. Thus, although no copying is done during operator application, intermediate states can be maintained in subgoals during a search. These copies are created deliberately by productions, and are under control of the problem solver.

3.3 When are changes made to the state?

Once the decision is made to maintain only a single state, the issue remains as to when changes to the state should be made. Two obvious possibilities are to make the changes incrementally as they are suggested by productions and the sensor system, or to bundle the changes together and make them *en mass* when the operator terminates. For strictly internal processing, there need be no functional difference between the two alternatives because none of the actions are time-dependent. Soar 4 made changes *en mass* because it first created a new state symbol and then built up the state by attaching structure to the symbol. Only when the operator was completed did the new operator get selected, essentially jumping to the new state.

However, once the architecture is extended to tasks requiring complex interaction with unpredictable and dynamic external environments (Constraints 4 and 5), the timing and order of actions becomes critical so that incremental changes to the state are necessary.

Design Decision 2 *Changes are made to the state when suggested by perception or productions.*

Therefore, changes to the state can occur incrementally and in parallel as an operator is being applied. Because there is no conflict resolution in selecting productions, it is possible for the actions of productions to conflict. We will address this issue in Section 3.5.

A second issue is that during the application of an operator, the state may take on intermediate values so that it is not a legal state of the problem space. For example, if the system was playing a game of chess, during the movement of a piece, the piece might be lifted in the air so that it is no longer on the board. These intermediate situations should occur only during operator application, not when the operator has terminated. This is true in Soar 5 as will be described in the next section.

A related problem is that productions that modify the state when the operator is first selected can potentially reapply incorrectly to the intermediate state. This is only a problem when incremental changes to the state are allowed. It is easily fixed by modifying the conditions of the productions and possibly introducing some additional intermediate changes to the state. This does not require an architectural solution, but it is one way in which productions had to be modified once we eliminated the assumption that all changes to the state occur at once.

3.4 How is an operator terminated?

For systems such as STRIPS, an operator terminates after its actions are performed, at which point a new operator is selected. Thus, successful completion is implicit in performing the actions. However, for operators that involve interaction with external environments, completion of the operator may be problematic and can only be detected by feedback from the environment (Constraints 4 and 5).

In Soar 4, an operator was terminated whenever a new state was selected. However, in Soar 5, there is no state change to signal completion of an operator. The simplest solution, and the one adopted here, is to allow productions to signal that the current operator is complete. This allows for simple tests where a production directly tests whether the current state is an appropriate result of the current operator, or for more complex tests, where a production tests that the problem solving of a subgoal tested for termination..

This approach is sufficient for terminating operators, however, there is a related issue that should be considered at the same time. One of the features of Soar 4 is that the selection of the current operator can change whenever the preferences for the current operator preferred a new operator at a decision. In Soar 4, the preferences for the current operator would not change during operator application because the contents of the state did not change. However, in Soar 5, the contents of the state change during the application of an operator (which may take many decisions in a subgoal), and thus, so can the available preferences. Thus, in Soar 5 the selection of the current operator changes only when an operator is terminated, and at that time, a new decision is made based on the current preferences.

Design Decision 3 *New decisions for operators are made only when a termination signal is generated for the current operator.*

3.5 How are other types of knowledge represented and used?

Up to now, the emphasis has been on representing and using knowledge to apply and terminate operators. Other types of knowledge that must be represented include control knowledge to select operators, as well as refinement knowledge that computes simple inferences based on the current state (but independent of the current operator) such as an evaluation of the state relative to the goal. Surprisingly, the design decisions we have made for operator application have a significant impact on the representation and use of non-operator application knowledge.

3.5.1 Representing non-operator-application knowledge

There are many alternatives for representing non-operator-application knowledge:

1. **No explicit represention.**
   One design goal of STRIPS was to have a general problem solver based only on operator descriptions. All control knowledge was implicit in the operator descriptions. This approach makes it difficult to represent special-case knowledge, and thus violates Constraint 1.
2. **Separate representation language.**
   GPS had its table of connections for encoding control knowledge, while PRODIGY has inference rules. In both cases, these use different representation languages than those used to represent operators.
3. **Operator representation language.**
   Soar 4 used productions to represent both control and refinement knowledge. Productions allow for the context-dependent encoding of knowledge useful in satisfying Constraint 1, and they can be automatically learned by chunking (Constraint 3).

Just as in Soar 4, Soar 5 represents all long-term knowledge as productions.

3.5.2 Persistence of knowledge

Soar 4 hid a basic distinction in how knowledge should persist in working memory. When applying an operator, the system commits itself to the changes that the operator makes to the state.[1] This knowledge should persist until changed by another operator. We will call this *O-persistence.* However, other types of knowledge are not commitments to change, but instead are simple monotonic inferences that are based on the contents of current state. This knowledge may become invalid if the state changes, either through the actions of an operator or changes in perception. For example, if productions create preferences for operators, and those preferences are maintained after an operator is applied, the preferences may later be incorrect. Soar 4 avoided this problem because it always created a completely new state whenever an operator applied. Thus, all control information, refinements, etc. were recomputed from scratch for each state. In Soar 5, a new state symbol is not created, so that non-operator application knowledge should persist only as long as its retrieval conditions are satisfied.

Design Decision 4 *Changes due to operator applications persist until explicitly modified.*

Design Decision 5 *The actions of non-operator application knowledge persist only as long as that knowledge is relevant to the current situation.*

Surprisingly, Soar's underlying RETE match algorithm [Forgy, 1982] automatically computes not only when productions match, but also when they no longer match, and thus, this design decision did not require any major addition to the underlying architecture, Thus, the production instantiation determines persistence and we will call this *I-persistence.*

The persistence scheme for non-operator application knowledge is essentially the same as a justification-based truth-maintenance systems (JTMS) [Doyle, 1979]. The productions act as justifications and maintain their actions only as long as the conditions of

[1]We will use operator application as a title for all such non-monotonic knowledge which also includes some types of operator creation and instantiation.

the production are satisfied. When one of the working memory elements of a production instantiation is removed (or a working memory element is created that would match a negated condition), the action of the production is retracted.

This design decision, together with other features of the Soar 5 architecture has interesting ramifications. For example, a production that suggests operators, may fire in the middle of the application of an operator because of intermediate values of the state. If the state continues to change so that the operator is no longer appropriate, the production will retract the operators and they will not be considered when the current operator finally terminates. If the conditions for operators are still met at termination, the decision for a new operator is ready to be made without any additional computation. This leads to a qualitative difference in Soar's behavior. In Soar 4 there was a phase of operator application, followed by state selection and then operator proposal and selection. In Soar 5, the state selection is eliminated and operators are proposed and compared in parallel with the operator application.

3.5.3 Conflicting knowledge

One danger in a parallel production system is that the actions of productions will conflict. This was not a problem in Soar 4 because all productions actions were monotonic additions to working memory and the only non-monotonic changes were the selections of operators and states by the decision procedure. In Soar 5, productions are used for applying operators directly, and so must be able to modify or delete values, thus conflicts seem inevitable. In systems that assume complete consistency in their knowledge, conflict would be taken as a sign that the current problem solving path is invalid and should be abandoned and thus, some form of dependency-direct backtracking should be invoked. In contrast, one assumption (not explicitly stated in our list of constraints) is that long-term knowledge may not be completely consistent so that conflicting actions are diagnostic of a possible inconsistency that should be probed further if it impedes problem solving.

Given this approach to conflicting action, how should it be handled in Soar 5? We can draw inspiration from Soar's preference scheme in which conflicting preferences lead to an impasse. The actions of the productions do not determine the selections for operator but instead create preferences. If there is a conflict, it is selecting between the alternatives suggested by the preferences. More preferences can then be created which in turn resolve the conflict (this depends in part on the details of the preference scheme [Laird *et al.*, 1990a]). In Soar 5 we have extended the preference scheme to all of the contents of working memory. Thus, productions create preferences for changes to working memory, and the preferences persist depending on the type of knowledge. The active preferences are combined by a decision procedure that determines the actual contents of working memory. If these preferences conflict, a structure is built in working memory that describes the conflict so that other productions can fire to create preferences that can resolve the conflict.

Design Decision 6 *The contents of working memory are determined by preferences created by productions.*

The decision procedure for selecting operators differs from the one used for working memory in that it is run only at quiescence when a termination signal is present for the current operator. The decision procedure for a working memory element is run whenever there is a change to the set of relevant preferences.

3.5.4 Determining knowledge persistence

Given the need to have different persistence of preferences, how should the distinction between the two classes of persistence be made, i.e., how is it determined whether the actions of a production are O-persistent or I-persistent? Below we review the alternatives in light of underlying behavior constraints and previous design decisions:

1. **Explicit production declaration.**
   The first alternative to consider is that the user gives some sort of type declaration when writing the production. Another alternative is to label which conditions of a production must be satisfied to preserve persistence. An operator application production would thus have its persistence determined by only a subset of its conditions that test for working memory elements that do not change during the problem solving. Both of these conflict with the constraint that knowledge can be created through learning (3).
2. **Type of learning.**
   If we had separate learning mechanisms for operator application knowledge and all other knowledge, we could simply classify productions based on the learning mechanism used to create it. However, in Soar, chunking can acquire either type of knowledge, and there is nothing in the chunking process that distinguishes the type of knowledge that is learnied.
3. **Inheritance.**
   If we assume that a production is created through chunking, the production actions could inherit the persistence type of the production actions that were created in the subgoal. Thus, if an O-persistent action in a subgoal is a result, the chunk built for that result will have an O-persistent action. This incorrectly assumes that the problem space function performed in the subgoal to create the result is the same as the one being performed in the supergoal. For example, within a subgoal, an evaluation of the state in the supergoal may be computed by operators that count certain properties of the state. The count is computed through operator applications, but the final evaluation is a refinement of the superstate, and thus should be retracted in the supergoal whenever any of the data it is based on is modified.
4. **Explicit data declaration.**
   Instead of depending on the structure of the computation, we could base the persistence on the structure of the data in working memory.[2] Thus, we could have separate representations for the "core" of the state that is modified and maintained by operators and are O-persistent, and the other structures that have a separate representation and are I-persistent (instantiation-presistent). This approach requires that data that plays different roles in different problem spaces (and thus has different persistence) must be explicitly translated from one representation to the other.

[2]This approach was suggested by Paul Rosenbloom.

This approach has the double-edged property in that it gives explicit control of persistence to the system when it chooses representations. The advantage is that the system can intelligently manage persistence, but the disadvantage is that it requires that the system develop a theory of persistence, and possibly learn when a piece of information should or should not be persistent.

5. **Structure of the production instantiation.**
   An alternative approach is to examine the structure of the production instantiation to determine the persistence of its actions. The theory is that the function of the action can be determined by the types of structures it tests and modifies. For example, if an action modifies the state while the conditions test the state and the operator, the action would be O-persistent because the production performs an operator-application function. The advantage of this scheme is that persistence is not based on either the process or data used to create the production, both of which we have argued do not necessarily determine the function of the production. This final alternative is the one used in Soar 5.

Design Decision 7 *Persistence of an action is determined automatically based on the structure of the knowledge used to generate it.*

3.5.5 Persistence of Results

The main justification for basing persistence on production structure was that the persistence of a result of was independent of the process and structures used to generate it. But how does this solve the persistence issue for results? If a preference is created in a subgoal, it will get the appropriate persistence for its existence in that subgoal from the production that created it. However, if it is a result, where is the production instantiation that gives it the appropriate persistence in the supergoal? The obvious choice (and the one made in Soar 5) is to use the compiled dependency structure that is the basis for building a chunk. This *justification* contains in its conditions all of the working memory elements that were necessary for creating the result, and the result is its action. Thus, in Soar 5, justifications are created for every result of a subgoal. This justification is used both to determine the support of the result and as a basis for creating a chunk.

We have yet to describe what happens when a preference receives persistence from more than one source, such as from a production in a subgoal and a justification. Since persistence is only a positive thing, a preference is considered as long as it has any support. However, one refinement must be made concerning O-persistence. Originally we stated that a preference with O-persistence is maintained until it is changed by a subsequent operator. This is true, but only within a subgoal. As should be obvious, if a preference gets O-persistence within a subgoal, but receives only I-persistence in the supergoal, it should not continue to receive O-persistence. Thus, O-persistence is goal-relative and is maintained only as long as the goal in which it was created exists in working memory leading to a change in Design Design 4.

Design Decision 4' *Changes due to operator application persist within a subgoal until explicitly modified.*

Design Decisions	C1. Knowledge-Dependent Action	C2. Arbitrary Problem Solving	C3. Learning	C4. Complex Operators	C5. Reactive Environment	C6. No External State Selection	DD1. Single State Principal	DD2. Incremental Changes	DD3. Termination Signal	DD4. Operator Persistence	DD5. Instantiation Persistence	DD6. Preferences for WM	DD7. Persistence Determination
Single State					●	●							
Incremental Changes				●	●		●						
Operator Decisions	●			●	●		●	●					
Operator Persistence	●	●	●				●	●					
Instantiation Persistence	●	●	●	●	●		●	●					
Preferences for WM								●		●	●		
Persistence Determination		●	●	●	●		●						

Figure 1: Dependencies between design decisions and behavior constraints. The dots signify that the design decisions on the left is dependent on a constraint or earlier design decision across the top.

The determination of persistence concludes the list of major design decisions required to extend Soar to external environments. The whole persistence issue was the trickiest part of the Soar 5 implementation, possibly because it is dependent on so many other issues, and also because of its novelty.

4 Discussion

Figure 1 summarizes the dependencies of the individual design decisions of Soar 5 on the behavioral constraints and other design decisions. This is of necessity an imprecise reconstruction of the actual design process, but for the most part it accurately reflects the development of Soar 5. This figure makes clear the impact that the choice of a single state (Design Decision 1) had on the complete design.

Given that there is a working implementation of Soar 5, there should be some significant results to report. Qualitative descriptions of the capabilities of Soar 5 have been reported for integrating execution, planning and learning in external environments [Laird and Rosenbloom, 1990]. All new development of Soar systems in the U.S. has switched over to Soar 5. Quantitative comparisons of systems implemented in both Soar 4 and Soar 5 show that Soar 5 significantly reduces the number of decisions (to as little as 50% because of the elimination of state selection), production firings (to as little as 13% because of the elimination of copying to create new states), and work by the matcher (to as little as 8% because operators change state incrementally). However, in spite of these improvements, Soar 5 can run up to a factor of three times slower than Soar 4. This is because many of Soar 5's algorithms for determining persistence and maintaining preferences are suboptimal, and Soar 5 was implemented within the data structures and software organization optimized for Soar 4. We are currently rewriting Soar 5 from scratch to improve its efficiency.

Two potential omissions from our analysis are that no mention is made of real-time bounded behavior or temporal reasoning. Issues of bounded response were not addressed in Soar 5, but will have impact on the match component of the architecture. These are currently being studied by others [Rosenbloom, 1989; Tambe *et al.*, 1990]. In contrast, temporal reasoning appears to be more appropriate as a domain for knowledge and not the architecture. Thus, we expect that problem spaces, operators, and control knowledge will encode temporal information, but there will be no direct architectural support.

Finally, there is one "burr" in the design of Soar 5 that has not yet been resolved. This burr arises when chunking is applied to a subgoal in which multiple values from a single sensors are tested to produce a result. For example, when identifying a cup using sonar, many readings may be required. If a chunk is built that summarizes the complete process, it will include tests for all of the sonar values occurring at once. This is clearly incorrect and the chunk will never fire. The problem is that there is a difference in representational power between problem solving in a subgoal, where multiple sensor readings can be tested and integrated over time, and the matching of a production. Chunking ignores this distinction, leading to useless (but harmless) chunks. In many cases, this problem can be avoided through recasting the problem solving in the subgoal so that incremental results are created that depend only on single sensor values and there is an explicitly maintained sensor history (Gervasio discusses a related problem and solution in learning reactive plans through EBL [Gervasio, 1990]). However, to date we have no domain-independent architectural approach to this problem.

5 Acknowledgments

Thanks to Karen McMahon for implementing Soar 5, as well as Brian Milnes and Gary Pelton for help in debugging the implementation and conceptual details of Soar 5's persistence scheme. Special thanks go to Paul Rosenbloom and Allen Newell for many hours of discussion on the ideas relating to this paper and the development of Soar 5.

References

[Brooks, 1987] R. A. Brooks. Intelligence without representation. In *Proceedings of the Workshop on the Foundations of Artificial Intelligence*. MIT, June 1987.

[Doyle, 1979] J. Doyle. A truth maintenance system. *Artificial Intelligence*, 12:231–272, 1979.

[Fikes *et al.*, 1972] R. E. Fikes, P. E. Hart, and N. J. Nilsson. Learning and executing generalized robot plans. *Artificial Intelligence*, 3:251–288, 1972.

[Forgy, 1982] C. L. Forgy. Rete: A fast algorithm for the many pattern / many object pattern match problem. *Artificial Intelligence*, 19:17–38, 1982.

[Gervasio, 1990] M.T. Gervasio. Learning general completable reactive plans. In *Proceedings of AAAI-90.* Morgan Kaufmann, 1990.

[Hendler *et al.*, 1990] J. Hendler, A. Tate, and M. Drummond. AI planning: Systems and techniques. *AI Magazine*, 11(2):61–77, 1990.

[Laird and Rosenbloom, 1990] J. E. Laird and P. S. Rosenbloom. Integrating execution, planning, and learning in Soar for external environments. In *Proceedings of AAAI-90*, July 1990.

[Laird *et al.*, 1987] J. E. Laird, A. Newell, and P. S. Rosenbloom. Soar: An architecture for general intelligence. *Artificial Intelligence*, 33(3), 1987.

[Laird *et al.*, 1990a] J. E. Laird, C. B. Congdon, E. Altmann, and K. Swedlow. Soar user's manual: Version 5.2. Technical Report CSE-TR-72-90, Electrical Engineering and Computer Science Department, The University of Michigan, October 1990. Also available from The Soar Group, School of Computer Science, Carnegie Mellon University, as technical report CMU-CS-90-179.

[Laird *et al.*, 1990b] J. E. Laird, K. Swedlow, E. Altmann, and C. B. Congdon. *Soar 4.5 User's Manual.* The University of Michigan, 1990. Unpublished.

[Minton *et al.*, 1989] S. Minton, J. G. Carbonell, C.A. Knoblock, D.R. Kuokka, O. Etzioni, and Y. Gil. Explanation-based learning: A problem solving perspective. *Artficial Intelligence*, 40(1–3):163–118, 1989.

[Newell and Simon, 1972] A. Newell and H. A. Simon. *Human Problem Solving.* Prentice-Hall, Englewood Cliffs, 1972.

[Newell *et al.*, 1957] A. Newell, J. C. Shaw, and H. A. Simon. Empirical explorations of the logic theory machine: A case study in heuristics. In *Proceedings of the 1957 Western Joint Computer Conference*, pages 218–230. Western Joint Computer Conference, Western Joint Computer Conference, 1957. (Reprinted in Feigenbaum, E. and Feldman, J. (Eds.) Computers and Thought, New York: McGraw-Hill, 1963).

[Newell, 1980] A. Newell. Reasoning, problem solving and decision processes: The problem space as a fundamental category. In R. Nickerson, editor, *Attention and Performance VIII.* Erlbaum, Hillsdale, NJ, 1980.

[Nilsson, 1971] N. Nilsson. *Problem-solving Methods in Artificial Intelligence.* McGraw-Hill, New York, 1971.

[Rosenbloom *et al.*, 1990] P. S. Rosenbloom, J. E. Laird, A. Newell, and R. McCarl. A preliminary analysis of the foundations of the Soar architecture as a basis for general intelligence. In *Foundations of Artificial Intelligence.* MIT Press, Cambridge, MA, 1990. In press.

[Rosenbloom, 1989] P. S. Rosenbloom. Towards real-time general intelligence in soar. 1989.

[Suchman, 1987] L. Suchman. *Plans and Situated Action.* Cambridge University Press, 1987.

[Tambe *et al.*, 1990] M. Tambe, A. Newell, and P. S. Rosenbloom. The problem of expensive chunks and its solution by restricting expressiveness. *Machine Learning*, 5(4), 1990.

CHAPTER 64

Integrating Knowledge Sources in Language Comprehension

J. F. Lehman, R. L. Lewis, and A. Newell, Carnegie Mellon University

Abstract

Multiple types of knowledge (syntax, semantics, pragmatics, etc.) contribute to establishing the meaning of an utterance. Immediate application of these knowledge sources is necessary to satisfy the real-time constraint of 200 to 300 words per minute for adult comprehension, since delaying the use of a knowledge source introduces computational inefficiencies in the form of overgeneration. On the other hand, ensuring that all relevant knowledge is brought to bear as each word in the sentence is understood is a difficult design problem. As a solution to this problem, we present NL-Soar, a language comprehension system that integrates disparate knowledge sources automatically. Through experience, the nature of the understanding process changes from deliberate, sequential problem solving to recognitional comprehension that applies all the relevant knowledge sources simultaneously to each word. The dynamic character of the system results directly from its implementation within the Soar architecture.

Introduction

Language comprehension is the process by which knowledge is used to map an utterance to a meaning. Many sources of knowledge contribute to this process: morphology, syntax, semantics, pragmatics, and discourse conventions are those most often considered. In addition to providing knowledge that may be critical in finding the correct mapping, each source may contribute significantly to reducing the effects of local ambiguity on the search for a meaning. Reducing search is a computational necessity; without multiple knowledge sources even common constructions such as prepositional phrase attachment can lead to an exponential number of interpretations. More important, search reduction is necessary to satisfy the real-time constraint of 200 to 300 words per minute required to model adult comprehension. To guarantee the correct mapping we need all knowledge sources. To guarantee a minimal search space we must be able to bring each type of knowledge to bear as soon as it is relevant.

Immediate application of multiple knowledge sources is a key component in many psychological theories of comprehension and parsing (e.g., [Altmann and Steedman, 1988, Marslen-Wilson and Tyler, 1980, Thibadeau *et al.*, 1982]). However, constructing a system to bring its knowledge to bear at the right moment is difficult. There seems to be a trade-off between search efficiency and ease of engineering. At one end of the spectrum is a pipeline design in which knowledge sources are ordered (morphology, syntax, semantics, etc.), and each source generates a set of structures based on the previous phase's output. A system with separated knowledge sources is relatively easy to create and extend, and exhibits few surprising or inconsistent behaviors as the grammar becomes large. Yet, by delaying the application of a type of knowledge, initial stages overgenerate, producing extra interpretations and unnecessary search[1]. At the other end of the spectrum is a fully-integrated design which encodes all the knowledge in the generator. In short, all knowledge sources contribute at once to the meaning structure produced as each word is comprehended. Although overgeneration is prevented, building such a system requires anticipating and keeping track of all

This research was sponsored in part by the Avionics Laboratory, Wright Research and Development Center, Aeronautical Systems Division (AFSC), U.S. Air Force, Wright-Patterson AFB, Ohio 45433-6543 under Contract F33615-90-C-1465, ARPA Order No. 7597 and in part by The Markle Foundation, and a National Science Foundation Graduate Fellowship.

The views and conclusions contained in this document are those of the authors and should not be interpreted as representing the official policies, either expressed or implied, of NSF, The Markle Foundation or the U.S. government.

[1]The work in principle-based parsing [Fong and Berwick, 1990] is an attempt to control the overgeneration in a syntactic pipeline while preserving its ease of engineering. However, since there is no single optimal ordering of modules, computing the optimal ordering for each sentence, while inexpensive, is heuristic. Consequently, overgeneration may still result. Similarly, blackboard models like Hearsay [Erman *et al.*, 1980] and READER [Thibadeau *et al.*, 1982] may reduce inefficiency by allowing for more flexible interaction than the pipeline approach, but cannot guarantee against overgeneration to the same degree full integration can. Furthermore, the same flexibility that can increase efficiency makes creating and extending the knowledge sources difficult.

the points at which each type of knowledge is relevant. With multiple knowledge sources, fully specifying the points of interaction becomes quite complex, and unexpected inconsistencies tend to arise as the grammar becomes large. In fact, no fully-integrated system has been attempted to date. Instead, most attempts at integration have combined only syntax and semantics, generally through the use of semantic grammars [Birnbaum and Selfridge, 1981], domain-specific syntactic grammars [Sager, 1981], or semantic annotations to syntactic rules [Shieber, 1986].

We believe that NL-Soar [Lehman *et al.*, 1991], the model of language comprehension we have implemented in Soar [Laird *et al.*, 1987, Lewis *et al.*, 1990, Newell, 1990], is a significant step toward a fully-integrated system. It comes closer to achieving ideal search behavior than previous approaches by bringing all sources of knowledge to bear as soon as possible. At the same time, the system maintains the modularity of a pipeline design. We achieve this combination of advantages by virtue of Soar's learning mechanism, *chunking*. Initially, comprehension proceeds by deliberate problem solving using independently represented knowledge sources. Through chunking, new knowledge is added to the system that applies all these sources in a single processing step for each word.

Overview of NL-Soar

Soar distinguishes between knowledge made available through search in problem spaces and knowledge available immediately through recognition. The computational model underlying Soar supports this view by committing to a long-term *recognition memory* (realized as a parallel production system) that yields knowledge in constant time. Problem solving proceeds recognitionally when Soar can select or apply operators in a problem space by simply drawing on this memory. Given the mapping of Soar onto human cognition [Newell, 1990], there is time for only a few (1-3) operators per word within the 200-300 millisecond per word constraint. Therefore, achieving recognitional comprehension is cast as the problem of creating a *comprehension operator* [Newell, 1990] that is directly implemented by productions in the recognition memory. A comprehension operator applied to a word must simultaneously bring to bear all the knowledge necessary to understand the word in the given context. Thus, the comprehension operator is a realization of the *immediacy of interpretation principle* [Thibadeau *et al.*, 1982]. Fully-integrated comprehension for the whole sentence proceeds via word-by-word application of comprehension operators.

Comprehension operators map an utterance to its meaning. The representation for meaning used in NL-Soar is a *model* of the situation that the utterance is about [Johnson-Laird, 1983, Newell, 1990, Polk *et al.*, 1989]. The essential property of models is that the elements in the representation map one-to-one into the situation. The right-hand side of Figure 1 shows the situation model that results from comprehending the sentence *The star above the circle is red.* To aid in building the situation model, NL-Soar also constructs an *utterance model* (Figure 1, left-hand side). This model is

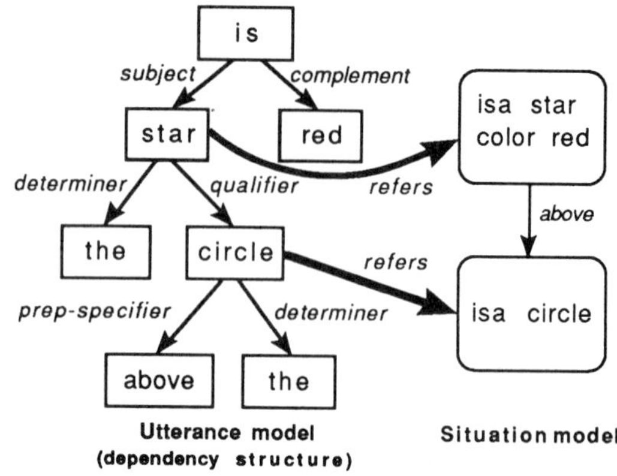

Figure 1: **The models for** *The star above the circle is red.*

a type of dependency structure [Hays, 1964, McCord, 1989, Mel'čuk, 1988], in which nodes correspond to words, and arcs label grammatical relations between words. Thus, the utterance model reflects the syntactic structure of the utterance, while the situation model reflects the structure of the situation being discussed. The relationship between the two models is one of *reference*; parts of the utterance model may refer to objects in the situation. Both models provide context for the comprehension process[2].

If models come from the application of comprehension operators, where do comprehension operators come from? As noted above, hand-coding fully-integrated operators for each word is an extremely difficult and complex task. In NL-Soar, however, hand-coding is unnecessary—comprehension operators arise automatically. To understand how, examine the system's problem spaces in Figure 2. The Comprehension space is where the recognitional comprehension capability is to reside. When Soar first attempts to apply the comprehend operator for a word in a new context, however, an *impasse* arises because the knowledge is not immediately available in recognition memory. Soar responds to this impasse (as it does all impasses) by creating a new subgoal to acquire the needed knowledge through search in another problem space. Knowledge in NL-Soar then chooses the Language space to deliberately implement comprehension by searching the space of partial utterance and situation models. For the operators in the Language space to construct and modify the two models, various syntactic, semantic, and pragmatic constraints on those operators must be satisfied. Ensuring that the constraints are met happens through the sequential application of operators in the Constraint space. If an impasse arises while checking semantic constraints, the Semantics space accesses the current situation model or general world knowledge to deliberately justify a semantic relation.

The result of the deliberate problem solving in the lower three spaces is to resolve the impasse for the comprehend

[2]Additional models may be needed (e.g. a discourse model) as new knowledge sources are added to the system.

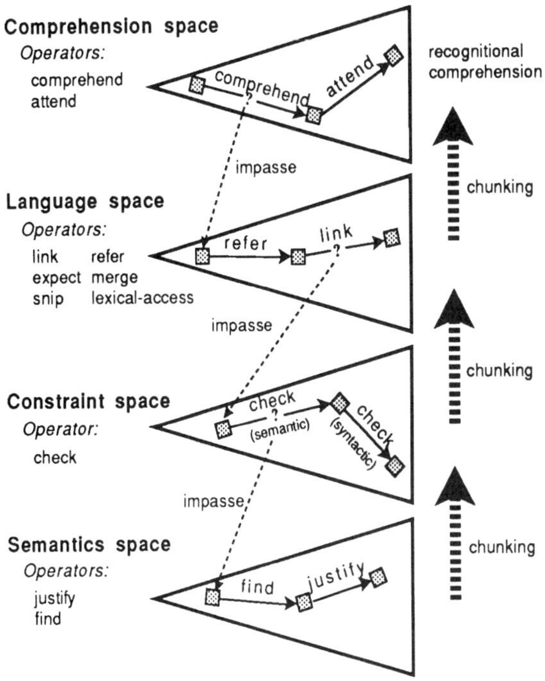

Figure 2: **The NL-Soar tower of problem spaces.**

operator, that is, to determine the appropriate changes to the two models in response to the word being comprehended. As these changes are made, Soar's chunking mechanism stores away the results of the problem solving and their pre-impasse conditions in the form of new productions (chunks) in recognition memory for the Comprehension space. These chunks form a recognitional comprehension capability, so that in future similar situations, comprehension can proceed without deliberate search. The chunks simultaneously bring to bear all the knowledge sources that were sequentially accessed in the lower problem spaces[3].

Examples of NL-Soar's behavior

The description of NL-Soar's problem spaces given above says little about the specific knowledge in the system or the particular type of processing that results. In this section, we make these ideas concrete by tracing the system's behavior with three simple examples. The characterization that emerges is that of a single-path comprehension system that combines both *bottom-up* (data-driven) and *top-down* (expectation-driven) knowledge with a limited capability for repairing misinterpretations.

[3]We have concentrated on how chunking creates new productions in the Comprehension space. However, chunking takes place whenever an impasse is resolved. Thus, knowledge is constantly moving up the tower of problem spaces in Figure 2, making processing more efficient in all spaces.

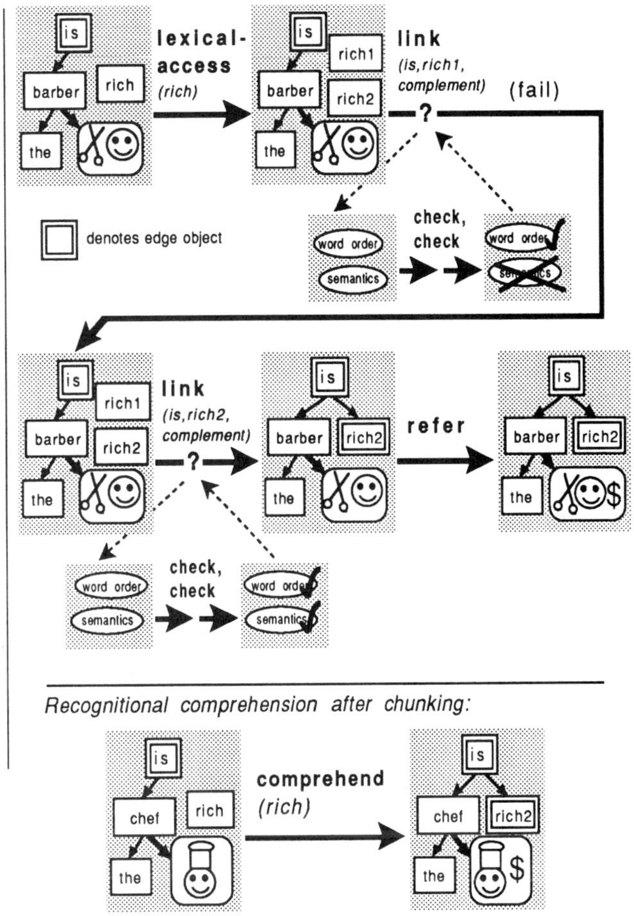

Figure 3: **Deliberate and recognitional comprehension of *rich*.**

Constructing the utterance and situation models

Consider comprehension of the word *rich* in *The barber is rich*. When the system cannot recognitionally implement the comprehend operator for *rich*, an impasse arises and problem solving continues in the Language space. Figure 3 illustrates the chain of operator applications that follows the creation of the Language space's initial state. As shown in the first grey box, the state consists of a partial utterance model and a single object in the situation model representing the barber. The first operator to be applied is lexical-access which retrieves two senses of *rich*: an adjective describing food (*rich1*), and an adjective meaning wealthy (*rich2*). Next, link operators are proposed for each sense. A link operator specifies a relationship between the word being comprehended and a word on the active edge of the utterance model[4]. Thus, functional, structural, and lexical ambiguity contributes to the parallel generation of multi-

[4]The active edge is a subset of the nodes in the utterance model corresponding to non-closed constituents. When *rich* is

ple link operators. In the absence of other knowledge, the system arbitrarily chooses which link operator to try.

In this case an attempt is made to link the first sense of rich (food). Associated with each link operator is a set of constraints which must be met before the operator can be applied. When knowledge of the success or failure of these constraints is not immediately available, the constraints are checked independently in the Constraint space. The current link operator evokes only two constraints: one for word order (the verb assigning a predicate complement must come before the complement), and another requiring semantic consistency between the predicate and the subject. Semantic consistency may be justified by using pragmatic knowledge (finding an appropriate referent already in the situation model) or by simple inference in the Semantics space. Since *rich1* describes food and not people, there is neither a barber who is rich (in the food sense) in the model, nor a justifying inference available from world knowledge. Thus the semantic constraint fails, and the link operator terminates with failure as well.

Next, the link for *rich2* is tried. Again, word order passes, and this time the semantic check passes as well (although no instance of a rich barber could be found in the model, knowledge exists in Semantics that allows a referent that isa person to be rich in the sense of wealthy). Since both constraints pass for *rich2*, this link operator succeeds, making the correct addition to the utterance model. This new piece of structure then triggers the refer operator, which updates the situation model by adding a "wealthy" property to the barber object. In general, the refer operator may create new objects, properties, and relations or resolve a reference to an existing object in the situation.

These changes to the utterance and situation models complete the application of the top-level comprehend operator for *rich*. Soar's chunking mechanism now integrates all four types of knowledge—lexical, syntactic, semantic, and pragmatic—used in the lower spaces into new productions in recognition memory. Figure 4 shows an example of one of these productions. These new productions directly im-

IF comprehending *rich*	[lexical]
and there is a verb on the edge,	[syntactic]
and the verb has an unfilled pred-complement role,	[syntactic]
and the subject of the verb isa person,	[semantic]
and the subject's referent isn't already wealthy	[pragmatic]
THEN the sense of *rich* is wealthy,	[lexical]
assign *rich* to be the pred-complement of the verb,	[syntactic]
assert the wealthy property of the subject's referent	[pragmatic]

Figure 4: **A new production learned for *rich*'s comprehension operator.**

plement the comprehension operator for *rich* in utterances similar to the example. As shown at the bottom of Figure 3, this part of *rich's* comprehension operator will transfer to all predicate complement utterances in which the subject has a referent in the model with the appropriate semantic features.

comprehended, only *is* is in the edge set available for attachment.

NL-Soar differs from previous attempts at integration (e.g., semantic grammars, domain-specific syntactic grammars, and syntactic grammars augmented with selectional restrictions) in three important ways. One, the single comprehension operator avoids generating any of the intermediate structures of the deliberate search. Two, the integration of referent resolution permits the context (the situation model) to aid in disambiguation. Three, the system is designed to be extendible to other knowledge sources while maintaining both modularity and recognitional comprehension.

Adding expectations and top-down knowledge

Often it is impossible to link an incoming word directly into the dependency structure. Consider the word *the* in *Mary loves the barber*. It does not properly attach to either *Mary* or *loves*; it must attach to an as yet unseen noun. Rather than buffer such words, NL-Soar uses expectations to maintain a connected utterance model. Figure 5 shows the creation

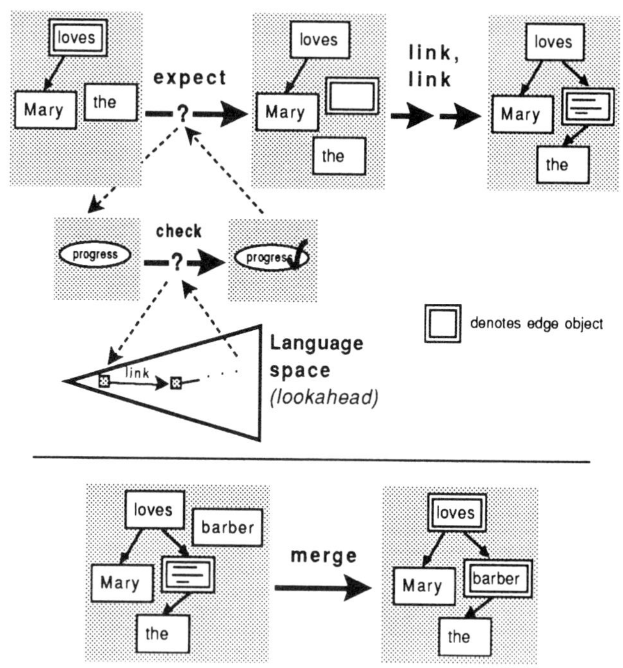

Figure 5: **Creating and merging expectations.**

of an expectation during comprehension of *the* (we omit the situation model in this and subsequent figures). Ignore for the moment the impasse on the expect operator and follow the states along the top row of the figure. First, expect produces an empty node—the expectation—that reserves a place for the future word. Next, two link operators are applied sequentially: the first assigning *the* as the specifier of the expectation, and the second assigning the expectation as the object of *loves*. As the links are made, the expectation accretes the properties necessary to satisfy the constraints of the links. Thus, there is no special knowledge encoded in the expect operator about what to expect; instead, this knowledge is generated dynamically as a side effect of linking the expectation into the existing model. When the expected word finally arrives, the merge operator (Figure 5, bottom) merges it with the expectation, making sure that the new word is consistent with the constraints previously recorded.

How does the system know *when* to create an expectation? There are no specific conditions for proposing the expect operator—it may be attempted at any time. But it is only appropriate when it makes progress toward the successful comprehension of the incoming word as a cohesive part of the utterance to this point. This idea is cast as a *progress* constraint in the Constraint space (the impasse on the expect operator in Figure 5). To determine whether positing an expectation makes progress, NL-Soar searches in a copy of the Language space. This lookahead search reveals that *the* can be linked to the expectation, and the expectation linked to *loves*. Therefore a cohesive structure integrating *the* is possible. Chunks learned during lookahead search encode the conditions that determine when an expectation is needed.

All operators in the Language space use local, bottom-up knowledge. But like expect, all operators in the Language space also have a progress constraint. Thus, the scheme outlined above provides a general mechanism for automatically acquiring top-down knowledge in a comprehension operator via lookahead to pass the progress constraint. If an expectation is created in order to comprehend the current word, then the creation of the expectation and its links is combined with the necessary syntactic, semantic, and pragmatic constraints in the chunks that define the comprehension operator for that word. By integrating over all available knowledge sources, this conception of "top-down" subsumes and moves beyond that found in standard syntactic parsing strategies.

Adding recognitional repair

Since NL-Soar maintains a single interpretation during comprehension of a sentence [Altmann and Steedman, 1988, Frazier and Rayner, 1982, Pritchett, 1988], some mechanism is needed to recover if the system is led astray by a local ambiguity. Consider the sentence *Mary knows Sharyn loves the barber*. *Sharyn* is initially assigned the object role of *knows*. At the point of comprehending *loves*, *Sharyn* must be reassigned to be the subject of *loves* so that the embedded clause may serve as the object. When a previous interpretation proves to be incorrect, the snip operator is applied to undo part of the utterance model. An interpretation was incorrect if no link or expect operator can make progress. A snip operator is proposed for each link connected to a node in the edge set (lookahead may be evoked to determine which snip will be successful). Figure 6 shows the processing during comprehension of *loves*. First, snip cuts the object link between *knows* and *Sharyn*. Next, link operators apply, attaching *Sharyn* as the subject of *loves* and then *loves* as the clausal direct object of *knows*. The snip operator itself only disconnects a piece of the utterance; the

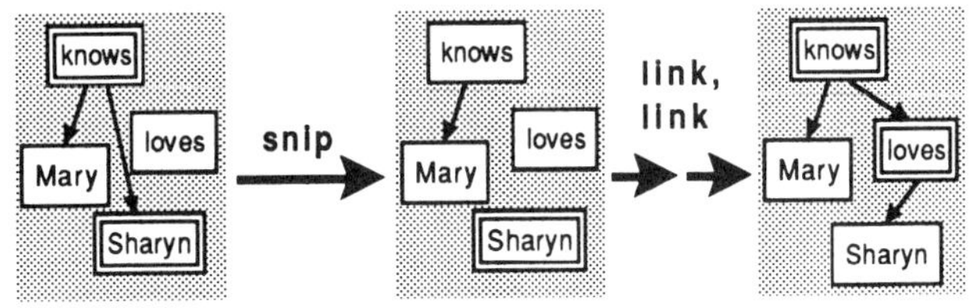

Figure 6: **Repairing a misinterpretation in** *Mary knows Sharyn loves the barber.*

actual repair is carried out by the same link and refer operators we saw above. In contrast to an arbitrary backtracking scheme, the repair mechanism does not require maintaining a complete memory of previous choice points[5].

As in the case of creating expectations, if the comprehension of a word in the current context requires a repair, the effects of all the separate actions that went into making the repair will be captured in new productions for a single operator in the Comprehension space. In this way, limited *recognitional repair* becomes another part of NL-Soar's comprehension capability.

Summary

We have seen examples of sentences in which NL-Soar's processing proceeded strictly bottom-up (*The barber is rich*), included a top-down component (*Mary loves the barber*), or required repair (*Mary knows Sharyn loves the barber*). In each case, the operators that were applied accessed many different types of knowledge at different times. What is important to note about these examples is that the modularity of both the search control strategies and the knowledge sources is irrelevant in the Comprehension space. The comprehension operators produced by chunking are fully integrated, simply making changes to the models directly (and without search) for each word. Currently in NL-Soar, chunking is a compilation mechanism rather than a language acquisition mechanism. What changes is not the set of utterances that can be assigned meaning structures but the process by which a meaning is assigned. Chunking transforms the mapping process from a search-intensive sequential application of operators representing different but necessary types of knowledge, to the simultaneous application of all knowledge sources by a single operator.

Up to this point, the system's development has been driven by two types of demands. The first type of demand has been the satisfaction of basic psychological criteria: word-by-word, incremental comprehension under the real-time constraint. The second (and related) type of demand has been functional: how to compose meaning structures, how to prevent overgeneration, how to commit to structures before all relevant information is available, how to undo incorrect commitments. As a result of this emphasis, certain knowledge sources have been completely ignored to

[5]The limited nature of the repair means that garden path phenomena may arise. We are currently investigating NL-Soar's predictions in this area.

date (the discourse level, for example). Given the automatic way in which comprehension operators arise within NL-Soar, however, we believe the system can be extended to include additional knowledge sources without sacrificing the benefits of fully-integrated processing. In addition to the lack of some knowledge sources, both the system's syntactic and semantic coverage remain underdeveloped. The system's grammatical coverage is currently limited to about 75% of Allen's basic English grammar [Allen, 1987]. Its world model is a simple class hierarchy in the Semantics space. So far this degree of coverage has been adequate for preliminary work in three areas: a natural language interface to a robot arm [Laird *et al.*, 1990], instruction taking for simple reasoning experiments in psychology [Lewis *et al.*, 1989], and predicting garden path phenomena. To continue to extend the system's coverage in realistic and useful ways, we are exploring integrating NL-Soar with other Soar systems. For a more detailed description of the system, see [Lehman *et al.*, 1991].

Acknowledgements. The content and clarity of this paper were improved by the comments of Angela Kennedy Hickman. The integration of NL-Soar with the Robo-Soar project at the University of Michigan was done by Scott Huffman.

References

[Allen, 1987] J. Allen. *Natural Language Understanding*. Benjamin/Cummings, Menlo Park, CA, 1987.

[Altmann and Steedman, 1988] G. Altmann and M. Steedman. Interaction with context during human sentence processing. *Cognition*, 30:191–238, 1988.

[Birnbaum and Selfridge, 1981] L. Birnbaum and M. Selfridge. Conceptual analysis of natural language. In R. C. Schank and C. K. Riesbeck, editors, *Inside Computer Understanding*. Lawrence Erlbaum Associates, Hillsdale, New Jersey, 1981.

[Erman *et al.*, 1980] L. D. Erman, F. Hayes-Roth, V. R Lesser, and D. R. Reddy. The Hearsay-II speech-understanding system: Integrating knowledge to resolve uncertainty. *Computer Surveys*, 12(2), 1980.

[Fong and Berwick, 1990] S. Fong and R. Berwick. The computational implementation of principle-based parsers. In M. Tomita, editor, *Proceedings of the First International Workshop on Parsing Technologies*, pages 75–84, Pittsburgh, PA, 1990. Carnegie Mellon University.

[Frazier and Rayner, 1982] L. Frazier and K. Rayner. Making and correcting errors during sentence comprehension: eye movements in the analysis of structurally ambiguous sentences. *Cognitive Psychology*, 14:178–210, 1982.

[Hays, 1964] D. G. Hays. Dependency theory: a formalism and some observations. *Language*, 40(4):511–525, 1964.

[Johnson-Laird, 1983] P. N. Johnson-Laird. *Mental Models*. Harvard, Cambridge, MA, 1983.

[Laird *et al.*, 1987] J. E. Laird, A. Newell, and P. S. Rosenbloom. Soar: An architecture for general intelligence. *Artificial Intelligence*, 33(1):1–64, 1987.

[Laird *et al.*, 1990] J. E. Laird, E. S. Yager, M. Hucka, and C. M. Tuck. Robo-Soar: An integration of external interaction, planning, and learning using Soar. To appear in Van de Velde (ed.) *Machine Learning for Autonomous Agents*, 1990.

[Lehman *et al.*, 1991] J. F. Lehman, R. L. Lewis, and A. Newell. Natural language comprehension in Soar. Technical report, School of Computer Science, Carnegie Mellon University, 1991. Forthcoming technical report.

[Lewis *et al.*, 1989] R. L. Lewis, A. Newell, and T. A. Polk. Toward a Soar theory of taking instructions for immediate reasoning tasks. In *Proceedings of the Eleventh Annual Conference of the Cognitive Science Society*, pages 514–521, 1989.

[Lewis *et al.*, 1990] R. L. Lewis, S. B. Huffman, B. E. John, J. E. Laird, J. F. Lehman, A. Newell, P. S. Rosenbloom, T. Simon, and S. G. Tessler. Soar as a unified theory of cognition: Spring 1990. In *Twelfth Annual Conference of the Cognitive Science Society*, pages 1035–1042, 1990.

[Marslen-Wilson and Tyler, 1980] W. Marslen-Wilson and L. K. Tyler. The temporal structure of spoken language understanding. *Cognition*, 8:1–71, 1980.

[McCord, 1989] M. C. McCord. A new version of slot grammar. Technical Report RC 14506, IBM Research Division, Yorktown Heights, NY 10598, 1989.

[Mel'čuk, 1988] I. A. Mel'čuk. *Dependency Syntax: Theory and Practice*. State University of New York Press, Albany, 1988.

[Newell, 1990] A. Newell. *Unified Theories of Cognition*. Harvard University Press, Cambridge, Massachusetts, 1990.

[Polk *et al.*, 1989] T. A. Polk, A. Newell, and R. L. Lewis. Toward a unified theory of immediate reasoning in Soar. In *Proceedings of the Eleventh Annual Conference of the Cognitive Science Society*, pages 506–513, 1989.

[Pritchett, 1988] B. L. Pritchett. Garden path phenomena and the grammatical basis of language processing. *Language*, 64:539–576, 1988.

[Sager, 1981] N. Sager. *Natural Language Information Processing*. Addison-Wesley, Reading, MA, 1981.

[Shieber, 1986] S. M. Shieber. *An Introduction to Unification-Based Approaches to Grammar*. Center for the Study of Language and Information, Stanford, CA, 1986.

[Thibadeau *et al.*, 1982] R. Thibadeau, M. A. Just, and P. A. Carpenter. A model of the time course and content of reading. *Cognitive Science*, 6:157–203, 1982.

CHAPTER 65

A Constraint-Motivated Lexical Acquisition Model

C. S. Miller and J. E. Laird, University of Michigan

Abstract

A cognitive model for learning associations between words and objects is presented. We first list basic constraints to which the model must adhere. The constraints arise from two sources. First they stem from observed psychological phenomena including typicality effects, extension errors observed from children and belief-dependent behavior. Secondly they arise from our choice to integrate the model in a unified theory of cognition. In presenting the constraints to the model's construction, we motivate our design decisions while describing our algorithm that takes a symbolic, production-based approach. The model's adherence to the constraints is further supported by some empirical results.

Introduction

In this paper, we present a model for concept acquisition similar to the learning tasks in systems such as ID3 [Quinlan, 1986] and COBWEB (when used to predict features) [Fisher, 1987]. However, our model has been subjected to further constraints in its role of a psychological model. In particular, we account for phenomena observed in children acquiring new words as well as the more general robust phenomena observed in conceptual acquisition. Furthermore, in order to ground our model in a broader, existing theory, we propose to implement the model in a unified theory of cognition.

In this paper, the task requires our model to predict object names of unlabeled objects based upon training examples that include the object name. For our task, we choose to represent object instances as lists of attribute-value pairs. For example, a particular instance of a ball may be represented as follows: [shape:spherical color:blue texture:smooth size:large]. While limiting instance descriptions to lists of attribute-value pairs admittedly restricts expressibility, the representation still permits specifications for an adequate assortment of objects and easily suffices for illustrating some of the model's interesting behaviors.

Design constraints

In this section, we present the major constraints that led us to the model's current design. The psychological motivations are discussed for each constraint. In the next section we will explain our model and how these constraints influenced its design.

Constraint 1 *The word-learning model must be consistent with a unified theory of cognition.*

A unified theory of cognition is a proposed system of mechanisms capable of producing the full range of human cognition [Newell, 1990]. Ideally a model should not operate in isolation but rather play an integral and cooperative role with other cognitive activities. By conforming to a unified theory, the relationship of the various cognitive faculties becomes more apparent.

Constraint 2 *Learning must be incremental.*

A child learning words does not have the opportunity to learn her entire vocabulary before applying it. Instead, learning and performance are interleaved. The learning of words is an ongoing, *incremental* process. For our purposes, we will consider a learning model to be incremental if the computational complexity of integrating a new instance into the system's knowledge is roughly constant relative to the number of training trials.

Constraint 3 *The model must exhibit typicality effects.*

Typicality effects include: 1) typical instances are generally processed faster than less typical ones, 2) typical instances lead to fewer errors in category prediction and 3) typical instances are frequently given as an example to a category [Rosch, 1978]. In this paper, we limit ourselves to showing how typical instances are processed faster than less typical ones.

Constraint 4 *The model must exhibit underextension errors in the early stages of learning.*

*A similar version of this paper appeared as [Miller and Laird, 1991].

Underextensions result when the child's application of a label is too narrow in contrast to the full adult category. In regard to our model, an underextension occurs when no object name prediction is delivered for a particular object instance even though objects of the same category have been previously encountered. For example, a child may be able to identify that a softball is a 'ball' but fail to identify a football as being one. These underextension errors often occur during the early stages of lexical development [Dromi, 1987].

Constraint 5 *The model must be sensitive to knowledge as determined by the system's beliefs, goals and theories.*

It is well documented that beliefs, goals and theories play an important role in human categorization [Murphy and Medin, 1985, Schank *et al.*, 1986]. Our model addresses this constraint by operating at the deliberate level, i.e. it can potentially bring to bear all pertinent knowledge in guiding its decisions.

Constraining the design

In applying our first constraint, we choose to construct our model within the confines of Soar, a proposed unified theory of cognition [Newell, 1990]. Soar presents its theory in the form of an architecture—a system of mechanisms that applies knowledge, represented as productions, in creating intelligent behavior. We will further motivate our choice of Soar, but first let us focus on the new constraints that result from this choice. They include: 1) all learning occurs through an experience-based learning mechanism, 2) the system does not have direct access to its long-term memory and 3) processing is fully symbolic with no native support for frequency counts or probabilities. A basic understanding of the system and its assumptions follow within this section. In particular, a short review explains some of the basic ideas of how induction should proceed in Soar. We will then explain our model and how it coincides with the rest of our constraints.

Learning in Soar

Problem solving in Soar [Laird *et al.*, 1987] consists of the sequential selection and application of operators to a representational state within a problem space. Both the selection and application of operators is determined by the knowledge represented in a long-term recognition memory encoded as productions. Learning involves the construction of new productions, called chunks, which summarize the results of a subgoal. A chunk in Soar is similar to an operationalized result in explanation based learning [Mitchell *et al.*, 1986, Dejong and Mooney, 1986]. Subgoals are born out of impasses caused by conflicting knowledge or a lack of knowledge. Subgoaling relies on additional knowledge to consider the alternatives, often requiring further search. During subgoaling, the system may try out the alternatives or it may recast the problem. In any case, the subgoal resolves the problem that caused the impasse. Furthermore, the architecture traces back through the conditions that led to the impasse's resolution. Using these conditions, a new production is created that summarizes the subgoal's result so that, in analogous applications, the summarizing information is retrieved. This avoids the impasse and thus the costly search encountered when the chunk was first created. In this scenario, the knowledge in the problem space has been partially operationalized in that an increase in efficiency has occurred. Although counterintuitive, previous work with Soar has demonstrated that this technique can also increase the total knowledge of the system [Rosenbloom *et al.*, 1988]. This approach, called data-chunking, is a precurser to the work we present here.

Describing the model

For our approach, we rely exclusively on chunking to monotonically add productions that predict a concept name given a partial description of an object. The definition of a concept is not localized to a single production, or even a small set of productions. Instead, a concept definition is distributed across the set of productions that predict the concept name, plus a process that creates abstractions of object descriptions, attempting to find an object description that can be matched by the productions. The search plays an integral role in defining the concept; for it is here that Soar brings to bear its knowledge in determining which abstractions should be considered and in what order. In the model presentation that follows, we will see how this fully symbolic learning process adheres to the constraints described in the previous section.

When attempting to predict the object's category, the object's description serves as the initial state in a problem space. For example, if we want to classify a blue, smooth, spherical object as a ball, the initial state would contain the following object description: [shape:spherical color:blue texture:smooth].

The operators of the problem space recognize descriptions and predict categories. Initially, the system will have very few operators and be able to predict only a few categories, but with experience, more operators will be learned. For our example, let's assume that the system already has acquired the following productions for creating word-prediction operators:

```
[spherical, red, smooth] -->
  create-operator(predict word:ball)
[spherical, red] -->
  create-operator(predict word:ball)
[spherical] -->
  create-operator(predict word:ball)
```

If one of these productions exactly matched the object description, it would fire, create an operator which would then be selected and predict a word and we would be done. However, for a production to apply, we insist that it matches every feature in the object description, so that a general production will only match an abstracted description.[1] This means that even the third production is not applicable for our initial object description because it has no feature match for color and texture.

If an object can not be classified by the existing knowledge, no operators are created and an impasse results. Within the ensuing subgoal, a search is performed to find an abstraction that modifies the object description in such a way as to allow it to be categorized. For our example, the abstraction operators render an object description more general by removing one of the attribute-value pairs from the description. Let us assume the chosen operator removes the texture feature from the description, producing the description (spherical, blue). Following an abstraction, there is the potential that the new description can be categorized. However in this example, no match occurs, and another impasse and subgoal are created. Only after the color has been abstracted out, will the object description be recognized by the third production and a prediction for the word will be made. For performance trials, the correctness of the prediction will depend on the object recognition productions store in long-term memory, as well as the abstraction performed during the search for a match.

In this formulation, there is no explicit abstraction hierarchy; instead the abstractions are generated dynamically. This allows knowledge to be used to determine which abstractions should be made first. The ramifications of this approach are that novel objects will be classified into existing categories if it differs only in features that are abstracted early on.

For training trials, the purpose is not to predict a word, but instead to learn the association between an object description and a word. Consistent with earlier work in data chunking, our approach is to treat a training trial like a performance trial, so that the system will attempt to predict which word it already would associate with the given object. The prediction will be verified by comparing it against the given word before accepting it. If necessary, abstraction will continue until a very abstract production for predicting the word is found. When the correct prediction is finally made, the training trial is finished.

How has the training resulted in any learning? Recall that in Soar, learning happens when a result is produced in a subgoal. In this case, the result is the correct prediction created in the final subgoal where the object is correctly categorized. For a performance trial, when no word accompanies the description, there is no attempt at verification and no chunk is created. For training, learning occurs for the subgoal lying just above the subgoal where recognition was achieved and verified. There the object description [spherical, blue] eventually led, following abstraction, to the results created in the lower subgoal (predict word:ball). Chunking summarizes the abstraction and recognition processing in the subgoal, and builds a new production:

```
[spherical, blue] -->
  create-operator(predict word:ball)
```

In future training trials, this production will be available and allow a prediction to be made even earlier, and thus allow an even more specific production to be learned. As practice continues, more and more specific productions are acquired. So that, although the search for a category proceeds from a specific example through varying levels of abstraction, the learning proceeds from most abstract to more specific. Thus, this learns the same way as discrimination learning and previous data-chunking work in Soar [Rosenbloom *et al.*, 1988] (abstract to specific), but this scheme attempts to perform classification by moving from specific to general (through abstraction operators) while in a discrimination test it is from general to specific (through successive tests for the values of more and more features).

Before continuing with our model's description, let us address how the approach already fulfills some of our initial constraints. First of all, since training and performance runs can be interleaved, learning is incremental, thus fulfilling our second constraint. In a sense, the Soar architecture already enforces this by disallowing direct access to long-term memory, i.e. productions cannot directly access, delete or modify productions. This simply prohibits any action of massively reorganizing the long-term memory every time a new learning instance is encountered. The model itself has a surprising consequence in that learning time per instance can potentially decrease as new instances are acquired. This is a result of having each learning trial build upon chunks acquired on previous learning trials. The more instances the system has encountered, the less likely a new object description will have to be fully abstracted in order to be integrated with the current set of productions.

The typicality effects (Constraint 3) are also a result of how the model searches for the best and most specific match first and then slowly generalizes until a match is found. Here queries using frequent and typical objects will find a match that is not only a better match, but they will also find it quicker. This assumption stems from the notion that typical instances will already have several stored exemplars that nearly (if not completely) match them. Therefore little abstraction is required in order to find the match.

So far we have assumed that there was always some way of classifying an object correctly, even if it had not been seen before. Within our model, that translates into productions that do not test any features and

[1] Although Soar's production matching generally does not have this property, by representing object descriptions appropriately (i.e., as linked lists), the object recognition productions will have this property.

predict the words. Thus, the system must be "bootstrapped" with productions of this form:

```
[] --> word:ball
[] --> word:book
[] --> word:apple
```

Where do these productions come from? They in turn must be learned from lower-level components such as phonemes. This recursion bottoms out in some primitive set of components that the system can inherently generate.

The consequences of starting with these very general productions could cause one to think that many over-generalized predictions during performance would initially result, thereby contradicting our fourth constraint, that underextensions must initially result. Some overextensions will be produced for this reason, but surprisingly, the choice of these very generalized productions actually lead to many initial underextensions. During performance, these very general productions will often suggest conflicting predictions. Since the system has no way to choose which prediction is correct, *no prediction is made whenever there is a conflict in predictions.*[2] Because the productions are so general, initially there will be many abstractions in trying to categorize a word, and thus there will be many conflicts. Therefore, there will initially be many underextensions.

We have already discussed how our choice of Soar has led to an incremental learning model. Our choice has also contributed to fulfilling some of our other constraints. First of all, we argue that placing the task on Soar's deliberate processing level is the appropriate for modeling typicality effects. In several psychological experiments, it was shown that differences in response times due to differences of similarity varied on the order by several hundreds of milliseconds [Rosch *et al.*, 1976]. Results from other research and analysis of Soar has led us to conclude that the application of a primitive operator in Soar corresponds to a human time of approximately 50 milliseconds [Newell, 1990, Wiesmeyer and Laird, 1990]. Since difference in response times in our model vary by several operator applications, these results suggest that we are in the ball park and that our explanation of typicality effects on an *algorithmic* level is reasonable. This contrasts with other previous work that seeks a quantitative approach (i.e. typicality is represented in the form of frequency counts or probabilities) for explaining typicality effects. In taking these approaches, strong assumptions are required concerning the underlying implementation in order to explain similarity-dependent response times. For example, in COBWEB, category prediction involves traveling to a node that explicitly represents the instance's category. Typicality timing effects come only with the strong implementational assumption that "the time required to reach a node is inversely proportional to the total predictiveness towards that node." [Fisher, 1988].

Finally Soar provides us with the support of fulfilling our last constraint—goal and belief dependent behavior in categorization. In Soar, the selection of an operator is a deliberate act, i.e. all applicable knowledge can potentially influence the choice of an operator. This knowledge, expressed through productions preferring some operators over others, can also be learned through the result of subgoaling. Although this paper does not emphasize the learning of this knowledge, the issues presented here remain a central concern of our research work. Briefly we can say that we are concentrating on three kinds of knowledge: 1) default preferences that prefer abstracting out some features before others, 2) abstraction preferences learned from prediction failures and 3) abstraction preferences favoring features that lead to the system's goals.

Empirical results

In this section, we present two experiments that confirm our predictions on extensional errors and typicality effects. For both of these, we chose an assortment of objects that are simply described by attribute-value pairs, similar to the examples given so far. For all our data, we chose objects that roughly correspond with physical objects children are likely to encounter. The abstraction operators generalize the instance descriptions by removing a feature. Furthermore, we have included additional heuristics that guide the selection of these abstraction operators.

Our first experiment demonstrates the effect that similarity has on response time. A training set was presented twice to the system. It is a collection of object descriptions, all of them representing different kinds of balls. With each description, the appropriate French word for ball was given (either *ballon* or *balle*). In French, *ballon* is used to refer to balls that are inflated (basketballs, volleyballs, footballs, etc.), while *balle* refers to solid balls (baseballs, golf balls, tennis balls). Thus, the system must learn to distinguish between objects in the two categories even though the critical feature (inflatable or not) is not included in the input. Between the training trials, a set of object descriptions were run on the system. For each of the performance object descriptions, the similarity was mathematically calculated based upon the number of shared features the object description has with the training object descriptions of the same category. We have divided the performance descriptions into three groups of low, medium and high similarity and average their response times in terms of decision cycles. Table 1 shows that the instances with a lower similarity measure require a longer response time. This table also shows how learning times can improve as new

[2]Conflicting predictions do not arise during training because operators that suggest incorrect predictions are rejected. This is possible because the correct answer is provided.

Training Trials	Average time in decision cycles		
	Similarity groups		
	$S <= 2.0$	$2.0 < S <= 3.0$	$3.0 < S$
1	23.0	18.2	17.0
2	23.0	12.2	9.8

Table 1: Response time according to similarity group

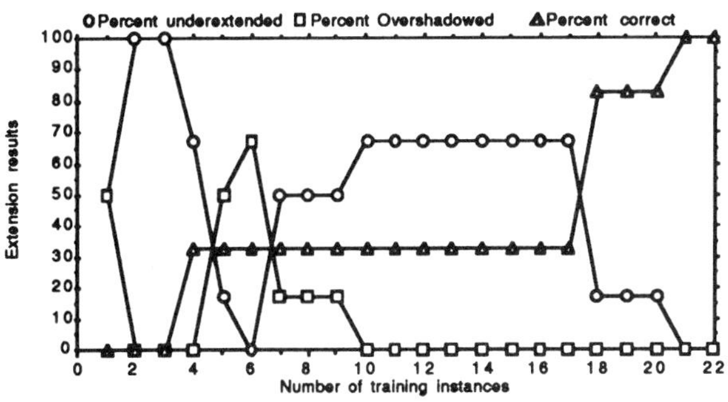

Figure 1: Trace of extensional errors

knowledge is acquired. The performance is faster after the second training trial because more specific chunks have been acquired. This means less abstraction need occur in order to make a prediction.

In the second experiment, we trace extensional errors by testing performance on one category of objects. Here training instances drawn from several categories are given one at a time. Between each training instance, a set of testing instances, all from the same category, are run on the system. Figure 1 shows the results of the trace. Here we see an initial onslaught of underextensions and overextensions before correct predictions dominate. We consider the category to be *underextended* whenever the system fails to make a prediction. The category is *overshadowed* by another category whenever a wrong response is given for the category we are testing. The latter is a case of *overextension*, and we have included in our figure a trace of these errors for the sake of completeness. The particular conclusion that can be drawn from this figure is that several initial underextensions result from our model even though the system starts by learning more general productions first. As we have said before, this is the result of several general conflicting rules matching at the same time.

Future work

The model we have presented here is a first pass at a system which conforms to our selected set of constraints. For future work, we intend to improve the model by expanding its capabilities while also having it adhere to more constraints. The expansion of capabilities include the learning of abstraction heuristics, extending learning to predict missing features, and increasing instance description expressibility. For adding more constraints, we are looking at covering additional typicality effects and basic-level effects.

Acknowledgements This work was supported by a grant from the W.K. Kellogg Foundation through The Presidential Initiative Fund of The University of Michigan. We would like to thank Melanie Mitchell, Steve Lytinen and Mark Wiesmeyer for their helpful comments on earlier drafts of this paper.

References

[Dejong and Mooney, 1986] G. Dejong and R. Mooney. Explanation-based learning: An alternative view. *Machine Learning*, 1:145–176, 1986.

[Dromi, 1987] E. Dromi. *Early Lexical Development*. Cambridge University Press, New York, 1987.

[Fisher, 1987] D. H. Fisher. Knowledge acquisition via incremental conceptual clustering. *Machine Learning*, 2:139–172, 1987.

[Fisher, 1988] D. H. Fisher. A computational account of basic level and typicality effects. In *Proceedings of the Seventh National Conference on Artificial Intelligence*, pages 233–238, 1988.

[Laird *et al.*, 1987] J. E. Laird, A. Newell, and P. S. Rosenbloom. Soar: An architecture for general intelligence. *Artificial Intelligence*, 33:1–64, 1987.

[Miller and Laird, 1991] C. S. Miller and J. E. Laird. A constraint-motivated model of lexical acquisition. In L. Birnbaum and G. Collins, editors, *Machine Learning: Proceedings of the Eighth International Workshop*, San Mateo, CA, 1991. Morgan Kaufman.

[Mitchell *et al.*, 1986] T. M. Mitchell, R. M. Keller, and S. T. Kedar-Cabelli. Explanation-based generalization: A unifing view. *Machine Learning*, 1:47–80, 1986.

[Murphy and Medin, 1985] G. L. Murphy and D. L. Medin. The role of theories in conceptual coherence. *Psychological Review*, 92:289–316, 1985.

[Newell, 1990] A. Newell. *Unified Theories of Cognition*. Harvard University Press, Cambridge, MA, 1990.

[Quinlan, 1986] J. R. Quinlan. Induction of decision trees. *Machine Learning*, 1:81–106, 1986.

[Rosch *et al.*, 1976] E. Rosch, C. Simpson, and R. S. Miller. Structural bases of typicality effects. *Journal of Experimental Psychology: Human Perception and Performance*, 2:491–502, 1976.

[Rosch, 1978] E. Rosch. Principles of categorization. In E. Rosch and B. B. Lloyd, editors, *Cognition and Categorization*, pages 27–48. Erlbaum, Hillsdale, NJ, 1978.

[Rosenbloom *et al.*, 1988] P. S. Rosenbloom, J. E. Laird, and A. Newell. The chunking of skill and knowledge. In B. A. G. Elsendoorn and H. Bouma, editors, *Working Models of Human Perception*. Academic Press, London, 1988.

[Schank *et al.*, 1986] R. C. Schank, G. C. Collins, and L. E. Hunter. Transcending inductive category formation in learning. *Behavioral and Brain Sciences*, 9:639–686, 1986.

[Wiesmeyer and Laird, 1990] M. Wiesmeyer and J. Laird. A computer model of 2d visual attention. In *The Twelfth Annual Conference of the Cognitive Science Society*, pages 582–589, 1990.

CHAPTER 66

Formulating the Problem Space Computational Model

A. Newell, G. R. Yost, J. E. Laird, P. S. Rosenbloom, and E. Altmann

11.1 Introduction

The *foundation paradigm* of computer science is the application of computational operations to data structures to perform semantically meaningful computations, as specified by a program. The great utility of this arrangement depends on the existence of programming languages that humans can use to specify the computations that perform tasks of interest. This utility is enhanced many-fold by the generality of these computations and the immense rapidity with which they can be carried out and their results communicated over large distances. But the basic paradigm is key—a human with a task that he or she can cast as a computation and express in a programming language that a computer can interpret and perform.

The revolutionary productivity of this paradigm—economically, socially, and intellectually—is apparent to us all. An important element in its success is situating the task in the mind of the human, without explicit representation in the paradigm. All that need exist to make the paradigm work is the program embodied in a program-language expression for some computer. The relation of the task to the program is a conceptual invention in the mind of the human user that need never be made manifest. This was a great divide and conquer. Society could understand and automate one type of intellectual activity (instruction following) without automating another more difficult type (task definition). In the event, it has yielded immense rewards.

Immediately, of course, the enterprise commenced to understand and automate the bypassed intellectual activity. The intellectual agent that conceives a task, designs the algorithm, embodies it in programming-language expressions, and maintains the connection between task and interpretable structure should be realizable as a computational process. Conceivably, no such extension is possible—task creation cannot be automated in general. However, many indicators contravene this conservative reaction, among them the universality of computers and the successful psychological analysis of human task creation and task definition. Indeed, much progress has already occurred in this enterprise. In many limited, though interesting, ways, programs write other programs. These keep the basic paradigm of the human creating the task, but make the task be that of creating programs. More far reaching are the efforts in artificial intelligence (AI) to create intelligent agents that have the essential characteristic of creating and representing their own tasks and the operational structures to accomplish them.

The key question to be asked in opening up task creation to understanding and automation is how tasks are to be *formulated*. Before an agent can even begin on a task, that task must be given form. Enough elements of the task—givens, goals, constraints, resources, background, whatever—must be assembled in a way that permits processing to commence. This is exactly what the basic paradigm avoids—it leaps directly to accomplishment by a program, taking the formulation to be something already accomplished by the human.

The conundrum is that the agent must at once begin to do something—it must take steps to accomplish the task—yet it cannot know what to do at the beginning, because that would imply that the task was already accomplished in its essentials. This is exactly what the program provides—it lays out the steps to be done (possibly conditional on data in specified ways). But it never says how it was known to do just *these* steps rather than others. The problem for the agent is how to get started before knowing what to do.

For computer scientists, the immediate impulse for how to get something for nothing is to recurse—deciding the first step is just another task. Alas, the impulse is in vain. It is reminiscent of the old Pat-and-Mike story. Pat offered Mike a million dollars a year just to solve problems for him. That seemed to Mike a fantastic deal, and he accepted with alacrity. Knowing Pat to be a man of modest means, Mike said "Where will you find all that money to pay me?" "That," said Pat, "is your first problem."

What seems to be needed is the adoption of some kind of *framework* that permits bringing in all the considerations necessary to get a task sufficiently formulated to get off the ground. There is no magic, so the framework must be

1. **Operationality.** The framework must permit the agent to work, i.e., it must be grounded in some version of the basic paradigm, with data structures and operations.
2. **Scope.** The framework must be usable on the full range of tasks that the agent can attempt. The interest is at human scale, corresponding to the range of tasks humans cast into computer programs.
3. **Initialization.** The framework must not pose significant difficulties or require significant effort to get started formulating and attempting a task from whatever initial fragments exist. The point of a framework is to help get started.
4. **Openness.** The framework must easily admit the incorporation of whatever resources, knowledge, considerations and constraints the agent and the environment bring to the task, and in whatever form.
5. **Bias.** Frameworks will necessarily impose something of their own structure on how they are used. As with programming languages, they will make some things easy and other things hard. But a framework should inject as little bias as possible into how task accomplishment proceeds.

EXHIBIT 11.1
Criteria for a task-formulation framework.

adopted without knowledge of the specific task. Thus, the framework must be essentially domain independent. The best that can be hoped for is that it satisfy some very general criteria.

The criteria are described in Exhibit 11.1. The few task-formulation frameworks that have emerged as candidates to meet them are listed in Exhibit 11.2.[1] These frameworks all define an arena in which task accomplishment can proceed. With a cunning reminiscent of Pat, they all hire a hall before knowing what entertainment is to play.

It is difficult to evaluate such candidates abstractly. Each candidate does provide an operational computational framework that permits tasks to be formulated and work to commence. Likewise, most have an extremely broad scope. Indeed, most can, in some technical way, incorporate the others, so their scopes are all formally equivalent and computationally universal. The exceptions are

[1]There is no received list of candidates, so we may have missed some. Some other plausible candidates do not seem viable at the present time. Natural language and sensory images seem difficult to complete with appropriate operations in their own terms. Blackboard architectures [6] seem to specify too little of an entire framework. Production systems and object-oriented programming systems, although they make many things easier, remain within the foundation paradigm of humans doing the task formulation. Connectionist systems have not yet matured to a broad enough scope.

1. **Problem spaces**. A space of states with a set of operators on states, where a task is formulated as starting at an initial state and searching for a desired state.
2. **Logics**. A set of clauses that describes the task situation with rules of inference to derive new clauses, where a task is formulated as proving a given theorem from a set of axioms.
3. **Constraint satisfaction**. A set of variables of given (often discrete) ranges subject to a set of constraints of fixed types, where a task is formulated as finding the values of the variables that satisfy the constraints and (often) optimize various functions of the variables.
4. **Schemas**. A hierarchical attribute-value structure with values determined by inheritance hierarchies, defaults, constraints, and attached procedures, where a task is formulated as filling out the slots of a given schema.
5. **Programs**. A programming language, where a task is formulated as synthesizing a program to meet a specification on the inputs, outputs and behavior. The specification is given in some formal language.
6. **Plans**. A (large) data base of highly abstract variabilized procedures containing subgoals to be obtained by other plans, where a task is formulated as attaining a given partially instantiated plan.
7. **The big switch**. A (large) data base of programs with a big index on task-relevant features, where a task is formulated by sorting it through the index and applying whatever program is obtained.

EXHIBIT 11.2
Candidate frameworks for formulating tasks.

plans and the big switch, which depend on a pre-existing data base. These sacrifice scope for practicality, relying on the fact that the data bases can be built to cover the most frequently occurring tasks for an agent. They can of course be augmented by a capability for automatically adding to the data base, which then requires another framework to do the plan or program synthesis.

Initiation, in some sense the most important criteria, is even harder to assess. Within their scopes plans and the big switch are clearly built to be easy. The others have not been used extensively to formulate tasks in a context that requires going from nothing to something, i.e., from an environment that contains dispersed, fragmented, and hidden bits of knowledge, difficulties, and goal indications, to a formulated task. Instead, in the tradition of the basic paradigm, humans formulate the tasks within these frameworks. However, the intellectual efforts required for this are much less than to produce programs to do the specific tasks. The systems employing these frameworks—theorem provers and problem solvers—formulate for themselves the many subtasks that are needed to complete a task. Some work on initial formulation has occurred, of course, but only in simple situations.

Bias is a second-order concern, since the primary requirement is to be able to do something at all. But there is plenty of evidence that bias will be an issue. In AI this often shows up as the *representation problem*, namely, that much depends on the representation that is chosen for a task. Changing the representation (though staying within a framework) may make orders of magnitude differences in the effort required. A recent example showed up in the N-Queens task [19].[2] The best constraint-satisfaction and heuristic search programs solve on the order of the 1,000-Queens task. A shift to searching in the space of repairs of faulty but complete solutions has been able to solve the million-Queens task, limited only by space. Nonetheless, it will be a while before issues of bias become paramount in evaluating task frameworks.

It should be evident we are still at the stage of exploring each framework in its own terms to discover how it well works out. In fact, that is what we see happening. Research groups and subfields adopt one framework or another, in order to get on with their work. And indeed, each framework can be made to work reasonably well in limited situations.

Against this background, we wish to focus on the *problem-space* framework, the candidate listed at the top of Exhibit 11.2. Problem spaces have a long history in artificial intelligence (AI), growing out of the concept of heuristic search in a combinatorially expanding state space. Most early AI systems used a search space. Indeed, this was true of all the problem-solving systems described in *Computers and Thought* [7], the famous early compendium of AI research. The continuing central role of problem spaces can be traced through the major textbooks of the field [23,24,28,33,34]. However, the search space has seemed conceptually simple, and has not attracted theoretical attention. Its ubiquity is often noted, as is its entailment of combinatorial search. It has also been used to epitomize a paradigm era in AI (search-based) in contrast to other newer paradigms, e.g., knowledge-based [8]. But that is about all the attention it has garnered.

In fact, there is more to problem spaces than meets the eye. Our own involvement with problem spaces began with the Logic Theorist, our first AI system [27], moved though observing their centrality [20,26], demonstrating that they describe human problem-solving [25], extending them to routine as well as problematical situations [21], and taking them as the foundation of an architecture for general intelligence (Soar) [14]. New aspects of problem spaces have continued to emerge throughout, convincing us of their fundamental nature.

[2]Placing N queens on an $N \times N$ chessboard so that no Queen can capture any other Queen.

As they stand, problem spaces are incomplete as a task framework. They specify that search occurs in a space, but they leave open almost everything else—how to specify operators, how to specify the heuristics that guide search, how to specify detection of the desired state. In our work on Soar we combined problem spaces with a significant number of organizing principles in order to fashion a complete framework (production systems, preference-based decision making, universal subgoaling, and chunking to name the main ones). However, our continuing experience with Soar has moved us more and more toward treating the problem space as a self-contained level. In particular, it seems that users should view Soar as consisting entirely of problem spaces, whatever that might mean. The gradual emergence of a problem-space level as a way of describing Soar can be traced through our recent history (e.g., by comparing succeeding versions of its manuals).

To anyone grounded in computer science, this indicates that the problem space should be cast as a complete level, i.e., as a self-contained computational model. Doing so is not entirely straightforward, because of all the unspecified aspects mentioned above. The present chapter is our attempt at a complete formulation. This attempt will occupy the entire chapter, leaving little room to analyze and elaborate the formulation or to discuss its ramifications.

In Section 11.2 we lay out the general scheme of analysis in terms of computational models, and provide an overview of how we will proceed. Section 11.3 describes the *knowledge-level computational model* (KLCM), the first of the computational models we will need. Section 11.4, the main one, describes the *problem space computational model* (PSCM) in a sequence of three stages: defining the problem space, implementing the KLCM by means of problem spaces, and generating multiple problem spaces. Section 11.5 provides a brief discussion.

11.2 Computational Models and the Overall Scheme

To describe problem spaces we use the notion of *computational model*, which is just an articulation of the foundation paradigm stated at the beginning. A *computational model* is a description of a class of systems in terms of a set of operations on entities that can be interpreted in computational terms, to wit, that have a computational semantics. A computational model permits the description of particular systems. The description can be *complete* in that the system's structure, its behavior, and how the behavior is determined by its structure, can all be described without appeal to any constructs outside the computational model.

Such a framework is implicit in any discussion of computation, but becomes explicit when multiple models are under consideration. This occurs in

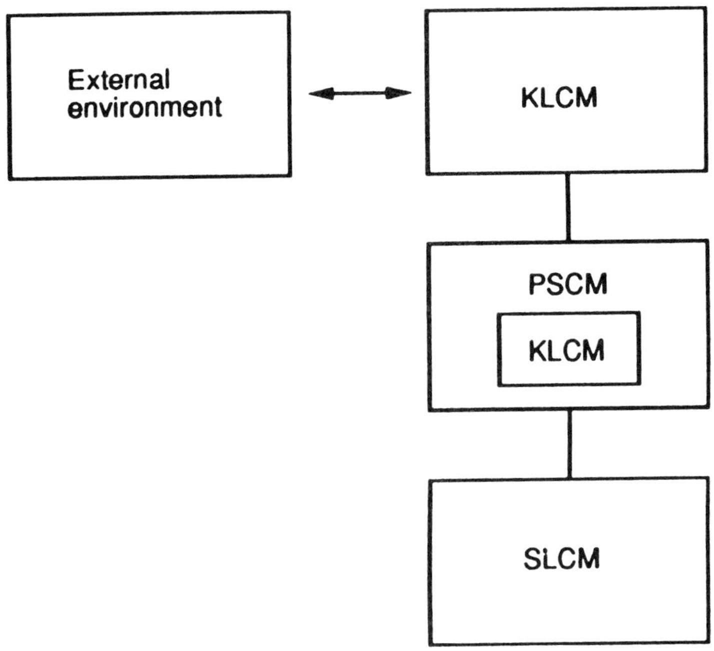

EXHIBIT 11.3
Computational models involved in defining problem spaces.

many places in computer science. One computational model is often specified or implemented within another, for example, the hierarchy of system levels that governs the way we construct computers, and also the programming-language systems that tower unendingly upward. As these examples illustrate, the bottom of a hierarchy can be a system without a computational interpretation—indeed, it must be if the hierarchy grounds the systems in the world of physics. Although completeness is of the essence, system levels are often realized only approximately. In programming systems, especially, higher levels often leave much to be described by the lower level, as in packages of subroutines. Computational models are also a standard device in the study of algorithms, where they provide the bases within which algorithms can be described and their computational costs assessed [1]. Turing machines and random-access machines are familiar computational models for these purposes. Computational models play a strong role in parallel computer systems, where simplified computational models of parallel computation are adopted for programming purposes, which are realized in an underlying, more complex hardware architecture. The LINDA computational model is a typical example [3].

Exhibit 11.3 shows the computational models needed to provide a formulation of problem spaces. At the top we define the KLCM. This will provide a model for a system capable of goal-oriented rational behavior, i.e., capable of intelligent action in interaction with an external environment. A knowledge-level (KL) system is implemented by a PSCM system, i.e., by a system described in the problem-space computational model. The PSCM describes a class of symbolic processing systems. However, it remains abstract in essential ways. Hence, a PSCM system must still be implemented in a symbol-level computational model (SLCM) of the standard kind, with memory, representations, and operations. Though the PSCM is defined as an autonomous level (as with any computational model), it is shaped by both the functional constraints of being suitable to realize KL systems to a useful approximation and the structural constraint of being physically realizable in a standard SLCM.

The abstract character of the PSCM shows up in some of its components being defined as KL systems. That is, certain aspects of a PSCM will not be defined by specific symbolic mechanisms and structures, but only by the knowledge they make available. This knowledge, of course, is not knowledge about the external task environment, which is the knowledge in the top KL system; rather, it is about the problem space. Nevertheless, the result is that the KLCM shows up in our analysis in two ways and plays two distinct roles.

11.3 The Knowledge-Level Computational Model (KLCM)

The notion of a KL system is already familiar in AI and expert systems [5,12,22, 29] and a closely corresponding notion of intentional systems is familiar in philosophy [4]. We use the simplest version sufficient for our purposes, which has a single goal, discrete errorless actions and perceptions, and a deterministic discrete environment.

Exhibit 11.4 records the essential definition. A *knowledge-level system* is defined as an *agent* behaving in an *environment (E)*. The agent is defined as a set of *actions (A)*, a set of *perceptual devices (P)*, a *goal (G)*, and a *body of knowledge (K)*. The environment is in one of a set of states at each instant of time, and the state changes with time. The agent interacts with the environment at various times by taking actions, which affect what next environment state occurs, and by using its perceptual devices, which acquire knowledge about the environment (adding to K). The state of the environment, the state of the agent, and the interactions determine the joint behavior over time of the environment and the agent. The goal is a preference function on behavior, i.e., the agent prefers some joint behaviors to others. The agent's knowledge is about the environment, the agent, and their joint behavior. The agent's behavior is determined by the *principle of rationality* that if the agent knows that one of its actions leads to a preferred situation according to its goal, than it will *intend* the preferred action, which will then occur if it is possible. In the application of this principle, the entire body of knowledge is brought to bear on determining the action. Knowledge once acquired continues to be available forever, the *principle of permanence*. The source of new knowledge is perception.[3] Thus, knowledge in the system grows with each perception and increases monotonically throughout the life of the system. The KLCM defines a class of systems, each situated in a specific environment and with specific actions, perceptual devices, goal, and initial knowledge.

This is a model of goal-directed behavior, because all actions intend to attain the goal of the agent. It is a model of rational behavior, because everything the agent knows serves the agent's interest. This is a narrow concept of rationality. It takes the goal of the agent as given, so there is no issue of whether the agent's goal is rational or not, in terms of any larger considerations (e.g., the agent's survival). What determines the agent's behavior is the agent's knowledge of its goal, rather than the objectively defined preference function. Thus, the only thing that distinguishes the agent's own goal from other things the system knows about is that the principle of rationality operates in terms of the agent's goal.

Actions must be intended rather than just taken. The agent's knowledge need not necessarily include whether an action is possible. Thus, the principle of rationality can determine an action to be taken that cannot in fact occur. In our simple model, where an action cannot produce an errorful result, this implies that no action on the environment then occurs. However, knowledge may be acquired about the situation that leads to different actions being determined subsequently.

Knowledge can be taken to be an abstract set of states with the properties necessary to fulfill the principles of rationality and permanence for the range of environments and goals that characterize the agent. At any moment, the agent's body of knowledge is one of these states and each act of perception changes the state of knowledge. To be in a given state of knowledge (including knowledge of the goal) is to determine the set of actions that move toward maximally preferred behaviors. Knowledge has certain general properties that hold whatever the content domain involved and there have been attempts to formally axiomatize it [9,10,12]. Two properties are needed here. First, knowledge is *about* something. Each knowledge state has associated with it a set of entities to which the content of the knowledge refers (often called its *ontology*). KL systems are often restricted to be about some specific set of entities, and hence have nothing

[3] Perception is taken to be equivalent to acquisition. Elaboration of the definition is required to accommodate that only a fraction of what is perceived generally becomes part of the long-term body of knowledge.

E: An external environment
Exists in some state at each time t
The agent is an object in the environment

The agent

A: A set of actions
Can be evoked at time t
May or may not be applicable, depending on state of E
Affect state of E at next time t+1

P: A set of perceptual devices
Adds knowledge of E to K at time t
This is the only source of new knowledge

G: A goal

K: A body of knowledge
About the environment, goal, actions, perceptual devices

Principles of operation

Rationality: Take actions that know lead to attaining goal
Take A_t such that K_t and K(G) imply will-attain(A_t, G)

Permanence: Knowledge once acquired is available ever after
$P_t{:}K_t \rightarrow K_{t+1}$, where K_{t+1} includes K_t

EXHIBIT 11.4
The definition of a knowledge-level (KL) system.

to say about any of the other things in the universe. Second, there is relation of *inclusion* on knowledge states. One state of knowledge can include another. So, when knowledge is added by perception, thus leading to a new knowledge state, the knowledge of the previous state is still available, because the new state includes the old.

At any specific moment, either no action, a unique action, or a set of actions may be intended. Intending no action or a unique action uniquely determines the behavior of the agent. However, intending a set of actions is indeterminate.

This can occur from multiple causes, e.g., knowledge can be incomplete so that the agent does not know which of several actions leads toward the goal; or any action of the set suffices so the agent does not need to resolve the indeterminacy. In any event, it is sufficient for our purposes to leave unresolved the possibility of indeterminism.

The KLCM specifies an agent without commitment to specific internal mechanisms. It is a description entirely in terms of the external environmental situation. True, both the agent's goals and knowledge are internal to the agent. However, both constructs are expressed entirely in terms of the external situation, so do not require positing structures and mechanisms internal to the agent. Despite this lack of internal mechanisms, the description of a KL system can be complete, so that behavior is completely determined by the internal state of the system, namely by its goals and knowledge, in conjunction with the state of the environment.

KL systems are useful for two distinct but equally important purposes. The first purpose is to describe systems capable of intelligent action. A sufficiently intelligent system must appear to the external world as a KL system. The more effectively a system realizes its goals, the more its behavior conforms entirely to the actual relations of means to ends in the external environment, and the less its behavior reflects any inner mechanisms or structure. To state the matter negatively, if some inner structural characteristic of a system determines some aspect of its external actions (so the action gives evidence that the system has the given internal characteristic), the system will fail to attain its goals when the environment demands a different characteristic. This is the basic argument through adaptation [32] and it applies to all adaptive agents, animal, human, or machine. It is what justifies taking a perfect KL agent as the appropriate model of an intelligent system—intelligence has done all it can do if it perfectly relates means to ends, subject to the knowledge available.

By way of example, Exhibit 11.5 shows a simple situation involving an intelligent system whose internal mechanisms we hardly know, namely a human. By viewing the human as a KL system, positing some knowledge and a goal, the human's behavior can be predicted. We have no idea how Louie has represented his knowledge that St. Louis is a city, the routes to get there, and what one does to travel those routes, nor how he processes these representations to actually call up an airline, get a ticket, call a taxi, go to the counter, or whatever. But it is a good prediction that Louie will indeed get there, if we have agreement from him to meet us (hence having evidence of his goals). There is no issue of design here, just prediction of a goal-oriented system's behavior.

The second useful purpose of KL systems is for design of computational systems. In design, systems are specified prior to determining the structures and mechanisms that meet their specifications. A KL description goes beyond specifying the inputs and outputs to provide necessary and sufficient conditions on what must be available internally, without committing to mechanism. In fact,

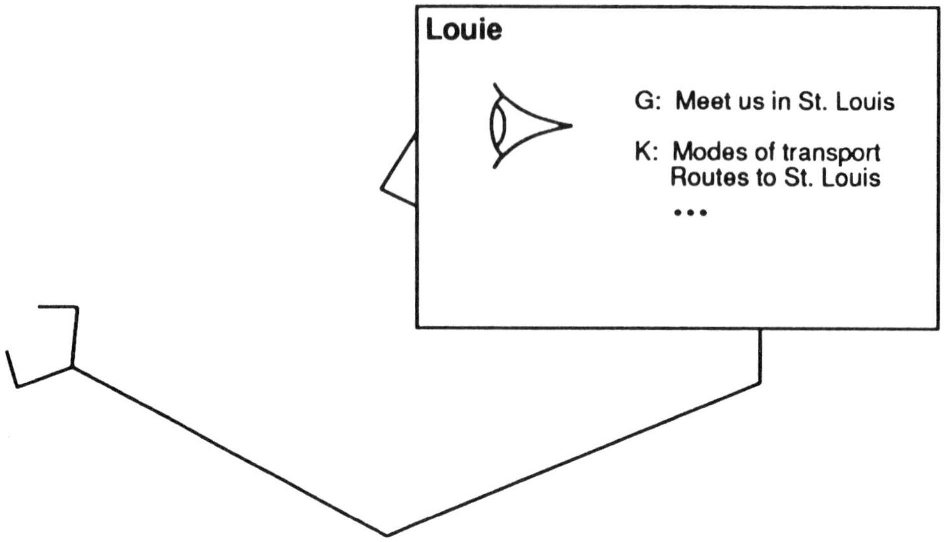

EXHIBIT 11.5
Example KL system: an intelligent system.

the knowledge level of description provides the maximal specification that can be given without making commitments to internal structure.

By way of example, Exhibit 11.6 shows a simple design specification for a data base application, in a form that is familiar to everyone in computer science. In particular, the various components are specified at disparate levels of detail. K is specified in general terms, leaving it to the programmer to choose how to structure the data base, given that the relevant database concepts are understood. P is specified in greater detail, partly as a convenient way to clarify the demands on K and A. Here, the behavior is taken for granted, and the primary issue is design of a system.

The same feature of KL systems underlies both uses, namely, the ability to work from a description given entirely in external terms. In the case of prediction, an internal system exists, but nothing is known about it. In the case of design, nothing internal exists to be described.

In the definition of problem spaces, KL systems will appear in both roles. The KL system at the top of Exhibit 11.3 is intended to be an intelligent system. Therefore, it is appropriately modeled as a KL system. On the other hand, the KL systems that are part of the PSCM are intended to perform specific functions, but to be specified in as general a manner as possible. Therefore they are also appropriately modeled as KL systems.

E: Personal computer

G: Prompt for a query, then respond to it

K: A database relating townships, electoral districts, zip codes
The ability to retrieve on each key

P: Strings that represent queries
Format: "I ; Q"
Where I is an index, of the form:
"D = d" or "T = t" or "Z = z"
Where:
d is a district number
t is a township
z is a zip code
and Q is a query, of the form:
"D = ?" or "T = ?" or "Z = ?"
Examples:
Q1: "D = d; Z = ?"
(Given district number, what are all zip codes in it?)
Q2: "Z = z; D = ?"
(Given zip code, what districts is it in?)

A: Responses sent to the printer
Examples (corresponding to above):
R1: List of zip codes
R2: List of districts

EXHIBIT 11.6
Example KL system: a design specification.

That KL systems are an appropriate model for both rational behavior and design specification has important consequences. The enterprise of automating task formulation is driven by a mixture of motives. On the one hand, we want to be able to construct computer systems that formulate their own tasks. Not only do we want this for its own sake, in order to understand the nature of intellectual activity, but from an applications point of view we want to create devices that can face problematic situations without us around and still succeed. On the other hand, we still want to create systems where we can specify as much of the behavior as we care to and let the rest of the formulation happen within the system we are designing. The two faces of KL systems, toward rational behavior and toward design specification, match well these two different motivations for computational systems.

11.4 The Problem Space Computational Model (PSCM)

An agent described at the knowledge level must be realized by a system that has representations of the agent's body of knowledge, and processes that represent new knowledge from perception and determine the actions according to the principle of rationality. In short, KL systems are realized by symbol-level systems. For a sufficiently large and diverse body of knowledge and a sufficiently wide range of goals, no physically realizable system (whether a symbol-level system or any other) can do this in bounded time. This is simply another way of reading the results on undecidability for universal computing systems. Symbol-level systems can, of course, approximate such realizability. This is where the adoption of a framework comes in (see Exhibit 11.2). For us it means problem spaces.

11.4.1 Problem Spaces

The conceptual unit of the PSCM is the *problem space*, whose definition is given in Exhibit 11.7. A problem space consists of a space of *states (S)* and a set of *operators (O)*. Each operator is an effective procedure for a function from a subset of states to states. Thus, for each state there is a set of *applicable* operators, each of which, when applied to the state, produces a new state. Overall, the application of operators to states remains within the space.

A problem-space system generates *behavior* in a problem space, consisting of an indefinite sequence of *steps*, each a state-operator pair, (s_i, o_i), where i indexes the sequence. At each step, the system is at some *current state* s_i. It first selects a *current operator* o_i and then applies the operator to the current state s_i. If it succeeds (the operator is applicable to s_i), the current state for the next pair in the sequence (i+1) is the result, $s_{i+1} = o_i(s_i)$. If it fails (the operator is not applicable to s_i), then the system remains at state s_i, attempting to select an operator.

A problem space is a framework within which to attempt many tasks. A task is *formulated* in a problem space as starting at an *initial current state* (s_0) to produce a *desired state* in a specified set D, by the successive application of operators to the current state. The task is accomplished if, at some step, the current state is a desired state. Any applicable operator of the space can be used at any step to produce the next current state. Thus the requirement for task accomplishment is that a connected *path* of states and operators exist from the

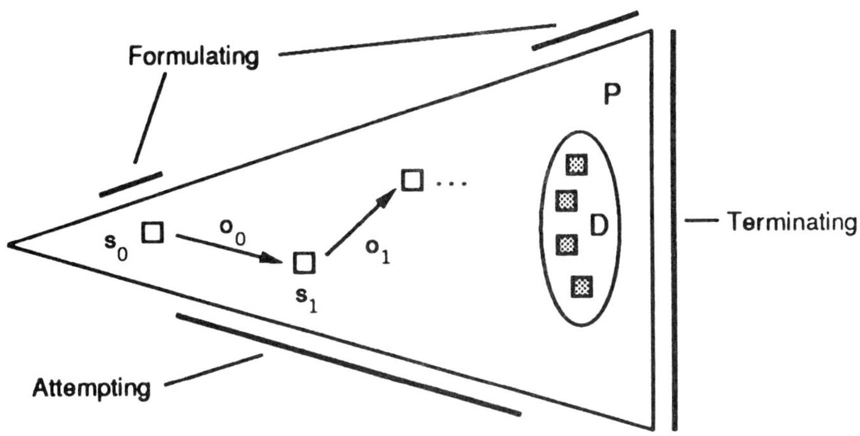

A problem space P is **defined** by:

S A set of states

O A set of operators on S
Each o in O is applicable to a subset S_o of S
Each o realizes a function: $o:S_o \rightarrow S$
Applying o to a state in S_o produces a new state in S

Behavior occurs in problem space P by consecutive steps:

The step at i starts with the system at current state s_i

Each step has two phases:

Selecting: The current operator o_i is selected from O
Applying: The operator o_i is applied to s_i
If o_i is applicable, the current state at i+1 is $o_i(s_i)$
If o_i is not applicable, still remain at s_i

A task is **formulated** using a problem space by:

Determining-space: A problem space P is adopted
Goal-setting: A set of desired states D is adopted
Initializing: The state s_0 becomes the current state

A formulated task is **accomplished** by:

Attempting: Steps are taken in the space
Independence principle: Any operator that can be applied, may be applied
Terminating: The task attempt is terminated
If the current state s_i is in D
If s_i cannot be brought to be in D

EXHIBIT 11.7
Definition of a problem space

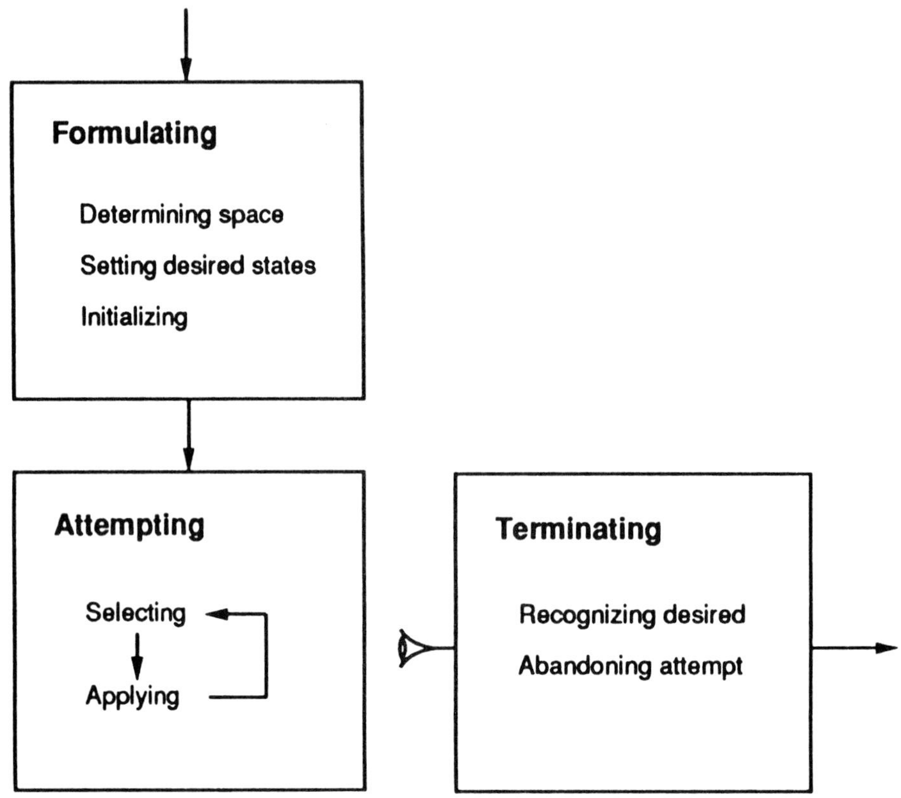

EXHIBIT 11.8
Problem space processes.

initial state to a desired state—and that the system traverse such a path, where it has access at any moment only to a single state (the current one). A given problem space can only be used for tasks that can be formulated in its terms; but given a task a problem space can be fashioned in whose terms the given task can be formulated.

For a problem-space system actually to behave, the states and operators must be represented and a set of processes adequate to imply Exhibit 11.7 must be carried out effectively. Exhibit 11.8 shows these processes in a simple flow diagram. The processes of formulating the task come first: determining the problem space, and then the desired states and the initial state. Then the processes of attempting the task occur: an unending loop of selecting the next operator, and applying it. Finally, there must be processes of terminating the task attempt: detecting the current state to be a desired state or terminating the attempt without accomplishing the task.

Terminating processes proceed concurrently with attempting processes and take the running results of the attempt as their input. Thus the process of determining if s_i is in D must occur concurrently with select-operator for s_i. D itself is not given explicitly as part of the state, but is incorporated in the terminating process. This process can be said to *recognize* that s_i is in D, in the sense of being an immediate action. Such a recognition must always exist. One could imagine an expensive test to determine if a state was in D. This could be embodied in an operator o_D and applied to every state produced by any other operator. Thus, even states (say) would be the result of a task operator and odd states would contain an additional mark *yes* or *no*, which would be the result of o_D. It would still be necessary to recognize whether *yes* or *no* occurred on the state to convert this symbolized knowledge into the action to stop the attempt. Thus, the real set of desired states would be the set of all states marked *yes*.

The activities of Exhibit 11.8 may be encapsulated into four component processes by putting together those that use common knowledge and separating those with data dependencies: *formulate-task*, *select-operator*, *apply-operator*, and *terminate-task*. These processes require further specification. We will do this by making each a KL system (these are the KL systems internal to the PSCM in Exhibit 11.3). Exhibit 11.9 sets out for each its goal, actions, perceptions, and knowledge. The environment of these components is the internal computational environment of an agent, not the external environment of Exhibit 11.3. It is not specified yet, because we are just defining the problem space itself, but we can call it the *current context*. The impulse to formulate a task can be taken to have just arisen in this current context. But this impulse situation and all other aspects of the current context are not in terms of the problem space or its parts, since no problem space has yet come into existence.

The goal of formulate-task is to determine the problem space P, the set of desired states D, and the initial state s_0. Formulate-task is to be evoked at the point when a task is to be formulated, before any formulation has occurred. This contrasts with what might seem more natural, namely, to take the problem space as given. This would take the problem space as an input to formulate-task. However, all aspects of a task formulation—the problem space, desired set, and initial state—call on the same body of knowledge and are interrelated. Formulate-task has knowledge about the current context and perceptual access to it. In particular, it perceives the situation that gave rise to its evocation and it has knowledge about possible problem spaces that might be useful.

The goal of select-operator is to produce the operator to be applied to the current state that will lead to successful performance of the task. It operates in the context of each current state as it occurs. Select-operator generates the control knowledge for moving through the problem space. It has knowledge about the problem space (the states and operators), the task, and the relation

Environment	The inner computational context of an agent.
Formulate-task	
Goal	To formulate a task by using a problem space
Actions	Produce P (the problem space), D, and s_0
Perceptions	Of the current context and the impulse situation
Knowledge	About problem spaces and the current context
Select-operator	
Goal	To select o_i to reach a state in D
Actions	Produce o_i
Perceptions	Of s_i
Knowledge	About P, s_0, and D
Apply-operator	
Goal	To apply o_i to s_i
Actions	Produce $o_i(s_i)$
Perceptions	Of o_i and s_i
Knowledge	About the conditions of applicability of o_i and the function $o{:}S \rightarrow S$
Terminate-task	
Goal	To stop attempt if s_i in D or if cannot succeed
Actions	Stop processing
Perceptions	Of P, D, o_i, and $o_i(s_i)$ for the current i
Knowledge	About the current context

EXHIBIT 11.9
Knowledge-level specification of problem-space components.

between the two—exactly what it knows determines how effective it can be in selecting operators, hence how intelligent the processing can be.

The goal of apply-operator is to produce the next state by applying the operator. Operators are context-limited effective procedures, so that nothing besides the state and operator needs to be known to produce the result. Determining whether the operator is applicable is part of apply-operator and requires only the same knowledge.

The goal of terminate-task is to stop work in the problem space. It should stop the attempt as soon as the task is accomplished, i.e., on the first occasion when s_i is a member of D. Success cannot be assured, of course, so terminate-task must also stop for other reasons as well. Terminate-task might come to know that the task cannot be accomplished, but there are indefinitely diverse other reasons, for instance, that time or some other resource has run out. These depend on aspects of the current context.

The reason for defining the component processes as KL systems is to characterize them as generally as possible, without regard to what processing must occur within them to accomplish their functions. Even with such an abstraction, these processes are limited by the knowledge they have available, especially the entities they can know about, and by their being goal-oriented.

Exhibit 11.10 provides a simple example of a problem-space system and its behavior. The system is a subset of a simple job-shop scheduler [18]. The task is to schedule a series of machining operations on a collection of objects. The customer supplies the objects and their desired characteristics, and also a time constraint in the form of a bound on how long the system has to satisfy the order.

From a description of the objects, formulate-task produces an initial state that contains the objects to be processed and their initial characteristics. Characteristics include shape, surface condition, and number of holes. The operators correspond to a particular machine operating on a particular object at a particular time. Interactions between operator preconditions and effects constrain the order in which operators can be executed. Select-operator has some knowledge of these constraints, and tries to select an operator that will prove to fit into a final schedule. Apply-operator also has knowledge of operator effects, which it uses to change the state when an operator has been selected. In particular, apply-operator updates the developing schedule with a new triple that ties an object to a time slot and a machine, and updates the characteristics of the object affected by the machine.

The behavior of the system is depicted at the bottom of the exhibit. Operator selection knowledge guides the system to apply the lathe to object B and the punch to object A, both during time slot 1. By scheduling early time slots first, the system attempts to maximize concurrency. After polishing B to bring it to its final state, the system tries to roll A, but because this heats the object the polisher cannot be used. The system backtracks from this failure by returning to the previous state. Backtracking is enabled by a history of states maintained by the system. From the previous state, the system first lathes and then polishes A. Terminate-task recognizes that this is a desired state, and the task halts with success.

A problem-space system is a partially specified symbol system. It is a symbol system because it describes the processing that is required to accomplish a task and because what it processes are representations. But it is only partially specified. The component processes are only determined up to KL systems. This

System Specification

Name: Job-shop-scheduler
State:
  Time slots: 1, 2, 3
  Objects: A, B
  Schedule: { ($object_i$, $machine_i$, $timeslot_i$) }
s_0:
  A: rough, triangular, no holes
  B: spherical, no holes, surface undetermined
D:
  A: cylindrical, polished, size 2 hole
  B: cylindrical, polished, no holes

Operators:
  Lathe (what when)
    Preconditions: none
    Effects: cylindrical, rough
  Punch (what when size)
    Preconditions: unheated or rectangular
    Effects: rough, hole
  Polish (what when)
    Preconditions: unheated or rectangular
    Effects: smooth
  Roll (what when)
    Preconditions: none
    Effects: cylindrical, hot, surface undetermined

Operator selection:
  Rule out all unhelpful operators
    Those that do not achieve a desired characteristic
  Punch before rolling
    Rolling heats the object so it cannot be punched
  Punch or lathe before polishing
    Punch and lathe leave an object rough
  Try earlier time slots first
  Choose randomly among undifferentiated candidates

Behavior on the task

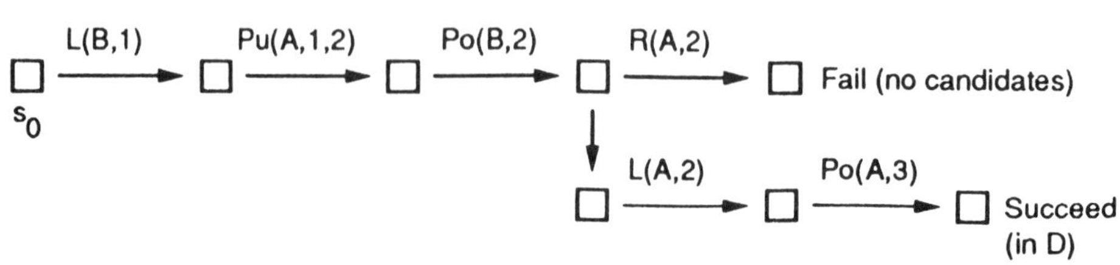

suffices as far as determining the system's behavior is concerned, providing that an external notation exists in which to express the knowledge, for then the behavior can be derived. But the problem space must also be realized computationally. If only a small body of knowledge is involved this might be a detail, for any number of mechanisms could be used to realize the component KL systems. But problem spaces are intended to be used with arbitrarily large and rich bodies of knowledge. Then constructing the KL systems for the component becomes problematical.

There are two additional minor ways in which a problem-space system is only partially specified. One is the representation of the states and the operators that apply to them. The other is the operating structure of the current context, which permits the four components to execute, produce actions, and communicate with each other. These are left to be specified in the symbol-level computational model that supports the problem space. Any way of realizing these that meets the functional specification of a problem space with its four components will suffice. No critical implementation issues are hidden within these two aspects.

11.4.2 Implementation of a Knowledge-Level System

For those familiar with problem spaces for the last 30 years, the treatment to this point may seem a bit labored. We now enter upon new ground. The problem space has been described as an autonomous system level, without reference to adjacent levels (once a task is formulated in it). However, problem spaces are intended to implement KL systems.

Exhibit 11.11 shows how this occurs. The exhibit depicts a simple agent described as a KL system implemented by a problem space. The top panel depicts the agent's knowledge and goal embodied in the knowledge of the four components of the problem space: formulate-task (Ft), select-operator (So), apply-operator (Ao), and terminate-task (Tt). The middle panel depicts the operation of the agent's perception and action. The bottom panel indicates which parts of the problem space realize the various parts of the KL system. The situation is a simple reactive arc from perception through the KL system to action. This bypasses many issues of dynamic interaction with a concurrently dynamic and reactive environment, but it will suffice for this chapter.

The key to the implementation is the middle panel. KL perceptions are realized partly by formulate-task, which creates an initial state that corresponds to relevant aspects of the external environment, and partly by apply-operator, which generates the changes due to a KL-action operator. KL actions are realized by operators in the problem space. When an operator is applied, the corresponding

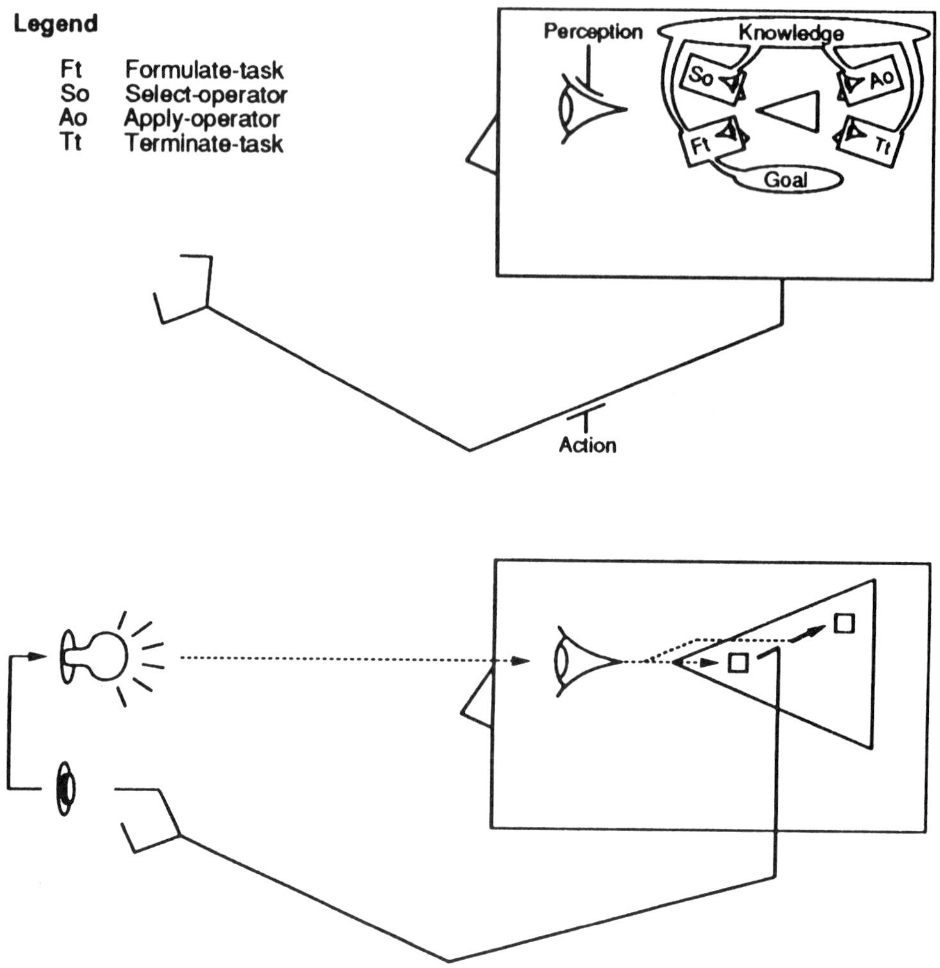

KL system		Problem space
Action	⟷	Operator
Perception	⟷	Ft sets s_0 Ao sets new state
Goal	⟷	Ft sets D
Knowledge	⟷	Knowledge in Ft, So, Ao, and Tt Behavior in problem space

EXHIBIT 11.11
The problem-space implementation of a KL system.

external action occurs.[4] The new state produced by apply-operator in the problem space is the result of doing the KL action in the environment. Perception reflects those changes in the new state.

The agent's knowledge is embodied in the knowledge of the four problem space components. However, this latter knowledge is about the problem space, states, and operators; hence it cannot of itself be the knowledge of the agent, which is about the goal, actions, and environment. It becomes the agent's knowledge by means of the relationships just described. That is, states are about the external world because of KL perception; operators are about the external world because of KL actions; the desired states are about the goal of the KL agent because of formulate-task; and the means-ends knowledge of select-operator is about performing tasks in the environment because it links environment-referring operators on environment-referring states to descriptions of environment-referring desired states.

Behavior of the KL agent happens as follows. We imagine a changing environment, which is mostly irrelevant to the agent but which from time to time creates a situation relevant to the agent's goal. This external situation is perceived by formulate-task defining a set of states in this space to be desired states, expressing the agent's goal. Formulate-task also encodes the current external situation as an initial current state in the space. Select-operator proposes an operator to change this state. It knows something about the current state and the desired states and uses this knowledge to select an appropriate operator, which apply-operator then executes by the corresponding action, which affects the environment, which is then perceived, which then produces a new state, which becomes the current state. (If the action could not take place in the external world, then the operator was not applicable.) If the new state is a desired state, then both the agent's goal in the external environment and the task in the problem space have been accomplished and terminate-task lapses the agent back into inactivity. If the situation does not attain the goal and the current state is not desired, then another step is taken. This continues until the internal task and external goal are accomplished, or until terminate-task abandons the agent's attempt to attain its goal. After all, there is nothing in the nature of things to assure success. The agent remains quiescent until the environment again presents a situation in which the agent's goal is perceived as not satisfied. Thus, behavior in the problem space realizes the principle of rationality to the extent that the tasks formulated in it are accomplished.

This is a simplistic scenario. It even has some glitches. For instance, it assumes (unrealistically) that the environment changes autonomously until it provokes the agent, but then ceases autonomous change while the agent acts

[4] As discussed above, the action is actually only intended; whether it occurs depends on the state of the external world, which includes the state of the agent as object in that world.

upon it, even through multiple actions. However, the glitches are not worth fixing at this point. Our aim has been solely to show how a problem-space system implements or realizes a KL system. Putting the glitches to one side, what we get is a reactive agent that operates directly coupled to its environment, something like a Brooks critter [2].

11.4.3 Lack of Knowledge and Multiple Problem Spaces

The KL agent of Exhibit 11.11 is to be a rational goal-oriented agent. Implicit in this is the requirement for unlimited scope for the agent's knowledge and goal—problem spaces are to be a general implementation of KL agents. Though an unlimited KL agent cannot be perfectly realized, problem spaces are to be the symbol-level processing scheme to approximate pure knowledge-based behavior indefinitely closely.

Against this aspiration, the scheme of Exhibit 11.11 appears totally inadequate, well beyond any glitches. Suppose we take the system to be a reactive agent, analogous to a Brooks critter. Then the problem-space components (formulate-task, select-operator, apply-operator, terminate-task) are primitive processes that embody some fixed, limited knowledge of the environment. But we know that only extremely simple behavior can be so realized. Suppose, instead, we take the problem space in Exhibit 11.11 to be the arena to deal with really difficult tasks of goal attainment. Then we see that our example doesn't even permit any internal processing within the problem space to create and verify plans. Every internal operator executes as an external operator. What has happened to the problem space as a means for doing problem solving?

We can extend Exhibit 11.11 to take care of this latter difficulty. We add operators to the space whose application produces only an internal state. This provides for internal heuristic search before executing an external action. With a mechanism for saving states, this extends to planning and even the mixing of planning and execution. Some elaboration is required to provide for inner/outer correspondences, i.e., pairs of operators that produce the same internal change of state, but only one of which intends a KL action; and states that describe the same external situation, but with various modalities such as perceived, expected, imagined, or desired. Such elaboration, if done correctly, removes the glitches, permitting the external situation to change continuously and the state to be modified continuously by perception.

All the above, while essential and not entirely without interest, does not touch the essential difficulty—the component problem-space processes are themselves described only at the knowledge level. They remain without realization in terms of symbol-level mechanisms. It is not that *no* reduction has occurred in going from the KL agent to the problem space that realizes it, only that the reduction is small. Only if the components are simple enough to be realized by fixed mechanisms can the scheme of Exhibit 11.11 be taken to be operational. In terms of KL systems, we might describe this as the components having their knowledge *immediately available*. That is, if the components have knowledge immediately available, the system of Exhibit 11.11 is operational. We have not yet explored what is implied by knowledge being immediately available. Nevertheless, we can see that in some definite, if small, set of circumstances, reduction to symbol-level mechanisms can occur.

Now is the time to yield to the impulse to recurse. Let us be in a problem space with its four components: formulate-task, select-operator, apply-operator, and terminate-task. Let there be some symbol-level scheme that permits their implementation if the knowledge they contain is immediately available. Suppose, on the contrary, for some component, C, knowledge is not available. In this circumstance, let C's behavior be realized by means of a problem-space system, P_C. If appropriate knowledge becomes available, C will attain its goal, and behavior in the original problem space proceeds. P_C has its own four components, each characterized as a KL system. The knowledge may be available for these components. But if not—if some knowledge is not available—then the lacking component is implemented by yet another problem-space system.

We have recursed. The recursion bottoms out when the knowledge required by a component of a problem-space system is immediately available. This aspect is the primitive mechanism, and remains undefined. For the moment, however, we should contemplate what has been attained. We now have a *multiple problem-space system*. This brings us a long ways toward having an adequate definition of a PSCM. Exhibit 11.12 gives its specifications. Not surprisingly, problem spaces are related as means to ends. However, the relationship between problem spaces is the general one of *lack of knowledge*. Whenever in a problem space there is a lack of knowledge, then another problem space is created that obtains that knowledge.[5] The generality of this relationship should be noted. For computer science, the natural relationship on which to establish a multiple problem-space system is operator implementation, i.e., procedure hierarchy. Not only does the present scheme encompass the additional functions of formulating tasks, selecting operators, and terminating tasks, but the means-ends linkage is defined by whatever lack of knowledge has occurred.

We now have a symbol-level process that operates to approximate a given KL system. Whenever knowledge is missing the system operates so as to acquire it. It ceases to set up processes to acquire more knowledge when its available knowledge suffices. It almost seems too good to be true—as if we really have gotten something for nothing, because we seem to have avoided forcing the system into definite representations and processes that would compromise the

[5]This includes conflicting knowledge, since the fundamental way of dealing with contradictions is by adding knowledge, e.g., explanations, determinations of what knowledge is in error, etc.

A multiple problem-space system consists of:

A KL system (EKL) situated in an external environment

A set of problem spaces PS: $\{P_\alpha\}$

Each component of P_α is a KL system

A top problem space (TPS) that implements EKL

Each P_α (except TPS) supports another space P_β in PS

P_α implements a component of P_β

Components (hence their spaces) may have many supporting P_α

The P_α that have no support are the primitive spaces of PS

The components of a primitive P_α have available knowledge

EXHIBIT 11.12
Multiple problem space system.

generality. Nevertheless, it certainly is the right shape for a symbol-level system that is supposed to implement a KL system, hence a rational goal-oriented agent.

Such systems are a little unwieldy to be laid out in full detail within the confines of a chapter. Nevertheless, Exhibit 11.13 shows a system, Browser-Soar [11], which operates through many different problem spaces (the triangles). The small circled numbers are the order in which the system generated the spaces. The task is one of using a browser[6] on an interactive computer system called cT. Browser-Soar is simulating a human using the browser at the workstation display, the whole being about a minute's worth of human behavior, although that is not relevant here. Almost all the relations among spaces in the exhibit are due to apply-operator. That is, the results of operators in the space are not immediately known, with the consequent need to go into a subproblem-space to implement the operator. However, in the upper part of the figure there is an operator that is proposed independent of what space the system is in, which acts as an interrupt from perceived information from the display; and in the lower right corner select-operator was unable to select any operator at all, so another problem space (back-up) had to be entered to change the situation to where an operator could be selected.

[6] A browser is an interactive tool that lets a user move from place to place in a data base by displaying a continuously changing accessing structure. Hypermedia are a type of browser.

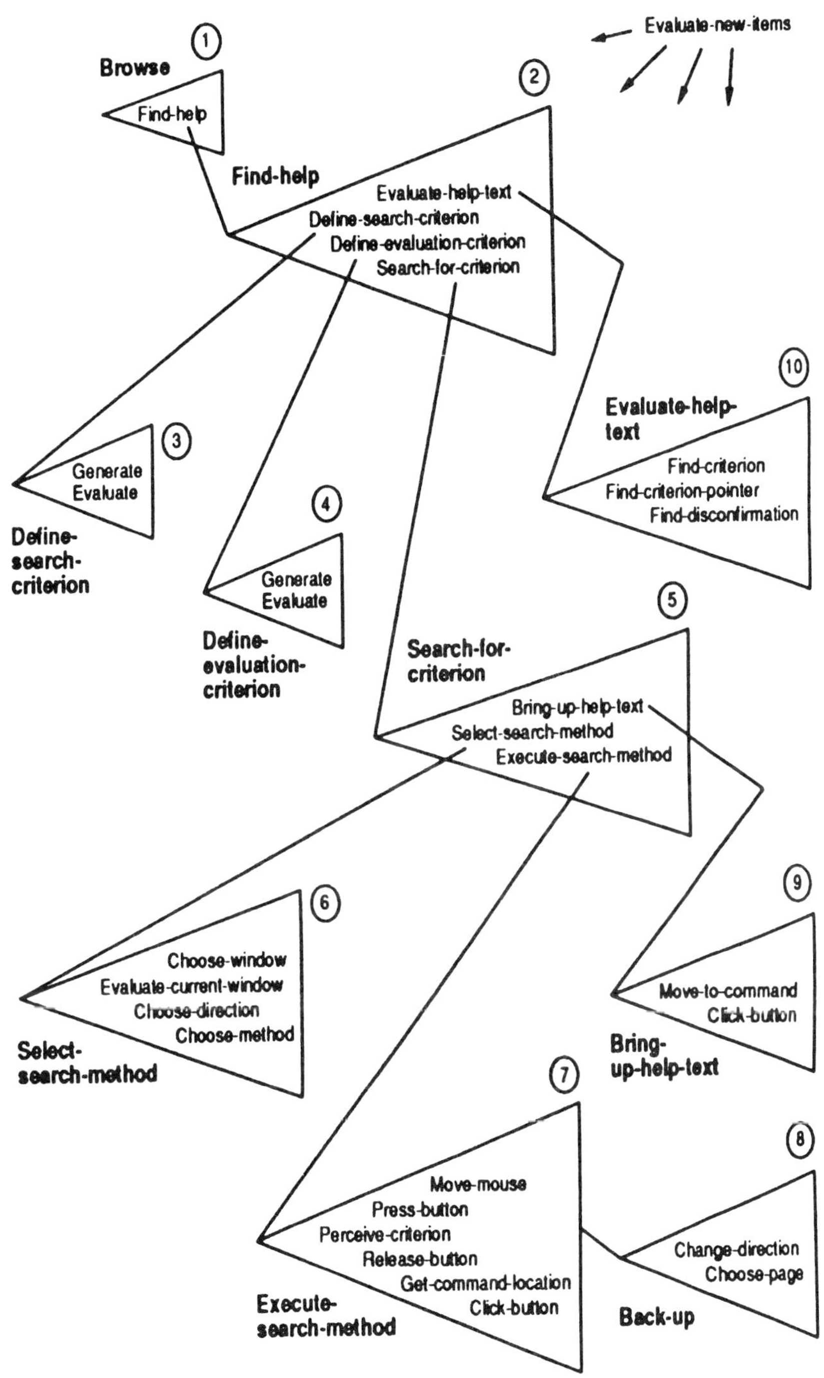

EXHIBIT 11.13

Several aspects remain to be pinned down before the PSCM is defined. The first is available knowledge, which serves to ground the recursion of problem spaces. For the knowledge in a component to be available means both that a representation of the knowledge exists that determines the actions, given the goal of that component and the principle of rationality, and that the component will actually behave in accordance with it within some definite time. Although the symbol mechanisms that produce the behavior are not specified, they must operate as a primitive, finite mechanism—there can be no possibility of internal exponential problem-solving or of failing to reach a definite termination. Thus, if the knowledge of a component is available, the component will perform its function in some finite time, otherwise it will indicate that the knowledge is not available. Each component could have its own internal mechanisms, so each could have its own distinct time bound. However, we will assume there is a uniform *time constant* for the system, within which the bounds of all individual components fit. The available knowledge itself need not be adequate in terms of the goals of the system as a whole. Nothing guarantees that a system must be able to actually meet its goals, only that the system's capability to attain its goals can be expressed as knowledge about its goals, environment, and actions, so that limitations in the system's capability show up as limitations in knowledge, not as limitations in whether available knowledge can be brought to bear.

The second aspect demanding attention consists of some details of operation. Exhibit 11.14 shows a set of problem spaces as generated by a problem-space system. This is a dynamic trace, starting with the top problem space (TPS) and proceeding to P1, then P2, and finally to P5. Around each problem space (the triangles) cluster its four components. Most components have knowledge immediately available and respond immediately. Some, such as the apply-operator of TPS, require a problem space in order to perform (the double arrow). Expansion to a subproblem space occurs for formulate-task (at P5), select-operator (at P1), and apply-operator (at TPS, P1, and P3). However, no such expansion is possible for terminate-task, which operates as a concurrently acting recognizer, hence is never required to produce a result. Only part of the structure in Exhibit 11.14 exists at any one time. The trace of the active spaces is given at the right of the exhibit; it is a typical stack discipline.

The trace assumes that all components succeed, although they may require the support of processing in subspaces. Failure is also possible, since not all tasks can be accomplished. Failure is determined by terminate-task, which can stop an attempt in a problem space before the desired state is reached. This can cause the component being supported by the given problem space to fail (though it need not, because formulate-task could formulate another task using a different space). If a formulate-task fails then the component it supports fails. If a select-operator fails, then there is nothing more to do in the space and terminate-task stops the attempt (with failure, since the current state will not

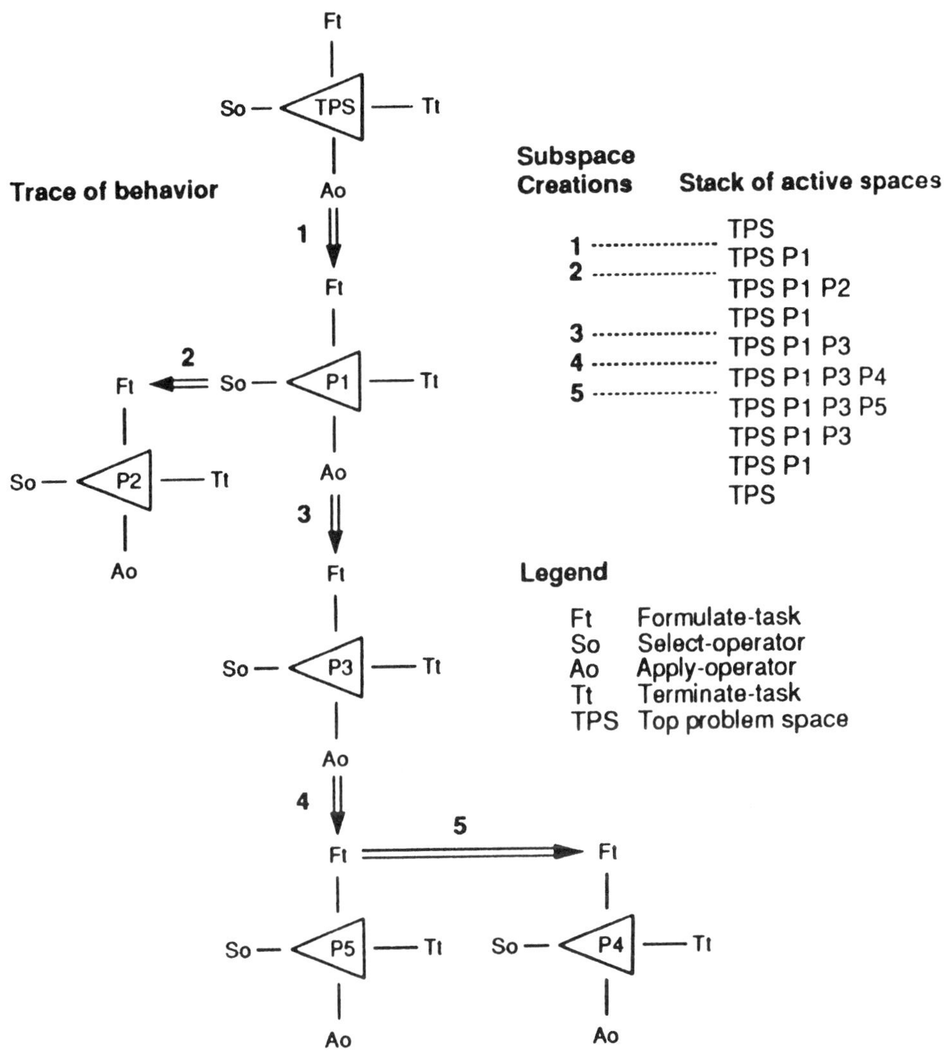

EXHIBIT 11.14
Details of PSCM operation.

be in D). If an apply-operator fails, this simply leaves the system at its current state, attempting to select an operator to apply.

The third aspect requiring attention is the possibility of unending operation. This occurs in two forms. One is infinite descent in the recursion of problem spaces because no knowledge is ever immediately available. The other is infinite search through a problem space because terminate-task never stops the proceedings, even though the task can never be accomplished. These infinities are to be avoided by the components having specific immediate knowledge, not by anything built into the PSCM structure. General default knowledge can avoid most of them. For example, let formulate-task know to fail if the component for which it is formulating a task is formulate-task and if it itself doesn't even know a problem space in which to cast this task. Then nothing is to be served by recursing further. This will avoid all infinite descent except loops.[7] For another example, let terminate-task have an upper bound on the number of steps it will permit in a problem space. This will avoid infinite search (though there are more task-sensitive ways to keep search under control).

We now have a complete performance system. Given available knowledge for some components of various problem spaces, the system will attempt to realize a KL system behaving in its external environment. The knowledge that this KL system will exhibit cannot be described simply as the union of the available knowledge of these components. Many (indeed, most) of these components do not have knowledge about the external environment of the top KL system, but rather possess knowledge about the internal computational environment; this knowledge is not included. However, the tasks attempted in all these internal problem spaces serve to generate knowledge in the components of higher spaces, which ultimately serve to generate knowledge in the top KL system. It is the immediately available knowledge in the top KL system plus the generated knowledge arising from the activity in all the problem spaces that forms the total knowledge of the top KL system.

11.5 Discussion

The formulation of the PSCM is now complete in its essentials. Many elaborations, issues, and questions should follow in its wake, but we will only be able to hint at them here. We will do that first. Then we will discuss briefly the PSCM as a task formulation, the issue raised as an opener. Finally, we will expand a little on the relation of the PSCM to Soar.

11.5.1 Elaborations, Caveats, and Missing Aspects

It is important not to take the *search view* of problem spaces (and the PSCM) exclusively, although that is the role it has played in AI. There is also the *control view*. The problem space is a *least-commitment* programming control

[7] Soar has an analogous default rule.

construct. It delays as long as possible determining what operations to execute, namely to the moment of execution. This arises from the complete separation of select-operator from apply-operator. Programming languages in general intermix control and application, thereby giving up flexibility (and buying efficiency). There is also the *error-recovery view*. Any error occurs in a context (the problem space) that permits recovery from error and the consideration of alternative behaviors. Furthermore, any failure of the system to have the knowledge to deal with errors leads to the formulation of tasks to gain that knowledge. Programming languages in general do not have the context available to recover from error and must settle for communicating the error to some appropriate intelligent agent. In sum, the PSCM incorporates many of the characteristics needed by an autonomous agent.

The problem space, as given in Exhibit 11.7, has no automatic state saving and advances entirely from the current state. Thus as it stands, it can perform none of the weak methods, such as depth-first search and means-ends analysis. In fact, state saving is important, but in our formulation of PSCM it is to be done by the task encoded in the PSCM rather than automatically by the PSCM. States can be saved in several ways, e.g., by having the current state incorporate related prior states, or by reconstructing past states from history descriptions stored in the current state, or by spreading the search across many problem spaces so each space stores a single state (Soar usually saves state this way).

The problem space is a form of generate and test, the most fundamental problem solving method of them all. Sequences of operators generate candidate states for testing by terminate-task. This identification helps to understand why many features of the PSCM are the way they are. Encapsulating more knowledge of a task in the operators and less in the desired state shifts knowledge from the test to the generator (almost always improving efficiency). The existence of multiple problem spaces, as opposed to a single large space, implies putting more knowledge in the generator. The independence principle of operator application guarantees that extensive memory of paths need not be maintained automatically to verify path constraints.

The definition of problem spaces sets no limits on the complexity or number of states or operators. There clearly are some limits, although it makes sense to consider them as additional specifications, rather than complicating the basic definition. For instance, operators can be finitely generated. Each state that becomes current must be a finite structure. The space can have an infinite number of states, since only the current state is present in the agent at one time, hence an infinite number of states need never be realized simultaneously.

The PSCM contains an implicit requirement for mechanisms of experiential learning in its implementation. A PSCM system faces the external environment as a KL system. As it performs a sequence of tasks, the problem spaces evoked generate knowledge, which is exhibited in the behavior of this KL system (indeed, that is what the problem spaces are for). According to the permanence principle, this knowledge should then be available ever after. But there is no guarantee the knowledge will be available on later tasks, even if it is relevant. The problem space may have no way of generating it again in the different circumstances. Thus the KL system appears inconstant, exhibiting knowledge on one occasion, then failing to exhibit it, then perhaps exhibiting it again. This condition may be viewed simply as a facet of the necessarily approximate nature of all implementations of KL systems. However, if it were required that the knowledge generated by a problem space for the KL system it implements becomes part of that KL system's immediately available knowledge, then the inconstancy would be ameliorated. The matter is not entirely simple, because the knowledge to be added is underdetermined by the KL system's performance—the KL system may induce beyond the minimum knowledge necessary for the task. Consequently, many different learning mechanisms may be able to fulfill this requirement, with varying characteristics. In any event, we see that the principle of permanence strongly implies that experiential learning be a feature of PSCM systems.

The PSCM must be implemented in a symbol-level computational model (recall Exhibit 11.3). This SLCM must provide an operational arena within which all the activities of the PSCM occur and intercommunicate. It must also provide the symbol-level mechanisms that realize all the sources of immediately available knowledge. We have not attempted to treat the SLCM in this chapter, since it does not affect the definition of the PSCM, just as long as the entire scheme is realizable. As for the latter, Soar provides a concrete and useful demonstration of an operational system organized along PSCM lines.

11.5.2 The PSCM as a Task Formulation Framework

The PSCM incorporates the complete act of task formulation in the formulate-task component. If formulate-task is primitive, it knows (immediately) what problem space, desired states, and initial state to put into effect. If formulate-task is not primitive, it formulates the task of determining the problem space, desired states and initial state—doing so, of course, in another problem space, namely, one for determining formulations (or more precisely, for determining whatever part of the formulation cannot be immediately produced). And if this latter formulation cannot be done immediately, this formulation task itself (i.e., how to formulate the task of formulating a problem space) can be formulated. In short, the PSCM is reflective enough to cast the formulation problem in its own terms.

The PSCM also incorporates the instigation of task creation—the going from nothing to something. Creation occurs at the moment when the system becomes dependent on a component that does not have the appropriate available knowledge. Thus the PSCM not only creates its own subtasks but determines the circumstances in which to do so. The temptation is to say the PSCM *decides* when to create a new task, but that is not correct. The PSCM creates a new task when it has to, because knowledge is unavailable to do what it wants to do. Positive knowledge is not required to initiate creating a task; the system itself does it autonomously.

Of the five general criteria for evaluating task frameworks mentioned in the introduction, three require little comment: operationality, scope, and bias. The PSCM is implementable with an appropriate symbol-level computational model (such as Soar) and is fully operational. The scope of PSCM is universal, which can again be seen from the Soar implementation, but is also apparent on its face given appropriate state saving. As for bias, not much can be said at this stage (as noted more generally at the beginning of this chapter).

A potentially interesting feature of PSCM with respect to openness is multiple problem spaces. Problem spaces can be created in response to whatever things are in the environment, reflecting their structure in such a way as to make their incorporation easy. That is, problem spaces invite the creation of special representations for special purposes. This contrasts with a framework such as logic that specifies the form of the representation, thus forcing the encoding of all external things into its own terms. We describe this feature only as potential, because there are as yet no substantial demonstrations of its use. Indeed, on the other side of the ledger, problem spaces do not seem to lend themselves to embodying declarative information (e.g., geographical information) and this is an active research issue in Soar.

With respect to initialization, problem spaces have the property of being almost indefinitely easy to formulate a task within. The space is simply made larger and larger until it is believed to encompass both the initial state and the projection of the desired states into the space. A price is to be paid for this, of course. As the space gets larger, the search for a desired state gets more expensive, in general, combinatorially so. Concomitantly, the test for the desired state can be left more and more to be the unassimilated and uninterpreted initial problem statement. This also increases the ease of task formulation. The corresponding price is the expense of detecting that the current state is a desired state. These costs can be very real. But the fundamental point is that at least by paying them, task formulation occurs and an attempt gets underway. Moreover paying a heavy price need only occur if no knowledge is available to use a smaller space or a less expensive goal test.

The formulation of tasks arises in a variety of contexts. At one extreme is the *autonomous* agent, which has its own high-level goals and concerns. It needs to formulate tasks in its encounters with its environment. This is (mostly) the situation with us humans. As we construct systems capable of task formulation, this will be the situation for many robotic systems. We have described the PSCM mostly as an autonomous agent. This flows naturally from the fact that the topmost level is a rational, goal-oriented KL agent.

At the other extreme is the *instrumental* agent, coupled to an autonomous agent. The autonomous agent wishes to formulate a task it has formulated only partially or perhaps has not formulated at all beyond some fragmentary goal statement. It wishes to use the instrumental agent to help in the formulation, getting the instrumental agent to formulate whatever does not seem critical, but reserving to itself the important parts of the formulation, including final review. This instrumental situation, of course, is the extension of the foundation paradigm of programming, described at the beginning of the chapter.

An indication of how this instrumental relation might develop is given by a hypothesis that has emerged in the Soar effort [36]. In attempting to realize a typical expert system within PSCM (i.e., using Soar as a PSCM system) it appears that no knowledge of methods needs to be provided. That is, starting from a specification of the task in English in entirely domain-oriented terms, it is necessary for the human knowledge engineer to: (1) map the parts of the spec (literally, in terms of short sections of text) into the elements of the PSCM (spaces, operators, desired states); (2) decide on the representation of the elements (in Soar's basic representation of attributes and values); and (3) determine the communication requirements for results between spaces and within spaces at different points in time. The rest takes care of itself, namely, the knowledge engineer does not have to design the methods to be used to accomplish the task or an executive system for carrying out the task. These are provided by the PSCM. This avoidance of method design is possible because (typically) expert systems explicitly specify how they want things done (not just what they want done), though in domain-oriented terms. The PSCM is able to capitalize on this characteristic of expert systems to make formulation easy. The domain-oriented structures are reflected directly in the PSCM structure. We are currently engaged in a major experimental effort to explore how robust our initial findings are, using a task-acquisition language, TAQL, that treats Soar as a PSCM [35].

Another indication of the power of PSCM for task formulation is that it provides for what might be called *goal programming*. The face that a PSCM system shows to the human is that of the top KL system. If the user can specify the goals desired, the knowledge available, and the actions whereby the goal is to be effected, this should be enough for the PSCM system to formulate the task of attaining the goal. More precisely, it provides the framework in which knowledge can be provided to do that formulation. Small experiments are underway in Soar that operate at about this level [13]. Soar is first given some general instructions, as shown in the sentences 1 to 4 of Exhibit 11.15. Then it is given a specific task in sentences 5 to 9, whereupon it answers *true*, as required. The form of the instructions is program-like, but it is a far cry from a program in a procedural language. The knowledge that the PSCM system has so it can formulate a task from the instructions is given in its knowledge of English, both syntax and semantics. But the entire act of task formulation occurs within the PSCM, including the comprehension of the specification and the creation of

Instructions:

1. Read four premises.
2. Then read a statement.
3. If the statement is true say "true".
4. Then stop.

The specific task:

5. A plate is left of a knife.
6. A fork is left of the plate.
7. A jug is above the knife.
8. The fork is below a cup.
9. The cup is left of the jug.

The system should answer:

10. True.

EXHIBIT 11.15
Simple instruction-taking (by Soar).

problem spaces to do the task. This experiment is quite rudimentary, but it gives a glimpse of how a PSCM might actually support task formulation.

11.5.3 The Role of Soar in the Development of the PSCM

Although, as noted in the introduction, problem spaces have been around for a long time, both in AI and in our own research, Soar has been the major catalyst in the formulation of the PSCM. Prior to Soar there were no multiple problem-space systems. Problem spaces remained a system-organizing principle rather than a complete system level (computational model). For one, much was missing in the notion of problem spaces, so it required completion in some way. But also problem spaces were seen as appropriate only for problematical situations requiring search. They provided a reduction to something nonproblematical, namely, the operators. Necessarily, then, operators should be specified in a more computationally effective way, i.e., in a standard programming language. This kept the problem space as a single level of organization, with the parts (the PSCM components) specified in another programming formalism.

The first break in this relatively fixed picture seems to have been the extension of problem spaces to be an organizing scheme for all goal-oriented activity, in what was called the *problem-space hypothesis* [21]. This was motivated largely by psychological concerns. It did, however, open the way for the construction of Soar as a multiple problem-space system [15]. This system developed a series of symbol-level mechanisms, first for combining problem spaces and production systems (the universal weak method), then for doing universal subgoaling and then for chunking. The result was a tightly integrated system that combined all these organizational constructs.

As Soar has evolved we have more and more come to separate a problem-space level from the set of symbolic mechanisms that supports it. This evolution has been driven by three forces. First, people seem to find Soar hard to understand and we keep changing the description to find ways to make the system clearer. Second, in designing a more general specification language for Soar we have moved toward the PSCM as the appropriate level of generality [36]. Third, in moving to a new implementation based on some low-level considerations (whether to copy states or modify them) we found we needed to describe a distinct problem-space level in order to understand the effects of the symbol-level changes [17]. All of this has moved us toward the PSCM, though still drawing on the symbol-level aspects of the Soar architecture to fill in the missing details.

The final ingredient in creating an autonomous PSCM has been our growing use of the knowledge level. Ever since the knowledge level was introduced as a system construct [22] it has provided a useful definition of an intelligent agent, namely one that closely approximates a KL system. We have continually tried to use the knowledge level as a way of organizing and understanding Soar [29,30,31]. This has had as a primary focus analyzing Soar as an agent in an external world (knowledge-level learning) and how close the mechanisms of Soar could be seen to support a knowledge-level description of that agent.

The present chapter takes the important step of creating the PSCM as a genuine systems level, independent of Soar. Soar has informed this effort at every point along the way and a direct mapping can be made between the constructs of the PSCM and Soar. As should be evident, Soar is the one system we can draw upon to illustrate a number of features of the PSCM. However, it would be wrong to think of the PSCM as simply Soar in disguise. A genuine act of abstraction has occurred, and multiple implementations of the PSCM are certainly possible. Indeed, in the Soar project we have had two quite distinct symbol-level implementations, Soar4 [16] and Soar5 [17], and expect additional ones to follow. As a final point of dependence of this PSCM effort on Soar, we are able to detect inadequacies in the PSCM by noting features of the Soar architecture that have no reflection in the PSCM. The primary example is the way Soar is able to make decisions at any level of the context at any time and to communicate freely among all active problem spaces. The PSCM described here does not seem to have this property, but to be a more classically stack-like structure.

11.6 Conclusion

We have attempted in this chapter to describe the PSCM, a computational model of multiple problem spaces. This task goes beyond simply having the concept of problem spaces around as an organizing principle for AI systems. It implies an act of abstraction to define a complete system structure in its own terms, i.e., without embedding it in another computational model. As it turns out, the PSCM requires another computational model, the knowledge level computational model (KLCM). However, this is not an implementation model for the PSCM, but one that is co-defined with it. The entire structure is grounded in a more conventional symbol-level computational model (SLCM), but one whose character is quite constrained. Most of what is novel in this effort comes from the use of the PSCM and KLCM to realize each other.

Although the PSCM is necessarily abstract, and properly so, this effort arises from extremely practical motivations. Generally stated, it is the need in computer science to extend the foundation paradigm to systems that formulate their own tasks. As such, this is an attempt to advance programming systems and languages as much as AI. It seeks to get work in programming systems to raise its sights from variations of the foundation paradigm, even those as rich as object-oriented programming, to organizations that permit computer systems to take on more of the total intellectual task of helping humans get their computational work done.

We started by describing the several task-formulation frameworks that have emerged as possibilities (see Exhibit 11.2). At this stage of understanding, none can be eliminated in favor of the others. We know too little about any of them in the face of realistic task formulation. We hope that these other frameworks will continue to be developed. We have been sufficiently encouraged by our work with the PSCM that we will continue to pursue it.

11.7 Acknowledgments

We would like to acknowledge the entire Soar research community, which has provided the environment in which the ideas of the PSCM have matured.

This research was supported in part by the Defense Advanced Research Projects Agency (DOD), and monitored by the Avionics Laboratory, Air Force Wright Aeronautical Laboratories, Aeronautical Systems Division (AFSC), Wright-Patterson AFB, Ohio 45433-6543 under Contract F33615-87-C-1499, ARPA Order No. 4976, Amendment 20; in part by DARPA under Contract

N00014-89-K-0155; in part by the National Aeronautics and Space Administration under Contract NASA Ames NCC2-517; in part by the Natural Sciences and Engineering Research Council of Canada and the Alberta Heritage Scholarship Fund; and in part by the Digital Equipment Corporation.

The views and conclusions contained in this chapter are those of the authors and should not be interpreted as representing the official policies, either expressed or implied, of the Defense Advanced Research Projects Agency, the National Aeronautics and Space Administration, the U.S. government, the Canadian Government, or the Digital Equipment Corporation.

References

[1] A. V. Aho, J. E. Hopcroft, and J. D. Ullman. *The Design and Analysis of Computer Algorithms*. Addison-Wesley, Reading, MA, 1974.

[2] R. A. Brooks. A robust layered control system for a mobile robot. *IEEE Journal of Robotics and Automation*, RA-2:14-23, 1986.

[3] N. Carriero and D. Gelernter. How to write parallel programs: A guide to the perplexed. *ACM Computer Surveys*, 21:232-357, 1989.

[4] D. C. Dennett. *The Intentional Stance*. Bradford Books: MIT Press, Cambridge, MA, 1988.

[5] T. G. Dietterich. Learning at the knowledge level. *Machine Learning*, 1:287-316, 1986.

[6] *Blackboard Systems*, Addison-Wesley, Reading, MA, 1988.

[7] *Computers and Thought*, McGraw-Hill, New York, 1963.

[8] I. Goldstein and S. Papert. Artificial intelligence, language and the study of knowledge. *Cognitive Science*, 1:84-124, 1977.

[9] J. Hintikka. *Knowledge and Belief*. Cornell University Press, Ithaca, NY, 1962.

[10] J. Hintikka. *Logic, Language-games and Information*. Oxford, London, 1973.

[11] B. E. John, A. Newell, and S. Card. Browser-soar: A goms-like model of a highly interactive task, 1990 (in preparation).

[12] H. J. Levesque. Foundations of a functional approach to knowledge representation. *Artificial Intelligence*, 23:155-212, 1984.

[13] R. L. Lewis, A. Newell, and T. A. Polk. Toward a soar theory of taking instructions for immediate reasoning tasks. In *Proceedings Cognitive Science Eleventh Annual Conference, 1989*. Cognitive Science Society, 1989.

[14] J. E. Laird, A. Newell, and P. S. Rosenbloom. Soar: An architecture for general intelligence. *Artificial Intelligence*, 33:1-64, 1987.

[15] J. Laird, P. Rosenbloom, and A. Newell. *Universal Subgoaling and Chunking*. Kluwer Academic Publishers, Boston, MA, 1986.

[16] J.E. Laird, K.R. Swedlow, E.M. Altmann, C.B. Congdon, and M. Wiesmeyer. Soar 4.5 User's Manual. School of Computer Science, Carnegie Mellon University and Department of Electrical Engineering and Computer Science, University of Michigan, 1989. Unpublished.

[17] J.E. Laird, K.R. Swedlow, E.M. Altmann, and C.B. Congdon. Soar 5 User's Manual. School of Computer Science, Carnegie Mellon University and Department of Electrical Engineering and Computer Science, University of Michigan, 1989. Unpublished.

[18] S. Minton, J. G. Carbonell, C. A. Knoblock, D. R. Kuokka, O. Etzioni, and Y. Gil. Explanation-based learning: A problem solving perspective. *Artificial Intelligence*, 40:63-118, 1989.

[19] S. Minton, M. D. Johnston, A. B. Philips, and P. Laird. Solving large-scale constraint-satisfaction and scheduling problems using a heuristic repair method. In *Proceedings of IJCAI-90*. American Association of Artificial Intelligence, 1990 (in press).

[20] A. Newell and G. Ernst. The search for generality. In W. A. Kalenich, editor, *Proceedings of IFIP Congress 65*, pages 17-24, Spartan, Washington, DC, 1965.

[21] A. Newell. Reasoning, problem solving and decision processes: The problem space as a fundamental category. In R. Nickerson, ed., *Attention and Performance VIII*. Erlbaum, Hillsdale, NJ, 1980.

[22] A. Newell. The knowledge level. *Artificial Intelligence*, 18:87-127, 1982.

[23] N. Nilsson. *Problem Solving Methods in Artificial Intelligence*. McGraw-Hill, New York, 1971.

[24] N. Nilsson. *Principles of Artificial Intelligence*. Tioga, Palo Alto, CA, 1980.

[25] A. Newell and H. A. Simon. *Human Problem Solving*. Prentice-Hall, Englewood Cliffs, 1972.

[26] A. Newell and H. A. Simon. Computer science as empirical inquiry: Symbols and search. *Communications of the ACM*, 19(3):113-126, 1976.

[27] A. Newell, J. C. Shaw, and H. A. Simon. Empirical explorations of the logic theory machine: A case study in heuristics. In *Proceedings of the 1957 Western Joint Computer Conference*. Western Joint Computer Conference, 1957.

[28] E. Rich. *Artificial Intelligence*. McGraw-Hill, New York, 1983.

[29] P. S. Rosenbloom, J. E. Laird, and A. Newell. Knowledge-level learning in soar. In *Proceedings of AAAI-87*, Morgan Kaufman, Los Altos, CA, 1987.

[30] P. S. Rosenbloom, J. E. Laird, and A. Newell. The chunking of skill and knowledge. In B. A. G. Bouma and H. Elsendoorn, ed., *Working Models of Human Perception*, pp. 391-410. Academic Press, London, 1988.

[31] P. S. Rosenbloom, A. Newell, and J. E. Laird. Towards the knowledge level in soar: The role of the architecture in the use of knowledge. In K. VanLehn, ed., *Architectures for Intelligence*. Erlbaum, Hillsdale, NJ, 1990 (in press).

[32] H. A. Simon. Cognitive science: The newest science of the artificial. *Cognitive Science*, 4:33-46, 1980.

[33] J. Slagle. *Artificial Intelligence: The heuristic programming approach*. McGraw-Hill, New York, 1971.

[34] P. H. Winston. *Artificial Intelligence*. Addison-Wesley, Reading, MA, 1977.

[35] G.R. Yost and E.M. Altmann. Taql 3.0: Soar task acquisition system user's manual, 1989. School of Computer Science, Carnegie Mellon University, December, 1989. Unpublished.

[36] G. Yost and A. Newell. A problem space approach to expert system specification. In *Proceedings of IJCAI-89*. American Association of Artificial Intelligence, 1989.

CHAPTER 67

A Computational Account of Children's Learning about Number Conservation

T. Simon, A. Newell, and D. Klahr

1. Introduction

This chapter focuses on the conceptual domain known in developmental psychology as "conservation of quantity". Acquisition of quantity conservation constitutes a fundamental part of cognitive development, and hundreds of studies have been published in which children's "naturally acquired" conservation concepts are assessed, or in which attempts are made to teach such concepts to children. We review some of the major regularities emerging from this literature, and then we describe one particular training study in detail. Following that, we describe Q-SOAR, a computational model that simulates the acquisition of number-conservation knowledge.

The particular study that we examine is Gelman's (1982) training of three and four year old children, and we use Q-SOAR to model the learning behavior exhibited by children in this study. This model is constrained by a unified theory of cognition, which is the SOAR architecture (Lewis et al., 1990; Newell, 1990). The version of Q-SOAR to be described in this chapter accounts only for the learning that occurs in Gelman's study. However, we will suggest that chunking, SOAR's learning mechanism, which is the only learning process included in Q-SOAR, could account for the acquisition of all conservation knowledge.

Our study of conservation learning and human development can be viewed as an instance of research in concept formation. The nature of knowledge acquisition in cognitive development is consistent with the concerns of work on incremental processing. In addition, the feedback that is naturally available during development rarely has the explicit nature that is assumed in supervised learning models (Fisher & Pazzani, Chapter 1, this volume). In fact, studies of conservation training (such as Gelman's) demonstrate that more explicit forms of feedback considerably accelerate the acquisition of conservation concepts. However, even under training conditions, the type of learning that is discussed here is in line with theory-driven approaches to concept formation (Fisher & Pazzani, Chapter 6, this volume), notably the construction of *ad hoc* concepts (Barsalou, 1983) and *explanation-based* methods (Mooney, this volume). We now turn our attention to conservation learning, and then to the particular system that we have developed to model it.

2. The Phenomenon of Conservation

A central tenet of Piagetian theory (Piaget, 1952, 1970) is that the acquisition of conservation knowledge is a crucial step in the child's development of mature conceptual capabilities. Piaget (1968, p. 978) defines conservation as follows:

> We call "conservation" (and this is generally accepted) the invariance of a characteristic despite *transformations* of the object or of a collection of objects possessing this characteristic. Concerning number, a collection of objects "conserves" its number when the shape or disposition of the collection is modified, or when it is partitioned into subsets.

Children's knowledge about the effects of transformations must be empirically derived in the first instance because all transformations have different effects on different physical dimensions of the transformed material. For example, whether or not the *pouring* transformation conserves quantity depends on what is poured and what is measured:

> If we pour a little sugar into red sugar water, we do not change temperature, amount, height, width, or redness, but we increase sweetness. If we add more of an identical concentration, we do not change temperature, redness or sweetness; however the

> amount increases, as does liquid height, but not width (in a rigid container). On the other hand, if we add water, we increase two extensive quantities (amount, liquid height), reduce two intensive quantities (redness, sweetness), and leave one unchanged (temperature) (Klahr, 1982, pp. 68–69).

Therefore, a central component of what must be learned, either in training studies or "naturally acquired" by the child outside the laboratory, are the linkages between transformational attributes and their dimensional effects as measured in a wide variety of contexts.

The centrality of conservation concepts to most theories of cognitive development has produced a vast database of empirical results. Nevertheless, a computational model that can account for the regularities has yet to be fully specified. There have been both structural and processing accounts of the knowledge *used* by a child who "has" conservation, as well as global characterizations of the acquisition of that knowledge, such as Piaget's assimilation and accommodation processes, Klahr and Wallace's (1976) time-line processing, and Halford's (1982) levels of cognitive systems. However, neither these nor any other accounts have completely stated a set of operations and their interaction with a specified learning mechanism and shown this to produce the pattern of behavior observed in children acquiring conservation knowledge.

Q-Soar is a model of the acquisition of conservation knowledge designed to meet several desiderata for computational models of developmental phenomena:

1. Such models should be based on a principled cognitive architecture, rather than as a set of arbitrary and ad hoc mechanisms. For Q-Soar, the architecture is Soar, to be described in Section 5.

2. Computational models should be constrained by the general regularities in the relevant empirical literature. There are a number of such regularities, i.e., findings that are consistently reported and for which there is little or no disconfirming evidence.

   (a) Young children in the three to four year age range can consistently obtain accurate specific quantitative values for small sets of objects (up to four) (cf. Fuson, 1988).

   (b) Young children in this age range cannot consistently obtain accurate specific quantitative values for large sets of objects (more than five or six) (cf. Fuson, 1988).

(c) Children from three years of age are able to correctly produce a cardinal value for three or four items in under one second by the process of subitizing[1] (Campbell, Cooper, & Blevins-Knabe, 1988; Chi & Klahr, 1975; Svenson & Sjoberg, 1983).

(d) Subitizing has a limit of four items in these children (Campbell et al., 1988; Chi & Klahr, 1975; Svenson & Sjoberg, 1983).

(e) Children who have not fully acquired conservation knowledge can still correctly answer conservation questions when they can obtain a specific quantitative value for the objects concerned (cf. Siegler, 1981).

(f) Children who have not fully acquired conservation knowledge do not correctly answer the conservation question when they cannot obtain a specific quantitative value for objects concerned (cf. Halford & Boyle, 1985).

(g) Young children can respond correctly and provide explanations for tests of conservation of quantity when discrete materials are used (such as counters or cookies) before they can do this on tests involving materials with continuous properties, such as columns of water or areas of space (cf. Gelman & Baillargeon, 1983).

3. Computational models should generate the same behavior as do the children in the specific domain being modeled. More specifically, they should compute an approximation of subjects' final knowledge states, given an approximation of initial states and external inputs like those imposed by experimental and/or natural conditions.

Although more than 20 years have passed since Klahr and Wallace (1970) proposed an information-processing approach to cognitive development, as yet there are no computational models of any major developmental transitions that satisfy all of these criteria. The Klahr and Wallace work on the development of quantitative concepts (Klahr, 1973, 1984; Klahr & Wallace, 1973, 1976) consists of verbal descriptions, flow charts, and production-system models of distinct performance levels in the general domain of quantitative reasoning, including subitizing, counting, estimation, class inclusion, transitive reasoning, and quantity conservation. However, with respect to transition processes, their most

1. Subitizing is a fast and accurate process of determining the numerosity of small sets of entities.

fully developed model (Wallace, Klahr, & Bluff, 1987) goes only as far as a partially specified architecture for supporting developmental transitions.

More recent computational accounts of developmental phenomena have been of two kinds:

1. One type of account is highly constrained by data from empirical studies of children's acquisition of knowledge in a domain, but the computational model itself is not constrained by any theoretical principles. Instead, it is based on pragmatic decisions about how to implement a set of assumed mechanisms (e.g., Siegler, 1991).

2. The other type of account is based on a very broad set of theoretical assumptions that are consistent with a wide range of specific implementations, such as the adaptive production system used by Halford et al. (1991) to model the acquisition of transitive inference or the connectionist model used by McClelland (1991) to model the acquisition of balance scale rules. Computational models of this type, while suggesting interesting learning mechanisms, tend to be relatively unconstrained by any particular empirical results on children's knowledge acquisition.

The purpose of our approach is to formulate a model that is tightly constrained by both a general theory of the cognitive architecture and a specific set of empirical results. Q-SOAR's challenge is to demonstrate that it can model the learning reported in Gelman's (1982) training study, which we describe next. The further issue of explaining the general developmental regularities listed above is addressed in the final section of the chapter.

3. A Training Study

In constructing a simulation of training studies, we were faced with the choice of modeling either our own arbitrary view of the essential properties of a typical training situation, or one specific training situation chosen from the vast conservation training literature. The problem with the former choice is that there is no "typical" training study. Detailed examination of the literature on conservation training studies reveals that they vary along so many potentially relevant dimensions that it is nearly impossible to get agreement even on a prototypical training study, let alone a set of defining properties. For example, Field's (1987) review organizes a collection of 25 recent conservation training studies with preschoolers along nine dimensions and three theoretical orientations.[2] Without any principled basis on which to construct a typical study, we chose to simulate a specific training study with well-defined procedures and clear quantitative outcomes.

3.1 Gelman's Training Procedure

As noted, we chose a training study reported by Gelman (1982) in which three and four year olds were trained in a brief session using small collections of discrete objects ($N = 3 - 4$) in both equivalence (two rows of equal number) and inequivalence (two rows of unequal number) relations, and in which the transfer test included both small ($N = 4 - 5$) and large ($N = 8 - 10$) collections. Gelman trained one group and used two types of control groups. Children in the Experimental group were trained with two types of collections in counterbalanced order. Half the children were first shown an equivalence relation (two rows of four items each), and the other half were first shown an inequivalence relation (one row of four and one row of three). In both equivalence and inequivalence collections, the items were initially placed in one-to-one correspondence.

For each type of collection there were nine steps, as illustrated in Figure 1: (1) The display was presented in one-to-one correspondence and the child was instructed to count the number of items in one of the rows. (2) That row was covered by the experimenter and the child was asked, "How many are under my hands?" (3) The child was instructed to count the number of items in the other row. (4) That row was covered by the experimenter and the child was asked, "How many are under my hands?" (5) The child was asked to judge whether the two uncovered rows contained "the same number or a different number" of items. (6) While the child watched, the length of one of the rows was spread or compressed. (7) The experimenter pointed to the altered (or unaltered) row and asked, "Are there still N here?" (8) The experimenter pointed to the other row and asked the same question. (9) The child was asked

2. The procedural dimensions were design, pretest, training, materials, reinforcements, verbal rule instruction, post-test, justifications, and delayed post-test. The theoretical orientations were specific experience, cognitive readiness, and perceptual readiness. Space does not permit an elaboration of these "guiding models", as Field calls them, but it is clear that training studies vary widely along both procedural and theoretical dimensions.

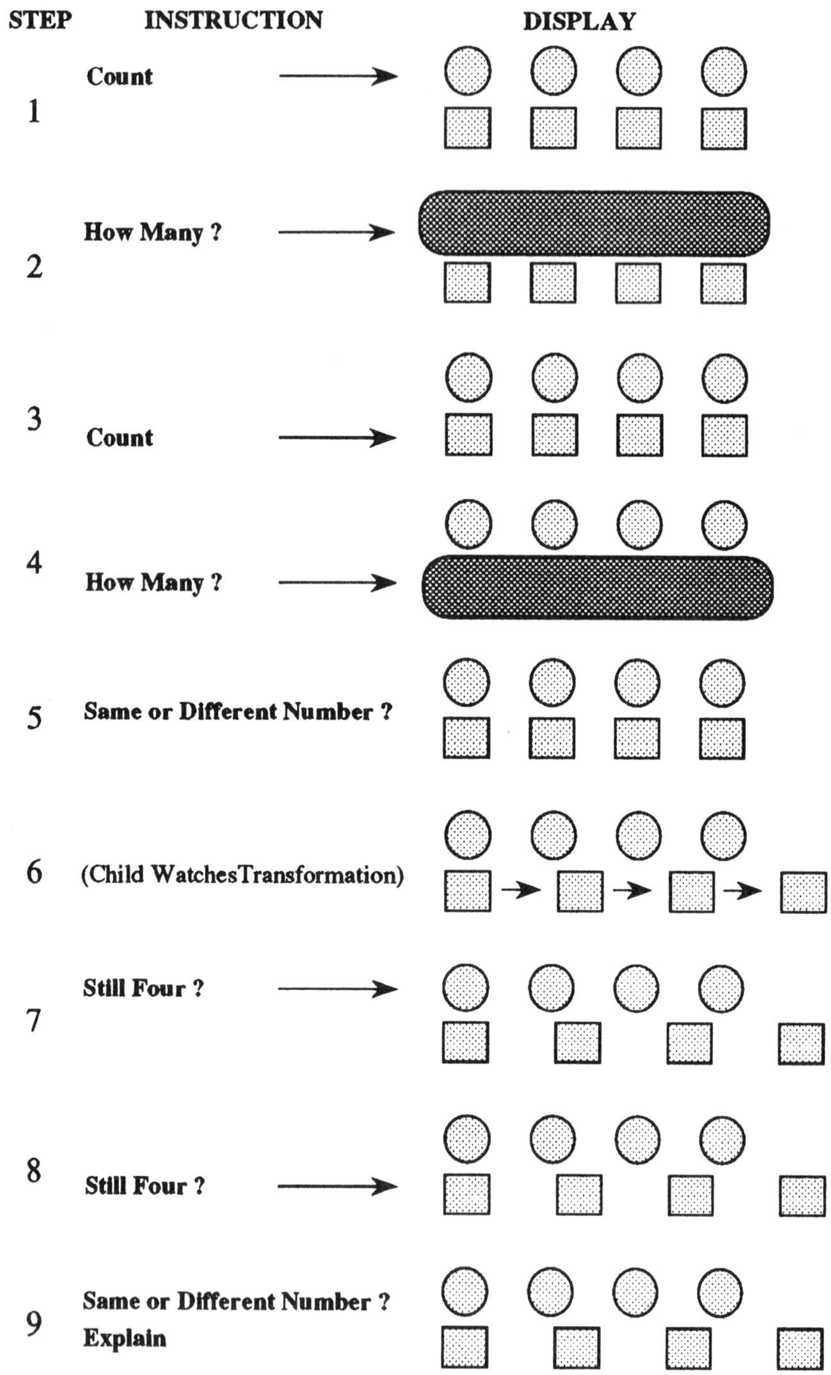

Figure 1. Graphical representation of the Experimental procedure.

whether the pair of rows had the same number or a different number of items, and to explain his/her judgment. All children answered the questions above correctly (except for one three year old who needed a slight extra prompt).

Gelman used two control groups. Children in the Cardinal-Once group were exposed to only one row (of three or four items). For that one row, they were exposed to steps 1–2 and 6–7 listed above. (Each row was altered four times to provide a comparable number of counting trials between the Experimental and control groups.) The other control group (No-Cardinal) simply counted single rows of three or four items, but the children in that group were not asked to "indicate the cardinal value rendered by the count".

3.2 Conservation Test

Immediately following the Experimental or other procedures, conservation tests were administered. Each child was given four different conservation tasks (large or small set size, and equal or unequal numbers of items in the two rows). Small sets included either four and five or five and five items, and large sets included either eight and ten or ten and ten items.

> The order of presentation of large and small set sizes was counterbalanced as was the order of conservation of equality and inequality tasks within a set-size range. The equal arrays were equal in length prior to the transformation and unequal in length after being transformed. The reverse was true for the nonequivalent arrays: before being transformed they were unequal in length and then equal in length after the transformation. The conservation trials were run in the standard way older children are tested, and *included requests for explanations*. Likewise, children were discouraged from counting. (Gelman, 1982, p. 213)

Because children were discouraged from counting, and because one or both of the rows had at least five items, and because children of this age do not count beyond three or four items very reliably (Fuson, 1988), it is likely that the equivalence (or non-equivalence) of both large and small arrays was established by one-to-one correspondence.

Table 1. Proportion of correct conservation judgments (over all four judgments and all subjects) in each condition, derived from Table 1 in Gelman (1982).

AGE & SET SIZE	EXP'L (N=32)	CARD'L-ONCE (N=24)	NO-CARD'L (N=16)
3'S ON SMALL SET SIZE	71	11	13
4'S ON SMALL SET SIZE	75	58	16
3'S ON LARGE SET SIZE	72	8	0
4'S ON LARGE SET SIZE	65	34	13
OVERALL THREES	71	9	6
OVERALL FOURS	70	46	15

3.3 Results

For both the large and small sets, there was almost no difference in the equal and unequal set sizes, so those results will be collapsed in the following discussion. Table 1 shows the overall proportion of correct judgments on conservation tasks. The effect of condition is striking: overall, the Experimental groups passed about 70% of the conservation trials, compared to passing rates from 0% to 15% for the "untrained" (No-Cardinal) groups. Trained threes and fours did equally well on large and small sets.

The interesting difference between the threes and fours occurred in the Cardinal-Once groups. For threes, Cardinal-Once training had no effect, but for fours it had a substantial effect when tested on both small and large set sizes. This is important, because the children in the Cardinal-Once group were trained only in identity conservation (transforming a single row), rather than equivalence conservation (transforming one of a pair of rows).[3] That is, they were never trained to notice that the relation between two different collections remained the same under a perceptual transformation, nor could they use one-to-one correspon-

3. See Klahr (1984) for a full discussion of the difference between identity conservation (IC) and equivalence conservation (EC). Note that Klahr's account of the acquisition of conservation rules is presented entirely in terms of the simple IC situation.

Table 2. Reference to transformation or one-to-one correspondence of Gelman's explanation categories.

	Transformation	One-to-One
Irrelevant Transformation	×	
Addition/Subtraction	×	
Initial Equality/Inequality	×	
One-to-One Correspondence		×

dence to reason about the effects of the transformations to which they were exposed. Instead, they could only learn that the initial and final cardinal value of a collection remained unchanged under certain kinds of transformations (i.e., spreading and compressing). Apparently, many four year olds, though few three year olds, were able to learn about transformations without the further help of one-to-one correspondence.

Gelman's categorization of children's explanations for their correct responses are presented in Table 2 in terms of (our interpretation of) whether the explanation makes reference to the transformation or to one-to-one correspondence. Gelman gives examples of two categories: *Irrelevant transformation* ("They just moved.") and *Addition/Subtraction* ("You need another one to make them the same.") explanations. *Initial equality/inequality of number* explanations presumably stated that the original value still held, while the content of *One-to-One Correspondence* explanations is obvious. The majority of the children's explanations referred to the transformation, and there were many more of these transformationally referenced explanations than there were explanations in terms of one-to-one correspondence. More specifically, for the Experimental threes, Experimental fours, and Cardinal-Once fours, the proportion of transformationally referenced explanations was 61%, 81%, and 65%, respectively, while for the same groups, one-to-one correspondence was used for only 21%, 9%, and 15% of the explanations.

Three year olds did not benefit from Cardinal-Once training, and four year olds in the Experimental group benefited more than did their age-mates in the Cardinal-Once group. Rather than attribute these differences to the role of one-to-one correspondence, we note that subjects in the Experimental group, but not in the Cardinal-Once group, got repeated exposure to observations of the following transitive relation. When, for example, two rows of objects have the same number, and after spreading the transformed row has the same number as before, then the untouched row and the transformed row still have the same number of objects.

Note that it is not difficult for the child to compute the effect of the transformation. First, each set was counted before and after the transformation for the Experimental trials, rendering one-to-one matching redundant. Second, in Experimental trials, the pre- and post-transformation information is visible in the form of a transformed and an untransformed row after the transformation has taken place. However, in the Cardinal-Once trials, memory of the pre-transformation information is always required to compute the transformation's effect. All of the three year olds and some of the four year olds apparently needed this additional information (and reduction of processing) that was provided to the Experimental group.

4. A Theory of Number Conservation Knowledge

We can summarize our view of the important difference between the Experimental group and the Cardinal-Once group as follows. Subjects in the Experimental group were exposed to equivalence (or inequivalence) conservation trials in which they observed and encoded an initial quantitative relation between two collections, and then observed a quantity-preserving transformation on one of the collections. They then requantified both collections and noted that the relation had not changed. In contrast, subjects in the Cardinal-Once group, because they were dealing with only one collection, rather than two, were in an identity conservation situation. That is, they had to judge, after observing a spreading or compressing transformation, whether the quantity following the transformation was the same as the quantity preceding it; they could not simply requantify and compare the two rows.

In both situations, acquired knowledge stemmed primarily from the discovery that certain types of transformations have no effect on the numerosity of an object set, even though the transformations may affect other properties, like the spatial density or length of the set. This conclusion is independent of the number of objects in the set that was measured when the new knowledge was created. In other words, what was learned was a characterization of the quantity-preserving aspects of the transformation in question.

Q-SOAR was built to model this piece of knowledge acquisition. In order to do this, the system must be able to specify:

1. The knowledge state prior to the training (i.e., a non-conserving child);
2. The encoding of the collection(s) prior to transformation. This will include salient features such as number, length, and density, as well as other features that may ultimately be irrelevant for the task at hand;
3. The encoding of the relation between collections (for the Experimental group);
4. The encoding of the collection(s) following transformation;
5. The encoding of the physical aspects of the transformation (e.g., salient motion, how objects were moved, how many were moved, direction of movement); and
6. New knowledge acquired from repeated trials of the kind presented to both the Experimental group and the Cardinal-Once group.

The model will have two variants, and each variant will be exposed to the three kinds of stimulus presentations (corresponding to the Experimental, Cardinal-Once, and No-Cardinal groups): Q-SOAR-4 will model the four year olds, who learn from both the Experimental manipulations and the Cardinal-Once manipulations. Q-SOAR-3 will model the three year olds, who learn only from the Experimental condition.

This set of general hypotheses about the essential mechanisms involved in the child's acquisition of number conservation can be called Q Theory, to distinguish it from Q-SOAR, which conjoins Q Theory with the assumptions of a particular cognitive architecture (SOAR) to form a more complete operational theory. A full theory of conservation will ultimately contain assumptions about the nature of the environments in which development takes place. Indeed, it is the lack of justifiable assumptions that can be made about naturally occurring conservation experiences that forces us to focus entirely on training studies.

5. The SOAR Architecture

This section describes the relevant aspects of the SOAR architecture. More detailed accounts of it exist elsewhere (Laird, Newell, & Rosenbloom, 1987; Laird, Swedlow, Altmann, & Congdon, 1989; Newell, 1990). Besides being an operational architecture, SOAR is also a theory of cognition that has been shown to explain a wide variety of psychological phenomena. No attempt can be made to describe that wider background here (cf. Lewis et al., 1990; Newell, 1990).

All tasks are formulated in SOAR as search in *problem spaces*, where operators are applied to states in an attempt to attain a goal state. Problem spaces can be thought of as packages of knowledge about different tasks. The operators within a given space (and knowledge about constraints on legal states) define the problem solver's competence for a task. For example, a complete problem space for the Missionaries and Cannibals puzzle contains the necessary operators to carry out moves, knowledge about the goal state, and knowledge about legal and illegal moves. Problem solving proceeds sequentially by decisions that select *problem spaces*, *states*, and *operators*. This processing gathers knowledge from a long-term recognition memory that is implemented as a production system. This memory matches structures in working memory and retrieves knowledge that elaborates the existing state and suggests preferences for the next step to take.

If SOAR cannot make a decision, an impasse occurs. In this case, SOAR automatically generates a subgoal in which a new problem space can be used to find the required knowledge. A major reason that SOAR exhibits the impasse and subgoal pattern is that not all of the knowledge required to carry out a task can be searched for within a single problem space. For example, should the goal arise in the Missionaries and Cannibals context to explain why the boat does not sink, there will be no knowledge in the problem space to implement that process. In response, an impasse will arise and in the resulting subgoal, SOAR will select a problem space for solving such an explanatory problem, since this is a different task requiring different knowledge. Once that knowledge is found, subgoals are resolved and processing continues where it left off (Newell, 1990).

SOAR has a single learning mechanism, called *chunking*, that learns new productions, or *chunks*, for resolved impasses. When similar situations are encountered, the knowledge generated by the previous subgoal processing is retrieved automatically so that the impasse is not recreated. The chunk will apply in a wider set of circumstances than the exact conditions under which it was created. This is because the chunking mechanism carries out an analysis that is a form of explanation-based learning (Mitchell, Keller, & Kedar-Cabelli, 1986; DeJong & Mooney, 1986; Rosenbloom & Laird, 1986; Mooney, this volume) to determine the critical features of the situation that led to the creation of the new knowledge. In future situations these act as cues to make the new knowledge available. The behavioral implication of chunking is that SOAR exhibits a shift from deliberate to automatic processing as the situations that it encounters become increasingly familiar. In other words, knowledge becomes compiled from search-based retrieval to recognition-based retrieval (Anderson, 1987; Rosenbloom & Newell, 1986).

6. The Acquisition of Number Conservation Knowledge

The knowledge and processes that enable Q-SOAR to acquire number conservation knowledge are implemented as a set of problem spaces that are depicted in Figure 2. The figure shows the problem spaces that are selected to carry out processing in response to given deficiencies in available knowledge; these deficiencies are stated as labels on the downward-pointing sides of the arrows. Once sufficient knowledge is returned (as depicted by the upward-pointing side of the arrows), the original processing can continue. The new knowledge becomes immediately accessible on later occasions in the form of chunks. The top panel depicts the knowledge required to interpret task instructions and to establish initial values before a transformation is applied. The lower panel depicts the knowledge involved in determining the quantitative effects of transformations.

The figure also distinguishes between task-motivated problem spaces (unshaded) and theory-motivated problem spaces (shaded). The unshaded spaces contain those operations that any task analysis of the training studies would deem to be necessary for its successful completion. These processes include the ability to understand instructions, create responses, and determine relative or absolute values for the objects used in training and testing. The shaded problem spaces contain operations that we, as theorists, assert are necessary to enable the cognitive architecture, SOAR, to achieve the behavior and learning that constitute the attainment of number conservation as shown by children in the three to four year old age range.

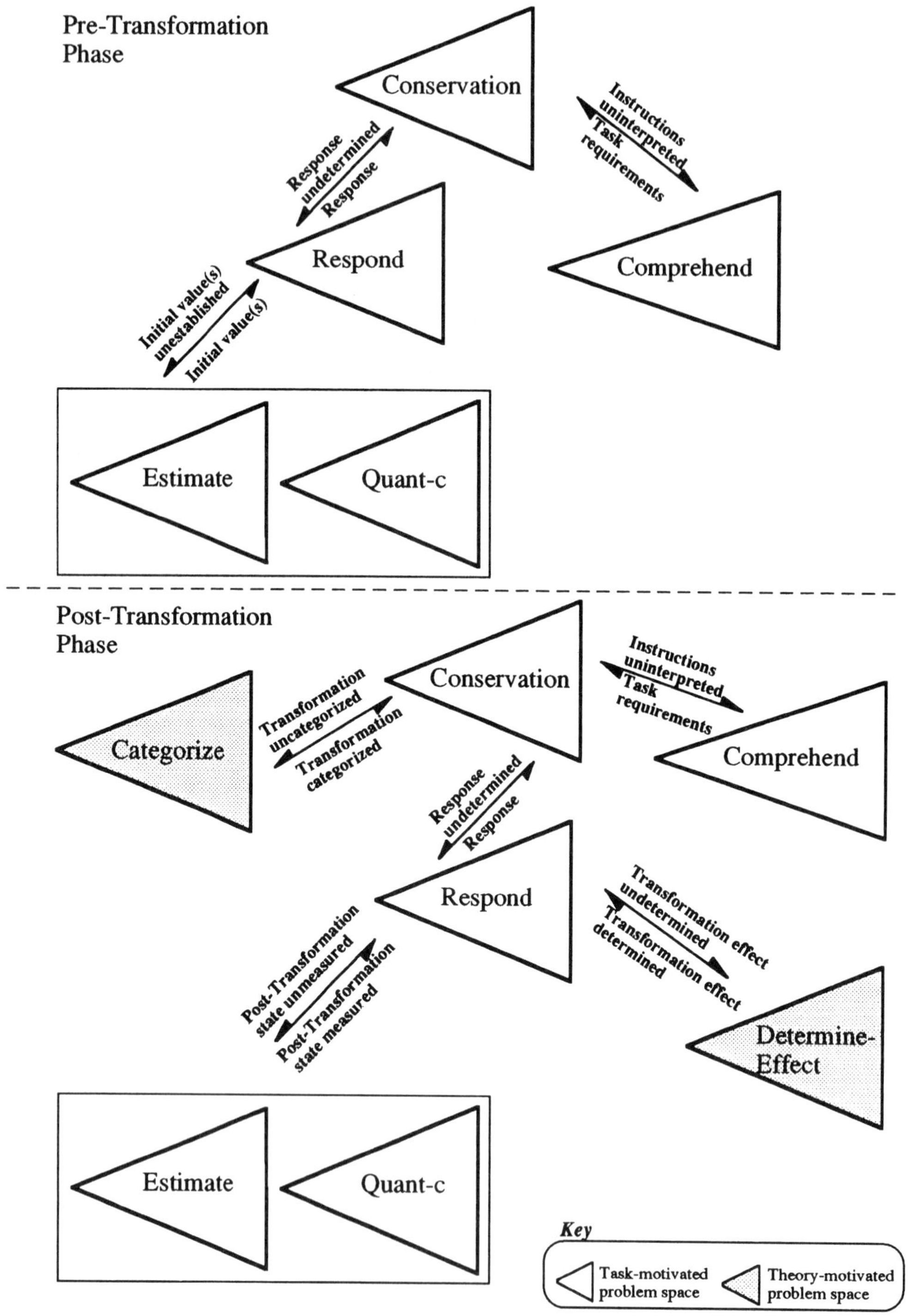

Figure 2. Problem spaces for the Q-SOAR model of conservation behavior.

Q-SOAR's design presumes that young children acquire number conservation knowledge by measurement and comparison of values to determine the effects of transformations on small collections of discrete objects. Having been shown a transformation to a set of objects, the child first categorizes the transformation and then initiates a conservation judgment about the transformation's effect. Ideally, categorization will identify the observed transformation as an instance of a larger class, with effects that are known to be associated (through chunking) with this class. If not, then pre- and post-transformation values created by measurement processes are compared to determine the effect of the transformation. The learning over this processing creates new knowledge about this kind of transformation, which will become available on future occurrences in similar contexts.[4] Now the transformation's effects can be stated without the need for any empirical processing. In other words, the necessity of the effects is recognized.

6.1 Theoretical Assumptions

The behavior exhibited by Q-SOAR is determined, in part, by five assumptions that we make about the knowledge and strategies used by three and four year old children in the context of conservation experiments. The five assumptions are:

1. *The numerical value of a row of objects will not change if the row is not transformed.* Gelman (1977) has shown in her "magic studies" that children as young as two years of age operate with the assumption that the numerical value of a set of objects will remain constant in the absence of any observable manipulation of the set.

2. *The numerical value of a row of objects is very likely to change if the row is visibly transformed by an experimenter.* Many experiments, notably those of Donaldson (1978), have shown that the act of an experimenter making explicit physical changes to a set of objects suggests to young children that some significant change will result from the action.

3. *Four year olds have the knowledge that they can verify whether assumption 2 is true or false where measurement is possible.* By mea-

4. The notion of similarity involved is the occurrence in the new situation of the same essential features used in the prior situation. There is no similarity metric involved.

suring the numerical value of the objects before and after the transformation, a determination can be made as to whether the action changed the number of the objects.

4. *Three year olds do not have the knowledge that a transformation's effects can be verified but they may be motivated to measure a transformation's effects if faced with two conflicting sources of evidence.* If one source of information suggests that the value of the objects has changed while another suggests that it has not, three year olds will attempt to determine the true effect of the transformation where measurement is possible.

5. *Three and four year olds have the capacity to store and recall pre- and post-transformation values but only four year olds do so systematically.* Four year olds have the knowledge that it is important to do this in order to determine the effect of a transformation. There is a sizable literature on young children's strategic use of their mnemonic capacity which indicates that, even if three year olds have the same capacity for remembering as older children and adults, they have little knowledge about how to exploit that capacity and thus their untutored memory performance is poor (Brown, Bransford, Ferrara, & Campione, 1983).

Q-SOAR's behavior in simulating the training study is described below in sections that correspond to the problem spaces involved. References will be made to the example procedure in Figure 1 so that the reader can keep track of both the current subproblem that Q-SOAR is attempting to solve and the arrangement of the objects concerned. The description will be presented using the Experimental procedure since it is a superset of the other two control conditions. The actual behavior that Q-SOAR produces during this procedure, and its subsequent behavior on one of the test conditions, is presented in the appendix to this chapter. (Recall that the Cardinal-Once group only experienced steps 1–2 and 6–7 and the No-Cardinal group experienced only step 1.)

6.2 Conservation Task Operations

To carry out a conservation task, five basic processes are required. These correspond to SOAR operators in the CONSERVATION problem space: COMPREHEND-INSTRUCTION, CATEGORIZE-TRANSFORMATION, DETERMINE-RESPONSE, RETURN-RESPONSE, and WAIT.

All operators process internal representations in working memory. These representations correspond to aspects of the external situation to which the model is attending. There is a focus of attention, which is determined partly by external sources, such as the experimenter asking questions or drawing attention to the experimental materials. It can also be determined by internal processing, such as attention to individual items during counting. The internal representations are in the form of *annotated models* (Lewis, Newell, & Polk, 1989), which are descriptions of attended aspects of the external situation expressed symbolically as objects with parts, properties, and relations to other objects. These models are manipulated by operators and augmented with knowledge from memory and from the external situation via perception.

Each step in the Experimental (and other) procedures is carried out in response to an instruction or request from the experimenter; we shall refer to these as *instructions*. When an instruction is perceived, its meaning must be represented as an annotated model. This model is constructed by a COMPREHEND-INSTRUCTION operator in the manner of an existing system, called NL-SOAR, which is implemented in the COMPREHEND problem space; Lewis, Newell, and Polk (1989) give a description of this process. COMPREHEND-INSTRUCTION operators produce a representation of a request called a *behavior-model object*. In step 1 of Figure 1, for example, the child is requested to count the row of circles. In this case, the COMPREHEND-INSTRUCTION operator would produce a behavior-model object representing the operation "measure", the argument "circles", and the dimension "number". Thus a behavior-model object is a child's representation to himself/herself of what behavior should be carried out to achieve the task. In general, the child is perfectly capable of behaving without such a plan, but in the case of an experiment, he/she must represent (and remember) the instruction to be carried out. These representations also play a role in mediating the speed of acquisition of conservation knowledge.

Once the instruction has been comprehended and represented, Q-SOAR must still produce a response. To do so, it selects the DETERMINE-RESPONSE operator. Q-SOAR implements steps 1 and 2 (and then steps 3 and 4) in Figure 1 with a single DETERMINE-RESPONSE operator, which is augmented with the instructions represented on the behavior-model object. If the response is not immediately available, then there will be an impasse and other problem spaces will be selected to compute the response. When the system has created a response that satisfies the instructions (such as the value "four" for steps 1 and 2), it selects the RETURN-RESPONSE operator to output the answer and then waits for the next instruction by selecting the WAIT operator.

Q-SOAR's first response to observing a transformation (step 6) is to categorize it. This is done before responding to post-transformation questions by selecting the CATEGORIZE-TRANSFORMATION operator. The categorization process is described in Section 6.6.

6.3 Response Determination

If the DETERMINE-RESPONSE operator in the CONSERVATION space cannot immediately produce a response to the counting instructions of steps 1 and 2, there will be an impasse. The RESPOND space will always be selected when the DETERMINE-RESPONSE operator impasses, since it contains the three operators that are required to create responses in the conservation task: MEASURE, COMPARE, and RECALL. In the case where steps 1 and 2 have been comprehended as requiring a measurement, the MEASUREMENT operator is selected. Depending on the number of objects and their representation (see Section 6.5.1), either the QUANT-C or ESTIMATE space is selected to carry out this measurement. That measurement is returned as the result of the MEASURE operator and, in turn, it is also returned as the result of the top-level DETERMINE-RESPONSE operator.

Once Q-SOAR has created and returned a measurement for the circles and squares, it perceives and comprehends the question "same or different number?" in step 5. The resulting DETERMINE-RESPONSE operator will be augmented with the instruction "compare", the arguments "circles" and "squares", and the dimension "number". Since this is the first time the instruction has been encountered, there will be no immediately available response and, in the resulting subgoal, the COMPARE operator will be selected in the RESPOND space. This operator tests whether the values for the measurements of the two rows match, since only a "same" or "different" response is required. In the current example, that processing will be carried out in the QUANT-C space if a value for that comparison is not immediately available.

Once the comparison has been created and returned, and the transformation has been observed and categorized (step 6 and lower panel of Figure 2), the experimenter asks, "Are there still *N* objects?" for each row (where N is the number of objects in the row). These instructions are treated in a similar way to steps 2 and 4, by selecting a DETERMINE-RESPONSE operator. However, the operator is now augmented with the operation "recall". If no answer to the question is immediately available, that operator will impasse and the RECALL operator will be selected in the RESPOND space. The implementation of this operator differs when it is applied to rows that have been transformed. The alternatives depend on the model variant (Q-SOAR-3 or Q-SOAR-4) and training condition (Experimental or Cardinal-Once), as discussed in Section 6.4. Responses to the "Are there still N?" question with respect to an untransformed row (e.g., step 7 in Figure 1) are dealt with in the following way. Recall that assumption 1 (in Section 6.1) stated that the numerical value of a row of objects will not change if the row is not transformed. This means that the value for the row in question is assumed to be the same before and after the transformation of the other row. Q-SOAR-4 is able to recall the pre-transformation value and return it as the answer to this question. This is not the case for Q-SOAR-3 (see assumption 5 in Section 6.1). However, even without retrieving the correct value with the RECALL operator, Q-SOAR-3 can answer the question correctly by requantifying the objects in question. This can be done by subitizing since no row has more than four objects.

6.4 Effect Determination

The way that Q-SOAR responds to the "Are there still N?" question for transformed rows is not only to produce a post-transformation value but also to determine the effect of the transformation. The DETERMINE-EFFECT problem space is selected if the RECALL operator impasses, because no effect of the transformation is immediately available. In order to learn about the effect of the transformation, the system must compare the pre- and post-transformation values for the row. Also, some role must be attributed to the transformation for the value of that comparative judgment. This can be as simple as identifying it as the action that created the post-transformation array. In other words, this process creates the knowledge to answer the implicit question, "What change did the transformation make to the number of objects?" This new knowledge states that, whenever such a transformation is applied, the relation between the pre- and post-transformation values that have just been computed will hold for the dimension in question. For example, the response to step 9 in Figure 1 is that a spreading transformation causes no change because it produces an identical value to the one that existed before it was applied, namely "four squares" in both cases.

6.4.1 Effect Determination in Q-Soar-4

Q-Soar-4 determines the effect of transformations in the same way for both the Experimental and Cardinal-Once conditions. Although assumption 2 in Section 6.1 stated that children believe that the value of a row will change when it is transformed, assumption 3 stated that four year olds have the knowledge that this can be verified when it is possible to measure the materials before and after a transformation is applied. This is the case in both of these conditions because of the small number of discrete objects. Thus, in all cases, Q-Soar-4 makes a pre- and post-transformation value comparison to determine the effects of observed transformations.

6.4.2 Effect Determination in Q-Soar-3

Q-Soar-3 behaves differently in the Experimental and Cardinal-Once conditions. In the Experimental condition its behavior is like that of Q-Soar-4, due to assumption 4. This assumption stated that three year olds do not possess knowledge about verifying a transformation's effect but may be induced to do so if they are faced with two conflicting sources of evidence. This is always the case with the Experimental condition. Before transformations, the two rows are in one-to-one correspondence so equal trials have equal-length rows and unequal trials have unequal-length rows. In other words, perceptual information and quantitative information are not in conflict. However, "transformations on unequal trials yielded rows of the same length; equal trials involved rows of different lengths" (Gelman, 1982, p. 212). In other words, after transformation, quantitative information, which was available via subitizing, and perceptual information were in conflict: unequal rows were the same length and equal rows were different lengths. This conflict leads Q-Soar-3 to recall the pre-transformation value it measured and check it against the post-transformation value of the row.

In the Cardinal-Once condition, no such conflict exists. There is a single row of objects which, when transformed, takes on a new visual appearance. There is nothing in the visual array to suggest that the assumed change in its numerical value should be doubted. Thus Q-Soar-3 makes no attempt to compare pre- and post-transformation values of rows. As with the untransformed row, it answers the question "Are there still N?" by requantifying. Since no comparison is made to the original value, no learning can take place as to whether the transformation has had any effect on the numerical value of the row.

6.4.3 Effect Determination Operations

There are two operators in the Determine-Effect space. The Recall operator recalls a pre-transformation value for comparison to the post-transformation value. The Determine-Effect operator matches pre- and post-transformation values for the transformed row as described above. The process is a simple match that tests whether the values are the same or not. A requested determination of the magnitude or direction of the change will require accessing quantification knowledge. The result of this match is returned by the Determine-Effect operator as the effect of the transformation, and the basis of its determination (e.g., that pre- and post-transformation values matched) constitutes an explanation. This will be the result of the Recall operator in the Respond space and, ultimately, the Determine-Response operator in the Conservation space. The chunks that are built when this new knowledge is returned enable immediate retrieval of the effect of the current transformation. These chunks will fire in response to selection of the Determine-Response operator, letting Q-Soar immediately return the effect and explanation of the transformation. This demonstrates the shift in conservation performance from empirical examination of materials to direct explanation of the transformation's effects.

6.5 Quantification and Estimation

In the preceding sections we showed how the acquisition of number conservation knowledge in Q-Soar is founded on empirical processing, whose results are then used by the effect determination process. In this section we examine the quantification and estimation abilities available to Q-Soar that implement the measurement and comparison processes.

6.5.1 QUANTIFICATION

The primary measurement capability that is possessed by young children is quantification. This quantification subsystem, which we call *Quant-C*, for "quantification in conservation", includes only capabilities that produce cardinal values for small sets of entities. Thus it includes subitizing and counting of small sets.

In cases where values are to be determined in terms of number, the QUANT-C problem space may be selected to implement the measurement. Selection of the space depends on two factors. The first is whether the conservation property represented on the MEASURE operator suggests the use of Quant-C processes (e.g., in the case of discrete objects but not liquid). The second is the suitability of the representation for the application of operators in the QUANT-C problem space.

Even in cases where the conservation property suggests Quant-C processes for determining equivalence, the problem solver may still be unable to use it. In order to select the QUANT-C space, the representation of objects to be measured must be in the form of symbols representing discrete objects that are in one-*onto*-one mapping (hereafter *onto*) with their external referents. We assume such representations are only possible for set sizes within the range that young children can subitize: a limit of four objects. Above this limit, a much looser one-*into*-one mapping (hereafter *into*) is used.

The process of subitizing in the QUANT-C space is not controlled by an operator: it is simply that of creating an *onto* representation of up to four external referents. This approach is based on the view that there is a special code for the representation of discrete quantities which is primitive to the architecture and which differs from the formal code used to communicate about numbers with words such as "three" or symbols like "3". We call this primitive representation the *basic quantitative code* (Simon & Newell, 1990) and assume that it provides the agent with an ability to represent quantity in a primitive form.

There are six operators in the QUANT-C space: ATTEND, INITIALIZE, FETCH-NEXT, COUNT-NEXT, COMPARE, and MEMORIZE. The ATTEND operator attends to the objects specified in the behavior-model object and sets up an *onto* representation. All of the other operators are involved only if counting and not subitizing is to be carried out. The INITIALIZE operator selects a mark for identifying objects to be counted, selects an initial word from the counting string to be used, and selects an initial object to be processed. The Count-Next operator assigns a selected count word to a marked object and, where cardinal responses (Fuson, 1988) are to be returned, assigns that label to the cardinality of the set. Fetch-Next obtains a next item to be counted, marks it, and obtains a next count word to be assigned. The Compare operator can be used to test either the relative similarity or difference of values created by Measure operators. The Memorize operator carries out a deliberate act of memorization on the final response to a pre-transformation and post-transformation instruction, so that the results are stored in long-term memory and are available for the processes that determine the effect of the transformation.

None of these operations can be directly applied to *into* representations. However, one can count large collections of objects if perceptual and motor operations can be carried out to serially map individual items onto their external referents, thereby creating transitory *onto* representations for up to four items at a time. If this cannot be done or if a decision is made against doing so, the only recourse is to use estimation operations.

6.5.2 Perceptual Estimation

Perceptual estimation in the children modeled by Q-Soar is unidimensional — the relative number of two numerous rows of objects is determined either by length or by density, but not both. Siegler (1981) showed that a child's ability to integrate more than one dimension to solve a range of problems does not develop until around eight years of age. Thus, estimation in conservation settings is inaccurate, since one dimension is often inadequate for an accurate quantitative judgment.

The Estimation problem space is selected to obtain values for materials under a number of conditions. As discussed in Section 6.5.1, Q-Soar may be requested to create a relative quantity judgment where there are too many objects to create an *onto* representation. In this case the model uses perceptual estimation, in which the primary cue as to quantity is the length of the rows. A Match operator carries out a type of one-to-one matching called *end matching* (Klahr & Wallace, 1976), which tests whether the end items of each row are above or below the end items of the other row. If this is not the case, the longer row is assumed to be more numerous. A Memorize operator stores the result of this processing, just as in the Quant-C space.

6.6 Categorization

As mentioned earlier, Q-SOAR categorizes observed transformations.[5] This means that it identifies critical features that are common to individual transformations, such as that all spreading actions move things further apart irrespective of the objects in question. Chunks created from processing in the DETERMINE-EFFECT problem space associate the new effect with the category of the transformation, not to the specific instance. As a result, invariance effects will be cued by any new transformation that can be identified as a member of that category. This enables novel situations to cue knowledge acquired about other members of the same category. Thus we assume that all novices, especially young children, form concepts to facilitate plausible generalizations about novel instances. Chunking models this desirable behavior, as do some other methods of explanation-based learning. As noted by Mooney (this volume), categorization need not be limited to a single dimension, but it should be sensitive to current goals. For example, when confronted with studies of number conservation like Gelman's, Q-SOAR may "CATEGORIZE" spreading, compressing, piling, and distributing together since they have no numeric effect. In contrast, if the concern is with spatial density, then compressing and piling would constitute a category with the opposite effect of spreading and distributing. The imposition of conceptual cohesiveness by goals or effects is related to *ad hoc* categorization introduced by Barsalou (1983) and discussed by Fisher and Pazzani (Chapter 6, this volume).

Q-SOAR selects the CATEGORIZE problem space when there is a transformation represented on the state and the CATEGORIZE-TRANSFORMATION operator in the CONSERVATION space cannot retrieve a type for it. The categorization process identifies in the representation of the transformation a set of features that are predictive of a certain classification. It is implemented as a recognition task. If a new instance is not immediately recognized as a member of a known class, features are progressively abstracted out of the instance description until the instance is recognized as a known class member. If no class is retrieved, then a new one is formed using the set of features in the new instance. For example, when all the features common to all spreading transfor-

5. The current version of Q-SOAR does not fully implement this process. Instead, the structures that would be created by an existing system called AL-SOAR (Miller & Laird, 1990) are fed into working memory.

mations are present, and none that are indicative of some other type of action (like compressing) are represented, the transformation will be treated the same way that other spreading transformations would be in the current context. This strategy is straightforward and sufficient to model Gelman's study, though a more general theory of conservation development will likely require more flexible principles of feature-discriminating power, like those found in Chapters 1 through 5 of this volume.

6.7 Learning Conservation Knowledge in Q-SOAR

The above subsections presented the problem spaces and operators that comprise Q-SOAR. How then do these components combine to create the number conservation knowledge that is the result of the effective training procedures? The answer is that they are called upon to contribute knowledge as Q-SOAR experiences impasses during problem solving. These impasses arise dynamically from the particular task that Q-SOAR is working on and the knowledge it brings to bear on each task at a given time. Thus, the conservation knowledge that the system has depends of what problems it has tried to solve and what knowledge it had available when it tried to solve them.

For example, if the knowledge required to respond to the question about the relative quantity of the two rows of objects in the initial array is not available, an impasse will arise. Q-SOAR will have already quantified the two values, but no comparative value will exist. The resulting series of impasses ground out in the selection of the COMPARE operator in the QUANT-C space. The successful creation of that comparative value resolves the impasse and creates a new piece of information that is available for later instances of the same problem. This kind of processing is repeated for every impasse that the system encounters. Some of these chunks simply reduce the amount of search that Q-SOAR engages in on subsequent trials (such as chunks that implement the instruction comprehension operators). Other chunks, such as those that arise from compare operators in the QUANT-C space, not only reduce search but also directly contribute to the ultimate conservation judgments that the system makes.

The result of one such impasse is the chunk (hereafter the *conservation* chunk) marked in the appendix that produces the conservation response. Due to the explanation-based nature of chunking, some generalization will occur with respect to the applicability of the chunk. Specifically, only features that existed before the impasse arose can become conditions for chunks. This is to ensure that an impasse for the same problem will not recur. However, not all of the pre-existing features will become conditions; only those that are used to compute the result in the subgoal will be selected. This means that the chunked result will be retrieved in a wider set of circumstances than the one in which it was formed. However, it does not mean that Q-SOAR exhibits conserving responses after one trial. When simulating human cognition, SOAR builds chunks only for the results created from the lowest goal in a subgoal stack. This *bottom-up* chunking causes the architecture to exhibit a gradual progression from deliberate (search-based) to automatic (recognition-based) behavior.

In the case of Q-SOAR, the conservation chunk at first only implements the response to the DETERMINE-EFFECT operator because that was the operator that led to the final impasse from which the chunk was created. Only after a series of trials is there a single subgoal caused by the top-level DETERMINE-RESPONSE operator. Then the information in the original chunk becomes available to implement that operator and thus enable a recognitional response to the effect of an observed transformation, as in the case of a conserving child.

By acquiring conservation knowledge in this way, Q-SOAR does not create any single knowledge structure that represents a "conservation concept". Instead, it builds a series of chunks that, when appropriately cued, enable the system to exhibit number conservation. In other words, rather than learning concepts that define the features of conserving transformations, Q-SOAR acquires generalized knowledge about the effects of observed transformations that is cued by other, similar transformations in similar contexts. As already described, these pieces of knowledge are acquired incrementally as problems are solved by the system with different amounts of available knowledge. In this particular modeling study, Q-SOAR was led to acquire its conservation knowledge by the use of a training regime. However, this was not a supervised concept-learning situation in which pre-classified examples of concepts are presented for the system to learn. Indeed, Q-SOAR is never presented with the concept of conservation; it is merely asked to solve a series of problems that were experimentally demonstrated to result in the acquisition of conservation knowledge. These kinds of problems can be encountered and solved without supervision and, as can be seen in the next section, we claim that Q-SOAR should be capable of learning conservation knowledge without training but at a slower speed than demonstrated here.

7. Toward a Full Theory Of Conservation

Q-SOAR successfully models the acquisition of conservation knowledge attained by subjects in Gelman's training study in an implementation within SOAR's unified cognitive theory. In this final section, we describe the behavior of Q-SOAR before and after training. We also describe what we anticipate as the necessary steps toward a full theory of conservation in other domains.

Ultimately, one can evaluate an enterprise such as the one presented here in terms of Piaget's (1964) well-known criteria for "real" conservation:

> But when I am faced with these facts [that *learning* of structures seems to obey the same laws as the *natural development* of these structures], I always have three questions which I want to have answered before I am convinced.
>
> The first question is, "Is this learning lasting? What remains two weeks or a month later?" If a structure develops spontaneously, once it has reached a state of equilibrium, it is lasting, it will continue throughout the child's entire life. When you achieve the learning by external reinforcement, is the result lasting or not and what are the conditions for it to be lasting?
>
> The second question is, "How much generalization is possible?" ... When you have brought about some learning, you can always ask whether this is an isolated piece in the midst of the child's mental life, or if it is really a dynamic structure which can lead to generalizations.
>
> Then there is the third question, "In the case of each learning experience what was the operational level of the subject before the experience and what more complex structures has this learning succeeded in achieving?"

To these three questions, we add a fourth: How can subjects (and Q-SOAR) learn so rapidly from a brief training study, when untrained subjects take several years to acquire the same knowledge?

7.1 Durability and Robustness of Learning

With respect to Piaget's first question, Q-SOAR makes a specific theoretical claim: a chunk, once learned, is always available, and will be evoked whenever the context-specific information that was included in the original chunk is recognized and encoded. For the SOAR architecture, chunking is an automatic acquisition mechanism that is applied to all processing that takes place. Thus, by undertaking the processing that is induced by the externally driven training procedure, the learning of conservation knowledge will occur.

The empirical prediction associated with this claim is not straightforward. The general pattern of results with increasingly remote post-tests is that, for a while, performance declines as a function of intervening time between training and testing, but then performance improves as one would expect with the "natural" acquisition of conservation. At present we have no principled explanation of this in terms of chunking.

7.2 Generalization

The second question refers to the specificity of learning from experience. This is a well-established empirical fact and is predicted by the chunking mechanism (Laird, Rosenbloom, & Newell, 1986). In the context of Q-SOAR, chunking predicts little generalization from learning about certain transformations of discrete objects to other transformations of different materials (e.g., the pouring of water). Indeed, this is what one usually finds from conservation training studies: very little generalization to other kinds of quantity conservation.

Transfer from small to large number tasks is achieved by the generalization inherent in SOAR's chunking mechanism. The actual objects that are measured in determining a conservation judgment are not tested when it is retrieved from memory. There are tests for the kind of transformation and the conservation property (in this case, number) and these delimit the scope of transfer. If that were not so, Q-SOAR would predict unrealistically fast learning: to transformations of quantities that are not affected in the same way as the one measured.

In addition, transfer is also limited with respect to continuous quantities such as volumes of liquid. Acquiring knowledge about continuous quantity is not addressed by Q-SOAR. Nevertheless, having acquired conservation knowledge based on small number measurement, a problem solver must come to appreciate what is common to transformations like lengthening and the pouring of liquids. This requires that these transformations be represented as actions that neither add nor remove any of the materials that they manipulate.

Finally, we suggest that the problem solving that enables the identification of the common features of different transformations and materials can best be described as a discovery process. The learner operates with a set of expectations based on current knowledge. This will at some point create a violation of the expected effects of a transformation. The learner's task then is to generate an hypothesis of what caused that violation, to devise ways of testing that hypothesis, and to integrate the results either into new hypotheses or modified knowledge. Research on scientific reasoning (Klahr & Dunbar, 1988), instructionless learning (Shrager, 1987), and analogy (Gentner, 1983) provides good explanations of the nature of such processes. Mediating factors in the effectiveness of that problem solving are the selection and combination of features that are considered for inclusion in the analysis (Bransford, Stein, Shelton, & Owings, 1981).

7.3 Operational Level and Structural Change

With respect to Piaget's third question, Q-SOAR makes explicit statements about the "complex structures" arising from the training of conservation responses. These can be seen by examinations of Q-SOAR-3 and Q-SOAR-4 before and after training.

7.3.1 Q-SOAR-3 AND Q-SOAR-4 BEFORE TRAINING

Before experiencing the three conditions of Gelman's training study, both versions of Q-SOAR are able to execute all the steps of the three experimental conditions. The only difference between the two versions is that Q-SOAR-3 does not start out with the knowledge that the effects of transformations can be verified by comparing pre- and post-transformation values. Apart from this difference, both versions have all the capabilities described in Section 6.

However, since neither variant has undergone any training and has not learned about the effects of any transformations, both versions of Q-SOAR fail all of the conservation tests that Gelman used. Neither system can accurately measure the large number of objects in the tests to yield the correct comparative answers. They must use estimation, a process that results in the assertion that a longer row contains more objects than a shorter row. Finally, both untrained variants of Q-SOAR-3 and Q-SOAR-4 are unable to determine the effects of the transformations and so cannot state an explanation. Before training, then, both are true non-conservers. We will now examine their behavior after training. Since the No-Cardinal condition is not expected to induce any change in behavior, we will discuss only the results of the other two conditions.

7.3.2 Q-SOAR-3 AFTER CARDINAL-ONCE TRIALS

Without employing its memorization capability to recall and compare pre- and post-transformation values, Q-SOAR-3 cannot learn anything about the numerical effect of observed transformations. Thus, based on assumption 2 in Section 6.1, it always assumes that the value of the row changes. Since this is never the case in the experiment, Q-SOAR-3 is always wrong and it fails the conservation tests. As can be seen in Table 1, three year olds produced few correct responses.

7.3.3 Q-SOAR-3 AFTER EXPERIMENTAL TRIALS

As explained in Section 6.4, the conflicting information in Experimental trials after a transformation induces Q-SOAR-3 to recall and compare values in the same way as Q-SOAR-4. Thus, Q-SOAR-3 can construct a correct comparison and explanation from such trials. These can then be recalled later, enabling it to pass the conservation tests. The behavior of Q-SOAR-3 after the Experimental condition produces correct responses and explanations, and thus is consistent with the pattern of results in Table 1. It seems likely that the experience of this conflict and the resulting recall and comparison of values provide the means by which three year olds acquire the effect-verification knowledge that we have assumed to be available to four year olds and which we provided for Q-SOAR-4.

7.3.4 Q-SOAR-4 AFTER BOTH TRIALS

Having produced a quantitative response before a transformation (e.g., step 4 in Figure 1), Q-SOAR-4 selects the MEMORIZE operator to store the computed values in long-term memory. Then, in the DETERMINE-EFFECT problem space, it selects the RECALL operator to enable it to compare pre- and post-transformation values to determine the effect of the transformation and create an explanation. This knowledge can then be recalled in the tests, enabling Q-SOAR-4 to pass the conservation tests after experiencing both the Experimental and Cardinal-Once procedures. This pattern of results is also consistent with that in Table 1. The higher proportion of correct responses in the Experimental group may reflect the fact that not all four year old children had acquired the effect-verification knowledge that we assumed for Q-SOAR-4. Those that had not would be expected to perform less well in the Cardinal-Once condition, just as was the case for three year olds.

7.4 Learning Speed

In Section 4 we stated that Q Theory is designed to account for the natural development of conservation, while Q-SOAR simulates only conservation learning in a single training study. Therefore, we should explain how the same processes can learn very quickly under experimental situations and yet take a few years to reach the same point during natural development. Two obvious factors are the differences in exposure and the availability of feedback. Intensive exposure to important features and informative feedback are characteristic of training studies, but neither of these is the case in unsupervised everyday activity.

However, we suggest that the greatest influence on learning speed is what we shall call the goal versus encoding interaction. A learner may activate the goal of measuring the effects of transformations. Alternatively, that learner's processing may be in the service of some other goal, such as building towers out of blocks. Even if the measurement goal has been activated, the learner may not attend to a property of the transformed materials that will reveal any number-invariance knowledge, such as the spatial density of a pile of blocks. Only if the child simultaneously has the goal of measurement and the encoding of number as the feature to be measured will he/she acquire number conservation. Well-designed training studies, such as Gelman's, foster just such optimal conditions, and in Q-SOAR these aspects are explicit in the representation of comprehended instructions. Similar directiveness appears to be provided for the child in relatively natural mother-child interactions, as set up by Saxe, Gearhart, and Guberman (1984). We know of no evidence to suggest that the goal and property combination optimal for number conservation learning would be chosen by the child any more or less often than any other, although it is evident that children often set themselves the goal of counting things. Thus, three of the four types of opportunities for learning number conservation knowledge would not produce conservation learning in Q-SOAR.

8. Conclusion

In this chapter we presented Q-SOAR, a computational model of the acquisition of conservation knowledge as reported in a single experimental training study. This is the first such account to present a set of mechanisms, constrained by a unified theory of cognition, that can be shown to acquire conservation knowledge. Furthermore, we demonstrated not only that Q-SOAR can account for the rapid learning observed in the Gelman (1982) training study but also that, without modification, it may also be able to explain the slower, more opportunistic acquisition of invariance knowledge that is characteristic of a young child's everyday unsupervised learning experiences. Much remains to be done before we can claim that Q-SOAR gives a complete account of the acquisition of conservation knowledge. There exist many other training studies (Field, 1987) whose results should also be explicable by the mechanisms of Q Theory. The transfer to conservation of continuous quantity remains to be explained, and an account of "natural" conservation development is still an important goal. Nevertheless, we believe that the work reported in this chapter represents real progress in the creation of computational theories of conceptual development.

Acknowledgements

We thank Bob Siegler for comments and access to his experimental data and Rochel Gelman for further explication of her experimental procedures. In addition, the first author wishes to thank members of the SOAR group for invaluable help, Richard Young for comments, discussions, and support, and Doug Fisher for helpful suggestions on earlier drafts. This work was supported by Contract N00014-86-K-0678 from the Computer Science Division of the Office of Naval Research.

References

Anderson, J. R. (1987). Skill acquisition: Compiling weak method problem solutions. *Psychological Review*, *94*, 194–210.

Barsalou, L. W. (1983). Ad hoc categories. *Memory and Cognition*, *11*, 211–227.

Bransford, J. D., Stein, B. S., Shelton, T. S., & Owings, R. A. (1981). Cognition and adaptation: The importance of learning to learn. In J. Harvey (Ed.), *Cognition, social behavior, and the environment*. Hillsdale, NJ: Lawrence Erlbaum.

Brown, A. L., Bransford, J. D., Ferrara, R. A., & Campione, J. C. (1983). Learning, remembering and understanding. In J. H. Flavell & E. M. Markman (Eds.), *Handbook of child psychology: Cognitive development* (Vol. 3). New York: John Wiley.

Campbell, R. L., Cooper, R. G., & Blevins-Knabe, B. (1988). *The development of subitizing in preschool and early elementary school children* (Tech. Rep. No. 63254). Yorktown Heights, NY: IBM, T. J. Watson Research Center.

Chi, M. T. H., & Klahr, D. (1975). Span and rate of apprehension in children and adults. *Journal of Experimental Child Psychology*, *19*, 434–439.

DeJong, G., & Mooney, R. (1986). Explanation-based learning: An alternative view. *Machine Learning*, *1*, 145–176.

Donaldson, M. (1978). *Children's minds*. Glasgow, Scotland: Fontana.

Field, D. (1987). A review of preschool conservation training: An analysis of an analysis. *Developmental Review*, 7, 210–251.

Fuson, K. C. (1988). *Children's counting and concepts of number*. New York: Springer Verlag.

Gelman, R. (1977). How young children reason about small numbers. In N. J. Castellan, D. B. Pisoni, & G. R. Potts (Eds.), *Cognitive theory* (Vol. 2). Hillsdale, NJ: Lawrence Erlbaum.

Gelman, R. (1982). Accessing one-to-one correspondence: Still another paper about conservation. *British Journal of Psychology*, *73*, 209–220.

Gelman, R., & Baillargeon, R. (1983). A review of some Piagetian concepts. In J. H. Flavell & E. M. Markman (Eds.), *Handbook of child psychology: Cognitive development* (Vol. 3). New York: John Wiley.

Gentner, D. (1983). Structure mapping: A theoretical framework for analogy. *Cognitive Science*, *7*, 155–170.

Halford, G. S. (1982). *The development of thought*. Hillsdale, NJ: Lawrence Erlbaum.

Halford, G. S., & Boyle, F. M. (1985). Do young children understand conservation of number? *Child Development*, *56*, 165–176.

Halford, G. S., Smith, S., Mayberry, M., Stewart, J., & Dickson, J. C. (1991). *A computer simulation model of acquisition of transitive inference*. Paper presented at the Biennial Meeting of the Society for Research in Child Development, Seattle, WA.

Klahr, D. (1973). Quantification processes. In W. Chase (Ed.), *Visual information processing*. New York: Academic Press.

Klahr, D. (1982). Nonmonotone assessment of monotone development: An information processing analysis. In S. Strauss & R. Stavy (Eds.), *U-shaped behavioral growth*. New York: Academic Press.

Klahr, D. (1984). Transition processes in quantitative development. In R. J. Sternberg (Ed.), *Mechanisms of cognitive development*. New York: W. H. Freeman.

Klahr, D., & Dunbar, K. (1988). Dual space search during scientific reasoning. *Cognitive Science*, *12*, 1–48.

Klahr, D., & Wallace, J. G. (1970). An information processing analysis of some Piagetian experimental tasks. *Cognitive Psychology*, *1*, 358–387.

Klahr, D., & Wallace, J. G. (1973). The role of quantification operators in the development of the conservation of quantity. *Cognitive Psychology*, *4*, 301–327.

Klahr, D., & Wallace, J. G. (1976). *Cognitive development: An information processing view*. Hillsdale, NJ: Lawrence Erlbaum.

Laird, J. E., Newell, A., & Rosenbloom, P. S. (1987). SOAR: An architecture for general intelligence. *Artificial Intelligence*, *33*, 1–64.

Laird, J. E., Rosenbloom, P. S., & Newell, A. (1986). Chunking in SOAR: The anatomy of a general learning mechanism. *Machine learning*, *1*, 11–46.

Laird, J. E., Swedlow, K. R., Altmann, E. M., & Congdon, C. B. (1989). *SOAR 5 User's Manual* (Tech. Rep.). Ann Arbor: University of Michigan, Department of Electrical Engineering and Computer Science.

Lewis, R. L., Huffman, S. B., John, B. E., Laird, J. E., Lehman, J. F., Newell, A., Rosenbloom, P. S., Simon, T., & Tessler, S. G. (1990). SOAR as a unified theory of cognition. *Proceedings of the Twelfth Annual Conference of the Cognitive Science Society* (pp. 1035–1042). Cambridge, MA: Lawrence Erlbaum.

Lewis, R. L., Newell, A., & Polk, T. A. (1989). Toward a SOAR theory of taking instructions for immediate reasoning tasks. *Proceedings of the Eleventh Annual Conference of the Cognitive Science Society* (pp. 514–521). Ann Arbor, MI: Lawrence Erlbaum.

McClelland, J. L. (1991). *Connectionist models of developmental change.* Paper presented at Biennial Meeting of the Society for Research in Child Development, Seattle, WA.

Miller, C. S., & Laird, J. E. (1990). *A simple, symbolic model for associative learning and retrieval.* Unpublished manuscript, Artificial Intelligence Laboratory, University of Michigan, Ann Arbor.

Mitchell, T.M., Keller, R.M., & Kedar-Cabelli, S.T. (1986). Explanation-based generalization: A unifying view. *Machine Learning*, *1*, 47–80.

Newell, A. (1990). *Unified theories of cognition.* Cambridge, MA: Harvard University Press.

Piaget, J. (1952). *The child's conception of number*. New York: W. W. Norton.

Piaget, J. (1964). Development and learning. In R. E. Ripple & V. N. Rockastle (Eds.), *Piaget rediscovered*. Ithaca, NY: Cornell University Press.

Piaget, J. (1968). Quantification, conservatism and nativism. *Science*, *162*, 976–979.

Piaget, J. (1970). *Structuralism*. New York: Basic Books.

Rosenbloom, P. S., & Laird, J. E. (1986). Mapping explanation-based generalization into SOAR. *Proceedings of the Fifth National Conference on Artificial Intelligence* (pp. 561–567). Philadelphia, PA: Morgan Kaufmann.

Saxe, G. B., Gearhart, M., & Guberman, S. R. (1984). The social organization of early number development. In B. Rogoff & J. V. Wertsch (Eds.), *Children's learning in the zone of proximal development*. San Francisco, CA: Jossey-Bass.

Shrager, J. (1987). Theory change via view application. *Machine Learning*, *2*, 1–30.

Siegler, R. S. (1981). Developmental sequences within and between concepts. *Monographs of the Society for Research in Child Development*, *46*, 1–74.

Siegler, R. S. (1991). *Variation and selection as cognitive transition mechanisms*. Paper presented at the Biennial Meeting of the Society for Research in Child Development, Seattle, WA.

Siegler, R. S. (1989). Mechanisms of cognitive development. *Annual Review of Psychology*, *40*, 353–379.

Simon, T., & Newell, A. (1990). *Subitizing is faster than you think — If you don't ask 'How Many?'* Unpublished manuscript, Department of Psychology, Carnegie Mellon University, Pittsburgh, PA.

Svenson, O., & Sjoberg, K. (1983). Speeds of subitizing and counting process in different age groups. *Journal of Genetic Psychology*, *142*, 203–211.

Wallace, J. G., Klahr, D., & Bluff, K. (1987). A self-modifying production system model of cognitive development. In D. Klahr, P. Langley, & R. Neches (Eds.), *Production system models of learning and development*. Cambridge, MA: MIT Press.

Appendix: Sample Q-SOAR Run

Here we illustrate how the problem spaces described in Section 6 generate behavior when Q-SOAR is presented with a task. The following trace is an abstracted version of the steps presented in Figure 1, which show Q-SOAR in operation for the first time. The second trace shows the model's successful performance on a conservation test.

The traces retain only the critical information, showing the problem spaces (denoted by P) and operators (denoted by O) that are selected in response to the impasses that arise. An impasse is shown by processing in a subgoal (G) being indented under the operator that produced the impasse. When an impasse is resolved, processing continues at the highest level at which an operator can be selected. The operators are augmented with the instruction that led to their initiation or by the objects on which they are focused.

External arrays and instructions are depicted to the right of the trace in lower case and Q-SOAR's output is given in the center in upper case. The trace is marked with '**' at the points in the run where the key conservation chunk is acquired and where it is evoked. Chunks are created continually throughout the run (one or more when returning from each impasse), but these are not shown.

ABSTRACTED RUN OF Q-SOAR DURING ITS FIRST OPERATION

```
                                                  () () () ()
                                                  [] [] [] []
P: (CONSERVATION)
                                    How many circles?
O: (COMPREHEND-INSTRUCTIONS)
O: (DETERMINE-RESPONSE)
==>G: (OPERATOR NO-CHANGE)
   P: (RESPOND)
   O: (MEASURE)
   ==>G: (OPERATOR NO-CHANGE)
      P: (QUANT-C)
      O: ((CIRCLE) ATTEND)
      O: (INITIALIZE)
      O: ((CIRCLE) COUNT-NEXT) Counting item: ONE
      O: ((CIRCLE) FETCH-NEXT)
      O: ((CIRCLE) COUNT-NEXT) Counting item: TWO
      O: ((CIRCLE) FETCH-NEXT)
      O: ((CIRCLE) COUNT-NEXT) Counting item: THREE
      O: ((CIRCLE) FETCH-NEXT)
      O: ((CIRCLE) COUNT-NEXT) Counting item: FOUR
      O: (MEMORIZE)
O: (RETURN-RESPONSE)                Answer FOUR
                                    How many squares?
O: (COMPREHEND-INSTRUCTIONS)
O: (DETERMINE-RESPONSE)
==>G: (OPERATOR NO-CHANGE)
   P: (RESPOND)
   O: (MEASURE)
   ==>G: (OPERATOR NO-CHANGE)
      P: (QUANT-C)
      O: ((SQUARE) ATTEND)
      O: (INITIALIZE)
      O: ((SQUARE) COUNT-NEXT) Counting item: ONE
      O: ((SQUARE) FETCH-NEXT)
      O: ((SQUARE) COUNT-NEXT) Counting item: TWO
      O: ((SQUARE) FETCH-NEXT)
      O: ((SQUARE) COUNT-NEXT) Counting item: THREE
      O: ((SQUARE) FETCH-NEXT)
```

```
      O: ((SQUARE) COUNT-NEXT) Counting item: FOUR
      O: (MEMORIZE)
O: (RETURN-RESPONSE)           Answer FOUR
                               Same or different number?
O: (COMPREHEND-INSTRUCTIONS)
O: (DETERMINE-RESPONSE)
==>G: (OPERATOR NO-CHANGE)
   P: (RESPOND)
   O: (COMPARE)
   ==>G: (OPERATOR NO-CHANGE)
      P: (QUANT-C)
      O: (COMPARE)
O: (RETURN-RESPONSE)           Answer SAME
                                             () () () ()
                                             []   []   []   []
                               Still four circles?
O: (CATEGORIZE-TRANSFORMATION)
O: (COMPREHEND-INSTRUCTIONS)
O: (DETERMINE-RESPONSE)
==>G: (OPERATOR NO-CHANGE)
   P: (RESPOND)
   O: (RECALL)
O: (RETURN-RESPONSE)           Answer FOUR
                               Still four squares?
O: (COMPREHEND-INSTRUCTIONS)
O: (DETERMINE-RESPONSE)
==>G: (OPERATOR NO-CHANGE)
   P: (RESPOND)
   O: (RECALL)
   ==>G: (OPERATOR NO-CHANGE)
      P: (DET-EFFECT)
      O: (RECALL)
      O: (DETERMINE-EFFECT)**
O: (RETURN-RESPONSE)           Answer FOUR
                               Same or different number?
O: (COMPREHEND-INSTRUCTIONS)
O: (DETERMINE-RESPONSE)
==>G: (OPERATOR NO-CHANGE)
   P: (RESPOND)
   O: (COMPARE)
O: (RETURN-RESPONSE)           Answer SAME
      VALUES MATCH BEFORE AND AFTER THIS TRANSFORMATION.

End -- Explicit Halt
```

The following rule paraphrases the chunk that Q-SOAR learns at the point marked '**' in the run above and that applies at the point marked '**' in the following trace. Pattern-match variables are preceded by question marks.

```
If Goal ?G1 has State ?S1 and Operator ?O1,
   and State ?S1 has Transformation ?T1 marked on it,
   and Transformation ?T1 is Spreading,
   and Operator ?O1 is Determine-Response,
Then mark State ?S1 with Effect ?E1 of Transformation ?T1,
   where ?E1 states that ?T1 has the effect NONE on the
   property Number, because pre- and post-transformation
   numerical values matched.
```

Q-SOAR RUN ON A CONSERVATION TEST AFTER LEARNING

```
                                                  () () () () ()
                                                  [] [] [] [] []
 P: (CONSERVATION)
                                      Same or different number?
 O: (COMPREHEND-INSTRUCTIONS)
 O: (DETERMINE-RESPONSE)
 ==>G: (OPERATOR NO-CHANGE)
    P: (RESPOND)
    O: (COMPARE)
    ==>G: (OPERATOR NO-CHANGE)
       P: (ESTIMATE)
       O: (MATCH-1-TO-1)              One-to-one end-match: SAME
       O: (MEMORIZE)
 O: (RETURN-RESPONSE)                 Answer SAME
                                                  () () () () ()
                                                  []  []  []  []  []
                                      Same or different number?
                                      Explain
 O: (CATEGORIZE-TRANSFORM)
 O: (COMPREHEND-INSTRUCTIONS)
 O: (DETERMINE-RESPONSE)**
 O: (RETURN-RESPONSE)                 Answer SAME

 VALUES MATCH BEFORE AND AFTER THIS TRANSFORMATION.

End -- Explicit Halt
```

CHAPTER 68

Attentional Modeling of Object Identification and Search

M. Wiesmeyer and J. Laird, University of Michigan

1 Introduction

In this paper we present two applications of an operator-based model of human covert visual attention.[1] Unlike overt visual attention, in which eye movements provide evidence of shifting attention, evidence for shifting attention in covert visual attention is inferred through reaction times. Task models of experiments presented in this paper show that a single model of covert visual attention can account for reaction times in two major classes of tasks. In *identification tasks*, the location of an object to be identified is cued and the goal is to identify the cued object. Reaction times in identification tasks have been shown to decrease if a cue for the location of the object is presented prior to the object's presentation. In *search tasks*, the identity of a potentially present object is given and the goal is to determine its presence or absence. Reaction times for search tasks fall into two major categories. In the first, reaction time is linearly dependent upon the number of distracting elements in a display. In the second, reaction time is faster and nearly independent of the number of distracting elements. We introduce our model in basic form as an explanation of reaction time behavior in object identification experiments that employ target precuing [Colegate *et al.*, 1973]. We then incrementally expand the model and show how it can also be used as an explanation of reaction times in visual search [Treisman and Gelade, 1980; Treisman and Gormican, 1988; Wolfe *et al.*, 1989]

Our model is based on the Model Human Processor (MHP) [Card *et al.*, 1983]. It capitalizes on the architecture and basic timing parameters of MHP in order to specify visual operators and memories and provide reaction time predictions for tasks requiring visual attention. It employs an attentional "zoom lens" controlled by cognition in order to both locate features in visual space and improve the quality of featural information delivered to short-term memory [Treisman and Gelade, 1980]. Reaction time accounts are based on sequences of deliberate acts in the 50 msec range that are expressed as operator traces. The model is implemented in the Soar cognitive architecture and task models are verified by simulations that produce operator traces [Laird *et al.*, 1987].

The goal of our research is the construction of a task-independent model of covert visual attention that is capable of predicting *average reaction time behavior* in a wide range of visual tasks. Currently, we limit application of our model to tasks requiring only covert visual attention in two dimensions (hereafter simply "visual attention"). Our model is task independent in that—with the exception of task-specific control—the operators, memories and the information flow assumed by our model are unchanging across the range of tasks it seeks to cover.

We verify our model through *coverage*. Coverage in terms of our work means testing the model on a large number of tasks, while only allowing for small variations in its specification for task-specific control to occur. In addition to the tasks covered in this paper, we have applied our model to rapid counting tasks [Chi and Klahr, 1975; Klahr and Wallace, 1976; Wiesmeyer, 1991], tasks that produce illusory conjunctions [Treisman and Schmidt, 1982], as well as experiments from Sperling [Sperling, 1960] and LaBerge [LaBerge and Brown, 1989]. The application of our model to these experiments is described in [Wiesmeyer, Forthcoming].

*This research was sponsored by grant NCC2-517 from NASA Ames.

[1] A portion of this paper appeared in an earlier work [Wiesmeyer and Laird, 1990].

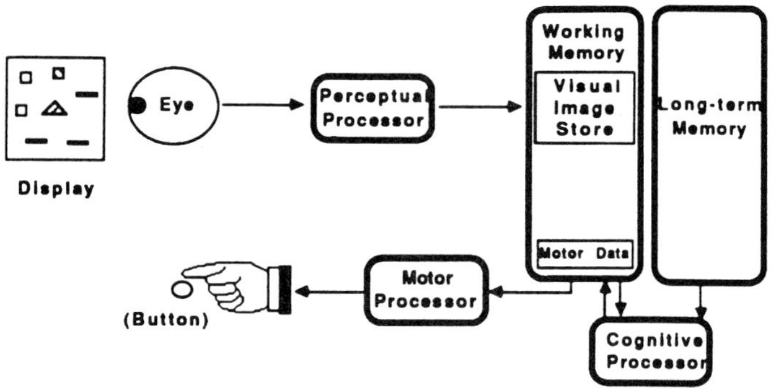

Figure 1: The Model Human Processor

2 The Model Human Processor and Soar

The MHP was designed to be a cognitive model of human behavior. It has been most successfully used for estimating the timing of man and machine interactions [John, 1988; John and Newell, 1989]. Figure 1 shows a simplified representation of the MHP from Card et al. (1983). On the top left-hand side of the figure is the Perceptual Processor or Perception, which consists of sensory modalities, such as vision and audition. (For clarity of presentation, the figure only shows vision.) Each modality delivers a limited amount of information at a particular rate to Working Memory. On the bottom left-hand side of the figure is the Motor Processor or Motor, while on the right-hand side of the figure is Cognition, which consists of Working Memory, Long-Term Memory, and the Cognitive Processor. In the MHP, tasks are decomposable into deliberate actions that take place in the form of discrete, sequential operator applications in Cognition. Some operators require input from the Perception, others initiate external acts using Motor, and still others use existing data in Working Memory for internal calculations that are independent of Perception and Motor.

Each subsystem in the MHP has a range of nominal *cycle times*. Perceptual (visual) cycle time is defined to be the time required for Perception to convert a visual stimulus at the retina into features in Working Memory; cognitive cycle time is defined to be the time required for an operator to apply; and motor cycle time is defined to be the time required for a change in Working Memory to effect an overt, external response. Thus, timing of internal calculations is solely dependent upon the cognitive cycle time; timing of deliberate acts involving Perception is dependent upon both perceptual and cognitive cycle times; and timing of deliberate motor acts is dependent upon both cognitive and motor cycle times. The cycle times that we use in our model for Perception and Motor are MHP median figures. The cycle time that we employ for Cognition is taken from John (1988) and is 20 msec faster than the MHP median figure for Cognition, but well within the range of nominal cycle times for Cognition in the MHP.

Perceptual (vision) cycle time (τ_p)	= 100 msec	(Range: 50-200 msec)
Cognitive cycle time (τ_c)	= 50 msec	(Range: 25-170 msec)
Motor cycle time (τ_m)	= 70 msec	(Range: 30-100 msec)

In the MHP, total time required to perform a task is calculated by creating a "operator trace" (our term) and then summing the durations of component operator applications, perceptual dependencies, and motor cycle times. We define a perceptual dependency to be a situation in which the creation of a critical operator in a trace is dependent upon visual stimuli that are not yet converted into features by Perception. In the MHP, perceptual dependencies occur strictly as the result of stimulus presentation latencies or eye movements. One of our major extensions to the MHP is a characterization of perceptual dependencies that are due to the latencies of covert attentional shifts. Motor cycle times contribute to reaction time calculations in all tasks, because all tasks end in some motor operator that causes an external, observable response. Finally, since the Perception, Cognition, and Motor processors operate independently for the most part, there is often overlap between their activities that reduces reaction times.

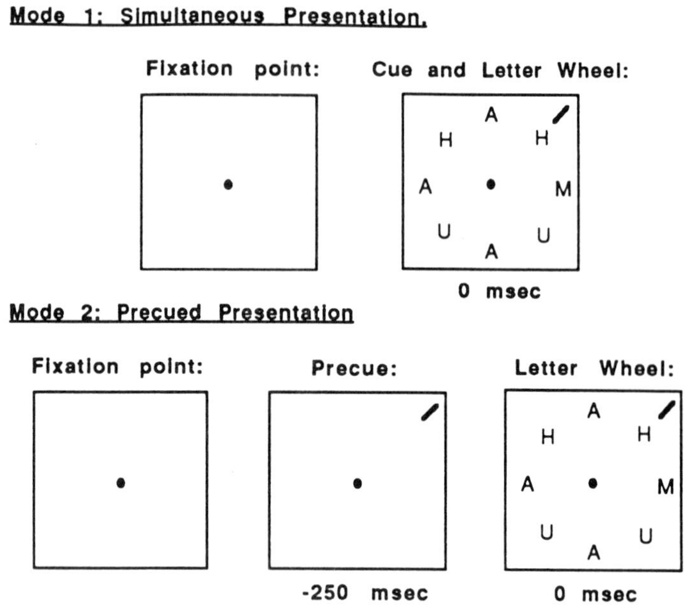

Figure 2: Example letter wheel stimuli from Colegate, et al. (1973)

We use Soar [Laird *et al.*, 1987] as the underlying architecture for implementing operator traces for task models. Soar has all of the basic subsystems of the MHP, including Perception, Cognition, and Motor. In Soar there is a Working Memory and a Long-term Memory, and deliberately selected operators provide the basis of action. Soar's Long-term Memory is a parallel production system. In the Soar implementation of our model, Perception is implemented as Lisp functions that transduce simulated environmental stimuli and send input to working memory, while Motor is implemented as Lisp functions that receive output from Working Memory and then produce simulated actions in the environment. In Soar, low-level perception and motor actions occurs in parallel with the firing of productions.

The basic deliberative act in Soar is the selection of an operator to apply. Thus the operators in the MHP map directly onto operators in Soar. Both the selection and application of operators are performed by productions matching against Working Memory and suggesting changes to it. Thus, productions control which operators are selected, and once selected, how they apply. In Soar, specific operators (that is, instantiations of operator types) are created as soon as the data needed to instantiate them are available. In general, this means that new operators will be created, and ready for selection, during the application of the currently selected operator. However, only one operator can be applied on any given cycle.

3 Identification Experiment

Colegate, Hoffman and Eriksen (1973) (hereafter "CHE") is a typical example of an object identification task that involves precuing. Other such experiments have yielded similar results under slightly different conditions [Eriksen and Hoffman, 1972; Eriksen and Hoffman, 1973]. In CHE, subjects were presented with displays similar to those shown in Figure 2. The task was to identify the cued letter. Subjects responded vocally. Letters from the set A,H,M,U were systematically distributed over the various locations in 8 and 12 letter displays so that the effects of letters neighboring the target on reaction time could be studied. Displays were 2 degrees in visual angle and presented with a tachistoscope—2 degrees is the extent of the fovea and approximately the diameter of the entire letter wheel on the right of the figure if this paper is held at arm's length.

There were two basic modes of stimulus delivery, simultaneous presentation and precued presentation. In both modes subjects were told to fixate on a point in the center of the visual field until a cue for the location

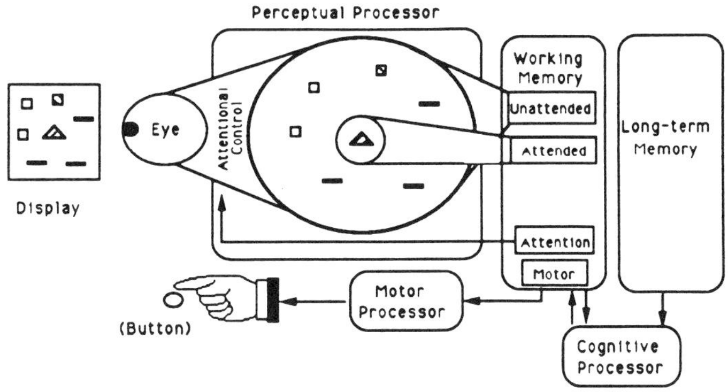

Figure 3: The model human processor with visual attention extension

of a letter to be identified was presented. In simultaneous presentation the cue and the letter arrived at the same time, while in precued presentation the cue preceded the letter wheel by an interval of up to 350 msec. In both modes, subjects were required to identify the cued letter. CHE's data showed that reaction times improve at a constant rate as the precue period increases up to 250 msec. With a 250 msec precue there was a 100 msec improvement in reaction time with respect to the simultaneous presentation condition. Response times for 8-letter displays were always slightly faster than for 12-letter displays (about 8 msec). We do not account for the differences between the 8 and 12 letter displays in this paper, since we posit that these differences are due to mechanisms below the operator level (50 msec).

4 Basic Model of Visual Attention

Our model of visual attention is an early selection model [Broadbent, 1958], because attentional selection occurs before semantic categorization. We have capitalized on the general organizational and timing specifications of the Model Human Processor (MHP) and sought to further define timing, operators, memories, and information flow within the MHP that are required to support an attentional model. The MHP is a much richer and complete theory than was shown earlier, however our extensions to the theory are only dependent upon those aspects presented. In this exposition of our model, only details relevant to explaining reaction times in the letter wheel experiment (which is typical of object identification paradigms) will be presented. In a later section, additions will be made to the model to aid in explaining the mechanisms and reaction times involved in visual search.

With reference to the letter wheel tasks, we assume that

- Visual attention is required for object identification, otherwise there would be no difference between reaction times in the simultaneous and precued trials.
- Cognition can control the spatial locus and extent of visual attention and thus the portions of the visual field that are attended or unattended.
- Unattended features are used to cue new shifts of attention, but cannot be used for identification.
- Shifting of visual attention is a deliberate act.
- Attended features are used in object identification.
- Since features are iconic representations, object identification involves a transformation in working memory from an iconic to a semantic representation.
- Object identification requires access to long-term, semantic representations and is also a deliberate act.

Similar assumptions are found scattered throughout the attention and perception literature. Let us take a moment, however, to expand on these simple assumptions as they relate to our model.

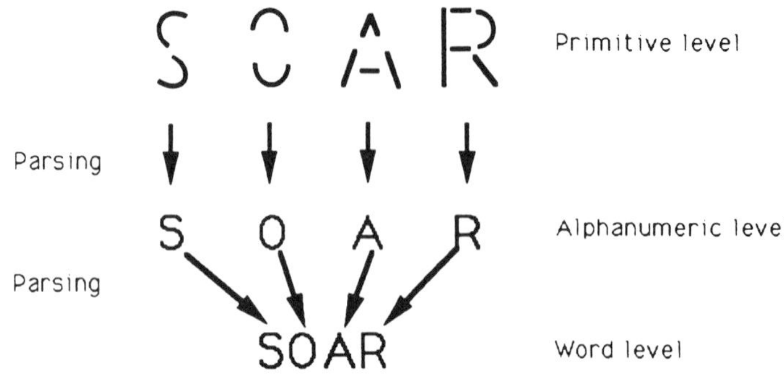

Figure 4: Parsing as a candidate method of visual identification

4.1 Properties of Attention

In our model, visual attention is controlled by Cognition, as shown in Figure 3. A single ovoid region of attentional focus, as in Eriksen's "Zoom Lens Theory" [Eriksen and Yeh, 1985; Eriksen and St. James, 1986], separates the visual field into attended and unattended stimuli. Perception delivers both attended features, which derive from the attended region, and unattended features, which derive from the unattended region, into immediate visual memory, which is part of the Visual Image Store.

Because visual attention is a deliberate act, it must be controlled through an operator, the **ATTEND** operator. A separate operator is created for each unattended feature in the visual field and application of a **ATTEND** operator shifts the region of attention to its corresponding feature. In shifting attention, the new region of attention may also include other features that are near the selected feature. The **ATTEND** operator can be further specialized to shift to the *nearest* feature (with respect to the current region of attention) of a given type. For example, in the letter wheel task, it is critical that the **ATTEND** can be used to shift attention to the shape feature nearest the cue.

4.2 Visual Features

Visual features are simply defined to be iconic representations of visual stimuli. For the letter wheel tasks, features need only correspond to shape attributes in the visual field. We assume a model in which alphanumeric features are directly available from Perception and **RECOGNIZE** operators transform alphanumeric features into semantic representations (e.g., symbols, names).

Other theories take an opposing view in which there is a cannonical set of simple, primitive features [Treisman and Gelade, 1980] and that primitive features are "parsed" into complex objects, as shown in Figure 4. The complex objects are then transformed into semantic representations. Unfortunately, in spite of a large body of research, no definitive set of primitive features has yet been found and there are reaction time phenomena that a naive parsing model cannot explain.

As shown in Figure 4, a parsing model of complex object identification predicts that identifying substructure (e.g., primitive features) should always require less time than identifying objects (e.g., characters or words). But precisely the opposite seems true! For instance subjects were able to determine the categories of letters and numbers faster than they were able to determine if the same sets of letters and numbers had curved or straight lines [Bundesen *et al.*, 1984]. In another experiment, Hoffman showed subjects large letters that were composed of smaller letters [Hoffman, 1980]. Their task was to identify the smaller letters that composed the larger letters. When the larger letter was different from the smaller letters that formed it, reaction times were slower. This can be interpreted as an interference effect caused by identification of the larger, incompatible letter prior to the smaller target letter.

The above behavior indicates that access to substructure features is often not possible before the access to object identities. There are two explanations: either substructure features either do not exist in Working Memory or access to them is inhibited during and after parsing. We take the former, more parsimonious stance to simplify our model, although there is no conclusive evidence for doing so. We allow features of varying complexity with attention determining the grain size of features. When an individual attends to an object in the visual field, that object stimulus is delivered by Perception to Working Memory *directly* as a feature. Attention is required to gain access to substructure and Perception will not deliver both an object and its substructure to Working Memory simultaneously.

Of course, this discussion about the interaction between features and attention is an oversimplification. For instance, due to rapidly diminishing visual acuity with retinal eccentricity, there must be a limit to the visual angle that objects can subtend and still be directly converted into features. Evidence for this assertion is to be found in Hoffman (1980). When objects exceed this limit, shifts of covert attention and perhaps even eye movements are necessary for component attributes to be integrated and identification to occur. Also, some objects subtending a small visual angle are identifiable only through fine internal detail. In these cases attention to and integration of substructure will again be necessary for identification. Multifixation feature integration is not a part of any of the task models that we present.

4.3 Timing in general

We assume that τ_c (50 msec) is the time required for an average cognitive operator to be created or selected and applied—creation being separate from selection and application; τ_p (100 msec) is the time required for a stimulus to get from the retina to working memory; and τ_m (70 msec) is the time required for a new Working Memory element to effect a motor command. Neither operator creation nor operator selection play any part in the MHP, its emphasis being wholly on operator application. The concepts of creation and selection in our model are derived from Soar which has been proposed as a unified theory of cognition [Newell, 1990]. Extending both the MHP and Soar, we propose that operator creation is independent of operator application and requires time. However, since next operator creation most often takes place during current operator application, these functions often overlap in a pipelined manner. Thus, creation times often are not included in operator trace timing calculations. Operator selection time is assumed to be minimal and not to affect timing.

4.4 Timing of shifting attention

We assume that shifts of visual attention require constant time regardless of the visual angle traversed during the shift. This assumption contradicts the findings of some researchers [Shulman *et al.*, 1979; Tsal, 1983] and is supported by others [Hughes and Zimba, 1985]. In the latter work, latencies proportional to visual angle from the fovea were shown to be attributable to a simple decrement in stimulus processing rate that occurs with retinal eccentricity. We do not compensate for retinal eccentricity effects in our model, because the slowdown is on the order of 1.8 msec per degree, and therefore negligible in small displays.

Shifts of attention as mediated by the **ATTEND** involve interaction between Cognition and Perception, which makes determining its time course problematic. We decompose its time course into the three stages required for Cognition to (1) react to a new stimulus, (2) shift visual attention to that new stimulus, and (3) then receive new features in Working Memory that reflect the change in visual attention. The only unknown component of this series of events is the time required for a visual stimulus to travel from the locus of action of attention to Working Memory.

Visual attention has been shown to act at a location in the brain called V4 [Moran and Desimone, 1985]. From V4 attended stimuli go to the inferior temporal cortex and then to the amygdala and the hippocampus [Mishkin and Appenzeller, 1987]. The amygdala and hippocampus are known to be involved in visual memory and are thus assumed to be the beginnings of Cognition (Working Memory). Since V4 is physically located about half way between the retina and the amygdala and hippocampus, we estimate that it should take about 1/2 of τ_p (or 50 msec) for the effects of visual attention to be reflected in the contents of Working Memory. Thus, we estimate the amount of time required for the entire process as:

100 msec	τ_p for propagation of data from the retina to working memory
50 msec	τ_c for **ATTEND** creation
50 msec	τ_c for **ATTEND** selection and application
50 msec	$\frac{1}{2}\tau_p$ for propagation of attended data from V4 to working memory
250 msec total	

An example of shifting attention to a new stimulus in the visual field appears in the first 250 msec of the operator trace shown in Figure 6. Often, shifting attention requires less time, however. For instance, if a stimulus has been in the visual field for τ_p, the time required for a shift of attention to that stimulus can be as little as 150 msec (the last three steps above), since unattended features that the **ATTEND** operator requires for creation are already in Working Memory. Further, shifts of attention can appear to require as little as 100 msec, since **ATTEND** creation can be pipelined with the application of a previous operator. An example of this pipelining behavior appears between 100 and 250 msec in the operator trace shown in Figure 8.

Admittedly, it would be preferable to use an empirically derived time in our model rather than these estimates, but we have not been able to locate a suitable one in the literature and have found this time to work well in our operator traces. Bearing this model in mind, the job at hand in creating operator traces to explain the letter wheel task is to fit operators together so that the task may be done and known time constraints may be satisfied.

5 Modeling the Letter Wheel Task

The minimum additions to the MHP in order to implement the model are:

- A notion of what features can be.
- An immediate memory for features.
- An operator that allows objects to be identified (**RECOGNIZE**).
- An operator that allows attention to shift (**ATTEND**).

In addition, two operators that key off of semantic representations are required. The **VERIFY** operator is required to assure that the cue has been identified and, thus, the target is the next nearest letter. The **RESPOND** operator is required in order to convey an overt response for the task (i.e., voicing the letter's identity). We list them separately since although they are required for the complete task models, they are not part of our model of covert visual attention. Figure 5 shows our model with details of memories, operators, and information flow in Cognition. Arrows pointing to operators indicate the regions of Working Memory that they are dependent upon, while arrows pointing from operators indicate regions of Working Memory where their effects are felt.

RESPOND operators are representatives of a class of operators that elicit motor responses. **RESPOND** operators vary according to the requirements of each task, and their duration depends upon the specifics of the response required (e.g., pushing a button or voicing a response). **VERIFY** operators are also specific for that tasks in which they are required, since they are used to check that task expectations.

5.1 Operator Traces

We have implemented our model in Soar and have produced operator traces for both the simultaneous presentation and 250 msec precue conditions. Both task model simulations use a single set of productions that controls the selection of operators based on the contents of Working Memory—there is no explicit selection strategy programmed for the two tasks.

Observed mean response times from CHE are 574 msec (483 – 635 msec) for the simultaneous presentation condition and 491 msec (427 – 569 msec) for the 250 msec precued presentation condition. Our operator traces predict 570 msec and 470 msec, respectively, and are thus both within the range of times obtained from experimental subjects. Additionally, the improvements due to precuing predicted by our model (100 msec) correlate closely with those of actual subjects (mean 83 msec).[2] Details of the both operator traces follow. Selection of operators in the traces is not shown, but occurs for each operator immediately preceding its application.

[2] There is a great deal of variation in experimental results for precuing in object identification experiments. The CHE experiment was chosen simply on the basis of its typicality.

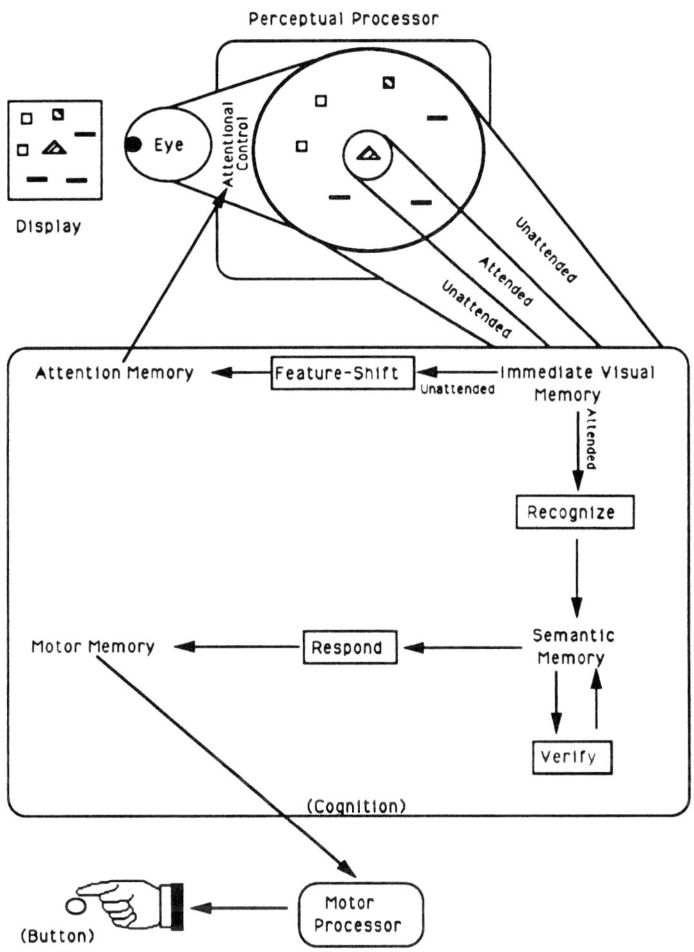

Figure 5: Details of Cognition in the Extended Model Human Processor

Time	Operator Event	Event/Comment
		Attention centered on fixation point
0 msec	None	Wheel and cue at retina
0+ msec	None	Wheel and cue in P
100 msec	ATTEND created	Wheel and cue in WM
150 msec	ATTEND applies	Shift to cue and letter
200 msec	ATTEND completed	Attentional message at V4
250 msec	RECOGNIZE (cue) created RECOGNIZE (letter) created	Cue and letter attended in WM
300 msec	RECOGNIZE (cue) applies VERIFY (cue) created	
350 msec	VERIFY (cue) applies	
400 msec	RECOGNIZE (letter) applies RESPOND created	Letter identified
450 msec	RESPOND applies	
500 msec	RESPOND completed	Motor output begins
570 msec		Motor command completed

Figure 6: Operator trace of the simultaneous presentation of the letter wheel

The simultaneous presentation operator trace is shown in Figure 6 and visual field and Working Memory changes for the trace are shown in Figure 7. In the trace, a single shift of attention is made to the cue. Both the cue and the letter are in the region of attention and their features are in Working Memory by 250 msec. Operators to identify both the cue and the letter in the region of attention are created (250 – 300 msec). The cue is identified (300 – 350 msec) and verified (350 – 400 msec). The target letter is identified (400 – 450 msec). The response then ensues (450 – 570 msec). In Figure 7, Working Memory changes are shown at the bottom of the figure. Shaded areas of the panels represent the unattended region, while unshaded areas represent the attended region.

The precued presentation operator trace is shown in Figure 8 and visual field and Working Memory changes for the trace are shown in Figure 9. The cue is presented at -250 msec, a shift of attention is made to the cue, and it is attended in Working Memory by 0 msec. (This is the same sequence of steps that occurs from 0 – 250 msec in the simultaneous presentation trace.) Following the shift, the cue is identified (0 – 100 msec) and verified (100 – 150 msec). At the same time, the letter wheel is being processed by perception and becomes available in Working Memory at 100 msec. At this point, a second shift is performed to the nearest letter (150 – 250 msec) followed by the letter's identification (250 – 350 msec) and finally the response (350 – 470 msec).

In the simultaneous presentation condition, only one shift of attention is required, while in the precued

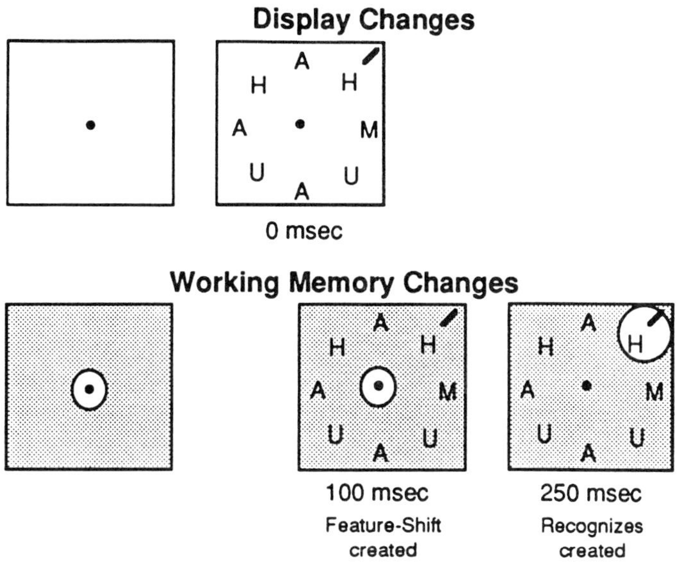

Figure 7: Display and Working Memory changes in the simultaneous presentation

condition two shifts are required. In spite of this, the precued condition is still faster. There are two reasons for this: (1) The first shift of attention for the precued condition finishes before the wheel is presented and timing starts. (2) The RECOGNIZE and VERIFY operators for the cue occur during the period in which the wheel stimulus is traveling from the retina to working memory (labeled "overlap" in the second operator trace).

The CHE results show that there is no improvement in reaction time when precuing exceeds 250 msec. The response time of our implementation does not improve either, since the shift to the target letter is contingent upon its shape feature appearing in Working Memory, which time will never change from 100 msec after the stimulus is presented.

The success of results of the model for precue between 0 and 250 msec are less clear. One of the assumptions of our model is that operators always take the same amount of time to apply and the application of one operator cannot overlap the application of another in time. As the precue extends from 0 to 250 msec there is about a 100 msec improvement in reaction time. Unfortunately, the model cannot account for the improvement, since all operators in the trace are required and operator application time overlap, which might account for the improvement, is not allowed. It is possible that the non-overlap assumption should not be held. However, allowing operator overlap, would only increase the number of degrees of freedom of the model, which should be avoided.

6 Summary of the Model

So far in this paper, we have developed a basic model of visual attention and used it to produce operator traces that explain mechanisms and latencies in object identification tasks where the target is precued by various intervals.

Summary of the model developed so far:

- Cognition can control the spatial locus and extent of visual attention through the ATTEND operator.
- Attention is manifest as a single ovoid region of attention that separates stimuli in the visual field into attended and unattended regions.

Time	Operator Event	Event/Comment	
		Attention centered on fixation point	
-250 msec	None	Cue at retina	
-200 msec	None	Cue in P	
-150 msec	ATTEND created	Cue in WM	
-100 msec	ATTEND applies	Shift to cue	
-50 msec	ATTEND completed	Attentional message at V4	
0 msec	RECOGNIZE (cue) created	Cue attended in WM	O
		Wheel at retina	v
50 msec	RECOGNIZE (cue) applies		e
	VERIFY (cue) created	Wheel in P	r
			l
100 msec	VERIFY (cue) applies	Wheel in WM	a
	ATTEND(s) created		p
150 msec	ATTEND applies	Shift to nearest letter	
200 msec	ATTEND completed	Attentional message at V4	
250 msec	RECOGNIZE (letter) created	Letter attended in WM	
300 msec	RECOGNIZE (letter) applies	Letter identified	
	RESPOND created		
350 msec	RESPOND applies		
400 msec	RESPOND completed	Motor output begins	
470 msec		Motor command completed	

Figure 8: Operator trace of the 250 msec precued presentation

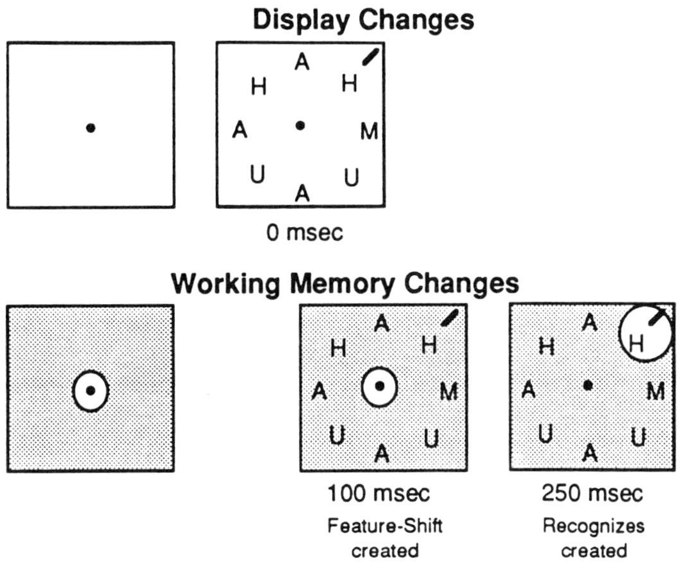

Figure 9: Display and Working Memory changes in the precued presentation

- Perception converts stimuli into shape features that are deposited in an immediate visual memory in Working Memory.
- Unattended features are used to cue new shifts of attention.
- Attention can shift to a particular type of unattended feature that is nearest the current region of attention.
- Attended features are used in object identification.
- Object identification is mediated by the **RECOGNIZE** operator.
- Since features are iconic representations, object identification involves a transformation in working memory from an iconic to a semantic representation.

In addition, we defined non-visual operators for checking task expectations and making motor responses. We now discuss several search experiments, so extensions to the theory can be suggested that will allow them to be modeled.

7 Search Experiments

Search is the opposite of identification. The reader may recall that in identification tasks, the location of a target is known and the goal is to identify the target. On the other hand, in search, the identity of the target is known and the goal is to determine its location or if it is present at all in a field of distractors. In *feature search,* the target possesses a unique attribute, such as a color or shape that the distractors do not share. In *conjunctive search,* the target is defined by both a shape and a color and the distractors share the attributes of the target but in different combinations. We survey results from three papers that show the representative range of reaction time behaviors for search tasks.

Experiment I of Treisman and Gelade (1980) (hereafter TG80) tested both feature and conjunctive search conditions: Distractors for both conditions were brown Ts and green Xs that were evenly distributed both in type and location in the display. Distractor numerosity varied from 1 to 30 items. In the feature search condition, the target was either the color blue (blue T or blue X) or an S (green S or brown S). In the conjunctive search condition the target was a green T.

TG80 found extremely robust linear relationships in conjunctive search between the response time and the number of distractors for both target present and target absent cases. (Response behaviors are typically graphed as linear or near linear relationships of response time (ordinate) to the number of distracting items (abscissa); we call them "slopes.") Additionally, the ratio of target present slopes to target absent slopes was always about 1:2. From the linearity and relationships between the slopes TG80 concluded that conjunctive search is serial, item-by-item, and self-terminating. In feature search, results were vastly different. In target present conditions, targets seemed to "pop out" since response times were very fast and seemed practically independent (very shallow slopes) of the number of distractors. In target absent conditions, the relationship between the number of distractors and response time (slope) was positive as in conjunctive search but not as linear. The fact that "pop out" only occurred during feature search, which did not seem to involve attention, since response times were independent of the number of distractors, led TG80 to conclude that some visual attributes are available as features "preattentively." The existence of illusory conjunctions of shapes and colors and the frequent inability of subjects to identify locations of identified features in a display when time was limited (also discussed in TG80) led to their pivotal "Feature Integration Theory." In this model, features float free in the absence of attention (i.e., have no locational information) and focused attention is required for proper localization and conjunction of features. Actual figures from TG80 appear below:

Experiment #1		Experiment #2	
Conjunctive search:		Difficult Conjunctive:	
Positive slope	28.7 (99.7)	Positive slope	55.1 (99.8)
Negative slope	67.1 (99.6)	Negative	92.4 (99.9)
Feature search:		Easy Conjunctive:	
Positive slope	3.1 (67.9)	Positive slope	20.5 (99.8)
Negative slope	25.1 (96.6)	Negative slope	39.5 (99.9)

Numbers in parentheses are percent variance with display size that is due to linearity.

Treisman and Gormican (1988) surveyed many examples of feature search and found response times were basically linear in the number of distractors but varied widely (2 – 128 msec) in slope.

Wolf, Cave, and Franzel (1989) (hereafter WCF) found that under some conditions subjects could do conjunctive searches when the target was present (even for targets defined by triple conjunctions) at about the same level of performance (3 – 6 msec per item) as seen in target present feature search conditions of TG80.[3] The ratio of target present slopes to target present slopes was often found to be less than 1:2 (maybe as low as 1:1.55) and there was some evidence of nonlinearity in response slopes—our model will not account for these findings. The fact that the same performance was achieved for both feature and conjunctive search led WCF to theorize that there is no qualitative difference between different types of search. WCF propose a "Guided Search Model" in which subjects make use of identity and location information that is available without attention, to guide their attentional search for a target.

8 Expanded Model for Search

In order to extend our previous model we have borrowed heavily from WCF's "Guided Search Model," since that model is able to explain (at least in our interpretation) a range of search results that subsumes those covered by Treisman's "Feature Integration Theory." We assume that in addition to the assumptions required for the letter wheel tasks that

- There are color features.
- Some features have locational information.
- Attention improves both identity and location information for both shape and color features.

[3] The particular condition that they discovered was when the background was dark and the targets and distractors were colored shapes (e.g., red and green Xs and Os).

- Features derived from attended stimuli are guaranteed to have good identity and locational information.
- Features derived from unattended stimuli have poor identity and locational information.
- Attention can shift to a feature within the current region of attention.

There is evidence from psychology and neuroscience that color features are represented separately from shape or other features [Treisman and Schmidt, 1982; Livingstone and Hubel, 1984; Livingstone and Hubel, 1987]. So, in our model Perception delivers color and shape features separately into Working Memory. This, however, presents a problem. If shape and color features are deposited separately in Working Memory, how are the objects that they represent identified?

In our model, differences in the quality of attended and unattended featural information create the need for attention. We posit that attention improves identity and location information for color and shape features so that identification can take place. Therefore, we extend the **RECOGNIZE** operator such that if a color and a shape feature are in the current region of attention, they can be transformed into a unitary semantic representation; that is, they can be identified. This makes our model appear to be similar to Treisman's "Feature Integration Theory" (FIT). However, there are differences.

The FIT is a late selection theory of attention in which the featural information present in Working Memory (not Treisman's terminology) is not affected by attention. In our model, identity and location information for features is affected by attention, since it is an early selection model. Also, in the FIT, location information is not available without focussed attention. In our model, we depend upon identity and location information outside of the current attentional region in order to account for conjunctive pop out. Since conjunctive pop out is a relatively rare phenomenon, we assume that simultaneously good identity and location information for large displays is relatively uncommon except for certain types of stimuli (e.g., those with black backgrounds). However, attention in our model always improves featural information for groups of features that are near to the current attention focus.

Since groups of objects may be attended, does attention need to be focussed exclusively on a single shape/color feature pair for identification to take place? In the previous letter wheel tasks, we assumed that attended shapes could be identified even if they were not attended to separately. However, with identification that involves both shapes and colors, complications arise. The model requires that the **ATTEND** key off of location information, but does not require **RECOGNIZE** operators to have access to location information. If location information is not available to **RECOGNIZE** operators, then illusory conjunctions of shape and color features can occur when identifying objects within attentional regions containing several different colors and shapes. This has been shown to happen in time-limited tasks [Treisman and Gelade, 1980; Treisman and Schmidt, 1982]. Thus, we assume that for identification involving both shapes and colors that the attentional region must only contain the shape and color to be conjoined. Since attention can be focussed on groups of objects at a time, this creates the need for attention to be able to shift to objects that are within the current attentional region.

9 Modeling Search Tasks

Our primary research emphasis is to develop a unified model of visual attention. This requires a high degree of consistency of operators, memories and information flow across task models. For search tasks, the layout of memories and information flow is the same as in the letter wheel tasks. With reference to operators, however, there are a few extensions to the model. First, the power of **RECOGNIZE** is expanded for search, since color features are now relevant. We assume that the **RECOGNIZE** operator can join attended color ("**GREEN**") and shape ("**T**") features and produce corresponding unitary semantic representations ("**GREEN-T**"). Second, since features now include both shapes and colors which may or may not have identity and location information, **ATTEND** operators should be able to be selected on the basis of this information. This is essential in conjunctive search. When target features (e.g., "**GREEN**" and "**T**") appear in Working Memory at the same location, attention should shift to them, so that they can be identified. Whether or not identity and location information is good enough for conjunctive pop out to occur is strictly a function of the stimulus presented. The **VERIFY** operator is used in modeling target absent search, and will be discussed further later. Finally, of course, the **RESPOND** operators are different, since the responses required for search tasks are not those

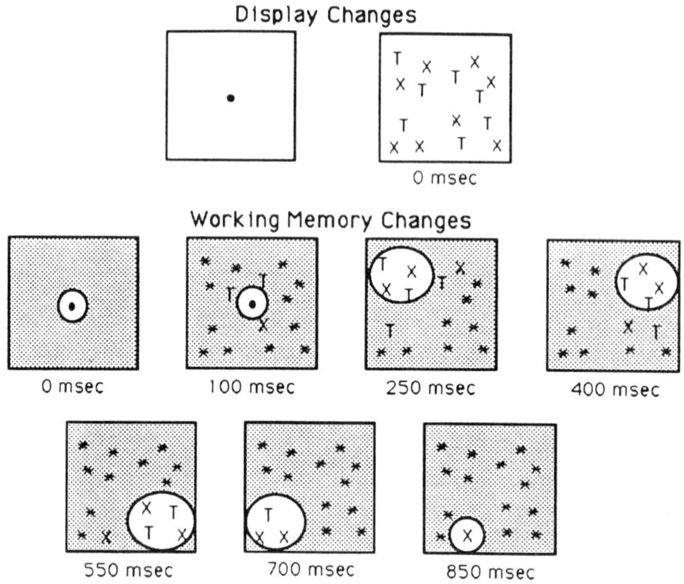

Figure 10: Group-by-group search

required for letter wheel tasks. Other than these minor changes, all operators identical to those used in the letter wheel tasks, although the conditions under which operators are selected vary due to the task control. The expansions of the definitions of **RECOGNIZE** and **ATTEND** do not affect the explanation of letter wheel task mechanisms or latencies.

9.1 Interpretation of Guided Search Model

The assertion by WCF that there is no qualitative difference between feature and conjunctive search is affirmed by our model, since the same operator traces account for reaction times in both conjunctive and feature search. Our interpretation of the "Guided Search Model" is as follows: At one extreme, when very good identity and location information for the target object is available, "pop out" should occur. At the other extreme, when such information is poorest, focused attention will be critical and serial, self-terminating, item-by-item search should occur. When moderately good information is available, when search will still appear to be serial and self-terminating, but attention will move across groups, not items. Figure 10 shows Working Memory changes for group-by-group search, where the distractors are target brown Ts and green Xs and the target is a green T (imagine color, please). The stars represent unidentifiable features, that is, features without good identity information. (Actually, these features would be expected to not have good location information either, since we posit that location information always breaks down before identity information.) Attention, denoted by the circles, is shown improving the identity and location information of each group in turn (imagine color improving, please). Letters inside of the regions of attention represent features with good identity and location information (by definition), while and letters outside of the regions of attention represent features with good identity and *possibly* good location information. The last two panels of the figure show how improved information in a small group of attended features allows the attention to shift to the target so it can be identified. This type of behavior in the terminal stage of group-by-group search is very similar, if not identical to that which Treisman found in her investigations of localized "pop out" [Treisman, 1985]. In these localized pop out experiments, objects did not pop out until attention was shifted to the subgroup of which they were a part.

9.2 Operator Traces

We implemented the extensions to the model required by search tasks in Soar and produced operator traces similar to those for the letter wheel tasks. In the implementation, search proceeds according to a horizontal scanning pattern as shown in Figure 10, however the particular attention shifting strategy is unimportant in the operator traces that we present.

Figure 11 shows the target present operator trace for either feature or conjunctive pop out. For feature pop out, the target feature in Working Memory must simply have good identity information and, for conjunctive pop out, the all component target features must have both good identity *and* good location information. Figure 12 shows the operator trace for target present search conditions in which identity and/or location information is not very good and there is a large enough number of distracting items in the display to warrant multiple shifts of attention.

In order to speed search, it is critical to avoid wasting time identifying distracting objects in the visual field. Therefore, in the traces, **ATTEND** operators are preferred to **RECOGNIZE** operators, except if there is an attended group of features at the same location that matches the search specification exactly. Because shifting attention requires time, however, **RECOGNIZE** operators can sometimes apply during the dead time that is required for new features to arrive in Working Memory (shown in Figure 12). This is precisely the way that the Soar implementation behaves and is a possible explanation for impression that some distracting objects are identified as search proceeds. Thus, during search, identification occurs only after the next shift of attention is initiated. When the target is found, the corresponding **RECOGNIZE** operator is preferred to all possible **ATTEND** operators and the target is identified. A **RESPOND** operator indicating success applies following the application of the **RECOGNIZE** operator for the target.

In the case of target absent trials, the story is a bit more complicated. The end of a target absent trial is detected if there are no remaining unvisited features. Given the fact that, when searching, **RECOGNIZE** operators are suppressed unless the target itself is to be identified, it should also be the possible that they can be suppressed when the target is absent, thus speeding the negative response. That is, there should be no terminal **RECOGNIZE** operators for target absent trials as in operator traces for target present conditions. Thus, target absent trials should always be approximately 50 msec faster than target present trials. However, experimental results show that both target present and target absent intercepts are usually nearly identical.

In our model, all reaction times must be accounted for by summations of operator applications or perceptual dependencies. In this particular case it is clear that the potentially missing 50 msec cannot be made up by a perceptual dependency. One possibility, however, is that target absent cases end with another form of the **VERIFY** operator. In this case the **VERIFY** operator would not be needed to determine if some event had happened, rather it would be required to determine that an event did not happen (i.e., the target was not present). We do not show operator traces including the **VERIFY** operator, since they can be easily created by replacing the terminal **RECOGNIZE** operator from the target present traces with a **VERIFY** operator. If we accept this explanation, all operator traces have the same intercept of 470 msec.

9.3 Analysis of Operator Traces

The total time for either operator trace to complete with only one shift of attention is 470 msec, which is in the middle of the observed range (397 – 682 msec). For the target absent case, the predicted response time is $470 + 150(x - 1)$ msec, where x is the expected number of shifts of attention. The expected number of shifts of attention should be the number of items in the display divided by the average number of items per attended group, where group size is dependent on the quality of the identity and location information available. The average number of items per attended group should be relatively constant for any particular type of display and individual differences in these constants account for individual differences in response times. For the target present case, the predicted response time is $470 + 150\frac{(x-1)}{2}$ msec, since on the average only 1/2 of the locations in the display will need to be searched.

For any stimulus condition, we assume that the existence of a positive reaction time slope implies a finite (although in many cases a very small) probability that multiple shifts of attention occur for that condition.[4] The inherently random nature of the arrangement of stimuli and their potentially noisy transduction by Per-

[4] In just about all search experiments response time slopes are positive. In the few cases where they are flat or negative it is possible that some sort of "object superiority" effect is at work [Weisstein and Harris, 1974].

Time	Operator Event	Event/Comment
0 msec	None	Stimulus at retina
0+ msec	None	Stimulus in P
100 msec	ATTEND created	Stimulus in WM
150 msec	ATTEND applies	Shift to blob/group
200 msec	ATTEND completed	Attentional message at V4
250 msec	RECOGNIZE created	Target attended in WM
300 msec	RECOGNIZE applies RESPOND created	Target identified
350 msec	RESPOND applies	
400 msec	RESPOND completed	Motor output begins
470 msec		Motor command completed

Figure 11: Operator trace for target present search with single shift of attention

```
      Time          Operator Event            Event/Comment
      ----          --------------            -------------

     0 msec             None              Stimulus at retina

    0+ msec             None              Stimulus in P

   100 msec      ATTEND(s) created        Stimulus in WM
                                                                 -
150 + 150x msec  ATTEND applies           Shift to blob/group    |C
                                                                 |y
200 + 150x msec  ATTEND completed         Attentional message at V4 |c
                 RECOGNIZE applies (sometimes)                   |l
                                                                 |e
250 + 150x msec  ATTEND(s) created        New attended data in WM _|
                 RECOGNIZE created        (On last cycle)

300 + 150x msec  RECOGNIZE applies         Target identified

                 RESPOND created

350 + 150x msec  RESPOND applies

400 + 150x msec  RESPOND completed        Motor output begins

470 + 150x msec                           Motor command completed
```

Figure 12: Operator trace for target present search with multiple shifts of attention ception forces us to discuss shifting attention in terms of probabilities. Unfortunately, we cannot determine the exact probability that multiple shifts of attention occur for any condition. We can, however, use our model to make a semi-quantitative estimate of the likelihood of multiple shifts.

For target absent conditions, we know that for there to be a positive slope that $\frac{Items}{GroupSize} > 1$. If the Item/GroupSize quotient it is not greater than one, the probability of multiple shifting should be low. We now solve this inequality for slope and the number of distracting items: Given our model, slopes can be estimated by dividing the time required to shift attention (150 msec) by the group size. Solving for group size and substituting this relationship into the inequality yields $Items(Slope) > 150$. If this inequality is satisfied, multiple shifts are likely to occur. This relationship is exactly what we would expect: Since attended groups are of a fixed average size, the greater the number of items, the more likely it is that multiple shifts should be required. Since positive slopes imply the possibility of multiple feature shifts, the more positive the slope, the more likely that multiple feature shifts should occur. For target present conditions, the number 150 can be replaced by 75, to yield the analogous inequality.

Our model and operator traces are capable of accounting for the full range of search response behaviors. Using the inequality above we can predict which searches are likely to require multiple shifts of attention. For instance, the target present searches with very shallow slopes (3 – 6 msec per distractor) from TG80 (feature) and WCF (conjunctive) are likely to be accomplished without multiple shifts of attention. The inequality $Items(Slope) > 75$ is not satisfied for the slope of 3 until there are 25 items and is not satisfied for the slope of 6 until there are 12. Only after the number of items exceeds these cutoffs, are multiple shifts of attention likely to occur for any particular search task. This prediction partially confirms the conclusions of both TG80 and WCF, however those researchers imply more that shifts of attention do not occur rather than that they are unlikely. For searches with large products of items and slopes, the inequality predicts that shifts of attention must occur. All of the conjunctive search conditions and the target absent feature search condition of TG80 fall into this category. The feature shift conditions surveyed in Treisman and Gormican fall into both the single and multiple shift categories. The final prediction based on this operator trace is that 150 msec per item should be the upper bound for target absent slopes and that 75 msec per item should be the upper bound for target present slopes. Of the work we have surveyed, the largest slopes observed were 124 and 82 msec per distracting item, respectively, from a feature search condition in Treisman and Gormican (1988).

A topic of future research is to develop a principled way of calculating items per group a priori. The solutions may be found in theories that seek to quantify object complexity [Leeuwenberg, 1971].

10 Discussion

The core of our research strategy is to provide converging evidence that our model of visual attention is capable of accounting for reaction times in visual tasks requiring attention. We concentrate on accounting for reaction times, because there are few overt, observable, events that occur in most of the tasks that we model, besides the final response. We employ a coverage strategy in which the model is incrementally extended to account for ever wider ranges of visual phenomena. And, in doing this, we hope that the computational model that emerges to generate timing predictions will reflect the actual mechanisms behind human visual behavior.

We first presented a basic model of visual attention in order to account for reaction times in object identification tasks and then augmented the basic model in order to account for reaction times in a range of search experiments. The characteristics of the expanded model are a superset of those of the basic model, such that the cycle times for subsystems of the model, memories, and visual operators and specifics of their behavior including timing are essentially the same as in the basic model. The fact that there is so much commonality between the basic and the expanded models is evidence that a task independent model of visual attention is being realized. The only major model changes were that task control knowledge had to be replaced, which is reasonable since the tasks are different.

So far the Soar architecture has been shown to be a worthy computational vehicle for verifying the model. It is interesting to note that the explicit control structure of operator traces is not programmed into Soar as a set of sequential steps, but arises reactively in response to visual input. Also, the set of productions, which supports visual operator creation and application does not change for any of the letter wheel or search trace implementations. These are exactly the sort of characteristics that one would expect in a human implementation.

References

[Broadbent, 1958] D.E. Broadbent. *Perception and Communication.* Pergamon, Oxford, 1958.

[Bundesen *et al.*, 1984] C. Bundesen, L.F. Pedersen, and A. Larsen. Measuring efficiency of selection from briefly exposed visual displays: A model for partial report. *Journal of Experimental Psychology: Human Perception and Performance*, 10:329–339, 1984.

[Card *et al.*, 1983] S.K. Card, T.P. Moran, and A. Newell. *The Psychology of Human-Computer Interaction.* Erlbaum, Hillsdale, NJ, 1983.

[Chi and Klahr, 1975] M.T.H. Chi and D. Klahr. Span and rate of apprehension in children and adults. *Journal of Experimental Child Psychology*, 19:434–439, 1975.

[Colegate *et al.*, 1973] R. Colegate, J.E. Hoffman, and C.W. Eriksen. Selective encoding from multielement visual displays. *Perception and Psychophysics*, 14:217–224, 1973.

[Eriksen and Hoffman, 1972] C.W. Eriksen and J.E. Hoffman. Some characteristics of selective attention in visual perception determined by vocal reaction time. *Perception and Psychophysics*, 11:169–171, 1972.

[Eriksen and Hoffman, 1973] C.W. Eriksen and J.E. Hoffman. The extent of processing noise elements during selective coding from visual displays. *Perception and Psychophysics*, 14:155–160, 1973.

[Eriksen and St. James, 1986] C.W. Eriksen and J.D. St. James. Visual attention within and around the field of focal attention: A zoom lens model. *Perception and Psychophysics*, 40:225–240, 1986.

[Eriksen and Yeh, 1985] C.W. Eriksen and Y.Y. Yeh. Allocation of attention in the visual field. *Journal of Experimental Psychology*, 11:583–597, 1985.

[Hoffman, 1980] J.E. Hoffman. Interaction between global and local levels of a form. *Journal of Experimental Psychology: Human Perception and Performance*, 6:222–234, 1980.

[Hughes and Zimba, 1985] H.C Hughes and L.D. Zimba. Spatial maps of directed visual attention. *Journal of Experimental Psychology: Human Perception and Performance*, 11:409–430, 1985.

[John and Newell, 1989] B.E. John and A. Newell. Cumulating the science of HCI: From S-R compatibility to transcription typing. In *Proceedings of CHI*, pages 109–114, Austin, Texas, April 30–May 4 1989.

[John, 1988] B.E. John. *Contributions to engineering models of human-computer interaction.* PhD thesis, Carnegie Mellon University, 1988.

[Klahr and Wallace, 1976] D. Klahr and J.G. Wallace. *Cognitive Development: An Information-processing View.* Erlbaum, Hillsdale, NJ, 1976.

[LaBerge and Brown, 1989] D. LaBerge and V. Brown. Theory of attentional operations in shape identification. *Psychological Review*, 96:101–124, 1989.

[Laird *et al.*, 1987] J. E. Laird, A. Newell, and P. S. Rosenbloom. Soar: An architecture for general intelligence. *Artificial Intelligence*, 33, 1987.

[Leeuwenberg, 1971] E.L.J. Leeuwenberg. A perceptual coding language for visual and auditory patterns. *American Journal of Psychology*, 84:307–349, 1971.

[Livingstone and Hubel, 1984] M.S. Livingstone and D.H. Hubel. Anatomy and physiology of a color system in the primate visual cortex. *Journal of Neuroscience*, 4:309–356, 1984.

[Livingstone and Hubel, 1987] M.S. Livingstone and D.H. Hubel. Psychophysical evidence for separate channels for the perception of form, color, movement, and depth. *Journal of Neuroscience*, 7:3416–3468, 1987.

[Mishkin and Appenzeller, 1987] M. Mishkin and T. Appenzeller. The anatomy of memory. *Scientific American*, June:80–89, 1987.

[Moran and Desimone, 1985] J. Moran and R. Desimone. Selective attention gates visual processing in the extrastriate cortex. *Science*, 229:782–784, 1985.

[Newell, 1990] A. Newell. *Unified Theories of Cognition*. Harvard University Press, Cambridge, MA, 1990.

[Shulman *et al.*, 1979] G.L. Shulman, R.W. Remington, and J.P. McLean. Moving attention through visual space. *Journal of Experimental Psychology: Human Perception and Performance*, 5:522–526, 1979.

[Sperling, 1960] G. Sperling. The information available in brief visual presentations. *Psychological Monographs*, 74:1–29, 1960.

[Treisman and Gelade, 1980] A. Treisman and G. Gelade. A feature integration theory of attention. *Cognitive Psychology*, 12:97–136, 1980.

[Treisman and Gormican, 1988] A. Treisman and S. Gormican. Feature analysis in early vision: Evidence from search asymmetries. *Psychological Review*, 95:15–48, 1988.

[Treisman and Schmidt, 1982] A. Treisman and H. Schmidt. Illusory conjunctions in the perception of objects. *Cognitive Psychology*, 14:107–141, 1982.

[Treisman, 1985] A. Treisman. Preattentive processing in vision. *Computer Vision, Graphics, and Image Processing*, 31:156–177, 1985.

[Tsal, 1983] Y. Tsal. Movements of attention across the visual field. *Journal of Experimental Psychology: Human Perception and Performance*, 9:523–530, 1983.

[Weisstein and Harris, 1974] N. Weisstein and C.S. Harris. Visual detection of line segments: An object superiority effect. *Science*, 186:752–755, 1974.

[Wiesmeyer and Laird, 1990] M.D. Wiesmeyer and J.E. Laird. A computer model of visual attention. In *Twelfth Annual Conference of the Cognitive Science Society, Boston*, 1990.

[Wiesmeyer, 1991] M.D. Wiesmeyer. An operator-based model of rapid visual counting. In *Thirteenth Annual Conference of the Cognitive Science Society, Chicago*, 1991.

[Wiesmeyer, Forthcoming] M.D. Wiesmeyer. *An Operator-Based Model of Covert Visual Attention*. PhD thesis, The University of Michigan, Ann Arbor, Forthcoming.

[Wolfe *et al.*, 1989] J.M. Wolfe, K.R. Cave, and S.L. Franzel. Guided search: An alternative to the feature integration model for visual search. *Journal of Experimental Psychology: Human Perception and Performance*, 15:419–433, 1989.

Index

Artificial Intelligence
Patrick Henry Winston, founding editor
J. Michael Brady, Daniel G. Bobrow, and Randall Davis, current editors

Artificial Intelligence: An MIT Perspective, Volume I: Expert Problem Solving, Natural Language Understanding, Intelligent Computer Coaches, Representation and Learning, edited by Patrick Henry Winston and Richard Henry Brown, 1979

Artificial Intelligence: An MIT Perspective, Volume II: Understanding Vision, Manipulation, Computer Design, Symbol Manipulation, edited by Patrick Henry Winston and Richard Henry Brown, 1979

NETL: A System for Representing and Using Real-World Knowledge, Scott Fahlman, 1979

The Interpretation of Visual Motion, by Shimon Ullman, 1979

A Theory of Syntactic Recognition for Natural Language, Mitchell P. Marcus, 1980

Turtle Geometry: The Computer as a Medium for Exploring Mathematics, Harold Abelson and Andrea di Sessa, 1981

From Images to Surfaces: A Computational Study of the Human Visual System, William Eric Leifur Grimson, 1981

Robot Manipulators: Mathematics, Programming, and Control, Richard P. Paul, 1981

Computational Models of Discourse, edited by Michael Brady and Robert C. Berwick, 1982

Robot Motion: Planning and Control, edited by Michael Brady, John M. Hollerbach, Timothy Johnson, Tomás Lozano-Pérez, and Matthew T. Mason, 1982

In-Depth Understanding: A Computer Model of Integrated Processing for Narrative Comprehension, Michael G. Dyer, 1983

Robotic Research: The First International Symposium, edited by Hideo Hanafusa and Hirochika Inoue, 1985

Robot Hands and the Mechanics of Manipulation, Matthew T. Mason and J. Kenneth Salisbury, Jr., 1985

The Acquisition of Syntactic Knowledge, Robert C. Berwick, 1985

The Connection Machine, W. Daniel Hillis, 1985

Legged Robots that Balance, Marc H. Raibert, 1986

Robotics Research: The Third International Symposium, edited by O.D. Faugeras and Georges Giralt, 1986

Machine Interpretation of Line Drawings, Kokichi Sugihara, 1986

ACTORS: A Model of Concurrent Computation in Distributed Systems, Gul A. Agha, 1986

Knowledge-Based Tutoring: The GUIDON Program, William Clancey, 1987

AI in the 1980s and Beyond: An MIT Survey, edited by W. Eric L. Grimson and Ramesh S. Patil, 1987

Visual Reconstruction, Andrew Blake and Andrew Zisserman, 1987

Reasoning about Change: Time and Causation from the Standpoint of Artificial Intelligence, Yoav Shoham, 1988

Model-Based Control of a Robot Manipulator, Chae H. An, Christopher G. Atkeson, and John M. Hollerbach, 1988

A Robot Ping-Pong Player: Experiment in Real-Time Intelligent Control, Russell L. Andersson, 1988

Robotics Research: The Fourth International Symposium, edited by Robert C. Bolles and Bernard Roth, 1988

The Paralation Model: Architecture-Independent Parallel Programming, Gary Sabot, 1988

Concurrent System for Knowledge Processing: An Actor Perspective, edited by Carl Hewitt and Gul Agha, 1989

Automated Deduction in Nonclassical Logics: Efficient Matrix Proof Methods for Modal and Intuitionistic Logics, Lincoln Wallen, 1989

Shape from Shading, edited by Berthold K.P. Horn and Michael J. Brooks, 1989

Ontic: A Knowledge Representation System for Mathematics, David A. McAllester, 1989

Solid Shape, Jan J. Koenderink, 1990

Expert Systems: Human Issues, edited by Dianne Berry and Anna Hart, 1990

Artificial Intelligence: Concepts and Applications, edited by A. R. Mirzai, 1990

Robotics Research: The Fifth International Symposium, edited by Hirofumi Miura and Suguru Arimoto, 1990

Theories of Comparative Analysis, Daniel S. Weld, 1990

Artificial Intelligence at MIT: Expanding Frontiers, edited by Patrick Henry Winston and Sarah Alexandra Shellard, 1990

Vector Models for Data-Parallel Computing, Guy E. Blelloch, 1990

Experiments in the Machine Interpretation of Visual Motion, David W. Murray and Bernard F. Buxton, 1990

Object Recognition by Computer: The Role of Geometric Constraints, W. Eric L. Grimson, 1990

Representing and Reasoning With Probabilistic Knowledge: A Logical Approach to Probabilities, Fahiem Bacchus, 1990

3D Model Recognition from Stereoscopic Cues, edited by John E.W. Mayhew and John P. Frisby, 1991

Artificial Vision for Mobile Robots: Stereo Vision and Multisensory Perception, Nicholas Ayache, 1991

Truth and Modality for Knowledge Representation, Raymond Turner, 1991

Made-Up Minds: A Constructivist Approach to Artificial Intelligence, Gary L. Drescher, 1991

Vision, Instruction, and Action, David Chapman, 1991

Do the Right Thing: Studies in Limited Rationality, Stuart Russell and Eric Wefeld, 1991

KAM: A System for Intelligently Guiding Numerical Experimentation by Computer, Kenneth Man-Kam Yip, 1991

Solving Geometric Constraint Systems: A Case Study in Kinematics, Glenn A. Kramer, 1992

Geometric Invariants in Computer Vision, edited by Joseph Mundy and Andrew Zisserman, 1992

HANDEY: A Robot Task Planner, Tomás Lozano-Pérez, Joseph L. Jones, Emmanuel Mazer, and Patrick A. O'Donnell, 1992

Active Vision, edited by Andrew Blake and Alan Yuille, 1992

Recent Advances in Qualitative Physics, edited by Boi Faltings and Peter Struss, 1992

Machine Translation: A View from the Lexicon, Bonnie Jean Dorr, 1993

The Language Complexity Game, Eric Sven Ristad, 1993

The Soar Papers: Research on Integrated Intelligence, edited by Paul S. Rosenbloom, John E. Laird, and Allen Newell, 1993